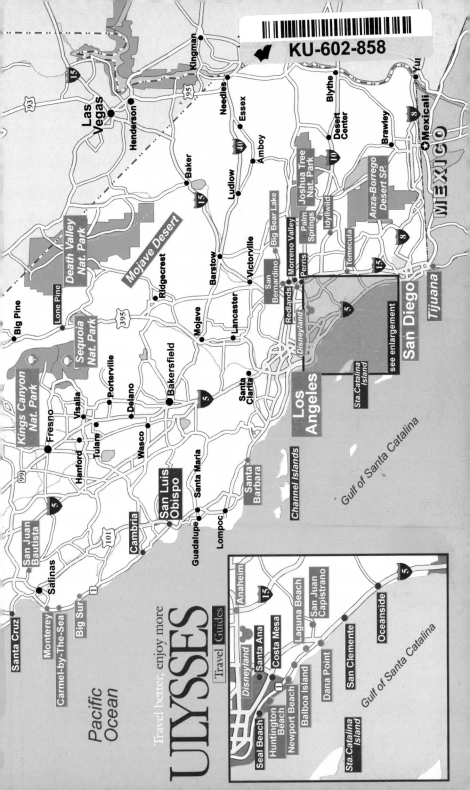

The urban conglomerate of Los Angeles stretches along the Pacific coast from Ventura County, northeast of the city, to Orange County in the southeast, reaching out to the mountains and desert. - *LACVB*

The large and varied collection displayed at the Los Angeles County Museum of Art is most impressive. This museum's goal is to showcase art from all of the world's major cultures, from ancient times to the modern era. - *LACVB*

The beaches on the coast of L.A.—Santa Monica, Malibu and Venice Beach—are covered with the tanned, muscle-bound sun-worshippers for which California is famous. - *Michele & Tom Grimm/LACVB*

Since its creation in 1960, the Hollywood Walk of Fame has immortalized more than 2,000 actors and musicians with small, black-and-gold plaques set in concrete along Hollywood Boulevard.
- *Anne Gardon*

Many visitors come here specifically to admire the unique desert flowering, which lasts for one week in April. Each year, the natural combination of rain, sun, wind and temperature creates this phenomenon. The result can be spectacular, but is occasionally disappointing, as some years have fewer flowers than usual.
- *Claude Hervé-Bazin*

The Gaslamp district, named after the gas lamps that still illuminate its streets, is without a doubt San Diego's most popular neighbourhood. Here, you will find some of the most splendid examples of Victorian architecture.
- *J. Greenberg/ Camerique*

The legendary Hotel Del Coronado is definitely the main feature of Coronado Island. This impressive establishment is easily recognizable thanks to its white facade and red, octagonal roof.
- *Tibor Bognár*

California

Travel better, enjoy more

ULYSSES
Travel Guides

Offices

CANADA:
Ulysses Travel Guides, 4176 St-Denis, Montréal, Québec, H2W 2M5,
☎(514) 843-9447 or 1-877-542-7247, Fax: (514) 843-9448, info@ulysses.ca,
www.ulyssesguides.com

EUROPE:
Les Guides de Voyage Ulysse SARL, BP 159, 75523 Paris Cedex 11, France,
☎01 43 38 89 50, Fax: 01 43 38 89 52, voyage@ulysse.ca, www.ulyssesguides.com

U.S.A.:
Ulysses Travel Guides, 305 Madison Avenue, Suite 1166, New York, NY 10165, ☎1-877-542-7247, Fax: (514) 843-9448, info@ulysses.ca, www.ulyssesguides.com

Distributors

CANADA:
Ulysses Books & Maps, 4176 Saint-Denis, Montréal, Québec,
H2W 2M5, ☎(514) 843-9882, ext.2232, 800-748-9171, Fax: 514-843-9448, info@ulysses.ca,
www.ulyssesguides.com

GREAT BRITAIN AND IRELAND:
World Leisure Marketing, Unit 11, Newmarket Court, Newmartket Drive,
Derby DE24 8NW, ☎1 332 57 37 37, Fax: 1 332 57 33 99, office@wlmsales.co.uk

SCANDINAVIA:
Scanvik, Esplanaden 8B, 1263 Copenhagen K, DK, ☎(45) 33.12.77.66,
Fax: (45) 33.91.28.82

SPAIN:
Altaïr, Balmes 69, E-08007 Barcelona, ☎454 29 66, Fax: 451 25 59,
altair@globalcom.es

SWITZERLAND:
Havas Services Suisse, ☎(26) 460 80 60, Fax: (26) 460 80 68

U.S.A.:
The Globe Pequot Press, 246 Goose Lane, Guilford, CT 06437 - 0480,
☎1-800-243-0495, Fax: 800-820-2329, sales@globe-pequot.com

Other countries, contact Ulysses Books & Maps, 4176 Saint-Denis, Montréal,
Québec, H2W 2M5, ☎(514) 843-9882, ext. 2232, 800-748-9171,
Fax: 514-843-9448, info@ulysses.ca, www.ulyssesguides.com

Cataloguing-in-Publication Data (see page 5)
© February 2001, Ulysses Travel Guides.
All rights reserved
Printed in Canada
ISBN 2-89464-390X

"It was always a wild, rocky coast, desolate and forbidding to the man of the pavements, eloquent and enchanting to the Taliesans. The homesteader never failed to unearth fresh sorrows...Though young, geologically speaking, the land has a hoary look. From the ocean depths there issued strange formations, contours unique and seductive. As if the Titans of the deep had labored for aeons to shape and mold the earth. Even millenia ago the great land birds were startled by the abrupt aspect of these risen shapes...And ever the sea recedes. Moon drag. To the west, new land, new figures of earth. Dreamers, outlaws, forerunners. Advancing toward the other world of long ago and far away, the world of yesterday and tomorrow. The world within the world."

Henry Miller,
From *Big Sur and the Oranges of Hieronymus Bosch*

Publisher
Pascale Couture

Editors
Caroline Béliveau
Stéphane G. Marceau

Copy Editing
Eileen Connolly
Anne Joyce
Cindy Garayt

Page Layout
Typesetting
Anne Joyce
Visuals
Isabelle Lalonde

Translation Coordination
Caroline Béliveau
Jacqueline Grekin

Cartography
André Duchesne
Patrick Thivierge
Yanik Landreville
Bradley Fenton

Photography
Cover Page
Grant V. Faint/
The Image Bank
Inside Pages
Claude Hervé-Bazin
Patrick Escudero
Anne Gardon/
Reflexion
James Blank/
Reflexion
J. Greenberg/
Camerique/Reflexion
Tibor Bognár/

Reflexion
Carrie Grant/
Eureka! Humboldt Bureau
Don Leonard/
Eureka! Humboldt Bureau
Arnesen Photography/
LACVB
Michele and Tom Grimm/
LACVB

Design
Patrick Farei
(Atoll Direction)

Illustrations
Valérie Fontaine
Myriam Gagné
Jenny Jasper
Josée Perreault
Lorette Pierson
Richard Serrao

Authors:
Portrait, The Sierra Nevada, Central Coast : François Hénault; *translation* : Suzanne Murray, Danielle Gauthier, Renata Isajlovic;
Los Angeles : Eric Hamovitch;
Orange County, Mojave National Preserve and Death Valley, Inland Empire and Palm Springs : Clayton Anderson;
San Diego and Surroundings: Caroline Béliveau, *translation* : Cindy Garayt, Francesca Worrall, Danae Lambros;
San Francisco and Surroundings : Alain Legault, *translation* : Cindy Garayt, Danielle Gauthier, Renata Isajlovic;
Wine Country, The North Coast, Northeastern California, Sacramento, the Delta and Gold Country : Jenny Jasper and Matthew Von Baeyer.

Thanks to:
Debbie Barber, Fred Sater, Chris Taranto, Lulu Lopez, Janis Flippen, Malei Jessee, Kelly Edmunston, Vida Smart (Los Angeles), Bonnie Tregaskis, Melissa Centano, Tonya Stephan, Jim Timko (San Diego Tourism and Convention Center), Loïc Hamon, François Béliveau, Jean-Marie Colle, Laurie Armstrong (San Francisco Convention & Visitors Bureau), Julie Brodeur, Jean Dumont, Alexandra Gilbert, Jean Roger, Laurence Wegscheider, Jan Austerman, Karen Whitaker, Jim Rairdon and Tony Smithers.

We acknowledge the financial support of the Government of Canada through the Book Publishing Industry Development Program (BPIDP) for our publishing activities.

We would also like to thank SODEC (Québec) for its financial support.

Cataloguing-in-Publication Data

Main entry under title:

California

(Ulysses travel guide)
Includes index.

ISBN 2-89464-390-X

1. California - Guidebooks. I. Series

F859.3.C33 2001   917.9404'54   C2001-940019-5

Table of Contents

Map List

Map Symbols

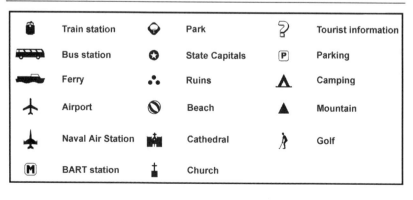

Train station	Park	Tourist information
Bus station	State Capitals	Parking
Ferry	Ruins	Camping
Airport	Beach	Mountain
Naval Air Station	Cathedral	Golf
BART station	Church	

Symbols

⛵	Ulysses's favourite
≡	Air conditioning
bkfst incl.	Breakfast included
♠	Casino
tv	Television
⊗	Fan
⇄	Fax number
⊘	Fitness centre
fb	Full board (lodging + 3 meals, usually quoted for one person)
½ b	Half board (lodging + 2 meals, usually quoted for one person)
K	Kitchenette
pb	Private bathroom
≈	Pool
ℝ	Refrigerator
ℜ	Restaurant
△	Sauna
sb	Shared bathroom
✿	Spa
☎	Telephone number
♿	Wheelchair access
⊛	Whirlpool

ATTRACTION CLASSIFICATION

★	Interesting
★★	Worth a visit
★★★	Not to be missed

The prices listed in this guide are for the admission of one adult.

HOTEL CLASSIFICATION

$	$40 or less
$$	$40 to $80
$$$	$80 to $130
$$$$	$130 to $200
$$$$$	$200 or more

The prices in this guide are for one standard room, double occupancy in high season.

RESTAURANT CLASSIFICATION

$	$10 or less
$$	$10 to $20
$$$	$20 to $30
$$$$	$30 to $40
$$$$$	$40 or more

The prices in the guide are for a meal for one person, not including drinks and tip.

All prices in this guide are in U.S. dollars.

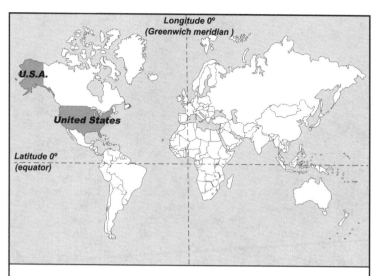

 Where is California?

California

Capital: Sacramento
Population: 29,760,025 inhab.
Currency: US dollar
Area: 411,000 km² (158,646 sq mi)

©ULYSSES

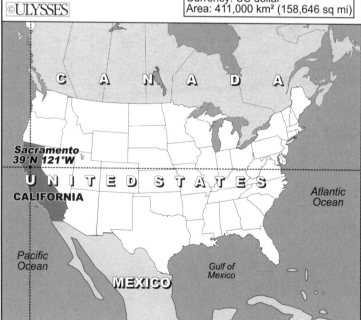

America on Two Tracks

The United States was emerging from its devastating Civil War, during which the Union was on the brink of collapse. Anxious to strengthen ties between East and West, officials threw their full support behind an ambitious undertaking: to link the two coasts with a transcontinental railroad. Engineer Theodore Judah had already conceived of a 22mi (35km) line in the Sacramento Valley, and the idea of one day extending it across the daunting Sierra Nevada was obviously an exciting one. He sat down at the drawing board and sketched out the plans for the Transcontinental Railroad. Now, all that was needed was money.

Charles Crocker, Mark Hopkins, Collis Huntington and Leland Stanford, four wealthy businessmen from Sacramento, took care of this aspect of the project. With excellent political connections, the "Big Four" founded the Central Pacific Company and persuaded U.S. Congress to throw its support behind the undertaking. On July 1, 1862, the Pacific Railroad Act granted the new company huge land concessions, generous credits and subsidies. In collaboration with the Union Pacific, the projected rail line was to link Omaha, on the Missouri River and Sacramento. The Central Pacific was to be responsible for the west-to-east section from Sacramento, while the Union Pacific was to complete the east-to-west portion from Omaha.

The four men thus took complete control of the situation, pushing Judah to leave the Central Pacific, despite the fact that he had come up with the original plans. Dissatisfied with the rate of progress and unable to find cheap labour, Crocker brought over by boat more than 15,000 Chinese "coolies" who worked relentlessly and in miserable conditions.

On May 10, 1869, after numerous fatalities from dynamite blasts, and following the plans of the unfortunate Judah who died some time earlier, the Sierra Nevada was conquered and the dream became reality. The two sections of railroad were joined at Promontory Point in Utah. From then on, it would take a mere five days to travel from San Francisco to New York. The settlement of the West could begin in earnest.

Portrait

Revered by some,
disliked by others, California is a land of extremes and extravagancy that certainly leaves no one indifferent.

A true blend of the best and the worst the U.S. has to offer, this mythical state on the United States' West Coast has made millions of people dream for generations. Since its creation, the Golden State has emitted an immeasurable force of attraction like no other land in the Americas, or the world for that matter. Pioneers, prospectors, great poets, singers, actors and athletes have come here over the years to strike it rich, change the world, find true love or simply enjoy its mild climate, turning California into the legend so well defined by the cliché "opposites attract."

I nitially drawn by the mild and intoxicating weather as well as the fertile land, the first Californian pioneers created a territory in their image; today, it is populated by all kinds of entrepreneurs seeking that all-too-often-elusive goal: the American Dream. If there exists a heavenly place on earth where everything and anything seems possible, where the poor can become rich in a snap of the fingers, or a total unknown can become an adulated celebrity, it's surely here in California! It's not surprising that thousands of people around the world fantasize about this legendary state with its big shiny cars, money growing on trees, perennial surfing and shapely blondes strolling on sandy beaches. In the eyes of many, California evokes a very particular aspect of the United States with its bevy of fairytale success stories.

E ven people who have never even set foot in California are familiar with it. We entertain a loving, almost lustful relationship with this state. For generations, we've been bombarded with words and images showing us the many faces of this grandiose land. Brought to life by the greatest authors, acclaimed in song, painted and filmed by generations of artists moved by its unique character, California definitely wins top honours as one of the earth's mythical lands. Who hasn't seen, at one time or another, John Wayne or another famous cowboy riding a horse across the Mojave Desert? Is there still anyone in the Western World who hasn't watched a television show shot in Los Angeles or witnessed a car chase in the streets of San Francisco on television or the big screen? Very few people can say they've never seen a surfer or a stunning blond share their life stories with millions of television viewers. California seems so closely within our grasp but in reality, its impressive dimensions and numerous, hard-to-define facets render it elusive. In appearance, it symbolizes the simplicity of the American Dream, of Eldorado. Yet it remains so immensely complex that many are engulfed by it, losing their own identity. Welcome to California...

Geography

Located on the western seaboard of the United States, California has a surface area of 158,693 sq mi (411,012km²), ranking it the third largest state after Alaska and Texas. Resembling a boomerang tossed towards Asia, the Californian territory stretches from the vast pine forests in the state of Oregon in the north to the arid lands of Mexico in the south; from the mountains and deserts of Arizona and Nevada in the east, all the way to the majestic Pacific Ocean and 1,180mi (1,900km) of coastline. The ocean exerts just as strong an influence on the lifestyle of the inhabitants as it does on the climate; not a single point in this immense state which, incidentally, is larger than Germany, is more than 250mi (400km) from the

coast. Some 33.8 million people (approximately the population of Canada), increased by some 200,000 immigrants every year, currently inhabit California—the most populous state in the Union since the 1960s. One American out of eight lives in this legendary land and one third of them dwell in the megalopolis of Los Angeles.

Geology

Over the course of several thousand years, glacial and seismic activity sculpted the Californian landscape and created a place where, in very little time, arid deserts give way to damp conifer forests and limpid lakes lead to vast expanses of salt water. California was created by the movement of two giants, the Pacific and North American plates, which have been grinding against each other for millions of years, forming the mountain ranges we know today, but also causing the seismic activity that terrorizes so many Californians. Recently formed in geologic history, California occupies an unstable land located at the junction of these plates, which unfortunately slide in opposite directions about 0.4in (1cm) every year. In fact, the world-famous San Andreas Fault results from the movement of these plates: the Pacific plate moves in the northwestern direction while the North American plate moves towards the west. Like a Sword of Damocles hanging over the region, this terrible fault extends over 559mi (900km) from north to south, from Cape Mendocino on the northern coast to Imperial Valley in the southeast. On a periodic basis, California

endures the after-effects of this tectonic movement and occasionally, like the terrible earthquake in 1906, the phenomenon takes on dramatic proportions. That year, the ground shook so hard that very few buildings in San Francisco remained standing and the city was practically reduced to ruins. The earthquake measured 8.3 on the Richter Scale, the highest level ever recorded in California. More recently, in 1994, the earth trembled in the Los Angeles region, driving meters up to 6.8.

While the South is vulnerable to seismic movements, the North has been afflicted by intense volcanic activity for the past thousands of years. Many national parks allow visitors to observe the environment and marvel at the natural beauty of volcanoes, lava beds, hot springs and geysers through a haze of smoke and gas.

This intense tectonic activity on the West Coast has created spectacular and varied scenery in California, ranging from rainforests, arid deserts, snow-covered mountain caps to fine-sand beaches. Geographically, the territory is divided into four principal regions: the Coast Range, Central Valley, Sierra Nevada and the deserts.

Coast Range

Forming a border measuring between 50 and 75mi (80 and 120km) wide beside the Pacific Ocean, the Coast Range extends from Northern to Southern California and provides absolutely spectacular landscapes. Summits ranging from 1,968 to 5,249ft

(600 to 1,600m) high compose this mountain range, which literally dips its big toe into the water where tall sheer cliffs suddenly fall into the ocean. Its eastern side, however, gently slopes down to the Central Valley and the high peaks gradually lose their majestic character as they slowly melt into the valley's rich soil. Acting as a physical barrier between the ocean and the valley, the Coast Range pauses only for San Francisco Bay, which is the only region at sea level that provides access to the centre of the state.

The fairly unpopulated North Coast has a humid climate and is famous for its gigantic sequoias, the most impressive conifers on the planet. The central part, from San Francisco to Ventura, features a milder climate and myriad sandy beaches which are propitious for hotel resorts. South of Los Angeles, the Coast Range changes a little and gives birth to the Peninsular Range which continues into Mexico. The latter gives a good idea of the kind of landscape to expect in the southern neighbour's Baja California Peninsula. Extending west to east, the Transverse ranges take shape in the southern part of the Coast Range, joining the Sierra Nevada just as it begins to fork slightly towards the west. It is these Transverse ranges that form the spectacular alpine scenery in the background of Los Angeles... that is, when there isn't any smog blocking the view!

Central Valley

The Central Valley is an impressive tectonic trough measuring 50mi (80km) wide and nearly 372mi (600km) long, featuring some extremely favourable agricultural land. Endowed with incredibly rich sediments, this fertile valley located east of the Coast Range is the most fruitful territory with the most diverse agriculture in the United States. Cotton, peaches, almonds, grapes and other market produce grow in abundance throughout its entire area. Though the Central Valley is often referred to as a unique entity it is, in fact, constituted of two water basins: Sacramento Valley in the north and San Joaquin Valley in the south. These two fluvial networks meet in San Francisco Bay to form the Sacramento Delta.

The San Francisco region includes two bountiful valleys famous for their fruits and vines. Although they are part of the Coast Range, both the Napa and Santa Clara valleys have been blessed with the distinctive richness and great fertility of the neighbouring Central Valley. Almost all the wine produced in California, becoming more and more renowned among connoisseurs, comes from the Napa Valley which, like its counterpart, is unfortunately threatened by the expansion of urban centres and the proliferation of high-tech companies.

Sierra Nevada and Cascade Ranges

The Sierra Nevada (in Spanish, snow-covered mountains) spreads over 400mi (650km) along California's eastern border. Its stately granite cliffs, high plateaus, majestic canyons and snow-capped summits literally isolate the state from the rest of the country. The towering Cascade Range is the northern extension of the Sierra, extending northwest of the Pacific all the way to British Columbia. These grandiose and inseparable mountain ranges encompass an incredible number of natural attractions, which are enhanced by numerous national parks. Every year hundreds of thousands of visitors are drawn to these parks to witness their splendour.

On the western side of the Sierra Nevada, the intense activity of glaciers and torrential rivers has shaped splendid natural sculptures and canyons, notably in the famous Yosemite and Kings Canyon national parks. Another of the Sierra's major attractions, Mount Whitney lords over the Californian landscape at 14,495ft (4,418m).

The Cascade Range--its highest peak, Mount Shasta, culminates at 13,937ft (4,248m)--was formed approximately five million years ago by exceptionally intense volcanic activity. Today, volcanic cones, endless conifer forests as well as the nerve centre of the region, the Klamath and Trinity rivers, dominate its wild landscape.

Deserts

California includes three major desert expanses in its territory: the Colorado Desert in the south, the Mojave Desert northeast of Los Angeles and finally, a section of the immense Great Basin Desert, east of the Sierra Nevada. Completely cut off from the humid, cooler masses of the Pacific by the physical barriers formed by the Peninsular Range, Transverse ranges and Sierra Nevada, the vast desert lands contrast sharply with the snow-covered peaks and lush forests that border them. The Colorado Desert, west of the river of the same name, extends in southeast California at altitudes varying between sea level and 1,968ft (600m). Considered a low, or southern, desert, it receives less than 5in (13cm) of precipitation per year.

The Mojave Desert is adjacent to the neighbouring state of Nevada and covers one fifth of the Californian territory. Rising over 3,280ft (1,000m), it is considered a high, or northern, desert. Greater precipitation ranging from 10 to 16in (25 to 40cm) yearly, lower temperatures and lower levels of evaporation distinguish it from its neighbour to the south, the Colorado Desert.

Lastly, the Great Basin Desert, considered by some as more of a semiarid land than a real desert, principally spreads out in neighbouring Nevada; California only has a tiny but oh-so-famous section of it: the notorious Death Valley. Forming a deep depression approximately 282ft (86m) below sea level at its lowest point, and squeezed be-

Water: an Ongoing Struggle

The bone of contention between agricultural, environmental and urban groups, managing the water supply was and continues to be a major challenge for California's government. Subject to periodic dry spells, the state has had to adopt an efficient management plan that involves ecological groups, suppliers and government agencies. Through awareness-raising campaigns, officials have more or less succeeded in conserving water and creating reserves that can be drawn on during heat waves. Increasingly, cities are recycling used water, and several have initiated desalination programs.

There is no denying the fact that in California's development flies in the face of the absence of water resources. About 75% of the state's precipitation falls north of Sacramento, while 75% of the demand for water comes from the coastal region. During the 1930s, a network of reservoirs, dams and aqueducts had to be built to maintain the Central Valley's productivity and to develop the urban centres of Southern California. Major challenges remain, since the southern areas are experiencing major population growth, with a large influx of retired Anglos as well as Latinos from Mexico.

tween the Paramint and Amargosa mountain ranges, this extremely arid territory, contrary to the rest of the Great Basin, constitutes the lowest point in all of the U.S. In the summer, daytime temperatures can exceed 122°F (50°C). This valley certainly lives up to its name!

Climate

On the whole, California enjoys a mild, humid Mediterranean climate, with temperatures hovering around 50°F (10°C) in the winter and 75°F (24°C) in the summer. The summer

is relatively dry, since most of the rainfall occurs between November and April. The California Current, a cool air mass from Northern Canada, brings its fair share of humidity to the vast expanses in Northern California, well-known for their relatively cooler temperatures, persistent clouds, heavy winter fog and abundant precipitation. However, to the delight of Southern Californians, a break in the coast by Point Conception and the Santa Barbara Channel pushes this cool current away, making the temperatures more gentle in the southern part.

Although the coast has a mild, humid climate with stable temperatures, the mountains in the interior and the deserts are another story altogether. While several feet of snow coat the mountains in the winter, deserts in the South receive an infinitesimal quantity of precipitation. Fortunately, milder summer conditions allow these great wild regions to be appreciated. The Central Valley can also be scorching in the summer yet besieged with colder temperatures and fog during the winter. This very same fog shrouds San Francisco and is caused by hot air from the continent meeting colder oceanic masses.

Urbanization and its Consequences

Other than the capital of Sacramento, which is located in the interior, the majority of the population lives on the coast. San Diego, San Francisco and Los Angeles are the largest urban centres with respective populations of 2 million, 3.2 million and 11 million inhabitants, the latter coming in second after New York as largest U.S. city.

A stream of immigrants in search of a better life invades California every year. Having increased by 26% between 1980 and 1990, the population is expected to reach 38 million by 2010. However, the net increase in population is not the greatest challenge facing authorities. The problem lies in the density of the population in urban centres and the resulting urban sprawl. Moreover, this urban and often well-to-do population frequently subscribes

to a whirlwind of consumerism where quality of life does not necessarily go hand-in-hand with energy conservation. As one of the most urbanized states in the United States, the urban population in California increases at a phenomenal rate. About eight out of every 10 Californians live in a city. Not to mention the fact that, because of the climate, Californians have the unfortunate habit of flocking to Southern California, an arid environment where living conditions are not well suited to sustain large populations. Consequently, numerous engineering projects have been set in motion, to build dams and aqueducts which collect water flowing from the northern mountains to supply populations in the south, entailing all the imaginable consequences on the environment. Avid city-dwellers also have to be housed and fed. The result is the overexploitation of forests, overgrazing and the urbanization of zones endowed with a rich agricultural potential. Finally, all these city residents have to get around, leading to air and ground pollution caused by the construction of endless highways and the almost religious use of energy-consuming automobiles. California includes a network of over 161,556mi (260,000km) of highways and roads, more than six and a half

times the circumference of the Earth!

Fortunately, state authorities have implemented a series of policies to protect the environment. But California has yet to catch up with the rest of the country in such matters, and the American Dream surely won't die any time soon.

Portrait

Flora

Adapted to the ecosystems of the territory, Californian flora is extremely diversified. More than 40% of the country's wild plants are indigenous to California. From the coasts, forests and deserts to the alpine regions, you'll see a tremendous variety of vegetation.

The special charm of Northern California is generally attributed to its immense conifer forests. Legendary **sequoias**, **great pines** and **Douglas firs** grow along the Coast Range and Sierra Nevada. Dating back to prehistoric times, sequoias are gigantic evergreen coniferous trees with a very distinctive red bark, which can grow up to 20ft (6m) in diameter. Known as the biggest trees on the face of the earth, these giants prefer the inland to the coast and can live for several hundreds of years in favourable conditions. For their part, the pines

Sequoia

are more modest in size and are more comfortable in the salty ocean air on the western side of the Coast Range. Here, they mix with Douglas firs, another coniferous tree of inordinate dimensions.

The coast and southern mountains welcome a more sparse, tropical vegetation called **chaparral**. Its bushes and shrubs enter a period of dormancy during the hot and dry season but explode in a rapid growth spurt after forest fires thanks to bulbs located in their roots that react to high temperatures. **Eucalyptuses** and **umbrella pines**, species which are characteristic to tropical regions, also grow on this poor and arid soil.

Sparse forests of **oaks** compose the scenery in the valleys. Having to survive in difficult conditions, the trees maintain a fair distance between one another since they must extract their nutritive elements from a poor soil. Another distinctive element of these vast expanses, the ubiquitous **herbaceous species** gorge themselves on water and proudly display their rich green colour in summer, but dramatically turn golden yellow in winter.

Finally, plant species have magnificently adapted to the extreme conditions found in the unavoidable Californian desert. Species like the **creosotebush**, which is endowed with strong, waxy leaves and a pungent odour, have roots that extend deep into the earth to draw on water reserves. This is also the case for the **Joshua tree**,

which, contrary to popular belief, does not uniquely grow in Joshua Tree National Park but also in the Mojave Desert. Its very particular name originates from the first Mormon immigrants who, upon seeing this tree, likened it to Joshua welcoming them to the Promised Land.

Ocotillo

Although it's typically found in southern deserts, the **ocotillo** plant with its long, willowy, dried-up branches doesn't look like it can survive the aridity of the environment. Yet as soon as a few drops of rain fall from the sky, the seemingly lifeless branches suddenly and miraculously burst into bloom. Another native desert species, the vibrantly coloured **cholla** cactus stores water in its spongy and fatty tissues, and is surrounded by a luminous halo. Unfortunate herbivores beware! This cactus is armed with extremely sharp thorns. Last but not least, made famous by countless westerns, the **tumbleweed** is a type of amaranth originally from Europe that forms resistant balls of branches fixed to the ground by a fragile stem which is broken by desert winds. And so the tumbleweed rolls,

blowing across the dusty streets of towns in the Far West.

Fauna

Like its flora, California's fauna is rich and diversified. Sadly, many species have disappeared over the course of generations or are seriously threatened by the increasing human population and consequent pressure on the environment. Fortunately, thanks to governmental "green" policies, a number of seriously threatened species have been successfully reintroduced into their natural habitat.

The coast and humid zones are home to many feathered species, such as the **pelican**, **goose**, **mallard**, **heron**, **ibis** and **swan**. Sadly, pelicans are threatened by the use of pesticides along the coast which have contaminated fish stocks, the main source of food for these large waterfowl. Other types of birds have had their vital space strongly limited by urbanization, the draining of humid zones and dam construction.

At first glance, you might not think that the desert is conducive to the development of animal life. However, many species have succeeded in adapting to such arid conditions. Hardy representatives of these animals, mostly furtive and nocturnal, include the **lynx**, **coyote**, **hare**, **kangaroo rat**, **snake** and **lizard**.

Numbering only 27 individuals in captivity in 1987, **condors** have almost completely disappeared from the Californian landscape. To ward off the frequent attacks on their livestock by valley coyotes, farmers used poisoned meat as bait. But the condor, a well-known carrion eater, was attracted to these pieces of red meat and became an unsuspecting victim of the eradication campaign. Fortunately, biologists have been able to reintroduce the condor into its natural habitat and preserve this species whose 10ft (3m) wingspan is the greatest of any bird in North America.

Formerly found everywhere except in the desert, the **grizzly bear** was once the symbol of California but has since completely disappeared from the territory. The last local representative of this species is said to have been hunted down in 1922. Another member of the Ursidae family, **black bears** proliferate high in the Sierra Nevada between 2,953 and 7874ft (900 and 2,400m).

On the verge of extinction at the turn of the 20th century, numerous species of **deer** once again wander in the valleys and mountains of California thanks to stringent protection policies and rehabilitation programs.

Although rarely encountered by visitors, **pumas** still inhabit the Central Valley. However, disturbed by the extensive human development infringing on its habitat, this feline has become increasingly aggressive, and a few dramatic deadly accidents have occurred in recent years.

With its hundreds of miles of coast, California inevitably features a wealth of marine life. **Walruses**, **seals**, **sea lions**, **otters** and **whales** live in an environment that still isn't entirely free of problems related to human activities. Grey whales can be observed in several places along the coast during their winter migration to the warmer waters of Baja California, Mexico. If you don't have the opportunity to see these spectacular sea mammals in their natural habitat, you can admire them in several zoos in coastal cities.

History

In the Beginning

Before the arrival of the first Europeans, as is the case with many great U.S. spaces, Native American peoples had already been living on the land that would become California for thousands of years. After crossing the Bering Strait during a major period of glaciation some 20,000 years before, these first nations originating from the confines of Siberia led a peaceful life and formed a Pacific community devoid of social classes. When the first explorers from the other side of the Atlantic arrived, several hundreds of

Pumas

Native Americans inhabited the territory of present-day California, communicating in about 300 different dialects. Unfortunately, very little is known about these first inhabitants of the land, and estimates of their numbers when the first conquerors landed remain imprecise. However, most historians agree that between 200,000 and 300,000 indigenous people populated this land which was fertile and abounding with game, though still arid and inhospitable. The majority of Native Americans hunted, fished and gathered, and their nomadism partly explains the limited number of objects found that could help shed light on the lifestyle of these first peoples. For them, the arrival of the Europeans was only the beginning of a long and painful period marked by harsh treatment, slavery and deadly epidemics.

Early European Expeditions

The European saga in California began on September 28, 1542, when Portuguese explorer Juan Rodríguez Cabrillo, working for the Spanish navy, landed on the shores of San Diego Bay. This adventurer was originally in search of gold, precious spices and, of course, the Strait of Anian said to provide a rapid passage from the Atlantic to the Pacific. A few years earlier, fellow conquistadors had been the first to land on the peninsula of Baja California and claim it for the Spanish crown. Upon their arrival, these Spaniards believed they were *on* California, a mysterious and idyllic island covered in gold and precious stones which was described in 1510 by author García Ordóñez de Montalvo in his novel *La Sergas de Esplandián*. Therefore, these emissaries sent by Hernán Cortéz simply gave it the same name—California. For their part, Cabrillo and his men set foot on the actual territory of California, but set off again without even founding a village. In the same vein, English explorer Sir Francis Drake reached the shores of San Francisco Bay in 1579, took possession of the land in the name of sovereign Elizabeth I and christened it Nova Alvus. Just like his Spanish-Portuguese predecessor, he departed from the region without leaving the least trace of colonization.

In 1602, the Spaniard Sebastián Vizcaíno pushed the exploration of this land a little further and navigated along the Pacific coast for many long weeks. Sundry actual names, such as San Diego, Monterey, Santa Barbara and Carmel, show signs of the explorer's sojourn here, since he baptized a number of natural sites as he made his way along the coast. However, because the Spanish crown still manifested very little interest in these lands so far from the motherland, Vizcaíno and his men returned to Spain, bringing with them maps and log books, but without having introduced any form of colonization.

The Spanish Period

It wasn't until the second half of the 18th century that Spain began to consider the strategic importance of Californian land. Already possessing the Philippines colony in the Pacific for over 200 years, Spanish navigators saw the natural ports meticulously described by Vizcaíno as favourable areas to pull into port during their numerous and exhausting expeditions around Cape Horn. What's more, the Spanish crown frowned upon the increasing presence of the English in the Pacific region and the installation of fur-trading posts by the Russians who shuttled between Californian lands and their colonies in Alaska in the north. The time had come for the Spanish to settle down in California and colonize the land that was still only populated by Native Americans. But as was the custom of the day, colonization was synonymous with evangelization. Hence, it wasn't surprising that the Spanish crown designated a Franciscan priest, Juníperro Serra, to head this mission on Californian soil. Aided by a military man, Gaspar de Portolá, the Catholic priest was given the clear mandate to evangelize the "barbaric" tribes and establish permanent settlements.

In 1769, Father Serra founded the first Catholic mission on Californian soil, San Diego de Alcala,

which would much later become the big city we know today as San Diego. Missions were comprised of a modest wooden chapel surrounded by a few shacks that served as dwellings. These missions soon became important centres of community life for Spanish settlers and recently converted Native Americans. Subject to attacks by other Native Americans nations who rejected the European presence, the missions required military protection and Gaspar de Portolá erected the first *presidios*, groups of fortified barracks, administrative buildings and warehouses for munitions and supplies. The very first of these defensive groups was built on the actual site of Monterey in 1770.

By 1823, a string of 21 missions was established along the Californian coastline, from San Diego to Sonoma, linked by a meandering dirt road called El Camino Real (the royal road), which roughly corresponds to the current US 101. This was how the San Francisco de Asis and Los Angeles de Porciuncula missions were founded in 1776 and 1781 respectively. These missions enjoyed peaceful times for over a century until a demographic boom turned them into the huge metropolitan centres that we now know them as. Small Native American and Spanish towns, called *pueblos*, formed along this major artery; large estates, the *ranchos*, were granted to settlers to raise livestock. The Franciscans, aided by Native Americans who converted to the Catholic faith, the loyal *vaqueros*, were the most important ranchers until the Mexican Revolution.

Strangely enough, the first cowboys were in fact... "Indians"!

Mexican Revolution and U.S. Takeover

The Mexican Revolution in 1821 represents an important date in the history of California. Once the former colony was free, it cut off all links with its former motherland, Spain, and appropriated all its possessions. This was how the new Mexican leaders made official the annexation of Upper California and Lower California to their new country. Opposing the revolutionary ideas of the Mexican authorities, the Franciscans abandoned their missions in the U.S. to return to Spain, but not before destroying all their buildings, leaving nothing for the new masters. As early as 1833, missions were dismantled and deconsecrated and the vast pieces of land that belonged to the Franciscans were handed over to those occupying positions of power.

Although California was now under Mexican protection, the Americans, English and Russians continued to show interest in this far-reaching territory and began to analyze the strategic and economic potential of the region. Concerned about expanding and strengthening the Union, countering the expansionist designs of the English who were already in Oregon, and isolating the Russian colony Fort Ross north of San Francisco, President Andrew Jackson offered Mexican authorities $300,000 to purchase the coveted territory in 1830. The offer was refused. In spite of this, thousands of pioneers left the central and eastern regions of the country to settle down next to the Pacific. Although attracted to the fertile land of the Central Valley, they were more encouraged to migrate by the concept of Manifest Destiny. This almost religious doctrine was very popular at the time, and stipulated that it was necessary, good and right for the United States to colonize all the territories in North America. First by sea—the Sierra Nevada and deserts were deemed insurmountable—then by land, entire families came to colonize the Mexican pieces of land, some going as far as to offer to buy the vast domains on the former Franciscan property.

Jedediah Strong Smith had the honour of being the first settler to reach California by land, shortening the three-month sea expedition around Cape Horn by several weeks. Leaving St-Louis, Missouri in 1826, he crossed the Sierra Nevada and reached the Californian coast, opening the way for thousands of pioneers who, in the 1830s and 1840s, travelled thousands of miles through hostile regions on board strange-looking wagons full of supplies, personal objects, even livestock. If most succeeded this arduous journey, others were not so fortunate and died along the way, such as the 47 unfortunate souls of the Donner Expedition who, in 1846-1847, remained prisoners of the snowed-in mountains of the Sierra Nevada. Miraculously, resorting to cannibalism saved 40 members. Johann (or John) Sutter is certainly the most famous of the lucky adventurers. Originating from Switzerland, he settled down in California in 1839, bought a domain of 62,000 acres (25,000ha) in the Sacramento Valley and then founded New Helvetia. Nine years later, a significant event in Californian history would immortalize him...

In 1845, expansionist president James Polk snatched Texas from Mexico and unilaterally declared its annexation to the Union. By the same token, under increasing pressure from the population, he offered $40,000,000 to buy California. For a second time, the Mexican government refused, but the affront was too great and the United States's will, too strong. Already embittered by the conflict in Texas, the two countries embarked on a territorial war in 1846, a confrontation that ended with the defeat of Mexico after two years of intermittent fighting. On February 2, 1848, the Guadalupe Hidalgo Treaty officially handed over to the victors all Mexican territory north of the Rio Grande: New Mexico, Arizona and, of course, California. After bitter negotiations, Mexico managed to keep the peninsula of Baja California, and the border between the two countries was drawn south of San Diego.

The Gold Rush...

A few weeks before the 1848 treaty signing, an employee on one of John Sutter's properties, James Marshall, made a stunning discovery in the American River that would inflame all of California: gold nuggets! Sutter tried to keep this discovery secret for a while, out of fear of potential dramatic repercussions for his possessions, but his men were too excited to keep quiet. Some began to show off their small booty in the

Portrait

A Brief History

1542
Serving in the Spanish navy, Portuguese explorer Juan Rodríguez Cabrillo lands on the shores of San Diego Bay.

1579
English explorer Sir Francis Drake first sets foot on the shores of San Francisco Bay.

1602
Spanish explorer Sebastián Vizcaíno presses on a little further, following the Pacific Coast.

1769
With the help of Gaspar de Portolá, the Spanish Fransiscan priest Juníperro Serra founds the Catholic mission of San Diego de Alcala, the first on Californian soil.

1770
The first presidio is erected in Monterey.

1776
Founding of San Francisco de Asis.

1781
Founding of Los Angeles de Porciuncula.

1821
Mexico becomes independent. California is under the jurisdiction of the new nation.

1826
Jedediah Strong Smith leaves Saint Louis, Missouri and crosses the Sierra Nevada, becoming the first person to reach California by land.

1833
Franciscan missions are disbanded and secularized.

1846
Beginning of the territorial war between Mexico and the US.

1848
Mexico is defeated. Under the Treaty of Guadalupe Hidalgo, New Mexico, Arizona and California fall to the United States.

James Marshall, an employee of John Sutter, discovers the first gold nuggets in the American River.

1849
The gold rush begins. Arrival of more than 55,000 prospectors, known as the "Forty-niners."

1850
California becomes the 31st state to join the Union.

1869
The transcontinental railroad is inaugurated.

1876
The coastal line of the Southern Pacific railroad is built.

1885
The coastal line of the Santa Fe railroad is built.

1906
The great San Francisco earthquake practically destroys the city.

1915
San Francisco's Panama Pacific International Exhibition marks the city's reconstruction, as well as the opening of the famous Panama Canal several months before.

1920
This is the decade marking the beginning of the great era of Hollywood film.

1965
Racial riots break out in Los Angeles's Watts district.

1967
San Fransisco's hippie movement proclaims this year the "Summer of Love."

1992
Fifty people lose their lives in the Los Angeles race riots.

1998
The election of Governor Gray David marks the Democrats' return to power after a 12-year interval.

town shops. This was all that was needed to launch one of the most fantastic and euphoric periods in the history of California: the gold rush! Not just an isolated stroke of luck, the gold nuggets Marshall found really belonged to a gold-bearing vein, known as the Mother Lode, measuring over 118mi long (190km). The news spread like wildfire across the continent and beyond the U.S. borders. Hoping to find Eldorado, thousands of people from every walk of life came from all over the U.S. In addition, to German, French, Italian and even Chinese adventurers flocked to Northern California in droves for years to come. But only the first to arrive, nicknamed the forty-niners were able to fulfill their dreams. The rush started in 1849 and attracted 55,000 newcomers that very year. However, from 1850 on, the remaining deposits were often located in deep mines which could only be accessed by the heavy and costly equipment of big mining companies. More often than not, poor gold prospectors in search of fortune ended up simple employees of one of the big businesses. At the peak of the rush, between 1849 and 1851, an estimated 300,000 people came to Northern California. Although 1853 was the beginning of the end of this extraordinary period, transformations to the state's social and economic landscape were irreversible.

... and its Consequences

Facing the unfolding events, U.S. authorities made California the 31st state of the Union in 1850. San Jose was designated as the capital, but would be replaced four years later by Sacramento.

Even though the gold rush ended in the 1850s, California was now a rich and well-populated state. Heavenly images of the region with its fertile land, high standards of living and mild climate continued to attract numerous newcomers, market gardeners, vine growers and, of course, simple tourists. All this movement in population and merchandise

dramatically emphasized the state's transportation shortcomings. Indeed, even though the legendary Pony Express had provided mail delivery by stage coach since 1860 as well as transportation services for passengers, it took at least 10 days to get from San Francisco to St. Louis. Not to mention that shipping merchandise by sea took forever. This favourable context caused the Union Pacific and Central Pacific railway companies to unite and create an ambitious railroad project to link Sacramento, California to Omaha in the Midwest by passing through the majestic Sierra Nevada. Benefiting from the support of political authorities wanting to strengthen the Union after the devastating American Civil War, the impossible project saw the light of day in 1869. After years of hard work, the East and West were finally brought together. The construction of the southern lines of Southern Pacific and Santa Fe Railroad, in 1876 and 1885 respectively, encouraged development in Southern California which, until then, had been fairly limited. Previously a peaceful little town, Los Angeles saw its population

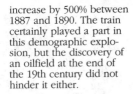

Gold rush statue

increase by 500% between 1887 and 1890. The train certainly played a part in this demographic explosion, but the discovery of an oilfield at the end of the 19th century did not hinder it either.

A Euphoric Start to the 20th Century

The 20th century confirmed the mythical and idyllic character of California but did not, however, get off to a good start. On April 18, 1906, the San Francisco earthquake killed 452 people and left nearly 300,000 homeless. But the inhabitants, proud descendants of the first pioneers, kept their chins up and rebuilt, brick by brick, their devastated city. In 1915, to underline the reconstruction of the city, in addition to the opening of the famous Panama Canal a few months before, a huge celebration was organized: the Panama Pacific International Exhibition.

From that year on, the New York-based movie industry left the East Coast and moved to the Los Angeles region. The steady flow of money and the very mild climate attracted the first studios who, as early as the 1920s, created the world's first Hollywood movie stars. The Californian dream continued. In fact, it was this dream, projected onto the silver screen in a big way, that attracted thousands of country dwellers fleeing the arid and sterile plains of the Midwest during the Great Depression in the 1930s. Just like Steinbeck's heroes, they came looking for a better life, but the road to happiness was unfortunately studded with difficulties for many of them. All these factors, coupled with an inflow of Mexican immigrants during the revolutionary years from 1910 to 1921, created a demographic boom exceeding 60% in the 1920s and 1930s, twice as much as in the rest of the country.

The Second World War also had important repercussions. Soldiers, military factory workers and war services agents moved to towns along the coast and many decided to stay once peace returned. Consequently, the population increased by 53% in the 1940s and again by 49% in the following decade.

The post-war years spurred a considerable growth, anarchical some would say, in urban development. Where the discovery of gold and the movie industry had a major impact on the development of California, it was the advent and subsequent proliferation of the automobile that revolutionized its urban landscape. Symbol of wealth and success, the car became a true object of worship and oriented future urban-planning policies. Responding to the needs of a relatively well-to-do population that was tired of big cities, suburbs multiplied and urban sprawl surfaced in the 1950s. Innumerable endless highways were built in this state apparently ruled by the car. Residential development often followed the construction of a fast lane that literally dictated the road. Like many other places, California enjoyed periods of growth and expansion where consumerism and material comfort were utmost. And yet...

The Flower Children

The Beatniks of the 1950s paved the way for the baby boomers who took up the cause at the end of the 1960s, clamouring for social change. Born into an era of prosperity, these children were the products of a comfortable middle class, but rejected the values of their parents, following instead the example of Timothy Leary by experimenting with drugs and abandoning their studies to enjoy the bohemian life. This pacifist hippie movement, which viewed love as a source of liberation, reached its height when the colourful residents of San Francisco's Haight-Ashbury district proclaimed the summer of 1967 as the "Summer of Love." The flower children, who, more often than not, lived wild and carefree lives in communes, envisioned a world without war and condemned U.S. military involvement in the Vietnam War, among other issues. Their anti-military stance was summed up in their slogan "Flower Power"—symbolized by a flower placed in the barrel of a gun. Still, with the new left wing gaining ground, the increasingly militant opposition to the Vietnam War and the emergence of the Black Panther protest movement, the ideology of "flower power" and non-violence suddenly seemed naïve. The loss of cult artists like Jim Morrison, Janis Joplin and Jimi Hendrix, whose names were associated with both disillusionment and excess, brought about the death of the movement at the beginning of the 1970s.

Countercultures

On the fringe of this consumerism frenzy, writers, artists and intellectuals of all sexual orientations from all around the country and the world gathered in this welcoming land. Congregating in different regions according to their affinities and lifestyles, they brooded over a world that seemed to turn too quickly for them and founded a movement that preached a return to basic values. This was the birth of the beatnik movement which, with leaders like Jack Kerouac and Allen Ginsberg, blossomed in North Beach, near San Francisco. Going against the current, this intellectual movement inspired the following generation in its quest for happiness and rejection of its parents' society. In came the hippie period which, with Timothy Leary as guru, advocated love and drugs as sources of liberation. "Flower power" was on everyone's lips. Mostly congregating in the Haight-Ashbury neighbourhood of San Francisco, this protest generation decreed the summer of 1967 the "summer of love." It openly defied the authorities and strongly denounced the U.S.'s military involvement in Vietnam. Although it communicated laudable values, this movement nonetheless lost its momentum at the turn of the decade after suffering numerous disillusions and falling victim to its own abuses.

Racial Tensions

Heavenly, liberal and tolerant on the surface, California remains a fragmental and rather conservative society in which several poles cohabitate uneasily, which sometimes results in open clashes. Dualities, such as rich-poor, White-Black and English-Hispanic, are strongly anchored, and dialog between groups can be difficult. History shows that these tensions are not new and that they go as far back as the 19th century, when anti-Chinese demonstrations took place in San Francisco in the crises years of the 1870s. During the Great Depression, Mexican immigrants, tolerated until then, were considered a nuisance and abruptly sent home, packed in wagons like livestock. The years of war when the United States confronted Japan in the Pacific revived latent anti-Asian sentiments. More recently, the black civil rights movement, which was very active in the 1960s, derailed and led to racial uprising that culminated in violence. You need only think back to riots in the Watts district

of Los Angeles in 1965 or the events in 1992 during which 50 people lost their life in clashes with law enforcement agents in the same city. Finally, there is the eternal tension with illegal Spanish-speaking immigrants who, for many Californian Anglo-Saxons, represent a threat and considerable economic burden. As idyllic as it may seem, California is far from being immune to the tensions that stir the rest of the world.

Politics

Colonial Political System

Under the yoke of the Spanish, California already benefited from a complex political system. Power was divided into three sections that controlled all-important aspects of colonial life. Firstly, the colonial administration that managed daily affairs lay with the Franciscan religious community. With the mission system, these great landowners exerted a religious power of an administrative nature. Secondly, civil power was attributed to a governor who was named by the viceroy in Mexico who, in turn, was appointed by the Spanish sovereign. As for the third section of power, the military was ruled by a commanding officer who resided in *presidios*, groups of barracks dedicated to the defence of the territory. The implementation of this system dated back to 1777 with the creation of the first *pueblos*, colonial municipal entities controlled by the new capital, Monterey. It wasn't until 1779 that the first laws that governed the territory for a

few decades were established.

The Mexican Revolution and the annexation of California to revolutionary Mexico obviously put an end to this system. Despite California officially becoming a Mexican territory in 1824, fierce resistance by influential U.S. and European *rancheros* forced the Mexican authorities to reconsider introducing a new system that would upset politics in the region. After a period of hesitation, the Mexican-American War began in 1846, and California was annexed to the Union two years later.

California, U.S. State

After the official creation of the State of California, 31st star on the U.S. banner, the present-day political institutions were instituted and a constitution was signed in 1879. Like the Union's 49 other states, Californians have two levels of government: the state controls daily affairs while the federal government oversees national business like defence and foreign affairs. Both levels operate similarly in the executive and legislative spheres.

At the federal level, executive power is given to the president who is elected for a four-year term by the electoral college—in other words, a body of representational voters that proportionally represents each state based on the number of representatives and senators. At the regional level, executive power goes to the governor of the state who is elected by universal suffrage. The two major federal parties, the Republicans and the Democrats, battle at the regional level. For the first time since 1986, California has a Democrat governor, Mr. Gray David, who was elected in 1998.

As for the legislative power, California, like all the other states, is represented by two senators in the Senate and 52 deputies in the House of Representatives, a number determined in proportion to the state's population. The Senate and the House of Representatives form the Congress, a bicameral entity that holds the legislative reins in the nation's capital, Washington. At the state level, Californian citizens elect the 40 senators and 80 members of the Legislative Assembly by universal suffrage; the latter also holds bicameral legislative power but pays special attention to issues that closely affect the population.

California's considerable demographic weight has allowed it to play an important role in presidential elections, especially since the 1950s. Its important contribution to the formation of the electoral college has enabled it to promote the candidacy and election of two Republican presidents from California in the past 20 years: Richard Nixon (1968 to 1974) and Ronald Reagan (1981-1989).

Tendencies of the Electorate

Associated with the traditional inclinations of the two main parties, the conservative Republicans and the more liberal Democrats, the Californian vote appears divided. On the one side, the older, white middle class, composed of families who arrived in the 19th century and of elderly people who came to California for the mild climate, usually support the first. Principally grouped in the southern part of the state, mainly around Los Angeles, this vote contrasts with the more liberal voice of Northern California. Having as its fief the city of San Francisco, forever reputed for its open-mindedness, the Democrats enjoy a strong support from the young and not-so- young with marginal and non-conformist ideas, vaguely reminiscent of the counterculture movements of the 1950s and 1960s. Because of its demographic weight, the conservatism of voters in the South generally manifests itself in the elected representation.

If voters take few risks at the federal and regional polls, municipal elections are often a different story. Here, the vote can be very audacious, leading to disparaging, sometimes violent movements. For instance, in 1977, San Francisco elected Harvey Milk, the first openly gay advisor; the following year, he was murdered by a homophobe. Although not going so far as to provoke bloodshed, ferocious opposition often surfaces in communities who elect African- American or Hispanic mayors. Some movie stars have embarked on a career in politics and succeeded in holding the reins of their town. Clint Eastwood, mayor of Carmel from 1986 to 1988, is the best example, not to mention Ronald Reagan, former B-movie actor turned state governor and then U.S. president.

Direct Democracy

The importance of individual rights in Californian society has led to the development of a widespread form of direct democracy where the referendum is king. Any citizen who has collected 5% of the population's support can submit a proposal to the government, which then presents it to the electors at the polls. Added to the Californian constitution in 1911, direct democracy can involve big stakes, such as the construction of a dam, or smaller, rather insignificant debates like obligatory collars for dogs. Despite this procedure, which implies that voters sometimes have dozens of boxes to tick off on their ballot, most of the important legislation is established by the government and does not reflect the results of a referendum. In the 1990s, a couple of proposals stirred the population, among others. These two were proposals 187 and 209, viewed by some as xenophobic in character. In proposal 187, all social services were forbidden to illegal immigrants. Proposal 209 stipulated that all preferential treatment be removed from State programs and employment in fields such as public education, for example. After the University of California applied this proposal, the number of admissions from Hispanic and Asian minority groups fell dramatically the following year...

Economics

On the economic front, California has very little to envy of the major industrialized countries. Its vitality and diversity in all sectors—the exploitation and transformation of raw materials or the services sector, for example—give it an extremely advantageous position in the world arena. If California was a sovereign country, it would rank ahead of Canada and slightly behind France with regards to its gross national product (GNP) which, per capita, is one of the highest in the world. Several factors explain the remarkable economic performances that have resulted in California contributing to 13% of the U.S.'s gross national product (GNP). First of all, the incredible growth brought by the gold rush created fabulous wealth which, since this period of effervescence, has evolved into powerful dynasties. Contrary to what you might think, it wasn't the valorous and adventurous gold prospectors who struck it rich during this period; rather it was the merchants and entrepreneurs who, upon seeing this golden opportunity, invested capital and lent equipment to support the exploitation. California, as much for its climate as for its economic vitality, has always attracted young and dynamic people determined to make their dreams come true in this new promised land. This continuous inflow of an often highly qualified workforce is the mainstay of an innovative economy. Providing a solid foundation for this economic power, universities shape the rising generation and are always on the lookout for new ideas; thanks to their research centres, they are leading the way in making today's dreams tomorrow's realities. If human beings contribute substantially to California's dynamism, the land has also been very generous to its inhabitants. The rich and fertile valleys have always more than adequately nourished the population and today play a vital role in the inner workings of the state's economy. Finally, California is lucky to have a most strategic geographic situation. In a world where international exchanges are becoming increasingly important, its position on the Pacific Rim, proximity to Latin American countries, and especially to the Asian market with its enormous potential, once again favours this territory which seems blessed with every imaginable advantage.

Environmental Stakes

Immigration is not the only issue weighing on the minds of Californians. Since the 1960s, residents have been concerned about the environment, which has been stressed by the presence of human development. Though California's legislation is among the strictest in the country, it will still take the state a long time to catch up, and the obstacles will be difficult to surmount. Under pressure from well-organized citizens groups, officials have established a number of parks and nature preserves, and are attempting to control the ongoing smog problem, to regulate development along the coast and to manage the water supply, one of the greatest challenges in the years to come. Water management proved to be a critical and thorny issue at the end of the 19th century, when the Wright Act of 1887 regulated irrigation in the Central Valley. The development of coastal cities, in near desert conditions, keeps this serious problem in the spotlight for governments from Sacramento to Washington. It is sure to determine California's social, environmental and economic future.

Agricultural Production

Leading the way in the United States in terms of production, as well as types of harvests, California has over 8 million acres (3.2 million ha) of cultivable land. A favourable climate, rich soil and an extensive land-irrigation system have allowed the state to take the lead in this sector of the economy. Over 200 different crops grow in California. Half of all fruits and vegetables consumed in the United States come from California, whether it be the Central Valley, Salinas Valley or other fertile stretches of land in the southeastern part of the state. Especially renowned for their citrus fruits and vines (the famous Navel oranges and Napa valley

wines), farmers intensively cultivate sugar beet, cotton and rice as well. In addition, all of the country's artichokes, almonds, dates, figs, kiwis, olives and pistachios grow on Californian soil. And on the high non-irrigated plateaus where large-scale cultivation is difficult, livestock is raised.

Despite all this, the agricultural domain is not without its share of major challenges looming in the future. Steep demographic growth in urban centres, which continue to spread beyond control, poses a serious threat to fertile lands in the Central Valley. Driven by productivity demands, farmers must increasingly turn to new production technologies and the massive use of chemical fertilizers, causing other harmful consequences on the environment.

Natural Resources

Natural resources are another area in which California has been blessed by the gods, and have been a driving force in the economy from day one. For that matter, was it not gold mines in the north followed by the discovery of oilfields in the south that spurred an extraordinary growth and shaped modern-day California? Although there only remain a few opencast goldmines and oil supplies must be exploited at great cost on oil rigs at sea, these two sectors have created powerful enterprises, notably the Standard Oil Co., which have a strong impact on the economic and financial landscape of the country. Nowadays, industries are turning to natural gas, silver and other more

prosaic minerals like sand, gravel and borates.

Once very important but now losing speed, the forestry industry is still an important cog in the state's economic wheel. Hard hit by overexploitation and deforestation, coupled with mounting pressure from ecological groups, this industry nonetheless ranks second after Oregon in terms of production and provides the country with one tenth of its wood cuttings. Commercial fishing of salt-water fish and seafood, in which California is the nation's leader, also suffers from overexploitation and fish stocks are dwindling.

Transportation Industry

Having on average the greatest number of vehicles per inhabitant in the entire United States, California is a paradise for the automotive industry. All the major companies in Michigan, such as Daimler-Chrysler, Ford and General Motors, operate factories or research centres here as well. The West Coast's presence in the Pacific Rim has led to the construction of Japanese car factories in California. What's more, hundreds of thousands of Japanese and Korean vehicles exported to the United States transit through Californian ports.

Aeronautics

The aeronautics industry dates back to the inter-war years when venturesome companies turned up in California and found a favourable climate all year long for test flights, plenty of capital as well as a qualified workforce. During the Second World War, the military industry gained the upper hand on more traditional businesses like General Dynamics, Dominion Douglas and Lockheed, which had dominated until that time. Fruits of the U.S. war efforts, the new industries profited from the post-war boom and began manufacturing missiles, rockets, satellites and other types space equipment. Still, the end of U.S.-Soviet tensions created a transition period for the aeronautics industry. After suffering massive job losses, companies are now increasingly reorienting themselves towards civil production.

Software and State-of-the-Art Technology

In the eyes of the entire world, California is synonymous with Silicon Valley, a hotbed of high-tech companies that mould tomorrow's world. Once a simple orchard in the Santa Clara Valley, this territory embodies the Californian success story and counts over 13,000 high-tech industries including famous names like Microsoft and Apple. With its luxurious buildings and wealthy companies flanked by parking lots filled with gleaming cars, this valley in the Coast Range, southeast of San Francisco, exudes success and money. Because of the explosion of the Internet and new means of communication, Silicon Valley will certainly remain a spearhead in this industry which is in full expansion and comparable to the gold rush. Point of interest: such companies prepare the young blood and invest in leading-edge research centres, the most renowned being the

California Institute of Technology in Pasadena and Stanford University in Palo Alto.

Film and Television

Formerly a quiet suburb of Los Angeles, Hollywood has become the Mecca of U.S. and international movies since the 1920s. Generating astronomical profits of several billion dollars per year, the film-making business in Hollywood sustains half of the major productions in the United States. Now intimately linked with this industry, the CBS television network has associated itself with major studios that supply it with state-of-the-art equipment, seasoned technicians and stars whose faces are familiar to the general public, in its battle against its New York rival, ABC.

Tourism

Lured by the wonderful Mediterranean climate, endless beaches coated with fine sand, remarkable natural attractions and surprising cities, millions of foreign and local visitors travel the roads of California every year. Tourist infrastructures are everywhere, in the deserts, in the mountains or along the coast, and provide jobs for hundreds of thousands of people. Every year, the State of California attracts about 50 million U.S. and foreign visitors, who spend over 60 billion dollars, making it the most visited state in the U.S.

Population

Since its first colonial settlements in the mid-18th century, California has

Hollywood: the Stuff of Legend

The origins of U.S. cinema date back to the first decade of the 20th century. Independent directors in New York produced the first works in this medium, which was just taking its first tentative steps. All films were shot outside at the time, so production was forced to stop in winter because of the weather. Determined to gain control of this new industry, which was already raking in healthy profits, the mafia began to harass small producers so they could buy out their businesses and take over. As a result, some producers left the East Coast in search of a more favourable climate, where they would be safely out of the grasp of organized crime, and where the weather would allow them to shoot year-round. In 1911, David Horsley rented (for $30 a month) the Blondeau Tavern, located at the corner of Sunset Boulevard and Gower Street, set in the peaceful rural suburb of Hollywood. Here he produced The Law of the Range, the first Hollywood film to be shot in a studio. Other entrepreneurs recognized the possibilities of this new location and founded production studios on Sunset Boulevard. Hollywood's legendary reputation was born.

always been a popular choice for millions of people in search of a better life. All the significant periods in its history have provoked the massive arrival of foreigners who today compose a diverse and heterogeneous population in this land of contradictions and extremes.

It seems as if California was created to make people dream. No other land has fascinated and attracted foreigners to such an extent. The epic began some 250 years ago when the first Spanish settlers set up camp near the Franciscan missions and established the first villages, or *pueblos*. The Spanish-speaking populating continued to thrive with the annexation of the territory by revolutionary Mexico in 1821. In 1848, the loss of California to the Union provoked a wave of immigration from the Eastern U.S., driven by the desire to find fertile lands, but even more so to populate the American West in accordance with the doctrine of Manifest Destiny. The gold rush saw rivers and mines overflow with brave prospectors from the world over, giving rise to an unprecedented demographic explosion. During the roaring years of the gold rush, from 1849 to

1851, the Californian population increased by 565%! Following this, the railroads facilitated the circulation of goods and people from east to west, in addition to bringing in thousands of workers. The Great Depression of the 1930s drove poor peasants from the arid plains of the Midwest to the West Coast. These farmers, who were mainly from Oklahoma —hence their nickname "Okies"—enlarged the population of California, which became the state with the strongest demographic growth in the United States. The success of the movie industry in the 1920s, the post-war aeronautics companies followed by the outburst of software and technology in the 1980s and 1990s also attracted thousands of people in search of the American Dream. Add to this a lovely Mediterranean climate and you'll understand why California currently receives nearly 30% of the country's immigrants.

Close to 90% of the Californian population lives in coastal cities and in the Napa, Santa Clara and San Bernardino valleys of the Coast Range. Mainly because of its milder and dryer climate, the south welcomes more newcomers—well-off retirees, young and dynamic executives as well as legal (or illegal) immigrants from the other side of the Rio Grande. California's heterogeneous population can, however, flare up palpable tension, especially in the Los Angeles district. Land of contrasts and paradoxes, it became a haven of tolerance in the 1950s and 1960s notably on account of its gay population. This now includes nearly 200,000 individuals

in San Francisco, or roughly a quarter of the urban population. However, racial tension and problems related to exclusion and ghettos have sullied relations between the various ethnic groups for several years. Up until the 1960s, when the civil rights movement claimed major victories, minority citizens suffered from institutionalized discrimination. And yet, riots in Los Angeles in the recent years and the incessant tension with Hispanic immigrants reveal the magnitude of the challenges facing this cultural mosaic, of which nearly one third does not speak English at home.

Native Americans

Afflicted by illnesses introduced by the first colonizers in addition to harsh treatment and discrimination practiced by their descendants, the Native American people of California almost disappeared at the turn of the 20th century. When the first Europeans arrived, 300,000 individuals inhabited the land, yet only 58,000 remained at the end of the 19th century. Thanks to policies, eliminating discrimination and reducing assimilation, as well as an increased awareness of the Native American community, California is now the state with the largest number of First Nations' representatives. The Native American population includes 300,000 people, about 1% of the total population of the state.

Asians

Asians of all origins represent nearly 10% of California's population. Although they originate from the

same continent, Californian Asians come from various countries and different backgrounds. Principally encompassing Chinese, Japanese, Vietnamese, Filipinos and Koreans, Asian people came to California throughout different eras, and presently constitute the most expansive group after Hispanic people.

The Chinese, undeniable builders of California, were among the first prospectors in the 1849 gold rush. Driven by the need to quickly find a numerous workforce that was not very demanding with regards to salary or working conditions, the heads of the Central Pacific Railway company chartered whole boats to bring Chinese workers to California. More than 15,000 coolies participated in the creation of the transcontinental railroad, often in miserable conditions that bordered on slavery. Yet these pioneers and builders received very little recognition from the inhabitants of their adopted land. Victims of harassment and sometimes violent discrimination, the Chinese congregated in typical neighbourhoods, such as San Francisco's Chinatown, the largest concentration of the Chinese population in the U.S. More recently, the retrocession of Hong Kong to the People's Republic of China in 1997 provoked a wave of immigration from the former British colony. The climate, economic prosperity, long-standing presence of the Asian community and the feeling of remaining part of the Pacific world influenced their decision to choose California as a refuge.

Arriving in California at the turn of the 20th century, the Japanese had fleeting success in agriculture as early as 1900, but this flourishing period was cut short by the advent of the Second World War. The attack on Pearl Harbour by their former countrymen and the declaration of war by the U.S. government marked the beginning of a difficult period for Japanese-Americans. In 1942, as a result of Executive Order 9066, all Japanese citizens became suspicious and were considered the enemy, even those who were born in the United States. Stripped of all their possessions and interned in prisoner-of-war camps, they were freed only in 1944. The scars took a long time to heal after the war and bitterness riddled the community. Somewhat of a rare occurrence in the U.S., the Japanese isolated themselves from the Anglo-Saxons and formed distinctive neighbourhoods in big cities, notably Japantown in San Francisco and Little Tokyo in Los Angeles. Over the past few years, rich and ambitious Asian newcomers have been flocking to Southern California and taking over the movie industry and high-tech technology.

Fleeing the regimes instituted after conflicts involving the U.S. forces, Koreans and Vietnamese have been increasing California's Asian population since the 1950s. The most substantial wave of immigrants from these two countries victimized by Sino-U.S.-Soviet conflicts arrived in the second half of the 1970s. Fleeing the Communist regime introduced after the U.S. debacle in Vietnam and the dramatic evacuation from Saigon in 1975, thousands of Vietnamese embarked on fragile crafts and sailed for the new land of prom-

ise. Although many died en route, numerous refugees, sadly known as the boat people, reached the shores of the United States. Thanks to their dedication and hard work, this community has become an integral and successful part of this society.

The Filipinos form a particular group. Although they're Asian, they also possess a Spanish legacy that was handed down to them by their former Spanish colonizers. Indeed, this overlap of two cultures would occasionally allow them to bridge the gap between these two communities on Californian soil. Long associated with ungratifying domestic work, Filipinos are now starting to enjoy success in the business world.

Latin-Americans

Today's California cannot deny its Spanish heritage, which is omnipresent in its historical sites and in the names of its cities, towns and natural attractions. This is sweet revenge indeed for a group that saw Mexico bow to the Anglo-Saxon giant in 1848. Massive immigration from countries formerly belonging to the Spanish results in the current Hispanic population that includes 28% of Californians. Two distinct groups form this population: the *Hispanos*, descendants of the first Spanish settlers who remained in California after 1848, and the more numerous *Chicanos*, immigrants from Mexico, Guatemala and Cuba for the most part. The considerable growth of the latter group predicts that within a few decades, over 50% of the Californian population will be of Spanish

origin. This situation worries some Anglo-Saxons who are doing their best to stop the phenomenon of illegal immigration from the other side of the Rio Grande. Although difficult to estimate, about two million illegal immigrants are currently living in miserable conditions resembling shantytowns.

African-Americans

Contrary to other populous states in the U.S., African-Americans in California form only 7% of the population. As free slaves from the Old South, they also attempted to make their fortune during the gold rush in 1849. However, like their unfortunate Asian companions, they were quickly pushed away from the best opportunities. Simple railroad employees, farm hands or workers in military factories, they made California their home despite the open discrimination and racism that they were subjected to. Since the 1960s, thanks to the civil rights movement, the black community has enjoyed a certain social ascension. Today, it isn't uncommon to see a mayor, judge or police chief from this community. Yet, recent racial tensions in Los Angeles show that the majority of African-Americans still live under difficult conditions and need to claim their rightful place in society.

Non-Hispanic Whites

California has invariably attracted scores of adventurers, prospectors, scientists, entrepreneurs, intellectuals and artists from all over the Western world. Italians, Irish, Germans,

French, Russians and even Americans from the U.S.'s East Coast have come here to fulfil their dearest dreams. This diversified group came to California for very different reasons, and non-Hispanic whites represent about 54% of California's population.

Arts and Society

Home to 32.5 million inhabitants, considerable available capital and an inexhaustible number of artists from across the U.S. and around the world, California dominates the world's cultural scene. Responsible for the best and the worst made in America, it represents a microcosm of the U.S. values that forged this complex society—admirable and hateful at all the same time. With California's ability to make people dream like no other place on earth, its artists convey U.S. culture throughout the world. If a movement, fashion or style is born here, you can be sure that it will be copied across the Western world and further still.

Since the end of the First World War, California has proved itself to be a land of predilection, attractive and dreamlike for artists who've found the necessary capital here to realize their wildest ambitions. Less dependent on old traditions than European countries, California has few reference models to guide its artists. This youthfulness has opened creative floodgates and allowed artists to work without restraint. Still, long intimidated by European and even U.S. artists from the East Coast, Californians, in a conscious or unconscious burst of com-

petition, have constantly sought new avenues in the name of continual progress.

In this land of excess where individualism and liberalism rule, it's often difficult to distinguish art and culture on the one hand and industry and finance on the other. Indeed, do we not still refer to the movie "industry" when it is unanimously considered an "art form"? Capital invested into cultural events creates an intimate relationship between these spheres which in turn gives birth to very real, very Californian art forms.

The Californian artistic world is a reflection of its people and places— complex, fragmental, paradoxical, extremist, detestable, admirable and sublime. A complete portrait of all the twists and turns of this endless maze would require a book in itself. Thus, we have humbly limited ourselves to painting a quick portrait of the main realms of cultural activities in which California distinguishes itself, such as movies, literature, music and architecture, with emphasis only on the most significant periods.

Films

Having initially blossomed in New York, most of the film-production business migrated to the West Coast around 1911. Hollywood movies, silent productions at the time, began appearing in Paris, London and Berlin in the late 1920s. The world of cinema already had its figureheads: Charlie Chaplin, Mary Pickford, Douglas Fairbanks Jr. and Rudolf Valentino.

Some consider the period between the 1930s and the 1950s as the golden age of West Coast cinema. Hollywood was projected onto big screens around the world and hallowed as the universal movie capital. Today's impressive system (Academy Awards, world distribution networks and movie theatres owned by studio subsidiaries) began in this era. Colossal production companies (Universal Pictures, Metro-Goldwin-Mayer, Paramount, Twentieth Century Fox and Columbia Pictures) took absolute control of the industry and introduced the star system. Consecrated stars like Bette Davis, Greta Garbo, Marlon Brando, James Dean and Marilyn Monroe not only became untouchables and objects of worship, but true demigods.

Although strict rules and censure prevented the more daring creators from tackling certain taboo subjects until the 1960s, these years gave birth to a whole new generation brimming with innovative ideas. In the wake of social unrest, the 1960s and 1970s witnessed the rise of original and imaginative directors and actors. The likes of Dustin Hoffman, Paul Newman, Jack Nicholson, Robert Altman and Steven Spielberg opened the way to a whole new Hollywood cinema.

Literature

As with film, Californian literature has always conjured up the dream and nourished the mythical element of the West Coast. A pivotal event in history, the gold rush impelled unprecedented hordes of men to find their fortune

On the Road...

After the Second World War, California experienced a period of great economic prosperity accompanied by insatiable consumerism. It is in this affluent context that two young, idealistic students, disheartened by an indifferent New York, left the East Coast and headed to the Pacific Coast. Disillusioned by the conformity and banality that characterized the society of that time, they ended up in San Francisco, a city with a sense of freedom reminiscent of the courageous pioneers who actually founded it a century earlier, at the height of the gold rush. Here, they frequented cafés, listening to jazz and engaging in earnest discussions about literature, poetry and philosophy. The two students who had left New York soon emerged as leaders from this group of marginal North

Beach drifters, becoming known for their terse, lively and scathing writing style. Jack Kerouac, a Franco-American writer from Massachusetts whose family originally came from Québec, published his most important work, *On the Road*, in 1957. Written in stream-of-consciousness prose, this pseudo-documentary became the bible of the Beat generation, which took its name from a jazz term used to describe a state of absolute bliss that seemed close to the state of supreme happiness preached by Jesus in the Beatitudes. In the realm of poetry, Allan Ginsberg produced a veritable revolutionary outcry in the Beat generation with *Howl & Other Poems*, published in 1956. Pioneers in the truest sense, the Beatniks brought a breath of freedom to other forms of expression, leaving their mark on generations to come.

American and Spanish heritage brought to life by author Mary Austin.

The Great Depression in the 1930s and the migratory flow from the barren plains of the Midwest brought tension to the community. Torn by the social demands of the newcomers, society became polarized. Thousands of poor workers and people from the country had great difficulty adjusting to the exploitation and miserable living conditions they endured; in their eyes, California was supposed to be a heavenly world. Indeed, this was the fabled image projected by Hollywood movies and acted out by magnificent stars who were both rich and beautiful. In fact, the Hollywood movie industry refused to portray the sadder side of Californian society. What the movies refused to show, however, the day's literature did not shy away from. It became the voice of marginal groups. It was during these times that John Steinbeck published his writings whose biting social commentary shook rigid Californian society.

A period of growth and opulence marked the post-war period. However, disappointed writers and intellectuals gathered in the San Francisco region to criticize the capitalistic society of consumerism that surrounded them. With leaders like Jack Kerouac and Allen Ginsberg, the "beat generation" questioned the values of this carelessly materialistic society.

Thereafter, Californian literature appeared to branch off. As a reflection of the multi-ethnic society, more and more room was given to Asian and Af-

in this land of milk and honey. As witnesses to this remarkable chapter of history in which they sometimes played important roles, some writers found words to express their experiences in this Eldorado. Among them was Mark Twain, celebrated journalist, novelist and humorist. Propelled by

the febrility of the times, he became a gold prospector and lived in San Francisco in the early 1860s. In his signature humorous tone, his writings depict the life of the courageous pioneers. The next generation, at the end of the 19th century, rediscovered California's past by examining its Native rican-American writers and to their work, which evoked the realities of their communities.

Music

All the big musical trends that impressed the U.S. included great Californian performers who flaunted their myriad talents on the stages of big cities. Conceived in steamy Mississippi, jazz came to the West Coast in the 1940s. As the cradle of great African-American musicians, Los Angeles witnessed the birth of Dexter Gordon, Charles Mingus and Art Pepper, among others. The following decade saw Dave Brubeck, Chet Baker and others adapt this music to the laid-back mentality of the Pacific, spawning the Cool Jazz phenomenon.

As a parallel to the birth of Californian jazz, blues and rhythms 'n blues, two more musical trends linked with African-Americans, created more and more noise in and around Los Angeles. From the hot music scene in the Watts neighbourhood emerged, among others, the famous Johnny Otis. And John Lee Hooker was the renowned torchbearer of the blues.

If jazz and blues shook music scenes in San Francisco and Los Angeles, it was mostly rock and pop music that put California on the map. In fact, the West Coast has been a breeding ground for pop groups since the 1960s. From the Beach Boys and The Mammas and The Pappas personifying the Californian sounds in the 1970s, to contemporary rap, by way of the psychedelic madness of the late 1960s embodied by The

Doors, The Grateful Dead, Jefferson Airplane and Janis Joplin and the punk movement led by the Dead Kennedys, California has always called the tunes in Western popular music trends.

Architecture

In light of California's never-ending artistic effervescence, it comes as no surprise to discover that the state has always been a fertile land of architectural experimentation. The mild temperatures, the rich and varied natural setting, and a considerable number of well-off artists have all merged to create a daring, fragmental and original style of architecture. Even though the individualism and liberalism of this society are reflected in its structural heritage, they have in no way created a structured and harmonious urban framework. The most flagrant example is undoubtedly Los Angeles, a concentration of independent suburbs and neighbourhoods, each with its own distinctive design, with no other link than miles and miles of highways which, more often than not, are blocked with traffic.

In the early days of the colony, the Spanish used elements found on location to make houses, churches and institutional buildings. Inspired by the Pueblo and Navajo Native Americans, they used limestone, dried herbs and adobe (sun-dried clay bricks), and built wooden frames as support. However, the flight of the Franciscan fathers following Mexican independence and the loss of the territory to the United States marked the end of this

period and its structures eventually crumbled under the weight of time.

The gold rush once more instigated a period of rapid development. Camps were hastily erected here and there, and houses were built using the overturned hulls of boats which had transported prospectors to California's coasts. Detecting a good opportunity, forestry companies on the East Coast began building prefabricated houses and shipping them by boat to the other side of the continent. Boom towns spread like wildfire everywhere in Northern California. Featuring wooden houses with false facades and vaguely Victorian ornamentation as well as plank sidewalks, towns like these have been projected thousands of times on the silver screen and now constitute part of the legend.

San Francisco was inundated by a flurry of rich prospectors, causing it to grow at a frenetic and anarchical pace. Without any urban-development knowledge or heed paid to the terrain or geographical constraints, these nouveaux riches created a city without any planning. The results are surprising and sometimes incongruous, such as the city's famous streets with unbelievable height variations that were totally unadapted to the carriages and horses of the epoch. Of a vaguely Victorian inspiration, luxury residences and small bourgeois palaces, kitsch and ostentatious at the same time, proliferated in the city. The more sober, wooden houses painted in the colours of the rainbow and known as the Painted Ladies, so evocative of San Francisco's urban landscape, also date back to this period.

The first half of the 20th century was marked by different, often contradictory trends. Many architects drew their inspiration from the past and designed Spanish residences with Plateresque facades, white-stucco facing, baroque interiors, terracotta-tiled roofs and, of course, alfresco courtyards and colonnades. At the same time, the more classic beaux-arts style began appearing. Synthesizing French architecture from the Renaissance to the end of classicism, it reached its apotheosis when San Francisco was rebuilt in 1915.

And yet, over and above all these dominant trends, it was the folly and fantasy of this part of the country that moulded the environ

ment. Influenced by the illusory yet omnipresent world of cinema, architects did not hesitate to recreate this illusion in the urban landscape. Thus was a New England town was created in Los Angeles, and a Henry VIII villa and a Roman palace in Santa Monica, in addition to many other extravagant edifices. It was during this era, in 1905 to be more precise, that an architect came up with the idea of designing a copy of Venice on the shores of Los Angeles. Today, Venice personifies Southern California's cult of the body. In the 1920s, the celebrated Chinese Theater saw the light of day in Hollywood. On premiere nights, glamorous stars driving flashy

cars flock to this reproduction of a Chinese theatre, which is the nerve centre of the movie world. Most leave their handprint in the ground, forever marked for future generations.

Yet another grassroots movement characterized the architectural scene of the 1950s and 1960s. Concerned about reusing traditional materials, architecture returned to a very Californian design inspired by barns and country ranches. Along with this glorification of the past when designing new buildings, the community began to pay more attention to the wealth of its heritage. From the 1960s on, renovating old buildings became all the rage.

Chinese Theater

Practical Information

T his chapter contains all the information you need to plan your trip to California, and to make the most of each area you visit.

H ere you will find helpful addresses and phone numbers, as well as other information that will be useful to you. Have an excellent trip to California.

Entrance Formalities

Travellers from Canada, the majority of western European countries, Australia and New Zealand do not need visas to enter the United States. A valid passport is sufficient for stays of up to three months. A return ticket and proof of sufficient funds to cover your stay may be required. For stays of more than three months, all travellers, except Canadians and citizens of the British Commonwealth, must obtain a visa (*$120*) from the U.S. embassy in their country.

N.B.: as medical expenses can be very high in the United States, travel health insurance is highly recommended. For more information, see the section entitled "Insurance" on p 44.

Customs

Foreigners may enter the United States with 200 cigarettes (or 100 cigars) and duty-free purchases under US$400, including personal gifts and 33,8fl oz (1l) of alcohol (the legal drinking age is 21). There is no limit on the amount of cash you can carry, although you must fill out a form if you are travelling with more than US$10,000.

Prescription medication must be placed in clearly marked containers (you may have to present a prescription or a written statement from your doctor to customs officials). Meat and meat by-products, all kinds of food, grains, plants, fruit and narcotics cannot be brought into the United States.

If you are travelling with your cat or dog, you will have to show a health certificate (provided by your veterinarian), as well as certification of rabies vaccination. Note that the vaccine must be administered at least 30 days before the date of departure and cannot be over one year old.

For more information, contact:
United States Customs Service
1301 Constitution Ave. NW
Washington, DC 20229
☎*(202) 566-8195*

Getting There

By Plane

From Canada

Air Canada offers five to 10 flights per day from Montréal to San Francisco via Chicago or Toronto.

Travel time varies from 7 tp 9hrs depending on stop-overs. The same companies have a few direct flights every day from Montréal to Los Angeles, as well as a few flights per day to Los Angeles via Chicago or Toronto. These companies offer daily flights to San Diego from Montréal via Chicago, Toronto and Los Angeles.

From Europe

All major airline companies offer flights to San Francisco and Los Angeles from the large European metropolises. The duration of the trip, without stop-over, is 11hrs. Add approximately 1hr for each stop-over; 2hrs if you have to change planes.

San Francisco International Airport

Located 25km (15mi) from the city centre, San Francisco International Airport ranks as the seventh busiest airport on the planet, averaging 40 million passengers each year. This modern airport is currently being expanded and revitalized at a cost of $2.4 billion. It serves numerous airlines and has currency-exchange offices, as well as several small, unpretentious restaurants. There are different options for getting into town: limousines, taxis and buses will take you pretty much anywhere in the metropolitan region. For information concerning flight arrival and departure times: ☎736-2008 or 800-736-2008 (or visit the Web site: *www.flysfo.com*).

The airport has three terminals. The **International Terminal** serves most international flights by foreign companies like Air France, KLM, Lufthansa, Aeroflot,

LACSA, Japan Airlines and United Airlines (North Terminal also). The **North Terminal** serves American Airlines and United Airlines. The **South Terminal** mainly receives domestic flights from companies like Delta, US Airways, Continental, Northwest, TWA and Air Canada.

Los Angeles Airport

The Los Angeles area has five airports that all serve regular commercial flights (several smaller airports in the surrounding area are used only by private or military planes).

The largest and busiest airport by far is **Los Angeles International Airport**, often referred to by its three-letter international code, **LAX**. Its huge facilities southwest of the city, not far from the Pacific Coast (most eastbound fights fly briefly over the ocean before heading inland), serve almost all international flights destined for Southern California as well as a large number of continental flights. The airport buildings are arranged in a horseshoe shape and are numbered from one to seven. An eighth, more recent building, the Tom Bradley International Terminal (named in honour of the former city mayor), is situated between Terminals 3 and 4.

LAX services impressive numbers of international carriers; almost all the large transatlantic and transpacific airlines in the world offer regular daily service to it. It is among the busiest airports in the western hemisphere in terms of international air traffic, and stands out as *the* busiest by far in terms of transpacific air traffic. Additionally, it serves a

vast spectrum of Canadian and Latin-American carriers, and there is a long list of cities on five continents that offer direct flights to LAX.

Most carriers from outside the United States (but certainly not all) are based at the spacious, well-lit Tom Bradley International Terminal. However, some are located elsewhere. For example, Air Canada, KLM, Virgin Atlantic and Air New Zealand are among the airlines that use Terminal 2. Bear in mind that the wave of mergers and takeovers currently affecting the airlines industry means that it would be risky to guess, even a few months after this is written, which terminal will be assigned to one carrier or another at the time of your flight's arrival or departure. Make sure you check the exact location written on your ticket or boarding pass to prevent any confusion; and if the information isn't clear, don't hesitate to consult your airline or travel agent. If you have to change terminals to make a connection, free buses marked "A" circulate counterclockwise through the complex, stopping every few minutes at all lower terminal levels beside signs reading "LAX Shuttle."

LAX also services a significant number of continental flights. All large U.S. airline companies, as well as a few smaller ones, offer frequent service to Los Angeles from their respective cities, or even to other destinations (including the large cities on the East Coast). The most common short flights, notably those along the very congested San Francisco corridor, are provided by two rivals: United Airlines and Southwest Airlines.

Table of distances (km/mi)
Via the shortest route

1 mile = 1.62 kilometres
1 kilometre = 0.62 mile

	Bakersfield	Eureka	Fresno	Las Vegas (Nev.)	Los Angeles	Medford (Or.)	Monterey	Palm Springs	Pasadena	Redding	Reno (Nev.)	Sacramento	San Diego	San Francisco	San Luis Obispo
Eureka	889/549														
Fresno	175/108	738/456													
Las Vegas (Nev.)	466/288	1368/844	638/394												
Los Angeles	179/110	1060/654	351/217	444/274											
Medford (Or.)	944/583	310/191	772/477	1412/872	1128/696										
Monterey	401/248	632/390	245/151	859/530	543/335	745/460									
Palm Springs	369/228	1237/764	532/328	457/282	184/114	1318/814	731/451								
Pasadena	181/112	1062/656	356/220	440/272	14/9	1130/698	555/343	181/112							
Redding	711/439	253/156	534/330	1170/722	890/549	240/148	513/317	1072/662	898/554						
Reno (Nev.)	659/407	687/424	488/301	721/445	838/517	719/444	526/325	1031/636	849/524	477/294					
Sacramento	438/270	483/298	261/161	908/560	628/388	510/315	301/186	810/500	635/392	268/165	219/135				
San Diego	384/237	1258/777	547/338	543/335	200/123	1322/816	750/463	232/143	210/130	1086/670	1045/645	829/512			
San Francisco	459/283	449/277	289/178	921/569	616/380	588/363	178/110	800/494	621/383	353/218	366/226	146/90	819/506		
San Luis Obispo	198/122	824/509	206/127	762/470	310/191	936/578	234/144	506/312	322/194	700/432	712/440	495/306	517/319	372/230	
Tijuana (Mex.)	399/246	1283/792	573/354	566/349	225/189	1350/833	773/477	255/157	237/146	1111/686	1070/660	857/529	28/17	845/522	546/337

Example: the distance between Los Angeles and San Francisco is 616 km or 380 mi.

Although the restaurants and shops at LAX have improved slightly in recent years, they still offer few choices compared to those at many of the world's other great airports. A single retailer has a monopoly on duty-free products, and their prices are very high.

San Diego Airport

To get to San Diego's international airport (☎291-3100), located 2mi (3km) northwest of the city centre, take Route 163 South to 10th Avenue. Turn right and stay on Market Street until Harbor Drive, which takes you directly to the airport in less than 10min.

Luggage

The maximum luggage weight allowed into an airplane varies from one airline to the next. On chartered flights, it is restricted to a minimum, and charges are applied for excess weight. Remember that you are usually only allowed one piece of hand luggage on the plane, and it must fit under the seat in front of you.

Be sure to securely fasten all bags and suitcases and to carefully wrap all packages, since they could get damaged by the trolley's mechanism as they go into or come out of the baggage hold. Some airlines and airports supply sturdy plastic bags for backpacks, boxes and other pieces of luggage.

Before boarding the plane, you might be asked whether or not you left your luggage unattended, or if you packed it yourself. The reason for this is to prevent strangers from slipping illegal merchandise into your bags, which you would then unknowingly carry with you.

You are not allowed to bring dangerous objects, such as knives and pocket knives, into the plane; these items can, however, be kept in luggage that will go in the baggage hold. Outdoor enthusiasts should note that oxygen tanks cannot be carried into airplanes and that bicycle tires must be deflated. If you are travelling with unusual items, it is best to inquire with the airline before packing.

By Car

If you are approaching Los Angeles, San Francisco or San Diego by car, please refer to each of these chapters, respectively, in the "Finding Your Way Around" section, for detailed information on highways and roads.

Car Rentals

In San Francisco

Most of the companies listed below have rental locations at the airport and in other parts of the San Francisco area.

Alamo Rent-A-Car
687 Folsom St.
☎(415) 882-9440
or
750 Bush St.
☎(415) 693-0191

Budget Rent-A Car
321 Mason St.
☎(415) 292-8400
or
1600 Van Ness Ave.
☎(415) 775-6602

Thrifty Car Rental
520 Mason St.
☎(415) 788-8111

In Los Angeles

Most of the companies listed below have rental locations at Los Angeles International Airport and in other parts of the L.A. area.

Avis
☎800-331-1212
☎(213) 977-1450
☎(310) 646-5600

Beverly Hills Rent A Car
☎(310) 337-1400

Bob Leech's Auto Rental
☎800-635-1240
☎(310) 673-2727

Budget
☎800-221-1203

Dollar
☎800-800-4000
☎(310) 645-9333

Enterprise
☎800-736-8222

Fox Car Rental
☎800-225-4369
☎(310) 641-3838

Hertz
☎800-654-3131

Los Angeles Rent-A-Car
☎(310) 670-9945

Lucky
☎800-400-4736
☎(310) 641-2323

Midway
☎800-824-5260
☎(310) 445-4355

National
☎800-227-7368

Payless
☎310-645-2100

Shooshani's Avon Car Rental
☎(323) 650-2631

Thrifty
☎(310) 645-1880

In San Diego

Alamo Rent-a-Car
☎297-0311 or 800-GO-ALAMO

Avis
☎688-5030 or 800-852-4617

Bob Baker Ford Rental
☎297-5001 or 297-3106

Budget
☎800-826-2090

Entreprise Rent-a-Car
☎(858) 457-4909
☎800-RENT-A-CAR

Thrifty
☎702-0577 or 888-297-8844

By Bus

To obtain schedules and destinations, call your local **Greyhound** office at ☎800-231-2222.

Smoking is forbidden on almost all bus lines. In general, children five and under travel for free, and travellers 60 and over are also eligible for discounts. Pets are not allowed.

By Train

In the United States, the train is not always the most economical means of transportation and is definitely not the fastest. However, it can be an interesting experience for long distances since it is quite comfortable (try to get a seat in a car where you can really enjoy the view). For schedules and destinations, call **AMTRAK**, which owns the U.S. railroad network: ☎800-872-7245, *www.amtrak.com*.

Hitchhiking

Hitchhiking is not recommended.

Embassies and Consulates

U.S. Embassies and Consulates Abroad

AUSTRALIA
Moonah Place, Canberra, ACT 2600
☎(6) 214-5600

BELGIUM
27 Boulevard du Régent
B-1000 Brussels
☎(02) 512-2210
≈(02) 511-9652

CANADA
2 Wellington St., Ottawa
Ontario K1P 5T1
☎(613) 238-5335
≈(613) 238-5720

Consulate:
Place Félix-Martin
1155 Rue Saint-Alexandre
Montréal, Québec, H2Z 1Z2
☎(514) 398-9695
≈(514) 398-9748

Consulate:
360 University Ave.
Toronto Ontario, M5G 1S4
☎(416) 595-1700
≈(416) 595-0051

Consulate:
1095 W. Pender, Vancouver, British Columbia, V6E 2M6
☎(604) 685-4311

DENMARK
Dag Hammarskjölds Allé 24
2100 Copenhagen Ø
☎(35) 55 31 44
≈(35) 43 02 23

FINLAND
Itaïnen Puistotie 14B
FIN-00140, Helsinki, Finland
☎358-9-171-931

GERMANY
Clayallee 170, 14195 Berlin
☎(30) 832-2933
≈(30) 8305-1215

GREAT BRITAIN
24 Grosvenor Square
London W1A 1AE
☎(171) 499-9000
≈(171) 491-2485

ITALY
Via Veneto 119-a
00187 Roma
☎(06) 467-41
≈(06) 467-42217

NETHERLANDS
Lange Voorhout 102
2514 EJ, Den Haag
☎(70) 310-9209
≈(70) 361-4688

NORWAY
Drammensveien 18
0244 Oslo
☎22448550

PORTUGAL
Avenida Das Forças Armadas
1600 Lisboa Apartado 4258
1507 Lisboa Codex
☎(351) (1) 727-3300
≈(351) (1) 727-2354

SPAIN
C. Serrano 75
Madrid 28006
☎(1) 577-4000
≈(1) 564-1652
Telex (1) 277-63

SWEDEN
Strandvägen 101
11589 Stockholm
☎(08) 783 53 00
≈(08) 661 19 64

SWITZERLAND
93 Jubilam Strasse
3005 Berne
☎31-43-70-11
≈31-357-73-98

Foreign Consulates in California

AUTRALIA
Century Plaza Towers
2049 Century Pk., E., 19th floor
Los Angeles, CA 90067
☎(310) 229-4800

Practical Information

1 Bush St., 7th floor
San Francisco, CA 94104
☎362-6160

BELGIUM
6600 Wilshire Blvd., Suite 1200
Los Angeles, CA 90048
☎(213) 857-1244
⇌(213) 936-2564

625 Third St.
San Francisco, CA 92106
☎(415) 882-4648
⇌(415) 957-0730

CANADA
550 S. Hope St., 9th floor
Los Angeles, CA 90071-2627
☎(213) 346-2700
⇌(213) 620-8827
lngls@dfait-maeci.gc.ca

DENMARK
10877 Wilshire Blvd., Suite 1105
Los Angeles, CA 90024
☎(310) 443 2090
⇌(310) 443 2099

20 California St., 4th floor
San Francisco, CA 94111
☎(415) 391-0100
⇌(415) 391-0181

FINLAND
1900 Ave. of the Stars, Suite 1025
Los Angeles, CA 90067
☎(310) 203-9903
⇌(310) 203-9186

Honorary Consulate
333 Bush St., 34th floor
San Francisco, CA 94104
☎(415) 772-6649
⇌(415) 772-6268

GERMANY
6222 Wilshire Blvd., Suite 500
Los Angeles, CA 90048
☎(323) 930-2703
⇌(323) 930 2805

1960 Jackson St.
San Francisco, CA 94109
☎(415) 775-1061
⇌(415) 775 0187

GREAT BRITAIN
11766 Wilshire Blvd., Suite 400
Los Angeles, CA 90025
☎(310) 477-3322
⇌(310) 575-1450

1 Sansome St., Suite 850
San Francisco, CA 94104
☎(415) 981 3030
⇌(415) 434 2018

ITALY
12400 Wilshire Blvd., Suite 300
Los Angeles, CA 90025
☎(310) 820-0622
⇌(310) 820-0727

2590 Webster St.
San Francisco, CA 94115
☎(415) 931 4924
⇌(415) 931 7205

NETHERLANDS
11766 Wilshire Blvd., Suite 1150
Los Angeles, CA 90025
☎(310) 268 1598
⇌(310) 312 0989

NORWAY
20 California St., 6th floor
San Francisco, CA 94111-4803
☎(415) 986-0766
⇌(415) 986-3318

PORTUGAL
3298 Washington St.
San Francisco, CA 94115
☎(415) 346-3400

SPAIN
5055 Wilshire Blvd.
Suite 960
Los Angeles, CA 90036
☎(323) 938-0158 or 938-0166
⇌(323) 938-2502

1405 Sutter St.
San Francisco, CA 94109
☎(415) 922-2995 or 922-2996

SWEDEN
10940 Wilshire Blvd., Suite 700
Los Angeles, CA 90024
☎(310) 445-4008
⇌(310) 473-2229

SWITZERLAND
11766 Wilshire Blvd., Suite 1400
Los Angeles, CA 90025
☎(480) 945-0000
⇌(480) 947-0020

Tourist Information

For all tourist information, contact the following organizations:

California Office of Tourism
801 K St., Suite 1600
Sacramento, CA 95814
☎800-862-2543
⇌(916) 322-3402

San Francisco Visitor Information Center
Hallidie Plaza, lower level
(corner Powell St. and Market St.)
San Francisco, CA 94102
☎(415) 391-2000

Los Angeles Visitors and Convention Bureau
633 W. Fifth St., Suite 6000
Los Angeles, CA 90071
☎(213) 624-7300

Getting Around

By Car

If you plan on discovering California by car, keep in mind the following guidelines:

Driver's License:
As a general rule, foreign driver's licenses are valid in the United States. Take note that certain states are linked by computer to provincial police services in Canada and that a ticket issued in the United States is therefore automatically transferred to your file in Canada.

Driving and the Highway Code:
Signs marked "Stop" in white against a red background must always be respected. Some stop signs are accompanied by a small sign indicating "4-way." This means that all vehicles must stop at the intersection. Come to a complete stop even if there is no apparent danger. If two vehicles arrive at the same time, the one to the right has the right of way. Otherwise, the first car to the intersection has the right of way.

Traffic lights are often located on the opposite side of the intersection, so make sure to stop at the stop line, a white line on the pavement before the intersection.

Turning right on a red light after a full stop is permitted, unless otherwise indicated.

When a school bus (usually yellow) has stopped and its signals are flashing, **you must come to a complete stop, no matter what direction you are travelling in.** Failing to stop at the flashing signals is considered a serious offense, and carries a heavy penalty.

Seat belts must be worn at all times.

There are no tolls on the highways, except on most Interstate highways that are indicated by the letter "I" followed by a number. Interstate highways are also indicated by a blue crest on a white background. The highway number and the state are written on the sign. "Interstate" is written on a red background at the top of the sign.

The speed limit is 55mph (88km/h) on most highways. These signs are rect-angular with a black border, white background and black writing.

The speed limit on Interstate highways is 65mph 104km/h.

Red and white triangular signs with the word "Yield" under them indicate that vehicles crossing your path have the right of way.

A round, yellow sign with a black X and two Rs indicates a railroad crossing.

Gas Stations: Since the United States produces its own crude oil, gasoline prices are less expensive than in Europe; gas is also less expensive than in Canada due to hidden taxes north of the border. Self-serve stations will often ask for payment in advance as a security measure.

Warning: Criminals looking to rob tourists have adopted a strategy to get you out of your car. Wether in moving traffic or not, these miscreants will starting bumping you from behind. Don't fall for this trick, and make sure you **do not** stop to argue with the other driver.

Do not stop for hitchhikers, always lock your doors and be careful.

Money and Banking

Money

The monetary unit is the dollar ($), which is divided into cents (¢).
One dollar = 100 cents.

Bills come in one, five, 10, 20, 50 and 100 dollar denominations; and coins come in one- (penny), five- (nickel), 10- (dime) and 25-cent (quarter) pieces.

Dollar and fifty-cent coins exist, as does a two-dollar bill, but they are very rarely used. Virtually all purchases must be paid in U.S. dollars in the United States. Be sure to get your traveller's cheques in U.S. dollars. You can also use any credit card affiliated with an U.S. institution like Visa, MasterCard, American Express, Interbank, Barclay Bank, Diners' Club and Discovery.

Please note that all prices in this guide are in US dollars.

Banks

Banks are open from Monday to Friday, 9am to 3pm.

There are many banks in the city, and tourists can take advantage of most services. Those who choose to stay for an extended period of time should note that a **non-resident** cannot open a bank account. To obtain cash, your best bet is always traveller's cheques. Withdrawing from your own account outside your home country can be costly since commission fees are high. However, most banks have ATMs, wich accept Canadian and European bank cards, allowing you to make a withdrawal. What's more, ATMs are often accessible 24hrs a day. Those who have resident status, permanent or non-permanent (immigrants, students), can open a bank account. To do so, all you need is your passport and a proof of your resident status.

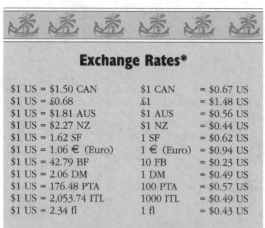

Exchange Rates*

$1 US = $1.50 CAN	$1 CAN	= $0.67 US
$1 US = £0.68	£1	= $1.48 US
$1 US = $1.81 AUS	$1 AUS	= $0.56 US
$1 US = $2.27 NZ	$1 NZ	= $0.44 US
$1 US = 1.62 SF	1 SF	= $0.62 US
$1 US = 1.06 € (Euro)	1 € (Euro)	= $0.94 US
$1 US = 42.79 BF	10 FB	= $0.23 US
$1 US = 2.06 DM	1 DM	= $0.49 US
$1 US = 176.48 PTA	100 PTA	= $0.57 US
$1 US = 2,053.74 ITL	1000 ITL	= $0.49 US
$1 US = 2.34 fl	1 fl	= $0.43 US

* Samples only—Rates Fluctuate

Exchanging Money

Several banks readily exchange foreign currency, but almost all charge a **commission**. While there are exchange offices that do not charge commission, their rates can be less competitive. These offices often have longer opening hours. It is a good idea to **shop around**.

Traveller's Cheques

It is always best to keep a certain amount of money in traveller's cheques, which are accepted in some restaurants, hotels and shops (those in U.S. dollars are most widely accepted). They are also easy to cash in at banks and exchange offices. Always keep a copy of the serial numbers of your cheques in a separate place; that way, if the cheques are lost, the company can replace them quickly and easily. Do not rely solely on traveller's cheques, however, as you should always carry some cash.

Credit Cards

Most credit cards, especially Visa, MasterCard, and American Express (in that order) are accepted in many businesses, including hotels and restaurants. While the main advantage of credit cards is that they allow you to avoid carrying large sums of money, using a credit card also makes leaving a deposit for a rental car much easier. In addition, the exchange rate with a credit card is usually better.

Credit cards also let you avoid service charges when exchanging money. By overpaying your credit card (to avoid interest charges), you can then withdraw against it. You can thus avoid carrying large amounts of money or traveller's cheques.

Withdrawals can be made directly from an automated teller if you have a personal identification number (PIN) for your card.

Taxes and Tipping

Taxes

A total tax (City and State) of 12% is applicable on accommodations, while the goods and services tax is 8.5%.

Tipping

In general, tips are applicable to all table services, that is, in restaurants and other places where you are served at the table (fast-food establishments do not fit this category). According to the quality of service, you should leave approximately 15% of the amount before taxes. Contrary to Europe, the tip is not included in the bill, so it is up to the customer to figure out how much to give the server. Airport baggage-handlers usually get $1. It is also proper to tip in bars and nightclubs, as well as bellhops, chambermaids and taxi drivers.

Insurance

Cancellation

Your travel agent will usually offer you cancellation insurance upon purchase of your airline ticket or vacation package. This insurance allows you to be reimbursed for the ticket or package deal if your trip must be cancelled due to serious illness or death.

Health

This is the most useful kind of insurance for travellers and should be purchased before your departure. Your insurance plan should be as complete as possible because health care costs add up quickly. When buying insurance, make sure it covers all types of medical costs, such as hospitalization, nursing services and doctor's fees. Make sure your limit is high enough, as these expenses can be costly. A repatriation clause is also vital in case the required care is not available on site. Furthermore, since you may have to pay on the spot, check your policy to see what provisions it includes for such situations. To avoid any problems during your vacation, always keep proof of your insurance policy with you.

Theft

Most residential insurance policies protect some of your goods from theft, even if the theft occurs in a foreign country. To make a claim, you are required to fill out a police report. It may not be necessary to take out further insurance depending on the amount covered by your current home policy. As policies vary considerably, you are advised to check with your insurance company. European visitors should take out baggage insurance.

Health

Vaccinations are not necessary for people coming from Europe or Canada. On the other hand, it is strongly suggested, particularly for medium or long-term stays, that visitors take out health and accident insurance (see above). There are different types, so it is best to shop around. Bring along all medication, especially prescription medicine. Unless otherwise stated, the water is potable throughout California.

The Sun

Despite its benefits, the sun also causes numerous problems. It is needless to say that the rising occurrence of skin cancer is due to overexposure to the sun's harmful rays. It is important to keep well protected and avoid prolonged exposure, especially during the first few days of your trip, as it takes a while to get used to the sun's strength. Overexposure to the sun can also cause sunstroke, symptoms of which include dizziness, vomiting and fever. Always use sunblock to protect yourself from the sun's harmful rays. Many of the sunscreens on the market do not provide adequate protection. Before setting off on your trip, ask your pharmacist which ones are truly effective against the UVA and UVB rays. For the best results, apply the cream at least 20 min before going out in the sun. Even after a few days, moderate exposure is best. A hat and pair of sunglasses are indispensable accessories in this part of the U.S.

First-Aid Kit

A small first aid kit can prove useful, and should be carefully prepared before leaving home. Bring along sufficient amounts of any medications you take regularly, as well as a valid prescription. Also bring along the prescription for your glasses or contact lenses. Your kit should also include:

- adhesive bandages
- a disinfectant
- an analgesic
- antihistamines
- tablets for upset stomach or mation sickness
- sanitary napkin and tampons.

Don't forget to include your contact lens solution, and an extra pair of glasses, if applicable.

Safety and Security

Unfortunately, U.S. society is still relatively violent. That said, there is no reason to panic and stay holed-up in your hotel room. However, it is always a good idea to avoid walking in parks or on poorly lit streets at night.

Be aware that pickpockets sometimes work in groups. A few of them will distract you momentarily, while others sneak away with your personal possessions.

Most good hotels have safes in which to leave your valuables, offering you a certain peace of mind. Be discreet when doing business in public. Don't expose a wad of bills when paying for an object or a service.

Lastly, be aware that the greatest cause of accidents involving tourists worldwide is driving... In the wonderful world of California, where the car is king, it is particularly important to be careful on the road.

Practical Information

In general, it is best to avoid being alone in the subway stations of San Francisco and Los Angeles outside of regular service hours, whether early in the morning or very late at night. In the same vein, you shouldn't even consider taking a nighttime stroll in one of the large parks in either city, unless there is some event taking place in it that draws a large crowd.

San Francisco

San Francisco is not a dangerous city, but it is always best to ask when you arrive about neighbourhoods that you should stay out of regardless of the time of day or night. If normal precautions are taken, there is no reason to be overanxious about safety. But should bad luck come your way, remember that the emergency phone number is **911**, or **0** when going through the operator.

Los Angeles

The crime rate in Los Angeles is fairly close to the U. S. average, at a level that falls between the relative security found in most of the world's industrialized cities and the greater danger present in certain third-world regions. As is true in many U. S. cities, violent crime here has decreased over the last few years, but it is still wise to take certain precautions. Vacationers often adopt a relatively carefree attitude, which can leave them more vulnerable to criminal attacks. Remember to keep your valuables out of sight in public places, and when withdrawing money from an

ATM, be sure to do so in a well-lit, busy place.

Some parts of Los Angeles are more dangerous than others. In general, the western section is relatively safe, but many areas to the south and east of downtown L.A. are much less so, since gangs of disreputable youths hang out in them. Some streets that appear safe in the daytime become quite eerie at night. This is particularly true of a large part of downtown L.A. and certain sections of Hollywood. Visitors on foot after sunset should use good judgement and avoid unfamiliar areas where there are few other pedestrians. L.A. has a large number of homeless people, some suffering from mental illness or drug problems. Though generally more deranged than dangerous, they can still be frightening to unsuspecting passers by. They are frequently seen in small groups to the east of the city centre and in certain neighbourhoods in Hollywood and Santa Monica.

Drivers too should take extra precautions when travelling late at night: be certain of your route and keep your car doors locked. The L.A. police force, tainted by many scandals, is not as inefficient as many critics would claim it to be, but it is still fairly spread out over a very vast territory. The number to call in case of emergency (from any public phone) is **911**.

Climate

When to Visit California

Southern California

Any region the size of California necessarily presents a variety of climates. When, additionally, the region in question stretches from the coast to the desert and on to the mountains, from below sea-level altitudes to higher than 13,900ft (4,250m), it goes without saying that things become even more complex.

In Southern California, you can surf and ski in the same day. The temperature change between the beaches and the mountains can sometimes be as much as 40°F (approximately 23°C). In the desert, the mercury can fluctuate just as much at a single location, with a 70°F (21°C) day giving way to a below-freezing night.

Along the Pacific Coast and on the coastal plains, where most visitors congregate, the climate resembles that of the Mediterranean, where the weather remains mild year-round.

Because the coast is regularly invaded by fog that quite naturally adds to its insulation and cools it, the mercury rarely falls below 39°F (4°C) and hardly ever exceeds 81°F

(27°C). September and October are the warmest months, while December and January are the coldest. In Los Angeles, the average temperature is 75°F (24°C) in the warm season and 50°F (10°C) in the heart of winter.

Spring, and perhaps especially autumn, are the best seasons for visiting the region. Winter, from November to March, can be quite rainy, with the heaviest rainfall occurring between December and February. But for the rest of the year there is practically no precipitation. It goes without saying that summer is the season that attracts most tourists, and the dramatic increase in local populations at that time of year can cause problems. In summer, just as in spring, fog often descends in the morning and at night. Patches of fog that form out at sea sweep over the coast and only dissipate around the middle of the day.

Most winter storms come from the north, so average precipitation and the length of the rainy season diminish as one goes further south. Santa Barbara receives 17in (432mm) of annual rainfall, Los Angeles, 15in (381mm), and San Diego, a scant 10in (254mm). On the other hand, the ocean air has relatively high humidity, averaging around 65%, and makes some regions seem cooler than the thermometer would indicate.

The fog is heaviest in August and September. Then, when autumn comes, the Santa Ana winds start blowing in from the desert. These hot, dry northeast winds can reach 33 to 48mph (55 to 80km/h), carrying sand, fanning forest fires and

making people more nervous than usual.

You won't be at all surprised to learn that the desert is very hot in the summer: the mercury can easily reach 100°F (38°C) and higher. However, spring is always a good time to visit since the air is cooler and the wildflowers are in full bloom. That said, autumn and winter are also pleasant.

As for the mountains, they are cold in winter, cool in the spring and astonishingly hot in summer. Precipitation is less abundant than on the coast, but the highest peaks get enough snow in winter for their much-admired ski resorts.

Northern California

Northern California stretches for nearly 390mi (650km) from Big Sur to Oregon and covers 192mi (320km) from east to west. This vast territory includes the Pacific coastline, a large inland valley and the high Sierra Nevadas, and its climate registers variations as extreme as those found on its relief map.

In Northern California, the temperature difference between the seasons is very slight. The ground hardly ever freezes, and sunburn is more often the result of harsh wind than torrid heat.

Temperatures vary only a few degrees over the course of the year (a deviation of 14°F or 8°C between January and July). One generalization can be made about this rather bizarre weather: the days are particularly pleasant (very sunny from April to September), while the nights are fairly cold.

Since winter is not severe, you will only have to worry about rain; so be sure to bring a raincoat and an umbrella. Although days are warm (you should still bring a sweater with you, however), it is highly recommended that you cover up well during the relatively cool nights.

Even summer is more springlike than suffocating, as evidenced by its July average high of around 73°F (23°C). Still, when night falls, you'll have to wear a sweater unless you're one of those people who never feels chilly.

The seasons are much more noticeable in the inland valleys, which make up a sort of climatic subzone. In Wine Country, the Delta and Gold Country, summer temperatures often exceed 90°F (32°C). There is less humidity, winters are cooler, and regions at higher altitudes occasionally get snow. Like the coast, this foothills region receives most of its precipitation in the winter.

The Sierra Nevada and the Cascade mountain ranges experience the greatest variations in climate. Summer days are hot and summer nights are cool. Spring and autumn bring colder temperatures and the trees even change colours (a phenomenon that is practically nonexistent on the coast, with its uniform seasons). Once winter arrives, the mercury plummets and snow falls in such abundance that the mountain ranges are transformed into spectacular ski centres.

Packing

For most stays, all you will actually need are walking shorts, light cotton shirts or

T-shirts, slacks, one or two bathing suits, a sweater or a windbreaker and a casual or dressy outfit to wear if you go out.

Remember to also bring an umbrella or a hooded, waterproof jacket to use in case of a sudden storm. If you visit California in the winter, a sweater is a good idea.

Flexible, comfortable, lightweight shoes are a must for travelling. If you plan to hike in the countryside, bring sneakers that you won't mind getting wet (the ground is often damp in places where you least expect it).

Don't forget to bring your camera (Pacific sunsets are fantastic!) and enough film to record all your memories.

The only other thing you might want to bring is a book or whatever essential items you wouldn't want to be without.

Mail and Telecommunications

The telephone system in the United States is extremely well designed. You will have no trouble finding pay phones using change ($0.35) or telephone cards.

By calling during certain specific periods, you can take advantage of substantial reductions, so you may want to inform yourself of these services.

Internet

Thanks to the Internet, keeping in touch with the folks back home has never been so easy. In fact, the growing popularity of this means of communication is in the process of relegating the good old postcard to the wastepaper basket. All you have to do is obtain an e-mail address before you leave.

Some hotels can also receive and transmit e-mail messages, but generally charge a higher fee than Internet cafés. For those concerned, the Microsoft boutique in the Metreon makes a few computers available without charge to Internet users who want to send messages or read their e-mail. However, the store limits user time to 15min.

Post Office

Post offices are open Monday to Friday from 8am to 5:30pm (sometimes until 6pm), and Saturday from 8am to noon.

Business Hours

Stores are generally open Monday to Wednesday from 9:30am to 5:30 (sometimes until 6pm), Thursday and Friday from 10am to 9pm, and Sunday from noon to 5pm. Supermarkets, on the other hand, close later or in some cases, even stay open 24hrs a day, seven days a week.

Public Holidays

The following is a list of public holidays in the United States. Note that most stores, government offices and banks are closed on these days.

New Year's Day
January 1

Martin Luther King Jr. Day
Third Monday of January

President's Day
Third Monday of February

Memorial Day
Last Monday of May

Independence Day (American National Holiday)
July 4

Labor Day
First Monday of September

Columbus Day
Second Monday of October

Veterans Day
November 11

Thanksgiving Day
Fourth Thursday of November

Christmas Day
December 25

Accommodations

No matter what your tastes or budget, this guide will surely help you find accommodations that suit you. Remember that rooms can be scarce and prices high in summer. Travellers who visit California in the summertime should therefore make reservations in advance.

The bed-and-breakfast formula is widespread in California. These establishments are often found in lovely, pleasantly decorated homes with fewer than 12 rooms.

What's more, an abundance of motels along the highways on the outskirts of cities makes it easy for travellers to find rooms that, while totally lacking in charm, offer very affordable prices.

In this guide, the stated prices for hotel establishments are for double rooms in high season and are as follows:

$	less than $40
$$	$40 to $80
$$$	$80 to $130
$$$$	$130 to $200
$$$$$	$200 or more

Restaurants

Apart from their many descriptions, the "Restaurants" section in each chapter will make it easier for you to find the type of establishment and cuisine you desire.

In this guide, the listed restaurant prices apply to a meal for one person, service and drinks excluded, and are as follows:

$	less than $10
$$	$10 to $20
$$$	$20 to $30
$$$$	$30 to $40
$$$$$	more than $40

Bars and Nightclubs

Some establishments charge admission, particularly if there is a show. Tipping is not required and is left to the discretion of each individual; of course, it's always appreciated. For drinks on the other hand, a tip of 10% to 15% is expected.

Note that the legal age for entering a bar or buying alcohol is 21. But always carry identification because in the States, you may be carded even if you look 40!

Identity and Culture Shock

Before going on vacation, we pack our luggage and get the necessary vaccinations and travel documents, but rarely do we prepare for culture shock. The following text explains what culture shock is and how to deal with it.

In a nutshell, culture shock can be defined as a certain

Note to Smokers

It is strictly forbidden to smoke in public places in the state of California, and the law is rigorously applied and carries heavy sanctions. As a result, you'll notice, first with surprise and then with a touch of amusement, that smokers light up in front of restaurants, bars and hotels. They find secluded spots, as though they were a little ashamed of themselves... It is true that smoking cigarettes in California is not really trendy. Strict measures and advertising campaigns seem to have worked since very few people have taken up the habit. Consequently, there is little tolerance towards smokers. If you absolutely have to smoke, note that cigars are a little more fashionable.

anxiety that may be experienced upon arriving in another country where everything is different, including the culture and language, making communication as you know it very difficult. Combined with jetlag and fatigue, the strain of orienting yourself in a new cultural context can lead to psychological stress that may throw you off track.

Culture shock is a frustrating phenomenon that can easily turn travellers setting out with the best of intentions into intolerant, racist and ethnocentric ones – they may come to believe that their society is better than the new, and seemingly incomprehensible, one. This type of reaction detracts from the whole travel experience.

People in other countries have different customs and lifestyles that are sometimes hard for us to understand or accept. We might even find ourselves wondering how people can live the way they do when their customs run contrary to what we deem to be "normal." In the end, however, it is easier to adapt to them than to criticize or disregard them.

Even though this is the era of globalization and cultural homogenization, we still live in a world of many "worlds," such as the business world, the worlds of different continents, suburbia, and the world of the rich and the poor. Of course, these worlds intersect, but each has its own characteristic set of ideas and cultural values. Furthermore, even if they are not in direct contact, each has at least an image of the other (which is often distorted and nothing more). And if a picture is worth a thousand words,

Practical Information

then our world contains million upon millions of them. Sometimes it is hard to tell what is real and what isn't, but one thing is certain: what you see on television about a place is not the same as when you get there.

When people interact with each other, they inevitably make sense of each other through their differences. The strength of a group, human or animal, lies in its diversity, whether it be in genetics or ideas. Can you imagine how boring the world would be if everyone were the same?

Travelling can be seen as a way of developing a more holistic, or global, vision of the world; this means accepting that our cultural fabric is complex and woven with many different ethnicities, and that all have something to teach us, be it a philosophy of life, medical knowledge, or a culinary dish, which adds to the richness of our personal experience.

Remember that culture is relative, and that people's social, technological and financial situations shape their way of being and looking at the world. It takes more than curiosity and tolerance to be open minded: it is a matter of learning to see the world anew, through a different cultural perspective.

When travelling abroad, don't spend too much energy looking for the familiar, and don't try to see the place as you would like it to be – go with the flow instead. And though a foreign country might seem difficult to understand or even unwelcoming at times, remember that there are people who find happiness and satisfaction in life everywhere. When you get involved in their daily lives, you will begin to see things differently—things which at first seemed exotic and mystifying are easily understood after having been ex plained. It always helps to know the rules before playing a game, and it goes without saying that learning the language will help you better understand what's going on. But be careful about communicating with your hands, since certain gestures might mean the opposite of what you are trying to say!

Prepare yourself for culture shock as early as possible. Libraries and bookstores are good places for information about the cultures you are interested in. Reading about them is like a journey in itself, and will leave you with even more cherished memories of your trip.

Seniors

In California, people 65 years and older can benefit from all sorts of advantages like significant reductions in entrance fees at museums and a variety of other attractions, and discounts at hotels and restaurants. These special rates often receive little publicity, so don't hesitate to ask.

On the other hand, be particularly careful in matters that concern health. In addition to medicines you regularly take, bring your prescriptions with you in case you need to renew them. Remember to also bring a copy of your medical history, as well as the name, address and telephone number of your doctor. Finally, make sure your insurance covers you in a foreign country.

American Association of Retired Persons
601 E. St.
Washington, D.C. 20049
☎ *(202) 434-2260*
The American Association of Retired Persons provides benefits that include discounts on organized trips offered by several companies.

Travellers with Disabilities

California is striving to make more and more places accessible to people with disabilities. Most tourist attractions are wheelchair accessible.

Travelling with Children

Travelling with children, however young they may be, can be a pleasant experience. A few precautions and ample preparations are the keys to a fun trip.

Aboard the Airplane

A good folding stroller will allow you to bring an infant or small child everywhere you go and will also be great for naps, if needed. In the airport, it will be easy to carry with you, especially since you are allowed to bring the stroller up to the plane's entrance.

Travellers with children can board the plane first, avoiding long line-ups. If your child is under the age of two, remember to ask for seats at the front of the plane when reserving your tickets since they offer more room and are more comfortable for long flights, especially if you've got a toddler on your lap. Some airlines even offer baby cribs.

If you are travelling with an infant, be sure to prepare the necessary food for the flight, as well as an extra meal in case of a delay. Remember to bring enough diapers and moist towels, and a few toys might not be a bad idea!

For older kids who might get bored once the thrill of taking off has faded, books and activities such as drawing material and games will probably do the trick.

When taking off and landing, changes in air pressure may cause some discomfort. In this case, some say that the nipple of a bottle can soothe infants, while a piece of chewing gum will have the same effect for older children.

In Hotels

Many hotels are well equipped for children, and there is usually no extra fee for travelling with an infant. Many hotels and bed and breakfasts have cribs; ask for one when reserving your room. You may have to pay extra for children, however, but the supplement is generally low.

Car Rentals

Most car rental agencies rent car seats for children. They are usually not very expensive. Ask for one when making your reservation.

The Sun

Needless to say, a child's skin requires strong protection against the sun; in fact, it is actually preferable not to expose toddlers to its harsh rays. Before going to the beach, remember to apply sunscreen (SPF 25 for children, 35 for infants). If you think your child will spend a long time under the sun, you should consider purchasing a sunscreen with SPF 60.

Children of all ages should wear a hat that provides good coverage for the head throughout the day.

Swimming

Children usually get quite excited about playing in the waves and can do so for hours on end. However, parents must be very careful and watch them constantly; accidents can happen in a matter of seconds. Ideally, an adult should accompany children into the water, especially the younger ones, and stand farther out in the water so the kids can play between the beach and the supervising adult. This way, he or she can quickly intervene in case of an emergency.

For infants and toddlers, some diapers are especially designed for swimming, such as "Little Swimmers" by Huggies. These are quite useful when having fun in the water!

Women Travellers

Women alone should not encounter any problems as long as they follow all the necessary precautions (see "Security," p ?). Keep in mind that it is dangerous to hitchhike and that it is better to avoid staying at accommodations located on the edge of town. Bed and breakfasts, youth hostels and YMCAs generally offer a more secure environment, as well as one that is conducive to meeting other travellers.

Miscellaneous

Time Difference

When it is noon in Montréal, it is 9am in California. The time difference for the UK is 8hrs. Don't forget that there are several time zones in the United States: California is 3hrs (and Hawaii 5hrs) behind New York.

Drugs

Recreational drugs are against the law and not tolerated (even "soft" drugs). Anyone caught

Practical Information

with drugs in their posses
sion risks severe conse-
quences.

Alcohol

You can purchase alcohol
24hrs a day. Liquor stores
are the best places to find
a wide selection of
products, but you can also
find wine and beer in
grocery stores. You must
be at least 21 years old to
drink.

Electricity

Voltage in the United
States is 110 volts and 60
cycles, the same as
Canada; to use European
appliances, you must have
a transformer/converter.

Electrical plugs are two-
pinned and flat; you can
find adapters in San Francisco, or purchase them at
a travel boutique or bookshop before your depar-
ture.

Cost of Living and Expenses

Typical Hotel and Restaurant Prices

Campsites vary from $11
to $18. Beds in youth
hostels cost from $7 to
$14. At bed and breakfasts,
prices for a double room
can range from $55 to
$185!

Lunch usually ranges from
$4 to $5. Lunch is the best
bet in terms of value for
your money. The same
size serving of a dish often
costs twice as much at
dinner. A sandwich or

Weights and Measures

Weights
1 pound (lb) = 454 grams (g)
1 kilogram (kg) = 2.2 pounds (lbs)

Linear Measure
1 inch (in) = 2.2 centimetres (cm)
1 foot (ft) = 30 centimetres (cm)
1 mile (mi) = 1.6 kilometres (km)
1 kilometres (km) = 0.63 miles (mi)
1 metre (m) = 39.37inches (in)

Land Measure
1 acre = 0.4 hectare (ha)
1 hectare (ha) = 2.471 acres

Volume Measure
1 U.S. gallon (gal) = 3.79 litres
1 U.S. gallon (gal) = 0.83 imperial gallons

Temperature
To convert F into C:
subtract 32, divide by 9, multiply by 5
To convert C into F:
multiply by 9, divide by 5, add 32.

hamburger, served with a
generous portion of fries,
varies from $5 to $10.

What to Buy

Bringing back souvenirs
and gifts is part of the
pleasure of travelling. But
pay attention to what you
buy. Try to find out how
an object was produced in
order to avoid encouraging
any kind of abuse. In
some countries, it is still
possible to obtain products
that are made with endan-
gered animal or plant
species, even though many

international agreements
ban this type of com-
merce.

Remember that objects
made from ivory, coral,
tortoiseshell and snake
skin are among those
which preferably should
not be purchased.

Also, restrictions on im-
porting animal or vegeta-
ble products exist to prevent the spread of epidemics. Fruits, vegetables,
plants and animals can't be
brought across borders
without special authoriza-
tion.

Outdoors

B ecause of its extensive territory and gorgeous, varied landscapes, California is a perfect place to enjoy all kinds of outdoor activities. We will therefore review a whole series of sports activities that can be practised in the Golden State.

G enerally concerned about their physical condition and appearance, Californians enjoy themselves to the full and spend a lot of time outdoors. You'll be amazed to see the sheer number of people jogging, cycling, in-line skating, golfing and engaging in myriad water sports. And who can blame them? You too will soon be swept up by this whirlwind of energy, so why not give in to the temptation?

I n short, California offers fitness buffs an infinite number of options, and this, in harmony with an ideal climate all year-round throughout must of the state.

T his list is, of course, only a sampling of the great variety of athletic pursuits to be enjoyed here. This chapter contains a few general comments in order to help you organize your activities. For more details, consult the "Outdoor Activities" section of each chapter.

Parks and Wildlife Reserves

There are close to 264 national parks in California, several of which are internationally recognized for their beauty and unique characteristics. Noteworthy among these are Death Valley National Park, Channel Islands National Park, Joshua Tree National Park, Redwood National Park, Sequoia and Kings Canyon national parks, Lake Tahoe and Yosemite national parks.

Throughout this guide, you'll find descriptions of most of these parks and wildlife reserves as well as the main outdoor activities that can be enjoyed in each of them.

For more information on the subject, contact:

California State Parks
P.O. Box 942896
Sacramento, CA 94296-0001
☎ *800-444-PARK*
www.cal-parks.ca.gov

Camping in the National Parks

There are several campgrounds in California's

national parks. Some are designed for RVs only, others welcome campers with tents, while still others admit both campers and trailers.

Services and facilities vary from park to park, but generally feature a campfire spot, picnic tables, showers, bathrooms and running water.

A few basic rules must be respected. For example, a maximum of two registered vehicles per campsite (with exceptions) is permitted, minors (under 18 years old) must be accompanied by an adult and dogs must be kept on a leash. Prices, which range from $10 to $25, generally vary with the campground and the season.

Most campgrounds are open year-round and some offer discounts during the low season. A few accept reservations, while others work on a "first come, first served" basis. To find out if reservations are accepted, call ☎(916) 653-6995. Whenever possible, it is strongly advised to make reservations, since most campsites fill up fast. Ideally, you must reserve seven months in advance and confirm by telephone two days prior to arrival. A non-refundable fee of $7.50 is charged for a reservation, which can be made by credit card, cheque or money order. You can also reserve by telephone, mail or e-mail. Cancellation: ☎800-695-2269.

For all additional information, contact the following service between 8am and 5pm:

California Department of Parks & Recreation
P.O. Box 942896
Sacramento, CA 94296-0001
☎*(916) 653-6995 or 638-5883*
☎*800-444-7275*

Information about road conditions
☎*800-427-7623*
www.cal-parks.ca.gov

Outdoor Activities

Hiking

A widely accessible activity, hiking is practised in many places in California. Several parks feature trails of varying lengths and levels of difficulty. Some even offer long-distance trails. Plunging into the wilderness, these trails can stretch over dozens of miles.

When taking these trails, hikers must of course respect the markers and be well equipped. Maps indicating the trails as well as wilderness-camping sites and shelters are available.

What's more, several local parks and reserves offer a multitude of well-maintained hiking trails abounding in natural riches of all kinds. Some parks even supply a pamphlet specific to a particular trail in order to guide you through your explorations (Anza Borrego Desert State Park, for example).

Most parks described in the "Parks" section of each chapter are brimming with possibilities. Depending on

your mood, you can explore magnificent salt marshes, majestic mountains or fascinating deserts. Head to each park's visitor centre, where the generally welcoming staff will give you the lowdown on the features of different trails, as well as their length and level of difficulty.

Finally, don't forget that California's numerous beaches also offer great opportunities for leisurely strolls in the refreshing sea air. Indeed, these are the favourite walking spots of many Californians.

Cycling

Cycling is a most enjoyable way of exploring the different regions of California.

Each chapter provides information about the best places to cycle, as well as the addresses of bike-rental shops.

In-line Skating

This still-nascent sport takes a little getting used to, but once you've gotten the hang of it, you'll appreciate how easily the miles fly by beneath your feet. In-line skating (or "roller-blading") is mainly practised in urban centres, on paved roads. A few companies rent out in-line skates. It is strongly advised to wear a helmet, knee pads, elbow pads and gloves.

California is known worldwide as the capital of

How to Survive the Desert: Some Tips

Water

Do not forget to take enough water and especially to stop and drink it at regular intervals. Over-economizing on water by hoarding it all for the return trip is not a good idea. It is better to drink it before leaving, during the trip and as you are returning.

Your Car

Make sure that your car is prepared for the desert. You must take water, a shovel, a canopy to protect you from the sun, a pump, a spare tire and food for emergencies. Ask yourself if you could survive 48 to 72hrs in your car in extreme heat.

And You

In addition to what you are carrying, do you have extra clothing to protect yourself from the sun, as well as sun screen, a hat and a good map?

Plan

Leave your itinerary with a friend, specifying your destination, the route you intend to take and when you plan to come back, as well as a description of your vehicle and the registration number. Do not count on being found by a park ranger if there is a problem. Have someone who can notify the authorities if you do not come back on the specified day.

Know your Enemies

There are three major symptoms of heat. Get to know and be alert for them.

Heat cramps: painful leg and abdominal cramps, heavy perspiration and weakness. Treatment: massage, drinking water with salt.

Exhaustion: occurs when the blood vessels dilate. Nausea, weakness, irregular pulse, headache, disorientation, change in skin colour. Same treatment as above.

Heat stroke: profoundly unstable body temperature. Sudden attacks, seizures, unconsciousness and even death. Dilated pupils, red blotchy skin, very rapid pulse, abnormal breathing, high fever. Treatment: lower the body temperature however you can. Protect the victim from injury during seizures.

If a member of your group suffers the symptoms of heat stroke, take them to a cool place in the shade. Do not continue walking and never leave the person alone; be sure to stay with them.

Stay Together

Do not split up. Emergency situations very often occur when a group seperates.

Leave Snakes Alone

Snakes attack when they are surprised and when they feel threatened. Do not try to catch or kill them. Be sure to make a lot of noise when you are walking so that they can hear you from a distance. If you are bitten, you must get medical care as soon as possible. Stay calm, not all snake bites are poisonous.

In Case of a Serious Accident

If there is an emergency, stay calm. Look for a shelter if you are hiking; if not, stay near your vehicle because you will be found much more easily. Open the hood and move your mirror around or shake a white garment to signal your location to any planes that might fly overhead.

Outdoors

in-line skating. Small wonder, since its climate and tarred roads which are maintained in tip-top condition make it a veritable roller-blading paradise. Many of these roads crisscross the cities and surrounding areas, running through breathtaking scenery. More than a mere sport, in-line skating is a true institution here, soon to be on par with surfing and cycling. In-line skaters share space with runners, walkers and cyclists in perfect harmony. Moreover, roads are not only very widespread, but irreproachably maintained.

Trying out this sport in California will undoubtedly make you a die-hard enthusiast. One more thing—practically all places that rent out bicycles also rent out in-line skates.

Rafting

River rafting, which consists of rushing down rapids in a rubber dinghy, is a thrilling sport to say the least. These crafts, which generally hold some 10 people, are resistant and flexible enough to withstand the raging rapids.

Rafting is especially enjoyed in the spring, when rivers are in spate and so feature much wilder currents. Needless to say, you must be in good shape to take part in such an activity, particularly since it's the strength of the rowers that steers the craft between the rapids. Nevertheless, a well-organized excursion in the company of an experienced guide is not inordinately dangerous. White-water rafting organizations usually supply the equipment necessary to participants' comfort and safety. So go ahead and embark on this adventure—let the rivers, finally free from the winter's ice, toss and spin you round in the midst of huge splashes!

Water Sports, Swimming and Beaches

A natural characteristic that sets California apart is its Pacific coast, which stretches from Oregon to the Mexican border. With a shoreline extending over more than 1,264mi (2,034km), the coastal landscape undergoes many transformations. The south coast, bordering on the cities of San Diego and Los Angeles, offers inviting

landscapes with warm water and waves perfect for swimming and water sports. The central coast, for its part, is wilder, with cooler waters and sparser populations.

Farther north, mist and fog cover dense sequoia forests. Water sports and swimming, however, are more dangerous here than in Southern California.

Surfing

California is a veritable surfers' Shangri-La, and a visit here may be the opportunity for neophytes to get acquainted with this mythic sport. You'll find good places to indulge in this activity on most beaches described in the "Beaches" section of each chapter. Surfboards are available for rent at several places near the main beaches.

Jogging

One of the things that may surprise you about Californians is their enthusiasm for running. Here, people of all ages and social spheres run at all hours of the day, wherever possible (and there's no shortage of places laid out for joggers, who share space with cyclists, in-line skaters and walkers). A likely reflection of a certain obsession with slimness in a land of plenty, jogging is unquestionably the most popular physical activity in this part of the country.

For more information, pick up a copy of *Raceplace*, a

monthly magazine that lists all running-related events, such as marathons, triathlons and walkathons, throughout Southern California. It is available in sports stores, sports centres and various public places.

A couple of Web sites for great and not-so-great runners:

www.raceplace.com
www.roadrunners-ports.com

Wildlife Observation

The Pacific coast is home to an abundance of wildlife, including sea lions, sea elephants, seals, California eared seals, whales and killer whales.

There's also a great variety of animal species inland due to the great diversity of habitats, such as deserts, dense forests, mountains, fertile valleys and urban landscapes, to name a few. You'll therefore get the chance to see mountain goats, foxes, stags, grizzlies, lynxes, coyotes and snakes, among others.

Golf

Golfers will be spoiled by the abundance of courses available in California. This sport occupies a choice place on both its territory and in the hearts of its residents, as evidenced by the impressive number of courses here, as well as the amount of specialized shops and services. Some offer a stunning view of the Pacific Ocean, others are nestled in the mountains or verdant valleys, while still others are set in the very heart of the desert. Most are well maintained, and the region's climate only adds to the pleasure of the experience. Several golf courses are linked to a hotel complex.

California is designed to please the most demanding of golfers. Indeed, the state and its courses have often been chosen as the site of various tournaments, including several at the national and international level. To book tee time, call or log on to this reservation service at (*www.selectteetimes.com;* ☎*877-486-GOLF, www.golfsocal.com*).

Horseback Riding

Several horseback-riding centres offer lessons or rides. A few even organize multi-day excursions. Centres usually offer one of two riding styles: classical (English saddle) or western. As the two are very different, it's best to check which is offered by a particular centre when making reservations. Some state parks also have riding trails.

Scuba Diving

Most regions have good scuba-diving sites, and California is home to several diving centres, schools and clubs.

Diving-centre addresses are listed in several chapters.

Suggested Tours

0   4   8km

0   2.5   5mi

Santa Clarita

N

Burbank

San Fernando Valley

170

5

Glendale

Pasadena

118

see Hollywood and surroundings

101

405

see Pasadena and surroundings

West Hollywood

Hollywood

University of California at Los Angeles

2

101

Alhambra

10

Bel Air

Beverly Hills

see Downtown Los Angeles

2

see Mid-Wilshire and Westside

East Los Angeles

see Santa Monica and Venice

Los Angeles

10

10

710

Santa Monica

Culver City

1

Maywood

5

110

Venice

Marina del Rey

Inglewood

Florence

Bell Gardens

see Airport and South Bay

Los Angeles International Aéroport

Westmont

710

Downey

El Segundo

1

Willow Brook

Lynwood

Hawthorne

Gardena

Lawdale

Manhattan Beach

405

Compton

Paramount

Hermosa Beach

1

Carson

Torrance

Redondo Beach

West Carson

710

Lomita

110

1

Palos Verdes Estates

Long Beach

Pacific Ocean

Rolling Hills Estate

Palos Verdes Peninsula

Lunada Bay

Palos Verdes Dr.

San Pedro

Port of Los Angeles

see Long Beach and San Pedro

Rancho Palos Verdes

Royal Palms State Beach

Cabrillo Beach

©ULYSSES

Santa Catalina Island

Los Angeles

L os Angeles ★★★ is a city of myths. For nearly a century, it has been one of the world's entertainment capitals.

Hollywood, once a modest suburb that quickly evolved into the undisputed centre of the world film industry, remains synonymous in the popular imagination with the glamour of the silver screen. Who could be better at spreading myths, both about themselves and the city they call home, than the producers of the great Hollywood epics?

Today, the entertainment industry—film, television, popular music, and various spinoffs—remains an important part of L.A.'s economy. (Scarcely anyone hesitates to call the city by its familiar initials.) The industry, and the aura of sun-drenched opulence that has led to the mildly pejorative "La-La Land" epithet, continues to dominate perceptions in the outside world. It remains a powerful magnet for visitors. But Hollywood and its glitzy veneer are only one element among many in the complex and fascinating scene that forms the second largest metropolitan area in the United States. (Only New York

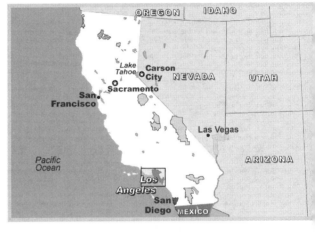

City and its surroundings have a bigger population.)

Contributing along with Hollywood to the La-La Land image are certain areas on the city's west side such as Beverly Hills, a place known for its serious wealth, as well as a number of beachfront communities, whose denizens seem to be portrayed almost invariably as blonde-haired, bronze-skinned, somewhat empty-headed surfers. In reality, parts of Hollywood are decidedly slummy; some of the big studios are located in less romantic-sounding suburbs like Burbank or Culver City.

And most Angelenos live far from any beach. Many have tawnier complexions, attesting to the city's fast-growing Latino and Asian communities, as well as its well established African-American population. L.A.'s vast ethnic variety is one of many facets that make the city more interesting, more real, and more sophisticated than its shallow cardboard-cutout image often suggests.

Following are some of the ways in which Los Angeles differs from its popular image:

Myth #1: Los Angeles is a city of glitz and glamour.

Reality: Los Angeles is largely a gritty, blue-collar industrial town with North America's heaviest concentration of manufacturing jobs, ranging from low-wage clothing production to advanced military aircraft assembly to cutting-edge ventures in various high-tech realms. The city is surrounded by a vast sprawl of white-collar, white-bread suburbs, many with their own share of industrial establishments. To the west and to the north are a few glitzy or quirky enclaves on which the city's rarified image has been built. Although this image is not totally unfounded, it bears no closer resemblance to total reality than do the products of Hollywood's film and television studios. Visitors who remain firmly ensconced on the west side of the metropolitan area may escape exposure to the more plebeian reality beyond, but it's definitely out there, along street after street of humble bungalows, bleak gas stations, and ubiquitous mini-malls. More than 16 million people live in the Los Angeles area. Only an infinitesimal fraction are movie stars. Many people work at jobs that pay little more than minimum wage. As in any other wealthy part of the world, the majority of the population lead humdrum, middle-class lives. In fact, most of the L.A. area has a startlingly "middle America" character, which surprises some travellers who come expecting to find a city with a zanier disposition. Its very ordinariness can come as a shock.

Myth #2: Los Angeles has no real downtown area.

Reality: Los Angeles has sometimes been characterized more as a cluster of villages than as a coherent city, but it does indeed have an area that is instantly recognizable as downtown, with office towers, public buildings, cultural attractions, shopping streets and an extensive skid road. Many first-time visitors are surprised to discover that downtown L.A. is nowhere near the coast. In fact, it lies 12.4mi (20km) inland, near the site where an early Spanish outpost was established in 1781. Because of the region's very decentralized character, downtown L.A. doesn't form as strong a central focus as do the downtown areas in more traditional cities, though it does lay claim to Southern California's highest concentration of office space. (When referring to downtown, it is useful to specify "downtown L.A." since several suburban municipalities have their own, more modest, downtown areas.) Lasrge parts of downtown L.A. are far from pretty and things can turn quite spooky at night. But downtown is for real and it's definitely worth visiting.

Myth #3: It's impossible to get around without a car.

Reality: L.A.'s extensive freeway network is more than myth, and it's true many Angelenos wouldn't dream of going beyond the next corner without jumping in the car. Alternatives do exist, however. Getting around car-ob-

sessed L.A. by public transit requires patience, but it's still quite possible. The author of a travel guidebook from a well-known New York publisher sneers: "I've heard rumors about visitors to Los Angeles who have toured the city entirely by public transportation, but they can't be more than that—rumors." The Los Angeles County Metropolitan Transportation Authority (mercifully abbreviated as MTA) is the butt of countless jokes: in fact, it is under court order to add more buses to relieve overcrowding on certain routes. But the MTA and other operators do offer a fairly comprehensive service. The mostly bus-based transit system is augmented by a small subway and light-rail network and by suburban trains. With a little planning, visitors wishing to avoid car expenses and freeway madness can reach most points of interest by bus, though late-evening service is spotty. (See p 69.) An unusual and very un-L.A. note: the Getty Center, a top cultural attraction in a remote hilltop setting, actually favours transit users. Visitors arriving by car require advance parking reservations, which may be hard to get at certain times. Bus passengers can arrive when ever they choose.

Myth #4: Culture in Los Angeles is all candy floss and superficiality.

Reality: There's substantially more to culture in L.A. than what emerges from the Hollywood studios and their amusement park adjuncts. Let's start with museums. By one

Smog—at Least You Can See what You're Breathing!

Smog is one of the curses of life in Los Angeles. The city's millions of motor vehicles and thousands of industrial establishments spew a noxious stew of gases that cannot disperse easily because of the city's walled-in saucer shape, creating a dull brown haze that varies in intensity from day to day. Smog alerts are issued on certain days, during which people with respiratory problems are urged to stay indoors. Exhaust gases and moisture (the word smog signifies smoke plus fog) are often held in place by layers of cooler air above and cooked to an unappealing consistency by hours of relentless sunshine. Some days, the result is highly visible to anyone approaching the city by air.

The South Coast Air Quality Management District, whose job it is to enforce regulations set by various levels of government, has clamped tighter controls on factories and ordered changes in the design of vehicle exhaust systems. These efforts have achieved modest success, and the number of smog alerts has declined. Lifestyle-infringing measures such as the restriction of private vehicle use appear to be unthinkable, however. Public policy seems aimed less at eliminating the problem than at keeping it from getting worse. To be sure, air pollution in L.A. is less severe than in many Third World cities, and even within the U.S. it has been eclipsed by Houston, under the Texas government's very lax environmental standards. Smog is nonetheless an element of local identity in L.A. that seems to be worn almost proudly as a badge of self-deprecation.

forms of music and theatre. While popular music tends to overshadow what esthetes may regard as more sophisticated forms like jazz and classical, variety is the key. A glance at the listings in weekly entertainment guides will amaze and delight culture lovers who come expecting little more than the one-dimensional scene that L.A.'s commercial image-builders have mischievously succeeded in conveying. Yes, there's life beyond Universal Studios and Disneyland.

Geography and Climate

To many, Los Angeles is associated almost automatically with the idea of suburban sprawl. A glance at any detailed map of southern California shows that the L.A. agglomeration spreads along the Pacific coast from Ventura County northwest of the city to the far end of Orange County to the southeast, and deep into Riverside and San Bernardino counties in the interior, where it encroaches on mountain and desert. If not for a stretch of relatively undeveloped territory in the northern part of San Diego County, Southern California would form a megalopolis extending beyond Tijuana, on the other side of the Mexican border. For an unfortunately large number of people living in the Los Angeles area, roundtrip commutes of 62mi (100km) or more are an endurance-testing, freeway-clogging part of everyday life.

This chapter concerns itself with Los Angeles County, the area centred around the City of Los Angeles and including

count, the L.A. area has nearly 300 museums, historic buildings, libraries with special collections, botanical gardens, and other sites with exhibits or collections open to public view. (Many, though not all of them, are explored in this chapter.) The Getty Center and the Los Angeles County Museum of Art both house extensive collections covering numerous periods and backgrounds. Together with the Museum of Contemporary Art, they reveal L.A. to be much more than an upstart in the world of art. In the domain of public performance, Los Angeles provides a broad array of venues offering many coastal areas stretching from Malibu to Long Beach. The neighbouring counties, which include outlying portions of the metropolitan area, are covered in other chapters. The total population of the five-county area was estimated in 1999 at 16.3 million. Los Angeles County, with a population of 9.7 million, encompasses 80 incorporated municipalities, of which the City of Los Angeles is by far the largest, with 3.7 million inhabitants. Certain well-known areas, among them Santa Monica, Beverly Hills, Pasadena and Long Beach, form separate municipalities, whereas others, including Hollywood, Venice and San Pedro, are part of the City of Los Angeles.

Much of Los Angeles County consists of a broad basin extending east and north from the coast, bound on the north by the San Gabriel mountain range. Dividing the northern and central parts of the county is a ridge of high hills known as the Santa Monica Mountains. The San Gabriel Valley, which includes Pasadena, lies beyond the hills to the northeast of downtown Los Angeles. The very populous San Fernando Valley, much of it included in the City of Los Angeles, lies to the northwest. The Los Angeles River, whose irregular flow caused serious flooding after heavy rains in the early 20th century, has since been channeled into a concrete-walled ditch, emptying into the Pacific near Long Beach. At times, it is almost completely dry.

The entire area lies near a shifting geological structure known as the San Andreas fault, and seismic activity is quite common.

Thousands of minor temors are recorded each year, and major earthquakes can be quite common (the last one in the 20th century occurred in 1994). Building codes insist on stringent design measures to protect structures, especially larger ones, against seismic shocks.

Los Angeles enjoys a semi-arid climate, with an average of 329 sunny days a year. Low clouds and isolated fog may greet the early riser, but these tend to burn off an hour or two after sunrise. Average annual rainfall is only about 14in (356mm), and most of this falls between November and March, although there may be occasional rain in other seasons. Temperatures are pleasant most of the year, with an annual average of 64°F (18°C). The proximity of the ocean and the shielding effect of nearby mountains keep temperatures from moving to extremes. Humidity is generally low, and frosts are unusual except at the highest elevations. Even in the summer, extreme heat is rare. In July and August, the average maximum temperature is 82°F (28°C), and the average minimum is 63°F (17°C). In January, the coolest month, an average day will see a high of 64°F (18°C) and a low of 45°F (7°C). Daytime temperatures are often several degrees cooler near the beaches and a few degrees warmer inland toward the desert.

History

Colony and Annexation

Before the arrival of the first European visitors, the area around present-day Los Angeles was very sparsely populated because its low rainfall made sustained agriculture difficult, though fishing and trading were conducted by scattered Native American groups distantly related to the Aztecs of central Mexico. In 1769, a Spanish expedition exchanged gifts with inhabitants of the village of Yang-na, near where downtown L.A. now stands. Two years later, a Catholic mission, one of a string of such missions in California, was established about 9mi (15km) away. On September 4, 1781, a group of settlers from western Mexico established a village they called El Pueblo de Nuestra Señora la Reina de Los Angeles, literally the Village of Our Lady the Queen of Angels. To this day some publicists use the term City of Angels to designate L.A.

When Mexico declared independence from Spain in 1810, the colony of Alta California (Upper California) followed suit, although it was virtually cut off from the rest of Mexico before fighting ended and independence was formalized 11 years later. In 1835, when the first Yankees from the eastern United States began arriving in the area, Los Angeles had a population of about 1,250. The Yankees showed great initiative in developing farms and workshops, and their numbers increased rapidly. Pío Pico, the Mexican governor, did little to stop them. War broke out between Mexico and the United States in 1846, with the U.S. amputating nearly half of Mexico's territory. When U.S. forces entered Los Angeles, hardly a shot was fired. A revolt in early 1847 was easily put down.

The city was formally incorporated under U.S. law in 1850 and became the rather lawless centre of a cattle ranching area. This era ended with a severe drought that began in 1862. The arrival of the railway in 1876 and the development of irrigated agriculture brought thousands of new settlers, and the city's population topped 50,000 by 1890, only to double in the following decade. Oranges and other crops that could survive long rail journeys to eastern markets provided a huge boon to the nearby countryside.

Overcoming Obstacles to Growth

Los Angeles, perennially short of water, would soon begin the first of the water wars. A grand scheme was hatched in 1904 to build an aqueduct from the Owens Valley, situated 249mi (400km) to the northeast at the base of the Sierra Nevada. This was later viewed as a massive swindle that hugely benefitted a small group of speculators (and formed the plot of the 1976 film *Chinatown*). Since that time, many battles over water resources have raged between city-dwellers and agricultural interests in California, as well as between the north and south of the state. Almost 100 years later, the Owens Valley still supplies most of L.A.'s piped water.

The absence of a natural seaport was overcome by the construction of a harbour at San Pedro, about 22mi (35km) south of downtown L.A., with the first wharf opening in 1914. One by one, the obstacles to growth were falling by the wayside.

Through most of the 19th century, San Francisco was California's dominant urban area, propelled in part by a massive gold rush that began in the late 1840s, and by favourable farming conditions in surrounding regions, especially compared to the more arid south. The city became the undisputed centre of transport, finance and much else. But when entire neighbourhoods were levelled by a severe earthquake in 1906, San Francisco's loss became L.A.'s gain. Thousands of San Franciscans, suddenly homeless, flocked to new homes in the Los Angeles area. This proved to be a decisive phase in L.A.'s gradual ascendency to its status as the largest and most powerful metropolitan area in the western United States.

Blessed by its sunny climate, Los Angeles attracted two of the 20th century's most glamorous nascent industries, cinema and aeronautics. The ability to film outdoors nearly every day of the year, together with the varied natural scenery available nearby, proved an irresistible lure to the pioneers of the modern film industry. And the founders of the Douglas and Lockheed aircraft companies set up production facilities close by, secure in the knowledge that skies would be mostly clear for test flights. World War II saw a huge increase in the production of military equipment, including aircraft and missiles. Military procurement played a major role in L.A.'s industrial growth right up to the 1980s.

The middle years of the century were a time when agriculture declined in relative importance as huge tracts of farmland were obliterated to make way for the suburban sprawl that would become an L.A. hallmark. A vast freeway network was built, and the area's extensive tramway network was dismantled after falling into the hands of a company controlled by General Motors. The model of the car-dependent city was born.

New Patterns of Population

At the same time, major shifts occured in migration patterns as large numbers of newcomers continued to arrive. L.A. was no longer being predominantly settled by light-skinned people from the eastern or midwestern U.S. The availability of jobs and affordable housing attracted large numbers of African-Americans from Texas, Louisiana and neighbouring states. An influx of wartime refugees enriched L.A. with the presence of some of Europe's leading creative talent, including writers Thomas Mann and Bertolt Brecht as well as composers Kurt Weill, Arnold Schoenberg, Béla Bartók and Igor Stravinsky.

The wartime *bracero* farm labour program brought thousands of Mexicans to Southern California, joining the descendants of inhabitants who were there before the U.S. annexation. In later decades, fresh waves of immigration from Mexico, as well as from Guatemala, El Salvador and other Latin American countries, transformed the character of large parts of the city. About one-quarter of Los Angeles residents speak Spanish as their mother tongue, and tacos are just as popular at local eateries as hamburgers. The U.S. may indeed

Los Angeles

have annexed California, but to L.A. residents it can sometimes seem that Mexicans are gradually reclaiming lost territory.

Helping round out the population mix is the strong Asian presence. Los Angeles has the largest concentration of Koreans outside Korea, as well as substantial Chinese, Japanese, Vietnamese, Philippine and other East Asian communities. India, Iran, the Middle East, and the Trans-Caucasus have also offered important contributions to the city's cultural blend. The very diverse nature of the local economy creates opportunities for low-skilled and high-skilled alike. The existence of a broad array of ethnic institutions acts as a further magnet to new arrivals.

The history of intercultural relations in Los Angeles has not been all sweetness and light. In 1943, a week-long outbreak of street fights ensued between English-speaking naval personnel and local Spanish-speaking youths. This episode became known as the Zoot Suit Riots, named after a style of clothing favoured by some Latinos at the time. In the mid-1960s, as dreams of prosperity turned to dust for many black residents in the face of job discrimination and other problems, frustrations rose to a boil in 1965 and spilled over into six days of burning and looting in the mostly black Watts neighbourhood, with dozens of deaths. Over the years, new tensions were created by heavy-handed policies that treated some lower-income neighbourhoods as military zones of occupation. In 1992, four white police officers were caught on

video savagely beating a black motorist stopped for speeding and were acquitted of assault charges by an all-white suburban jury. This caused pent-up pressures to break out into an even more violent and destructive orgy of rioting that started in the city's mixed-race South-Central district and spread beyond. Even after a change in command and approach at the Los Angeles Police Department, the force's problems were far from over. In 1999, a specialized anti-gang squad had to be dismantled after some officers were found to be engaging in patterns of violence and larceny that seemed more characteristic of the street gang members who were their intended targets.

These incidents grabbed headlines around the world, but they don't tell the whole story. Marriage statistics from recent years in Los Angeles County offer a more harmonious tale, with a steady rise in the number of interracial unions. Maybe people don't hate each other as much as we are sometimes led to believe.

Politics

A general rule of thumb is that Los Angeles County tends to show liberal and Democratic leanings in political matters, while the outlying counties, particularly Orange County, tend to support conservative, Republican candidates. However, Los Angeles lacks the political machine found in some eastern U.S. cities, and voting patterns are more fluid. Richard Riordan, the Los Angeles mayor first elected in 1993, is a wealthy Republican who knowns how to appeal to poorer,

Democratic-leaning voters. He succeeded long-time mayor Tom Bradley, a Democrat. Conversely, some more Republican-minded districts have sent Democrats to the U.S. Congress and the State Assembly because of unease with the moral preaching or anti-immigrant biases of certain Republican candidates. Some Republicans scorn the Hollywood show business establishment as a hotbed of pro-Democrat activism, but Hollywood also has its share of Republican firebrands.

Economy

The agricultural wealth on which Los Angeles was originally built gave way by the middle of the 20th century to almost wall-to-wall urban development. The local industry with by far the highest profile, sometimes referred to simply as The Industry, is, of course, the motion picture business, closely linked with other forms of mainstream entertainment such as television and popular music. The entertainment industry has contributed inestimably to L.A.'s development and employs many people. As mentioned earlier in this chapter, however, it is not as big a factor as the various manufacturing enterprises that have spread across the region.

Perhaps the most notable characteristic of the L.A. economy is its hugely diversified nature. On the manufacturing and technology front, it covers the gamut from Third World-style sweatshops in the downtown garment district to high-wage defence industry establishments to new-age firms working in a range of high-tech sectors. Los Angeles is also finance (those gleaming downtown office towers aren't as empty as they once were), transport (L.A. International Airport and the twin seaports of Long Beach and San Pedro are the busiest in the western U.S. in their respective domains), and tourism (readers of this guidebook provide living proof). One perhaps surprising source of wealth is crude oil production: although output has fallen well below peak levels, billions of dollars' worth of oil has been extracted over the decades, and working wells are easily visible within city limits, particularly in a barren, hilly area northeast of the main airport.

Like other parts of the U.S., Los Angeles has disparities of wealth and poverty that some western European visitors may find shocking. Recent immigrants, some of them illegals working at less than minimum wage, provide what amount to hidden subsidies for a range of businesses and even to homeowners doing renovations or maintenance. At certain street corners, and outside some stores where building supplies are sold, men forlornly gather early in the morning in the hope of being hired out for the day. On traffic islands in some parts of the city, men or women may be seen selling bags of oranges or peanuts to passing motorists. It is not a pretty picture, but it is a humble stepping stone to one aspect of the American Dream.

Finding Your Way Around

Getting to Los Angeles

By Plane

The Los Angeles area is served by five airports offering scheduled commercial flights. (Several smaller airports in the region handle only private or military flights.)

The biggest and busiest by far is the **Los Angeles International Airport**, often referred to by its three-letter international code, **LAX**. This gargantuan facility, located in the southwestern part of the city near the Pacific shoreline (most departing eastbound flights circle briefly over the ocean before turning inland), handles nearly all international flights destined for Southern California and a great many domestic flights as well. LAX's terminal buildings area laid out in a horseshoe shape and are numbered from 1 to 7. An eighth building, the newer Tom Bradley International Terminal (named after a former mayor), is located between terminals 3 and 4.

LAX is served by a very impressive roster of international carriers. Nearly all of the world's major trans-Atlantic and trans-Pacific airlines offer scheduled service here on a daily basis. It is among the busiest airports in the western hemisphere for international traffic and *the* busiest by far for trans-Pacific traffic. It is also served by

an impressive array of carriers from Latin America and Canada. A long list of cities on five continents are linked to LAX by non-stop flights.

Most non-U.S. carriers, but by no means all of them, operate from the bright, spacious Tom Bradley International Terminal. Some operate from other terminals. For example, Air Canada, KLM, Virgin Atlantic and Air New Zealand are among the airlines using Terminal 2. With a new wave of alliances and consolidations sweeping the global airline industry, it would be hazardous to guess, even a few months after these words are written, which terminal any given carrier is operating from. When arranging to have someone meet an arriving flight, or when catching a departing flight, it is essential for travellers to check their printed itineraries to avoid mixups. If the information is not clear, they should consult their airline company or travel agent. For connections between terminals, free buses, marked by the letter A and running every few minutes, circle the airport in a counter-clockwise direction, stopping near the lower level of each terminal building at stops marked "LAX Shuttle".

LAX is also served by a vast number of domestic flights. All major U.S. airlines, and some minor ones as well, provide frequent service to Los Angeles from their respective hub cities, as well as from additional points including the larger east coast cities. The most frequent service on short-haul routes, including the very busy corridor to the San Francisco area, is operated by rivals

United Airlines and South-west.

Although amenities such as food and shopping at LAX have improved some-what in recent years, the choice remains slim in comparison to many other major airports around the world. One retailer holds a monopoly on duty-free goods, and prices are not cheap.

The other commercial airports serving the Los Angeles area are:

• **Ontario International Airport**, in the far eastern suburbs, with domestic flights serving points in the western U.S. plus some key midwestern and eastern airline hubs, as well as a small handful of international flights from Mexico and Canada.

• **John Wayne Airport** (named after the Holly-wood cowboy), in Orange County southeast of Los Angeles, with a fairly heavy schedule of flights to points in the western U.S. and some airline hubs further east.

• **Burbank Airport**, in the northern part of the metropolitan area, convenient to Hollywood and Pasadena, served by a handful of airlines offering busy schedules of mostly short-haul domestic flights.

• **Long Beach Municipal Airport**, near the southern tip of Los Angeles County and the quietest of the five main airports, with a small array (this is relative, of course) of domestic flights.

By Train

Amtrak (☎800-872-7245; www.amtrak.com) operates regional services as well as long-distance trains from

the beautiful and ornate Union Station at the edge of downtown Los Angeles. (Union Station is worth a visit even if rail travel is not in your plans: see p 82.) The station is served by Metrolink suburban trains, by the Metro Red Line (subway), and by numerous local bus routes. Long-haul trains, offering coach, sleeping-car and dining-car service, include the *Coast Starlight* to Seattle via Oakland and Portland, the *Southwest Chief* to Chicago via Flagstaff (near Arizona's Grand Canyon), Albuquerque and Kansas City, and the *Sunset Limited* to Tucson, Houston, New Orleans and Orlando. Regional service from San Diego to Los Angeles (trip time: 2hrs, 40min) operates 11 times daily along a scenic route with many intermediate stops in San Diego County and Orange County. Four of these trains continue north to Santa Barbara, with one going as far as San Luis Obispo. Daily service between Los Angeles and Las Vegas was set to begin operation in 2001. Amtrak also runs buses from Union Station to Bakersfield, connecting there with its four daily trains to the San Francisco Bay area via the San Joaquín Valley.

By Bus

Scheduled intercity bus service to and from Los Angeles is dominated by **Greyhound Lines** (☎800-231-2222; www.greyhound.com). The main Los Angeles terminal is located along Sixth Street about 1.2mi (2km) east of the downtown area (served by MTA bus route 60) in a bleak industrial zone. The surrounding streets are not safe at night, and taxis are scarce. The terminal, although built recently, is

cramped and uncomfort-able—not the best way to begin or end a journey. Greyhound seems determined to pursue its sad and relentless downmarket thrust. That said, hourly service is provided to San Diego and across the border to Tijuana. Greyhound also runs several buses a day to San Francisco and serves Las Vegas, as well as points as near as Santa Barbara or Palm Springs and as distant as Boston or Miami. A Mexican company operating under the names Crucero and Golden State (☎213-627-2940) operates from the same terminal, offering competing service to Tijuana and to certain points in the California interior. Another Mexican company called Americanos (☎213-688-0044) operates to points in Mexico and Texas from an even more unpleasant terminal directly across the street.

By Car

Motorists approaching Los Angeles from the north (or heading north) have three main alternatives. Interstate Highway 5 (or I-5) provides the fastest link to or from the San Francisco area through the rather dull scenery of the San Joaquín Valley deep in the interior. The same highway continues north to Oregon, Washington state, and the Canadian border near Vancouver. A slower but more interesting route is U.S. Highway 101, also known as the 101 Free-way, that hugs the coast in some spots near San Luis Obispo and Santa Barbara. Slowest but most scenic is the Pacific Coast Highway, designated Highway 1, a narrow, curvy road that clings to the coast most of the way (but is prone to fog and occasional wash-outs).

South to San Diego and Tijuana, Interstate 5 is really the only direct route. Interstate 405, running along the west side of Los Angeles and then turning east past Long Beach, meets the I-5 in the southern part of Orange County. Going east from L.A., Interstate 10 runs through southern Arizona, New Mexico and Texas all the way to Florida. To reach Las Vegas, the I-10 connects with the I-15 near San Bernardino. Because much of the territory north and east of Los Angeles is uninhabited mountain or desert, there are fewer road links than might otherwise be expected given the city's size. Sunday evening traffic into L.A. can often be very slow.

Getting Around in Los Angeles

By Car

Los Angeles has a world-wide reputation for its extensive freeway network. Indeed, the city and its suburbs became the prototype soon after the Second World War for the car-dependent U.S. model where hardly anyone would dream of going anywhere without hopping into an automobile, and distant places could be reached swiftly and effortlessly along multi-lane ribbons of controlled-access highway. This began in 1940 with the opening of the Pasadena Freeway (initially known as the Arroyo Seco Parkway and now designated a historical monument—you take your

history where you can find it), snaking through the hills northeast of downtown L.A. The network later expanded throughout the metropolitan area and beyond.

L.A.'s urban freeway network is probably the most extensive anywhere, although there are not quite as many freeways as some first-time visitors may imagine. Indeed, in parts of the city it's possible to travel fairly long distances without encountering a freeway. Some other U.S. cities have denser networks, at least in relation to population. In L.A., the early dream has turned into a nightmare for many motorists, who have to put up with ever-lower speeds and massive traffic jams on a daily basis, and not just at rush hours. Some radio stations devote a significant part of their programming to traffic reports. Often, it's possible to avoid the freeway system altogether. But when entering Los Angeles, or when going long distances

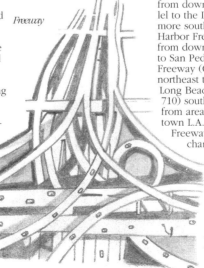

Freeway

within the metropolitan area, chances are that anyone going by car will spend at least part of their trip on a freeway.

The freeways are identified both by name and by highway number. Some, but not all, are officially designated as part of the interstate highway network. Several freeways change names along the way. For example, Interstate Highway 10 (I-10 for short) is an east-west highway that is named the Santa Monica Freeway west of downtown L.A. but the San Bernardino Freeway east of downtown. The north-south I-5 is called the Hollywood Freeway north of downtown L.A. but becomes the Santa Ana Freeway south of downtown.

Other major freeways include the San Diego Freeway (I-405) that branches off from the I-5, following a more westerly route through the L.A. area (and passing near the airport) before rejoining the I-5; the Pomona Freeway (California 60) running east from downtown L.A. parallel to the I-10 but along a more southerly route; the Harbor Freeway (I-110) from downtown L.A. south to San Pedro; the Pasadena Freeway (California 110) northeast to Pasadena; the Long Beach Freeway (I-710) south to Long Beach from areas east of downtown L.A.; the Hollywood Freeway (U.S. 101, changing to California 170 in North Hollywood) from downtown L.A. northwest through Hollywood and the San Fernando Valley) and the Ventura Freeway (U.S. 101), picking up where the Hollywood Freeway leaves off in North Hollywood and running west to Ventura county. Keep in mind that this list is by no means comprehensive.

Of course, there's a lot more to the road network than just freeways. Some of the main roads run for very long distances, forming a solid rectangular grid across much of the metropolitan area. Perhaps the best known of L.A.'s urban boulevards is Wilshire Boulevard, running from the western part of downtown west through what has become known as the mid-Wilshire district (home to several museums), and then on through Beverly Hills and Westwood to Santa Monica. Sunset Bouelvard, further north, runs west from the northern edge of downtown L.A. in an occasionally meandering route through Hollywood, West Hollywood, Westwood, Brentwood (passing near the Getty Center), and then through the hills of Pacific Palisades before reaching the coast.

To get between Los Angeles International Airport and Hollywood or downtown L.A., Fairfax Avenue and La Brea Avenue, parallel north-south arteries, can be handy time-savers, with short freeway-type stretches over part of their length south of the Santa Monica Freeway. They run through a hilly area with working oil wells clearly visible near the roadsides.

Parking is not often a problem in most of L.A. This is a city built for cars, and an astounding portion of the landscape is covered with parking lots. Many of the more expensive restaurants and hotels, and even a few of the

medium-priced ones, offer valet parking. Parking can be more difficult in downtown L.A. and downtown Santa Monica, as well as near Venice Beach and parts of Hollywood or Beverly Hills. What this usually means, however, isn't that it's impossible to find any sort of parking but that visitors have to use paying parking lots rather than being able to count on free street parking. This may even mean having to walk a couple of blocks, something that could horrify some Angelenos but that most visitors will take in stride.

Car Rental

Most of the companies listed below have rental locations at Los Angeles International Airport and in other parts of the L.A. area.

Avis
☎ *(213) 977-1450*
☎ *(310) 646-5600*
☎ *800-331-1212*

Beverly Hills Rent A Car
☎ *(310) 337-1400*

Bob Leech's Auto Rental
☎ *(310) 673-2727*
☎ *800-635-1240*

Budget
☎ *800-221-1203*

Dollar
☎ *(310) 645-9333*
☎ *800-800-4000*

Enterprise
☎ *800-736-8222*

Fox Car Rental
☎ *(310) 641-3838*
☎ *800-225-4369*

Hertz
☎ *800-654-3131*

Los Angeles Rent-A-Car
☎ *(310) 670-9945*

Lucky
☎ *(310) 641-2323*
☎ *800-400-4736*

Midway
☎ *(310) 445-4355*
☎ *800-824-5260*

National
☎ *800-227-7368*

Payless
☎ *(310) 645-2100*

Shooshani's Avon Car Rental
☎ *(323) 650-2631*

Thrifty
☎ *(310) 645-1880*

Motorcycle Rental

EagleRider
☎ *(310) 320-4008*
☎ *800-501-8687*

By Taxi

Taxis, as a general rule, are used not by motorists but by people on foot. Since most people in L.A. who have enough money to take taxis are rarely far from their own vehicles, there is little demand for taxis and hence not many taxis for a city this size. Although there is no rule against flagging taxis on the street, it is rare to see unoccupied taxis cruising along. There are stands with waiting taxis in a handful of places, for example at the airports, the main railway station, outside some (but not all) of the bigger hotels, especially downtown, and near several spots with heavy pedestrian traffic downtown and in Hollywood or Santa Monica. Otherwise, it's necessary for passengers to phone a taxi company and hope the dispatcher can locate a vehicle not too far away. Sometimes the wait can be quite long. Among the companies with citywide fleets are Yellow Cab (☎800-808-1000), L.A. Taxi (☎800-652-8294) and Independent Taxi (☎323-462-1088). Fares start at $1.90 and rise by $1.60/mi ($1.00/km). Since the distances to be covered are sometimes quite considerable, taxis can be an expensive proposition. There is a surcharge of $2.50 on trips originating at Los Angeles International Airport.

By Public Transit

Despite its well deserved reputation as a car-obsessed city that seems to spread out endlessly, Los Angeles does have a fairly comprehensive public transit system. Hundreds of bus routes link various parts of the city and the surrounding suburbs, augmented by a small network of subway and light rail lines called Metro Rail and a commuter rail system called Metrolink.

Few people brag about L.A.'s public transit system except in a pejorative sense. Some trips by bus seem to take forever, with long waits and long travel times. But things aren't as bad as they are often portrayed, and visitors who aren't in a huge hurry will find the transit system to be an economical and entirely feasible way of getting around. Most points of interest to visitors (with the notable exception of Dodger Stadium) are reasonably well served, although reliability is sometimes a problem, and service on most routes drops to infrequent intervals by mid-evening. A few bus routes operate 24hrs a day. Most others run from about 5am to midnight, seven days a week. Some do not operate in the late evening or

A Recent History of Public Transit in L.A.

Until just after the Second World War, the Los Angeles area had one of the world's most extensive networks of streetcars and electric railways connecting the city to its far-flung suburbs. Starting soon after the war, the system was totally dismantled under pressure from the automobile industry, which was able to influence local and state politicians to direct massive public investment into developing a major urban freeway network. This established a prototype that was subsequently imitated in other U.S. cities.

For several decades, transit users in the U.S.'s second largest metropolitan area relied on a totally bus-based system that operated on a shoestring budget. Then, in the 1980s, along came federal funds aimed at promoting public transit development. The MTA, picking up where a predecessor agency left off, devised expensive plans for new rail systems that appeared to place the interests of consultants and contractors above those of the eventual users. The result is a very limited urban rail network that nonetheless developed huge cost overruns and long construction delays.

Nor did it escape notice that heavy subsidies were being directed to comfortable suburban trains serving affluent commuters, while buses serving urban working-class areas were becoming increasingly decrepit and overcrowded. Legal action by a public interest group led to federal court orders calling for a rapid expansion of the bus fleet. Despite some foot-dragging by the MTA, service has slowly been improving. It is less common now to see crowded buses having to skip stops and strand passengers waiting to board, although this does still happen sometimes.

on weekends, while some others run only at rush hours. Most buses, and the entire rail network, are accessible to passengers in wheelchairs.

L.A.'s dominant transit operator is the Los Angeles County Metropolitan Transportation Authority, commonly known as MTA. Several suburban municipalities have their own bus operations that serve as part of a coordinated network in conjunction with the MTA. Service within

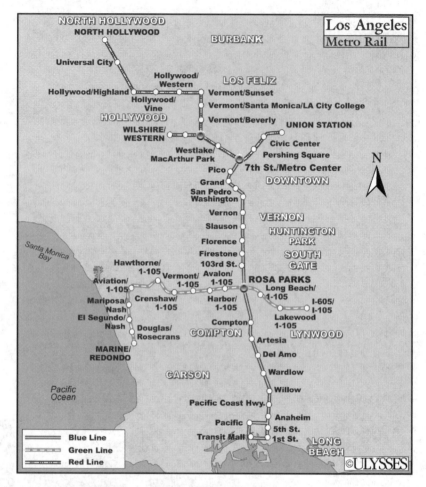

downtown Los Angeles and in several other parts of the city is supplemented by short and sometimes circuitous bus routes forming the separate DASH system.

Here are a few pointers on getting around by public transport. Remember that a little advance planning can save plenty of time. The route network is quite complex, and some routes offer faster or more frequent service than others. Once you've decided where you want to go, consult (if you have

Internet access) the MTA website at www.mta.net. This site provides a customized trip planning service, with detailed route and schedule information. It also provides links to the websites of other transit operators in the region.

Of course, not everyone has easy Internet access away from home. Another solution is the information service provided by telephone, reached by dialing 800-COMMUTE (☎800-266-6883). Voice prompts (in English or Spanish) direct callers to the pertinent

transit operator and route number or service. Bus routes serving many points of interest are indicated in the "Exploring" section of this chapter. Printed information is also available. Tourism information offices and MTA customer centres sometimes have route maps available and can usually provide printed timetables for specific routes. MTA customer centres are located at Union Station (east portal); downstairs in the Arco Plaza building at Fifth and Flower streets downtown; in the mid-Wilshire district at the corner of Wilshire and La Brea; and in several other locations. With a few rare exceptions, schedules are *not* posted at MTA bus stops.

The standard MTA fare (at press time) for bus or Metro Rail is $1.35 per trip anywhere within Los Angeles County. From 9pm to 5am the fare is $0.75. Tokens, sold in bags of 10, cost $0.90 each. Weekly passes, valid for unlimited travel on the MTA system from Sunday until the following Saturday, cost $11 and have become very popular. Monthly and semi-monthly passes are also available. Children under five travel free.

Transfers for connections between buses or between bus and rail cost $0.25 per use and are valid until the time marked on them. Express buses with route numbers in the 400s or 500s require fare supplements of $0.50 or $1, or sometimes higher, depending on the distance travelled on express portions of the route. No supplement is required for portions of these routes providing local service. Exact change is required when boarding any bus: drivers are not allowed to provide change. (Obviously, it's important to keep a good supply of 25-cent coins and $1 bills or coins.) Pass holders do not require transfers but do have to pay express supplements.

At Metro Rail stations, tickets for individual trips are sold by vending machines, which provide change. Bills, coins and tokens are all accepted. Passengers with valid transfers or passes can proceed directly to the boarding area. Fare collection on Metro Rail works on the honour system, subject to occa-

sional inspections: passengers caught without a valid ticket, transfer or pass are subject to heavy fines. Tokens and passes are sold at MTA customer centres, at some food stores and pharmacies, and at the ubiquitous cheque cashing shops that dot the L.A. landscape. Tokens and passes are *not* available at Metro Rail stations!

As if this weren't complicated enough, the MTA isn't the only show in town. A parallel system called DASH operates some short-distance local routes within downtown L.A. and in certain other areas, including Hollywood. The fare is only $0.25, though downtown DASH buses do not accept MTA transfers or passes. The DASH system can be a useful way of getting around the downtown area, within a perimeter extending from Chinatown in the north to Exposition Park in the south. Service on most routes is frequent, with buses at 5min intervals.

In addition, some municipalities in L.A. County have their own bus systems. The system most likely to be of use to visitors is Santa Monica Municipal Bus Lines, with a base fare of $0.50 (or $1.25 for the No. 10 express bus between Santa Monica and downtown L.A.). The Culver City system has a base fare of $0.60. Both companies accept MTA transfers but not MTA tokens or passes. Transfers valid for connections to the MTA cost $0.25.

Tour buses can be a way of getting around certain parts of the city. Limited information on bus tours is

provided in the "Exploring" section of this chapter.

By Bicycle

Getting around the sprawling L.A. area by bicycle is no longer as preposterous an idea as it once was. Many MTA buses now have front-end racks carrying up to two bicycles each, available for use at no additional fare. Leaflets describing procedures and listing the bus routes providing this service are available from MTA customer centres or by Internet at www.mta.net. This enables passengers to enjoy the flexibility of cycling at either end of their journey while using the bus for the longer hauls. Bicycles are accepted outside rush hours on the Metro Rail subway and light rail lines, but only to holders of special permits, making this less practical for visitors.

Los Angeles has a network of what are described as bike routes, although only a small part of this network consists of true cycling paths separated from motor traffic. In many cases, the so-called bike routes consist of little more than signage alongside busy streets. One notable exception is the coastal bike path extending from the northwestern tip of Santa Monica all the way south to Redondo Beach (see p 118 for a description).

Bicycle rentals are available at several easy-to-spot locations along or near the beach in Venice and Santa Monica.

By Foot

Among the joys of travel is being able to walk to

Los Angeles

where you're going or finding places that are conducive to a pleasant stroll. In many parts of Los Angeles, people have developed a heavy physical and psychological dependance on automobiles, making pedestrians notable by their scarcity. In certain places, walking is regarded as a sign of eccentricity.

But fear not: pedestrians are far from extinct even in this stronghold of automobile culture.

Much of downtown L.A. is eminently walkable, with a vibrant pedestrian scene along Broadway Avenue and the streets immediately to its west. In Santa Monica, a very lively three-

block stretch of Third Avenue is closed to motor traffic and provides one of the world's great pedestrian experiences by day and by night (see p 111). And, of course, several long stretches of beach provide ideal opportunities for a leisurely stroll, with Venice Beach providing a particularly interesting

A Glimpse at Metro Rail and Metrolink

Metro Rail, with hefty construction costs and controversial route planning, provided an inauspicious start to the era of modern mass transit in Los Angeles. But parts of the system are now being used quite heavily. Its biggest drawback is that it doesn't cover more territory. Metro Rail consists of three lines: the Red Line subway, with trains running underground, and two light rail lines, the Blue Line and Green Line, running mostly at surface level or along elevated track.

The **Red Line** runs west from Union Station across downtown L.A., and then northwest to Hollywood and North Hollywood. A shorter branch runs west to Wilshire and Western. Trains from downtown alternate between these two branches, so pay attention when boarding. The **Blue Line** runs south from downtown L.A. to Long Beach, connecting with the Red Line downtown at Seventh Street

and with the Green Line at Rosa Parks station in the Watts district, about halfway to Long Beach. The **Green Line** looks more than anything else like an afterthought to accompany the new east-west Century Freeway in the southern part of the city, running mostly along the median of this freeway (station platforms are not protected from noise or fumes). It runs essentially from nowhere to nowhere, passing *near* LAX airport (but not *to* the airport) and then turning south to the municipality of Manhattan Beach (without going anywhere near the beach).

While station design on the Blue and Green lines is very ordinary, each Red Line station features large-scale works of art, some of which are quite imaginative. These works, each by a local artist, form part of the decor at the mezzanine level and are not visible

from track level, but they offer pleasant surprises to passengers entering or leaving stations. Unlike many public installations in Los Angeles, Metro Rail stations are kept spotlessly clean and free of graffiti.

Metrolink is the name given to the suburban rail network. Six lines radiate from Union Station in downtown L.A., serving points as distant as Oxnard, Lancaster, San Bernardino and Oceanside. A seventh line provides a direct link between distant suburbs in Orange, Riverside and San Bernardino counties. Rolling stock consists of modern double-deck coaches. Some lines operate only at rush hours. Saturday service is very limited, and there is no service at all on Sundays or holidays. Tickets are sold from vending machines at each station, and all passengers must hold tickets or passes before boarding.

scene. This list is far from exhaustive: parts of Hollywood, Beverly Hills and Westwood draw large numbers of people on foot, as do some other spots.

Motorists generally tend to yield to pedestrians at intersections and at designated crossings, although care is still advised. Police enforce traffic laws regarding pedestrians and will issue tickets to pedestrians who cross against the signal or to motorists who fail to yield the right of way. One minor annoyance: at some intersections, pedestrians actually need to ask permission to cross; they are required to push a button before the pedestrian signals can be activated. This is not a serious inconvenience, but it does reinforce the second-class status of people without vehicles.

Getting to or from LAX

There's often no way around it. Countless travellers each day must confront the muddle and confusion involved in getting to or from Los Angeles International Airport. Travellers armed with a few bits of information have the battle half won. Following are the main alternatives:

By Private Car

A broad bi-level ring road circles the terminal buildings, with departure areas at the upper level and arrivals at the lower level. At peak holiday periods traffic moves very slowly. Motorists waiting outside the terminal buildings must remain in their vehicles. Unattended vehicles are often ticketed or towed. Huge long-term parking lots are situated near the airport, while short-term (very expensive) parking is available right on the airport grounds, within easy walking distance of each terminal building. Free buses, marked by the letters B, C or D, serve the three largest off-site parking lots. Running every few minutes, they circle the airport in a counter-clockwise direction, stopping near the lower level of each terminal building at the stops marked "LAX Shuttle". After arriving at the respective parking lots, they run in a fixed circuit to drop off or pick up passengers at clearly marked stops.

By Rental Car

Most of the major car rental companies have their offices and drop-off points clustered in a small area just northeast of the airport. Each company operates buses (referred to, for some bizarre reason, as "courtesy trams" even though they are clearly buses and not trams) that fetch passengers from fixed stops near the lower level of each terminal building. Next to illuminated panels in the baggage claim areas, free phones are provided to contact the various car rental companies.

By Hotel Bus or Van

Some hotels located near the airport provide free pickups for guests. It is wise to check with the hotel in advance.

By Taxi

Taxis are easy to find near the lower level of each terminal building. Fares are high and are augmented by a $2.50 airport surcharge (applying to trips from the airport but not *going to* the airport). To downtown L.A. or Hollywood, the total fare (without tip) comes to about $30; to the mid-Wilshire district or West Hollywood about $25; to Santa Monica about $20.

By Shared-Ride Van

Several companies, among them Super Shuttle (☎800-554-3146, 323-775-6600 or 310-782-6600; www. supershuttle.com) and Xpress Shuttle (☎800-474-8885; www.xpressshuttle. com), operate vans that provide door-to-door service with set fares to specific parts of the metropolitan area. Normally, vans carry several passengers going to the same general area, meaning there may be intermediate stops along the way and an indirect routing. On the other hand, fares for single passengers are typically about one-third less than the corresponding taxi fare, with discounts for additional passengers going to the same destination. For three or more people travelling together, taxis may often cost less, however. Van services can be arranged in advance or upon arrival at the airport by using a pay phone or the free phones in baggage claim areas attached to the illuminated panels advertising hotels and car rentals. Some van companies compete on price, and it may not hurt to compare. Vans can also be flagged at the appropriately marked stops near the lower level of each terminal building and are identified by signs on each vehicle showing the area served. There is no central collection point. Shared-ride van services are

Los Angeles

Pay Attention to those New Phone Codes!

It seems to be a matter of dogma in North America that all local telephone numbers must have seven digits, regardless of how big or small the locality may be. For decades, this worked quite well. More recently, however, an explosion in the use of cellphones, pagers, fax machines and computer modems has caused most large metropolitan areas to run out of numbers.

Rather than switch to eight-digit local numbers, as telecom authorities have done in several parts of the world, the private-sector agency that decides on such matters in North America opted instead to chop up local calling areas and add new three-digit area codes. This means that many local calls, even if no toll charge applies,

have to be treated as long-distance calls, prefixed by the numeral 1 and the three-digit code.

All numbers shown in this chapter are prefixed by the area code. When calling another number starting with the same code, only the last seven digits have to be entered.

The old 213 area code that once covered all of Los Angeles County now applies only in downtown L.A. and areas within a radius of 5km (3mi) of downtown. Surrounding this zone like a doughnut is the new 323 code, covering much of the inner city, including Hollywood, and some of the nearby suburbs. A few years ago, the 310 area code was created to cover the west side, including Santa Monica, Beverly Hills and

LAX airport. This zone later started running out of numbers, and the new 424 code was superimposed, meaning that some people have to enter 11 digits to call their next-door neighbours!

Other telephone area codes in the Los Angeles area are 818 for the San Fernando Valley, 626 for Pasadena and surrounding areas, 562 for Long Beach and areas to its north, 714 and 949 for Orange County, and 909 for Riverside and San Bernardino counties.

Note that long-distance charges apply on certain calls within the metropolitan area. Callers paying by coin at public phones will be advised by a recorded message of the additional amount to be deposited.

available for travel to the airport as well but require reservations many hours in advance.

By Scheduled Bus

Several points in Southern California, among them Disneyland, Van Nuys and Santa Barbara, are served by direct scheduled bus services from LAX. Information and tickets are available from the Ground Transportation kiosks located outside some of

the terminal buildings at the lower level.

By Public Transit

There is no direct rail or local bus service from Los Angeles International Airport, although both are available nearby.

The geniuses who planned the Green Line, part of L.A.'s rail transit system, chose a routing that serves areas near the airport but manages to skirt the air-

port entirely. The Green Line's Aviation station and the airport are linked by a free bus, marked by the letter G, that runs at intervals of 10 to 15min, stopping at the LAX Shuttle stops near the lower level of each terminal building. The trip normally takes about 10min, but can be slower in heavy traffic. Green Line tickets are sold at vending machines near station entrances, with change provided. The Green Line itself runs from nowhere to nowhere, mostly along a highway median, but it does connect with the Blue Line running between downtown L.A. and Long Beach.

The bus situation is somewhat better. Numerous local bus routes radiate from the LAX Transit Center, located adjacent to Parking Lot C, a short distance from the airport. Free buses marked by the letter C stop near the lower level of each terminal building at the stops marked "LAX Shuttle" and after circling the airport run in a long loop through the parking lot before stopping next to the transit centre. To save time, passengers can disembark at the first stop after leaving the airport and walk the block-and-a-half to the transit centre. (Going back to the airport, buses leave directly from a point next to the transit centre.) Scheduled departure times for each bus route are displayed on a large panel at the transit centre. Some routes are run by the MTA, the region's main transit operator, and other routes by suburban systems. Passengers must have the exact fare (see p 69). Among routes most likely to be useful to visitors are the MTA 42 local to downtown L.A.; MTA 439 express (premium fare) northeast to downtown L.A.; MTA 439 south to Manhattan Beach, Hermosa Beach and Redondo Beach; MTA 561 express (premium fare) north to the San Fernando Valley, stopping en route at the U.C.L.A. campus and the Getty Center; Santa Monica (blue bus) No. 3 northwest to Venice and Santa Monica, and Culver City (green bus) No. 6 north to U.C.L.A. with useful transfer connections along the way to various MTA east-west bus routes.

Practical Information

Tourist Offices

The **Los Angeles Convention & Visitors Bureau** (☎*213-689-8822 or 800-228-2452*) provides assistance by telephone and also operates two visitor information centres. One is located downtown at 685 South Figueroa Street between Wilshire Boulevard and Seventh Street (*Mon to Fri 8am to 5pm, Sat 8:30am to 5pm*). The other is in Hollywood at 6541 Hollywood Boulevard near Cahuenga Boulevard (*Mon to Sat 9am to 1pm and 2pm to 5pm*). Both these centres offer a wide range of leaflets (including transit information) and multilingual staff to help with inquiries.

Other visitor centres include those run by the **Santa Monica Convention and Visitors Bureau** (*every day 10am to 4pm, in the park along Ocean Ave. between Santa Monica Blvd. and Broadway*), the **Beverly Hills Visitors Bureau** (*239 S. Beverly Dr.,* ☎*310-248-1015*), and the **Pasadena Convention and Visitors Bureau** (*171 S. Los Robles Ave.,* ☎*626-795-9311*).

Personal Safety

Crime rates in Los Angeles are pretty close to the U.S. average, which is to say somewhere along a continuum between the relative security found elsewhere in the industrialized world and the higher levels of danger that characterize

parts of the Third World. As in much of the U.S., rates of violent crime have been falling in recent years, but it is still a good idea to take certain precautions. People on vacation often want to embrace a carefree attitude, and this can make them more vulnerable to criminal attack. Remember to keep valuables well hidden in public areas. When taking cash from an automated banking machine, do so only in a well-lit, well-trafficked area.

Bear in mind that some parts of Los Angeles are more dangerous than others. Generally speaking, the west side is fairly safe, while many areas to the south or east of downtown L.A. are much less secure, plagued by some of the city's notorious youth gangs. Certain streets that feel entirely safe by day may turn quite frightening at night. This is especially true in much of downtown L.A. and certain parts of Hollywood. Visitors on foot after dark should use common sense and avoid unfamiliar areas where there are few other pedestrians. L.A. has a substantial number of homeless people, some of whom suffer from mental illness or drug problems. Usually they are more deranged than truly dangerous, but they can still throw a scare into unsuspecting passersby. Clusters of them may be found on the east side of the downtown area and in parts of Hollywood and Santa Monica.

Motorists also should take extra precautions and, when travelling late at night, be quite sure they know where they're going and keep their doors locked. The scandal-wracked Los Angeles Police Department is not as

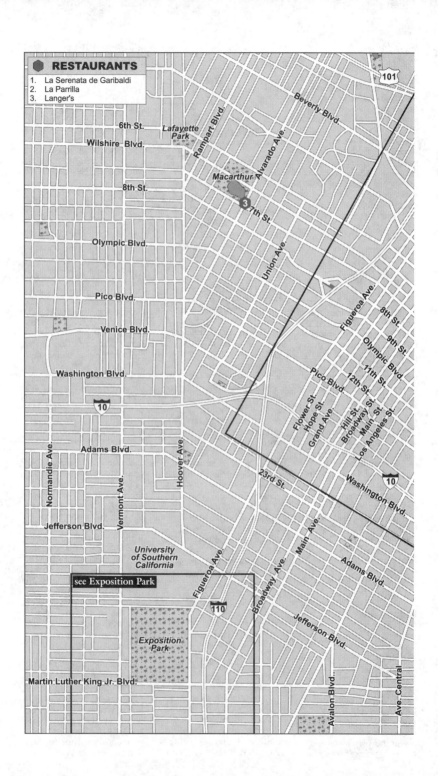

RESTAURANTS

1. La Serenata de Garibaldi
2. La Parrilla
3. Langer's

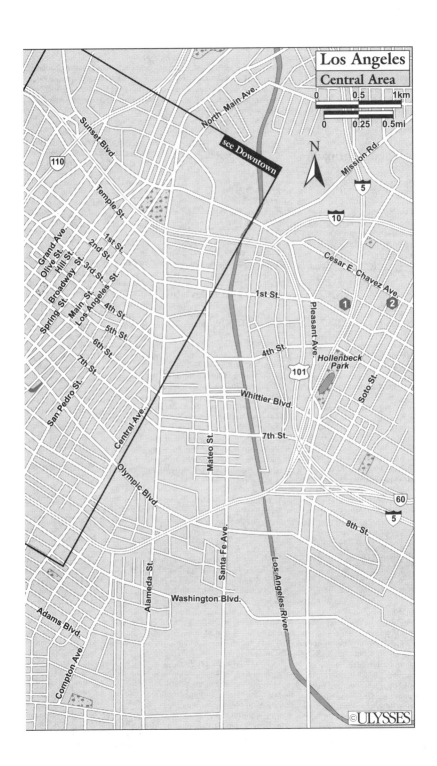

Los Angeles
Central Area

ineffective as some critics suggest, but it is stretched rather thinly over a very large territory. The emergency phone number (free from public phones) is 911.

General Information

Internet Sites

Several Internet sites provide useful information for visitors and up-to-the-minute listings of events and attractions. The Los Angeles Convention & Visitors Bureau provides a wide range of information on its site at *www.lacvb.com*. The *Los Angeles Times* newspaper has a very useful site for cultural listings of all sorts at *www.calendarlive.com*. Another good source of listings and other information is *www.at-la.com*.

Newspapers

The city's dominant newspaper is the *Los Angeles Times*, by far the most distinguished daily newspaper in the western U.S., with many news bureaus across the country and abroad as well as comprehensive local coverage. Its main local competition comes from the Spanish-language daily *La Opinión* and a number of very locally-oriented suburban dailies, the most important of which is the *Daily News*, published at Van Nuys in the San Fernando Valley.

The *L.A. Times* publishes movie and cultural listings in its daily "Calendar" section, as well as thorough listings for the coming week in its Sunday edition and for the following weekend in its Wednesday edition. Other excellent sources of listings and suggestions are two weekly papers, the *L.A. Weekly* and the slimmer but more informative *New Times*. Both are distributed free from racks near the entrances to various stores, restaurants and public buildings as well as from some street boxes.

Large selections of magazines, as well as some foreign newspapers, are available at certain newsstands in Hollywood and Santa Monica as well as from bookstore chains such as Borders and Barnes & Noble.

Radio and Television

Los Angeles offers an interesting variety of radio stations. Many stations stick to the Top 40 or "adult contemporary" formulas, but other tastes are also catered to. There are two all-news stations, found at 980 and 1070 on the AM band. On the FM band, jazz and blues may be heard at 88.1 and classical music at 91.5 or 105.1. Programs of National Public Radio can be picked up at 89.9.

L.A. has television stations affiliated with all the major networks (including PBS at Channel 28, or Channel 3 on some cable systems), in addition to several unaffiliated local channels. CNN and a vast variety of other cable channels are available at most hotels.

Exploring

Los Angeles has sometimes been described as more of a cluster of villages than a coherent city. In many urban areas around the world, the main attractions tend to be grouped in or around the city centre, with remaining points of interest easily reachable by a short trip to the suburbs. In Los Angeles it's the other way around: the downtown area offers its share of curiosities, but visitors are likely to spend most of their time elsewhere.

Far-flung parts of the metropolitan area offer their own special charms. Getting a varied taste of Los Angeles means not only a fair bit of moving around but also some careful planning. Because of the distances involved, touring can't really be done haphazardly. Congested freeways and slow public transit can make for long travel times. You can't just hop from Pasadena over to Santa Monica, for instance, because even in light traffic it could take close to an hour. Many points of interest are clustered in a few small areas, but these areas are widely scattered.

Because accommodations in the downtown area often tend toward extremes of lavish expense or desperate gloom, and because downtown L.A. is generally not very pleasant after dark, most leisure travellers are likely to end up staying in other parts of the city. It is a good idea to try to coordinate lodging and sightseeing plans, if only to cut down on travel time.

This entire chapter covering Los Angeles is divided into seven tours, each corresponding to a particular geographic zone of the city. Each zone has a distinctive character that provides certain unifying themes. We start with downtown Los Angeles and then proceed northeast to Pasadena, continuing from there in a counter-clockwise direction that takes us through Hollywood, the Wilshire corridor, Santa Monica and Venice, the airport and South Bay areas and, finally, Long Beach and its surroundings.

If you look at a map of the entire region, it immediately becomes evident that large swaths of territory receive no mention in this guidebook. Not all parts of Los Angeles are created equal, and some areas are simply more interesting than others. As in cities almost everywhere, there are large areas that may seem important to people living or working there but that offer little to entice most visitors.

Tour A: Downtown Los Angeles

To travellers who have experienced some of the world's great urban centres, downtown Los Angeles may come across as a big disappointment. Like the central areas of many U.S. cities, it has been drained of much of its vitality over the decades. It enjoyed a heyday in the 1920s and then sank into torpor during the Great Depression of the 1930s. As the suburban boom took hold and gained momentum in the decades following the Second World War, downtown L.A. fell into in a long era of relative decline, interrupted by brief periods of revival and stabilization. These periods included a massive bout of office construction in the 1980s, although several of the glittering new towers remained half-empty for

years afterwards until they were rescued by strong economic growth in the mid- and late-1990s.

Downtown L.A. has a decidedly schizophrenic character. On its western side are groups of office towers and high-rise hotels, hemmed in by a busy expressway. This area, part of it known as the financial district, is not without its attractions, although activity at street level is minimal except at noon hour or immediately after work. Part of it is set on a high promontory known as Bunker Hill.

In the middle of the downtown area is the traditional retail district, with Broadway Avenue as its spine and Seventh Street, perpendicular to Broadway and the former home of several big department stores, as a major cross street. Decades ago, business trickled away to the suburbs, leaving behind rows of empty storefronts.

New waves of Mexican and Central American immigration later revived the Broadway retail district. Listening to people talk and seeing the range of merchandise displayed in store windows and entrances over a bustling multi-block stretch, it's easy to imagine yourself on the main shopping street of a prosperous provincial centre in Mexico. (Much of Seventh Street, on the other hand, remains boarded up.)

Further east, downtown L.A. takes on an almost other-worldly persona. This is home to an extensive garment-manufacturing and wholesaling district. (It is no secret that some of the labourers hidden away from public view are undocumented immigrants paid at less than minimum wage.) Several of the streets north of the garment district form a massive skid row area with several seedy hotels and bands of

Downtown Los Angeles

homeless people visible at most hours of the day and night, many of them looking drunk or dazed or just plain unwell. This is definitely *not* Beverly Hills. A little beyond is the small but prim Little Tokyo district.

Some first-time visitors are surprised to discover that downtown L.A. is nowhere near the beaches of the Pacific. It lies about 12mi (20km) inland, closer to the geographic centre of the sprawling metropolitan area. Downtown is bound on the north by the Civic Centre, comprised of a rather sterile and lifeless collection of public buildings, including City Hall and the federal courthouse. The friendlier Chinatown district lies just beyond, several blocks further north. On the southern fringe of downtown are the gleaming

new Staples Center arena and the recently expanded Convention Center, although the surrounding streets are rather desolate, even after some rush landscaping was done to greet delegates to the national Democratic Convention held several months prior to the controversial 2000 presidential election. About 2mi (3km) south of downtown lies the campus of the University of Southern California and, immediately adjacent, Exposition Park, home to a couple of interesting museums (though the area is not especially safe after dark).

The preceding description probably makes downtown L.A. sound less appealing than it really is. This is a little unfair. It is true that downtown is shunned and even despised by many people living in other parts of Los

Angeles, perhaps influenced in part by race or class prejudice. But there is also plenty to admire downtown. Readers should not hesitate to visit this area, since it is full of character and quite walkable, at least by L.A. standards. It is also home to several architectural gems and numerous cultural attractions.

A good place to begin a tour is where the city began, not far from the banks of the diminutive Los Angeles River (except after heavy rains, this "river" forms just a tiny trickle channeled through a massive concrete-walled ditch skirting the eastern fringe of the downtown area). This is where Spanish explorers arriving from central Mexico discovered a small Native American settlement and where they established one of their

● **ATTRACTIONS**

1. El Pueblo de Los Angeles Historic Monument
2. Olvera Street
3. Union Station
4. City Hall
5. Music Center
6. Los Angeles Children's Museum
7. Japanese American National Museum
8. Japanese American Cultural and Community Center
9. Geffen Contemporary at MOCA
10. Museum of Contemporary Art
11. Grand Central Market
12. Angels Flight
13. Pershing Square
14. Central Library
15. Wells Fargo Museum
16. Museum of Neon Art
17. Convention Center
18. Staples Center

◐ **ACCOMMODATIONS**

1. Best Western Dragon Gate Inn
2. Figueroa Hotel
3. Hotel Inter-Continental Los Angeles
4. Hyatt Regency Los Angeles
5. Kawada Hotel
6. Metro Plaza Hotel
7. Miyako Inn
8. New Otani Hotel
9. Regal Biltmore Hotel
10. Stillwell Hotel
11. Westin Bonaventure Hotel
12. Wyndham Checkers Hotel

● **RESTAURANTS**

1. Café Pinot
2. Empress Pavilion
3. Engine Company No. 28
4. Grand Central Market
5. Maria's Pescado Frito
6. Mon Kee
7. Original Pantry Café
8. Philippe the Original
9. Shabu Shabu House
10. The City Pier
11. Yang Chow

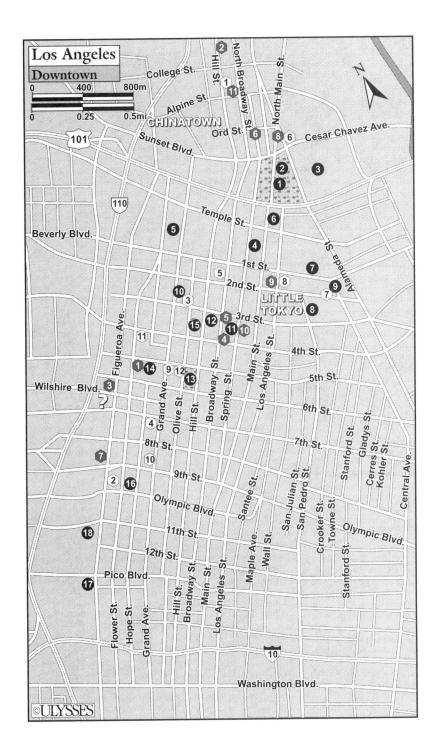

own a few years later, in 1781. The oldest surviving structure, built in 1818, now forms part of **El Pueblo de Los Angeles Historic Monument ★**, a small cluster of buildings and plazas occupying a 44 acre (18ha) site bisected by Main Street in the northeastern part of downtown L.A. between Union Station and the Civic Center. Designated a state park, the site includes a **visitors centre** *(Mon to Sat 10am to 3pm, 622 N. Main St., ☎213-628-1274)* housed in the Sepulveda House at the entrance to the Old Plaza. Brochures and general information are available, as are exhibits depicting the area's history and culture, including a 20min video. It is the departure point for free guided tours of the park offered hourly from 10am to 1pm from Tuesday to Saturday. Nearby is the **Avila Adobe ★** *(free admission; Mon to Sat 10am to 5pm)*, the aforementioned oldest building in L.A. This thick-walled structure was home to a wealthy family during much of the 19th century, and visitors can see several rooms furnished in the style of that period as well as a leafy courtyard. Other buildings of note include **Firehouse No. 1**, built in 1884 and displaying historic fire-fighting equipment *(free admission; every day 10am to 3pm, Sat to Sun until 4:30pm)*, as well as the stylish Pico House (a former hotel) and the former Merced Theatre. The two latter buildings, both erected in 1870, lie vacant while they await new uses.

By far the liveliest part of the historic park is **Olvera Street ★★**, a short pedestrian-only street that attempts to mimic some undefined period in Mexican history. It is lined with numerous Mexican handicrafts stalls and several restaurants. It is popular not only with tourists but also, perhaps surprisingly in view of its unauthentic character, with members of L.A.'s sizable Mexican community, some of whom are drawn to the area by the 19th-century **Iglesia de Nuestra Señora la Reina de Los Angeles** (Church of Our Lady Queen of Angels), on the other side of Main Street. Besides numerous masses celebrated in Spanish, this church is a favoured spot for weddings and baptisms. Family celebrations often spill into nearby public areas. Olvera Street, along with the church and the Old Plaza, is a central venue for the Cinco de Mayo celebrations that bring many Mexicans together on May 5, as the festival's Spanishname suggests. At the top of Olvera Street is the **Instituto Cultural Mexicano ★** that includes a bilingual (Spanish and English) bookshop, a consulting library, and a famous mural depicting the blessing of the animals. It is located in the historic Biscailuz Building that once housed the Mexican consulate.

One block east, on the other side of Alameda Avenue, lies **Union Station ★★**, opened in 1939 and the last of the truly grand railway stations constructed in the United States. Currently served by Amtrak intercity trains and Metrolink suburban trains, this magnificent structure is well worth a short visit even if rail travel is not part of your plans. With its bell tower and soaring arched windows, it imitates the early California-mission style on an enormous scale, also incorporating Moderne elements.

Inside, it features tiled floors in earth tones, wood-beamed ceilings nearly 52ft (16m) high, massive chandeliers and, in the waiting area, most of the original heavy wooden furniture. Hidden away (but freely accessible to the public) are two spacious and pleasant patios with gardens, shade trees and comfortable seating—a minor treasure that few people seem to have discovered. The north patio is partly occupied by a small café and restaurant with outdoor tables. The pedestrian tunnel providing passenger access to the trains also leads to the Patsaouras Transit Plaza, served by many city bus routes. This is more a showplace than a bus terminal, covered in marble and granite with trees, fountains and artwork that includes several large murals.

To the north, past Cesar A. Chavez Avenue (named after a Mexican-American farm union leader who achieved world fame in the 1960s after calling for grape boycotts to protest dismal working conditions), lies the **Chinatown ★** district, covering an area roughly four blocks wide and four blocks deep, and centred on North Broadway Avenue. This area is not nearly as picturesque as its San Francisco counterpart, and it is home to only a minuscule portion of L.A.'s large Chinese population (most live in the suburbs), but its countless food stores, restaurants and souvenir shops serve as a magnet, especially on weekends, for many people of Chinese and other origins. The Chinese New Year, which falls in late January or early February, is a time of celebration, with the

Golden Dragon Parade as a special highlight.

South of Chinatown and southwest of El Pueblo de Los Angeles historic district, the **Civic Center** occupies a multi-block area centred around Temple Street, an east-west artery running across the northern part of downtown L.A. It is occupied mostly by undistinguished government office buildings and courthouses fulfilling various functions at the city, county, state and federal levels. The key word here is bland. The only true landmark is the 28-storey **City Hall** (*200 N. Spring St. near Temple St*). Opened in 1928, the building will be familiar to some film buffs: it has often been used as a backdrop. Recently, it was undergoing a massive and costly facelift.

The **Music Center**, along Grand Avenue between First and Temple streets, lies at the western edge of the Civic Center and comprises three halls set around a plaza adorned by a large Jacques Lipschitz sculpture and a massive fountain. The largest of the halls, the Dorothy Chandler Pavilion, seats 3,200 (see p 138). The two smaller halls are the Ahmanson Theater and the Mark Taper Forum. They will be joined at some point by the on-again, off-again Walt Disney Concert Hall.

The **Los Angeles Children's Museum ★** (*$5; year-round, Sat and Sun 10am to 5pm; late June to early Sept Mon to Fri 11:30am to 4pm; rest of the year by special arrangement only; 310 N. Main St. near Temple St., ☎213-687-8800*), around the corner from City Hall and not far from El Pueblo de Los Angeles Historic Monu-

ment, was intended as a temporary facility when it opened in 1979 and has hopes of moving to larger quarters once the politically sensitive issue of location is settled. This is a hands-on sort of place where children are encouraged to touch the exhibits, many of which have an educational theme in addition to being entertaining. They range from the Cave of the Dinosaurs to Sticky City with its large velco forms, and Club Eco, which teaches about recycling. The museum also has a performance space with storytellers, musicians or dancers.

The **Little Tokyo ★** district, southeast of the Civic Center, occupies much of the area bounded by Temple, Los Angeles, Fourth and Alameda streets. Like Chinatown, it has only a tiny residential population and serves more as a meeting place for shopping, eating and certain cultural pursuits. With the exception of a handful of buildings, the area is not especially attractive, and there is little that people from the real Tokyo would find familiar. The district contains several shopping malls, the biggest of which is the Japanese Village Plaza (see p 141), in the form of a winding pedestrian-only zone meant to resemble a village street in Japan. The **Japanese American National Museum ★★** (*$4; Tue to Sun 10am to 5pm, Thu until 8pm; 369 E. First St. at Central Ave., ☎213-625-0414*)

Little Tokyo

occupies two buildings, one a former temple and the other a much bigger annex opened in 1998 and acclaimed for its design. The museum features a rotating series of exhibitions depicting the Japanese immigrant experience in the United States as well as certain home communities in Japan. One of the saddest chapters in U.S. history was the Second World War internment of approximately 100,000 U.S. citizens for no reason except their Japanese ethnic background. This facet of history is presented in certain exhibits and in the interactive Legacy Center, where visitors can trace family internment files through a computer link. The **Japanese American Cultural and Community Center ★** (*244 S. San Pedro St. between Second and Third sts., ☎213-628-2725*) is built around a plaza and a rock garden at the lower level

Los Angeles

A Taste of History: Walking Tours
Presented by Los Angeles Conservancy ★★

To most Europeans and even to many North Americans, Los Angeles comes across as a thoroughly modern city with only faint reminders of the past. Because the city's history doesn't go back very far, with the area not emerging as a major metropolis until early in the 20th century, historical consciousness is not firmly rooted among local inhabitants, and historical buildings, such as they are, have been vulnerable to abandonment or demolition. A volunteer organization that calls itself Los Angeles Conservancy has fought, often successfully, to preserve older buildings with architectural or symbolic value. Some of its demands have stirred controversy, including a campaign to save the earthquake-damaged Saint Vibiana cathedral (closed since 1994) against the wishes of the Catholic archbishop. (A new cathedral is under construction.)

Nobody can object to the extensive program of walking tours the Conservancy offers each Saturday morning *($8; most tours start at 10am; reservations required: Mon to Fri 9am to 5pm; 523 W. Sixth St., Suite 1216, ☎213-623-2489).* Most tours last from 2 to 2.5hrs and depart from the entrance to the Biltmore Hotel *(515 S. Olive St. facing Pershing Sq.),* with group size usually limited to 15 people. Tours are led by trained docents, some of whom are very effective at conveying their knowledge of local architectural history. Several

different tours operate on any given Saturday. The most popular tour visits the spectacular old movie palaces along Broadway Avenue, some of which are still in operation (it is useful to reserve places for this tour well in advance). Another popular tour, which also runs each week, visits some of the impressive Art Deco office buildings that dot downtown L.A., each with fine ornamental detail. Some tours operate only one or two Saturdays each month: these include tours of Union Station, Little Tokyo and the former financial district along Spring Street. For further information, please consult Los Angeles Conservancy at the address or phone number above.

that make for a pleasant stroll *(every day 9am to 6pm).* The centre is a focal point for cultural and educational activities. Its 841–seat theatre serves as a venue for both Japanese and non-Japanese music, dance and theatre presentations.

The **Geffen Contemporary at MOCA ★★★** and the **Museum of Contemporary Art (MOCA) ★★★** form a single museum housed in

two buildings that are situated eight blocks apart *($6 valid at both sites on the date of purchase; Tue to Sun 11am to 5pm, Thu until 8pm; Geffen Contemporary: 152 N. Central Ave. near First St. in Little Tokyo; MOCA at California Plaza: 250 S. Grand Ave. between Second and Third sts. in the financial district;* ☎213-626-6222, www.moca-la.org). Named for David Geffen, a music producer and benefactor of the arts, the Geffen Contemporary occupies a former ware-

house adapted to exhibition space by Los Angeles architect Frank Gehry. When it opened in 1983, it was dubbed the "Temporary Contemporary" because it was expected to close following the completion in 1986 of the new building on Grand Avenue designed by Japanese architect Arata Isozaki and consisting of two red sandstone pavilions in highly original shapes straddling an open plaza. Because of its size, the Geffen is well suited to large-scale installations, and a decision was thus made to keep it open. Together, the two buildings house a very impressive permanent collection, augmented in recent years by numerous acquisitions and bequests. They also showcase many temporary exhibits. (The two sites are connected by DASH bus route A.)

If only minor vestiges remain of 19th-century Los Angeles, the same cannot be said of the early decades of the 20th century. Spring Street and Broadway, two parallel streets a block apart, contain many architectural reminders of downtown L.A's heyday. In the 1920s, **Spring Street ★** was the centre of finance and proudly bore the title of Wall Street of the West. Nowadays the street conveys a rather seedy, bedraggled air, although it remains lined with many handsome buildings, some of them boarded up but others restored to their former glory or rumoured as candidates for restoration. At 300 South Spring Street, at the corner of Third Street, is an office building recently converted for use by the State of California (and named after former governor and president Ronald Reagan), which has a very exuberant large-scale mural in the lobby by artists Carlos Almaraz and Elsa Flores. Other buildings of note along Spring Street include the Title Insurance Building at No. 433 with its attractive Art Deco lobby and the somewhat rundown Alexandra Hotel at the corner of Fifth Street with its old-fashioned interior palm court.

Broadway ★★, one block west, finds itself in better circumstances, with a very vibrant Mexican-accented retail trade bringing life to the street, especially between Third and Ninth streets. It too has many handsome buildings from the early 20th century, although some of the interiors behind the impressive facades have been gutted. For instance, some of the grand old movie palaces along this stretch of the street (more than a dozen of these structures survive) have been converted to retail stores or evangelical churches, but others continue to operate as cinemas, mostly showing films in Spanish. The best way to catch a glimpse of their very ornate interiors is to take a Los Angeles Conservancy tour (see box). Several office buildings along Broadway have noteworthy architectural features. These include the Bradbury Building *(No. 304, corner of Third Street)*, with its five-storey glass-roofed atrium, and the gorgeous Art Deco Eastern Columbia Building *(No. 849, between Eighth and Ninth sts.)* with its distinctive turquoise exterior topped by large clock faces.

One of the most fascinating sights in downtown L.A. is **Grand Central Market ★**, covering the block bound by Broadway, Third, Hill and Fourth streets. This public market has been a beehive of activity since it opened in 1917 to serve the food needs of Los Angeles, with dozens of stalls selling fresh produce, meats, fish, dairy products and other types of food that reflect the city's ethnic diversity. It also includes several restaurants and snack counters.

Behind the market, on the Hill Street side, is the lower station of the **Angels Flight ★** funicular railway *($0.25; every day 6:30am to 10pm; ☎213-626-1901)* that climbs one steep block at a 33-degree angle to Olive Street atop Bunker Hill. When service was inaugurated in 1901, Bunker Hill was regarded as a very desirable residential neighbourhood, and people living there used the railway to reach their homes from the commercial district below. Service provided by the railway's very distinctive bright red carriages was halted in 1969 and resumed in 1996. Today, this beloved anachronism is used mostly, but not exclusively, by tourists. It runs every few minutes.

One of downtown's focal points is **Pershing Square**, a park (set atop an underground parking garage) covering the block bound by Hill, Fifth, Olive and Sixth Streets. (Hill is one block west of Broadway.) A public park since 1886, it was remodeled at great cost in 1994. Although not as heavily crime-ridden as it once was, Pershing Square (named after a First World War general) is not especially appealing despite the resources that went into fountains and public art, some of it in the form of whimsically coloured geometric shapes. With its absence of shade trees or comfortable seating, it is more a place to traverse than to linger in.

The **Central Library ★★** *(Mon, Thu to Sat 10am to 5:30pm; Tue to Wed noon to 8pm; Sun 1pm to 5pm; 630 W. Fifth St. between Grand and Flower sts., ☎213-228-7000)* is the hub of L.A.'s extensive public library system and a major reference library, with close to three million books and other documents. Most of

Los Angeles

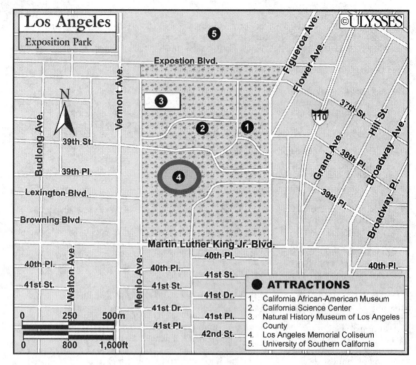

Los Angeles
Exposition Park

©ULYSSES

N

Expostion Blvd.

Figueroa Ave.
Flower Ave.
Vermont Ave.
Budlong Ave.
39th St.
39th Pl.
Lexington Blvd.
Browning Blvd.
37th St.
Hill St.
110
Grand Ave.
38th Pl.
Broadway Ave.
39th Pl.
Broadway Pl.

Martin Luther King Jr. Blvd.

40th Pl.
40th Pl.
41st St.
41st St.
40th Pl.
41st St.
41st Dr.
41st Dr.
41st Pl.
41st Pl.
42nd St.
40th Pl.

Walton Ave.
Menlo Ave.

0   250   500m
0   800   1,600ft

● **ATTRACTIONS**
1. California African-American Museum
2. California Science Center
3. Natural History Museum of Los Angeles County
4. Los Angeles Memorial Coliseum
5. University of Southern California

the books are accessible in open stacks. Designed in 1922, the building was extensively renovated and expanded following two disastrous fires in 1986; it reopened in 1993. The addition of a new wing and new underground levels doubled the library's capacity, and the creation of a skylit atrium added to the aesthetic appeal of the building, with its vaguely Egyptian motifs. Built-up grime actually saved the library's precious murals from heavy fire damage; these include tableaus in the main rotunda dating from 1933 that depict four eras in California history. One section of the library is devoted to children. The library grounds include the **Maguire Gardens** ★, named after a major benefactor, with abundant shade trees and seating (unlike Pershing Square). On the other side of Fifth Street

are the **Bunker Hill Steps**, with a broad stairway and watercourse winding around a modern office tower, flanked by sculptures and outdoor cafés, and providing a shortcut to the Museum of Contemporary Art. Local boosters say this is L.A.'s answer to Rome's Spanish Steps.

Two small downtown museums that perhaps deserve more attention than they receive are the **Wells Fargo History Museum** ★ *(free admission, Mon to Fri 9am to 5pm; 333 S. Grand Ave. between Third and Fourth sts.,* ☎*213-253-7166),* sponsored by the bank of the same name, depicting elements of mid-19th-century California history, including stagecoaches used to cross the western U.S., and the **Museum of Neon Art** ★★ *($3.50; Tue to Sat 11am to 6pm; 501 W.*

Olympic Blvd. at Hope St., ☎*213-489-9918)* this second museum is a weird and wonderful place where the only lighting comes from the art itself, part of a collection of old neon commercial signs rescued by artist Lili Lakich, as well as some contemporary creations using the same medium.

In the following section are several museums that lie outside the downtown area, but are still not far from downtown.

The **Southwest Museum** ★★★ *($5; Tue to Sun 10am to 5pm; 234 Museum Dr. in Highland Park northeast of downtown L.A.; by car, Pasadena Freeway to Avenue 43 exit, turning right onto Figueroa and up the hill; by bus from downtown L.A., MTA routes 81 or 83, about 15min;* ☎*323-221-2164,* *www. southwestmuseum.org)*, founded in 1907, is the oldest museum in Los Angeles. Perched on a remote hillside in a mostly residential area, it holds one of the world's most extensive collections of Native American artifacts, with an emphasis on the cultures of California and other parts of the U.S. Southwest. Indigenous cultures of the Great Plains, the U.S. Northwest, Mexico and Central America are also represented, ranging from prehistoric to contemporary periods. The exhibits of Navaho textiles is especially impressive. Pottery, clothing, baskets and teepees help round out the collection. Unfortunately, exhibition space is very limited, and only a tiny part of the collection can be showcased at any time. (A satellite location in the Wilshire corridor near the Los Angeles County Museum of Art allows some additional items to be displayed; see p 102.)

Exposition Park, south of downtown L.A. (connected by DASH bus route F) and facing the campus of the University of Southern California, is home to four museums. One of these, the Aerospace Museum, is closed for the time being pending decisions on renovations, although some of the outdoor exhibits remain in place, including a four-engine Douglas DC-8 jetliner painted in United Airlines colours clearly visible at the southwest corner of Exposition Boulevard and Figueroa Avenue. Exposition Park also encompasses the mammoth 106,000-seat Los Angeles Memorial Coliseum (the site of major events at the 1932 and 1984 Olym-

pic Games) and the adjacent Sports Arena.

The **California African-American Museum** ★★ *(voluntary contribution; Tue to Sun 10am to 5pm; 600 State Dr., Exposition Park, ☎213-744-7432)* presents mostly temporary exhibitions portraying various aspects of African and African-American culture and historical experiences, including historical artifacts and contemporary art.

The **California Science Center** ★★ *(free admission; every day 10am to 5pm; 700 State Dr., Exposition Park, ☎213-744-7400, www.casciencectr.org)* is a family favourite that invites participation by children at its many interactive displays exploring physics and biology as well as certain aspects of human technology. Among the more popular areas of the museum are an earthquake simulator and the Bodyworks theatre, which enables visitors to see the inside of a 50ft (15m) human-shaped creature named Tess. The museum also includes an IMAX cinema *(admission charge)*.

The **Natural History Museum of Los Angeles County** ★ *($6; Tue to Sun 10am to 5pm; 900 Exposition Blvd., ☎213-763-3466, www.nhm.org)* attracts many visitors who come to see its dinosaur hall, which includes a complete tyrannosaurus skull. Other sections of the museum present mammals of North America and Africa, birds, insects, marine life, and gems and minerals. Elsewhere, there are displays of Native American cultures, including Navaho textiles. At the lower level, California history is portrayed in detail.

Tour B: Pasadena and Surroundings

Every New Year's Day, Pasadena plays host to the Tournament of Roses Parade, an extravagant affair featuring hundreds of lavishly flower-adorned floats whose stately progress is transmitted live to millions of television viewers across the United States. This is followed by the Rose Bowl college football championship game held at the namesake stadium. Then the crowds depart and Pasadena can revert to its usual elegant tranquility, so close and yet so far from the smog-choked metropolis on the other side of the hills.

Nestled in the San Gabriel Valley northeast of downtown L.A., Pasadena and some of the surrounding communities have managed to retain an old-fashioned, small-town atmosphere without forsaking cultural and commercial amenities that match the best the big city has to offer. As far as some residents are concerned, this is close to idyllic. First promoted in the 1880s by railway companies as a winter retreat for wealthy midwesterners, Pasadena has never quite abandoned its semi-aristocratic roots. Many of the old mansions have been lovingly maintained, several of which are open to the public.

Cultural attractions include two institutions that have achieved worldwide fame: the Norton Simon Museum in Pasadena and the Huntington Library, Art Collections and Botanical Gardens in nearby San Marino. Several smaller museums add to the scene, such as Pasadena's Pacific Asia Museum. But what probably draws the greatest number of visitors is pedestrian-friendly Colorado Boulevard, as well as some of the neighbouring streets in gentrified Old Pasadena with their Victorian ambiance and many original shops and restaurants. In addition to some of the more obvious attractions, the Pasadena Convention and Visitors Bureau offers several suggestions for walking tours.

Colorado Boulevard is the main east-west avenue crossing downtown Pasadena. It forms an inverted "L" with South Lake Avenue—another shop-lined street—toward the eastern edge of downtown Pasadena. Numerous parking lots dot the area, particularly along the streets behind South Lake Avenue and behind Colorado Boulevard in the Old Pasadena area between Arroyo Parkway and Pasadena Avenue. A free bus service (look for the stops marked ARTS) operates at intervals of 15 to 20min along this L-shaped loop, running west along Colorado Boulevard as far as Orange Grove Boulevard near the Norton Simon Museum, then east along Green Street one block to the south, and down South Lake Avenue. Further north along Orange Grove Boulevard lie the Pasadena Historical Museum, the Gamble House and the Rose Bowl.

To reach Pasadena by car from downtown Los Angeles, the most obvious route is the Pasadena Freeway, numbered California Highway 110 and also known as the **Arroyo Seco Parkway**. Opened in 1940, this 10km (6mi) stretch of

highway was the first freeway in the L.A. area and has been designated a historical monument! With its meandering path through the hills of the San Gabriel range and the pleasant greenery beyond its shoulders, it bears little resemblance to newer parts of the urban-freeway network.

By bus, MTA express route no. 401 runs north along Olive Street in downtown L.A., taking about 25min to reach the corner of Colorado Boulevard and Los Robles Avenue in downtown Pasadena. Service is twice an hour on weekdays, more frequent at rush hours and once an hour on evenings and weekends. From Hollywood, MTA routes 180 and 181 run along Hollywood Boulevard, through Los Feliz and Glendale, and then along Colorado Boulevard. Several other bus routes also serve the area.

The very helpful **Pasadena Convention and Visitors Bureau** (Mon to Fri 9am to 5pm, Sat 10am to 4pm, 171 S. Los Robles Ave. between Green and Cordova sts., ☎626-795-9311) offers many useful leaflets and maps as well as information and suggestions. The leaflets include suggested self-guided **walking tours** of historic residential areas featuring architectural designs that have had a significant impact in California and beyond.

One place to begin your visit is the **Old Pasadena** district, centred around Colorado Boulevard between Arroyo Parkway on the east and Pasadena Avenue on the west, also extending south along Fair Oaks Avenue to Central Park and north along Ray-

mond Avenue to Memorial Park.

This was the main business district a century ago, and its many shops and former warehouses have been revived to create a quaint sense of traditional small-town U.S.A. (not often found in the western part of the country) that many people find appealing for shopping, dining out, movie-going, or simply strolling along the broad, café-lined sidewalks. Several of the buildings display whimsical architectural features, particularly along Raymond Avenue near Green Street.

A little further west along Colorado Boulevard, beyond Freeway 210 but before Orange Grove Boulevard, is the **Norton Simon Museum of Art** ★★★ ($6; Wed to Sun noon to 6pm, Fri until 9pm; 411 W. Colorado Blvd., ☎626-449-6840, www.nortonsimon.org). Named for a food-processing magnate and arts benefactor whose personal collection of works by Degas, Renoir, Gauguin, Cézanne and several of the Old Masters now forms an important part of the museum's permanent collection, the Norton Simon occupies an airy, attractive building with uncluttered lines and sensible layout flanked by a sculpture museum and garden café. The collections of European art, covering most major periods from Renaissance to modern, are supplemented by substantial selections of East-Indian and Southeast-Asian art. The museum shop offers a vast array of art books, cards, maps and gift items.

A couple of blocks north along Orange Grove Boulevard, at the corner of Walnut Street, is the small **Pasadena Historical**

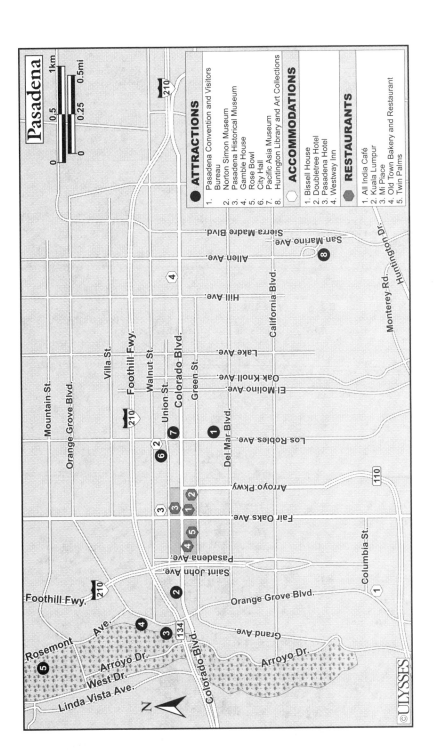

Pasadena

0 | 0.5 | 1km
0 | 0.25 | 0.5mi

ATTRACTIONS

1. Pasadena Convention and Visitors Bureau
2. Norton Simon Museum
3. Pasadena Historical Museum
4. Gamble House
5. Rose Bowl
6. City Hall
7. Pacific Asia Museum
8. Huntington Library and Art Collections

ACCOMMODATIONS

1. Bissell House
2. Doubletree Hotel
3. Pasadena Hotel
4. Westway Inn

RESTAURANTS

1. All India Café
2. Kuala Lumpur
3. Mi Piace
4. Old Town Bakery and Restaurant
5. Twin Palms

© ULYSSES

Museum ★ *($4; Thu to Sun 1pm to 4pm; 470 W. Walnut St., ☎626-577-1660)*. Far more interesting to many visitors than the collections of photographs and assorted period mementos is the 1906 mansion, called the Feynes House, that houses the museum and forms part of Pasadena's original Millionaire's Row. Features include mahogany pillars at the entrance, oriental rugs and silk damask wall coverings. A small building in the mansion's lavish gardens contains, of all things, a collection of Finnish folk art.

A block further north, just off Orange Grove Boulevard is the **Gamble House** ★★ *($5; Thu to Sun noon to 3pm; group tours offered at other times with advance notice; 4 Westmoreland Pl., ☎626-793-3334, www.gamblehouse. org)*. Designed by architects Charles Sumner Greene, and Henry Mather Greene and built in 1908 for one of the founding families of the Procter and Gamble Company, it is widely regarded as a masterpiece of the Arts and Crafts movement. Visitors are taken on 1hr guided tours that run every 15min. Although the design relies heavily on traditions of wooden architecture using a blend of many exotic and native species, it also has a strongly Southern California character, with wide terraces and open sleeping porches to bring the indoors and outdoors together. Broad overhanging eaves and a studied effort to capture cross-ventilation adapt to the climate rather than attempt to conquer it. What is perhaps most

impressive is the architects' attention to detail in the articulated joinery, built-in cabinetry and panelling, stained-glass doors, and careful integration of lighting, rugs and various furnishings. The site includes a bookstore and museum shop.

Just northwest of the Gamble House is Brookside Park, home to the famous 98,000-seat **Rose Bowl** football stadium.

Back in downtown Pasadena, one of the most striking public buildings in all of California is the red-tile-domed 1927 **City Hall** ★ *(Garfield Ave. at Union St.)*, which blends Spanish, Moorish and Italian Renaissance influences. Two blocks behind, on Walnut Street, is Pasadena's Central Library.

City Hall

The **Pacific Asia Museum** ★★ *($4; Wed to Sun 10am to 5pm; 46. N. Los Robles Ave. between Union St. and Colorado Blvd., ☎626-449-2742)* is housed in a jewel of a building designed in the 1920s in Chinese imperial-palace style, with an enticing courtyard garden and pond. Its very limited exhibition space allows for only small rotating displays from its own permanent collection of mostly Chinese and Japanese art from various periods, though other countries are also represented. It makes for a brief but interesting visit.

The **Playhouse District**, named for the famed Pasadena Playhouse (see p 138), is a shopping and entertainment area centred along Colorado Boulevard between Los Robles Avenue on the west and **South Lake Avenue** of the east. The latter avenue features several blocks of shops, restaurants and cafés, some of them located in European-style arcades in the block between Cordova Street and Del Mar Avenue.

San Marino, directly south of Pasadena, is home to the fabulous **Huntington Library, Art Collections and Botanical Gardens** ★★★ *($8.50; free first Thu of each month; late May to early Sep Tue to Sun 10:30am to 4:30pm, early Sep to late May Tue to Fri noon to 4:30pm, Sat to Sun 10:30am to 4:30pm; 1151 Oxford Rd. near Huntington Dr., ☎626-405-2100, www.huntington.org)*. A bookshop, tea room and restaurant serving light meals are located on the premises.

As the name suggests, this sprawling cultural institution comprises three entities, each of which can be described in superlative tones. It is set on an 207-acre (84ha) former ranch once owned by railway magnate Henry E. Huntington, who collected books and art with the same fervour with which he built his numerous businesses.

Today, the **library** holds about four million items, including half a million rare books, as well as many maps, prints, drawings and photographs. The collection is noted for its many early quartos and folios of Shakespeare plays, as well as early editions of many later British and U.S. writers, and documents penned by several leading U.S. historical figures. A continuous series of rotating exhibitions presented in the library's Exhibition Hall draws upon the extensive archives, going back to the Middle Ages and including illustrated Books of Hours and Bibles.

The **art collections** are housed in a former Huntington family residence that was later augmented by an extensive gallery wing. The earliest collec-

tion amassed by Huntington, who died in 1927, and his second wife, Arabella, centred around Old Masters. To this they later added collections of 18th-century British and French paintings, as well as sets of Beauvais tapestries and Savonnerie carpets. The British paintings include many full-length portraits, among them famous works by Thomas Gainsborough. Nor is American art neglected: one wing of the gallery focuses on the Arts and Crafts movement of the early 20th century.

The extensive grounds are shaded by more than 1,000 mature oaks and numerous specimens of other trees. A carefully planned series of **gardens**, some of them formal in the European tradition, others more bucolic, provide a graceful setting for the buildings and a thoroughly delightful area for visitors to stroll or rest. Winding pathways are lined with various species of flowers. Other areas include a desert garden and conservatory, as well as Japanese, Australian, subtropical and jungle gardens.

Getting here can sometimes be tricky, though parking is rarely a problem. By car from downtown L.A., take Highway 110 (the Pasadena Freeway), exit at California

Street and turn east. By bus from downtown L.A., MTA route 79 runs north along Olive Street and takes about 35min to reach Huntington Drive and San Marino Avenue, several minutes' walk from the main entrance. Buses run 30min apart (40min on Sun). By bus from downtown Pasadena, the relatively short hop actually takes longer because there is no direct link: MTA bus 260 southbound along Los Robles Avenue connects with the No. 79 at Huntington Drive.

Tour C: Hollywood and Surroundings

No name evokes the magic of the movies the way Hollywood does. Mention Hollywood to people almost anywhere on earth, and what comes to mind is the glamour of the silver screen and the romantic lives of movie stars. Hollywood isn't the only place in the world where movies are made, but its prodigious production and its heavily hyped stars have dwarfed everything else, in box office receipts if not always in quality. This has been the case since "the industry" (in L.A., this is shorthand for the entertainment industry) set roots early in the 20th century in what had been a semi-rural suburb northwest of downtown L.A. It was drawn here by the mild California climate and the variety of scenic backdrops nearby. Later, Hollywood also became the world's top production centre for popular music and television programming.

Shrine Auditorium

Los Angeles

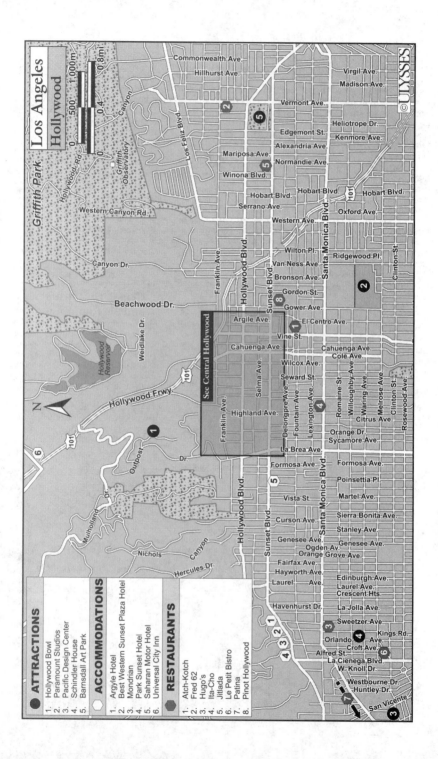

What visitors to Hollywood will now see is a far cry from what existed in the glory days. The Hollywood name sticks to the entertainment industry even though all but one of the major studios have relocated to more spacious facilities in other parts of the L.A. area. Much of the Hollywood urban area has fallen on hard times, and Hollywood Boulevard, its fabled thoroughfare, is only beginning to re-emerge from the decades of neglect that gave it a decidedly seedy character. In the last several years, redevelopment efforts have switched into higher gear. The aim—as with the clean-up of New York's Times Square—is once again to make Hollywood safe for suburbanites. Abandoned theatres are being rebuilt, office buildings are being spruced up, and several down-at-the-heels apartment buildings are being resuscitated. In addition, a large luxury hotel is under construction, one or two landmark restaurants are being restored, and some of the porn shops and tacky souvenir emporiums are beginning to give way to more presentable retailers. A modern and suitably glitzy new home for the Academy Awards is set to open in 2002 near the legendary corner of Hollywood and Vine. Hollywood Boulevard could again become the throbbing heart of entertainment in the region. It still has a long way to go, however, and getting rid of the accumulated grime (both literally and figuratively) will not be accomplished overnight.

Visitors in search of glamour may have to wait a while longer. But the signs are hopeful.

Meanwhile, Hollywood continues to trade on its image and star-studded past. Some of the attractions are decidedly kitsch, like the names of long-ago denizens of the silver screen cast in tiny terrazzo and bronze plaques planted in neat rows at pavement level. Other attractions aim a little higher, though nearly always with entertainment as the central theme. Some visitors may find that, apart from walking around and soaking up a little atmosphere, there isn't really very much to see or do in Hollywood.

This tour covers not only central Hollywood and the Hollywood Hills (which form the eastern part of the Santa Monica range), giving some sense of identity to local topography, but also to neighbouring areas—West Hollywood, Los Feliz, Griffith Park and, just beyond the hills, North Hollywood. The Los Angeles Convention & Visitors Bureau operates a visitor information centre in Hollywood (*Mon to Sat 9am to 1pm and 2pm to 5pm, 6541 Hollywood Blvd. near Cahuenga Blvd.*), which offers a wide range of pamphlets (including transit information) and multilingual staff to help with inquiries.

Hollywood sign

Perhaps the most familiar landmark of all is the **Hollywood sign** whose 50ft (15m) letters are perched on 1,640ft-high (500m) Mount Lee in an off-limits section of Griffith Park. This sign is easily visible (except on the smoggiest days) from a great distance over much of Los Angeles. Originally, the sign read Hollywoodland. It was erected in 1923 to publicize a housing development. In 1945 it was deeded to the Hollywood Chamber of Commerce, which lopped off the last four letters. As it was decaying badly, the sign was rebuilt in 1978.

Many visitors come to Hollywood expecting to see film or TV studios. As already noted, most of the studios are now located elsewhere. Please see the box for information on studio tours. And yes, bus tours with guides spouting corny remarks about the stars and their lavish abodes really do exist.

First, we take a look at Hollywood Boulevard, beginning at the corner of Vine Street, where passengers emerging from the gleaming new Metro Red Line station are greeted by the sight of the **Pantages Theater ★** across the street. Following extensive restoration work carried out by

the Walt Disney Company, this 2,700-seat landmark reopened in September 2000 with a stage production of *The Lion King* that appears set to run for years.

Want to see your favourite Hollywood star from the past? His or her name just might be embedded in the sidewalk along the **Hollywood Walk of Fame ★**. More than 2,000 actors and musicians have been remembered in this way since the program began in 1960. The tiny black-and-gold, star-shaped monuments decorate the sidewalks along Hollywood Boulevard from Gower Street all the way west to La Brea Avenue (a distance of more than 15 blocks), and along three blocks of Vine Street between Sunset Boulevard and Yucca Street. A leaflet published by the Hollywood Chamber of Commerce *(7018 Hollywood Blvd., ☎323-469-8311)* and also available from the tourism office *(6541 Hollywood Blvd.)* provides a complete list with exact locations.

On Vine Street, a half-block north of Hollywood Boulevard, is the **Capitol Records Tower ★**, a circular building erected in 1956 in the shape of a stack of vinyl records with a stylus on top. (Like most vinyl albums, the Capitol label has faded from view.) Another distinctively shaped Hollywood landmark from that period is the **Cinerama Dome**, a couple of blocks south on Sunset Boulevard between Vine and Ivar streets, built in 1963 as a futuristic

movie theatre and still the world's only geodesic dome built entirely of concrete.

Back on Hollywood Boulevard, three of the truly grand old movie palaces have made stirring comebacks. These are the **Egyptian Theatre ★** *(6712 Hollywood Blvd. at Las Palmas Ave.)*, **El Capitan ★** *(6838 Hollywood Blvd. at Highland Ave.)* and **Mann's Chinese Theater ★** *(6925 Hollywood Blvd. near Orange Dr.)*, all located within two blocks of each other. The Egyptian, built in 1922, reopened in 1998 following extensive restoration work that maintained the original kitschy elements such as hieroglyphs and sphinx heads while dramatically improving sight lines and technical equipment. It is now home to the non-profit

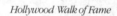

Hollywood Walk of Fame

American Cinematheque, which presents retrospective series. El Capitan, built in 1926 with an ornate Spanish colonial exterior and opulent interior decor, has been restored by the Disney organization and is now showing first-run films. Mann's Chinese Theater, probably the most

famous of all with its giant pagoda-shaped exterior, not only shows films but also displays the cement footprints of about 150 stars from Hollywood's golden era.

At the same corner as the Egyptian, three tourist-trap museums—the Hollywood Wax Museum, the Guiness World Records Museum and Ripley's Believe It or Not—are wholly forgettable and ludicrously over-priced. All three are commercial rip-offs... believe it or not!

One block west of Mann's Chinese Theater, the **Hollywood Entertainment Museum ★** *($7.50; Thu to Tue 11am to 6pm; 7021 Hollywood Blvd. at Sycamore St., ☎323-465-7900)* is a light-hearted celebration of movie-making and its history. Opened in 1996, it is located in a space at the Galaxy cinema complex once occupied by an unsuccessful food court. Visitors enter through a rotunda gallery, where they can see sets and other memorabilia from favourite movies and TV shows, as well as exhibits on costumes and makeup. A timeline presents the industry's century-long history, and a 7min multiscreen show every 30min presents voices and faces from the past. Then the second part of the visit begins, with a guide leading groups through other rooms where various techniques like sound effects are presented from a historical view point. Another part of the tour demonstrates the various departments found in a typical

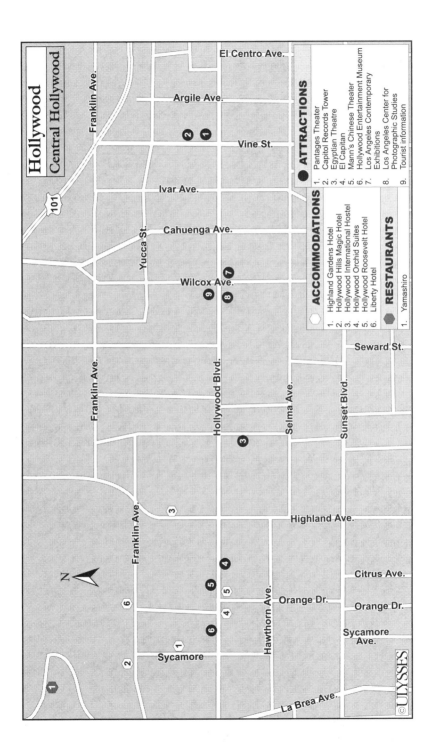

Hollywood
Central Hollywood

El Centro Ave.

Argile Ave.

Vine St.

Ivar Ave.

Cahuenga Ave.

Wilcox Ave.

Franklin Ave.

Yucca St.

Hollywood Blvd.

Selma Ave.

Sunset Blvd.

Seward St.

Franklin Ave.

Highland Ave.

Citrus Ave.

Orange Dr.

Orange Dr.

Hawthorn Ave.

Sycamore Ave.

Sycamore

La Brea Ave.

101

N

● ATTRACTIONS

1. Pantages Theater
2. Capitol Records Tower
3. Egyptian Theatre
4. El Capitan
5. Mann's Chinese Theater
6. Hollywood Entertainment Museum
7. Los Angeles Contemporary Exhibitions
8. Los Angeles Center for Photographic Studies
9. Tourist Information

⬡ ACCOMMODATIONS

1. Highland Gardens Hotel
2. Hollywood Hills Magic Hotel
3. Hollywood International Hostel
4. Hollywood Orchid Suites
5. Hollywood Roosevelt Hotel
6. Liberty Hotel

⬢ RESTAURANTS

1. Yamashiro

© ULYSSES

Studio Tours

Publicity-conscious "Hollywood" studios (most of them located outside Hollywood) are always happy to peddle their wares and to squeeze a little extra cash out of their adoring fans in the process. All cynicism aside, studio tours enable visitors to get behind-the-scenes glimpses of the daily operations of major film and television facilities. Because of a continuously changing mix of productions, no two tours are exactly alike. It may be possible on occasion to see a well-known film or TV personality, though visitors are not always taken to areas where filming is underway. Reservations are always recommended, and good walking shoes are often suggested.

Paramount Studios ★ *($15; Mon to Fri, every hour from 9am to 2pm; 5555 Melrose Ave. near Gower St., parking entrance on Bronson St., south of Melrose, ☎323-956-1777)* is the only major Hollywood studio actually located in Hollywood, though it is in the quiet southeast corner of Hollywood far from much of the action. This lends the 2hr tour a sense of history that may be less apparent in some of the other studios. Children under 10 are not admitted. (By bus: MTA routes 10 or 11 from downtown L.A. or West Hollywood, or MTA route 210 along Vine Street from Hollywood Boulevard or Crenshaw Boulevard, get off at Melrose and walk east.)

Sony Pictures Studios ★ *($20; tours start Mon to Fri at 9:30am, 11am, 12:30pm and 2pm; 10202 W. Washington Blvd., east of Overland Ave., Culver City, ☎323-520-8687)* offers 2hr walking tours (children under 12 not admitted) that provide glimpses of historic sound stages, current film and TV productions, and future advances in production technology. Among the TV shows filmed here is Jeopardy. Tours leave from the Sony Pictures shopping plaza. Culver City lies in the western part of the L.A. area, southwest of Hollywood and east of Venice. (By car: Overland Avenue exit from the Santa Monica Freeway, or Venice Boulevard exit from the 405 Freeway. By bus: Culver City Route 1 along Washington Boulevard from Venice or the West L.A. Transit Center, or MTA route 33 along Venice Boulevard from downtown L.A. or Santa Monica, get off at Madison Avenue and walk two blocks south.)

Warner Bros. Studios ★★ *($30; tours Mon to Fri only, Jun to Sep every 30min 9am to 4pm, Oct to May every hour 9am to 3pm; 4000 Warner Blvd., near Hollywood Way and Olive Ave., Burbank, ☎818-972-8687)* is considered by some connoisseurs to offer the best of the studio tours, with the least gimmickry and the most realism, as well as the greatest chance of witnessing a live filming. The tour runs 2hrs, 15min, partly on foot, partly by electric cart. It begins with a 15min film and continues with a visit to the Warner Bros. Museum, which features archival material celebrating the stars. Visitors are then taken around the vast backlot with its many sound stages, with stops at some of the technical departments. Warner Bros. and NBC Studios (below) are located in Burbank, at the southern edge of the San Fernando Valley. Children under eight are not admitted. (By car from downtown L.A.: 101 Freeway, Burbank Boulevard exit. By public transit from downtown L.A. or Hollywood: Metro Red Line to Universal City station, connect to MTA bus 96 or 152 eastbound.)

NBC Studios Tour ★ *($7; tours depart at regular intervals Mon to Fri 9am to 3pm, open later and on weekends in summer;*

3000 W. Alameda Ave.,
Burbank, entry via
California St. south of
Olive Ave., ☎818-840-
3537) provides a 1hr,
15min tour starting with a
brief history of NBC radio
and television. This is
now strictly a television
studio, but it has sound
stages and technical
departments similar to
many of those at the film
studios. Visitors can
request tickets to be part
of the studio audience at
tapings of popular pro-
grams such as the
Tonight Show with Jay
Leno. (By car from down-
town L.A.: 101 Freeway,
Burbank Boulevard exit.
By public transit from

downtown L.A. or
Hollywood: Metro Red
Line to Universal City
station, connect to MTA
bus 96 or 152 east-
bound.)

Universal Studios Hollywood
is more of a theme park
than a true studio tour
and is covered separately
on page 100.

For a list of film shoots
around town, and the
opportunity to sneak a
peek and maybe get an
autograph, visitors may
request the free "shoot
sheet" from the **Motion
Picture Coordination Office**
(Mon to Fri 8am to 6pm;
7083 Hollywood Blvd.,

fifth floor, ☎323-957-
1000).

For tickets to TV-show
tapings, sources include
CBS (☎323-852-2458),
NBC (☎818-840-3537),
Audiences Unlimited (preferred distributor for
ABC, ☎818-506-0043), or
Television Tickets (☎323-
467-4697). Requests for
popular shows should be
made well in advance,
although tickets are
sometimes available on
the day of the taping.
Sometimes several episo-
des are shot back to
back, requiring extra
audience stamina.

studio backlot. Original
items from popular movies
including *Star Trek* are integrated with the other displays.

Across the street lies the
Hollywood Roosevelt Hotel
(7000 Hollywood Blvd.), an
integral part of Hollywood
lore in the early decades
after its 1927 opening. It
was briefly home to the
Academy Awards, and has
been renovated and
stripped of the "modern-
izing" touches that once
concealed its impressive
Spanish-colonial design,
including intricately carved
columns and painted ceil-
ings.

On a very different note,
**Los Angeles Contemporary
Exhibitions (LACE)** (free admission; Wed to Sat noon to
6pm; 6522 Hollywood Blvd.
at Wilcox St., ☎323-957-
1777) is an artist-run gallery with a reputation for
conceptual works that

move toward new fron-
tiers, using painting and a
variety of other media.
Some of its exhibitions
have won enthusiastic
critical acclaim. Next door,
**Los Angeles Center for
Photographic Studies** (free
admission; Wed to Sat 11am
to 6pm; 6518 Hollywood
Blvd. at Wilcox St., ☎323-
466-6232) presents a con-
tinuing series of exhibi-
tions in a small storefront
space.

The **Hollywood Bowl**, located
off Highland Avenue
0.75mi (1.2km) north of
Hollywood Boulevard,
partway to North Holly-
wood, is a popular venue
for summer concerts (see
p 139).

West Hollywood, as the name
suggests, lies to the west
of Hollywood. With its
varied and often funky
shopping opportunities
and its eclectic selection of
hotels, restaurants, cafés

and night spots, it is regarded as one of L.A.'s
hipper areas. The substantial number of elderly residents does not seem to
deter from this image. It is
also the main centre of the
gay and lesbian social
scene.

Although it is difficult to
pinpoint many specific
attractions in West Hollywood, some streets have
special character and are
thus worth a drive or a
stroll. **Sunset Boulevard** follows a sinuous path along
the base of the Hollywood
Hills between Fairfax Avenue and Doheny Drive to
the west. Once referred to
as the Sunset Strip, it connects discontinuous rows
of shops and restaurants.
Further south, **Melrose Avenue** between La Brea Avenue and La Cienega Boule-
vard was, for a long time,
the place to go for avant-
garde fashions. Although
its popularity has led to

Los Angeles

the arrival of more mainstream retailers in recent years, the scene still has a certain edge.

One of the most interesting buildings in West Hollywood is the **Pacific Design Center** ★ (*8687 Melrose Ave. near San Vicente Blvd.*), a giant seven-storey bubble clad in curving cobalt-blue glass. A later bright green addition was equally controversial. Designed by Argentinian architect Cesar Pelli, it has become known locally as the Blue Whale. It houses interior design showrooms for the wholesale trade.

The **Schindler House** ★ (*835 N. Kings Rd., 1½ blocks north of Melrose Ave.*) is regarded as a landmark of Modernist architecture. Named for Rudolph Schindler, the Austrian-born architect who designed this building in the early 1920s as his personal residence, this house has a flat roof and large concrete-walled studio rooms with sliding doors opening to the outdoors. These and other elements were to influence California architecture in the succeeding decades. Heavy alterations after the architect's death were subsequently reversed in a restoration project, and the house is now the site of a small museum established in partnership with Vienna's Museum of Applied Arts (MAK in its German initials). The **MAK Center for Art** (*$5; Wed to Sun 11am to 6pm, ☎323-651-1510*) features exhibitions dealing with current issues in art and architecture.

Los Feliz is a neighbourhood to the east of Hollywood that appears to have picked up where Melrose Avenue left off in terms of new horizons in style, particularly along a stretch

of Vermont Avenue between Hollywood Boulevard and Franklin Avenue. Occupying a large hilltop estate extending from the southwest corner of Hollywood and Vermont

Mann's Chinese Theater

is the **Barnsdall Art Park**, named for oil heiress Aline Barnsdall whose grandiose plans for the site never took full shape. The site is home to the **Los Angeles Municipal Art Gallery** (*free admission; Wed to Sun 12:30pm to 5pm; 4804 Hollywood Blvd., ☎213-485-4581*), operating as an extension of Junior Arts Center with its extensive program of studio classes. The gallery presents temporary exhibitions of works by students and professional artists. Next door is the **Hollyhock House** ★ (*$2; guided tours every hour Wed to Sun noon to 3pm; ☎323-913-4157*), an architectural landmark designed by Frank Lloyd Wright in the late 1910s. Hollyhocks, an abundant flower, form a theme in parts of the design, which incorporates a variety of elements and innovates through the clever use of varied ceiling heights from room to room.

Griffith Park ★★, north of Los Feliz in the Hollywood Hills, provides the most significant area of green

space in Los Angeles. Occupying 4,200 acres (1,700ha), this massive and very hilly park (see p 99) encompasses many attractions, including golf courses, hiking trails and numerous picnic grounds, as well as the Forest Lawn Cemetary (immortalized in Evelyn Waugh's novel *The Loved One*), an outdoor theatre, the Griffith Observatory and Planetarium, the Los Angeles Zoo, Travel Town Museum and the Autry Museum of Western Heritage. (By bus: MTA route 96 skirts the eastern side of the park, near the main attractions, running north from downtown L.A. along Olive Street and continuing to North Hollywood.)

The **Griffith Observatory** ★★ (*free admission; Tue to Fri 2pm to 10pm, Sat to Sun 12:30pm to 10pm, summer: every day 12:30pm to 10pm; children under five restricted; planetarium shows: $4; 3pm, 7:30pm, also Sat to Sun 4:30pm; laserium shows: $7; Fri to Sat*

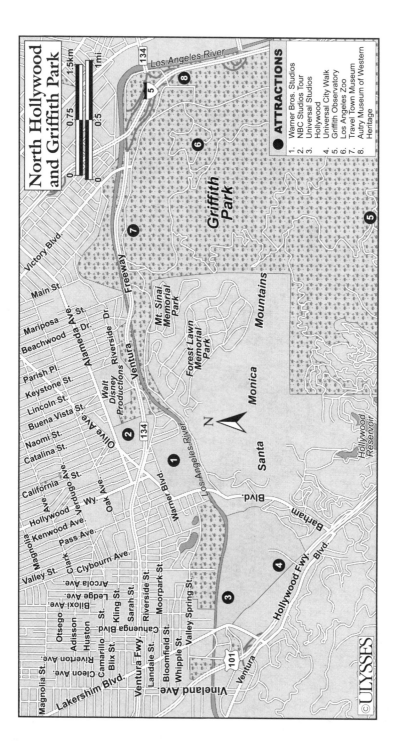

North Hollywood and Griffith Park

ATTRACTIONS

1. Warner Bros. Studios
2. NBC Studios Tour
3. Universal Studios
4. Universal City Walk / Hollywood
5. Griffith Observatory
6. Los Angeles Zoo
7. Travel Town Museum
8. Autry Museum of Western Heritage

Los Angeles River

Griffith Park

Mt. Sinai Memorial Park

Forest Lawn Memorial Park

Santa Monica Mountains

Hollywood Reservoir

Victory Blvd.

Main St.

Mariposa

Beachwood Ave.

Parish Pl.

Keystone St.

Lincoln St.

Buena Vista St.

Naomi St.

Catalina St.

California

Hollywood Ave.

Kenwood Ave.

Pass Ave.

Clybourn Ave.

Magnolia Ave.

Valley St.

Clark

Arcola Ave.

Ledge Ave.

Biloxi Ave.

Otsego

Adisson

Huston

Camarillo St.

Blix St.

Cahuenga Blvd.

Kling St.

Sarah St.

Riverside St.

Moorpark St.

Valley Spring St.

Landale St.

Bloomfield St.

Whipple St.

Ventura Fwy.

Magnolia St.

Cleon Ave.

Riverton Ave.

Lakershim Blvd.

Vineland Ave.

Ventura

Warner Blvd.

Oak Ave.

Verdugo St.

Wy.

Olive Ave.

Alameda Dr.

Riverside Dr.

Walt Disney Productions

Freeway

Ventura

Los Angeles River

Barham Blvd.

Hollywood Fwy. Blvd.

Blvd.

N

0   0.75   1.5km
0   0.5   1mi

134

5

101

© ULYSSES

6pm, 8:45pm, 9:45pm; other days 3pm, 7:30pm; 2800 E. Observatory Rd., Griffith Park, enter via Los Feliz Ave., ☎323-664-1191, www.griffithobs. org) is housed in a landmark triple-domed building high on a hilltop. Even for those who aren't astronomy buffs, it's worth a visit for the extraordinary view over Los Angeles from the terrace. One dome conceals a triple-beam solar telescope, another a 12in (30cm) Zeiss refracting telescope and, in the middle, the planetarium. The building, which opened in 1935, also houses a science museum that includes displays of meteorites and interactive computer stations where visitors can explore advances in astronomy. On clear evenings visitors can observe the heavens from one of the observatory's telescopes. The 1hr-long planetarium shows narrate aspects of astronomy. Laserium shows, popular with teenagers, feature laser lights set to popular music.

Los Angeles Zoo ★ ★ *($8.25; every day 10am to 5pm, Jul to Aug until 6pm; 5333 Zoo Dr., Griffith Park, ☎323-666-4090, www.lazoo.org)* features more than 400 species spread over its 80-acre (32ha) grounds linked by winding pathways through abundantly landscaped areas. Not all animals are caged, with moats or space used instead as barriers. The zoo has gradually been reducing its collection to allow the animals more roaming room. Special collections include the Great Ape Forest, the Ahmanson Koala House, Adventure Island (for children) and an aviary.

Almost next door is the **Travel Town Museum** ★ ★ *(free admission; Mon to Fri 10am to 5pm, Sat to Sun 10am to 6pm, Jul to Aug closes 1hr later; 5200 Zoo Dr., Griffith Park, ☎323-662-5874)*, of particular interest to railway buffs. This partly outdoor museum features a miniature railway *(rides $1.75)* and 14 full-sized steam locomotives, the oldest of which dates back to 1864. Among other exhibits are passenger cars (including luxurious sleeping cars and club cars), freight cars, cabooses and an extensive model railway layout. Antique fire engines are also on display.

The **Autry Museum of Western Heritage** ★ ★ *($7.50; Tue to Sun 10am to 5pm; 4700 Western Heritage Way, Griffith Park, ☎323-667-2000)* adopted a cowboy and lasso as its emblem, but the museum's scope is far broader, presenting many aspects of the settlement of the western U.S. by citizens of British heritage and the displacement of earlier inhabitants. The mural-lined galleries do include a section devoted to the Spirit of the Cowboy, but Native American populations and Spanish settlers also receive their due. One gallery presents the bar and other furnishings created in 1880 for a saloon in Montana and portrays some of the wilder aspects of life in the Wild West.

North Hollywood lies at the southern edge of the San Fernando Valley just beyond the Hollywood Hills. It includes Universal City and lies adjacent to Burbank, home to several of the ex-Hollywood studios (see box). A new extension to the Metro Red Line speeds access from downtown L.A. and central Hollywood.

Universal Studios Hollywood *($39; every day 9am to 7pm, summer 8am to 10pm; off the Hollywood Freeway, Universal Center Dr. exit, ☎818-622-3801, www.universalstudios. com)* is one of the world's most popular tourist attractions, situated on the grounds of the world's largest movie and television studio and replete with throwbacks to hit-animation features like images of dinosaurs from the film *Jurassic Park*. Obviously, somebody is doing something right. If we haven't given this flashy and heavily hyped theme park a star rating, it's because opinions can vary so wildly. Adolescents will certainly clamour for their parents to fork up the hefty admission price that does, admittedly, include all rides (although the waits can be long, especially in summer). The lavish commercial development of what used to be a simple studio tour has created an interesting phenomenon: movie sets are, by definition, simulations of real scenes. What we see here are simulations of movie sets—in other words, simulations of simulations. The special effects are very special indeed, including simulations of an earthquake in New York and a bridge that collapses practically beneath the wheels of the huge electric carts that ferry visitors around on an introductory 45min tour. Needless to say, food and drink are offered in abundance (although it's not a bad idea to bring along some bottled water). Besides the fake (and a few real) movie sets that visitors can see, there are the rides, some of them suitably stomach-churning, others more tame. Repeat visitors have their favourites. By common consensus, one of the best is the

Organized Tours

Tour D: Mid-Wilshire and Westside

Sometimes the hassle of getting around on your own in an unfamiliar city may seem a bit much. Organized tours can provide an introduction to parts of the city and, if this sort of thing interests you, a chance to glimpse the mansions of certain Hollywood celebrities and pick up bits of gossip from chatty tour guides. The most popular tour programs are the half-day "City Tour and Movie Stars' Homes" offerings—the names vary slightly from one company to the next—typically priced at $40 to $45. Some tour companies provide visits to various theme parks or to the Getty Center, but in reality this is little more than a transporta-

tion service. Shopping tours, nightlife tours and full-day tours to out-of-town places like San Diego are also available.

Companies operating these tours include **Starline Tours of Hollywood** *(☎800-959-3131)*, **Guideline Sightseeing Tours** *(☎800-604-8433 or 323-465-3004)*, **Go West Adventures** *(☎310-216-2522, www.gowestadventures.com)*, **Euro Pacific Tours** *(☎310-574-0595 or 800-303-3005)*, **Hollywood Sightseeing** *(☎323-469-8184)* and **L.A. Tours** *(☎323-937-3361)*. The bell captains at some hotels have arrangements with particular tour companies.

This tour covers the broad area west of downtown Los Angeles, east of Santa Monica, and south of Hollywood. Moving from east to west, it includes the Koreatown district, Wilshire Boulevard's Miracle Mile with its impressive row of museums, the very swank City of Beverly Hills, the Westwood-UCLA area and, finally, Brentwood, crowned by the attention-winning Getty Center, one of the world's most richly endowed art institutions. The Los Angeles County Museum of Art, along the Miracle Mile, is a more than worthy rival.

Wilshire Boulevard, in some respects the most important street in Los Angeles, stretches from downtown L.A. to Santa Monica Beach and is the central artery serving the territory covered here. (It may horrify some wealthy Westsiders to learn that this important thoroughfare, crossing their elegant neighbourhoods, was named for a social reformer and publisher of socialist newspapers. But Gaylord Wilshire, who came from a well-to-do family, also had his capitalist side: he made an astute investment in real estate west of downtown L.A. in the 1880s, in an area that was subsequently developed as a fashionable residential district. More than a century later, the boulevard bisecting this and other districts continues to bear his name.)

Wilshire Boulevard starts at Grand Avenue downtown and runs west past

Jurassic Park ride, a sort of slow-moving indoor roller coaster whose riders are confronted at every turn by prehistoric monsters. It may all seem superficial, but it can be fun for those in the right frame of mind and it does present an important element of California culture.

Universal City Walk, adjacent to Universal Studios, is a shopping and entertainment mall designed to look like a traditional shopping street, minus the intrusive automobile traffic

and any elements that make real urban streets so creepy. First the suburban malls suck the commercial life from downtown areas, and now they pay the ultimate compliment by simulating city life. Universal City Walk, with its many shops, restaurants, cinemas and even nightclubs, is a security-controlled area where cleancut suburbanites can walk around outdoors in an environment made to appear less artificial than the typical enclosed mall. Top marks, though, for design.

MacArthur Park, one of the few significant and appealing patches of greenery in inner-city L.A. A few blocks further west, it crosses through part of **Koreatown ★**, an unofficially designated area that is home to part of the city's large and growing Korean community. It covers an extensive zone reaching from Beverly Boulevard south to Pico Avenue between Vermont Avenue on the east and Western Avenue on the west, and it spills even beyond these limits. While by no means everyone inhabiting this area is of Korean descent, this is a living, working, thriving immigrant neighbourhood (quite unlike the more fossilized Chinatown and Little Tokyo, which have lost most of their residents). Many of the businesses here cater to a mostly Korean clientele, and some have signs in Korean only. The most intensely developed commercial strip lies along Olympic Boulevard between Vermont and Western, with hundreds of shops and restaurants, most located in two-storey mini-malls plagued by a perpetual shortage of parking space. This is where to come for anything Korean, including food and decorative items. The **Korean American Museum of Art and Cultural Center** *(free admission; Tue to Sat 11am to 4pm; 3333 Wilshire Blvd. between Vermont and Normandie Aves., ☎213-388-4229)* presents photos, memorabilia and other items portraying the Korean-American immigrant experience, along with some traditional works of art.

Several interesting buildings, with no relation to Koreatown, are located in this general area. They include the **Wiltern Theater** *(Wilshire Blvd. at Western Ave.)*, a gorgeous turquoise-coloured Art Deco structure erected in 1931; **Saint Sophia Cathedral** *(Fri to Wed 10am to 2pm; 1324 S. Normandie Ave. near Pico Blvd.)*, spiritual home to the local Greek Orthodox community, a Byzantine structure built in 1952 and noted for its fabulously lavish interior with numerous icons, murals and crystal chandeliers; and the former **Bullocks Wilshire Department Store** *(3050 Wilshire Blvd. near Vermont Ave.)*, an elegant 1929 Art Deco landmark, its five storeys topped by a tower, that was closed in 1992 but rescued intact a few years later to serve as the law library of Southwestern University.

The **Miracle Mile**, covering the stretch of Wilshire Boulevard between La Brea and Fairfax avenues, was originally developed as a shopping area in the 1920s to serve the rapidly growing residential areas nearby. Many of the buildings from that period show Art Deco features in various *moderne* styles. Today, the area has lost its importance as a retail zone, and the first few blocks east of Fairfax have been taken over instead by at least a half-dozen museums, dominated by the mammoth Los Angeles County Museum of Art.

The newer and flashier Getty Center has certainly garnered more attention in the art world over the last few years, but the breadth and depth of the collection at the **Los Angeles County Museum of Art ★ ★ ★** *($6; Mon, Tue, Thu noon to 8pm; Fri noon to 9pm; Sat to Sun 11am to 8pm; closed Wed;* *5905 Wilshire Blvd., three blocks east of Fairfax Ave, ☎323-857-6000, www.lacma.org)* is impressive by any standards. LACMA has set itself the ambitious aim of presenting the art of all major cultures from the ancient world to the present. Generous bequests, along with the recent acquisition of a former department store building to provide added exhibition space, bring it closer to this goal. As with any large museum that takes an encyclopedic approach, a thorough visit can stretch the visitor's time and stamina. Many visitors may choose to focus on the periods or cultures that most interest them. The museum's more than 200,000 works (only a fraction of which are on display) fall under 10 curatorial departments:

• European paintings and sculpture from the Renaissance to the 19th century, including works by Titian, El Greco, Rembrandt, Millet, Degas and Cézanne;
• American art that focuses on the 18th and 19th centuries;
• Ancient and Islamic art, with valuable collections from ancient Egypt, the Near East and the Greek and Roman Empires, as well as ancient Islamic art and objects from the pre-Columbian cultures of the western hemisphere, including sculptures, ceramics and gold masks;
• Far Eastern art (one of the museum's true strengths), with a Chinese collection spanning 3,000 years of bronzes, pottery, porcelain, calligraphy and painting; the Japanese collection (housed in its own pavilion) contains painting, sculpture, lacquerware, ceramics, textiles, painted screens and small ivory carvings; Korean and

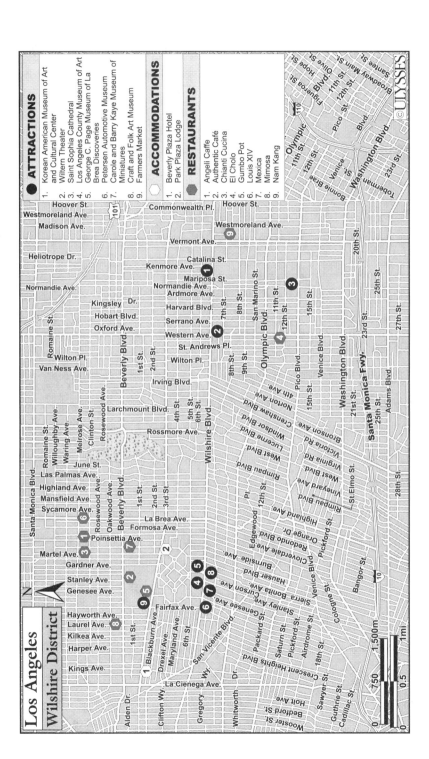

Central Asian art are also represented;

• Indian and Southeast Asian art (another strong section), including Indian religious sculpture in stone and bronze, wood carvings, decorative arts and Buddhist objects from Nepal, Tibet and Cambodia;

• Twentieth-century art, including works by Braque, Picasso, Magritte and several top U.S. artists;

• Prints and drawings, encompassing etchings and woodcuts spanning the centuries from Goya to Picasso;

• Photography, with European and U.S. artists well represented;

• Decorative arts, running the gamut from 14th-century French cathedral windows to early U.S. glass and furniture and including Italian renaissance porcelain, German glassware, French tapestries, and French and English furniture, porcelain and silverware;

• Textiles and costumes, with ancient and modern items from many parts of the world.

Even this doesn't tell the whole story. In 1997, for example, the museum received the donation of a sizable collection of Mexican modernist art. The museum has been in its current location since 1965 and has grown with the addition of new buildings. It is laid out in campus style, with five buildings set around a central court.

The largest structure is the Ahmanson Building, with exhibition space on four levels housing the real heart of the permanent collection (visitors should be sure to obtain a floor plan at the entrance to orient themselves more accurately). The Hammer Building is home to prints and photography, as well

as to some late 19th- and early 20th-century European art. The Anderson Building is dedicated to 20th-century art, with the more recent objects on the upper level. Finally, the Japanese Pavilion

A Note on Transit Service

Wilshire Boulevard is one of the city's main transit corridors, but the Red Line subway branch serving Wilshire from downtown L.A. extends only as far west as Western Avenue. An express bus, MTA route 720, identified as "Metro Rapid" service, operates from Santa Monica along Wilshire Boulevard to downtown L.A., continuing east to Montebello. Buses on this route, with their own special red-and-white livery, offer faster service than the other routes running along Wilshire, but they make only a limited number of stops. Visitors to the Los Angeles County Museum of Art, for instance, have to disembark at Fairfax and walk several blocks to reach the museum entrance, while the slower local routes 20, 21 and 22 stop a little closer. The express bus (no supplement payable) is usually faster overall. Transfers between the subway and Wilshire Boulevard buses are free.

obviously houses the Japanese collection.

An additional building, the former May Company department store, located a couple of blocks west at the corner of Fairfax Avenue, has been named **LACMA West** and, for the time being, is used mainly for special exhibitions. It also houses a children's gallery and a satellite of the **Southwest Museum** (see p 86), whose main harder-to-reach site is seriously short of space. The LACMA West location presents special exhibitions and rotating shows from the permanent collection. The admission charge varies; sometimes it is free (☎323-933-4510).

George C. Page Museum of La Brea Discoveries ★ *($6; Tue to Sun 10am to 5pm; 5801 Wilshire Blvd. at Curson Ave., four blocks east of Fairfax Ave., ☎323-857-6311)* is situated next to a small expanse of bubbling tar-like ooze, known as La Brea tar pits, in which a huge variety of animals, large and small, became trapped over a period of more than 40,000 years. The site has been under excavation by archeologists since 1906 and has yielded a rich treasure trove of bones. Some of these are on display in the form of reconstructed skeletons in a bright, attractive exhibition hall at the museum, named for George C. Page, a local businessman, amateur scientist and philanthropist. The museum (worth an additional star for children) includes a small botanical garden and a 15min film documenting the discoveries. Visitors can sometimes watch archeologists at work in the museum's research wing.

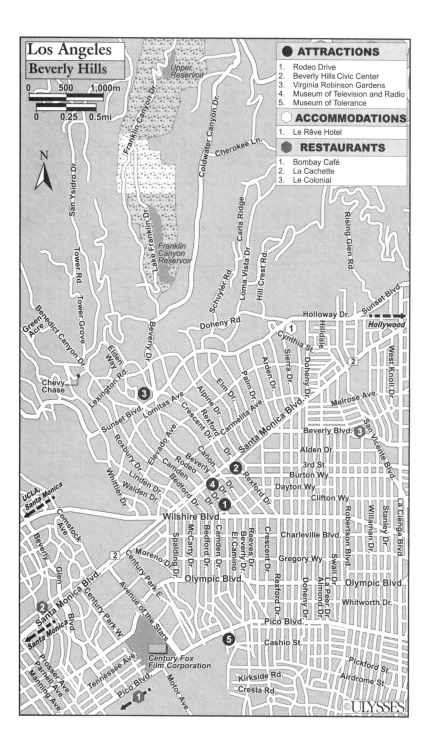

Los Angeles
Beverly Hills

0   500   1,000m

0   0.25   0.5mi

N

Upper Reservoir

Franklin Canyon Dr.

Coldwater Canyon Dr.

Cherokee Ln.

Carla Ridge

Lake Franklin Dr.

Franklin Canyon Reservoir

Schuyler Rd.

Loma Vista Dr.

Hill Crest Rd.

Rising Glen Rd.

San Ysidro Dr.

Tower Rd.

Tower Grove

Benedict Canyon Dr.

Green Acre

Sunset Blvd.

Holloway Dr.

Hollywood

Doheny Rd.

Cynthia St.

Hildale

Sierra Dr.

Doheny Dr.

West Knoll Dr.

Chevy Chase

Elden Way

Lexington Rd.

Beverly Dr.

Arden Dr.

Palm Dr.

Elm Dr.

Alpine Dr.

Crescent Dr.

Rexford Dr.

Carmelita Ave.

Melrose Ave.

San Vicente Blvd.

Sunset Blvd.

Lomitas Ave.

Roxbury Dr.

Elevado Ave.

Cañon

Beverly

Rodeo

Camden

Bedford

Linden Dr.

Walden Dr.

Whittier Dr.

Santa Monica Blvd.

Beverly Blvd.

Alden Dr.

3rd St.

Burton Wy.

Dayton Wy.

Clifton Wy.

Rexford Dr.

La Cienega Blvd.

Stanley Dr.

Willaman Dr.

Robertson Blvd.

UCLA
Santa Monica

Comstock Ave.

Beverly

Glen

Wilshire Blvd.

McCarty Dr.

Spalding Dr.

Bedford Dr.

Camden Dr.

El Camino

Beverly Dr.

Reeves Dr.

Crescent Dr.

Charleville Blvd.

Gregory Wy.

Swall Dr.

La Peer Dr.

Almond Dr.

Doheny Dr.

Olympic Blvd.

Whitworth Dr.

Santa Monica Blvd.

Santa Monica

Moreno Dr.

Century Park E.

Avenue of the Stars

Olympic Blvd.

Rexford Dr.

Pico Blvd.

Cashio St.

Century Park W.

Century Fox Film Corporation

Tennessee Ave.

Prosser Ave.

Parnell Ave.

Manning Ave.

Pico Blvd.

Motor Ave.

Kirkside Rd.

Cresta Rd.

Pickford St.

Airdrome St.

©ULYSSES

The **Petersen Automotive Museum** ★★ *($7; Tue to Sun 10am to 6pm; 6060 Wilshire Blvd. at Fairfax Ave., ☎323-930-2277, www.petersen.org)* provides a fascinating historical portrayal of L.A.'s love affair with the automobile. The museum, set on three floors in a former department store building, goes beyond a mere collection of automobiles from various decades and presents mock-ups of Los Angeles streetscapes from the pertinent periods to place these vehicles in context. One section documents the role of the automobile in the development of the city. The collection includes large, flashy vehicles once owned by particular Hollywood celebrities.

Carol and Barry Kaye Museum of Miniatures ★ *($7.50; Tue to Sat 10am to 5pm, Sun 11am to 5pm; 5900 Wilshire Blvd., two blocks east of Fairfax Ave., ☎323-937-6464, www.museumofminiatures.com)* is named after the founders whose collection it houses, augmented by many pieces from the personal collection of Walt Disney, the great animator and film producer. It presents a fantasy world of palaces and monuments intricately pieced together by many hundreds of artists. Objects include a replica of the Vatican Palace more than 10ft (3m) high and a model of the Titanic made of 75,000 toothpicks.

Craft and Folk Art Museum ★ *($3.50; Tue to Sun 11am to 5pm; 5814 Wilshire Blvd. four blocks east of Fairfax Ave., ☎323-937-4230)* is set in a charming old house with only limited exhibition space. A series of rotating shows present contemporary and historic displays

City Hall

from different parts of the world.

The **Farmers Market** at the corner of Fairfax Avenue and Third Street, anchored by its distinctive clock tower, has outgrown its original role as a place where farmers can sell their goods directly to city people. It has developed into what marketing people refer to as a "festival marketplace", with food stalls and restaurants accompanied by crafts shops (see p 143). Further north along Fairfax, particularly between Melrose and Beverly avenues, is an area sometimes known as the **Fairfax District**. Forming the spine of L.A.'s largest traditional Jewish neighbourhood, Fairfax Avenue is here lined with shops and restaurants reflecting this character. One of the most imaginatively named establishments is a Chinese restaurant called Genghis Cohen!

Beverly Hills is one of the world's wealthiest municipalities. Lying at its heart is an ultra-swank shopping district known as the **Golden Triangle** (see p 143), bound by Wilshire Boulevard, Santa Monica Boulevard and Crescent Drive, with **Rodeo Drive** running through the

centre. Wealth is so obvious here that it doesn't have to be flaunted in the architecture, which observes low heights and restrained lines.

At the apex of the Golden Triangle is the Beverly Hills **City Hall** ★ *(Rexford Dr. at Santa Monica Blvd.)*, built in 1932 in Spanish-revival style with a high tower and a gilded cupola. It forms part of the Beverly Hills **Civic Center** ★, also encompassing other public buildings, most built or expanded in the 1980s and set around an attractive oval plaza. Even the post office has attracted architectural notice, as has the public library. On restricted-access streets north of Santa Monica Boulevard lie the mansions of those with serious money. The **Virginia Robinson Gardens** *($6; by reservation only; 1008 Elden Way, ☎310-276-5367)* cover most of the almost 6-acre (3ha) estate bequeathed by the widow of a department store magnate. Visitors are taken on tours of the gorgeously landscaped grounds, with their terrace hillsides, shaded footpaths and many hundreds of varieties of plants and flowers.

The **Museum of Television and Radio** (*suggested donation $6; Wed to Sun noon to 5pm, Thu until 9pm; 465 N. Beverly Dr. at Little Santa Monica Blvd., Beverly Hills,* ☎*310-786-1000*) is less a museum than a series of private viewing rooms where visitors can view long-ago TV shows contained in extensive archives.

The **Museum of Tolerance** ★★ (*$8.50; tour departures: Mon to Thu 10am to 4pm, Fri 10am to 1pm, Apr to Oct until 3pm, Sun 11am to 5pm, closed Sat and on Jewish and civic holidays; 9786 W. Pico Blvd. at Roxbury Dr., south of Beverly Hills and east of Century City; by bus: Santa Monica Route 7,* ☎*310-553-8403, www.wiesenthal.com*) is part of the **Simon Wiesenthal Center**, established by the famed investigator of Nazi war crimes. The museum aims to get people thinking about racial or ethnic prejudice and the violent extremes to which it has escalated. Visitors are taken on a 1hr-long tour of exhibits portraying the rise of Nazism in Germany in the 1930s and the calamitous events that followed.

Elsewhere in the museum, visitors can wander on their own through a series of interactive displays relating to the Second World War Holocaust and to more recent tragedies. Each visitor is given a document bearing the name of a Jewish child born in Europe before the war; later in the visit, the child's fate is revealed (in most cases, it is tragic).

The sprawling campus of the University of California at Los Angeles, known everywhere as **UCLA**, encompasses more than 100 buildings set on 419 acres (170ha) of landscaped grounds west of Beverly Hills. First developed in 1919, it's not especially noteworthy in itself, although it is the site of many special events, and some of its libraries are open to the public. It's also home to the **Fowler Museum of Cultural History** ★ (*$5; Thu free; Wed to Sun noon to 5pm, Thu until 8pm;* ☎*310-825-4361*), which presents rotating exhibitions of art from Asia, Africa and Latin America, the **Franklin D. Murphy Sculpture Collection** ★, with more than 50 works

Getty Center

including objects by Lachaise and Rodin, and the **Mildred Mathias Botanical Garden**. Locations are clearly marked on large maps at campus entrances. Just south of the campus, **Westwood Village** features a large concentration of cinemas, fast-food restaurants, and shopping. (Many bus routes pass by the UCLA campus, including MTA routes 2, 21, 302, 429, 561 and 576 and Santa Monica Routes 2, 3, 8 and 12.)

The **Skirball Cultural Centre and Museum** ★ (*$8; Tue to Fri 10am to 4pm, Sat noon to 5pm, Sun 10am to 5pm; Sepulveda Blvd. off the 405 Freeway north of Mulholland Dr.; by bus: MTA route 561,* ☎*310-440-4500*), set on lavish grounds in the remote Sepulveda Pass between the Getty Center and the San Fernando Valley, portrays Jewish life through the centuries in many parts of the world, including the arrival of Jewish immigrants to the United States. Exhibits are drawn from an extensive collection of Judaica, with many stressing the theme of religious tradition. Designed by architect Moshe Safdie and opened in 1996, this centre also has an auditorium, conference hall and restaurant.

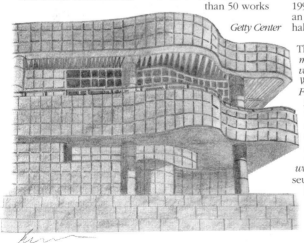

The **Getty Center** (*free admission; parking $5; reservations required; Tue to Wed 11am to 7pm, Thu to Fri 11am to 9pm, Sat to Sun 10am to 6pm; 1200 Getty Center Dr., by car: 405 Freeway to Getty Center Dr. exit, by bus: MTA Rte. 561 or Santa Monica Rte. 14,* ☎*310-440-7300, www.getty.edu*) is the museum the art world has been talking about for years, among the most elaborate and richly endowed museums ever built. The

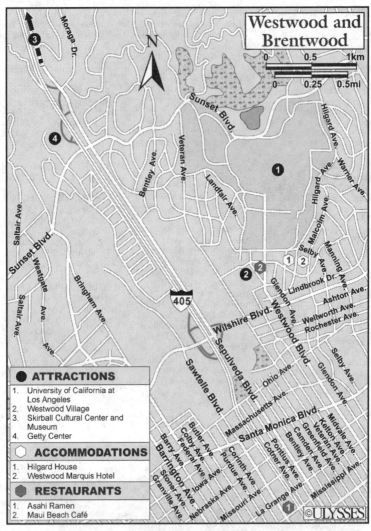

Westwood and Brentwood

0   0.5   1km

0   0.25   0.5mi

N

● ATTRACTIONS

1. University of California at Los Angeles
2. Westwood Village
3. Skirball Cultural Center and Museum
4. Getty Center

⬡ ACCOMMODATIONS

1. Hilgard House
2. Westwood Marquis Hotel

⬢ RESTAURANTS

1. Asahi Ramen
2. Maui Beach Café

©ULYSSES

museum's billion-dollar campus, designed by architect Richard Meier, opened amid much fanfare in 1997 after 14 years of planning and construction. The collection is impressive, but what most visitors will notice first is the magnificence of the site, perched on a hilltop like a medieval fortress.

The Getty Center is endowed by a trust fund established by oil magnate and art collector J. Paul Getty, who died in 1976. Besides the museum, the centre houses various research and educational institutions, including the Getty Research Institute for the History of Art and the Humanities, the Getty Conservation Institute, the Getty Education Institute for the Arts and the Getty Grant Program. The work done by these organiza-

tions helps conserve artworks and archeological sites worldwide and creates arts education programs in schools across the United States.

Preparations for a visit may seem inauspicious. People arriving by car at the museum's remote location in the hills at the northern edge of the exclusive Brentwood district must reserve parking

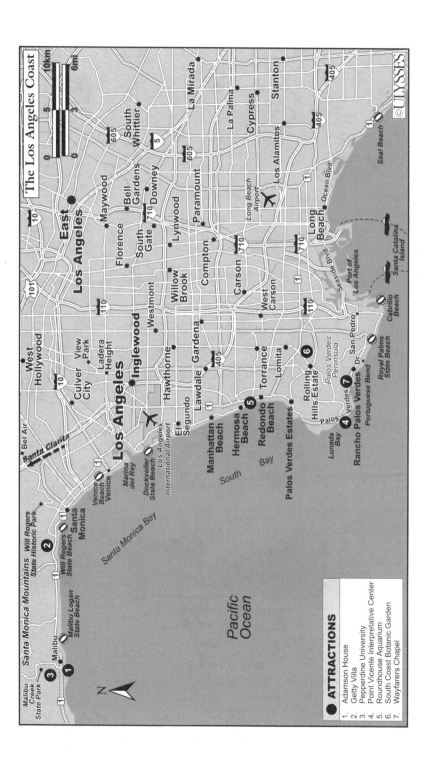

The Los Angeles Coast

ATTRACTIONS

1. Adamson House
2. Getty Villa
3. Pepperdine University
4. Point Vicente Interpretative Center
5. Roundhouse Aquarium
6. South Coast Botanic Garden
7. Wayfarers Chapel

© ULYSSES

ahead of time. Bus passengers can (and usually do) arrive without advance notice, but there is a slight risk of having to wait in line or, at especially busy periods, of being turned away (reservations are possible). For some, this may be the only experience riding a bus in L.A.

After that, things improve. Visitors are whisked up the hillside by a small railway that offers stunning views of the city and valley. You'll emerge on a broad plaza surrounded by gardens, terraces and a cluster of buildings in white Italian travertine with glass and curved metal forming a harmonious blend of geometric shapes. The entrance pavilion offers a brief orientation film as well as activities for children.

The actual museum consists of a group of five two-storey pavilions set around an open courtyard with trees, fountains and reflecting pools. Four are devoted to specific periods while the fifth houses rotating exhibitions. Other buildings house an auditorium, a café and restaurant, and the research institute, which presents exhibitions of rare books and other archival material. Between the museum and the research institute lies the central garden, designed by artist Robert Irwin, that combines trees, flowers and a cascading stream.

The museum's permanent collection includes works gathered by Getty himself over nearly half a century as well as numerous acquisitions. Galleries vary enormously in size and lighting to suit the works they display. Many on the upper floor have sophisticated skylight systems. Some of the galleries containing French furniture and decorative arts include rooms with 18th-century wood panelling.

The European Paintings collection covers the 14th to 19th centuries and includes important works by Rembrandt, Titian, Rubens, Veronese, Cézanne, Van Gogh, Monet, Renoir and Manet. The Decorative Arts collection is one of the museum's strengths, with particular emphasis on French items from the mid-17th to early 19th centuries, including furniture, tapestries, carpets, clocks, porcelain and chandeliers. The Drawings collection contains many works by Van Gogh and by earlier artists including Rubens and Leonardo. The Manuscripts collection features illuminated books from Ottoman, Byzantine and Gothic sources. Other collections include Photography and European Sculpture.

Items from the Getty Trust's very extensive collection of classic antiquities are to be exhibited at the Getty Villa in Malibu starting in 2002 once renovations there are complete. Prior to the opening of the Getty Center, the Getty Villa was the main repository for the other collections.

Tour E: Santa Monica and Surroundings

This is the area of Los Angeles that best fits so many Southern California clichés. Here we find broad beaches extending as far as the eye can see, merry crowds, surfers with beautiful bronzed bodies, muscle builders with rugged physical routines, rollerbladers with unimaginable body piercings and barely imaginable hair colours, more sunglasses than you can shake a stick at, the *dolce vita* of casual café society and, something almost shocking in car-obsessed L.A., two lively but very different streets where cars are banned.

Santa Monica is best known for its beach, its famous pier and its eccentric local politics. Just a couple of blocks from the beach are bookshops and other outward signs of cerebral activity. Few places combine beaches and urban life quite the way Santa Monica does. Besides Santa Monica, this tour covers secluded Malibu to the west and zany Venice to the south. We'll begin in Malibu and follow the curvature of the coastline east and south from there.

Malibu ★, west of Santa Monica near the western edge of Los Angeles County, projects an image of a hedonistic lifestyle centred around beaches with unmatchable surf, perfect tanned bodies, superb sunsets and a relaxing sense that all is well with the world. It is also a community with large pockets of exclusive wealth and closely guarded enclaves (some of them blocking access to the beach). On a slightly ominous note, Malibu has figured in the headlines over recent years in connection with natural disasters, particularly the late-summer brush fires that routinely ravish arid cliffside areas where exclusive mansions have been built in obvious defiance of nature. The area has also been hit by earthquakes, mudslides and tidal waves. But the many miles of natural splendour along the wild Pacific shore that are the very essence of Malibu have long proven an irresistible lure to visitors and residents alike.

One of the most famous local landmarks is the **Getty Villa**, which was the home of the Getty Museum until its move to its splendid new quarters in Brentwood (see p 107). The villa is currently closed to the public but is expected to reopen in 2002 as the venue for the Getty Trust's extensive collection of classical antiquities.

Another landmark is **Pepperdine University**, with a gorgeous campus that at first glance looks like an upper-crust country club, set in rolling hills overlooking the sea. The university has been denigrated by people on the political left, in part because of its links with conservative political and religious organizations. In 1998, the Pepperdine Law School offered its deanship to Kenneth Starr, the special prosecutor who attempted to hound President Bill Clinton from office.

The **Adamson House** *($2; by guided tour only, Wed to Sat, first tour 11am, last tour 2pm; 23200 Pacific Coast Hwy., ☎310-456-8432)* is situated along one of Malibu's finest stretches of beach next to a lagoon that is an important bird-breeding ground. Built in 1928 for a member of the last family to hold a Spanish land grant in Malibu, this gorgeous house is set on a landscaped, pine-shaded estate. The building shows Spanish and Moorish influences and makes abundant use of a type of ceramic

tile produced in the area at the time. The adjacent **Malibu Lagoon Museum** *(free admission; Wed to Sat 11am to 3pm)* presents elements of local history, including Chumash Indian artifacts and a display on the history of surfing.

Santa Monica ★, 13mi (21km) from downtown L.A., is what some people imagine all of California to be. An independent municipality with a strong sense of community, Santa Monica is best known to the outside world for its broad, sandy beach with a palm-fringed linear park perched above and a lively, alluring pier protruding into the surf. Sometimes denigrated as the People's Republic of Santa Monica by right-wing critics who are alternately appalled and amused by the municipal council's occasional forays into deep matters of social conscience (for example, homeless people are treated more humanely than in most other suburban areas), this is a place where an above-average number of people take politics seriously and where the candy floss atmosphere of the beach belies the existence of a more substantial side to local life. (Municipal boundaries do extend more than 30 blocks inland.)

Santa Monica has its own downtown area, extending from Ocean Avenue, parallel to the beach, east to Lincoln Boulevard, and from Pico Boulevard north to Wilshire Boulevard. In addition, interesting retail strips line Montana Avenue, a few blocks north, between Seventh and 20th streets, and Main Street from Pico Boulevard all the way south to Venice Beach. Main Street also

features a large number of quaint cafés. An electric bus service called the "Tide Shuttle" *($0.25)* runs at 15min intervals afternoons and evenings between downtown Santa Monica and the Main Street area. The approximately 2mi (3km) between Santa Monica Pier and the heart of Venice Beach make for a wonderful stroll along a beachside footpath. A separate path accommodates cyclists and rollerbladers.

Santa Monica pier ★, at Ocean and Colorado avenues, was built in 1916 and is immediately recognizable by the large Ferris wheel standing guard near the entrance. This Ferris wheel, worth riding for the aerial views of Santa Monica and the Pacific shore, is part of a small amusement area called **Pacific Park** *(rides range from $1 to $4; hours vary by season; ☎310-260-8744)* that also includes a roller coaster and a beautifully restored carousel dating from 1922. The pier is quite enormous and houses many commercial establishments, including souvenir stalls, pinball arcades, and a variety of snack bars and restaurants with offerings ranging from hot dogs to seafood. It's also possible to rent fishing rods and try your luck right from the edge of the pier. In general, the atmosphere is lively and fun though just a bit tacky. In the summer, free concerts featuring top world musical artists *(☎310-458-9800)* are presented Thursday evenings starting at 7:30pm (arrive early to be near the stage).

Third Street Promenade ★★★ in downtown Santa Monica is one of North America's

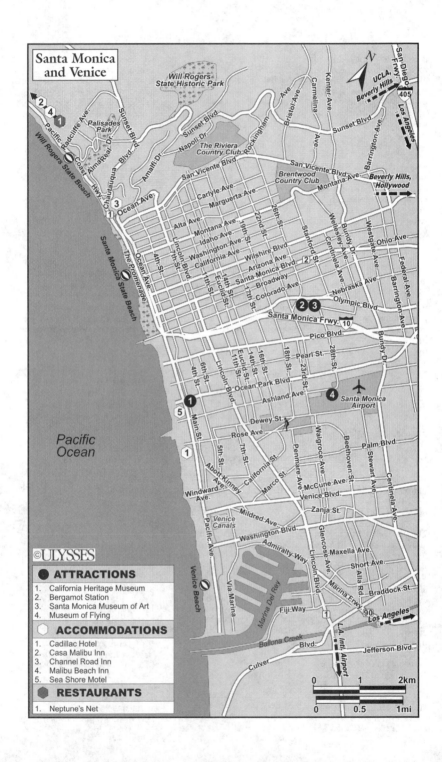

Santa Monica and Venice

Pacific Ocean

ATTRACTIONS
1. California Heritage Museum
2. Bergamot Station
3. Santa Monica Museum of Art
4. Museum of Flying

ACCOMMODATIONS
1. Cadillac Hotel
2. Casa Malibu Inn
3. Channel Road Inn
4. Malibu Beach Inn
5. Sea Shore Motel

RESTAURANTS
1. Neptune's Net

©ULYSSES

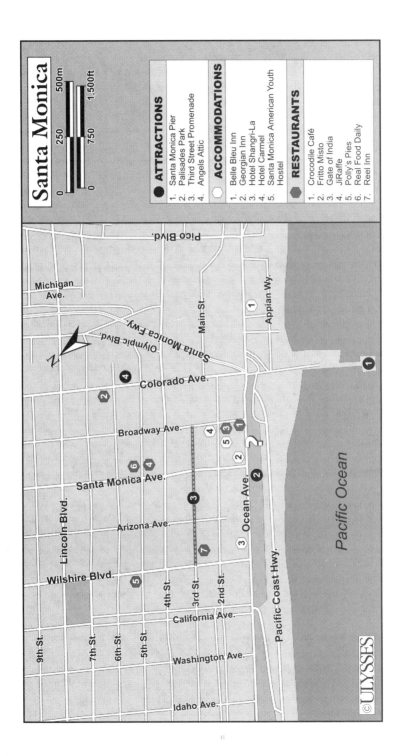

Santa Monica

0   250   500m

0   750   1,500ft

Pico Blvd.

Michigan Ave.

Main St.

Appian Wy.

Santa Monica Fwy.

Olympic Blvd.

Colorado Ave.

Broadway Ave.

Santa Monica Ave.

Lincoln Blvd.

Arizona Ave.

Ocean Ave.

Pacific Coast Hwy.

Wilshire Blvd.

4th St.

3rd St.

2nd St.

California Ave.

9th St.

7th St.

6th St.

5th St.

Washington Ave.

Idaho Ave.

Pacific Ocean

© ULYSSES

liveliest pedestrian-only streets. Covering three long blocks from Broadway to Wilshire Boulevard, the Third Street Promenade succeeds for a variety of reasons. Its mixture of businesses include many restaurants, cafés, cinemas, bookshops, music stores and other establishments that draw large crowds until late in the evening. It is designed with small kiosks, benches and other installations that facilitate pedestrian movement while palliating any sense of physical emptiness. Musicians and other street performers contribute to the vibrant atmosphere. This is justifiably one of the most popular streets in California and well worth a visit.

Angels Attic ★ *($6.50; Thu to Sun 12:30pm to 4:30pm; 516 Colorado Ave. near Fifth St., ☎310-394-8311)* is a museum of antique dollhouses set in a lovingly restored Victorian house. About 50 dollhouses are on display at any given time, along with toy trains, miniature animals and, of course, dolls.

California Heritage Museum *($3; Wed to Sat 11am to 4pm, Sun 10am to 4pm; 2612 Main St. at Ocean Park Blvd., ☎310-392-8537)*, set in a house built in 1894, presents late 19th-century decorative arts on the ground floor and rotating exhibitions on particular aspects of California history upstairs.

Bergamot Station ★ *(2525 Michigan Ave. near Olympic Blvd. and 26th St.; by bus: Santa Monica Rte. 5)* is a former transit station from the days when L.A. was served by an extensive tramway network. It was later expanded for industrial use and then aban-

doned. However, it reopened in 1994 after its ramshackle buildings were resurrected and redeveloped to house numerous art galleries, as well as some architecture and design offices. It has become a major hub in the L.A. art scene, with a number of the top local galleries as well as several smaller galleries specializing in particular types of art. A bright, attractive space in this same complex houses the **Santa Monica Museum of Art** ★ *(suggested contribution $3; Wed to Sun 11am to 6pm, Fri until 10pm; ☎310-586-6488)*, which has no permanent collection but presents varied shows by contemporary artists. Its Friday evening discussion series draws many people from the local art scene.

The **Museum of Flying** ★ *($7; Wed to Sun 10am to 5pm; 2772 Donald Douglas Loop N. at 28th St. about 1,312ft or 400m east of Ocean Park Blvd.; by bus: Santa Monica Rte. 8; ☎310-392-8822, www.mof.org)* is located at Santa Monica municipal airport, which was the headquarters of the Douglas Aircraft Company and birthplace of the legendary DC-3. This specific airplane is represented in the museum's collection along with Spitfires, a Grumman Bearcat, a P-47 Thunderbolt and more than 20 other vintage aircraft—sure to stir the blood of aviation history buffs. Some of these planes look as if they are ready to roll out and fly. Docents, some of them retired military pilots, are happy to show visitors around. For an extra $2, visitors can spend several minutes in a flight simulator. The museum also has an interactive children's section.

Venice ★★, directly south of Santa Monica, is where individuals of all sorts come to see people who are just slightly weird—or to be a little weird themselves. For decades this has been L.A.'s haven of counterculture. People who were emblematic of the Beat generation of the 1950s, the hippie movement of the 1960s, and various cults and New Age trends since then have felt right at home along Venice's colourful shoreline. It's no different today.

Ocean Front Walk ★★★, also known as the Boardwalk (although there are no boards), is one of the zaniest, most effervescent, most kaleidoscopic, most carnivalesque spots in all of North America. Running alongside **Venice Beach** (and banned to vehicular traffic), this delightfully loopy pedestrian thoroughfare is a scene unto itself. Maybe it's the colourful assortment of merchandise at the countless street stalls radiating from the corner of Ocean Front Walk and Windward Avenue—tie-dyed T-shirts, nose rings, amazing assortments of sunglasses, psychedelic posters, tattoos, palms readings, you name it; maybe it's the physical culturists who put on a continuous show nearby in a small area called **Muscle Beach** between 17th and 18th streets, where bodybuilders with gigantic muscles pump iron for all to see, next to the basketball and volleyball courts; maybe it's the varied and distinctive residential architecture of the buildings, mostly two or three storeys high, that form a backdrop to the beach from the northern tip of Venice all the way to Santa Monica; maybe it's the street performers, some of whom

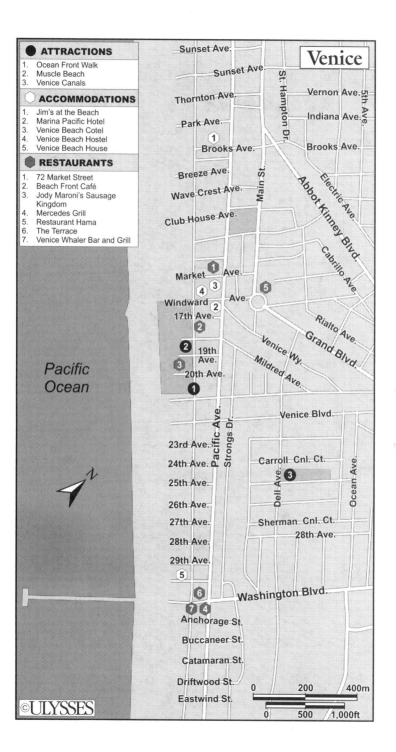

ATTRACTIONS
1. Ocean Front Walk
2. Muscle Beach
3. Venice Canals

ACCOMMODATIONS
1. Jim's at the Beach
2. Marina Pacific Hotel
3. Venice Beach Cotel
4. Venice Beach Hostel
5. Venice Beach House

RESTAURANTS
1. 72 Market Street
2. Beach Front Café
3. Jody Maroni's Sausage Kingdom
4. Mercedes Grill
5. Restaurant Hama
6. The Terrace
7. Venice Whaler Bar and Grill

Venice

Sunset Ave.
Sunset Ave.
Thornton Ave.
Park Ave.
Brooks Ave.
Breeze Ave.
Wave Crest Ave.
Club House Ave.
Market Ave.
Windward Ave.
17th Ave.
19th Ave.
20th Ave.
23rd Ave.
24th Ave.
25th Ave.
26th Ave.
27th Ave.
28th Ave.
29th Ave.

St. Hampton Dr.
Vernon Ave.
Indiana Ave.
Brooks Ave.
Main St.
Electric Ave.
Abbot Kinney Blvd.
Cabrillo Ave.
Rialto Ave.
Grand Blvd.
Venice Wy.
Mildred Ave.
5th Ave.

Pacific Ocean

Venice Blvd.
Pacific Ave.
Strongs Dr.
Carroll Cnl. Ct.
Dell Ave.
Ocean Ave.
Sherman Cnl. Ct.
28th Ave.
Washington Blvd.
Anchorage St.
Buccaneer St.
Catamaran St.
Driftwood St.
Eastwind St.

0   200   400m
0   500   1,000ft

©ULYSSES

The Canals of Venice

Venice, a separate municipality until it was annexed by the City of Los Angeles in 1925, takes its name from the city on Italy's Adriatic coast famed for its numerous canals. The marshland that once covered much of present-day Venice (the one on the Pacific coast) was drained at the turn of the 20th century by tobacco heir Abbot Kinney, who built a network of 16mi (26km) of canals as the foundation for what he hoped would become a centre of artistic and cultural inspiration for U.S. citizens. He even brought over gondoliers from Italy for the opening ceremonies in 1905, but his project soon floundered. A couple of decades later, with

Venice in deep decay, most of the canals were paved over, though about 3mi (5km) of canals survive, still traversed by some of the original narrow bridges. These can be seen in the area east of Pacific Avenue and south of Venice Boulevard. What was until recent times a badly rundown residential area has undergone a quiet gentrification, and real estate values have soared. It would take a huge leap of the imagination to see any resemblance to its Adriatic counterpart, but, for anyone who cares to wander any distance from the beach, this corner of Venice provides a fascinating century-old reminder of California eccentricity.

stretch the limits in ways that defy description; but more than anything, it's the passing parade of people who aren't there to perform but who provide a constant pageant of wild clothing, improbable hair colours, dazzling bikinis, rippling muscles, peculiar sunglasses, or just about anything else to look different. The scene is especially lively on weekend afternoons, when middle-class visitors and their children come to watch the local fauna strut their stuff, creating almost a spontaneous symbiosis with them. There is also a broad sandy beach, a long

cycling trail, and the footpath up to Santa Monica. **Windward Avenue**, perpendicular to Ocean Front Walk in the centre of the action, is interesting for its arcaded sidewalks, its murals, and its assortment of cafés and bars.

Tour F: South Bay and Surroundings

This tour takes us along the Pacific shoreline from Marina del Rey south to Palos Verdes. It includes the area around Los An-

geles International Airport as well as the communities of Manhattan Beach, Hermosa Beach and Redondo Beach, which together form an area known as South Bay. Here we find great expanses of beach, some of it excellent for surfing, along with some of those famous Pacific sunsets. In terms of cultural stimulation, however, this area is decidedly tepid.

Marina del Rey, extending from Venice in the north to the community of Playa del Rey in the south, is notable chiefly for its enormous small-craft harbour carved out of the coastal lowlands in a hand-like shape with several fingers. Primarily a residential area with streets named after South Sea islands and lined with large apartment buildings, Marina del Rey is also home to several hotels and restaurants. Some additional residents live aboard their boats. The only real attempt at a tourist attraction, apart from the marina itself, is a cluster of shops and restaurants in a commercial zone called **Fishermen's Village** (13755 Fiji Way). Set by the edge of the marina, it is meant to imitate the look of a New England fishing village, although it doesn't quite succeed. Harbour cruises and fishing expeditions can be booked here.

Los Angeles International Airport (see p 65 in the "Practical Information" chapter) covers a vast area extending almost—but not quite—to the shoreline. The beach runs uninterrupted past the airport grounds. Cyclists using the beachside trail between Santa Monica and South Bay who happen to like planes will enjoy close-up

Airport area and South Bay

Marina del Rey

Jefferson Blvd.

Culver Blvd.

Pershing Dr.

Vista Del Mar

83rd St.
Manchester Ave.

La Tigra Blvd.

Airport Blvd.

90th St.

405

Inglewood

Century Blvd.

Los Angeles International Airport

Imperial Hwy.

105

120th St.

Manhattan Ave.

Sepulveda Blvd.

El Secundo Blvd.

Douglas St.

Aviation Blvd.

Inglewood Ave.

Hawthorne Ave.

Prairie Ave.

N

Rosecrans Ave.

Marine Ave.

Manhattan State Beach

Manhattan Beach

107

Manhattam Beach Blvd.

Robinson Blvd.

Santa Monica Bay

Artesia Blvd.

91

Grant Ave.

Hermosa Beach

Pier Ave.

Pacific Coast Hwy.

Hermosa Ave.

Ripley Ave.

190th St.

Hermosa Beach

Del Amo Blvd.

● ATTRACTIONS
1. Roundhouse Aquarium

⬡ ACCOMMODATIONS
1. Continental Plaza Hotel Los Angeles
2. Crowne Plaza Los Angeles Airport
3. Grandview Motor Hotel
4. Marina International Hotel & Bungalows
5. Sea Sprite Motel
6. Skyways Airport Hotel

⬡ RESTAURANTS
1. Kincaid's Bay House
2. Reed's
3. The Kettle

Redondo Beach

Torrance Blvd.

Maple Ave.

Carson St.

Redondo State Beach

Harbour Dr.

Sepulveda Blvd.

Lomita Blvd.

©ULYSSES

0   1.5   3km
0   1   2mi

views of low-flying aircraft taking off over the sea. The area to the east of the airport is characterized by airport-related activities. On the southern side are cargo sheds and aircraft maintenance hangars, while further north lies a large cluster of hotels. There is really little of special interest in this area, which has surprisingly few restaurants considering the number of overnight guests.

Manhattan Beach is the first, and most upscale, of the three beach towns that form the South Bay area between the airport and the Palos Verdes Peninsula. The Pacific Coast Highway, running parallel to the coast but several blocks inland, is the principal thoroughfare in the mainly residential South Bay area, distinguished by its long, wide strand of superb sandy beach, replete with the trademark California symbols of surfers and volleyball players, especially on summer weekends, when the beach can be quite crowded (and parking hard to find). By bus, the best bet is MTA route 439 from downtown L.A. via the LAX Transit Center (near the airport) and the Green Line's Aviation station, despite the infrequent service (only once an hour, slightly more often during weekday

rush hours). Pedestrian and cycling paths run for many miles along the edge of the beach.

In Manhattan Beach itself, the main perpendicular thoroughfare is Manhattan Beach Boulevard, which is lined with boutiques and restaurants, ending in a long pier. Near the tip of this pier is the **Roundhouse Marine Studies Lab and Aquarium** *(voluntary contribution; Mon to Fri 3pm to sunset, Sat to Sun 10am to sunset; Manhattan Beach Pier, ☎310-379-8117)*, with several aquarium tanks of interest mainly to children.

Hermosa Beach is a traditional rival to Manhattan Beach. Long considered a more casual and youth-oriented spot, Hermosa Beach has gradually become move upscale, as some of the grand new beachfront villas suggest. It too has its pier, about 1.5mi (2.5km) south of its Manhattan Beach counterpart. The Hermosa Beach pier is an extension of Pier Avenue, whose intersection with the beach has been converted to an attractive pedestrian-only area with numerous snack bars, cafés, restaurants and shops.

Redondo Beach, regarded as a more family-oriented leisure spot, was also a

commercial seaport for a brief time, until fierce storms destroyed the main wharf in the early 20th century. A small marina is perched near the north end of this community. Closer to the centre of town, at the end of Torrance Avenue, are Monstad Pier and Fishermen's Wharf, two large and not especially attractive piers that meet at the seaward end. Both house numerous souvenir shops, restaurants and bars, as well as a fishing dock.

Further south lies the **Palos Verdes** Peninsula, where the beach gives way to high bluffs with surf pounding below. Although housing (mostly quite exclusive) has been built in inland zones, this area is surprisingly undeveloped, with only traces of urban influence. A scenic roadway called **Palos Verdes Drive ★** runs near the perimeter, linking Redondo Beach to the north and San Pedro to the east. Along this drive lies the **Point Vicente Interpretative Center ★** *($2; every day 10am to 5pm, summer until 7pm; 31501 Palos Verdes Dr. W., ☎310-377-5370)*. Marked by a lighthouse, this spot features displays on local history but is most interesting as an observation point for the grey whales that pass here on their annual migration between the Arctic and northwestern Mexico (south from December to February, north from February to April). The **Wayfarers Chapel** *(free admission; every day 7am to 5pm; 5755 Palos Verdes Dr. W., ☎310-377-1650)* is something of a curiosity. A high glass structure built in 1949 by the Swedenborgian church to resemble the

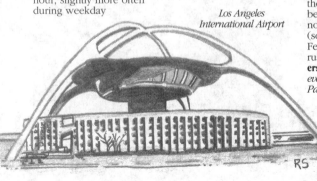

Los Angeles International Airport

RS

surrounding redwoods and pines, it forms an enchanting setting and is a popular spot for weddings. The **South Coast Botanic Garden** ★ *($5; every day 9am to 5pm; 26300 Crenshaw Blvd., ☎310-544-6815)* is built on a reclaimed garbage dump and is often cited as an imaginative example of land recycling. Its 150,000 plants representing 2,000 species include many from southern Africa, Australia and the Mediterranean. Bisected by a stream, it has several specialized gardens, among them a cactus garden and a fuchsia garden.

Tour G: Long Beach and Surroundings

The southern tip of Los Angeles County, bound by the Palos Verdes Peninsula to the west and Orange County to the east and south, is serious commercial-port territory. The twin ports of San Pedro and Long Beach are the busiest in the western United States, and parts of their massive installations can be seen from the high Vincent Thomas Bridge that links the two. Both of these communities, known mainly for their carefully zoned residential and industrial areas, also attempt to draw tourists, though some of the offerings may seem rather bland with the exception of two truly outstanding aquariums, the Cabrillo Aquarium in San Pedro and the Aquarium of the Pacific in Long Beach. The latter also includes a pair of interesting art museums. Santa Catalina Island (often locally referred to simply as Catalina Island) lies 22mi (35km) offshore

and provides an interesting getaway.

San Pedro, about 22mi (35km) south of downtown L.A., is a largely working-class area of broad ethnic diversity noted chiefly for the vast marine installations officially designated as the Port of Los Angeles. Pacific Avenue, an unremarkable commercial street, is the main thoroughfare in downtown San Pedro. It does have at least one interesting building, however, the 1,500-seat **Warner Grand Theater** *(478 W. Sixth St. at Pacific Ave.)*, with its huge neon sign, opulent Art Deco lobby, and intricate wood carvings. Rescued by the City of Los Angeles (to which San Pedro was annexed in 1909) and reopened in 1996, this theatre is open only for special performances. Gaffey Street, a couple of blocks west, is another important thoroughfare.

The **Los Angeles Maritime Museum** ★★ *($1; Tue to Sun 10am to 5pm; Berth 84 at the foot of Sixth St., ☎310-548-7618)* fills seven galleries in the former Municipal Ferry building and explores contemporary port activity as well as various aspects of the nautical past. Displays include models of more than 700 vessels, including an 18ft (5.5m) replica of the *Titanic*, with a detailed cutaway view of the interior. Among other vessels similarly showcased are the *Golden Hind*, the *Bounty*, the *USS Constitution* ("Old Ironsides") and the *Poseidon*. The museum also has a floating collection of real vessels as well as displays of seafaring artifacts and memorabilia. **Ports O'Call Village**, just south of the Maritime Museum, is a

forgettable tourist trap where souvenirs and snacks are sold at numerous stalls in a silly attempt to recreate a New England fishing village.

One of the biggest draws in San Pedro is the **Cabrillo Marine Aquarium** ★ *(free admission; parking $6.50; Tue to Fri noon to 5pm, Sat to Sun 10am to 5pm; 3720 Stephen White Dr. off Pacific Ave., ☎310-548-2631)*, located next to Cabrillo Beach near the southeastern tip of San Pedro. Built in 1981, the aquarium doesn't compare in size to the newer Aquarium of the Pacific in Long Beach, but it does contain 38 saltwater tanks displaying a broad variety of marine habitats, with many colourful fish as well as birds and marine mammals. Special children's programs are offered.

A few blocks southwest, **Point Fermin Park** covers a large cliffside area above the shore and the tide pools that form a sanctuary for marine life. The park provides good vantage points for views of the ocean below, with migrating grey whales passing close by, and the port installations to the east. Besides picnic grounds and footpaths, it boasts a picturesque lighthouse built in 1874. Further up the hill is **Angel's Gate Park**, site of the **Korean Friendship Bell** ★. Weighing 16.7 tons (17 tonnes), this U.S. bicentennial gift from the Korean government, installed here in 1976, is sheltered by a colourful and ornate pagoda-style structure. What is perhaps most attractive about this site is its pervasive sense of tranquility, with the ocean stretching out below. Also located in this park is the

Los Angeles

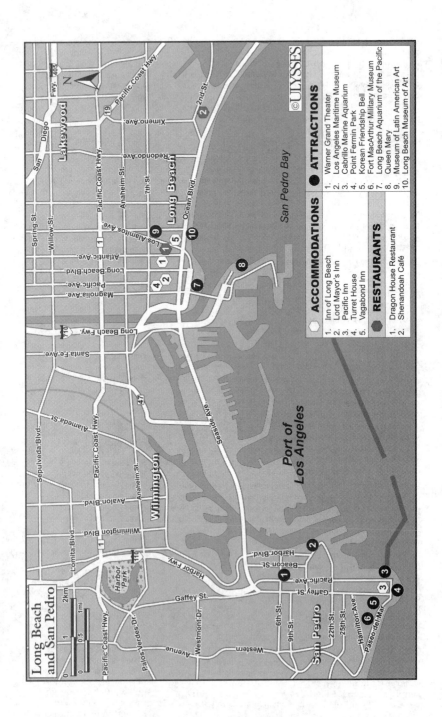

Long Beach and San Pedro

ACCOMMODATIONS
1. Inn of Long Beach
2. Lord Mayor's Inn
3. Pacific Inn
4. Turret House
5. Vagabond Inn

RESTAURANTS
1. Dragon House Restaurant
2. Shenandoah Café

ATTRACTIONS
1. Warner Grand Theater
2. Los Angeles Maritime Museum
3. Cabrillo Marine Aquarium
4. Point Fermin Park
5. Korean Friendship Bell
6. Fort MacArthur Military Museum
7. Long Beach Aquarium of the Pacific
8. Queen Mary
9. Museum of Latin American Art
10. Long Beach Museum of Art

© ULYSSES

San Pedro Bay

Port of
Los Angeles

Fort MacArthur Military Museum *(free admission; Tue, Thu, Sat, Sun noon to 5pm;* ☎*310-548-2631)*, housed in a military installation built in 1916 to watch for enemy attacks. Exhibits portray the defence of Los Angeles harbour and various civilian and military aspects of the war effort. Visitors can also see an artillery battery.

Long Beach is a prim community with a picture-perfect, pedestrian-friendly downtown area that often looks as if a neutron bomb had hit. Everything is clean and tidy, and big money went into refurbishing the waterfront following the closing of a naval base. Despite this, somehow it all seems peculiarly lifeless, as if it were early Sunday morning all week long. All the same, Long Beach does attract a sizable number of visitors (but why do so many of them seem invisible?), drawn to the numerous meetings held at the gargantuan convention centre, as well as to the Aquarium of the Pacific and Queen Mary Seaport.

Downtown Long Beach lies just east of where the diminutive Los Angeles River flows into the Pacific. Ocean Boulevard runs parallel to the shore across the entire length of Long Beach. Shoreline Drive runs a little closer to the shore in the downtown area, while Pine Avenue is a major perpendicular street, lined with many shops and restaurants over a stretch of several blocks extending up to Sixth Street. Long Beach Boulevard runs parallel, one block further east. The free Passport shuttle bus ser-

vice operates along four routes, connecting all major attractions with each other and with parking areas. The Long Beach Freeway, bearing route number 710, links Long Beach and downtown L.A. Another way to reach Long Beach from downtown Los Angeles is the Blue Line light rail system,

Queen Mary

which has its southern terminus in downtown Long Beach. There is no bus or rail service to Long Beach Airport.

Opened in 1998, **Long Beach Aquarium of the Pacific** ★ ★ *($14.95; every day 9:30am to 6pm; 100 Aquarium Way, off Shoreline Dr.,* ☎*562-590-3100, www.aquariumofpacific.org)*, is distinguished from the outside by its curved glass walls and undulating roofline. Nearly 1,000,000 gallons (more than 3,000,000L) of sea water fill the 17 major habitat tanks and the 30 smaller "focus tanks" that together house more than 550 species of marine life. Using a familiar U.S. metaphor, the aquarium's exhibition space is supposedly the size of three football fields. Visitors enter by the Great Hall of the Pacific and are wowed by a full-scale

model of a blue whale, our planet's largest creature. Three distinct parts of the Pacific are represented in the temperate Southern California and Baja section, the frigid Northern Pacific and Bering Strait section, and the warm Tropical Pacific section. Simulated waves and special sound and atmospheric effects add to the experience. Charming marine mammals such as sea otters can be seen alongside sharks, barracudas and giant spider crabs, who also share quarters with many of the sea's smaller and meeker creatures.

Long Beach's other landmark tourist attraction is the **Queen Mary** ★ ★ *($15; every day 10am to 6pm, until later in summer; Pier J, 1126 Queens Hwy.,* ☎*562-435-3511, www.queenmary. com)*. This great relic of the golden era of trans-Atlantic crossings, launched in 1934 and weighing in at more than 71,832 tons (73,000 tonnes), easily qualifies as a shameless tourist trap. Indeed, she has drawn in suckers by the millions since she was moored permanently at Long Beach in 1967, three years after her retirement from service. But this is as close as most of us will ever get to reliving the special ambiance of a bygone period. From lavish hardwood-panelled staterooms to the stunning Art Deco observation lounge, she is a statement in splendour and elegance. With her 12 decks and her 984ft (300m) length, she was the largest passenger vessel of her time. The vessel houses a 385-room hotel and countless gift shops. A former Soviet submarine moored next to the *Queen Mary* can be visited for an extra charge.

The **Museum of Latin American Art** ★ *($5; Tue to Sat 11:30am to 7:30pm, Sun noon to 6pm; 628 Alamitos Ave. at Sixth St.,* ☎*562-437-1689)* has a small permanent collection focusing mostly on contemporary artists and also offers a continuing series of temporary exhibitions. Housed a few blocks northeast of downtown Long Beach in a former roller skating rink dating from 1920, the museum makes an effort to achieve geographic diversity and to move away from the Mexican dominance of the Latin American art scene in the United States. The museum includes a book and crafts shop as well as a small restaurant with a delightful outdoor terrace and a menu reflecting this same geographic diversity. Several private art galleries are located nearby.

The **Long Beach Museum of Art** ★ *($2; Wed to Sun 10am to 5pm, Fri until 8pm; 2300 E. Ocean Blvd. between Junipero and Temple aves.,* ☎*562-439-2119)* focuses on works by contemporary California artists and has developed a reputation for experimental video works, although the exhibition program is far broader than this may suggest. The museum is housed in a historical mansion on a bluff overlooking the Pacific Ocean a few blocks east of downtown Long Beach.

Santa Catalina Island ★★, often referred to simply as Catalina Island, offers Angelenos and their visitors an opportunity to escape urban living without having

to travel very far. Although it would be an exaggeration to call it an island paradise, this hilly outcropping with its many coves and its sense of remoteness has its own special laid-back charm and offers plenty of outdoor activities as well as a range of accommodations for overnight stays. The island was purchased in 1919 by chewing gum magnate William Wrigley, who developed part of it as an exclusive fishing club. Later, the island became accessible to a broader group of visitors, and in 1975 a newly established conservancy gained control of 88% of the island's territory with the mandate to protect its unique ecosystem from further development.

Most of the island's 300 permanent residents (the population multiplies in the summer) live in the village of **Avalon**, which has a faintly Mediterranean flavour and really does feel like a small seaside town, with many quaint restaurants, shops and hotels radiating from the pier. Its most noticeable building is the circular, white-walled, red-tile-roofed **Casino**, built by Wrigley in 1929 not as a gambling hall but as a dance hall upstairs with a large theatre below; it now serves as a cinema. The building also

houses a small museum. Other parts of the island provide opportunities for hiking, swimming, snorkelling, kayaking, fishing, cycling and golf. Only a handful of residents are allowed to operate regular motor vehicles, and anyone wanting to penetrate the island's interior by bicycle or golf cart requires a specil permit. Several companies operate minibus tours of the island along its very limited road network.

Visitor information is available from the **Catalina Island Chamber of Commerce** *(☎310-510-1520, www.catalina.com)*, which maintains an information booth on the main pier in Avalon. Located 22mi (35km) south of San Pedro or Long Beach and forming part of the Channel Island group, it can be reached in about 1hr by the passenger ferries operating frequently from Long Beach and San Pedro. Catalina Express *($38 round-trip; ☎562-519-1212 or 800-464-4228)* provides the most frequent service, with departures from the Queen Mary Landing in Long Beach and the well-marked Sea-Air Terminal at Berth 95 in San Pedro. Catalina Cruises *($25 round-trip, ☎800-228-2546)* operates bigger, slower vessels that take slightly under 2hrs for the

Avalon Casino

crossing. Island Express Helicopter Services *($66 each way,* ☎*310-510-2525)* offers a faster (15min) but rather expensive alternative.

Accommodations

Choosing accommodations in a big city is often a daunting task. In a sprawling, decentralized city like Los Angeles, distance poses an added consideration.

In most cities, staying downtown would be an obvious choice for many travellers, but this is less true in Los Angeles. After dark, downtown L.A. offers few attractions, and some areas can be a bit scary. Furthermore, many downtown hotels are skewed toward either extreme of the price scale, with a selection of high-end establishments catering mainly to business travellers and, at the opposite end, faded skid-row hostelries where most guests pay by the week or month—or by the hour. For travellers seeking a modicum of comfort and security but lacking the benefits of a generous expense account, the choice is narrower, although we do offer several suggestions within this chapter.

That leaves several other parts of the city. Venice Beach will be a natural choice for many young budget travellers both because of its attractive ambiance and the ready availability of low-priced accommodations. There are also some possibilities in Hollywood. The overall choice is broader for mid-range and higher-end travellers. With the great strength of the U.S. dollar in recent years, prices across the whole spectrum may seem high to some visitors from abroad.

Even for the most impecunious of travellers, time is money. It doesn't make sense to waste it unnecessarily on L.A.'s clogged freeways or tortoise-like public transit. Before deciding on accommodations, readers may wish to consider which parts of the city they are most likely to visit and make their choice accordingly.

Downtown Los Angeles

Stillwell Hotel
$$
≡, *tv*, ℜ
838 S. Grand Ave.
between Eighth and Ninth sts.
☎*(213) 627-1151*
☎*800-553-4774*
≈*(213) 622-8940*
H.STILLWELL@aol.com
This is an older but refurbished 250-room hotel located about midway between the convention centre and the heart of the downtown area. Although far from luxurious, it is a friendly spot offering a decent level of comfort for the price and interesting decorative touches.

Metro Plaza Hotel
$$
≡, *tv*
711 N. Main St.
at Cesar Chavez Ave.
☎*(213) 680-0200*
☎*800-223-2223*
res@metroplazahotel.com
Conveniently located near Union Station, Olvera Street and Chinatown, this hotel has 80 plain but functional rooms.

Best Western Dragon Gate Inn
$$-$$$
≡, *tv*, ℜ
818 N. Hill St. between Alpine St. and College St.
☎*(213) 617-3077*
☎*800-282-9999*
≈*(213) 680-3753*
www.bestwestern.com
This hotel, located in the heart of Chinatown, includes a shopping gallery that was set around a central atrium following renovations in 1999. The 57 rooms are simply furnished, most with refrigerators and coffee-makers. A light breakfast is included in room rates.

Figueroa Hotel
$$$
≡, *tv*, ≈, ℜ
939 S. Figueroa between Ninth and 10th sts.
☎*(213) 627-8971*
☎*800-421-9092*
≈*(213) 689-0305*
This is a high-rise version of classic L.A.-style Spanish revival architecture. Built in 1927, it features ceramic tiles, wrought-iron chandeliers and wood-beamed ceilings in the common areas. The 285 rooms are spacious and comfortable, although decorators have chosen a curious blend of styles. The main restaurant is next to the garden-lined pool area; upstairs is a coffee shop for lighter fare. Located near the convention centre, the hotel tends to be fully booked during major events.

Kawada Hotel
$$$
≡, *tv*, ℜ, K
200 S. Hill St. at Second St.
☎*(213) 621-4455*
☎*800-752-9232*
reservations@kawadahotel.com
Located in the northern part of the downtown area near city hall, this hotel looks from the outside like an old low-rise office

Los Angeles

building, but inside the 115 mainly small rooms are bright, pleasant and highly functional, most with kitchenettes.

Miyako Inn
$$$-$$$$
≡, tv, ☺, ℛ
328 E. First St. between San Pedro and Central aves.
☎*(213) 617-2000*
☎*800-228-6596*
⇛*(213) 617-2700*
miyakola@earthlink.net
Located in the Little Tokyo district, this establishment includes a fitness club and karaoke lounge. Many of the 174 rooms have mats, screens and low beds in the Japanese style.

Hyatt Regency Los Angeles
$$$-$$$$$
≡, tv, ℑ
711 S. Hope St. at Seventh St.
☎*(213) 683-1234*
☎*800-233-1234*
⇛*(213) 612-3179*
bregencyl@aol.com
Located near the heart of the financial district, adjacent to Macy's Plaza, this 24-storey, 482-room hotel offers the standard comforts of a business-style establishment and panoramic views from many rooms.

New Otani Hotel
$$$$-$$$$$
≡, tv, ☺, ℛ
120 S. Los Angeles St.
between First and Second sts.
☎*(213) 629-1200*
☎*800-421-8795*
⇛*(213) 253-9269*
www.newotani.com
Housed in a 21-storey building located in the heart of Little Tokyo, this hotel offers a blend of American and Asian styles in its common areas and its 414 rooms. Features include a large Japanese garden and a two-storey shopping arcade. Special Japanese cultural packages are available.

Westin Bonaventure Hotel
$$$$-$$$$$
≡, tv, ≈, ☺, ℑ
404 S. Figueroa St. at Fourth St.
☎*(213) 624-1000*
☎*800-228-3000*
⇛*(213) 612-4800*
A 35-storey landmark with 1,356 rooms in five gleaming cylindrical towers perched like a spaceship on the western side of the downtown area, this vast convention hotel is almost a city within a city. On the premises are more than 40 shops, restaurants and bars. The rooms are large and comfortable, many with wonderful views.

Wyndham Checkers Hotel
$$$$-$$$$$
≡, tv, ☺, ℑ
535 S. Grand Ave.
between Fifth and Sixth sts.
☎*(213) 624-0000*
☎*800-996-3426*
⇛*(213) 626-9906*
checkersla@aol.com
This hotel offers 188 very comfortable rooms and suites. Elegant touches include a rooftop spa, wood-panelled library, and marble bathrooms. Built in 1927 and classed as a historical monument, the hotel has an intricate stone facade.

Regal Biltmore Hotel
$$$$$
≡, tv, ≈, ☺, ℑ
506 S. Grand Ave. at Fifth St.
☎*(213) 624-1011*
☎*800-245-8673*
⇛*(213) 612-1545*
www.thebiltmore.com
A landmark hotel in the heart of the downtown area, this 11-storey building, built in 1923, has an elegant marble-lined lobby with a truly palatial atmosphere. The hotel's Crystal Ballroom was the setting of the Academy Awards in the 1930s and 1940s. The 683 rooms and suites are grandly furnished and very comfortable.

✿ Hotel Inter-Continental Los Angeles
$$$$$
≡, tv, ≈, ☺, ℑ
251 S. Olive St.
between Second and Third sts.
☎*(213) 617-3300*
☎*800-327-0200*
⇛*(213) 617-3399*
Located on Bunker Hill near the Museum of Contemporary Art, this 17-storey, 434-room establishment is the newest of the big downtown hotels, conservative but chic in style, with attention to service. Features designed for business travellers include two phone lines in each room and a business centre. Weekend specials are sometimes offered.

Pasadena

Westway Inn
$$
≡, tv, ≈
1599 E. Colorado Ave.
across from Pasadena City College
⇛*(626) 304-9678*
⇛*(626) 449-3493*
This 61-room motel is one of the more attractive places to stay along Pasadena's motel row. Its rooms are modern, with refrigerator, and service is friendly.

Pasadena Hotel Bed & Breakfast
$$$-$$$$ bkfst incl.
sb/pb, ≡, tv
76 N. Fair Oaks Ave.
between Union and Holly sts.
☎*(626) 568-8172*
☎*800-653-8886*
⇛*(626) 793-6409*
This establishment offers 12 guest rooms in a historic house located in Old Pasadena. Rooms are small but comfortable (in most cases, the bathroom is down the hall). They are complemented by an elegant sitting room downstairs. Breakfast and afternoon tea, served in a

courtyard, are included in room rates.

Bissell House
$$$-$$$$ bkfst incl.
≡, ≈
201 Orange Grove Ave.
at Columbia St.
☎(626) 441-3535
☎800-441-3530
⇌(626) 441-3671
www.virtualcities.com
This historical gingerbread house, built in 1887, is located along Pasadena's traditional millionaire's row. Tall hedges provide shelter from the busy street outside. The five rooms have antique furnishings, including old-fashioned bathtubs. A large breakfast and afternoon snacks are included in room rates.

Doubletree Hotel
$$$$-$$$$$
≡, tv, ≈, ☉, ℥
191 North Los Robles Ave.
near Walnut St.
☎(626) 792-2727
☎800-222-8733
⇌(626) 795-7669
This modern hotel is adjacent to the very picturesque city hall near the Old Pasadena district. Set on wide landscaped grounds with a Mediterranean theme, this 12-storey, 360-room hotel offers large, comfortable rooms with a range of amenities. Special rates apply most weekends.

Hollywood and Surroundings

Hollywood International Hostel
$16/pers.
sb
6820 Hollywood Blvd.
near Highland Ave.
☎(323) 463-0797
☎800-750-6561
⇌(323) 463-1705
Hollywood International Hostel offers multi-bunk rooms each with three or four beds as well as a handful of private rooms at $40 per room. Facilities for guests include a kitchen, a TV lounge, a laundry room and a game room with pool tables. Check-in is available 24hrs a day, and the general atmosphere is lively. The majority of guests are from abroad.

Saharan Motor Hotel
$-$$
≡, tv, ≈
7212 Sunset Blvd. at Poinsetta Place
four blocks west of La Brea Ave.
☎(323) 874-6700
⇌(323) 874-5163
sahara-jaco@worldnet.att.net
This is a garish, 1960s-style motel whose 63 rooms are better than they look from the outside. The immediate area can be noisy at night.

Liberty Hotel
$$
≡, tv
1770 Orchid Ave. near Franklin Ave.
☎(323) 962-1788
This spot is located in downtown Hollywood near Mann's Chinese Theater. Recently renovated, it offers 21 bright, spacious rooms as well as a communal kitchen and laundry facilities.

Highland Gardens Hotel
$$
7047 Franklin Ave.
near Sycamore Ave.
☎(323) 850-0536
☎800-404-5472
⇌(323) 850-1712
This spot provides 70 pleasant rooms and suites set around a lush courtyard. Multi-bedroom suites with private kitchen are available at higher rates. The hotel is located near downtown Hollywood toward the Hollywood Hills.

Hollywood Hills Magic Hotel
$$-$$$
≡, tv, K, ≈
7025 Franklin Ave.
near Sycamore Ave.
☎(323) 851-0800
☎800-741-4915
⇌(323) 851-4926
www.magichotel.com
Offering 49 spacious rooms and suites with modern decor set around a courtyard and large heated pool, this spot is considered family-friendly and provides great value for the money. Located near downtown Hollywood at the base of the Hollywood Hills, it takes its name from the Magic Castle, a private club just up the hill where top-rated magicians perform. (The hotel can arrange reservations.)

Universal City Inn
$$-$$$
≡, tv, ≈
10730 Ventura Blvd. between Lankershim Blvd. and Vineland Ave.
in Studio City
☎(818) 760-8737
⇌(818) 762-5159
This 37-room motel is located just off the Ventura Freeway in North Hollywood within walking distance of Universal Studios. Rates here provide substantially better value than at hotels directly adjacent to the park. The rooms are modern and spacious.

Hollywood Orchid Suites
$$-$$$
≡, tv, K, ≈
1753 N. Orchid Ave. between Hollywood Blvd. and Franklin Ave.
☎(323) 874-9678
☎800-537-3052
⇌(323) 467-7649
www.orchidsuites.com
Set in a former apartment building on a quiet side street in downtown Hollywood, this hotel offers 36 pleasant rooms of various sizes. Each has kitchen facilities, and a few have

Los Angeles

balconies. The lobby is not very appealing.

Park Sunset Hotel
$$$
≡, *tv, K, ≈*
8462 Sunset Blvd.
just east of La Cienega Blvd.
☎*(323) 654-6470*
☎*800-821-3660*
(323) 654-5918
Located along a busy part of the famous Sunset Strip, this three-storey, 82-room hotel is set well back from the street and the noise. Rooms are pleasantly decorated, and a few have kitchens or balconies.

Best Western Sunset Plaza Hotel
$$$ bkfst incl.
≡, *tv*
8400 Sunset Blvd.
two blocks east of La Cienega Blvd.
☎*(323) 3654-0750*
☎*800-421-3652*
(323) 650-6146
This hotel offers 88 spacious and pleasantly decorated rooms, some with full kitchen. A light breakfast is included in room rates. This Sunset Strip spot is friendly for families.

Hollywood Roosevelt Hotel
$$$-$$$$
≡, *tv, ≈, ☺, ☒*
7000 Hollywood Blvd. at Orange Dr.
☎*(323) 466-7000*
☎*800-950-7667*
(323) 462-8056
sales@hollywoodroosevelt.com
This landmark establishment is a step back in time to a more romantic Hollywood era. Located in downtown Hollywood across from Mann's Chinese Theater and built in 1927, the 12-storey Roosevelt is a restored Art Deco monument displaying a Spanish revival influence. It is surrounded by lush gardens. The original home of the Academy Awards, it is replete with Hollywood lore and was once a

hangout for literary figures. Its 328 rooms and suites are rather ordinary, however, in contrast to the magnificent lobby.

 The Argyle Hotel
$$$$-$$$$$
≡, *tv, ≈, ☺, ☒*
8358 Sunset Blvd. three blocks east of La Cienega Blvd.
☎*(323) 654-7100*
☎*800-225-2637*
(323) 654-9287
www.argylehotel.com
Dating from 1929, this 15-storey Art Deco gem has 64 exquisitely decorated rooms, each with Art Deco reproductions and distinctive furniture, as well as modern conveniences like VCRs and CD players. Rooms are a little on the small side, but many offer superb city views.

Mondrian
$$$$$
≡, *tv, K, ≈, ☺, ☒*
8440 Sunset Blvd.
two blocks east of La Cienega Blvd.
☎*(323) 650-8999*
☎*800-525-8029*
(323) 650-5215
This a masterpiece of design was created from what was once an ordinary apartment building in West Hollywood. Guests in the 53 rooms and 185 suites enjoy superb city views (the designer set out to create a "hotel in the clouds") along with elegant minimalist decor and a sophisticated, if somewhat overbearing, level of service. Suites include kitchenettes.

Mid-Wilshire and Westside

Park Plaza Lodge
$$
≡, *tv*
6001 W. Third St. near Martell Ave.
between La Brea and Fairfax
☎*(323) 931-1501*
(323) 931-5863
This hotel is located near the Farmers Market in the Fairfax district and lies within walking distance of the Los Angeles County Museum of Art. Rooms are spacious and decently furnished. Good value.

Hilgard House
$$$ bkfst incl.
≡, *tv*
927 Hilgard Ave. between Weyburn Ave. and Le Conte Ave.
☎*(310) 208-3945*
☎*800-826-3934*
(310) 208-1972
reservations@hilgardhouse.com
This 53-room hotel is located near UCLA and Westwood Village.

Beverly Plaza Hotel
$$$-$$$$
≡, *tv, ≈, ☺, ☒*
8384 W. Third St.
at La Cienega Ave.
☎*(323) 658-6600*
☎*800-624-6835*
(323) 653-3464
info@BeverlyPlazaHotel.com
This spot offers 98 rooms in a six-storey building near the Beverly Center. Rooms are spacious and very pleasantly decorated.

Le Rêve Hotel
$$$$-$$$$$
≡, *tv, K, ≈, ☒*
8822 Cynthia St. one block north of Santa Monica Blvd.
☎*(310) 854-1114*
☎*800-835-7997*
(310) 657-2623
Located between West Hollywood and Beverly Hills, this spot offers 80 suites with a floral motif and French influence.

Most have balconies and kitchenettes. The rooftop garden and pool area provides panoramic views.

Westwood Marquis Hotel
$$$$-$$$$$
≡, *tv*, ℑ
930 Hilgard Ave. between Weyburn Ave. and Le Conte Ave.
☎ *(310) 208-8765*
☎ *800-421-2317*
↪ *(310) 824-0355*
www.wbotels.com
This elegant 257-room all-suite establishment is located near UCLA and Westwood Village. The hotel is set on beautifully landscaped grounds and offers a sophisticated level of service.

Santa Monica, Venice and Malibu

Venice Beach Hotel
$15-$17.50/pers.
sb
25 Windward Ave.
one block from the beach
☎ *(310) 399-7649*
↪ *(310) 399-1930*
This hostel offers a total of 98 beds, most of them in dorms with three to six beds each, the remainder in 16 private rooms *($36 sb, $48 pb)*. Accommodations are simple but satisfactory. The entrance is upstairs.

Jim's at the Beach
$15-$20/pers., bkfst incl.
sb
17 Brooks Ave.
half a block from the beach
☎ *(310) 399-4018*
hostel_info@yahoo.com
This is the author's choice as the best hostel at Venice Beach. The atmosphere is just a little friendlier, the rooms more appealing, and the common areas more comfortable. Beds are mostly six to eight per dorm, and breakfast is included in the price. On Sundays a special barbecue is offered. Guests have

the use of a spacious kitchen, laundry facilities and computers. There is no curfew.

Venice Beach Hostel
$17-$21/pers.
sb
1515 Pacific Ave. at Windward Ave.
one block from the beach
☎ *(310) 452-3052*
↪ *(310) 821-3469*
vbb@caprica.com
Venice Beach Hostel offers dorms with four to six beds as well as smaller dorms and a few private rooms *($45-$55 pb, tv)*. Some dorms are set aside for women only. Amenities include laundry facilities and refrigerators with private locked compartments. The hallways are lined with murals and posters. Facilities are plain and a bit tattered, although the atmosphere is friendly. There is no curfew.

Santa Monica American Youth Hostel
$19-$24 /person, $3 surcharge for non-members of Hostelling International
sb
1436 Second St.
south of Santa Monica Blvd.
☎ *(310) 393-9913*
This spot offers about 200 beds mostly in dorms as well as some private rooms *($28/pers. for two or more)*. Housed in a large brick building that was once a town hall, this well managed spot includes a pleasant courtyard, big kitchen, laundry room, library and travel store. It is located near the Third Street Promenade and the beach.

Sea Shore Motel
$$
≡, *tv*
2637 Main St. at Hill St.
fácing the beach
☎ *(310) 392-2787*
↪ *(310) 392-5167*
This German-run spot is popular with European

visitors. The hotel is located by the sea, although it is some distance from downtown Santa Monica. Rooms are comfortable if somewhat ordinary. Good value.

Cadillac Hotel
$$-$$$
tv, ☺
8 Dudley Ave. facing Venice Beach
☎ *(310) 399-8876*
↪ *(310) 399-4536*
www.thecadillachotel.com
This is a restored hotel dating back to 1905. Many of its 34 rooms have sea views. The lobby shows Art Deco influences, while the rooms, redecorated several times over the decades, manage to be both funky and a little tired-looking.

Hotel Carmel
$$$-$$$$
≡, *tv*
201 Broadway Ave.
at Second St., Santa Monica
☎ *(310) 451-2469*
↪ *(310) 393-4180*
This establishment is ideally located around the corner from Santa Monica's lively Third Street Promenade and near Santa Monica Beach. However, despite the recent renovation of some rooms this aging hotel does not live up to its potential. The 104 rooms vary in size and decor, and some of them are located down long hallways. Most offer a reasonable level of comfort, although the decor tends to be quite plain. Rooms on the street side can be noisy. The lobby is spacious but mostly empty, and there is just one creaking elevator to serve this four-storey building.

Los Angeles

Marina Pacific Hotel
$$$-$$$$
≡, tv
1697 Pacific Ave.
one block from the beach
☎ *(310) 452-1111*
☎ *800-421-8151*
⊷ *(310) 452-5479*
www.mphotel.com
This imposing spot offers 96 spacious but rather nondescript rooms near the heart of the action at Venice Beach. Double windows cut down on noise. Service is friendly.

🏊 **The Venice Beach House**
$$$-$$$$ bkfst incl.
sb/pb
15 30th Ave. near the beach
☎ *(310) 823-1966*
This delightful spot is located on a quiet pedestrian-only street about 200 feet (60m) from the beach and a few blocks south of the central scene in Venice Beach, although there are several restaurants nearby. This lovingly maintained property is listed on the National Register of Historic Places. Its nine guest rooms vary in size; all provide a warm, cozy atmosphere and are adorned with antique furniture. The large verandah, facing a garden, is a wonderful place to relax. A light breakfast is included in room rates.

🏊 **Casa Malibu Inn**
$$$-$$$$
tv
22752 Pacific Coast Hwy., 0.25mi (400m) from the Malibu pier
☎ *(310) 456-2219*
☎ *800-831-0858*
⊷ *(310) 456-5418*
casamalibu@earthlink.net
Offering 21 tastefully decorated rooms in a two-storey motel-style structure set around a garden, this hotel has a sparkling private beach. Some of the rooms have kitchenettes or private balconies.

Belle Bleu Inn
$$$-$$$$$
≡, tv, K
1670 Ocean Ave.
near the Santa Monica pier
☎ *(310) 393-2363*
⊷ *(310) 393-1063*
This spot offers 26 suites in a central location close to the beach. Rooms feature hardwood floors, kitchen or kitchenette, and, in most cases, patios facing the beach.

Hotel Shangri-La
$$$$
≡, tv
1301 Ocean Ave., Santa Monica near Wilshire Blvd.
☎ *(310) 394-2791*
☎ *800-345-7829*
⊷ *(310) 451-3351*
www.shangrila-hotel.com
This hotel is ideally located overlooking the Pacific at the edge of downtown Santa Monica. Most of the 55 rooms are set around a verdant courtyard, and many have ocean views. Much of the decor reflects an Art Deco influence, although some of the furniture is more mid-20th-century suburban.

🏊 **Channel Road Inn**
$$$$-$$$$$ bkfst incl.
tv
219 W. Channel Rd.
one block from the beach
☎ *(310) 459-1920*
⊷ *(310) 454-9920*
www.channelroadinn.com
This charming spot offers 14 rooms in a carefully restored house. Full breakfast, afternoon tea and hors d'œuvres are included in room rates. Rooms, some with sea views and several with fireplaces or whirlpool baths, are furnished mostly in wood with decorative touches like Amish quilts. Guests are generally pampered.

Malibu Beach Inn
$$$$-$$$$$ bkfst incl.
tv, ☺
22878 Pacific Coast Hwy.
near Malibu pier
☎ *(310) 456-6444*
☎ *800-462-5428*
⊷ *(310) 456-1499*
reservations@
malibubeachinn.com
This hotel offers 46 rooms facing a quiet beach that is ideal for bathing. The building and grounds are laid out in early Mexican style. Rooms are pleasingly decorated in deep colours, and each has a balcony or porch facing the sea.

The Georgian Inn
$$$$-$$$$$
≡, tv, ≈, ☺, ❆
1415 Ocean Ave. between Santa Monica Blvd. and Broadway Ave.
☎ *(310) 395-9945*
☎ *800-538-8147*
⊷ *(310) 451-3374*
www.georgianhotel.com
Superbly located overlooking the Pacific Ocean at the edge of downtown Santa Monica, this eight-storey Art Deco treasure, built in 1933, has a bright pastel exterior, Miami Beach-style. The breakfast room was once a speakeasy, popular with some Hollywood stars of the era. Most of the 84 rooms offer ocean views, and guests are catered to with a wide range of services.

Airport Area and South Bay

Skyways Airport Hotel
$$
≡, tv, K
9250 Airport Blvd. several blocks north of Century Blvd.
☎ *(310) 670-2900*
☎ *800-336-0025*
This is one of the more economical hotels among the cluster of establishments immediately to the east of LAX Airport. Some of the 69 rather nonde-

script rooms have kitchenettes.

Continental Plaza Hotel Los Angeles
$$$-$$$$
≡, tv, ≈, ☉, ℨ
9750 Airport Blvd. 600ft (200m) north of Century Blvd.
☎*(310) 645-4600*
☎*800-529-4683*
⁓*(310) 645-7489*
This hotel offers 570 large, nondescript rooms near the airport. The fitness center is open 24 hours a day.

Crowne Plaza Los Angeles Airport
$$$-$$$$
≡, tv, ≈, ☉, ℨ
5985 W. Century Blvd. near Airport Blvd.
☎*(310) 642-7500*
☎*888-315-3700*
⁓*(310) 417-3608*
www.crowneplaza.com/hotels/laxap
Offering 615 corporate-style rooms near the airport, this spot has the usual business-oriented amenities.

Sea Sprite Motel
$$-$$$$
≡, tv, R, ≈
1016 The Strand at 10th St. Hermosa Beach
☎*(310) 376-6933*
⁓*(310) 376-4107*
Well suited to beach-goers, this family-oriented spot is located just a few steps from the golden sands. It offers a playground and volleyball court as well as refrigerators and microwave ovens in the rooms.

Grandview Motor Hotel
$$$
≡, tv
55 14th St., off Hermosa Ave. Hermosa Beach
☎*(310) 374-8981*
⁓*(310) 374-8983*
Located just a few steps from the beach, this three-storey hotel is grand in name only: it totals just 17 rooms, but they are spa-

cious and reasonably comfortable, with refrigerators and balconies. The atmosphere is friendly.

Marina International Hotel & Bungalows
$$$$-$$$$$
≡, tv, ≈, ☉, ℨ
4200 Admiralty Way at Palawan Way, Marina del Rey
☎*(310) 301-2000*
☎*800-882-4000*
⁓*(310) 301-8867*
This establishment provides views of a vast marina from the 110 large, pleasant rooms in the main tower and the 25 bungalows with private patios or balconies.

Long Beach and San Pedro

Vagabond Inn
$$
≡, tv, ≈
150 Alamitos Ave. near First St. Long Beach
☎*(562) 435-7621*
Located between downtown Long Beach and Sunset Beach, this friendly spot offers 62 ordinary-looking motel-style rooms, some with refrigerator and microwave. Room rates go higher on summer weekends.

Inn of Long Beach
$$-$$$$ bkfst incl.
≡, tv, ≈
185 Atlantic Ave. at Broadway Long Beach
☎*(562) 435-3791*
☎*800-230-7500*
⁓*(562) 436-7510*
This friendly place offers renovated rooms set around a central courtyard and pool.

Pacific Inn
$$-$$$
≡, tv
516 W. 38th St. at Pacific Ave. San Pedro
☎*(310) 514-1247*
⁓*(310) 831-5538*
This spot offers 24 pleasantly furnished rooms in a motel-type setting. Some have kitchenettes. Several attractions are within easy walking distance.

Lord Mayor's Inn
$$$-$$$$ bkfst incl.
435 Cedar Ave. between Fourth and Fifth sts., Long Beach
☎*(562) 436-0324*
www.lordmayors.com
This bed and breakfast is set in a carefully restored Edwardian house built in 1904 in a residential neighbourhood a couple of minutes' walk north of downtown Long Beach. A baby grand piano stands guard at the entrance. Each of the five rooms is furnished with period antiques and fine linens. Seven additional rooms, most with private bath, are set in adjacent cottages. Breakfasts (included in room rates) are considered something special.

The Turret House
$$$-$$$$ bkfst incl.
556 Chestnut Ave. between Fifth and Sixth sts., Long Beach
☎*(562) 983-9812*
☎*888-488-7738*
www.turrethouse.com
Set is set in a beautifully restored 1906 mansion located on a quiet residential street just north of downtown Long Beach, this spot offers five guest rooms, each with its own name, decorated fastidiously with antique furnishings. A player piano shares duties with a VCR. A

sumptuous breakfast and evening refreshments are included in room rates.

Restaurants

Dining in a certain type of Los Angeles establishment is more about seeing and being seen than about friendly service and quality food. An entire subculture of Hollywood agents, scriptwriters and assorted wannabes seems to set great store by the table they get at some of these spots, if indeed they can obtain reservations without booking months in advance. Sneering condescension by restaurant staff toward less-exalted patrons has been elevated to an art form at some eateries, with stratospheric prices demanded for dishes that are good but not exceptional.

Fortunately, most L.A. restaurants are entirely different from this all-too-real stereotype. Restaurants with cheerful staff and good value exist in abundance. Attitude problems do creep up occasionally, exemplified by staff at almost-empty restaurants shaking their heads sadly and promising to see what they can do for diners who arrive without reservations. However, this sort of approach seems to be going out of style.

L.A.'s diversified ethnic base contributes enormously to the very evident variety in the local dining scene. This accounts, for example, for the profusion of fine Asian restaurants and the ready availability of good Mexican fare. Fine Italian cooking is also part of the scene. Although the

local French population is smaller, French cuisine is far from absent. The "fusion cuisine" (sometimes referred to as "confusion cuisine"!) that was all the rage a few years ago, with cooking styles and ingredients from different continents blended holus-bolus, has mercifully passed its peak and now exists in more restrained form.

The emphasis in this chapter is on value. Not every establishment listed here is cheap, but an effort has been made to select restaurants that provide an enjoyable experience for the price, in various budget categories. Diners who are willing to put up with abuse in hopes of catching a glimpse of some Hollywood celebrity will have to look elsewhere for guidance.

As any visitor will quickly observe, the L.A. area is one of the world's great strongholds of fast-food culture, with a plethora of hamburger, pizza, taco and fried chicken joints. Among the various fast-food chains, the author's favourite is El Pollo Loco (literally, "The Crazy Chicken"), whose numerous branches offer Mexican-style grilled chicken served with tortillas, rice and a wide choice of condiments.

Downtown Los Angeles and Surroundings

Far more interesting than any bland modern food court is the **Grand Central Market** (bound by Broadway, Third, Hill and Fourth sts.), where the produce vendors and meat counters are joined by a small cluster of restaurants providing cheap and tasty

dishes in atmospheric surroundings, from early morning to late afternoon. Among the favourites is **Maria's Pescado Frito ($)**, offering simple Mexican-style fish and seafood dishes, including *ceviches*.

Original Pantry Café
$
every day 24hrs
877 S. Figueroa St. near Ninth St.
Almost a local landmark, this spot may appear a bit down at the heels, but it serves up old-time American favourites ranging from breakfast pancakes to a late-night steak at bargain prices.

The City Pier
$
Mon to Fri 10:30am to 3:30pm
333 S. Spring St.
between Third and Fourth sts.
☎*(213) 617-2489*
This unpretentious spot, with indoor and outdoor seating areas, is popular with office workers and has a menu centred around sandwiches, including those made with fish or seafood.

Philippe the Original
$
every day 6am to 10pm
1001 N. Alameda St. at Ord St.
☎*(213) 628-3781*
Open since 1908, this is one of the oldest restaurants in town, serving a broad cross-section of local society. The owners claim this is where the "French dip" sandwich was invented. This style of sandwich, which is probably unfamiliar to anyone from France, involves placing slices of roast meat (there are several to choose from) on a baguette that has been dipped in meat juices. Beef stew is another favourite. Food is served cafeteria style, with seating at long communal tables.

Langer's
$
Mon to Sat 8am to 4pm
704 S. Alvarado St. at Seventh St.
☎*(213) 483-8050*
This is a traditional Jewish delicatessen, with seating in booths and at a long counter. It is a popular spot despite its slightly seedy location. Many of the old favourites are available, including matzoh ball soup, pastrami (served several ways), and chopped-liver sandwiches.

La Parrilla
$-$$
every day 8am to 11:30pm
2126 Cesar Chavez Ave.
Boyle Heights
☎*(213) 262-3434*
This casual and cheerfully decorated spot, located in a largely Mexican neighbourhood east of downtown, offers authentic Mexican specialties in a festive atmosphere. Dishes include a variety of charcoal-grilled meats, seafood items such as shrimp in garlic sauce, *tamales* (cornmeal cakes with savoury stuffings), and *pozole* (a stew of large-grained corn with meat).

Shabu Shabu House
$$
Japanese Village Plaza
127 E. Second St.
near Los Angeles St.
☎*(213) 680-3890*
This popular spot in Little Tokyo specializes in a variety of fondues, with meat and vegetables dipped into pots of boiling broth. Other items are also available.

Yang Chow
$$
every day 11:30am to 2:30pm and 5pm to 9:30pm, Fri to Sat until 10:30pm
819 N. Broadway near Alpine
Chinatown
☎*(213) 625-0811*
This old-style Chinatown favourite, with functional decor, offers a wide range of Mandarin and Szechuan dishes as well as some distinctive seafood specialties, including the popular fried "slippery shrimp" with a sweet-and-hot sauce. Steamed pork dumplings served on a bed of spinach are a signature appetizer.

Mon Kee
$$
every day 11:30am to 9:45pm, slightly later on weekends
679 N. Spring St., Chinatown
☎*(213) 628-6717*
This spot in the heart of Chinatown forsakes some of the trendy advances in decor, but offers a broad selection of Chinese seafood specialties, including soups. Main-course items include stir-fried scallops with ginger and fresh squid with garlic and pepper.

Empress Pavilion
$$
every day 9am to 10pm
988 N. Hill St., Chinatown
☎*(213) 617-9898*
Situated near the northern edge of Chinatown, this vast and modern upstairs Hong Kong-style eatery, with sliding dividers to create a greater sense of intimacy, offers an extensive *dim sum* selection earlier in the day (with various sorts of dumplings and other small items served from roving trolleys) and a full traditional menu throughout the day with a special emphasis on fresh fish and seafood dishes.

Engine Company No. 28
$$-$$$
Mon to Fri 11:15am to 9pm, Sat to Sun 5pm to 9pm
644 S. Figueroa St.
between Sixth and Seventh sts.
☎*(213) 624-6996*
Modern versions of traditional American comfort foods like crabcakes, meatloaf and burgers fill the menu at this restored downtown fire station. The American wine list is interesting.

La Serenata de Garibaldi
$$-$$$
Tue to Sat 11am to 10:30pm, Sun 10am to 10pm
1842 E. First St., East L.A.
☎*(213) 265-2887*
This intriguing Mexican seafood restaurant comes as something of a surprise in a rather undistinguished neighbourhood. Dishes and decor reflect both modern and traditional tastes, with whole snappers and other fresh fish and seafood grilled and served on its own or with simple sauces.

Café Pinot
$$$-$$$$
Mon to Fri 11:30am to 2:30pm, every day 5pm to 9pm
700 W. Fifth St. at Hope St.
☎*(213) 239-6500*
This interesting spot, combining French and California cuisines, is located on the grounds of the central library, with both indoor and outdoor dining areas in a garden setting. Service includes free transport to the Music Center, making this a popular spot for pre-concert suppers. One of the favourite items here is rotisserie-grilled chicken in a three-mustard sauce,

Los Angeles

always available even though many menu items rotate through the seasons. Soups and desserts come recommended.

Pasadena and Surroundings

Old Town Bakery and Restaurant
$
every day 7:30am to 10pm, Fri to Sat until midnight
166 W. Colorado Blvd.
at Pasadena Ave.
☎*(626) 792-7943*
This cheerful bakery shop and café, set in a pleasant courtyard, offers an array of light dishes including sandwiches, salads and pastas, as well as pancakes and omelets at breakfast.

All India Café
$-$$
Mon to Sat 11:30am to 10pm, Fri to Sat until 11pm
39 S. Fair Oaks Ave.
near Colorado Ave., Pasadena
☎*(626) 440-0309*
This simple Old Pasadena café, enlivened by Indian tapestries, offers a broad range of Indian dishes, including vegetarian items, tandoori preparations, and several Bombay specialties like lamb frankie (pieces of seasoned lamb wrapped in a soft tortilla-like bread).

Kuala Lumpur
$$
Tue to Fri 11:30am to 2:30pm, Sat to Sun noon to 3:30pm, Tue to Sun 5:30pm to 10pm
69 W. Green St. near Fair Oaks Ave.
☎*(626) 577-5175*
As its name suggests, this bright and pleasantly decorated restaurant offers Malaysian cuisine, showing influences from Thailand, China and India. Items include a variety of noodle dishes as well as aromatic curry items, including vegetarian selections.

Mi Piace
$$-$$$
every day 11:30am to 11:30pm, until 12:30am Fri and Sat night
25 E. Colorado Blvd.
near Fair Oaks Ave., Pasadena
☎*(626) 795-3131*
This popular Italian eatery offers a bright, high-ceilinged interior and a few tables lining the sidewalk. Specialties include a sautéed chicken breast in a garlic and white wine sauce, mushroom capellini, veal *saltimbocca* with prosciutto, and risotto with seafood and ginger.

Twin Palms
$$-$$$
Mon to Sat 11:30am to 2:30pm, every day 5pm to 10:30pm
101 W. Green St. at De Lacey Ave.
☎*(626) 577-2567*
This vast but friendly outdoor restaurant (with a retractable tent for protection against rain; an indoor seating area is also available) is built around two enormous palm trees and includes a bandshell as well as a row of rotisserie spits. The menu focuses on California cuisine, which is to say a blend of Mediterranean, Asian and other influences. Dishes include pan-seared salmon with Asian vegetables, warm lamb salad with couscous and feta, and garlicky grilled chicken. Musical entertainment includes gospel singers during Sunday brunch.

Hollywood

Fred 62
$-$$
every day 24hrs
1854 N. Vermont Ave.
near Franklin Ave., Los Feliz
☎*(323) 667-0062*
This ultra-hip diner, with a lime-green exterior and vinyl booths inside, offers a wide range of comfort foods to a diverse clientele. Some very original sandwiches, as well as burgers, noodles, salads and desserts, provide an intriguing selection. Service tends to be erratic.

Ita-Cho
$-$$
Mon to Sat 6:30pm to 11pm
6775 Santa Monica Blvd.
☎*(323) 871-0236*
Although it looks dingy and unappealing from the outside and not much better inside, the fresh fish and Japanese home-style cooking here have been winning adepts from across L.A. Most dishes are small, allowing diners to sample several items. Specialties include eggplant in ground shrimp, a selection of sashimi (raw fish), tofu in a soy and ginger sauce, and marinated pork.

Atch-Kotch
$-$$
Mon to Sat 11:30am to 10pm
1253 N. Vine St.
☎*(323) 467-5537*
With its black-lacquer decor, this snug Japanese spot offers an interesting variety of sushi, noodle dishes, and other specialties.

Jitlada
$-$$
Tue to Sun 11:30am to 3pm, 5pm to 10pm
5233 W. Sunset Blvd.
☎*(323) 667-9809*
Authentic Thai cuisine and two pleasant dining rooms covered with artwork form an agreeable contrast to the dreary mini-mall exterior. Spring rolls and lemon-grass and seafood soup are among the openers. The main-course meat, seafood and noodle dishes are expertly sauced and seasoned.

Le Petit Bistro
$$
*Mon to Fri 11:30am to 3pm,
every day 5:30pm to 1am*
631 N. La Cienega Blvd.
West Hollywood
☎*(310) 289-9797*
This atmospheric and inexpensive French bistro offers old-fashioned decor and some new and old favourites on the menu, including goat cheese salad and duck confit.

Hugo's
$$
every day 7:30am to 10:30pm
8401 Santa Monica Blvd.
West Hollywood
☎*(323) 654-4088*
This casual spot, with bright and rather plain decor as well as some tables on the sidewalk, offers an extensive selection of breakfasts and a lunch and dinner menu centred around pastas and other Italian dishes. This is augmented by health-food items such as vegetarian burgers.

Yamashiro
$$$
*Sun to Thu 5:30pm to 10pm,
Fri and Sat 5:30pm to 11pm,
bar open until 2am*
1999 N. Sycamore Ave.
in the Hollywood Hills
☎*(323) 466-5125*
Although the food and service are good at this very romantic Japanese restaurant, the real reason to come here is for the extraordinary view over the city below. Finding the way isn't easy: the restaurant is located along a narrow, twisting road up a hill, but it's worth the effort, especially if a window table is available. It is set in a replica of a Japanese palace, with elaborate gardens rounding out the atmosphere. Grilled tuna is a specialty, as are various sushi, sashimi and tempura dishes.

Pinot Hollywood
$$$
*Mon to Fri 11:30am to
2:30pm, every day 6pm to
10:30pm*
1448 N. Gower St.
☎*(323) 461-8800*
Popular with those who work in the middle echelons of the film industry, this sprawling but comfortable mid-Hollywood spot offers a selection of French and American dishes. Specialities include foie gras ravioli, lamb with goat cheese polenta, and chicken with mustard sauce.

Patina
$$$$$
*Sun to Thu 6pm to 9:30pm,
Fri 6pm to 10:30pm, Sat
5:30pm to 10:30pm*
5955 Melrose Ave.
west of Cahuenga Blvd.
☎*(323) 467-2208*
Regarded by some as one of L.A.'s best restaurants, Patina is a warm, elegant and surprisingly low-key spot, noted for the French cooking of Joachim Splichal and his selected chefs. The decor is modern and subdued, the menu varies by season, and most dishes are inventive without going off the deep end.

Westside and
Mid-Wilshire

Gumbo Pot
$
*Mon to Sat 8:30am to
6:30pm, Sun 9am to 5pm*
Farmer's Market, 6333 W. Third St.
near Fairfax Ave.
☎*(323) 933-0358*
This is one of several self-service food counters at the bustling Farmer's Market in the Fairfax district. As its name suggests, hearty chicken, sausage and shrimp gumbo is a specialty, along with other Louisiana

items, including sandwiches, sweet-potato salad and beignets (doughnuts).

Asahi Ramen
$
*Fri to Wed 11:30am to 9pm
closed Thu*
2027 Sawatelle Blvd., West L.A.
☎*(310) 479-2231*
This is a simple and delightful Japanese noodle house. Various noodle dishes and dumplings dominate the short menu.

Nam Kang
$$
every day 11:30am to 9:30pm
3055 W. Seventh St.
near Vermont Ave., Koreatown
☎*(323) 380-6606*
The bland decor is not much to brag about, but the authentic Korean dishes, in particular some of the small side dishes make it worth the trip. Savoury mixtures of meat, vegetables and rice, accompanied by spicy *jimchee* (marinated cabbage) are among the items available. Fish and seafood dishes also appear on the menu.

El Cholo
$$
*Mon to Thu 11am to 10pm,
Fri and Sat 11am to 11pm,
Sun 11am to 9pm*
1121 S. Western Ave.
near Olympic Blvd.
☎*(323) 734-2773*
Open since 1927, this is one of the oldest Mexican restaurants outside Mexico. Located in a neighbourhood that is now largely Korean, this warm and cozy spot continues to appeal to a broad cross-section of L.A. society. The menu is vast and authentic, although the seasoning is toned down to appeal to American tastes.

Angeli Caffe
$$
Mon to Thu noon to 10:30pm, Fri and Sat noon to 11pm, Sun 5pm to 10pm
7274 Melrose Ave.
between La Brea and Fairfax
☎(323) 936-9086
Part of the attraction here is the original architecture, with steel beams and simple furniture. The menu centres around pizzas, pastas, salads and grilled chicken. Fish soup is a specialty.

Authentic Café
$$
Mon to Thu 11am to 10pm, Fri 11am to midnight, Sat 8:30am to midnight, Sun 8:30am to 10pm
7605 Beverly Blvd. east of Fairfax
☎(323) 939-4626
This noisy and brightly decorated spot specializes in U.S. southwestern cuisine. Specialties include wood-grilled chicken and variations on tacos. A number of vegetarian items are available.

Mexica
$$
Mon to Fri noon to 2:30pm, every day 5pm to 10pm, Fri and Sat until 11pm
7313 Beverly Blvd.
three blocks west of La Brea
☎(323) 933-7385
This spacious, artsy spot offers a version of nouvelle Mexican cuisine along with regional dishes such as *cochinita pibil* (Yucatan-style roast pork) and *mole poblano* (chicken with bitter, spicy chocolate sauce).

Bombay Café
$$
Tue to Thu 11:30am to 10pm, Fri 5pm to 11pm, Sat 4pm to 11pm, Sun 4pm to 10pm
12113 Santa Monica Blvd. near Bundy Dr., West L.A.
☎(310) 820-2070
Set in an unpromising location upstairs in one of L.A.'s countless mini-malls, this spot has built a reputation for creative Indian cuisine, with a constantly changing menu that includes excellent curries and tandoori items, as well as some interesting appetizers.

Maui Beach Café
$$
every day 11:30am to midnight, Fri and Sat until 1am
1019 Westwood Blvd., Westwood
☎(310) 209-0494
Popular with students from nearby UCLA and with assorted members of the Westwood crowd, this brassy and buoyant spot offers Hawaiian cuisine in its current manifestation as a blend of Asian and American dishes, running the gamut from sashimi to steak.

Le Colonial
$$-$$$
Mon to Fri 11:30am to 2:30pm, Sun to Thu 5:30pm to 11pm, Fri and Sat 5:30pm to midnight
8783 Beverly Blvd. near La Cienega
West Hollywood
☎(310) 289-0660
This charming spot aims to recreate the atmosphere of Vietnam during the French colonial period, with plenty of rattan, tiled floors, and old black-and-white photos of pre-war Vietnam. The menu offers a sophisticated range of Vietnamese dishes with a few French items or influences thrown in.

Louis XIV
$$-$$$
Mon to Sat 6pm to midnight
606 N. La Brea Ave. at Melrose
☎(323) 934-5102
Romantic, rustic decor provide an introduction to this simple, relaxed French bistro where typical menu choices include steak and *frites* (fries) or grilled salmon.

Chianti Cucina
$$-$$$
Mon to Thu 11:30am to 11:30pm, Fri and Sat 11:30am to midnight, Sun 4pm to 11pm
7383 Melrose Ave.
☎(323) 653-8333
This small, bright Italian spot is as good a place as any for a simple pasta dish or something a bit more elaborate. Specialties include beef carpaccio, linguine with seafood, and a grilled vegetable platter with polenta.

Mimosa
$$$
Mon to Sat 11:30am to 3pm and 5:30pm to 11pm, Fri and Sat until midnight
8009 Beverly Blvd. west of Fairfax
☎(323) 655-8895
This traditionally decorated bistro offers an authentic French menu that includes *cassoulet* (a bean stew with various meats) with duck confit, steamed mussels and roast pork.

La Cachette
$$$$
Mon to Fri 11:30am to 2:30pm, Mon to Thu 6pm to 10:30pm, Fri and Sat 5:30pm to 11pm, Sun 5:30pm to 9:30pm
10506 Santa Monica Blvd., West L.A.
☎(310) 470-4992
This is one of the top French restaurants in L.A., with a light California touch. Ugly on the outside, it is all flowers, paintings and light on the inside, with banquette seating. Staff say some of the traditional French classics such as roast duck and *cassoulet* are prepared here in lower-fat versions. The menu ranges broadly and includes foie gras, *bouillabaisse* (Marseille-style fish soup), and *tarte tatin* (caramelized apple pie).

Santa Monica, Venice and Surroundings

Jody Maroni's Sausage Kingdom
$
every day 9am to 6pm
2011 Ocean Front Walk
Venice Beach
☎*(310) 822-5639*
This is one of several snack stands along the Venice Beach boardwalk, but it stands out for the originality of its menu, consisting entirely of sausages served on crispy rolls with selections like orange-garlic-cumin chicken and duck sausage, Bombay bangers (made with curried lamb) and Louisiana *boudin* hot links. Jody Maroni's is expanding into a chain, though this outlet is where it all began. Outdoor picnic-style seating nearby.

Polly's Pies
$
Mon to Thu 6:30am to 11pm, Fri 6:30am to midnight, Sat 7am to midnight, Sun 7am to 11pm
501 Wilshire at Fifth St.
Santa Monica
☎*(310) 394-9721*
This traditional American diner is not the least bit trendy, unless the attached outdoor terrace qualifies. Nonetheless, it offers large, wholesome breakfasts and, later in the day, sandwiches, burgers, fried or grilled chicken, salads and, as the name suggests, a wide variety of pies.

🌿 Real Food Daily
$-$$
Mon to Sat 11:30am to 10pm
514 Santa Monica Blvd.
near Fifth St., Santa Monica
☎*(310) 451-7544*
This has to rank as one of the top vegetarian restaurants in California. The menu is strictly vegan, with no dairy or egg products used (for example,

the Parmesan-style dressing on the Caesar salad is soy-based), and great care is taken to provide good nutritional balance. The main menu selections offer various combinations of beans, grains and vegetables.

Reel Inn
$-$$
Sun to Thu 11am to 10pm, Fri to Sat 11am to 11pm
1220 Third St. near Wilshire
☎*(310) 395-5538*
Located along the Third Street Promenade, this big barn of a place has seating at long benches and a small outdoor terrace. On offer are a very substantial variety of fresh fish and seafood, including some Mexican-accented items.

Beach Front Café
$-$$
every day 6:30am to 6pm
17th Ave. at Speedway, Venice Beach
☎*(310) 399-6558*
This casual spot, located half a block from the Muscle Beach area of Venice Beach, offers big portions and what it bills as bodybuilder specials. The menu includes simple items such as pork chops, grilled fish and fried noodles, along with salads and other vegetarian items.

The Terrace
$-$$
Mon to Fri 11am to 11pm, Sat and Sun 9am to 11pm, bar open later
7 Washington Blvd.
at Ocean Front Walk
☎*(310) 578-1530*
Bordering the south end of Venice Beach, this casual

spot has a bright, pleasant dining room and a small terrace outside. The menu focuses on sandwiches, pizza, pasta and salads but also contains a number of interesting seafood appetizers.

Neptune's Net
$-$$
Mon to Thu 9am to 8pm, Fri and Sat 9am to 9pm, Sun 9am to 8:30pm
42505 Pacific Coast Hwy., Malibu
☎*(310) 457-3095*
Located across the highway from the beach at the western edge of Malibu not far from the border of Ventura County, this extremely casual self-service shack-like establishment makes up in value what it lacks in finesse. Clam chowder is a favourite. Steamed fresh seafood is remarkably inexpensive.

Gate of India
$-$$
every day 11:30am to 11pm
115 Santa Monica Blvd.
near Ocean Ave., Santa Monica
☎*(310) 656-1664*
This very welcoming spot is tastefully decorated with Indian fabrics and art and features a copious lunch buffet until 3pm. The menu items include a broad range of curries, as well as tandoori dishes.

Fritto Misto
$$
Mon to Thu 11:30am to 10pm, Fri and Sat 11:30am to 10:30pm, Sun 5pm to 9:30pm
601 Colorado Ave. at Sixth St.
Santa Monica
☎*(310) 458-2829*
This simple Italian restaurant offers basic decor, a friendly atmosphere, and a menu that ranges from a mix-and-match selection of pastas and sauces to more interesting meat or seafood items, including the restaurant's namesake dish prepared here with shrimp, calamari and vegetables.

Los Angeles

Crocodile Café
$$
*Sun to Thu 11am to 10pm,
Fri and Sat 11am to 11pm*
101 Santa Monica Blvd.
at Ocean Ave., Santa Monica
☎*(310) 394-4783*
This casual yet comfortable spot offers the archetypal California eating experience, with touches of Asia, Mexico, New Mexico and Italy. The menu ranges from pizzas (from a wood-burning oven) to chilis to burgers to moo shu chicken calzone and tostada salad with corn, black beans and chicken. Somehow, it seems to work.

Venice Whaler Bar and Grill
$$-$$$
every day 11am to 2am
10 Washington Blvd.
at Ocean Front Walk
☎*(310) 821-8737*
With a breezy dining room overlooking the southern end of Venice Beach, this attractive spot offers a varied menu centring around sandwiches, pizzas, salads and meat dishes but also including more elaborate items such as shrimp Alfredo and fresh albacore tuna with pear sauce.

Mercedes Grill
$$-$$$
Mon to Thu 7:30am to 10:30pm, Fri and Sat 8:30am to 11:30pm, Sun 8:30am to 9:30pm
14 Washington Blvd.
near Ocean Front Walk
☎*(310) 827-6209*
Located near the southern end of Venice Beach, this restaurant bills itself as Cuban-Californian. The dining room is bright and open, with big skylights. The menu offers an imaginative selection of starters and salads, as well as several vegetarian dishes. Feature items include cilantro papaya chicken, shrimp Florentine enchiladas and mango-almond halibut. Full breakfast menu also available.

Restaurant Hama
$$-$$$
Mon to Fri 11:30am to 2:30pm, Mon to Thu 6pm to 11pm, Fri and Sat 6pm to 11:30pm
213 Windward Ave., Venice Beach
☎*(310) 396-8783*
Facing the small traffic circle across from the Venice Beach post office, this friendly, casual spot specializes in sushi. Seating is in two attractive rooms with tables and a long sushi bar. The sushi list changes daily. The menu also includes tempura and teriyaki items.

72 Market Street
$$$-$$$$
Mon to Fri 11:30am to 3pm, Mon to Thu 6pm to 10pm, Fri and Sat 6pm to 11pm
72 Market St., Venice Beach
☎*(310) 392-8720*
This is one of the more elegant spots at Venice Beach, but it still manages to maintain a casual air, with an attractive dining room and above-average background music. Appetizers include selections of sushi and oysters, as well as other items like lobster cakes. Main courses include wild mushroom risotto, pan-roasted lamb loin and jerk chicken.

JiRaffe
$$$-$$$$
Tue to Fri noon to 2pm and 6pm to 11pm, Sat 5:30pm to 11pm, Sun 5:30pm to 9pm
502 Santa Monica Blvd. at Fifth St.
Santa Monica
☎*(310) 917-6671*
Decorated like a French bistro and offering a blend of traditional French and new American cooking, this spot appears to have developed a large and loyal clientele, meaning it can be noisy and cramped, but local food critics give it high marks. The menu changes frequently according to season and the quality of fresh ingredients. Recent selections have included spiced whitefish with ginger-carrot sauce and rabbit with polenta gnocchi and baked tomatoes.

Airport Area and South Bay

The Kettle
$-$$
every day 24hrs
1138 Highland Ave.
Manhattan Beach
☎*(310) 545-8511*
This friendly spot carries the American coffee shop concept to a new level, with a good assortment of sandwiches, salads and burgers served in a nondescript indoor dining room and a much more appealing outdoor terrace.

Reed's
$$-$$$
Mon to Fri 11:30am to 2:30pm, Mon to Sat 5:30pm to 10:30pm
2640 N. Sepulveda Blvd.
Manhattan Beach
☎*(310) 546-3299*
Despite its shopping mall location, this spot is elegant inside, with high windows and pale wooden walls. The menu changes regularly and recently offered newish American dishes such as tuna *tartare*, smoked salmon ravioli and an interesting take on chicken pot pie.

Kincaid's Bay House
$$$-$$$$
Mon to Thu 11am to 10pm, Fri and Sat 11:30am to 11pm, Sun 10am to 10pm
500 Fisherman's Wharf
at Harbor Dr., Redondo Beach
☎*(310) 318-6080*
The sedate atmosphere and soothing ocean views at this classy spot along the rejuvenated Redondo

Beach pier are a good introduction to the nouveau Hawaiian-influenced menu, which includes items like marinated pork brochettes grilled over apple wood, crab-and-shrimp hash with sherry cream sauce, and simpler fresh fish dishes.

Long Beach and Surroundings

Dragon House Restaurant
$-$$
every day 11am to 1am
101 Alamitos Ave. at First St.
Long Beach
☎*(562) 437-3303*
This great cavernous place, with a brighter area facing the street, offers a wide variety of Chinese and Thai dishes. Excellent value.

Shenandoah Café
$$-$$$
every day 5pm to 9pm or later (hours vary), Sun brunch 10am to 2pm
4722 E. Second St., Long Beach
☎*(562) 434-3469*
Decorated New Orleans style, this friendly spot offers Louisiana specialties such as blackened fish, shrimp in beer batter, and specially seasoned steaks.

Entertainment

As might be expected in the home of the entertainment industry, Los Angeles is a leading centre for popular music as well as for various alternative styles ranging from blues to techno. The city has an extremely lively club scene that caters to a wide variety of tastes. Some clubs seem to be perennial favourites, while others move in and out of trendy

acceptance with bewildering speed. We hesitate to venture opinions as to what's hot at any given moment, and thus provide only general guidance here, along with suggestions (two paragraphs below) as to where to look for more detailed and up-to-the-minute information. In addition to its unique local scene, including live theatre and a number of comedy clubs, L.A. also offers more run-of-the-mill entertainment. The area is dotted with multi-screen cinema complexes showing recent Hollywood releases as well as a few repertory or art cinemas. (Again, the sources indicated below provide detailed listings.) Spectator sports provide an additional option for an evening (or afternoon) outing.

Contrary to the image it sometimes conveys, Los Angeles is also home to what some would consider more serious forms of cultural endeavour, including live theatre, classical music, jazz, and ballet or modern dance. Although these tend to attract less attention than popular music and some of its newer variants, they do exist in abundance.

Helpful sources of information on the L.A. entertainment scene include the *Los Angeles Times* daily newspaper, which publishes movie and cultural listings in its Calendar section. Comprehensive listings for the coming week appear in its Sunday edition and for the following weekend in its Thursday edition. Other excellent sources of listings and suggestions are two weekly papers, the *L.A. Weekly* and the slimmer but more informative *New Times*. Both are distributed

free from racks near the entrances to various stores, restaurants and public buildings, as well as from some street boxes. For visitors with Internet access, useful sources of entertainment information include the L.A. Times' www.calendarlive.com and the rival www.at-la.com.

In Los Angeles, as elsewhere in California, smoking is allowed only in outdoor areas at bars and clubs, and last call for alcohol is at 2am. Bars with live entertainment often have a cover charge, which may vary according to the day of week, with higher prices on weekends. As in most cities, ticket prices for movies are often lower in the afternoon than in the evening.

Downtown Los Angeles

Many downtown L.A. streets become nearly deserted by early evening, creating an almost eerie atmosphere that seems anything but conducive to enjoyable night life. Even so, the variety of things to do is quite surprising, from spectator sports to classical concerts to theatre.

Perhaps a bit surprisingly for a city as decentralized as Los Angeles, the major **professional sport** venues are concentrated near the downtown area. **Dodger Stadium**, set atop a panoramic but isolated ravine about 1.5km (1mi) north of downtown L.A., is one of the great temples of major league **baseball** and home to the National League's legendary Dodgers since soon after the team's controversial move from Brooklyn in 1957. More than four decades

Los Angeles

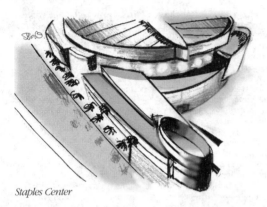

Staples Center

after its construction, this magnificent 56,000-seat open-air stadium is still regarded as one of the finest baseball venues in the land. The six-month regular season opens in early April. At the time of writing, no game here had ever been postponed because of rain, a great tribute to Southern California's climate. (The Los Angeles area's other major league baseball team, the Angels of the American League, play at Anaheim Stadium in Orange County.) Dodger Stadium is easy to reach by car and is surrounded by many acres of free parking. (In a less flattering reflection of Southern California, it's not served by public transit. The nearest bus stop is at the corner of Sunset Boulevard and Elysian Park Avenue, about a 10min walk from the stadium. Taxis are usually available after each game directly behind the centre field wall.) Tickets are easy to obtain for most games *(information: ☎323-224-1400, www.dodgers.com).*

Two professional **basketball** teams (the Lakers and Clippers) and one professional **hockey** team (the Kings) share the gleaming new 19,300-seat indoor

Staples Center *(Figueroa St. at 11th St., adjacent to the Convention Center)*. Named after an office-supply retailer that paid a sponsorship fee, the Staples Center opened in 1999. The regular season in both the National Basketball Association and the National Hockey League begins in early October and runs until April, followed by interminable playoff series. For schedule and ticket information, contact the Lakers *(☎213-480-3232, www.nba.com/lakers),* the Clippers *(☎213-742-7555, www.nba.com/clippers),* or the Kings *☎888-546-4752, www.lakings.com).*

The L.A. area is home to vast numbers of football fans, but for some strange reason its two National Football League teams both departed in 1995 and nobody rushed in to fill the vacuum. That leaves **college football**, which has a very wide following. The top venue is the venerable **Los Angeles Coliseum** in Exposition Park, home to the University of Southern California Bruins and their heated rivalry with the Trojans of the University of California at Los Angeles (UCLA).

The Music Center *(Grand Ave. between First and Temple sts., across from the Civic Center)* is L.A.'s most important venue for classical music as well as other types of musical performance and theatre. This multi-hall complex comprises the **Dorothy Chandler Pavilion**, home to the Los Angeles Philharmonic *(☎213-850-2000, www.laphil.org),* along with the Ahmanson Theater and the more intimate Mark Tapper Forum, each the scene of numerous theatrical productions. The **Japan Cultural Arts Center** *(244 S. San Pedro St. between Second and Third sts., Little Tokyo, ☎213-628-2725)* hosts both Japanese and non-Japanese ensembles that include children's theatre groups, dance troupes and the Los Angeles Chamber Orchestra.

For jazz and lighter music, several of the larger hotels offer live bands most evenings, though audiences tend mostly to be hotel guests. One long-surviving independent club downtown is **Al's Bar** *(305 S. Hewitt St. at Third St., two blocks east of Alameda, ☎213-625-9703)* in a somewhat grungy neighbourhood favoured by artists. This dark, graffiti-covered spot attracts bands (and audiences) that seem to have a knack for zeroing in on the next trend.

Pasadena

The **Pasadena Playhouse** *(39 S. El Molino Ave. near Green St., ☎626-356-7529),* built in 1924 and refurbished in the 1980s, is one of California's top theatrical venues. Registered as a national landmark, it has also built a reputation for the high quality of its productions. Several multi-screen **cine-**

mas are clustered along Colorado Boulevard in Old Pasadena, with restaurants close by, making this a favoured area for an evening out.

Hollywood and Surroundings

Hollywood is synonymous with entertainment and it certainly lives up to its reputation. Several of the major **film studios** offer tours (see box in the "Exploring" section), and some of their wares can be seen at historical venues that are landmarks in themselves. These include Mann's Chinese Theater and the Egyptian Theater along Hollywood Boulevard (see p 142), where current films can be seen amid a lavish decor that evokes the splendour of Hollywood's golden era. In a rather different style, Universal City Walk in North Hollywood is the setting for a gigantic 18-screen cinema and entertainment complex.

Needless to say, Hollywood is much more than cinema. Local actors also work in **live theatre**. The newly refurbished Pantages Theater *(6233 Hollywood Ave. near Vine St., ☎323-468-1770)* is a massive Art Deco classic that's often used to stage Broadway-style musicals. A stretch of Santa Monica Boulevard running west from Vine Street is home to several smaller theatres, including the Actor's Gang Theater *(6201 Santa Monica Blvd. near Vine St., ☎323-465-0566)* and the Hudson Avenue Theater *(6539 Santa Monica Blvd. near Wilcox Ave., ☎323-856-7012)*, which is divided into several small venues. The James A. Doolittle

Theater *(1615 Vine St. between Hollywood and Sunset Blvds., ☎323-462-6666)*, operated by UCLA, has showcased several top productions. Several other theaters are located in West Hollywood and in the Los Feliz area.

The **Hollywood Bowl** *(2301 N. Highland Ave., off the Hollywood Freeway, ☎323-850-2000, www.hollywoodbowl. org)* is a giant outdoor amphitheatre nestled in a canyon in the Hollywood Hills. Built in the early 1920s, it remains a popular venue for classical, jazz or popular concerts and serves as the summer home of the Los Angeles Philharmonic. The grounds outside the amphitheatre are ideal for a pre-concert picnic, a fine local tradition.

The ever-changing **club scene** in Hollywood remains very active, both in central Hollywood and outlying areas, with offerings ranging from traditional jazz in a dinner club setting to underground dance rhythms in what look like abandoned garages. West Hollywood has become known for its **comedy clubs**, including the Comedy Store *(8433 Sunset Blvd., ☎323-656-6225, www.comedystore.com)*, featuring a range of stand-up comics, and the Groundling Theater *(7307 Melrose Ave., ☎323-934-9700)*, noted for improvisation and biting satire.

Westside and Mid-Wilshire

Westwood Village, in particular a short stretch of Westwood Boulevard near Wilshire Boulevard a few short blocks south of the UCLA campus, is a popu-

lar evening hangout among a younger crowd, with numerous multi-screen **cinemas**, a multitude of fast-food restaurants (along with a few sit-down places) and a generally boisterous atmosphere. The **Geffen Playhouse** *(10886 Le Comte Ave. near Westwood Blvd., Westwood Village, ☎310-208-6500)*, noted for excellent acoustics and sight lines, is a top theatrical venue. It's run by UCLA, although it's not on the campus.

Santa Monica and Surroundings

The car-free **Third Street Promenade** in downtown Santa Monica is one of the L.A. area's liveliest and most pleasant places to be after work hours, with its numerous **cinemas**, restaurants, cafés, bookshops and other establishments that attract large and generally well-behaved crowds late into the evening. Street entertainers add to the atmosphere and many people come just for a stroll. A couple of kilometres to the south, the boardwalk at **Venice Beach** remains spirited after dark, retaining its younger, funkier ambiance. A selection of casual restaurants, bars and cafés keep the area around Windward Avenue near the beach hopping well into the night.

The tiny **Santa Monica Playhouse** *(1211 Fourth St. at Wilshire Blvd., ☎310-394-9779)* offers varied programs and a cozy atmosphere. Several small **clubs** nearby (check the newspaper listings) help round out the Santa Monica night life scene.

Los Angeles

South Bay

Hermosa Beach's oceanfront walk and the adjacent Pier Plaza have become known for a lively bar scene that draws a young and sometimes rowdy crowd, reaching a crescendo on summer weekends. The Fishermen's Wharf area of Redondo Beach provides an alternative; a couple of the bars here provide live music on weekends.

The **Redondo Beach Performing Arts Center** *(1935 Manhattan Beach Blvd., Redondo Beach, ☎310-372-4477)* is the South Bay area's major venue for theatrical and musical presentations.

Long Beach

On Pine Avenue near Broadway in downtown Long Beach lies the epicentre of what passes for evening activity in this very sedate community. Pine Avenue has a restaurant row with establishments catering to a variety of tastes, interspersed with a few bars and cafés.

Shopping

Downtown Los Angeles

Like almost every other aspect of life in Los Angeles, shopping follows the dictates of a very decentralized geography, and the often neglected downtown area is not necessarily where the action is, especially now that the grand old depart-

ment stores are all gone. The big suburban malls, as well as some of the tonier shopping streets in districts like Beverly Hills and Hollywood, account for larger shares of consumer spending, particularly for trendy or fashionable items. But even if downtown L.A. is not the region's top shopping destination, it does offer quirky and original experiences that should not be neglected, especially by bargain-hunters and seekers of the exotic.

A shopping tour could begin in the southeast corner of downtown L.A., in the extensive **garment district**, whose promoters call it the **Fashion District**, though the emphasis is more on everyday, down-to-earth items than on pricier fashions. Hundreds of shops—some run independently, others operated as outlets for nearby factories—offer a broad range of name-brand and generic goods, often at substantial savings compared to the big chain stores.

The garment district covers much of an often grimy area seven blocks wide and eight blocks long, bound by Broadway Avenue on the west, Seventh Street on the north, Wall Street on the east, and Pico Boulevard on the south. What you find here is miles removed from your average shopping mall environment and light years distant from the sunny Southern California stereotypes. Many shops operate on a cash-and-carry basis, with no credit cards accepted and no returns or exchanges. Some specialize in overruns or in goods that are slightly flawed—it's important to pay attention. Dressing rooms are often rudimentary or nonexis-

tent. And haggling over price may sometimes be part of the experience, particularly in the outdoor bazaar known as Santee Alley near Olympic Boulevard and 12th Street. Elsewhere, certain establishments cater exclusively to the wholesale trade.

For the less adventurous, a good place to look for women's clothing is the eight-storey Cooper Building at the corner of Ninth and Los Angeles streets. This former industrial building is filled with outlet shops for small manufacturers, with some shops selling brand-name items. For men's clothing, there is a cluster of shops along Los Angeles Street between Seventh and Ninth. Wall Street offers selections of fabrics as well as extra-size and children's clothing.

Another specialized shopping area downtown is the **jewellery district**, centred around Hill Street between Sixth and Seventh streets. Many dozens of small establishments offer a vast selection of jewellery and watches at often cut-rate prices, some produced locally and others imported from Asia. Prices and quality tend to be lower to middle range. Some shops face the street directly, but many others are hidden away along indoor passageways at several buildings in the immediate area. Signage at the entrances makes these buildings easy to spot.

Broadway lies at the heart of downtown L.A's historic shopping district. Its character has changed immensely over the decades, and the ornate stone facades of many buildings pay homage to an earlier, more prosperous era. Today, the street has

Where to Shop for Books and Music

Some L.A. residents recently arrived from New York or Boston have been known to complain that the city has a paucity of serious bookshops for a place its size, but visiting bibliophiles should have little trouble finding something to whet their appetites.

One of the better parts of town to look for books is the Third Street Promenade in Santa Monica which, besides large outlets of national chains **Borders** and **Barnes & Noble**, has several well-stocked independent bookshops, among them the **Midnight Special Bookstore**, with many authors readings on site and an obvious sense of political commitment, and **Hennessy & Ingalls**,

specializing in books on art, design and architecture. All are just a couple of blocks apart.

Two of the most noted independent bookshops in L.A. are **Book Soup** *(8818 W. Sunset Blvd., West Hollywood)* and **Dutton's Brentwood Books** *(11975 San Vicente Blvd. in Brentwood, west of Montana Ave.)*. Both have very extensive collections and knowledgeable staff.

For travel guidebooks and maps, places to look include **Thomas Bros. Books and Maps** downtown *(521 W. Sixth St. near Grand Ave.)* and **Traveler's Bookcase** on the west side *(8375 W. Third St. near La Cienega)*. The latter also offers a selection of

travel narratives. Two of the biggest second-hand bookshops, both with immense selections, are **Acres of Books** in Long Beach *(240 Long Beach Blvd.)* and **Book City** in Hollywood *(6627 Hollywood Blvd.)*.

For music, the two biggest mainstream CD shops are located a flew blocks apart on the Sunset Strip, **Tower Records** *(8801 W. Sunset Blvd.)* and the **Virgin Megastore** *(8000 W. Sunset Blvd.)*. **Rhino Record** *(1720 Westwood Blvd., north of Santa Monica Blvd.)* is something of a local institution and is noted for its selection of independent music. It also has a second-hand section.

recovered much of its former vitality, although the dominant language is Spanish rather than English. Many of the businesses cater to L.A.'s large Mexican and Central American immigrant communities, particularly along an extremely vibrant stretch between Third and Ninth streets. This is a good place to look for low-end electronic goods, assorted luggage, and cheaper items of clothing and footwear. The **Grand Central Market** (see p 85), bordering Broadway

between Third and Fourth streets, offers food in various forms, ranging from bulk produce to freshly cut meat to cheap and satisfying sit-down or take-out meals.

Downtown L.A. also offers a range of ethnic shopping experiences that straddle the divide between the authentic and the touristy. **Olvera Street**, located at the northern edge of the El Pueblo de Los Angeles historic district between the Civic Center and Union Station, is a block-long pedestrian-only street lined

with **Mexican** handicraft stalls and restaurants. Interesting selections of leather items, textiles, clothing, jewellery, paintings and carvings are available. **Little Tokyo** boasts dozens of shops, with the biggest concentration found in the **Japanese Village Plaza** covering part of the block bound by First Street, San Pedro Street, Second Street and Central Avenue. Items include Japanese crafts, toys and clothing. **Chinatown**, north of the Civic Center, is dotted with shops selling

Los Angeles

items ranging from heavy porcelain planters to light silk scarves. There are also many food shops.

More recent additions to the shopping scene, located toward the western edge of the downtown area, include the attractive open-air **Seventh Market Place**, Seventh Street at Figueroa Street, built around a distinctive three-storey circular atrium, with two department stores among its approximately 50 retail establishments. **Macy's Plaza**, a block away at Seventh Street and Flower Street, contains a branch of the namesake department store chain and about 30 other shops. These outlets, however, hardly compare in scale to the grand downtown department stores they replaced.

Pasadena

Old Pasadena has been revived and gentrified. A pleasant area for strolling and shopping, it's characterized by an eclectic mix of shops selling books, home furnishings, crafts, clothing, and a wide range of other items. Many are original one-of-a-kind shops, although some of the national chains have begun to intrude. The main shopping streets are Colorado Boulevard over a seven-block stretch between Pasadena Avenue and Los Robles Avenue, parallel portions of Green Street one block south, and a four-block section of South Lake Avenue running south from Colorado Boulevard, portions of which are lined with London-style arcades.

The **Rose Bowl Flea Market** is held the second Sunday of each month at the name-sake football stadium (*$6 after 9am, $10-$15 before 9am; 6am to 3pm, 991 Rosemont Ave., Pasadena, ☎323-560-7469*) which bills itself as the biggest flea market in the U.S., with more than 1,500 vendors offering antique furnishings, clothing, assorted knick-knacks and more. The **Pasadena Antique Mall** (*free, Mon 10am to 5pm Tue to Sun 10am to 9pm, 35 S. Raymond St. between Colorado Blvd. and Green St., ☎626-304-9886*) has about 50 exhibitors offering a wide range of antiques.

Hollywood and Surroundings

Hollywood Boulevard, the central artery in a district synonymous with the film industry, is going through a difficult period of revival. Still, amid the garishness and tackiness that have come to characterize parts of the area are several first-rate shops offering posters, books, scripts, videos, tasteful souvenirs and assorted memorabilia. The stretch between Gower Street and La Brea Avenue is the main shopping area.

Melrose Avenue between Fairfax and La Brea Avenues has developed a reputation for cutting-edge fashion. The street is lined with hundreds of boutiques and restaurants appealing to a moneyed crowd but also to people with an eye for some of the hipper trends in clothing and jewellery. It's also fun just for a stroll.

The **Los Felix-Silver Lake** area at the eastern edge of Hollywood has emerged as a leading centre of Bohemian life, with numerous cafés, nightclubs and funky shops scattered over a vast area. Some shops are clustered in smaller areas, in particular along Vermont Avenue between Hollywood Boulevard and Franklin Avenue and nearby along Sunset Avenue between Vermont and Hillhurst avenues. This is where to look for vintage clothing, trendy modern clothing, strange items of furniture and household accessories (as an example, a store named Plastica, 4685 Hollywood Boulevard east of Vermont Avenue, focuses on plastic objects from the 1950s), and music shops appealing to specialized tastes in CDs and vinyl.

The **Sunset Strip** in West Hollywood has achieved fame for the eccentric characters of some of its denizens and commercial establishments, but this long stretch of Sunset Avenue between La Cienega Boulevard and Doheny Drive is also home to the two largest mainstream record shops in L.A., Tower Records (*8801 W. Sunset Blvd.*) and Virgin Megastore (*8000 W. Sunset Blvd.*). A varied selection of shops offer clothing, jewellery, books, stage props and diverse other items.

On a completely different note, **Universal City Walk** in North Hollywood, adjacent to the Universal Studios theme park, is a sanitized recreation of a traditional shopping street for people who want to escape from the modern mall environment without exposing themselves to some of the harsher realities of urban life. Nonetheless, among its several dozen shops are a few selling original Native American crafts, antique toys, ecologically sensitive gifts and science fiction memorabilia.

Westside and Mid-Wilshire

Rodeo Drive in Beverly Hills is one of the best known and most elegant shopping streets in the United States. Many of the famous names—Tiffany, Louis Vuitton, Giorgio, Hermès, Gucci, Ralph Lauren—along with others that are less famous but no less classy are clustered along a short three-block stretch between Wilshire and Santa Monica Boulevards. The street runs through the heart of what has become known as the **Beverly Hills Golden Triangle**, bound by the above two boulevards and Crescent Drive, with Beverly Hills City Hall at its apex. This small triangular area forms a shopping district for the seriously wealthy and the seriously pretentious, but also for ordinary folk out on a splurge.

Beverly Hills is flanked by two major malls located outside its municipal limits. The **Century City Shopping Center** *(10250 Santa Monica Blvd. in Century City just west of Beverly Hills)* is a generally up-scale mall open to the outdoors, with two department stores and a multi-screen cinema complex. The **Beverly Center** *(Beverly Blvd. and La Cienega Ave., a short distance east of Beverly Hills)* is a high-end, multi-storey mall that also includes two department stores and a multi-screen cinema complex as well as a food court. With about 160 stores, it differs from most other L.A.-area malls with its vertical structure and multiple layers of indoor parking.

A little further east, at Fairfax Avenue and Third Street, is the partly open-air **Farmers Market** with numerous stalls selling fresh produce, meat, seafood or other unprepared items and other stalls selling prepared dishes or various gift items.

Santa Monica and Venice

Santa Monica's **Third Street Promenade** is one of North America's most successful pedestrian-only shopping streets. It succeeds because it contains a mixture of businesses that include many restaurants, cafés, cinemas, bookshops, music stores and other establishments that draw large crowds until late in the evening. It also has many clothing stores. Covering three long blocks from Broadway to Wilshire Boulevard, the Third Street Promenade is designed with small kiosks, benches and other installations that ease pedestrian movement without creating feelings of agoraphobia. Large directories at each corner can help shoppers find their way. Musicians and other street performers contribute to the lively atmosphere. This is justifiably one of the most popular streets in California. At its southern end is the stylish Santa Monica Place indoor shopping mall.

Another popular shopping street in Santa Monica is **Montana Avenue**, where a 10-block stretch from Seventh to 17th streets is home to many original boutiques offering interesting selections of home furnishings, as well as clothing, jewellery, items for children and other merchandise. A long section of **Main Street**, stretching from Pacific Street in Santa Monica to Rose Avenue in Venice, is sprinkled with art galleries, funky boutiques, small cafés and restaurants, antique shops and stores selling beach supplies ranging from surfboards to swimsuits.

Ocean Front Walk, running alongside Venice Beach, gives new meaning to "hip." If you ever need tie-dyed T-shirts, weird sunglasses, leather bikinis, or almost any sort of personal ornament that tickles your sense of the outrageous, this is where to come, especially on weekends.

South Bay

Hermosa Beach Pier Strand, along Pier Avenue between Hermosa Avenue and the pier in Hermosa Beach, has been spruced up and converted to an attractive palm-lined walkway with shops and restaurants. Although serious shoppers may not find the selection of fashions and other items especially interesting, the setting is distinctive.

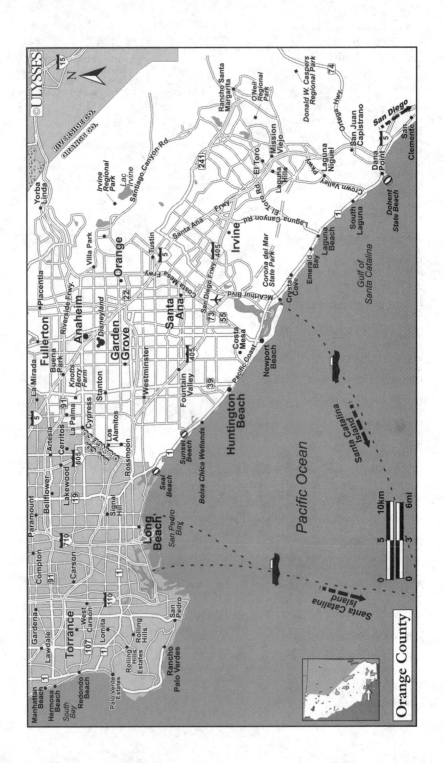

Orange County

Orange County

The pleasures of Orange County have changed over the years.

Early Spanish explorers and missionaries were the first to set foot on this untamed land, finding the Native Americans thriving in a near-perfect climate and on bountiful soil. A series of missions were erected and slowly spread along the California coast. The land was divided by the King of Spain into vast *ranchos*, and then divided again when California became a state.

The gold rush brought a flood of immigrants to the state, many of whom settled in what is known today as Orange County. Despite this population explosion, Orange County continued to serve as an agricultural community well into the middle of the 20th century, supplying wine, fruit and vegetables to the burgeoning metropolis of Los Angeles.

In the middle of the 20th century, several things were happening at once—Orange County was becoming increasingly important as an area of commerce, young G.I.'s were returning from the war, and a man named Walt Disney had a dream. Over the past half-century,

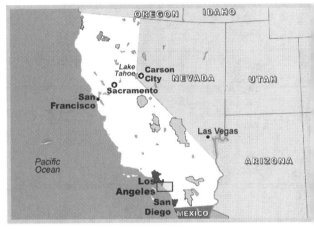

Orange County has reinvented itself as the land of fun and sun. Three of the most popular tourist attractions in the state are here: Disneyland, Knott's Berry Farm and Mission San Juan Capistrano. The unique personalities of its 32 cities offer diverse cultural attractions just waiting to be explored, and there are 42mi (68km) of stunning coastline all within a short drive.

There are two tours outlined in this chapter. "Tour A: Inland Orange County" uses Anaheim as a base to explore the surrounding region and its many attractions. "Tour B: The Beaches of Orange County" starts at Seal

Beach and works its way down the magnificent Pacific Coast Highway, stopping at the many beach towns along the route.

Finding Your Way Around

The **Metrolink** (☎800-371-LINK, *www.octa.net*) is a commuter service that runs from Oceanside to Anaheim. This service will take you to Union Station in Los Angeles. Stops are made in Oceanside, San Clemente, San Juan Capistrano, Irvine, Santa Ana, Orange and Anaheim. A full-day unlimited pass is just $2.50. Contact Metrolink for detailed times and fares.

Tour A: Inland Orange County

By Car

The inland Orange County area is reached by way of the I-5 Freeway from either the north or south. The exit for Disneyland is very clearly marked and leads to the centre of Anaheim.

By Train

Amtrak
☎*800-872-7245*
www.amtrak.com
2150 E. Katella Ave.
Anaheim
☎*(714) 385-1448*
1000 E. Santa Ana Blvd.
Santa Ana
☎*(714) 547-8389*

By Bus

Greyhound
1000 E Santa Ana Blvd # 105
Santa Ana
☎*(714) 542-2215*

Tour B: The Beaches of Orange County

By Car

The Pacific Coast Highway makes for a wonderful drive down the coast, passing through each of the beach cities in this tour. The PCH as it is known locally, can be reached via Highway 55 from inland Orange County or via Highway I-710 out of Los Angeles.

By Train

Amtrak
☎*800-872-7245*
www.amtrak.com
North Beach Station
1850 Avenida Estacion
San Clemente
☎*800-872-7245*
26701 Verdugo St
San Juan Capistrano
☎*(949) 240-2972*
235 Tremont St.
Oceanside
☎*800-872-7245*

By Bus

Greyhound
☎*800-229-9424*
www.greyhound.com
2421 S El Camino Real
San Clemente
☎*(949) 366-2646*
Transit Centre
235 Tremont St.
Oceanside
☎*(760) 722-1587*

Practical Information

Area Codes:

Seal Beach: **562**
Anaheim/ Huntington Beach : **714**
Newport Beach/ Laguna Beach: **949**

Tour A: Inland Orange County

Tourist Information

Anaheim / Orange County Visitor & Convention Bureau
800 W. Katella Ave., Box 4270
Anaheim, CA 92803
☎*888-598-3200*
☎*(714) 765-8888*
⇄*(714) 991-8963*
www.anaheimoc.org

Tour B: The Beaches of Orange County

Tourist Information

Seal Beach

Seal Beach Chamber of Commerce
311 Main St., Suite 14A
Seal Beach, CA 90740
☎*(562) 799-0179*
www.sealbeachchamber. com

Huntington Beach

Huntington Beach Conference and Visitors Bureau
417 Main St.
Huntington Beach, CA 92648
☎*(714) 969-3492*
☎*800-729-6232*
www.hbvisit.com

Newport Beach

Newport Beach Conference and Visitors Bureau
3300 W. Coast Hwy.
Newport Beach, CA 92663
☎*(949) 722-1611*
☎*800-942-6778*
⇄*(949) 722-1612*
www.newportbeach-cvb.com

Laguna Beach

Laguna Beach Visitors Bureau
252 Broadway, Box 221
Laguna Beach, CA 92652
☎*800-877-1115*
⇄*(949) 376-0558*
www.lagunabeachinfo.org

Dana Point

Dana Point Chamber of Commerce
24681 La Plaza
Dana Point, CA 92629
☎*800-290-3262*
⇄*(949) 496-5321*
www.danapoint-chamber. com

San Clemente

San Clemente Chamber of Commerce
1100 N. El. Camino Real
San Clemente, CA 92672
☎ *(714) 492-1131*
⇌ *(714)492-3764*
www.scchamber.com

San Juan Capistrano

San Juan Capistrano Chamber of Commerce
31781 Camino Capistrano
Franciscan Plaza, Suite 306
San Juan Capistrano
CA 92693-1878
☎ *(949) 493-4700*
⇌ *(949) 489-2695*
www.sanjuanchamber.com

Oceanside

Oceanside Chamber of Commerce
928 N. Coast Hwy.
Oceanside, CA 92054
☎ *(800) 350-7873*
www.oceansidechamber. com

Exploring

Tour A: Inland Orange County

Anaheim

Long before Disneyland ever existed, the city of Anaheim was established by German immigrants as an important wine-producing colony for the budding metropolis of Los Angeles. Anaheim, though best known for Disneyland, features a multitude of other attractions nearby as well as fantastic shopping, dining and entertainment

Sleeping Beauty's Castle

possibilities. Most visitors choose to stay in Anaheim when visiting inland Orange County due to its wide spectrum of accommodations and its central location. Most area attractions are within a short drive on Interstate 5, which runs through the city. Alternatively, the hotels listed in this guide also provide a free or low-cost shuttle to all the region's attractions. The city of Orange is only a few minutes east of Anaheim and features both charming antique shopping and the newest outdoor mall in the county.

Disneyland ★ ★ ★ *(adults $41, children $31; 1313 Harbor Blvd.; ☎ 781-4565; www.disneyland.com)* was Walt Disney's vision of the "happiest place on earth" and has been the main attraction in California for the past 45 years. What started as a mere 18 rides has grown to over 60, with plans for many more. The Magic Kingdom, however, is more suited to young children than teenagers. Teenagers will probably enjoy Knott's Berry Farm better, with its intense rides and slightly more mature attractions. For young children though, Disneyland is a dream come true.

Passes are available for one, two or three days and allow unlimited re-entry into the park. During the low season, it is possible to ride everything in one day. If you are visiting in the summer, however, two days may be more realistic as lineups are common. A new feature of the park is Fastpass, allowing guests to use their entry pass to "reserve" a time to come back to the ride. This is an invaluable service as it helps you avoid the majority of lineups. The Fastpass is currently available at Space Mountain, Splash Mountain and Roger Rabbit's Car Toon Spin.

Disneyland consists of eight different "lands," each with their own distinctive theme.

Main Street, U.S.A. features a variety of shops in an early 20th century atmosphere. Make sure to check out the main street cinema to see Mickey's first cartoon, *Steamboat Willy.*

Tommorrowland ★ ★ ★ is the highlight of the park, including attractions like Star Tours, Space Mountain, and Autotopia. Lineups can last up to 1hr or more at the rides, but Innoventions is both fun

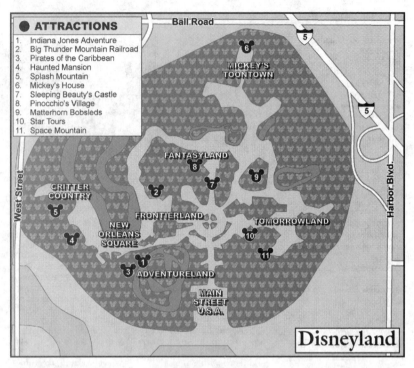

ATTRACTIONS

1. Indiana Jones Adventure
2. Big Thunder Mountain Railroad
3. Pirates of the Caribbean
4. Haunted Mansion
5. Splash Mountain
6. Mickey's House
7. Sleeping Beauty's Castle
8. Pinocchio's Village
9. Matterhorn Bobsleds
10. Star Tours
11. Space Mountain

Disneyland

and educational without the wait.

Mickey's Toontown ★★ is a especially popular attraction with the very young. Rides such as Gadget's Go Coaster and Goofy's Bounce House cater to children as young as three.

Fantasyland ★★ has a theatre offering live entertainment and several fun rides with very little waiting involved. Popular spots include the Sleeping Beauty Castle and King Arthur's Carousel.

Frontierland ★★ transports you back to the Wild West with attractions like a full-sized riverboat, the Big Thunder Mountain Railroad ride and a shooting gallery, to name a few. After dark, the Fantasmic show pits Mickey and his friends against the usual Disney villains.

Adventureland ★★★ is home to Tarzan's 70 ft (23m) treehouse and a great jungle cruise, complete with hippos and headhunters. The Indiana Jones ride is also worthwhile, but the lineups are sometimes daunting.

New Orleans Square ★★ has the classic Pirates of the Caribbean, as well as the famous Haunted House. The Blue Bayou Restaurant here is the most popular (and expensive) in the park. It is also the only restaurant with table service. Same-day reservations should be made by calling ☎956-6755. **Critter Corner ★★** is enchanting as characters from the world of Winnie the Pooh come to life. Hit the water on the Davey Crocket Canoes or get wet at Splash Mountain.

If you want to get to know the history behind Anaheim, try the **Anaheim Museum ★** (241 S. Anaheim Blvd.; ☎778-3301), located in the beautifully restored 1908 Carnegie Library Building. In addition to a series of changing exhibits, the museum also chronicles the changes that have occurred in the Anaheim area over the past 150 years, from vineyards to orange groves to Disneyland.

If sports are your passion, Anaheim has two professional teams. The newly-renovated **Edison Field** (200 Gene Autry Way; ☎940-2240) is home to baseball's **Anaheim Angels**, who slug it out April through October. The trademark Outfield Extravaganza features six water geysers, dramatic lighting and pyrotechnics. Across Highway 57 is the

Disneyland U.S.A.

Construction is currently underway on Disney's California Adventure and Downtown Disney, scheduled to be completed in 2001. The California Adventure will be a sampling of all that California has to offer. The Hollywood Back Lot will give visitors a chance to get a behind-the-scenes look at the movie business. At Paradise Pier, visitors can catch a few rays while experiencing a classic seaside amusement park. Also planned are white-water rafting and hang-gliding rides that should set the standards for extreme-sport simulation. Also included in the plans is a 750-room hotel, the Grand Californian, to be built within the park grounds.

Downtown Disney will be located adjacent to the California Adventure and offer shopping, dining and entertainment à la Disney. Since Anaheim doesn't really have a downtown as such, the new development should enjoy incredible popularity.

Arrowhead Pond of Anaheim *(2695 E. Katella Ave.; ☎704-2500)*, home to NHL's **Anaheim Mighty Ducks**, who take to the ice October through April.

Adventure City ★ *($5, unlimited rides $11; daily 10am to 5pm; 1238 S. Beach Blvd.; ☎236-9300)* is an affordable little theme park aimed at two to 12 year olds. Seventeen rides from rollercoasters to merry-go-rounds are complimented by face painting, puppet shows, a petting farm and a children's theatre. You should definitely spring for the unlimited pass. Next door, at the **Hobby City Doll & Toy Museum** *(free; 1238 S. Beach Blvd.; ☎527-2323)* visitors can browse through a variety of craft, art, and collectibles shops and explore a half-scale model of the White House and over 4000 antique and foreign dolls and toy soldiers.

Just south of Anaheim in nearby Garden Grove, the 3,000-seat **Crystal Cathedral** ★★★ *(13280 Chapman Ave., Garden Grove; ☎971-4069)* is an incredible sight to behold. Designed by architect Philip Johnson, this fascinating structure is comprised of over 10,000 panes of mirrored glass that shine brilliantly in the California sun. The 236 ft (79m) steeple houses a 52-bell carillon and a 24hr prayer chapel. Throughout the expansive grounds of the church is a collection of biblically-inspired statues that are set amid reflecting pools, fountains and myriad flowers. The "Glory of Christmas" and "Glory of Easter" shows are famous for their high production value, complete with flying angels, special effects and orchestral sound.

★★
Buena Park

The highlight of Buena Park is Beach Boulevard,

known as the "entertainment corridor." Most of the main attractions are located on this street, interspersed with various dining and shopping opportunities.

For the ultimate in high-speed, adrenaline-pumping rides, head to **Knott's Berry Farm** *(Adults $38, children $28; 8039 Beach Blvd.; ☎220-5200; www.knotts.com)*, just 10min northwest of Disneyland. From its humble beginnings as a chicken restaurant and roadside produce stand, Knott's is now the second most visited tourist site in California. The two newest attractions are the Supreme Scream, which drops its riders 30 storeys in three seconds, and the Ghost Rider, a colossal wooden roller coaster. There are 165 rides, shows and attractions in all, covering 150 acres (61ha). The park is divided into six themed areas: the Wild West Ghost Town, Indian Trails, Fiesta Village, The Boardwalk, Wild Water Wilderness and Camp Snoopy. At Camp Snoopy, children can experience smaller versions of the adult rides.

Right next to Knott's is **Soak City U.S.A.** ★★ *($20; 8039 Beach Blvd.; ☎220-5200)*, harbouring 15 acres (7ha) of water rides with a California surf theme. With its huge wave pool, tube slides and children's water lagoon, this is a great place to enjoy the California sun.

The **Mott's Miniature Museum** ★★ *(7900 La Palma Ave.; ☎527-1843)* is adjacent to the park. Several great exhibits are showcased here, including the History of American Living, which features six scale homes, ranging from the 18th century to modern day, complete with a miniature working television. The highlight here is the Microscopic Miniature display, where visitors must use magnifying glasses to see fully dressed fleas or "The Last Supper" painted on a pinhead.

The **Movieland Wax Museum** ★ *($13; 7711 Beach Blvd.; ☎522-1155)* is home to almost 300 celebrity wax figures on display in 115 realistic sets. Everyone featured in here, from Michael Jackson to John Wayne, is life-size and incredibly life-like. While the static displays are interesting and of amazing quality, Ripley's Believe It Or Not Museum is less expensive and far more intriguing.

Though not for the faint-of-heart, the **Ripley's Believe It Or Not Museum** ★★ *($9; 7850 Beach Blvd.; ☎522-1152)* is an interesting and, at times, shocking adventure into the strange, the amazing and the wonder

ful. Through a 10,000 sq ft (930m^2) collection of artifacts, wax sculptures and displays, visitors can observe some of the strangest things the world has to offer. Robert L. Ripley, born in nearby Santa Rosa on Christmas Day 1893, visited 198 countries during his lifetime, searching for just the things you now see in his museum. The work still continues in his memory, with more unbelievable exhibits added every year.

★
Santa Ana to Costa Mesa

Santa Ana and Costa Mesa are situated just south of Anaheim on Harbor Boulevard. This area is considered by many to be the artistic and cultural centre of Orange County, since it is home to the Bowers Museum, Orange County Theatre District and the Artist's Village. Costa Mesa has the added advantage of being conveniently located a quick 20min drive from the sands of Newport Beach.

The **Artist's Village** in downtown Santa Ana *(Broadway to Sycamore St. on Second St.)* is home to more than 55 studios and galleries that showcase their works at 7pm on the first Saturday of the month. Stroll through the village and take in the local artwork hanging in windows and displayed in the various galleries.

The **Bowers Museum of Cultural Art and Kidseum** ★★ *($8; 2002 N. Main St., Santa Ana; ☎567-3600)* is dedicated to the

Crystal Cathedral

preservation, study and exhibition of the cultural arts of the Americas, Africa and the Pacific Rim. Inside the museum walls and warm, open-air space, 85,000 objects are showcased including many one-of-a-kind and historical artifacts. Next door, the Kidseum offers interactive displays and activities for children to learn about local history and world cultures.

Learning is actually quite entertaining at the **Discovery Science Centre** ★★★ *($9.50; 2500 N. Main St., Santa Ana; ☎542-CUBE; www.discoverycube.org)*. Eight different areas feature interactive exhibits highlighting everything from the principles of flight and space exploration to human performance and perception. A 3-D laser theatre show is also included with admission. Kids will especially love the musical floor, bed of nails and mini-tornadoes.

Costa Mesa

Modern and contemporary U.S. art is featured at the **Orange County Museum of Art** ★ *(3333 Bristol St., Suite 1000; ☎662-3366)*. A lecture series takes place on Tuesday and Friday nights and features screenings of classic films. Sculptures, a meditative garden and a beautiful stained-glass enclosure are hidden here amid the shops and restaurants of South Coast Plaza.

The **Orange County Theatre District** offers over 3,000 seats overall at its various venues. The **Orange County Performing Arts Centre** *(600 Town Center Dr.; ☎556-2787)* features national and international selections of ballet, opera ballet, opera, musical theatre, classical

Edison Field

music, and jazz throughout the year. The bold-looking building is a local landmark with its gigantic window providing a view of the elegant, modern interior.

The Tony Award-winning **South Coast Repertory** *(655 Town Center Dr.; ☎708-5500)* stages creative new and classic drama and has drawn national attention for productions such as David Henry Hwang's *Golden Child,* which was first produced at South Coast Repertory and is now on Broadway.

The **Santa Ana Zoo in Prentice Park** ★★★ *($3.50; 1801 Chestnut Ave., Santa Ana; ☎647-6575; www.santaanazoo.org)* is home to more than 250 exotic animals from various habitats around the world. The highlight here is definitely the monkeys who never fail to entertain. An extensive rainforest exhibit, walk-through aviary and children's petting zoo add to the list of attractions.

The annual Orange County Fair takes place in the last two weeks of July at the **Orange County Fair & Exposition Center** *(88 Fair Dr.; ☎708-1567)* in Costa Mesa. During the rest of the year, the grounds host a **Farmer's Market** *(Thu*

8:30am to 1pm; ☎723-6616) and **International Speedway Racing** *($9; Sat. 7:30pm to 10pm; ☎492-9933).*

Tour B: The Beaches of Orange County

★
Seal Beach

Seal Beach is a small, attractive town that seems to have been forgotten in the rush to develop the Californian coast. The pace of life here is slower, the locals friendlier, and visitors return year after year hoping that their secret will still be safe. The small town atmosphere is best experienced in a short walk down charming Main Street, past the unique shops and casual restaurants. There are less than 100 beds available in Seal Beach, so visitors should make their reservations well in advance.

The **beach** ★★★ is the main attraction in town. A handful of shops along main street rent surf boards, boogie boards and sailboards for the water. Landlubbers will find kites and bicycles available. Over 30mi (48km) of bike paths wind throughout the area.

Seal Beach Pier is one of the longest wooden piers in the United States. Originally constructed in 1938, it was destroyed by a violent Pacific storm in 1983. The pier was rebuilt in 1984 through the concentrated efforts of the entire community. Fishing is available along the pier. Ruby's Diner (see p 172) is at the end of it, looking out onto the ocean.

The **Seal Beach Historical and Cultural Society** *(second and fourth Sat of each month 1pm to 4pm; ☎683-1874)* is located in a red, 1925 railway car on Electric Avenue, just west of Main Street. This small museum features photographs of early Seal Beach, sea shells, Native American artifacts and a small reference library.

The **Anaheim Bay National Wildlife Refuge** is accessible to visitors on the last Saturday of the month *(☎598-1024),* when a shuttle runs through the 1000-acre (404ha) reserve. The refuge is a salt marsh habitat that is a breeding ground for various fish and migratory birds. The tour is free and departs from the main gate of the naval base at 9am. There is only limited access to the refuge because it is located within the **U.S. Naval Weapons Support Facility** *(www.sbeach.navy.mil).* Giant naval vessels can be seen coming in and out of Anaheim Bay.

The main event in Seal Beach is the **Seal Beach Car Show** *(info ☎799-0179)* at the end of April. Thousands of people from all over California come to this sleepy beach town to watch the hotrods and vintage cars compete for prizes.

★★
Huntington Beach

In the 1920s, oil was discovered in Huntington Beach. This led to a population boom as speculators and residents drilled in their backyards looking for the coveted "black gold." By the 1950s, however, the oil had run dry, and Huntington began to develop its present claim to fame as "Surf City USA." In the downtown core, surf shops dominate the commercial area. Scores of bronzed surfers can be found lounging on the beaches and in the sidewalk cafés or, more likely, catching one of Huntington's famous waves by the pier. Huntington is home to the US Open Surfing Championship and the Bud Surf Tour. It was recently rated the "most heavily surfed beach on the West Coast" by *Surfer's Almanac*.

There are fabulous shopping, dining and nightlife opportunities to be had here. Huntington Beach is a laid-back, vibrant town, where "no shirt, no shoes, no service" doesn't necessarily apply.

The **beaches** of Huntington are the city's main attraction, stretching for 8mi (13km) east and west of downtown. Just west of the city, **Bolsa Chica Beach ★★★** tends to be less crowded than its counterparts, and fronts the ecological reserve of the same name (see p 153). The **Huntington City Beach ★★** surrounds the pier, and is a popular place to watch local surf-

ers. **Huntington State Beach ★★** is a 2mi-long (3.2km) sandy beach with six wheelchair ramps that reach almost to the water. All beaches include picnic facilities, outdoor showers and free parking nearby. Rangers and lifeguards are on duty year-round at both the state and city beaches.

The **Huntington Beach Pier ★★** is the longest concrete municipal pier in California, extending 1,850ft (616m) into the Pacific. Originally built as a wooden pier in 1903, it has been rebuilt twice after storm damage. The current pier was opened in July 1990. This is a Mecca of activity during the day, the perfect place to see and be seen, lounge in the sun, or watch the surfers tackle the waves. Fishing is allowed from the pier and doesn't require a licence. Ruby's Diner (see p 172) sits at the end of the pier, a busy but friendly spot for a meal at sundown.

Some of the most revered artifacts in the history of surfing can be found at the **International Surfing Museum ★★** *($2; Wed to Sun noon to 5pm; 411 Olive Ave.; ☎960-3483; www.surfingmuseum.org).* The music of the Beach Boys pervades the museum and surf videos help set the mood. A permanent display chronicles the

evolution of the surfboard, and an original Duke Kahanamoku hardwood board hangs among other treasures of its kind. The north wall of the museum is covered with a beautiful mural depicting surfers in action—a favourite photo opportunity for visitors.

The **Huntington Beach Surfing Walk of Fame ★** pays homage to the heroes of Surf City. Granite stone is inlaid in the sidewalk that extends outward from the corner of Main Street and the Pacific Coast Highway.

Huntington Central Park *(☎960-8895)* consists of over 350 acres (142ha) of majestic trees, grassy lawns, ponds and fountains. Throughout the park there are several great playgrounds, barbeques, sports facilities and 6mi (9km) of trails. The park is located on both sides of Golden West Street, near Talbert. The **Shipley Nature Centre** and **Central Library and Cultural Centre** are also located in the park.

In the north end of the park, near Slater Avenue and Golden West Street is the **Shipley Nature Centre ★★** (free; 9am to 5pm; ☎960-8847). The centre consists of an 18-acre (7.2ha) forest with a variety of wildlife habitats that are home to a community of raccoons, snakes, turtles, opossums and coyotes. Guests can explore the half-mile interpretive trail that will take them through the forests, grasslands and freshwater marsh of the park's centre.

The **Huntington Beach Cultural Centre and Central Library ★** *(7111 Talbert Ave.; ☎960-8839)* serves as the city's main library, but also houses the Huntington Beach Playhouse Community Theatre group and the Children's Storytime Theatre. The impressive lobby is adorned with fabulous fountains, pools and cascading waterfalls.

At Center Avenue, just off the San Diego freeway, is the **Old World Village ★** *(7561 Center Ave.)*. This shopping, dining and entertainment centre is an attempt to recreate a German alpine town. Wander down the cobbled streets and check out the European-inspired shops, have a little wiener schnitzel and sauerkraut and, when night falls, there are drinks and dancing. In late September and early October, this is the epicenter of the Oktoberfest celebrations.

The **Newland House Museum** *($2; Wed and Thu 2pm to 4:30pm, Sat and Sun 12-4pm; 19820 Beach Blvd.; ☎962-5557)* is a Queen Anne-style Victorian farm house, located a fair distance from downtown on the corner of Beach Boulevard. and Adams Avenue. The house has a wonderful view of the Santa Ana Gap, a marshy lowland between Huntington Beach and Costa Mesa. Inside, the furnishings and decor have been lovingly preserved for visitors.

The **Bolsa Chica Ecological Reserve ★★** *(tours 9am and 10:30am, first Sat of the month, Sep to Apr; Warner Ave. at the Pacific Coast Hwy.; ☎800-628-7275 ext.119)* is a protected wetland reserve that serves as a rest area for birds migrating along the Pacific Flyway. Its 530-acres (214ha) are also home to a variety of wildlife that is relatively easy to spot. The reserve has limited access to pro-

tect its flora and fauna, but there is a 1.5mi (2.5km) interpretive loop trail, with informative signs posted along it. Note the oil pumps that continue to operate in the reserve.

★★
Newport Beach

Every weekend, thousands of Orange County residents flock to Newport Beach for the fine restaurants, festive atmosphere and vibrant nightlife. Much more than just a beach, the Newport area is comprised of several small and distinct villages that compliment what most people refer to as Newport Beach. Stretching for 6mi (9km) along the Californian shoreline, this area has some of the most expensive real estate in Orange County and is a popular spot for Californians to unwind. Newport harbour is also one of the largest small-yacht harbours in the world, home to over 9,000 boats and the famous *Dory Fishing Fleet* (see p 156). Shoppers will delight in the upscale Fashion Island shopping centre (see p 183). The tourism industry is well developed in Newport Beach, but the adjacent community of Corona del Mar *(www.cdmchamber.com)* provides some respite with its quaint, small town atmosphere. Newport is also a convenient gateway to Catalina Island, 26mi (42km) offshore.

The stretch of Pacific Coast Highway between Newport Boulevard and Dover Drive is known as **Mariners Mile ★★**. Along this mile is a great collection of restaurants, shops and galleries that all share a common nautical theme. This is also a good area to charter a cruise and get a

terrific view of the harbour.

Just off Newport Boulevard from the Pacific Coast Highway, visitors will discover the **Lido Marina Village**. This charming sector of Newport brings to mind a European open-air marketplace as you stroll down the cobblestone street of **Via Oporto**, browsing through the many galleries, boutiques and antique shops. There are also several quaint cafés and restaurants that look out on the bay.

A few blocks east of the Lido Marina Village is **Cannery Village ★★**, which covers eight square blocks in an area that was once the centre of the Newport commercial fishing industry. In the early 1900s the area was filled with boat repair shops, boat yards and, of course, canneries. Today the village retains its nautical atmosphere, but the old buildings now house an eclectic collection of art galleries, antique shops and restaurants. Aspiring local artists converge on **Cannery Wharf Park** *(where 30th St. meets the bay)* Sunday afternoons to sell their latest works.

The **Newport Municipal Beach ★** stretches from the Santa Ana River Jetty and along the Balboa Peninsula to the Entrance Channel of Newport Harbor. Sun seekers are best to stay to the west end of the beach to avoid the considerable crowds that invade this beach on the weekends. Beach parking is available at either of the piers, or at one of the numerous beachfront lots *($7 maximum)*. **The Wedge**, by the Entrance Channel, is an excellent surfing spot, but once again, it fills up quickly. Inexperienced surfers and swimmers should try to remain within sight of the lifeguard towers. Beach volleyball courts and campfire spots are available. Numerous small beaches run along the inland shore of the Balboa Peninsula. At Bay Avenue, between 18th and 19th Streets is a calm **beach** that is lifeguard-supervised.

Big Corona and Little Corona Beaches ★★ are found just east of the Entrance Channel, in front of Corona del Mar. These smaller, less crowded beaches are great for families, watching yachts come into the harbor, and scuba diving.

The large, imposing structure of the **Orange County Museum of Art ★** ($5; Tue to Sun 11am to 5pm; 850 San Clemente Dr.; ☎759-1122; www.ocma.net) hosts temporary exhibits of various contemporary paintings, sculpture and photography, with emphasis on Californian art from the 19th century to the present. The bookstore specializes in contemporary art books. Lunch is served in the lush Sculpture Garden Café from 11:30am to 2:30pm weekdays. Work-

shops and classes are available.

The **Newport Harbor Nautical Museum ★** ($4; Tue to Sun, 10am to 5pm; 151 E. Pacific Coast Hwy.; ☎673-7863; www.newportnautical.org) celebrates all things nautical aboard the riverboat Pride of Newport in the Newport Harbor. A collection of historical photographs, videos and maritime paintings by renowned artist Arthur Beaumont serve to educate visitors on Newport Harbor and the surrounding area. Also exhibited is an interesting display of ships in bottles and navigational instruments. The museum shares the ship with the Riverboat Restaurant (see p 174).

Sports fans will be amazed by the **Newport Sports Collection Foundation** (free; Mon to Fri 10am to 6pm, Sat 10am to 3pm; 620 Newport Center Dr.; ☎721-9333). Over 10,000 game-worn jerseys, helmets and equipment cover the walls of the 10 rooms in this unique museum. The aim of the museum is to promote sports as a way to keep children away from gangs and

drugs. Baseball, football, basketball, golf, hockey and the Olympics are all represented. Professional athletes come here occasionally to speak to the visiting children.

The **Upper Newport Bay Ecological Reserve** (2400 Irvine Ave.; ☎646-8009) is a 752-acre (304ha) coastal wetland reserve that supports six ecological habitats. A variety of fish, mammals and over 200 species of birds call this reserve home. Fishing is available year round, with the best spots being near Big Canyon and North Star Beach. Canoe and kayak tours, sunset cruises and family campfire programs are offered throughout the year from the **Newport Aquatic Centre** (☎714-644-3151) at North Star Beach. There is also a 10mi (16km) loop trail that winds through the reserve. Free naturalist-guided walking tours are offered the first and third Saturday of the month.

An entire city block in Corona del Mar is devoted to the **Sherman Library and Gardens ★★** (daily 10:30am to 4pm; 2647 E.

● ATTRACTIONS	
1. Mariners Mile	9. Balboa Island
2. Lido Marina Village	10. Newport Harbor Nautical Museum
3. Cannery Village	11. Environmental Nature Center
4. Cannery Wharf Park	12. Orange County Museum of Art
5. Newport Pier	13. Newport Sports Collection Foundation
6. Balboa Pier	14. Sherman Library and Gardens
7. Balboa Pavilion/Balboa Fun Zone	15. Big Corona and Little Corona Beaches
8. Balboa Island Car Ferry	

◯ ACCOMMODATIONS	
1. Balboa Bay Club	5. Newport Channel Inn
2. Balboa Inn	6. Newport Classic Inn
3. Doryman's Inn	7. Portofino Hotel
4. Four Seasons Hotel	

▦ RESTAURANTS	
1. Alta Coffee	7. Roy's Newport Beach
2. Alysia 101	8. Spaghetti Bender
3. Blue Beet Café	9. Tale of the Whale
4. Chart House	10. Tutto Mare Ristotrante
5. Hornblower Cruises	11. Veg a GO-GO
6. Riverboat Restaurant	

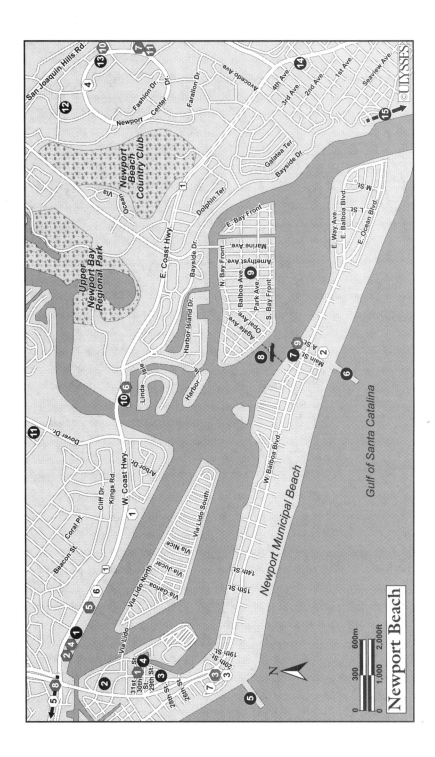

Newport Beach

Pacific Coast Hwy.; ☎*673-2261).* The facility was named for Moses H. Sherman, an educator and California pioneer. The historical research library (weekdays only) is an important repository of information on the Pacific Southwest over the past 100 years. The luxuriant gardens feature over 2,000 plant species from rare desert cacti to exotic tropical bromelia and orchids, highlighted by fountains and sculptures. The **Discovery Garden** ★ is designed for those with impaired vision, relying on the sense of touch, and is wheelchair accessible.

Newport Pier *(McFadden Pl. between 20th and 22nd Pl.)* is on the site of historic McFadden Wharf, which was destroyed by a violent storm in 1939. The original wharf was an important stop for coal steamers in the early 1900's. The **Balboa Pier** *(Main St. and E. Balboa Blvd.)* was built in 1909 and is the site of the first water-to-water hydroplane flight, in 1912, to Santa Catalina Island and back. Today, both piers have become a popular hangout for tourists and locals alike. Fishing is allowed from the piers without a licence.

Newport Beach's **pleasure craft harbor** is one of the largest of its kind in the world and provides avid boaters with the opportunity to admire some extravagant yachts. The harbour is also home to the **Dory Fishing Fleet**, which pulls in promptly at 9am every morning. Started in 1889, this fleet is the last beachside cooperative of its kind in the United States. Upon their return, the local chefs crowd in to get their pick of the freshest seafood. It's hard not

to get caught up in the marine atmosphere and you'll want to get out on the water yourself. **Balboa Boat Rentals** *(beside the Balboa Ferry dock;* ☎*673-7200)* rents by the hour or half day at reasonable prices. Double kayaks and pedal boats cost $50/half-day, while motor and fishing boats run $100 and more. Alternatively, bay cruises are available from Newport Harbor Sightseeing *($6; Daily 10am to 7pm;* ☎*673-5245)* leaving from the **Balboa Pavilion**.

The **Environmental Nature Center** *(daily 9am to 5pm; 1601 16th St.;* ☎*645-8489)* is a great way for children aged five and over to experience nature firsthand. Guided walking tours are available of the 2.5 acre (1.2ha) wildlife habitat that also supports 13 Californian plant communities.

In 1905, the Newport Investment Company erected the **Balboa Pavilion** *(400 Main St.)* as an open-air building with a Victorian-era balustrade edging the second floor. In 1906, it became the southern terminus for the Pacific Electric Railway, which connected the beach to downtown Los Angeles. Today it is home to **The Tale of the Whale** restaurant (see p 174), a snack bar and a number of fishing and cruise services. The pavilion also serves as the centre of the **Balboa Fun Zone** *(daily 10am to 10pm;* ☎*673-0408),* which has been a tradition in Newport since 1936. Admission is free, but there is a small cost to ride the Ferris wheel, carousel and bumper cars. Kids love the festive atmosphere, and some of the best views of the harbor are to be had from atop the restored Ferris wheel.

★★
Balboa Island

Be sure to catch the **Balboa Island Car Ferry** *($1/car or .35/pers.)* to get to the island. Alternatively, you can reach the island by car off the Pacific Coast Highway at Jamboree Road, but parking is in such short supply that it is better to explore the island on foot. The island is primarily residential, with a wonderful architectural mix of Cape Cod and modern Californian homes packed into its tight little streets. Along **Park Avenue** ★★ is a colourful collection of gift shops, galleries and restaurants. The North Bay front walkway is a nice stroll that allows some great views of the harbor.

★★★
Laguna Beach

Laguna Beach is a small, eclectic town and the heart of the artistic community on Southern California's coast. An artist's colony was established here amidst the 30 white-sand beaches and bays of Laguna Beach in 1917. The varied topography and numerous ocean lookouts continue to inspire the works of the Californian impressionist school. Laguna is the centre of the Californian Plein-Air movement, artists influenced by Monet-style French impressionism. During the 1920's, Laguna Beach was a haven for some Hollywood's superstars, from Charlie Chaplin and Douglas Fairbanks to Mary Pickford and Bette Davis. For a town this size, it has a surprising number of quality restaurants, yearly festivals, and quaint boutique shops. Almost everything in town is within a few

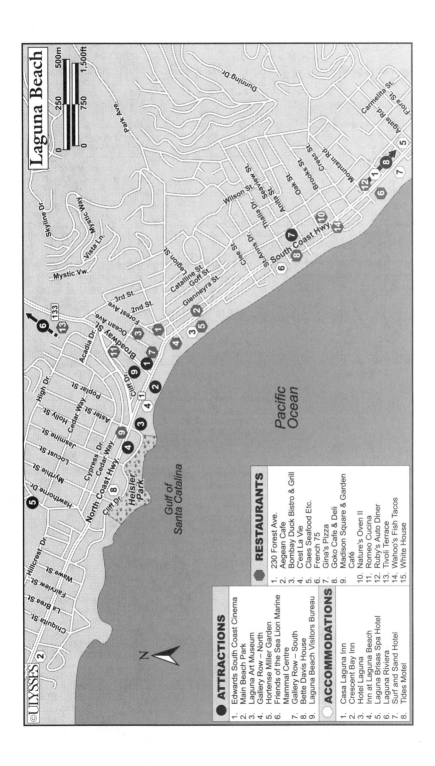

Laguna Beach

ULYSSES

Pacific Ocean

Gulf of Santa Catalina

Heisler Park

● ATTRACTIONS

1. Edwards South Coast Cinema
2. Main Beach Park
3. Laguna Art Museum
4. Gallery Row – North
5. Hortense Miller Garden
6. Friends of the Sea Lion Marine Mammal Centre
7. Gallery Row – South
8. Bette Davis House
9. Laguna Beach Visitors Bureau

◇ ACCOMMODATIONS

1. Casa Laguna Inn
2. Crescent Bay Inn
3. Hotel Laguna
4. Inn at Laguna Beach
5. Laguna Brisas Spa Hotel
6. Laguna Riviera
7. Surf and Sand Hotel
8. Tides Motel

⬡ RESTAURANTS

1. 230 Forest Ave.
2. Aegean Cafe
3. Bombay Duck Bistro & Grill
4. C'est La Vie
5. Claes Seafood Etc.
6. French 75
7. Gina's Pizza
8. Goko Cafe & Deli
9. Madison Square & Garden Café
10. Nature's Oven II
11. Romeo Cucina
12. Ruby's Auto Diner
13. Tivoli Terrace
14. Wahoo's Fish Tacos
15. White House

minutes' walk from the beach.

A fascinating pastime in Laguna Beach is touring the many **art galleries** in the area. During the depression, members of the Laguna Beach artistic community would display their works by the sides of the Pacific Coast Highway or hanging from the eucalyptus trees, hoping to make a sale to one of the passing motorists. Today, a multitude of art galleries line the highway where the artists once stood. In north Laguna, **Gallery Row** ★★★ covers the 300 and 400 blocks of the North Pacific Coast Highway. These two blocks are home to over 20 galleries, that proudly display their original artwork. In South Laguna there is a complete palate of galleries, crafts and artists studios waiting to be explored between the 900 and 1800 blocks of the South Pacific Coast Highway. The first Thursday of each month is the **Laguna Beach Artwalk**, when the multitude of area art galleries remain open until 9pm.

The Mediterranean-revival style **Edwards South Coast Cinema** (*156 Pacific Coast Hwy.; ☎497-1711*) was built in 1934 and was the first building in Laguna to be constructed of steel and concrete. It currently has two theatres showing recent releases.

Main Beach Park ★★ is located in the middle of downtown Laguna Beach, at the intersection of Laguna Canyon Road and the Pacific Coast Highway. The beach area has two half-court basketball courts, sand volleyball courts, benches, picnic tables, public showers and restrooms. A walk

along the wooden boardwalk will take you into the **Heisler Park Area** ★★.

The walking trails of **Heisler Park** ★★★ wind along the bluffs of Cliff Drive past public art displays, striking ocean views and through the **Glenn E. Vedder Ecological Reserve**. The reserve is a beautiful diving spot, and the natural tide pools are fascinating. Natural tide pool tours are available from Laguna Outdoors (*☎874-6620*). This is a perfect way to explore the incredible Californian coastline, but be careful not to remove anything from the protected areas of the beach.

The **Laguna Art Museum** ★★ (*$5; Tue to Sun 11an to 5pm; 307 Cliff Dr. at Pacific Coast Hwy.; ☎494-8971; www. lagunaartmuseum.org*) focuses on the art of California, but also has exhibitions of historical, modern and contemporary American art.

The **Friends of the Sea Lion Marine Mammal Centre** ★ (*donations welcome; daily 10am to 4pm; 20612 Laguna Canyon Rd.; ☎494-3050*) is a volunteer, non-profit organization that has been providing medical care to sick or wounded seals and sea lions since 1971. Visitors can take a guided tour of the facility,

watch a slide show, and see the recovering animals. Very little human interaction is allowed, however, as the centre tries to keep these animals wild, for a more successful re-release to their natural habitat.

The **Hortense Miller Garden** ★★ (*22511 Allview Terrace; ☎497-0716, ext.6; no children under 13*) can be found on the upper slopes of Boat Canyon and features over 1,500 plants from around the world on 2.5 acres (1ha) of superbly landscaped grounds. Hortense, who is 91 years old, still greets guests as they arrive. A feast for the senses, tours last 2hrs and must be booked in advance.

The **Bette Davis House** (*1991 Ocean Way*) is an English Tudor home which overlooks beautiful Wood's Cove. Built in 1929, it was the home of Bette Davis during the early 1940s.

★★
Dana Point

In the early days, Dana Point was called San Juan Point and served as an anchoring place for mission supply ships. It was also an important site in the hide trade, as hides tanned on the local ranches were thrown over the cliffs to trade ships from New England. Richard Henry Dana, a seaman aboard the *Pilgrim*, one of these trade ships, called the area "the only romantic spot in California" in his book *Two Years Before the Mast*. The town of Dana Point is indeed a romantic place, as

Sea lion

the dramatic cliffs and secluded Pacific lookouts attest. The place has somehow managed to retain its small town charm while developing a decent tourism industry with the local harbour.

The focal point of the community, **Dana Point Harbor** *(www. danapointharbor.com)*, houses two marinas which can accommodate for 2,500 small craft inside a 1.5mi (2.4km) jetty. In addition to the usual harbour facilities, the area offers windsurfing, jet skiing and certified dive charters. Dana Wharf Sportfishing *(34675 Golden Lantern; ☎496-5784; www.danawharfsportfishing. com)* offers sportfishing charters and whale-watching cruises (Dec to Mar). The harbour is also host to the Festival of Whales (February), the Tallships Festival (September) and the Holiday Boat Parade (December).

The west end of the harbour is home to the **Tallship** *Pilgrim* ★ ★ *(free admission; Sundays 10am to 2:30pm; 24200 Dana Point Harbor Dr.; ☎496-2274)*, which is a full-sized replica of the square-rigged vessel that Richard Henry Dana first sailed into this cove in 1835. Tours of the ship are led by docents in period costume, who explain what life was like aboard one of these seafaring vessels. During the summer months, there are children's programs as well as a "musical marine theatre" series.

The *Pilgrim* also marks the site of the **Orange County Marine Institute** ★ ★ ★ *(24200 Dana Point Harbor Dr.; ☎496-2274; www.ocean-institute.org)* which operates the 70 ft (23m) *R/V*

Sea Explorer, a marine educational vessel with a fully equipped floating laboratory dedicated to environmental education. A variety of programs are offered to allow visitors to get hands-on experience of the challenges faced by marine biologists. Programs are a very reasonable $20 and include a blue whale safari, bioluminescence night cruise (during the new moon only), and a marine wildlife cruise.

Doheny State Park ★ ★ *($5/car; 25300 Dana Point Harbor Dr.; ☎496-6172; camping $17 -$22 - no hook-ups)* is 62 acres (25ha) of green grass and white sand under grand palm trees. The interpretive centre at the park entrance has a small group of aquariums that display the fish found in this area. There are also exhibits about local animals, fossils and skeletons. The **beach** ★ ★ at Doheny Park is a beautiful stretch of well-tended white sand with volleyball courts and fire pits scattered throughout its 1mi (1.6km) length. Towards the west end of the beach is a rocky area that attracts divers and anglers. The nearby estuary is a great place for spotting flocks of migrating birds.

For one of the most picturesque views on the California Coast try **Heritage Park** *(corner of El Camino and Old Green Lantern)*, a lovely terraced park overlooking the marina and the Pacific. Only a block to the west on El Camino, the **Lantern Lookout Park** provides another panoramic vista.

For more information on the surrounding area, check out the small mu-

seum of the **Dana Point Historical Society** *(free admission; 34085 Pacific Coast Hwy.; ☎248-8121)*. The society has a small collection of old photos and artifacts from early Dana Point.

★
San Clemente

Visitors to San Clemente will notice that this town, just south of Dana Point on the Pacific Coast Highway, is subtly different from its neighbours. The town's founder, Ole Hanson, envisioned a Spanish city by the sea, with white stucco walls under red tiled roofs. The city has continued to follow this architectural style, turning San Clemente into a charming and popular beach town. The city offers almost 10mi (16km) of beach and a 1,200-ft (400m) long fishing pier reaching out into the Pacific.

The **beach** ★ ★ is the real draw here, since the town has few other interesting attractions. It is a good place, however, to relax and enjoy the surf and sand. Going north or south from the pier, the land rises and paths wind down from the bluffs to the sand.

Step back in time at the **San Clemente Heritage Centre** ★ *($2.75; Mon to Sat 10am to 5pm; 415 North El Camino Real; ☎369-1299)*, which has several rooms highlighting different aspects of the town's history. Exhibits include a tribute to the legends of surfing, the Nixon years, and an art gallery showcasing local artists.

The most popular festival in San Clemente is the **Ocean Festival**, held at the

Orange County

base of the pier on the third weekend of July. The festival features a fishing derby, lifeguard competitions, an art show and sand castle competition, as well as live entertainment.

★★
San Juan Capistrano

The historic city of San Juan Capistrano is the oldest settlement in Orange County, with three adobe houses in the Los Rios district that date back to 1794. The community here treasures its connections to the past, working to promote and protect the many historically significant structures in the area. Walking the streets of town will give visitors a sense of what early Southern California was like, where the great Mission was the centre of the community, just as it is today in San Juan Capistrano.

The **Mission San Juan Capistrano** ★★★ *($6; daily 8:30 to 5pm; corner of Camino Capistrano and the Ortega Hwy.; ☎248-2048; www.missionsjc.com)* is the third most visited attraction in Orange County—after Disneyland and Knott's Berry Farm—drawing over 500,000 visitors per year and dubbed the "Jewel of the Missions." Stepping onto the grounds evokes a sense of awe as centuries-old bells toll off the slow passage of time. The mission is at once beautiful and romantic, spiritual and spellbinding. Preservation and restoration efforts have left just enough undone to convey a sense of nostalgia within the adobe walls. Inside, Moorish fountains sit among lush gardens. Visitors can wander through the early soldier's barracks, friar's quarters and cemetery to get a look at the small Serra

Chapel, the oldest building in California. Inside the chapel is a magnificent gold baroque altar, which is 350 years old. Guides are available to tour the mission, but should be reserved in advance.

Just west of the mission, a beautiful white dome sits four storeys above San Juan and marks the site of the **Train Depot** *(26701 Verdugo St.)*, completed October 8, 1894. This historic landmark is served by Amtrak and the Metrolink and is home to Sarducci's restaurant (see p 178) and the Freight House Saloon (see p 182). A lovely mural depicting life in San Juan has been restored in the bar area of the saloon.

Across the tracks from the depot is the **Los Rios Historical District** ★★, with houses ranging from five decades to two-centuries old. The Montanez, Rios, and Silvas adobes are all that remain of the 40 adobes that once lined this

street. The **O'Neill Museum** *(31831 Los Rios St.)* dates back to the late 1800s and is now home to the offices of the San Juan Capistrano Historical Society. For those who wish to explore this area fully, self-guided walking tour maps are available from the society and at many establishments downtown.

Children will love the **Jones Family Mini-Farm**, behind the Olivares House at Los Rios and River Streets. This 3 acre (1.2ha) farm is home to the largest horse in Orange County, as well as other farm animals. Children can take a pony ride *($2)* or feed and interact with the barnyard animals at the petting zoo *($0.50)*. The farm strives to recreate life in San Juan in the early 1900s.

Photography buffs will really enjoy the **House of Photographic Arts** *(27182 Ortega*

Mission San Juan Capistrano

Hwy.; ☎494-1257) which showcases historical and modern photography by established as well as up-and-coming photographers.

★
Oceanside

Over the past two centuries, local missionaries and ranch workers have been saying "let's go to the ocean side" on warm days, and thus this quaint resort was born. Oceanside is situated halfway between Los Angeles and San Diego. The small town serves as the area's transportation hub, with trains and buses heading for destinations to the north, south and east. This makes it a good home base to explore the region. The 3.6mi (5km) of wide, white beaches provide an excellent location for all types of water sports, whether it be surfing, sailing, fishing or just plain lounging on the beach. The San Luis Rey Mission acts as the cultural centre of Oceanside, and offers a chance to explore the rich history and culture of the region.

The clean, white-sand **beaches ★★** of Oceanside fortunately don't draw the same crowds as its counterparts. There is, however, plenty to do here. **The Strand ★** is a paved path running parallel to the water that is perfect for jogging or in-line skating. The beachfront is divided into eight beaches even though it is one continuous stretch of sand. The beaches north of the pier have much more sand and more room to play. Most of the beaches have firepits, volleyball courts, public restrooms and showers. There is paid parking on both sides of

the pier and metered parking on the street.

At 1,942 ft (647m), the **Oceanside Pier ★★** (Pier View Way and Pacific St.) is the longest wooden pier in Southern California. As with most of the piers along the coast, it is alive with activity from sunrise to sunset. No license is required for pier fishing and there are snack shops along the way if you don't make a catch. An electric tram service is available for those with limited mobility, who can't make the considerable walk to the end.

Over 1,000 boats make their home at the **Oceanside Harbor ★★** (1540 Harbor Dr. N; ☎966-4580). A variety of services are available here, including whale-watching tours, deep-sea fishing trips and boat rentals. Around the harbour lighthouse is a quaint, Cape-cod style village with a fine selection of shops and restaurants.

Fifty-two trains pass through the **Oceanside Transit Centre** (235 Tremont St.), making Oceanside one of the easiest beaches to reach by public transit. This also makes Oceanside a great home base for those who don't want to battle with traffic. The **Metrolink** (☎203-808-LINK) service is intended for commuters but is useful for tourists as well. Commuter trains head north as far as Los Angeles Union Station in the early morning, Monday through Friday. The same trains run south in the evening, but there is no service during the day, so contact Metrolink to plan your travels ahead of time. The **Coaster Beach Train** ($3.00 - $3.75 one way; ☎800-262-

7837) operates throughout the day in both directions as far as San Diego (1hr), making stops along the coast. The last train back from San Diego runs at 6:42pm. **Amtrak** (☎800-872-7245) and **Greyhound** (☎722-1587) also serve Oceanside from this terminal.

The **Oceanside Historical Society** (Thurs, Fri, Sat 10am to 2pm; 305 N. Nevada St.; ☎722-4786) is located in the historic Gill Fire Station building. The museum has a collection of images from early Oceanside and the staff is very knowledgeable. The society sponsors a monthly historical walking tour of the downtown area on the third Saturday of the month, April through September. Alternatively, a self-guided tour and map are available.

The **Star Theater ★** (402 N. Pacific Coast Hwy.; ☎721-5700) has been lovingly restored to its 1956 grandeur, with its classic neon facade that is visible for blocks. Inside is the largest screen in the county and a seating capacity of 920.

The Spanish-revival style **Oceanside Museum of Art ★** ($3; Tue to Sat 10am to 4pm, Sun 1pm to 4pm; 704 Pier View Way; ☎721-2787) is across from **City Hall** in the **Civic Centre Plaza ★** (300 N. Pacific Coast Hwy). The museum features exhibitions on loan from major art museums around the world and showcases their own collection of regional, ethnic and local artists. The prime emphasis is on art education for children, and every effort is made to ensure they enjoy the visit. If you are in the area on a Thursday, check out the **Oceanside Farmers' Market** (Thurs 9am to 12:30pm; Corner of N. Pa-

cific Coast Hwy and Pier View Way) in the plaza, a chance to taste legendary Californian produce straight from the farm.

For an enlightening perspective on surfing culture and history, check out the **California Surfing Museum ★** *(free admission; closed Tue; 10am to 4pm; 223 N. Coast Hwy.; ☎721-6876)*. In addition to the many photos, surfboards and memorabilia, the museum features a new exhibit every six months that pays homage to one of surfing's legends.

Along the north side of Oceanside is **Camp Pendleton** *(Oceanside Harbor/Camp Pendleton ramp off Interstate 5; ☎725-5569)*, the world's largest U.S. Marine Corps Amphibious Training Base. The base is home to 37,000 people, more than 75 head of buffalo, and a few attractions. An 1827 adobe ranch house serves as the home of the commanding general. The adobe Chapel and Bunkhouse Museum have period rooms that depict early life on the ranch. Visitors can take a self-guided walking or driving tour of the base, but check with the guard shack for a map to find out the "rules."

Nicknamed the "King of the Missions," the **San Luis del Rey Mission and Museum ★★★** *($4; every day 10am to 4:30pm; 4050 Mission Ave.; ☎757-3651; www.sanluisrey.org)* was founded on June 13, 1798 by Father Fermin Francisco de Lausen and is located about 3mi (5km) east of town. Named after St. Louis IX, King of France and patron of the Secular Franciscan order, it was the 18th Spanish mission in California and also the largest. The present

The Orange: Symbol of California's Vitality

The first orange grove was created in 1804 on the San Gabriel Mission, east of San Francisco. Shoots from that grove were then used to create others, including the first commercial grove near Los Angeles in 1841.

But the real starting point of this industry was the discovery of gold in 1849, as the uncontrollable population growth increased the demand for fresh produce.

One variety of oranges called Navel was responsible for this industry's success throughout the country. Large, juicy and seedless, in addition to being easy to peel, this delicious fruit quickly became another symbol for the state, representing California as a

haven of peace and vitality.

There are many orange groves north of San Diego. Take the time to stop and admire the beauty of the orange tree, filled with its sun coloured fruit. Don't forget to respect private land limits, however.

You should also sample the different varieties of citrus fruits offered at nearby stands. There are actually more than 160 kinds in California. Among them are 18 types of Navels and 11 Valencias, five kinds of blood oranges, 29 mandarins, 16 types of grapefruit and 16 kinds of lemons. Also try the kumquat, limequat, mandarinquat and citrange (hybrid varieties).

structure was built between 1811 and 1815 with timbers from Mt. Palomar and adobe made on site. Since the 1890s the building has been under constant restoration and the brilliant white walls and perfect arches look better today than ever. The mission provides guided and self-guided tours through the sunken gardens and along the arched colonnade after a visit to the museum. Visitors are also

welcome to take part in weekend mass.

Behind the mission, the **Heritage Park Village and Museum ★★** *(free admission; grounds open daily 9am to 4m; ☎966-4545)* awaits visitors. The park is a collection of buildings from the late 19th and early 20th century that have been carefully brought in and assembled as a recreation of an old Californian town. Take a stroll back through time as you pass the town's first General Store, the Portola Inn, the Blacksmith Shop and even the old City Jail. Each building is period-furnished and faces onto a lovely park and gazebo. Unfortunately, the buildings are only open on Sundays from 1pm to 4pm. Guided tours are also available during the summer.

Outdoor Activities

Hiking

Tour B: The Beaches of Orange County

Newport Beach

The **Upper Newport Bay Ecological Reserve** *(2400 Irvine Ave.; ☎646-8009)* has a 10mi (16km) loop trail that winds through the reserve. Free naturalist-guided walking tours are offered the first and third Saturday of the month.

Huntington Beach

The **Bolsa Chica Ecological Reserve** *(tours 9am and 10:30am, first Sat of the month, Sep to Apr; Warner Ave. at the Pacific Coast Hwy.; ☎800-628-7275 ext.119)* has a 1.5mi (2.5km) interpretive loop trail, with informative signs along it. Keep an eye open for the many birds that make this reserve their temporary home.

Surfing

Tour B: The Beaches of Orange County

Surfing is the most popular water activity in California, and has spawned a rich and vibrant culture of its own. Any area with access to the beach has a surf shop or two nearby that will rent surf boards and wetsuits, as well as give you some pointers as to where the surf is good that day. **Huntington Beach** calls itself "Surf City U.S.A." and has a plethora of surf shops where you can rent a board at a reasonable price. Most of the surfing takes place near the pier, which is excellent for beginners, as there are generally lifeguards on duty in case you run into trouble. Great spots include the **Huntington Pier**, **The Wedge** at Newport Beach and **The Strand** at Oceanside.

Cruises

Tour B: The Beaches of Orange County

Newport Beach

Balboa Boat Rentals *(beside the Balboa Ferry dock; ☎673-7200)* rents by the hour or half day at reasonable prices. Double kayaks and pedal boats cost $50/half-day, while motor and fishing boats run at $100 and more.

Adventures at Sea *(3101 W. Pacific Coast Hwy., Suite 209; ☎650-2412;*

www.boatcharter.com) offers dinner cruises, sailing and sportfishing and Catalina Island excursions from the Newport Harbor.

Fishing

Tour B: The Beaches of Orange County

Visitors can fish from the piers in most beach towns without a licence.

Newport Beach

Davey's Locker Sportfishing *(400 Main St., Balboa; ☎673-1434)* offers individual ticket sales for half-day, 3/4 day, full-day and shark fishing trips year round. Whale-watching excursions are also available January to March.

Dana Point

Dana Wharf Sportfishing *(34675 Golden Lantern; ☎496-5794)* offers half-day, full-day and week-long sportfishing trips.

Bird-Watching

Tour B: The Beaches of Orange County

Many of the parks and wildlife reserves on the coast are in the path of the Pacific Flyway, serving as welcome stops for the numerous species of birds migrating along this route. There are also several species that make these wildlife refuges their home year round.

The Swallows of San Juan

In San Juan Capistrano, the "Miracle of the Swallows" is celebrated on March 19, St. Joseph's Day. It is with an odd punctuality that each year, the swallows of Goya, Argentina complete their 7,500mi (12,000km) migration northward. Crowds gather, a parade winds through the historic streets and the fiesta begins. The guests of honour are always on time as the first scouts arrive, setting down on the familiar arches and roofs of the mansion. Over the course of the day, their numbers swell as the swallows descend, lending their music to that of the festivities. Up to 20,000 people make the migration themselves to San Juan to take part in this event.

In the early part of the 20th century, the "Mi-

racle of the Swallows" attracted its share of media attention. Songwriter Leon René penned the song *When the Swallows Come Back to Capistrano* after being inspired by the event.

The swallows stay all summer, nesting and mating about the town, but mainly settling in the beautiful angles and recesses of the Mission. They generally make the trip back on October 23, the feast of San Juan of Capistrano. They have been leaving earlier in the pas few years due to a dwindling insect population. By the time they reach their winter home again in Argentina, these swallows will have travelled 15,000mi (24,000km)—equivalent to travelling half-way around the world!

birds migrating along the Pacific Flyway. The 530 acres (214ha) are also home to a variety of wildlife that is relatively easy to spot. (See "Exploring," p 153)

Newport Beach

The **Upper Newport Bay Ecological Reserve** *(2400 Irvine Ave.; ☎646-8009)* is a 752-acre (304 ha) coastal wetland reserve that supports six ecological habitats. A variety of fish, mammals and over 200 species of birds call this reserve home.

San Juan Capistrano

Every year the swallows of Goya, Argentina, return to their nests at Mission San Juan Capistrano, drawing the largest crowd of birdwatchers in California (see box).

Accommodations

Tour A: Inland Orange County

Anaheim

Desert Inn
$$
≡, *tv*, ≈, ☉
1600 S. Harbor Blvd.
☎772-5050
☎800-433-5270
≈778-2754
www.anabeimdesertinn.com
Right beside the park gates, the Desert Inn has large rooms, complete with fridge and microwave. The indoor heated pool and hot tub are great on cloudy days, plus there is a terrific rooftop sundeck that is perfect for watching the fireworks

Seal Beach

The **Anaheim Bay National Wildlife Refuge** is accessible to visitors on the last Saturday of the month *(info ☎598-1024)*, when a shuttle runs through the 1000-acre (404ha) reserve. The refuge is a salt marsh area that is a breeding ground for various fish and migratory birds. The tour is free and leaves from the main gate of the base at 9am. There is only limited ac-

cess to the refuge because it is located within the **U.S. Naval Weapons Support Facility** *(www.sbeach.navy.mil)*. Giant naval vessels can be seen coming in and out of Anaheim Bay.

Huntington Beach

The **Bolsa Chica Ecological Reserve** *(Warner Ave. at the Pacific Coast Hwy.; ☎800-628-7275 ext. 119)* is a protected wetland reserve that serves as a rest area for show at Disneyland. Get a room above the ground floor as they are much more accessible. Two- or three-bedroom suites with separate living areas are also available and are ideal for families.

Tropicana Inn & Suites
$$
≡, *tv*, ≈, ⊛
☎*635-4082*
☎*800-828-4898*
⇋*635-1535*
www.bei-hotels.com
The Tropicana is a motel-style property right at the gates of Disneyland. Rooms are rather generic with kitschy tropical art. The large heated pool and spa are a nice amenity at this budget establishment. Also on site is a guest laundry, convenience store and two take-out restaurants.

Holiday Inn at the Park
$$$
≡, *tv*, ≈, ⊛, ⊘, ℜ
1221 S. Harbor Blvd.
☎*758-0900*
☎*800-545-PARK*
⇋*917-0794*
This five-storey Holiday Inn provides a convenient free shuttle service to the park. Rooms are comfortable and family oriented, with pull-out couches. A decent pool and spa area are open to guests 24hrs. As an added bonus, kids eat free all day, up to four children per adult.

Park Inn
$$$
≡, *tv*, ≈, ⊛
1520 S. Harbor Blvd.
☎*635-7275*
☎*800-828-4898*
⇋*800-828-4898*
This Swiss-chalet style hotel is owned by the same company as the Tropicana but is slightly more upscale. The large rooms are furnished with care. Their heated pool and spa are on the fourth

floor for a great night view of the park's fireworks show.

Mariott Fairfield Inn
$$$
≡, *tv*, ≈, *spa*, ℜ
460 South Harbor Blvd.
☎*772-6777*
☎*800-228-2800*
⇋*999-1727*
The Marriot Fairfield goes out of its way to be kid-friendly: a magician entertains Monday, Wednesday and Friday; there's a large video arcade and McDonald's can be delivered right to your room. Their restaurant, Millie's, serves classic American fare and provides room service. The ample rooms feature a small fridge and pull-out couches.

The Hyatt Alicante
$$$$
≡, *tv*, ≈, ⊛, ⊘, ℜ
100 Plaza Alicante
at Harbour and Chapman
☎*750-1234*
☎*800-233-1234*
⇋*720-0465*
www.hyatt.com
The Hyatt features a huge, 17-storey atrium that encloses the restaurant, bar, towering live trees and fountains. Rooms are large and well laid out, with coffee makers, dataports and tasteful furnishings. On the third floor there is a heated pool, hot tub and fitness area. The service is excellent and they provide shuttle service to Disneyland. Parking is extra.

Disneyland Hotel / Disneyland Pacific Hotel
$$$$-$$$$$
≡, *tv*, ≈, ⊛, ℜ, ⊘
1150 West Cerritos Ave.
☎*778-6600*
☎*800-225-2024*
⇋*956-6508*
www.disneyland.com
For the ultimate Disney experience, stay right beside the park at the one of the two Disney hotels.

Though the warm, cozy rooms are decorated with classic Disney animation, guests will have little time to spend in them. The wonderfully landscaped grounds abound in fountains and waterfalls, with plenty of photo spots along the way. The recreation area is shared with the Pacific Hotel below and includes a gigantic free-form pool with Captain Hook's ship in the centre. An additional pool and spa are located on the landscaped roof, offering perfect views of the nightly fireworks. Add to this the singing bellhops, live poolside shows and a variety of great restaurants and you'll easily be caught up in the magic of Disney.

Buena Park

Guest House International Inn at Buena Park
$$
≡, *tv*, ≈, ℜ
7878 Crescent Ave.
☎*527-1515*
☎*888-782-9752*
⇋*527-2469*
Directly across from Knott's Berry Farm, the Guest House offers clean, comfortable rooms equipped with a fridge and microwave. A large, square pool dominates the inner courtyard. Pet friendly.

Embassy Suites Buena Park
$$-$$$ bkfst incl.
≡, *tv*, ≈, ⊛
7762 Beach Blvd.
☎*739-5600*
☎*800-362-2779*
⇋*521-9560*
The Embassy Suites features two room mini-suites, with a living room and private bedroom. Fridges, microwaves and coffee makers are also standard. A landscaped tropical courtyard gives way to the pool and spa.

Extra amenities include a full, cooked-to-order breakfast and 2hrs of complimentary beverages each evening. A free shuttle service to Disneyland is provided.

Holiday Inn Buena Park
$$$-$$$$$
≡, tv, ≈, ⊛, ⊘, ℜ
7000 Beach Blvd.
☎ 522-7000
☎ 800-HOLIDAY
⇄ 522-3230

A recent multi-million dollar renovation is evident from the new fountains, updated decor and the enormous European-style lobby, with a polished granite floor and baby grand piano. Rooms are available for a variety of budgets, from standard doubles to the poolside terrace room with private courtyard. The fourth floor is business-oriented and offers an executive lounge, complimentary breakfast, late night snacks, and upgraded rooms.

Santa Ana

Quality Suites
$$$ bkfst incl.
≡, tv, ≈
2701 Hotel Terrace Dr.
☎ 957-9200
☎ 800-228-5151
⇄ 641-8936
www.hotelchoice.com

An excellent budget choice that is long on amenities. Two-room suites are standard and include a full breakfast, nightly happy hour and dinner Tuesday through Thursday. A shuttle service is provided to area attractions.

Costa Mesa

Residence Inn Costa Mesa
$$$$
≡, tv, ≈, ⊛, ⊘
881 Baker St.
☎ 241-8800
☎ 800-331-3131
⇄ 546-4308
www.residenceinn.com

Part of Marriott family, the Residence Inn is an all-suite hotel close to the South Coast Plaza district. A choice of lodging includes studios, one bedroom/one bathroom and two bedroom/two bathrooms. All rooms feature fully equipped kitchens and some offer wood-burning fireplaces.

🏆 The Westin South Coast Plaza
$$$$
≡, tv, ≈, ⊛, ⊘, ℜ
686 Anton Blvd.
☎ 540-2500
☎ 800-WESTIN-1
⇄ 662-6608
www.westin.com

The Westin is in a prime location in Costa Mesa, steps away from the South Coast Repertory and South Coast Plaza shopping center. The luxurious, elegant atmosphere extends to the rooms, which

have incredibly comfortable beds and dark hardwood furniture. A full-service day spa is also available to guests. The Pinot Provence, an upscale Mediterranean bistro, is conveniently located at the hotel.

Tour B: The Beaches of Orange County

Seal Beach

Radisson Seal Beach
$$$-$$$$
≡, tv, P, ⊛, ⊘
600 Marina Dr.
☎ 493-7501
☎ 800-333-3333
⇄ 596-3448
www.radisson-seal.com

This lovely, three-storey Radisson is a short walk from the beach. The rooms are quite sterile, but all have balconies and most have a view of the water. An open atrium features a heated swimming pool and hot tub. The hotel also has a fleet of bicycles for rent. Small dogs are welcome.

🏆 Seal Beach Inn and Gardens
$$$-$$$$$ bkfst incl.
≡, tv, P
212 Fifth St.
☎ 493-2416
☎ 800-HIDEAWAY
⇄ 799-0483
www.sealbeachinn.com

The Seal Beach Inn is an elegant bed and breakfast nestled in an idyllic garden setting one block from the beach. The gardens themselves bear special mention—a sea of fragrant flowers overflows into every nook and cranny. Each room is uniquely decorated and furnished with hand-picked antiques and Victorian accents. Breakfast is a delight and tea is served in the lovely tea room.

Huntington Beach

 Colonial Inn Hostel
$
sb, tv, K
421 Eighth St.
☎*536-3315*
☎*536-9485*
www.colonialinnhostel.com
This pretty yellow hostel served as one of the few hotels in Huntington in the early 1900s. Today, it's the best deal in Huntington Beach with shared rooms for $16 and doubles for $18. Guests are welcome to use the large kitchen, T.V. room, laundry, garden and patio. An internet kiosk is also available. Toast and jam is served at breakfast and there is free coffee and tea all day. The beach is four blocks away.

Pacific View Motel
$$
≡, *tv, P,* ⊛
16220 Pacific Coast Hwy.
☎*592-4959*
☎*800-726-8586*
The Pacific View is north of downtown, on Bolsa Chica Beach. For those who want to avoid the centre of town, this is a bargain. For an extra $20, guests can upgrade to one of the whirlpool suites, which have ocean views. The staff is friendly and the rooms are clean and comfortable.

Quality Inn
$$$
≡, *tv,* ⊛, ℜ
800 Pacific Coast Hwy.
☎*536-7500*
☎*800-228-5151*
⇥*536-6846*
www.hotelchoice.com
The Pacific Coast Highway is all that separates the Quality Inn from the beach. Rooms are a good value and range from modest to extravagant, as some of the suites have in-room spas and fireplaces.

Unfortunately, the hotel lacks a pool, but there is an outdoor spa on the rooftop. Centrally located close to downtown.

Hilton Waterfront Beach Resort
$$$$-$$$$$
≡, *tv,* ℜ, *P,* ⊛, ☉
21100 Pacific Coast Hwy.
☎*845- 8000*
☎*800-822-7873*
⇥*845-8424*
www.hilton.com
The Hilton Waterfront is just across the street from the beach and well-located downtown. Each of the 290 bright and comfortable rooms have ocean views from their private patios while a large, freeform pool area overlooks Huntington City Beach. The Palm Court restaurant specializes in Mediterranean-style cuisine. Hilton is expanding in the area and should have an additional 250 rooms open by late 2001.

Newport Beach

Newport Channel Inn
$$-$$$
≡, *tv*
6030 W. Pacific Coast Hwy.
☎*642-3030*
☎*800-255-8614*
www.newportchannelinn.com
The Newport Channel Inn is an excellent budget choice for a normally costly destination. Though it is short on amenities, the beach is just across the road, and the staff is very friendly. A variety of rooms are offered, with everything from king-sized beds to family-oriented oversized rooms that sleep up to seven. While the inn doesn't have a pool, there is a rooftop sundeck where you can catch some sun or watch the birds on the adjacent channel.

Newport Classic Inn
$$-$$$
≡, *tv, P,* ⊛, ☉, ℜ, △
2300 W. Coast Hwy.
☎*722-2999*
☎*800-633-3199*
⇥*631-5659*
The Newport Classic is located right on Mariner's Mile, in the heart of the restaurant and entertainment district. On first glance, the large glass and concrete structure resembles a shopping mall. The rooms are clean but rather kitschy and nondescript. For the price, however, this hotel is full of amenities such as a pool, hot tub, sauna and small gym. Above the lobby is a the Tsuru restaurant featuring a sushi bar and great Japanese/Chinese cuisine.

Balboa Bay Club
$$$$
≡, *tv, P,* ⊛, ☉, △, ℜ
1221 W. Coast Hwy.
☎*645-5000*
☎*800-882-6499*
⇥*642-6947*
The Balboa Bay Club is a complete resort destination with 121 guest rooms and 14 suites on Newport Harbor. The list of amenities is impressive – two swimming pools, a private beach, men's and women's spas, indoor basketball and outdoor volleyball, racquetball and tennis courts. The guest rooms are equally impressive, bright and airy, with live plants and private balconies with ocean views. The Bay Club also has its own 140-slip private marina with guest- and charter-boat docking. The cheerful staff will help you arrange boat rental or charters. The First Cabin restaurant serves fine fresh seafood while the Shell Bar and Lounge is the place for nightly entertainment.

Orange County

Portofino Hotel
$$$$-$$$$$ bkfst incl.
≡, tv, ⊛, ℜ
2306 W. Oceanfront
☎*673-7030*
☎*800-571-8749*
⇌*723-4370*
www.portofinobeachhotel.com
The Portofino offers sincere European hospitality in this charming Oceanside bed and breakfast. The stunning rooms have been elegantly decorated with fine European antiques and many have exceptional views of the Pacific. Most rooms include in-room marble whirlpool tubs and all have private sundecks. Rates are negotiable for extended stays. True to their European atmosphere, English, French, German and Spanish are spoken.

Balboa Inn
$$$$-$$$$$ bkfst incl.
≡, tv, P, ⊛, ℜ
105 Main St.
☎*675-3412*
☎*877-225-2629*
⇌*673-4587*
www.balboainn.com
The Balboa Inn is a beautiful Old World bed and breakfast conveniently located on the boardwalk in Balboa. The inn itself is a historical landmark. Built in 1929, Hollywood celebrities used to flock to the Balboa for dancing at the Rendezvous Ballroom. The historic ambiance is alive and well today in the Balboa and its location on the boardwalk makes for a multitude of shopping and dining possibilities. Standard rooms are warm and inviting, though they lack an ocean view. Their famous suites start at $295 and include a fireplace, jacuzzi tub and views of the ocean.

Doryman's Inn
$$$$-$$$$$
≡, tv, ⊛, ℜ
2102 W. Oceanfront
☎*675-7300*
Doryman's is in the place in Newport Beach for intimate, pampering service. Each of the 10 unique rooms features a fireplace, sunken Italian marble tub and luxurious American and French antiques surrounding the inviting canopy bed. A rooftop patio and sundeck overlook the ocean. The staff is extremely knowledgeable and all serve as concierges, making your stay worry-free. A full breakfast can be enjoyed in the parlour or on the ocean-view patio.

Four Seasons Hotel
$$$$$
≡, tv, P, ⊛, ⊘, ℜ
690 Newport Center Dr.
☎*759-0808*
☎*800-332-3442*
⇌*759-0809*
www.fourseasons.com
For the most upscale experience in Newport Beach, many choose the Four Seasons Hotel, the only five-star establishment in Newport Beach. This oasis of casual elegance and impeccable service is adjacent to the Fashion Island shopping centre, nestled among majestic palms, sparkling pools and verdant gardens. Views from the upper floors of this 19-storey hotel are nothing short of breathtaking. Oversized guest rooms are comfortable and inviting while the Pavillion restaurant is one of the finest in Newport, overlooking a dense garden. Golfers will enjoy choice tee times and exclusive rates at the nearby Pelican Hill Golf Club.

Laguna Beach

Crescent Bay Inn
$$-$$$
≡, tv
1435 N. Pacific Coast Hwy.
☎*494-2508*
☎*888-494-2508*
⇌*497-1708*
This small, 29-room inn has ocean views and provides convenient access to Crescent Bay Park, Heisler Park, and the beach. The reasonable rates make this an attractive choice, though the beach is a short walk away and there is no swimming pool. The rooms are very clean and comfortable and half the rooms have kitchen facilities. Located about 1mi (1.6km) north of downtown.

Tides Motel
$$-$$$$
≡, tv, K, P
460 N. Coast Hwy.
☎*494-2494*
☎*497-5209*
The Tides is an intimate, 20-room hotel located a half-block from the beach just north of downtown. Ocean views and rooms with kitchens are available, some with patios. A colourful garden surrounds the barbeque, picnic and pool area.

Hotel Laguna
$$$-$$$$$
≡, tv, ≈, ℜ
425 S. Pacific Coast Hwy.
☎*494-1151*
☎*800-524-2927*
⇌*497-2163*
www.hotellaguna.com
The Hotel Laguna is the most historic hotel in Laguna Beach. With roots dating back to the late 1800s, the present Spanish-colonial-style building was constructed in 1931. Many of the rooms face the hotel's private beach, but unfortunately, none have balconies. The rooms are rather plain but neverthe-

less maintain some of their historic charm. The location is fantastic, however, right in the middle of downtown Laguna Beach. Three wonderful restaurants are in the hotel: Claes Seafood Etc. (see p 176), The Wine Cellar and the Terrace Café.

The Inn at Laguna Beach
$$$-$$$$$
≡, tv, P, ⊛
211 N. Pacific Coast Hwy.
☎497-9722
☎800-544-4479
⇌497-9972
www.innatlagunabeach.com
This hotel has an enviable position on a bluff overlooking the Main Beach. The pool and spa area looks onto a bright patch of flowers and a short path winding down to the white-sand beach. Rooms are tastefully furnished with eclectic accents. A continental breakfast is served in-room, as it may be difficult to pull yourself out of the feather beds and duvets. Private balconies look out over the ocean from 52 rooms while the other 18 have a view of downtown Laguna Beach.

Laguna Riviera
$$-$$$$
≡, tv, P, ⊛, K
825 S. Pacific Coast Hwy.
☎494-1196
☎800-999-2089
⇌494-8421
www.laguna-riviera.com
The Laguna Riviera is a fabulous beachside hotel. Its rooms range from the budget-conscious street views, to the luxurious oceanfront suites. Whichever room you choose, the multi-tiered terraces are the perfect place to enjoy Californian surf and sun. The unique "tropical pavilion" houses a heated swimming pool, sauna bath and whirlpool under a partially retractable roof. The main lounge is the

hub of the action with it's fireplace, grand piano and guest library. The Riviera is located in South Laguna, at the beginning of the shopping/gallery area.

Casa Laguna Inn
$$-$$$$$ bkfst incl.
≡, tv, P, K, ♥
2510 S. Coast Hwy.
☎494-2996
☎800-233-0449
⇌494-5009
The Casa Laguna is a lovely Spanish-style inn set on a terraced hillside in South Laguna. Guests have a choice of standard rooms, family suites with kitchens, or one of the two cottages with fireplaces. Each room is charming, with a mix of antique and contemporary furnishings. In addition to the scrumptious breakfast, afternoon tea, wine and snacks are provided in the library. Pet-friendly.

Laguna Brisas Spa Hotel
$$$-$$$$$
1600 S. Pacific Coast Hwy.
☎497-7272
☎877-503-1466
⇌497-8306
www.lagunabrisas.com
Just across the Pacific Coast Highway from the beach, the Laguna Brisas Spa Hotel is a charming villa overlooking the Pacific in South Laguna. Each of the 64 attractive guest rooms has a wonderful marble spa for two as the main attraction, while wicker furniture and generous windows complete the decor. Not all rooms have a balcony, however, so be sure to ask.

Surf & Sand Hotel
$$$$$
≡, tv, ℜ, P, ⊛, ☺
1555 S. Pacific Coast Hwy.
☎497-4477
☎800-LAGUNA-1
⇌494-7653
The beautiful Surf & Sand Hotel has been family

owned and operated for the past 50 years. All 157 rooms have fantastic ocean views. The rooms are bright, comfortable and cozy, with large glass doors opening out onto private balconies. Compact-disc players are an added bonus. A lovely pool area overlooks the pounding Pacific surf. Their two restaurants, Splashes and Towers, provide oceanfront dining ranging from casual to elegant, with Mediterranean and Pacific accents. Valet parking is extra and required to park at the hotel.

Dana Point

The Best Western Marina Inn
$$$
≡, tv, P, ☺
24800 Dana Point Harbor Dr.
☎255-6843
☎800-255-6843
⇌248-0360
The Best Western is the only hotel located right at the marina on the beautiful Dana Point Harbor Drive. There is a small pool and the rooms are generic but comfortable. Within walking distance to the Marine Institute and Doheny State Beach.

Blue Lantern Inn
$$$$ bkfst incl.
≡, tv
34343 St. of the Blue Lantern
☎661-1304
☎800-950-236
⇌496-1483
This New England-style inn has a great location on a bluff overlooking the harbour. The main lobby features a large fireplace and stairs overflowing with stuffed animals. Each of the 29 airy, spacious rooms has a marble fireplace and whirlpool bath. A full buffet breakfast is provided every morning and wine and snacks are served in the afternoon.

Orange County

Even if you're not staying here, check out the great view from the adjacent lookout. Bikes are available for guests use.

San Clemente

San Clemente Beach Hostel
$
sb, K
233 Avenida Granada
☎800-909-4776
☎492-2848
A member of Hostelling International, this seasonal hostel is open May 1 through October 31, when it's the best deal in town. Forty beds are available in either dorms or private rooms. There is a large kitchen and common room as well as two outdoor patios. The beach and the pier are five blocks away. A favourite with surfers and backpackers.

The Beachcomber Motel
$$$
≡, tv, K
533 Avenida Victoria
☎492-5457
☎888-492-5457
⇒492-5476
www.beachcombermotel.com
The Beachcomber is a cute, casita-style motel overlooking the beach and San Clemente Pier. Barbecue grills and picnic tables can be found on the grassy grounds surrounding the motel. Each room is different, so take a look before you commit. The rooms are modest but the motel has a fun atmosphere and a beach-house feel.

San Clemente Inn
$$$$
≡, tv, ≈, ⊛, ⌂, ☉, K
2600 Avenida del Presidente
☎492-6103
⇒498-3014
www.sanclementeinn.com
From this resort, the beach is just a short walk through San Clemente State Park.

Extra amenities include saunas for men and women, lit tennis courts and a children's play area. The rooms are modern and spacious and can accommodate up to six adults. Superb landscaping and the adjacent park make this a great choice.

🌴 Casa Tropicana
$$$-$$$$ bkfst incl.
≡, tv, ⊛, ℜ
610 Avenida Victoria
☎492-1234
☎800-492-1245
⇒492-2423
www.casatropicana.com
This lovely Spanish-style inn makes for an unforgettable stop in San Clemente. Choose one of their nine intricate theme rooms, such as the Emerald Forest with its vine ceiling or the Bali Hai with its mirrored bamboo canopy bed. Most rooms feature a spa and fireplace. The Tropicana Bar & Grill on the beach level features Mexican and Californian favourites. Champagne and a full breakfast are also included.

San Juan Capistrano

Mission Inn
$$
≡, tv, P
26891 Ortega Hwy.
☎493-1151
This small, 21-room motel, is designed after the mission itself. The affordable rooms are clean, comfortable, and within walking distance of the mission and downtown.

Best Western Capistrano Inn
$$$
≡, tv, ≈, ⊛
27174 Ortega Hwy.
☎493-5661
☎800-441-9438
www.capoinm.com
This Best Western is located just two blocks from the mission, downtown and the Los Rios Historical

district. Shuttle service is available to most other major attractions in the area. A variety of rooms are available, including some with kitchenettes.

Oceanside

Guesthouse Inn & Suites
$$-$$$
≡, tv, ≈, ℜ
1103 N. Pacific Coast Hwy.
☎722-1904
☎800-914-2230
⇒722-1168
The Guesthouse is a modest inn overlooking a nearby estuary and the ocean from a distance. The rooms are bland but clean, with decent balconies. The location is within walking distance of downtown, the harbor and Camp Pendleton. This is an excellent budget choice as rates can dip as low as $45 off-season.

Best Western Oceanside Inn
$$-$$$$
≡, tv, ≈, ⊛, ☉, K
1680 Oceanside Blvd.
☎722-1821
☎800-443-9995
⇒967-8969
www.bestwestern.com
This Best Western is well located, with lovely views of the ocean from its spacious rooms. A large pool and spa area is set among the palms and plants of the inner courtyard. Within walking distance to the beach, restaurants and shopping.

Oceanside Marina Inn
$$$$-$$$$$
≡, tv, ≈, ⊛, K, ℜ
2008 Harbor Dr. N.
☎722-1561
☎800-252-2033
⇒439-9758
www.omihotel.com
The Marina Inn is in a wonderful secluded location that makes visitors feel as though they are staying on a small island in the middle of the Pacific.

The one- or two-bedroom suites are spacious, with either marina or ocean views. A variety of rooms are available, with fireplaces, spas or kitchens. The friendly staff will help arrange any cruises or tours that may interest you. Sailboats and jet-skis are also available for rent.

Restaurants

Tour A: Inland Orange County

Anaheim

Spire's
$
990 S. Euclid St. at Ball Rd.
☎635-5730
Spire's is a family-style restaurant offering traditional American food. Six breakfast specials under $3 and daily dinner specials are perfect for those on a budget.

Millie's Restaurant
$-$$
1480 S. Harbor Blvd.
☎535-6892
Located just across from the park gates, Millie's is a great inexpensive way to feed an army of kids. Classic diner fare is available as well as a decent breakfast or dinner buffet.

The Spaghetti Station
$-$$
999 West Ball Rd.
☎956-3250
In an old rustic building two blocks north of Disneyland, a stagecoach and life-sized horses sit on the roof of this Wild West restaurant. Choose from steaks, ribs, or 14 kinds of spaghetti as you examine the vast collection of antique art and mining mem-orabilia of the Old West that covers the walls. Live entertainment is offered most nights of the week.

Breakfast with Minnie and Friends
$$
1717 S. West Ave.
☎956-6755
Head to the Disneyland Pacific Hotel before going into the park to have an all-you-can-eat breakfast with Minnie and her friend Merlin the Wizard. The interactive show is full of song and dance, sure to start off a great day at Disneyland.

J.T. Schmid's Brewhouse and Eatery
$$-$$$
2610 E. Katella Ave.
☎634-9200
Across from the Pond and Edison Field, J.T. Schmid's gets packed before and after a game. A brewery is on site, offering a selection of ales and lagers to accompany the Californian cuisine. The giant display kitchen serves up wood-fired pizza, Angus steaks, seafood and pasta in a fun, open-concept dining room. After dinner, relax in their comfortable bar.

Cuban Pete's
$$-$$$
1050 W. Ball Rd.
☎490-2020
Authentic Cuban and Caribbean cuisine is served in a 1940s Havana decor. Live music is featured every day but Monday, with everything from jazz to salsa. Flamenco shows accompany dinner on weekends with two performances on Saturdays at 6pm and 8pm. Reservations are recommended.

Charley Browns Steakhouse
$$$
1751 S. State College Blvd.
☎634-2211
Here, steaks and tender prime rib are complimented by an amazing selection of soups and salads. Steps away from Anaheim Stadium and the Pond. They also have a cozy little bar area that spills out onto a shaded patio.

The Anaheim White House Restaurant
$$$$
887 S. Anaheim Blvd.
☎714-722-1381
This restored 1909 Victorian home has consistently been ranked among the best restaurants in Orange County for its scrumptious Italian specialties and seafood. Eight different dining rooms feature crackling fireplaces, romantic lighting and elegant Victorian decor. Every choice on the menu is a winner, artistically arranged and flawlessly served. Reservations are highly recommended and a jacket and tie is suggested, but not required.

Orange

Gameworks
$$
The Block in Orange - City Dr.
☎939-9690
Gameworks is the kind of place where you are encouraged to play with your food. American classic cuisine is served, and

usually gulped down in a rush to get to the numerous pool tables and extensive video arcade.

The Lotus Cafe
$$
1515 W. Chapman Ave.
☎385-1233
The Lotus Cafe offers authentic Chinese vegetarian cuisine. There's not a trace of meat in the place, but some of the favourites include decent approximations of meatballs, pork dim sum and hot wok beef. Health-conscious cooking is combined with fresh ingredients and served with a smile.

Café TuTu Tango
$$-$$$
The Block in Orange- 20 City Dr.
☎769-2222
www.cafetututango.com
The brick interior and artwork seemingly displayed at random make this the perfect artist's café. A large patio is usually full of beautiful people watching the crowd go by. Try one of their "starving artist" specials, the fried alligator or barbecue salmon spears.

Wolfgang Puck
$$-$$$
The Block in Orange - 20 City Dr.
☎546-9653
Wolfgang Puck offers Asian-fusion cuisine as well as pizza, steaks and sushi—something to please almost anyone. The busy mosaic tile-motif walls preside over comfortable booths. Try their signature grilled tuna burger.

PJ's Abbey
$$$
182 S. Orange St.
☎771-8556
PJ's Abbey is housed in a centennial Victorian church with vaulted ceilings, rich woodwork and beautiful stained-glass windows. Hand-cut filet mignon with tiger shrimp, chicken cordon bleu and a marinated rack of lamb are just a few of the highlights. Friday and Saturday nights feature jazz from 6 to 9pm.

Buena Park

Bernie's Diner
$
6086 Beach Blvd.
☎739-4504
Bernie's is an inexpensive option along the "entertainment corridor" of Buena Park. The classic diner-style menu is offered from 5am to 3am daily.

The Train McDonald's
$
7861 Beach Blvd.
☎521-2303
The McDonald's restaurant in Buena Park merits special mention. Inside the early 20th-century exterior is the first high-tech amusement ride in a McDonald's. The McThriller simulates roller-coaster rides, jet-fighter acrobatics or downhill skiing. There are also five trains that make their way throughout the establishment, the largest McDonald's in America.

PoFolks
$-$$
7701 Beach Blvd.
☎521-8955
This friendly home-style restaurant serves generous helpings of classic American fare. A 500ft (160m) model railroad chugs its way through the restaurant. (See p. 179.)

Santa Ana

Ruby's Diner
$-$$
2800 N. Main St.
☎836-7829
This 1940s style diner has everything you could ever want in the way of burgers, fries and shakes. For an authentic experience, pop a quarter in the jukebox and settle into one of the vinyl booths.

Jerry's Famous Deli
$$
3210 Park Centre Rd.
☎662-3363
Located a half-block from the Orange County Performing Arts Centre, Jerry's Deli boasts a menu of over 600 items, ranging from traditional deli-style to Californian Cuisine. Just about anything you can imagine is on the menu, including a large kosher selection.

Shelley's Courthouse Bistro
$$-$$$
Mon to Fri 11am to 4pm
Thu to Sat 5pm to 9pm
400 Fourth St.
☎543-9821
Shelley's offers Cajun cuisine in a charming, bistro-style atmosphere. Try the signature alligator or the spicy seafood gumbo.

The Bluewater Grill
$$-$$$
1621 W. Sunflower Ave. Suite D-50
☎546-3472
The Bluewater Grill is reminiscent of casual New England seafood restaurants with it's wood decor and paper placemats. Over 20 varieties of fresh fish can be enjoyed either inside or on the patio. The oyster bar is also quite popular.

Costa Mesa

 The Gypsy Den Cafe
$$
2930 Bristol St.
☎*549-7012*
Located in the Anti-mall
shopping centre, the
Gypsy Den is a perfectly
eclectic spot where thrift-
store paintings line the
walls and the furniture has
been scrounged from
garage sales. They offer a
great selection of giant
sandwiches, vegetarian
delights, and their famous
gooey lasagna.

Memphis Soul Cafe & Bar
$$-$$$
2920 Bristol St.
☎*432-7685*
The Memphis Soul Cafe
offers a casual, funky at-
mosphere and a menu
featuring southern-style
meatloaf, Cajun gumbo,
Creole shrimp and other
inspiring dishes. The pre-
sentation is wonderful and
the cozy bar is great for an
after-dinner drink.

Antonello Ristorante
$$$$
1611 W. Sunflower Ave.
☎*751-7153*
Fantastic, well-presented
northern Italian specialties
are accompanied by an
award-winning wine list of
300 foreign and domestic
labels. Guests
dine amidst
frescoes of
hanging vines
and fine art.
President
Clinton dined
at Antonello
during a recent
visit, and the
restaurant is
often filled with
famous person-
alities.

Tour B: The Beaches of Orange County

Seal Beach

Hennessey's Tavern
$
143 Main St.
☎*598-6456*
Inside this lovely stone
building is a pub-style
restaurant/bar, a great spot
for a beer on a hot day.
The restaurant serves clas-
sic yet uninspired pub
grub, including a good
selection of sandwiches
and burgers. The bar heats
up after dark and is open
for breakfast as well.

BJ's Pizza & Grill
$
209 Main St.
☎*594-9310*
This open-air pizza joint
features deep-dish pizza,
hot subs, burgers and
pasta. Try the honey-crisp
chicken salad and the
chunky vegetarian deep-
dish pizza.

Finbars Italian Kitchen
$-$$
550 Pacific Coast Hwy. #111
☎*430-4303*
Swing and big band music
plays in the background of
this lovely family restaurant. Daily specials compliment the Italian-American
fare of pasta, pizza,
shrimp, chicken and sal-
ads. Try the chicken
tequila fusilli or design
your own pizza.

**"Kinda" Lahaina
Broiler**
$$-$$$
901 Ocean Dr.
☎*596-3864*
The "Kinda" Lahaina
Broiler has a wonderful
seaside location over-
looking Seal Beach. Its
extensive menu features
a wide selection of fresh
seafood, but also offers
Angus beef, pasta and
salads. Breakfast is served
until 2:30pm, with incredible omelets, fresh fruit and
seafood.

Bayou St. John
$$-$$$
dinner only
320 Main St.
☎*431-2298*
Bayou St. John is famous
in Seal Beach for its Creole
and Louisiana cuisine. A
definite break from the
ordinary, try the spicy
jambalaya, blackened red-
fish or prime rib. The service is friendly and the
atmosphere is comfortable.

The Glide'er Inn
$$$
1400 Pacific Coast Hwy.
☎*431-3022*
The Glide'er Inn combines
fresh seafood with a taste
of history. First established
in 1930, this restaurant
borders the local airstrip
and used to be a popular
hangout for the area's pi-
lots. Fresh clam chowder,
local seafood and thick,
juicy steaks highlight the
menu. Over 100 model
airplanes hang from the
ceiling and hundreds of
historical photos line the
walls.

Huntington Beach

**The Longboard Restaurant
and Pub**
$
217 Main St.
☎*714-960-1896*
www.longboard-pub.com
A true salute to the surf
heritage of Huntington
Beach, the Longboard
serves a great variety of
salads, sandwiches and
seafood in a bar that looks
like it's "in the through of
the wave," decorated with
surfboards and old surf
photos. It also has an
outdoor patio and happy
hour from 3 to 7pm.

Ruby's Surf City Diner
$
End of the Huntington Beach Pier
☎**969-7829**
After you've walked all the way to the end of the pier, some refreshments may be in order. Ruby's is a1950s-style diner that serves up a giant burger with a thick milkshake and slice of pie. Many come for the view alone, through the glass wall that looks out onto the Pacific.

Huntington Brewery
$$
201E. Main St. second floor
☎**960-5343**
The Huntington Brewery serves pasta, pizza, burgers, and of course, beer! Try their own brews, made in the stainless kettles right behind the bar. $1 "tasters" of their 10 on-tap selections are available. Exposed brick inside gives way to the beach view patio. Also try the Cajun jambalaya and grilled salmon with dill sauce.

Louise's Trattoria
$$$
300 Pacific Coast Hwy.
☎**714-960-0996**
Louise's offers Italian specialties, including pizza and pasta, in a perfect location overlooking the ocean. Dine on the beautiful open patio or in one of the comfy booths. The Sunday brunch will start off the day in style with champagne and an expansive buffet.

Chimayo
$$-$$$
317 Pacific Coast Hwy.
☎**374-7273**
Chimayo offers fine Mexican food, imaginatively prepared and presented, with incredible ocean views to match. Located below Duke's, the menu ranges from traditional

Mexican specialties like *queso fundido* (Mexican cheese, chicken sausage and chiles served in a skillet) to sage-crusted sea bass and grilled proscuitto. At night, guests sip a margarita and gather around a cozy beach fire pit. Impeccable service.

Duke's of Hawaii
$$$
317 Pacific Coast Hwy.
☎**374-6446**
Duke's is right on the beach with grand, panoramic views of the ocean. The decor is fun and interesting with *koa*-wood walls, tropical plants, Hawaiian artifacts and Huntington Beach memorabilia. Dine outside on one of their two dining areas or have a drink at the palapa-covered beach bar. In addition to the Hawaiian-inspired steaks, pastas and seafood, try the *huli-huli* chicken or a generous fillet of *mahi-mahi*.

Newport Beach

Alta Coffee
$
506 31st St.
☎**675-0233**
Alta Coffee is a good place to take a quick break with a coffee and pastry or a light meal. Live impromptu entertainment is often supplied by local artists, poets and musicians.

Veg A Go-Go
$
401 Newport Center Dr.
☎**721-4088**
A fantastic vegetarian restaurant where even carnivores won't mind dining. The trendy decor highlights tasty veggie burgers, intriguing salad combinations and some tofu delights.

Alysia 101
$-$$
Newport Beach2901 W. Pacific Coast Hwy.
☎**722-4128**
A variety of tempting Asian tastes is available at Alysia 101 in its many themed dining rooms. Choose from 1930s Shanghai, the Java or Bali Terraces or sip some saki at the Tiger or Dragon Bars. Sushi and sashimi are available at the Yuyake Sushi Bar. Prices are very reasonable, and the restaurant offers panoramic views of Newport Harbor.

The Blue Beet Cafe
$-$$
107 21st Place
☎**675-BEET**
The Blue Beet is a local favourite for thick, juicy steaks. Built in 1912, this is also the oldest commercial structure in Newport. Live music can be enjoyed nightly, as it has for the past several decades. For the quality of food and entertainment, the Blue Beet is ridiculously underpriced.

The Tale of the Whale
$$
400 Main St, Balboa Peninsula
☎**673-4633**
The Tale of the Whale is located in the historic Balboa Pavilion overlooking Newport Harbor. This family-style restaurant has a wide variety of seafood dishes prepared just about any way you like it. The lunch menu has a good selection of wraps and sandwiches to eat in or take out on one of the harbour cruises departing from the pavilion.

The Riverboat Restaurant
$$-$$$
closed Mon and Tue
151 E. Pacific Coast Hwy.
☎**673-3425**
Dine aboard an actual riverboat in Newport Har-

bor at this unique Louisiana-inspired restaurant. Try the macadamianut crusted *mahi mahi*, southern fried catfish or the "Dr. Voodoo" jambalaya while enjoying views of the harbour. Live entertainment and brunch is provided on weekends. After lunch you can also explore the Newport Harbor Nautical Museum, also on board (see p 154).

Tutto Mare Ristorante
$$-$$$
545 Newport Center Dr.
☎**640-6333**
Meaning "everything from the sea", Tutto Mare specializes in coastal Italian seafood. The exhibition kitchen produces succulent fish and pasta baked in a wood-fire oven. Chicken and beef are roasted over a mesquite grill. Eat inside or, preferably, on the garden patio. Sunday brunch features classical guitar. Reservations are highly recommended.

The Chart House
$$-$$$
dinner only
2801 W. Pacific Coast Hwy.
☎**548-5889**
Deep wood accents and comfortable booths compliment panoramic harbour views at the Chart House. The restaurant is built over the water, with boat parking available underneath. Inside, enjoy the teriyaki beef medallions, pan-fried sea scallops or choose your meal from the oyster and salad bars.

The Spaghetti Bender
$$$
dinner only
6204 W. Pacific Coast Hwy.
☎**645-0651**
Having a meal at the Spaghetti Bender is like eating in every room of an old Italian home, with its

many small rooms accented by dark carpeting, myriad candles and slightly kitschy floral wallpaper. Their gnocchi, which is handmade on the premises, has developed an almost religious following in the city over the past 30 years. Combination platters are also available, featuring veal, chicken and beef dishes accompanied with pasta and salad. The kids can choose anything on the menu with half portions for half price.

Roy's Newport Beach
$$$
453 Newport Center Dr.
☎**640-7697**
Roy's caused quite a stir when it landed in Newport. The menu was created by Roy Yamaguchi, who made this restaurant nationally famous in Hawaii. His unique fusion of fresh seafood, classic French sauces and Asian seasonings is given a Hawaiian twist and then artfully delivered to your plate. The casual upscale environment, near-perfect service and an extensive wine list compliment the meal. Reservations are usually necessary.

Hornblower Cruises
$$$$$
Fri to Sun
2431 W. Pacific Coast Hwy.
☎**646-0155**
Perhaps one of the best ways to spend an evening in Newport Beach is to go on a dinner-and-dancing cruise out into the ocean. Hornblower offers fixed-menu dinner cruises ($58 for 2.5hrs),that feature three-course meals with dancing to follow. Sunday champagne brunch cruises ($40 for 2hrs) offer a full buffet and a chance to admire the coastline. Reservations must be made in advance.

Laguna Beach

Wahoo's Fish Tacos
$
1133 S. Pacific Coast Hwy.
☎**497-0033**
www.wahoos.com
Wahoo's has become a Californian institution for semi-healthy fast-food. Choose from one of their many fish tacos, from tuna to *mahi-mahi*.

Gina's Pizza
$
217 Broadway
Gina's looks a little like a dive but serves generous portions of pizza and pasta that definitely won't break the bank. Vegetarian to "meatsa" pizza is offered as well as lasagna, manicotti and a selection of sandwiches and salads.

Madison Square & Garden Cafe
$
320 N. Pacific Coast Hwy.
☎**494-0137**
This lovely floral café is a great stop for a pastry and a cappuccino while strolling through the shops at Madison square.

Ruby's Auto Diner
$
30622 S. Pacific Coast Hwy.
☎**497-7829**
www.rubys.com
One of a chain of diners in California, this is a great place to travel back to the 1950s and enjoy a burger and a malt. Play some tunes on the jukebox or relax on the sunny, ocean-view patio.

Goko Cafe & Deli
$-$$
907 S. Pacific Coast Hwy.
☎**494-4880**
The Goko Cafe is a vegetarian- and vegan-friendly stop in South Laguna. Choose from one of its many soups, salads and sandwiches.

Orange County

Nature's Oven II
$$
1100 S. Pacific Coast Hwy.
☎*376-2026*
Nature's Oven is another great spot to find high-quality vegetarian dining in a comfortable setting.

 230 Forest
$$
230 Forest Ave.
☎*494-2545*
Right in downtown Laguna, this sidewalk café is one of the trendiest spots in town. Contemporary Californian cuisine is complimented by a well-chosen selection of California wines.

Romeo Cucina
$$
294 Broadway St.
☎*497-6627*
Romeo Cucina features 16 different pastas and 15 wood-fired pizzas at reasonable prices. Live music fills the restaurant every night but Sunday. Watch the open kitchen prepare authentic carpacio and wonderful *frittura mista* (deep fried calamari, shrimp, tuna and swordfish).

Bombay Duck Bistro & Grill
$$-$$$
231 Ocean Dr.
☎*497-7307*
The Bombay Duck serves fine Indian cuisine inside their tiny, intimate restaurant, or on their two-table patio. Try the whole turkey (*$40*) which serves at least six. The smoked baby back ribs are delightful as are their tandori specialties.

The White House
$$$
340 S. Coast Hwy.
☎*494-8088*
The White House is a landmark in Laguna Beach, built in 1918 and once-popular with the "in" Hollywood crowd. Today,

the menu offers a funky combination of giant Californian salads and pasta and sandwiches for lunch. Dinner features well presented meats and seafood with a Californian twist. At night, the White House provides live entertainment and dancing. Breakfast is available on weekends.

C'est La Vie
$$$
373 S. Coast Hwy.
☎*497-5100*
Imaginative French cuisine is served indoors or outside on the award-winning patio overlooking the ocean. There is also a French bakery on site to pick up some picnic supplies. Extensive wine list.

Claes Seafood Etc.
$$$
425 S. Coast Hwy.
☎*376-9283*
Located in the Hotel Laguna, Claes offers creative seafood selections with international accents. Though seafood is the main attraction, it also features lamb chops and steaks from the grill. Over 250 vintages of wine are available to accompany your meal, and the intimate "Wine Cellar" caters to groups of 10 or less. Panoramic views of the ocean are included at no extra charge.

Tivoli Terrace
$$$
650 Laguna Canyon Rd.
☎*494-9650*
www.tivoliterrace.com
The Tivoli Terrace is located on the Festival of Arts grounds, making it a convenient but over-crowded choice during the festival. Reserve in advance, however, and enjoy Cornish hen, tenderloin beef brochettes, or an extensive brunch menu in a beautiful French garden setting.

Aegean Cafe
$$$
closed mon
540 S. Pacific Coast Hwy.
☎*494-5001*
The Aegean Cafe features authentic Greek classics such as mousaka and chicken souvlaki in a lively Mediterranean environment. Belly dancers wander about the tables, waiters spontaneously break into dance, and there is live entertainment nightly. Fridays and Saturdays have a $20 minimum per person, which you'll have no problem reaching.

French 75
$$$-$$$$
1464 S. Coast Hwy.
☎*494-8444*
A fireplace accents the giant leather booths and the moody interior of French 75. This French bistro and champagne bar tries to recreate an ambiance of Paris in the 1940s, with some success. Reservations recommended.

Dana Point

The Inca Amazon Grill
$-$$
closed Mon
25001 Dana Point Harbor Dr.
☎*489-1900*
This small Peruvian restaurant has a slightly kitschy decor with leopard-skin accents on the booths and chairs. Spicy selections are available in chicken, pasta, beef and seafood. You should also try the fresh ceviche. Live Spanish music on Saturday and Sunday nights.

Yama Teppan House
$$-$$$
5pm-10pm
24961 Dana Harbor Rd.
☎*240-6610*
Sizzling teriyaki and teppan specialties are cooked right before your eyes and the large, communal tables make for a friendly, socia-

ble atmosphere. You can also enjoy sushi, chicken and steak delicacies either indoors or out on their patio. Karaoke "entertainment" is available on weekends.

Ristorante Ferrantelli
$$-$$$
25001 Dana Harbor Rd.
☎*493-1401*
This beautiful Italian restaurant is accented with classical busts and pillars. Chef Ligi Mazzaro serves up authentic cuisine amid the live operatic arias and songs in Italian, French, Spanish and English each evening. Try the amazing *cartoccio di mare* which combines a sampling of lobster, scallops, mussels, shrimp and fish of the day in a saffron, garlic and wine sauce.

The Chart House
$$-$$$
34442 Green Lantern St.
☎*493-1183*
A beautiful panoramic view of the harbour is the main attraction of this restaurant, perched atop a promontory overlooking the ocean. Inside, comfy booths are surrounded by a naval motif with copper accents. Try a thick-cut steak or fresh seafood.

San Clemente

Beach Garden Cafe
$
*Mon to Fri 7am to 2pm,
Weekends 7am to 3pm*
618 ½ Avenida Victoria
☎*498-8145*
This is a great place for breakfast or lunch across from the San Clemente Pier. During the summer, hours are extended for sunset dining. Inside, sidewalk and patio dining are available. Reasonable prices make this a good stop to grab some take-out for the pier.

The Shore House Cafe
$-$$
201 Avenida del Mar
☎*498-3936*
So you're hungry for meatloaf at 5am? No problem. Bacon and eggs for dinner? Sure thing. The Shore House Cafe offers 24hr service and an 11-page diner-style menu. Comfortable booths and high-back stools invite you to stay all day. There's something for everyone here, including a decent vegetarian section.

The Tropicana Grill
$$
610 Avenida Victoria
☎*498-8767*
The panoramic ocean views are the major draw of the Tropicana. The menu features Mexican selections, Californian-style fare, seafood and ribs. The restaurant is fun and lively, with its bamboo ceiling and bright tropical-colour scheme. Reservations are suggested, especially in the summer.

Vintage Restaurant & Bar
$$-$$$
110 N. El Camino Real
☎*492-3236*
Elegant surroundings are complimented by affordable prices at Vintage. Wraparound leather booths hug white tablecloths under soft lighting. The daily specials include prime rib, braised lamb or veal, served with ample side dishes. Dine inside or out on the garden patio.

Carbonara
$$-$$$
111 Avenida Del Mar
☎*366-1040*
"It's not a table without bread and wine" is the motto at Carbonara Trattoria Italiana. With an extensive (and affordable) wine list and freshly baked

focaccia bread upon arrival, very few tables are without bread and wine. The atmosphere is casual and family oriented, but there are still some cozy corners available. The menu features authentic northern and southern Italian pasta, veal and seafood. Reservations are suggested, especially on weekends.

San Juan Capistrano

Mollies Famous Cafe
$
32033 Camino Capistrano
☎*240-9261*
With over 150 items on the menu to choose from, deciding is the hardest thing to do here. Try their enormous breakfast specials, all priced at $3.75, or stop in for a soup and sandwich at lunch. The patio, unfortunately, is a little too close to the parking lot, but the food makes up for the view.

The Tea House on Los Rios
$-$$$
Wed to Sun
31731 Los Rios St.
☎*443-3914*
The Tea House on Los Rios is a true gem, full of lace, and crammed with more antiques than is truly necessary. With the staff in proper 19th-century attire and light classical music in the background, the illusion is almost complete. Enjoy world-class Herney loose-leaf tea, delicious scones and assorted finger sandwiches. For more substantial fare, classics like shepherds' pie and prime rib with Yorkshire pudding will not disappoint. The last seating is at 4pm, so make it a point to get there early to enjoy the ambiance.

Orange County

Sarducci's
$$-$$$
7am to 9pm daily
26701 Verdugo St.
☎493-9593

Sarducci's offers contemporary Californian cuisine in the historic Capistrano Depot, across from the mission. Live jazz fills the restaurant Thursday through Saturday evenings. The menu offers a delicious variety from breakfast through dinner, with seafood omelets, cobb salads, rich cream pastas and seared *ahi* tuna. Dine inside or on the patio.

 L'Hirondelle
$$$
closed Mon
31631 Camino Capistrano
☎661-0425

Pink bougainvillea caress the walls of this lovely adobe-style restaurant. Inside, French and Belgian specialties are served in a lovely patio garden within view of the mission. Enjoy braised duckling in a green peppercorn sauce, fresh bouillabaisse or veal medallions *aux champignons*, all beautifully presented with impeccable service.

Oceanside

 The 101 Cafe
$
631 S. Pacific Coast Hwy.
☎722-5220

The 101 Cafe is the oldest restaurant in Oceanside, built in 1928 and last remodeled in the 1950s. Old photos of the area and a well-stocked jukebox provide the entertainment. Full menu, diner-style food is available from 6:30am to midnight every day. The staff is incredibly knowledgeable about the town and will be happy to give you some suggestions and even some tourist pamphlets on area attractions. Try a classic burger, shake

and fruit cobbler, but leave your credit card at home since it's cash only.

The Longboarder Cafe
$-$$
228 N. Pacific Coast Hwy.
☎721-6776

The Longboarder is in the middle of downtown, just a few blocks from the beach. It has a fun, friendly atmosphere with its muraled walls and surfboards hanging from the rafters. Try it for breakfast, lunch or dinner, with huge omelets, salads and black Angus beef.

La Mission
$-$$
3232 Mission Ave.
☎760-435-9977

La Mission is a local favourite for authentic Mexican food but also serves American classics for those who aren't so bold. Live mariachi music accompanies the meal and a champagne brunch is served on Sundays.

Harbor Fish & Chips
$$
276-A Harbor Dr. S.
☎722-4977

This family-owned and operated restaurant is also home to the largest display of mounted fish in the county. This is a great place to enjoy a generous helping of beer-battered fish while enjoying views of the harbour.

The Caribbean Grill
$$
311 N. Tremont
☎722-3334

Owner Mark Cameron serves up gigantic plates of soul-pleasing Jamaican and Cajun cooking. The walls of this casual restaurant are covered by his original works of art, and jazz and reggae play in the background. Try the jerk chicken, tender ribs and spicy combination platters.

Chart House
$$$
dinner only
314 Harbor Dr. S.
☎722-1345

Beef, pasta, fresh fish and seafood dishes are accompanied by wonderful views of the ocean and harbour. This is a great place to slip into a comfy booth and watch the sun go down over the water with a bottle of wine. Brunch is offered on Sundays.

Entertainment

Tour A: Inland Orange County

Anaheim

Sun Theatre
2200 E. Katella Ave.
☎712-2700

The Sun Theatre offers an intimate venue to catch some of the top names in the music industry. Dinner and show tickets are available which include a full three-course meal and the show.

Good Ol' Boys Saloon & Sports Bar
10624 Katella Ave.
☎535-4355

At the Good Ol' Boys Saloon & Sports Bar you'll be equally comfortable in cowboy boots or a ball cap as you catch a game on one of the big-screen TVs. Drink specials and a happy hour make this a popular spot.

Linda's Doll Hut
107 S. Adams
☎879-8699

Linda's Doll Hut is one of the most crowded clubs in Orange County. The size of a small apartment and with no stage, Linda's has had bands such as The Offspring, Weezer and Brian Setzer play in the corner of the bar.

Alcatraz Brewing Company
20 City Dr., Block in Orange
☎939-8686
The Alcatraz Brewing Company has a prison motif and a fun bar atmosphere with its many micro-brewed beers. Live blues and jazz are presented on the weekends.

Dave and Buster's
20 City Dr., Block in Orange
☎769-1515
Dave and Buster's is a combination restaurant, bar and arcade. Try one of their golf simulators, 150 video games or shoot some pool.

Crooner's Lounge
12911 Main St., Garden Grove
☎638-3790
Elvis fans will have to stop into the Crooner's Lounge in the Azteca Mexican Restaurant. The walls are covered with photos and memorabilia of the King himself, and the music, of course, suits the decor. A fun place for a night out, but get here early to avoid a lineup.

El Calor
2916 W. Lincoln Ave.
☎527-8873
El Calor is a Latin dance favourite and tends to get crowded on Wednesday, which is gay night, when a fun drag show is presented.

Buena Park

Wild Bill's Wild West Dinner Extravaganza
7600 Beach Blvd.
☎522-6414
Wild Bill's Wild West Dinner Extravaganza offers a 2hr show nightly that features Western-style

singing, dancing and even a comical magician. The price of admission includes the show plus an all-you-can-eat chicken and rib dinner including beer, wine and all the fixin's. Yeehaw! Reservations are required.

The Medieval Times Dinner & Tournament
7662 Beach Blvd.
☎521-4740
The Medieval Times Dinner & Tournament is a unique experience. Inside an 11th-century European-style castle, guests are encouraged to eat with their hands and cheer on the jousting and sword-fighting knights as they battle in the centre arena. One price includes a veritable feast of ribs and chicken, plus two rounds of beer, wine or soft drinks, and the show. Dinner shows take place nightly, and there is also a Sunday matinee. Reservations are required.

The Ozz
6231 Manchester Blvd.
☎522-1542
The Ozz is a high-quality gay club in Buena Park that offers fantastic dancing and a live cabaret show.

Costa Mesa

Orange County Performing Arts Center
600 Town Center Dr.
☎556-2787
Orange County Performing Arts Center features national and international selections of ballet, opera ballet, opera, musical theatre, classical music, and jazz throughout the year.

South Coast Repertory
655 Town Center Dr.
☎708-5500
The Tony-Award-winning South Coast Repertory

provides creative new and classic drama and has drawn national attention for productions such as David Henry Hwang's *Golden Child*, first produced at South Coast Repertory and now on Broadway. Same day, half-price tickets can be purchased at the box office.

Yard House
1875 Newport Ave.
☎642-0090
The Yard House has an incredible 250 beers on tap and a dark and inviting bar. Classic rock fills the bar, but not to the point that it drowns out conversation.

Shark Club
841 Baker St.
☎751-6428
The Shark Club is a beautiful club whose most striking feature is a 2,000-gallon (8,000L) shark tank in the middle of the 27 pool tables downstairs. A small, ambiance-filled room behind the bar spins techno beats. Happy hour Thursday and Friday.

Chester Drawers' Inn
179 E. 17th St.
☎631-4277
The Chester Drawers' Inn is a fun place to dance, with a friendly, energetic crowd and a relaxed dress code. Things get started pretty late, with the DJs spinning everything from alternative to dance and disco.

Santa Ana

Crazy Horse Saloon
1580 Brookhollow Dr.
☎549-1512
The Crazy Horse Saloon features live shows nightly by some up-and-coming and established country music acts.

Orange County

Tour B: the Beaches of Orange County

Seal Beach

Besides a few taverns like **Henessey's** (143 Main St.; ☎598-6456) and **O'Malley's** (140 Main St.; ☎598-0843), most of the nightlife is found in Long Beach to the north or Newport Beach to the south.

Huntington Beach

Huntington Beach Playhouse
$13-15
Thu to Sat 8pm, Sun 2pm
7111 Talbert Ave.
☎*375-0696*
Huntington Beach Playhouse, has been entertaining Southern Californians since 1963 with their wide repertoire of musicals, dramas and comedy. Aside from their stage shows, the company also presents Shakespeare in the Park, weekends at 2pm (*$7*) throughout the summer.

Gallagher's
300 Pacific Coast Hwy., Ste. 113
☎*536-2422*
In the mood for a laugh? Check out Gallagher's on Thursday nights for their comedy show. Admission is free before 8:30 and $3 after.

Rhino Room
7979 Center Ave.
☎*892-3316*
For a fun night out, try the Rhino Room on Wednesdays with a full orchestra and free swing lessons. When your feet get sore, relax in the Martini Lounge upstairs.

The Laguna Art Festivals

Summer is the time to experience the artistic character of Laguna Beach. During July and August, several separate events take place, turning Laguna Beach into the artistic nexus of California. A single-price ticket can be purchased at any of the events for $15, which allows entry into all events.

Since 1932, **The Festival of Arts** (*650 Laguna Canyon Rd., ☎800-487-3378; www.foapom.org*) has featured original works by 160 area artists, from photography and oil painting to sculpture and mixed media, all judged by a panel of experts.

The **Pageant of the Masters** (*650 Laguna Canyon Rd., ☎800-487-3378; www.foapom.org*) pre-

sents live, tableaux-style re-creations with models of famous contemporary and classical works of art. The shows are presented nightly in the canyon amphitheatre and are accompanied by a full orchestra.

The **Art-A-Fair Festival** (*777 Laguna Canyon Rd., ☎949-494-4514; www.art-a-fair.com*) showcases the works of 130 artists and craftspeople from around the world. This is a chance to meet the artists and see them at work.

The **Sawdust Fine Art and Crafts Festival** (*935 Laguna Canyon Rd., ☎949-494-3030; www.sawdustfestival.org*) runs through July and August but also during the weekends from mid-

November to mid-December. The festival grounds are located in a wonderful shady canyon where visitors enjoy entertainment, food, and art-and-crafts shopping. Workshops are also available. In early April, tour the artist's studios during the Sawdust Festival Art Walk.

The **Laguna Plein Air Painters Association** (*☎949-494-8971*) is a unique competition during the second week of July. Fifty of the top U.S. landscape painters have a week to paint the natural beauty of Laguna Beach, which is later displayed at the Laguna Art Museum. The art-appreciating public is encouraged to watch these artists at work all throughout the town.

Gecko's
7887 Center Dr.
☎*892-0294*
Fridays are big at Gecko's, with a high-energy, unpretentious crowd. A little bit of everything gets spun by the DJ, from Top 40 to brand-new alternative. Minors (18+) are admitted but can't drink.

Newport Beach

Newport Beach International Jazz Festival
☎*650-LIVE*
The Newport Beach International Jazz Festival takes place in May at selected venues around the city including the Hard Rock Cafe and Fashion Island. The week long festival attracts acts from around the world.

Newport Theater Arts Center
2501 Cliff Dr.
☎*631-0288*
The Newport Theater Arts Center is known as the "theatre on the cliff" due to its envious position. Community theatre productions run throughout the year.

Newport Beach Brewing Company
2920 Newport Blvd.
☎*675-8449*
www.nbbrewco.com
The Newport Beach Brewing Company is the only micro-brewery in Newport Beach and offers a selection of homemade beers to enjoy inside or out in the gardens. A decent menu accompanies the original brews.

Margaritaville
2332 W. Coast Hwy.
☎*631-4110*
Margaritaville offers award-winning margaritas and live entertainment on Mariners Row.

The Blue Beet
107 21st Pl.
☎*675-BEET*
The Blue Beet is a favourite jazz and blues club near the Newport Pier. A lively mix of tourists and locals pack the club most nights of the week.

Woody's Wharf
2318 W. Newport Blvd.
☎*675-0474*
For live rock'n'roll, try Woody's Wharf with its great waterfront location.

Laguna Beach

Laguna Playhouse
$30-$40
606 Laguna Canyon Rd.
☎*497-ARTS*
www.lagunaplayhouse.com
The oldest continuously running theatre on the West Coast is the Laguna Playhouse, founded in 1920. This award-winning professional theatre company claims such alumni as Harrison Ford and has performances every night except Monday at 8pm, with two shows on the weekend at 2pm and 8pm. Dinner and brunch packages are available.

Ocean Brewing Company
237 Ocean Ave.
☎*497-3381*
The Ocean Brewing Company beside the Bombay Duck is a great place for after-dinner drinks. An enormous copper kettle dominates the bar area while a small fireplace gives it a slightly homey glow. They have a fine selection of local micro brews and are quite busy on weekends.

Laguna Beach Brewery
$6-$10
422 S. Coast Hwy.
☎*499-BEER*
The Laguna Beach Brewery is a second-floor brewpub right across from the Hotel Laguna. If you

choose the right seat you can even get a good view of the ocean. Try the Thai chicken pizza and the artichoke chicken pasta. Burgers are available in beef, turkey and vegetarian. Try the sampler of their seven beers brewed on site.

Sandpiper Lounge
1183 S. Pacific Coast Hwy.
☎*494-4694*
The Sandpiper Lounge is a popular place with locals and gets jammed with gyrating locals on Tuesday, Thursday and Saturday.

Dana Point

Renaissance
24701 Del Prado Ave.
☎*661-6003*
For the best in jazz and blues, stop by the Renaissance, which has live shows seven nights a week with little or no cover charge. Shows start at 8pm, but on weekends get there early as it can get packed.

Hennessey's Tavern
34111 La Plaza
☎*488-0121*
Hennessey's Tavern has a familiar pub-style atmosphere and some imported beers on tap.

San Clemente

China Beach Canteen
2371 S. El Camino Real
☎*492-6228*
The China Beach Canteen offers a casual night out with live music, dancing and a fun atmosphere.

Jonny James Steakhouse and Lounge
301 N. El Camino Real
☎*492-5666*
In addition to fine cuts of meat, the Jonny James Steakhouse and Lounge, offers jazz, swing and

Orange County

blues Wednesday through Saturday.

Cabrillo Playhouse
$12
202 Avenida Cabrillo
☎*492-0465*
For community theatre, check out what's happening at the Cabrillo Playhouse. The playhouse itself is in a historic 1926 white stucco house with Spanish tile roof.

San Juan Capistrano

The Swallows Inn
31786 Camino Capistrano
☎*493-3188*
The Swallows Inn is a cowboy saloon that features live music and dancing six nights a week. Grab your boots and head in for some line dancing and cheap beer. Happy hour 4pm to 6pm.

Freight House Saloon
26701 Verdugo St.
☎*493-9593*
The Freight House Saloon is a comfortable bar located in the historic train depot. Live music is provided most nights of the week. Note the restored mural depicting life in San Juan.

Coach House Concert Theatre
33157 Camino Capistrano
☎*496-8930*
The Coach House Concert Theatre hosts a variety of live events from jazz and blues to rock and reggae. B.B. King and Chris Isaak have graced this intimate venue in the past. A full bar and dinner service are also available. Call for the latest events.

Oceanside

Oceans 11 Casino
121 Brooks St.
☎*439-6988*
If you're feeling lucky, you might want to try out the Oceans 11 Casino with an

assortment of card games, from blackjack to seven card stud. Live entertainment and a full meal service is available in the Rat Pack Lounge.

La Mission
3232 Mission Ave.
☎*435-9977*
In addition to its authentic Mexican food, La Mission is also home to the Las Fuentes Cantina, with Spanish music and dancing, as well as top dance hits until 2am.

Strand Bar
608 N. Pacific Coast Hwy.
☎*722-7831*
The Strand Bar is a popular watering hole in Oceanside with pool tables, live rock and roll on weekends and an omnipresent jukebox.

Shopping

Tour A: Inland Orange County

Anaheim

Anaheim Plaza
530 N. Euclid St.
☎*429-3002*
The Anaheim Plaza is an open-air shopping centre located a few minutes north of Disneyland at the I-5 Freeway and Euclid Street. Major department stores are represented, as well as a few specialty shops.

Hobby City
1238 S. Beach Blvd.
☎*527-2323*
Hobby City is 6 acres (3ha) of hobby, collector and craft shops located beside Adventure City.

Orange

The Block at Orange
City Dr. at I-5
☎*769-4001*
Just a few minutes to the east of Anaheim is the city of Orange and its multitude of shopping possibilities. The Block at Orange is Orange County's newest outdoor mall. Amid the neon lights, The Block is an attraction in itself, with a full city block of restaurants, cafés, shopping and entertainment. The open air concept takes advantage of California's sunny climate.

Old Town Plaza Heritage District
At Chapman Ave. and Glassel St.
For a more nostalgic experience, the Old Town Plaza Heritage District is home to the largest block of buildings on the National Register of Historic Places. These late 19th- and early 20th-century buildings are home to more than 40 antique stores.

Santa Ana

MainPlace
2800 N. Main St.
☎*547-7800*
MainPlace is Santa Ana's main shopping centre and home to 190 stores, a sixplex theatre and four restaurants. A free shuttle service is available by contacting the front desk of your hotel.

Costa Mesa

South Coast Plaza
3333 Bristol St.
☎*435-2000*
The South Coast Plaza is visited by 23 million people every year. Hundreds of stores in this beautiful, modern shopping centre are complimented by excellent dining choices. It is

also home to the Discovery Launch Pad, a preview of the Discovery Science Centre (see "Exploring," p 150). Located in the Orange County Theatre District.

Lab Anti-Mall
2930 Bristol St.
☎*996-6660*
If you're not looking for the Lab Anti-Mall, you'll probably miss it. The one-storey, renovated factory is an eclectic mix of 16 second-hand boutiques, funky clothing stores and intimate cafés.

Farmer's Market
Thu 8:30am to 1pm
88 Fair Dr.
☎*723-6616*
The grounds of the Orange County Fair & Exposition Center hosts a Farmer's Market every Thursday with a selection of locally grown produce as well as crafts.

Tour B: The Beaches of Orange County

Laguna Beach

Laguna is famous for its art galleries, boutiques and local craft stores which can all be found along the Pacific Coast Highway. The

main areas are in the 300-400 north block and from 900 to 1800 south.

Huntington Beach

The **Farmer's Market** and **Art A-Faire Street Faire** takes place Fridays from noon to dusk at Pier Plaza, beside the Huntington Pier. In addition to the local produce, there is also a great selection of handmade art and collectibles.

Loehmann's Five Points Plaza
18593 Main St.
☎*841-0036*
Loehmann's Five Points Plaza has a collection of fashion and specialty stores including the full spectrum of Gap stores, Bath & Body Works and Old Navy.

Newport Beach

The stretch of Pacific Coast Highway between Newport Boulevard and Dover Drive is known as **Mariners Mile**. Along this mile is a great collection of shops and galleries that all share a common nautical theme.

Fashion Island
Mon to Fri 10am to 9pm, Sat 10am to 7pm, Sun 11am to 6pm
☎*800-495-4753*
www.fashionisland-nb.com
Fashion Island can be reached by Newport Center Drive from the Pacific Coast Highway. A unique upscale American shopping centre, Fashion Island is a collection of over 200 specialty shops and department stores, and over 40 cafés and restaurants. There is also a farmers market in the main plaza and plenty to keep the kids occupied. The open-air plazas and Mediterranean ambiance make for a wallet-draining experience.

Dana Point

The harbour in Dana Point is home to a variety of small boutiques, galleries and specialty stores all within a short walk.

San Clemente

Posh Peasant
220 Avenida del Mar
☎*498-7813*
The Posh Peasant is a charming antique and collectible store. While you're there, stop for a break in the tea room.

San Juan Capistrano

Downtown San Juan Capistrano features antique, craft and collectible shopping in many of the old historic buildings that surround the mission.

San Juan statue

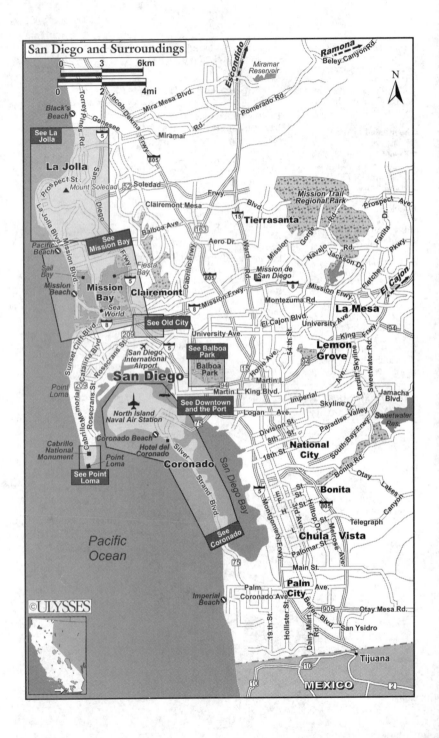

San Diego and Surroundings

San Diego

Birthplace of California,
the city of San Diego ★★★ enjoys an incomparable climate. As the first settlement site of Spanish explorers in Alta (Upper) California, it seemed destined for a brilliant future.

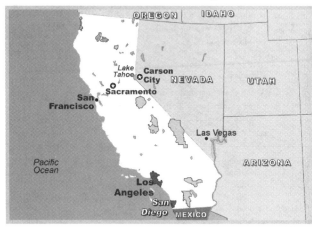

San Diego could have benefitted from its strategic situation as the future border between the United States and Mexico but was, however, overtaken at the beginning of the 20th century by its future famous neighbours, Los Angeles and San Francisco. Several factors explain its delayed development: irrigation difficulties—still a problem to this day—and the fact that it did not benefit as much as its rivals from the results of the gold rush.

At the time of its discovery by the Spanish in 1542, the site of San Diego was inhabited by the Dieguenos, a Pacific Amerindian people that for centuries had lived from hunting and gathering, but especially from fishing, sinice fish and shellfish were the staple of their diet.

The first European boat to enter the Bay of San Diego was that of Juan Rodriguez Cabrillo, a Portuguese commissioned by the court of Spain to find the legendary Strait of Darien which was supposed to link the Pacific Ocean to the Atlantic. The explorer arrived on the feast day of Saint Michael the Archangel and therefore baptized the place San Miguel.

It was, however, not until six years later that three boats commanded by Sebastian Vizcaino returned to the bay. Vizcaino rebaptized the site "San Diego" to mark the feast of Saint Didacus of Alcala.

No one returned to this site again until 1769. This time it was to establish a mission, a garrison and the beginnings of a colony at the location referred to today as Presidio Hill. The first colonists, about forty in number, were guided by Captain Gaspar de Portala and Father Junipero Serra. Mission San Diego de Alcala was the first of 21 Franciscan missions subsequently founded in Alta California. A few years later, the mission was moved a few miles away, closer to the water. Between 1790 and 1820, the colony's population tripled from 200 to 600 souls. New families settled further down, in the district known today as Old Town.

San Diego became a Mexican territory in 1821, owing to that country's independence. The new regime introduced a system of *ranchos*, immense pastures offered to the leaders' family and acquaintances and to deserving soldiers.

In 1848, the United States won the war against Mexico and annexed California. San Diego again saw its economic, political and social systems undergo tremendous upheaval.

The hunt for the grey whale, which migrates close to the Pacific coastline, constituted the main economic activity at the beginning of the 1800s. Later on, the city became wealthy thanks to the presence of prospectors and fur merchants. The arrival of the Santa Fe Railway in 1880 brought new life to the economy of San Diego, but this diminished when the railway network moved northwards.

In 1867, an astute property promoter from San Francisco, Alonzo Erastus Horton, purchased a vast piece of land bordering San Diego Bay which he then resold in plots for the construction of houses. This contributed to the birth of a new urban centre and to the decline of

Old Town, which the great fire of 1872 destroyed.

San Diego did not experience the demographic boom at the beginning of the 20th century in the same way as the rest of the state. However, two large-scale expositions, the Panama-California Exposition of 1915-1916, marking the opening of the Panama Canal, and the California Pacific International Exposition, 20 years later, were to highlight the beginning of this century. They made San Diego known throughout the country, in addition to favouring the development of the city's main park, Balboa Park.

The city did not truly boom until the construction of the Pacific naval forces district (Pacific Naval Headquarters) in the 1940s, the largest naval base during the Second World War. The end of the Cold War, at the beginning of the 1980s, brought about a new economic slow-down.

The last decade has seen a new era of economic and demographic growth in San Diego. The proximity of Mexican labour and the development of tourism have contributed to this expansion.

Today San Diego is home to 1.2 million inhabitants, making it the seventh largest city in the United States. It ranks 36th in the world for economic

output, just after Singapore.

In the last few years San Diego has appealed to the older sector of the population. Numerous well-to-do retirees, attracted by San Diego's quality of life and climate, have chosen to reside there. Safe, less expensive and less polluted than Los Angeles, San Diego offers the modern lifestyle of a new city, in a sun-drenched setting of dream beaches. Revenge is sweet...

Culture-loving tourists will discover a city endowed with a rich heritage, teeming with cultural activities and museums. Families will also appreciate the San Diego Zoo, the country's most prominent, as well as Sea World and Wild Animal Park, to say nothing of Legoland. Water sports enthusiasts and golf lovers will not be disappointed either.

Finding Your Way Around

Getting to San Diego

By Plane

This is the most expensive means of transportation. However, some airlines (particularly regional air

Airplanes and Skyscrapers

If you are travelling by plane, something might surprise you when you touch down in San Diego: the feeling that the aircraft is actually grazing the city's skyscrapers! This is due to the proximity of the downtown area to the airport, and it's enough to make you break into a cold sweat. This is why there aren't any extremely tall skyscrapers here, unlike in other major U.S. cities. Indeed, to prevent airline disasters, it is forbidden to erect a building of more than 50 storeys in San Diego.

As though the city wanted to remind us it was once the cradle of U.S. aviation, you will constantly hear the roar of airplanes over your head. And here's an unusual fact: the outdoor stage in Balboa Park is actually equipped with a system, not unlike traffic lights, which indicates to the actors when to stop and then proceed with the play if an airplane is flying nearby.

lines) regularly offer special rates (for example, during low season or for short stays).

It is worth taking the time to inquire at several travel agencies and compare rates.

San Diego International Airport

The San Diego International Airport (Lindbergh Field) is just over 3mi (5km) northwest of downtown San Diego. You may experience a strange impression when you land because it seems so close to downtown.

This is a modern airport with two terminals. There is a foreign exchange office, an information centre and several unpretentious little restaurants. To get downtown there are sev-

eral options: limousines, taxis, shuttles and buses will take you to just about every part of the metropolitan region.

Most airlines have stopovers at this airport.

To Leave the Airport

By Taxi

Taxis working out of San Diego airport use metres. The trip downtown only lasts 5min and the fare vaires from $7 to $10.

By Shuttle

Several shuttle bus companies meet passengers at the exits to take them to the main downtown hotels. Prices vary between $5 and $9. If you are alone, this is the most economical option. Otherwise, it's better to share a taxi.

By Car

A car can be a good way to get to the city, depending on the distance involved. From Eastern Canada or the U.S., it is an extremely long trip, so you'll need a lot of time. If you do have the time, however, what better adventure could there be than to follow in Jack Kerouac's footsteps, especially since the roads are excellent and you'll pass through wonderfully varied countryside.

Two major north-south routes, both starting at the Canadian border, converge toward San Diego. The I-5 goes through Los Angeles, then along the coast for some distance to end up at the Mexican border.

The I-15 crosses the country more toward the interior. It goes from the Canadian border down to Mexico, but through Riverside County and Las Vegas to Nevada and the Mohave Desert.

The I-8 is a east-west highway that starts in San Diego and goes along the Mexican border through Yuma in Arizona.

However, if you have the time and are coming from the north, Route 1, which goes along the coast through the small towns, is much more scenic and picturesque.

San Diego is 2.5hrs from Los Angeles.

Getting Around San Diego

By Car

For getting around the city of San Diego there are

San Diego

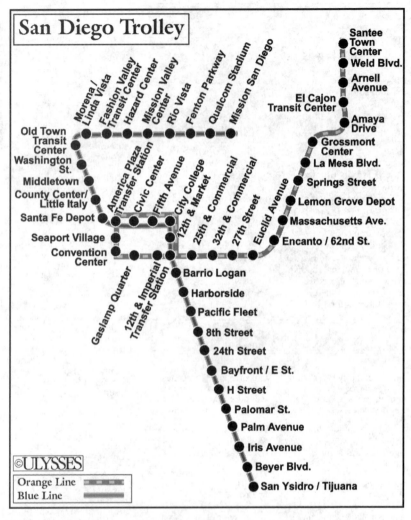

San Diego Trolley

Santee Town Center
Weld Blvd.
Arnell Avenue
El Cajon Transit Center
Amaya Drive
Grossmont Center
La Mesa Blvd.
Springs Street
Lemon Grove Depot
Massachusetts Ave.
Encanto / 62nd St.

Morena / Linda Vista
Fashion Valley Transit Center
Hazard Center
Mission Valley Center
Rio Vista
Fenton Parkway
Qualcom Stadium
Mission San Diego

Old Town Transit Center
Washington St.
Middletown
County Center/ Little Italy
Santa Fe Depot
Seaport Village
Convention Center

America Plaza Transfer Station
Civic Center
Fifth Avenue
City College
12th & Market
25th & Commercial
32nd & Commercial
27th Street
Euclid Avenue

Gaslamp Quarter
12th & Imperial Transfer Station

Barrio Logan
Harborside
Pacific Fleet
8th Street
24th Street
Bayfront / E St.
H Street
Palomar St.
Palm Avenue
Iris Avenue
Beyer Blvd.
San Ysidro / Tijuana

©ULYSSES

Orange Line
Blue Line

several options. It is relatively easy to find your way around the city by car, since traffic is not as dense as in Los Angeles and San Francisco (although it can sometimes be on major arteries during rush hours).

Car Rentals

If you wish to rent a car here are a few companies:

Alamo Rent-a-Car
☎297-0311
☎800-GO-ALAMO

Avis
☎688-5030
☎800-852-4617

Bob Baker Ford Rental
☎297-5001
☎297-3106

Budget
☎800-826-2090

Rent-a-Car
☎(858) 457-4909
☎800-RENT-A-CAR

Thrifty Car Rental
☎702-0577
☎888-297-8844

By Public Transportation

A well-developed public transportation system serves the centre of San Diego and vicinity. However, if you're planning outings to places that are outside the city, such as Anza-Borrego National State Park or Julian, a car is very practical.

The Metropolitan Transit System
1255 Imperial Ave.
☎*233-3004*
☎*231-8549 (trolley)*
This is a bus and trolley public transportation system that provides service for downtown San Diego and its surroundings. The ticket price includes free transfers for all connections. Rates vary between $1 and $3, according to the distance you're travelling.

You can take the red trolley, for example, to get across the city of San Diego, to Old Town, Tijuana or East County. A trolley departs every 15min daily. Rates vary between $1 and $3. You can also get a daily pass that costs between $5 and $12.

The ticket price is calculated according to the number of stations you pass through. Twenty stations costs $2.25. The tickets are sold from machines found in every station. Some require the exact amount, but most provide change. Some also accept credit cards.

Coast Express Rail
1050 Kettner Blvd.
☎*800-COASTER*
The Coast Express Rail is the ideal way to visit the communities along the north coast of San Diego. The ticket price includes transfers for the San Diego bus and trolley. The Coast Express Rail leaves from the Santa Fe depot downtown and passes through Old Town, Sorrento

Valley, Solona Beach, Encinatas, Carlsbad and Oceanside. The pricing operates by zone. If you cross one zone, the price is $3, while two zones is $3.25, three zones $3.50 and four zones $3.75. The service operates from Monday to Saturday, year round.

Note that the tickets are purchased from machines that are easy to use. Simply select the type of ticket (regular, senior, etc.) and your destination, insert payment (cash or credit card), take your ticket and change and validate your ticket before boarding.

Coronado Island Ferry

To get to Coronado Island, there is a ferry that leaves hourly every day from Broadway Pier in San Diego's port, and lands at Ferry Landing Market Place on Coronado Island. It costs $2 and bicycles are welcome on the boat.

www.sdcommute.com
This Web site provides information about public transportation in San Diego.

By Taxi

All taxis operate on a meter, and the price for one to five people is $1 to $2.80 plus $1.30 to $1.60 for each additional miles (0.62mi).

By Bus

To get schedules and find out which destinations are served, call the local Greyhound office at ☎*800-231-2222*.

Practical Information

San Diego

The area code for the city of San Diego is *619*. For the north coast of San Diego, starting from Mission Beach, the code is 858. For the north, the code is *760*. However, in this chapter, to avoid confusion, the code will only be indicated when it is other than 619.

Tourist Information

Downtown Information Center
225 Broadway, 1100
San Diego, CA 92101
☎*235-2222*
≈*236-9148*

International Visitor
11 Horton Plaza
San Diego, CA 92101
☎*236-1212*

Balboa Park Visitor Center
1549 El Prado
(House of Hospitality)
San Diego, CA 92101
☎*239-0512*

Coronado Visitors Bureau
1047 B Ave.
Coronado, CA 92118-3418
☎*437-8788*
≈*437-6006*

San Diego East Visitors Bureau
5005 Willows Rd, Suite 208
Alpine, CA 910901
☎*445-0180 or 800-463-0668*
www.visitsandiegoeast.com

San Diego North Convention & Visitors Bureau
720 North Broadway
Escondido, CA 92025
☎*(760) 745-4741*
☎*800-848-3336*
≈*(760) 745-4796*
www.sandiegonorth.com

Practical Web Sites

www.infosandiego.com
The San Diego Visitor Information Centre

www.sandiego.org
The San Diego Convention and Visitor Bureau

www.sandiego-online.com
San Diego Magazine

www.sdreader.com
San Diego Reader, a cultural weekly

www.gaslamp.com
The historic Gaslamp Quarter

www.coronado.ca.us
The City of Coronado

www.accessandiego.com
An organization promoting access to San Diego for travellers with disabilities

Borrego Springs Chamber of Commerce and Visitors Center
622 Palm Canyon Dr.
Borrego Spring, CA 91941
☎*(760) 767-5555*
☎*800-559-5524*
≈*(760) 767-5976*

Excursions and Guided Tours

Although it's fun to travel without any established structure or time constraints, you might consider going through a travel agency to plan a visit to certain sites. It would be pointless to list all the agencies operating in San Diego because there are far too many and the quality of their services is too uneven. Many options are available to visitors who want to see the town on a guided tour. We have listed a few of them here, but since there are frequent changes, you should contact all of the organizations directly to find out more detailed information on their programs, schedules and rates.

Old Town Trolley Tours
☎*298-8687*
This company offers guided tours of the city on an old trolley. It is a continuous service that allows you to get on and off at different points in the city. The company also offers theme tours such as one on the ghosts of San Diego or a visit to the city's military installations.

Cinderella Carriage Co.
☎*239-8080*
Various tours are offered that allow you to discover the historic districts of Gaslamp, the port and several other areas in the city.

Art Tours
☎*459-5922*
www.art-tours.com
This tour offers a 5hr tour of the most beautiful parts of the city, giving you a thorough general overview.

Out of the Ordinary Group Adventure
☎*(619) 487-3418*
This company offers various adventure packages like four-wheel-drive vehicle or mountain bike tours in the desert, as well as several other activities.

The following three companies offer several packages by coach or boat to see the city and its surroundings.

San Diego Scenic Tours
☎*234-4111*

Contactours
☎*477-8687*

Gray Line
☎*491-0011*

An original and very popular way to get to know the city is by taxi bike, and several companies offer guided tours on a three-seater bike. You can also keep them in mind as a pleasant alternative to taking a taxi.

San Diego Scenic Bike Tours
☎*888-424-5362*

Bike Tours San Diego
☎*238-2444*

Exploring

Like an immense playground, San Diego is filled with attractions just waiting to be discovered. You might think that this city is primarily a family destination that mainly offers amusement parks (such as the San Diego Zoo, Legoland, Wild Animal Park and Seaworld), but take a closer look; although these kinds of theme parks have largely contributed to the city's reputation with tourists, San Diego has much more to offer.

Tour A: Downtown and Gaslamp

(one day on foot)

In 1867, Alonzo Horton had a vision: he would build a new urban centre. He bought an empty lot facing San Diego Bay for $0.33 per acre. What would later become San Diego's downtown and Gaslamp district then began developing at a rapid pace. Although this is not where history began, it is where history is still made. This tour will allow you to discover the heart of San Diego.

The tour begins at the Hyatt Regency, at the corner of Harbor Drive and State Street.

The **Hyatt Regency San Diego** *(1 Market Place, ☎232-1234)* is one of the most famous and, with its 40 storeys, tallest buildings in San Diego. Conveniently located near the downtown area, between Seaport Village and the San Diego Convention Center on the bay shore, it is one of the most prestigious hotels in town (see p 218). Take some time to walk in and admire its splendid modern hall with a Victorian touch. Its wide bay-window, overwhelming greenery, imposing central staircase and marble-decorated walls give it a most luxurious feel. But the main point of interest is the bar on its top floor, the **Top of the Hyatt ★★** (see p 232), which offers one of the best views of the city. From

there, you can even see as far as Mexico. Take a break and enjoy a snack or a beverage; even though prices are a little steep, the location makes it all worthwhile.

Leave the hotel towards the bay, follow the path along the shore to the left and stop at the Embarcado Marina Park.

You will get to admire many luxurious yachts at the **Embarcado Marina Park**. This marina, which belongs to the San Diego Marriott Hotel & Marina, features no less than 446 pontoons. Take a look at the **promenade ★★** along the shore. Not quite 0.3mi long (0.5km), this pleasant alley connects the San Diego Convention Center, the Marina, the Hyatt and Seaport Village, and leads to the port (see p 197) along the shore. This is a lovely place for a stroll among cyclists, joggers and in-line skaters.

From the marina, head towards the hotel behind you. Walk in to admire its decor and come back out through the front entrance on Harbor Drive.

The **San Diego Marriott Hotel and Marina** *(333 W. Harbor Dr.; ☎234-1500)* is an imposing hotel (see p 218) with two unusually shaped, angular towers of

25 storeys. If you stand facing them, you will see what the architect had in mind: to create the illusion of two ships coming into port. The effect is rather well done. This ultra-modern structure is covered with mirrors, which gives a stunning look to the building. As a result, the hotel has become, just like its neighbour the Hyatt, one of the symbols of modern architecture of downtown San Diego.

Turn left on Harbor Drive and walk up to the San Diego Convention Center, which is easy to recognize thanks to its unusual shape.

Evoking a large cruise ship, the **San Diego Convention Center ★** *(111 W. Harbor Dr.; ☎525-5000)*, is one of the most modern convention centres in the world. Its roof, resembling white sails, makes it a unique structure, and both its interior and exterior are remarkable. This site was named one of the three best convention centres in the world for two consecutive years by *Meetings & Incentive Travel Magazine*, the most important European convention-industry magazine.

Since its opening in 1989, the San Diego Convention Center has gained an international reputation. It has

San Diego Convention Center

generated investments of nearly $3 billion in the region's economy, making the convention industry one of the most important in the city. Indeed, in the last 10 years, San Diego has attracted more than seven million business people. And it doesn't stop there: the centre will soon double its capacity, as renovations are scheduled to be completed in September 2001.

Retrace your steps until you reach Fifth Avenue, then head north to the entrance to the Gaslamp district. You will see a sign above your head that reads "Gaslamp Quarter Historic Heart of San Diego."

★★★
The Gaslamp District

The Gaslamp district *(between Boadway to the north and Harbor Dr. to the south, and between Third St. and Sixth St.)* was named after the gas lamps that are still found in its streets, and is no doubt San Diego's most famous sector. And for good reason. This historic area was developed around the 1870s, and most of its buildings were built between the Civil War and the First World War. Here you will find some of the finest examples of Victorian-style architecture.

In 1880, when the city's commercial activities moved north to the new suburbs, the neighbourhood gradually became the Red Light District. There were illicit goings-on here until a law passed in 1912 put an end to these activities.

Commerce has always been the main economic resource in this district and, although there were difficult periods (for exam-

ple, the suburban exodus of the 1980s, 100 years after the first flight of businesses), the area has been in full expansion since the 1990s. A good number of abandoned buildings have been renovated and turned into businesses. In fact, this is the most frequented and lively place in town. Its many trendy restaurants and bars, show venues, art galleries and hip stores will certainly seduce visitors.

Walk back up Fifth Avenue and turn left on Island Avenue. You will notice a beautiful hotel to your left, at the corner of Fourth Avenue.

The **Horton Grand Hotel** *(311 Island Ave.; ☎544-1886)* is actually two hotels in one. Both the Horton Grand and the Brooklyn Kahle-Saddlery hotels were supposed to be demolished in the late 1970s, but the city saved them from destruction and bought them back for $1 each. The sequoia frame of the Horton Grand Hotel was disassembled piece by piece and stored until it was reconstructed in 1986, and the two buildings were erected side by side, as one. The Horton Grand Hotel is on the left side.

The Horton Grand Hotel was originally built by a German immigrant in 1886 during the tourist boom that followed the completion of the transcontinental railroad. This elegant building was inspired by the Innsbruck Inn in Vienna, Austria.

The Brooklyn Kahle-Saddlery Hotel, on the other

hand, displays a more modest architecture, blending the Victorian and Far West styles. It was also built in the 1880s and was originally called the Brooklyn Hotel. The name of the saddlery that was housed on the main floor in the early 20th century was later added to the establishment's name.

Continue along Island Avenue, turn left on Third Avenue and walk up to the corner of J Street.

The Chinese population of San Diego has grown considerably in the last 10 years. According to the latest surveys, it includes approximately 50,000 people. But despite its relative importance, there aren't many traces of the cultural and historical heritage of this community in San Diego.

Horton Plaza

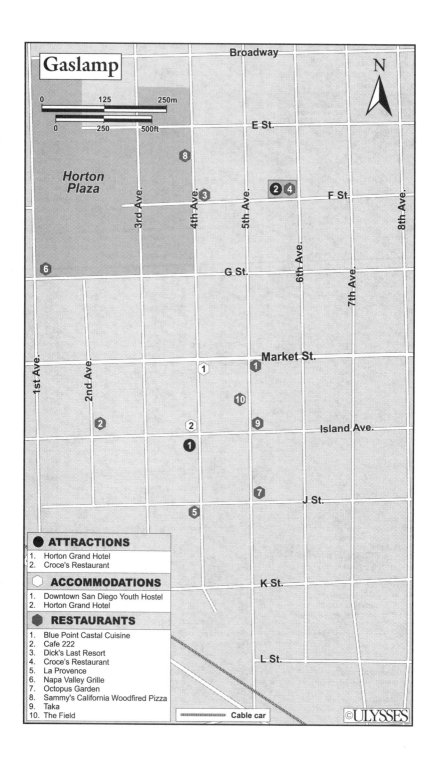

Gaslamp

0   125   250m

0   250   500ft

Broadway

N

E St.

Horton Plaza

3rd Ave.

4th Ave.

5th Ave.

F St.

6th Ave.

7th Ave.

8th Ave.

G St.

1st Ave.

2nd Ave.

Market St.

Island Ave.

J St.

K St.

L St.

San Diego
Downtown and the Port

0   250   500m
0   750   1,500ft

Date St.
Cedar St.
Beech St.
Ash St.
A St.
B St.
C St.
Broadway
E St.
F St.
G St.
Market St.
Island Ave.
Harbor
Drive

Columbia St.
State St.
Union St.
1st Ave.
2nd Ave.

Horton Plaza

Harbor Dr.
Belt St.
Pacific Hwy.
Kettner Blvd.

B St. Pier
Navy Pier
(Ferry Landing)
Tuna Ln.
G St. Pier
West G St.

Marina
Embarcadero Marina Park
Marina Park Wy.

San Diego Bay

● **ATTRACTIONS**
1. Hyatt Regency San Diego
2. Embarcadero Marina Park
3. San Diego Marriott Hotel
4. San Diego Convention Center
5. Broadway Street
6. Whydham Hotel
7. Museum of Contemporary Art
8. Maritime Museum
9. Broadway Pier
10. Seaport Village

⬡ **ACCOMMODATIONS**
1. Hyatt Regency San Diego
2. Pickwick Hotel
3. San Diego Marriott
4. The Inn at the YMCA
5. USA Hostel San Diego
6. Wyndham Emerald Plaza Hotel

⬡ **RESTAURANTS**
1. Antony's Fishette
2. Antony's Fish Groto
3. Brickyard Coffee & Tea
4. Bruegger's Bagels
5. Lael's Restaurant
6. Sally's
7. San Diego Pier Cafe
8. The Fish Market
9. Top of the Market

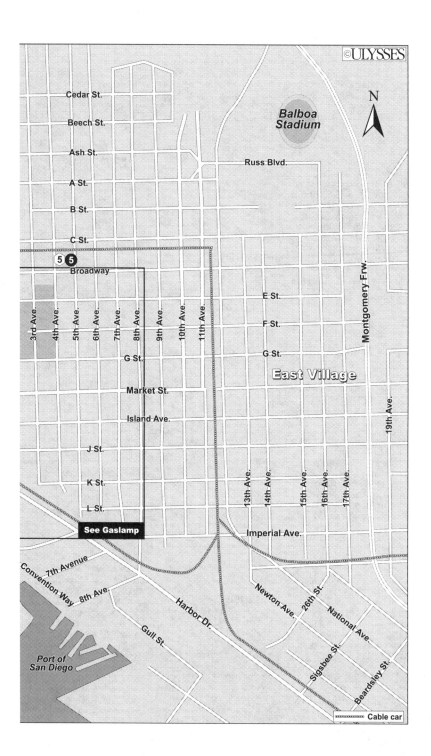

To fill this void, a group of Chinese-Americans created the Chinese Historical Society and the **Chinese Historical Museum** ★ *(donations appreciated; Tue to Sat 10:30am to 4pm, Sun noon to 4pm; 404 Third Ave.; ☎338-9888)* in 1986. This museum is housed in a former Chinese mission which, in 1992, moved to a site on Third Avenue that was generously donated by the City of San Diego. A fundraising campaign allowed the renovation of this building, originally built in 1927 at 645 First Avenue by reputed architect Irving Gill. It was home to a Chinese mission until 1960.

The museum's main goal is to teach the Chinese community in the United States, and the general population, about the Chinese cultural heritage and to promote exchanges and a better understanding between the different communities.

Here you will find a lovely exhibit of various objects relating to the Chinese community's history and heritage. The explanations are clear and easy to understand, and the very friendly staff is happy to answer any questions. Behind the museum is a small Chinese garden where stands a statue of Confucius, a gift from China. The museum also has a small library with some 700 books. This is unquestionably the best place to learn about the impact of the Chinese community on the city of San Diego.

Retrace your steps and go back to Fifth Avenue. Walk back to the corner of F Street.

Croce's Restaurant *(802 Fifth Ave.; ☎233-4355)* is note-worthy for the fact that it is owned by the widow of famous folk singer Jim Croce, who tragically died in a plane crash in the 1970s. To honour his memory, his wife Ingrid opened this restaurant-cabaret where various folk and jazz bands perform. She was one of the first restaurateurs in the Gaslamp district (see p 192).

Head north to reach Broadway Street.

Broadway Street ★★ is the heart of San Diego's business district. A number of important companies such as Pacific Bell, Home Saving and Washington Mutual, as well as most major banks, have their headquarters here. This is also where San Diego's **City Hall** is located. We suggest you walk along Broadway Street and notice the effervescence of busy San Diego residents amidst strolling tourists.

Continue along Broadway up to the corner of G Street.

Horton Plaza ★★ *(Mon to Fri 10am to 9pm, Sat 10am to 7pm, Sun 11am to 6pm; 324 Horton Plaza; ☎238-1596, ≈239-4021)*, is a brand-new outdoor shopping centre in the heart of downtown, which displays a most interesting architecture. Its designers blended San Diego's many architectural styles with a modern and efficient concept. This gigantic mall includes seven storeys and stretches along six blocks. With 140 shops and restaurants, this complex offers a most pleasant environment for shopping.

Head back to Broadway Street, turn left and walk to the corner of Columbia Street.

The main feature of the **Wyndham Hotel** *(400 W. Broadway St.; ☎239-4500 or 800-WYNDHAM)* is its unique architecture. What makes it unusual is the hexagonal towers that look like the pipes of a huge organ, topped with green neon lights. This building has become, along with the Hyatt and Marriott hotels, an architectural symbol of the town. It is found on many postcards and photographs.

Star of India

Continue along Broadway Street to reach Kettner Boulevard.

The **Museum of Contemporary Art** ★ *(free admission; Thu to Tue 11am to 5pm; 1001 Kettner Blvd. at Broadway St.; ☎234-1001, ≈234-1070)* is the second section of the Museum of Contemporary Art in La Jolla (see p 212). In a luminous environment, it showcases a highly interesting collection of contemporary works by Californian artists. There is also a lovely shop offering a wide array of books on contemporary art.

Tour B: San Diego's Port and Seaport

(half a day on foot)

The tour begins at the **Maritime Museum** ★ ★ ★ *($5; every day 9am to 8pm; 1306 Harbor Dr.; ☎234-9153)*, which is a most interesting attraction. It is composed of three ships, the *Bark Star of India* (1863), the *Steam Yacht Medea* (1904) and the *Ferryboat Berkeley* (1898). Visitors can circulate from one ship to the next and explore the many aspects of the region's maritime history. Visiting the *Star of India* will also allow you to familiarize yourself with a real ship dating from the days of the great discoveries.

Visitors then head to the *Ferryboat Berkeley*, built in 1898 as a ferry for San Francisco Bay. It houses an interesting exhibit on various subjects related to San Diego's rich maritime history: the first explorers,

whale-hunting, the tuna industry, and the role of the navy in the town's development.

The third ship is the *Steam Yacht Medea*. Built in Scotland in 1904, it once belonged to an aristocrat who used it as a pleasure boat and for fishing. It was then used as a war ship for military purposes during the two world wars.

In 1927, the *Star of India* was donated to a group of San Diego historians who dreamed of restoring it. But despite their good intentions, they lacked the funds to properly maintain the ship, and nothing happened until 1957. It was then that Alan Villiers, famous navigator and author, came to San Diego and, upon seeing the ship's neglected condition, publicly chided the City for its irresponsibility. He showed the city's residents the valuable heritage they were abandoning, and after this public denouncement, many suddenly concerned citizens donated funds. Soon afterwards, enough money was raised to begin its restoration, which was completed in 1976.

The museum was founded in 1948 by a committee of the Maritime Research Society, a

subdivision of the Zoological Society. It was expanded in 1973 when it purchased the *Ferryboat Berkeley* and the *Steam Yacht Medea*.

There are plans to move the museum in the next few years to allow for further expansion. The exact date of this move is unknown, but will probably take place before 2003. Extra land would allow the building of a library, an exhibit area, a shop and a cinema.

Walk along the shore by heading to your right after leaving the museum.

The port is the point of departure for many **boat excursions** (see p 190). It is also here that the **Coronado Island ferry** (see p 198) leaves. Right next to this is the **Broadway Pier**, where you will find many cruise ships.

Continue south but this time, take the waterfront promenade.

Seaport Village ★ ★ *(849 W. Harbor Dr. Suite D; ☎235-4041, ☎696-0025)* is a very pleasant commercial complex located on the bay shore, next to the Hyatt Regency, featuring shops, restaurants and entertainment. It includes some 28 buildings whose architecture is inspired by fishing houses and features various stores as well as a superb carousel dating from the early 19th century. It is quite pleasant to stroll the paved trails around the stores and discover what they have to offer. In addition, the area is enhanced by ponds, lakes and fountains.

Seaport Village

San Diego

Tour C: Coronado Island

(one day on foot or by car)

Rich in history and landscape, the city of Coronado Island is truly deserving of its nickname, Crown City. Bordered by the Pacific Ocean and San Diego Bay, this lovely maritime town is actually located on a peninsula that is attached to the mainland by a stretch of land known as the Silver Strand. It is also linked to San Diego by the imposing Coronado Bridge.

Coronado Island, with its 30,000 residents and more than 2 million annual visitors, has put a lot of effort into blending its commercial, tourist and residential aspects. Along a few quiet streets, away from the commercial hustle and bustle, you can, for example, admire splendid Victorian and modern homes. The lifestyle of island residents—almost a third of them are married military personnel with children—is relatively high, with an average annual income of $53,000.

Coronado Island has also had its share of famous inhabitants. Charles Lindbergh is said to have left from Rockwell Field in North Island (now a naval base) to go to New York and embark on his famous non-stop journey across the Atlantic. It is here that L. Frank Baum wrote the well-known *The Wizard of Oz*, in a house that still exists today. It is also said that King Edward VIII met Miss Wallis Simpson here, and out of love for her, abdicated the throne. Marilyn Monroe also ap-

parently stayed here during the filming of *Some Like It Hot*.

The **Coronado Walking Tour ★★** *($6; ☎435-5892)*, departing from the Glorietta Bay Inn on Tuesdays, Thursdays and Saturdays at 11am, should not be missed if you want to learn all about this island whose history is filled with anecdotes of all kinds.

From downtown, drivers must follow the directions for the Coronado Bridge. It costs $1 per car to cross the bridge.

The **San Diego Coronado Bay Bridge ★** proudly stands amidst the urban landscape with its imposing structure, which reaches nearly 213ft (65m). Built in 1969, this 1.8mi (3km) bridge links downtown San Diego to Coronado Island. Pedestrians and cyclists cannot use the bridge and must take the ferry, which will give you a glimpse into the daily lives of the many workers who, morning and night, travel from Coronado Island to San Diego and vice versa.

The **Coronado Ferry ★** *($2; departures every 30min)* allows pedestrians and cyclists to travel between Coronado Island and downtown San Diego. The ferry leaves the port of San Diego and arrives at Ferry Landing Market Place in Coronado Island. Crossing San Diego Bay is very pleasant, allowing passengers to admire the city from a different angle.

You will discover **Ferry Landing Market Place ★** *(1201 First St. at B Ave.; ☎435-8895)* as soon as you step off the ferry. Drivers need only turn right when exiting the bridge and take Glorietta Boulevard to

reach it. Parking spaces are easy to find. Ferry Landing Market Place is actually a group of restaurants, fast-food counters and shops made to look like a seaside resort. Many savvy visitors take this opportunity to rent a bicycle or in-line skates and go for a spin on the nearby bike path. There is also an outdoor market on Tuesdays between 2:30pm and 6pm.

Walk up First Street, then take Orange Avenue.

Historic **Orange Avenue ★** is Coronado Island's main thoroughfare. Take a minute to admire its splendid buildings; both shop-owners and the general community work together to preserve their charm. We suggest you walk along the avenue to take in its lovely architecture and discover its many shops.

Take a short detour by Star Park Circle, facing Spreckels Park.

It's in the lovely, small, Victorian home at **1101 Star Park Circle** that L. Frank Baum, author of the famous *The Wizard of Oz*, wrote many of his works.

*Continue along Orange Avenue, then take B Avenue. Follow the directions to the **tourist information centre** (1047 B Ave.; ☎437-8788). It is worthwhile to stop in here, especially since the staff is most helpful. Retrace your steps and continue along Orange Avenue until you spot the Hotel Del Coronado.*

The **Hotel Del Coronado ★★★** *(1500 Orange Ave.; ☎800-HOTELDEL)* is definitely the main feature on Coronado Island. This fabulous hotel is easily recognizable thanks to its white facade

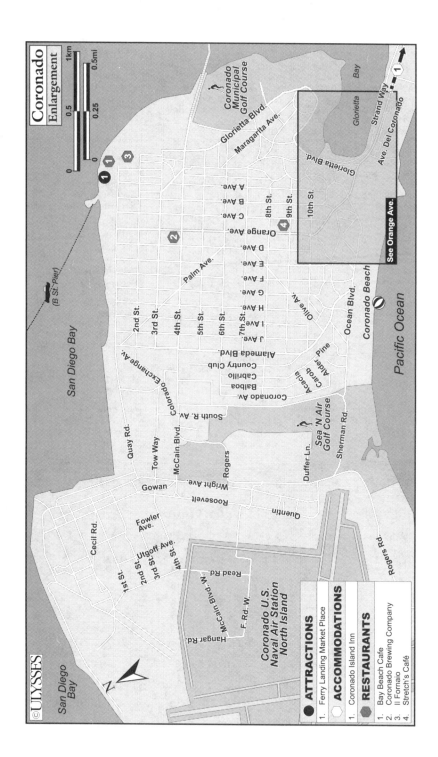

© ULYSSES

Coronado
Enlargement

0   0.25   0.5   1km

0   0.5ml

San Diego Bay

(B St. Pier)

Coronado Municipal Golf Course

Glorietta Blvd.

Maragarita Ave.

A Ave.
B Ave.
C Ave.
Orange Ave.
D Ave.
E Ave.
F Ave.
G Ave.
H Ave.
I Ave.
J Ave.

8th St.
9th St.
10th St.

Glorietta Bay

Strand Way

Ave. Del Coronado

Glorietta Blvd.

See Orange Ave.

Palm Ave.

2nd St.
3rd St.
4th St.
5th St.
6th St.
7th St.

Olive Av.

Alameda Blvd.

Pine
Alder
Carob
Acacia
Cabrillo
Balboa
Coronado Av.
Country Club

Colorado Exchange Av.

South R. Av.

Quay Rd.

Tow Way

McCain Blvd.

Rogers

Wright Ave.

Gowan

Roosevelt

Quentin

Duffer Ln.

Sea 'N Air Golf Course

Sherman Rd.

Ocean Blvd.

Coronado Beach

Pacific Ocean

Rogers Rd.

Fowler Ave.

Cecil Rd.

1st St.
2nd St.
3rd St Utgoff Ave.
4th St.

McCain Blvd. W.

Read Rd.

Hangar Rd.

F. Rd. W.

Coronado U.S. Naval Air Station North Island

San Diego Bay

N

ATTRACTIONS
1. Ferry Landing Market Place

ACCOMMODATIONS
1. Coronado Island Inn

RESTAURANTS
1. Bay Beach Cafe
2. Coronado Brewing Company
3. Il Fornaio
4. Stretch's Café

and red, octagonal roof. You can see by its unique architectural style that its creator specialized in designing train stations. Although they have been modernized, the hotel's 339 rooms have preserved their original charm. The establishment is currently being expanded.

In 1885, financiers Elisha Babcock and H.L. Storu bought an empty lot on Coronado Island for $111,000 to build the Hotel Del Coronado. During the depression of 1887, the Coronado Beach Company fought to keep the project alive and meet the deadline. John D. Spreckels, a 34-year-old multimillionaire from San Francisco, arrived just in time to lend the money needed to finish the project. Today, this hotel is known throughout the world.

During your tour, take the time to admire the superb **entrance hall ★★**, its rich ceiling, balconies and columns made of Illinois oak.

Don't miss the main dining room, the **Crown Room ★★**, which is also used as a ballroom. Its gigantic octagonal ceiling and chandeliers are absolutely remarkable. Then take the hallway, which features elegant jewellery, clothing and gift shops, to reach the **outdoor terrace ★★**. Enjoy this exceptional site by sipping an apéritif and admiring the view of the Pacific, as once did Marilyn Monroe, Frank Sinatra, Henry James, the Prince of Wales and the Duchess of Windsor, as well as 14 U.S. presidents, including John F. Kennedy.

Go back to the hotel entrance. Cross Orange Avenue towards the pavilion in Glorietta Bay.

This structure, which is known as the **Chart House** and was built in the same style as the hotel, used to be a boathouse. Workers assigned to the hotel's construction first practised on the boathouse before beginning work on the

hotel. The place has since been transformed into a restaurant (see p 226).

Take Glorietta Bay Boulevard up to the Glorietta Bay Inn.

The **Glorietta Bay Inn ★★** *(1630 Glorietta Bay Blvd.;* ☎*435-3101)*, a historic house that was once the home of John D. Spreckels, is now a luxury hotel. The building is basically the same as it was when the baron and his family called it home. Take a few minutes to visit the entrance hall and the Music Room. There are interesting photographs of Spreckels hung on the entrance walls, near the staircase.

Once again, retrace your steps to reach Ocean Boulevard.

Coronado Central Beach ★★ stretches along Ocean Boulevard. Bordered to the north by the U.S. Army naval and aviation base and to the south by the historic Hotel Del

John D. Spreckels

Although Elisha Babcock and H.L. Storu, initiated the Hotel Del Coronado project, it was completed by another man, John D. Spreckels, son of San Francisco sugar magnate Claus Spreckels. Indeed, the hotel's construction came to depend on the fortune of this millionaire, a sugar industrialist like his father. When he came to Coronado Island in 1887, at the age of 34,

the city was experiencing a severe economic depression, and the value of real estate was rapidly declining. In spite of this, two years later, Spreckels decided to invest $500,000 in the Hotel Del Coronado project, which had already begun but was by then in trouble. This investment made him the main shareholder, not only of the hotel, but also of North Island,

the ferry, the trolley and the aqueduct system. Coronado Island essentially belonged to him!

In 1906, fearing an earthquake, Spreckels left San Francisco and moved to a home on Glorietta Bay, which today is the Glorietta Bay Inn. For the next 20 years, he was considered as the most influential man on Coronado Island.

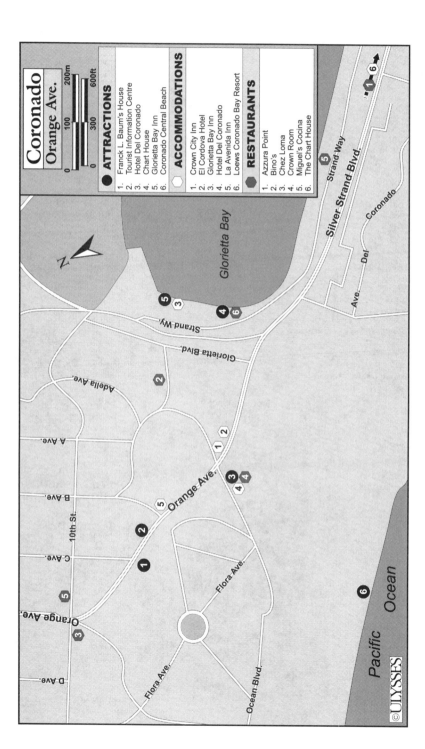

Coronado
Orange Ave.

0   100   200m
0   300   600ft

Glorietta Bay

Strand Wy.

Glorietta Blvd.

Silver Strand Blvd.

Ave.   Del   Coronado

Adella Ave.

A Ave.

B Ave.

10th St.

C Ave.

Orange Ave.

Flora Ave.

D Ave.

Orange Ave.

Flora Ave.

Ocean Blvd.

Pacific   Ocean

© ULYSSES

N

Coronado, it is one of the most beautiful beaches in the region. It is located right on the Pacific Ocean and is surrounded by splendid homes. The view here is unique, and you might even spot Navy officers doing their morning jogging at 7am. South of the Del Coronado, if you look carefully at low tide, you will also get the chance to see the hull of the *Monte Carlo* shipwreck, which sank in 1936.

The walking tour stops here. Take Ocean Boulevard towards the hotel, then take Silver Strand Boulevard up to the sign indicating Silver Strand Beach State Park, some 10-20mi (20-30km) from the Hotel Del Coronado.

Located on the northern tip of the island, the **North Island Naval Air Station** is one of the major military naval bases in the country. Birthplace of U.S. aviation, it is from this aerodrome that Charles Lindbergh set off, on May 9, 1927, in his monoplane *The Spirit of Saint-Louis* for his historic solo journey from New York to Paris. For the past few years, visitors have not been allowed into U.S. military bases, which is unfortunate when you consider how important the army has been in San Diego's history. The only way to access the military world is by taking part in the **Old Town Trolley Bus** ★★ guided tour (*$24;* ☎298-8687) which leaves every Friday at 9:30am from Ferry Landing Market Place.

Tour D: Old Town and Presidio Hills

(one day on foot)

Old Town San Diego State Historic Park is located at the corner of San Diego Avenue and Twiggs Street. To reach it by car from downtown, take Pacific Highway up to San Diego Avenue and turn right. There are many parking spaces around the park.

In 1542, the Spanish landed on the site of the future city of San Diego for the first time, but it was only in 1769 that a settlement was established. The district known today as Old Town was the first European settlement in California.

In 1821, Mexico won its independence from Spain, and life in the Old Town took on a new turn. The new leaders divided the territory into properties and distributed these parcels of land among their friends, marking the beginning of the *ranchos* period,

which lasted until the war against the United States began in 1848.

At first, life in San Diego gravitated around the Old Town. In 1868, however, a businessman named Alonzo Horton decided that a site near the bay shore was a much better location to develop the city. He then bought an immense piece of land and sold it in smaller lots until, gradually, a new city was born a few miles away from the present-day Old Town. This was the beginning of the end for the former urban core; the final blow came in 1872 when a major fire destroyed a large section of the Old Town.

The site was abandoned until 1968, the year that marked San Diego's bicentennial. Considered a cultural landmark of great value, the area was restored and reopened to the public for this milestone anniversary. The Old Town then became a state historic park.

★★★
Old Town San Diego State Historic Park

Old Town San Diego State Historic Park (☎858-220-5422) re-creates life the way it was during the Mexican period and at the beginning of the U.S. take-over of Mexican possessions, between 1821 and 1872. The park covers six blocks and features no less than 20 reconstructed or renovated historic buildings. Many of these homes used to belong to rich, influential Mexicans. Today, they house museums, shops and restaurants.

Mexican Art

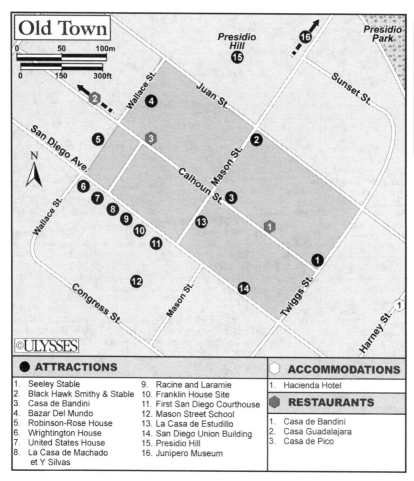

ATTRACTIONS

1. Seeley Stable
2. Black Hawk Smithy & Stable
3. Casa de Bandini
4. Bazar Del Mundo
5. Robinson-Rose House
6. Wrightington House
7. United States House
8. La Casa de Machado
   et Y Silvas
9. Racine and Laramie
10. Franklin House Site
11. First San Diego Courthouse
12. Mason Street School
13. La Casa de Estudillo
14. San Diego Union Building
15. Presidio Hill
16. Junipero Museum

ACCOMMODATIONS

1. Hacienda Hotel

RESTAURANTS

1. Casa de Bandini
2. Casa Guadalajara
3. Casa de Pico

After visiting the city, the suggested tour will take you to nearby Presidio Hill. This is where, even before the Old Town appeared, settlers first established themselves and founded the Mision de Alcala.

Be sure not to miss the **guided tour ★ ★ ★** (☎293-0117) beginning at 11am and 2pm every day at the park's entrance, facing the tourist information centre. This tour is essential if you wish to learn all about the first settlers and life in the early days. The staff is friendly and well informed, and will be happy to answer your questions.

San Diego offers another must-see attraction: the **Old Trolley Tour ★ ★ ★** (☎298-TOUR; www.historictours. com). As you sit aboard an old trolley converted into a bus, the driver will tell you about the city's history, peppered with loads of anecdotes and amusing facts. The trolley does the same tour over and over, with eight stops: Old Town, the port of San Diego, the Hyatt Regency and Marriott hotels, Horton Plaza, Coronado, the San Diego Zoo and Balboa Park. It is therefore possible to begin the tour wherever you please, to get on and off at your leisure, or simply take the complete 2hr tour. This is a pleasant way to get a general overview of the city and its history. For those who want to learn even more, this tour company also offers guided tours with different themes, such as the ghosts of San Diego or the importance of the army in the city.

The tour begins at the entrance of Old Town San Diego Historic Park, at Seeley Stable, to your right when entering the park.

In 1867, Albert Seeley went into business, founding a carriage-transport company offering trips of less than 100mi (160km) in less than 24hrs. In 1875, his company was doing so well that he was able to offer daily trips. However, the appearance of railroads put an end to his prosperity, and the business was shut down. **The Seeley Stable ★** building now houses a captivating museum dedicated to carriages. Its collection, displayed on two floors, includes different models of old-time carriages accompanied by descriptions. There is also a lovely collection of Native American everyday objects.

You will find the small stable behind the main building.

In the 1860s, J.B. Hinton opened the **Black Hawk Smithy and Stable**, located right next to La Casa de Bandini. He offered shelter for horses and rooms for their owners, and also sold food for the animals.

Head back to Mason Street on your right. At the corner, you will spot the Casa de Bandini restaurant.

Born in Peru, Juan Bandini came to California in 1819 with his father, a rich shipowner. His mansion, **La Casa de Bandini ★**, completed in 1829, rapidly became the social centre of the Old Town. Bandini was always involved in the city's affairs; for instance, when California was annexed to the United States, it was Bandini who supplied residents with provisions and horses. In the

early 1850s, however, financial difficulties forced him to sell many of his belongings. The second owner, Albert Seeley (see above), gave a new vocation to the sumptuous balcony-decorated home by turning it into a hotel. Today, this beautiful building, filled with rich furnishings and art, is a most lively Mexican restaurant (see p 227). Here, patrons can enjoy margaritas and nachos in the large interior courtyard, under parasols of many colours.

Continue on Calhoun Street, along the Plaza.

The **Bazar del Mundo ★★** (**☎296-3161**) features adobe-style structures surrounding a large garden. At the heart of it, you will find a Mexican restaurant (see p 227) with a terrace and fountain. Each building offers lovely shops and stands selling Spanish- or Native American-style art at prices that are a little steeper than elsewhere, but the pieces are quite unique and exquisite. You will often hear the sound of *mariachis* here, and maybe even get to see folk dancers perform. This bazaar is one of San Diego's most lively and colourful.

Upon exiting the Bazar del Mundo, go straight ahead and stop at the second home on your right.

Texas native James W. Robinson came to San Diego in 1850, and for seven years, was quite involved in the city's development. Possessing a good knowledge of both U.S. and Mexican laws, Robinson was a successful lawyer. In 1853, he built the **Robinson-Rose House**, a lovely single-storey home, not only for his family but also to house the offices of

the *San Diego Herald* and the railroad company, as well as other businesses. In fact, in the early days of the U.S. period, this was the commercial heart of the Old Town. Today, this house features an information and interpretation centre dedicated to the history of the Old Town.

Leaving the Robinson-Rose House, turn right and head towards the first house at the corner of Wallace Street and San Diego Avenue.

Wrightington House, a long, adobe-style home, was built in 1852 and was the residence of the Wrightington family. After the death of Thomas Wrightington in 1853, his widow Juana lived here until she was forced to leave in 1890. Many families lived here afterwards, and this was also the office of dentist George McKinstry Jr. for 30 years.

The next homes on the tour are found along San Diego Avenue, facing the Plaza.

Charles Noell and John Hayes managed a general store in the 1850s, set up in the pre-fabricated, wooden, single-storey building next to Wrightington House. In March 1854, Hayes bequeathed the business to Robert Lloyd and Edward Kerr, who kept the store open under the name **U.S. House**.

The **Casa de Machado y Silvas**, built by José Nicasio Silvas in 1843, remained in the Silvas family for more than a century. Quite long, this adobe-style house with a tiled roof was successively a boarding house, a lounge, a restaurant, an art studio, a souvenir shop, a museum and even a church. Today, it has been converted into a house-museum to allow visitors to learn about homes of that period.

Juan Rodriguez, a Presidio Hill soldier, was granted a piece of land as payment for his military services. He built a small home (**Racine and Laramie**) in 1830, but unfortunately, it burned in the fire of 1872. It was then rebuilt and furnished in order to re-create the cigar and tobacco store it became in 1869.

On the empty lot located right before the First San Diego Courthouse (see below), is where Franklin House used to stand.

In 1855, Lewis Franklin built a large, two-storey hotel, which he named Franklin House. The *San Diego Herald* declared it the biggest hotel in Southern California. However, the entire time it was open, the hotel experienced more financial difficulties than success. Although a bar, a pool room and a stable were added, the business just wouldn't take off, and finally closed its doors in 1858. It then belonged to Joseph Mannasse, who had some success, but the building burned down in 1872 and was not rebuilt. Today, all you will find here is an empty space that is known as **Franklin House Site**.

In January 1847, in the middle of the Mexican-American War, a large group of Mormons came to San Diego to support the U.S. Army. Although they did not participate in military operations, they did bring a helping hand to the community. For example, they helped build the first brick structure in town, the **First San Diego Courthouse** ★, which

served as both the school and town hall. In 1850, California's legislature named San Diego the state's first town, and from then until it was destroyed in the fire of 1872, this building was used as the first courthouse in the state. It was rebuilt in 1992 thanks to a fundraising campaign by the First San Diego Courthouse Association.

The next building on the tour is a school located behind the San Diego Courthouse.

The **Mason Street School** ★ was first used in 1865. Prior to that year, classes had been taught at the First San Diego Courthouse. Its first teacher was Mary Chase Walker, a woman from Massachusetts whose monthly salary was $65. When she came to San Diego, she described the town as being the most miserable place she had ever seen. After working as a teacher for 11 months, she quit to marry the school's president.

The most popular adobe-style home in the park is undoubtedly the **Casa de Estudillo** ★. Its construction began in 1827 and was completed in June 1829. It belonged to Captain José Maria de Estudillo, commander of the Presidio. When he died in 1830, the home was left to his son José Antonio. This home is one of the park's few original buildings; indeed, erosion makes it difficult to preserve the clay walls that characterize adobe architecture. Note the horseshoe shape of this structure, which surrounds a wide garden, as did many homes of that style and era. The thickness of the walls varies between 30 and 60in (75 and 150cm)

in order to support the heavy beams and the tiled roof. In those days, the thicker the walls, the richer the family. Furthermore, thick walls and materials protected rooms from the summer heat. Retrace your steps on San Diego Avenue and continue straight ahead.

The **San Diego Union Building** ★ was built in Maine and shipped here by boat. This pre-fabricated, wooden structure housed the *San Diego Union*'s first presses. Now restored, visitors can observe a typical, reconstructed press room and editor's office.

To reach Presidio Hill, you can either walk or drive. If you're in the mood for an uphill walk, you will enjoy a pleasant, brief stroll. Go to the Bazar del Mundo then take Juan Street to your right. Turn left on Mason Street and follow it until you get to Jackson Street, which you will cross to enter Presidio Hill Park.

Presidio Hill Park is located 164ft (50m) above the Old Town. This is where the first settlers established themselves and where the Mision de Alcala (see p 209), the first of the 21 Californian missions, was built. It was later moved 5mi (8km) east to be closer to the water and also, apparently, to keep the garrison's Native American women away.

Many soldiers and their families preferred to build their homes at the foot of the hill, founding the Old Town. Presidio Hill Park was abandoned in 1830. A few years ago, students from San Diego University began digging and found the remains of the fort and the Alcala mission.

The Junipero Museum *(Tue to Sat 10am to 4:30pm; ☎297-3258)*, a white, adobe-style building, is home to the Historical Society and displays exhibits on Native Americans, Spaniards and the Mexican period.

Tour E: Balboa Park

(two days on foot; access to the park by car or bus)

To reach the park from downtown, take Sixth Avenue up to Laurel Street. You can park at the entrance.

Located a few minutes from downtown by car, Balboa Park is a large municipal park where you will find the ubiquitous bike paths, hiking trails and play areas for children. Its main features, however, are its 15 museums and internationally renowned zoo. The park is named after the Spanish explorer who, after having crossed the Panamá isthmus, discovered the Pacific Ocean.

Culture is also well represented in this park thanks to, among other things, the Old Globe Theater, which stages quality shows year-round. Many of the museums along the El Prado walkway are set up in beautiful colonial homes that were built especially for the 1915-1916 Panama-California Exposition.

Admission fees to these museums vary between $3 to $8 for adults, with the usual reductions for chil-

dren, visitors with disabilities, seniors, students and military personnel. If you plan on visiting more than six museums, it might be wise to purchase the $25 passport that will give you access to a dozen establishments. Unfortunately, not all museums are included on the passport, but it will allow you access to the main ones. The passport is available at the tourist information centre. For more information, call ☎239-0512. You can also visit some of the museums for free on Tuesdays (see box).

As soon as you walk into the park, you'll no doubt be impressed by the imposing colonial buildings, dominated by the **California Tower ★**. At the top of the building is a weather vane shaped like a Spanish vessel, the same kind that carried explorer Cabrillo to what is now San Diego. The tower's chimes ring every 15min and for 5min at noon. The system rings automatically, but occasionally, a bell ringer does the honours in person.

To plan your visit, it is best to stop at the **tourist information centre** *(every day 9am to 4pm; ☎239-0512)*, located in the souvenir shop in the **House of Hospitality ★**, which also features an elegant restaurant (see p 227).

The original building was demolished and then rebuilt in 1997 because it did not meet today's anti-earthquake requirements. Headquarters of the 1915-1916 Panama-California Exposition organization, the House of Hospitality's facade features a lovely sculpture of an Aztec woman, *Woman of Tehuantepec*, by artist Donal Hord.

Located in the former Casa de Balboa pavilion, the **Museum of Photographic Arts ★★★** *($6; every day 10am to 5pm; ☎238-7559, www.mopa.org)* is dedicated to photography and art films and, since its opening in 1983, has become one of the most interesting of its kind in the world. This is a unique opportunity to see the works of some of the most famous photographers and filmmakers, all in one place. The book, poster and postcard shop is also worth a visit.

Adjoining the Museum of Photographic Arts, the **San Diego Historical Society Museum & Research Archives ★★** *($5; Tue to Sun 10am to 4:30pm; ☎232-6203, www.sandiegohistory.org)* showcases collections of visual archives. The San Diego Historical Society, which is very involved in the research and promotion of the city's historical heritage, owns

Balboa Park

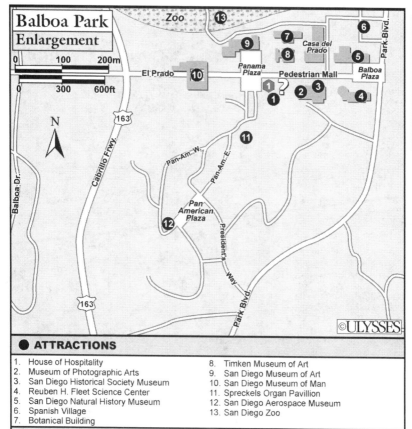

Balboa Park Enlargement

| 0 | 100 | 200m |
| 0 | 300 | 600ft |

N

163

163

Zoo ⑬

⑥ Park Blvd.

⑦

Casa del Prado

⑨

⑧

Panama Plaza

⑤

El Prado ⑩

Pedestrian Mall

Balboa Plaza

① ?

① ② ③

④

⑪

Pan-Am. W.

Pan-Am. E.

Pan American Plaza

⑫

President's Way

Park Blvd.

Cabrillo Frwy.

Balboa Dr.

©ULYSSES

● **ATTRACTIONS**

1. House of Hospitality
2. Museum of Photographic Arts
3. San Diego Historical Society Museum
4. Reuben H. Fleet Science Center
5. San Diego Natural History Museum
6. Spanish Village
7. Botanical Building
8. Timken Museum of Art
9. San Diego Museum of Art
10. San Diego Museum of Man
11. Spreckels Organ Pavillion
12. San Diego Aerospace Museum
13. San Diego Zoo

○ **RESTAURANTS**

1. El Prado

an impressive collection of nearly one million images of San Diego, dating from 1867 to the present. The museum includes five galleries and an archive section for research.

The next building is where you will find the **Reuben H. Fleet Science Center ★★★** *($6.50; museum plus two Imax movies $15, children $12; Mon to Thu 9:30am to 6pm, Thu to Sun 9:30am to 9pm; El Prado, Balboa Park, ☎238-1233, www.rhfleet. com)*. A cross between an entertainment centre and a science museum, the Reu-

ben H. Fleet Science Center offers a stimulating high-tech environment. Without question, this will be the favourite of young and old alike. The centre's new **SciTours Simulator Ride**, for example, takes visitors on a highly realistic space journey. Also featured here is the first dome-shaped **OMNIMAX** cinema.

Across from the centre, the **San Diego Natural History Museum ★★** *(☎232-3821, www.sdnhm.org)* will allow you to familiarize yourself with San Diego and Baja

California's natural habitat. The collection includes more than seven million species of animals, plants and fossils, as well as many mineral samples. The permanent collection also features reproductions of dinosaur and whale skeletons.

Behind the San Diego Natural History Museum is the Spanish Village.

The **Spanish Village ★★** *(every day 11am to 4pm; 1770 Village Place)* houses a group of studios shared by some of the region's artists. Every day, visitors can enjoy demonstrations of pottery, painting, sculpting, silver and enamel work. This is one of the best places to admire regional art and purchase a souvenir. Built for the 1935-1936 California Pacific International Exposition, this pavilion with interior courtyard, was designed to recreate the charm of Spanish villages. It was so popular with the public that it was kept after the exposition. It is the artists themselves who are in charge of maintaining and beautifying the site.

The **Botanical Building** ★★ *(Fri to Wed 10am to 4pm)*, a building made of wooden boards and shaped like a hat, will certainly catch your eye. Its greenhouse contains more than 2,000 tropical plants. The **Lily Pond**, which was cleverly designed to reflect the building, also includes a variety of water lilies that blossom from spring to fall.

Nearly half a million annual visitors come to the **San Diego Museum of Art** ★★★ *($8; Tue to Sun 10am to 4:30pm;* ☎*232-7931)*, making it one of the busiest in the country. Dedicated to art from the Italian Renaissance period, as well as Spanish and Dutch baroque art, the museum also showcases contemporary paintings and sculptures.

The **San Diego Museum of Man** ★★ *($6; every day 10am to 4:30pm; 1350 El Prado;* ☎*239-2001, www.museumofman.org)* contains veritable treasures of anthropology. Each section covers a specific period in the history of humankind. Here, you will learn about such ancient

The Panama-California Exposition

In 1915, the Panama-California Exposition was launched to celebrate the completion of the Panama Canal. Organizers wished to illustrate, through various exhibits, the progress and possibilities of humankind. The pavilions of Spanish colonial inspiration were designed by Bertram Grosvenor Goodhue, a well-known architect. At first, only the California Building and the Spreckels Organ Pavilion were supposed to

remain after the exposition, but in the end, new uses were found for the other buildings as well. As a result, most of the event's structures are still on site, such as the Cabrillo Bridge, the California Building (Museum of Man), the House of Charm, the House of Hospitality, the Casa de Balboa, the Casa del Prado, the Balboa Park Club, the Spreckels Organ Pavilion, the Botanical Building and the Alcazar Garden.

civilizations as the Egyptians, of course, but also get better acquainted with Native American culture.

The **Old Globe Theater** *(*☎*239-2255, www.oldglobe. org)* is one of the most important and oldest theatres in the country. Each year, some 30 plays are presented on its three stages.

The **Mingei International Museum** ★ *($5; Tue to Sun 10am to 4pm;* ☎*239-0003, www.mingei.org)* is named after the Japanese word meaning "art of the people," referring to art that is created in the daily lives of different peoples. This museum lets you discover art forms that are hidden in the simple everyday objects used by different peoples throughout the ages. Some of the many

displayed works are true masterpieces.

The **Spreckels Organ Pavilion** ★★ *(*☎*702-8138, www.serve.com/sosorgan)* houses one of the largest outdoor organs in the world, a gift to the city of San Diego from John D. and Adolph Spreckels in 1914 during the Panama-California Exposition. The organ was built by the Austin Organ Company of Hartford, Connecticut. A beautiful decorated vault protects and highlights this unique instrument of 4,500 pipes. Free concerts are presented throughout the year from 2pm to 3pm.

The **San Diego Aerospace Museum** ★ *($8; Sep to May every day 10am to 4:30pm, May to Sep 10am to 5:30pm, last admission 30min before closing; 2001 Pan American Plaza;* ☎*234-8291)* will teach you all about the aviation industry that played an important role in the development of San Diego. There are 65 aircraft displayed here, from the Wright brothers' plane to the space shuttle. One section of the museum honours the memory of engineers, pilots and companies that played a significant role in aviation history.

The San Diego Zoo is located on Zoo Drive in Balboa Park.

The **San Diego Zoo** ★★★ *($18, children 3-11 $8; admission to two parks, the zoo and the Wild Animal Park $38.35, children $23.15; everyday 9am to 5pm; 2920 Zoo Dr.; ☎234-3153)* was founded in 1916 by Dr. Harry Wegeforth. With only some 50 animals when it first opened, the zoo now covers 98 acres (40ha) and is home to 3,800 animals of 800 species. Throughout the years, the San Diego Zoo has acquired an international reputation. It is known and praised for having recreated the animals' habitats out of concern for their well-being. In fact, there are nearly 6,500 plant species from around the world here, some of

which are used to feed the animals, such as bamboo, eucalyptus and agacia. The zoo also has quite a reputation for its births in captivity and preservation of endangered species, such as Galapagos turtles, koalas, gorillas and pandas. The pandas are actually the zoo's main feature. A great way to start your visit is by climbing aboard the train that offers regular guided tours of approximately 30min. To find out about show schedules, consult the brochure. Furthermore, to fully enjoy this experience, you can rent a "zoophone" *($4)*, an audioguide that is available in English, Spanish, French, Japanese and German.

To reach the Mision San Diego de Alcala, take Highway 8, exit at Mission Gorge Road and turn left on Twain Avenue, which then becomes Mission Road.

The **Mision San Diego de Alcala** ★★ *(☎283-7319 or 281-8449)* was founded in July 1769 by Father Junipero Serra in honour of Saint Didacus de Alcala. Explorer Sebastian Vizcaino had already given that name to the bay which would later become San Diego Bay. Father Luis

Jayme was assigned to build the mission while Father Serra continued his explorations toward Monterey to establish a second mission. Originally located on Presidio Hill, the mission was moved in 1774. It was the first of 21 missions in California.

After the annexation of California by the Mexicans, the missions were abandoned, and when the Mision San Diego de Alcala was later bequeathed to the Church, it was in ruins. It was not before 1880 that Father Anthony Ubach began restoring it. He died in 1907, well before it was completed in 1931.

In 1941, the mission became a parish church. In 1976, Pope Paul VI gave the mission the title of basilica, which was considered a great honour. Today, the mission is still used as a parish church, even though it has been declared a historical monument. A small museum located in the temple tells the mission's history.

Tour F: Point Loma

(half a day by car)

From downtown, follow Harbor Drive. After the airport, head north on Nimitz Boulevard and then take Chatsworth Boulevard on your left, which will then become Catalina Boulevard and Cabrillo Memorial Drive.

Before coming to the end of Point Loma, you will see, to your right, an immense 74 acre (30ha) cemetery with rows and rows of identical white

Mision San Diego de Alcala

headstones. This is **Fort Rosecrans National Cemetery**, where more than 49,000 U.S. military personnel and their families are laid to rest.

You will then reach the Cabrillo National Monument Park.

★★★
Cabrillo National Monument Park

The park is open every day from 9am to 5:15pm. You must leave your car at the visitor center parking lot, but you can easily walk to the main attractions, such as the Cabrillo statue, the Old Point Loma Lighthouse and the whale observation deck. To visit the Tidespool, however, you can take your car and park in the designated area. Along the various walking trails, you will find descriptions of the park's plants, wildlife and history. There is no restaurant here, but it is a great place for a picnic.

The **Visitor Center ★** *(1800 Cabrillo Memorial Park)* is without question the best place to begin your visit. You will find information, a small exhibit and a movie about the park. The panorama that can be admired from its huge bay windows is quite impressive. The shop, located in the middle of the building, offers many interesting reference books as well as countless souvenirs.

Exit the centre and head towards the Cabrillo statue.

The **Cabrillo National Monument ★★**, which proudly stands on the highest point of the Point Loma Peninsula, commemorates the arrival of explorer Juan Rodriguez Cabrillo (see p 185) in

1542. The statue, which measures more than 13ft (4m) and was completed in 1939 by Portuguese sculptor Alvaro DeBree, is one of the most photographed attractions in the city. From this observation point, you will get a stunning view of the county. On site is a sign that will allow you to identify far-away landmarks.

Next, take the trail leading to the Old Point Loma Lighthouse by following the directions.

In 1851, one year after California joined the Union, the *U.S. Coastal Survey* chose a promontory located 423ft (129m) above sea level to build a lighthouse, the **Old Point Loma Lighthouse ★**. Its construction began a few years later and was completed in 1854. However, more than one year went by before they received, from France, the engine that would make it work. However, the thick fog that often covered the area made it very difficult to see the light. In March 1891, the keeper turned off the light for good, after only 36 years of operation. A century later, the relic is still standing, attracting curious visitors. The interior has remained the same as when the keeper and his family called it home.

Head to the second observation point, known as Whale Overlooking.

Whale Overlooking ★ is an observation deck that will allow you to witness, especially in December and February, the migration of grey whales. At certain times, up to 200 whales pass by this area. This is the best place to view them, aside from boat excursions.

You now have the option of taking a trail of a few miles long or heading back to your car to go down to the Tidespool.

Along the shore, the tides control the rhythm of marine life. At the foot of the peninsula, facing the Pacific Ocean, is a rocky environment where plant and animal species have adapted to the harsh conditions of the tides, of prolonged exposure to the sun and wind, and to the abrupt changes of weather and salinity. This **tidespool** is home to, anemones, crabs and a variety other species. Observe them, but do not attempt to remove them from their habitat. We recommend you wear rubber-soled shoes and be cautious, as the rocks are quite slippery. The best time to observe these specimens is at low tide; ask the staff about tide schedules.

Orca

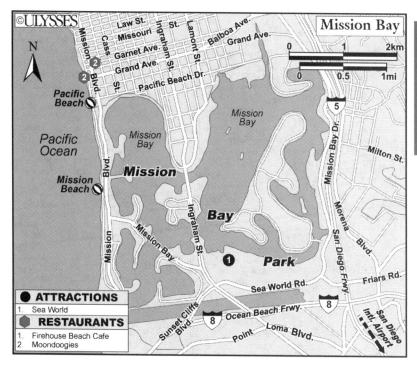

©ULYSSES

Mission Bay

San Diego

ATTRACTIONS
1. Sea World

RESTAURANTS
1. Firehouse Beach Cafe
2. Moondoogies

Tour G : Mission Bay Park, Mission Beach and Pacific Beach

(half a day by car or on foot)

From Highway 5, take the Sea World Drive exit.

★
Mission Bay Park

An immense playground, Mission Bay Park is a paradise for swimming, sailing, fishing, boating, surfing and water-skiing. It is also the ideal place for cycling, golf, hiking and picnicking, and features countless hotels and restaurants. Without a doubt, however, its main attraction is the famous Seaworld amusement park.

Seaworld ★★★ *($40; early Sep to mid-Jun opens at 10am, mid-Jun to early Sep opens at 9am, closing time varies;* ☎*226-3901, www.seaworld.com)* is an amusement park that truly stands out. Whether or not you're travelling with family, if you can only visit one of San Diego's many attractions, Seaworld is the one to choose. Dedicated to the sea and marine life, this site offers an unforgettable whirlwind of sensations.

The park's newest acquisition and first adventure ride, **Seaworld's Shipwreck Rapids** takes visitors on a ride through the rapids while comfortably seated in a small, circular boat that holds nine passengers. Be prepared: the caverns, waterfalls and other obstacles will more than likely

get you soaked to the bones.

The park's best-known attraction is the **Shamu Adventure** ★★ whale show. Marvellously animated and extremely humorous, this show is sure to impress. The whales' skills are particularly stunning. The dolphin show, **Dolphin Discovery** ★★, is just as entertaining, as these agile mammals are simply dazzling.

Another must-see attraction, although it doesn't relate to the sea, is **Wings of the World** ★★, an impressive bird display including no less than 55 species from around the world.

In addition to its entertainment aspect, Seaworld endorses the **Manatee Rescue** program, which is dedicated to researching and preserving manatees. Seaworld is one of the only places in the United States where visitors can admire this endangered species. You can observe these rescued creatures under water as they swim, eat and interact with their keepers.

For a cool trip to the Great North, don't miss **Wild Arctic**. Just getting there is an adventure, as you climb aboard for a ride in a helicopter simulator. Upon exiting the simulator, you'll find yourself in the land of polar bears, beluga whales and seals.

A few steps from the Wild Arctic pavilion is another pavilion, **Shark Encounter ★★**, which features an underwater glass tunnel. A walk through this tunnel allows for up-close observation of many sharks of various species and sizes. Guaranteed chills!

The Seaworld **Aquarium**, for its part, will get you better acquainted with more than 1,000 marine species kept in large tanks and reservoirs that re-create their natural habitat. Quite popular in this region, it's not surprising that Seaworld also features a "tactile tank." Here, you'll be able to see and touch starfish, sea urchins, unusual algae and other similar specimens.

Shamu's Happy Harbor is a large play area for kids with more than 20 activities such as nets, rides, slides, fun ships and water games. This is a great way to end the day.

Of course, Seaworld also has a wide array of services and installations,

restaurants and many shops. If you wish to take full advantage of this site's educational aspect, we recommend the **guided tour ★★** *($8)*, which lasts 90min. The guide will tell you about different aspects of the park, such as the research, training and rescue operations that are conducted here.

Tour H: La Jolla

(one day on foot or by car)

From San Diego, follow Highway 5 towards Los Angeles and take the La Jolla exit. Then take Torrey Pines Road and Prospect Street. You can park on Prospect Street near the Contemporary Art Museum.

A 15min car ride from San Diego is all it takes to reach the lovely, well-to-do town of La Jolla, whose name means "jewel" in Spanish. La Jolla is one of the towns that were developed in the 1940s to provide homes for the gradually increasing number of military personnel in the region. It is especially renowned for its elegant hotels, chic boutiques and great restaurants. To give yourself a better idea of what La Jolla is like, think of it as the Beverly Hills of San Diego. At one time, this town had the reputation of being a haven for retired millionaires, but the creation of the Salk Institute and a University of California campus has now given it a more intellectual and culturally dynamic image.

The tour of the city begins at the **Museum of Contemporary Art – La Jolla ★★** *($4; Sep to May every day 11am to*

7pm, Thu until 11pm, May to Sep Mon to Fri 11am to 11pm, Sat and Sun 11am to 5pm, closed Wed; 700 Prospect St., ☎858-454-3541). This nationally known museum, housed in an beautiful, immaculate building, offers a lovely space to admire its collection. Many Californian artists exhibit their work here. The museum is divided into two pavilions, the second of which is located in downtown San Diego. We strongly recommend the guided tour, offered to groups of five or more, to help you better understand the messages conveyed by the works you'll see. Tours are held on Tuesdays at 2pm and 3pm, Thursdays at 6pm and 7pm, and weekends at 2pm and 3pm. A great way to end the tour is by stopping at the gift shop, which offers an excellent selection of various items and reference books.

Right next to the museum is the Children's Pool.

The **Children's Pool** is a small bay surrounded by a pier. The site was donated to the city by Ellen Scripps to allow children to swim in a safe place. Seals and sea lions are often spotted here.

Go back to Prospect Street and turn left.

Prospect Street and **Girard Avenue** are the town's two main thoroughfares, featuring most of its shops and businesses. Elegant, unique boutiques can be found along with all kinds of restaurants.

Continue along Girard Avenue to reach Coast Boulevard. If you're travelling by car, you'll find, at the end, a parking lot which is often quite packed.

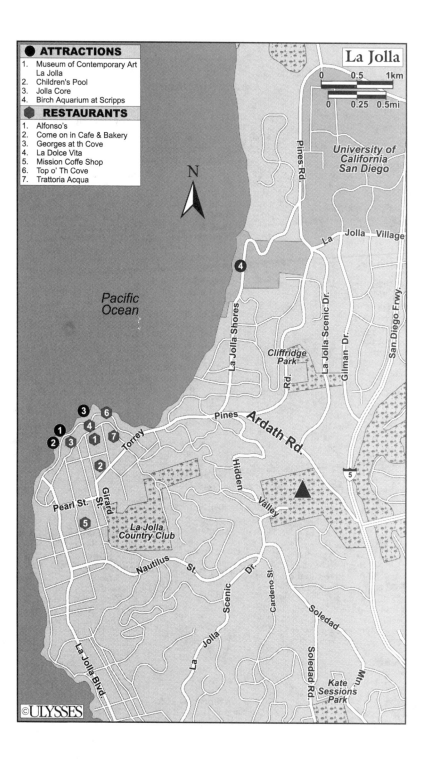

● ATTRACTIONS

1. Museum of Contemporary Art La Jolla
2. Children's Pool
3. Jolla Core
4. Birch Aquarium at Scripps

⬣ RESTAURANTS

1. Alfonso's
2. Come on in Cafe & Bakery
3. Georges at th Cove
4. La Dolce Vita
5. Mission Coffe Shop
6. Top o' Th Cove
7. Trattoria Acqua

La Jolla

0   0.5   1km
0   0.25   0.5mi

N

Pacific Ocean

University of California San Diego

Pines Rd.

La Jolla — Village

La Jolla Scenic Dr.

Gilman Dr.

San Diego Frwy.

La Jolla Shores Rd.

Cliffridge Park

Pines   Ardath Rd.

Torrey

Hidden

5

Pearl St.

Girard St.

Valley

La Jolla Country Club

Nautilus St.

La Jolla Scenic Dr.

Cardeno St.

Soledad

Soledad Rd.

Mtn.

La Jolla Blvd.

Kate Sessions Park

©ULYSSES

La Jolla Cove is a popular beach for swimming and snorkelling, since the water here is very clear. You might even get the chance to see seals and sea lions.

We suggest that you use your car to continue this tour. Take Prospect Drive, Torrey Pines Road and La Jolla Shores Drive, then turn left on Expedition Way. Follow the directions leading to the Birch Aquarium at Scripps.

The first thing you'll see upon arriving at the aquarium are the magnificent bronze statues of grey whales at the entrance. The **Birch Aquarium at Scripps** ★ ★ *($8.50, parking $3; every day 9am to 5pm; 2300 Expedition Way)* is part of the University of California, San Diego. Its mission is threefold: education, research and the promotion of ocean preservation. To reach these goals, the aquarium's administration uses various tools, such as interactive and educational exhibits, programs and special activities.

The Birch Aquarium at Scripps surrounds a central hall which is actually the entrance to three interactive exhibit areas. The first is the fish pavilion, containing 33 tanks; the second is the oceanographic pavilion, dedicated to the science of oceans; and the third is an outdoor exhibit which includes a tidespool, promoting discovery. To learn all about marine life on the coast of California and about oceans in general, this place is a must.

Tour I:
Around San Diego

(two days by car)

From Highway 76, head east on the S6 and follow the signs to the San Diego Wild Animal Park.

Although it belongs to the owners of the San Diego Zoo, the **San Diego Wild Animal Park** ★ ★ ★ *($21.95, parking $5, inquire about prices for both Wild Animal Park and zoo; every day 9am to 4pm; 15500 San Pasqual Valley Rd., Escondido, ☎760-747-8702)* is much larger than the zoo and offers a completely different experience.

This huge amusement park has gone to great lengths to reproduce the natural habitat of animal species from Asia and Africa. It first opened nearly 30 years ago and has been expanding ever since. Today, the park is home to more than 3,500 animals representing 260 species.

Upon arrival, most visitors opt for the **Wgasa Bush Line Trailway**, a slow, 4mi (7km) train ride that lasts 55min. This option allows you to get a good general overview of the site and to get a little closer to the animals than if you were using your car, as is the case for many parks of this type around the country. It is also much less stressful. Furthermore, the guided tour offers lots of information on the animals you will encounter. However, if you prefer to do things differently, a number of options are available.

If you can't travel to Africa, **Photo Caravan Tours** offer a great opportunity to experience a safari that is just like the real thing. A four-

wheel-drive vehicle takes you the heart of the park, and lets you see the animals up close. This tour, obviously more expensive, is by reservation only.

But without a doubt, the most unusual activity offered here is the chance to sleep in a tent on site, only a short distance away from the wildlife. These camping adventures take place on Fridays, Saturdays and Sundays from mid-April to October. The demand is high, so reserve in advance. For more information, call ☎800-934-CAMP.

There are also many interesting shows presented in this park. **Rare and Wild America** *(1pm and 3:45pm; Village Amphitheater)* will give you an interesting overview of many unusual animal species from the wild regions of America. There is also a **bird show** *(11am, 2pm and 4:30pm; Benbough Amphitheater)*. Finally, the **Elephant Show** is, you guessed it, a show that displays the strength, vitality and intelligence of this impressive pachyderm.

The next attraction is located next to the San Diego Wild Animal Park.

The **Pasqual Battlefield** ★ ★ *(free admission; Fri to Sun; 15808 San Pasqual Valley Rd., Escondido, ☎220-5430)* commemorates the bloody battle that took place here in 1846, when the war between Mexico and the United States was at its peak. The U.S. had just lost Los Angeles to the Mexican army and, before dawn, 160 U.S. soldiers decided to attack the Mexicans while they still slept. The battle took place in what was then a Native American village. Because of the more or less equal loss of life on both sides,

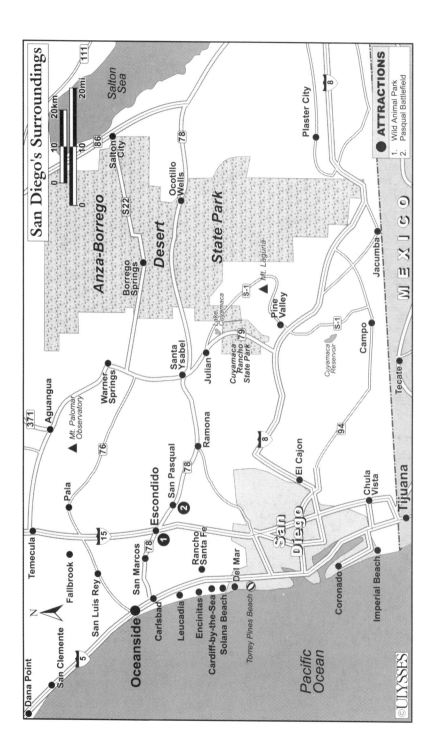

San Diego's Surroundings

ATTRACTIONS

1. Wild Animal Park
2. Pasqual Battlefield

© ULYSSES

both declared victory. On site, you will find an exhibit, a movie and a slide show explaining the battle and its history.

★★
Tijuana

To reach Tijuana, we suggest you leave your car in San Diego and take the San Diego Trolley, which leaves from downtown and takes you straight to the Mexico border for $4.50 (return). You can also drive to the border and leave your car at one of the many parking lots designed for that purpose, on the U.S. side. Although not strongly recommended, driving in Tijuana requires Mexican insurance, which you can purchase at the many agencies on each side of the border.

Located approximately 15.5mi (25km) from San Diego, the Mexican border town of Tijuana is one of the most visited in the world, with more than 50 million annual visitors. It does not really offer an extraordinary array of attractions, except perhaps for the simple fact that it is in such contrast with its neighbour, San Diego. San Diego is clean, rich, organized; Tijuana is lively, untidy, poor, dizzying. However, the destiny of these two cities has always been closely linked.

Strolling down the city's main thoroughfare, the Avenida Revolución, visitors will be dazzled by its animated atmosphere; here, peddlers, beggars, tourists, shop-owners and nightclubs of all kinds exist side by side in a profusion of sounds, smells and colours.

Tijuana is also known as the favourite "playground" of U.S. residents in search

of a rocking good time. The many nightclubs that remain open until the wee hours of the morning and blast their decibels into the main street can certainly attest to that.

U.S. and other tourists are also quite keen on the deals they can find in Tijuana. The many shops and markets are filled with a variety of objects imported from all over Mexico, but also from Taiwan, Beijing and Thailand—items such as trinkets, watches, bags, clothing, alcohol, and various arts and crafts. These items are not always of top quality, but with a little digging, you might find some real treasures. Another advantage is the fact that Tijuana is a free zone, but the merchants' pushy attitude will soon remind you that you have indeed crossed the border. Note that U.S. dollars are accepted everywhere.

To cross into Mexico without problem, U.S. citizens must carry identification, while Canadians and other visitors must show their passport.

Since the downtown area is located a little farther than the border, upon crossing, an impressive number of taxi drivers will insist on offering their services. You can either accept their offer or walk a distance of 0.6mi (1km) to get there. Taking a taxi can be a good way to familiarize yourself with the town, but be sure to ask ahead of time how much the fare will be to prevent an unpleasant surprise. Adventurous visitors who choose to walk downtown should exercise caution, avoid flashing their belongings and not walk alone at night. Here, like everywhere else, being a

tourist can make you more vulnerable.

The **Tijuana Tourism and Convention Bureau** *(P.O. Box 434523, Tijuana, ☎011-52-66/84-0537)* has three offices: one is located near the parking lot where the taxis are found, near the border, and the two others are on Avenida Revolución. A visit to one of these offices will provide you with a few brochures. The staff is not particularly helpful but does speak English.

Accommodations

There are nearly 45,000 hotel rooms in San Diego county, ranging from luxurious equipped suites to more economical rooms. The downtown core has seen a boom in the past decade, and several hotels have been constructed very recently. Room rates are generally quite high, but note that they are lower during the winter months.

Downtown and Gaslamp

USA Hostel San Diego
$15/dormitory, $34/private room
K, sb/pb
72 Sixth Ave.
San Diego
☎*232-3100 or 800-438-8622*
≈*232-3106*
www.usahostels.com
This is an establishment that will definitely suit travellers on a tight budget. It is not a member of Hostelling International, but it is along the same lines. Very conveniently located near the lively Gaslamp district, its rooms

San Diego

are clean and it offers facilities and services such as equipped communal kitchens, washing machines and safes. It also offers guests coffee and tea. They organize several activities and there is a shuttle service that goes regularly to the main beaches.

Downtown San Diego Youth Hostel
$19/nonmembers
$17/members
sb/pb, K
7am to midnight
(24hr access)
521 Market St., corner Fifth Ave.
San Diego, CA 92101
☎*525-1531 or 800-909-4776*
⇌*338-0129*
www.hostelweb.com/sandiego
Located in the heart of the charming Gaslamp district, the San Diego Youth Hostel has everything for people who are looking for action. It is surrounded by a multitude of stores, cafes and bars, each more interesting than the last. The three-storey building is especially charming, as are the other buildings in the area, and the interior has recently been renovated. There are 134 beds in dormitories or private rooms, well-equipped kitchens, a lounge and even a pool room with a superb view over the lively neighbourhood. The rooms are simple but clean and they have safes. In addition to the traditional youth hostel clientele, a large number of convention delegates stay here, mostly for the location. The polite staff will be pleased to inform you about the area's activities and businesses to help you get the most out of your stay. Internet access and bicycle rentals are available.

Pickwick Hotel
$$
tv, ℜ, ⊗
132 W. Broadway
San Diego, CA 92101
☎*234-9200*
☎*(800) 826-0009*
⇌*544-9879*
This little hotel, built in 1926 and located not far from the port, has an interesting appearance. Its rooms are clean and comfortable, it is affordable, and children under 16 stay free. A popular spot with families.

The Inn at the YMCA
$$
ℜ, ☉, △, *tv*, ≈, ⊗
500 W. Broadway
San Diego, CA 92101
☎*234-5252*
⇌*234-5272*
Do not mistake this for one of those residences that you often see managed by the YMCA. Rather, as the name indicates, this hotel is located in the same building as that famous organization. The Inn at the YMCA is located in a beautiful historic downtown building and its location is very convenient. The clientele consists of young people and sailors, which gives the place a convivial atmosphere. It offers good quality, and you can use the YMCA's facilities. The rooms are simple and clean and there is a restaurant available.

Wyndham Emerald Plaza Hotel
$$$$
tv, ≡, ≈, ☉, △, ℜ, ⴳ
400 W. Broadway
San Diego
☎*239-4500*
☎*800-WYNDHAM*
www.wyndham.com
With its hexagonal towers topped with glowing green crowns, this hotel belonging to the Wyndham chain

evokes the magic of the circus. It has, moreover, adopted the image of the Cirque du Soleil for its marketing. Located in the heart of downtown San Diego, it is visible from far away and has become one of the architectural symbols of the city. The rooms are comfortable and clean, although they are less impressive than the hotel itself. They have all the amenities, such as a coffee machine, hair dryer, ironing board and iron. Depending on the orientation of your window, you can admire the city centre or San Diego Bay. In spite of appearances, the prices are very competitive considering the quality of the service, the comfort of the hotel and its location.

Horton Grand Hotel
$$$$
≡, *tv*, ℜ, K, ⴳ
311 Island Ave.
San Diego, CA 92101
☎*544-1886 or 800-542-1886*
www.hortongrand.com
This is one of the most picturesque hotels in the city (see p 192). Completely renovated in 1986, both the architecture and the decor are essentially inspired by the Victorian period. Do take the time to admire this hotel's beauty and architectural details; it blends perfectly into the historical Gaslamp district, where it is located not far from the convention centre.

The 132 rooms and suites each have their own look, with Victorian-style furniture, carved cupboards, a fireplace and curtains. They are for the most part equipped with an iron and ironing board, a hair dryer and coffee machine, and the suites also have kitchenettes. From the balconies you can either look out onto the interior courtyard or the Gaslamp district. The establishment also has an excellent restaurant and piano bar, and on some days of the week you can have tea in the interior courtyard.

San Diego Marriott
$$$$$
tv, ≡, ⊛, ☉, *K*, ✪, ℜ, △, ⚲
333 W. Harbor Dr.
San Diego, CA 92101-7700
www.marriott.com
The Marriott is a splendid 25-storey building with two wings and no fewer than 1,354 rooms. Next to the conference centre, it is conveniently located close to downtown, the Gaslamp, the ocean and Seaport Village. It has its own marina at the rear of the hotel.

The building's architecture is particularly interesting. The architect wanted to symbolize two boats coming into the port. The striking result has made this one of the most beautiful and prestigious hotels on San Diego Bay.

The interior is also spectacular, with its lobby and lounges, restaurants, two bars, yacht club and conference rooms. The rooms, which are not as luxurious as the rest of the hotel, are nevertheless basically well equipped. Some have a balcony with a magnificent view over the bay.

The hotel has various recreational facilities (exercise room, health club, tennis courts and pool). It is not far from the ocean and a bike path, and you can rent boats and bicycles.

San Diego Hyatt Regency
$$$$$
ℜ, ✪, *K*, ☉, ≈, △, ⚲, *tv*
1 Market Pl.
San Diego, CA 92101
☎*232-1234*
≈*233-6464*
www.travelweb.com/hyatt.html
The Hyatt Regency, with its imposing architecture, is probably one of the first hotels you will see as you head downtown from the airport. It stands majestically on the bay just near Seaport Village, the city centre and the Gaslamp.

Geared toward business people and convention delegates, it offers them the whole range of collective and individual services aimed at facilitating their work (meeting rooms, fax machines, computer hook-ups, etc.). It is an easy walk to the convention centre from this hotel, which is one of the most luxurious in the area and is frequently featured in the city's publicity material. Moreover, expect to be as impressed by the interior as you are by the exterior.

This hotel has several bars and restaurants, the best known being Sally, which specializes in sea food. Laels is simpler, but it is especially popular for its brunches. For a drink and a breathtaking view, go to the Top of the Hyatt, where you can overlook the city at a height of almost 500 ft (150m). The hotel's facilities also include a billiards room and a bookstore.

All the rooms are very comfortable and have a view over the bay. From the south-facing rooms you can sometimes see Mexico, while from those facing north you can admire the town of La Jolla.

The 819 rooms and 56 suites are tastefully and simply decorated in the Victorian style. They are all generally equipped with, among other things, a hairdryer, a refrigerator, a mini-bar, a coffee maker and of course, the newspaper.

Coronado Island

Coronado Island Inn
$$
≡, *tv*, ℝ, *P*
301 Orange Ave.
Coronado
☎*435-0935*
☎*888-436-0935*
This unpretentious hotel-motel has the considerable advantage of being central while also being relatively affordable. Since its rooms have refrigerators, you can also save on dining-out expenses. Coffee is offered all day.

San Diego Hyatt Regency

El Cordova Hotel
$$$

tv, ≡, ≈, K, ℜ, P

1351 Orange Ave.
Coronado, CA 92118
☎*435-4131*
☎*800-229-2032*
⇌*435-0632*
www.elcordovahotel.com

The El Cordova Hotel was built in 1902 as a mansion and converted into a hotel in 1930. Its Spanish-colonial style architecture has been preserved, and the spacious rooms have recently been renovated. The interior courtyard—with its little tables, patio next to the restaurant and heated pool—invites relaxation. Conveniently located close to the beach and downtown.

Crown City Inn
$$$

tv, ≈, ≡, ℜ

520 Orange Ave.
Coronado, CA 92118
☎*435-3116*
☎*800-422-1173*
⇌*435-6750*

Like several of the neighbouring establishments located close to downtown, the Crown City Inn is an honest little hotel-motel that offers clean, comfortable rooms at competitive rates. The style of the building is reminiscent of a *hacienda*, but overall it is modern, with a swimming pool and restaurant.

La Avenida Inn
$$$$

tv, ≡, ≈, K

1315 Orange Ave.
Coronado, CA 92118
☎*435-3191 or 800-437-0162*
⇌*435-5024*

The simple but clean hotel-motel is well located between the beach and the Coronado city centre, and it is also near the famous Hotel Del Coronado. You will find all the facilities here to help make your stay pleasant. Coffee is served throughout the day.

Glorietta Bay Inn
$$$$

K, ≈, ⊛, ≡, tv, &

1630 Glorietta Blvd.
Coronado, CA 92118-2998
☎*435-3101 or 800-283-9383*
⇌*435-6182*
www.gloriettabayinn.com

The Glorietta Bay Inn is a distinguished hotel that dates back to 1950. The building was the personal home of John Spreckels, the famous visionary and founder of the Hotel Del Coronado, who built this magnificent house on 7.5 acres (3ha) of land on Glorietta Bay (see p 200). Designed by the architect Harrison Albright in 1906 and completed as a house in 1908, the building is unquestionably an important part of the history of Coronado Island and San Diego. Here you will have an opportunity to enjoy the luxury and comfort of the large neighbouring hotels, with the added bonus of this hotel's own unique style.

This hotel consists of two wings. The original building, called the Mansion, was originally occupied by John Spreckel's family and now has 11 rooms and suites. The new wing is similar to a luxury motel; its rooms are more modern and therefore have less character. All the rooms are tastefully decorated in the Victorian style and offer views of the bay or the swimming pool in front. Breakfast is served every morning on the veranda or in the Music Room. You can rent bicycles and boats, and guided tours of the island are offered daily.

Loews Coronado Bay Resort
$$$$$

&, ≡, ⊛, ⊘, K, ℝ, ✿, ℜ

4000 Coronado Bay Rd.
Coronado, CA 92118
☎*424-4000 or 800-815-6397*
www.loewshotels.com

Located a little out of the way on a private peninsula on San Diego Bay, but not far from the city centre and beaches, the Loews Coronado Bay Resort is one of the most chic hotels in the area.

Its pink façade, cream walls and tile roofs set the tone right from the first glance: this is a classic seaside resort. The hotel complex has three pools, terraces sprinkled with lounging chairs and palm trees, a health club and an 80-berth marina for recreational boats. You can sail or out-board motor, take out a personal watercraft or a pedalo, and bicycle or in-line skate. A complete fitness centre and five tennis courts complete the picture. Wow!

The lobby, with its double staircase complete with wrought-iron balustrades and copper railings, its chandelier and overstuffed armchairs, could be the set of a Hollywood musical. The hotel has four excellent restaurants, including San Diego's premier restaurant, the Azzura Point (see p 226), and a café-grocery store.

The rooms are decorated in a refined but simple style that harmonizes well with the coastal scenery. They look out onto San Diego Bay and have all the usual amenities plus a few extras: a minibar, two telephones, fax machine and computer hookups as well as a spacious bathroom.

Hotel Del Coronado
$$$$$
👤, ≡, ⊛, ⊘, *K*, ≈, ℝ, ✪, ℜ, ◯
1500 Orange Ave.
Coronado, CA 92118
☎*800-HOTEL-DEL*
www.hoteldel.com
The symbol of a whole island and emblem of San Diego, the Hotel Del Coronado is more than just a hotel. It figures among the most prominent hotels in the world. Its extraordinary architecture—a blend of Victorian inspiration and railway station design—as well as its unique history (see p 198) undoubtedly account for much of this fame. If you are willing to pay the price and want to treat yourself to the luxury of sleeping in a very famous hotel, the Hotel Del Coronado, also called the Del, is definitely the right choice.

Now a legend thanks to visits by hundreds of celebrities and dignitaries like Marilyn Monroe, John F. Kennedy and Frank Sinatra, the hotel is constantly cited in the media. It has 10 restaurants, scores of stores and galleries, in addition to all the necessary facilities for business people and convention delegates. A health club, an immense terrace, tennis courts and every service imaginable add to the luxurious atmosphere. The only sobering note is that several of the rooms are not of the same calibre as the rest; nevertheless all offer the full range of expected comforts. There are various activity programs for children, and the hotel's location, a stone's throw away from the ocean and near the most beautiful beach in the area, completes its charm.

Tent City

In 1900, sugar magnate Baron John D. Spreckels invested in the construction of the grandiose Hotel Del Coronado. Since the project cost more than expected, he decided to establish a camping resort to raise extra funds. On the beach, south of the hotel, he erected hundreds of tents and cottages that he rented out in summer. Tent City became an autonomous mini-town with, among other things, its own newspaper, specialized shops and a beauty parlour. A number of activities were also offered to vacationers. Tent City outlasted the hotel's construction period by nearly 40 years, during which time it attracted an impressive number of people. It was replaced by a highway in 1939.

Old Town and Presidio Hills

For those who are looking for a lively area or some Latin American culture, or for history buffs, it might be pleasant to stay right near the Old Town, even if there is less choice here than in other parts of the city.

Hacienda Hotel
$$$$
ℜ, ≡, *tv*, ⊛, ≈, ⊘, *K*
4041 Harney St.
San Diego, CA 92110
☎*298-4707 or 800-888-1991*
The Hacienda Hotel is constructed in a most picturesque architectural style that blends in well with the rest of the old city. The place is undeniably beautiful and looks more like a seaside resort than a simple hotel, with its pool, fitness centre, sauna and whirlpool tubs. The rooms are tasteful, just like the rest of the hotel, and in addition to the usual amenities they have coffee machines and balconies. With a bit of luck you will get a room with a view of the bay (several of the balconies look out onto the interior courtyard). This establishment offers a good quality/price ratio.

Balboa Park and Mission Valley

🏠 **Park Manor Suites**
$$$$
ℜ, *tv*, ⊗
525 Spruce St.
San Diego, CA 92103
☎*291-0999 or 800-874-2649*
⇍*291-8844*
www.parkmanorsuites.com
This lovely hotel, built in 1926 and classified as a historical monument by the city of San Diego, is one of the most interesting options. It was designed by the architect Frank P. Allen Jr., the architect who designed the buildings for the Panama-California Exposition.

Its 80 comfortable and elegant rooms are furnished with antiques, and they also have kitchenettes. The view from the rooms is either of Balboa Park or downtown San Diego. A continental breakfast is served every morning near the lobby.

There is a decent restaurant here, a bar offering regular live shows and a rooftop terrace that is frequently used for weddings. For its style and quality, the prices are among the most reasonable in town. Highly recommended.

Town and Country Resort and Convention
$$$$
ℜ, ≈, ✪, ☺, *tv*, ♿, ≡, ®, *K, P*
500 Hotel Circle N.
San Diego, CA 92108
☎*691-7131 or 800-77-ATLAS*
www.towncountry.com
For those who want everything in one spot without having to go anywhere, the Town and Country Resort and Convention is the place to stay. This vast hotel complex, aimed at business people and convention delegates, is a veritable little community unto itself. It consists of no fewer than 30 buildings, a total of 1,000 rooms, a health club, two large show rooms, several large-capacity conference halls, and five restaurants and bars; in short, everything you could possibly need.

The atmosphere here is pleasant with its several landscaped gardens, pools and terraces. The overall effect is attractive and modern. The rooms are very comfortable, the decor is warm and they are equipped with all the necessities. There is golf and a racket ball and tennis club just next door. All in all, this is an attractive option that will appeal to a wide variety of clients, and particularly to business travellers.

Point Loma

Point Loma Hostel
$16/non-members
$14/members
K, pb/sb, tv
3790 Udall St.
San Diego, CA 92107
☎*223-4778*
≈*223-1883*
www.hostelweb.com/Sandiego
In contrast with its downtown counterpart, the Point Loma youth hostel, located in a large house, will appeal to those who are looking for a quiet place. Only 4.5 mi (7km) from the city centre, it is easily accessible by car or public transportation. The lovely Ocean Beach is barely 1.25 mi. (2km) away. With its 61 beds and six private rooms, the hostel offers all the usual facilities, such as a kitchen and a lounge. You can also take advantage of a sunny terrace and ping pong table. The employees frequently organize activities like barbeques and fires on the beach for the guests. There are several markets in the vicinity that sell fresh and organic products for your evening meal or your beach picnic. Internet access and bicycle rental are available.

Restaurants

With its great selection of restaurants (almost 2,500 in the county), San Diego is without question one of the top gastronomic capitals of the Unites States. Here you will find all types of cuisine, everything from Ethiopian to traditional Native American. The most popular types, however, are California cuisine (fusion), seafood, Italian, Asian and Mexican. There are also many excellent French restaurants in San Diego.

Downtown and Gaslamp

It is in this neighbourhood, more specifically in Gaslamp, that you will find the most hip and popular restaurants in the San Diego area. You will also find a great choice of multiethnic establishments. Their lively atmosphere, from early evening until the wee hours, is sure to please everybody.

Brickyard Coffee & Tea
$
open for lunch and dinner
G St., corner Kettner
☎*(619) 696-7220*
Located in the downtown area but slightly set back from the noise and traffic, Brickyard Coffee & Tea looks like a quaint neighbourhood restaurant and is the kind of place where you feel right at home. The menu is quite simple, featuring bagels, sandwiches, salads and quiches, and this is the perfect spot for those who simply feel like relaxing, reading or writing.

Bruegger's Bagels
$
326 Broadway
☎*239-2243*
Although this is actually a chain, the place offers an interesting concept where you can enjoy a good, quick and inexpensive meal. You guessed it: fresh bagels are the house specialty. There are a dozen varieties to choose from, including cranberry, jalapeño pepper, sun-dried tomato and chocolate chip. And of course, there's plenty of cream cheese. You can also opt for a homemade bagel sandwich. The decor is rather

unexciting, which will probably encourage you to take out and enjoy your bagels in a park or on the beach.

Cafe 222
$-$$
222 Island Ave.
☎236-9902
"The man who gets breakfast in bed is probably in the hospital" are the words that will greet you at this charming little restaurant, a few steps away from the Gaslamp district near the downtown area. Housed in a building that, at first glance, is really nothing special, this small café has managed to spread its joyous atmosphere throughout the entire neighbourhood. This is undoubtedly due to its small sidewalk terrace, always packed with businesspeople discussing worldly matters or reading the paper, as well as the tempting aroma of fresh coffee in the air. Many workers flock to this haven of peace during rush hour, and on weekends, wandering tourists mix in with the regulars. The menu offers delicious and unusual dishes such as pumpkin waffles and pesto-and-goat-cheese omelets, served with foccacia bread. Excellent value.

Dick's Last Resort
$-$$
open for lunch and dinner
300 Fifth Ave., corner J and K sts.
☎231-9100
Everything is so aesthetically pleasing and proper in a city like San Diego that stopping by a place like Dick's Last Resort can become a necessity, just to maintain some kind of equilibrium. Nicknamed "The Shame of the Gaslamp District," this Irish pub-like establishment brags about being the most casual place in town,

and as such, is an ideal place to just take it easy. No fuss, no dress code, no fancy service or ultra-refined dishes here; only simple cuisine, loud music and friendly staff. The terrace is also quite pleasant. You're guaranteed to have a great time here!

Hob Nob Hills
$-$$
2271 First Ave.
☎239-8176
Open since 1944, Hob Nob Hills is a San Diego classic. Many generations have come here to enjoy traditional-style meals, either for breakfast (the place is packed on weekends, though), lunch or dinner. This establishment serves fine meals at honest prices, in a simple but warm setting. If it weren't so big, it would almost look like a diner, with its traditional red booths. In spite of its old-fashioned appearance, this is one of those places that never go out of style, and still remains a great spot to appreciate the many tastes of America.

The Field
$$
544 Fifth Ave., corner Market and Island sts.
☎232-9840
This great Irish pub is ideal for having a beer with friends or enjoying folk performances (Sundays between 5pm and 9pm). In fact, this establishment is quite involved in the promotion of Irish culture and organizes many cultural events. Incidentally, did you know that St. Patrick's Day is the most celebrated day in the United States? The Field also serves excellent homemade dishes prepared with fresh products. Lunch and dinner are served every day and delicious breakfasts on weekends only. In spite of a

somewhat cavernous setting, there is a fun atmosphere here.

Sammy's California Woodfired Pizza
$$
770 Fourth Ave.
☎230-8888
In a simple but lovely decor, you will be offered a variety of woodfired pizzas that have made this place popular. In fact, Sammy has become so well known and appreciated over the years that he has opened five new restaurants. The service isn't fantastic but the food is very good and the prices are reasonable. Portions are quite generous. This restaurant also serves calzones, pasta, salads and a few more elaborate dishes such as lamb chops. Perfect for families and for those on a tight budget.

Napa Valley Grille
$$$
502 Horton Plaza
☎238-5440
≈238-9591
This elegant restaurant on the third floor of the Horton Plaza shopping centre, in the heart of downtown, serves lunch and dinner. The decor and reception give the impression that the prices here are sky-high, but you're in for a pleasant surprise: an excellent selection of salads, sandwiches, apetizers, pasta and main dishes at relatively affordable prices. Fish dishes such as salmon and tuna are particularly appreciated. The wine list, as you might have guessed by the restaurant's name, is quite elaborate.

La Provence
$$$-$$$$
708 Fourth Ave.
☎544-0661
The first thing you notice when you walk into this restaurant, located near the

San Diego

heart of San Diego, is its well-designed Provençal setting. The place is divided into two sections: the first, somewhat formal, has soft colours that evoke summers in Provence, with chairs and booths covered in the area's signature fabric, patterned tablecloths and curtains, bouquets of flowers, and ploughing implements hanging on the walls. Obviously, the specialty here is French cuisine, and escargots, bouillabaisse, cassoulet and coq au vin are all offered at reasonable prices. The table d'hôte changes every day. The owner, a Frenchman who emigrated many years ago, makes it clear through his establishment's style that he has not forgotten the lifestyle of his native homeland. The second room acts as a bar and is also Provence-inspired, in a way that is more quiet but just as lovely. Here you can enjoy a *pastis*, just like they do in the old country.

Blue Point Coastal Cuisine
$$$$
565 Fifth Ave.
☎233-6623
⇌233-1931
Blue Point Coastal Cuisine is a very chic restaurant-bar that specializes in seafood. It features a sumptuous sea-theme decor with wide, comfortable seashell-shaped booths, as well as a beautiful bar area where the sound of clinking martini glasses resonates. The terrace, not as busy, faces the street. The clientele is mostly composed of businesspeople, tourists and wealthy locals, and the staff is friendly, although slightly stiff. The fish served here is a real treat! Take this opportunity to sample a regional specialty: the oyster martini, which consists of a raw oyster served in a schnapps glass with a dry martini that you must swallow in one shot. Another safe bet is their famous clam chowder.

Croce's Restaurant
$$$$
803 Fifth Ave., Corner F St.
☎233-4355
This restaurant is more than a gastronomic institution; it represents the story of a woman who, for love of the man she lost in an plane accident, opened a restaurant in his memory. This woman is Ingrid Croce and the man is famous folk-singer Jim Croce. In his lifetime, he performed in many countries, and he died while returning from a tour in 1973. Ingrid opened the restaurant about 10 years later and became one of the pioneers in developing the Gaslamp district. Since then, thanks to the devotion of this woman who is both owner and head chef, the establishment has become one of the neighbourhood's favourites.

The food here is excellent. In fact, Ingrid has even published a recipe book in which she writes about the inspiration she finds in

The Tuna Industry

At one time, San Diego's tuna industry was apparently the largest in the world. Descendants of Portuguese immigrants were the first to develop this type of business in San Diego, around 1910. The industry continued to expand until the early 1970s. At that time, the flotilla included nearly 130 boats measuring between 164ft and 262ft (50m and 80m) which criss-crossed the bay and the Pacific Ocean. Each crew had some 20 men who went to sea for four to five months and returned with 1,600 tonnes of tuna.

Today, many fishing families still live in San Diego, but it is very rare to see a fishing boat at sea. The increase of fishing in Asia, which contributed to the closing of two canneries in the 1980s, has resulted in fewer boats stopping in San Diego. Now, fishers go to the Samoa Islands or Puerto Rico. There is a cannery in Los Angeles, which brings some business to San Diego, but all that is left of this industry is fishing families who ply their trade in different ports along the Pacific coast.

places and people she has known and loved over the years. The decor is rather bare, but is accentuated by family photographs, gold records and guitars (the place is almost a small shrine to Jim). There are two floors here, as well as exterior tables set out on the street. A pleasant way to finish the evening is to cross over to the bar, where jazz, blues and folk shows are presented.

San Diego Pier Cafe

Lael's Restaurant
$$$$
Hyatt Regency Hotel
☎232-1234
≈239-5678
As one of the imposing Hyatt Regency's restaurants, Lael's is mainly known for its all-you-can-eat buffet that changes every day. The large bay window lets in plenty of sunlight and the enormous sculpted-wood chandeliers complete the sober Victorian-style decor. The adjacent terrace is located near the ocean and Seaport Village, amidst birds of paradise and magnolias. The sound of cell phones ringing everywhere is a pretty good sign that the clientele is mostly made up of businesspeople, but honeymooners and wealthy families also enjoy dining here. However, this restaurant is not as impressive as the rest of the hotel.

Taka
$$$$
555 Fifth Ave.
☎338-0555
≈338-0898
With Asia so close by, successive immigration waves have made San Diego a great city in which to enjoy authentic Japanese cuisine. In fact, Californians have a bit of a penchant for it. Over the years, Taka has acquired an excellent reputation with connoisseurs; the place is actually known as the best sushi bar in town. However, this popularity has its drawbacks, such as interminable waiting lines and rather uptight service.

Sally's
$$$$-$$$$$
Hyatt Regency Hotel
☎232-1234
≈239-5678
Located next to Seaport Village, Sally's is the pride and joy of the Hyatt Regency Hotel. The menu offers many different dishes but it is seafood that gets top billing. The idea here is to prepare fresh, high-quality delights of the sea accompanied with unusual side dishes and food combinations. The elegant terrace provides a beautiful view of the bay and the marina, and the open kitchen allows diners to watch the cooks in action. This establishment has received many awards, especially for its seafood dishes; the bouillabaisse and crab cakes are absolute musts.

The Port and Seaport

Seaport was designed with tourists in mind, which is why, at certain hours of the day, the place is practically deserted. However, you will certainly find some decent restaurants here.

San Diego Pier Cafe
$$-$$$
Seaport Village
☎239-3968
The photograph of the San Diego Pier Cafe actually serves as the promotional logo of Seaport Village. This is not surprising: with such a location, it's hard to get any closer to the water. The view here is unique. Although this place principally attracts passing tourists, it can still be quite pleasant to sit here and enjoy one of its many seafood dishes. The menu offers such safe bets as clam chowder, fish and chips, fried squid, seafood fettuccini and fish tacos. A lovely spot for families.

Anthony's Fish Grotto
$$$
1360 North Harbor Dr.
☎(619) 232-5103
Right in the port, this restaurant offers seafood, salads and fish and chips. Portions are generous and reasonably priced. Because of its proximity to the port, freshness is guaranteed. This is a safe bet for tourists and their families.

Death Valley reveals deep reds, golds, greens and browns under a beautiful blue sky. Heat waves rise and fall above the desert as one descends the mountains to the depths of the valley. However, the site's main draw is its absolute emptiness, which creates an unusual and unwelcoming landscape amidst a world that is otherwise so full of life.
- *Patrick Escudero*

La Purisma Lompoc Mission is one of the most completely reconstructed missions in California, which once belonged to the Franciscans.
- *Claude Hervé-Bazin*

Along the Pacific coast, it is not rare to see the silhouette of a wooden pier jutting out into the deep blue sea.
- Claude Hervé-Bazin

California's coastal landscapes are simply breathtaking. Big Sur, for example, is known throughout the world for the spectacular beauty of its coastline and dramatic cliffs, sandy beaches and the lush vegetation of its many state parks.

The murals decorating these houses demonstrate the creativity of San Franciscans.
- *J. Ducange*

One of the most photographed scenes in San Francisco, this row of six beautiful Victorian homes has been nicknamed "Postcard Row."
- *P. Escudero*

The superb Golden Gate Bridge, the city's symbol *par excellence,* crosses the strait where San Francisco Bay flows into the choppy waters of the Pacific.

The craze generated by the California gold rush attracted people from as far away as China; today, San Francisco's Chinatown is one of the largest in the United States.
- *Claude Hervé-Bazin*

Anthony's Fishette

$

Harbor Dr. at Ash

☎232-5105

A simplified version of Anthony's Fish Grotto, Anthony's Fishette is a counter serving a variety of fast-food-style seafood and fish. Although it is mostly crowded with tourists, this place is an excellent choice. Don't hesitate to try the clam chowder, the mixed-fries plate or the fish taco. The simple pleasure of sitting on the terrace, observing passersby, boats, slightly voracious seagulls and even seals, while enjoying the sun's warm rays and breathing the fresh sea air is definitely worth the detour. It will cost you less than most other activities and is guaranteed to leave you with sweet memories.

The Fish Market

$$

Top of the Market

N. Harbor Dr.

☎232-3474

Always filled with regulars and businesspeople, as well as fascinated tourists, this address is strictly for seafood-lovers. Indeed, here you will find great selection and absolute freshness. The sushi and oyster bars are quite popular.

On the third floor is the Top of the Market restaurant, which is in fact a dining room that is a little more sophisticated than the second floor, with a great view of the bay and the Coronado Bridge. This place is pricier but still a great value.

Coronado Island

Stretch's Cafe

$

943 Orange Ave.

☎435-8886

One almost finds this place by chance; there is no big sign or bright neon lights at the entrance. However, this is a small, warm café-restaurant that is really not expensive and offers fresh and simple dishes. The specialties here are soups, breakfasts, unusual sandwiches and frozen yogurt. Most of the ingredients are homemade.

Bino's

$-$$

1120 Adella Ave.

Coronado Island, CA 92118

☎522-0612

Slightly set back from the main street, Bino's is the best-kept secret in Coronado. Only recently opened, it is a great place to discover. The Mexican owner has replaced the inevitable tacos with a fabulous crepe recipe he picked up in Brittany. He prepares them in a delicious way, mixing in all kinds of fresh ingredients. Delectable! You won't find such outstanding crepes anywhere else in San Diego.

In addition, the service is very friendly and considerate, and the decor, although modest, is conducive to relaxation. An ideal spot to sit and read or write postcards, with lovely music in the background. You also have the choice of sitting outside on the terrace set out on a small street. The clientele is mostly made up of regulars, as workers from the area come here for take-out breakfast or lunch. You can also treat yourself to some delicious coffee, fresh croissants or tasty sandwiches. This is truly the kind of place that makes life a little sweeter.

Miguel's Cocina

$-$$

1351 Orange Ave.

☎437-4237

A Mexican restaurant facing the Coronado Hotel, Miguel's Cocina offers, in addition to an interesting and affordable menu, both an exterior and interior decor that is highly colourful and will definitely make you feel like you're on vacation.

Coronado Brewing Company

$$

170 Orange Ave.

☎437-4457

It is not rare to see this place packed with revellers, including Marines, who give the place a particularly festive atmosphere. This establishment is actually a micro-brewery that offers ribs, pizza and sandwiches. The terrace is quite lively and provides a magnificent view of San Diego's skyscrapers.

Bay Beach Cafe

$$$

1201 First St.

☎435-4900

⇄435-6641

This elegant family restaurant is located in Ferry Landing Park. Although it's a rather impersonal andunexciting place in terms of menu, decor and service, it is not necessarily a bad dining choice, since it is still quite pleasant in attractive, modern pastel shades. The Bay Beach Cafe is mainly a good place to stop after a day of shopping, while waiting for the ferry back to San Diego. Here you can enjoy a drink or a meal and admire the view of the port and the lively promenade. There is also a nice heated terrace.

Il Fornaio
$$$
1333 First St.
☎437-4911

Viva Italia! For those who just can't get enough of the refinement that embodies this country, Il Fornaio, which recently opened, is just the place. This is the newest of a chain that includes about 20 restaurants in the United States.

At the entrance, to the right, is a counter where fresh bread (note that Il Fornaio is first and foremost a bakery), imported goods and sandwiches are served. To the left is a fantastic bar where you can relax before your meal. But it's the dining room that will really catch your eye. It is a long, narrow room that has huge windows overlooking the bay and the bright lights of San Diego on one side, and on the other, an open kitchen where cooks are busy working their magic.

The interior decoration is both sober and sumptuous, with white walls, high woodworked ceilings and rattan chairs that add an Asian touch to the ensemble. The fireplace in the centre, the gigantic chandeliers and the beautiful table candlesticks contribute to this discreet ambiance. The terrace is also quite lovely.

Another feature that makes this place unique is its menu. Each month, a different specialty from Italy is offered, while the regular menu is filled with marvellously prepared, classic and, quite surprisingly, affordable dishes. For an elegant dinner that won't cost you an arm and a leg, keep this address in mind.

The Chart House
$$$
1701 Strand Way
☎435-0155

The history of the Del Coronado is fascinating, and the Boathouse, built in 1887, is an important part of it (see p 200). This is why The Chart House steak and seafood chain has definitely found a prime location in this historic building. The view of Glorietta Bay is gorgeous. Here, the meat dishes are adequate though the seafood dishes are somewhat uneven, especially considering the price. Location, location, location: that's what makes this restaurant special. And that is, after all, part of the fun of eating out in restaurants.

Chez Loma
$$$$
1132 Loma Ave.
☎435-0661

Open since 1974, this small French bistro is housed in a beautiful Victorian home on a street near the Hotel Del Coronado. The place has acquired quite a reputation for its fine dining, so much so that it doesn't even require any advertising. Many critics rank it among the best restaurants in the region. Try the Atlantic salmon with sun-dried-tomato vinaigrette or the succulent duck.

Azzura Point
$$$$$
Loews Coronado Bay Resort
4000 Coronado Bay Rd.
(Silver Strand Blvd.)
☎424-4000

Fit for a prince, this restaurant atop the Loews Hotel has been the recipient of many awards. The view is breathtaking, as is the colonial-style decor: you'll think you've just stepped into a Karen Blixen novel! Entering this establishment, you first walk through the exquisite cocktail room, followed by the dining room.

As you can imagine, the atmosphere and the setting are what truly make this dining experience unique: rattan chairs, fake giraffe-skin centrepieces, wide booths and chairs covered in soft velvet leopard-print, not to mention the lamps that are shaped like African animals and the spectacular chandeliers. The service and the Mediterranean-inspired menu are equally flawless; obviously, the price is in keeping with the elevated standards set by this restaurant. But if you're looking for an unforgettable evening, this is the right place.

Crown Room
$$$$$
Hotel Del Coronado
☎522-8490

This restaurant is without question the most luxurious of all. There is even a grand piano in the middle of the large, exquisitely decorated dining room with a 33ft-high (10m) ceiling. Here, dinner and dancing are on the menu, making it the ideal location for special occasions. Many critics say that thequality of the dishes doesn't live up to expectations one might have of such a place, but as we all know, elegance has a way of making things taste better...

The Crown Room mostly serves California coastal cuisine. The Sunday brunch is quite popular, as are the ballroom-dancing nights.

San Diego

Old Town and Presidio Hills

Although quite touristic, this sector is filled with very lively restaurants, mostly Mexican establishments that offer more or less the same concept. Tables with coloured parasols are set up around a central square with a fountain where diners are served by staff in traditional costumes.

These restaurants serve a variety of Mexican dishes, tortillas and margaritas. You will find a whole slew of these places and they are all basically equal; however, a visit to San Diego would not be complete without trying at least one of them. Here are a few suggestions.

Casa de Bandini
$$
2754 Calhoun St.
☎297-8211
Located in a historic building, (an original adobe from 1829), Casa de Bandini was once the home of Juan de Bandini, a politician at the time. Although a "tourist trap," it is still pleasant and prices are reasonable. Dishes are not especially refined but the servings are huge. You might have to wait in line for a while; at the door, a device is given to you which will vibrate to signal that your table is ready. In the meantime you can enjoy a margarita in the waiting area. The service is not extraordinary but since the place is constantly filled with both tourists and locals, there isn't much room for personalized service. The multicoloured exterior and interior decor, for its part, is charming.

Casa Guadalajara
$$
4105 Taylor St., corner Juan St.
☎295-5111
The latest of all the old town's restaurants, this place stands out for the folk-art objects that fill the dining room and lend it a unique atmosphere. Here you can sample a nourishing meal along with a tasty margarita, all to the sound of *mariachis*... you might even be tempted to try a few dance steps. The service can be a little disappointing, however.

Casa de Pico
$$-$$$
Bazar del Mundo
☎296-3267
The Bazar del Mundo restaurant is located in the highly animated market of the same name. Although most restaurants in the old town are alike, this one is a great choice for its prime location, as you find yourself at the heart of the market, near a lovely water fountain. There are also lots of activities, colours and entertainment here; for example, *mariachis* often perform Mexican music. To accompany your appetizer of tortillas and salsa, try one of their many margaritas. The setting is a true festival of colours, with parasols, servers dressed in traditional garb and many store displays around the square.

Balboa Park

The Prado
$$$-$$$$
House of Hospitality
Balboa Parque
☎557-9441
If you're looking for a decent place to eat in Balboa Park, aside from fast-food outlets, you won't find that great a selection: The Prado is basically the only restaurant. Here, the owners have ingeniously managed to cater to tourists as well as to locals looking for a touch of class. The colourful decor is as elaborate as it is amusing. The two-in-one menu features affordable Mexican dishes as well as more refined meals that will please all palates and pocketbooks. The Mexican food is slightly disappointing, however; you will soon realize that it's not really a specialty but rather a way to attract a specific clientele. But what makes this establishment notable is its desserts, which you really should try: the pecan-chocolate pie, the tajetas, the pear cheesecake and the coconut cake are simply delightful.

Hillcrest

The large gay community in this neighbourhood contributes to a certain commercial dynamism in all sectors, including the restaurant industry. As a result, there are plenty of fun and unusual places to choose from.

Bronx Pizza
$
111 Washington St.
☎291-3341
Don't expect out-of-this-world service or decor here. However, in this small, unpretentious 16-seat restaurant, you will find heavenly pizza. The rest is secondary. Some even say that this place has the best pizza in the entire county! Despite the hard chairs, it's definitely worth a try.

Corvette Diner
$
3946 Fifth Ave.
☎542-1001
This is a San Diego institution. If you're nostalgic for

the 1950s, come here and enjoy a milkshake and fries in a Happy Days setting. The menu, without exactly offering fine dining, proposes a great variety of reasonably priced dishes. Not surprisingly, people come back year after year. Among other things, you'll find a wide selection of hamburgers and sandwiches, typical U.S. dishes like fish and chips and meat loaf, as well as some 30 varieties of soft drinks and milkshakes. Families will no doubt have a great time here.

The Vegetarian Zone
$$
2949 Fifth Ave., corner Quince St.
☎298-7302
Sports fans, outdoors-lovers and vegetarians alike will adore this little restaurant located near Balboa Park, next to Karen Krasne's Extraordinary Desserts pastry shop. Since there isn't much room for sitting, the place is always crowded and the atmosphere is casual. The service is good, but what makes The Vegetarian Zone unique is the food. The dishes are all vegetarian and simply mouthwatering. To satisfy both your taste buds and your body, it doesn't get any better than this.

Karen Krasne's Extraordinary Desserts
2929 Fifth Ave.
☎294-7001
✄294-7032
For true dessert-lovers, this is an absolute must; they will probably have difficulty hiding their joy upon viewing the array of treats found here. The place essentially offers cakes but also cookies, great coffee and a variety of teas from around the world. The head pastry chef has studied culinary arts in top

schools such as Le Cordon Bleu and Le Nôtre in France. You can enjoy her delicacies either inside or outside on the lovely terrace. A great way to end an evening.

Kemo Sabe
$$$$
3958 Fifth Ave.
☎220-6802
✄220-6801
"Wow!" is the only way to describe this absolutely unique establishment, since it really is one of the most interesting gastronomic experiences you can enjoy in all of North America. Upon entering, you may think this is just another hip California spot, but look again, because the place is actually quite exceptional. Is it perhaps due to that unmistakable feeling that everything here, the service, the decor and the menu, has been designed with the customer in mind?

The menu is clearly the winner. Indeed, chef Deborah Scott has become an expert in the art of combining ingredients and culinary trends, as well as being a real pro in matters of food presentation. The restaurant's decor, like the dishes, is Asian, American and Native American inspired, and features touches of other world communities. In terms of fusion cuisine, this establishment features the best of what Californian gastronomy has to offer. Many people have recommended this place by adding that it offers the best meals in the city, and the presentation and flavour of the dishes prove to be well worth the detour. The service is cordial and the staff know their menu well. On account of the gigantic servings, they'll automatically suggest you share a plate; if you don't

finish it, they'll offer a doggie bag. The only disadvantage: the steep prices. Still, Kemo Sabe should not be missed.

Mission Bay Park, Mission Beach and Pacific Beach

Firehouse Beach Cafe
$$
722 Grand Ave.
☎272-1999
This part of San Diego has a certain *je-ne-sais-quoi* that is conducive to lots of fun… perhaps it is the hordes of youths flocking to the beach in search of good times. Whatever the reason for this lively atmosphere, this restaurant really fits in with the festive scene. Its immense terrace is filled with a mixed clientele and is a great spot to enjoy a meal and some distraction after a busy day. Great for families.

Moondoogies
$$
919 Garnet Ave.
☎(858) 581-1100
Moondoogies is a bar-restaurant with a large television screen. People come here to hang out with friends, make acquaintances or just people-watch. The terrace is pleasant.

La Jolla

Mission Coffee Shop
$-$$
1109 Wall St.
☎(818) 454-2819
The Mission Coffee Shop is a charming little restaurant nestled in the heart of La Jolla, slightly off the beaten track, and known only to a handful of lucky customers. Only breakfast and lunch are served here. The decor has a metallic,

futuristic touch but is still warm and inviting. It is clear that the emphasis is put on atmosphere and menu instead of interior design.

The place is rather small, with a dozen tables inside and about 10 more set right out on one of La Jolla's main streets. It is still possible to find a table without too much waiting, but that might not be the case for long, unless the place expands. The clientele is composed of regulars, mainly surfers. There is even a menu especially for them, featuring high-protein dishes to get them off to a good start.

La Dolce Vita
$$
1237 Prospect St.
☎ *(858) 454-2524*
≈ *(858) 454-3761*
If you feel like enjoying an Italian meal at a reasonable price, this quaint little restaurant offers a mouth-watering selection of pizza, pasta and meat dishes. Come lunch time, their *paninis* steal the show.

Alfonso's
$$-$$$
1251 Prospect St.
☎ *454-2232*
This is *the* Mexican restaurant in La Jolla, a lively place with an immense heated terrace. This area is sunny and cheerful-looking, with checkered tablecloths. The interior section is equally entertaining, featuring a bar and televisions, but the atmosphere is more fun on the terrace. This spot is enjoyed by families, tourists and young locals who simply wish to spend some time with friends.

Come On In Cafe & Bakery
$-$$
1030-B Torrey Pines Rd.
☎ *551-1063*
≈ *551-1863*
Located in a shopping centre, this very charming café looks onto the street. There are as many seats inside, around the counter, as there are on the exterior flower-filled terrace. Service would probably be less hurried if the place weren't so popular. Here, many couples and their little ones come to grab a bite and discuss amongst themselves, making for a lively atmosphere. During rush hour, however, the clientele is quite different, but the place is still packed. And you'll quickly understand why when you see your plate: servings are generous, dishes are well prepared and made with fresh ingredients, while the prices are more than reasonable. House specialties are breakfasts, waffles, salads, sandwiches, focaccia and freshly squeezed fruit juices.

Trattoria Acqua
$$$-$$$$
1298 Prospect St.
☎ *(858) 454-0709*
≈ *(858) 454-0710*
In a romantic decor bathed in shades of blue, you can enjoy excellent, innovative Italian cuisine. The Mediterranean atmosphere is enhanced by the proximity of the ocean, the terrace and the rustic but modern setting. The many tables provide a view of the bay and beach.

Georges at the Cove
$$$$$
1250 Prospect Ave.
☎ *(818) 454-4244*
Highly romantic, this restaurant is where you'll find one of the best ocean views in all of San Diego.

Combined with classy service, a flawless menu and an elaborate wine list, this establishment attracts, not surprisingly, the city's jet-set. On the second floor is the Ocean View Room, a distinguished dining room with huge bay windows that reveal a splendid panorama of the bay of La Jolla. Everything here will make you feel special, from the candles and orchids on the table to the ultra-considerate service to the elegant and sober decor.

The menu features what is called "creative regional cuisine," which consists of serving fresh regional products in unusual dishes: a feast for both the eyes and taste buds! Don't miss the chocolate soufflé, a pure marvel.

However, our favourite feature in this restaurant is the third floor, the Ocean Terrace, with its bar and magnificent terrace. Here the menu is more modest and, consequently, less expensive. A great meal in a great setting.

Top O' the Cove
$$$$-$$$$$
1216 Prospect St.
☎ *(858) 454-7779*
In a high-class, Mediterranean-inspired setting, this restaurant offers an elaborate menu of French cuisine where seafood and steak have pride of place. This establishment has acquired a reputation for, among other things, its impeccable service and great food. On the second floor is a superb terrace with an ocean view, what they call a "cocktail room," with a lighter and more affordable menu that in the main dining room. This place is said to have one of the most complete wine lists in the region.

San Diego

Entertainment

After the sun sets on San Diego, the city is a happening and exciting place to be.

Indeed, the arts and culture scene is rather well established here, with many shows and performances in venues and nightclubs. However, San Diego locals seem to prefer going out to bars and pub-restaurants and just meeting people. In the evening, certain neighbourhoods such as the Gaslamp District and La Jolla are packed with a colourful crowd searching for a place to relax and enjoy a fine meal with, of course, a nice bottle of wine or a martini.

Classical music, jazz, blues, rock, hip-hop, Latino or slightly more exotic concerts are presented in most of San Diego's establishments. You will therefore have plenty of opportunities to enjoy them in concert halls or while savouring a meal in restaurants that also offer shows.

Those who wish to do a little gambling are also in luck, with three casinos are conveniently located near the downtown area.

To find out what's going on in terms of arts and culture, check out the weekly *San Diego Weekly Reader* and *D-Town*, the San Diego downtown magazine that is found in many area businesses. For the gay and lesbian scene, the *San Diego Gay and Lesbian Times* provides information on events and activities taking place in the city's gay establishments. Finally, the *San Diego Performing Arts League* is an organization whose goal is to promote arts and culture in San Diego, and every two months publishes the cultural guide *What's Playing*. This guide lists all shows in the city and surroundings. It's free and you can find it in restaurants, cafés, theatres and other similar establishments. Those who prefer the Internet should visit the *www.sandiegotheatre.com* site, an excellent source of information.

All in all, San Diego has a lot to offer in terms of arts and culture. This chapter will guide you through, among other things, the city's nightlife. You will find suggestions for bars and nightclubs, as well as addresses for movie theatres and concert venues.

Theatres, Cinema and Concerts

Tickets

Arts Tix
Horton Plaza, corner Third St. and Broadway
☎*497-5000 or 238-0700*
≈*(619) 238-0710*
www.sandiegoperforms.com
This is the place to purchase affordable tickets for dance, music and theatre performances. The box office is operated by the San Diego Performing Arts League, the same organization that publishes *What's Playing*.

Visit a Museum on a Tuesday!

To attract a new clientele, some museums can be visited for free on certain Tuesdays of each month.

First Tuesday of the Month
San Diego Natural History Museum
Reuben H. Fleet Science Center
San Diego Model Railroad Museum

Second Tuesday of the Month
San Diego Historical Society Museum
San Diego Hall of Champions Sports Museum

Third Tuesday of the Month
San Diego Museum of Art
San Diego Museum of Man
Mingei International Museum

Fourth Tuesday of the Month
San Diego Aerospace Museum
San Diego Automotive Museum
House of Pacific Relations
International Cottages & Hall of Nation

Fifth Tuesday of the Month
San Diego Aerospace Museum

Venues

Forever Plaid
4040 Twiggs Ave.
☎*688-2494*
688-0960
This theatre, located in the heart of the Old Town, features a 90min show that is sure to please the entire family. This musical comedy stars four performers singing hits tunes from the 1950s and 1960s. Shows are from Tuesday to Sunday; variable hours.

La Jolla Playhouse
La Jolla
☎*(858) 550-1070*
(858) 550-1075
www.lajollaplaybouse.com
Located on the University of California, San Diego (UCSD) campus, this venue is one of the most prestigious in the United States.

Triple Espresso
Horton Grand Theatre
444 Fourth Ave.
☎*234-9583*
www.tripleespresso.com
Several times a week, Triple Espresso presents, as it has for many years, a comedy where laughter and music come together to offer a highly entertaining show. Sure to be a hit with the whole family.

Old Globe Theatre
El Prado Way
Balboa Park
☎*239-2255*
☎*231-5879*
www.oldglobe.org
Located in Balboa Park, this magnificent theatre comprises three halls and was built during the California Pacific International Exposition in 1935. It is one of the oldest theatres in the state and the largest in the city. Here, a wide selection of shows is presented throughout the year, from Shakespeare to contemporary works, in-

cluding some large-scale productions.

Lamb's Players Theatre
1142 Orange Ave.
Coronado
☎*437-0600*
Housed in the historic Spreckels Building on Coronado's main thoroughfare, the Lamb's Players Theatre offers excellent shows throughout the year.

Reuben H. Fleet Science Center
OMNIMAX
☎*238-1233*
www.rhfleet.org
3D movies shown on a giant screen.

Gaslamp 15
701 Fifth Ave.1
☎*232-0400*

UA Horton Plaza
457 Horton Plaza
☎*234-4661*

Hillcrest Cinema
3965 Fifth Ave.
☎*299-2100*

Casinos

There are three casinos in the eastern part of San Diego county.

Barona Casino
☎*888-7-BARONA*
www.barona.com
This is one of California's largest casinos, and is reminiscent of those found in Las Vegas.

Viejas Casino
☎*800-84-POKER*
www.viejasnet.com
The Viejas complex includes a large casino, 33 designer boutiques and three restaurants. In addition to many special events, variety shows are presented here on a regular basis.

Pechanga Entertainment Center
45000 Pala Rd.
Temecula
☎*888-PECHANGA*
www.pechanga.com

Dinner Cruises

San Diego Harbor Excursion
1050 North Harbor Dr.
☎*234-4111*
This company offers a dinner and dancing evening on a 2.5hr cruise.

Bars and Nightclubs

Downtown and Gaslamp

Sing Sing
655 Fourth Ave.
☎*(619) 231-6700*
A simply decorated room, two pianos facing one another at the front of the stage, two singer-emcees who try to warm up the audience with popular songs and jokes… this is basically what you'll find at this cabaret, located next to the Rock-Bottom microbrewery. You're sure to have a lively, entertaining evening here, singing along to such classics as The Beatles, Frank Sinatra, Elton John and others.

The Bitter End
770 Fifth Ave.
☎*233-4603*
This two-storey bar is one of the most well known and popular places in town. On the first floor is The Underground, strictly for dancing, while the second floor features the sumptuous Upper Lounge, with a distinguished decor, exquisite furnishings, a marble bar, fireplaces and a reading room. This establishment is unique in

the city. Try the house specialty, the famous martini, which is extremely popular in this area.

Croce's
Corner Fifth Ave. and F. St.
☎233-4355
Adjacent to the restaurant of the same name and dedicated to Jim Croce (see p 196), this bar offers jazz or blues shows every night in a casual atmosphere. Those who enjoy this genre will be delighted.

Blue Point Coastal
565 Fifth Ave.
☎233-6623
Although this establishment is better known for its acclaimed restaurant, the bar is also a popular spot for a drink; the decor's sea theme certainly contributes to the trendiness of the place. Many locals come here to meet friends and sip a martini. It is also said that this is *the* place to see and be seen.

A great spot to get a real feel for the city.

Gaslamp Billiards Place
379 Fourth Ave.
☎230-1976
Perfect for billiards-lovers.

Lips, The Ultimate Drag Dining
2770 Fifth Ave.
☎295-7900
Here you'll have the opportunity to watch a highly entertaining drag-queen show while enjoying a fine meal. A gospel brunch is also offered on Sundays. (Just the songs, not the service!)

Sevilla
555 Fourth Ave.
☎233-5979
In a lively atmosphere, this restaurant-pub has a Spanish-inspired decor and menu. Shows are featured every night, and you can

also enjoy salsa and flamenco dancing. Lessons are even offered to the uninitiated.

Dick's Last Resort
300 Fifth Ave. between J and K Sts.
☎231-9100
This place is well known by those who are looking for a place to relax. This large, unpretentious bar-restaurant (see p 222) has a big terrace, and there are rock shows here every night.

Top of the Hyatt
Hyatt Regency
One Market Pl.
☎232-1234
☎239-5678
Located on the 40th floor of the imposing Hyatt Regency Hotel, the Top of the Hyatt is a place where you can have a drink in a casual, discreet atmosphere, and enjoy one of the best views of San Diego's surroundings at the same time.

The Field
544 Fifth Ave.
☎232-9840
Those who can't get enough of Irish music, dance and culture will be happy to discover this establishment. Here, the beer, fine Irish food and shows all contribute to what is guaranteed to be a great evening. Come join the fun!

Bayou Bar & Grill
329 Market St.
☎696-8747
Established in the neighbourhood since 1989, way before it became the hottest district in town, the Bayou Bar & Grill is here to stay. The New Orleans French touch is found everywhere: in

the menu, the drinks and the atmosphere; it truly feels like the real thing! Mardi Gras is celebrated here every month.

Coronado Island

Azzura Point
Loews Coronado Bay Resort
4000 Coronado Bay Rd. (Silver Strand Blvd.)
☎424-4000
Azzura Point is first and foremost an upscale restaurant, but its cocktail room has a splendid bar and a few tables. The beauty of the decor and the view makes it the perfect place to enjoy your favourite drink. Expect high prices, however.

Coronado Brewing Company
170 Orange Ave.
☎437-4452
The Coronado Brewing Company is the only microbrewery on the island of Coronado. In addition to sampling the delicious house beer, you can partake of fine dishes in a lively and relaxed atmosphere.

Crown Coronet Room
Hotel Del Coronado
☎522-8490
This historic restaurant (see p 200) is particularly interesting on Sunday nights when dinner and dancing are offered.

Hillcrest

The Flame
☎295-4163
The Flame is the gay bar par excellence in the colourful Hillcrest neighbourhood. It is well known for, among other things, the DJ's great musical selections.

Mission Bay Park, Mission Beach and Pacific Beach

Canes Bar & Grill
3105 Oceanfront Walk
☎ *(858) 488-1780*
Canes Bar & Grill is only a few steps away from Mission Beach. This bar-restaurant with a rooftop terrace is one of the most popular spots in town. The atmosphere is red-hot, especially on nights when music shows of various genres are featured.

Moondoogies
919 Garnet Ave.
☎ *(858) 273-8440*
This bar-restaurant located near the beach is dedicated to surfing, and regulars gather here mainly for its particularly casual atmosphere. They come here to meet friends, sip a cold beer, enjoy a good meal or shoot some pool.

La Jolla

George's at the Cove
1250 Prospect St.
☎ *(858) 454-4244*
Frequented by many celebrities, this excellent restaurant is also known for its bar-terrace on the third floor. You can sip an aperitif while admiring the sun setting on the Pacific. Definitely one of the best places in the city for a drink.

Tijuana (Mexico)

Tijuana is a popular destination for those in search of action and hot nights. In the downtown area, especially along Revolución and New Rio avenues, a number of nightclubs start blasting their loud music as soon as night falls. There are usually no cover charges, and beer and alcohol, especially margaritas, are less expen-sive than on the other side of the border. This place is great to simply breathe in the Latino *joie de vivre*. Be careful, however, especially if you're by yourself.

Shopping

When it comes to shopping, San Diego is undoubtedly on par with all the big U.S. cities. There is a vast selection of huge shopping malls in the city centre and surrounding areas, and all the big fashion names have factory outlets here. Everything is designed so that the simplest purchase becomes an event. After all, this is the United States—land of consumer preferences! Stores, theatres, large restaurants and attractions are usually grouped together in the same space to form a huge mega-complex. Seaport, Old Town, Ferry Landing Market Place, Vieja Outlet Center, Horton Plaza, Legoland, the Zoological Gardens and Seaworld are good examples of this.

For those who like exclusive little boutiques and neighbourhoods with a more human face, places like the Gaslamp, downtown Coronado Island, the Spanish Village in Balboa Park, and the centre of La Jolla as well as Hillcrest are undoubtedly preferable to the immense shopping malls, where everything seems to be a bit over-rated.

Gaslamp

This charming, completely renovated historical sector of San Diego is crammed with all kinds of treasures. You will find a whole array of original shops and art galleries, most of which are located between Broadway and Harbor and between Fourth Street and Sixth Streets. It is a real pleasure just to wander around wherever your fancy takes you.

Seaport

It is true that the village is completely geared toward tourism. Nevertheless, among the 75 stores in this area there are some that are small and quite original, often focusing on specific themes such as kites, hats, hammocks, the sea and chilli peppers. There are some interesting products to be found here, all in a very pleasant setting. Not much is made in San Diego, but still, you'll find things that you've never seen before.

Coronado Island

The stores on the island are divided into three sectors. First, the main historical neighbourhood of Orange Avenue, then the Ferry Landing Market Place, right where you get off the ferry, and finally, the stores at the Del Coronado Hotel, a cluster of 30 businesses.

Do not miss Art-In-The-Park, the bimonthly event organized by the Coronado Art Association, which gives craftspeople in the region the opportunity to display their works. This exhibit takes place on the first and third Sunday of the month, from 9am to 4pm, at Spreckles Park, between Seventh Street and Orange Avenue.

San Diego

Old Town

Again, this part of the city does appear to be a tourist trap. However, if you take your time you can find some interesting pieces, especially Mexican crafts, because this is the theme of this historic neighbourhood. The shops, restaurants and hotels, many of them tucked away in adobe-style buildings, are a reminder that Mexico is just a hop, skip and a jump away.

Bazar del Mundo
Juan St.
Old Town
☎296-3161
This is a string of very colourfully decorated little boutiques surrounding a central square occupied by a restaurant that pulsates with the sound of *mariachis*. Although the presence of wealthy tourists has pushed up the prices of the products sold here, you can find some interesting objects. Most of the items come from Latin America, especially Mexico, and there is also some pretty Native American jewellery, among other things.

Balboa Park

Apart from the museum boutiques along El Prado Avenue, which are so full of interesting things, there are few places for shopping in Balboa Park. However, the **Spanish Village Art Center** *(every day 11am to 4pm)*, at the far northeastern section of the park behind the Museum of Man, is an obligatory stop, as it is unquestionably one of the best places to unearth art works and crafts. This area is a concentration of 36 artists who have established their studios

here to display and sell their works. It is possible to uncover real treasures and it is also the best introduction to what can be called San Diegan art. This excellent initiative helps the artists to become better known and make a living through their art. Take some time to look at the magnificent paintings as well as the famous carved gourds made of hollowed out squash. This is also one of the few art centres where you can watch the artists at work.

Hillcrest

The district of Hillcrest runs the length of Fifth Avenue near University. This is where you will find antique dealers and stores specializing in interior decorating. The sector is filled to the brim with fashion boutiques of all kinds and shops selling all the latest crazes.

Mission Beach and Pacific Beach

These two neighbouring municipalities feature a host of stores, especially if you're looking for sports clothing or equipment, and reasonably priced funky or casual clothing. Considering the proximity of the beach, you'll find beach items that are heavily influenced by the surfer style that is currently sweeping across the whole planet. You'll also find everything you need for that indispensable cool look you'll desire to have when strolling on the beach and the promenade.

La Jolla

A few miles north of downtown San Diego is the

prosperous little town of La Jolla. Scattered along the main arteries of Prospects, The Coast Walk, Girard, Pearl Street, Fay Street and La Jolla Boulevard, there are several well-known art galleries and boutiques offering high-quality products for those who are looking for a certain distinction.

Tijuana (Mexico)

Tijuana, on the Mexican coast, is a perfect place for the collector. Here you can unearth all sorts of objects at lower prices than on the other side of the border. It is not surprising that U.S. citizens cross the border specifically to find bargains. It is true that the items are not always of high quality and some of the stores look exactly the same. Nevertheless, it's worth working your way through the many stores along the main road, Revolucion, and the little avenues in the vicinity to see what they offer. You can sometimes discover some very interesting items.

The crafts and bottles of local drinks are especially highly rated among visitors, but you can also find jewellery, blankets, bags of all kinds and hammocks. Don't worry about the salespeople being rather insistent as they provide a true contrast to the cold politeness of salespeople in the neighbouring country. Remember that you are in Mexico and bargaining is acceptable. Don't forget also that you are allowed to bring a maximum of $400 worth of purchases back into the United States.

Do not miss the **Bazar de Mexico Tijuana Art and Crafts**

Center *(corner of Avenida Revolucion and Calle 7,* ☎*011-52-66-38-4737),* a permanent exhibition bringing together 40 artists from all regions of Mexico.

Music

Here are a few addresses for your musical souvenirs:

Croce's Store
Corner of Fifth St. and F St.
802 Fifth Ave.
☎*233-4355*
Various products relating to Jim Croce and Croce's Restaurant, such as sweaters for the whole family, Croce's wife Ingrid's cookbook and especially CDs of this famous folk singer's music.

Music Trader
931 Fourth Ave.
Gaslamp
☎*(619) 232-2565*
A good place to buy all kinds of music.

Clothing

Urban Outfitters
665 Fifth Ave.
Gaslamp
☎*231-0102*
This boutique is part of a chain of more than 40 stores. They sell a host of eccentric items, mostly clothing, but also accessories and decorative objects. The style that emerges is a subtle blend of urban fashion and the beatnik style that was popularized in this part of the world.

Fresh Produce
1274 Prospect St.
La Jolla
☎*(858) 456-8134*
In spite of the ambiguous name, this is not a fruit and vegetable market, but a line of lively, colourful and comfortable clothing with fun themes for the whole family. Since its

inception, this company has opened a dozen stores across the state and another in Las Vegas. The theme of the collection evokes the sea, the sun and nature. It suits the very young ones beautifully.

Crazy Shirts
853 Harbour Dr.
Seaport Village
☎*595-0468*
To find a sweater that matches your mood, come and browse in this original store, part of a chain of no less than a hundred across the country.

Hats

The Village Hat Shop
Seaport Village
853 W. Harbor Dr.
☎*233-7236*

Hillcrest
3821 Fourth Ave.
☎*(619) 683-5533*
Quite an amusing shop that is completely devoted to hats. You'll find a surprising selection ranging from the chic to the comical. This is the store to visit if you want to stand out in a crowd, or if you just want to protect yourself from a sun that is rather too intense.

Western Hat Works
868 Fifth Ave.
☎*234-0457*
This place offers a complete range of cowboy hats. After all, this is the Far West, isn't it?

Toys

Warner Bros. Studio Store
90 Horton Plaza
☎*233-3058*
Although these toy stores, designed around cartoon themes, are all over the country, they are always very popular among the

young and the not so young.

Bookstores

Bay Books & Café
Mon to Sat 8am to 8pm, Sun 8am to 6pm
1029 Orange Ave.
Coronado
☎*435-0070*
A pleasant bookstore offering a wide selection of books as well as stationary.

Perkins Book Worm
Oldest Book Store
930 Orange Ave.
Coronado
☎*435-5775*
This bookstore has been around since 1923 and offers an excellent selection of works.

B. Dalton Booksellers
407 Horton Plaza
☎*615-5373*
A large bookstore located in the impressive Horton Plaza mall.

Libros Bookstore
Bazar Del Mundo
☎*299-1139*
Located in the very lively Bazar Del Mundo central square, this little bookstore is a pleasure to visit and offers a vast selection of books devoted, among other things, to Mexican and Native American cultures.

John Cole's Book Shop
780 Prospect St.
La Jolla
☎*(858) 454-4766*
Part of a little house that has been converted into businesses, this bookstore has a large space for consulting the numerous works distributed around the various rooms. The house is near the La Jolla Museum of Contemporary Art.

San Diego

Posters

Chuck Jones Studio Gallery
2501 San Diego Ave.
Old Town
☎294-3489
An excellent selection of original posters by animated-film artists that is sure to please comics fans.

Art Galleries

Robson Gallery
535 Fourth Ave.
☎234-7356
Watercolours, oil paintings and sculptures by emerging regional artists. The carefully selected pieces allow you to discover the talents of these exceptional artists.

Spirits in Stone Galleries
Carlsbad Company Stores
Hwy. 5
5600 Paseo del Norte
Suite 138
☎888-774-6627
Judging by the number of San Diegan galleries exhibiting sculptures by Shona artists from Zimbabwe, we clearly seem to be witnessing a real craze for this sculptural style. This is quite understandable, since the Shona have made sculpture an art form for several generations. There are some incomparable works here, all the more so because there are still few opportunities to admire them outside southern Africa. This gallery gives you an excellent opportunity to get to know the works of more than 300 Shona artists.

Galerie Adrienne
1205 Prospect St.
La Jolla
☎456-4560
The Galerie Adrienne exhibits the works of nearly 20 well-known Californian painters and sculptors.

Thomas D. Mangelsen's Image of Nature Gallery
7916 Girard Ave.
☎(858) 551-9553
A visit to this gallery, which displays the works of one of the most famous nature photographers in the world, is an absolute must. Mangelsen has a unique way of capturing the magnificence of fauna, flora and wide-open spaces. The artist spends more than nine months of the year crisscrossing these wide-open spaces to capture all their beauty and splendour. You can admire his photographs in all the biggest magazines like *National Geographic* and *Life*, as well as in several U.S., Canadian and European galleries.

Gifts

Mex-Art
1155 Morena Blvd.
☎276-5810
As you know, San Diego is just near the Mexican border, which presents an opportunity to discover Mexican arts and crafts at good prices. This is particularly true of this large store, which brings together a vast quantity of objects selected from all across Mexico. An excellent address if you want to take back this type of souvenir.

Miranda's Courtyard
2548 Congress St.
Old Town
☎296-6611
A pretty store that sells a host of objects from Mexico at reasonable prices. You can also find all sorts of decorative and garden-related articles.

Authentic Old Ship Relics
1891 San Diego Ave.
Old Town
☎574-1891
With the sea and the marine military base just nearby, this store specializing in old boat relics is a veritable little museum with loads of stories to tell about the area's maritime history. You'll find all sorts of amazing objects in this store, a thrilling place for collectors.

Kite Flite
Seaport Village
☎234-KITE
In countries that have beaches and gentle breezes, there is definitely a place for this kind of store. You'll find kites for beginners and professionals flyers alike, since there are many enthusiasts of this activity in the region. There are also some very amusing kites for beginners of all ages.

Green Field Paper Company
1330 G St.
☎338-9432, ext. 13
Jeff Lindenthal created this little business eight years ago as a hobby. His knowledge of and interest in recycled materials inspired him to create his own wedding invitations. Then he took courses on papermaking and built a workshop in his garage, and this is how his little business was born. Since then, Jeff has been creating note books, block notes and agendas out of recycled paper or fibres. You will have no problem picking out the unique style of his product designs. An excellent and original souvenir to take home.

Trails West
821 W. Harbor Dr.
Seaport Village
☎*232-0553*
A variety of objects inspired by the spirit of the Far West. This store has an interesting selection of jewellery, belts and belt buckles, leather items and, above all, Native American decorative objects and crafts.

Cost Plus World Market
372 4th Ave.
Gaslamp
☎*236-1737*
☎*233-7517*
This enormous store specializes in exclusive imports from all over the world. You'll find a huge choice of decorative objects and a large selection of original food products. This has to be one of the best addresses in the Gaslamp for gifts.

The Gallery
Bazaar del Mundo
☎*296-3161*
The Gallery specializes in Native American jewellery and silk-screens.

Fabrics & Finery
Bazaar del Mundo
☎*256-3161*
As soon as you walk into this store, you'll be dazzled by the brightly coloured displays of fabrics from Latin America.

Shopping Malls

Westfield Shoppingtown Horton Plaza
*Mon to Fri 10am to 8pm
Sat 10am to 7pm, Sun 11am to 6pm*
between Broadway and G St. and between First and Fourth aves.
☎*238-1596*
This five-storey complex, which is the pride of downtown San Diego, offers a very pleasant setting for shopping. In this building, which is architecturally inspired by both contemporary and adobe styles, there are 140 stores and restaurants. Here you can enjoy shopping in large chains like Macy's and Mervyn's and there is also a cinema on the premises. As well, it is useful to know that if you buy something here, the first 3hrs of parking are free.

Macy's
Horton Plaza, Second floor
Fashion Valley
Macy's is a department store that offers exceptional products and personalized service, which is what the chain has become famous for.

Fashion Valley
Hwy. 163, Friars Rd. West exit
you can take the San Diego Trolley and get off at Fashion Valley
☎*688-9113*
With nearly 200 stores and restaurants on two floors, Fashion Valley is the largest shopping mall in the whole region. Among others, there are six department stores, including JC Penney, Macy's, Neiman Marcus and Nordstrom—shopaholics will be in seventh heaven.

Weatfield Shoppingtown UTC
La Jolla Dr., between the I-5 and the I-805
More than 155 stores in a setting enhanced by floral arrangements, fountains and a central exterior promenade. Because this is a posh neighbourhood of San Diego, there are quite a few big names, including Nordstrom, Banana Republic, Bebe, Charles David, Ann Taylor, Guess, Godiva Chocolaterie and Chanel. There are also several restaurants and an ice-skating rink.

Factory Outlets

Carlsbad Company Stores
take the I-5, Palomar Airport Road exit, turn right, and then left at the first light on Paseo Del Norte
You'll find this large and elegant open-air shopping complex just next to Flower Field, in the direction of Orange County. Around 60 big fashion names have boutiques here, including Adidas, Calvin Klein, Jones New York County, Polo Ralph Lauren, Reebok and Tommy Hilfiger. You'll also find everything you need to quench your thirst.

Viejas Outlet Center
Highway 8 east, Willows Rd. exit
☎*659-2070*
Built by a Native American nation, this factory outlet houses 35 of the best-known manufacturers and designers in the United States. You'll shop in a spectacular setting with fountains, lush vegetation, rock formations and Native-American-inspired decor in an adobe style building, all just 30min by car from San Diego. There is also a casino and entertainment is featured on the premises.

Travel

Rand MacNally Map and Travel Store
243 Horton Plaza
☎*234-3341*
Guides, maps, globes, and travel accessories and games.

Specialty Stores

The shops connected to museums and theme parks are among the best places to pick up that something special. They usually offer items that are carefully selected according to the theme of the place and are hard to obtain elsewhere. You can also find books that will help enrich your visit to San Diego. Here are a few suggestions.

Wild Animal Park
☎(760) 747-8702
Since this amusement park is oriented around a safari theme, there are numerous stores offering imports from Africa and Asia. Many of the objects here are cheap trash but, if you look hard, you may find some interesting pieces.

Legoland
☎(760) 918-LEGO
Here the child is king. The stores in Legoland naturally offer the things you'd expect them to, but you'll also find all types of Meccano sets imaginable, many of which you can't find anywhere else.

Seaworld
☎800-23-SHAMU
Each attraction at Seaworld has its own store. In the Arctic park module, you'll find polar bears, penguins and seals of all kinds. Dolphins and whales also have their own stores near their show areas. Many stuffed toys, T-shirts and key-rings, but definitely a few knick-knacks that will enchant the very little ones.

San Diego Zoo
Balboa Park
☎(619) 231-1515
This zoo, one of the biggest in the world, has a worthy number of stores. Many of them specialize in imports, as well as traditional souvenirs. They often feature themes relating to the zoo, like the panda, Australia, the Arctic and so on.

Museum of Photographic Arts
1649 El Prado
☎238-7559
The store in this fascinating museum will tempt you with its intriguing selection of books about photography, as well as cards reproducing works exhibited in the museum.

Museum of Contemporary Art
1001 Kettner Blvd.
☎234-1001
This shop offers a wide selection of books devoted to contemporary art. You'll also find other interesting items inspired by this type of art.

San Diego Maritime Museum
1306 N. Harbor Dr.
☎234-9153
The shop in this museum offers all kinds of articles relating to navigation. It has a very interesting selection of books, some of which will give you a better understanding of the importance of the sea in the region's history.

Whole Foods Market
8825 Villa La Jolla Dr., corner Nobel Ave.
☎(858) 642-6700
Hillcrest
711 University Ave., corner Seventh Ave.
☎294-2800
This Californian grocery chain, which has some 20 stores scattered all over the state, is a typical example of what the U.S. does best. Excesses of all kinds (consumption, pollution, obesity) have given rise to a collective awareness of the importance of eating well while maintaining harmony with the environment. This has made possible the opening of an enormous grocery store completely devoted to organic and environmentally friendly products. It is a real pleasure to wander through the numerous aisles and find a host of diverse products, each more interesting than the last. The large section of prepared foods makes this store an obligatory stop for organizing a picnic.

Panda

The Inland Empire and Palm Springs

T he Inland Empire comprises Riverside and San Bernardino counties and is rich in both cultural and recreational attractions.

A variety of climates can be sampled in one day travelling throughout the area due to the great rise in elevation toward the San Bernardino Mountains.

V isitors can enjoy a variety of activities from touring the vineyards of Temecula Valley and visiting the historic Riverside Mission to skiing at Big Bear Lake. The central location also provides convenient access to the beaches of Orange County and the Palm Springs area, both within an hours' drive. This is also one of the fastest-growing regions of the United States, as people are attracted by the clean air, perfect weather and friendly atmosphere.

J ust east of the Inland Empire, Palm Springs has a history of attracting Hollywood's movie crowd. Many of the establishments around town lovingly remember the days when the Brat Pack used to call this desert oasis home.

Today, the city continues to attract the rich and famous, providing world-class resorts and attractions. The Coachella Valley also has a rich cultural heritage as the ancestral home of the Agua Caliente Cahuilla Indians.

Finding Your Way Around

Tours A through D cover the Inland Empire region from Temecula to Big Bear

Lake. **Tours E and F** bring you out of the mountains of Idyllwild to Palm Springs and Joshua Tree National Park.

Practical Information

Area Codes

Inland Empire: **909**
Palm Springs and Anza-Borrego National Park: **760**

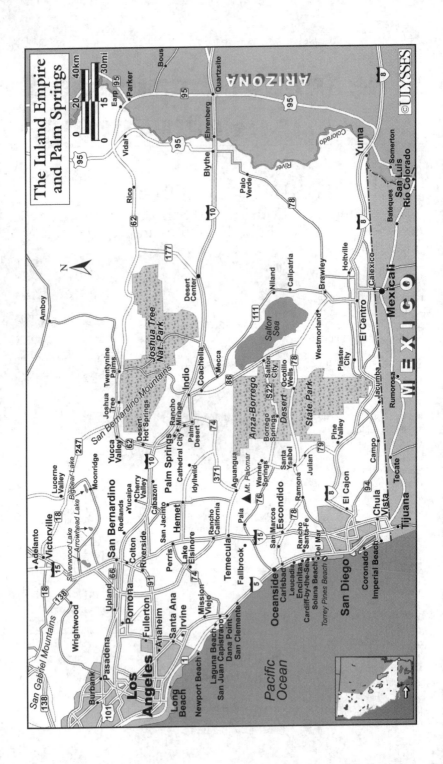

The Inland Empire and Palm Springs

Tourist Information

The Inland Empire Tourism Council
301 E. Vanderbilt Way, Suite 100
San Bernardino 92408
☎*890-1090*

Palm Springs Visitor Information Center
2781 N. Palm Canyon Dr.
☎*778-8418*
☎*800-347-7746*
www.palmsprings.com

Temecula Valley Chamber of Commerce
☎*676-5090*

Perris Valley Chamber of Commerce
☎*657-3555*

Moreno Valley Chamber of Commerce
☎*697-4404*

Greater Riverside Chamber of Commerce
3985 University Ave.
☎*683-7100*
⇒*683-2670*
www.riverside-chamber.com

San Bernardino Convention and Visitors Bureau
200 N. 'E' St., Suite 103
☎*889-3890*
☎*800-867-8366*
www.san-bernardino.org

Redlands Chamber of Commerce
☎*793-2546*

Big Bear Lake Visitors Center
630 Bartlett Rd.
☎*866-7000*
☎*800-424-4232*
www.bigbearinfo.com

Idyllwild Chamber of Commerce
☎*888-659-3259*

Borrego Springs Chamber of Commerce and Visitors Center
622 Palm Canyon Dr.
Borrego Spring, CA 91941
☎*767-5555 or 800-559-5524*
⇒*767-5976*

Exploring

★★

Tour A: Temecula, Perris and Moreno Valley

★★
Temecula

The name Temecula comes from a Native American word meaning "Valley of Joy," though it has a less-than-joyous past. The town was the sight of the Temecula Massacre in the 1700s: a battle between the Cahuilla and Temecula Indians. During the 1800s, the town was one of the original cowboy towns of the Old West, with several shootouts and a widely publicized bank robbery. Today, however, light jazz and blues follow you down **Old Town Front Street ★★**, thanks to an audio system built into the replica street lamps. Old Town is known as one of the premier antique shopping centres of Southern California, as the rustic storefronts pay homage to a bygone era that is reflected in their wares. The Old West ambiance and myriad antique treasures are sure to loosen even the tightest of purse strings— even the McDonald's is dressed up as an old train station. On the second weekend of February, over 1,200 antique cars and hot rods descend on Old Town for the annual Rod Run. **Guided walking tours** of Old Town are hosted by Bob and Bea Taylor *(☎676-4614)* who will explain the history behind the area.

Butterfield Square is the heart of Old Town's Temecula Historical Preservation District. It was also the site of the Butterfield Overland Coach Stagecoach Stop and California's first inland post office. A beautiful **mural ★** covers a wall across from the **Temecula Stage Stop** *(28464 Old Town Front St.; now a Greyhound stop)*, depicting the natural beauty in the vineyards surrounding Temecula.

The **Temecula Valley Museum ★** *($2; closed Mon; 28315 Mercedes St.; ☎676-0021)* can be found at the north end of Old Town, in Sam Hicks Monument Park. The first floor features displays depicting the history and peoples who lived in the region. On the second floor, the "Touch History" exhibits are an interactive discovery area where children have a chance to visit the general store, dress up in period clothes and get their photos taken.

The Temecula Valley is also the largest wine producer in Southern California, with over 17 different wineries to be found just east of town, along Rancho California Road. (See box)

★
Perris

Downtown Perris is really just a food-gas-lodging town along Highway 235. The main attraction is the **Orange Empire Railway Museum ★** *(free; rides $7; 2201 S. "A" St.; ☎657-2605; www.oerm.mus.ca.us)*, if you have a little extra time. The museum is rather haphazardly laid out, but does contain a great selection of railcars

The Inland Empire and Palm Springs

The Wineries of Temecula Valley ★★★

With a unique microclimate, well-drained soil and an elevation of 1,500ft (500m), the Temecula Valley provides an ideal location for growing premium winegrapes. Most of the wineries are open daily for guided tours of the vineyards and production facilities, ending in a wine tasting. The Mount Palomar, Baily, Maurice Cafrire and Van Roekel wineries also feature a selection of cheeses and deli products to accompany the tastings. A small fee *($2-$4)* covers the tour, the tasting and a souvenir glass. There is no finer way to spend a California afternoon than with a glass of local wine to enjoy among the vineyards.

To reach the wineries, exit Highway 15 or follow Old Town Front Street to Rancho California Road and head east for approximately 10min. Most of the wineries are found on this road and there are signs indicating the rest.

Alternatively, tours can be arranged by Toth Tours (☎*909-677-3372*) or through the Temecula Shuttle (☎*909-695-9999*).

Baily Winery
every day 10am to 5pm
33833 Rancho California Rd.
☎*(909) 695-1895*

Callaway Vineyard and Winery
every day 10:30am to 5pm
32720 Rancho California Rd.
☎*(909) 676-4001*

Cilurzo Vineyard and Winery
every day 9:30am to 5pm
41220 Calle Contento
☎*(909) 676-5250*

Filsinger Vineyards and Winery
Sat and Sun 10am to 5pm
39050 De Portola Rd.
☎*(909) 676-4594*

Hart Winery
every day 9am to 4:30pm
41300 Avenida Biona
☎*(909) 676-6300*

Keyways Vineyard and Winery
every day 10am to 5pm
37338 De Portola Rd.
☎*(909) 676-1451*

Maurice Carrie Winery
every day 10am to 5pm
34225 Rancho California Rd.
☎*(909) 676-1711*

Mount Palomar Winery
every day 10am to 5pm
33820 Rancho California Rd.
☎*(909) 676-5047*

Santa Margarita Winery
Sat and Sun 11am to 4:30pm
33490 Madera de Playa
☎*(909) 676-4431*

Stuart Cellar's Wine
10am to 5pm
33514 Rancho California Rd.
☎*888-260-0870*

Temecula Crest Winery
every day 10am to 5pm
40620 Calle Contento
☎*(909) 676-8231*

Thornton Winery
Sat and Sun 10am to 5pm
32575 Rancho California Rd.
☎*(909)699-0099*

Van Roekel Vineyards and Winery
every day 10am to 5pm
34567 Rancho California Rd.
☎*(909) 699-6961*

from the past 150 years, in varying condition. Their gift shop has an extensive selection of railway related books, toys and clothing. Rides are available on weekends only. Unless you're a real train buff, this may not be worth the trip.

Just north of Perris, exiting Highway 215 at the Ramona Expressway, you will find the **Lake Perris Fairgrounds** (*18700 Lake Perris Dr.*; ☎*657-4221*), just before the entrance to the Lake Perris State Park. The fairgrounds are home to

the **Satellite Sports Wagering**, the **Perris Area Speedway** (☎*800-976-RACE*) and go-cart and BMX bicycle racing tracks. A variety of racing events are held on the grounds throughout the year.

The **Lake Perris State Park** (*$6/vehicle; ☎657-0676*) offers an artificial lake, camping and hiking. By the lake, visitors will find a marina, waterslide and campgrounds. There is also a little coffee shop restaurant by the marina if you didn't pack a picnic. Plan stopping at the golden beach on the calm waters of the lake. Camping is available for $21/night, $15 without hookups (*☎800-444-7275*). The park's hidden gem among the boulder-strewn mountains is the **Ya'i Heki' Regional Indian Museum ★ ★** (*Wed 10am to 2pm, Sat and Sun 10am to 4pm; 17801 Lake Perris Dr.; ☎657-9739*). This museum overlooking the lake has wonderful displays highlighting Native American art, history, and artifacts.

★
Moreno Valley

Moreno Valley is a very young city, incorporated on December 3, 1984. What was once a thriving citrus farming community in the late 1800s virtually disappeared, as years of drought were exacerbated by the diversion of precious water resources to nearby Redlands. Some of the more expensive homes in the Moreno Valley were moved in their entirety by steam-powered tractors to the nearby city of Riverside. By 1901, few people resided in the Moreno Valley, and those who remained turned primarily to the dry farming of hay, grain, and grapes. In the latter part of the 20th century, the population has exploded, from a mere 18,000 in 1970 to almost 150,000 by the year 2000.

The highlight of Moreno Valley is the **March Field**

Museum ★ ★ (*$5; I-215 at the Van Buren Offramp; ☎697-6600; www.marchfield.org*). Over 50 airplanes are on display, from 1918 to the present. Visitors can see everything from the giant B-52 bomber to the super-secret SR-71 Blackbird. There is also a section dedicated to the 475th fighter group, Satan's Angels, and their fleet of P-38s. The surrounding airbase was established in 1918, just south of the city and brought new life to Moreno Valley. March Field was established at a time when the United States was anticipating entry into World War I and was rushing to build up its military forces. Today, the base serves as an air force reserve. AirFest takes place at March Field during the second weekend of May when hundreds of new and vintage planes are on display, and a variety of acrobatic shows are presented.

Tour B: Riverside

Riverside was once known as "the city of trees" due to the palm-lined avenues, and wide array of subtropical shade trees, such as eucalyptus, pepper, and sycamores, that were imported and planted throughout the city. The architecture of Riverside is another pride of the city – from the early 1900s to the Second World War, Riverside concentrated on creating a Mediterranean-style atmosphere, with excellent examples of California Mission Revival and Spanish Colonial buildings throughout the city. The crowning glory of the California Mission Revival style is the Historic

Mission Inn, in downtown Riverside.

The tour starts at the Fox theatre at the corner of Mission Inn Avenue and Market Street.

Each spring and fall, the historic **Fox Theater ★** (*3801 Mission Inn Ave.; ☎784-3686*) is host to the Riverside Film Festival, showcasing a series of 10 films every other Thursday. Open since 1929, the Spanish-Colonial-Revival-style theatre served as a cinema/vaudeville house and attracted such well-known performers as Bing Crosby and Judy Garland. The Fox was also a popular location for motion picture previews, and was the site of the first public screening of *Gone with the Wind* in 1939.

Walk east down Mission Inn Avenue to the Main Street Pedestrian Mall.

The beautiful **Loring Building** (*3685 Main St.*) was originally built in the Richardson Romanesque style in 1890 and housed the city hall, library, jail and municipal courts. Later it would serve as the headquarters of the Riverside Fruit Exchange (parent company of Sunkist brand) and a popular theatre venue. In 1918 the building was remodelled to the current Mission Revival structure.

Across the street from the Loring Building is the elegant **Mission Inn Hotel ★ ★ ★** (*3649 Mission Inn Ave.; ☎784-0300*). The hotel comprises an entire city block and took 30 years to complete, built in several stages between 1902 and 1932. Owner Frank A. Miller used the hotel to showcase the art and artifacts he collected

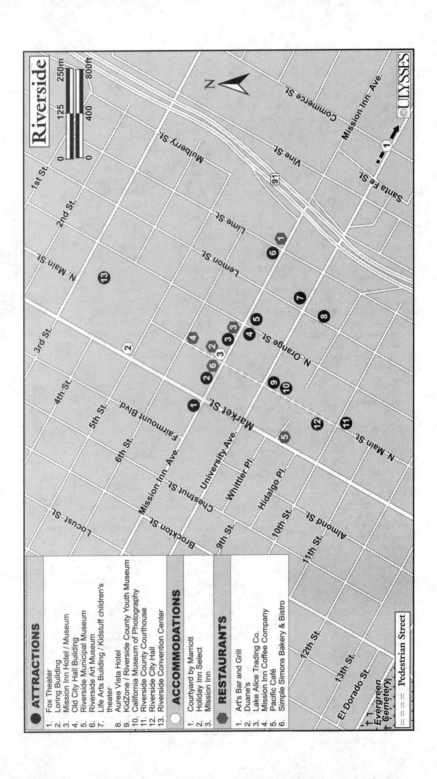

Riverside

0 · 125 · 250m
0 · 400 · 800ft

● **ATTRACTIONS**
1. Fox Theater
2. Loring Building
3. Mission Inn Hotel / Museum
4. Old City Hall Building
5. Riverside Municipal Museum
6. Riverside Art Museum
7. Life Arts Building / Kidstuff children's theater
8. Aurea Vista Hotel
9. KidZone / Riverside County Youth Museum
10. California Museum of Photography
11. Riverside County Courthouse
12. Riverside City Hall
13. Riverside Convention Center

⬡ **ACCOMMODATIONS**
1. Courtyard by Marriott
2. Holiday Inn Select
3. Mission Inn

● **RESTAURANTS**
1. Art's Bar and Grill
2. Duane's
3. Lake Alice Trading Co.
4. Mission Inn Coffee Company
5. Pacific Café
6. Simple Simons Bakery & Bistro

= = = Pedestrian Street

© ULYSSES

Mission Inn

on his many travels around the world. The architecture is truly impressive, blending Mission Revival style with modern influences as seen by the interior courtyards, flying buttresses, domes and clock towers. Over $5 million worth of antiques and artifacts are on display throughout the hotel and charming surprises can be found at every turn. President Nixon was married in the elegant Presidential Suite in 1940, which is now a bar and lounge. Public tours of the hotel (*$8; 75min;* ☎*781-8241)* are led by trained guides of the Mission Inn Foundation and leave from the museum.

The **Mission Inn Museum** ★★ (*$2; Mon to Sun 9:30am to 4pm 3696 Main St.;* ☎*788-9556)* is located within the Mission Inn and displays and impressive collection of artifacts from around the world. Most of the collec-

tion was gathered by the hotel's founder, Frank Miller, on his travels. Craftsman period furniture, lacquered Asian temple guardians, lifesized papal court figures and 19th and early 20th-century paintings are just a few of the offerings here.

Continue down Mission Inn Avenue to Orange Street.

On the Southwest corner of Mission Inn Avenue and Orange Street is the **Old City Hall Building.** This Spanish Renaissance Revival style edifice served as city hall from 1924 to 1975.

Across Orange Street is the **Riverside Municipal Museum** ★★ (*free; Mon 9am to 1pm, Tue to Fri 9am to 5pm, Sat and Sun 1pm to 4pm; 3580 Seventh St.* ☎*826-5273)* where dinosaur bones, woven baskets and sparkling gemstones await. The Italian Renaissance style building was formerly a post office, built

in 1914. Today the museum strives to preserve and display the diverse communities and cultural heritage of the Riverside area. Of particular interest is the natural history section, which features static displays of the plants and animals in the area's desert and mountain regions.

Continue east along Mission Inn Avenue.

A block down from the Municipal Museum is the **Riverside Art Museum** ★★ (*$1; Mon to Sat 10am to 4pm; 3425 Seventh St.;* ☎*684-7111)*, built in 1929 as the YWCA. The museum purchased this Hispanic Revival building in 1966 and it now exhibits a changing selection of classic and contemporary Southern California art. The Museum's Atrium Court Restaurant is surrounded by a lovely garden and makes a great stop.

Turn right (south) on Lime Street and walk one block to University Avenue. Turn right (west).

Originally built in 1909 as a YMCA, the historic **Life Arts Building** ★★ now houses artists' studios for the Riverside Community Arts Association and a few small galleries. The **Kidstuff** children's theater (see p 270) also occupies this 1909 Italian Renaissance building.

Across the street from the Life Arts Building is the **Aurea Vista Hotel.** The upper floor ballroom is now the home of the California Riverside Ballet.

Follow University Avenue to the Main Street Pedestrian Mall. Turn left (south).

The **KidZone/Riverside County Youth Museum** ★★ *($4; closed Mon, Tue to Fri 10am to 5pm, Sat to Sun 10am to 4pm; 3800 Main St.; ☎683-3800)* features over 28 hands-on activities and interpretive exhibits plus regular arts and crafts workshops. Kids can play with everything from Fender guitars to fire department equipment in a safe, supervised environment.

The **California Museum of Photography** ★★ *($2; Wed to Sat 11am to 5pm; 3824 Main St; ☎784-FOTO; www.cmp.ucr.edu)*, a facility of the University of California, Riverside, explores politics, art and society as represented by photography. Exhibits include Ansel Adams photographs, examples of cameras from 1839 to the digital present, and a unique, world-famous collection of stereoscope cards. For the children, there is also a fun, interactive display gallery and a giant camera obscura. The gift shop has a great selection of books, chldren's educational toys and jewellery.

At the end of the pedestrian walk stands a beautiful **sculpture of Martin Luther King** with the words "I have a dream" emblazoned below. It truly is a spectacular work with some of the great people and moments in black history molded into the figure.

Across the street from the end of the pedestrian mall, stands the **Riverside County Courthouse** ★ *(4050 Main St.)*. Constructed in 1904, the county's first courthouse was designed by Franklin P. Burnam in classical Beaux Arts style to duplicate the facade of

the 1900 Paris Exposition's Grand Palace of Fine Arts.

Other attractions in Riverside include the following:

Fairmont Park ★ *(2601 Fairmount Blvd.)* was designed by Frederick Law Olmsted, of Central Park, New York City fame. The park features two tennis courts, a playground, picnic facilities and rose gardens. Lake Evans and Fairmount Lake provide fishing and a restored historic boathouse rents paddle boats.

The **1873 Parent Navel Orange Tree**, from which the navel orange industry grew, is at the corner of Magnolia and Arlington avenues.

Castle Amusement Park ★★ *(3500 Polk St., ☎785-4140)*, is on a 25-acre (10.1ha) site filled with rides, games, arcades, and highlighted by four 18-hole championship miniature golf courses. The three-level arcade area has over 400 games. Miniature railroads, a log ride and a 90-year-old carousel round out the attractions.

The **Botanic Gardens at the University of California Riverside** ★★ *(free admission; everyday 8am to 5pm; 900 University Ave ; ☎787-4650)* are a welcome escape from city life. Stroll among the 39 acres (15.8ha) of flowers, trees, woods, and gardens. Hiking trails and secluded picnic spots abound. A gentle pathway for wheelchair access winds through the main features of the gardens. Twice a year, the Gardens hold their popular plant sale.

The **Jensen-Alvarado Ranch** ★ *(4350 Briggs St.; ☎369-6055)* has been re-

stored to portray rural life. A variety of farm animals roam among the citrus groves, the peach, apricot and plum orchards, and the vineyard. Horses are hard at work plowing the fields. The staff is all dressed in period clothing and will explain the various historical aspects of the farm. The Winery Museum and Gift Corner are open 10:00am to 4:00pm on weekends.

Tour C: San Bernardino and Redlands

★★
San Bernardino

The city of San Bernardino originally served as an outpost for the San Gabriel Mission and was founded May 20, 1810 on the feast day of St. Bernadine, hence its name. In 1860, San Bernardino experienced a brief gold rush and began to grow in both importance and population, first as an east-west wagon stop, and later as a link between the two trans-continental railroads. The historical remnants of the town are few, however, as many of the old structures were razed to make way for "progress." Now, sadly, only historical signs remain to mark San Bernardino's previous grandeur.

The tour starts at the convention and visitors bureau.

The **San Bernardino Convention and Visitors Bureau** *(201 N. E St., suite 103; ☎889-3980, ☎800-867-8366; www.san-bernardino.org)* is a great place to stop to find out about local events and activities.

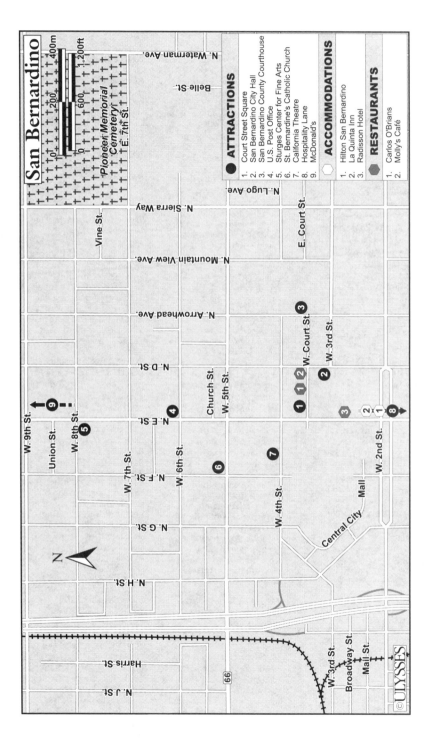

San Bernardino

ATTRACTIONS

1. Court Street Square
2. San Bernardino City Hall
3. San Bernardino County Courthouse
4. U.S. Post Office
5. Sturges Center for Fine Arts
6. St. Bernardine's Catholic Church
7. California Theatre
8. Hospitality Lane
9. McDonald's

ACCOMMODATIONS

1. Hilton San Bernardino
2. La Quinta Inn
3. Radisson Hotel

RESTAURANTS

1. Carlos O'Brians
2. Molly's Café

© ULYSSES

San Bernardino Festivals

The **Renaissance Pleasure Faire** (☎800-525-2473) is held each spring in Glen Helen Regional Park just north of San Bernardino, and presents a historically accurate English market and festival. Eat with your hands, watch the knights joust, and toast the queen among acres of shady trees and lakes.

The **Stater Brothers Route 66 Rendevous** (☎888-5998, www.route-66.org) is San Bernardino's signature event. On the third weekend of September, 2,448 hot rods, as well as custom and classic cars roll into town—one car for every mile (1.6km) of Route 66. The classic-car exhibition covers 14 square blocks of downtown and draws over 400,000 spectators who come for the cars, the concerts and the nostalgia.

Just north of the visitors bureau, past the towering Radisson Hotel is the **Court Street Square** (Court St., between D and E Sts.). This was originally the site of the 1892 court house but is now more of a "concrete beach" which hosts outdoor concerts, Shakespearean festivals, and local events. Call ☎381-5037 for

event information. The **Earl Buie Memorial Clock** (E St., in front of the Radisson) was originally mounted on the tower of the 1873 court house and was dismantled in 1927, only to be remounted in its current location in 1972 thanks to the efforts of Earl Buie.

The **San Bernardino City Hall** ★ (340 N. D St.) is located on the east side of Court Street Square and is an interesting example of modern architecture. The black cubic building is supported for three quarters of its length by thick pillars. A many-tiered waterfall runs beside the building and past a sculpture of Martin Luther King.

Follow Court Street east to Arrowhead Avenue and the court buildings.

The neoclassical **San Bernardino County Courthouse** ★ (418 N. Arrowhead Ave.) stands on the site of the original Mormon Stockade Site. The Mormons, fearing an Indian attack, built a stockade on this site out of split cottonwood and willow logs which became the home of over 100 families. The attack never came, and the Mormons eventually moved out. The park beside the courthouse is a great place to have a picnic and admire the many monuments, fountains and works of art.

Head North on Arrowhead Avenue and turn west (left) on Fifth Street.

The **U.S. Post Office** ★★ (Fifth St. and D St.) is San Bernardino's best surviving example of Spanish-Italian revival architecture, built in 1931. In 1993 the original marble, plaster, terrazzo, brass and mahogany were meticulously

restored from underneath 60 years of "improvements." The interior recaptures another era with its restored 1930s post boxes, brass chandeliers and carved corbels in the lobby's ceiling.

If you are an art lover, follow E Street north to Eighth for the Sturges Center—otherwise continue west on Fifth Street to F Street.

The **Sturges Center for Fine Arts** ★ (Tue, Thu, Fri 11am to 3pm; 780 N. E St.; ☎384-5415) is home of the San Bernardino Art Association and the Community Concert Association. A small art gallery features local exhibitions and a variety of cultural performances are held throughout the year.

St. Bernadine's Catholic Church ★★ (Corner of F and Fifth sts.) is a Romanesque church that stands on the site of two previous churches. Note the ornate stained grass windows imported from Germany in the early 1900s. The building originally had a bell tower which was demolished in 1957 as it began to lean precariously. St. Bernadine's Rectory stands just north of the church and was built in 1865 as a makeshift fort for local Confederate Sympathizers in the Civil war.

Turn left (south) on F Street and continue two blocks to Fourth St. Turn left.

The **California Theatre** ★★★ (562 Fourth St.; ☎885-7969) was built in 1928 and was the site of Roger's last performance in 1935. The elegant old theatre is now home to the Civic Light Opera, Inland Empire Symphony Orchestra and a community theatre. The Spanish-mansion style architecture and gilded accents have been lovingly restored over the years.

Around San Bernardino

The very first **McDonald's** *(1398 N. E St.; ☎885-6324)* was opened in San Bernardino in 1948 on historic Route 66. Early photos and memorabilia are on display.

A Special Place, Children's Hands-On Museum ★★ *($2; Mon 9am to 5pm, Tue to Fri 11am to 3pm, Sat 1pm to 5pm; 1003 E. Highland Ave.; ☎881-1201)* features antiques, face-painting, costumes, a shadow room and hand-puppets in an old classroom setting.

Hospitality Lane can be found south on E Street near the I-10 freeway. This area has an extensive collection of hotels, restaurants and bars.

Old West buffs will want to visit the **Roy Rogers – Dale Evans Museum ★★**, *(everyday 9am to 5pm; 15650 Seneca Rd.; ☎243-4547)* 40min north on Interstate 15 in Victorville. A larger-than-life trigger rears at the main entrance and inside is an extensive collection of movies, pictures, posters and items donated by the famous couple. Two exclusive movies are shown in the main theatre. Reservations are suggested for guided tours.

★
Redlands

Redlands is a picturesque community with the small town charm of yesteryear. Named for the colour of the adobe soil, this area was once known as the "Navel Orange Capital of the World." Today Redlands is known as the

"museum without walls," due to its interesting architecture and several carefully restored Victorian homes. As you enter town you will feel the pace of life slow down quite noticably. Many small boutiques, shops and eateries are scattered throughout the downtown area.

Smiley Park *(Vine St. and Eureka)* is home to two of Redland's attractions. The **A.K. Smiley Public Library ★★** *(Mon to Thu 9am to 7pm, Fri and Sat 9am to 5pm)* was named for the twin brothers who moved to Redlands in 1889 and donated the building. The beautiful architecture and colourful gardens are worth a quick visit. The **Lincoln Memorial Shrine ★** *(free; Tue to Sat 1pm to 5pm; 125 W. Vine St.; ☎798-7632)* is dedicated to Abraham Lincoln and the Civil War era. A large collection of manuscripts, books and artifacts is available.

The French chateau-style **Kimberly Crest House and Gardens ★★** *(Thu to Sun 1pm to 4pm; 1325 Prospect Rd.; ☎792-2111)* was built in 1897 and features terraced Italian gardens and a unique gift shop. Guided tours are available through the elegantly furnished interior which remains as it was 75 years ago.

Just west of Redlands off the I-10 Freeway is the **San Bernardino County Museum ★★** *($4; closed Mon; 2024 Orange Tree Lane; ☎888-BIRD-EGG)*. Three floors feature a wide variety of exhibits on the Inland Empire Area and the Southwest in general. The museum is internationally renowned for its collection of over 40,000 bird eggs. Other attractions include the exhibits of fossils and minerals that

have been found in the area. Kids will love the hands-on discovery hall.

Pharaoh's Lost Kingdom ★★ *(1101 N. California St.; ☎335-7275)* is a decent theme park also located west of Redlands on the I-10 Freeway. Visitors enter through a giant sphinx and can spend the day riding the midway, shooting it up in the laser tag arena, or beating the heat in the River of The Nile water park.

Tour D: Big Bear Lake

A picturesque drive through the mountains is rewarded by majestic Big Bear Lake. This quaint village sits at an elevation of 7,000ft (2300m) and experiences a refreshing seasonal climate. The village itself is a pedestrian-friendly shopping and dining area full of old-fashioned charm. Clean mountain air and the active outdoor lifestyle of Big Bear are the main attractions here, (see p 259), making this a favourite vacation spot for Southern Californians. Throughout the area, a variety of outdoor activities are possible, from skiing and hiking to canoeing and fishing. Over 300 sunny days a year ensure beautiful weather during your stay. Big Bear is also renowned for the rainbow of wildflowers that bloom each spring as the snow begins to melt. During the winter, heavy snowfalls can make the winding, single lane road slow, so check conditions before you start your trip.

The **Big Bear Visitors Center ★** *(630 Bartlett Rd.; ☎800-424-4232;*

The Inland Empire and Palm Springs

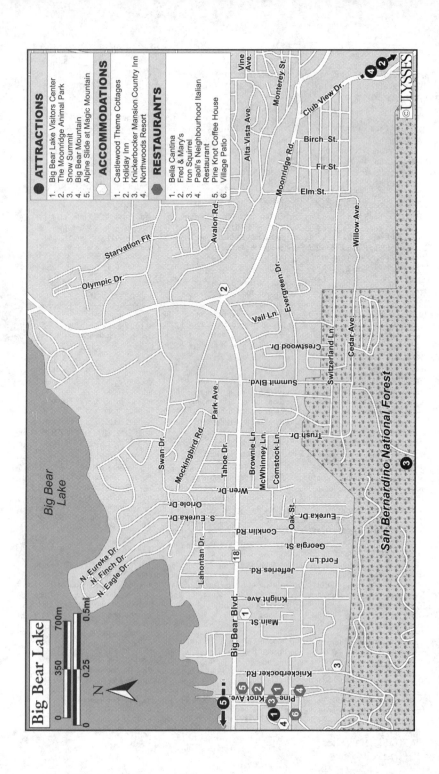

Big Bear Lake

Big Bear Lake

N

| 0 | 350 | 700m |
| 0 | 0.25 | 0.5mi |

ATTRACTIONS
1. Big Bear Lake Visitors Center
2. The Moonridge Animal Park
3. Snow Summit
4. Big Bear Mountain
5. Alpine Slide at Magic Mountain

ACCOMMODATIONS
1. Castlewood Theme Cottages
2. Holiday Inn
3. Knickerbocker Mansion Country Inn
4. Northwoods Resort

RESTAURANTS
1. Bella Cantina
2. Fred & Mary's
3. Iron Squirrel
4. Paoli's Neighbourhood Italian Restaurant
5. Pine Knot Coffee House
6. Village Patio

San Bernardino National Forest

© ULYSSES

www.bigbearinfo.com) is located in the heart of the village and is an invaluable resource with friendly, courteous staff. Pick up one of their *Visitor Guides* or order it online.

Star gazers will be enthralled with the **Big Bear Solar Observatory** ★ *(summer only, Sat; ☎866-5791 ext. 10)*, one of only six in the world. The observatory is located on North Shore Drive, across the lake from the village. Tours are available on weekends during the summer only.

The **Moonridge Animal Park** ★★ *($2.50; everyday 10am to 4pm; ☎866-0183; www.moonridgezoo.com)* is home to a variety of orphaned or injured animals that are being rehabilitated before re-release into the wild. Visitors can enjoy a stroll through the pines and marvel at the coyotes, deer and even a bald eagle. A family of grizzlies, a pair of bison and a snow leopard are among the park's permanent residents. A tour is held at noon daily while the feeding tour is at 3pm on weekends.

The **Big Bear Discovery Center** ★★★ *(donations; ☎866-3437)* is an excellent place to learn about the history, wildlife and outdoor activities of Big Bear. The centre supplies guides or maps for a number of hikes into the surrounding forest. There are also several nature tours available *($18-$35)*, including canoe tours of Big Bear Lake, guided wildflower tours, and historic mining tours. Naturalists at the centre are familiar with the flora, fauna and history of the area and would be glad to share their knowledge. Attend one of their many talks *($4)* that educate

visitors on the area's natural attractions. The Adventure Outpost Shop carries a wide selection of books and souvenirs.

Due to the seasonal climate at Big Bear, skiing is still possible into early April, at **Big Bear Mountain** ★★★ *($32; 43101 Goldmine Dr.; ☎585-2519; www.bearmtn.com)* and **Snow Summit** ★★ *($34; Summit Blvd.; ☎566-5766; www.snowsummit.com)*. The two resorts offer 60 runs up to 1000 vertical feet (300m) in altitude and 2mi (3.2km) long. Non-skiers can choose to ride the lift up to the top of the mountain for the spectacular panoramic views. Big Bear Mountain is also the site of the U.S. Adaptive Recreation Center, catering to persons with disabilities, and they have specialized equipment and instructors available. During the summer, the centre focuses on the lake, providing sailing, canoeing and waterskiing.

For a day of pure fun, try the **Alpine Slide at Magic Mountain** ★★★ *(Big Bear Blvd. Just west of the village; ☎866-4626)* where you careen down a bobsled style track during the summer. Miniature golf, go-carts and video games are also available. When the snow falls, a chairlift or the "magic carpet" will transport you and your toboggan or inner-tube to the top of the mountain so you can plummet right back down.

Just east of the Big Bear City Airport, you will find the **Big Bear Historical Museum** *(weekends, May to Oct; Greenway Dr.; ☎585-8100)*. This small museum explores the history of the first miners and hunters who settled in Big Bear

and traces the village's evolution from its inception to the vacation paradise that it is today.

Tour E: Idyllwild, Palm Springs and the Coachella Valley

★★
Idyllwild

The scenic route to Palm Springs takes Highway 243 through the mountains to Idyllwild, a beautiful little mountain town in the San Bernardino National Forest. The evergreens make a nice change from the omnipresent palms in lower altitudes. The air is cleaner, the smog is gone, and a fresh pine scent wafts through the air. These attractions have made Idyllwild a vacation retreat for desert dwellers in the surrounding area. Idyllwild sits at over 5000 ft (1700m) and temperatures at night tend to drop off, so pack some warm clothes. While you're here, check out **Lily rock**, a huge granite rock with an 800 ft (266m) sheer face that is visible from all over town. Hiking is a popular activity here, and the best point of departure is at the ranger station, where they have maps and information for each of the many trails. The streets are confusing, but the people are friendly, so ask anyone for directions to the restaurants or hotels listed. Idyllwild is not the place for nightlife and action, but rather for some relaxation and communion with nature. Keep in mind that the drive from any direction can be challenging, especially at night or during the winter months. From Idyllwild, Highway

The Inland Empire and Palm Springs

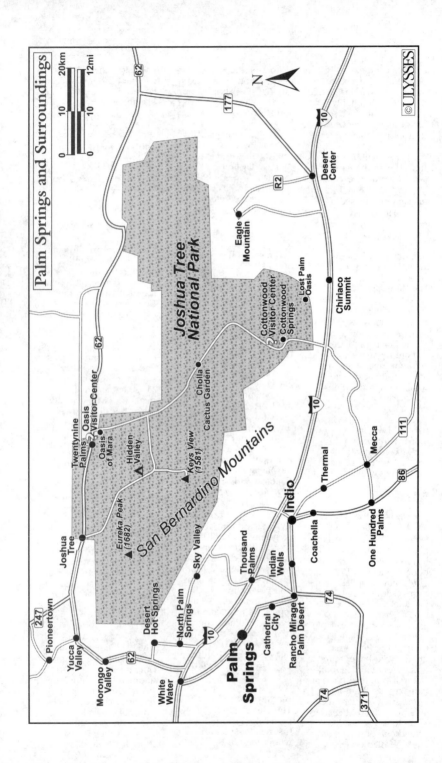

Palm Springs and Surroundings

243 continues down out of the mountains into the Coachella Valley and Palm Springs.

★★★
Palm Springs

The Agua Caliente Cahuilla Indians were the first people to settle in the Palm Springs area. They were attracted by the ample flora and fauna of today's Indian Canyons and the bubbling hot springs in the area were said to have magical healing powers. By the mid-1800s the Mormons of San Bernardino had made their way to this area, bringing with them smallpox which decimated the Cahuilla population. Even today the tribe numbers under 300. In 1884 John McCallum became the first white settler to the area, building the now-famous McCallum Adobe that still stands today. By 1940, the population numbered just over 5,000, and swelled seasonally to almost 9,000 as tourists and the Hollywood film community began to discover this oasis in the desert. After the Second World War, the secret was out and Palm Springs became the "playground of the stars," with regular visits from the Brat Pack and other Hollywood celebrities. Bob Hope was appointed honorary mayor. Until the early 1990s, Palm Springs had a reputation as a party resort town, and thousands of students descended on the town during spring break. After a small riot one year, Mayor Sonny Bono created new laws to discourage this influx of students, much to the dismay of local bar and hotel owners. Today Palm Springs has adopted a more subdued atmosphere, but continues to attract visitors in record numbers. The warm, dry climate and cosmopolitan restaurants, shopping and hotels keep visitors coming back year after year.

The tour starts at the world-famous Desert Museum.

A must-see on your visit is the **Palm Springs Desert Museum** ★★★ *($7.50; Tue to Sat 10am to 5pm, Sun noon to 5pm; 1101 Museum Dr.; ☎325-0189)*. Art exhibits include a large permanent collection of contemporary and Western American art, with special emphasis on California. The natural science galleries are the most interesting, however, focusing on the history and culture of the local indigenous peoples, the flora and fauna of the desert and containing a special wing devoted to Death Valley. Here you can learn about the Cahuilla Indians as well as the rattlesnakes, desert tortoises and lizards that inhabit the desert around you, while a seismograph records earthquake activity all over Southern California. A wonderfully landscaped **sculpture garden** awaits after the galleries. Also located in the museum is the **Annenberg Theater**, *(☎325-4490)*, a 450-seat, state-of-the-art theatre facility that presents ballet, opera and classical music.

Walk north to Amado Road and turn right (east).

Stop in to the **Palm Springs Chamber of Commerce** ★ *(190 W. Amado Rd.; ☎325-1577)* for more information, a free map, and coupons to the area's attractions. The friendly staff would be happy to recommend some attractions to you.

Continue east to Palm Canyon Drive and turn right (south).

Palm Canyon Drive ★★★ is the main street and the heart of Palm Springs. Walking down this street you will find all sorts of small boutiques, opulent hotels and art galleries. Also of interest is the Palm Springs walk of stars, with gold stars inlaid in the sidewalk to honour such Palm Springs regulars as Frank Sinatra and Marilyn Monroe.

Across from the Mercado Plaza shopping centre, is the **Plaza Theater** ★ *(128 S. Palm Canyon Dr.; ☎327-0225)*, which is home to the critically acclaimed Palm Springs International Film Festival. The **Fabulous Palm Springs Follies** *(☎864-6514)* also perform here, a group of actors 50 years of age and over that present a music, dance and humour of the 1930s and 40s.

Some of the greatest works of Southwest and Latino art are showcased at **Adagio Galleries** ★★ *(193 S. Palm Canyon Dr.; ☎320-2230)*. The gallery has recently been expanded and hosts major showings throughout the year of such artists as Frank Howell, Nivia Gonzalez and John Nieto.

Learn about the original people of Palm Springs at the **Agua Caliente Cultural Museum Information Center** ★ *(free admission; Mon to Sat 10am to 4pm, Sun noon to 3pm; 213 S. Palm Canyon Dr. ☎323-0151)*. Displays highlighting the history and accomplishments of the Agua Caliente Cahuilla Indians feature artifacts, music and photographs. The Flora Patencio Basketry exhibit highlights her famous work and a

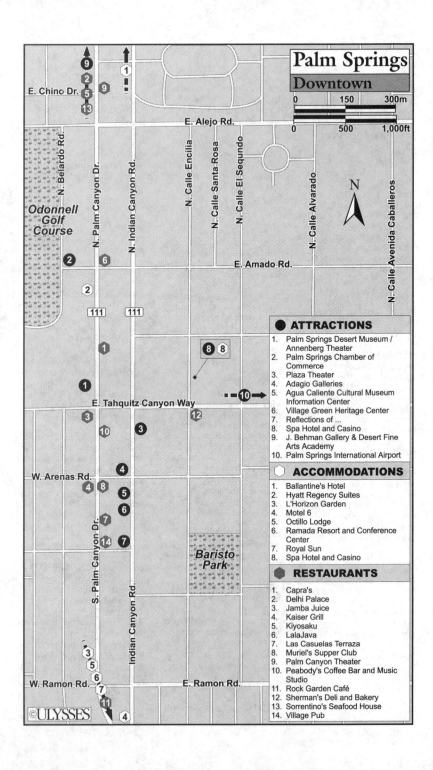

Palm Springs
Downtown

| 0 | 150 | 300m |
| 0 | 500 | 1,000ft |

E. Chino Dr.

N. Belardo Rd.

Odonnell Golf Course

N. Palm Canyon Dr.

N. Indian Canyon Rd.

E. Alejo Rd.

N. Calle Encilia

N. Calle Santa Rosa

N. Calle El Segundo

N. Calle Alvarado

N

N. Calle Avenida Caballeros

E. Amado Rd.

111   111

E. Tahquitz Canyon Way

W. Arenas Rd.

S. Palm Canyon Dr.

Indian Canyon Rd.

Baristo Park

W. Ramon Rd.

E. Ramon Rd.

©ULYSSES

● ATTRACTIONS

1. Palm Springs Desert Museum / Annenberg Theater
2. Palm Springs Chamber of Commerce
3. Plaza Theater
4. Adagio Galleries
5. Agua Caliente Cultural Museum Information Center
6. Village Green Heritage Center
7. Reflections of ...
8. Spa Hotel and Casino
9. J. Behman Gallery & Desert Fine Arts Academy
10. Palm Springs International Airport

⬡ ACCOMMODATIONS

1. Ballantine's Hotel
2. Hyatt Regency Suites
3. L'Horizon Garden
4. Motel 6
5. Octillo Lodge
6. Ramada Resort and Conference Center
7. Royal Sun
8. Spa Hotel and Casino

⬡ RESTAURANTS

1. Capra's
2. Delhi Palace
3. Jamba Juice
4. Kaiser Grill
5. Kiyosaku
6. LalaJava
7. Las Casuelas Terraza
8. Muriel's Supper Club
9. Palm Canyon Theater
10. Peabody's Coffee Bar and Music Studio
11. Rock Garden Café
12. Sherman's Deli and Bakery
13. Sorrentino's Seafood House
14. Village Pub

desert landscape diorama that shows how the Cahuilla Indians lived and worked with their environment.

The **Village Green Heritage Center** ★★ *(221-223 S. Palm Canyon Dr.)* is dedicated to the pioneers that helped build Palm Springs out of rough desert country. The centre is a collection of heritage buildings that strives to educate visitors on the rich history of the area.

The **McCallum Adobe** was the first pioneer home in Palm Springs, built in 1885. It is now home to the **Palm Springs Historical Society** ★ *($0.50; Oct to May; 221 South Palm Canyon Dr.; ☎323-8297).*

Next to the adobe is **Miss Cornelia White's house** ★, built nine years later out of railway ties and home to Palm Springs' first telephone. Both contain personal memorabilia of the original owners and are worth a quick visit.

Ruddy's General Store Museum ★★ *($.50; Oct to Jun, Thu to Sun 10am to 4pm Jul to Sep Sat and Sun 10am to 4pm; ☎327-2156)* is probably the most fun of the three museums. Inside, over 6,000 *unused* items line the shelves. Take a minute to wander through and marvel at the collection of everyday goods from the late 1930s.

Reflections of... *(285 S. Palm Canyon Dr.; ☎800-921-7787)* has one of the largest collections of Art Glass in the United States. Over 300 artists are featured, who were chosen for their skill in creating vases, sculptures, paperweights and oil lamps. You might want to leave the kids outside.

Turn left (east) on Baristo Road to South Indian Canyon Drive. Turn left (north on Indian Canyon.

Three blocks north of Baristo Road is the **Spa Hotel and Casino** *(24hrs; 100 N. Indian Canyon Dr.; ☎325-1461).* Here you can try your luck at the slots or sit in on a hand of poker or blackjack. The interior doesn't meet Vegas standards, but it's a great place to spend a rare wet afternoon.

Other Palm Springs Attractions

If you need to beat the desert heat, grab your bathing suit and head over to the **Oasis Water Park** ★★ *(1500 Gene Autry Trail; ☎327-0499).* Thirteen water slides with such intimidating names as the Black Widow and the Scorpion provide the thrills while the giant wave pool and lazy Whitewater River are perfect for relaxing and catching some rays.

For cutting-edge contemporary art, stop by the **J. Behman Gallery & Desert Fine Arts Academy** *(1103 N. Palm Canyon Dr.; ☎320-6806).* The gallery showroom displays pieces created by the students of this full-time art school and is a refreshing change from the classics. Drop in on Saturdays for a children's craft class or on Friday for an adult figure drawing workshop.

Over 50 years in the making, **Moorten Botanical Gardens** ★★ *(everyday; 1701 S. Palm Canyon Dr.; ☎327-6555)* features over 3,000 varieties of desert plants. Several different habitats have been constructed to provide for the differing needs of the plants. Stroll through and marvel at the

incredible diversity of desert fauna.

On the north side of the Palm Springs airport is the **Palm Springs Air Museum** ★★ *($7.50; everyday 10am to 5pm; 745 N. Gene Autry Trail; ☎778-6262).* This gigantic museum is dedicated to preserving the fighters, bombers and trainers from the U.S. armed forces. Two main display hangars house everything from the B-17 *Flying Fortress* to the P-38 *Lightning.* Climb up the many ladders and take a look in the cockpit. Get some hands-on experience in one of their flight simulators. Flight demonstrations are held occasionally and there is a unique gift shop

Hadley Fruit Orchards ★★ *(free admission; every day 9am to 5pm 122 La Plaza; ☎325-2160)* is a working farm that grows a variety of fruits, dates and nuts. Walk through the orchards then sample some of their goods including their signature date shakes. Stop by their store and pick up some fresh supplies for a trip to Indian Canyons.

★★★
Indian Canyons

Indian Canyons are so named because centuries ago, ancestors of the Agua Caliente Cahuilla (pronounced Kaw-we-ah) Indians developed several flourishing communities in the Palm, Murray, Andreas, Tahquitz and Chino canyons. A natural oasis, water was plentiful and the canyons were a natural habitat for a variety of flora and fauna on which these people depended. The Cahuilla were accomplished farmers and grew a variety of crops in the fertile valleys. Throughout the canyons, evidence of these settlements can still be found in the rock art, building foundations, irrigation system and well-worn trails. The entrance to Indian Canyons can be found 3mi (5km) south of East Palm Canyon Drive. The $6 entrance fee is payable at the ranger station. Get there early as the area is locked down after 6pm.

Palm Canyon ★★★ is 15mi (24km) long and lined with majestic palms on either side of a meandering stream. A paved foot path leads down into the canyon, through the abundant cacti and desert shrubs. The Trading Post stocks maps, refreshments and souvenirs.

Tahquitz Canyon is currently off limits, but may open soon as the new site of the Agua Caliente Cultural Museum. This canyon is famous for its many waterfalls and pools.

The verdant oasis of **Andreas Canyon** ★★ supports more than 150 different species of plants. Picnic tables are provided along the scenic walking trail for a welcome rest stop. Examples of Cahuilla rock art can be seen on some of the striking rock formations found along the trail.

Not far from Andreas Canyon is **Murray Canyon** ★, home to a few wild horses and the endangered peninsula big horn sheep. This canyon seems to attract fewer visitors, making it an ideal destination for some natural solitude.

The **Palm Springs Wind Energy Farms** ★★★ (*N. Indian Canyon Dr.*) can be found in the hills just north of the city. Taking advan-

tage of the strong winds that blow down out of the mountains, hundreds of giant windmills make for a surreal sight on the desert landscape. Visitors can drive into the area and look around, but they are best seen with a tour. **Palm Springs Windmill Tours** (*$23; ☎251-1997; www.windmilltours.com*) offers electric vehicle tours with expert guides that explain the awesome capabilities of these giant turbines.

The **Palm Springs Aerial Tramway** ★★★ (*$19.35; every 1/2hr.; Tramway Rd. off SR-111; ☎888-515-TRAM; www.pstramway.com*) is an opportunity to experience another environment and get a break from the desert heat. The tram starts at 2,643ft (881m)and rises to the Mountain Station summit at 8,516ft (2838m). Two rotating cars provide a 360-degree view of the ascent. The views of the desert and the surrounding mountains are absolutely stunning. There is cross-country skiing here (weather permitting) and ski rentals are available. Be advised that the temperature can drop sharply

so be sure to bring a light jacket with you. The last car leaves Mountain Station and returns to the valley at 9:45pm.

Other Attractions in Coachella Valley

The surrounding communities in Coachella Valley are home to several major attractions, spectacular resorts and myriad golf courses. Rancho Mirage and Palm Desert are more upscale communities and have some fabulous houses owned by the rich and famous. If Palm Springs is your primary destination, however, make sure to choose a hotel near the city centre. The surrounding communities of Rancho Mirage, Cathedral City and Indio are close by, but the traffic and multitude of stop lights on Highway 111 make for slow going.

Palm Springs Wind Energy Farms

Palm Springs Aerial Tramway

Rancho Mirage

A unique attraction in Rancho Mirage is **Heartland—The California Museum of the Heart** ★ *($2.50; Mon to Fri 7am to 7pm, Sept to May Sat 8am to noon; Bob Hope Dr., Rancho Mirage; ☎32-HEART)*. Learn all about the heart and its function, walk through a giant model or get an in-depth view at the Happy Heart Cinema.

The **Children's Discovery Museum of the Desert** ★★ *($5; Tue to Sat 10am to 5pm, Sun noon to 5pm; 71-701 Gerald Ford Dr., Rancho Mirage; ☎321-0602)* encourages children to interact with over 50 hands-on activities. They can participate in their very own archaeological dig, paint a Volkswagen beetle or create their own simple inventions. The museum store has a selection of educational gifts and toys.

Palm Desert

The Living Desert ★★★ *($7; everyday 9am to 5pm, closed Mid-Jun to Aug; 47-*
900 Portola Ave., Palm Desert; ☎346-5694) covers over 1,200 acres (487ha) and serves as both a zoo and botanical park. Scenic trails through the park take you through a collection of native and exotic animals from deserts around the world. The new Watutu Village is a recreation of a traditional African village that is home to leopards, camels and hyenas. Children will enjoy the "Petting Kraal" where they can pet and feed sheep, goats and cattle.

The powerful **Desert Holocaust Memorial** *(Palm Desert Civic Center Park, San Pablo and Fred Waring; ☎325-7281)* is an outdoor tableau of seven towering bronze figures within a row of trees representing the concentration camp walls. Dramatic lighting and cobblestone walks highlight the effect.

Avid golfers will want to check out the **Jude E. Poynter Golf Museum** *(free; everyday 8am to 8pm; Fred Waring Dr. and San Pablo Ave. ☎341-2491)* with exhibits featuring the history and personalities of the game.

The **McCallum Theater for the Performing Arts** *(73-000 Fred Warring Dr.; ☎340-2787)* is located inside the Bob Hope Cultural Theater. This impressive concert hall presents everything for symphonies to musicals.

Indio

The history, artistry and handiwork of the valley's first people is presented at the **Coachella Valley Museum & Cultural Center** ★ *($1; Wed to Sat 10am to 4pm, Sat 1pm to 4pm; 82-616 Miles Ave.; ☎342-6651)*.

Tour F: Joshua Tree National Park

The ancient Pinto people were the first to inhabit the area now known as the Joshua Tree National Park. These hunter-gatherers lived along a stream that ran through the now-dry Pinto Basin. Over the years, many other groups of Native Americans have made the oases of the park their homes, leaving behind rock paintings, pottery and small dams.

The park comprises 794,000 acres (321,000ha) of the Colorado and Mojave deserts. The Colorado Desert occupies the eastern half of the park, at elevations under 3,000ft (914m) and is inhabited by the creosote bush, spidery ocotillo and jumping cholla cactus. As the elevation rises toward the western half of the park, you enter the cooler, moister climate of the Mojave, where the extensive stands of Joshua trees dominate the landscape. The park is not completely arid, however, as five palm oases scattered throughout its terrain are teeming with local wildlife. The main attractions here are the clean air, panoramic vistas and unusual rock formations that dot the landscape. Impressive granite monoliths, smoothed by the passage of time, are found throughout the park, and are a favourite for rock-climbers. An excellent time to visit Joshua Tree is after an infrequent rain when the desert wildflowers, after waiting patiently, spring to life in a rainbow of colour. In the spring and fall, the park rangers conduct a

The Inland Empire and Palm Springs

series of walks, hikes and campfire talks. Visitor wishing to stay close to the park can stay in the town of **Joshua Tree** or **Yucca Valley** (see p 264).

Joshua Tree National Park is about a 45min drive east from Palm Springs via the I-10 Freeway, then on Highway 195 to the Cotton-wood Visitor Center. This route allows you to drive north through the park and return to Palm Springs from the northwest.

Stop into the **Cottonwood Visitor Center** and pay the $10 fee for entering the park. Keep your receipt as it allows for unlimited entry into Joshua Tree and Death Valley for a seven-day period. Some small exhibits relating to the park can be found in the centre and the park rangers will be happy to answer any questions you may have. **Cottonwood Springs** ★★, the first palm oasis in the park is 1mi (1.6km) to the west and features camping and picnic facilities. This is also a great place to spot a variety of desert birds who frequent the spring.

Continuing north you will enter Pinto Basin, a dry lake bed. The Pinto Basin Road passes a patch of tall, flame-tipped ocotillo plants on the right before reaching the **Cholla Cactus Garden** ★. This unique desert garden has a short interpretive trail featuring the plants and animals of the Colorado Desert.

As you leave the Cholla Garden, the road begins to rise and you enter the Mojave section of the park. Notice the Joshua trees are

more populous and the temperature begins to drop.

Pinto Basin Road becomes Utah Trail that leads up to the Oasis of Mara and the Oasis Visitor Center.

Joshua tree

The **Oasis Visitor Center** ★ is home to the park head-quarters and contains various informative resources regarding Joshua Tree National Park. Just behind the centre, a short interpretive trail winds through the **Oasis of Mara** ★★ which was home to various Native American settlements and the original homesteaders of the area.

Head back south along Utah Trail and veer right through Sheep Pass.

Interesting granite rock formations are found in the **Jumbo Rocks** ★★ area, as well as well marked hiking trails and several picnic sites. Just past Jumbo Rocks is the **Geology Tour Road**, which is only accessible by four-wheel-drive. The dirt road winds 18mi (29km) through many impressive rock structures.

Continuing west, you will find the trail head to the summit of Ryan Mountain (5,461ft or 1660m). Following the moderately strenuous 1.5mi (2.4km) trail is rewarded by beautiful vistas of the valley.

At the intersection of Park Boulevard, turn left (south) towards Keyes View.

Keyes View ★★★ is the most popular attraction in the park and is an easy drive up to the 5185ft (1581m) lookout. Here you get a chance to look out over the desert floor for miles in every direction from the Little San Bernardino Mountains.

Turning right (west) on the dirt road before Hidden Valley will take you to the **Barker Dam** ★★. The dam was built in the early 20th century to support herds of cattle raised by the homesteaders of the area. Local wildlife can often be seen here taking advantage of the collected rain-water. The road can be rough at times but is manageable by car.

Head north along Park Boulevard through Lost Horse Valley.

Hidden Valley ★★ was originally a cattle-rustlers hideout, taking advantage of the massive boulders that line the interpretive trail through the valley. Picnic facilities are available.

Exit the park via Park Boulevard to Joshua Tree. Highway 62 heads back to Palm Springs through Yucca Valley and Morongo Valley.

Tour G: Anza-Borrego National Park

Located approximately 1hr away from San Diego, Anza-Borrego National Park is an absolute must. In terms of size, this is the largest national park in the United States. It is simply splendid, with vast desert-covered mountains where unique fauna and flora live peacefully side by side. In summer, the temperature can soar to levels that are difficult for humans to handle; we therefore suggest that you visit it in spring, during flowering time, or after August.

The tranquil town of **Borrego Springs ★★★** (*☎767-5555 or 800-559-5524*), located in the heart of Anza-Borrego National Park, is surrounded by 600,500 acres (243,000ha) of desert-like wilderness. It is the park's only town. The small community offers many hotels, campgrounds, restaurants and shops, as well as loads of activities such as four-wheel-drive rides, bike rentals, horseback rides and hot-air balloon rides that let you explore the region's treasures. Borrego Springs is basically the safest gateway to this incredible, indescribable natural park.

Stop by the **information centre ★★** (*Oct to May every day 9am to 5pm, Jun to Sep Sat and Sun 10am to 5pm; 200 Palm Canyon Dr., ☎767-4205*). In addition to collecting pertinent information and perusing a lovely shop selling typical products and interesting reference books, there is an exhibit offering the ideal introduction to the park, which will help you better understand and appreciate this unique environment. A 15min slide show is a pleasant way to end your visit.

Outdoor Activities

Hot-Air Ballooning

Temecula

A Natural High Balloon Charters (*☎888-323-5987; www.anaturalhigh.com*) offers balloon flights over the vineyards of the Temecula Valley with a post-flight champagne continental breakfast on the patio of their launch site.

Palm Springs

Balloon Above the Desert (*$155; ☎800-342-8506, ☎776-5785*) offers customized balloon flights not only in Palm Springs, but all over California. The flight lasts 60-75min and departs at 6am or 3pm. Hotel pickup and drop-off is available.

Cycling

Big Bear Lake

Big Bear Bikes (*$6/hr, 41810 Big Bear Blvd.; ☎866-2224*) rents high quality mountain bikes with front or full suspension for use in town or on the North Shore Bike Path. This is by far the best way to travel around Big Bear. In the winter they

also rent snowshoes (*$10/day*).

Palm Springs

Bighorn Cycles (*302 N. Palm Canyon Dr.; ☎325-3367*) offers mountain bikes for as low as $29/day, with kids' bikes and city cruisers also available. Bighorn also leads tours through Indian Canyons (*$49*) and the estates of Palm Springs (*$35*).

Anza-Borrego National Park

There are more than 250mi (402km) of cyclable routes in this park. Whether on rocky slopes, sandy roads or along panoramic routes, all paved roads and roads reserved for four-by-fours are open to cyclists. It is, however, forbidden to go off the roads or on hiking trails.

One very popular route for mountain bikes is the Blair Valley Road which, in addition to being relatively flat, has some striking view points. The Oriflamme Canyon is for more seasoned cyclists. There are a number of other options, all of which the staff at the visitor centre will explain. A warning, however: remember that you should not venture into the desert without taking certain precautions (see box in the "Outdoors" chapter).

Mountain Bike Rentals
☎767-3872

Bicycle Rentals
☎800-824-1884

Guided Downhill Adventure Bike Tours
☎742-2294

Boat Tours and Rentals

Big Bear Lake

Sailboats, speedboats and fishing boats can be rented from one of the many facilities in Big Bear Lake. Try **Pine Knot Landing** (☎866-2628), the **Big Bear Marina** (☎866-3218; *www.bigbearmarina.com*) or **Holloway's Marina** (☎866-5706). Jet-skis and water-skiing are also available.

The Mississippi-style paddle boat *Sierra Belle* (*$10; 866-2628*) leaves Pine Knot Landing several times a day for a tour of Big Bear Lake.

Golf

Palm Springs

Palm Springs has dozens of fantastic golf courses to choose from in both a desert and classical layout. Here are a few resources for last minute tee times.

Next Day Golf (☎345-8463) and **Stand-by Golf** (☎321-2665) offer a good selection of guaranteed tee times at public, semi-public and private golf courses in Palm Springs. Call a day in advance.

Hiking

Big Bear Lake

The **Big Bear Discovery Center** (*42300 N. Shore Dr.; ☎866-3437*) is a hotspot for hiking enthusiasts. The naturalists at the centre can suggest which hikes are best for the time of year. Decent maps are available and all hikes are graded by level of difficulty. The easy **Bluff Mesa Trail** of under a mile round trip is great for beginners while the **Castle Rock Trail** is extremely popular and offers a chance for a little rock climbing along the way. Attend one of their nature talks first to get the most out of the experience. Note that an Adventure Pass is required to park at the trail heads and is available at the centre for a modest fee.

Palm Springs

Exploring **Indian Canyons** is a popular route for hikers, as are the trails that lead from **Mountain Station** into San Jacinto State Park. Maps are available at the Indian Canyons Ranger Station and in the Mountain Station gift shop.

Joshua Tree National Park

A variety of well-marked hiking trails are located in Joshua Tree National Park. The Cottonwood and Oasis ranger stations have maps and can provide sound advice for those wishing to hike

through the park. Always remember, however, that this is desert country, so make sure to bring plenty of fluids and protect yourself against the sun.

Horseback Riding

Big Bear Lake

Baldwin Lake Stables (☎585-6482) offers horseback riding year-round and has a variety of outings from 1hr to overnight camp rides. The pony rides and petting zoo are a hit with the kids.

Palm Springs

Smoke Tree Stables (*2500 Toledo Ave.; ☎327-1372*) specializes in equestrian tours of Indian Canyons. Rides are available by the hour or by the day.

Skiing and Snow Boarding

Big Bear Mountain (*$32 lift ticket; 43101 Goldmine Dr.; ☎585-2519; www.bearmtn.com*) and **Snow Summit** (*$34; ☎566-5766*) cater to both skiers and snowboarders. The two resorts offer 60 runs up to 1,000 vertical feet in altitude (305m) and 2mi (3.2km) long. Quicksilver pro rider Nick Drake designed Big Bear's extensive snowboard park. Up-to-date ski reports are available at ☎888-786-6481 for Snow Summit and ☎800-232-7686 for Big Bear Mountain.

Rock Climbing

Palm Springs

Uprising *($25 with lessons, $15 with prior experience for all day climbing; 1500 S. Gene Autry Trail; ☎320-6630, ☎800-CLIMB-ON; www.uprising.com)* is the only outdoor artificial rock climbing centre in the country. Instructional packages are available for those new to the sport. They also offer guided rock climbing trips to Joshua Tree and Idyllwild as well as mountain biking and hiking adventures. Children six years and up are welcome.

Accommodations

Temecula

Butterfield Inn
$$
≡, tv, ≈, ⊛
28718 Old Town Front St.
☎ 676-4833
The Butterfield provides basic but adequate accommodation. Rooms are clean and generous in size but lack any sort of real appeal. The location is fantastic, however, right in Old Town Temecula. The pool and hot tub are quite small and not always in service.

Ramada Inn
$$-$$$
≡, tv, ≈, ⊛
28980 Front St.
☎676-8770
☎800-228-2828
≈699-3400
www.ramada-temecula.com
The Ramada is within easy walking distance of Old Town Temecula. Clean but bland rooms feature a fridge, microwave and coffee maker. The outdoor pool and hot tub are as bland as the rooms, but will serve when the weather heats up.

Loma Vista Bed And Breakfast
$$$-$$$$ bkfst incl.
≡, tv, ⊛
33350 La Serena Way
☎676-7047
≈676-0077
Loma Vista is located right in the heart of Temecula Wine country, next to the famous Callaway Vineyards. The beautiful Mission Style home sits on 5 acres (2ha) of lush citrus groves and vineyards. A full champagne breakfast is served in the morning and wine and cheese is offered each evening. Each of the charming rooms is individually decorated with a different theme and named after a local wine. Smoking is not permitted.

Embassy Suites
$$$$ bkfst incl.
≡, tv, ⋈, ⊘, ℜ
29345 Rancho California Rd.
☎676-5656
☎800-362-2779
≈699-3928
The Embassy Suites is an all suite hotel located conveniently close to Highway 15, with easy access to golf, the vineyards and Old Town Temecula. Each of the two-room suites features a fridge, microwave and VCR. A complimentary beer and wine reception is held each evening. Pet friendly.

Riverside

Courtyard by Marriott
$$-$$$
≡, tv, ≈, ⊛
☎276-1200
☎800-321-2211
≈787-6783
The Courtyard is just a few miles from downtown and the historic Mission Inn district. The rooms are comfortable and include a large desk and in-room coffee. The outdoor heated pool and spa are a welcome feature. Friendly service.

Holiday Inn Select
$$$
≡, tv, ≈, ⊛, ⊘, ℜ
3400 Market St.
☎784-8000
☎877-291-7519
≈369-7127
Spotless rooms include a small sitting area with couch and dark hardwood furniture. Oversized desks with dataport phones are a nice option. A recent renovation has provided upscale suites with a large marble whirlpool tub as the centrepiece. The location is unbeatable, within the Mission Inn district and beside the convention center. A busy lounge and decent restaurant are located at lobby level.

Mission Inn
$$$$
≡, tv, ≈, ⊛, ℜ, ⊘
3649 Mission Inn Ave.
☎784-0300
☎800-344-4225
≈784-5525
What began as a two-storey adobe guesthouse in 1876 has grown to encompass and an entire city block in downtown Riverside. The architecture is truly impressive, with interior courtyards, flying buttresses and clock towers. Many of the rooms are absolutely unique, with domed ceilings, stained

glass windows and carved pillars. Over $5 million worth of antiques and artifacts can be found on display throughout the hotel. A fully equipped health club, Olympic-sized swimming pool and two wedding chapels round out the amenities. Also on site is the Mission Inn Museum, Duane's Prime Steaks and Seafood and the Mission Inn Restaurant.

San Bernardino

La Quinta Inn
$$
≡, tv, ≈, ☉, 🐾
205 E. Hospitality Lane
☎888-7571
☎800-531-5900
⇆884-3864
www.laquinta.com
An excellent budget choice on Hospitality Lane is the La Quinta Inn. Kids stay free and a complimentary continental breakfast is served each morning. Pets are welcome.

Hilton San Bernardino
$$$
≡, tv, ≈, ◉, ☉, ℜ
285 E. Hospitality Lane
☎889-0133
www.sanbernardino.hilton.com
The Hilton San Bernardino is located in the "Hospitality Lane" district and offers newly renovated rooms with coffee makers and oversized work desks. An outdoor heated pool and hot tub are the perfect way to spend the early evening. Martini's Bar and the Potiniere Restaurant are located onsite or there are many other bars and restaurants nearby.

Radisson Hotel
$$$$
≡, tv, ◉, ☉, ℜ
295 N. E St.
☎381-6181
www.radisson.com
The Radisson is the latest in a line of hotels that have occupied this site since 1887. The 230 rooms are plush and comfortable after a recent renovation. Free Internet access is offered to guests in the hotel lobby. On weekends stay away from the rooms facing Court Street Square as they can be rather noisy due to Carlos O'Brians across the street.

Big Bear Lake

🌴 Castlewood Theme Cottages
$$$
≡, tv, ◉
547 Main St.
☎866-2720
The Castlewood Cottages are truly unique. Eight of the twelve rooms feature intricate themes such as: Anthony and Cleopatra, the Enchanted Forest and the Cave. Most rooms feature a hot tub which is expertly designed to match the decor. Costumes are also available to complete the experience. For those not looking for theme rooms, Castlewood also has a wonderful two bedroom A-frame cabin and a private wood cabin. An excellent bargain with attentive service.

🌴 Knickerbocker Mansion Country Inn
$$$
869 Knickerbocker Rd.
☎878-9190
☎800-388-4179
⇆878-4248
This wonderful three-storey log mansion is a great find in Big Bear. In the 1920s, Bill Knickerbocker, logger and damkeeper, felled the trees himself, constructing this impressive home overlooking the lake for his wife and five children. The home has been lovingly restored and innkeepers Stanley and Thomas provide a warm reception. The original fieldstone fireplace is highlighted by lustrous wood paneling. The rooms are perfect, with full marble baths and inviting down-filled beds and comforters. Two luxurious suites are also available. The large patio is perfect for enjoying an intimate breakfast or relaxing on late summer evenings.

The Holiday Inn
$$$$
≡, tv, ≈, ☉, ℜ
42200 Moonridge Rd.
☎866-6666
☎800-Holiday
⇆(909)866-8988
These rooms are outstanding for the Holiday Inn chain. The carpets are a busy country floral pattern, gas fireplaces are included and the decks are of weathered wood. Victorian-style furniture and brass beds complete the decor. The pool, however, is rather small and only open seasonally. Their restaurant, Le Bistro ($$-$$$), has a selection of pasta in addition to the chicken, lamb and beef dishes.

Northwoods Resort
$$$$
≡, ≈, ◉, ☉, △, ℜ
40650 Village Dr.
☎866-3121
☎800-866-3121
⇆ 878-2122
www.northwoodsresort.com
Entering the chateau-style lobby, guests are greeted by antler chandeliers and stone accents. The rooms are spacious and rustic, with log furniture and a wood decor. Rooms facing the pool have a balcony,

while those on the roadside do not. Try the king-bed rooms which include a fireplace. A heated pool and spa are and added attraction. Unfortunately, the resort does not have a lake view. Stillwells restaurant serves up hearty American fare including steaks, pasta and wild game dishes. This hotel is conveniently located right next to downtown and two blocks from the lake. In the summer, Northwoods also rents mountain bikes and runs an off-road adventure tour (www.offroadadventure.com).

Idyllwild

Strawberry Creek Inn
$$$-$$$$ bkfst incl.
≡
26370 Hwy. 243
☎659-4707
☎800-262-8969
www.strawberrycreekinn.com
The Strawberry Creek Inn is a charming bed and breakfast just outside Idyllwild, perfectly located among the pines. Each of the 10 rooms is unique, and is lovingly prepared for the visitor. Only some of the rooms have TVs though most have cozy fireplaces for the chilly mountain nights.

Palm Springs

Motel 6
$$
≡, ≈, ⊛, tv
606 S. Palm Canyon Dr.
☎327-4200
The Motel 6 features clean, spartan rooms for those on a tight budget. Reserve early as it's one of the cheapest hotels within walking distance of downtown. A pool and small hot tub are available.

The Royal Sun
$$-$$$ bkfst incl.
≡, tv, ≈, ⊛, K
1700 S. Palm Canyon Dr.
☎(760) 327-1564
☎800-619-4SUN
≈(760) 323-9092
Located just south of downtown, this family hotel has bright rooms furnished with a small desk, stove top, microwave and fridge. The pool and hot tub are ample and spotless. A full buffet breakfast is included. This is a definite bargain in Palm Springs.

Ramada Resort and Conference Center
$$$$ weekend
≡, tv, ≈, ⊛, ℜ
1800 E. Palm Canyon Rd.
☎323-1711
☎800-245-6907
www.ramadapalmsprings.com
The balconies on the Ramada's 241 rooms surround a 2 acre (0.8ha) lawn and courtyard area with a large pool and hot tub. Rooms are spacious and cute, with natural wood furnishings and king or double queen beds.

Ocotillo

Octillo Lodge
$$$-$$$$
≡, tv, ≈, ⊛, ⊘
1111 E. Palm Canyon Dr.
☎416-0678
Daily weekly and monthly rates are available. While the hotel may not look like much from the outside, the suites are homey and well laid-out with a sofa, loveseat and full kitchen. There is no bath tub, however. They have an above average fitness room, plus two outdoor hot tubs and a heated pool.

Ballantine's Hotel
$$$$ bkfst incl.
1420 N. Indian Canyon Dr.
☎800-780-3464
≈320-5308
www.palmsprings.com/ballantines
Ballantine's has 14 theme rooms based on 1950s musicals, and 1950s France, complete with artwork by Léger and Miro. Every room features an authentic period fridge and a secluded patio. Try the all-pink Marilyn Monroe suite ($199) where she actually stayed at one point. Brat Pack music fills the air around the comfortable pool area. No children allowed.

L'Horizon Garden
$$$$
≡, K, ≈, tv
1050 E. Palm Canyon Dr.
☎(760) 323-1858
☎800-377-7855
William Cody, a modernist architect of the 1950s, designed this two bedroom house and seven bungalows. Each open-concept studio bungalow includes a full kitchen plus king-size bed. The unique showers face outside, but are protected from prying eyes by a wall and a bouquet of flowers. Marilyn Monroe refused to use these showers for fear of photographers coming over the fence. Rooms

without a kitchen are $30 less. Two acres (0.8ha) of landscaped gardens surround a popular pool in the center. Nicky, the friendly owner, will be happy to fill you in on the history of the hotel and it's famous guests. No children allowed.

Hyatt Regency Suites
$$$$
≡, *tv*, ≈, ◉, ⊘, ℜ
285 N. Palm Canyon Dr.
☎*322-9000*
☎*800-633-7313*
⇒*325-4027*
www.hyatt.com
Each of the spacious, two-room suites at the Hyatt Regency feature a private patio or balcony, marble bath and live plants. The elegant open-air atrium is rich in marble and brass and a half-block-long swimming pool is set among the impeccable landscaping. Located right in the heart of Palm Springs, the Hyatt is step away from all the major downtown attractions. Ask for a mountain-view rooms, as they are quieter.

Palm Desert

The Embassy Suites
$$$$$ bkfst incl.
≡, ≈, ◉, ℜ
74700 Hwy. 111
☎*340-6600*
☎*800-EMBASSY*
⇒*340-9519*
The Embassy is a beautiful, all-suite hotel that is now part of the Hilton chain, and features fountains, a free form pool and a whirlpool. Each two-bedroom suite is done in neutral colours, and has a living room, a microwave and fridge. Full cooked-to-order breakfast. The Sonoma Grill restaurant serves your choice of grilled chicken, and meats with a southwestern flair.

Note the beautiful stained glass in the lobby.

Marriot Desert Springs Resort
$$$$$
≡, *tv*, ≈, ◉, ⊘, ℜ
74-855 Country Club Dr.
☎*341-2211*
☎*800-331-3112*
⇒*341-1872*
The Marriot Desert Springs is a spectacular resort in Palm Desert. Elegant, oversized guest rooms overlook the water which surrounds the entire property. It is even diverted into the enormous lobby where it falls over five-tiered waterfalls. Gondola tours also leave from the lobby, taking guests on tours of the resort or to one of its many restaurants. Two 18-hole championship golf courses and miles of jogging trails are located on the property. The award-winning spa facility covers over 30,000 sq ft (2,787m^2). The only problem with the Marriot Desert Springs is that you may never leave the resort!

Joshua Tree

Safari Motor Inn
$$
≡, *tv*, ≈
61959 29 Palms Hwy.
☎*366-1113*
One of the only options in Joshua Tree, the Safari Motor Inn is about 6mi (10km) from the park's northern entrance. The motel is simple but clean and friendly. The rooms have showers only.

High Desert Motel
$$
≡, *tv*, ≈
61310 29 Palms Hwy.
☎*(760) 366-1978*
Slightly better quality than the Safari, the High Desert retains it s 1970s-style shag carpet in the sparsely-furnished rooms.

Yucca Valley

Oasis of Eden Inn and Suites
$$, theme rooms $$$-$$$$
≡, ≈, ◉
56377 29 Palms Hwy.
☎*365-6321*
⇒*365-9592*
www.oasisofeden.com
The Oasis of Eden in Yucca Valley is a fun place to spend the night. Fourteen theme rooms are available, ranging from the jungle room with its rock floor, imitation trees and rattan furniture to the cave, complete with stalactites, bats, cobwebs and spiders (fake ones!). All theme rooms have in-room hot tubs. The standard rooms are also distinctly different from 1950s art deco, to kitschy 1970s or modern European styling. Studio and full-kitchen rooms are available.

Anza-Borrego National Park

If you are seeking an adventure in the splendid Anza-Borrego Park, the town of Borrego Springs is one of the few places where you can find a room. In addition to the numerous camping options, there are also a few hotels ranging from huge luxurious complexes to simple, reasonably priced motels. Here are a few.

Borrego Valley Inn
$$$ bkfst incl.
ℜ, ◉, *K*, ≈
405 Palm Canyon Dr.
Borrego Springs, CA 92004
☎*767-0311 or 800-333-5810*
⇒*767-0900*
www.borregovalleyinn.com
This inn, which could be called a bed and breakfast, is particularly welcoming and undoubtedly will give you a good taste of the

unique desert atmosphere. The rooms are decorated in Santa Fe style, as is the entire establishment, and each offers a private patio and a magnificent view of the desert scenery. Every morning the hosts welcome you to a copious breakfast, which you will savour in enchanting surroundings.

Palm Canyon Resort
$$$
tv, ≈, ≡, ℜ, ⊛, K
221 Palm Canyon Dr.
P.O. Box 956
Borrego Springs, CA 92004
☎767-5341 or 800-242-0044
Palm Canyon Resort offers simple, clean and tasteful rooms with a view over the valley. With its old-saloon look, this establishment recalls hotels of the Old West, and the interior is warmly decorated with woodwork and a pastel colour scheme.

Borrego Springs Resort & Country Club
$$$
tv, P, ⊘, ≡, ⊛, ℜ, K, ℝ,⑤
1112 Tilting T. Dr.
Borrego Springs, CA 92004
☎767-5700
The San Diego county tourist industry is clearly aimed at business travellers. This is evident even in the wild Anza-Borrego, where you will find establishments largely oriented towards this clientele. The Borrego Springs Resort & Country Club is one such example, with its numerous banquet halls and convention rooms. Moreover, workaholics can also take some time to relax here thanks to a golf course, swimming pool, tennis courts, health club and fitness centre. The establishment has 100 fully equipped rooms, each with its own terrace. The decor is unoriginal, but the rooms are comfortable and clean.

La Casa Del Zorro
$$$$$
ℜ, ⑤, ℑ, tv, ≡, K, ≈, △
3845 Yaqui Pass Rd.
Borrego Springs, CA 92004-5000
☎767-5323 or 800-824-1884
☎760-767-5963
www.lacasadelzorro.com
The Casa Del Zoro is a magnificent hotel complex in the heart of the desert, an oasis of luxury and comfort. As soon as you arrive you will be struck by the opulent architecture of the establishment, which recalls a Spanish colonial house. Among the 30-odd adobe-style buildings that house the rooms and the communal areas, there is also a garden, pools, terraces, a tennis court and a golf course.

The rooms, of which there are various categories, are not to be sneezed at either. Their decor is reminiscent of an old Mexican *casa*, and the rich, comfortable furniture, verandas opening onto the courtyard and, in some, the fireplace, give the rooms a very romantic aura. Some even have a piano. All the rooms offer amenities such as a coffee machine, minibar, hair dryer, ironing board and iron and, let's not forget, the newspapers under the door in the morning.

The hotel, with its numerous conference and meeting rooms, is designed for a business clientele as well as passing tourists, and patrons have access to all the services and facilities necessary for a successful stay. There is also everything you need to get into shape or pamper yourself, thanks to the exercise rooms, whirlpool tubs, health club and hairdressing salon.

Restaurants

Temecula

The Swing Inn Café
$
28676 Front St.
☎676-2321
Start off your day with one of the 10 breakfast specials, all priced under $5. The Old West exterior gives way to a diner-style interior. This café has been a local favourite since 1927. Ask for one of their take-out menus that features a brief history of Temecula as well as a sort walking tour of town.

The Bank
$-$$
28645 Front St.
☎676-6160
The Bank serves delicious Mexican food in the Old Town Bank Building. Dine inside where the neon contrasts with the centennial walls or on the small patio which spills out onto Front Street. Try the crab quesadillas or, if you're starving, one of their giant combination platters.

Texas Lil's
$$
28495 Front St.
☎ 699-5457
What would an old town be without a Texas style restaurant/bar? Texas Lil's has a slightly kitschy interior, complete with giant bullhorns and cattle skulls. They have a great selection of steaks and ribs—a definite carnivores delight! As an added bonus, you can cook your own steak on one of their indoor grills to save yourself a

few bucks. If you fast all day you may be able to get through their 24oz (680g) porterhouse steak.

County Garden Restaurant and Bakery
$-$$
2900 Front St.
☎695-2421
The Country Garden is a charming little restaurant where the aroma of fresh baking is all the appetizer you'll need. The offerings are impressive, from blueberry stuffed french toast with ice-cream sauce for breakfast, to a generous Reuben melt for lunch and sizzling swordfish for dinner.

The Vineyard Terrace
$$$-$$$$
Thu to Sun, lunch 11:30am to 4pm
Fri and Sat, dinner 5pm to 10pm
32720 Rancho California Rd.
☎308-6661
Located at the Callaway Winery in the heart of wine country, the Vineyard Terrace offers outdoor dining with a lovely view of the vineyards. Enjoy fresh California cuisine and, of course, a bottle of wine. Reservations are suggested.

Riverside

Simple Simons Bakery & Bistro
$
3639 Mission Inn Ave.
Simple Simons has an astounding variety of different breads and pastries, sandwiches and soups, but is only open for breakfast and lunch.

Mission Inn Coffee Company
$
3649 Mission Inn Ave.
☎341-6789
Built onto the back of the Mission Inn, this coffee shop is a great alternative

to the omnipresent Starbucks, and has better coffee. Their patio on the pedestrian walk is a great spot for people watching.

Lake Alice Trading Co.
$$
3615 University Ave.
☎(909) 686-7343
This great little restaurant is an excellent value. Start with one of their extensive appetizers then move on to halibut tacos, stuffed lemon chicken breast or filet mignon. Live music is provided Wednesday through Saturday nights.

Art's Bar and Grill
$$
3357 University Ave.
☎(909) 683-9520
Art's offers traditional American fare from thick burgers to pastas, prime rib and lobster tail, all at reasonable prices. The patio is perfect for enjoying the afternoon with one of their microbrew beers.

Pacific Café
$$-$$$
Closed Sun
3770 Ninth St.
☎782-8088
Located conveniently in downtown Riverside, the Pacific Café offers sushi in addition to such tantalizing specialties as halibut a la Ken and *mahi mahi* Mediterranean.

Duane's
$$$$
3649 Mission Inn Ave.
☎784-0300 ext. 6780
Duane's has an upscale steakhouse decor in the heart of the Historic Mission Inn. The menu features a variety of hand-cut steaks, in addition to veal chops grilled with lemon and herbs, lamb chops in mint glaze or grilled swordfish. A well-chosen wine list, first-class service and the beautiful architec-

ture of the Mission Inn make this an excellent choice.

San Bernardino

Molly's Café
$
Mon to Fri 6am to 3pm, Sat to Sun 7am to 2pm
350 N. D St.
☎888-1778
Molly's is a great spot for breakfast, served in one of their comfy booths. Vinyl records and movie posters are the extent of the decor. Try one of their delicious daily specials that range from pork chops to sirloin steak sandwiches to chicken fajitas for under $5. Brown bag lunches are available if you're going on a road trip.

Carlos O'Brians
$$
440 W. Court St.
☎384-8765
Situated just behind the Radisson, Carlos O'Brians is housed in a historic building dating back to 1931 and inspired by the city hall in Seville, Spain. They offer high-class Mexican entrees and combination platters and serve up award-winning tacos and salsas. Friday and Saturday nights they open their club upstairs, with dancing and pool tables. Make sure to check out the hand-painted ceilings and beautiful turn-of-the-century architecture.

Redlands

Soul Sipp Café and Records
$
19 E. Citrus St.
☎335-1600
Located downstairs, the Soul Sipp bills itself as a "house-techno-trance-jungle-hip-hop café." They

have a comfortable couch area, reminiscent of homey, laid-back living room... fantastic for relaxing and enjoying the music while sipping one of their exotic teas, coffees and juices.

Katalina's Mexican Grill
$
328 Orange St.
☎793-0102
Check out Katalina's for their limited yet delicious Mexican menu within simple brick walls on their two-table patio. Located downtown across from the Redlands mall.

The Downtown Redlands Brewery and Restaurant
$$
19 E. Citrus St.
☎307-5980
The Redlands Brewery has 10 distinct house brews to compliment such dishes as artichoke lasagna and Hungarian goulash. They have a spacious bar area and small but classy restaurant with pressed tin ceilings.

The Great Gatsby Dining and Wine Bar
$$$$
Dinner only
19 E. Citrus St.
☎792-9448
A must for fine dining in Redlands, this basement restaurant is finished in a 1920s motif, right down to the period-dressed serving staff. An extensive wine list features 88 different wines to accompany the imaginative cuisine.

Big Bear Lake

The Pine Knot Coffee House
$
535 Pine Knot Ave.
☎866-3537
This great bakery and coffee house can be found

in the center of the village and presents live entertainment on the weekends. Wednesdays are open-mike night and there are occasional poetry readings in a comfortable, loungy atmosphere. They also sell books.

Bella Cantina
$
Thu to Mon only
625 Pine Knot Ave.
☎866-873
In among the quilts, decorations and gifts, you'll find the Bella Cantina, a great mid-day stop for a cocktail and a sandwich. Take a break from your shopping while you enjoy one of the region's fine wines or beers.

The Village Patio
$
40766 Village Dr.
☎(909) 866-9575
The village patio serves a limited selection of sandwiches and soups plus a respectable variety of hard ice creams. A good spot to sit and watch the people stroll by.

Paoli's Neighbourhood Italian Restaurant
$$
40821 Village Dr.
☎866-2020
Paoli's is an under-appreciated Italian restaurant bar in the middle of downtown. The decor is rustic with fruit tablecloths, but the Italian food is popular with the locals.

Fred & Mary's
$$-$$$
607 Pine Knot Ave.
☎866-2434
This small, 14 table restaurant serves a great selection of California's signature cuisine. Everything from their rosemary scented pork tenderloin to the sesame-nori wrapped

blue tuna is fresh and wonderfully spiced. They also have popular pastas and interesting appetizers. Reservations are recommended on weekends.

The Iron Squirrel
$$$
646 S. Pine Knot Ave.
☎(909) 866-9121
The Squirrel offers upscale dining in Big Bear, but only requires casual dress. The wood paneled decor is light and in keeping with the style of town. Leather booths and extensive brass round out the decor. Try the roasted orange duckling or the veal marsala.

Idyllwild

The Bread Basket
$
54710 N. Circle Rd.
☎659-4700
This is the place for breakfast and it gets jam-packed on weekend mornings. Freshly baked breads and pastries meet an array of omelets and typical American fare. The restaurant is in a converted house and feels like breakfast at home.

Goodtimes Pub & Grill
$-$$
Hwy. 243
☎659-7746
A small restaurant and even smaller bar in what constitutes downtown Idyllwild, the Goodtimes is friendly and cooks up a variety of barbequed goodies.

Restaurant Gastronome
$$-$$$
54381 Ridgeview Rd.
☎659-5055
The Gastronome is a cross between a mountain lodge and steakhouse with a

patio opening out onto the forest floor. The most upscale establishment in the area, it serves the classics from surf & turf to baby back ribs. An extensive wine list is available.

Palm Springs

Jamba Juice
$
111 S. Palm Canyon Rd.
Jamba Juice has over 20 fruit smoothies with a huge selection of fresh ingredients that are meals in themselves. Various "boosts" are available to increase the vitamin and protein content. They also offer a selection of fresh juices including citrus, wheatgrass, carrot and any mix in-between. Vegetarian salads and soups are available as well as a selection of energy bars and health foods.

LalaJava
$
300 N. Palm Canyon Dr.
☎(760) 325-3484
Lalajava is a trendy corner coffee shop with a popular street side patio. Stop in for the organic coffee or a frozen mochaccino and a quick bite.

Sherman's Deli and Bakery
$-$$
401 Tahquitz Canyon
☎325-1199
Sherman's is an all-kosher, premium-quality deli in the heart of Palm Springs. They have an incredible array of soups, sandwiches, pastries and desserts all served with their famous dill pickles and sauerkraut. The patio is always busy.

Village Pub
$-$$
226 S. Palm Canyon
☎323-3265
The Village pub features live daily music on the

patio all day on weekends and at 9pm during the week. Their internationally-inspired pub menu gives credit to the countries where their sandwiches, pastas and salads originated. The heat of the patio is somewhat moderated by the great volumes of mist that characterize the outdoor patios of Palm Springs. The interior is decorated with cheesy art and dollar bills from customers gone-by.

Peabody's Coffee Bar and Music Studio
$-$$
134 S. Palm Canyon Dr.
☎322-1877
Peabody's is the place for breakfast. Try their "eggs benny," which are the best in the city. Live local jazz and blues is presented Thursday to Sunday, accompanied by snacks, desserts and alcohol-laden coffees. They also have an impromptu gallery that changes every month, showcasing local artistic talent.

The Rock Garden Café
$-$$
777 S. Palm Canyon Dr.
☎(760) 327-8840
Just south of downtown, the Rock Garden Café has a rock-walled patio enclosing many fountains, flowers, fruit and palm trees. The rock motif continues inside, where the casual dining room is bounded by stone walls. The menu is varied, from moussaka to shrimp fajitas with chicken marsala and burgers in between. They also have a small bakery providing the freshly baked breads and desserts.

Capra's
$-$$
204 N. Palm Canyon Dr.
☎325-7073
Capra's bills itself as "a wonderful Italian ristorante and deli" and is owned by

Tom Capra, son of legendary director Frank Capra. Inside is a 1940s movie star motif, with Capra posters adorning the walls and an actual academy award. Capra's offers a wide array of sandwiches and salads in addition to their extensive daily specials. The patio is misted to ward off the desert heat.

Las Casuelas Terraza
$$
225 S. Palm Canyon Dr.
☎325-2794
Las Casuelas is a wonderful Mexican restaurant with a palapa covered bar and heated patio. They serve grilled steak, chicken, and shrimp meals in an authentic Mexican style. Choose their spicy *camarones diablos* a simple burrito or one of their combination platters. The margaritas are legendary, and this place gets packed every night of the week. Wandering mariachis provide impromptu entertainment. They also have the largest selection of tequilas in the desert valley.

Kiyosaku
$$
closed wed.
5:30pm to 10:30pm
1418 N. Palm Canyon Dr.
☎ 327-6601
Kiyosaku is an authentic and unpretentious Japanese tepanyaki and sushi restaurant with a classic Japanese decor.

The Delhi Palace
$$
11:30am to 2:30pm, 5pm to 10pm
1422 N. Palm Canyon Dr.
☎325-3411
Inexpensive and cheerful, this place may not look like much, but it is rumored to have the finest Indian cuisine in Palm Springs.

The Kaiser Grill
$$-$$$
205 S. Palm Canyon Dr.
☎*779-1988*

The Kaiser Grill has an almost overwhelming metallic-red interior that becomes more subtle as the evening progresses. Their specialty is anything and everything that comes out of their woodburning ovens or off of their mesquite grill, from fresh fish to marinated chicken and thick-juicy steaks. The heated patio is alive with greenery that separates diners from the busy street. Get a seat near the kitchen to watch you meal prepared through the glass, indoor fountain.

Sorrentino's Seafood House
$$$
1032 N. Palm Canyon Dr.
☎*325-2944*

The dark, Italian-style interior of Sorrentino's was a favourite of Sinatra and the Brat Pack. The historic piano bar was the sight of many impromptu performances over the years. Settle into one of the leather booths and enjoy fantastic steaks and seafood.

Muriel's Supper Club
$$$-$$$$
210 S. Palm Canyon Dr.
☎*325-8839*

Muriel's is *the* place in Palm Springs for fine dining in a fun and interesting atmosphere. The menu is created from scratch every evening and has featured such delicacies as braised venison shank over wild mushroom and truffle crepes, pan seared rare ahi tuna and roasted quail. The interior is Art Deco in its styling and features high-quality live entertainment from salsa to blues every evening. The patio is the hip place to be see and be seen at night.

Anza-Borrego National Park

Pablito
$$
590 Palm Canyon Dr.
☎*767-5753*

The only Mexican restaurant in the area, Pablito welcomes you in the typically colourful setting that seems to be the norm is this kind of dining establishment. The menu offers a good selection of Mexican specialties, as well as an affordable Mexican breakfast menu. The outdoor terrace is quite enjoyable.

Palm Canyon Resort Restaurant
$$$
Open from 11am to 2pm and 5pm to 9pm
221 Palm Canyon Dr.
☎*767-5342*

Time seems to stand still at the Palm Canyon Resort, within the Indian Head Hotel, which was once a refuge for Hollywood stars. Here you will have the opportunity to enjoy a fine meal at the hotel's restaurant, in the dining room or on the terrace, next to the pool and surrounded by the arid mountains. The place will make you feel like a 1940s- or 1950s-style movie star, in the manner of Marlon, Bing and Marilyn, who actually set foot here. To get a little more in the mood, we suggest you visit the room near the reception that is filled with many vestiges and yellowed photographs of the establishment's golden days. The decor and food are not exceptional but the place is bathed in an aura that gives it a unique charm.

Casa del Zoro
$$$$$
3845 Yaqui Pass Rd.
☎*767-5323*

Located in a very elegant resort, this restaurant is slightly disappointing compared to the rest of the services offered here. The dining room, however, does complement the magnificent, warm adobe style, with fireplace, exquisite furnishings and table settings, candles and classical music. On the walls you will notice beautiful paintings depicting horse-drawn carriages crossing the West, which perfectly suit the atmosphere. The service is impeccable, as two servers cater to your every need, dramatically presenting each dish on a folding table they carry about. But in spite of all this, something is lacking. The food is average and without surprise, and the decor could be a little less conventional. All of this wouldn't be so bad if prices were a little lower; but we mustn't forget this is the only restaurant of the kind for many miles. We are, after all, in the middle of the desert...

Entertainment

Temecula

Temecula Beer & Wine Garden
28464 Old Town Front St.
☎*(909) 506-4474*

The Temecula Beer & Wine Garden in Old Town has a selection of over 50 beers and is the only bar to serve all 17 area wines. The outdoor patio is heated at night.

Club Odyssey

28822 Front St.
☎506-9931
The hottest nightclub in town is Club Odyssey with two bars, a great light show and dancing Thursday through Saturday.

Temecula Stampede

28721 Front St.
☎695-1760
Squeeze into those cowboy boots and head down to the Temecula Stampede, a gigantic country and western nightclub. Live entertainment is often featured and dance lessons are available.

Tour B: Riverside

Riverside County Philharmonic

☎787-0251
The Riverside County Philharmonic performs a series of five concerts and two free children's concerts at the Municipal Auditorium in downtown Riverside. In addition, the orchestra tours Riverside County performing in Moreno Valley, Temecula and twice yearly for the Fallbrook Music Society.

Kidstuff

☎684-4555
Kidstuff, presents puppetry, mime, story telling and other quality family entertainment every weekend, year-round in the YMCA building in downtown Riverside.

San Bernardino

Carlos O'Brians

440 W. Court St.
☎384-8765
Carlos O'Brians is housed in a historic building dating back to 1931 and inspired by the city hall in Seville, Spain. Fridays and Saturday nights they open their club upstairs with dancing and pool tables.

Tour D: Big Bear Lake

Bear Paw

664 S. Pine Knot Ave.
☎866-9883
The Bear Paw features a wide demographic dancing to a mix from rock to funk and house. You might want to stay away from karaoke Thursdays.

The **Village Theater** *($7; 40789 Village Dr.)* has two screens showing recent films while the **Village Theater North** *(602 Pine Knot Ave.)* has three more theatres.

Idyllwild, Palm Springs and the Coachella Valley

Casinos

Spa Hotel and Casino

24hrs
100 N. Indian Canyon Dr.
☎325-1461
At the Spa Hotel and Casino you can try your luck at the one of 1,100 slots or sit in on a hand of poker or blackjack.

Palm Springs Villagefest

The late Sonny Bono created the Palm Springs Villagefest *(☎320-3781)*, which is held year-round every Thursday evening from 6pm to 10pm. Palm Canyon Drive is closed to traffic from Amado Road to Baristo Road as the street becomes a huge block party. Fresh fruit stands, artisans' works and restaurant samplings line the street, and live music is presented. This Palm Springs tradition is a must-see for visitors.

Theatre

Palm Canyon Theatre

538 N. Palm Canyon Dr.
☎323-5123
The Palm Canyon Theatre is the only professional theatre company in the Coachella Valley. Check out one of their Broadway-style plays or musicals.

Annenberg Theater

1101 Museum Dr.
☎325-4490
The Annenberg Theater in the Desert Museum presents ballet, opera and classical music in a 450-seat, state-of-the-art theatre facility.

Plaza Theater

128 S. Palm Canyon Dr.
☎327-0225
The Plaza Theater is home to the critically acclaimed Palm Springs International Film Festival.

Bars and Nightclubs

Hair of the Dog
238 N. Palm Canyon Rd.
☎*323-9890*
The Hair of the Dog is a little hole-in-the-wall English pub across from the Hyatt Downtown. They have plenty of international bottled beers and great happy-hour specials.

Zeldaz
169 N. Indian Canyon Dr.
☎*325-2375*
Zeldaz may not look like much from the outside, but has been a local hotspot for the past 22 years. Dancing, comedy and live entertainment are presented.

Banana'z
72291 Hwy. 111, Palm Desert
☎*776-4333*
Banana'z is a sports bar during the day with over 40 TVs catching all the action. At night it's a lively dance bar.

Blue Guitar
125 E. Tahquitz Canyon Way
☎*327-1549*
The Blue Guitar is an intimate concert nightclub that presents local and international blues and jazz artists. The balcony on the second floor is perfect for people watching.

Peabody's Coffee Bar
134 S. Palm Canyon Dr.
☎*322-1877*
Peabody's Coffee Bar offers java and jazz in a comfortable lounge setting.

Shopping

Temecula

Farmers Market
Sat
Front St. and Sixth St.
☎*728-7343*
A farmers market is held each Saturday where shoppers can pick up local produce and crafts.

Chaparral Center
28465 Old Town Front St.
The Chaparral Center is a giant old-style building that is home to a number of antique stores as well as a hair salon and massage parlour.

Ol' Town Antique Faire
28601 Front St.
☎*694-8786*
The Ol' Town Antique Faire has a wonderful Old West front that houses four antique shops and a coffee bar.

Riverside

Downtown Bookstore
3582 Main St.
☎*682-1082*
The Downtown Bookstore is a family run store that has an outstanding selection of used books on two levels. Thousands of books are in perfect order on the shelves, a rarity for used book stores. It is located around the side of the building, through the arch.

Dragon Marsh
3744 Main St.
☎*276-1116*
Dragon Marsh is one of those freaky stores that's a lot of fun to look around in. They call themselves "a historical store," carrying everything from herbs and teas to artisan creations and alternative literature. They have one of the largest selections of herbs and spices in Southern California.

San Bernardino

Carousel Mall
295 Carousel Mall
☎*884-0106*
The Carousel Mall features over 100 stores plus the signature carousel for the kids.

Heritage Antique Mall
1520 S. E St.
☎*888-3377*
The Heritage Antique Mall offers an almost limitless selection of antiques and collectibles.

Redlands

Simple Elegance
19 E. Citrus St.
☎ *798-3771*
Simple Elegance is a unique shop that has both a casual clothing line and a wooden flower galley, with excellent hand crafted flowers, guaranteed not to wilt.

Sisters
21 E. Citrus St.
Sisters specializes in "antiques and home embellishments" and offers a selection of classiccal and modern home decorating ideas.

The Inland Empire and Palm Springs

Big Bear Lake

Village Mall
40729 Village Dr.
The Village Mall has a selection of specialty stores including a deli, an ice cream shop, the Big Bear Candle Company, and several clothing shops.

Wild Wings Unlimited
42656 Moonridge Rd.
☎*684-4295*
Wild Wings Unlimited is a cute shop that has everything for the amateur or professional ornithologist. They offer guidebooks, seed, birdhouses, binoculars and feeders. The owners are knowledgeable about the fowl in the area and even lead guided bird or wildflower walks.

Bear Mountain Trading Company
42646 Moonridge Rd.
☎*585-9676*
Right beside Wild Wings is the Bear Mountain Trading Company. Its wonderful smells emanate from an assortment of candies, candles, sauces, decorations, country goods and curiosities.

Leather Depot
40794 Village Dr.
☎*866-5120*
The Leather Depot sells everything you can think of made of leather, MOO!!!! They also sell skins.

Edelweiss Books
40804 Village Dr.
☎*866-7734*
Edelweiss Books is the only bookstore in town and has mainly bestsellers.

Palm Springs

Desert Walk
123 N. Canyon Dr.
☎*320-8282*
The Desert Walk shopping center features some of the most upscale fashion stores in Palm Springs including a Saks Fifth Avenue. There are also several restaurants to choose from.

Modern Way Mid-Century Furniture
Tue and Wed
by appointment only
1426 N. Palm Canyon Dr.
☎*320-5455*
Modern Way Mid-Century Furniture has everything to suit your retro and Art-Deco furnishing needs. They were also instrumental in furnishing the retro-styled Ballantine's Hotel. (see p 263)

Adagio Galleries
closed Wed and Thu
193 S. Palm Canyon Dr.
☎*320-2230*
The Adagio Galleries has a wonderful collection of Southwest, Californian, and Native American art on display and for sale.

G. Wm. Craig Bookseller
33 N. Palm Canyon Dr.
☎*323-7379*
G. Wm. Craig Bookseller is a small bookstore that deals in used but also rare and first edition books.

Dazzles
1414 N. Palm Canyon Dr.
☎*327-1446*
Dazzles sells 1950s furniture, antiques and decorations.

Natures RX
555 S. Sunrise Way
☎*323-9487*
Natures RX has a wide selection of natural and homeopathic vitamins, herbs and health food.

Outlaw Lingerie
245 S. Calm Canyon Dr.
☎*322-1675*
Outlaw Lingerie has a wide assortment of things to get a little more (or less) comfortable in.

Anza-Borrego National Park

There are not many stores in Borregos Springs. However, the few stores there are have the advantage of offering products that you will not find in San Diego, especially when it comes to literature about this impressive desert, its art (the desert seems to have inspired quite a few painters) and Native American art, which is so rich and distinctive.

Mojave National Preserve and Death Valley

T he desert parks
of California have a unique charm.

F irst-time visitors will be amazed by majestic landscapes and the incredible diversity of life in one of the world's harshest environments. Bighorn sheep, coyotes, and eagles can be spotted among the hearty cacti and fragile wildflowers. Death Valley National Park and the Mojave National Preserve consist of almost five million acres (2,023,500ha) of protected land, much of which has remained untouched for eons.

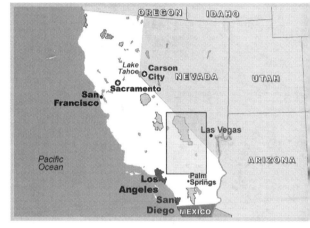

T he Mojave National Preserve is the newest addition to the California park system and lays claim to some impressive geological structures ans the world's largest Joshua tree. In addition, it is easily accessible and there are no admission fees. There is little in the Mojave in the way of touristic development, which helps to heighten its natural attractions. Death Valley is more developed and offers a wider array of tourist attractions, many of which

revolve around the valley's surreal desert vistas. Death Valley also presents a variety of environments, from the Badwater salt flats at 282ft (86m) below sea level, to the snow-covered Telescope Peak at 11,049ft (3,368m). Temperatures during the summer regularly reach well over 100°F (38°C), with a record-setting temperature of 128°F (53°C) on July 15, 1972. As a result, the majority of visitors avoid the summer months. Don't let the heat deter you, however, be-

cause the deserts of California can be a rewarding destination all year-round. Both deserts are so vast, with so many natural attractions, that visitors will be pleasantly surprised by the lack of crowds. Indeed, when you reach some of the more out of the way attractions, you'll feel like you have the entire desert to yourself.

T his chapter is divided into two tours: Tour A explores the Mojave National Preserve while Tours B explores Death

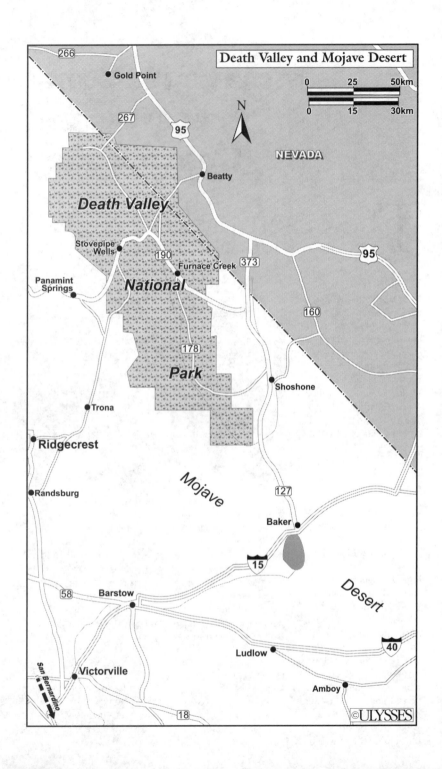

Valley. Each can be completed in a day.

Finding Your Way Around

By Car

The only way to see the Mojave National Preserve and Death Valley is by car. A four-wheel-drive vehicle is required for some of the roads that wind through these parks, but most of the major attractions can be reached by way of the paved roads, between 1 to 3mi (1.6 to 4.8km) of dirt road travel. If you plan to attempt some of the four-wheel-drive roads by car, make sure you let the rangers know where you are going, and opt for full insurance on your rental. If your car overheats in Death Valley, there are numerous radiator water stations marked on the park map. The rangers recommend that you stay with your car in the event of a breakdown.

Practical Information

Keep in mind, when planning a trip to the desert, that summer temperatures can reach over 120°F (49°C) and that facilities within Death Valley and the Mojave are extremely limited. Plan to bring at least a gallon (4l) of water person (or pet) if you plan on doing some hiking, plus extra for the car radiator, as it is common to

overheat in these temperatures. The lack of shade makes sun an important concern, so bring your sunscreen and a hat. Restroom facilities in the desert are not only rare, but of poor quality, normally just outhouses simmering under the 100°F (37.7°C) heat.

Area Codes

Mojave National Preserve and Death Valley Area: **760**
Beatty, Nevada: **775**

Tourist Information

Tour A: Mojave National Preserve

Mojave National Preserve Headquarters
222 E. Main St., Suite 202
Barstow, CA 92311
☎ **255-8800**

Mojave National Preserve/ Death Valley Information Center
72157 Baker Blvd./ P.O. Box 241
Baker, CA 92309
MOJA_Baker_Interp@nps.gov

Baker Information Center
☎ **733-4040**

Needles Information Center
☎ **326-6322**

Hole-in-the-Wall Ranger Station
☎ **928-2572**

Tours B: Death Valley

Death Valley National Park

Furnace Creek Visitor Center
Death Valley, CA 92328
☎ **786-2331**
www.nps.gov/deva

Mojave National Preserve/ Death Valley Information Center
72157 Baker Blvd./ P.O. Box 241
Baker, CA 92309
MOJA_Baker_Interp@nps.gov

Exploring

Tour A: Mojave National Preserve

Three of North America's four deserts—the Sonoran, Great Basin and Mojave—meet to form the Mojave National Preserve. The preserve was created on October 21, 1994, protecting 1.6 million acres (647497ha) of sand dunes, volcanic cinder cones and mountain-top forests. Far from being a desolate pile of sand, this rugged territory is home to nearly 300 species of animals including coyotes, desert bighorn sheep and the protected desert tortoise. The fauna is equally diverse, ranging from the hardy creosote bush to Joshua trees and, when conditions are just right, a rainbow of wildflowers. Within the park there are also numerous abandoned and still-active mines as well as a few ghost towns. Many of these, however, are only accessible by four-wheel-drive. Admission to the preserve is free, and it is open 24hrs. The only completely paved roads running through Mojave are the Kilbaker Road, Morningstar Mine Road, Kelso-Cima Road and Cima Road. Other roads throughout the preserve range from gravel and graded dirt to those passable by four-wheel-drive

Mojave National Preserve, Death Valley

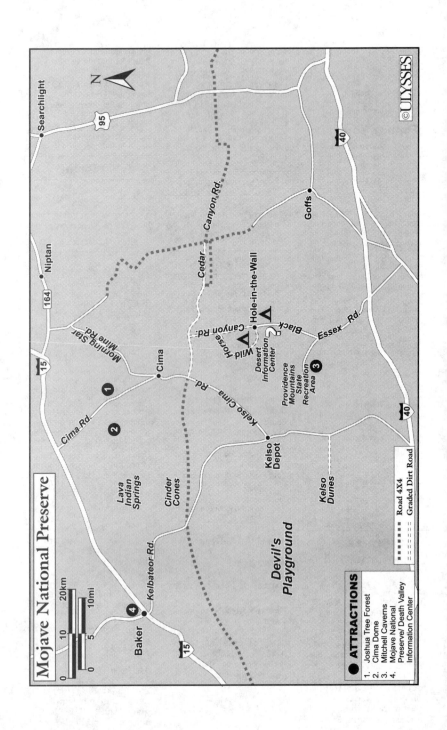

Mojave National Preserve

Searchlight

95

Niptan

164

15

Cima Rd.

Morning Star Mine Rd.

Cima

①

②

Lava Indian Springs

Cinder Cones

Kelbateor Rd.

Baker

④

15

20km

10mi

0   10

0   5

Devil's Playground

Kelso Cima Rd.

Kelso Depot

Kelso Dunes

Cedar Canyon Rd.

Wild Horse Canyon Rd.

Hole-in-the-Wall

Desert Information Center

Providence Mountains State Recreation Area

③

Black

Essex Rd.

Goffs

40

40

N

© ULYSSES

● **ATTRACTIONS**

Road 4X4
Graded Dirt Road

1. Joshua Tree Forest
2. Cima Dome
3. Mitchell Caverns
4. Mojave National Preserve/ Death Valley Information Center

only. Pick up a map at the Baker ranger station, which outlines road conditions, before entering the Mojave.

The Mojave Preserve is bordered on the north by Highway I-15 and to the south by Highway I-40. The driving tour starts at Baker, where you should pick up any supplies before getting underway.

An essential stop before entering the Mojave is the **Mojave Desert Information Center** (*Everyday 9am to 5pm; 72157 Baker Blvd., Baker, ☎ 733-4040; www.nps.gov/moja*). Here you can pick up a free map and browse the many books available on the region. The centre also has information on Death Valley. Helpful rangers can give you information on area accommodations and out of the way sites within the parks. A few small exhibits feature the area's wildlife, and a variety of movies are shown in the small theatre. Stop a moment to marvel at the world's largest thermometer right in front of the visitor centre.

Take Kelbaker Road south from Baker to Aiken Mine Road.

The first attraction you will find in the Mojave is the lunar-like landscape of the **Cinder Cones** ★★, 18mi (29km) from Baker. More than 30 young volcanic cones sit among the black basalt lava flows. The cones are the product of low-pressure eruptions that allowed the lava to solidify almost instantly as recently as 1000 years ago. Aiken Mine Road is a rough, graded dirt road, but is passable by car if you take it slowly. It is approximately 3mi (5km) to the heart of the cinder cones.

Head South on Kelbaker Road, 18mi (29km) to Kelso Depot.

The Spanish-style **Kelso Depot** is all that remains of the small town of Kelso that once served as a stop between Los Angeles and Salt Lake city. Built in 1924 by the Union Pacific Railroad, this depot is one of only two left in existence. The building once served as overnight accommodations for the railroad employees, a telegraph office, and a waiting room for passengers. It was later converted to a restaurant and community centre nicknamed the "Beanery" by the 2,000 residents that lived here in the 1940s. With the advent of the diesel engine, the demand for the water supplied by this depot dwindled, the population likewise dwindled down to nothing, and it was closed in 1985. Some remnants of the town can still be found.

Continue South 7mi (11km) to Kelso Dunes.

To reach **Kelso Dunes** ★★★, take the gravel turnoff marked Kelso Dunes parking. From here it is 4mi (6km) to the dune site. You'll have no problem finding the dunes, as they rise 700ft (233m) from the desert floor and cover 45 sq mi (117km²). Rose quartz particles in the sand are responsible for the incredible golden colour of the dunes. A popular activity here is to cause sand slides, as the sand makes a peculiar, low frequency "booming" sound when it slides (see box). A hike to the top of the dunes is rewarded by a view of the Mojave Desert and the Devil's Playground expanse of sand to the northwest. The round trip hike

from the parking lot takes approximately 2hrs. Though most of the dune occupants are nocturnal, this is a good spot to see some lizards, birds and wildflowers in the late spring.

From Kelso Dunes, backtrack up to Kelso Depot and turn on Kelso-Cima Road. Continue for 14mi (22km). Turn right on Cedar Canyon Road for 4mi (6km) then head south on Black Canyon Road for 7mi (11km). Alternatively, you can take Wild Horse Pass to circumvent part of Black Canyon Road, which makes for an exciting drive among the mesas and canyons in the area. This road, however, is in worse condition than Black Canyon Road.

Getting to Hole-in-the-Wall and the Mitchell Caverns involves negotiating the 11mi (18km) of graded dirt roads by way of Cedar Canyon Road and Black Canyon Road. Drive slowly and admire the beautiful mountains, vistas and fauna along the way. When you reach pavement once again, you will have found Hole-in-the-Wall.

The unusual rock formations at **Hole-in-the-Wall** ★★ were formed over millions of years as eruptions spewed layer upon layer of lava and ash over the area. Due to uneven cooling and gasses trapped within the rock, numerous holes were formed in the rock. Wind and rain erosion has expanded these holes into the great caverns that are found today. The wonderful reddish colour in the caverns' volcanic walls is due to their high iron content. Climbing the rock walls is not advised as the rock is very porous and brittle. Some areas, however, have metal rings attached to the walls to

Mojave National Preserve, Death Valley

Singing Sands

The Kelso Dunes were formed over the past 10,000 to 20,000 years from particles of ancient mountains, eroded and transported by wind and the Mojave River. The particles were originally deposited at the river delta, which became dry and dusty as the climate changed. Prevailing winds from the west picked up the dry, portable grains and carried them along a 35mi (57km) path, creating a vast sand sea called the Devil's Playground. Eventually, the westerly winds were confronted by winds from the north and east. The windborne sand grains tumbled down and piled up to form the Kelso Dunes. The dunes are dynamic, constantly moving a few feet back and forth, but remaining in relatively the same location due to the duelling winds. The various wind-shaped patterns on the dunes are called *eolian* (also *aeolian*) after Aeolus, the mythical Greek ruler of the winds.

When the sand slides, the dunes are known to "sing" as the grains rub against each other resulting in characteristic loud, deep tones. This is a rare phenomenon that occurs only in certain places on the planet. You can hear the sounds from up to 1mi (1.6km) away, and even feel them due to their low frequency. This phenomenon has to do with the unique shape of the grains of sand, having been altered in their long travels by wind and water.

1:30pm, 3pm; reduced summer hours; ☎805-942-0662 or 928-2586). Tours of this underground limestone world last 1.5hrs and a 1.5mi (2.4km) hike is required to reach the caverns. Inside, visitors enter another world, with impressive stalactites, stalagmites, cavern coral and flowstone. Stairs, railings and lighting make for a safe experience. Jack Mitchell was the first spelunker to descend into these depths and his signature still survives on a wall in the "Dog Leg Room," dated July 1, 1931. Reservations can be made, but take two to three weeks to process and are subject to a $2 fee.

Return north on Black Canyon Road to Cedar Canyon Road (you may want to take Wild Horse Pass on the return) and turn left to find the Kelso-Cima Road. Turn right and head north 5mi (8km) to Cima. Turn left and follow Cima Road to the Cima Dome.

The drive along Cima Road is spectacular. As the road begins to rise, Joshua trees start to line the sides, gradually becoming the world's largest **Joshua tree forest ★★★** with over two million trees covering 48,000 acres (19,425ha). These beautiful trees are actually part of the lily family, making these the world's largest flowers. The trunk is not wood, but a spongy material where the plant stores water. The trees are so named because their outlines reminded early settlers of the biblical story of Joshua holding out his hands while the sun stood still.

The attraction here is easily missed due, surprisingly, to its immense size.

allow you to descend into some of these "holes". Hiking is popular here (see p 285) and the picnic area makes for a good rest stop before continuing on. Camping facilities are also available (see p 286).

The **Desert Information Centre ★** *(Tue to Fri 10am to 2pm; Sat and Sun 8am to 4pm; closed Mon; ☎928-2572)* at Hole-in-the-Wall sells books and postcards and offers advice on where to visit in the park. This is also the only source of potable water in the park, so refill your containers.

Travelling south 10mi (16km) will bring you to Essex Road. Turn right to the Providence Mountains State Recreation Area and Mitchell Caverns (5mi or 8km).

The **Providence Mountains State Recreation Area ★★** is open for camping, hiking and picnicing year-round. The highlight of this area, however, is are the **Mitchell Caverns ★★★** *(weekdays 1:30pm; weekends 10am,*

The **Cima Dome** is the largest round rock structure in the Western Hemisphere, covering over 75 sq mi (194km^2). The symmetrical dome shape was created by enormous amounts of magma rising to the surface, but without enough force to explode as a volcano. Over the millennia, wind and rain eroded the quartz monzonite that covers the rock, exposing the near-perfect dome. While the dome may be a geological marvel, the main attraction in this area is the forest that surrounds it. The Teutonia Peak trail is a 4mi (6.4km) round-trip hike through the Joshua tree forest.

Joshua tree

Cima Road continues north out of the park to Highway 40, 24mi (37km) east of Baker.

★★★

Tour B: Death Valley

Death Valley is painted with a masterful palette of red, gold, green and brown under a beautiful sky of blue. Heat shimmers off the desert floor as you descend out of the mountains and down into its depths. The attraction here is the complete nothingness, the utterly alien and inhospitable landscape in a world so full of life. When you take a closer look, and have a little patience, you will find that Death Valley isn't so dead after all. In the spring especially, visitors will discover desert wildflowers, eagles, lizards, coyotes and other hearty wildlife. Death Valley was proclaimed a national monument by President

Herbert Hoover on February 11, 1933. There is plenty to explore in the park, and wonderful vistas to be seen. Some of the more remote regions can only be reached by four-wheel-drive, though everything in this tour can be done in an economy rental car. Check with the ranger station for road conditions. Entrance to the park is $15 for a seven-day pass, which is payable at any of the ranger stations throughout the park. Keep your receipt, as it will be checked at various locations.

Panamint Springs to Wildrose

The driving tour starts at Panamint Springs, which can be reached by taking Interstate 395 to Highway 190 or by taking Highway 178 to Panamint Valley Road.

Panamint Springs (pop. 18) is a place where the road widens just enough for a hotel, restaurant and campground. This is also a good place to top off your tank before heading deeper into the valley. The Panamint Springs Motel was built in 1937 by the niece of Buffalo Bill Cody, while the restaurant (see p 288) offers the best food

in the valley. From the restaurant patio, visitors can watch the airplanes from China Lake Air Force Base (an experimental flight facility) fly by. The planes sometimes swoop down low, close to the desert floor, raising huge dust clouds in their wake.

Head east on Highway 190.

Emigrant is the next destination on the Death Valley map, but it is really only an average view from the 2,100ft (700m) elevation. There is also a picnic area, a phone and a seasonal campground.

Turning right at Emigrant leads to Wildrose, a 42mi (67.6km) round-trip. This detour is recommended only if you have extra time. The drive is enjoyable, and the high country is decidedly different than the lower desert.

As you rise up out of the valley through **Emigrant Canyon** ★, the countryside takes on a new look. The desert springs to life as you rise in elevation and the ground turns green as bushes grow closer together, taking advantage of the increased rainfall in this region.

The first turnoff to the **Skidoo** townsite can easily be ignored, as all that remains now of the town of 700 is an interpretive sign, reached after a tough drive on a high-clearance, four-wheel-drive road. This was, however, the site of the largest producing gold mine in Death Valley in the early 1900s.

About 14mi (22km) from the Emigrant Intersection you will come upon the first turnoff that leads to **Aguereberry Point**. Along

Mojave National Preserve, Death Valley

this rough dirt road is the Harrisburg townsite, an abandoned mine and, of course, Aguereberry Point. Just before you reach the mine, you will find the **Harrisburg townsite** on the right hand side, where three decrepit structures are still standing. This site was home to a tent city and a population of 300 after Shorty Harris struck gold in 1905. Pete Aguereberry, one of the original strike finders, was later awarded the rights to the Eureka mine and worked it for the next 40 years. Pete's original cabin is the first of the three surviving structures, built in 1907, where he lived until his death in 1945. The **Eureka Gold Mine ★★★** can be found just beyond the town site, and the entrance still has narrow-gauge tracks coming out of it. The entrance is sealed in the winter to protect the bat habitat inside. During summer, however, visitors can enter the mine as the walls have been stabilized. Bring a flashlight if you plan on exploring. Next to the mine are the remnants of a storage building and the Cashier Mill, a large wooden structure that was used in processing the ore. Be careful of shafts and adits, most are covered, but some are not.

Aguereberry Point ★★ (6,422ft or 1,961m) is about 4mi (6km) further along a rough, narrow road. The view at the end is spectacular, but is comparable to **Dantes View** (see p 284) which is much easier to get to. The advantage here is that very few people make this journey, so you may have the view all to yourself.

Follow the paved road through Wildrose to the Charcoal Kilns.

The **Charcoal Kilns** are a series of interesting conical kilns that were built over 100 years ago to smelt ores from the surrounding mines. The kilns are surrounded by a beautiful section of pinyon pine and juniper woodland and also mark the trail to Wildrose Peak (9,064ft or 2,763m, see p 285). However, unless you are here for the hike, the kilns are hardly worth the detour.

Return to the Emigrant Junction and continue north to the Mosaic Canyon road. Turn right to reach Stovepipe Wells.

★★
Stovepipe Wells to Scotty's Castle

This tour starts at Stovepipe Wells Village. Take the turnoff to Mosaic Canyon 0.25mi (400m) west of the village.

Mosaic Canyon ★★★ is considered a geologic "outdoor museum." A 2mi (3.2km) gravel road rises 1,000ft (333m) from Highway 190 to the parking area. A 2mi (3.2km) hike through the canyon ends at a dry waterfall. The marble walls of the canyon have been polished and smoothed by centuries of running water and flash floods. The canyon gets its name from the fragments of colourful rock that give the canyon its unique look. Some visitors are lucky enough to spot one of the occasional bighorn sheep that call this area home.

Stovepipe Wells Village is the one place to stop for gas, food, some desert souve-

nirs and maybe a night's stay. There is also a campground available for pitching your tent of parking your RV. The main attraction is the hotel, and the chance to pick up some supplies before heading back out into the desert.

Just north of Stovepipe Wells, turn left (north) off the pavement onto the unpaved road heading to the sand dunes.

The golden sand of the **Death Valley Dunes ★★** is continually being re-sculptured by the wind and occasional flash flood. Take a moment to examine the distinctively different shapes created by the wind. The winds blowing through the valley are blocked by the towering Tucki Mountains and cannot carry their sand any further; their load of wind-swept sand is therefore deposited in this small area. Complex wind patterns have created three distinct types of dunes here: crescent, linear and star shaped. The crescent and linear are formed by winds blowing in predominantly one direction while the star-shaped dunes are caused by winds blowing from a variety of directions. Hardy mesquite trees dot the dunes, providing stable habitats for wildlife.

Old Stovepipe Well is the only watering hole in the sand dune area of Death Valley, and originally sat at the junction of two trails originally forged by aboriginals. During the bonanza days of Rhyolite and Skidoo it was the only water source on the cross valley road, and, when sand obscured the site, a length of stovepipe was inserted as a marker, hence the town's name.

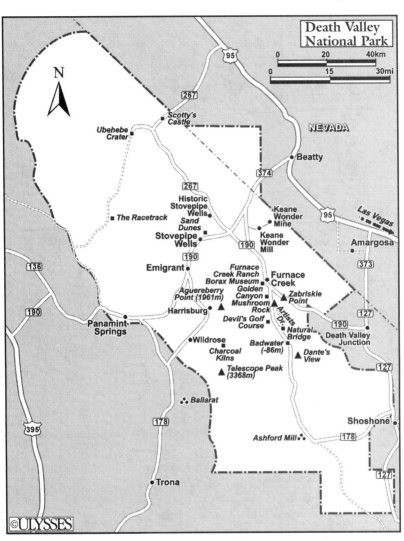

Death Valley National Park

Mojave National Pre-
serve, Death Valley

*After Old Stovepipe Well, con-
tinue north to rejoin the pavement.*

Heading north you will
reach Titus Canyon after
14mi (23km) and Scotty's
castle and the Ubehebe
Crater after 33mi (53km).

Driving through **Titus Canyon ★★** is like taking a
trip back through time, as
evidenced by the exposed
layers of sedimentary rock.

The colourful rock depos-
its in this area contain
fossil beds 30-35 million
years old. One such fossil
unearthed was the skull of
the huge, rhino-like
titanothere, which was excavated in the canyon of
the same name in 1933.
The **Leadfield** ghost town
can be found within Titus
Canyon, though it is now
only a collection of abandoned mines and shacks.
Klare Spring is a small wa-

ter source that supports a
handful of bighorn sheep.
Native Americans came
here to hunt and have left
behind petroglyphs in the
rock. A small dirt road off
Highway 190 leads to the
mouth of the canyon,
where you start hiking
further into the canyon. If
you have sufficient ground
clearance (economy rental
cars need not apply), you
can take the full, one-way
loop from Highway 374. If

you plan on taking the loop, check with the ranger station to ensure that your vehicle and the road conditions are satisfactory.

Continue north and bear left at Grapevine to reach Ubehebe Crater.

Thousands of years ago, rising magma came into contact with shallow groundwater, turning it instantly to steam. This process creates what is known as a Maar volcano. The energy produced was more powerful than a nuclear blast and created the spectacular **Ubehebe Crater** ★★★ with its beautifully coloured rock strata. The blast scattered debris over 6 sq mi (15km²) and up to 150ft (50m) deep in places. Most of the surrounding area is the surreal black remnants of volcanic material expelled 3,000 years ago. The crater is about 500ft (152m) deep and approximately 0.5mi (0.8km) wide from rim to rim. The wind at the top of the crater can be quite strong at times. Visitors can easily walk down the trail to the bottom of the crater—getting back is more of a challenge. Walk around the rim to the west from the parking area to find **Little Hebe** and a few other small craters.

Return down the road and turn left at the fork in the road towards Scotty's Castle.

The towers of **Scotty's Castle** ★★ (*$8, various times for tours*) look oddly out of place after seeing so much of nothing. Originally built by Albert Johnson in the late 1920s, desert rat Death Valley Scotty was able to convince the public it was his, and took possession of it (see box). Tours last 50min, though there can be a wait of up to 2hr on the weekends. Buy your tickets as soon as you arrive and walk around the grounds, as there is plenty to see. The castle itself is an amazing sight and extremely well preserved, while inside the furnishings, books and decor are completely original, circa 1939. Check out the exhibits next to the castle and grab a bite to eat while you are waiting. While exploring the grounds you will see a natural spring that has created a mini-oasis of grass, Joshua trees and palms. The stable in the back is home to some old vehicles, from an 1890s stagecoach to a 1936 Dodge. The bookstore, gift shop, snack bar and gas pump are open from 9am to 5pm.

Death Valley Scotty

Walter Scott (a.k.a. Death Valley Scotty) is the valley's most famous legend. Born in 1872 in Kentucky, he eventually worked his way west. In 1890, he was discovered by a talent scout for Buffalo Bill Cody, and would spend the next 12 years travelling the world as a cowboy in the Wild West show. By 1902, Scotty had returned to the valley and began his gold-prospecting career. It's unclear whether Scotty ever did strike gold, though he convinced several prominent businessmen that all he needed were the funds necessary to extract his fortune from the earth. Chicago insurance magnate Albert Johnson was one of Scotty's principal sponsors. After investing thousands of dollars and getting nothing but excuses from Scotty, he decided to make the trip to Death Valley and check on his investment. Though Johnson never saw any gold on that or any other visit to Death Valley, the climate did wonders for his health, and he and Scotty became great friends.

Over the next ten winters, Johnson often returned to Death Valley, eventually deciding to build a more permanent vacation home. Scotty, the perpetual story-teller, began to circulate word that the immense castle under construction was his, built from the profits of his lucrative gold mine. Johnson did nothing to dispel these rumours and reporters from around the country ran stories about the castle of one of the world's richest gold miners. Scotty lived his last few years in the castle and is now buried on the hill overlooking the same structure that bears his name.

Scotty's Castle

*If you aren't staying in Stovepipe Wells or Furnace Creek, you may want to consider staying in **Beatty, Nevada**, which is south on Highway 190 and then east on Highway 374, 62mi (100km) from Scotty's Castle.*

★★★
Beatty to Dantes View

This tour starts in Beatty, Nevada.

Many visitors to Death Valley choose to stay in the small town of **Beatty, Nevada ★**, as it lies just 10mi (16km) from the park limits and 19mi (31km) from Hell's Gate. In addition to plentiful budget accommodations, Beatty has several casinos, a few restaurants and inexpensive gasoline. See the hotel and restaurant listings at the end of this chapter. This is also an excellent home base to explore the park.

The **Rhyolite Ghost Town ★★** can be found 4mi (6km) southwest of Beatty off Highway 374. From 1905 to 1911 this was the largest town in the Death Valley area with a population of almost 10,000. The town had 50 saloons, two churches, a stock exchange, an opera house and two undertakers. Today the town is in ruins, but makes for an interesting stop due to its easy access from the highway. The Bottle House is famous, constructed almost entirely of multi-coloured bottles. The remains of the train depot, three storey bank and the jail are also worth a look.

Two miles (3.2km) past the Rhyolite turnoff is the turnoff for the Titus Canyon road. High clearance is recommended.

Descending down through Daylight Pass, the road winds it's way down to **Hell's Gate ★**. This fork in the road has a small, self-serve information kiosk and fantastic panoramic views of the valley. This is a great place to watch the sun rise and set.

Turn left at Hell's Gate on the Beatty Cutoff towards the Keane Wonder Mine and Mill.

The **Keane Wonder Mine and Mill ★** was one of the largest-producing gold mines in Death Valley with over $1 million worth of ore extracted during its operation. Jack Keane and Domingo Etcharren struck the gold vein in December 1903, Keane's first strike in eight years of prospecting. They dubbed it the "Wonder" mine and were soon rich beyond their dreams, expanding their empire to 22 claims on 240 acres (97ha) of land. The ruins of an old aerial tramway that operated by gravity are still visible. Carts filled with ore would make the 4,700ft (1,432m) journey down the hill, carrying the empty carts back up. There is a trail up to the main mine complex, along the tramway.

Continue down the Beatty Cutoff to Highway 190.

The **Old Harmony Borax Works ★★** can be found just before entering the tiny town of Furnace Creek and a sign marks the short road up to the site. Borax was discovered in 1881 in the marshlands of Mustard Canyon, which takes its name from the distinctive mustard-yellow hills nearby. The works were built in 1882 and the work of collecting the ore (called "cottonballing") was done by Chinese workmen. Processed Borax was hauled by a 20-mule train 165mi (266km) to the railroad at Mojave. On the site there is a short interpretive trail that winds around the ruins of the old buildings and partially restored equipment. There is also a short hike to the site where the ore was collected. The Borax works is in Mustard Canyon.

Furnace Creek ★★ is a true oasis in the heart of Death Valley, as the scrub and sand gives way to palm trees and grass. This is the hub of the action in the valley, but it gets very busy on the weekends, so if you plan on staying at one of the two hotels here, make your reservations months in advance (see p 288). Golfing is also available at Furnace Creek if you are brave enough to face the scorching temperatures. At 214ft (71m) below sea level, these are the lowest 18-holes in the world.

Mine Hazards

Hundreds of abandoned mines can be found throughout Death Valley. While they may seem like an opportunity for adventure, they are extremely dangerous. Most of the entrances have been closed off, but some remain open. When exploring around these sites, be especially careful if you're with children. The ground surrounding the mines hides numerous open shafts, prospect holes and adits, which may be hidden by overgrowth. Occasionally, forgotten caches of explosives can also be found, and these should be reported to the park rangers.

At the **Visitor Center/ Death Valley Museum ★★** in Furnace Creek you can pay the park fee (*$10/car for 7 days*) and also get information on the history, climate, and wildlife in the park. Make sure to pick up the free map of the valley. The centre also has an extensive set of exhibits with information and artifacts, as well as a large model of the entire valley. Fantastic guides will enthusiastically answer any questions you have. An orientation slide show is presented every half hour.

The **Borax Museum ★** (☎783-2345 x.215) has everything you ever wanted to know about borax—plus they have a nice selection of other minerals that can be found in Death Valley. The mining tools and artifacts display presents equipment dating back to the late 1800s. Pick up a few samples in the small gift shop. Most of the museum is outside, behind the main building where a selection of mining machinery is on display.

The **general store** in Furnace Creek is a great place to stock up on souvenirs, sundries and clothing. There is also a small **post office** where you can mail postcards home with the Death Valley postmark.

Dating back to the late 1920s, **The Furnace Creek Inn ★** is about 1mi (1.6km) down the road from the town of Furnace creek, set into the hillside with panoramic views of the valley below. Intricate stonework, and old-fashioned elegance make this inn worth a visit. A series of tunnels run throughout the property, and can get confusing at times, but add to the charm. Wonderful lounging nooks in the lobby and elsewhere are perfect for a welcome drink and a chance to appreciate the landscape.

Right next to the Furnace Creek Inn is a marker commemorating the **Death Valley 49ers**. This famous group of emigrants from Salt Lake City, Utah, travelled through a nearby mountain pass, following what they thought was a short cut to the gold fields of central California. They entered in December, 1849 and suffered from thirst and starvation while making the trip, though only one person perished. Local legend maintains that one of the members of the party turned back and said "good-bye Death Valley," thereby giving the area its name.

Follow Highway 190 en route to Zabriskie Point.

Zabriskie Point ★★★ is a stunning location in Death Valley, and one of the most popular lookouts. Atop a small mesa, visitors will marvel at the rainbow of colours in the erosion-sculpted rolling hills that surround the lookout on all sides. The 360-degree panorama is absolutely breathtaking. This is an excellent spot to watch the sunset in Death Valley.

Just after Zabriskie Point is the entrance to **Twenty Mule Team Canyon**. This is a beautiful drive among the weathered and multi-coloured cliffs and can be done in an ordinary car, but drive slowly due to the rough road. The road is one-way, so if you intend on driving it, take on the way to Dantes View.

Approximately 3mi (5km) past the exit of Twenty Mule Team Canyon is the cutoff to Dantes View on the right.

Dantes View ★★ sits at an elevation of 5,475ft (1,669m) and offers a birds-eye view of the valley below. From this point you can see the salt flats, badlands and the endless miles of rolling, colourful hills. Walk down along the ridge for some quiet contemplation while enjoying the fantastic views. Note that motor homes are not allowed to the summit of Dantes View due to the narrow road.

Return to Furnace Creek and turn left onto Highway 178 towards Badwater. On the way to Badwater you will pass the entrance to Artist's Canyon. This is a great drive but one-way in the opposite direction and best taken on the way back.

The **Devil's Golf Course** is interesting if you are a geologist or have some extra time. This protected salt bed features crystallized salts which form jagged formations with a strange, unearthly appearance. Salt continues to be deposited by recurring floods that occasionally submerge this region that sits below sea level. Some delicate conical salt formations are hidden among the jagged formations, but they are located further back, out of reach of all but the most curious.

Badwater ★ has the distinction of being the lowest point in the western hemisphere with an elevation of 282ft (94m) below sea level. Unless there has been a recent rain or flooding, there will be little water to be seen, but the salt flats themselves are worth a look, as is the view to be had by walking a little into the valley. If there is any water, however, the still surface perfectly reflects the snow capped Telescope Moun-

tain in the distance. The hike, out from Badwater to the salt flats is approximately 0.5mi (0.8km).

Everything in **Shoshone** (pop. 71) is owned by one person—the hotel, restaurant, everything...

Outdoor Activities

Hiking

Tour A: Mojave National Preserve

The Teutonia Peak Trail can be found 6mi (10km) north of Cima on Cima Road. The 4mi (6.4km) round-trip trail winds through a scenic Joshuatree forest strewn with granite boulders.

Bighorn sheep

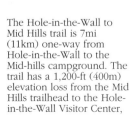

The Hole-in-the-Wall to Mid Hills trail is 7mi (11km) one-way from Hole-in-the-Wall to the Mid-hills campground. The trail has a 1,200-ft (400m) elevation loss from the Mid Hills trailhead to the Hole-in-the-Wall Visitor Center,

so if you like hiking downhill start at Mid Hills. The trail requires some bouldering and climbing down metal rings set into the rock, and is recommended for experienced hikers only.

Tour B: Death Valley

Hiking is the most popular activity in Death Valley. To fully explore many of the desert attractions, a short hike is required. The Furnace Creek Visitor Center has numerous handouts and maps that outline a variety of excursions for both the novice or experienced hiker. **Titus Canyon** (see p 281) provides an excellent variety of hiking possibilities from a short hike through the Narrows to the challenging climb up Thimble Peak (6,381ft or 2,127m).

Another popular hike leaves from the charcoal kilns at Wildrose to **Wildrose Peak** (9,604ft or 2763m). This is a moderately strenuous hike with an elevation gain of 2,000ft (666m) over 4.2mi (6.7km) one-way. During the winter months the trails near the peak can be snow covered.

Highly recommended is the hike through **Mosaic Canyon** (see p 280). This great 2mi (3.2km) hike winds through the polished marble walls of the canyon and ends at a dry waterfall.

Spelunking

Tour A: Mojave National Preserve

Guided tours are offered by the park rangers at Mitchell Caverns.

Mojave National Preserve, Death Valley

Four-Wheel-Drive Touring

Tour A: Mojave National Preserve

For those with four-wheel drive, there is a whole other world waiting to be explored. The **historic Mojave Road** runs east-west through the length of the preserve. It was originally part of a trail that connected the military barracks in Wilmington, California with the new town of Prescott, Arizona. The going can be quite slow at times and can test the skills of even an experienced off-roader, but it provides a great opportunity to see the remote and pristine parts of the reserve. The route is featured on the official map of the preserve and the park rangers can give up-to-the-minute tips on the road conditions.

Tour B: Death Valley

Death Valley also has numerous four-wheel-drive roads that wind through the park. Some of the attractions, such as the **Racetrack** are only accessible this way. Check with the park rangers for road conditions and maps.

Golf

Tour B: Death Valley

Furnace Creek Golf Course
$50
☎786-2301
The Furnace Creek Golf Course is the only place to golf in the area. At 214ft (71m) below sea level, it is also the lowest golf course in the world. The 18 holes set in rolling, green grass look rather out-of-place, but the surrounding landscape is beautiful. Cart rental is $20 and indispensable in the desert heat.

Horseback Riding

Tour B: Death Valley

Furnace Creek Stables
☎786-3339
The Furnace Creek Stables organizes moonlight horseback riding in Death Valley with experienced desert guides. Hayrides and day tours are also available.

Accommodations

Baker

Wills Fargo
$$
≡, *tv*, ≈
72252 Baker Blvd.
☎733-4477
⇌733-4680
In the tiny town of Baker, this small hotel lies just off the Highway. Rooms are larger, but rather bare in the new section. You can save $10 if you get one of their older rooms, which have a shower only, and are a little smaller, but of the same quality.

Gambel Quail

The Bun Boy Motel
$$
≡, *tv*, ≈, ℜ
72155 Baker Blvd.
☎733-4363
⇌733-4365
The Bun Boy looks more like a rest stop on the highway than a motel. It is popular, however, and shares a pool with the Wills Fargo, a block down the road. The rooms are clean but basic with showers only.

Hole-in-the-Wall

Two campgrounds are located at Hole-in-the-Wall; the main campground *($10 per night)* is on a first-come, first-served basis and the Equestrian & Group Campground is available by reservation. *($20 per night;* ☎733-4040). Both campgrounds are well maintained with running water and toilet facilities. Camping is also allowed on the roadside throughout the park and at Providence Mountain.

Death Valley

Panamint Springs to Wildrose

Camping is available at the **Panamint Springs Resort** *(*☎482-7680, ⇌775-482-7682)* for $10/night with a tent or $20/night for a recreational vehicle with hookup. Both **Emigrant** and **Wildrose** offer free tent camping and are open year round on a first-come, first-served basis. Emigrant doesn't allow fires but has flush toilets, while Wildrose allows fires but offers only pit toilets.

Panamint Springs

Panamint Springs Resort
$$
≡, ℜ
☎482-7680
↝(775) 482-7682
This charming motel was
built in 1937 by the niece
of Buffalo Bill Cody. The
old wooden exterior of the
rooms has been retained,
but the interiors have been
remodeled. Escape from
the world in one these
comfortable rooms which
mercifully lack tv's and
telephones. As a result, the
large porch becomes an
international meeting place
at night, jammed with a
friendly collection of the
motel's guests. This is a
truly different type of ho-
tel, with all the electricity
being supplied by genera-
tor only. Also available is a
two-bedroom cottage
(with a TV), for $130. The
owner, Jerry Graham is the
man to see for information
on the valley.

Stovepipe Wells Village to Scotty's Castle

Camping is available year
round at Mesquite Spring,
just south of the Grapevine
junction. Thirty sites are
available for $10/night.
Fires are allowed, and the
flush toilets are a bonus.

Stovepipe Wells Village

Stovepipe Wells Village
$$
≡, tv, ≈, ℜ
☎786-2387
↝786-2389
The rooms vary as to size
and furnishings so you
may want to look at one
first. Some have TV, some
do not. All rooms, how-
ever are comfortable and
clean and arranged in a
motel-like fashion. They
have their own dining
room (7am to 2pm, 6:30pm

to 10pm), and saloon
(4:30pm on). Their pool is
usually quite busy. It's the
only place to stay in
Stovepipe.

Beatty to Dante's View

Camping is available year
round at Furnace Creek for
$16/night. The facilities are
well developed and the
campground is adjacent to
Furnace Creek Village. The
Texas Spring campground
is open October to April at
a cost of $12 and is a
much smaller area. Both
campgrounds allow fires
and provide flush toilets.
Reservations can be made
up to five months in ad-
vance (☎800-365-2267;
reservations.nps.gov).

Beatty, Nevada

**The Stagecoach Hotel and
Casino**
$
≡, tv, ≈, ℜ
Hwy 95
☎(775) 553-2419
☎800-4-BIGWIN
↝(775) 553-9054
The Stagecoach has large
rooms that are clean but
generic. Get one of the
upgraded rooms for an
extra $5 as they include a
fridge and have been re-
cently renovated. The ca-
sino has craps, blackjack
and slots and the restau-
rant is open 24 hrs. Very
friendly service.

**The Exchange Club Motel &
Casino**
$$
≡, tv, ℜ
119 Main St.
☎(775) 553-2333
☎888-561-2333
↝(775) 553-9348
The Exchange Club has
average rooms that have a
little more style than the
Stagecoach. The building
itself dates back to 1906,
built during the prosper-

ous gold rush days. All
rooms feature a full bath
and fridge. Try their exec-
utive rooms with a hot tub
for $68. The casino is
smaller than that of the
Stagecoach and has only
one blackjack table.

Shoshone

Shoshone Inn
$$
≡
☎852-4335
↝852-4107
The tiny town of Shoshone
lies just outside of the park
limits to the east along
Highway 190. The Sho-
shone Inn features a warm
spring-fed pool that stays
at 85-90°F (29-32°C) year-
round. Basic rooms feature
showers only and kitchen-
ettes are available. Check
out the caves nearby
where, up until a few
years ago, miners used to
live.

Death Valley Junction

**Amargosa Opera House and
Hotel**
$$
☎852-4441
↝852-4138
amargosa@kay-net.com
These rustic rooms provide
only the bare essentials, in
a beautiful old adobe
building built in 1923.
Across the road is the Op-
era House where Marta
Becket performs her desert
skits and ballets. Some
rooms have only baths,
others only showers. The
nearest food is 7mi (11km)
away at the Longstreet
Casino in Nevada.

Longstreet Inn & Casino
$$
≡, ≈, ⊛, ℜ
Hwy 373 at State Line
☎(775) 372-1777
↝(775) 372-1280
The Longstreet is just over
the border in Nevada, a
few minutes' drive from
Death Valley Junction

**Mojave National Pre-
serve, Death Valley**

Hedgehog cactus

along Highway 127. Rooms are a much better value than the nearby California options. The rooms are clean and neat, with patios on the pond and rooms facing the mountains. King suites feature a fireplace. Also on site is an RV park *($16/night)* with full-service hookups. The casino features blackjack from Thursday to Saturday and the steakhouse is open on Saturdays only. The regular restaurant serving typical American fare is open daily.

Furnace Creek

The Furnace Creek Ranch
$$$
≡, *tv*, ≈, ℜ
☎786-2345 or 800-236-7916
⇌786-2514
www.furnacecreekresort.com
The ranch is part of the same company as the inn, but offers less expensive accommodations. Rooms range from the wooden cabins with shower only, to the main building with more expensive, better appointed rooms with bathtubs and fridges. All rooms are clean and neat, with comfortable beds. Golf packages are available on their 18-hole course. Other amenities include a pool, tennis

courts, a children's playground and a large grassy lawn.

Furnace Creek Inn
$$$$$
≡, *tv*, ℜ
☎786-2345 or 800-236-7916
⇌786-2514
www.furnacecreekresort.com
The more upscale Furnace creek Inn is about 0.5mi (0.8km) down the road from the town of Furnace Creek. The historic building is was built in 1927 and features great stonework and a series of tunnels throughout the property. Its envious position overlooking the valley provides for spectacular views. Wonderful lounging nooks in the lobby and elsewhere allow visitors to fully appreciate the landscape. The inn's dining room is simple but the food is elegant, and the lobby bar has a cozy fireplace to ward off the cool desert nights.

Restaurants

Tour A: Mojave National Preserve

Baker

Bun Boy
$-$$
72159 Baker Blvd.
☎733-4660
The Bun Boy is oddly decorated, with an ornate marble wall that opens onto an open kitchen and a lunch counter. Booth and table seating is also available. The Bun Boy has diner-style food with a twist: the usual gigantic burgers, plus stir-fry's, fajitas and several salads.

Strawberries are the local produce and find their way into fresh cheesecakes, shakes and pies.

The Mad Greek Cafe
$-$$
72146 Baker Blvd.
☎733-4354
The Mad Greek is a crazy, busy, confusing restaurant with a little something for everyone. They offer burgers, huge breakfasts and a complete selection of Greek food. The restaurant is loud with a pervasive blue and white decor. Large, generous helpings provide excellent value.

Tour B: Death Valley

Panamint Springs to Wildrose

Panamint Springs

Panamint Springs Restaurant
☎(775) 482-7680
www.deathvalley.com
The best restaurant in Death Valley, you can choose to dine indoors with the air conditioning or out on their lovely porch overlooking the valley. The roadhouse-style restaurant features hearty portions of steak, pastas and ribs. The friendly service is complimented by micro-brewery beers and a small wine list.

Beatty to Dante's View

Beatty

Ye Olde Fashioned Ice Cream Shoppe
$
Main St. and Hwy 95
☎(775) 553-9008
Decent ice-cream will help you beat the heat in Death Valley.

Sourdough Saloon
$-$$
106 W. Main St.
☎*(775) 553-2266*
The Sourdough Saloon serves great pizza among the slots, darts and pool tables. At night the bar caters to tourists who have developed a thirst in the desert.

The Stagecoach Hotel
$-$$
Hwy 95
☎*(775) 553-2419*
The small restaurant at the Stagecoach serves diner-style food 24hrs. From the comfortable booths you can hear the fortunes being won and lost in the adjacent casino.

The Exchange Club Motel & Casino
$-$$
119 Main St.
☎*(775) 553-2333*
The exchange club has a small restaurant and bar

on the ground floor serving typical American fare.

Furnace Creek

Forty Niner Café / Corkscrew Saloon
$-$$
7am-9pm
The dark wood interior of the Forty Niner Café features comfortable booths lit by old mining lamps. The menu has an ample mix of soups, salads, sandwiches, fried chicken and steaks. Next door, the Corkscrew Saloon is the only bar in town, with a pool table and a good selection of draft beers. Pizza and bar munchies are also available.

The Wrangler Steakhouse
$$-$$$
The Wrangler has a selection of steaks, from prime rib to filet, hand-cut and served with all the fixin's. A limited wine list is available. It also features a hot

and cold breakfast and lunch buffet (11am-2pm) for $10.

Entertainment

Tour B: Death Valley

Beatty to Dante's View

Beatty

Beatty is the heart of the nightlife in Death Valley. Besides the Sourdough Saloon (see p 289), there are also three casinos in town: The Stagecoach, the Burro, and the Exchange Club. All three are located along Highway 95; just follow the neon and flashing lights.

Ocotillo

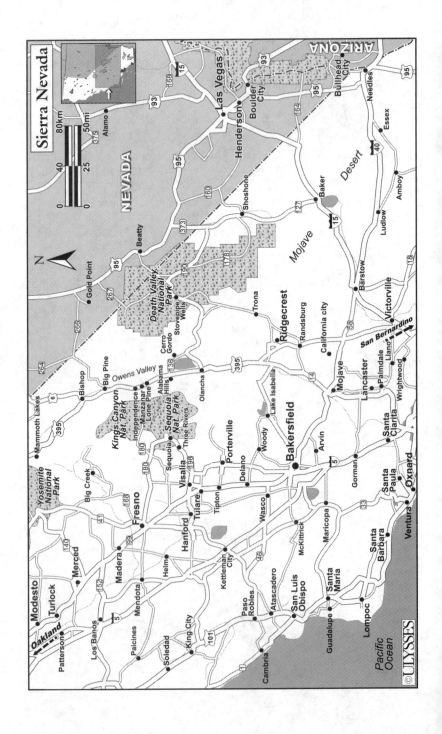

The Sierra Nevada

The Sierra Nevada (Spanish for "snow-covered mountain range") extends over more than 400mi (650km) along the eastern border of California.

Its imposing granite cliffs, high plateaus, monumental canyons and snow-capped summits literally cut the state off from the rest of the country.

Created by the movement of tectonic plates over 10 million years ago, it is a region of majestic splendour and humbling 13,125ft (4,000m) summits. Each side of California's principal mountain range has a distinct character, the result of its geological past and marine air currents. While the western Sierra Nevada slopes down gently over several miles, the east face drops sharply and the rocky, jagged sides of the high, snow-covered peaks create spectacular alpine landscapes. Barely visible from the San Joaquin Valley to the west, the heights of the Sierra Nevada tower above the Owens Valley below and form an enchanting setting for the towns of the eastern Sierra. The west face, caressed by damp oceanic air masses, favours the growth of vast, very dense forests. The mountain

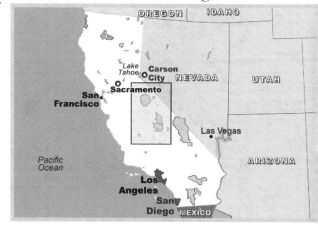

range's jagged summits break up clouds drifting in from the west, leaving the eastern side dry as a bone.

The proximity of the small towns on the east side, linked by US Highway 395, to the lake- and meadow-rich alpine area draws thousands of campers, climbers, hikers and photographers every year. Most of the hiking trails cross the Sierra Nevada's watershed and continue into the national-park areas on the west side.

On the west side of the Sierra Nevada, the intense activity of glaciers and torrential rivers has carved out magnificent

natural sculptures and canyons, most notably in the famous Yosemite, Sequoia and Kings Canyon national parks. Another of the Sierra's main attractions in the Sequoia National Park is Mount Whitney, whose 14,494ft (4,418m) summit dominates the entire California landscape. These three parks rank among the country's greatest natural riches and are a must-see during a stay in California, giving visitors the chance to practise a wealth of outdoor activities while surrounded by grandiose scenery.

Finding Your Way Around

By Car

Two major access roads lead to both sides of the Sierra Nevada. US Highway 395 links all the towns on the east side and provides easy access to Yosemite National Park in summer via Highway 120. US Highway 99 runs through the San Joaquin Valley on the west side and leads to Sequoia, Kings Canyon and Yosemite national parks from the valley's main towns.

Sequoia and Kings Canyon National Parks

Drivers can reach Kings Canyon National Park via Highway 180, while Highway 198, less well-maintained than the former, leads to Sequoia National Park. The Generals Highway links the two roads and therefore facilitates transit between the two parks. Note that no road runs through the parks, so there is no access from Highway 395 and the eastern Sierra Nevada. Also, there are no gas stations within the parks, so be sure to fill your gas tank before venturing in. Cedar Grove-bound Highway 180 is closed from late November to mid-April. To find out about road and weather conditions, you can call ☎559-565-3341 at any time of day.

Yosemite National Park

Several roads lead to the four entrances to Yosemite National Park. Eastbound Highway 120 leads to the Big Oak Flat entrance, which opens out onto the Hetch Hetchy area. The Arch Rock entrance is on Highway 140 farther south and primarily leads visitors to the Yosemite Valley. From the south, the Wawona entrance is on Highway 41 and leads to the area of the same name. Lastly, from May to November only, visitors coming in from the eastern Sierra Nevada can take Highway 120 and cross the park from east to west via the Tioga Pass entrance, 12mi (19km) from Lee Vining and Highway 395. To find out about road and weather conditions, you can call ☎209-372-0200 at any time of day. There are no gas stations within the Yosemite Valley, but some can be found near the entrance to Arch Rock, in the Wawona area, in Crane Flat and, in the summer season, on Tioga Road.

By Bus

Below is a list of the main bus stations:

Lone Pine
126 W. Post St.
at Lone Pine Locksmith
☎760-876-5300
☎800-231-2222

Bishop
201 S. Warren St.
behind J.C. Penney
☎760-872-2721

Mammoth Lakes
bus stop in the McDonald's parking lot, opposite the Visitor Bureau, Highway 203
☎800-231-2222

Lee Vining
bus stop at the supermarket, US 395
☎800-231-2222

Yosemite National Park
Greyhound bus stop at the Yosemite Lodge and VIA Bus Lines stop at Curry Village, on the way to Fresno and Merced
☎800-VIA-LINE

Practical Information

Like most regions in the United States, the Sierra Nevada has a most efficient tourist information network. Even the smallest town has its own visitor center, with a gracious staff and a wealth of highly pertinent information on the area. To reach these tourist information centres, simply follow the roadsigns along the major access roads. Below is the contact-information of a few such centres, listed by city and by park:

Lone Pine

Visitor Bureau
126 S. Main St.
☎760-876-4444
info@lone-pine.com
www.lone-pine.com

Interagency Visitor Center
at US Hwy. 395 and Hwy. 136
☎760-876-6222

Mount Whitney/Inyo National Forest Ranger Station
640 S. Main St.
☎760-876-6200

Bishop

Visitors Bureau
690 N. Main St.
☎760-873-8405
www.bishopvisitor.com

**White Mountains
Ranger Station**
798 N. Main St.
☎ *760-873-2500*
www.r5.fs.fed.us/inyo

Mammoth Lakes

**Visitors Bureau and Ranger
Station**
north of the village, Hwy. 203
☎ *760-924-5500*
☎ *800-466-2666*
www.visitmammoth.com

Lee Vining

**Mono Lake Committee Visitor
Center and Lee Vining Chamber of Commerce**
US 395, at Third St.
☎ *760-647-6595*
☎ *760-647-6629*
www.monolake.org
www.leevining.com

**Mono Basin Scenic Area
Visitor Center**
US 395, north of the village
☎ *760-647-3044*
www.r5.fs.fed.us/inyo

Bridgeport

Ranger Station
US 395, south of the village
☎ *760-932-7070*

Sequoia and Kings Canyon National Parks

The Sequoia and Kings
Canyon national parks
offer three visitor centers
open year-round, including one in Grant Grove
(Hwy. 180), one in
Lodgepole *(at Generals
Hwy. and Hwy. 198)* and
another in Foothills *(Hwy.
198)*. The small-scale Cedar Grove *(May to Sep; Hwy.
180)* and Mineral King
*(June to Sep; access via Hwy.
198, Mineral King Rd.)* visitor centers are only open
in summer *(☎ 559-565-3341,
www.nps.gov/seki,
www.visitsequoia.com)*. A

$10 admission fee is
charged at the park entrances.

Yosemite National Park

Yosemite National Park
has a total of four visitor
centers: in Valley *(Northside
Dr., Yosemite Valley)*,
Wawona *(Wawona Rd.,
Hwy. 41)*, Big Oak Flat
(Hwy. 120) and Tuolumne
Meadows *(May to Nov;
Tioga Rd., Hwy. 120)*. Admission to the park costs
$20/vehicle *(☎ 209-372-
0200, www.nps.gov/yose,
www.yosemite.org)*. Complimentary shuttle-bus service
is provided between the
park's main attractions
which are accessible by
car. Organized bus tours
for a fee are also offered.

Exploring

Lone Pine

Founded in the 1860s to
provide miners, then
ranchers and farmers, from
southern Inyo County with
a supply post, Lone Pine
leads a quiet existence,
sheltered by the imposing
Sierra Nevada, which
provides the town with
fantastic vistas and a natural barrier against the
humid air coming in from
the west. A quiet little
community of 1,800 souls
with a dry and sunny
climate, Lone Pine is traversed only by US Highway 395, which turns into
Main Street in its compact
town centre. With a solitary traffic light, at the
corner of Whitney Portal
Road, the main drag has

retained a bygone cachet,
with its few typically western wooden facades. However sleepy, this burg has
experienced and occasionally still experiences, the
thrill and excitement of
film shoots in the magical
Alabama Hills.

The highest point of the
Sierra Nevada and all of
California, **Mount
Whitney ★★** stands majestically some 12.5mi (20km)
west of Lone Pine, in the
heart of the **Inyo National
Forest**. Hiking trails of
varying levels of difficulty
allow you to explore the
environs of this 14,494ft
(4,418m) colossus. The
occasionally very steep
11mi (17.6km) Mt. Whitney Trail is the most-travelled in the entire Sierra
Nevada mountain range.
This magnificent but difficult trail, which leads to
elevations fluctuating
around 9,850ft (3,000m),
was laid out in 1904, some
31 years after the giant
was first climbed on August 18, 1873. Another trail
that is difficult but worth
the effort is the Meysan
Lake Trail, which, after a
4.6mi (7.5km) ascent, leads
to a magnificent alpine
lake and other trails running to various summits of
the Sierra. As for the Cotton Pass Trail, it extends to
the Pacific Crest Trail and
the northern area of
Golden Trout Wilderness
and the Kern Plateau. This
trail of medium difficulty
covers a hilly terrain in the
midst of subalpine meadows. All these trails are in
optimal condition during
the summer months
(snow-free from July to
October), and accessible
from Lone Pine via Whitney Portal Road. This same
road leads to **Whitney Portal**, the starting point of
several hiking trails and a
pleasant rest, supply,
snack and picnic area.

"America's Roof"

Mount Whitney is the highest summit in the continental United States, reaching 14,494ft (4,418m) at its highest point. The majestic granite peaks on the east side of the southern Sierra Nevada's snow-covered colossus drop down sharply more than 10,827ft (3,300m) into the Owens Valley below. The mountain is named after Josiah Dwight Whitney (1819-1896), a U.S. geologist and leader of an expedition that attempted to scale the summit in 1864. The exploit, however, only succeeded nine years later, on August 18, 1873. On July 17, 1904, the famous Mt. Whitney Trail opened to the first adventurers who set out to conquer "America's Roof."

Though Mount Whitney is part of Sequoia National Park, the wilderness of the western Sierra Nevada makes Lone Pine the easiest place from which to access most mountain roads.

But make no mistake, for although Lone Pine is just a small, isolated town with a population of 1,800 nestled deep in the Owens Valley, it is certainly worth the trip. The magical **Alabama Hills** ★★ (take Whit-

ney Portal Rd. from the centre of Lone Pine and continue for a few miles) alone make it worthwhile to linger a bit in Lone Pine. Dating back a few million years, these ancient rock formations feature a landscape strewn with masses of tumbled red rocks and outcrops surrounded by brushwood. This lunar landscape contrasts spectacularly with the backdrop of the Sierra's steep, snow-capped summits. In the 1920s, Hollywood discovered this magical region and shot many movies on site. Spend a few hours here and try to spot some famous film-shooting locations (including those of *High Sierra* with Humphrey Bogart, *Tycoon* with John Wayne and *Maverick* with Mel Gibson), or wander through the strange rock formations. A real thrill for photographers.

Bishop

One of the largest communities in the eastern Sierra Nevada, with a population of 3,500, Bishop has long been renowned as an outdoor-activities, fishing and camping centre. Founded by Samuel Bishop in the 1860s, when the Owens Valley was home to ranchers and miners, the village has retained a certain period cachet and seems frozen in time, with its few wooden facades, covered sidewalks and 1950s neon signs. US 395 runs through the village, where it turns into Main Street, Bishop's hub of commercial activity.

The **Owens Valley Paiute-Shoshone Indian Cultural Museum** (*free admission; Mon to Fri 9am to 5pm, Sat and Sun 10am to 4pm; 2301*

W. Ligne St., south of the village, ☎760-873-4478) showcases an impressive collection of woven baskets, jewellery and scores of other Native American crafts.

Only 15mi (24km) west of Bishop via Highway 168, **Bishop Creek Canyon** ★ offers the most spectacular of settings at the foot of the Sierra Nevada. A drive up a steep 5,000ft (1,500m-plus) incline leads to the base of the high summits, where you can relax, enjoy various outdoor activities or have a picnic in one of three areas, namely South Lake, Lake Sabrina or North Lake.

It's hard to believe that trees can grow under such harsh conditions, with constant winds, biting cold and minimal moisture at over 9,845ft (3,000m) in altitude. And yet, for more than 4,000 years, the amazing ancient bristlecone pines have flourished in the White Mountains, east of the Sierra Nevada. Squat, gnarled, with tentacular branches and exposed roots, these age-old pines have developed on barren soil that has eroded over the centuries. The **Ancient Bristlecone Pine Forest** ★ (*exit US 395 at Big Pine and follow northeast-bound Hwy. 168 for about 25mi (40km)*) has an information centre at Schulman Grove that showcases these fascinating conifers' history.

Mammoth Lakes

Located in the heart of a splendid region harbouring a wealth of natural wonders, Mammoth Lakes is a Mecca for nature-lovers. A small town with a population of 5,300, Mammoth Lakes bustles with activities in the winter season, when skiers flood the streets to storm the famous Mammoth Mountain, one of the most popular ski resorts in the country. Summer also draws a number of vacationers, hikers, fishers and others to discover this privileged region's many attractions.

Though Main Street *(Hwy. 203)* and Old Mammoth Road abound in all manner of shops and constitute the community's central hub, the cross streets, set up in a judiciously preserved pine forest, enjoy amazing peace and quiet. To avoid the drawbacks of heavy traffic, a shuttle transports visitors from the major hotels to the natural and tourist attractions. This inexpensive, well-organized means of public transportation makes frequent stops and attracts scores of commuters happy to leave their car behind in the parking lot during their stay in Mammoth Lakes.

Mammoth Lakes's ample recreational opportunities make us forget that its history dates back to 1878, when the discovery of gold and silver engendered a period of prosperity as spectacular as it was short-lived. In less than a year, 22 saloons, two breweries and 13 shops sprouted in Mammoth City (as Mammoth Lakes was known in its heyday) – before the town went belly up. Unfortunately, there remain very few traces of this not-so-distant past.

Housed in a log cabin, the **Mammoth Historical Society Museum** *(free admission; June to Oct 9:30am to 4:30pm; Old Mammoth Rd., ☎760-934-6918)* recounts the region's history from its mining days to the present.

Created by the joint forces of fire and ice, the stunning **Devils Postpile National Monument ★** *($8; shuttle service from the ski resort's Main Lodge; Hwy. 203)* stands majestically some 12.5mi (20km) west of Mammoth Lakes. About 100,000 years ago, a lava flow running down Mammoth Pass slowed its course, cooled off and solidified in a peculiar manner, creating this huge formation of 50ft-high (about 18m) basalt columns. The mass of blue-grey volcanic rocks, split vertically, cracked and was then polished to a glitter by later glacial activity. A short trail leads to the top of the columns from which you can admire this extraordinary volcanic formation. A shuttle bus provides access to the site from the Mammoth Mountain Ski Area's Main Lodge.

Two miles (3km) downstream from Devils Postpile, the San Joaquin River plunges over a 101ft (30m) ridge, forming the majestic **Rainbow Falls** *(Hwy. 203)*, famed for the delightful rainbows created by the fine mist and rays of sunshine. From Reds Meadow, a 1.5mi (2.5km)

Lights, Camera, Action!

Often considered a veritable living film museum, the magical Alabama Hills will revive long-lost memories for film buffs. Admiring these age-old rock formations conjures up a number of famous Hollywood movie scenes. The legend of the Alabama Hills dates back to the 1920s, when booming-Tinseltown producers discovered the quiet little burg of Lone Pine, at the foot of Mount Whitney. Attracted by its striking, arid moonscapes, directors shot over 300 movies here. Fortunately, the hordes of stars and film crews left no lasting mark on the wild scenery, which remains just as Fatty Arbuckle must have seen it during the shooting of the *The Roundup*, the very first movie shot here in 1920. Later, the biggest names in Hollywood came here on location, including Cary Grant, Kirk Douglas, Errol Flynn, Humphrey Bogart, Gregory Peck, Mel Gibson and, of course, the most famous cowboy of all time, John Wayne. Legend has it that the latter stayed at Lone Pine's Dow Villa Hotel. Today, some films and commercials are still shot on location in the Alabama Hills.

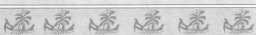

trail leads to a spot whose beautiful falls, roaring water and refreshing drizzle make it a great place for a picnic.

With 150 trails and 3,460 acres (1,400ha) of ski slopes with a vertical drop of 3,100ft (about 1,000m), the **Mammoth Mountain Ski Area ★** (see p 311) *(Minaret Rd., Hwy. 203)* will delight sliding-sports buffs. Both beginners and experts will enjoy optimal climatic conditions and abundant snowfall, very well exploited and shown to advantage by the excellent facilities first set up in 1955.

Mammoth stands in the huge **Inyo National Forest**, a boundless playground for outdoor activities, from hiking and mountain biking to horseback riding. At the end of Lake Mary Road, the Mammoth Lakes Basin area is a hiker's paradise.

Lee Vining

A tiny, sleepy community of scarcely 400 souls located some 8,860ft (2,700m) above sea level at the foot of the Sierra Nevada, Lee Vining is both the gateway to Yosemite National Park, via Tioga Road, and the start-off point for extraordinary Mono Lake.

Once again, Mother Nature has succeeded in creating a marvel that human beings cannot help but contemplate with humility. The fruit of glacial and volcanic activity, of fire and water, **Mono Lake ★** *(US 395, ☎ 760-647-3044, www.r5.fs.fed.us/inyo)* is one of California's most striking natural attractions. Located

May God Have Pity on their Souls!

"Goodbye God, I'm going to Bodie."

Since Bodie's heyday around 1880, 95% of its buildings have succumbed to the ravages of time, fire and the elements. These days, it is a typical California gold-rush ghost town. Bodie was named after Waterman Smith Body (a.k.a. William Bodey), who discovered gold here in 1859. The variant spelling, often attributed to an illiterate sign painter, was actually a deliberate change by the townspeople to ensure correct pronunciation. By 1879, Bodie was home to some 10,000 people, and its depravi-ty, scores of criminals and difficult climate had earned it a wicked reputation. Murders were a commonplace and sometimes daily occurrence. The fire bell, which tolled the victims's age, rang all too often. Robberies, stage holdups and street brawls provided entertainment, while the rowdy town's 65 saloons offered many temptations after a hard day's work in the mines. Outlaws, bad whiskey and horrible weather were endemic to this lawless gold-mining boomtown, which a minister once described as *"A sea of sin, lashed by the tempests of lust and passion."*!

over 8,860ft (2,700m) above sea level, the huge lake is actually a remnant of a prehistoric inland sea that dates back more than 760,000 years. The confluence of pure mountain water flowing into the lake's salty, alkaline waters has in fact created bizarre calcareous columns, tufa towers that poke through the surface of the water here and there. Resembling of steeple spires, these pure-white towers are framed by the lake's turquoise waters, giving the whole area an unreal appearance.

Mono Lake is a vital habitat for over 80 species of aquatic birds (including gulls, grebes and phala-ropes). The Mono Basin has a rich volcanic past, as evidenced by the volcanic formations surrounding the lake on three sides: Bodie Hills, to the north, and Anchorite Hills, to the east, are several million years old, while to the south, the Mono Craters (a series of 21 volcanic cones) form the youngest mountain range in North America. The northernmost of these volcanoes, the **Panum Crater**, erupted only 640 years ago. The latter is easily reached by car from Highway 120 East. **South Tufa** and **Mono Lake County Park** are the best places to enjoy this fabulous body of water. The Mono Lake Tufa State Reserve, the

United States Forest Service and the Mono Lake Committee organize free guided tours every day in summer and on weekends during the winter season. The Mono Basin Scenic Area visitor center offers beautiful views of the lake, but primarily features very interesting and instructive exhibits on this extraordinary natural area's geology, flora and fauna. Moreover, hiking trails of varying levels of difficulty crisscross the area. Ranging in length from 1mi to 5mi (1.5km to 8km), these trails feature vertical drops of close to 1,970ft (600m).

Bridgeport

Bridgeport first saw the light of day in 1859 when gold was discovered "in them thar hills," 6.2mi (10km) south of its present-day location. This discovery precipitated a genuine gold rush, leading thousands of prospectors and adventurers to swoop down on the desert-like plateaus. Founded then as a supply post for miners, the village gained considerable importance as a supplier of lumber for mining camps. A small village of 500 inhabitants, Bridgeport is certainly no longer the bustling centre it once was, but still offers rural charm, an Old West atmosphere and a few traces of its glorious past. Highway 395, which turns into Main Street in the town centre, exudes a typical western atmosphere, lined with

Bodie State Historic Park

stores still sporting their facades of yore and graced with an imposing, late-19th-century courthouse.

Bridgeport prides itself on having the oldest existing courthouse in all of California. Built in 1880, the impressive Victorian-style **Courthouse** *(Main St.)* stands majestically in the heart of the village and conveys Bridgeport's former standing.

In the late 1850s, the gold deposits in the western Sierra Nevada ran dry. Prospectors reached the east side in 1859, where they discovered the Comstock Lode in Virginia Creek, which precipitated a wild rush to the surrounding desert-like plateaus. Founded by prospector Waterman Smith Body, the village of Bodie peaked in 1879, when its population reached 10,000. When the lode ran dry, the inhabitants left, abandoning the place to the elements. Today, the **Bodie State Historic Park ★★** *($2; May to Sep every day 8am to 7pm, Oct to Apr every day 9am to 4pm; Hwy. 270, 12.5mi (20km) from Hwy. 395,* ☎ *760-647-6445)* is one of California's best-preserved ghost towns. Visitors will get the impression that the residents of this isolated village, designated a his-

toric park in 1962, left in a mad rush, leaving everything behind. Today, everything is just as time and the elements have left it! Though only a few buildings are open to the public, you can peer inside the shops and homes through the windows. Absolutely fascinating! A museum open in summer chronicles Bodie's history with maps and exhibits.

Fishers and hikers flock to **Twin Lakes**, two bodies of water by Yosemite National Park long renowned for their trout and salmon.

Sequoia and Kings Canyon National Parks

Located in the western Sierra Nevada, the jointly administered, adjoining Sequoia and Kings Canyon national parks are home to the most spectacular and grandiose mountains in the southern Sierra, notably majestic 14,494ft (4,418m) Mount Whitney, the highest peak in the continental United States. The parks also encompass the world's largest groves of giant sequoias, the largest trees on the planet.

Together, Sequoia and Kings Canyon national parks cover over 8,266,720 acres (345,496ha) of territory and offer nature-lovers 810mi (1,300km) of hiking trails, canyons more than 4,920ft (1,500m) deep

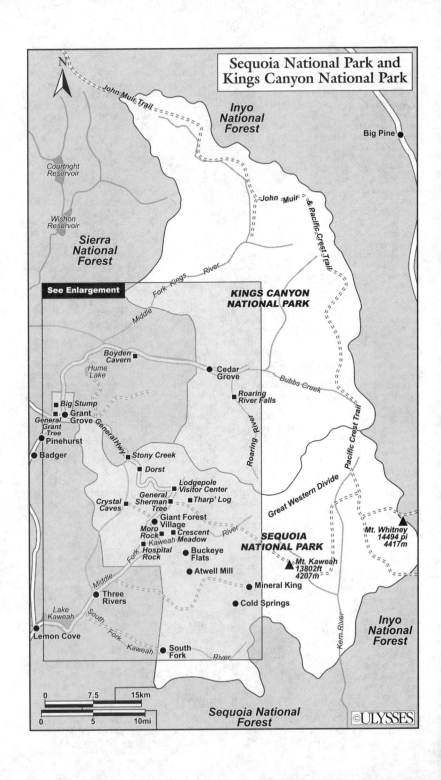

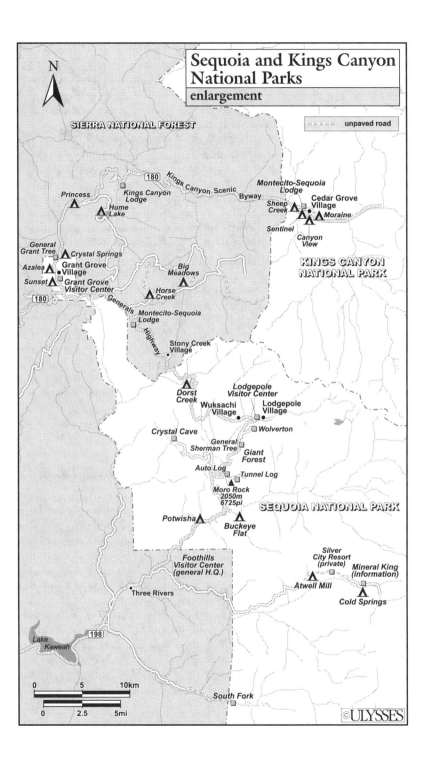

and summits almost 13,125ft (4,000m) high. The parks are not only a hiker's paradise, with a vast range of marked trails, but also a rider's and cross-country skier's playground. These vast expanses are also studded with streams and rivers, as well as a few trout ponds. Swimming is allowed in certain spots, but it is inadvisable to venture in when the river level is high.

Often wrongly considered "little Yosemites," the Sequoia and Kings Canyon national parks welcome much fewer visitors (1.5 million a year) than their famous counterpart, and so enjoy greater tranquillity. While scores of facilities and roads greet hordes of tourists in summer, and almost 4 million visitors annually in Yosemite, its two neighbours display nature in a more primal state. Some will even go so far as to say that these parks' administration has treated Mother Nature with greater respect and pays her the homage she deserves. This is evidenced by the fact that vast tracts of Sequoia and Kings Canyon national parks are only accessible on foot.

Reaching altitudes of 4,920ft (1,500m), the vast foothills are covered with manzanita, black oaks and large yuccas whose sweet-smelling flowers bloom in early spring. On a 200mi (320km) strip of land north of Kings River are eight clusters of giant sequoias. These expanses are home to stags, Douglas squirrels, coyotes and lynx. Beyond an altitude of 5,905ft (1,800m), austere granite

Sequoia

landscapes predominate, dotted with lakes, foxtail and pines. In total, this fabulous wilderness is home to over 200 species of birds, 75 species of mammals and 23 varieties of reptiles. The plant kingdom is represented by over 1,400 species of plants, 22 kinds of broad-leaved trees and 26 varieties of conifers.

The history of the two national parks dates back to 1858. Guided by the Kaweah and Potwisha peoples, a cowboy from Three Rivers named Hale Tharp ventured into the giant forest's dense sequoia groves. After meeting the rash adventurer, naturalist John Muir lost no time in chronicling his explorations, creating a

journal that was later published in magazines. The gold rush quickly led to excessive logging in the Grant Grove area as well as the exploitation of the Mineral King mine. At first, very few people denounced this sometimes brutal exploitation of the nation's natural heritage, save for a few journalists, notably editor George Stewart, one of the first to sound the alarm. In the late 1880s, the all-powerful forest industry intensely exploited the West Coast's dense forests. With their colossal trees, sequoias and other pines, these green expanses provided unscrupulous companies with considerable revenue.

Heeding conservationists' warnings and recognizing both the ecological importance and great natural beauty of these vast sequoia forests and their supporting environment, the U.S. Congress passed legislation protecting this wilderness from the forestry companies' infernal machinery. Thus was it that, on September 25, 1890, a small tract of the vast expanses encompassing sequoia groves and part of the hydrographic basin irrigating the San Joaquin Valley became Sequoia National Park. A week later, Congress increased the park's size threefold, spawning General Grant and Yosemite national parks. These three protected areas constitute the first national parks ever created in U.S. history, after Yellowstone National Park, in Wyoming.

In 1926, Sequoia National Park's surface area was doubled to include Mount

Whitney and Kern Canyon. Fourteen years later, Kings Canyon National Park was finally created, encompassing the former General Grant National Park in its entirety and other vast expanses of wilderness, notably Redwood Mountain, the Kings River basin and Grant Grove. At first, the great potential for hydroelectric power excluded spectacular Kings Canyon from the legal protection bestowed by the park's creation. Though the park bore its name, this natural wonder wasn't incorporated into the national park until 1965. The final step in protecting the region came in 1978 with the integra-

tion of Mineral King into Sequoia National Park.

The Sierran Foothills (Sequoia National Park)

Once home to the Potwisha, the **Hospital Rock** area now offers exhibits on this Native American society's way of life. A trail laid out by the Civilian Conservation Corps in the 1930s leads to the river.

A 3.7mi (6km) trail leads to **Marble Falls**, a lovely waterfall that flows right through chaparral. Departure from the Potwisha campground.

Paradise Creek, a steep trail, is a very pleasant way to enjoy the enchanting wilderness. Departure from the Buckeye Flat campground.

Eventually leading onto the high plateaus, the first few miles of the **Middle Fork** trail give hikers the opportunity to admire Kaweah Canyon, Moro Rock and Castle Rocks. Departure from the Buckeye Flat campground.

Ladybug is a fairly easy trail along the South Fork of the Kaweah River. Departure from the South Fork campground.

Green Giants

Known as being among the largest and oldest living organisms on the planet, sequoias are the survivors of a very distant time that goes back several million years, when the planet's vast forests were home to several varieties of these colossal trees. Only two types of these conifers still exist, namely the giant sequoia and the redwood, both of which are widely represented in California. However, there remain only 70 sequoia forests on earth. The sky-scraping trees are named after a Cherokee chief who devised a written alphabet for his people.

Redwoods abound on the Pacific coast, from central California to southern Oregon, where they thrive on the mild, humid and salty air. As for the giant sequoia, it prefers the western Sierra Nevada at altitudes ranging from 2950ft to 7875ft (900m to 2,400m). Though the latter does not attain the staggering heights of its cousin, which averages 295ft (90m) in height, its trunk appears much larger. Several have a circumference of close to 98.5ft (30m) at the base.

Impressive immune systems and very thick

bark make sequoias highly impervious to adverse conditions, old age, disease, insects and even forest fires. Small wonder then that most sequoias still standing are several hundred or thousand years old. And yet, even this forest giant is no match for humankind and its infernal heavy machinery, which has prompted the U.S. government to protect the most vulnerable representatives of this species. Only 8% of sequoias measuring over 10ft (3m) in diameter are on privately owned land.

The Sierra Nevada

A relatively abrupt trail leads to the **Garfield** sequoia forest. Departure from the South Fork campground.

★★★
The Giant Forest Area (Sequoia National Park)

Giant Forest ★★★, a breathtaking grove in the heart of Sequoia National Park, is home to four of the world's largest sequoias. Several highly popular trails run through this one-of-a-kind forest and wind around more than 8,000 scrupulously protected giant sequoias.

Named in 1879 in honour of an American Civil War hero, the **General Sherman Tree ★** is the world's largest tree in terms of volume.

Moro Rock/Crescent Meadow Road also serves as a cross-country-skiing trail in winter. Climbing a 400-step stairway judiciously set up by the Civilian Conservation Corps in 1931, the road continues on to **Moro Rock** (65,780ft or 2,050m). The striking granite dome offers spectacular panoramic views of the surrounding canyons and summits. On the way to this rock formation, you'll get the chance to drive onto the **Auto Log ★**, a gargantuan sequoia that fell several years ago. Nearby, you can also drive right through another fallen sequoia, now known as the **Tunnel Log ★**!

Carved out of limestone by an underground river and harbouring rock formations dating back more

than 10,000 years, the **Crystal Cave** *($5, guided tour, tickets on sale at the Lodgepole visitor center)* was discovered in 1918. Amazing stalactites and stalagmites of all shapes and sizes adorn miles of chambers

Attention!

The General Sherman Tree, which stands in Giant Forest, is unquestionably the most famous and spectacular sequoia in Sequoia National Park. Described as the largest living thing on Earth, the 2,100-year-old conifer is 274.9ft (83.8m) tall and its trunk is 52.5ft³ (1,487m³) in volume. Given its staggering size, it is difficult to fully appreciate the true dimensions of this 4,298,813.84lb (1,950,460kg) behemoth. The General Sherman Tree stands as high as a 26-storey building and measures over 36ft (11m) in diameter at its base. Over 30 train cars would be needed to move its trunk alone. Though a mature tree (to say the least!), it continues to grow at the rate of 40ft³ (1m³) a year, which in terms of biomass is equal to the overall volume of a tree some 12in (30cm) in diameter and 50ft (15m) tall!

and underground passages.

★★
Grant Grove Area (Kings Canyon National Park)

First described by Joseph Hardin Thomas, the giant sequoia known as the **General Grant Tree ★** is the third largest tree still standing on the planet. Held at the foot of the giant every second Sunday of December since 1925, the **Nation's Christmas Tree Ceremony** pays homage to those who died for their country.

Two-and-a-half miles (4km) west of Grant Grove Village, a 2,625ft (800m) trail leads to **Panoramic Point ★**, a fantastic lookout offering spectacular vistas of the High Sierra.

Highway 180, which links Grant Grove Village and Cedar Grove Village, runs through **Kings Canyon ★★**, a glacier-carved natural wonder. With an ultimate depth of 8,530ft (2,600m), this gargantuan natural sculpture formed by the South Fork and the Kings River is one of the deepest canyons on the continent.

Yosemite National Park

An immense natural area the size of Rhode Island, Yosemite National Park covers about 1,170 sq mi (3,030km²) of wilderness encompassing the Sierra Nevada's myriad splendours. Created on October 1, 1890, by an act of Congress, it has since become one of the most famous

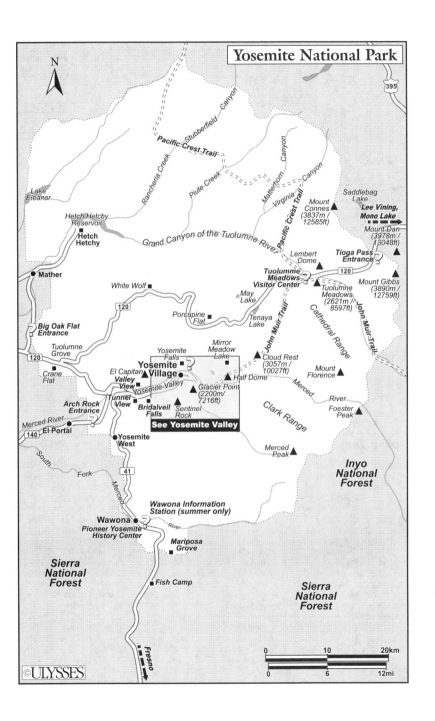

Yosemite National Park

395

Stubberfield Canyon

Pacific Crest Trail

Rancheria Creek

Piute Creek

Matterhorn Canyon

Virginia Canyon

Pacific Crest Trail

Lake Eleanor

Hetch Hetchy Reservoir

● **Hetch Hetchy**

Grand Canyon of the Tuolumne River

Saddlebag Lake

Lee Vining, Mono Lake

Mount Connes (3837m / 12585ft) ▲

Mount Dan (3978m / 13048ft) ▲

● **Mather**

White Wolf ■

Lembert Dome ▲

Tioga Pass Entrance ▲

120

Tuolumne Meadows Visitor Center ▲

Tuolumne Meadows (2621m / 8597ft)

Mount Gibbs (3890m / 12759ft) ▲

120

Porcupine Flat ■

May Lake ■

Tenaya Lake

John Muir Trail

John Muir Trail

Big Oak Flat Entrance

Tuolumne Grove

Cathedral Range

120

Crane Flat ■

Yosemite Falls ■

Mirror Meadow Lake ■

Cloud Rest (3057m / 10027ft) ▲

Mount Florence ▲

Yosemite Village ●

El Capitan ▲ **Valley View**

Yosemite Valley

Half Dome ▲

Tunnel View

Glacier Point (2200m / 7216ft) ▲

Merced

River

Foester Peak ▲

Arch Rock Entrance

Bridalveil Falls

Sentinel Rock ▲

See Yosemite Valley

Clark Range

Merced River
140 ● **El Portal**

● **Yosemite West**

Merced Peak ▲

Inyo National Forest

South

Fork

41

Merced

Wawona Information Station (summer only)

Wawona ●
Pioneer Yosemite History Center

River

Mariposa Grove

Sierra National Forest

■ **Fish Camp**

Sierra National Forest

Fresno

© **ULYSSES**

0 — 10 — 20km

0 — 6 — 12mi

The Man of Sierra Nevada

Born in Dunbar, Scotland, in 1838, explorer, conservationist and author John Muir came to the United States with his father in 1849. After studying botany and geology at the University of Wisconsin, he joined expeditions to the Arctic and the Yukon, and notably "discovered" Glacier Bay in Alaska. A world authority on forest management, he visited such places as Russia, India and the Phillippines in order to study their forests. But above all, he devoted a major part of his life to the Sierra Nevada, studying its geology and flora. He discovered 75 glaciers and drew up their first maps. He led a campaign that established his beloved Yosemite as a "national park," and in 1892, founded the Sierra Club, a now-world-famous organization devoted to nature conservation. In the course of his very full life, Muir wrote several books, the best known being *The Mountains of California* (1894), *Our National Parks* (1901) and *Yosemite* (1912). He died on December 24, 1914, at the age of 76. The John Muir Trail, a 199ft-long (320km) trail that links the Yosemite Valley and Mount Whitney, pays homage to this man who devoted his life to the conservation of the Sierra Nevada and to Mother Nature herself.

and visited parks in the world. Resulting from the U.S. government's first gesture to preserve a site for its aesthetic and scientific value, as well as for the public's benefit Yosemite Park paved the way for the future concept of state and national park networks. The oval-shaped park features over 260mi (420km) of roads and 795mi (1,280km) of hiking trails laid out in the heart of the Sierra Nevada. Ranging in elevation from 1,970ft (600m) to 13,125ft (4,000m), this vast and varied protected area attracts more than 4 million visitors every year; hordes of tourists literally swarm the park during the summer season. Most of them head straight for the famous Yosemite Valley, which though fantastic and a must-see, only covers 7 sq mi (18km²) of this park, of which over 94% of the total area is designated as wilderness. With its exceptional rock formations, bare mountains, verdant valleys and majestic, glistening waterfalls, Yosemite Park is a unique, heavenly place to discover from all angles.

From semi-arid foothills to snow-capped peaks, the Yosemite National Park's wide range of environments allows it to harbour the richest and most varied of flora and fauna, including over 37 kinds of trees, hundreds of varieties of wildflowers and close to 250 bird species, 80 species of mammals and 40 species of reptiles and amphibians. California black oaks, ponderosa pines and incense cedars abound in the valleys, while Jeffrey and Douglas pines have adapted to the harsh conditions at high altitudes. Giant sequoias, though present, are only found in a few areas: Mariposa Grove, Tuolumne Grove and Merced Grove. Flowers bloom around April or May in the valley, and around May or June at high altitudes. The most beautiful wildflowers (including lupins, irises, monkey flowers and Mariposa lilies) mainly bloom around Tuolumne Meadows. After their near disappearance in the last few decades due to hunting and disease, some 20 California bighorn sheep have been roaming the heights of the park again since 1986, living in herds at the eastern edge of the park. Coyotes, mule deer, western gray squirrels, cougars, golden eagles, Steller's jays and other endangered bird species such as the peregrine falcon cohabitate in the park's vast expanses. Black bears, with golden-brown, dark-brown or black fur, abound and roam freely. Generally unaggressive, they will attack if they feel threatened or to protect their young.

Though Yosemite's existence as a national park only dates back a little over a century, the birth and transformation of its unique glacier-sculpted rock formations go back to the dawn of time. For more than 500 million years, alternating periods of glaciation and warming and the processes of glacial sedimentation, formation and retreat have shaped the earth's crust, creating the spectacular granite-rock configurations for which the park is famous. Gravity and water continue to shape the Yosemite Valley landscape, as events like the Happy Isles rockslide of July 1996 and the flood of January 1997 serve to remind us.

First Nations people lived in the Yosemite region for tens of thousands of years, well before the arrival of Europeans in the mid-19th century. The Miwok were the first to come into contact with the first non-Native American adventurers. The Miwok knew the Yosemite Valley as *Ahwahnee*, loosely translated as "place of the gaping mouth," and called themselves the *Ahwahneechee*. These first inhabitant subsisted on hunting, fishing and acorns, which, once ground, provided them with nourishing flour. They traded acorns and other goods native to the valley with the Mono Lake Paiute people for rabbit skins, pine nuts and obsidian. The Yosemite Valley was known to very few whites before 1851. Armed conflicts between First Nations peoples and American colonists and prospectors accidentally led a military regiment into

the valley, introducing them to its great, still-primal and secret beauty. Word of the Yosemite Valley's charms soon spread like wildfire, and in 1855, San Francisco journalist James Mason Hutchings led the first contingent of sightseers to the valley, after which the first pioneers, settlers and residents soon followed.

Nine years later, a group of influential Californians persuaded the federal government to bestow the territories of Yosemite Valley and Mariposa Grove to the state of California in order to create the first public nature reserve. This bequest, outlined in President Lincoln's *Yosemite Grant* decree of June 1864, is often considered the cornerstone on which future state and national parks were built. Bolstered by this initial victory, environmentalists then demanded the same protection for the vast wilderness surrounding the valley and Mariposa Grove. The group was steadfastly supported by influential editor Robert Underwood Johnson and famous botanist and geologist John Muir, who in 1869 began denouncing the devastating effects of colonization on the region. From 1889, the two men led a strong joint awareness campaign and, bolstered by political support, arranged in under a year for Congress to designate over 1,160 sq mi (3,000km²) of high-country woodlands as a protected area, which soon became Yosemite National Park. But it wasn't until John Muir met with President Theodore Roosevelt in 1903, and subsequent lobbying from railroad-magnate Edward Harriman, that the valley and Mariposa Grove areas were ceded by the state of

California and included in the Yosemite National Park we know today.

Yosemite National Park is made up of four large areas, each of which has its own entrance.

★★★
The Yosemite Valley Area

Measuring 7mi long and 1mi across (11km by 1.6km), **Yosemite Valley ★★★** is by far the most visited area of the park. In fact, the great majority of the 4 million visitors that flock to the park every year are only familiar with this small territory. The imposing rock faces that surround this deep glacial valley are draped with spectacular waterfalls. Visitors here enjoy fields of flowers in summer, a tapestry of colours in autumn and sparkling snow-capped peaks and relatively mild temperatures in winter. Scores of outdoor activities (hiking, cycling, skating, cross-country skiing) can be enjoyed here thanks to well-laid-out facilities. Yosemite Village offers a concentration of services, attractions and tourist infrastructures in the heart of the valley.

Next to the Valley Visitor Center, a museum complex houses the **Yosemite Museum Gallery** (*free admission; every day 9am to 4:45pm*), which welcomes temporary exhibitions, and the **Indian Cultural Exhibit** (*free admission; every day 9am to 4:45pm*), which features exhibits on the history of the Miwok and Paiute peoples from 1850 to the present day.

Bridalveil Falls was called *Pohono*, or "spirit of the

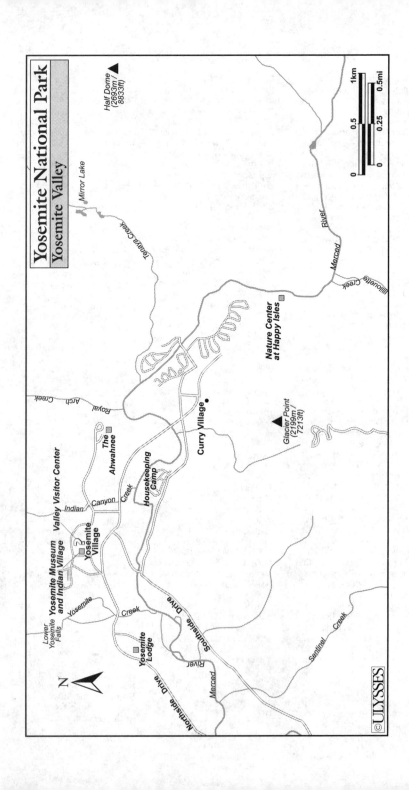

puffing wind," by the Ahwahneechee. The wind that swirls around the cliff often lifts and blows the water into a fine, rainbow-coloured mist. Surrounded by towering canyon walls, this waterfall appears to be of modest size but is actually 620ft (190m) tall, or as high as a 62-storey building!

An impressive two-tiered waterfall, **Yosemite Falls ★★★** is the fifth highest in the world and the tallest in North America. An easy trail a few miles long allows visitors to reach the foot of this giant and appreciate its splendour. Braver souls can tackle a sometimes very steep trail that, after a good 2hrs of occasionally very difficult climbing, leads to the top of the gigantic rock face from which the water rushes down over 2,300ft (700m). The effort is well worth it, as the panorama is truly breathtaking.

El Capitán ★★, a colossal granite monolith, stands majestically some 3,535ft (1,077m) above the valley floor. You can't miss it, on the left side of the Yosemite Valley-bound road. From spring to fall, a fair share of intrepid climbers set out to conquer its daunting rock face—one beyond the reach of most common mortals.

The symbol of Yosemite and the park's most remarkable natural rock monument, **Half Dome ★★★** dominates most of the valley's vantage points. Standing at the east end of the Yosemite Valley, this fledgling, metamorphic semi-spherical rock mass—it is a mere 87 million years old—rises to an elevation of 9,845ft (3,000m). In summer, hik-

ers can reach the giant's summit by taking the **John Muir Trail ★** or the Mist Trail to the Little Yosemite Valley, where they can camp (a permit is required). The difficult 17mi (27km) loop and daunting climb, made with the help of cables that have been permanently installed on the rock face, generally calls for a two-day hike.

Along Northside Drive, the road leading to the valley, you'll come across the **Valley View Turnout**, a peaceful spot on the banks of the Merced River that offers motorists a splendid panorama of El Capitán, Bridalveil Falls and Yosemite Valley.

Featuring one of the world's most photographed panoramas, **Tunnel View ★★★** stands at the east end of the Wawona Tunnel on Highway 41. From this popular turnout, visitors will marvel at the unobstructed view of El Capitán, Half Dome, Sentinel Rock, Cathedral Rocks and Bridalveil Falls. Offering an incredible medley of colours, sunsets here are particularly magnificent.

An absolutely spectacular vantage point on the south edge of the rock faces that surround the valley, **Glacier Point ★★★** offers awesome sweeping views of the area. Like an eagle perched on a promontory overlooking the valley 3,070ft (935m) below, sightseers will marvel at the natural wonders around them. This unique lookout is reached by one of two routes, though both are unfortunately closed from November to May. The first, which is easier, consists of driving along Glacier Point Road, which starts at Chinquapin on

Highway 41. The second, reserved for athletic types, provides access to Glacier Point via the difficult, steep **Four Mile Trail**, a three to 4hr climb starting from Southside Drive, near Sentinel Beach.

The forces of nature are constantly at work in Yosemite Park—something the **Happy Isles** area rockslide ★ proved all too conclusively on July 10, 1996, when a huge 3,884,540 cubic ft (110,000m³) slab of rock weighing several dozen tons broke loose between Washburn and Glacier Point, crashing down to the ground 1,970ft (600m) below at an estimated speed of over 155mph (250km/h). The blast of air produced upon impact generated winds in excess of 100mph (160km/h), the force of which uprooted hundreds of trees. Pulverized upon impact, the slab of rock disintegrated into a cloud of dust that covered a surface area of 50 acres (20ha). Guided tours of the area are organized by National Park Service rangers, and exhibits describing the natural phenomena that occur in the park are offered at the **Happy Isles Nature Center** (*free admission; May to Nov every day 10am to 4pm*). **Happy Isles** marks the starting point of one of the park's most popular hiking trails, the **Mist Trail**. This sometimes steep trail skirts the delightful Merced River and climbs up toward Vernal and Nevada falls. The 8.5mi (13.6km) **Panorama Trail**, another much appreciated but easier trail, runs to Glacier Point.

Accessible by a relatively easy trail, **Mirror Lake** is at its most beautiful in the spring, when the Tenaya Canyon's reflection

The Sierra Nevada

The Better Half

An imposing, semi-spherical rock mass and the symbol of Yosemite, Half Dome, as its name indicates, only makes up one half of a formation that dates back some 87 million years. Geologists agree that glacial activity is likely responsible for its unique appearance and near-vertical 93° face. As they receded, the huge glaciers likely split the metamorphic rock mass lengthwise along a vertical fissure, and eventually scattered its morainal debris along the valley.

Native Americans, on the other hand, have an altogether different—and much more romantic—explanation for this phenomenon. One day, a man came down from Yosemite Valley to Mono Lake, were he wed a woman named Tesaiyac. The trek back to the heights of the valley was so difficult for the young woman that she yearned to go back to her family at Mono Lake. An argument ensued and Tesaiyac fled into the forest, chased by her husband. Their quarrel so enraged the spirits that they turned them to stone: the man thus became the North Dome and the woman, the Half Dome. Tesaiyac wept so hard that her tears marked the rock face forevermore and formed Mono Lake.

appears in its crystal-clear waters. By summer's end, the lake dries up completely.

In the **Tuolumne Grove ★** giant-sequoia forest, located at the junction of Tioga Road (Highway 120) and Big Oak Flat Road, you'll come across the **Dead Giant**, one of only two trees in Yosemite Park through which you can still walk. The historic road that runs into the forest is now closed to traffic, leaving walkers and cross-country skiers free to enjoy this 6mi (10km) stretch of tranquillity, which displays a riot of colours in autumn.

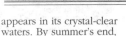

★★
The High Country (Tuolumne Meadows)

Though the scenery of the High Country *(Tioga Rd. closed Nov to May)* can be admired from your car during the summer and early fall, the best way of exploring this vast wilderness is on foot, skis or horseback. The area features countless verdant meadows, magnificent crystal-clear lakes, remarkable granite formations and an extensive network of hiking trails. Tuolumne Meadows lies the heart of the region, is over 8,200ft (2,500m) in altitude, and is the vastest area of subalpine meadow in the Sierra Nevada, as well as a very popular hiking spot.

Reaching 9,800ft (2,983m) at its highest point, **Tioga Pass** *(closed Nov to May)* is the highest pass open to motor vehicles in California. Many lookouts along Tioga Road (Highway 120) offer magnificent vistas of the area. Among them, **Tenaya Lake ★**, one of the largest and most beautiful lakes in the Sierra Nevada, is particularly noteworthy. Farther east, **Tuolumne Meadows ★★** is the largest subalpine meadow in the Sierra Nevada.

★
The Wawona Area

The park's historical centre, **Wawona ★** was once inhabited by Native Americans who called the neighbouring giant-sequoia forest *wawona*, "the sound of the call of the owl," who was the guardian spirit of the big trees. The headquarters of the park in its infancy, the area was home to Yosemite National Park's first tourist facilities. On site are the Wawona Hotel, a charming 19th-century hotel, and the Pioneer Yosemite History Center. Wawona is also home to the Mariposa Grove of Giant Sequoias.

At the south end of the park, on Wawona Road (Highway 41), is the **Pioneer Yosemite History Center ★**, a small museum that encompasses stagecoaches and a few of the park's first buildings, transported here from their original location. About 6mi (10km) farther south lies **Mariposa Grove ★**, the largest giant-sequoia forest in Yosemite National Park and home to the

Grizzly Giant, one of the largest giant sequoias on the planet. Housed in rustic log building, the

Mariposa Grove Museum features exhibits on the natural history of these venerable forest giants.

Fragile Mono Lake

"If I could bring everyone in Los Angeles to Mono Lake, they would all see its value." – David Gaines

Though stalagmite-like tufa "towers" give Mono Lake a mysterious and surreal appearance, these unusual calcareous formations actually developed underwater and are only exposed because water is pumped from this lake to supply Los Angeles with drinking water. For the last 60-odd years, the "City of Angels" has been carrying out major drainage that, coupled with natural evaporation, has lowered the lake's water level by 40ft (12m) and doubled its level of salinity. This dramatic drop naturally threatens the resident fauna's natural habitat and source of food. The toxic dust of the lake bed and its dried-up tributaries, stirred up and carried away by the wind, have caused serious damage to the lakeshore ecosystem. Grebes and phala-

ropes seem particularly affected by the extinction of their primary source of food, Artemia, a species of brine shrimp they feast on with relish. The drainage also caused Negit Island to become a peninsula, making gulls's nests easy prey for mainland predators like coyotes. Alarmed by the situation, a group of young scientists led by David Gaines formed the Mono Lake Committee in 1978. Through litigation and major public-awareness and education campaigns, this organization's efforts were crowned with success in 1994, when the State Water Board set limits on the amount of water diverted from the region so as to raise and stabilize the lake's water level in the following decades. The government and citizens's groups then came to an agreement on a conservation and revitalization plan for the fragile Mono Lake Basin. But the battle has yet to be won.

★
The Hetch Hetchy Area

At one time, the **Hetch Hetchy** ★ Valley looked much like the Yosemite Valley does today, with its original rock formations and waterfalls. All water sports are unfortunately prohibited in the reservoir, the product of the damming of the Toulumne River, as it is a source of drinking water for San Francisco residents. The building of the O'Shaughnessy Dam was the subject of a great battle pitting conservationists, led by John Muir, against the federal government. The great Yosemite-lover died a year after President Woodrow Wilson authorized the building of the dam.

The **Hetch Hetchy Valley** ★ is a 30min drive from the end of Hetchy Road, off Evergreen Road. On the north side of the reservoir are Tueeulala and Wapana falls, behind which stands the Hetch Hetchy Dome rock formation. The trail along the reservoir's north side runs past O'Shaughnessy Dam.

Outdoor Activities

Swimming

At **Mono Lake** *(US 395, Lee Vining)*, you'll have the immense privilege of diving into a fantastic 760,000-year-old saltwater lake!

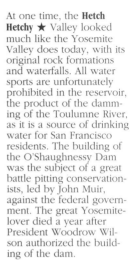

The Sierra Nevada

Kayaking and Canoeing

You can kayak or canoe down the Merced River and enjoy unique views of **Yosemite Valley**. Equipment is rented out at **Curry Village**.

The **Mono Lake Committee** (*US 395, at Third St., Lee Vining*, ☎ *760-647-6595*) organizes canoe trips on fabulous Mono Lake. If paddling on blue waters from which pure-white tufa columns emerge, while surrounded by countless aquatic birds appeals to you, you'll be enchanted by Mono Lake. One-hour outings are offered Saturday and Sunday mornings from June to September at a cost of $17 per person.

Fishing

Fishing enthusiasts visiting Bishop are duty-bound to take Highway 168 and head to the **Bishop Creek Recreation Area**, whose rivers and three lakes make it a very popular trout-fishing spot.

The Troutfitter (*Main St., at Old Mammoth Rd., in the Shell Mart Center, next to the Breakfast Club*, ☎ *760-924-3676, www.thetroutfitter.com*) organizes half-day and one-day guided fishing

trips for beginners and seasoned fishers alike. Rates vary from $100 to $190. Fishing gear is also rented out here.

Fishers can make their way to **Rick's Sport Center** (*Main St., near Center St., Mammoth Lakes*, ☎ *760-934-3416*), which offers half-day guided fishing trips to the most beautiful spots in the Mammoth Lakes area for $75 to $150 per person. Fishing gear is also available for rent.

Fishing is permitted in **Sequoia National Park** and **Kings Canyon National Park** for those with a California State Fishing Licence, available at tourist information offices.

Cycling

Yosemite National Park offers 12mi (19km) of bike paths in the valley area. Bicycles are available for rent at **Yosemite Lodge** (☎ *209-372-1208*) and **Curry Village** (☎ *209-372-8319*).

Horseback Riding

The **Rock Creek Pack Station** (*P.O. Box 248, Bishop*, ☎ *760-872-8331, www.rockcreekpackstation.com*) offers many packages to the eastern Sierra Nevada. Ranging from a few hours to several days, and from a few tens of to several hundred dollars, excursions include a wide choice of destinations.

Mammoth Lakes features several horseback-riding centres that organize excursions into the valleys of the majestic Sierra Nevada. Among them, **Reds Meadow Pack Station** (*Mammoth Lakes*, ☎ *760-934-2345 or 800-292-7758*), **McGee Creek Pack Station** (*The Roses, Rte. 1, Mammoth Lakes*, ☎ *760-935-4324*) and **Mammoth Lakes Pack Outfit** (*Mammoth Lakes*, ☎ *888-475-8747*) work in tandem with the Inyo National Forest authorities.

Two agencies organize summer excursions within the extraordinary Sequoia and Kings Canyon national parks. Working jointly, the **Wolverton Pack Station** (*north of Giant Forest*, ☎ *559-565-3039*) and **Mineral King Pack Station** (*at the end of Mineral Rd.*, ☎ *559-561-3039*) organize 1hr to one-day outings for $20 to $75.

The Yosemite National Park's **Yosemite Valley** (☎ *209-372-8348*), **Wawona** (☎ *209-375-6502*) and **Tuolumne Meadows** (☎ *209-372-8427*) areas have stables that offer 2hr, half-day and one-day guided excursions. More adventurous types can also make expeditions of up to six days, which include all meals and accommodations in one of the High Sierra camps.

Climbing

Yosemite National Park features some of the most beautiful rock faces in the world. The **Yosemite Mountaineering School and Guide Service** (*in Tuolumne Meadows in summer and Curry Village in winter, Yosemite National Park*, ☎ *209-372-8344 or 372-8435*) provides training workshops offering everything from basic rock-climbing techniques to guided climbs.

Downhill and Cross-Country Skiing

Note that winter activities are generally practised from November to March.

The **Mammoth Mountain Ski Area** (see p 296) (*Minaret Rd., Hwy. 203, Mammoth Lakes, ☎760-934-0745 or 800-MAMMOTH, woolly@mammoth-mtn.com, www.mammothmountain.com*) is a world-class ski resort where experts, beginners and families alike can indulge in their favourite sport. A one-day ski pass costs $52 per person. Packages of up to six days or more are also available.

The **Volcano Sports** shop (*126 Old Mammoth Rd., in Mammoth Mall, Mammoth Lakes, ☎760-924-3776*) rents out ski and snowboarding equipment.

You can rent snowboards as well as downhill and cross-country ski equipment at **Ski Renter** (*Main St., at Old Mammoth Rd., next to the gas station, Mammoth Lakes, ☎760-934-6560*).

Wave Rave (*3203 Main St., Mammoth Lakes, ☎760-934-2471*), a reputable local shop, specializes in the sale and rental of snowboards.

Snowshoes and cross-country skis can be rented at **Wolverton** (*Sequoia National Park*). Trails link this area to the General Sherman Tree Area.

Cross-country skiers will find trails in the **Grant Grove**, **Cherry Gap** and **Big Meadows** (*Kings Canyon National Park*) areas. Equipment is available for rent at the **Grant Grove Market**.

Snowmobiling

Mammoth Snowmobile Adventures (*on the other side of the ski resort's Main Lodge, Minaret Rd., Mammoth Lakes, ☎760-934-9645*) offers two to 5hr excursions in the Sierra Nevada for $70 to $260, snowmobile and helmet included.

Accommodations

Lone Pine

Inyo National Forest Campgrounds
$6-$12 per tent
May to Oct
☎*(760) 876-6200*
☎*800-280-CAMP*
www.reserveusa.com
www.r5.fs.fed.us/inyo
Outdoor enthusiasts should make a beeline for the Inyo National Forest, which offers campsites in an enchanting setting at the foot of Mount Whitney and the Sierra Nevada. The campgrounds generally have washrooms and drinking water and, above all, provide access to superb hiking trails of varying levels of difficulty (see p 293). Noteworthy campgrounds include Whitney Portal, Whitney Portal Trailhead, Cottonwood Lakes, Horseshoe Meadow Equestrian, Golden Trout Backpacker,

Lone Pine and Tuttle Creek.

Mt. Whitney Motel
$$
tv, ≈, ⅄
305 N. Main St.
Lone Pine, CA 93545
☎*(760) 876-4207*
☎*800-845-2362*
≈*(760) 876-8818*
A simple, unpretentious little establishment located north of the village, the Mt. Whitney Motel is a very decent option for budget travellers not in search of luxury or fancy accommodations. The place offers well-kept rooms with typical low-budget-motel decor and furnishings.

Best Western Frontier Motel
$$-$$$ bkfst incl.
≡, tv, ≈, ⅄
1008 S. Main St.
Lone Pine, CA 93545
☎*(760) 876-5571*
☎*800-528-1234*
≈*(760) 876-5357*
A quiet and well-kept establishment, the Best Western Frontier Motel has made the most of recent renovations to further improve its level of quality. Located at the south entrance to the village, on US 395, this small motel offers 73 soberly decorated rooms, some of which are adorned with a few photographs of film shoots in the Alabama Hills, and lovely mountain and valley views.

Dow Villa Motel / Historic Dow Hotel
$$-$$$
≡, tv, ℝ, ≈, ⅄
310 S. Main St.
Lone Pine, CA 93545
☎*(760) 876-5521*
☎*800-824-9317*
≈*(760) 876-5643*
www.dowvillamotel.com
An institution in Lone Pine that has been around for decades, the Dow Villa

The Sierra Nevada

Motel / Historic Dow Hotel has managed to keep its charm of yesteryear while providing all modern conveniences. The main building's facade, with its wooden planks and shingles, is reminiscent of the Old West. All the motel rooms feature comfortable furnishings and a private entrance, while the central historic building houses other, smaller, more rustic rooms as well as a very pleasant period lobby.

Bishop

Inyo National Forest Public Campgrounds
$11-$12 per tent
☎877-444-6777
www.r5.fs.fed.us/inyo
www.reserveusa.com
The Bishop Creek area offers more than a dozen campgrounds open during the summer season, most of which have washrooms and drinking water.

The Chalfant House Bed & Breakfast
$$-$$$ bkfst incl.
tv
213 Academy St., Bishop, CA 93514
☎*(760) 872-1790*
☎*800-641-2996*
⇒*(760) 872-9221*
www.chalfanthousebb.com
Fred and Sally Manecke welcome you to the charming Chalfant House, built in 1898 by the editor of the Owens Valley's first newspaper, P. A. Chalfant. Later turned into the Academy Hotel, an inn catering to area miners, the elegant house now offers eight rooms, three of which are set up in a more modern annex behind the main house. The decor and furnishings of the rooms, each of which is named after a member of the

Chalfant family, recall the Victorian era.

Rodeway Inn
$$-$$$
≡, *tv*, ≈
150 E. Elm St., Bishop, CA 93514
☎*(760) 873-3564*
☎*800-228-2000*
⇒*(760) 873-6936*
Slightly set back from Main Street, the Rodeway Inn offers 55 modest rooms, some of which feature a sofa and a work table. This simple, hospitable little motel has recently been upgraded.

Best Western Creekside Inn
$$$ bkfst incl.
≡, *tv*, ℝ, K
725 N. Main St., Bishop, CA 93514
☎*(760) 872-3044*
☎*800-273-3550*
⇒*(760) 872-1300*
Though part of the well-known Best Western chain, the Creekside Inn is particularly charming, with its retro-looking lobby. Well kept, this small hotel stands next to a creek bordered by a small flowery garden that can be viewed from some of the rooms. The 89 rooms, 12 of which come with a kitchenette, feature quality cherrywood furniture and offer a level of comfort and quiet that is much appreciated by guests.

Bishop Creek Lodge
$$$
ℝ, K
take Hwy. 168 (W. Ligne St.) from the Bishop town centre
2100 South Lake Rd.
Bishop, CA 93514
☎*(760) 873-4484*
⇒*(760) 873-8524*
bspcrk@schat.com
www.bishopcreekresorts.com
Benefitting from a choice location in the Bishop Creek Recreation Area, the Bishop Creek Lodge offers cabins that sleep two to eight people. Rustic but

comfortable, they are well equipped and offer a most pleasant stay deep in the country, where you will be charmed by the singing birds and murmuring river.

Mammoth Lakes

As Mammoth Lakes is a very popular outdoor-activities and ski area, those travelling with children and looking to extend their stay will be pleased to learn that there are several long-term condo rentals available here.

Inyo National Forest Public Campgrounds
$12-$13
☎877-444-6777
www.r5.fs.fed.us/inyo
www.reserveusa.com
The Mammoth Village, Mammoth Lakes Basin and Reds Meadow areas offer more than a dozen campgrounds, equipped with washrooms and drinking water.

Innsbruck Lodge
$$-$$$
tv, ℝ, K, ♿, △
913 Forest Trail
Mammoth Lakes, CA 93546
☎*(760) 934-3035*
www.innsbrucklodge.com
Reminiscent of an alpine cottage, the Innsbruck Lodge offers 17 simple rooms, some of which feature a balcony while others come with a kitchenette. The sloping grounds offer beautiful mountain views to guests in the back rooms. Located in the heart of a pine forest, this pleasant little hotel ensures the peace and quiet sought by many visitors to Mammoth Lakes.

North Village Inn
$$-$$$ bkfst incl.
tv, ℝ, K
103 Lake Mary Rd.
Mammoth Lakes, CA 93546
☎*(760) 934-2525*
☎*800-257-3781*
⇄*(760) 934-1466*
www.northvillageinn.com
The North Village Inn caters to all tastes and budgets, offering motel-style rooms in the main building, rooms with a kitchenette, some of which have a fireplace as well, and Swiss-chalet-like cabins. Yet another quiet, warm and friendly establishment redolent of pines.

Snow Goose Inn
$$-$$$ bkfst incl.
tv, K, ◊
57 Forest Trail
Mammoth Lakes, CA 93546
☎*(760) 934-2660*
☎*800-874-7368*
⇄*(760) 934-5655*
frnvegas@aol.com
www.snowgoose-inn.com
Rustic, affordable and welcoming, the Snow Goose Inn is located in a quiet spot set back from the main drag. Offering 19 simple rooms and a country-style dining room, the establishment exudes bucolic simplicity much appreciated by guests. Comfortable rooms featuring a kitchenette and fireplace are also available.

Mammoth Mountain Inn
$$$-$$$$ bkfst incl.
tv, K, ≈, ℛ, ᕕ, ◊
Minaret Rd., at the foot of the slopes
mailing address: P.O. Box 353,
Mammoth Lakes, CA 93546
☎*(760) 934-2581*
☎*800-228-4947*
⇄*(760) 934-0701*
the-inn@mammoth-mtn.com
www.mammothlodging.com
Skiers take note: at the foot of the slopes, in front of the Main Lodge and ski lifts, the Mammoth Mountain Inn is a dream choice for snow-sports buffs. This luxurious, alpine-style

stone-and-wood resort predictably offers a wealth of activities in the winter season, but also fills up with outdoor enthusiasts during the summer. Its 213 units (chalets, condos and motel rooms), several of which feature a fireplace and kitchenette, are all warmly decorated, as are its lounges. The result is an atmosphere that is congenial yet refined.

🏔 Tamarack Lodge & Resort
$$$-$$$$ bkfst incl.
K, ℛ
take Lake Mary Rd. toward Twin Lakes
mailing address: P.O. Box 69
Mammoth Lakes, CA 93546
☎*(760) 934-2442*
☎*800-237-6879*
⇄*(760) 934-2281*
www.tamaracklodge.com
Combining luxury, comfort and mountain charm, Tamarack Lodge has been a quality choice for visitors to Mammoth Lakes and outdoor enthusiasts since 1924. With its magnificent location a few miles south of town, deep in the forest on Twin Lakes, the establishment offers guests rooms in the cozy, picturesque main wooden lodge, and charming cabins spread throughout the countryside that are peaceful and intimate. In winter, cross-country-skiing and snowshoeing trails converge on Tamarack Lodge, while the summer season provides guests with a perfect home base for hiking, cycling and fishing.

Lee Vining

Besides the following establishments, the village of Lee Vining has a few rustic motels that lack charm but offer very affordable rooms.

Inyo National Forest Public Campgrounds
$6-$11
☎*877-444-6777*
www.r5.fs.fed.us/inyo
www.reserveusa.com
The Lee Vining and Mono Lake area offers six campgrounds, two of which are without drinking water.

El Mono Motel
$$
Apr to Oct
sb/pb, tv
Main St., at Third St.
Lee Vining, CA 93541
☎*(760) 647-6310*
Built in 1927 and restored a few times since, the El Mono Motel is a decent alternative for budget travellers. The old house with dormer windows—which could certainly use a facelift—contains two rooms, while seven others are located in an annex at the back. Though the exterior of the house is no indication, the rooms prove to be clean and bright. There is also a small café at the entrance.

Best Western Lake View Lodge
$$$
tv
30 Main St., Lee Vining, CA 93541
☎*(760) 647-6543*
Located at the south entrance to the village, in the Sierran foothills, the Best Western Lake View Lodge offers motel-style rooms. Spread out over two floors, each room has a private entrance. Guests enjoy understated but very comfortable rooms in a quiet, peaceful spot.

🏔 Tioga Lodge
$$$
Apr to Oct
US 395, Lee Vining, CA 93541
☎*(760) 647-6423*
A few miles north of Lee Vining, the Tioga Lodge is enviably located right on magnificent Mono Lake. Simple, rustic and intimate, a handful of white-painted

wooden cabins modelled after the two main houses offer guests accommodations by this beautiful lake. Additional cabins were built during the winter of 1999-2000.

Bridgeport

A few establishments close their doors during the winter season.

Humboldt-Toiyabe National Forest Public Campgrounds
$5-$10
☎877-444-6777
The Bridgeport and Twin Lakes area has 14 campgrounds, most of which offer washrooms and drinking water.

Bridgeport Inn
$$
sb/pb, tv, ℜ
Main St., P.O. Box 128
Bridgeport, CA 93517
☎(760) 932-7380
☞(760) 932-1160
www.thebridgeportinn.com
Built in 1877 as the Old Levitt House, then later turned into a hotel and a stagecoach stop favoured by prospectors and farmers for its jovial atmosphere, the Bridgeport Inn is an indisputable part of the community's history. The historic central building houses a friendly Irish pub, a very well-preserved Victorian lounge richly decorated with period furniture and objects, as well as a few 19th-century-style rooms. Unfortunately, most guestrooms are set up in a very mundane motel behind the venerable house.

Walker River Lodge
$$$
tv, ≈, &
100 Main St., Bridgeport, CA 93517
☎(760) 932-7021
☎800-688-3351
☞(760) 932-7914
A very pleasant motel set right near a small river, the Walker River Lodge offers soberly decorated but quite comfortable rooms. Some rooms feature a small terrace overlooking a little garden by the river.

Cain House Bed & Breakfast
$$$ bkfst incl.
Apr to Oct
340 Main St., Bridgeport, CA 93517
☎(760) 932-7383
The old Cain House has been welcoming guests since 1989. Located in the village's historic centre, this venerable 100-year-old wooden house offers rooms with period cachet.

Sequoia and Kings Canyon National Parks

Note that there are three hotels and restaurants in the Sequoia National Forest, which adjoins both national parks. These establishments are a choice alternative for those unable to find accommodations within Sequoia and Kings Canyon national parks.

Public Campgrounds
reservations May to Oct
☎800-365-2267
www.reservations.nps.gov
The two national parks encompass over 1,200 campsites scattered throughout some 20 campgrounds that stretch from gentle valleys to fresh conifer forests. A few of these campgrounds are

open year-round. Only those of Lodgepole Village and Dorst Creek accept reservations.

Grant Grove Lodge
$-$$
sb/pb, ℜ
Hwy. 180, Grant Grove Village
Kings Canyon National Park
☎(559) 335-5500
The Grant Grove Lodge stands at the entrance to Kings Canyon Park. Run by government funds, the establishment offers rustic cabins with kerosene lamps and wood-burning stoves, as well as more comfortable "housekeeping cabins" with electricity.

Kings Canyon Lodge
$$
May to late Nov
ℜ
Hwy. 180, 27km east of Grant Grove
Sequoia National Forest
☎(559) 335-2405
A private hotel, Kings Canyon Lodge provides guests with cabins and rooms offering good value for the price. Secluded, this establishment is sure to please those eager to enjoy the surrounding wilderness.

Montecito-Sequoia Lodge
$$
sb/pb, ½b, ℜ, ≈, &
Generals Hwy., 9mi (14.5km) south of Grant Grove
Sequoia National Forest
☎(559) 565-3388
☎800-227-9900
msreservations@montecitosequoia.com
Offering 26 rooms and 13 cabins, the Montecito-Sequoia Lodge is a good choice for those looking to take advantage of the many summer and winter activities in the area. The establishment is administered by private funds.

Silver City Resort
$$
May to Sep
ℜ
Mineral King Rd.
Sequoia National Park
☎*(559) 561-3223*
A private establishment, the Silver City Resort offers rustic cabins in a wild, secluded spot.

Stony Creek Lodge
$$
May to Sep
ℜ
Generals Hwy., between Grant Grove and Giant Forest
Sequoia National Forest
☎*(559) 335-5500*
This small hotel features a common room with a large stone fireplace, a dining room and a souvenir shop. The motel-style rooms are past their prime but attractive.

Cedar Grove Lodge
$$$
May to Nov
ℜ
Hwy. 180, Cedar Grove Village
Kings Canyon National Park
☎*(559) 335-5500*
This National Park Service-managed motel is unfortunately forced to shut down in winter as Highway 180 is closed due to snow and the risk of avalanches.

Wuksachi Village & Lodge
$$$-$$$$
tv, ℜ
Generals Hwy., 4mi (6.5km) north of the General Sherman Tree
Sequoia National Park
☎*(559) 253-2199*
☎*888-252-5757*
Managed by the park authorities, the brand-new Wuksachi Village & Lodge offers 102 comfortable rooms within three rustic yet upscale lodge buildings that blend in very well with their surroundings. Guests can take advantage of all the facilities and comforts of a major

hotel in a most enchanting setting.

Yosemite National Park

Public Campgrounds
☎*800-436-7275*
www.reservations.nps.gov
Yosemite National Park offers campers a grand total of 13 campgrounds. From May 1 to September 15, a maximum stay of seven days is permitted in the Wawona and Yosemite Valley areas, while the other areas allow a maximum stay of 14 days. Throughout the rest of the year, campers can stay for up to 30 days.

A stay in **Yosemite National Park** *(☎559-252-4848, www.yosemitepark.com)* must be planned in advance; reservations are essential. Please call the above-mentioned number to reserve for all of the following lodgings.

The Yosemite Valley Area

Housekeeping Camp
$$
May to Nov
sb
The Housekeeping Camp offers impressive views of Yosemite Falls and Half Dome, as well as a sandy beach on the banks of the Merced River. A total of 266 tent cabins with beds are available here.

Curry Village
$$-$$$
May to Nov, weekends and public holidays in winter
sb/pb, ≈
Created in 1899 as a budget alternative to other, more expensive establishments, Curry Village remains true to its roots. Nestled in the shadow of Glacier Point, it benefits

from the coolest temperatures on hot summer days. The establishment offers 18 motel-style rooms, 103 cottages with private bathrooms, 80 cabins and 427 tent cabins with beds and shared bathrooms.

Yosemite Lodge
$$-$$$
sb/pb, ≈, ℜ
☎*(209) 372-1274*
Yosemite Lodge occupies the former site of Fort Yosemite, the park headquarters of the U.S. Army Cavalry, which was in charge of managing and protecting the park from 1906 to 1914. In June 1915, a Los Angeles entrepreneur was hand-picked to set up new lodging facilities. Some military barracks remained until the 1950s, when the hotel was updated. Yosemite Lodge now features 245 comfortable rooms.

The Ahwahnee
$$$$$
≈, ℜ
Designated a National Historic Landmark, The Ahwahnee is a magnificent establishment in an enchanting forest setting. The quality of the service and facilities have gained the public's favour since the hotel first opened, in 1927. Designed by architect Gilbert Stanley Underwood, the establishment's six-storey facade of granite columns, stained to resemble redwood, is in perfect harmony with the surrounding forest set against the backdrop of the Royal Arches rock formation. Paintings, photographs and Native American handicrafts adorn the magnificent communal rooms. Would-be guests must often make reservations up to a year in advance to snag one of the hotel's 123 newly renovated rooms.

The Sierra Nevada

Water, Water Everywhere...

California is experiencing a phenomenal urban-population boom. Approximately eight out of 10 Californians are city-dwellers. And given the climate, Californians have an unfortunate tendency to end up in Southern California, in an arid territory where living conditions are the least favourable. With great ingenuity, a number of dam and aqueduct projects were launched to collect water from the mountains and thus to supply the southern populations. California's aqueduct system is the most extensive in the world.

The Colorado River is one of Southern California's principal sources of drinking water. From Lake Havasu, on the famous river, a 29-tunnel aqueduct system runs 242mi (389km) through the desert and the San Bernardino Mountains, delivering precious water into Matthews Lake in the San Diego area. The Colorado River Aqueduct, completed in 1939, carries a daily average 133,678,004ft³ (3,785,411m³) of water.

The city of Los Angeles has had an independent source of water since 1913. The Los Angeles Aqueduct, which draws its water from the Owens River in the Sierra Nevada, runs 338mi (544km) and supplies the megalopolis's residents with 534,712,016ft³ (15,141,644m³) of water a day.

As for San Francisco, it has primarily drawn its water from the Hetch Hetchy Reservoir in Yosemite National Park since 1934.

Last on the list and completed in 1972, the 444mi-long (715km) State Water Project Aqueduct links the Sacramento River Delta to the Perris Reservoir, south of Los Angeles.

The High Country

High Siera Camps
$$
Jun to Sep
sb, ½b
High Sierra Desk, Yosemite Reservations, 5410 E. Home Ave.
Fresno, CA 93727
Home-style meals and comfortable beds await guests of the five High Sierra Camps. Accessible on foot or horseback, each camp is well laid out in a beautiful wild setting. The tent cabins with beds sleep two to six people. Given the high demand, spaces are assigned by lottery, held in mid-December. Submissions are accepted from October 15 to November 30 only. Lottery

results reach "contestants" in late March.

Tuolumne Meadows Lodge
$$
May to Nov
sb, ℜ
Located in the very heart of Tuolumne Meadows, the rustic but hospitable Tuolumne Meadows Lodge is a favourite with hikers. It offers 69 tent cabins furnished with beds.

White Wolf Lodge
$$
May to Nov
sb/pb, ℜ
A popular base camp for day hikes to the Harden and Lukens Lakes area, the White Wolf Lodge is set in the wilderness of the High Country. Four cottages

with private bathrooms and 24 tent cabins with beds and shared bathrooms are available.

The Wawona Area

🚣 Wawona Hotel
$$-$$$
Apr to Nov,
Christmas holidays and
weekends year-round
sb/pb, ≈, ℜ
☎ **(209) 375-6556**
A National Historic Landmark, the Wawona Hotel and its predecessor have been welcoming visitors since the 1850s in the park's least-visited area. A fine example of Victorian architecture then in fashion, the wooden building has earned the recognition

of the California Trust for Historic Preservation. The venerable hotel offers 104 rooms with rustic cachet.

Restaurants

Lone Pine

PJ's
$-$$
24hrs
446 S. Main St.
☎*(760) 876-5796*
Adjacent to the Dow Villa Motel, the small PJ's eatery opens its kitchen, emitting the smell of cooking 24hrs a day for the pleasure of its local clientele. Filling home-style fare is featured on the menu, which offers salads, sandwiches, burgers, steaks and, of course, hearty breakfasts.

Totem Cafe
$$-$$$
131 S. Main St.
☎*(760) 876-1120*
A small establishment with seven to eight tables and a warm, long-standing decor, the Totem Cafe is the place to go for a thick, rare steak. Patrons here enjoy typically American fare, including fried food, ribs, chicken and seafood, to the sounds of country music.

Season's
$$$
N. Main St., at Whitney Portal Rd.
☎*(760) 876-8927*
As conservative and retro as the community of Lone Pine, Season's is the most popular restaurant in town for big Saturday nights out. Served here are simply prepared steaks and other grilled meats as well as seafood, some of which is fried.

Bishop

 Erick Schat's Bakery
$
Main St. (next to Cottonwood Plaza)
☎*(760) 873-7156*
A veritable Bishop institution, Erick Schat's Bakery has been turning out bread and pastries since 1938. This very popular local establishment also features a sandwich counter as well as a café offering baked goods fresh from the oven. Be sure to try the house specialty, sheepherder bread!

Bar-B-Q Bills
$$
187 S. Main St.
☎*(760) 872-5535*
With a name like Bar-B-Q Bills, it is hardly surprising that this establishment does not dabble in nouvelle cuisine. Ribs, chicken and burgers have been getting top billing here since 1966. Patrons are invited to sit in a typical Old West-style dining room, complete with booths, a salad bar, an old piano and western decor.

Imperial Gourmet Chinese Restaurant
$$
785 N. Main St. (Cottonwood Plaza)
☎*(760) 872-1144*
Specializing in Middle Kingdom cuisine, the Imperial Gourmet Chinese Restaurant will satisfy fans of the genre. In an unexceptional dining room, an all-you-can-eat Sunday brunch buffet is also served. The restaurant is located at the back of the Cottonwood Plaza parking lot, on the second floor.

The Upper Crust Pizza Co.
$$
1180 N. Main St.
(Smart & Final Center)
☎*(760) 872-8153*
The most popular Italian restaurant in Bishop, The

Upper Crust Pizza Co. dishes up simple fare in a laid-back, family-style ambiance. The red-painted wooden restaurant features a menu with an emphasis on pasta and pizza.

Whiskey Creek
$$-$$$
524 N. Main St.
☎*(760) 873-7174*
In business since 1924, the Whiskey Creek restaurant offers breakfast, lunch and dinner on the outdoor terrace, in the Saloon or in a more intimate dining room. The chef specializes in sandwiches, thick steaks, ribs and barbecued chicken, so popular in these parts. The charming wooden gabled house is also home to a souvenir shop.

Mammoth Lakes

Base Café Camp
$
Main St., next to Schat's Bakery
☎*(760) 934-3900*
Set up in a wooden house reminiscent of a mountain chalet, the Base Café Camp serves simple meals in keeping with the place. Sandwiches, salads and burgers take up most of the menu.

Breakfast Club
$
Old Mammoth Rd., at Main St.
near the gas station
☎*(760) 934-6499*
A favourite with both out-of-towners and locals for its delicious, lavish breakfasts and varied lunches, the Breakfast Club has been in business since 1986. In addition to his pancakes, omelets and other specialties, the chef is a past master at making cheesecakes whose renown extends far beyond the borders of Mammoth Lakes. On Sunday mornings, it is best to make

The Sierra Nevada

reservations—or keep in mind that patience is a virtue.

🌴 Café Vermeer/ Schat's Bakery
$
Main St., across from the post office
☎(760) 934-4203
A European-style café that serves breakfast and lunch, Café Vermeer offers simple fare for people on the go. Sandwiches with fresh-baked bread, pancakes, "glazed eggs Benedict à la Vermeer," French toast and Sierra-style shepherd's pie have made the café's name. Before sitting down to eat, you'll have to walk through Schat's Bakery, where the aroma of freshly baked bread and other goodies may just prove too tempting to resist!

🌴 Looney Bean Coffee Roasting Company
$
Main St., a little west of the intersection of Old Mammoth Rd.
☎(760) 934-1345
A tiny café where customers order espresso, pastries and excellent homemade muesli at the counter, the Looney Bean Coffee Roasting Company is the morning hangout of snow bunnies. The outdoor terrace is a great spot on which to discuss yesterday's good runs or those still to come!

Yodler Bar & Pub
$
Minaret Rd., next to the Mammoth Mountain Inn
☎(760) 934-0636
A sports pub and restaurant, as well as a perfect after-ski hangout, the Yodler Bar & Pub has a distinctly alpine character, with its Swiss-style architecture. Sandwiches, burgers, barbecued chicken and fish & chips make up the bulk of the conventional menu. Patrons and skiers enjoy the warm fire on cold winter days, while

spring sees the huge outdoor terrace fill up with a lively, good-natured crowd.

The Stove
$-$$
644 Old Mammoth Rd.
☎(760) 934-2821
Set up in a small, grey wooden house and aptly graced with an old wood-burning stove at the entrance, this lively, popular eatery has been offering patrons generous portions and friendly service for nigh on 30 years. The generous and simple family fare served here, including classic salads, burgers, pies and poultry, goes hand in hand with the place's character.

🌴 Alpenrose
$$$
343 Old Mammoth Rd.
☎(760) 934-3077
An authentic Swiss restaurant offering a friendly and laid-back yet romantic and intimate atmosphere, Alpenrose serves the finest of Helvetic dishes alongside house specialties such as lamb, fresh-fish and veal dishes. Homemade strudel, torte and crepes pleasantly round out a meal at this small restaurant, housed in a quintessential wooden mountain lodge.

Mogul Restaurant
$$$
Tavern Rd., at Old Mammoth Rd.
☎(760) 934-3039
Mogul's tasty, tender steaks are the key to its long-running success. In addition to an extensive menu featuring prime rib, fresh fish, seafood, poultry and rack of lamb, patrons appreciate the warm and rustic atmosphere of this charming wood-panelled chalet.

Shogun
$$$
Old Mammoth Rd.
upstairs at the Sierra Center Mall
☎(760) 934-3970
Established in 1980, Shogun offers classic Japanese cuisine at its finest, from teriyaki and tempura to sashimi and sushi. The second-floor dining room features large picture windows that offer stunning panoramic views of the neighbouring mountains.

Slocums American Grill & Bar
$$$
Main St., east of the intersection of Old Mammoth Rd.
☎(760) 934-7647
Featuring a dining room with a 19th-century decor, Slocums American Grill & Bar has been specializing in tender, juicy steaks since 1983. In addition to red meat, the chef skilfully prepares house specialties such as sautéed scampi, "escargot royale," Portobello chicken stuffed with feta and basil, fresh salmon and crab.

Mountain Side Grill
$$$-$$$$
Minaret Rd., at the Mammoth Mountain Inn
☎(760) 934-0601
The culinary complement to the swanky Mammoth Mountain Inn (see p 313), Mountain Side Grill offers a wide array of dishes, from the most traditional to the most elaborate, such as game and fresh fish. Located on the hotel's second floor, the establishment features a very pleasant outdoor terrace overlooking the ski slopes.

Lee Vining

The small supermarket located right next to the Best Western Lake View Lodge hotel can come in very handy when planning picnics by Mono Lake.

You can't miss it: it's housed in a red log structure.

Nicely's Restaurant
$$
Main St.
☎(760) 647-6477
Hearty breakfasts and generous portions draw patrons to Nicely's Restaurant all year-round. The down-to-earth fare served here, including burgers, sandwiches, salads, grilled meats and pasta, goes hand-in-hand with the simple, home-style decor, with booths and paper tablecloths.

The Yosemite Trails Inn Restaurant
$$
Apr to Oct
Main St.
☎(760) 647-6312
The appealing Yosemite Trails Inn Restaurant occupies a green-and-white house in the heart of Lee Vining. The food is typically American, simple and unoriginal but of indisputable quality.

Bridgeport

Most of the village's handful of dining establishments close their doors during the winter season.

Hays Street Café
$-$$
Apr to Oct
Main St.
opposite the Walker Lodge Motel
☎(760) 932-7141
For the first two meals of the day, the pleasant, convivial Hays Street

Coyote

Café, set up in a small green-and-white wooden house, serves decent fare in a laid-back atmosphere.

Virginia Creek Settlement
$$
Apr to Oct
US 395, a little north of Hwy. 270
☎(760) 932-7780
If you've built up an appetite exploring the Bodie ghost town, the Virginia Creek Settlement restaurant's filling home-style Italian cooking will satisfy your hunger. Pasta, pizza, steak and poultry make up the bulk of the menu at this eatery, located in a small wooden house some 12.5mi (20km) south of the village. With a barouche and wind turbine prominently displayed on the neighbouring land, you can't miss it.

Bridgeport Inn
$$-$$$
Main St.
☎(760) 932-7380
The historic Bridgeport Inn features a dining room with about 10 tables and a menu that emphasizes simple fare such as burgers, salads, steak and pasta. Unlike the charming adjacent pub, the decor here seems more commonplace, without many references to the past.

Sequoia and Kings Canyon National Parks

For breakfast and inexpensive light meals such as salads, pizza, sandwiches and burgers, summer visitors can turn to Lodgepole Village, Stony Creek Village, Grant Grove, Cedar Grove Village or the Giant Forest and Wolverton areas. In winter, from November to March, visi-

tors must make do with Grant Grove and Wolverton, as all other establishments are closed. Of course, you can always stock up on picnic supplies here and take advantage of the many picnic spots in the area while enjoying the beauties of nature.

Wuksachi Village & Lodge
$$$
year-round
Generals Hwy., 4mi (6.5km) north of the General Sherman Tree
Sequoia National Park
☎(559) 560-4070
The charming Wuksachi Village & Lodge serves all three daily meals in a dining room with mountain charm. The food is simple but top-notch.

Kings Canyon Lodge
$$
May to late Nov
Hwy. 180, 16.8mi (27km) east of Grant Grove
Sequoia National Forest
☎(559) 335-2405
The Kings Canyon Lodge's café serves breakfast and lunch daily in a warm and friendly atmosphere. Dinner is served on weekends only.

Yosemite National Park

Fast food and light meals are served at the Yosemite Lodge Swimming Pool, Curry Village Coffee Corner, Curry Village Hamburger Deck, Curry Village Pizza Ratio, Village Grill (Yosemite Village), Degnan's Delicatessen (Yosemite Village), Degnan's Fast Food (Yosemite Village), Happy Isles Snack Stand, Glacier Point Snack Stand, Wawona Golf Shop Snack Stand and Tuolumne Meadows Grill. Again, it is always a good idea to enjoy the beauties of nature and take advantage of the many picnic spots in the area. Opening hours and seasons can vary, so it is best to call ahead (☎209-372-1000, ext. 8). There are also a few small supermarkets in various areas of the park, the main one being the Village Store in Yosemite Village.

The Yosemite Valley Area

Yosemite Lodge Cafeteria and Coffee Corner
$-$$
The Yosemite Lodge Cafeteria and Coffee Corner serves all three daily meals.

Curry Pavilion
$-$$
Mar to Oct
The Curry Pavilion also serves breakfast, lunch and dinner.

Degnan's Pasta Plus
$$
May to Nov
☎(209) 372-8381
A cheerful, family-style eatery, Degnan's Pasta Plus dishes up fresh pasta, salads and roast chicken.

Garden Terrace (Yosemite Lodge)
$$
May to Oct
☎(209) 372-1269
A salad bar, soups, pasta, cuts of meat and desserts are offered at the Garden Terrace, a one-price, buffet-style eatery.

Mountain Room Restaurant (Yosemite Lodge)
$$$
Refurbished in 1997, the Mountain Room Restaurant now offers steak, prime rib, fish and various kinds of pasta as well as a wonderful view of Yosemite Falls.

The Ahwahnee Dining Room
$$$$
☎(209) 372-1489
Graced with 36ft-high (11m) ceilings, splendid chandeliers and huge picture windows that allow patrons to enjoy the surrounding wilderness from the comfort of a very posh dining room, the Ahwahnee Dining Room is often considered one of the most beautiful restaurants in the country. Though breakfast and lunch are casual affairs, patrons are requested to dress more formally for dinner.

The High Country

Tuolumne Meadows Lodge
$$
May to Nov
☎(209) 372-8413
Beneath a simple canopy tent in a forest setting by the Tuolumne River, patrons of the Tuolumne Meadows Lodge enjoy hearty breakfasts and lunches.

White Wolf Lodge
$$
May to Nov
☎(209) 372-8416
An establishment with a laid-back atmosphere located on Tioga Road, the White Wolf Lodge serves breakfast, lunch and dinner. Its large porch and rustic dining room make for a very pleasant dining experience.

Wawona Area

Wawona Hotel Dining Room
$$-$$$
Apr to Nov, Christmas holidays and weekends year-round
The Wawona Hotel Dining Room has built its reputation on simple, always-fresh home-style fare. Patrons here enjoy breakfast, lunch and dinner in a charming Victorian-style setting while treated to magnificent sunsets.

Entertainment

Lone Pine

Lone Pine's Main Street offers country-music-loving beer drinkers a few saloons.

Shopping

Bishop

Owens Valley Paiute-Shoshone Indian Cultural Museum
2301 W. Ligne St.
south of the village
☎(760) 873-4478
The Owens Valley Paiute-Shoshone Indian Cultural Museum houses a shop where you can purchase handmade Native American jewellery.

The proximity of Bishop Creek, a trout and freshwater-fish paradise, explains the great concentration of hunting and fishing shops in such a small community.

Lee Vining

Outfitters Fine Leather Goods
Main St., opposite the supermarket
Outfitters Fine Leather Goods sells Native American crafts. The shop not only carries leather goods, but also tapestries and jewellery made by local artisans.

Central Coast

T he Central Coast,
which is the cradle of modern California,
stretches nearly 373mi (600km) between San Jose
and Oxnard.

I ts green mountains, jagged cliffs, pine forests,
sandy beaches, and cities
that are both picturesque
and modern make the
Central Coast one of California's most impressive
regions.

T he Central Coast is the
California of our
dreams, where stunning
scenery borders fine-sand
beaches and where the
high-tech and entertain-
ment industries flourish.
Although these images are
so vivid, visitors should go
beyond these simple
clichés and completely
immerse themselves in
exploring this region,
which is so rich in every
sense. Let yourself be surprised by the facets of
mythical California that
have yet to be discovered.
Although the Central Coast
includes fabulously rich
San Jose and its famous
Silicon Valley, posh and
bourgeois Carmel and
opulent Santa Barbara with
its endless beaches, it also
features picturesque and
underrated agglomerations
full of history such as
Monterey and San Luis
Obispo, not to mention

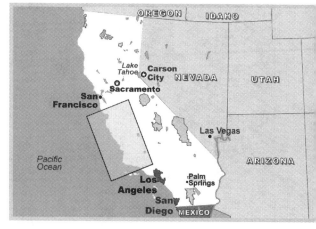

the free-spirited Santa Cruz
and peaceful Ventura.

I ts rich soil and favourable climate have
blessed the Central Coast
with, among other things,
several impressive vine-
yards, as evidenced by the
quality of wine they pro-
duce. Santa Ynez Valley
producers certainly mea-
sure up to their colleagues
of the famous Sonoma and
Napa Valleys, and their
wines are well represented
on store shelves.

A s if the list of attractions was not long
enough, the Central Coast
also includes several of
California's most under-

rated and wonderful architectural and historical treasures. Most Spanish mis-
sions erected by Francis-
can monks were built in
this region. The Camino
Real (what is today the US
101) linked the 21 mis-
sions of the network. To-
day visitors can admire
these gems, among which
San Juan Bautista, Carmel,
San Miguel, La Purísima,
Santa Inés and Santa
Barbara stand out.

W onders of nature are
certainly not lacking
on the Central Coast, and
the Big Sur region, which
is located south of the
Monterey Peninsula, can
attest to that. This jagged

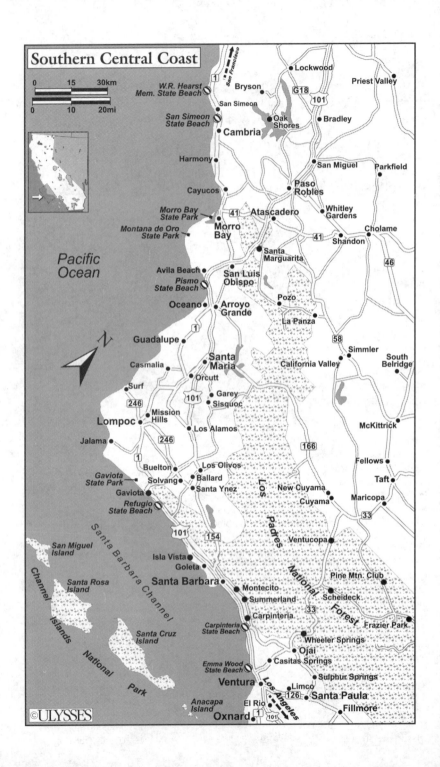

Southern Central Coast

0   15   30km
0   10   20mi

Pacific Ocean

Santa Barbara Channel

Channel Islands National Park

San Francisco

Lockwood
Priest Valley
W.R. Hearst Mem. State Beach
Bryson
San Simeon
G18
101
San Simeon State Beach
Oak Shores
Bradley
Cambria
Harmony
San Miguel
Parkfield
Cayucos
Paso Robles
Morro Bay State Park
41
Atascadero
Whitley Gardens
Cholame
Montana de Oro State Park
Morro Bay
41
Shandon
46
Santa Marguarita
Avila Beach
San Luis Obispo
Pismo State Beach
Pozo
Oceano
Arroyo Grande
La Panza
Guadalupe
58
Simmler
South Belridge
Casmalia
Santa Maria
California Valley
Orcutt
Surf
246
Garey
101
Sisquoc
Mission Hills
McKittrick
Lompoc
Los Alamos
246
Jalama
166
Fellows
Buelton
Los Olivos
Taft
Gaviota State Park
Solvang
Ballard
New Cuyama
Gaviota
Santa Ynez
Refugio State Beach
Cuyama
Maricopa
33
101
154
Los Padres National Forest
Ventucopa
San Miguel Island
Isla Vista
Goleta
Pine Mtn. Club
Santa Rosa Island
Santa Barbara
Montecito
Scheideck
Summerland
33
Santa Cruz Island
Carpinteria
Frazier Park
Carpinteria State Beach
National
Wheeler Springs
Park
Ojai
Emma Wood State Beach
Casitas Springs
Sulphur Springs
Ventura
Limco
126
Santa Paula
Anacapa Island
El Rio
Los Angeles
Fillmore
Oxnard
1
101

©ULYSSES

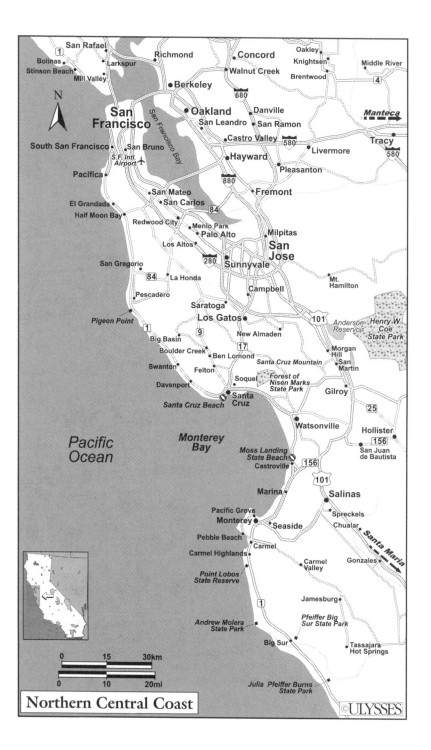

Northern Central Coast

©ULYSSES

For the Glory of Church and Crown

The real Spanish occupation of Alta California began in 1769 when Gaspar de Portolá led an expedition up the coast from Baja California to present-day San Diego. Junípero Serra, a Franciscan father originally from Majorca, was on board, and the expedition's objective was to affirm the Spanish presence on Californian soil and evangelize indigenous populations by establishing Catholic missions on their territory.

Beginning in 1697, the Jesuits had already set up a series of missions in Baja California. In 1767, in disgrace with the Spanish Crown, this religious community had to cede its place to the Franciscans, who were entrusted with continuing their work. Largely inspired by the model the Jesuits used on the California peninsula, Father Serra, known as the "Apostle of California" because of his role as first missionary, saw to the establishment of the first seven missions, starting in 1769.

Each mission consisted of a church, clerical residences, schools and dormitories for Amerindian converts to Catholicism and hundreds of acres of cultivated land. As they developed, the missions became more secular and served as centres of communal life for converted Amerindians and Spanish colonists. These agglomerations, the *pueblos*, were the foundations of modern California's main urban centres. In all, 21 missions were established between 1769 and 1823, from San Diego to Sonoma. Linked by a sinuous dirt road, El Camino Real (the royal road), that corresponds roughly to today's U.S. Highway 101, these missions were a backbone that would support California's future development. The Franciscans's original objective, after all, was to create an efficient network of religious institutions separated by no more than a day's journey on horseback.

Most of these missions were destroyed by an earthquake in 1812 or voluntarily reduced to ruins by the Franciscans at the time of their exodus after Mexico's independence. Today, after a huge restoration and reconstruction campaign over the past few decades, several of these period gems have been brought back to life and stand as proud reminders of the early Spanish presence on California soil.

region, which is without a doubt the most picturesque place on the Central Coast, features steep rocks and densely vegetated canyons, and is one of the most beautiful regions in the United States. The list of natural treasures definitely includes the Channel Islands, an archipelago located off the coast of Ventura and Oxnard that forms a natural reserve of paramount importance. These unexplored islands are a true paradise and harbour several endangered and unique species.

Finding Your Way Around

By Car

The US 101 is the fastest and most direct way to cover the 373mi (600km)

between San José and
Oxnard. Taking this north-
south expressway, how-
ever, seems absolutely
nonsensical, as you will
miss most of the region's
attractions. Route 1, from
Santa Cruz to San Luis
Obispo, is the narrowest
and slowest route, winding
up the sometimes steep
coast, and features some
of California's most breathtaking views.

By Bus

Here is a list of the main
bus stations:

San Jose
70 S. Almaden
☎ *800-231-2222*

Santa Cruz
425 Front St.
☎ *831-423-1800*
☎ *800-231-2222*

Monterey
Greyhound
1024 Del Monte Ave.
Monterey-Salinas Transit
1 Ryan Ranch Rd.
☎ *831-899-2555*

Pacific Grove
Monterey-Salinas Transit
☎ *831-899-2555*

Carmel-by-the-Sea
Monterey-Salinas Transit
☎ *831-899-2555*

Big Sur
Monterey-Salinas Transit
☎ *831-899-2555*

Cambria
Central Coast Area Transit
☎ *805-541-2228*

Morro Bay
Central Coast Area Transit
☎ *805-541-2228*

San Luis Obispo
Greyhound
150 South St.
☎ *805-543-2121*

Santa Barbara
Greyhound
34 West Cabrillo St.
☎ *805-962-2477*

Oxnard
Greyhound, Oxnard Transportation
Center
200 East Fourth St.
☎ *805-487-2706*

By Train

Train stations are located
at the following addresses:

San Jose
65 Cahill St.
☎ *408-287-7462*
☎ *800-USARAIL*

San Luis Obispo
1011 Railroad Ave.
☎ *805-541-0505*
☎ *800-USARAIL*

Santa Barbara
209 State St.
☎ *805-963-1015*
☎ *800-USARAIL*

By Plane

Airports are located at the
following addresses:

San Jose International Airport
1661 Airport Blvd., Coleman Ave.
exit off the I-80 or the Guadalupe
exit off the US 101
☎ *408-277-4759*

Monterey Peninsula Airport
Olmsted Rd., access by the 68
☎ *831-373-1704*

Santa Barbara Airport
500 Fowler Rd., 13km (8mi) east of
the city, near the US 101
☎ *805-683-4011*

Oxnard Airport
2889 W. Fifth St.
☎ *805-388-4211*

Practical Information

Like most regions in the
United States, the Central
Coast maintains an admirably efficient tourist information network. Even the
smallest towns have their
own visitor center, where
pleasant staff provide a
wealth of extremely pertinent information on the
area. Follow the signs on
the main roads, which will
clearly lead you to these
tourist information centres.
Here are the addresses and
phone numbers of a few
visitor centres, listed by
city and park:

San Jose

**Convention and Visitors
Bureau**
333 West San Carlos St., Suite 1000
☎ *408-295-9600*
☎ *800-SAN JOSE*
www.sanjose.org

Santa Cruz

**Conference and Visitors
Council**
1211 Ocean St.
☎ *831-425-1234*
☎ *800-833-3494*
www.santacruzca.org

Monterey

**Visitors and Convention
Bureau**
380 Alvarado St.
☎ *831-649-1770*
www.monterey.com

Pacific Grove

Visitors Center
corner Central Ave. and Forest Ave.
☎ *831-373-3304*

Carmel-by-the-Sea

Business Association
San Carlos St., between Fifth St. and
Sixth St., upstairs in the Eastwood
Building
☎*831-624-2522*

Big Sur

Chamber of Commerce
☎*831-667-2100*
www.bigsurcalifornia.org

Big Sur Station
0.6mi (1km) south of Pfeiffer Big
Sur State Park
☎*831-667-2315*

Cambria

Chamber of Commerce
767 Main St.
☎*805-927-3624*
www.thegrid.net/
cambriachamber

Morro Bay

Chamber of Commerce
880 Main St.
☎*805-772-4467*
☎*800-231-0592*
www.morrobay.org

San Luis Obispo

Visitors Center
1039 Chorro St.
☎*805-781-2777*
www.visitslo.com

Santa Barbara

**County Conference and
Visitors Bureau**
12 E. Carrillo St.
☎*805-966-9222*
www.santabarbaraca.com

Tourist Office
1 Garden St., corner Cabrillo Blvd.
☎*805-965-3021*

Hot Spots
36 State St.
☎*805-963-4233*

Ventura

Visitors & Convention Bureau
89 S. California St.
☎*805-648-2075*
☎*800-333-2989*
www.ventura-usa.com

**Channel Islands National Park
Visitors Center**
1901 Spinnaker Dr.
☎*805-658-5730*

Oxnard

Tourism Bureau
200 W. Seventh St.
☎*805-385-7545*
☎*800-2-OXNARD*

Channel Islands Harbor Visitors Center
810 W. Channel Islands Blvd.
Suite G
☎*805-985-4852*
☎*800-994-4852*

Exploring

San Jose

The *pueblo* of San José de
Guadalupe, which is the
oldest Spanish colonial
agglomeration on Californian soil, was founded in
1777 to supply provisions
and cattle to soldiers of the
Monterey and San Francisco *presidios*. The city of
San Jose was officially
founded in March 1850
and shortly thereafter
became the capital of the
new state of California.
Once a small rural community and later a grand
suburb of San Francisco,
San Jose has enjoyed
dramatic economic growth
since the 1980s, thanks to
the boom in the information technology and high-tech industries. Some liken

the emergence of this new
economy in the Silicon
Valley capital, a city that is
901,000 strong, to a new
gold rush. The shiny cars
that fill the parking lots of
ultra-modern plants and
the new and luxurious
downtown office buildings
are tangible proof of this
gold mine. Though it has
preserved a few traces of
its colonial past, northern
California's most populated city (it is bigger than
San Francisco) is without a
doubt geared towards the
future. A rich, clean and
safe city, San Jose has neither the cultural life nor
the liveliness of its neighbouring city, but is nevertheless worth a stop.

The Silicon Valley capital's
most popular attraction is
the **Technology Museum of
Innovation** ★ *($8; every day
10am to 5pm; 201 South
Market St.,* ☎*408-294-TECH,
www.thetech.org)*, which
allows visitors to explore
the latest technological
discoveries thanks to interesting, stimulating and
entertaining interactive
exhibits. Five theme rooms
feature the different facets
of technology, robotics,
genetic engineering and
space exploration, whose
high point is the
Hackworth IMAX Dome
Theater, the only one of its
kind in northern California.
The huge, striking orange-and-blue building houses
an institution whose quality is completely befitting
of a city like San Jose, a
world leader in the high-tech industry.

The simple Peralta Adobe,
which was built in 1797, is
the last remains of the first
pueblo of San José de
Guadalupe. You can visit
the small gardens and the
ancient residence, which is
built from sun-dried earth
and supported by wooden
beams. Fallon House,

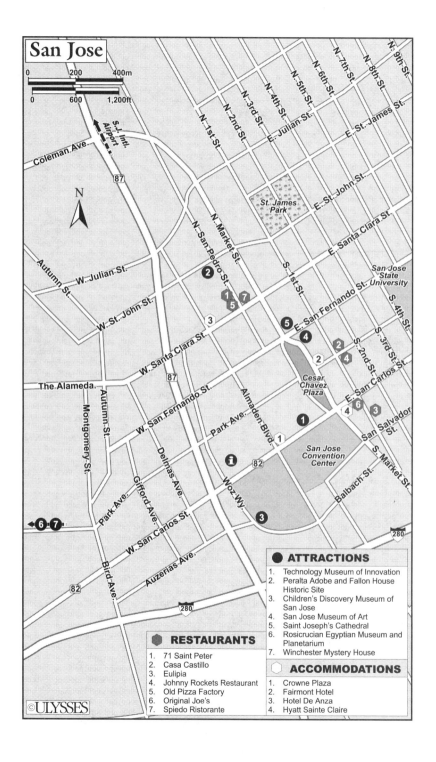

San Jose

0 200 400m
0 600 1,200ft

N

S.J. Intl. Airport
87
Coleman Ave.
Autumn St.
W. Julian St.
W. St. John St.
W. Santa Clara St.
The Alameda
Autumn St.
Montgomery St.
W. San Fernando St.
Delmas Ave.
Gifford Ave.
Park Ave.
Park Ave.
W. San Carlos St.
Bird Ave.
82
Auzerias Ave.
280

N. 1st St.
N. Market St.
N. San Pedro St.
N. 2nd St.
N. 3rd St.
N. 4th St.
N. 5th St.
N. 6th St.
N. 7th St.
N. 8th St.
N. 9th St.
E. Julian St.
E. St. James St.
St. James Park
E. St. John St.
E. Santa Clara St.
San Jose State University
S. 1st St.
S. 2nd St.
S. 3rd St.
S. 4th St.
E. San Fernando St.
E. San Carlos St.
S. Market St.
San Salvador St.
Balbach St.
Cesar Chavez Plaza
San Jose Convention Center
Almaden Blvd.
Park Ave.
Woz Wy.
87
82
280

© ULYSSES

● ATTRACTIONS

1. Technology Museum of Innovation
2. Peralta Adobe and Fallon House Historic Site
3. Children's Discovery Museum of San Jose
4. San Jose Museum of Art
5. Saint Joseph's Cathedral
6. Rosicrucian Egyptian Museum and Planetarium
7. Winchester Mystery House

⬡ RESTAURANTS

1. 71 Saint Peter
2. Casa Castillo
3. Eulipia
4. Johnny Rockets Restaurant
5. Old Pizza Factory
6. Original Joe's
7. Spiedo Ristorante

⬡ ACCOMMODATIONS

1. Crowne Plaza
2. Fairmont Hotel
3. Hotel De Anza
4. Hyatt Sainte Claire

which was owned by one of the city's first mayors, stands on the other side of the street. Built in 1885, this charming residence is an excellent example of the Victorian bourgeois architecture of the time. The two buildings, which have been restored and decorated with period furniture, are part of the **Peralta Adobe and Fallon House Historic Site** ★ *($6; Tue to Sun 11am to 4pm; 175 West St. John St., ☎408-993-8182).*

The **Children's Discovery Museum of San Jose** ★ *($6; Tue to Sat 10am to 5pm, Sun noon to 5pm; 180 Woz Way, ☎408-298-5437)* devotes its didactic exhibits to young budding explorers, who can test, climb, listen, feel, touch and smell as they please, without too many restrictions, in a non-traditional museum setting. One of the largest of its kind in the United States, this brightly coloured museum offers more than 150 interactive exhibits, which feature the many links between nature and human creations, as well as people from different cultures and times.

The **San Jose Museum of Art** *($7; Tue to Sun 10am to 5pm, Thu 10am to 8pm; 110 S. Market St., ☎408-294-2787)* presents temporary exhibits of contemporary American art, as well as a permanent collection that includes photographs, paintings, drawings and sculptures. The museum, which is mainly housed in a modern building, recently reopened its historical wing, a marvellous stone construction built in 1892.

Saint Joseph's Cathedral *(free admission; 80 S. Market St., corner Fernando St., ☎408-283-8100),* which is the city's first church, dates from 1803 and was originally built in adobe. It was in large part restored in 1877 following a devastating fire. This majestic site of worship, which features two church towers and a facade decorated with colonnades, is adorned with magnificent stained-glass windows and mural paintings.

The **Rosicrucian Egyptian Museum and Planetarium** ★ *($7; every day 10am to 5pm; 1342 Naglee Ave., corner Park, ☎408-947-3636)* owns the largest collection of objects from ancient Egypt and Assyria in the western United States. Visitors will discover, among other things, a mummy that is over 3,000 years old, as well as a replica of an underground Pharaonic tomb.

Built at the end of the 19th century according to the wishes of wealthy widow Sarah L. Winchester, who unfortunately did not live to see her dream house become reality, **Winchester Mystery House** *($13; Sun to Thu 9am to 6pm, Fri to Sat 9am to 9pm; 1525 S. Winchester Blvd., ☎408-247-2101)* is a vast Victorian residence surrounded by a sumptuous garden. With its 160 rooms and 47 fireplaces, this rich residence, which is the setting of strange supernatural phenomenons, features interesting collections of ancient objects, stained glass and firearms.

Santa Cruz

The history of Santa Cruz dates back to 1791, when the Franciscan community founded the 12th mission of its Californian network. At the end of the 19th century, the city enjoyed increasing economic growth related to the forest, agriculture, mining,

Rosicrucian Egyptian Museum and Planetarium

The Road to Happiness

The Cabrillo Highway, better known as Route 1, follows the Pacific Coast for more than 140km (84mi) and is one of the most spectacular stretches of road in the United States. Originally, this prestigious road was very modest-looking, and only an occasional wagon ventured upon the narrow, sinuous dirt road that ended south of the Big Sur Valley. Of course, this was in the 1880s, when the region had yet to experience the wave of agricultural and tourist development that was soon to occur. At the time only a few rather marginal adventurers dared to penetrate this wild,

isolated region. However, the natural attractions of Big Sur soon lead to the arrival of many tourists along the coast and many colonists began settling there. From then on, a safer, more efficient and faster road infrastructure became a necessity. However, building a road through dense pine forests, and sculpting the jagged coast with its overlooking vertiginous cliffs seemed like a very risky undertaking during that period. Nevertheless, a budget of $1.5 million, an astronomic sum for the time, was set aside in 1919 for the construction of this long-awaited road, which began three years

later. For more than 15 years, thousands struggled to complete the job, working in difficult and hazardous conditions. Provisions and materials were most often delivered on the backs of mules or deposited by barges on the shore. In June 1937, the road from the Monterey Peninusla to San Simeon was finally completed at a total cost of $10 million. Since its opening, thousands, even millions, of visitors have be able to explore the marvels of the Central Coast, thanks to human ingenuity and determination.

fishing and tanning industries. A university campus was founded in the mid-1960s, which soon drew a number of artists and intellectuals who would turn Santa Cruz into a tolerant and multi-cultural society. Celebrated for its popular surf beaches, bicycle paths and a huge amusement park, Santa Cruz manages to successfully combine nature, urban life, history, culture and architectural heritage. This city of 49,000-strong has a laid back and vaguely bohemian atmosphere, which makes for a very pleasurable stay, with plenty to do: stroll down Pacific Avenue, Santa Cruz's main street, which has many restaurants, terraces, cafés and shops, ride your bike

or go for a run along West Cliff Drive, which overlooks the ocean.

Between Santa Cruz and the Monterey Peninsula, we suggest you stop at the small village of **San Juan Bautista ★ ★**. With barely 2,000 residents, San Juan Bautista seems to be frozen in time with its grand main street and typically western facades. The town features a few historic buildings such as the **Plaza Hotel** and **Castro House**, which are part of the San Juan Bautista State Historic Park. This community is especially known for the splendid **Mission San Juan Bautista ★ ★** (*$1 donation; every day 9:30am to 4:30pm*), which is perched

slopeside on the famous San Andreas Fault. The 15th Californian mission, which stands next to California's only preserved authentic Spanish square, was founded in 1797, and the construction of its current church began in 1803. Other buildings had been previously built, but due to its vulnerable and precarious location on the outskirts of the Fault, and a series of earthquakes caused irreparable damage. Later buildings and the Franciscan institution's gardens and cemetery have been magnificently preserved. Part of the original Camino Real, a dirt road linking the 21 missions, was preserved on the site. After a visit to the mission you can recharge

Central Coast

your batteries at one of the few small establishments on Third Street, the town's main road, several hundred feet long.

The Misión la Exaltación de la Santa Cruz, better known as the **Mission Santa Cruz** *(donation recommended; Tue to Sat 10am to 4pm, Sun 10am to 2pm; 126 High St., ☎831-426-5686)* is a remnant of California's rich colonial past and Native American cultural heritage. Founded in 1791 by Fermín Francisco de Lasuén, the mission is marked by a stormy history that is punctuated by a series of natural disasters that damaged it greatly, often requiring its reconstruction. The latest episode occurred in 1857, when an earthquake and harsh winter completely destroyed the buildings and church. Another church was built on the site of the original mission 32 years later and replicas of the ancient buildings were erected in 1931. The State of California manages the **Santa Cruz Mission State Park** *(Thu to Sun 10am to 4pm; 144 School St., ☎831-425-5849)*, a small park

that is home to a museum, as well as the only original adobe building that still stands.

The **Santa Cruz City Museum of Natural History** *($2; Tue to Sun 10am to 5pm; 1305 E. Cliff Dr., ☎831-420-6115)* is an attraction the whole family will enjoy. It specializes in the natural and cultural history of Monterey Bay. First opened in 1904, the museum features, among other things, a basin where visitors can touch sea creatures, a room devoted to Native American culture, living exhibits on the regional ecosystem and a room devoted to palaeontology. Little ones can even climb onto the back of a grey whale skeleton! The Santa Cruz area is a winter refuge for monarch butterflies, which can be observed in the trees behind the Museum of Natural History from October to March.

The **Municipal Wharf** *(parking $1/hr; Beach St., ☎831-420-6025)* is a lively and must-see stop for visitors to Santa Cruz. The quay is open at the crack of dawn,

and closes late at night. You can rent fishing boats or enjoy ecological excursions and kayaking, as well as a number of restaurants whose specialty is sea food.

The **Santa Cruz Beach Boardwalk ★** *(free entry but admission fees for rides; May to Sep every day, Sep to May weekends and holidays; 400 Beach St., ☎831-426-7433)*, which is the main amusement park bordering the West Coast beaches, is an urban institution. Established in 1906, the park has around 30 games, miniature golf, a casino and many other attractions. The Giant Dipper wooden rollercoaster and the Looff game, which were built in 1923 and 1911, respectively, are true historical monuments. You can also enjoy the nearby beach.

Surfing enthusiasts should head to the **Santa Cruz Surfing Museum** *(free admission; Wed to Mon noon to 4pm; Mark Abbott Lighthouse, W. Cliff Dr., ☎831-429-3429)*, a small but unique museum dedicated to this sport, which is extremely popular in Santa Cruz.

● **ATTRACTIONS**	
1. Mission Santa Cruz	4. Municipal Quay
2. Santa Cruz Mission State Park	5. Santa Cruz Beach Boardwalk
3. Santa Cruz City Museum of Natural History	6. Santa Cruz Surfing Museum
	7. University of California Santa Cruz

◯ **ACCOMMODATIONS**	
1. The Babbling Brook Inn	5. HI Santa Cruz Hostel
2. Blackburn House Motel	6. Ocean Pacific Lodge
3. The Darling House	7. Sea and Sand Inn
4. Henry Cowell Redwoods State Park Campgroud	

● **RESTAURANTS**	
1. Clouds Downtown	5. Pearl Alley Bistro & Cafe
2. El Palomar	6. Sea Cloud Restaurant
3. Gabriella	7. Walnut Avenue Cafe
4. Oswald's	

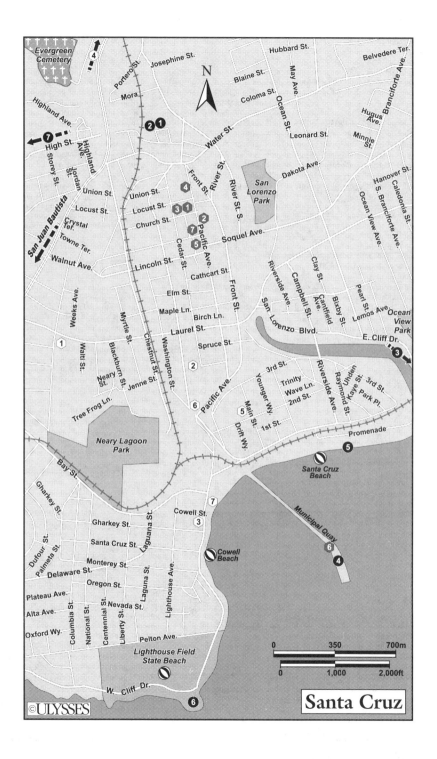

Santa Cruz

Photographs, old surfboards and videos document nearly 100 years of surfing in Santa Cruz.

The research lab at the **University of California Santa Cruz** (UCSC) ★ features interesting showrooms on the world of the sea. The **Long Marine Laboratory and Aquarium** *(Tue to Sun 1pm to 4pm; 100 Shaffer Rd., ☎831-459-4308)* allows visitors to get up close and personal with sea anemones, starfish, crabs and other creatures. You can also observe dolphins, seals and a huge whale skeleton. UCSC's **Arboretum** *(free admission; every day 9am to 5pm; 1156 High St., ☎831-427-2998)* is one of California's richest botanical gardens. Its collection includes countless numbers of vegetation specimens from as far as Australia, New Zealand and South Africa.

Monterey

In 1602, Sebastián Viscaíno became the first European to set foot on the small Monterey Peninsula, which is located around 125mi (200km) south of San Francisco Bay. The wealthy Spanish merchant named the place after Count Monte Rey, who managed Spanish colonies in Mexico. However, these lands that were inhabited by Native Americans were not colonized until 1770, when Father Junípero Serra and Major Don Gaspar de Portola built a mission and founded a *presidio*, guarded by Spanish troops. In 1777, Monterey became the capital of Upper and Lower California, a role it would play until Mexico's independence in 1821. Several years later, in the midst of the American-Mexican conflict, Commodore John Drake Sloat landed at Monterey and raised the American flag above Custom House on July 7, 1846, thereby putting an end to Mexican domination. This was followed by the famous meeting at Colton Hall, where 48 delegates from throughout California signed California's constitution on September 1, 1849. Following the official founding of the State of California in 1850, Monterey was incorporated as a city. In the second half of the 19th century, waves of immigrants from Europe and Asia, attracted by a booming fishing industry, came to Monterey. These Japanese, Chinese, Portuguese and Italians would create the rich cultural life that remains today. The construction of the first railway in the 1870s also marked an important step in the transformation of this peaceful fishing port, which is now linked to cosmopolitan San Francisco and other agglomerations. Today, the city numbers 33,000 residents and is marked by its rich colonial past. Its small town centre, with Alvarado Street as the main artery, features a surprising series of heritage buildings. Located on the bay whose name it shares, Monterey has a few extremely well laid out greenspaces and beaches. The Cannery Row neighbourhood, made famous by Nobel Prize for Literature winner John Steinbeck's novel of the same name, lies east of the city. This densely packed district is swarming with tourists and features a string of restaurants, hotels and shops adjacent to a few empty lots and disused warehouses.

● ATTRACTIONS

1. Monterey State Historic Park	8. Pacific House
2. Royal Presidio Chapel	9. Cooper-Molera Complex
3. Robert Louis Stevenson House	10. Monterey Peninsula Recreation Trail
4. Colton Hall	11. Monterey Museum of Art
5. California's First Theater	12. La Mirada
6. Larkin House	13. Maritime Museum of Monterey
7. Custom House	14. Fisherman's Wharf

◐ ACCOMMODATIONS

1. Casa Munras Garden Hotel	5. Sprindrift Inn
2. Merritt House Inn	6. Veterans Memorial Park Campground
3. Monterey Hotel	7. Victorian Inn
4. Monterey Plaza Hotel & Spa	

◉ RESTAURANTS

1. Britannia Arms Pub & Restaurant	5. Old Monterey Cafe
2. Café Abrego	6. Paradiso
3. Cibo Ristorante	7. Rosine's
4. Jugem Japanese Restaurant	

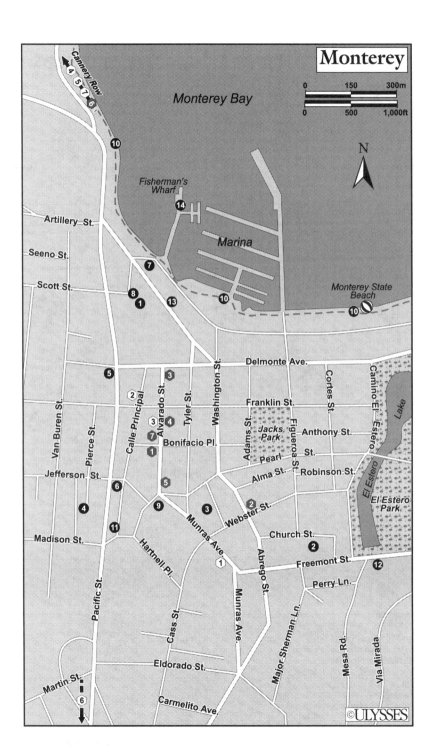

Monterey

Monterey Bay

| 0 | 150 | 300m |
| 0 | 500 | 1,000ft |

N

Cannery Row

4
5 7
6

10

Fisherman's
Wharf

14

Artillery St.

Marina

Seeno St.

7

Scott St.

8
1

13

10

Monterey State
Beach

10

Delmonte Ave.

Van Buren St.

Pierce St.

5

2

Calle Principal

Alvarado St.

3

3
4

Tyler St.

Washington St.

Franklin St.

Adams St.

Jacks
Park

Figueroa St.

Cortes St.

Camino El Estero

Lake

7

Bonifacio Pl.

Anthony St.

1

Pearl
St.

Jefferson St.

6

5

Alma St.

Robinson St.

El Estero

El Estero
Park

4

9

3

2

Webster St.

11

Munras Ave.

Church St.

2

12

Madison St.

Hartnell Pl.

1

Freemont St.

Pacific St.

Abrego St.

Perry Ln.

Cass St.

Munras Ave.

Major Sherman Ln.

Mesa Rd.

Via Mirada

Eldorado St.

Martin St.

6

Carmelito Ave.

©ULYSSES

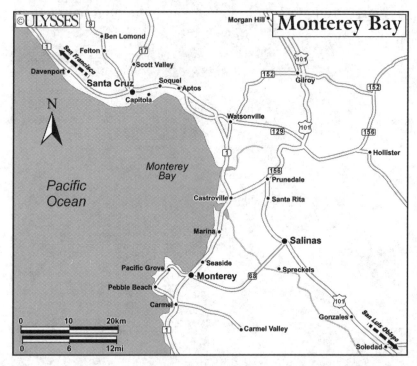

Monterey's rich history has left its mark on the city's architectural heritage. The **Path of History ★★** *(guided tour $5; departure from 20 Custom House Plaza; every day 10am to 5pm; ☎831-649-7118)*, which is a pedestrian trail managed by the California Department of Parks and Recreation, will lead you to the most beautiful architectural treasures in Old Monterey. Five guided tours are offered daily. The path, a section of which runs through **Monterey State Historic Park**, leads to, among other places, the **Royal Presidio Chapel**, **Robert Louis Stevenson House**, **Colton Hall**, **California's First Theater**, **Larkin House**, **Custom House**, **Pacific House** and the **Cooper-Molera Complex**. The **Royal Presidio Chapel**, which is the city's oldest building, was built by Spanish authorities in 1794 and has

been active ever since. It has been included in the national historical register since 1961. The original section of the **Robert Louis Stevenson House** dates back to the 1830s, during the Mexican presence. Robert Louis Stevenson moved into the residence in 1879. **Colton Hall**, which is where the 1849 California Constitutional Convention was held, was built under the supervision of Reverend Walter Colton and accommodated the 48 delegates who signed California's Constitution. **California's First Theater**, which is the only building to have been built in the 1840s, was originally a saloon with four small adjoining apartments that were divided by detachable walls. The building, which was built by English sailor Jack Swan, served as a meeting place where theatre pro-

ductions were staged for soldiers of the New York Volunteers, who were assigned to Monterey. **Larkin House**, which many consider to be the most beautiful example of colonial architecture in Monterey, was built in 1834 under the guidance of British merchant Thomas Oliver Larkin. By adapting the tradtional styles of eastern and southern United States residences and by using local materials such as the Douglas fir and adobe, he not only created a magnificent residence but developed a new architectural standard. In 1844, Larkin was named Mexican consul in Monterey and the building housed the consulat's main quarters. In 1822, the Mexican government opened the port of Monterey to international trade. Authorities built **Custom House**, where customs on imported goods from the United States, England and South America were paid. On July 7, 1846, John Drake Sloat raised the United States flag above Custom House, thereby putting an end to Hispanic domination in the region. Originally built to store the equipment of U.S. soldiers, **Pacific House** has played many roles. Having once served as a church, hotel, law firm office, ballroom and county office, this adobe building today houses a museum on the history of California. The **Cooper-Molera Complex**, which was built between 1827 and 1900, retraces the history of three generations of the Cooper family. Run by the State of Califor-

nia, it features a garden, an exhibition room with ancient objects and an information centre.

The **Monterey Peninsula Recreation Trail** ★ (☎831-646-3866), which is one of the loveliest seaside recreational paths in the entire United States, covers 18mi (29km) from Asilomar State Beach, to Pacific Grove, up to the small town of Seaside. It allows joggers, walkers, cyclists and roller-bladers to peacefully stroll past some lovely public beaches, the Monterey Bay Aquarium, Cannery Row, Fisherman's Wharf and the Custom House Plaza.

Acclaimed as one of the most interesting small-

town art museums in the United States, the **Monterey Museum of Art** ★ (*$3 donation; Wed to Sat 11am to 5pm, Sun 1pm to 4pm; 559 Pacific St., ☎831-372-5477*) paints an artistic portrait of California, as well as other regions of the world. This small private non-profit museum exhibits a number of primitive and popular art objects, paintings and photographs, in its seven rooms that house permanent and temporary collections. **La Mirada** (*$3 donation; Thu to Sat 11am to 5pm, Sun 1pm to 4pm; 720 Via Mirada, ☎831-372-5477*) is another wing of the museum that is housed in an old colonial adobe residence. Surrounded by magnificent gardens that are themselves encircled by a picturesque stone wall, the Hispanic residence takes visitors back in time to the colony's early days. In 1993, architect Charles Moore drafted the plans for an annex that today houses four contemporary art showrooms.

The **Maritime Museum of Monterey** ★ (*$5; every day 10am to 5pm; 5 Custom House Plaza, ☎831-373-2469*) presents exhibits on Monterey's rich maritime past. It houses, among other things, a collection of model boats in bottles and some interesting displays devoted to Monterey's history.

The venerable **Fisherman's Wharf** (*access from Del Monte Ave., www.montereywharf. com*), which is a tourist meeting place, was built in 1846 and today features a number of restaurants, shops and fishmarkets. It is also the departure point for several fishing, scuba diving and whale watching excursions.

The Greatness and Misery of the Sardine

The fish-farming industry in Monterey dates back to the 1850s when Chinese fishermen settled on the peninsula and began plying their traditional trade. However, it wasn't until the 1920s that the sardine industry really took off, and a row of fish canneries was established, known as Cannery Row. Until the 1940s, dozens of processing plants and canneries handled tens of thousands of tons of sardines harvested from Pacific waters annually. Monterey became the sardine capital of the world. Author John

Steinbeck (1902-1968), winner of the Nobel Prize for Literature in 1962, immortalized the region in his famous 1944 novel *Cannery Row*, which realistically described the deplorable working and living conditions of the workers. Then, in the 1940s, water pollution, climatic changes, warming waters and overfishing all contributed to the agonizing decline of Monterey's sardine industry. Today, Steinbeck wouldn't recognize the Cannery Row he once described so vividly.

Central Coast

The **Monterey Bay Aquarium** ★ ★ *($16; every day 10am to 4pm; 886 Cannery Row, ☎831-648-4860 or 800-756-3737, www.mbayaq.org)* has acquired an extremely enviable reputation on the national and international scene over the years. Open since 1984, it is located in Monterey's biggest sardine canning factory. The wonders of Monterey Bay's sea world will fascinate both young and old alike. The acquarium features more than 6,500 living creatures, including fish, birds and other marine life that is housed in more than 100 exhibition areas. The bird and sea-otter rooms, the kelp forest which sways in over 44,470 cu ft (1,260 m³) of water, and a basin where visitors can touch living specimens, are particularly popular. The new Outer Bay Wing, which is a huge indoor salt-water pool that features the many facets of marine life, and the "Mysteries of the Deep" exhibit, which depicts the abyssal splendours of Monterey Canyon, are a great way to end your visit. The aquarium greets more than two million visitors each year and line-ups can be long. We therefore recommend buying your tickets in advance.

Immortalized by writer John Steinbeck, **Cannery Row** ★ *(west of Coast Guard Pier, www.canneryrow.com)* was an important industrial sardine processing centre in the 1920s and 1930s. The appearance of this once industrial and odour-filled neighbourhood has changed a great deal over the years and few traces remain of that period. Today, the famous seaside street has become a tourist destination and features many restaurants, hotels and shops.

Discover the glorious history of Cannery Row thanks to the life-size char-

Butterfly Town

Each year, the Monterey Peninsula is host to thousands of monarch butterflies who fly here from Canada to spend the winter. From October to February, 40,000 to 60,000 of these splendid winged insects winter in warm George Washington Park and the Monarch Grove Sanctuary in Pacific Grove. Year after year, descendants of the same butterfly families go to the exact same trees in the park—an ever-fascinating phenomenon that is an innate part of this insect's life cycle.

The city of Pacific Grove, nicknamed the "City of Butterflies," is proud to greet the arrival of these unusual and famous guests each year with a parade and a bazar. But don't get so carried away by the monarchs's great beauty that you can't resist the urge to touch them. A strict Pacific Grove municipal regulation stipulates a $1,000 fine for anyone who molests the monarchs or interferes with them. You don't fool around with royalty!

acters and informative narrations at **Steinbeck's Spirit of Monterey Wax Museum** *($6; every day 10am to 5pm; 700 Cannery Row, ☎831-737-2469).*

Every September for the last 35 years, the best jazz musicians have gathered at the famous **Monterey Jazz Festival** ★ *(☎831-373-3366).* Over the years, both promising young talent and veritable jazz legends such as Miles Davis, Stan Getz, Dizzie Gillespie and Dave Brubeck have performed on the stages of the Monterey Fairgrounds, making this festival a world-famous event.

Pacific Grove

Founded by methodists over a century ago, Pacific Grove is a quiet and serene tourist resort that is perfectly located at the tip of the Monterey Peninsula. This simple agglomeration of 17,000 residents that is litterally surrounded by beaches and coastal parks, features, among other things, a few beautiful and well-preserved Victorian residences. Each winter, Pacific Grove, which is nicknamed the "butterfly city," is home to thousands of monarch butterflies who migrate there for the winter. The centre of activity for this charming little town is located at the intersection of Lighthouse Avenue and Central Avenue, where you will find many restaurants, hotels and shops.

Each year, thousands of monarch butterflies spend the winter in the Monterey Peninsula area. You can see them at the **Monarch Grove Sanctuary** ★ *(Grove Acre Ave., between Short Ave.*

and Lighthouse Ave.) from October to February.

Recognized as one of the most interesting museums of its kind and size in the United States, the **Museum of Natural History** *(free admission; Tue to Sun 10am to 5pm; 165 Forest Ave., corner Central Ave., ☎831-648-3116 or 648-3119)* presents exhibits on local fauna, Native American history and culture, as well as geology. A short report and slide show explain the migration phenomenon of monarch butterflies in Pacific Grove. Travelling exhibitions of the Smithsonian Institution are occasionally featured. *Sandy the Gray Whale*, a life-sized sculpture of a huge grey whale by Larry Foster, sits imposingly before the building's facade to the delight of photographers.

The **Point Piños Lighthouse** *(free admission; Thu to Sun 1pm to 4pm; at the end of Lighthouse Ave., ☎831-648-3116)*, a real city landmark, is the oldest operating lighthouse on the entire West Coast. It has helped boats steer clear of the peninsula's northern tip, which is a sailing hazard, since 1855. It also features an exhibit on the lighthouse's history and local shipwrecks.

Perfectly located on the tip of the Monterey Peninsula, Pacific Grove offers great spots for swimming, hiking, bike riding and even picnics. This area includes **Asilomar State Beach**, **Ocean View Scenic Drive** and **Lovers Point**.

Carmel-by-the-Sea

Founded as a holiday resort in around 1880,

Carmel-by-the-Sea quickly acquired a reputation as a somewhat bohemian and artistic vacation destination. While its artistic side has survived, the descendants of the 19th-century bohemians have greatly quieted down. Today, the small community of Carmel-by-the-Sea, simply called Carmel by residents, is one-of-a-kind in California. The wealthy residents of this precious agglomeration have built themselves a clean, highly civilized city where all symbols of urban life have been forbidden. Evoking an opulent and politically-correct atmosphere, residents wanted to create a place that enjoyed the advantages of the modern world, while maintaining a protective barrier against the more depraved aspects of urban life. In a way, Carmel is the dream come true of well-to-do, privileged people. The result is pleasant, nonetheless. A quiet community of 4,500 residents, Carmel has a small town centre which features a number of chic boutiques and art galleries, reputable restaurants and cafés, as well as charming hotels. The entire town is nestled in the shade of tall trees, and the landscaped settings of the picturesque residences are worthy of mention. An impressive seafront, inviting sandy beaches and a magnificent Spanish mission complete the picture. With a little luck, you might run into Carmel's most famous resident and former mayor, actor Clint Eastwood. That would certainly make your day!

When Father Junípero Serra landed on Monterey Bay in 1770, he founded a mission and named it San Carlos. The lack of rich soil and the great proximity to the *presidio* and sol-

City of the Rich and Famous

The wealthy folks who migrated to Carmel wanted to live out their fantasies by creating a little paradise which would include all the advantages of the modern world, yet stand like a fortress against everything they considered repugnant in urban life. Along these lines, Carmel, whose most famous resident, actor Clint Eastwood was mayor from 1986 to 1988, is a dream-come-true for the privileged well-to-do. A city of "Thou shalt not's," Carmel won't accept street numbers on houses, parking metres (don't worry, the police watch like hawks and count the minutes!), large chain stores, franchise restaurants, live music in bars or... eating ice cream on the street! Everything is straight, clean and according to the rules. That's how life is in Carmel.

diers, however, quickly convinced the good father that the chosen location was far from ideal. In August 1771, Father Serra relocated to the current site of Carmel and founded the **Misión San Carlos Borromeo del Río Carmelo**, better known as the **Carmel Mission ★★**

($2; Jun to Aug 9:30am to 7:30pm, Sep to May 9:30am to 4:30pm; 3080 Rio Rd., south of Carmel, near Rte. 1, ☎831-624-3600). The original church was built in wood and adobe, and the stone one that stands today was constructed two years later. As of 1834, the buildings and church were no longer used for religious purposes and fell into a state of neglect and disrepair. This only ended in the 1930s, when religious authorities in Monterey launched a campaign to restore the church and elevated the mission to parish status. In 1960, Pope John XXIII consecrated the historic role of this architectural and religious-heritage treasure by granting it minor basilica status. Today, the Carmel Mission is one of the most visited religious sites in the United States and is certainly one of the most impressive and moving California missions. The remains of Father Junípero Serra, who was beatified in 1988 by Pope John Paul II, rest in Carmel. The buildings of this elaborate Franciscan mission hold interesting museums related to the history of the mission's founding father.

Carmel Mission

The **Point Lobos State Reserve ★★** *($7; every day 9am to 5pm; Rte. 1, a little south of Carmel; ☎831-624-4909, http://pt-lobos.parks. state.ca.us)* is an extraordinary place where the riches of the sea meet the wonders of land. The reserve's spectacular scenery, an impressive mosaic of bare lands, emerging cliffs, irregular creeks and rolling meadows, was shaped by the collision of sea and land over millions of years. Underground rock formations surfaced and were carved by weather conditions and the perpetual rolling of the waves. The resulting sand and gravel, which are the products of the erosion of these rocks that were transported by the sea, formed long stretches of beaches. In total, this natural site, considered a jewel in the State of California, covers some 1,285 acres (520ha), 741 acres (300ha) of which are water. This aquatic section was added in 1960, making Point Lobos the country's first marine park. This aquatic area, which is considered one of California's richest marine habitats, is home to extremely diverse and remarkable fauna. Visitors can see seals, otters, grey whales and a number of sea birds. The convergence of currents of varying temperatures and the particular movement of air masses provide an ideal environment for a rich underwater world. Both novice and expert divers can discover a fascinating, though fragile environment beneath the surface of the waves (see p 355). In addition, more than 7mi (11km) of trails cut across the 692 acres (280ha) of protected land, allowing hikers to enjoy the beauty of countless fragrant and colourful plants and wild flowers, as well as the charm of the tall pine trees and cypresses. Over 300,000 people visit Point Lobos every year; in order to limit the impact humans have on this fragile environment, the reserve's authorities only grant 450 people access to this site each day.

Big Sur

El Sur Grande, the "Great South," is what the first Spanish colonisers named this wild and unknown region, located south of Monterey. Only inhabited at the end of the 19th century by brave and hardy adventurers, the region developed a prosperous forest industry at the turn of the 20th century. Today the Big Sur region comprises a dramatic and sensational stretch of 87mi (140km) on the Central Coast between Point Lobos State Reserve to the north and San Simeon to the south. Known world-wide for the spactacular beauty of its coast, and adorned with dramatic cliffs, sandy beaches and abundant vegetation protected by a number of state parks, Big Sur stands out as an exceptional destination on the California coast. Route 1, which is considered the most striking strech of highway in California, runs through the region and is flanked by the majestic Santa Lucia Mountains on one side and the jagged Pacific coast on the other. Fresh air reigns in this natural environment, where there are few commercial establishments and which is ideal for camping and picnicking. Your road map should indicate an agglomeration named Big Sur bordering Route 1; nevertheless, don't be surprised if you miss it. Far from being a village, Big Sur Center has only a few fundamental businesses and services.

The most photographed bridge on Route 1 is without a doubt **Bixby Creek Bridge ★**, which is one of the longest cement bridges of its kind in the United States. Completed in 1932 and initially called Rainbow Bridge, it is supported by 236 tons (240 tonnes) of iron and enough cenment to fill the equivalent of 825 cement trucks.

Erected in 1889 on a gigantic granite formation, **Point Sur Light Station** *(guided tour $5; Rte. 1, West Coast; summer Wed 10am and 2pm, Thu 10am, Sat 10am and 2pm, Sun 7pm; the rest of the year Sat 10am and 2pm, Sun 7pm; ☎831-625-4419)* shines its protective light up to 25mi (40km) away, and is the only centennial lighthouse open to the public today. Many courageous families lived and worked in this lighthouse up until 1974, when automation replaced human labour. In order to preserve the dramatic am-

biance and sense of isolation that permeates this place, the number of persons admitted per visit is limited and guided tours are required. These tours leave from the parking lot, which is at the foot of the imposing Point Sur rock formation.

The **Andrew Molera State Park** *(☎831-667-2315)* is one of the largest parks in the Big Sur region. A 500ft-wide (800m) path leads to a sandy beach at the mouth of Big Sur River, which is protected from the open-sea wind by a rocky slope. The path, which cuts through a flower meadow and offers beautiful views of the moutains to the east, is just as pleasant as the beach itself. Other paths lead to more isolated beaches.

A magnificent protected greenspace on the verdant hills surrounding Big Sur River, **Pfeiffer Big Sur State Park ★★** *($6; ☎831-667-2315)* has everything to delight outdoor enthusiasts: campgrounds, picnic spots, swimming areas in the river, and eight hiking paths through the pine forest. The Pfeiffers were the first European immigrants to permanently settle in the Big Sur region. Michael Pfeiffer and his wife Barbara built a house near Sycamore Canyon in 1869 and, thanks to their hard work, managed to survive despite difficult living conditions. Their son John settled on the north shore of Big Sur and, in 1884, moved to the site of Homestead Cabin. When Big Sur was becoming increasingly popular with visitors and the need for accommodations became obvious, John and his wife Florence opened Pfeiffer's Ranch Resort on the current site of Big Sur Lodge.

In 1933, the State of California acquired 672 acres (272ha) of woodland belonging to John Pfeiffer and named the new park after him. Today, the park covers 2,036 acres (824ha) and is home to a rich and diverse fauna and flora.

Another beautiful beach adorned with spectacular rock formations, cliffs, dunes and lagoons, **Pfeiffer Beach ★** *(access by Sycamore Canyon Rd.)* is unfortunately too dangerous for swimming. The area lends itself best to such activities as contemplating nature and photography.

Henry Miller, who is the most famous resident among the artists who moved to the region, lived in Big Sur in the 1940s. His work gave the coastal region world-wide notoriety. Emil White, an artist and friend of the writer, donated the residence and a collection of Miller's books and personal objects to found the **Henry Miller Memorial Library** *(10am to 7pm; ☎831-667-2574)*. The library, which is surrounded by gardens and sculptures, holds all of Miller's literary and pictorial works, as well as translations of his novels.

Open to day-visitors, **Julia Pfeiffer Burns State Park** is the perfect spot to have a picnic and discover the unique Saddle Rock Waterfall, which falls directly into the Pacific Ocean. The park stretches on each side of Route 1, over an area of 2mi (3km) starting from Partington Cove.

The **Esalen Institute** *(bath $10; 1:30pm to 3:30pm; ☎831-667-3000)*, which is the site of some spectacular hot springs, is home to the Human Potential Movement.

Central Coast

The Press King

Editor and California politician William Randolph Hearst was born on April 29, 1863 in San Francisco. Son of rich industrialist and senator George Hearst and philanthropist Phoebe Apperson, he replaced his father as the head of the *San Francisco Examiner* newspaper in 1887. As editor, he favoured sensational journalism and his methods, supported by a $20-million fortune, met with immediate success. In 1895, he acquired the *New York Morning Journal,* and the following year, he launched the publication of the *Evening Journal.* In a few months, these two papers reached circulations of 1.5 million copies, an astronomical figure for the time. By 1927, Hearst had expanded his journalistic empire and controlled a network of 25 newspapers published in the major U. S. cities.

Always stressing sensational journalism and scandals that caught the attention of the ordinary citizen, he included in his publications articles, cartoons, opinion columns and shocking revelations that created controversy and fanned its flames. Simultaneously, the already fantastically wealthy press magnate threw himself into magazine publication, creating such notable magazines as *International-Cosmopolitan* and *Good Housekeeping.* The Great Depression of the 1930s forced him to sell a few of his newspapers.

Although William R. Hearst was a colossus of publishing, he was less fortunate in his forays into politics. Elected to the House of Representatives from 1903 to 1905 under the political banner of the New York Democrats, he didn't succeed in being named the party's candidate in the presidential elections of 1904. Twice defeated in New York City municipal elections, in 1905 and 1909, he suffered the same fate in 1906 when he sought the necessary votes to become governor of the state. Despite repeated efforts, he was never elected governor.

Willian R. Hearst amassed one of the greatest fortunes in the history of the United States and his central role in the press world made him one of the most influential people of his period. Inspired by the larger-than-life press magnate, cinematic genius Orson Wells created one of the world's masterpieces of film, *Citizen Kane.*

Hearst died on August 14, 1951 in Beverly Hills at the respectable age of 88.

Limekiln State Park and Beach (☎*831-667-2403)* features a public beach and campground.

Cambria

Cambria was founded in 1866 following the construction of the first sawmill by William

Leffingwell, and it quickly became an important commercial and whale-hunting port. Mining, cattle raising and dairy production would later be added to the commercial activities of the prosperous community. However, the construction of a railway in 1894 was detrimental to the port industry, causing the community to enter an era of isolation and economic decline. Today,

Cambria enjoys quiet times and its 6,000 residents, many of whom are artists and craftspeople, claim they enjoy a good quality of life, despite the summertime tourist crowds that descend on the village. Cambria stretches over three unique sectors, allowing visitors to enjoy all the variety this town has to offer. The historic East Village neighbourhood, with its restaurants and accommodations, lies beside Route 1, which runs between the village and the sea. The West Village, situated 1.2mi (2km) away on the same side of the highway, features an impressive concentration of art galleries and shops. Finally, Moonstone Beach, on the western side of Route 1, is a sandy beach swept by the Pacific winds and features numerous hotels and restaurants on Moonstone Beach Drive. The village is the point of departure for those who want to discover the architectural follies of San Simeon, a few miles further north.

Though located a few dozen miles from Cambria, on the other side of the mountain range, the **Mission San Miguel Archangel** ★ *($1; every day 10am to 4:30pm; Rte. 101, take Rte. 46 from Cambria, north of Paso Robles, ☎805-467-3256)* is definitely worth a detour. Founded in 1797 as the 16th Spanish Franciscan mission, its main purpose was to facilitate the trip between the San Antonio mission in the north and San Luis Obispo in the south. The Franciscan monks were striving to create an efficient network of religious institutions, closely linked so that each one was not further than a day's travel on horseback from any of the others. Like many of its fellow missions, San Miguel experienced a turbulent history, and a fire ravaged the church and most of the buildings in 1806. Quickly rebuilt with the help of neighbouring missions, the church was again recon-

structed 12 years later, this time on a more solid stone foundation. In 1821, Esteban Munras arrived in San Miguel to supervise the work of decorating the interior, which became a true work of art created by Chumash Indians, residents of the mission. Taken by Mexican authorities in 1836, the mission was used for secular purposes until it was given back to the Franciscan community in 1928. Today the mission is the heart of an active parish, with its religious offices, noviciate and retirement home.

Today, San Miguel is one of the best preserved and most authentic missions in the entire Franciscan network. The church's mural paintings, which were created using mineral pigments nearly two centuries ago, are intact and magnificently preserved; they are especially noteworthy and have contributed greatly to San Miguel's reputation. As you explore its premises, you can imagine the lives of the first mis-

sionaries, since the buildings have an old-style feel to them and house historical and religious objects, among other things.

There are no words to describe **Hearst Castle** ★★★ *($14; every day 8:20am to 3:20pm; 750 Hearst Castle Rd., Rte. 1, Visitor Center, near San Simeon's quay, 9mi (14km) north of Cambria, ☎805-927-2020 or 800-444-4445, www.hearstcastle.com)*, the megalomaniacal construction of fabulously rich press baron William Randolph Hearst. As the only son of wealthy industrialist and senator George Hearst and Phoebe Apperson, in 1919 he inherited a vast domain of 247,100 acres (100,000ha) in the San Simeon region. Originally known as Camp Hill, this wild stretch of land served as a refuge for the family, where they entertained friends in complete privacy at their campsite. Hearst, however, quickly grew tired of these primitive, rustic conditions and contacted renowned San Francisco architect Julia Morgan, to let her in on his plans to build "a little something" on his property. And so began a staggering worksite that consumed $5 million, an absolutely astronomical sum at the time. In 1947, the completed project graced the hills of San Simeon, which were rechristened La Cuesta Encantada (the enchanted hill). Here stood an incredible 165-room palace, surrounded by 126 acres (51ha) of gardens, terraces, pools and promenades, not

Hearst Castle

including the vast stretches of land where cattle grazed and exotic animals pranced about. The main residence, Casa Grande, with its two imposing towers that were inspired by Spanish cathedrals, houses a superb European art collection. The reception room and dining room, with their sculpted solid-wooden ceilings and Flemish wall coverings, are absolutely stunning. The striking outdoor and indoor pools are surrounded by a neoclassical decor. Guests of Mr. Hearst, who included the biggest names in the art world at the time, Hollywood stars and jet-setters, stayed in three neo-Mediterranean residences. They could watch movies in complete peace in a large-screen movie room equipped with dozens of chairs, set up in the Casa Grande. Today, visitors can enjoy the splendours of this unique domain, nestled on top of San Simeon, a few miles north of Cambria. They are requested to leave their car at the visitor center, located at the foot of the hill, and to take part in one of five guided tours. Tour 1, which features a visit to Casa Grande, a guest residence, the pools, the esplanade and gardens, is ideal for a first visit. Visitors board a bus that climbs over 5mi (8km) up the enchanted hill on a narrow, winding road. Still at the visitor center, the **National Geographic Theater** (*$7; every day 9:30am to 5:30pm;* ☎*805-927-6811*) shows the *Enchanted Castle* movie on a gigantic five-storey screen. The 40min production illustrates how this incredible architectural dream became reality.

Morro Bay

Morro Bay's history can be traced back to 1542, when explorer Juan Cabrillo first described Morro Rock, which is the first of nine extinct volcanos that stretch from the coast to the current site of San Luis Obispo. The Spanish later took possession of this region and their ships profited from this narrow bay, which allowed them to cast off their moorings in complete safety. During the Mexican period, much land was granted to settlers who raised cattle on hundreds of rather dry acres in the area. It was not until 1870 that Franklin Riley built the first house, erected the first boarding quay and officially founded the village of Morro Bay. Today, the small city of 10,000 residents considers itself to be a rather lively vacation destination, since it is ideally located at the foot of Morro Rock, in a small bay rich in diverse marine life. A true marine sanctuary, Morro Bay shelters around 20 bird species threatened with extinction, notably the peregrine falcon. Blue herons, white pelicans, several kinds of seagulls and grebes faithfully visit this place and play among the seals and sea lions. Over 70 migratory-bird species also call the bay home during the winter months. Though the small town centre has a few basic businesses, restaurants and hotels, the port and marina are the heart of the town's action. Many people stroll along Embarcadero, a popular seaside street that has a number of tourist offices and restaurants.

The Nine Sisters, which are a series of extinct volacnos around 21 million years old, are practically perfectly aligned from Morro Bay to San Luis Obispo. These rounded rock formations plot the line between the Los Osos and Chorro valleys. This region was once inhabited by the Chumash tribe, which set up their camp at the foot of these ancient volcanoes and lived off the berries and roots that grew on their slopes. Described for the first time in 1542 by Spanish explorer Juan Rodríguez Cabrillo, **Morro Rock ★** is the most famous of the nine sisters. Nicknamed the Gibraltar of the Pacific, this stunning rock formation is a nature reserve and is nearly 656ft (200m) high. It is home to a colony of peregrine falcons, a bird species threatened with extinction. Its seaside location is a few minutes from town and the reserve is considered the symbol of Morro Bay.

Lovely hiking paths cut through the popular **Morro Bay State Park** (*south of town*) with its flower pastures, sandy beaches and sweet-smelling eucalyptus forests that were planted in the 1930s. Countless numbers of monarch butterflies come here in October to take refuge during the winter season. The park holds the **Morro Bay Natural History Museum** (*$3; every day 10am to 5pm;* ☎*805-772-2694*), whose interesting exhibits and audiovisual presentations are devoted to natural history and the region's environment.

San Luis Obispo

San Luis Obispo is located halfway between San Francisco and Los Angeles,

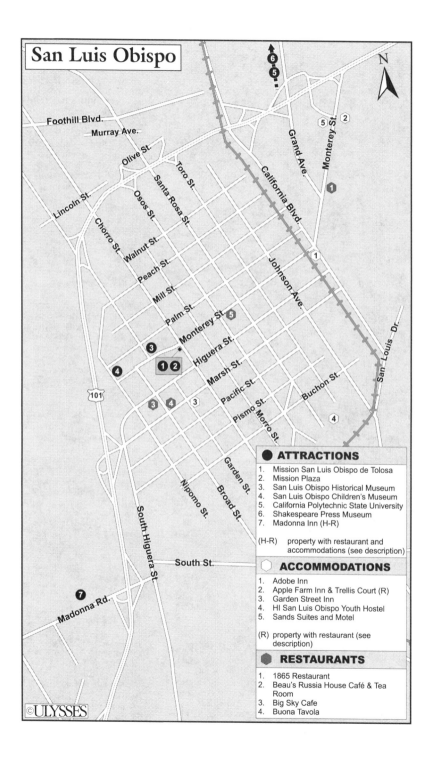

San Luis Obispo

● ATTRACTIONS

1. Mission San Luis Obispo de Tolosa
2. Mission Plaza
3. San Luis Obispo Historical Museum
4. San Luis Obispo Children's Museum
5. California Polytechnic State University
6. Shakespeare Press Museum
7. Madonna Inn (H-R)

(H-R)   property with restaurant and
        accommodations (see description)

▢ ACCOMMODATIONS

1. Adobe Inn
2. Apple Farm Inn & Trellis Court (R)
3. Garden Street Inn
4. HI San Luis Obispo Youth Hostel
5. Sands Suites and Motel

(R)   property with restaurant (see
      description)

▧ RESTAURANTS

1. 1865 Restaurant
2. Beau's Russia House Café & Tea
   Room
3. Big Sky Cafe
4. Buona Tavola

©ULYSSES

The Founding Father

Miguel José Serra was born on the Spanish island of Majorca in 1713. In 1730, he joined the Franciscan Catholic Order and took the name Junípero Serra. One year later, he began teaching philosophy at Lullian University, in Spain, and continued to do so for the next 15 years. In 1749, Franciscan authorities sent him as a missionary to Mexico, then a Spanish colony. On American soil, he first encountered the Sierra Gorda Amerindians and worked among them while teaching at the College of San Fernando in Mexico's capital city. Appointed Superior of the Alta California missions in 1767, he was entrusted with the task of continuing the work

of his predecessors the Jesuits, who had begun establishing Catholic missions in Baja California in 1697. Father Serra, known as the "Apostle of California" for his role as first missionary, founded the San Diego mission two years after his nomination. It was largely modelled after the example set by the Jesuits on the Californian peninsula. Subsequently, he would supervise the establishment of six more missions before passing away in Carmel, in 1784, at the age of 71. In recognition of the Franciscan's primordial role in the colonization and evangelization of California, Pope John-Paul II beatified Father Serra in 1988.

at the junction of Route 1 and the US 101. Surrounded by the green hills of the Santa Lucia Mountains a few miles from the Pacific, San Luis Obispo clearly enjoys one of the best locations. The history of this 42,000-strong city is both peaceful and lively, and can be traced back to 1772, when Father Junípero Serra founded the fifth Franciscan mission here. Today, this house is still the city's geographic centre and all urban activity revolves around this historic site. A rich agricultural community at first,

San Luis Obispo's economic development boomed with the arrival of the Southern Pacific Railway in 1894, and this rural community quickly became a regional centre for trade and merchandise transportion. If the old mission marks the city's geographic centre, California Polytechnic State University fuels, without doubt, the city's cultural life. It gives the otherwise quiet and reserved community a breath of fresh air and a youthful ambiance. The presence of this academic institution is

certainly responsible for the proliferation of Higuera Street cafés and pubs, which feature all types of music, and are the favourite meeting place of music lovers between September and May. It is also extremely pleasant to stroll through the small shaded town centre, which features several restaurants and shops. To make it easier to get around downtown and avoid frustrating traffic jams, a free trolley service was set up. For its part, Monterey Street, which is north of Mission Plaza, has several hotels and motels, restaurants and other services.

Founded in 1772 by Father Junípero Serra as the network's fifth mission, the **Mission San Luis Obispo de Tolosa** (*$1; summer every day 9am to 5pm, winter every day 9am to 4pm; Mission Plaza, corner Monterey St. and Chorro St.,* ☎805-543-6850) stands at the heart of the town centre in **Mission Plaza**. This is a picturesque shaded pedestrian area that surrounds San Luis Creek, which first served as a water source for mission residents and monks. Originally built in adobe by the Chumash and completely restored in the 1930s, the church, which is decorated with picturesque wood trim, remains the centre of a still active Catholic parish. The mission's buildings house an excellent museum, which features great collections devoted to the Chumash and the missionary period.

As of 1956, the original buildings of the Carnegie Library (built in 1905) were transformed to house the **San Luis Obispo Historical Museum ★** (*$2; Wed to Sun 10am to 4pm; 696 Monterey St., near the mission,* ☎805-543-0638), a small museum devoted to the region's history. Thanks to more than 17,000 old photographs and ancient objects, visitors can discover San Luis Obispo's rich past, from its nautical history to the Victorian era, with some Chumash history in between. The venerable stone building's interior was restored at the start of 2000.

The **San Luis Obispo Children's Museum** *($4; Mon to Tue and Thu to Sat 10am to 5pm, Sun 1pm to 5pm; 1010 Nipomo St., ☎805-544-5437)* is a spot that is entirely devoted to interactive exhibits that let children discover the wonders of the world that surrounds them. Kids will find these activities both fun and instructive.

California Polytechnic State University *(every day; take Grand Ave. N., ☎805-756-5734)*, Cal Poly to those who know it well, is known throughout the country for its architecture, agriculture and engineering programs, which are the most important in the western United States. You can stroll through the pleasant campus, which is located on the pretty hills north of the city, on your own or with the help of a tour guide. Make sure to stop at the **Shakespeare Press Museum** *(☎805-756-1108)*, which features a collection of printing presses and type settings from the gold rush. The collection belongs to Charles Palmer, a collector and poet who was known as "Little Shakespeare" in the California gold mines. Buildings devoted to horses and dairy production, as well as ornamental horticultural greenhouses are also extremely popular with the public.

The legedary **Madonna Inn ★** *(100 Madonna Rd., ☎805-543-3000)* (see p 365) accommodates strollers and the curious who want to discover this kitsch emporium.

The Saturday preceding Ash Wednesday, Higuera Street takes on a New Orleans ambiance for San Luis Obispo's **Mardi Gras ★** *(☎805-542-2183)*. The exuberant parade, which is no doubt the most colourful show west of the Mississippi, makes its way through the centre of town.

Santa Barbara

Chumash Indians prospered in the Santa Barbara region for thousands of years, building villages that were well organized societies on the coast, in inner valleys and on the Channel Islands. Rich fauna, fertile lands and abundant natural resources allowed them to lead a relatively peaceful and comfortable life. Their first contact with Europeans was in 1542, when explorer Juan Cabrillo penetrated the channel and took possession of the land in the name of the Spanish Crown. Cabrillo was warmly greeted by the Chumash and gifts were exchanged. It was not until 1602 that another Spanish explorer would venture down the waters of the channel. Under the command of Sebastián Vizcaíno, three frigates penetrated dangerous waters, swept by violent winds and tossed by a turbulent sea. A carmelite aboard one of the ships, attributed being saved from the storm to his prayers, beseeching the

saint who was honoured that day; he therefore named the bay and the surrounding coast in honour of that saint—Santa Barbara. In 1782, a group of Spanish soldiers led by Father Junípero Serra, captain José Ortega and governor Felipe de Neve, left the colony of Mexico to found a *presidio*, which is a military outpost assigned to protect the Franciscan missions between Monterey and San Diego. The Chumash chief gave them a warm welcome and his people actively took part in the founding and erection of the Santa Barbara mission less than four years later. Stirred by this relationship with the Natives, the Franciscans founded two other missions in the region, Santa Inés and La Purísima. However, the Chumash were never to assist the Spanish expansionist movement again, they succumbed to, among other things, diseases brought over by the Spanish, exacerbated by the new sedentary lifestyle and promiscuity that reigned in the missions. The Spanish governed the region until 1822, when High California passed under the control of independent and revolutionary Mexico. The missions were gradually put to secular use by mexican authorities and the vast lands were given to settlers who were close to power. Following the Mexican-American War, colonel John Fremont took possession of Santa Barbara in 1846, in the name of the United States of America. Santa Barbara remained a small peaceful community up until the end of the 19th century, when newspaper articles described its fabulous climate, invigorating thermal springs and natural beauty, and wealthy East Coast

Central Coast

residents began to take long holidays here. The tourist industry developed and cultural life flourished, which attracted distinguished visitors to Santa Barbara from around the world, such as heads of state, opera stars, kings and queens. In 1910, before movie-making activities were centralised in Hollywood, the American Film Company opened Flying A Studio, the most important studio of its kind in the world at the time, in Santa Barbara. More than 1,200 movies, mainly westerns, were shot over a decade. Even after the studio closed, Santa Barbara remained popular with movie stars and became home to big names such as Douglas Fairbanks, Mary Pickford, Charlie Chaplin, Ronald Colman and Alvin Weingand. Today, many celebrities own property in the surrounding areas, thus escaping the crowds of Los Angeles and Hollywood, which are less than 2hrs away by car.

A wealthy agglomeration of more than 90,000 residents, Santa Barbara's unique character is both lively and peaceful, historic and resolutely modern all at once. Proud of its origins, the city has managed to preserve and accentuate its architectural heritage, which will no doubt delight you during your walks. Among these marks of the city's colonial past stand cafés, restaurants, bars, theatres and cinemas, which abound here, in a town where culture, social gatherings and the art of living are sacred. If the city is bustling with activity, its residents nevertheless take time to relax and enjoy its enchanting Pacific setting. Its population takes great advantage of the green spaces and endless sandy beaches that let them enjoy such an enviable lifestyle. The heart of urban activity revolves around State Street, a large avenue flanked by shops, cafés and restaurants, which leads to Stearn's Wharf and the ocean. Perpendicular to State Street and running along the Pacific, Cabrillo Boulevard abounds in green spaces, and especially affordable motels and luxury hotels. It is a paradise for surfers, joggers, cyclists and volleyball enthusiasts, offering miles of beach that strech along the palm-lined boulevard.

The **Red Tile Walking Tour ★**, which is a walking route that runs through Santa Barbara's historic centre, lets visitors peacefully discover this wealthy city's 23 most beautiful heritage treasures. The 45min tour, which is clearly marked by the red sidewalk tiles, cuts across 12 of the town centre's quadrilaterals and links the main museums, notable institutional buildings and old colonial residences.

In April 1782, 42 Spanish soldiers, most of whom were accompanied by their families, arrived in the region and began construction of a military barracks complex, which would quickly become Santa Barbara's centre of activity. As the last Spanish outpost built in California, it served to protect the missions between Monterey and San Diego from attacks by the aboriginal people. With the end of the Spanish and Mexican presence in California, this *presidio* suffered a long period of decline, which

● ATTRACTIONS		
1. Red Tile Walking Tour	6. Gledhill Library	13. Sea Center
2. El Presidio de Santa Barbara Historic Park	7. Santa Barbara Museum of Art	14. Stearns Wharf
3. Casa de la Guerra	8. Contemporary Arts Forum	15. Yacht Harbor & Breakwater
4. Santa Barbara County Courthouse	9. Farmer's Market	16. Santa Barbara Zoological Gardens
5. Santa Barbara Historical Museum	10. Mission Santa Barbara	
	11. Santa Barbara Museum of Natural History	
	12. Santa Barbara Botanic Garden	

◎ ACCOMMODATIONS		
1. Banana Bungalow Guest House	4. Harbor View Inn	8. Simpson House Inn
2. Carpinteria State Beach Campground	5. Holiday Inn Express/Hotel Virginia	9. The Eagle Inn
3. El Capitán and Refugio State Beach Campgrounds	6. Hotel Santa Barbara	10. The Upham
	7. Los Padres National Forest Campgrounds	

◼ RESTAURANTS		
1. Arts & Letters Cafe	5. Bucatini	10. Wine Cask
2. Bistro Med	6. Ca' Dario	
3. Bouchon	7. Deli Sushi Gogo	
4. Brophy Brothers Clam Bar & Restaurant	8. The Natural Cafe	
	9. Waterfront Grill	

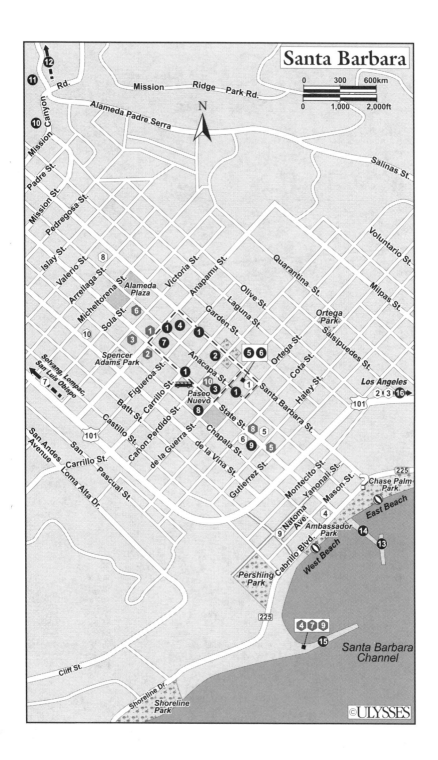

Grapes of Pleasure

The Santa Barbara region has seen an incredible expansion of its wine-making industry in the last few years. Since 1992, the number of wineries has increased by 60%, and the 56 current vineyards cover more than 17,791 acres (7,200ha). Already acknowledged as one of the largest regions producing Chardonnay and Pinot Noir, Santa Barbara County has now achieved a level of excellence that delights wine enthusiasts, who spent more than $10 million in wine-tastings alone in 1998. That same year, more than 861,000 cases of wine were sold, an increase in production of 85% since 1992. Winemaking is now the largest agricultural industry in Santa Barbara County and its 56 producers achieve annual sales in the order of $135 million.

Located 27mi (45km) northwest of Santa Barbara, the Santa Ynez and Santa Maria valleys benefit from a dry micro-climate that is ideal for growing several varieties of sturdy grapevines. Hot days give way to nights cooled by sea breezes that blow from east to west along the transverse mountain ranges.

There are two annual festivals held in honour of the nectar of the gods. In April, the Vintner's Festival offers wine-tastings and gourmet products in a lively bazar atmosphere, while the October grape harvest brings the Harvest Celebration. Visitors can crisscross the wine-making region on Route 101 and Route 154. The **Santa Barbara County Vintners Association** *(3669 Sagunto St., Unit 101, Santa Ynez,* ☎*805-688-0881 or 800-218-0881)* sells a *Winery Touring Map* and organizes wine-tasting tours of the leading wineries.

was heightened by natural disasters. Beginning in 1964, it was partially rebuilt under the aegis of the Santa Barbara Trust for Historic Preservation, and the Spanish military bases were resurrected at the heart of the **El Presidio de Santa Barbara Historic Park ★** *(free admission; every day 10:30am to 4:30pm; 123 E. Canon Perdido St.,* ☎*805-965-0093)*. The chapel and the commanders' and soldiers' quarters are worth a visit, which includes a 15min historical slide show. Restauration work and several archaeological excavations are still in progress.

José de la Guerra y Noriega, the fifth com-mander of the Santa Barbara *presidio*, had a large adobe residence built for his family in 1818. For decades, the **Casa de la Guerra** *(free admission; Thu to Sun noon to 4pm; 15 East De la Guerra St.,* ☎*805-965-0093)* was the heart of Santa Barbara's social, commercial and cultural life. The Santa Barbara Trust for Historic Preservation acquired it in 1971, and after much archaeological research, it was restored to its original state.

Completed in 1929 after the previous courthouse was destroyed by an earthquake, the **Santa Barbara County Courthouse ★★** *(free admission; weekends 10am to 4:45pm; Mon to Fri 8am to 4:45pm; 1100 Anacapa St.,* ☎*805-962-6464)* is one of the most fascinating old buildings in California. Surrounded by luscious tropical gardens, the splen-did Hispano-Moorish building features rich interior decorations. The hand-painted ceilings, gigantic central lights, imposing mural paintings and sculpted solid-wood doors give the building a monumental and opulent look. Visitors can go up the 82ft (25m) tower to enjoy a one-of-a-kind panoramic view of Santa Barbara.

A picturesque complex of old adobe buildings is home to the **Santa Barbara Historical Museum** *(free ad-*

mission; *Tue to Sat 10am to 5pm, Sun noon to 5pm; 136 East De la Guerra St., ☎805-966-1601).* It holds a rich collection of regional historical objects including magnificent old clothes, furniture and toys, as well as art. Permanent and temporary art exhibits help you relive Santa Barbara's glorious past, from the first European explorations to the Spanish, Mexican and America eras. The **Gledhill Library** *(admission; Tue to Fri 10am to 4pm, first Sat of the month 10am to 1pm; 136 E. De la Guerra St., ☎805-966-1601),* which is part of the museum, features a significant historical collection of books, photographs, maps and ancient manuscripts. Adjacent to the museum stand two 19th-century adobe buildings, which surround a shaded garden. The Casa Covarrubias, at 715 Santa Barbara Street, and its neighbour, the Historic Adobe, date back to 1817 and 1836, respectively.

The **Santa Barbara Museum of Art** ★ *($5, free admission Thu and first Sun of the month; Tue to Sat 11am to 5pm, Fri 11am to 9pm, Sun noon to 5pm; 1130 State St., ☎805-963-4364),* which is one of the most intersting regional art museums in the country, is housed in a magnificent historical adobe building; it features an excellent collection of American art, by artists such as O'Keeffe, Eakins, Sargent and Hopper.

French impressionist and post-impressionist painters, notably Monet, Matisse, Degas and Chagall, are well represented, as are Asian, classical, ancient, modern and contemporary art, photography, engravings and drawings.

Founded in 1976, the **Contemporary Arts Forum** ★ *(free admission; Tue to Sat 11am to 5pm, Sun noon to 5pm; 653 Paseo Nuevo, first floor, ☎805-966-5373)* is the heart of contemporary art in Santa Barbara. It organizes exhibits, performances and lectures year-round.

The **Farmer's Market** *(Sat 8:30am to 12:30pm, corner Santa Barbara St. and Cota St.; Tue 4pm to 7:30pm, levels 500 and 600 of State St.; ☎805-962-5354)* is a colourful outdoor market where fresh fruit, vegetables, flowers, honey, nuts and other fruits of the land are sold. The atmosphere here is reminiscent of a country fair. This market is much beloved by Santa Barbara residents.

The **Mission Santa Barbara** ★★ *($4; every day 9am to 5pm; 2201 Laguna St., ☎805-682-4713),* the network's tenth, was founded by the Franciscans on December 7, 1786. With its ideal location, 2,625ft (800m) above sea level and surrounded by the Santa Ynez Mountains, plus its unique twin towers and magnificent facade, the Mission Santa Barbara deserves its title as "Queen of the Missions." Greatly damaged by an earthquake in 1812, the original

buildings and adobe church underwent considerable restauration work. The current stone church dates from 1815 and the addition of a second bell tower completed the work 18 years later. Another earthquake levelled the religious buildings and it was not until 50 years later that their facades were rebuilt. Today the Spanish mission, which was built with the help of Chumash Indians, is the heart of an active Catholic parish. You can visit parts of the buildings that have been converted into a museum, the exotic indoor gardens, and the church. You can also explore the old cemetary, with its 4,000 Chumash tombs, and the richly decorated mausoleums of the first Californian settlers.

The **Santa Barbara Museum of Natural History** *($5; free admission last Sun of the month; Mon to Sat 9am to 5pm, Sun 10am to 5pm; 2559 Puesta del Sol, ☎805-682-4711)* presents exhibitions on the natural history of California and the North American West Coast. A slide show in Chumash Hall, a room that holds an important collection related to this Native American people, retraces the lives of the pre-Columbian Native American societies that lived in the Santa Barbara area. The museum features the region's only planeterium.

The **Santa Barbara Botanic Garden** ★ *($3; Mar to Oct weekends 9am to 5pm and Mon to Fri 9am to 6pm; Nov to Feb weekends 9am to 4pm and Mon to Fri 9am to 5pm; 1212 Mission Canyon Rd., ☎805-682-4726),* which was founded in 1926 by Anna Blaksley, is devoted to the study of California flora, as well as the deserts stretching to the Sierra Nevada, meridional mountains and large coastal islands. More than 5mi (8km) of trail cut through 64 acres (26ha) of instructive plantations which feature over 1,000 indigenous and rare species. You will have the chance to stroll through fields, canyons, cacti, and pine and sequoia forests, as you enjoy the magnificent view of the surrounding mountains. The trail also leads to the mission's old dam, which was built by the Chumash to irrigate the fields.

Santa Barbara abounds in superb coastal **beaches** ★ that stretch over 25mi (40km). Several of them are close to the centre of town, especially East Beach, which stretches from Stearn's Wharf to Montecito, West Beach, which lies between Stearn's Wharf and the Yacht Harbor, as well as Leadbetter Beach, located further west.

Managed by the Museum of Natural History, the **Sea Center** *($3; Oct to May Mon to Fri noon to 5pm, weekends 10am to 5pm, summer every day 10am to 5pm; Stearns Wharf, ☎805-962-0885)* offers a a fascinating look at the Santa Barbara Channel's marine life, thanks to instructive exhibits, a living animal reserve and a computerized learning centre.

Built in 1872 under the direction of John Peck Stearns, **Stearns Wharf** *(access from State St., ☎805-564-5518)* is one of the oldest jetties that is still active on the West Coast. A popular meeting place for visitors to Santa Barbara, the venerable footbridge features many shops, specialized stores,

restaurants and seafood markets.

Another spot that is popular with locals and tourists alike, the **Yacht Harbor & Breakwater** *(access by West Cabrillo Blvd.)* features a number of restaurants and businesses, and is also the point of departure for various marine excursions. A breakwater promenade lets you admire the city and the mountain backdrop.

More than 700 animals from all regions of the world are featured in the **Santa Barbara Zoological Gardens** ★ *($7; every day 10am to 5pm; 500 Niños Dr., near Cabrillo Blvd., East Beach, ☎805-962-5339)*, which is a theme park set in a vast 30 acre (12ha) seaside domain. Big cats, elephants, gorillas, antelopes, alligators, gibbons, lemurs, otters, giraffes and tropical birds live here in captivity, in a recreated natural environment that is rich and verdant. A miniature train and an amusement park will delight the little ones.

Between San Luis Obispo and Santa Barbara on Route 246 lies the unique community of **Solvang** ★, a corner of Northern Europe in the heart of California. A small village of 4,500 residents 45mi (72km)

northwest of Santa Barbara that was founded in 1911 by three Danish farmers, Solvang has managed to preserve a strong cultural identity with a rich cultural life, and has an undeniable Scandinavian feel to it. Its small, colourful half-timbered houses, gas lamps, windmills and restaurants specializing in Northern cuisine, (which feature delicious traditional pastries), give the city a picturesque style that draws many visitors every year. This pleasant community also features a heritage site that is a religious gem dating from the Spanish period: the **Mission Santa Inés** ★ *($3; summer 9am to 7pm, rest of the year 9am to 5:30pm; 1760 Mission Dr., Solvang, ☎805-688-4815)*, the 19th mission of the Franciscan-founded network, dates from 1804, when the missions' prosperity was at its peak. The belltower and the interior of the chapel were restored to their original grace and beauty. Visitors can discover antique furniture and accessories, and admire the colourful landscaped setting. The mission is the heart of an active parish and school.

On Route 246, 3mi (5km) northeast of the village of

Facade of a house in Solvang

Lompoc, visitors will come across one of the best restored missions. One of only two places once owned by the Franciscan missions that are today managed by State of California authorities, **La Purísima Mission State Park** ★ ★ *($5; every day 9am to 5pm; Rte. 246, ☎805-733-1303)* lets you discover the mission's socal and religious life, more than any other place. The buildings were completely restored in the 1930s and feature period furniture. Traditional Chumash medicinal plants grow in the gardens.

Once Chumash land, the vast **Los Padres National Forest** ★ *(Ranger Station, on Paradise Rd., access from Rte. 154, ☎805-967-3481)* starts at the foothills of Santa Ynez east of Santa Barbara and stretches northward and westward, covering more than 988,000 acres (400,000 ha). The territory contains many ecosystems, semi-alpine mountain chains with semi-arid deserts, conifer forests and a marine environment. The protected forest has several campgrounds, lakes and rivers, and many hiking trails. To get there from Santa Barbara, take Route 154 heading northwest.

Ventura

Over 1,500 years ago, the Chumash led a peaceful life in their village of Shisholop—peaceful, until the first Spanish explorers landed in the area and Franciscan monks founded the Mission San Buenaventura, in 1782. This date marks the start of the modern history of Ventura (whose name derives from that of the mission) and the begin-

ning of the decline of Native American society. The discovery of oil at the start of the 20th century caused the city to grow dramatically and in 1925, Ventura was one of the most productive sites in the entire country. Although its small town centre still features architectural marks from the past, its glory days and bustling activity seem to be long gone. The city is 93,000-strong and enjoys a tranquil existence on the shores of the Pacific. The sleepy town centre has given way to Ventura Harbor, the true heart of tourist activity, located 3mi (5km) south on the way to Oxnard. Ventura lives for the sea and this is one of the reasons you should visit.

Ventura has miles of sandy, sunny beaches. You will delight in hours of pleasure on **Emma Wood State Beach** and **San Buenaventura State Beach**.

Founded on March 31, 1782, the **Mission San Buenaventura** *($1; Mon to Sat 10am to 5pm, Sun 10am to 4pm; 211 E. Main St., ☎805-643-4318)* is the ninth mission of the Franciscan-founded network and is the last one to be established by founding father Junípero Serra. Destroyed by a fire in the 1790s, the original church was rebuilt after 12 years of hard work and reopened in 1809. Taken in 1834 by Mexican authorities, the mission was given back to the Catholic clergy on May 23, 1862, following a decree issued by U.S. president Abraham Lincoln. The buildings were restored in the decades that followed. Today, visitors can enjoy the small museum and green courtyard that is adorned with a lovely ceramic tile fountain. One of

the church's jewels are the paintings of the Stations of the Cross, painted 250 years ago, which have hung on the temple's walls since its reconstruction.

The **Ventura County Museum of History and Art** *($4; Tue to Sun 10am to 5pm; 100 E. Main St., ☎805-653-0323)* presents lovely exhibits on the region's history, which range from the Native American period to that of the Spanish, Mexican, U.S. and European settlers. One of the most notable exhibits is surely the "George Stuart" collection, which depicts small characters admirably dressed in clothes of different periods. The Hoffman Gallery is devoted to art.

The small, though interesting **Albinger Archeological Museum** *(free admission; summer Wed to Sun 10am to 4pm, winter Mon to Fri 10am to 2pm and Sat to Sun 10am to 4pm; 113 E. Main St., ☎805-648-5823)* covers more than 3,500 years of history. Its collection includes stone tools used by Native American peoples several centuries AD, objects found on the site of the Chumash city of Mitzkanakan, and a precious Spanish crucifix that is over 200 years old.

Ventura Harbor Village *(Spinnaker Dr., ☎805-644-0169)*, which is at the heart of the lively coastal region, abounds with restaurants, terraces, cafés and stores specializing in water sports equipment. In addition to these businesses, which are extremely popular with tourists, the port features activities such as games for children, craft fairs and outdoor concerts. **Channel Islands National Park Visitors Center** ★ *(May to Sep Mon to Fri 8am to 5pm, Sat to Sun 8am to 5:30pm; Oct to Apr*

Central Coast

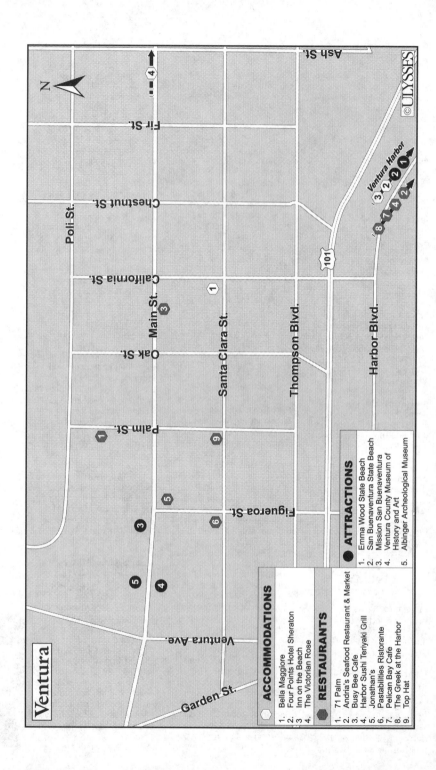

Mon to Fri 8am to 4pm, Sat to Sun 8am to 4:30pm; 1901 Spinnaker Dr., Ventura Harbor, ☎805-658-5730), located on the site of Harbor Village, is the main part of the fantastic land and marine national park located off of Ventura. A source of inexhaustible information on the five main islands that form the archipelago, the centre exhibits the replica of a pygmy mammoth found on Santa Rosa Island in 1992. A 20min educational movie is shown in the auditorium.

Ventura's most remarkable attraction lies 16mi (25km) off the coast. Established in 1980 following an act of Congress, the fantastic **Channel Islands National Park ★** *(1901 Spinnaker Dr., Ventura Harbor, ☎805-658-5730)* encompasses five of the archipelago's eight islands: Anacapa, Santa Cruz, Santa Rosa, San Miguel and the furthest island, Santa Barbara. In addition to the land on these rocky islands with jagged shores, the Channel Islands National Marine Sanctuary, an exceptional marine park, covers an aquatic territory of six nautical miles (11km) around the islands. Its section closest to the shore is part of the national park and is managed jointly between the National Park Service and the National Marine Sanctuary. This superb land and marine nature reserve, which is oftened nicknamed the Galápagos of the United States, features unique terrestrial wildlife species, exceptionally rich and varied marine life and bird species, and several endemic vegetation species (i.e. that do not grow anywhere else in the world). Movie master Alfred Hitchcock had noted this fact and it is not a coincidence that he chose to shoot a

few scenes of his famous movie *The Birds* on Anacapa Island. Once inhabited by the Chumash and Gabrielinos, the first European set foot here in 1542. Juan Rodríguez Cabrillo spent a winter here, and following injuries resulting from a bad fall, died on one of the islands. Legend says he was burried, but no tombstone has ever been found. Throughout the 18th and 19th centuries, Russian, British and U.S. hunters flocked to the island and caused the near extinction of sea otters, sea lions and seals, which were hunted for their fur and fat. During the same period, Spanish authorities tore the Natives from their native land and moved them to Catholic missions on the mainland, thereby leaving the place to the settlers, cattle raisers and European farmers. It was not until the 20th century that action was taken to protect these natural treasures. The first important administrative decision was made in 1938, when President Franklin D. Roosevelt designated the islands of Santa Barbara and Anacapa as the Channel Islands National Monument. A series of protective measures would follow and would culminate in 1980 with the creation of the Channel Islands National Park, the 40th national park in the United States. The islands offer great possibilities for hiking, diving and excursions to observe marine life. You can also pitch your tent for free in one of the **campgrounds** *(☎800-365-CAMP, http://reservations. nps.gov)* on each of the five islands. It is essential to make a reservation, however, as the number of spaces is limited. Campers must bring their own supply of drinking water, be-

Strawberry Country

Did you know that...

–Strawberry farming in Ventura County is a $100 million industry.

–In 1996, 5041 acres (2,040ha) were devoted to strawberries.

–The industry employs 13,000 people at harvest time.

–Ventura County produces 22% of the total California harvest.

–Strawberry season lasts from December to June.

–Strawberry growing in the Oxnard area alone has generated $4.8 million in revenue since 1996.

–Oxnard is the largest strawberry-producing region in the United States.

cause there is none on the islands. Only two official agencies are authorized to organize expeditions on national park territory: **Island Packers** and **Truth Aquatics Inc.** offer every kind of outing imaginable, from whale watching to diving, with kayaking, hiking and bird-watching, plus basic transportation on the islands, or between islands. Those who prefer making the visit by plane

Central Coast

or camping will opt for **Channel Islands Aviation**. See "Outdoor Activities" section for the complete addresses of these companies.

Oxnard

Although the Chumash occupied this region for thousands of years, the first U.S. settler only settled here in 1865, when Thomas Bard built Hueneme Port, which would quickly become an important transit terminal for grains and agricultural products. Agriculture remained at the heart of Oxnard's development at all times. It is therefore not surprising that the city, which has 159,000 residents, enjoys peaceful days, without too much hustle and bustle. Visitors seeking exuberance and ceremony should be on their way. Once described as the "land of the endless summer" by explorer Juan Rodríguez Cabrillo, Oxnard's Channel Islands Harbor, which is a marina and a lively tourist attraction during high season, is a gateway to the Channel Islands and the Pacific Ocean.

In 1985, the Oxnard Redevelopment Agency, which was backed by local investors, took an important step towards preserving the region's rich historical, agricultural and architectural heritage. After surveying the most impressive private residences and institutional buildings built at the turn of the 20th century, they decided to move them to a unique spot in Oxnard's town centre. Today, the precious four-sided and well laid out **Heritage Square ★** *(guided tour Sat 10am to 2pm; 200 W. Seventh St.,*

Heritage Square

☎805-483-7960 or 805-385-7545) houses 14 of the region's most beautiful heritage treasures. The residences house professional offices, the tourist information centre, a theatre and rooms, for special events. Visitors are more than welcome to take a look inside these impressive residences.

In 1906, wealthy industrialist Andrew Carnegie left a large sum to the municipality of Oxnard to build a library. The splendid neoclassical monument adorned with Doric colonnades today houses the **Carnegie Art Museum** *($3; Thu to Sat 10am to 5pm, Sun 1pm to 5pm; 424 S. C St., ☎805-385-8157)*. Devoted to education and entertainment through art, the institution presents temporary international art exhibits and holds a permanent collection of works from the Californian impressionist movement as well as some wonderful old Hollywood photographs.

Located between Harbor Boulevard, Peninsula Road, Victoria Avenue and Channel Islands Boulevard, the **Channel Islands Harbor** *(2731 S. Victoria Ave., ☎805-985-4852)* is the city's centre of activity, the hub of Oxnard's liveliness. Visitors will discover a number of restaurants and

specialized stores, as well as a marina. Several special outdoor events can also be enjoyed. The port is a point of departure for visits to the Channel Islands National Park (see p 354).

Each year in May, street performers, musicians and the curious pay hommage to the small red fruit during the **California Strawberry Festival** *($9; a weekend in May; 1621 Pacific Ave., ☎805-385-7578)*. The festival is a pleasant two-day fair and highlights the importance of Oxnard's strawberry industry.

Outdoor Activities

Channel Islands National Park

Only two official agencies are authorized to organize expeditions on national park territory. **Island Packers** *(1867 Spinnaker Dr., Ventura Harbor, Ventura,*

☎*805-642-1393; 3600 S. Harbor Blvd., Oxnard,* ☎*805-382-1779, www. islandpackers.com) and* **Truth Aquatics Inc.** *(301 W. Cabrillo Blvd., Santa Barbara,* ☎*805-963-3564, www. truthaquatics.com).* Those who prefer making the visit by air or camping will opt for **Channel Islands Aviation** *(305 Durley Ave., Camarillo,* ☎*805-987-1301, www.flycia.com),* a company specializing in air transport on the island of Santa Rosa.

Swimming

The Central Coast features magnificent sandy beaches. The section located between Santa Barbara and Oxnard is especially favoured by Mother Nature, as its orientation on the coast ensures the warmest currents and a calm sea.

Scuba Diving

Point Lobos State Reserve
Rte. 1, a little south of Carmel
☎*831-624-8413*
ptlobos@mbay.net, http://pt-lobos.parks.state.ca.us
The Point Lobos State Reserve is a diver's paradise (see p 338). However, divers must be aware of the environment's frailty and respect the rules established by marine park authorities. Since diving permits are limited to 15

The Island Gray Fox

A native species, found only on the Channel Islands, the island gray fox *(Urocyon littoralis)* is in serious danger of falling off the map. Preyed on to an extraordinary degree by eagles, attacked by parasites and struck down by illnesses, these foxes may become extinct in a few years.

Found on the Santa Cruz, Santa Rose and San Miguel islands, the island gray fox is the largest indigenous mammal on the islands. With a height of 12in (30cm) and weighing less than 4.4lbs (2kg), it appears more frail than its ancestor on the continent, the gray fox.

Fossils found on Santa Rosa show that the fox was established there nearly 16,000 years ago. During the last glacial period, ocean levels lowered, unifying the islets into one island and shortening the distance to the continent. It seems probable that gray foxes, clinging to some floating debris, were carried by the current to the large Santarosae Island. The new population would have adapted to its new setting and evolved into a species with different physical characteristics than its ancestors. When global warming brought the ocean back to a higher level, the Island of Santarosae separated into four parts: San Miguel, Santa Rosa, Santa Cruz and Anacapa. Lack of fresh water prevented the fox from surviving on Anacapa, but the three other islets had all the attributes the small animals needed to multiply. The Chumash, the Amerindian people who inhabited the islands, venerated the fox and probably used its fur for making clothing and quivers.

Since 1995, tallies show a dramatic decline in the island gray fox population. Biologists estimated that the number of adult foxes fell from 450 in 1994 to 40 in 1998. Since that time, funds have been earmarked to study the causes of this decline and to quickly adopt protective measures to ensure the survival of these foxes, an essential part of the rich wildlife heritage of Channel Islands National Park.

teams of two or three divers per day, it is essential that you make a reservation at least one day in advance, and a maximum of two months ahead of time. There is a $7 reservation fee.

Dive & Sport
1559 Spinnaker Dr., Suite 108, Ventura Harbor, Ventura
☎**805-650-6500**
Dive & Sport offers certification courses, organizes excursions and has a shop where you can rent and buy diving equipment. Complete training to receive the first level PADI costs $275.

Pacific Scuba Center
3600 S. Harbor Blvd., Channel Islands Harbor, Oxnard
☎**805-984-2566**
For $339, you can obtain PADI certification at Pacific Scuba Center. In addition to diving training, the company offers outings to the fantastic and richly diverse waters of the Channel Islands.

Snorkelling

AB Seas Kayaks *(32 Cannery Row, Monterey,* ☎*831-647-0147)* and **Beachside Sports** *(645 Cannery Row, Monterey,* ☎*831-647-0148)*, work together to offer excursions to discover the fascinating waters of Monterey Bay.

Surfing and Windsurfing

Steamer's Lane Beach in Santa Cruz attracts thousands of surfing enthusiasts every year.

Richard Schmidt Surf School
236 San Jose Ave., Santa Cruz
☎**831-423-0928**
A renowned training school for over 20 years managed by a master surfer, the Richard Schmidt Surf School offers an initiation to windsurfing course for people of all ages. A 2hr group lesson costs $70, whereas a private 1hr course costs $65, equipment included.

Sailing

Chardonnay Sailing Charters
west side of Santa Cruz Harbour, FF Dock, Santa Cruz
☎**831-423-1213**
Set off on a magnificent 72ft (22m) sailboat and discover Monterey Bay's marvellous marine life with Chardonnay Sailing Charters. This company offers a vast selection of excursions at $40/person.

Sea Kayaking and Boating

Kayak Connection
413 Lake Ave., Suite 4, Santa Cruz
☎**831-479-1121**
Kayak Connection rents kayaks and organizes excursions in Monterey Bay. Excursion rates range from $25 to $45 for a few hours.

Adventures by the Sea
299 Cannery Row, Monterey
☎**831-372-1807**
201 Alvarado St., Monterey
☎**831-648-7235**
You can explore the Monterey Peninsula's coast with Adventures by the Sea, which rents kayaks for $25 per excursion, and even organizes outings at a cost of $45/person.

From their two shops on Cannery Row, **AB Seas Kayaks** *(32 Cannery Row, Monterey,* ☎*831-647-0147)* and **Beachside Sports** *(645 Cannery Row, Monterey,* ☎*831-647-0148)* work in tandem to organize kayak excursions in Monterey Bay for $45/person.

Monterey Bay Kayaks
693 Del Monte Ave., Monterey
☎**800-649-5357**
Monterey Bay Kayaks offers a wide range of excursions in the waters of Monterey Bay, which feature rich marine life. A

3hr guided tour costs $50/person, while kayakers who opt to go solo pay $30 for a 4hr rental.

Sea for Yourself
2084 Main St., East Village
Cambria
☎ *805-927-1787*
Sea for Yourself offers excursions and rents kayaks.

Ka'nu 2U
699 Embarcadero Suite 9
Morro Bay
☎ *805-772-3349*
Ka'nu 2U rents both boats and kayaks. Rental rates go up to $39 and $29.50 for the day, respectively. Three-hour initiation outings cost $32.50 and $39.

Kayak Horizons
551 Embarcadero, Morro Bay
☎ *805-772-6444*
Discover Morro Bay's rich flora and fauna with Kayak Horizons. Rental rates are $8/hr and $19/half day.

Pedal & Paddle of Santa Barbara
Santa Barbara
☎ *805-687-2912*
Judy Keim has been exploring the Santa Barbara coast by bicycle and kayak for over 25 years. She has shared her great knowledge with paddling and pedalling enthusiasts since 1992, when she founded Pedal & Paddle of Santa Barbara. A 2hr excursion costs $42/person and a half-day excursion costs $72.

Channel Island Kayak Center
3600 S. Harbor Blvd., Suite 213, Oxnard
☎ *805-984-5995*
Channel Island Kayak Center, which rents and sells kayaks, and offers lessons and organized excursions, is one of the most complete agencies for novice and expert kayakers alike. A one-man kayak rental

costs $12.50/hr and a 2hr lesson costs $45. Excursions are varied and complete, and sometimes include a training session or snorkelling. Rates range from $45 to $140/person.

Fishing

Capitola Boat and Bait
1400 Wharf Rd., Capitola
Santa Cruz
☎ *831-462-2208*
The salmon and halibut better watch out, because Capitola Boat and Bait gives you every opportunity to catch them. Equipment, fishing rod and boat rental will run you $60/half day, and the company provides all services that are necessary for an enjoyable excursion.

Stagnaro's Fishing Trips
32 Municipal Wharf, Santa Cruz
☎ *831-427-2334*
Salmon fishers can leave with Stagnaro's Fishing Trips for $49/person per day.

High Sea Fishing

Stagnaro's Fishing Trips
32 Municipal Wharf, Santa Cruz
☎ *831-427-2334*
Stagnaro's Fishing Trips takes cod and mullet lovers to the high seas. The price tag is $40/person per day.

Virg's Landing
1215 Embarcadero, Morro Bay
☎ *805-772-1222*
☎ *800-ROCKCOD*
Cod fishing enthusiasts should go to Virg's Landing, where, for $36/person per day, you are brought to the open sea where the best catches await you.

WaveWalker Charter
Marina Gate 3
Santa Barbara Harbor
☎ *805-946-2946*
☎ *805-895-3273*
Abord the *Grady-White*, a speed boat that seats four to six passengers, WaveWalker Charter takes fishing lovers to the rich waters of the Santa Barbara Channel that abound with fish. Aside from fishing, you will also be able to enjoy the natural beauty of the area and observe its rich marine life.

Whale Watching

Stagnaro's Fishing Trips
32 Municipal Wharf, Santa Cruz
☎ *831-427-2334*
Stagnaro's Fishing Trips lets you search for big cetaceans. The expeditions last about 3hrs both in winter and summer and cost $20 and $25/person, respectively.

Monterey Bay Whale Watch
Fisherman's Wharf, Monterey
☎ *831-375-4658*
The renowned Monterey Bay Whale Watch organizes 3hr outings that leave from Sam's Fishing Fleet in Fisherman's Wharf. In addition to imposing grey whales, you will no doubt see seals, otters, dolphins and sea birds. Excursions cost $25/person and are led by experienced biologists and naturalists who have nearly 30 years of whale-watching experience.

Capt. Don's Whale Watching
Santa Barbara Harbor, next to the Brophy Brothers restaurant
☎ *805-969-5217*
Capt. Don's Whale Watching lets you discover cetaceans in the Santa Barbara Channel aboard the *Rachel G*, a powerful

149-passenger boat. In addition to blue and humpback whales, you will no doubt see dolphins and sea lions. The excursion costs $55.

Bicycling

Bicycle Rental & Tour Center
131 Center St., two blocks from the Municipal Wharf, Santa Cruz
☎*831-426-8687*
This means of transportation and recreational activity is becoming increasingly popular in Santa Cruz. Bicycle Rental & Tour Center lets you set out to discover the region on its many bike paths. You can rent bicycles of any kind and size from $7/hr to $75/week.

Adventures by the Sea
299 Cannery Row, Monterey
☎*831-372-1807*
201 Alvarado St., Monterey
☎*831-648-7235*
In addition to kayaking, Adventures by the Sea rents bicycles for $24/day, or $12 to $18/day for long-term rentals.

Sister enterprises **AB Seas Kayaks** (*32 Cannery Row, Monterey,* ☎*831-647-0147*) and **Beachside Sports** (*645 Cannery Row, Monterey,* ☎*831-647-0148*) offer tours on the bike paths of the Monterey Peninsula for $45/person. You can also rent bicycles for $22/day.

Sea for Yourself
2084 Main St., East Village Cambria
☎*805-927-1787*
Sea for Yourself rents bicycles that will let you enjoy the splendour of Cambria and its surrounding areas.

Bike Rentals
22 State St., Santa Barbara
☎*805-966-2282*
Discovering the heart and beaches of Santa Barbara by bicycle is a judicious choice that will let you avoid traffic problems and enjoy the city's beauty. Bike Rentals gives you this opportunity for $15/half day.

Horseback Riding

Rancho Oso
3750 Paradise Rd., access from Rte. 154, Santa Barbara
☎*805-683-5686*
Located in the magnificent Los Padres National Forest, Rancho Oso organizes outings in the Santa Ynez Valley and its surrounding areas. One hour of riding costs $22.

Golf

California's Central Coast has a countless number of golf courses of different calibres. Golfers will have no trouble finding a golf course that suits their level by asking at local information centres or hotels.

Accommodations

San Jose

San Jose might have fewer attractions than its neighbour San Francisco, but its location only a few miles from the latter makes it a good alternative for accommodations. In a bid to attract a clientele to the capital of Silicon Valley, many of the city's hotels offer unbeatable weekend rates, taking as much as 50% off the regular price. These advantageous rates easily justify the half-hour drive between the two neighbouring agglomerations. In San Jose, guests can enjoy comfortable, even luxurious, rooms at very decent rates.

Crowne Plaza
$$$$-$$$$$
≡, tv, ℝ, K, ≈, ℜ, ☺, ⊛, △
282 Almaden Blvd., CA 95113
☎*(408) 998-0400*
☎*800-2-CROWNE*
≈*(408) 279-1076*
Providing 239 rooms and a great location right downtown, the Crowne Plaza enjoys the reputation that precedes this world-class hotel chain. Spacious rooms with a classic, no-frills decor provide very appreciated comfort and tranquillity to guests. Like other superior hotels, the Crowne Plaza offers leisure and sports equipment as well.

Fairmont Hotel
$$$$-$$$$$
≡, *tv*, ℝ, K, ≈, ℜ, ☺, ⊛, △
170 S. Market St., CA 95113
☎*(408) 998-1900*
☎*800-527-4227*
≈*(408) 287-1648*
www.fairmont.com
A distinguished hotel in downtown San Jose, the Fairmont needs no introduction. Featuring a grandiose lobby, 500 very luxurious rooms and 41 equally advantageous suites, this 20-storey establishment is a judicious choice for visitors who don't mind digging a little deeper into their purse.

all of which are exquisitely decorated and furnished.

Silicon Valley: The Modern Gold Rush

Silicon Valley refers to an abstract region which has seen lightning-fast growth in high-tech industries during the past few years. The term originated with Don Hoefler, editor of the magazine *Micro-electronics News*. This Santa Clara engineer was referring to silicon chips used in microcomputers. He started popularizing the term in 1971, so Silicon Valley had its name long before the arrival of the yuppies of the 1980s!

The boom in the high-tech and computer chip industry arose during the 1960s in Santa Clara County, near the city of San José. Although the name Silicon Valley will never appear on a map, authorities and business-men generally trace its borders between San Mateo in the north, the Santa Cruz Mountains in the west, San Francisco Bay/Diablo Mountains in the east and Morgan Hill to the south of San José. This latter, the region's largest city, is known as the capital of Silicon Valley. The head offices of several large high-tech and computer compa-nies, such as Adobe, Cisco Systems, Netcom, Hewlett-Packard, Apple, Intel, National Semi-conductor, Advanced Micro Devices and dozens of others are found here. San José is located approximately 1hr south of San Francisco.

Santa Cruz

Henry Cowell Redwoods State Park Campground
101 N. Big Trees Park Rd.
☎*(831) 335-4598*
A few miles north of the city, the charming and verdant Henry Cowell Redwoods State Park features a pleasant camp-ground with over 110 summer sites.

 **HI Santa Cruz Hostel**
$
sb, ℝ, *K*
321 Main St., CA 95060
☎*(831) 423-8304*
≈*(831) 429-8541*
www.Hi-santacruz.org
Occupying an old cottage surrounded by a garden, the welcoming HI Santa Cruz Hostel youth hostel enjoys a great location in a quiet neighbourhood, only minutes away from down-town and the beaches. Managed by a friendly and original young crowd, this establishment includes some 40 beds in small dormitories. Reservations are essential.

Blackburn House Motel
$$-$$$$
≡, *tv*, ℝ, *K*
101 Cedar St., CA 95060
☎*(831) 423-1804*
≈*(831) 423-8233*
Situated only minutes away from the ocean, a little outside the down-town area, the Blackburn House Motel features 31 units, affordable cabins and slightly more expen-sive cottages built around a hundred-year-old house. A large English garden encircles this historical two-storey house which, unfortunately, is located in a rather dull residential neighbourhood.

Hotel De Anza
$$$$-$$$$$
≡, *tv*, ℝ, *K*, ≈, ℜ, ☉, ◉, ⌂
233 W. Santa Clara St., CA 95113
☎*(408) 286-1000*
☎*800-843-3700*
≈*(408) 286-0500*
www.HotelDeAnza.com
Well-known for its first-rate service, and featuring 106 comfortable rooms and suites, the Hotel De Anza enjoys an advanta-geous location downtown. Its classic and polished decoration highlights the architectural qualities of the building.

Hyatt Sainte Claire
$$$$-$$$$$
≡, *tv*, ℝ, *K*, ≈, ℜ, ☉, ◉, ⌂
302 S. Market St., CA 95113
☎*(408) 885-1234*
☎*800-824-6835*
≈*(408) 977-0403*
The prestigious Hyatt Sainte Claire flaunts the old-world charms of its historic building while providing all the modern comfort that guests expect from an establishment of this class. Located in downtown San Jose, this hotel features an impres-sive lobby in addition to 170 rooms and six suites,

Central Coast

Ocean Pacific Lodge
$$$-$$$$ bkfst incl.
≡, *tv*, ℝ, ≈, ⊛
120 Washington St., corner Pacific Ave., CA 95060
☎*(831) 457-1234*
☎*800-995-0289*
≈*(831) 457-0861*
Close to the sea, but unfortunately located in an uninspiring area surrounded by empty lots, the Ocean Pacific Lodge includes 57 basic but spotless rooms. Nearby traffic might inconvenience guests who choose this establishment for the quality of its service, good rates and proximity to interesting sights in the city.

The Babbling Brook Inn
$$$$ bkfst incl.
tv, ⊛
1025 Laurel St., CA 95060
☎*800-866-1131*
≈*(831) 427-2457*
www.babblingbrookinn.com
Embellished by a small waterfall, brook, charming garden and evergreen forest, the Babbling Brook Inn is the oldest and largest bed and breakfast in the Santa Cruz region. Named after grand masters of European painting, each of the 13 plush rooms in this hundred-year-old house provides a refined setting in which every element of the decoration contributes to the old-world ambience.

The Darling House
$$$$ bkfst incl.
314 W. Cliff Dr., CA 95060
☎*(831) 458-1958*
www.darlinghouse.com
The superb Darling House, a dignified residence built in 1910 on West Cliff Drive overlooking the ocean, features seven charming and uniquely decorated rooms garnished with antique objects and furniture. Some of the rooms provide unobstructed views of the ocean below. Caressed by ocean breezes and surrounded by fruit trees, this luxurious Victorian residence also includes a remarkable dining room and lounge area.

Sea and Sand Inn
$$$$-$$$$$ bkfst incl.
≡, *tv*, ⊛
201 W. Cliff Dr., CA 95060
☎*(831) 427-3400*
≈*(831) 466-9882*
www.santacruzmotels.com
All 20 rooms in the cliffside Sea and Sand Inn afford magnificent views of the ocean. The variously sized rooms provide more than adequate comfort, but do not display any particular cachet. Facing the bay, a lovely garden behind the building enhances guests' sojourn here. Unfortunately, traffic on West Cliff Drive might inconvenience people who are a little more sensitive to noise.

Monterey

Veterans Memorial Park Campground
$15 per tent
Via Del Rey, 1.5mi (2.5km) from downtown, south on Pacific St. and right on Jefferson St.
☎*(831) 646-3865*
In addition to 40 campsites with showers, this hillside campground affords lovely views of Monterey Bay. Reservations are not accepted, so arrive early in the summer.

Victorian Inn
$$$-$$$$ bkfst incl.
≡, *tv*, ⊛
487 Foam St., CA 93940
☎*(831) 373-8000*
☎*800-232-4141*
≈*(831) 373-4815*
www.victorianinn.com
Next to the Victoria Historical Residence, which houses the reception and administrative offices, the

17-Mile Drive

The opulence of the Monterey Peninsula is not a recent phenomenon. For generations, the rich and famous have visited and lived in this beautiful natural setting. The first prestigious visitors came to stay and play at the Original Del Monte Hotel, built in 1880 on the grounds of the present-day U.S. Naval Postgraduate school, in Monterey. The guests, comfortably seated in horse-drawn carriages, were no doubt charmed by the narrow gravel road that ran along the coast and through the Del Monte Forest. They stopped for refreshments, admired the scenery and turned around at the Carmel Mission further south. Seventeen miles (27km) long, this stretch of road still exists as part of the peninsula's landscape. For $7, you can take this magnificent panoramic road that crosses private properties in Pebble Beach that are crowned by luxurious residences, goes through lush forests and runs along the peninsula's superb coast.

Victorian Inn includes 68 rooms with a classic decor, some of which include a fireplace. Although it is located in the Cannery Row district, this inn provides no view of the ocean as it is slightly off the promenade. Guests enjoy breakfast in a charming Victorian dining room.

Casa Munras Garden Hotel
$$$$
≡, *tv*, ≈, ℜ
700 Munras Ave., CA 93940
☎*(831) 375-2411*
☎*800-222-2446*
⇌*(831) 375-1365*
www.casamunras-hotel.com
Guests of the Casa Munras Garden Hotel appreciate both the modern comfort and colonial charm of this establishment that was tastefully designed with respect to its integration and aestheticism. The hotel's 166 rooms are ensconced in little houses built of wood and cement which harmonize with the historical character of the main building which was erected in 1824. The dining room and lounge in this venerable Hispanic edifice are also reminiscent of the era.

The Monterey Hotel
$$$$
≡, *tv*
406 Alvarado St., CA 93940
☎*(831) 375-3184*
☎*800-727-0960*
⇌*(831) 373-2899*
www.montereyhotel.com
Designed by Harry Ashland Greene in 1904, the Monterey Hotel is part of the architectural heritage of downtown Monterey. Visitors will be pleasantly surprised by the facade and interior of this edifice, which was considered modern when first built. Its 45 rooms and suites, furnished in tune with the period, are equally endowed with

unparalleled old-fashioned charm.

Sprindrift Inn
$$$$-$$$$$ *bkfst incl.*
≡, *tv*, ℜ, ⊛
652 Cannery Row, CA 93940
☎*(831) 646-8900*
☎*800-841-1879*
⇌*(831) 646-5342*
www.sprindriftinn.com
Each of the 42 rooms in the Sprindrift Inn has a unique decor combining comfort, classicism and luxury. Wood floors, top-quality furniture, marble bathrooms and decorative art objects create a plush and soothing setting. Located right by the sea in Cannery Row, this hotel commands magnificent views of the ocean.

The Merritt House Inn
$$$$-$$$$$ *bkfst incl.*
≡, *tv*
386 Pacific St., CA 93940
☎*(831) 646-9686*
☎*800-541-5599*
⇌*(831) 646-5392*
www.merritthouseinn.com
Formerly the residence of Monterey County's first judge, the Merritt House Inn now contains three rooms decorated with the classic charm of the epoch. Surrounded by date and olive trees, this comfortable two-storey Victorian residence also includes annexes, which were built in the same architectural style, and feature 22 rooms and suites. Some have a private balcony overlooking the splendid gardens, which will certainly help you to forget its proximity to downtown.

Monterey Plaza Hotel & Spa
$$$$$
≡, *tv*, ℜ, ⊘, ⊛, △, ✪
400 Cannery Row, CA 93940
☎*(831) 646-1700*
☎*800-334-3999*
⇌*(831) 646-5937*
www.woodsidehotels.com
With its 290 ultra luxurious rooms, large European-

style whirlpool on the roof, unimpeded view of the ocean and splendid terrace, the Monterey Plaza Hotel & Spa is certainly the most prestigious hotel in the city. Perched on a promontory in Cannery Row, this hotel complex features rooms with a marble bathroom and mahogany furniture, and many have a balcony overlooking the ocean.

Pacific Grove

Pacific Grove Motel
$$-$$$
tv, ℝ, ≈
1101 Lighthouse Ave., corner Grove Acre, CA 93950
☎*(831) 372-3218*
☎*800-858-8997*
⇌*(831) 372-8842*
Gracious and helpful employees greet guests at the Pacific Grove Motel, a modest establishment located in the centre of Pacific Grove. This small motel includes 30 rooms that are simply decorated with no-frills, as well as a terrace and barbecue area. Without a doubt, this establishment provides quality accommodations at reasonable prices.

Asilomar State Beach & Conference Grounds
$$$ *bkfst incl.*
≈, ℜ
800 Asilomar Blvd., CA 93950
☎*(831) 372-8016*
⇌*(831) 372-7227*
Built on an immense, magnificent, wooded-estate encompassing 104 acres (42ha) by the ocean, the Asilomar State Beach & Conference Grounds can accommodate over 300 guests in 28 charming little houses made of stone and wood. Owned by the State of California since the 1950s, this institution combines rustic charm, comfort and family atmosphere with a dash of wild

beauty. Guests enjoy its grounds covered in pines and sand dunes, and have access to the far-reaching Asilomar State Beach.

🌴 Green Gables Inn
$$$-$$$$ bkfst incl.
tv
104 Fifth St., CA 93950
☎ *(831) 375-2095*
☎ *800-722-1774*
⇔ *(831) 375-5437*
Featuring large windows looking out to the ocean, the Green Gables Inn, a cozy Queen Anne residence, is one of Pacific Grove's brightest architectural gems. Each of the 11 rooms in this respectable home built in 1888 has been carefully restored and decorated with items and furniture of the period. The Chapel and Gable rooms as well as the Lucy suite are exceptionally sumptuous and luxurious. Finally, the richly furnished common room drenched in sunlight is a lovely place to unwind and admire the beautiful view of the ocean.

The Centrella Bed & Breakfast Inn
$$$-$$$$ bkfst incl.
tv
612 Central Ave., CA 93950
☎ *(831) 372-3372*
☎ *800-233-3372*
⇔ *(831) 372-2036*
www.centrellainn.com
Even though the Centrella Bed & Breakfast Inn occupies a venerable Victorian home dating back to 1889, its interior bears very little resemblance to the epoch. Rooms in the main residence as well as cottages in the back have a classic decor that is a little disappointing given the age of the edifice. There are 26 rooms and suites in this establishment, which is only a step away from Lover's Point Beach.

🌴 Seven Gables Inn
$$$$-$$$$$ bkfst incl.
555 Ocean View Blvd., CA 93950
☎ *(831) 372-4341*
www.7gables-grandview.com
Settled in a superb Victorian residence built in 1886 for the Chase family (of the Chase Manhattan Bank), the Seven Gables Inn features a rich and opulent period interior. Antique objects and furniture from Europe adorn this impressive first-class residence, which also has a few cottages in the back that can house up to 14 guests. Large windows allow the invigorating rays of sunshine to enter, so happy occupants can fully admire the immensity of the nearby Pacific. This sumptuous residence stands in the middle of a delightful garden embellished with roses and marble statues.

Carmel-by-the-Sea

🌴 The Happy Landing
$$$
tv
Monte Verde St. between Fifth St. and Sixth St., P.O. Box 2619, CA 93921
☎ *(831) 624-7917*
The adorable pink-and-green gable house nestled among the pine trees of Happy Landing certainly has all the earmarks of the adventures of Hansel and Gretel. Built in 1925, this charming little residence, with annexes in the back, includes seven rooms which have an old-fashioned decor and are furnished with antiques. The flower garden, with its small paths and a pond, provides a calm and bucolic setting.

Adobe Inn
$$$$ bkfst incl.
≡, *tv*, ℝ, ≈, ℜ
corner Dolores and Eighth St., P.O. Box 4115, CA 93921
☎ *(831) 624-3933*
☎ *800-388-3933*
⇔ *(831) 624-8636*
www.adobeinn.com
Located in the heart of the town, the Adobe Inn provides 20 comfortable rooms with a balcony and fireplace decorated in a classic manner, without excess luxury or superfluity. For 25 years, this small two-storey building, with a lovely flower garden at the entrance, has provided relatively affordable lodgings in Carmel, a notoriously expensive city.

🌴 Carmel Valley Lodge
$$$$ bkfst incl.
tv, ℝ, ≈, ☺, ☻, ⌂
Carmel Valley Rd., near Ford Rd., Carmel Valley, CA 93924-0093
☎ *(831) 659-2261*
☎ *800-641-4646*
⇔ *(831) 659-4558*
www.valleylodge.com
A few miles east of Carmel, the Carmel Valley Lodge stands in a lush and verdant valley. Combining comfort, warmth and country charm, the 31 rooms, some with fireplace, of this top-notch establishment are spread out in a few small houses. This setting creates a peaceful oasis far from the peninsula's whirlwind of activities.

The Green Lantern
$$$$
tv
corner Casanova St. and Seventh St., P.O. Box 1114, CA 93921
☎ *(831) 624-4392*
☎ *888-414-4392*
⇔ *(831) 624-9591*
www.greenlanterninn.com
A darling little establishment with rustic charm, the Green Lantern Inn lies slightly outside Carmel's centre of activity. Twenty uniquely decorated rooms,

each bearing a name evoking green forests, are scattered in a few small wooden houses surrounded by a delightful flower garden. Breakfast is served in a sunny dining area on a veranda.

Big Sur

In Big Sur, camping is king and campgrounds are legion. However, because it gets very crowded during the summer, it is necessary to reserve ahead of time with PARKNET (☎800-444-PARK). The three principal state parks are the most well known and popular places to camp: **Andrew Molera** *($3; at the mouth of the Big Sur River,* ☎831-667-2315), **Pfeiffer Big Sur** *($21;* ☎667-2315) and **Limekiln** *($6;* ☎831-667-2403). All three provide more or less the same services—drinking water, toilets, picnic tables, sometimes showers—in forested zones with access to hiking trails and beaches in some cases.

The Glen Oaks Motel
$$$
≡, ℝ, K, ℜ
Hwy. 1, east side, CA 93920
☎*(831) 667-2105*
⌐*(831) 667-1105*
The simple and rustic Glen Oaks Motel is tucked away in the green hills of Big Sur. It encompasses a series of small brick houses with a no-frills decor and kitchenettes in some cases. Scattered among the trees alongside Highway 1, the 17 little cottages, decorated in an old-fashioned country style, will suit visitors who wish to enjoy the beauty of the region while staying in an easily accessible area that provides acceptable comfort.

Big Sur Lodge
$$$-$$$$
ℝ, K, ≈, ℜ
Hwy. 1, Pfeiffer Big Sur State Park, CA 93920
☎*(831) 667-3100*
☎*800-424-4787*
⌐*(831) 667-3110*
www.bigsurlodge.com
In the heart of Pfeiffer Big Sur State Park, the Big Sur Lodge promises calm and serenity in the midst of pine and oak trees. The establishment includes 61 rustic but comfortable cottages, some with fireplace or kitchenette (or both), built around an outdoor pool. The housing units, accessible by a narrow road, are less than a hundred yards (90m) from the park entrance and are perfect for taking full advantage of the park's outdoor activities and hiking trails.

Ventana Inn & Spa
$$$$$
≡, *tv*, ≈, ℜ, ◉, ⌂, ✪
Hwy. 1, east side, CA 93920
☎*(831) 667-2331*
☎*800-628-6500*
⌐*(831) 667-2419*
www.ventanainn.com
A little south of Big Sur's Ranger Station, after driving a few hundred yards on a meandering road off Highway 1, you will find an extraordinary, very luxurious and classy hotel complex. Built on an immense and beautiful estate in the mountains, the Ventana Inn & Spa lords over the region and commands amazing views of the neighbouring verdant landscape and the blue Pacific Ocean. This luxurious establishment features rooms and suites of the highest quality, yet has managed to maintain a rugged mountain charm, thanks in part to the judicious use of untreated wood in both the interior

and exterior of the main buildings and cottages.

Cambria

San Simeon State Beach Campgrounds
$17
Hwy. 1, about 1mi (1.6km) north of Cambria
☎*(805) 927-2020*
☎*800-444-7275*
There are two campgrounds in San Simeon. The first, San Simeon Creek, has 133 campsites as well as showers and access to the ocean for swimming. The second, Washburn, is more rugged and features 67 campsites on a hill overlooking the ocean.

Creekside Inn
$$
≡, *tv*
2618 Main St., East Village, CA 93428
☎*(805) 927-4021*
☎*800-269-5212*
The Creekside Inn has no particular charm, but this motel remains a good choice for visitors with limited budgets. Impeccable comfort and a retro decor characterize the 21 rooms of this establishment, which just opened a few years ago.

Castle Inn
$$-$$$ bkfst incl.
≡, *tv*, ℝ, ≈, ◉
6620 Moonstone Beach Dr., CA 93428
☎*(805) 927-8605*
Well-kept and affordable for the oceanfront district, the Castle Inn Motel is neither particularly attractive nor original. However, the quality and cleanliness of its rooms as well as its judicious location make it a good place to keep in mind.

Central Coast

The Blue Bird Motel
$$-$$$
≡, *tv*, ℝ
1880 Main St., East Village,
CA 93428
☎*(805) 927-4634*
☎*800-552-5434*
≈*(805) 927-5215*
info@bluebirdmotel.com
www.bluebirdmotel.com
The Blue Bird Motel's
charming period-lobby
and reception are located
in the ravishing 1880s Lull
Mansion, the former home
of George Washington
Lull, one of the founding
fathers of Cambria. Sur-
rounding the mansion a
series of modern little
houses, simply and taste-
fully decorated, accommo-
date guests in a peaceful
and green environment.

Olallieberry Inn
$$$-$$$$ bkfst incl.
2476 Main St., East Village,
CA 93428
☎*(805) 927-3222*
☎*888-927-3222*
≈*(805) 927-0202*
olallieinn@olallieberry.com
www.olallieberry.com
In 1873, the Manderscheid
brothers built a residence
by the Santa Clara Creek in
the new town of Cambria.
Years later, they were of-
fered a Douglas fir tree,
which they planted in their
garden. Today, this stately
one-hundred-year-old co-
nifer and a splendid reno-
vated house of neoclassi-
cal style welcome guests
to the Olallieberry Inn.
Owners Peter and Carol
Ann Irsfeld take meticu-
lous care of their establish-
ment where each of the
rooms—six in the histori-
cal part and three more in
cottages in the
back—provide a particular
setting enhanced with old-
fashioned objects and fur-
niture. In the afternoon,
the smell of freshly baked
bread and pastries lingers
in the air and hints at the
quality of the breakfast

and hors d'oeuvres which
are prepared on the pre-
mises, to the great delight
of the guests.

Cambria's Pelican Suites
$$$$-$$$$$
≡, tv, ℝ, ≈, ☉, ⊛
6316 Moonstone Beach Dr.,
CA 93428
☎*(805) 927-1500*
www.cambriahotels.com
Classic, elegant and re-
fined are the kinds of
words used to describe
Cambria's Pelican Suites, a
chic establishment just a
few steps from the ocean.
All rooms include a fire-
place, balcony or terrace
and more importantly,
comfortable and luxurious
furniture, all of which cre-
ate a plush and comfort-
able setting. Attentive em-
ployees make staying in
this first-class establish-
ment very pleasant.

Morro Bay

Morro Bay State Park Campground
$18
South Bay Blvd.
☎*(805) 772-2560*
The popular Morro Bay
State Park features a camp-
ground with 133 sites,
including showers and
drinking water. Reserve
ahead of time.

El Morro Lodge
$$$
≡, *tv*, ℝ, ☉, ⊛
1206 Main St., CA 93442
☎*(805) 772-5633*
☎*800-527-6782*
≈*(805) 772-1404*
With its turret and tiled
roof, the El Morro Lodge
looks like a small Spanish
castle. Its 27 rooms, some
of which include a fire-
place, are decorated in a
Hispanic style which adds
a special charm to this
establishment located in
downtown Morro Bay. The

hotel's gem, the El Mirador
Suite, distinguishes itself
by its grand and comfort-
able style. Future guests
should keep in mind that
the El Morro Lodge is lo-
cated on the busy Main
Street and that the ocean is
a few minutes away on
foot.

Embarcadero Inn
$$$ bkfst incl.
tv, ≡, ℝ, ⊛
456 Embarcadero, CA 93442
☎*(805) 772-2700*
☎*800-292-7625*
Facing the ocean but on
the opposite side of the
street, the Embarcadero
Inn features 32 oceanview
rooms with private balco-
nies, 19 of which also in-
clude a fireplace. The de-
cor is not extravagant but
careful attention was given
to ensure the comfort of
the guests. Rooms on the
upper storey of this estab-
lishment with a wooden
facade obviously provide
the best views of the port
and ocean.

La Serena Inn
$$$ bkfst incl.
≡, *tv*, ℝ, ⌂
990 Morro Ave., CA 93443
☎*(805) 772-5665*
☎*800-248-1511*
≈*(805) 772-1044*
laserena@fix.net
www.laserena.com
Halfway between the
downtown area and the
ocean front, the lovely
pink La Serena Inn is a
top-quality establishment
offering its guests spa-
cious, sunny and comfort-
able rooms with private
balconies. Despite its size,
this large 37-room hotel
has managed to remain
personal and congenial. La
Serena Inn includes a
pleasant rooftop terrace
where guests can bask in
the rays of the warm Californian sun.

The Villager Motel
$$$
≡, tv, ℝ, ⊛
1098 Main St., CA 93442
☎ *(805) 772-1235*
☎ *800-444-0782*
www.villager-morrobay.com
A classic motel featuring 22 rather ordinary rooms, the Villager Motel is an economical alternative to downtown Morro Bay. This well-kept establishment, however, might be a little noisy for guests who are light sleepers.

San Luis Obispo

HI San Luis Obispo Youth Hostel
$ bkfst incl.
sb, ℝ, K
1617 Santa Rosa St., near the train station, CA 93401
☎ *(805) 544-4678*
⇌ *(805) 544-3142*
eslmer@slonet
The recently moved San Luis Obispo Youth Hostel emits a lovely and casual atmosphere while providing rudimentary comfort. Young guests can choose between spending the night in a dormitory or in a private room.

Apple Farm Inn & Trellis Court
$$-$$$$ bkfst incl.
≡, tv, ≈, ℜ, ⊛
2015 Monterey St., CA 93401
☎ *(805) 544-2040*
☎ *800-255-2040*
www.applefarm.com
Welcome to a very original and carefully perfected concept. The Apple Farm Inn and the Trellis Court are located on a superbly landscaped property overrun with 26 tree species, 92 kinds of plants and 50 varieties of flowers along the banks of the San Luis Creek. Standing next to an attractive souvenir and gift shop, an authentic working mill and a restaurant featuring a most enviable terrace, these two estab-

lishments have something for all tastes and budgets. Time stands still in these two delightful residences harbouring a total of 104 rooms, as the quaint and picturesque early 20th-century setting evokes calm and serenity. The rich design of the charming wooden buildings with gabled roofs, from the accessories and wall decorations to the furniture, creates a picturesque country ambience that will make you long for the days when people took more time to relax and enjoy life. Surprisingly, this haven of peacefulness is only a few minutes by car from downtown San Luis Obispo.

Adobe Inn
$$$ bkfst incl.
≡, tv, ℝ, K
1473 Monterey St., CA 93401
☎ *(805) 549-0321*
☎ *800-676-1588*
⇌ *(805) 676-1588*
www.adobeinns.com
Despite its plain appearance and disadvantageous location on a busy street, the Adobe Inn nonetheless offers 15 extremely well-kept rooms. The owners of this small motel—far more charming than others of its class—have done everything within their surely limited budget to provide maximum comfort to their guests.

Sands Suites and Motel
$$$ bkfst incl.
≡, tv, ℝ, ≈, ⊛,
1930 Monterey St., CA 93401
☎ *(805) 544-0500*
☎ *800-441-4657*
www.sandsuites.com
Providing excellent service and very affordable rates close to downtown, the lovely Sands Suites and Motel has the appearance of a Spanish residence with its tiled roof and immitation adobe walls.

Although it is located on a street where traffic can sometimes be quite heavy, some of its 70 rooms provide quieter accommodations in the back, with views of the pool and terrace. Of course, guests choose the Sands Suites and Motel for its very good quality/price ratio rather than its interior decoration which, although acceptable, isn't very original.

Garden Street Inn
$$$-$$$$ bkfst incl.
≡, ⊛
1212 Garden St., CA 93401
☎ *(805) 545-9802*
☎ *800-488-2045*
www.gardenstreetinn.com
Opened in 1990 by Dan and Kathy Smith, the Garden Street Inn is a dignified Queen Anne residence dating back to 1887. The owners have preserved the old-fashioned atmosphere by decorating each of the 13 rooms with sober and classic antique furniture. Located in the heart of downtown, this distinguished establishment also harbours a splendid library where guests can read quietly or simply relax.

Madonna Inn
$$$-$$$$
≡, tv, ℜ
100 Madonna Rd., CA 93405
☎ *(805) 543-3000*
☎ *800-543-9666*
⇌ *(805) 543-1800*
www.madonnainn.com
A unique establishment reaching new heights in kitsch and a veritable institution in San Luis Obispo for over 40 years, the very original Madonna Inn is located on a property of 1977 acres (800ha), a few minutes from downtown. The creators of this eccentric establishment, Alex and Phyllis Madonna, architect and interior designer respectively, wanted

to design a place that surpassed the common hotel. With the help of numerous artisans and unusual objects collected during their trips around the world, they shaped a virtually surreal universe. This hotel not only attracts guests for the night, but busloads of curious onlookers and tourists also flock here to have their picture taken in front of this monument to bad taste, that is both ludicrous and fascinating. Each of the 109 rooms has a unique name and decor; the most famous, The Caveman, recreates the insides of a cave with stone walls, ceilings and floors, a cascading shower and fake leopard skin! And this is only one of the many fabulous rooms with unbelievable decors evoking such themes as Hawaiian paradise, the Spain of toreadors, Imperial Austria or African safaris. But there's more. You can't leave without taking a look at the restaurant that will undoubtedly dazzle you with its dining room and seats in fake pink leather.

Santa Barbara

Los Padres National Forest Campgrounds
free - $15
Hwy. 154, NW of Santa Barbara
☎*(805) 967-3481*
☎*683-6711*
☎*688-4658*
The vast Los Padres National Forest includes several inexpensive, sometimes even free, campgrounds with attractive layouts, the closest of which is located about 20mi (30km) from downtown Santa Anna. The **Santa Ynez Recreation Area** *(Paradise Rd., accessible from Hwy. 154, ☎805-967-3481 or 683-6711)* has a few campsites along the banks of

the Santa Ynez River. At the base of the San Marcos Pass, the **Lake Cachuma Recreation Area** *(Hwy. 154, ☎805-688-4658)*, surrounded by oak trees, features a large campground including several hundred sites and all the necessary services.

El Capitán and Refugio State Beach Campgrounds
$15-$17
US 101, west of Santa Barbara
☎*(805) 968-1033*
☎*800-444-7275*
El Capitán and Refugio State Beach include campgrounds with 140 and 84 sites respectively. Both have beach access.

Carpinteria State Beach Campground
$18
US 101, 12mi (19km) SE of Santa Barbara
☎*(805) 684-2811*
☎*800-444-7275*
La Carpinteria State Beach has a campground of 262 sites with showers.

Banana Bungalow Guest House
$
tv, ℝ, K
210 E. Ortega St.,CA 93101
☎*(805) 963-0154*
☎*800-3-HOSTEL*
⇋*(805) 963-0184*
SBres@bananabungalow.com
The Banana Bungalow Guest House welcomes young, international and merrymaking travellers in a laid-back and friendly atmosphere. Amenities include a television room, video games and pool tables. Guests sleep in dormitories.

Hotel Santa Barbara
$$$-$$$$ bkfst incl.
≡, *tv*
533 State St., 93101
☎*(805) 957-9300*
☎*888-259-7700*
⇋*(805) 962-2412*
info@hotelsantabarbara.com
A long-standing institution situated right downtown,

the Hotel Santa Barbara is certainly a choice address, not only because of its centralized location but also because of its impeccable service and Mediterranean charm. You will surely appreciate the elegance of the spacious and illuminated lobby as well as the careful decoration of the 75 rooms. The comfortable and soft-coloured rooms gracefully blend in with the building's architecture.

Holiday Inn Express/Hotel Virginia
$$$$ bkfst incl.
≡, *tv*
17 W. Haley St., CA 93101
☎*(805) 963-9757*
☎*800-549-1700*
⇋*(805) 963-1747*
Positioned in the heart of the downtown area since the 1920s, the Holiday Inn Express/Hotel Virginia certainly has cachet. Soon to become a historical national monument, the building harbours beautiful decorative and artistic treasures, such as the superb mosaic fountain in the lobby. The hotel's 61 rooms, spread over three storeys, are furnished in the 1920s Art Deco style and provide guests with exemplary comfort.

✄ The Eagle Inn
$$$$ bkfst incl.
≡, *tv, ℝ, K*
232 Natoma Ave., CA 93101
☎*(805) 965-3586*
☎*800-767-0030*
⇋*(805) 966-1218*
The calm and intimate Eagle Inn is a lovely example of the Spanish colonial architecture which is so widespread in the historical part of Santa Barbara. This very well-restored old home of dried earth with a tiled roof provides a haven of peace in a quiet residential neighbourhood, close to downtown and the beaches. Each of the

establishment's 27 rooms prides itself on a unique and classic decor which, however, does not always reflect the inn's colonial past.

Harbor View Inn
$$$$-$$$$$
≡, *tv*, ≈, ⊙, ⊛
28 W. Cabrillo Blvd., CA 93101
☎ *(805) 963-0780*
☎ *800-755-0222*
⇝ *(805) 963-7967*
Combining the luxury of high-class establishments and the charm of neo-colonial villas, the Harbor View Inn is judiciously located within range of the beaches and the marina. Caressed by the winds of the open sea, its various buildings harbouring 80 rooms surround a lush interior tropical garden and pool. The commodious rooms, most with balconies and views of West Beach, provide a classic setting, that is refined and modern, with a touch of old-fashioned charm.

The Upham
$$$$-$$$$$ *bkfst incl.*
≡, *tv*
1404 De La Vina St., CA 93101
☎ *(805) 962-0058*
☎ *800-727-0876*
⇝ *(805) 963-2825*
www.vintagehotels.com
Founded in 1871, the Upham is Santa Barbara's oldest hotel which is still in business. Surrounded by colourful flower gardens, this venerable residence also includes a few cottages, which are more modern but designed to harmonize with the Victorian setting. The antique furniture in solid wood and sober decorations from the era respect the heritage and noble character of this 50-room establishment.

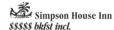 **Simpson House Inn**
$$$$$ *bkfst incl.*
≡, *tv*, ≈, ⊛
121 E. Arrellaga St., CA 93101
☎ *(805) 963-7067*
☎ *800-676-1280*
⇝ *(805) 564-4811*
The Simpson House Inn is in a class by itself for world-class inns. Set in an extraordinary aristocratic manor built in 1874, this unique establishment located north of downtown offers its privileged guests an unforgettable stay in a place rich with history. Encircled by a large English garden, far from the other homes in this residential neighbourhood, this fantastic residence includes 14 rooms decorated with incredible care and enhanced with the most beautiful antiques and furniture of the period. This five-star hotel also features a sumptuous parlour which will plunge you right into the golden age of the Victorian era.

Ventura

Bella Maggiore
$$-$$$$ *bkfst incl.*
≡, *tv*, ≈, ⊛
67 S. California St., CA 93001
☎ *(805) 652-0277*
☎ *800-523-8479*
⇝ *(805) 648-5670*
A breeze of Italy sweeps over the Bella Maggiore Inn, a charming two-storey Mediterranean hotel in the middle of downtown Ventura. From the bas-relief facade and interior courtyard, adorned with flowers and a fountain, to the 24 rooms with a sober but southern decor, the warmth of Southern Europe adds a special touch, both classic and tasteful, to this establishment.

Inn on the Beach
$$$-$$$$ *bkfst incl.*
≡, *tv*
1175 S. Seaward Ave., CA 93001
☎ *(805) 652-2000*
⇝ *(805) 652-1912*
If location constitutes one of the main factors to take into account when choosing a hotel, one might say that the Inn on the Beach has a winning start. This small and unpretentious hotel of 24 rooms with balconies has direct access to Ventura's far-reaching beaches. Sun and idle relaxation are guaranteed in this small, wooden three-storey establishment.

Four Points Hotel Sheraton
$$$$
≡, *tv*, ≈, ℛ, ⊙, ⊛
1050 Schooner Dr., CA 93001
☎ *(805) 658-1212*
☎ *800-229-5732*
⇝ *(805) 658-1309*
fourpointsvta@hotmail.com
http://fourpoints.com/ventura
Set on a 7acre (3ha) property near Ventura Harbor, the Four Points Hotel Sheraton provides all the services and comfort of a superior hotel. Forty-four of the 152 rooms occupy a separate building, which is right by the marina, with balconies affording views of breathtaking sunsets.

The Victorian Rose
$$$$ *bkfst incl.*
≡, ⊛
896 E. Main St., CA 93001
☎ *(805) 641-1888*
⇝ *(805) 643-1335*
www.victorian-rose.com
The Victorian Rose certainly distinguishes itself from other establishments on the Central Coast. This is mainly because the owners, Richard and Nona, had the wonderful idea of turning an old wooden Methodist church built in 1888 in the Gothic Revival style into an inn! After two years of work, the result is

Central Coast

clever, surprising, fascinating and original. The temple's unique structure is intact, with its 30ft-high (9m) ceilings, visible beams, steeple and stained-glass windows; inside, five fabulous rooms have been designed. A jumble of second-hand objects and antique furniture fill the majestic central room while a small parlour occupies a space under the amazing internal structure of the bell tower. The *pièce de résistance* is surely the magnificent room nestled in the heights of the former church, which is accessed by a massive spiral staircase. Rooms have all the modern comfort as well as a private bathroom, and are enriched with sumptuous furniture and decorative elements that create a luxurious and appeasing setting.

Oxnard

McGrath State Beach Campground
$22 per tent
☎(805) 654-4744
Only minutes away from the Channel Islands Harbor, the McGrath State Beach hosts a popular campground with 174 campsites near a long, sunny beach.

Casa Sirena Hotel & Marina
$$$
≡, tv, ℝ, ≈, ℜ, ☉, ⊛, △
3605 Peninsula Rd., CA 93035
☎(805) 985-6311
☎800-44-RELAX
⇥(805) 985-4329
Featuring 272 rooms with balconies and views of the marina or garden, in addition to 28 more luxurious suites, the Casa Sirena Hotel & Marina is a good choice for boating fans and ocean lovers. Comfortable and well-kept but not

pretentious, this hotel enjoys a favoured location in a very pleasing marine environment.

Country Inn & Suites at Port Hueneme
$$$-$$$$ bkfst incl.
≡, tv, ≈, ⊛
350 E. Hueneme Rd., Port Hueneme, CA 93041
☎(805) 986-5353
☎800-456-4000
⇥(805) 986-4399
Member of a reputable hotel chain, the Country Inn & Suites at Port Hueneme features 135 attractive rooms which exude simplicity and comfort. Guests of this establishment providing impeccable service in the port area only have to walk a few hundred yards to reach the sandy beaches around Oxnard.

Restaurants

San Jose

Johnny Rockets Restaurant
$
150 S. First St.
☎(408) 977-1414
If you are filled with nostalgia for the 1950s, you will surely enjoy Johnny Rockets, the quintessential American diner of that period. Wearing retro apparel, waiters serve classic hamburgers and no less classic milkshakes to guests seated in booths.

Casa Castillo
$$
200 S. First St.
☎(408) 971-8130
A welcoming staff greets guests at the friendly Casa Castillo, a typically festive Mexican restaurant. A large

choice of dishes, from *moles* and *chile relleno* to *burritos*, make up the exhaustive menu of this small restaurant with 15 or so tables and a simple, unpretentious decor.

Old Pizza Factory
$$
51 N. San Pedro Square
☎(408) 288-7488
In addition to a variety of delicious pizzas and savoury pasta dishes, the Old Pizza Factory provides a cozy setting in an old brick house with visible beams. The entrance to this pleasant restaurant is by a charming and beautifully landscaped lane on the side of the house.

Eulipia
$$$
closed Mon
374 S. First St.
☎(408) 280-6161
Serving creative Californian fine cuisine since 1977, Eulipia has made a name for itself as one of the best restaurants in San Jose. The sober and polished decor provides the perfect setting to appreciate the quality of the food, whether it be one of the savoury fish specialities, the couscous with scampi and saffron or the pork chops with sweet onion jam.

Original Joe's
$$$
301 S. First St.
☎(408) 292-7030
A popular institution with subdued lighting and an Italian decor, Original Joe's has prepared pasta and meat dishes with Mediterranean flavours for years. Customers dine in a warm, intimate room filled with plants and other decorative objects.

71 Saint Peter
$$$
71 N. San Pedro Square
☎*(408) 971-8523*
71 Saint Peter offers a cuisine of fresh Californian products highlighted with rich Mediterranean colours and perfumes. The European-inspired dining room is delightfully warm with its lovely woodwork. It is next to a small outdoor terrace, which is much appreciated on long summer days.

Spiedo Ristorante
$$$
151 W. Santa Clara St.
☎*(408) 971-6096*
A very classy establishment appreciated by the young professionals of Silicon Valley, Spiedo Ristorante serves the best Northern Italian dishes in a sober and modern setting. The very high ceilings and appreciable distance between the tables reduce the noise level and suit guests in wont of tranquillity. The chef artfully prepares grilled meats and fresh pasta.

Santa Cruz

El Palomar
$$
1336 Pacific Ave.
☎*(831) 425-7575*
The chef of the popular and lively El Palomar restaurant prepares the best Northern Mexican specialities in an inspired decor combining bright colours, high ceilings and visible beams. Customers savour *enchiladas, moles, ceviches* and other vegetarian dishes by a fireplace in the intimate dining room or on the sunny and animated terrace.

Walnut Avenue Cafe
$$
106 Walnut Ave.
☎*(831) 457-2307*
Every morning and noon, locals congregate at the very popular Walnut Avenue Café, a small establishment serving salads, sandwiches, hamburgers, fresh juices and espresso. Terrace in the back.

Clouds Downtown
$$$
110 Church St.
☎*(831) 429-2000*
Simple, family-style cooking awaits you at Clouds Downtown, a laid-back establishment located, not surprisingly, downtown. From juicy roast beef with mashed potatoes and spare ribs to grilled chicken, the chef does not indulge in superfluity. A maritime theme characterizes the vast and well-lit dining room.

Gabriella
$$$
910 Cedar St.
☎*(831) 457-1677*
Those who appreciate pâtés, duck, lamb, fish and meat prepared with the sun and perfumes of the Mediterranean gather at Gabriella, a friendly establishment with approximately 15 tables located in a charming old building made of dried earth. The chef uses fresh local products to prepare healthy and original dishes, which are complemented by a large selection of local and European wines.

Oswald's
$$$
closed Mon
1547 Pacific Ave.
☎*(831) 423-7427*
Oswald's is a warm and friendly restaurant serving continental Californian nouvelle cuisine. The renowned chef uses the tenderest meats and freshest fish to create refined dishes. Featuring a small verdant terrace set back from the street, this small brick establishment is accessed by a bridge leading down to the street.

Sea Cloud Restaurant
$$$
Municipal Wharf, local 49B
☎*(831) 458-9393*
Among the establishments on Municipal Wharf, the Sea Cloud Restaurant distinguishes itself by the quality of the fish and seafood it serves as well as by its very enviable location. Come evening, guests enjoy sunsets the colour of fire as they gaze at the Pacific from the dining room or terrace.

Pearl Alley Bistro & Cafe
$$$$
110 Pearl Alley
☎*(831) 429-8070*
The refined, varied and original menu of the Pearl Alley Bistro & Café draws its inspiration from Mediterranean fine cuisine. A splendid old terracotta house in rich yellows with a tiled roof, enfolds a very warm and distinguished dining room divided into two storeys. People in Santa Cruz will tell you that this reputable restaurant, which is located on a quiet alley, is one of the city's finest.

Monterey

If just thinking about seafood and fish makes you salivate, head to **Fisherman's Wharf**, a meeting place for both locals and visitors who come to experience the myriad establishments specializing in ocean delicacies.

**Britannia Arms
Pub & Restaurant**
$
444 Alvarado St.
☎**(831) 656-9543**
A quintessential pub where beer flows like water and fried food and other light meals are served, the Britannia Arms Pub & Restaurant notably distinguishes itself by its lovely wooden bar. Over 24 kinds of draught beer are served.

Old Monterey Cafe
$
489 Alvarado St.
☎**(831) 646-1021**
A well-established institution where regulars come for the first two meals of the day, the Old Monterey Café features an original decor composed of a thousand and one relics from the past showcased on the walls. Sandwiches, bagels and salads share the menu of this small bistro, which also serves espresso.

Rosine's
$$
434 Alvarado St.
☎**(831) 375-1400**
Popular with locals, Rosine's is an unpretentious family restaurant with a very varied menu covering the three meals of the day. From pasta and grilled meats to poultry and sandwiches, there is something for all tastes. Regulars appreciate the generous portions and lively ambience of this downtown eatery.

Jugem Japanese Restaurant
$$-$$$
409 Alavarado St.
☎**(831) 373-6463**
Across from the Monterey Hotel, the Jugem Japanese Restaurant serves delicious Japanese specialities. This small restaurant, containing about 10 tables and a sober decor, specializes in classic but always appreci-
ated Japanese cuisine. The menu features fantastic sushi and other vegetarian dishes, as well as seafood and meat. Interesting and affordable specials are served at lunchtime.

 Café Abrego
$$$
closed Mon night
565 Abrego St.
☎**(831) 375-3750**
A 5min walk from downtown, the Café Abrego is an oasis of peace where you can sample original Californian fine cuisine made with the freshest local products. The lamb, filet mignon and salmon are among the favourites on the inviting menu. Located in a small wooden house with soothing colours, it also features a very pleasant verdant terrace.

 Cibo Ristorante
$$$
301 Alvarado St.
☎**(831) 649-5042**
An elegant restaurant with a Mediterranean decor and muffled atmosphere, the Cibo Ristorante features classic but refined Italian cuisine. Chef Eric Melley artfully prepares fresh pasta, pizzas, meats, poultry and seafood with herbs and fresh local produce. The wine lists abounds in excellent Californian and Italian choices. Thursday through Sunday jazz musicians perform under the arches and low ceilings of this intimate establishment.

Paradiso
$$$
654 Cannery Row
☎**(831) 375-4155**
Settled on the main floor of the Sprindrift Inn in Cannery Row, Paradiso specializes in fresh seafood and fish. Oysters, salmon, tuna, halibut and mahi mahi hold a place of honour on a menu which also features a number of
Thai specialities, pizzas and *cioppinos* (fish in tomato sauce on linguini). Large bay windows in the elegant dining room afford pleasing views of the ocean below.

Pacific Grove

 Peppers Mexicali Cafe
$
closed Tue
170 Forest Ave., between Lighthouse Ave. and Central Ave.
☎**(831) 373-6892**
If you are attracted to Mexican and Latin American flavours, the Peppers Mexicali Café is the perfect place for you. Here, Latino dishes are prepared using local ingredients, that result in pleasant surprises, such as salmon tacos and swordfish fajitas.

 Toastie's Cafe
$
702 Lighthouse Ave.
☎**(831) 373-7543**
Regulars meet at Toastie's Café for the first two meals of the day. The familiar smells of cooking waft through the charming dining room with its relaxed ambience. Just like the restaurant itself, the honest and simple meals offer no surprises to guests who are familiar with these typically American small establishments, where sandwiches, salads, fried foods and eggs are honoured.

Fishwife
$$
1996^{1/2} Sunset Dr.
beside the Beachcomber Inn
☎**831-375-7107**
Chef Julio Ramírez adds a touch of the Caribbean to the Californian cuisine served at Fishwife. The menu features fresh seafood and fish, with favourites such as the Belize shrimp, grilled red mullet Cancún style, calamari,

fettuccini Alfredo with shrimp, scallops and crab. This popular unpretentious restaurant, with a simple decor, is next to Asilomar State Beach.

Crocodile Grill
$$$
closed Tue
701 Lighthouse Ave.
☎ *(831) 655-3311*
Chef Ted Walker creates imaginative and diversified dishes in which various types of savoury meat (lamb, duck, beef and game) are artfully prepared and served with the greatest freshness. Shunning colourful artifices, the downplayed sober decor takes a backseat to the cuisine, which is nicely accompanied by a well-stocked wine cellar.

 Fandango
$$$
223 17th St.
☎ *(831) 372-3456*
You'll rediscover the warmth of the Mediterranean in Fandango's polished decor as well as in its fragrant and colourful cuisine. The best dishes of Spanish, Italian and French regional cuisine fill the menu of this pleasant establishment occupying an attractive two-storey wooden house. The fresh lamb, delicious pasta, traditional paella, bouillabaisse and ubiquitous couscous are among the house specialities.

Old Bath House Restaurant
$$$$
620 Ocean Blvd.
☎ *(831) 375-5195*
A renowned establishment for over 15 years, the Old Bath House serves fine Californian nouvelle cuisine inspired by French and European traditions. Chef Sheri O'Connor has a gift for adapting traditional dishes to modern tastes

using the freshest products. This old Victorian house, within steps from the ocean and a coastal park, features a dining room whose classical style is both sophisticated and romantic.

Carmel-by-the-Sea

Britannia Arms Pub & Restaurant
$$
Dolores St., between Fifth and Sixth sts., in the El Prado de su Vecino Gallery
☎ *(831) 625-6765*
Like its cousin in Monterey, the Britannia Arms Pub & Restaurant is a classic and elegant pub featuring red velour chairs and green leather stools next to a solid wood bar. Regulars of such places where beer flows like water will recognize some of their favourite foods, such as meat pies, hamburgers and fish and chips. A small terrace opens onto the alley.

Café Gringo
$$
Paseo San Carlos, between Ocean Ave. and Seventh St.
☎ *(831) 626-8226*
The chef of the Café Gringo uses the best of Mexican and Californian culinary art to create an original nouvelle cuisine with sunny highlights. Of course, familiar names such as *quesadilla*, *enchilada*, *tamale* and *burrito* appear on the menu, but their preparation strays from tradition. This small café decorated in soothing orange tones enjoys a privileged location outside the hustle and bustle of the town, and has a little terrace in the adjoining alley.

Merlot! Bistro
$$$
Ocean Ave., between Lincoln St. and Monte Verde St.
☎ *(831) 624-5659*
A newcomer to Carmel's rich culinary scene, the Merlot! Bistro specializes in Californian fine cuisine served in a muted setting with soft colours and visible beams. Sunny Latin music bestows an even warmer dimension to this already inviting place. The kitchen serves original dishes ranging from crab and goat cheese *calzone* and Gorgonzola *gnocchi* to braised rabbit and lamb prepared with mustard and herbs.

PortaBella
$$$
Ocean Ave., between Lincoln St. and Monte Verde St.
☎ *(831) 624-4395*
Guests of Portabella savour dishes with local Mediterranean influences in a cozy southern atmosphere. Over the years, the enticing and intimate setting provided by the brick walls, beams and fireplace has turned this little bistro into a gastronomic mecca in Carmel acclaimed by critics and residents alike.

Summerhouse
$$$
6 Pilot Rd., near the Carmel Valley Lodge, Carmel Valley
☎ *(831) 659-8114*
Guests staying at the pleasant and peaceful Carmel Valley Lodge (see p 362) will find the perfect culinary complement in the Summerhouse. A classic and rustic atmosphere characterizes this establishment specializing in European and Californian cuisine. The inviting menu offers a number of daily specials in addition to the salmon skilfully prepared by the chef.

Central Coast

Village Corner Restaurant
$$$
corner Dolores St. and Sixth St.
☎*(831) 624-3588*
Established for over 50
years, this small family
bistro known as the Vil-
lage Corner Restaurant
provides a soft, Mediterra-
nean atmosphere bathed
in sunlight, where guests
dine on Californian fine
cuisine. The savoury lamb,
divine duck, grilled salmon
and other fresh fish, as
well as a variety of pasta
dishes share the spotlight
on the menu, without for-
getting the succu-
lent breakfasts.
Guests can savour
appetizing
dishes in a
peaceful set-
ting provided
by the ver-
dant ter-
race or
the
brightly
illumi-
nated
dining room.

Big Sur

Regardless of the season, it
goes without saying that
the natural beauty of the
surroundings is best en-
joyed by taking advantage
of the numerous picnic
areas in the region. Should
you decide on doing so,
we suggest you stock up
on food in Monterey, the
largest city in the region.

Cafe Kevah
$
Mar to Dec
Hwy. 1, west side, south of the
Ventana Inn & Spa
☎*(831) 667-2344*
Located below the Nepen-
the (see below), the Cafe
Kevah serves Tex-Mex
food and pastries on an
outdoor terrace; although
the view is not as spectac-
ular as that of its upstairs
neighbour, because it's not

as high, it is nonetheless
very pleasant and sunny.

Nepenthe
$$
Hwy. 1, west side, south of the
Ventana Inn & Spa
☎*(831) 667-2345*
A restaurant-bar on an
incredible terrace dominat-
ing the coast, the Nepen-
the merits a stop if only to
have a drink and feast
your eyes on the breath-
taking view. Bought by
Orson Wells for Rita
Hayworth, his wife at the
time, this property was
later sold to Bill and Lolly
Fassett, who opened the
famous Nepenthe. If the
panorama is stunning, the
food, however, is not
very original. Salads,
hamburgers and
sandwiches are
offered to
guests
who, to
be hon-
est, pay
mostly for the
view. The bar and
dining room feature se-
quoia beams, immense
bay windows overlooking
the ocean and a patio rising above the cliff. Stairs
from the parking lot lead
up to this establishment.

The Trail's Head Café
$$
Big Sur Lodge, Hwy. 1, Pfeiffer Big
Sur State Park
☎*(831) 667-3100*
The Trail's Head Café
draws a family crowd,
often guests of the Big Sur
Lodge or Pfeiffer Big Sur
State Park. Consequently,
it comes as no surprise
that it is a simple and
friendly restaurant, which
serves generous portions
of unpretentious fare. In
addition to steak, fish and
pasta *à la carte*, the chef
prepares daily specials
which are available at rea-
sonable prices.

The Glen Oaks Restaurant
$$$
closed Tue and Wed
Hwy. 1, west side, facing the Glen
Oaks Motel
☎*(831) 667-2264*
A warm dining room en-
dowed with a beneficent
chimney, pine tables and
chairs, as well as works by
local artists, welcomes
guests of the Glen Oaks
Restaurant. The chef offers
a limited but original menu
featuring duck, seafood,
steak, fresh pasta and
other Asian-inspired specialities.

Cielo Restaurant
$$$$$
Ventana Inn & Spa
Hwy. 1, east side
☎*(831) 667-2331*
In the image of the
Ventana Inn & Spa Hotel,
which manages it, the very
classy Cielo Restaurant
serves refined and widely
acclaimed Californian cuisine in an elegant and
warm setting. Its privileged
location in the middle of a
forest on the hills of Big
Sur provides exceptional
panoramic views that are a
divine complement to the
gastronomic meals.

Cambria

The Moonstone Beach
area lends itself particularly well to walks along
the ocean and picnics in
one of the designated
sites. Visitors of Hearst
Castle will rediscover the
same ocean pleasures at
the San Simeon wharf, in
the William Randolph
Hearst State Park.

Moonstone Beach Bar & Grill
$$
6550 Moonstone Beach Dr.
☎*(805) 927-3859*
On bright summer days,
crowds gather on the
large, breezy terrace of the
Moonstone Beach Bar &
Grill, which is certainly the

most interesting feature of this popular restaurant by the ocean. People come here to eat simple, typical American fare in a friendly ambience. Salads, steak and hamburgers form the greater part of the predictable menu.

Pablo's Mexican Restaurant
$$
2336 B Main St., East Village
☎*(805) 927-0175*
A darling little Mexican restaurant enriched by warm and peaceful colours, Pablo's emits a meridional and convivial atmosphere with its sunny dining room, terrace and ubiquitous tropical plants. The menu holds no surprises and limits itself to the classics of the genre.

 **Bistro Sole**
$$$
1980 Main St., East Village
☎*(805) 927-0887*
The Bistro Sole is certainly one of Cambria's lovely places to eat. Exuding a calm and relaxed ambience, this small bistro with 10 or so tables serves an innovative cuisine, healthy and refined, of Mediterranean inspiration. On the menu is a vast selection of original entrées and sophisticated dishes, ranging from assorted pasta and risotto to lamb and calamari. The chef adds a daring touch in the preparation of specialities combining traditional and nouvelle cuisine, and the results are surprising. Both the small dining room and outdoor terrace, adorned with flowers and greenery, are attractive.

Sow's Ear Café
$$$
2248 Main St., East Village
☎*(805) 927-4865*
A recipient of various culinary prizes, the reputable Sow's Ear Café has mastered the preparation of fish, seafood, pasta and

grilled meats. The low ceiling, woodwork, beams and chimney provide a certain cachet to the warm dining room of this restaurant, which also has daily specials.

 **The Sea Chest**
$$$
closed Tue
6216 Moonstone Beach Dr.
☎*(805) 927-4514*
Residents will tell you that this is the best fish and seafood restaurant in the region, and quite honestly, they aren't far from the truth. Freshness plays a major role at the Sea Chest, and the many guests who eat here on a regular basis greatly appreciate being served the best catches of the day. Other than its flawless cookery, this establishment embellished by a warm marine decor provides a festive and lively atmosphere.

Morro Bay

Lolo's Mexican Food
$
2848 N. Main St.
☎*(805) 772-5686*
Lolo's has been serving healthy Tex-Mex fare since 1985, and vegetarian guests are sure to find something to please their palate. Beans, rice and tortillas are cooked without fat. This small family restaurant is certainly a good place for a light meal.

Flying Dutchman
$$
701 Embarcadero, Dutchman's Landing Mall
☎*(805) 772-2269*
A small oceanfront restaurant built on supports, the Flying Dutchman enjoys a most enviable location. Simple and conventional meals are served in a dining room with large bay windows. The chef's

specialities include seafood, pasta and poultry.

 **Hoppe's Hip Pocket**
$$$
901 Embarcadero
☎*(805) 772-5371*
Hoppe's Hip Pocket might look like just another of Embarcadero's restaurants built on supports, but its original menu distinguishes it from its many neighbours. This plainly decorated bistro offers a varied menu composed of Mexican and Asian starters as well as creative main dishes. Fish, lamb, game and more traditional types of meat are prepared with originality by the chef who judiciously uses Madeira, coconut milk, peanut sauce and other condiments to give creations a remarkable perfume. Finally, the wine list features a good choice of local wines.

Rose's Landing
$$$
725 Embarcadero
☎*(805) 772-4441*
Yet another establishment built on supports using a veranda as a dining room, Rose's Landing devotes itself to conventional cuisine starring steak, fish and seafood. On Wednesdays, the house invites you to an "all you can eat scallops" evening.

San Luis Obispo

 **Apple Farm Restaurant**
$$
2015 Monterey St.
☎*(805) 544-6100*
On the charming Apple Farm Inn & Trellis Court estate, the Apple Farm emits the same rustic and convivial warmth as its hotel counterpart. Simple and generous family-style meals are served, in which homemade soups, salads, grilled meats and deserts

fresh out of the oven delight guests who also enjoy a peaceful terrace, overlooking a yard overrun with innumerable varieties of flowers and arborescent species.

🌴 Big Sky Café
$$
1121 Broad St.
☎(805) 545-5401
The Big Sky Café suggests a healthy and modern approach to American cooking with international accents. The chef adapts the best dishes of Cajun, Creole, Thai, Mediterranean and Mexican cuisine and masterfully concocts original and unique creations. Well-known as one of San Luis Obispo's more interesting restaurants, the popular and lively Big Sky Café provides a spacious dining room with a relaxed and festive ambience.

1865 Restaurant
$$$
1865 Monterey St.
☎(805) 544-1865
The 1865 Restaurant is a first-rate restaurant specializing in grilled meats, fish and seafood, with a pleasant terrace in the back, at the foot of the hills. The menu is not very innovative but the establishment nonetheless has a special character, occupying a large two-storey wooden building with beams and a fireplace.

Beau's Russia House Café & Tea Room
$$$
699 Higuera St.
☎(805) 784-0172
Specializing in traditional pre-Soviet cuisine, Beau's Russia House Café & Tea Room is a classy establishment, with a setting combining finesse and classicism. For starters, the chef suggests oysters or the obvious caviar, while the beef Stroganoff, chicken

Kiev and pirojkis are only a few of the outstanding dishes which are worth discovering on the extensive menu.

🌴 Buona Tavola
$$$
1037 Monterey St.
☎(805) 545-8000
Chef Antonio Varia skillfully and lovingly prepares Northern Italian fine cuisine at Buona Tavola, a charming new bistro already praised by critics. A large choice of starters, fresh pasta, imaginative main courses and irresistible deserts compose the menu of this typical restaurant with its unadorned dining room and small, verdant terrace in the back. Among the specialities, the chef recommends such refined dishes as the *agnolotti* pasta, shrimp dumplings with saffron sauce, *osso buco* of lamb as well as the *saltimboca alla fontina* (veal escalope stuffed with raw ham and cheese), which admirably lead in to desert: the succulent homemade *tiramisu*.

🌴 Gold Rush Steak House and Coffee Shop
$$$-$$$$
100 Madonna Rd.
☎(805) 543-3000
If you can stomach a shocking pink, extravagant and brilliantly kitsch retro decor, try the unique eating experience offered at the Gold Rush Steak House and Coffee Shop at the famous Madonna Inn. In the image of the hotel, the dining room juxtaposes fake leather and flashy objects in its bid to reach new heights in over-the-top excessiveness. As can be expected, the food isn't very innovative, falling back on the classic thick and rare steak as well as seafood prepared simply *à la American*.

Santa Barbara

🌴 Deli Sushi Gogo
$
119 Harbor Way
In front of the marina, right below Brophy Brothers, the Deli Sushi Gogo serves Japanese rolls to a young and alternative clientele seated around the four or five tables arranged here and there in front of the minuscule counter.

🌴 The Natural Cafe
$
508 State St.
☎(805) 962-9494
An institution devoted to healthy and vegetarian cuisine founded several years ago, the Natural Café attracts a faithful clientele who appreciate the originality of the many dishes and the convivial character of the place. Guests are invited to seat themselves, before informally ordering their meal at the counter in the back of the large room endowed with a very high ceiling. In the afternoon, you can sit on the terrace to savour a freshly squeezed delight from the juice counter.

Arts & Letters Cafe
$$
7 E. Anapamu St.
☎(805) 730-1463
At the back of the Sullivan Goss Books & Prints gallery and bookstore, you will be surprised and delighted to discover a charming, quiet bistro-terrace, far from the hustle and bustle of the street. Popular at lunchtime, this café dons a more peaceful style in the evening, when the food becomes more refined. Inspired by Asian, Latin American and Mediterranean flavours, the chef of the Arts & Letters Café creates a truly Californian, cleverly balanced

and imaginative nouvelle cuisine.

Bistro Med
$$
1129 State St.
☎*(805) 965-1500*
Bistro Med bears its name very well. Here, the warmth of the Mediterranean is felt everywhere, from the convivial dining room in the historical building with a lively and flowered patio, to the savoury Greek cuisine prepared without compromise. Famous and delicious starters open the way to succulent Hellenic specialities, such as lamb kebabs, fish, salads, moussaka and other fragrant vegetarian dishes.

Bucatini
$$
436 State St.
☎*(805) 957-4177*
The Bucatini admirably recreates the simple and laid-back atmosphere of an Italian trattoria. With a handful of tables, most of which are on the terrace, this small restaurant specializes in generous pasta and innovative pizzas, not to mention a few lamb and chicken dishes served in *secundi*.

Waterfront Grill
$$-$$$
113 Harbor Way
☎*(805) 564-1200*
The Waterfront Grill has something for all tastes and all budgets. Next to the Maritime Museum in Santa Barbara Harbor, this large establishment is really made up of two separate entities. Upstairs, guests enjoy succulent specialities from the sea in a comfortable dining room featuring a marine decor and lovely ocean views. At the marina level, the ambience unwinds, the meals become a little simpler and

a large terrace occupies most of the space.

🐟 Brophy Brothers Clam Bar & Restaurant
$$$
Harbor Way
Yacht Basin and Marina
☎*(805) 966-4418*
Brophy Brothers is part of Santa Barbara tradition. Known for its views of the marina as well as its generous portions of seafood and fish, this institution attracts scores of curious tourists and faithful regulars. A far cry from Californian fine cuisine, this restaurant dishes out honest and authentic meals for the whole family, accompanied by starchy, fried foods and rich sauces. Scampi, chowders, seafood salads and, of course, fresh catch of the day have top billing in this popular restaurant which doesn't accept reservations and, as a result, has interminable lineups on weekend evenings.

Ca' Dario
$$$
37 E. Victoria St.
☎*(805) 884-9419*
The secret behind Ca' Dario's success is none other than fine authentic Italian cooking. This small restaurant serves *antipasti*, *primi* and *secundi* featuring spicy aromas and well-balanced creamy sauces, in a warm, intimate and typically Italian ambience, with about 15 tables. Grilled meats (chicken, rabbit and duck) and fresh fish are only a few of the many specialities of this small bistro, offering you a truly Italian dining experience.

🐟 Bouchon
$$$$
9 W. Victoria St.
☎*(805) 730-1160*
Since opening in 1998, the chef and owner of the

Bouchon restaurant has been reaping successes and wildly passionate reviews. Refined, fragrant and fresh dishes are enhanced with local touches such as meat, vegetables and fruits direct from the farms and ranches of the region. The grilled rabbit, conserve of duck, red mullet and lamb in wine sauce are definitely worth lingering over, especially when accompanied by a large choice of the best wines of the neighbouring vineyards. This restaurant offers a refreshing ambience, both intimate and warm which, combined with the undeniable quality of the cuisine, explains its popularity.

Wine Cask
$$$$
813 Anacapa St.
☎*(805) 966-9463*
Certainly one of the finest restaurants in Santa Barbara, which also features one of the most impressive wine lists, the Wine Cask exudes refinement, good taste and elegance. The dining room, embellished by art works displayed on the walls, is advantageously connected to a splendid patio, providing a unique setting, downtown in an old Hispanic residence. The renowned chef prepares a Californian cuisine inspired by the land, generous and delicate at the same time, in the image of the establishment. The white fish in wine sauce, duck breasts and lamb fillet are but a few examples of the inviting menu. Wine lovers will find great vintages in the Wine Cask Wine Store, a boutique dedicated to this divine nectar, which is located right beside the restaurant.

Central Coast

Ventura

Top Hat
$
corner Palm St. and Santa Clara St.
Feeling a little hungry?
Why not stop at the
friendly Top Hat, a typical
fast-food place that has
been part of the urban
landscape since 1966. No
tables or chairs here, just a
counter poking out of a
smoky and fragrant little
house.

Pelican Bay Café
$
Schooner Dr., Ventura Harbor
☎(805) 658-2228
The convivial and simple
Pelican Bay Café serves
sandwiches, hamburgers
and salads by Ventura
Harbor. The terrace of this
small, sparsely decorated
restaurant is very popular,
especially for breakfast.

Andria's Seafood Restaurant &
Market
$
Schooner Dr., Ventura Harbor
☎(805) 654-0546
One of Ventura Harbor's
very popular institutions,
Andria's Seafood Restau-
rant & Market serves fish
and seafood, unfortunately
often fried, in a dining
room and on a terrace.
The atmosphere is very
relaxed and the food is
served with plastic plates
and utensils amid a persistent smell of cooking and
fish. Customers order at
the counter and then
patiently wait for their
number to be called.

Busy Bee Café
$-$$
478 E. Main St.
☎(805) 643-4864
The Busy Bee Café takes
you back 40 years, to a
time when the youth
danced to the sounds of
rock 'n roll and ended the
evening by wolfing down
a hamburger, sipping a

cherry coke and savouring
a high-calorie banana split.
With its raw lighting and
red booths covered in fake
leather, it perfectly recreates the quintessential
American diner of the
1950s. The menu is just as
faithful to this carefree
epoch, before the post-war
generation began counting
calories and neglecting to
refine its cereals.

Harbor Sushi Teriyaki Grill
$$
closed Mon and Tue
Schooner Dr., Ventura Harbor
☎(805) 339-0717
With a name that leaves
no doubt as to its special-
ities, the Harbor Sushi
Teriyaki Grill is a small,
friendly establishment,
with gracious service and
quality cuisine. The tal-
ented chef skillfully pre-
pares the best Japanese
dishes. You will surely
appreciate the family am-
bience of this modest res-
taurant whose small ter-
race opens onto the
Ventura Harbor prome-
nade.

The Greek at the Harbor
$$-$$$
Schooner Dr., Ventura Harbor
☎(805) 650-5350
The Hellenic world invites
you to the Greek at the
Harbor. In the evening
guests can sit in a classic
dining room with large
bay windows, while at
noon-time they can enjoy
the shade under a parasol
on the spacious terrace.
No matter what the time of
day, guests always find the
same delicious items on
the menu (moussaka,
lamb, grilled meats and
kebabs). In addition to its
sandwiches made with pita
bread, famous salads and
delicious typically Greek
specialities, the house pro-
poses a large choice of
mezedakia, a variety of
fragrant hot and cold start-
ers.

71 Palm
$$$
closed Sun
71 Palm St.
☎(805) 653-7222
In the almost one-
hundred-year-old Norton
Ranch House, the 71 Palm
restaurant offers its guests
authentic and honest
French food. Ever faithful
to traditions, the chef prepares starters with fish and
assorted cooked meats,
and simmers regional spe-
cialities from cassoulet and
sauerkraut to bouillabaisse.
The rustic yet distin-
guished interior sets the
tone and goes hand-in-
hand with the establish-
ment's gastronomic quali-
ties.

Jonathan's
$$$
closed Mon
204 E. Main St., in front of the
mission
☎(805) 648-4853
Having recently opened,
the chic and warm Jona-
than's has an original
menu that draws its inspi-
ration from the Mediterra-
nean basin. The menu of
this establishment, deco-
rated in warm and meridi-
onal tones, suggests invit-
ing specialities from Italy,
Spain, Portugal, France
and Greece. The interior
decoration highlights the
intrinsic features of the old
building in which the res-
taurant is housed. Its
bricks, wood and rich
colours all blend in per-
fectly.

Pastabilities Ristorante
$$$
185 E. Santa Clara St.
☎(805) 648-1462
A charming building of
Hispanic style accommo-
dates Pastabilities, a refined Italian restaurant
with an elegant and classic
decor. Located just a
stone's throw from the
Mission San Buenaventura,
this restaurant is famous
for its fresh pasta, pizzas

and appetizing *secundis* featuring veal, fish, seafood and poultry, all prepared according to traditions and enhanced by a touch of modernity.

Oxnard

 BG's Coffee Shop & Deli
$
428 A St.
☎*(805) 487-0700*
For breakfast and lunch, locals flock to BG's Coffee Shop & Deli, an institution in downtown Oxnard. This typical eatery, where regulars sit in booths covered in fake leather, probably hasn't changed very much over the course of its long life. The gracious and experienced waitresses have been serving classic omelettes, crêpes, sandwiches and hamburgers for eons.

The Lobster Trap
$$$
3605 Peninsula Rd.
at the extremity of the dead end
☎*(805) 985-6361*
Next to the Casa Sirena Hotel & Marina, the Lobster Trap specializes in fish and seafood fresh from the sea. The pleasant dining room is literally surrounded by bay windows, which give guests the impression of savouring ocean delights right in the marina.

The Whale's Tail
$$$
Harbor Blvd., Channel Islands Harbor
☎*(805) 985-2511*
The best seafood and fish restaurant in Oxnard, the Whale's Tail has a double personality. Upstairs, the Shellfish Bar is ideal for informal meals, whereas the large dining room downstairs is reserved for evening dining. Regardless of where they are seated, guests enjoy this pleasant,

familiar and convivial setting, surrounded by large bay windows overlooking the port. With a distinctively nautical theme featuring a salad counter shaped like a boat, and a boat hanging from the ceiling, the decor pleasantly complements the cuisine. Other than the seafood, which has made the reputation of this establishment, varied starters, such as oysters, cockles and crab cakes are offered, as well as main dishes consisting of delicious pasta, poultry or tender steak.

Entertainment

San Jose

San Jose's lively First Street features a number of movie theatres.

Ice Centre of San Jose
1500 S. 10th St.
☎*(408) 279-6000*
Hockey fans surely know that the area's Sharks play in the National Hockey League. The Ice Centre of San Jose, situated a few minutes from downtown, welcomes the valorous skaters and their fans.

Café Matisse
371 First St.
☎*(408) 298-7788*
Both the young and not so young, who wish to sip a coffee or a drink in an alternative, artistic ambience gather at the Café Matisse. The old furniture, art work on the walls and atmospheric music create a vaguely bohemian setting which lends itself well to existential discussions.

Shark and Rose
69 N. San Pedro St.
☎*(408) 287-6969*
The charming Shark and Rose is a very inspiring place to savour good draught beer in rustic and friendly surroundings. The wooden bar dominated by a huge deer head is only one of the decorative elements in this small British establishment which also serves light meals.

The Cactus Club
417 S. First St.
☎*(408) 280-0885*
Fans of all kinds of music meet at the Cactus Club to enjoy live shows.

The Usual
400 S. First St.
☎*(408) 535-0330*
Facing the Cactus Club, the Usual provides a stage for local artists to get the youth of San Jose dancing.

Santa Cruz

Blue Lagoon
admission fee
every day 4pm to 2am
923 Pacific Ave.
☎*(831) 423-7117*
A popular, hot dance club that welcomes a varied clientele, both gay and heterosexual, the Blue Lagoon is definitely an institution in Santa Cruz's nightlife scene. There is a bar, pool tables and several dance floors.

Caffe Pergolesi
418A Cedar St.
☎*(831) 426-1775*
As part of an old house, Caffe Pergolesi exudes a bohemian and serene air in a laid-back and welcoming setting. Young students come here for a coffee or beer as they write a few verses, read quietly, discuss how to change the world or relax on the sunny terrace,

Central Coast

without a care in the world.

Kuumbwa Jazz Center
tickets on sale at Logos Books and Music
1117 Pacific Ave.
☎*831-427-5100*
320-2 Cedar St.
☎*(831) 427-2227*
Locally known for its jazz nights when artists let inspiration guide them, the Kuumbwa Jazz Center also allows other forms of music to be expressed. This small and intimate bar is a perfect place to discover budding new talent.

Rosie McCann's Irish Pub & Restaurant
1220 Pacific Ave.
☎*(831) 426-9930*
Musicians get the regulars up and dancing at Rosie McCann's Irish Pub & Restaurant. Dancers can quench their thirst with any of the 29 kinds of draught beer offered, and satisfy their appetite with a choice of classic or original light meals.

Monterey

Blue Fin Cafe & Billiards
685 Cannery Row
☎*(831) 375-7000*
Fans of beer, music and pool flock to Blue Fin Cafe & Billiards to satisfy all their whims. Perched on the third floor of a building in Cannery Row, this restaurant-bar is a good place to hit the eight ball, enjoy a light snack and admire the ocean at your feet. Live music Thursday through Saturday.

San Luis Obispo

Linnaea's Cafe
1110 Garden St.
☎*(805) 541-5888*
A delightful little café with a terrace in the back, Linnaea's Café serves good

European-style coffee and pastries in a student and bohemian ambience. The smell of strong coffee, the pleasantly lax aspect of the place with its old furniture and piano, as well as acoustic musicians in the evening attract a young, intellectual and somewhat trendy crowd.

Mother's Tavern
$3-$4
725 Higuera St.
☎*(805) 541-8733*
Mother's Tavern is a superb two-storey tavern with sculpted woodwork and a majestic bar, which is a very popular gathering place for university students. In addition to the many kinds of beer and light meals, customers appreciate Wednesday disco nights and live music appearances in the evenings from Thursday to Saturday.

SLO Brewing Co.
$2
1119 Garden St.
☎*(805) 543-1843*
An long-established institution housed in a hundred-year-old building, the SLO Brewing Co. has been brewing blond, brown and red ales for years to the great delight of the city's beer drinkers. On the main floor, pool amateurs gather in a room seeped in old-fashioned cachet while reggae and rock devotees gather upstairs every Thursday, Friday and Saturday night to attend live musical stage performances. In this large room under the eaves, you can have a light meal, typical of these establishments where beer flows like water.

Tortilla Flats
cover charge
1051 Nipomo St.
☎*(805) 544-7575*
The popular Tortilla Flats is a restaurant by day and

a dance club night. The young crowd appreciates its Tex-Mex food, the warm and rustic setting furnished with beams and brick walls, as well as the many musical events presented in the evenings.

Santa Barbara

Club H₂O
cover charge
634 State St.
Club H_2O welcomes the youth of Santa Barbara who want to let loose and dance to the beat of their favourite music.

Fathom
cover charge
every day 5pm to 2am
423 State St.
☎*(805) 730-0022*
A dance club that draws a mostly gay clientele, Fathom is one of this city's most appreciated establishments, drawing devotees of all kinds of music. Theme nights (swing dance, the 1980s and others) are organized on certain evenings.

Old Kings Road
532$^{1/2}$ State St.
Fans of Jazz and Dixieland crowd together in the Old Kings Road, a tiny old-fashioned bar with an intimate, lively and warm ambience.

Q's Sushi A-Go-Go
cover charge
every day 4pm to 2am
409 State St.
☎*(805) 966-9177*
This place is as popular with people their 20s as its name is original. Q's Sushi A-Go-Go is a great place to savour the famous Japanese rolls and have a drink while listening to a variety of music, from the Jackson Five to Brazilian samba. The scarlet wallpaper, immense mirrors on the walls and dim lights

give this disco-bar-restaurant its unique style. The clientele can visit the three stories or enjoy sitting on a balcony overlooking the street.

Soho
cover charge
1221 State St.
☎*(805) 962-7776*
Jazz lovers gather at Soho where big names as well as young talent take the stage.

Wild Cat
15 Ortega St.
☎*(805) 962-7970*
With its heterogeneous, mysterious and 1970s inspired character, the Wild Cat plays a variety of music for a clientele from many different backgrounds.

Shopping

Santa Cruz

World Market Bazaar
1233 Pacific Ave.
☎*819-469-3872*
Curious and patient shoppers can find beautiful imported objects at the World Market Bazaar.

Monterey

Old Monterey Market Place
Tue
Alvarado St.
Every Tuesday throughout the year, residents and visitors gather downtown at the Old Monterey Market Place. The largest market of its kind in California, it provides space for over 130 vendors to display art pieces and crafts, and offer food and fresh products from the region. On average over the years, between 7,000 and 10,000 people come here every Tuesday.

Carmel-by-the-Sea

Carmel Art Association Gallery
Dolores St.
between Fifth and Sixth sts.
☎*831-624-6176*
The artistic community of Carmel plays host to many renowned art galleries. Taking over the country's second oldest artistic cooperative, which was founded in 1927, the Carmel Art Association Gallery continues the tradition and presents paintings and sculptures of over 120 of the region's best known artists. Vernissages, readings, films and concerts are periodically held in this venerable gallery.

Cambria

Cambria has declared itself an artistic town, and with good reason. This small community, particularly the West Village area, includes a surprising concentration of high-quality **art galleries** which are pleasant to discover as you while away the time.

Santa Barbara

Shopping is a favourite pastime of Santa Barbara residents who find what they are looking for in the elegant and chic **Paseo Nuevo Mall**. This shopping centre is located on Canon Perdido Street and on **State Street**, the city's main street, which is lined with innumerable art galleries and trendy boutiques.

Arts and Crafts Show
Sat and Sun 10am to nightfall
Cabrillo Blvd
On nice days, artists and artisans gather along the ocean front to sell their finest creations to passersby during the Arts and Crafts Show.

Ventura

Main Street abounds in second-hand shops and antique dealers where, with a little patience, buyers can find some good deals.

San Francisco and Surroundings

S an Francisco ★ ★ ★ has always exerted an almost mythical fascination on the unbridled imagination of pioneers, artists, writers, curious souls, tourists and all those who were once seduced by the invitation to "go west young man!"

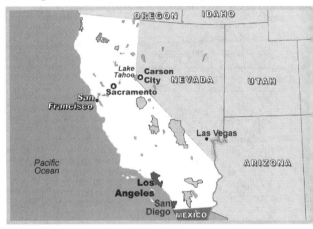

P irates and conquistadors imagined it like a ghost rising from the twilight fog where it had drowned; artists and poets pictured it as an elegant, sun-drenched metropolis; painters and photographers used it as a canvas on which the city blurred behind a veil of greyness and melancholy; dreamers and writers saw it as far-off land shrouded in mystery.

D elimited to the west by the Pacific Ocean and to the north by the Golden Gate Strait, San Francisco stretches across the tip of a peninsula bordered by a bay that covers 495 sq mi (1,280km²). The Golden Gate Bridge leads to Marin County, while the Bay Bridge links the cities of Oakland and Berkeley. The city of San Francisco barely covers 48 sq mi (125km²) and is dotted with some 40 hills, of

which the highest is Mount Davidson, reaching 985ft (282m). With the evident European touch that is the result of its many Victorian homes, the urban design of San Francisco is unlike that of any other typical U.S. city. Finally, another characteristic of this town is the dense fog caused by the meeting of the cold air from the ocean and the warm air of the coast.

L ocated in one of the planet's highly seismic regions, San Francisco is in the state of California, which is covered by many faults on a seismic belt. The city is situated on the

San Andreas fault. If you look at the history of California's major earthquakes during the 20th century, you will notice that they generally hit the northern section of the fault, in the San Francisco area. The best examples of this are the highly devastating quake of 1906, which started a fire that burnt down a large section of the town, and the quake known as the Loma Prieta, which shook the region during the third game of the 1989 baseball World Series between the San Francisco Giants and the Oakland A's.

For a long time, San Francisco was the most populated city in California, but in the mid-20th century it fell to fourth rank, behind Los Angeles, San Diego and San Jose. Today, San Francisco is home to approximately 750,000 people over an area of 46 sq mi (119km²). San Francisco is a veritable cultural melting pot; it is estimated that 250,000 of its inhabitants were born outside the United States.

History

Almost two centuries after the discovery of California, a ship navigated by Spaniard Juan Manuel de Ayala managed to cross the San Francisco Strait on August 5, 1775. Ayala then nick-named a pelican-populated island *isla de los alcatraces* ("pelican island," now known as Alcatraz). At that moment, the history of San Francisco's colonization began. The Spanish, accompanied by Franciscan priests, settled in the bay, establishing a military garrison (the Presidio), followed by a mission named Nuestra Señora de Dolores, dedicated to Saint Francis of Assisi.

The Gold Rush

The discovery of shiny nuggets of gold in a river east of Sacramento in 1848 obviously had a great impact on the city's future by guiding it to the path to prosperity, much to Mexico's dismay. Beginning in 1849, this discovery launched a glorious but violent chapter in the history of the western United States known as the "gold rush." Numerous pioneers in search of gold, named Forty Niners in remembrance of the year 1849, travelled in packed, covered wagons, seeking out the famous yellow metal they couldn't wait to get their hands on. Others feverishly set off from as far as Cape Horn, or the Panamá isthmus, or even Europe; packed like sardines in nearly unnavigable ships, they braved harsh waters as they set sail for the western United States, dreaming of happiness and wealth.

For many, this adventure represented a chance to start over, the opportunity to perhaps become richer and find a better life. Many of these people did strike it rich, but a large number failed completely. On a demographic note, suffice it to say that only one year after the discovery of gold, San Francisco's population reached 20,000 inhabitants.

By 1850, the city became a melting pot composed mostly of Europeans, but also including Asians, Mexicans and Latin Americans, with a grand total of 100,000 inhabitants. Its port became an important maritime traffic stop for both legal and illegal merchandise.

In April 1850, California was annexed to the Union and became the 31st state in the United States of America. The same year, San Francisco welcomed the country's first Chinatown. But in 1854, riches began to dwindle and immigration waves died down.

The "Iron Horse"

In 1862, the Pacific Railroad Act was signed. Two private railway companies, Union Pacific and Central Pacific, joined forces to connect the eastern coast of the United States to San Francisco.

Like a true hero of the western conquest, a rattling, back-firing train spitting clouds of thick, black smoke arrived in San Francisco in 1869. It was the first train to officially travel from East to West; the journey took one week.

The Earth Trembles, the City Burns

April 18, 1906, is a date that will forever remain in the collective memory of Californians. At 5:16am on that day, windows and objects suddenly began to tremble, giving a foretaste of the destruction that was to come: a violent quake measuring 8.3 on the Richter scale that for four days sparked a succession of fires and killed nearly 3,000 people. Smoky ruins as far as the eye could see, almost half the population decimated, no electricity, severed water pipes, looters executed on the spot… the city was in shambles, almost annihilated by what was undoubtedly one of the most devastating catastrophes in the country. The news quickly spread throughout the world and was followed by surprising displays of solidarity.

Despite this terrible blow, and thanks to a well-designed reconstruction plan that received generous and efficient outside support, the city rapidly rose from its ashes. Six years after the earthquake, San Francisco was practically rebuilt, redeployed and definitely improved.

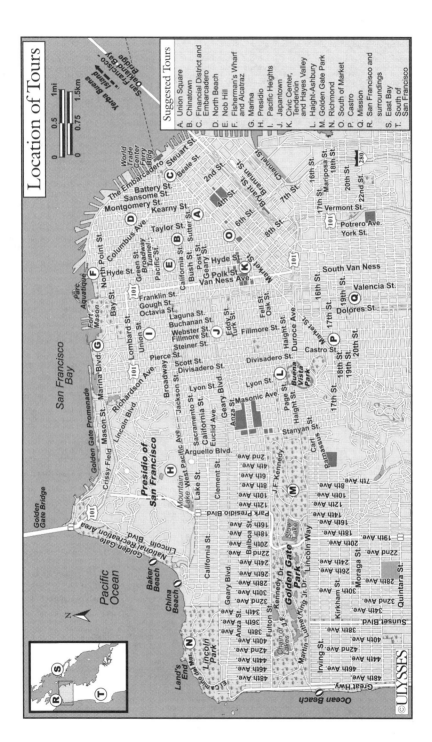

Location of Tours

San Francisco Bay

Golden Gate Bridge

Pacific Ocean

Yerba Buena Island

San Francisco Bay

Oakland Bay Bridge

| 0 | 0.5 | 1mi |
| 0 | 0.75 | 1.5km |

© ULYSSES

The Second World War

In December 1941, the attack on Pearl Harbor officially marked the beginning of war between the United States and Japan. Thanks to its strategic location, San Francisco became the main military port in the Pacific. Army factories quickly sprang up, as virtually all military equipment had to pass through its strait. When the war ended in 1945, the city was the stage for the signing of the Charter of the United Nations.

The 1950s: the Beatniks

When William Burroughs, Jack Kerouac and Allen Ginsberg left New York's Lower East Side, they established themselves in North Beach. Rejecting the grandiose ideas of U.S. society, this group threw themselves into the nihilistic Beat movement that had originally manifested itself in the mid-1940s. These brilliant writers rebelled against the taboos imposed by a puritanical country, seeking refuge in drugs, alcohol and sex. Kerouac's book, *On the Road*, became an outlet for an entire generation in search of its identity.

The 1960s: Social Unrest and the Psychedelic Era

If the 1950s were marked by the beatniks, the 1960s definitely belonged to the hippies who took over the Haight-Ashbury district. Unlike the dark, intellectual beatniks who listened to jazz and folk music while smoking marijuana, the younger and more jovial hippies lived in an atmosphere of carefree optimism, strolling to the psychedelic rhythms of rock music under the influence of LSD.

Protest Songs

Anthems for poets-cum-standard-bearers of counter culture, protest songs conveyed anti-establishment ideas. During the 1960s, a string of socially conscious singers desperately sought to pass on their message. But, despite himself, Bob Dylan was considered the leading spokesperson for this generation. He was involved in the beat era and embodied the values and ideology of a generation in turmoil (the Vietnam war, the cold war, the civil-rights movement, capitalism, pollution and so on with his simple yet vivid and powerful lyrics.

The 1970s: Gay Emancipation and the Murder of Harvey Milk

The 1970s are synonymous with the beginning of the gay rights movement. In 1977, Harvey Milk became the first openly gay politician to occupy a high-ranking electoral position.

Milk and San Francisco mayer George Moscone, who also fought for the rights of homosexuals, were both brutally murdered at city hall by Don White, an ex-civil servant.

The Late 20th Century

In the early 1980s, AIDS continued to spread in the city, devastating the gay population. But instead of becoming discouraged and giving up, the population banded together and created information and listening centres to counter the crisis.

In October 1989, in the middle of the third game of the World Series between the San Francisco Giants and the Oakland A's at Candlestick Park, the earth suddenly began to move. The Loma Prieta quake, measuring 7.1 on the Richter scale, shook all of Northern California. Slightly less destructive than the 1906 quake, the Loma Prieta still caused extensive material damage and killed approximately 60 people.

The following year, in 1990, Willie Brown became the first African-American mayor of San Francisco. During the decade that followed, the spread of AIDS continued to grow, becoming one of the leading causes of death in men in the city.

The 21st Century: the Era of New Technology

San Francisco began the new millennium under better auspices. Indeed, the city entered the 21st century by riding the wave of new technologies. Start-up and "dot-com" companies are so numerous here that a section of the South of Market district was nicknamed "Multimedia

Gulch." This great interest in the unlimited possibilities of the virtual world has also had an impact on other industries and is transforming the face of

San Francisco: neighbourhoods are being revitalized, rents are climbing tourism is flourishing... San Francisco is truly at the top of the "economically correct" list.

Finding Your Way Around

The area code for San Francisco is **415**. Unless indicated otherwise in this chapter, assume that all phone numbers have this area code.

Getting to San Francisco

By Plane

From Canada

From Montréal, Air Canada offers between five and 10 daily flights to San Francisco via Toronto or another U.S. city. The flight lasts between 7 to 9hrs, depending on stopovers. Remember that there is a CAN $10 departure tax for anyone leaving Canada.

From Europe

All major carriers fly to San Francisco from major European cities. The duration of the trip, without stopover, is 11hrs.

San Francisco International Airport

Located 15mi (25km) from downtown, San Francisco International Airport is the seventh busiest airport in the world, with an average of 40 million passengers each year. This modern airport is presently undergoing a $2.4-billion renovation and expansion. It is served by a large number of airline carriers and features currency exchange bureaus, as well as many modest restaurants. To

---

Important Dates in History

1492: Christopher Columbus discovers the New World.

1579: Privateer Sir Francis Drake drops anchor north of San Francisco Bay and raises the British flag.

1779: Spaniard Juan Manuel de Ayala reaches San Francisco Bay.

1821: Mexico, which owns California, is freed from the Spanish yoke.

1822: Englishman William Richardson settles in San Francisco in a cove that would later be named Yerba Buena.

1847: Yerba Buena is renamed San Francisco.

1848: Sam Brannan discovers gold nuggets in a river near San Francisco.

1849: The gold rush begins.

1869: The first transcontinental train reaches San Francisco.

1906: A violent earthquake sets off terrible fires, destroying most of the city.

1915: The Panama Pacific Exhibition is held in San Francisco.

1929: The stock market crash and economic crisis rattle the country.

1937: The Golden Gate Bridge is built.

1955: Allen Ginsberg recites his famous poem *Howl.*

1967: The Summer of Love festival is held.

1978: Harvey Milk and Mayor George Moscone are murdered, resulting in violent riots.

1989: The Loma Prieta quake hits the city.

1990: Willie Brown becomes the first African-American mayor.

2000: San Francisco's economy is in full expansion.

reach the city, you have various options, as limousines, taxis and buses will bring you practically everywhere in the metropolitan area. Information on departures and arrivals: ☎736-2008 or 800-736-2008, www.flysfo.com.

San Francisco International Airport has three terminals. The **International Terminal** receives most international flights from carriers such as Air France, Lufthansa, Aeroflot, LACSA, Japan Airlines and United Airlines (also at the North Terminal). The **North Terminal** welcomes flights from American Airlines, Canadian Airlines and United Airlines. The **South Terminal** is primarily for domestic flights from such carriers as Delta, US Airways, Continental, Northwest, TWA and Air Canada.

Airline Carriers

Air Canada
☎800-776-3000

Air France
☎800-237-2747

American Airlines
☎433-7300

British Airways
☎800-247-9297

Canada 3000
☎(310) 338-2201

Continental
☎871-1400
www.continental.com

Delta
☎448-7000
www.delta-air.com

Hawaiian Airlines
☎800-367-5320

KLM
☎800-374-7747

LACSA
☎800-225-2272

Lufthansa
☎800-645-3880

Mexicana
☎800-531-7921
www.mexicana.com

United
☎800-241-6522
www.ual.com

US Airways
☎800-428-4322

Singapore Airlines
☎800-742-333

TWA
☎800-221-2000

Taking a Taxi from the Airport

It can be more economical and comfortable to share a **taxi** with other passengers than to take the bus to get to your hotel. Taxis leaving the San Francisco Airport use their meter. The fare is not determined before departure and is non-negotiable.

From the airport to downtown San Francisco, the fare is approximately $30 to $35 (not including tip).

The **American Airporter Shuttle** (www.americanairporter. com) links the airport to the city's tourist areas. A one-way fare is $11. However, if you take the shuttle, remember to ask for the itinerary; you wouldn't want to be the last one off after a long and tiresome trek across the city.

If money is no object:

All City Limousine
161 Country Club Dr., Suite 11
☎(650) 873-3621
☎800-723-7854

Advanced Airport Shuttle
501 First St., Suite 207
☎550-1112

These two companies rent out long, shiny cars with tinted windows.

Oakland International Airport

Located approximately 7.5mi (12km) from Oakland and only 16mi (26km) from San Francisco, Oakland International Airport (☎510-577-4000, www.oaklandairport.com) is smaller than San Francisco International Airport. It receives mostly domestic flights and is a very popular point of entry for visitors. If your hotel is in San Francisco, however, you might have to travel 15 or 20min more than if you arrive at San Francisco Airport.

The taxi fare from Oakland Airport to San Francisco will cost you about $45.

You can also use the BART, which will bring you from Oakland Airport to San Francisco. From there, however, you will have to take a taxi to get to your hotel.

Airline Carriers

America West
☎800-235-929

Continental Airlines
☎800-525-0280

Corsair
☎800-677-0720
www.corsair-int.com

Delta Airlines
☎800-221-1212

Southwest Airlines
☎800-435-9792

United Airlines
☎800-241-6522

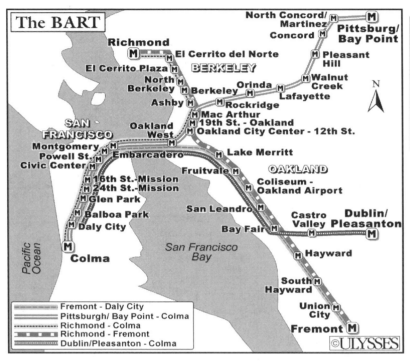

By Car

If you are coming from the east, take Highway 80 and the Bay Bridge to get to San Francisco. You will have to pay a $2 toll to cross the bridge.

From the north, Highway 101 runs through Marin County up to the Golden Gate Bridge. The toll for this bridge is $3.

Coming from the south, the simplest way is to follow Route 1 or US 101. These two highways lead to San Francisco. Note that Route 1 is less busy and stressful than the US 101.

Car Rentals

San Francisco Airport

Avis Rent-A-Car
☎800-831-2847
www.avis.com

Budget Rent-A-Car
☎871-3053
www.budget.com

Hertz Rent-A-Car
☎800-654-3331
www.hertz.com

Thrifty Car Rental
☎871-5050
www.thrifty.com

In San Francisco

Alamo Rent-A-Car
687 Folsom St.
☎882-9440
or
750 Bush St.
☎693-0191

Budget Rent-A Car
321 Mason St.
☎292-8400
or
1600 Van Ness Ave.
☎775-6602

Thrifty Car Rental
520 Mason St.
☎788-8111

By Bus

To obtain schedules and destinations, call your local **Greyhound** office at ☎800-231-2222.

Smoking is forbidden on almost all bus lines. In general, children five and under travel for free, and travellers 60 and over are also eligible for discounts. Pets are not allowed.

By Train

In the United States, the train is not always the most economical means of transportation and is definitely not the fastest. However, it can be an interesting experience for long distances since it is quite comfortable (try to get a seat in a car where you can really enjoy the view). For schedules and destinations, call **AMTRAK**, which owns the U.S. railroad network: ☎*800-872-7245*, *www.amtrak.com*.

AMTRAK does not have a station in San Francisco. You must get off in Oakland or Emerville, where a free shuttle will bring you to the Ferry Building, near Market Street.

AMTRAK station in Berkeley
Third St. at University Ave.

AMTRAK station in Oakland
Jack London Sq.

AMTRAK station in Emerville
65 Cahill St.

AMTRAK station in San Jose
5885 Landregan St.

Caltrain
Fourth St. at King St.
☎*800-660-4287*
Caltrain offers railway service to peninsula towns such as Palo Alto and San Jose.

Hitchhiking

Hitchhiking is not recommended.

Getting Around

By Car

Travelling by car is not really an efficient or pleasant way to visit San Francisco. Unless you are travelling outside the city, renting a car is not recommended. Aside from the orientation difficulties posed by the city's unusual urban layout, you should know that public parking lots are virtually non-existent, parking meters are rare, traffic jams are an everyday occurrence and valet parking is expensive

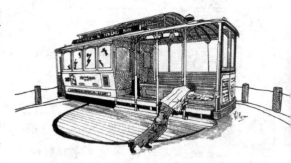

(between $12 and $18 per day).

By Public Transportation

Unlike other fragmented U.S. cities where having a car is absolutely necessary, this is not the case in San Francisco. Public transportation is relatively well developed, quite efficient and rather economical. However, if you wish to leave the city (to visit, for example, Napa Valley or the village of Half Moon Bay), you must rent a car.

The **San Francisco Municipal Railway** (Muni) (☎*673-6864*) is a public transportation system serving San Francisco and suburbs that features about 100 bus lines and includes the subway, Munis and cable cars. The fare per person is $1 for the bus and $2 for the cable car. Exact change is required.

If you plan on using the bus often, you can purchase a Muni Day Pass or a Muni Passport:

One day: $6
Three days: $10
Seven days: $15

The **BART** *(Bay Area Rapid Transit System;* ☎*992-2278)* is a safe, modern public transportation network serving the downtown and

Mission areas, and links San Francisco to East Bay cities such as Berkeley and Oakland.

By Cable Car

Invented by British engineer Andrew Smith Hallidie, the cable car, an ever-present symbol of the city, made its appearance in San Francisco in 1873. There is no engine inside cable cars; instead, they are linked by a steel cable (hence the name "cable car") that slides between the tracks to a central engine. A National Historic Landmark since 1964, the cable car rarely exceeds 9mi/hr (15km/h).

Out of the 12 original cable-car lines, only three are still in service: Powell-Mason, Powell-Hyde and California-Market.

By Taxi

For unknown reasons, it is often difficult to get a cab on the streets of San Francisco. They are easily recognizable and can be an economical means of transportation if you share them with other passengers; they can fit up to four people. The meter starts at $2 and adds $0.30 after each fifth of a mile (0.3km). Occasionally, taxi drivers may not know how to reach your destination, so be sure to have details on where you want to go. Finally, drivers expect a 15% tip on the fare. Here are a few taxi companies:

City Wide
☎ *920-0700*

Desoto Cab
☎ *970-1300*

Veteran's Cab
☎ *552-1300*

Yellow Cab
☎ *626-2345*

Practical Information

Foreign Consulates in San Francisco

AUSTRALIA
1 Bush St.
☎ *362-6160*

BELGIUM
625 Third St.
☎ *882-4648*

CANADA
5 Fremont St.
☎ *541-3900*

DENMARK
601 Montgomery St., Suite 400
☎ *391-0100*

FINLAND
Honorary Consulate
333 Bush St., 34ᵗʰ floor
☎ *772-6649*

GERMANY
1960 Jackson St.
☎ *775-1061*

GREAT BRITAIN
1 Sansome St.
☎ *981-3030*

ITALY
2590 Webster St.
☎ *931-4924*

NETHERLANDS
1 Maritime Plaza
☎ *981-6454*

NORWAY
20 California St.
☎ *986-0765*

PORTUGAL
3298 Washington St.
☎ *346-3400*

SPAIN
1405 Sutter St.
☎ *922-2995*

SWEDEN
120 Montgomery St.
☎ *788-2631*

SWITZERLAND
456 Montgomery St.
☎ *788-2272*

Tourist Information

San Francisco Convention & Visitors Bureau
201 Third St., Suite 900
San Francisco, CA 94103
☎ *391-2000*
~*974-1992*
For a message in Spanish:
☎ *391-2122*
For a message in Italian:
☎ *391-2002*
This is the best place to pick up all kinds of tourist information, brochures and maps. The San Francisco Convention & Visitors Bureau will send you a free information package if you call, fax or e-mail their office.

Other Places to get Brochures and Maps

San Francisco

Visitor Center
900 Market St. at Powell St. (in the basement), Hallidie Plaza
The friendly, multilingual staff here can help with your travel plans.

Berkeley

Berkeley Convention & Visitors Bureau
2015 Center St.
☎ *(510) 549-7040*
☎ *800-847-4823*
~*(510) 644-2052*
www.berkeleycvb.com
or
University of California (Berkeley) Visitor Center
220 University Ave. at Oxford St.

Oakland

Oakland Convention & Visitors Bureau
1000 Broadway, Suite 200
Oakland, CA 94607
☎ *(510) 839-9000*

Marin County

Marin County Convention & Visitors Bureau
1013 Larkspur Landing Circle
Landspur, CA
☎ *(415) 499-5000*
~*(415) 461-0965*
marincvb@marin.org

Half Moon Bay

☎ *(650) 726-8380*
www.halfmoonbaychamber.org

Guided Tours

Although it can be fun to travel without a pre-established itinerary or any time constraints, you might want to consult a travel agency to visit some of the city's attractions. San Francisco is filled with such agencies, which are of various levels of quality. A number of options are available to visitors who wish to discover the city through a guided tour. Here are a few, but because they often change, remember to call ahead to find out about tours, schedules and fees.

San Francisco Historical Walking Tours
☎252-9485
jay@victorianwalk.com
This is an excellent opportunity to get off the beaten track and discover San Francisco's beautiful Victorian homes.

Barbary Coast Trail
San Francisco Historical Society
P.O. Box 420569
☎641-5058
Barbary Coast Trail offers many excursions throughout the city, allowing visitors to learn more about San Francisco's history, its development, its architecture and its culture.

The Explorer's Club
1230 Willard St.
☎566-7014
setours@best.com
The Explorer's Club is an agency offering city tours designed especially for children. Parents can also participate.

3 Babes and a Bus
334 Thornton Ave.
☎552-2582
www.threebabes.com
This agency owns a luxury bus that will bring you to three or four nightclubs, with stops of about 45min at each one. The fee guarantees direct access to these clubs without having to wait in line or pay the cover charge.

Flower Power Haight-Ashbury Walking Tour
520 Shrader St.
☎221-8442
To hear all about the Summer of Love festival, the hippie movement and 1960s anecdotes, join the Flower Power tour.

Crusin' the Castro
375 Lexington St.
☎550-8110
trvrbailey@aol.com
Highly recommended for its interesting and instructive visits, Crusin' the Castro tells the history of gay life in San Francisco, from the gold rush to the gay bars of the 1940s to the emancipation of the 1970s to today.

Chinatown Adventure Tours
654 Commercial St.
☎981-8989
www.wokwiz.com
Why not combine a historical guided tour of parts of Chinatown with a gourmet stop to sample China's culinary traditions?

Dashiell Hammett Tours
Tours depart near the San Francisco Public Library
☎287-9540
Dashiell Hammett Tours will satisfy lovers of mystery novels who wish to discover the sites that inspired Dashiell Hammett to write *The Maltese Falcon*.

Green Tortoise
494 Broadway at Kearny St.
☎834-1000
www.greentortoise.com
Green Tortoise specializes in organized trips to national parks in buses equipped with platforms that passengers can sleep on.

Sfgaytours
173 Elsie St.
☎648-7758
www.sfgaytours.com
Sfgaytours is an agency that organizes city excursions as well as evenings in the gay bars and restaurants of San Francisco.

San Francisco Seaplane Tours
☎332-4843
www.seaplane.com
If money is no object for you, why not admire the city from above? San Francisco Seaplane Tours' airplanes leave from Pier 39 and Sausalito and fly over San Francisco Bay and its attractions, such as Alcatraz, the Golden Gate Bridge and Angel Island, among others.

A Few Web Sites about San Francisco

www.bayinsider.com
Bayinsider is a general-information site about the city.

www.sftravel.com
Sftravel covers San Francisco hotels, restaurants and tourist attractions, and provides practical information about the city.

Banks and Exchange Bureaus

Wells Fargo
1 Montgomery St.
☎396-7152

Union Trust Offices
2 Grant Ave.
☎800-864-3557
www.wellsfargo.com

Foreign Exchange Limited
429 Stockton St.
☎677-5100

Bank of America
1 Powell St.
☎953-5102
or
San Francisco International Airport
AFEX, Associated Foreign Exchange
221 Sansome St.
☎781-7683
www.afex.com

Telecommunications

For Berkeley and Oakland, on the other side of the bay, the area code is *510*.

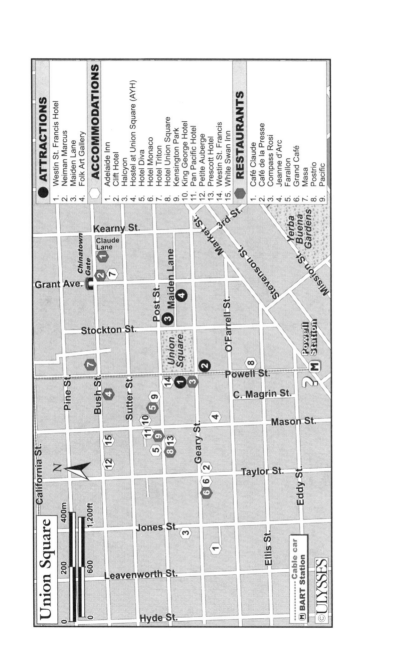

Union Square

● ATTRACTIONS
1. Westin St. Francis Hotel
2. Neiman Marcus
3. Maiden Lane
4. Folk Art Gallery

◆ ACCOMMODATIONS
1. Adelaide Inn
2. Clift Hotel
3. Halcyon
4. Hostel at Union Square (AYH)
5. Hotel Diva
6. Hotel Monaco
7. Hotel Triton
8. Hotel Union Square
9. Kensington Park
10. King George Hotel
11. Pan Pacific Hotel
12. Petite Auberge
13. Prescott Hotel
14. Westin St. Francis
15. White Swan Inn

● RESTAURANTS
1. Café Claude
2. Café de la Presse
3. Compass Rosi
4. Jeanne d'Arc
5. Farallon
6. Grand Café
7. Masa
8. Postrio
9. Pacific

© ULYSSES

M BART Station

Cable car

For Half Moon Bay and the area to the south the area code is *650*.

To reach San Francisco from Canada, dial *1-415*, then the number.

From Europe, dial *00-1-415*, then the number.

Phone Numbers to Remember

24hr pharmacy
☎*800-925-4733*

California Medical Center
☎*923-3333*

Cityline
☎*512-5000*
Information line for cultural or sports events.

Weather
☎*837-5000 ext. 1112*

Bass
☎*(510) 762-2277*
Information line that provides comprehensive listings of concerts and sporting events taking place in the San Francisco Bay area.

Exploring

Nestled between the sea and the mountains, San Francisco is a captivating city with a dramatic topography, where tradition, modernity and classicism come together in one fabulous setting.

Tour A: Union Square

As the stage of historic events, Union Square owes its name to popular pro-Union demonstrations that were held here during the American Civil War. One of San Francisco's busiest and most expensive districts, today it swarms with tourists, the down-and-out and residents of the city. A vast array of chic boutiques, luxury hotels and fashionable stores line this huge square. The place itself is not that spectacular, but the areas surrounding Union Square are commonly called the "downtown" of San Francisco.

The district is bordered by Bush Street to the north, Jones Street to the west, Eddy Street and Market Street to the south, and Grant Avenue to the east. All of the district's attractions are located around Union Square.

Inaugurated in grand style by millionaire Charles T. Crocker, the **Westin St. Francis Hotel ★★** *(355 Powell St.,* ☎*397-7000)* occupies the entire western side of Union Square and is a vacation stop for high society. The hotel unfortunately was seriously damaged by the fire caused by the 1906 earthquake, but was quickly rebuilt a few years later. In the 50 years that followed, people with money to burn and Hollywood stars were frequent patrons of this extremely upscale hotel. To adjust to the constraints and changes at the end of the century, panoramic elevators were added to the hotel's infrastructure, which was restored in 1972. The glass elevators offer great views of the city. Royalty and stars passing through never fail to make a stop. Movie buffs might remember the scene from Francis Ford Coppola's movie *The Conversation*, in which Gene Hackman watches couples

walk around Union Square from a room in this hotel.

Southeast of Union Square stands **Neiman Marcus** *(150 Stockton St., corner Geary St.)*, with a beautiful **rotunda ★** and its window.

A few blocks north of Neiman Marcus lies a small alley named **Maiden Lane**. Maiden Lane was once lined with disreputable brothels and bars, where, from their open windows, prostitutes solicited potential clients strolling down the street. Brawls were common and legend has it that on average two murders were committed here per week. The fire of 1906 purged Maiden Lane of its vices and residents acted quickly to give it a new look. Today, boutiques, café terraces and restaurants line both sides of the street. Fans of contemporary architecture will be interested to learn that the **Folk Art Gallery ★**, a prosperous and highly respected art gallery at 140 Maiden Lane, is the only building in the city to have been designed by renowned architect Frank Lloyd Wright.

Tour B: Chinatown

Spread out over an area largely delimited by Broadway Street to the north, Montgomery and Columbus streets to the east, California Street to the south and Powell Street to the west, San Francisco's Chinatown has around 90,000 residents and is one of the largest Chinese neighbourhoods outside of China, equal in size to those of New York and Vancouver. Strolling through Chinatown is a little like travelling back in

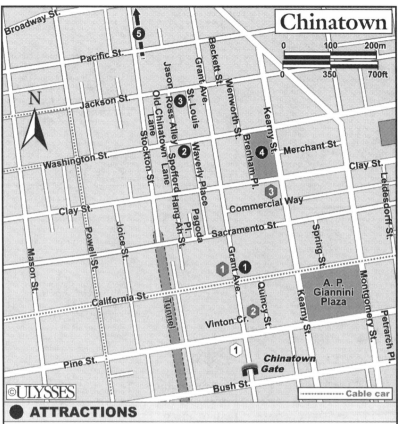

San Francisco and Surroundings

● ATTRACTIONS

1. Old St. Mary's Church
2. Tian Hou Temple
3. Golden Gate Fortune Cookie Factory
4. Portsmouth Square
5. Chinese Historical Society of America

○ ACCOMMODATIONS

1. Grant Plaza Hotel

◉ RESTAURANTS

1. Far East Café
2. Lotus Garden
3. R & G Lounge

time. A multitude of people of Asian origin live in the neighbourhood. Fabulous restaurants, most of which are Chinese, carry on the tradition of the feasts of yesteryear, characterized by animal carcasses hanging above stalls, subtle flavours that float in the air, and mythical dragons that adorn the facades covered by curved roofs.

The district can easily be visited on foot. The best place to start your tour is by the Chinese portal on Grant

Avenue, at the corner of Post Street.

Most visitors enter Chinatown by the **Chinatown Gateway**, which consists of an arch decorated with Chinese dragons. **Grant Avenue ★★** is both Chinatown's and the city's oldest street, and is the district's backbone and commercial centre. Exotic restaurants, kitsch souvenir shops and art galleries line the entire street, which is always swarming with tourists and locals.

To your right, at the corner of California Street, stands the Gothic Revival **Old St. Mary's Cathedral** ★ *(660 California St., corner Grant Ave.),* built in 1854 by Chinese workers. This religious bastion managed to survive the many earthquakes that have shaken the area for over a century.

Continue your stroll down Grant Avenue and turn left on Sacramento Street, then right onto Waverly Place. You'll notice the lovely wrought-iron balconies on both sides of the street. Stop at 125 Waverly Place. Climb the stairs to the Tian Hou Temple.

The **Tian Hou Temple** ★★ is a small Buddhist temple where the faithful solemnly gather. Enter politely to pay your respects to the smiling Buddha, located in the middle of the offerings.

As you leave, turn left and walk to Washington Street. Once there, turn left, then turn right onto Ross Alley.

You are very near the **Golden Gate Fortune Cookie Factory** ★ *(56 Ross Alley, ☎781-3956),* a small business that bakes the famous fortune cookies that hold proverbs and maxims.

Continue to Jackson Street, turn left, then turn left again onto Stockton Street, which is a much more picturesque commercial street than Grant Avenue. At the corner of Clay Street, turn left and keep walking until you reach Portsmouth Square.

Named after the U.S. ship that anchored in San Francisco Bay in 1846, **Portsmouth Square** is a green space where elderly Chinese residents like to meet to play cards. You'll also discover the sculpture of a ship in memory of writer Robert Louis Stevenson, who used to spend time in the square. For their part, curious tourists take advantage of the square to stop and catch their breath.

To further familiarize yourself with the Chinese community, the **Chinese Historical Society of America** ★ *(Tue to Fri, 10am to 4pm; 664 Broadway, ☎391-1188, www.chsa.org)* retraces the history of the arrival of Chinese citizens in the western United States through a small, but interesting collection of photographs and paintings from local archives.

Tour C: The Financial District and the Embarcadero

The Financial District roughly forms a triangle with Market, Kearny and Jackson streets. As the bustling centre through which money flows onto the city's prosperous streets, the Financial District is aptly named the Wall Street of the West. The district features glass and steel skyscrapers that hold a closely woven network of armoured banks, lively insurance company offices, opulent brokerage agencies and expensive law firms. This network is hidden at the heart of an impressive forest of skyscrapers that towers over criss-crossing streets and shiny cars.

The tour begins on Market Street, at the corner of Kearny Street.

Located near the junction of Market and Kearny streets, the **Sheraton Palace** ★ wears its facade proudly. At the time of its inauguration in 1875, the Sheraton Palace Hotel was a gleaming castle. Sharing the same fate as many buildings in the last quarter of the 19th century, it was destroyed by the fire that followed the earthquake of 1906, but was rebuilt a few years later. Between 1989 and 1991, the building underwent important renovations to bring it back to life. In fact, more than \$150 million were invested to restore its splendour. Writer Oscar Wilde and actor Sarah Bernhardt are among the celebrities to have stayed at the Sheraton Plaza. Don't miss the marvellous **Garden Court** ★★ and its stained-glass cupola.

Turn left onto Market Street, then right onto Post Street.

The **A. P. Giannini Plaza** ★ *(between Post St. and Sutter St.)* is a lovely shopping centre that honours the memory of the Italian banker who transformed a small savings bank into one of the meccas of finance: the Bank of America. This complex holds a range of exclusive boutiques and cafés on a central terrace that is covered by an enormous glass dome. Window-shoppers should know that these boutiques will definitely satisfy the most diverse and extravagant tastes.

As you leave Sutter Street, turn right and keep walking until you reach Montgomery Street. Turn left and stop between the

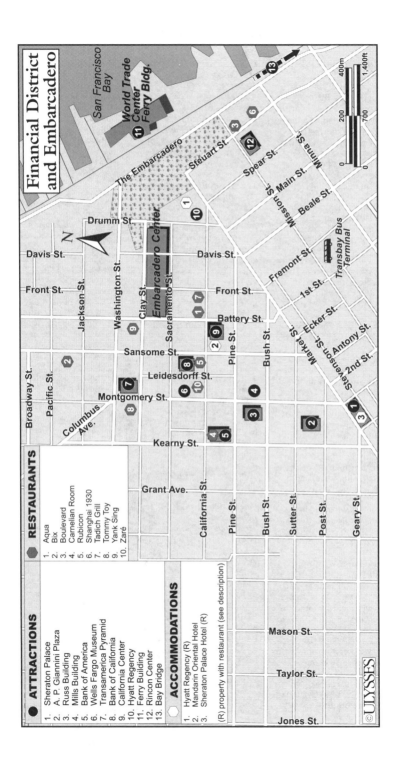

Financial District and Embarcadero

San Francisco Bay

World Trade Center Ferry Bldg.

The Embarcadero

● ATTRACTIONS

1. Sheraton Palace
2. A. P. Giannini Plaza
3. Russ Building
4. Mills Building
5. Bank of America
6. Wells Fargo Museum
7. Transamerica Pyramid
8. Bank of California
9. California Center
10. Hyatt Regency
11. Ferry Building
12. Rincon Center
13. Bay Bridge

● RESTAURANTS

1. Aqua
2. Bix
3. Boulevard
4. Carnelian Room
5. Rubicon
6. Shanghai 1930
7. Tadich Grill
8. Tommy Toy
9. Yank Sing
10. Zaré

○ ACCOMMODATIONS

1. Hyatt Regency (R)
2. Mandarin Oriental Hotel
3. Sheraton Palace Hotel (R)

(R) property with restaurant (see description)

© ULYSSES

Russ Building and Mills Building.

The 31-storey **Russ Building** ★ *(235 Montgomery St.)* has been here since 1927. Once the residence of a jeweller, it was transformed into a luxury hotel that was then ravaged by the fire that followed the earthquake of 1906. The Russ Building was for a long time considered the highest skyscraper in the western United States, before being dethroned by several recent structures. Today it fits perfectly into the skyscraper decor that makes up the financial district's characteristic silhouette.

Built in 1891, the **Mills Building** ★ *(220 Montgomery St.)* was partially damaged by the earthquake of 1906. It remains, however, one of the few buildings to have survived the terrible fire that followed and consequently only had to undergo a few repairs, around 1907. A 20-storey tower was added to the building in 1931, 40 years after its construction. It fits in surprisingly well with the surrounding decor.

One street farther stands the Bank of America, between Montgomerey, Kearny, Pine and California streets.

Located in a 781ft-tall (238m), 52-storey office building, the **Bank of America** ★ is the fruit of the perseverance of Amadeo Peter Giannini. In 1969 he founded the Bank of Italy for expatriate Italian clients, who did not have the means of borrowing money from banks at the time. The tower's top floor features the chic Carnelian Room restaurant (see p 443).

Follow Montgomery Street a little farther to the Wells Fargo Museum.

The **Wells Fargo Museum** ★★ *($5; every day 9am to 5pm; 420 Montgomery St., ☎396-2619)* exhibits the famous stagecoaches that once rode between the east and west coasts. The museum also holds false money that was issued by "Emperor Norton," gold nuggets, as well as a few photographs from the era. Founded in 1852 by Henry Wells and William G. Fargo, Wells Fargo ruled the roadways of yesteryear by ensuring the delivery of mail and money. As both a transport company and bank, Wells Fargo played an important role in developing the U.S. West Coast.

Probably the building with the most audacious architecture, the **Transamerica Pyramid** ★★ *(600 Montgomery St.)*, inaugurated in 1972, stands on the old historic site of Montgomery Block. It is 853ft (260m) high and towers over the city's skyscrapers.

Jackson Square lies right next to the Transamerica Pyramid.

Jackson Square is where the famous Barbary Coast district was once located. It was notoriously infested with merry sailors, seductive prostitutes and hooch drinkers. The district was almost completely destroyed by the devastating fire that followed the 1906 earthquake. The square was renovated in the mid-20th century and today features fashion boutiques, art galleries and antique shops.

Turn right onto Sansome Street and stop at the corner of California Street.

As you exit the Bank of California, turn left onto California Street and keep walking until you reach the California Center.

The **California Center** ★★ *(345 California St.)* soars spectacularly in the middle of historic buildings, like the Robert Dollar Building and the J. Harold Building. It stands out thanks to its two corner towers that are linked by a glass bridge. The chic Mandarin Hotel occupies the top 11 floors of the building.

In Spanish, the word *embarcadero* means "quay." A curious irony of sorts, the effervescence and development of the Embarcadero are closely linked to the 1989 earthquake, known as "Loma Prieta," which shook the district. In some ways, there was a silver lining to this earthquake, from the point of view of the Embarcadero's urbanization. The horrible cement highway that obstructed the

Transamerica Pyramid

view of the bay was so damaged that it was torn down. The resulting breathtaking view today makes people wonder why it wasn't levelled sooner.

You must visit the **Hyatt Regency** ★★ *(5 Embarcadero Center)*, if only to admire the fabulous 17-storey atrium that is adorned with a profusion of plants and trees, in addition to a giant Charles Perry sculpture entitled *Eclipse*. Panoramic elevators rise to Equinox, a revolving restaurant that makes a complete rotation every 40min.

As you leave the hotel, head towards the Justin Herman Plaza.

On the opposite side of the plaza, you will find the **Ferry Building** ★★ *(Embarcadero, corner Market St.)* is the district's hot spot, which makes it hard to miss. Soaring 233ft (71m) high, it was built in 1898 and is thus one of the few historic buildings to have survived the events of 1906. Its clock tower is modelled after that of Seville's cathedral. Every day of the week, early and late in the day, suburbanites pass through here on their way to and from Sausalito, Tiburon and Oakland.

The **Embarcadero** follows the seafront all along the bay. Its extension was recently named the **Herb Caen Way**, in honour of the famous editorialist, who wrote for the *San Francisco Chronicle*. The Herb Caen Way is bordered by lovely palm trees, under which cyclists and joggers mingle with business people.

Beatnik

The word "beatnik" was coined by San Francisco *Chronicle* columnist Herb Caen. The particle "nik" alludes to the first satellite launched into space by the Soviets in 1957: *Sputnik I*. In this time of uncertainty, beatniks were suspected of giving allegiance to communism. Beat not only means "tired" or "worn out," but also has manifold connotations, including resignation, rhythm and beatitude, or blessedness.

Take the Herb Caen Way, then turn right onto Mission Street and keep walking to Spear Street.

The **Rincon Center** ★ *(101 Spear St.)* is a modern building, whose two curved glass towers soar 280ft (85m) into the sky. A residential building, it also harbours business offices. Its interior features a lovely 89ft (27m) atrium that is surrounded by restaurants and businesses. Part of the Rincon Center overlaps into a former post office that is adorned with murals painted by artist Anton Refregier. The murals depict the events that marked the history of San Francisco.

Retrace your steps to the Herb Caen Way and enjoy the view of the Bay Bridge.

Resolutely less flamboyant and spectacular than the

Golden Gate Bridge, the **Bay Bridge** ★ is nevertheless one of the world's longest steel bridges. Inaugurated in 1936 to relieve traffic congestion, this bridge rests on Yerba Buena Island and stretches 8mi (13km) to Oakland. Despite the five lanes that run on each of its two levels (one level for traffic in each direction), traffic is still heavy and somewhat stressful. The 1989 earthquake damaged the bridge and caused the death of a motorist. Following this dramatic accident, the superstructure was quickly reinforced.

South of the Bay Bridge lies the **SS Jeremiah O'Brien** ★ *(Pier 32, audioguided tours)*, an old warship. It was part of the ship fleet that helped the Allies land on the beaches of Normandy, in France, in 1944.

Tour D: North Beach

Today, the old district, which was not long ago courted by Ginsberg, Kerouac and their retinue of beatniks, is roughly delimited by Fisherman's Wharf to the north, Telegraph Hill to the east, Russian Hill to the west and Chinatown to the south. Today, North Beach is undergoing a complete renovation, with upscale gourmet restaurants and trendy bars neighbouring porno movie theatres, sex-shops and brothels.

The tour starts on Columbus Avenue, at the corner of Kearny Street.

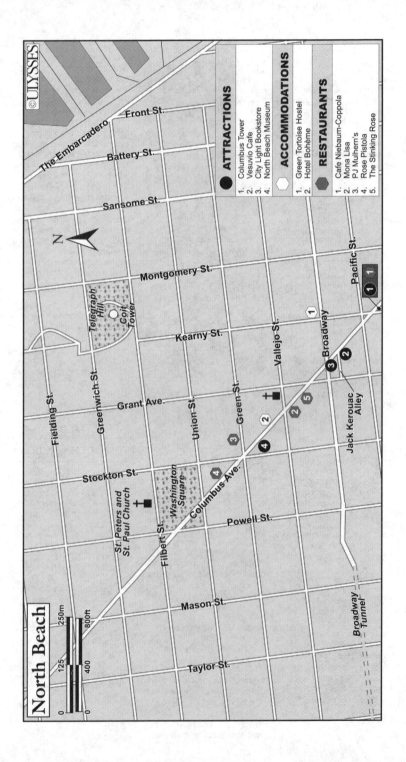

Easily recognizable thanks to its lovely green dome, the **Columbus Tower ★★** is one of the district's most beautiful buildings. Built at the start of the 20th century, the building has been owned by Francis Ford Coppola since the 1960s. Its upper floors hold the offices of his production company, Zoetrope, while the main floor was recently converted into the chic Café Niebaum-Coppola restaurant (see p 444).

Continue walking north on Columbus Avenue and stop at the Vesuvio Café.

The **Vesuvio Café ★★★** *(255 Columbus Ave., corner Jack Kerouac Alley, ☎362-3370)* is one of the few former beatnik hangouts still in existence today. Contrary to what its name suggests, it is a bar that today caters not only to its share of tourists, but to nostalgic poets and intellectuals in need of inspiration. In addition to the beatniks of years gone by, Welsh poet Dylan Thomas is among the celebrities that once courted the café. Take the time to stop in, if only to raise a glass in memory of Jack Kerouac or Allen Ginsberg.

As you leave the Vesuvio Café, you will notice the City Lights Bookstore on your left.

The **City Lights Bookstore ★★** *(261 Broadway, corner Columbus Ave., ☎362-8193, www.citylights.com)* was the first bookstore in America to sell only pocket books. It was also the first publishing house to publish Jack Kerouac. Open since 1953, it is still owned by the same man, poet and former beatnik, Lawrence Ferlinghetti. Here, the floors crack, dust covers

the shelves, but the place is loaded with charm. The quality of books and the service is excellent. Good poetry section. It is an ideal place to browse and maybe uncover an old classic lying incognito on a shelf.

Hippies

When Ronald Reagan was governor of California, he described a hippie as "someone who dresses like Tarzan, has hair like Jane and smells like Cheetah." A more pragmatic definition is that hippies were peace-loving people who settled in San Francisco's Haight-Ashbury district during the 1960s. Trademark traits included flared pants, multicoloured scarves, flowing, tie-dyed clothing and long hair—a symbol of freedom. Unlike beatniks, "flower children" advocated free love, respect and tolerance, and preferred LSD to marijuana.

Continue walking down Columbus Avenue until you reach the North Beach Museum.

The lovely photograph collection at the **North Beach Museum ★** *(Mon to Fri, 9am to 5pm; 1435 Stockton St., corner Columbus Ave., mezzanine, ☎626-7070)* depicts the events that have unfurled over the centuries and shaped the district.

A little farther down along Columbus Avenue, you will reach Washington Square.

Washington Square ★★, dominated by St. Peter and St. Paul Church, is bordered by Union, Powell, Filbert and Stockton streets. Washington Square has honoured the memory of the first U.S. president, George Washington, since 1852. A bronze statue of Benjamin Franklin stands in the middle of the park. Another monument honouring the city's volunteer firefighters lies northwest. This green space is swarming with tourists and locals on sunny days, and it isn't uncommon to see Asian people practising tai-chi here.

Completed in 1924, the **St. Peter and St. Paul Church ★★** features a painting of Santa María, the city's patron saint. Trivia buffs should note that Marilyn Monroe and Joe Dimaggio posed for photographers on the church steps in 1957.

Turn right onto Filbert Street and keep walking until Telegraph Hill.

Goat Hill, which gets its name from the many goats that once grazed here in complete safety, was later named Signal Hill, and then **Telegraph Hill ★** when a semaphore station was built atop its peak at 2,795ft (852m), in 1849. This station signalled the arrival of ships with the first morse code transmitter-receiver in the western United States. The semaphore was destroyed around 1890 and a castle adorned with an observation tower and cable-car was built in its place. Unfortunately, it was completely destroyed by a fire

Coit Tower

at the beginning of the 20th century. Today, Telegraph Hill has become a middle-class residential district.

Atop Telegraph Hill stands **Coit Tower** ★★, whose cylindrical silhouette stretches 213ft (64m) high. Built in 1934 in memory of an 1850 firehouse, this tower was donated by Lillie Hitchcock Coit. Crude gossip says that the tower's phallic form is related to Ms. Coit's love of firemen... As you might correctly suspect, the **lookout** ★★*($2)* at the top of the tower offers a breathtaking view of the city and its surrounding areas. The main floor features beautiful **murals** that depict episodes in the history of San Francisco.

Retrace your steps to Columbus Avenue. Turn right and continue until Lombard Street; keep walking until you come to Russian Hill.

As of the late 19th century, cable cars were already travelling up and down this hill. After the fire that followed the earthquake of 1906, architects decided to remodel the face of the hill by giving it Hispanic, colonial and even Art Deco architectural styles.

Located on the slope of Russian Hill, **Lombard Street** ★★★ *(between Hyde St. and Leavenworth St.)* is the world's most winding one-way street and has no less than eight hairpin turns to help vehicles tackle the steep 27% slope. The maximum speed limit is only 5mi/h (8km/h). The view from atop the hill is absolutely panoramic. You might have already seen it in movies shot in San Francisco, notably in *Bullit*, starring Steve McQueen.

Tour E: Nob Hill

The name Nob Hill derives from a distortion of the word *Nabab* (a name given to the pioneers who found fortune and glory in the Indies) and refers directly to the district's wealthy residents, who once built themselves magnificent Victorian and Edwardian residences. Unfortunately for these bold owners, the terrible earthquake of 1906 caused a devastating fire that ravaged every one of these beautiful residences, except the Italianate home of James C. Flood, which was built of sandstone. This house is today the headquarters of the **Pacific**

Union Club, which is open to members only *(no visits; 1000 California St.).*

The tour begins at the Fairmont Hotel on Mason Street at the corner of California Street.

The splendid, historic **Fairmont Hotel** ★★ *(950 Mason St.)* still enjoys an aura of the prestige and glory of yesteryear. Its construction began in 1902, but its framework was seriously damaged by the 1906 earthquake and the fire that followed. Despite this serious setback, it was quickly fixed up and finally re-opened its doors in grand style in April 1907. The reception area is simply spectacular.

As you leave the hotel, turn left, then right onto California Street, and stop at the corner of Taylor Street.

Grace Cathedral's ★ *(1051 Taylor St., corner California St.)* Gothic Revival silhouette towers over the horizon. Its nearly 16ft-high (5m) sculpted bronze doors are replicas of those of Florence's Santa Maria del Fiore Cathedral. The massive oak altar and organ, which has over 7,000 pipes, are worth a look. The stained-glass windows are somewhat incongruous, with some featuring individuals such as Albert Einstein and Robert Frost. People often practise tai-chi in front on the cathedral, in small **Huntington Park**.

The **Cable Car Museum** ★ *(free admission; every day 10am to 6pm; 1201 Mason St., corner Washington St.)* provides an opportunity to find out more about the functioning of San Francisco's famous cable cars.

Tour F: Fisherman's Wharf and Alcatraz

Let's be frank: Fisherman's Wharf has become a popular tourist trap that attracts no fewer than 10 million visitors a year. The place is so popular that any self-respecting resident avoids it like the plague. Fisherman's Wharf does, however, feature attractions worth mentioning and is the point of departure for visits to the famous Alcatraz penitentiary.

Pier 39, which was once a goods shipment jetty, features Underwater World, an Imax movie theatre and a colony of sea lions. The place has become an extremely popular and lively tourist destination ever since a **sea lion colony** ★ made it their home in 1989. The abundance of food and the absence of predators made it the perfect spot. Early on, merchants complained of the sea mammals' unpleasant, sometimes downright stinky, odour. They gladly accommodated the animals though, when they realized these pinnipeds attract more than 10 million tourists a year. The best time to see them is between August and late May; the sea lions head south in June and July to reproduce.

Also located at Pier 39 is **Underwater World** ★ *($8; every day 9am to 9pm;* ☎*623-5300)*, a theme park at the heart of which visitors sporting headphones travel on a moving walkway that runs along two huge aquariums, where colourful fish swim among sharks, fascinating jellyfish and other aquatic species belonging to this wonderful silent world. There is also an **Imax** theatre on site for those who enjoy movies shown on giant screens.

From Pier 39, go to Pier 41, from where you can enjoy a **cruise** ★★ in the bay that passes under the Golden Gate Bridge. Boats heading to the island of **Alcatraz** also weigh anchor from Pier 41.

The Blue and Gold Fleet *(Pier 41,* ☎ *705-5555, www.blueandgoldfleet.com)* and the **Red and White Fleet** *(Pier 43-1/2,* ☎*673-2900,* ≈*447-2794, www.redandwhite.com)* organize excursions to Alcatraz and the bay. All outings to **Alcatraz** *($20; duration: around 2hrs 30min)* set off from Pier 41. Take note that only 300 people at a time may visit the island of Alcatraz. We recommend you reserve your tickets

ahead of time (a few days, even a few weeks in advance during tourist season, which runs from June to October).

Immortalized in several movies, **Alcatraz** ★★★ is the famous San Francisco Bay island that owes its notoriety to the maximum security prison that once held the worst criminals in the United States. The island has an area of 1.85 sq mi (4.8km²) and is located approximately 1.5mi (2.5km) off the city's coast. Nicknamed "The Rock" because of the steep cliffs that hem the island in, its vocation is now essentially touristic.

Spaniards José de Canizares and Juan Manuel de Ayala had the honour of discovering the island in 1775. Exploring the island, they noticed numerous sea birds and decided to name it *Isla de los alcatraces*, or "pelican island."

The prison held 450 cells, but the average occupancy was only 265 prisoners. The small cells (barely 3ft or 1m wide by 9ft or 3m long) were enough to induce claustrophobia.

Among the many escape attempts, without a doubt, the most famous is that of Frank Morris and the Anglin brothers (Clarence and John). This incredible story was told in the movie *Escape from Alcatraz*, starring Clint Eastwood. On June 11, 1962, the prisoner trio disappeared without a trace. To fool guards, the prisoners made stunningly life-like dummies (with real hair) to make them believe they were sleeping. Authorities claim, however, that the prisoners must have drowned in their

PIER 39

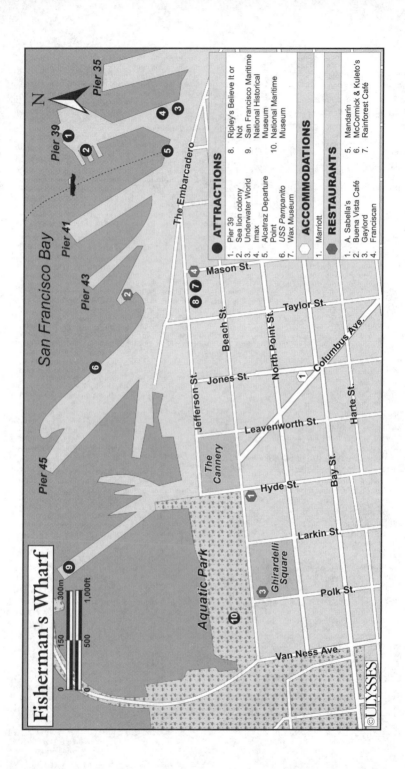

Fisherman's Wharf

San Francisco Bay

N

Pier 35
Pier 39
Pier 41
Pier 43
Pier 45

The Embarcadero

Aquatic Park
Ghirardelli Square
The Cannery

Mason St.
Taylor St.
Beach St.
North Point St.
Jefferson St.
Jones St.
Leavenworth St.
Columbus Ave.
Harte St.
Hyde St.
Bay St.
Larkin St.
Polk St.
Van Ness Ave.

● ATTRACTIONS

1. Pier 39
2. Sea lion colony
3. Underwater World
4. Imax
5. Alcatraz Departure Point
6. USS Pampanito
7. Wax Museum
8. Ripley's Believe It or Not
9. San Francisco Maritime National Historical Museum
10. National Maritime Museum

⬡ ACCOMMODATIONS

1. Marriott

⬡ RESTAURANTS

A. Sabella's
1. Buena Vista Café
2. Gaylord
3. Franciscan
5. Mandarin
6. McCormick & Kuleto's
7. Rainforest Café

0   150   300m
0   500   1,000ft

© ULYSSES

attempt. To this day, their fate remains a mystery.

The following year, in 1963, the prison closed its doors to criminals. The reasons for this, however, had nothing to do with the escape (or attempted escape). The building's infrastructure was deemed to be falling apart and dilapidated. Today, thousands of tourists flock here every year. The audioguided tour that recounts episodes in the lives of some of the prisoners is fascinating.

Returning from your visit to Alcatraz, head westward to Pier 45 to visit the USS Pampanito *submarine.*

The **USS Pampanito ★ ★** *($6, every day 9am to 6pm)* is the king of warships, a silent killer, a spy ship that sinks enemy convoys, that launches ballistic missiles that can destroy the world, that transports James Bond in the middle of a movie and picks him up at the end. As kids, we imagined the sub to be modern and spacious, our impressionable young minds having been marked by *20,000 Leagues Under the Sea* and *Journey to the Bottom of the Sea*. Nevertheless, submarines were surprisingly narrow in the mid-20th century. During your visit, you'll be able to walk on the deck and imagine having 10 seconds to reach the hatch before the vessel submerges. Inside, you can familiarize yourself with the cramped environment and grasp the degree of confinement of a space that was referred to as the "steel coffin." You can smell the diesel fumes and knock your head in the gangways, while the irregular reception of a recorded message that is supposed to guide you gives you the impression

of navigating several hundred feet under the sea. The *USS Pampanito* will help you appreciate the snug comfort of your own home, while giving you a clear idea of how nasty and horrible war is.

Ken Kesey

Ken Kesey is quite plainly one of the progenitors of the psychedelic movement. Born in Colorado in 1935, he was enrolled in Stanford University's creative-writing program when he volunteered to participate in government-sponsored studies on the effects of various hallucinogenic drugs conducted at Menlo Park Veterans Hospital. After his experience, he wrote his famous book *One Flew Over the Cuckoo's Nest*, and even voluntarily submitting to electroshock "treatments" in the name of research. In the early 1960s, Kesey formed a group known as the "Merry Pranksters," who lived communally. The Pranksters bought a school bus that they painted in psychedelic colours, rigged with a sound system and nicknamed "Further." In June 1964, he and friend Neal Cassady set off with the Merry Pranksters on a wild road trip across the United States, smoking pot and dropping LSD, and armed with hand-

held cameras. Thus equipped, Kesey and Cassady organized totally over-the-top multimedia happenings known as Acid Tests—events awash in drugs, music and humourous antics. In fact, Timothy Leary's "Turn on, tune in and drop out" credo was Kesey's clarion call. This trip manifestly set the stage for the psychedelic era and managed to influence a number of bands, including the Grateful Dead and Jefferson Airplane.

When the government outlawed LSD a few years later, a good number of bands continued to make subtle illusions to the drug in their lyrics. In fact, even the Beatles climbed on the bandwagon with *Lucy in the Sky with Diamonds*, while Bob Dylan's *Mr. Tambourine Man* is now considered a 1960s pop-culture reference. To find out more about Kesey's fascinating trip, read Tom Wolfe's *The Electric Kool-Aid Acid Test*.

After walking up Taylor Street to the corner of Jefferson Street, you'll find two flashy museums that just might make your kids smile.

The **Wax Museum** *(admission fee; 145 Jefferson St.)* holds a collection of some 300 wax figures. Among the

plethora of characters, visitors can admire former U.S. presidents, as well as celebrities like Elvis Presley, Andy Warhol, Mozart and even Mark Twain. You can also see a recreation of Tutankhamen's tomb. Right next door stands a tacky museum devoted to the weird, strange and uncouth: **Ripley's Believe It or Not Museum** *(admission fee; Jefferson St.).*

Keep walking westward on Jefferson Street to the district's next wonder, **The Cannery ★** *(between Leavenworth St. and Hyde St.).* Built in 1907, The Cannery is a former fruit-canning plant. It has been converted into a three-storey commercial building, featuring restaurants, boutiques and a small museum devoted to the city's history.

A detour towards the water will lead you to a quay where a fleet of ships from around the turn of the century is docked and make up the **San Francisco Maritime—National Historical Museum ★★** *($5; every day 10am to 5pm).* The admission fee gives you the right to board ships such as the imposing three-mast *Balclutha* (1886), the *C.A. Thayer* (1895) schooner, the *Eureka* (1890) steamship and the *Hercules* (1907) steam tugboat, just to name a few. Depending on your interest level, you could easily spend anywhere from 30min to more than 3hrs discovering these ancient ships at your own pace.

Go back up Hyde Street and turn right onto Beach Street to **Ghirardelli Square ★** *(between Polk St. and Larkin St.).* Ghirardelli Square is a former chocolate factory where the

world-famous Ghirardelli chocolates originated. The business still exists, but its old processing premises have been converted into a shopping centre whose vocation is to please as many shoppers as possible by offering a wide range of services. You'll find the same mix of boutiques, cafés and restaurants that are featured everywhere that business predominates.

The **National Maritime Museum** *(free admission; 10am to 5pm; 900 Beach St.)* is located in an Art Deco structure that looks like a steamship. Despite its rather pretentious name, it is a small, simple museum devoted to the area's maritime history.

Tour G: The Marina

The Marina district is today a bourgeois residential seafront neighbourhood. The district enjoyed its moment of glory during the Panama Pacific Exhibition, which was opened with a speech by President Wilson. The speech was rebroadcast coast to coast by telegraph, and announced the festivities surrounding the completion of the Panama Canal, the coming technological age and the rebuilding of San Francisco following the 1906 earthquake. All of the buildings were quickly torn down after the exhibition's closure, with the exception of the Palace of Fine Arts, in order to make room for residential buildings that would be sold to the highest bidders. The district was seriously damaged by the 1989 earthquake, but was quickly rebuilt.

The tour begins at the Marina Green.

Located between Scott Street and Webster Street, the **Marina Green ★** is a grassy park bordered by the bay. The area is popular with joggers, in-line skaters, walkers and kite flyers. As a bonus, visitors can enjoy exceptional views of the Golden Gate Bridge.

As you walk westward down Marina Boulevard, your vision will quickly be attracted to the multitude of yachts that fill the bay. Keep walking until you reach the end of the jetty.

The strange stone structure that stands before you is the **Wave Organ ★**, which was built at the same time as the Exploratorium (see below). Pipes installed partially in and out of the water produce sound when waves break on them. With a little imagination, you could probably hear anything...

Retrace your steps and take Palace Drive to get to the Palace of Fine Arts.

Designed by architect Bernard Maybeck, the **Palace of Fine Arts ★★★** *(free admission)* is the only pavilion of the 1915 Panama Pacific Exhibition that was not destroyed after the event. This neoclassical architectural specimen is easily recognizable thanks to its magnificent 108ft-high (33m) dome that is supported by impressive columns into which angel figures have been engraved. Standing in almost Olympian fashion at the heart of green spaces, this colossal structure borders an artificial lagoon. This attraction has become, like the Golden Gate Bridge and Transamerica Pyramid,

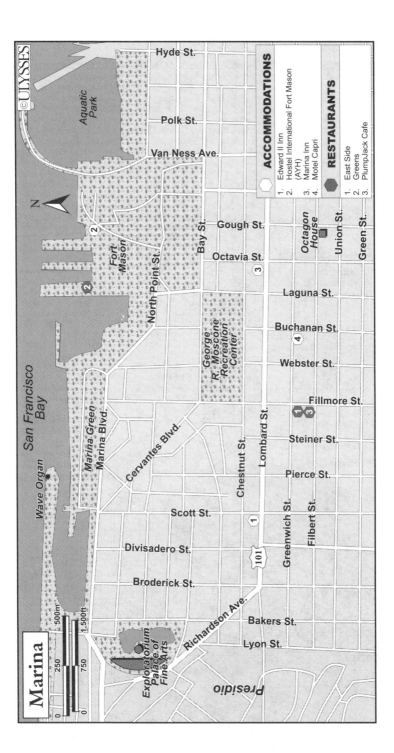

Marina

N

San Francisco Bay

Wave Organ

Aquatic Park

Fort Mason

Marina Green
Marina Blvd.

George R. Moscone Recreation Center

Exploratorium
Palace of Fine Arts

Presidio

Richardson Ave.

Hyde St.

Polk St.

Van Ness Ave.

North Point St.

Bay St.

Gough St.

Octavia St.

Laguna St.

Buchanan St.

Webster St.

Fillmore St.

Steiner St.

Pierce St.

Scott St.

Divisadero St.

Broderick St.

Bakers St.

Lyon St.

Cervantes Blvd.

Chestnut St.

Lombard St.

Greenwich St.

Filbert St.

Octagon House

Union St.

Green St.

101

1

2

2

3

4

ACCOMMODATIONS

1. Edward II Inn
2. Hostel International Fort Mason (AYH)
3. Marina Inn
4. Motel Capri

RESTAURANTS

1. East Side
2. Greens
3. PlumpJack Cafe

0   250   500m

0   750   1,500ft

© ULYSSES

one of San Francisco's most famous landmarks.

The **Exploratorium** ★★★ (*$9; Thu to Tue 10am to 6pm, Wed 10am to 9pm; 3601 Lyon St., ☎561-0360, www.exploratorium.edu*), a jewel among U.S. science museums, is located next to the Palace of Fine Arts. In 1969, the father of the atomic bomb, Frank Oppenheimer, saved the main pavilion's vast vacant lot from neglect and invading spider webs, and converted it into a technology museum, with the aim of familiarizing the general public with science through experiments of the natural world. Thus was born San Francisco's Exploratorium, and Oppenheimer remained its mentor as director until his death in 1985.

The Exploratorium is a science and technology museum that is unique in its originality and educational attractions. By assembling the contributions of scientists, artists and teachers, the museum features more than 650 remarkably ingenious interactive attractions. All exhibits are made on site in a workshop that is open to the public. Demonstrations are divided into three sections on two floors, and cover 13 general themes such as light, colour, movement, cognitive senses, waves and resonance, sound and music, and weather, which help initiate visitors to subjects as diverse as the chaotic forces that formed the ocean's sand, the principle of a car differential, or DNA structure and its use in legal investigations. Its innovative approach to bringing together technology and culture involves the invitation of six resident artists every year, who contribute to the established demonstrations by developing themes for temporary exhibits. One of the museum's avowed goals is to awaken the minds of children to the strange beauty of the world

Palace of Fine Arts

that surrounds them—a goal that it also achieves by sometimes awakening the minds of the adults that accompany them.

Wedged between Pacific Heights and the Marina, **Cow Hollow** ★ is a small, quiet residential neighbourhood that owes its name to the cows that grazed here in the late 19th century. No trace of its long forgotten past remains, but its territory is still dotted with numerous green spaces. The district's commercial activity now centres around Union Street, which is lined with many restaurants, cafés, antique shops, Victorian residences and chic boutiques.

Aside from Union Street, which is perfect for strolling, the district has few tourist attractions. The only one that is probably worth mentioning is Octagon House.

Octagon House ★ (*schedule varies; 2645 Gough St., ☎441-7512*) is an eight-sided residence, as you no doubt guessed. Built in 1861, the home's architecture aimed to provide each room with as much light as possible. This incongruous relic of the past today holds a small museum of decorative arts.

Tour H: Presidio

Once considered the oldest military garrison in the United States, the Presidio is today one of the country's largest urban parks. Founded in 1776 by the Spanish, this army base has had the Spanish, Mexican and U.S. flags flying over it at one time or another. It became a national park in 1994.

Tour I:
Pacific Heights

however. The view is spectacular.

The **Golden Gate Bridge** ★★★ was once considered impossible to build. Others maintained it would ruin the scenery. Before its construction began, no one, aside from a few silent visionaries, thought the Golden Gate Bridge would ever be realized—except for engineer Joseph Strauss. Not afraid to speak his mind, the swank, brilliant and perseverant Strauss was the perfect person to lead the project to completion. During construction, he installed safety nets under the bridge that ended up saving the lives of a few workers. Work began in January 1933 and the bridge was inaugurated with great pomp on May 27, 1937.

One of the most interesting and spectacular walks you can take in San Francisco is to cross the Golden Gate Bridge on foot, as long as you are not afraid of heights. A renowned suspension bridge, which stretches over the strait where San Francisco Bay meets the turbulent waters of the Pacific, it is an architectural marvel that lets you better take in the city as a whole. This superb Art Deco bridge is as much a symbol and icon of San Francisco as the Statue of Liberty is of New York. When fog gently envelops the bay and foghorns are sounded, the Golden Gate Bridge's orangy silhouette evokes fabulous images that will leave their mark on the souls of romantics.

Golden Gate Bridge

Lovers of green spaces can trek along one of the many trails that cut through the Presidio's bucolic hills.

The **Visitor Center** provides brochures and information on the park and its trails.

The **Presidio Museum** ★ *(free admission; Wed to Sun noon to 4pm; Funston Ave., corner Lincoln Blvd.)* is a small military museum located in a former hospital.

The **Cemetery** *(Lincoln Blvd.)* is a veritable city of the dead, as more than 15,000 soldiers have been buried here over the last 200 years or so.

Located beneath the Golden Gate Bridge, and responsible for guarding access to San Francisco Bay during the American Civil War, **Fort Point** ★★ is a former fortress whose cannons still point out to sea. No cannonball was ever fired from here,

Located between Cow Hollow and Japantown, Pacific Heights, according to many, is probably San Francisco's most stylish residential district. A walk through its wide, flowered streets, which are lined with magnificent Victorian or Tudor residences with shiny cars parked in front, is enough to fully justify this widespread opinion.

The tour starts at Alta Plaza Park.

Alta Plaza Park ★ *(delimited by Jackson St., Scott St., Clay St. and Steiner St.)*, a green space that is especially enjoyed by residents, is bordered by magnificent Victorian residences. Its location offers lovely views of the surrounding area.

Keep walking eastward on Washington Street and you will reach Lafayette Park four street corners down.

Lafayette Park ★ attracts dog walkers and couples out for an intimate walk. Its north side runs along the entire length of the magnificent Spreckels Mansion.

Owned by prolific novelist Danielle Steele, **Spreckels Mansion** ★ *(2080 Washington St.)* is obviously not open to the public. A symbol of prestige and splendour, this superb Victorian mansion was originally built for sugar magnate Adolph Spreckels at the beginning of the 20th century. Few people have had the privilege of seeing the interior, but rumour has it the mansion has no fewer than 26 bathrooms...

Keep walking down Washington Street until you reach Franklin Street, onto which you will turn left and stop in front of Haas-Lilienthel House.

Haas-Lilienthel House ★★
($5 guided tours only; 2007 Franklin St., ☎441-3004), a Queen Anne–style Victorian residence, is the former home of Alice Haas-Lilienthel, the daughter of a merchant, who lived here until 1972, when she donated it to San Francisco's Architectural Heritage Foundation. It is one of the few Victorian residences open to the public. You should know, however, that this beautiful residence is not up to par with the opulent and ostentatious villas that were destroyed by the fire that followed the 1906 earthquake.

Tour J: Japantown

Nihonmachi means "Japantown" in Japanese, but practically everybody uses the English term to designate this neighbourhood. Despite its exotic name, the district has nothing really outstanding to offer tourists. Bordered by Fillmore, Sutter and Laguna streets, as well as Geary Boulevard, Japantown is much quieter and much less interesting than the very lively Chinatown.

Indeed, there isn't much for visitors to see or do in Japantown. Its commercial activity mostly takes place around **Japan Center** *(bordered by Geary Blvd. and Laguna,*

Post and Fillmore streets), a huge, modern five-storey complex, with no particular charm, where you will find restaurants, boutiques, grocery stores, the AMC Kabuki 8 cinema and the Peace Pagoda. The five-level **Peace Pagoda** is currently under renovation. It was built to strengthen relations between Japan and the United States.

★★

Tour K: The Civic Center, the Tenderloin and Hayes Valley

Another district that is currently undergoing renovations, the **Civic Center** is making great efforts to improve its image with tourists, and the city is hoping it gets its second wind in the near future. Nevertheless, the neighbourhood is not without noteworthy attractions. For example, this is where you will find one the city's most beautiful buildings, city hall. In addition, the old San Francisco Public Library will soon house the magnificent Asian Art Museum (see p 414).

There are also a good number of quality restaurants here. Basically, the Civic Center's main

City hall

problem is its location next to one of the city's least reputable districts, the Tenderloin.

The tour begins at the city hall, around which you will find all the attractions.

An impressive building topped with a splendid dome modelled after St. Peter's Basilica in Rome, the **city hall ★★** *(400 Van Ness Ave.)* was built in 1915 for the Panama Pacific Exhibition after the first city hall was destroyed in 1906. An interesting fact for trivia-lovers: its dome measures 305ft (93m), barely an inch or two higher than the Capitol in Washington, D.C. The history of the city hall also has its share of fascinating facts: it is here that baseball player Joe Di Maggio and actress Marilyn Monroe were married in 1954; 24 years later, in 1978, Mayor Moscone and his colleague Harvey Milk were murdered here by Dan White.

City hall was renovated after the 1989 earthquake and reopened in 2000.

Inaugurated in 1996, the **San Francisco Public Library ★** *(100 Larkin St.)* welcomes bookworms in to peruse the many books in its inventory. The library is also equipped with some 300 computers that

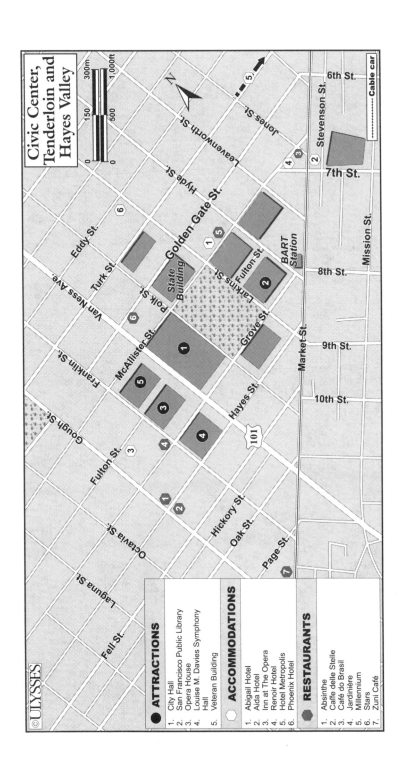

© ULYSSES

Civic Center, Tenderloin and Hayes Valley

ATTRACTIONS
1. City Hall
2. San Francisco Public Library
3. Opera House
4. Louise M. Davies Symphony Hall
5. Veteran Building

ACCOMMODATIONS
1. Abigail Hotel
2. Aida Hotel
3. Inn at The Opera
4. Renoir Hotel
5. Hotel Metropolis
6. Phoenix Hotel

RESTAURANTS
1. Absinthe
2. Caffe delle Stelle
3. Café do Brasil
4. Jardinière
5. Millennium
6. Stars
7. Zuni Café

you can use to consult CD-ROMs or surf the Internet. Its splendid atrium makes it worth the detour.

The **Opera House** ★ *(301 Van Ness Ave.)* welcomes world-class opera companies as well as the San Francisco Ballet Company. This is where the Charter of the United Nations was signed.

For those who prefer classical music, the **Louise M. Davies Symphony Hall** ★ *(201 Van Ness Ave.)* is home to the San Francisco Symphony Orchestra.

The **Veteran's Building** *(401 Van Ness Ave.)* houses the small Herbst Theater.

Located west of Union Square between the Civic Center and Market Street, the **Tenderloin** is a rather shady neighbourhood where greasy spoons stand next to run-down buildings and pornographic theatres. Homeless people sleep in its recesses and a

colourful crowd furtively wanders the alleys of this district, which is about to be cleaned up and revitalized. Indeed, the city is trying to gradually erase the more unpleasant aspects of its disreputable areas. Since this is one of the rare places in San Francisco where you can still find good deals on commercial rentals, many expanding businesses are establishing themselves here. For instance, more and more businesses specializing in multimedia and new technology are choosing this district to avoid the generally unaffordable rents in South of Market. Laotians, Vietnamese and Cambodians have also made this district their home, attempting to give it a new lease on life and make it as charming and vibrant as it used to be. Within a year or two, hip restaurants, renovated buildings and maybe even a few trendy coffee shops may even find their way here too.

A little off the beaten path, between the Civic Center to the east and Lower Haight to the west, lies the charming neighbourhood of **Hayes Valley**. A bohemian district, it features many art galleries, quaint cafés, cool restaurants and antique shops.

Tour L: Haight-Ashbury

Perhaps the most famous free-spirited neighbourhood in the country, Haight-Ashbury is synonymous with the festive, psychedelic Summer of Love event. Located east of Golden Gate Park, the Haight-Ashbury district is named after the intersection of Haight and Ashbury streets. Today, it has become more gentrified, thanks to the young professionals who have established themselves in the area, but there is still a colourful crowd living here, much as they did some 30 years ago.

The area can basically be divided in two sections: Upper Haight, which stretches from Golden Gate Park to Divisadero Street, and Lower Haight, from Divisadero to Webster Street.

Upper Haight ★ has few tourist attractions, and most of the action takes place on Haight Street. The majority of visitors combine this tour with the Golden Gate Park tour, while others enjoy spending time in its eccentric bookstores and newspaper stands, exploring second-hand shops, or simply discovering Haight Street and its Victorian homes while a musician casually

The City Pass

Designed for visitors, the **City Pass** *(adults $33.25, seniors $26.25, children aged five-17 $24.25)* is a kind of package deal that allows you to save up to 50% on admission fees to some of the most popular attractions in San Francisco. The pass can be used at the Exploratorium, the Blue and Gold Fleet Bay Cruise, the California Academy of Sciences

and Steinhart Aquarium, the San Francisco Museum of Modern Art, the California Palace of the Legion of Honor and the M.H. de Young Memorial Museum. In addition, the City Pass allows you to avoid long waiting lines to buy tickets. The pass is available at the box offices of the attractions mentioned above.

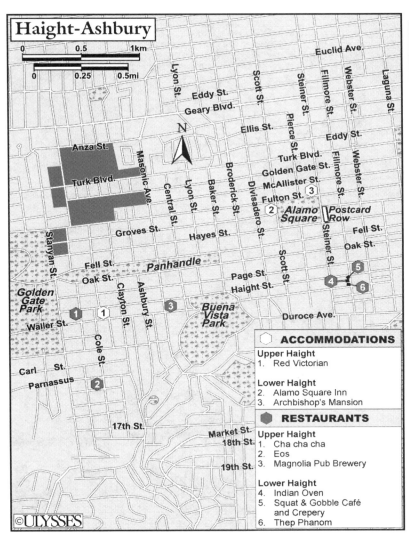

Haight-Ashbury

ACCOMMODATIONS

Upper Haight
1.   Red Victorian

Lower Haight
2.   Alamo Square Inn
3.   Archbishop's Mansion

RESTAURANTS

Upper Haight
1.   Cha cha cha
2.   Eos
3.   Magnolia Pub Brewery

Lower Haight
4.   Indian Oven
5.   Squat & Gobble Café
     and Crepery
6.   Thep Phanom

©ULYSSES

plays the guitar and hums a tune.

Although you will be unable to actually visit the former homes of Janis Joplin and other musicians who will live on in our memory, here are their addresses: **Janis Joplin**: 112 Lyon Street; **The Grateful Dead**: 710 Ashbury Street.

The summit of **Buena Vista Park ★** *(Haight St. and Buena Vista Ave.)* offers lovely views of the surroundings. Unfortunately, it has a bad reputation because of the presence of drug dealers, so avoid it at night.

The only real attraction in **Lower Haight** is **Alamo Square**, a charming park bordered by six fabulous

Victorian houses collectively called **Postcard Row ★★** because it is the most photographed row of Victorian homes in the city. This neighbourhood's activity is centred on Haight Street, between Steiner and Webster streets.

Not as popular as Upper Haight, Lower Haight is home to nonconformist students, artists in search of spiritual elevation and adults who refuse to grow old. This strange crowd fills the coffee shops and bars that abound on Haight Street between Steiner and Fillmore streets.

Tour M:
Golden Gate Park

As a great victory of humankind over nature, the beautifully designed green space that you see here today was a vast field of windswept dunes just 110 years ago. Created in 1870 to rival Manhattan's Central Park in size and reputation, Golden Gate Park today features some 31mi (50km) of trails, many lakes, a variety of bucolic landscapes and a number of tourist attractions. On sunny days, cyclists cross paths with in-line skaters and joggers, while other outdoor enthusiasts leisurely stroll about or picnic on one of the many patches of grass. Covering an area of 1,018 acres (412ha), 3mi (5km) long and 0.6mi (900m) wide, Golden Gate Park is the city's "green lung," and is actually the largest urban park in the United States.

Every Sunday, a section of John F. Kennedy Drive is closed to cars and reserved for cyclists, in-line skaters and pedestrians.

The suggested tour starts at McLaren Lodge.

McLaren Lodge *(everyday 8am to 5pm; 501 Stanyan St. and Fell St., ☎831-2700)* is where you will find information on Golden Gate Park.

The traditional itinerary for visiting Golden Gate Park

consists of taking John F. Kennedy Drive from McLaren Lodge up to the Conservatory of Flowers. However, if you wish to take a different route and bring your children along, opt for the southern section of the park and take Kezar Drive to reach the Children's Playground.

The **Conservatory of Flowers ★★** *(John F. Kennedy Dr.)* is the oldest building in Golden Gate Park. It dates back to 1875, when millionaire James Lick purchased a greenhouse in Ireland to beautify his San Jose home. However, Lick died in 1876 and the greenhouse was bought by a group of investors who donated it to Golden Gate Park. After a terrible fire in 1883, the original structure was replaced by an immense glass dome under which bloom a wide variety of flowers.

Built in 1888, the **Children's Playground ★** *(Kezar Dr.)* is a play area for children that features a carousel, swings, slides and many other fun things to entertain them. You will also find the Sharon Building, which has been rebuilt and renovated many times

and is home to a community of goats.

From the Conservatory of Flowers, turn back until you reach Middle Drive East, which you will then follow up to the AIDS Memorial.

As its name indicates, the **AIDS Memorial ★** *(John F. Kennedy Dr. at Middle Dr. E.)* is a small memorial for the victims of this disease.

Follow Middle Drive East up to the California Academy of Science.

The **California Academy of Science ★★** *(☎750-7100, ☞750-7346, www.calacademy.org)* is a venerable scientific institution that houses the Natural History Museum, the Morrison Planetarium and the Steinhart Aquarium. The **Natural History Museum ★** *($8.50; Mon to Fri 10am to 5pm)* makes it

Conservatory of Flowers

easy to understand the natural history of the United States thanks to interactive exhibits, dioramas, photographs and comic strips by Gary Larson, creator of *The Far Side*.

Exploring the **Steinhart Aquarium ★** *($8.50; 10am to 5pm)* will make you feel

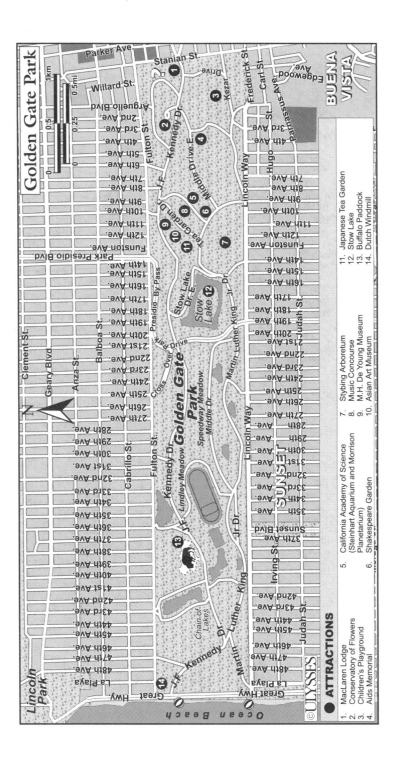

Golden Gate Park

BUENA VISTA

Lincoln Park

Golden Gate Park

SUNSET

Ocean Beach

© ULYSSES

● ATTRACTIONS

1. MacLaren Lodge
2. Conservatory of Flowers
3. Children's Playground
4. Aids Memorial
5. California Academy of Science (Steinhart Aquarium and Morrison Planetarium)
6. Shakespeare Garden
7. Stybing Arboretum
8. Music Concourse
9. M.H. De Young Museum
10. Asian Art Museum
11. Japanese Tea Garden
12. Stow Lake
13. Buffalo Paddock
14. Dutch Windmill

The Midwinter International Exposition

In 1893, realizing that the city's economy was in pretty bad shape, M.H. de Young, a *San Francisco Chronicle* editor, campaigned for an international fair be held in San Francisco. Thanks to his perseverance and perceptiveness, the Midwinter International Exposition was inaugurated on January 2, 1894 in Golden Gate Park. Most of the buildings that were built for the event were inspired by exotic and Asian themes in order to emphasize California's warm climate, even in January. Among these structures were the Japanese Tea Garden and the M.H. de Young Museum. This large-scale fair gave such a boost to the city's economy that it came completely out of its slump. To commemorate this victory over economic adversity, permanent museums were constructed in Golden Gate Park.

as though you have just begun a fantastic voyage to the unknown universe of the sea. The establishment was designed so that visitors could tour the various sections in a clockwise direction. There are more than 200 tanks here, containing placid manatees, friendly dolphins, sharp-toothed crocodiles and many other colourful fish species and crustaceans that will delight kids and grown-ups alike.

A true window on the sky, the **Morrison Planetarium ★** (*$3; Mon to Fri 10am to 5pm*) is named after Alexander Francis Morrison, a San Francisco lawyer and member of the California Academy of Science who lived here in the late 19th century. This is a great place for those who are fascinated by the stars.

At the corner of Middle Drive East and Martin Luther King Jr. Drive is the Shakespeare Garden.

The **Shakespeare Garden ★** (*Middle Dr. at Martin Luther King Jr. Dr.*) is a small garden whose every flower and plant is mentioned in one of this famous playwright's works.

Head for the southern section of Golden Gate Park by taking Martin Luther King Jr. Drive until you reach the corner of Lincoln Way and Ninth Avenue. You are now at the entrance to the Stybing Arboretum.

An arboretum is a nursery filled with many species of trees that are the subject of study. A stroll through the **Stybirg Arboretum ★★** will certainly please nature-lovers. Here, visitors can admire different species

from Asia, America and Australia.

Retrace your steps northwards by taking Martin Luther King Jr. Drive up to Hagiwara Tea Garden Drive, then turn right. Stop at the Music Concourse, facing the M.H. de Young Museum.

In summer, you can enjoy classical music concerts at the **Music Concourse ★**, an esplanade facing the M.H. de Young Museum.

In the left wing of the building that houses the M.H. de Young Museum is the **Asian Art Museum ★★★** (*$8.50; www.asianart.com*). However, because of the high risk of earthquakes and the reduced surface area that only allows visitors to see 15% of the collection, the museum is scheduled to move to the Civic Center's old library in the fall of 2002. It is closed until then. This is without question the largest American collection of Asian art. Although most of it comes from China, the exhibit rooms tell an amazing historical saga involving some 40 countries, including India, Tibet, Korea, Thailand, Nepal and Japan. Among the museum's gems is the bronze statue of a rhinoceros dating back to AD 338 that once belonged to the Chang dynasty. There are also early printed books, frescoes, sculptures and many other works of art that will undoubtedly pique your curiosity.

Leaving the Asian Art Museum, turn right to reach the Japanese Tea Garden.

Designed in 1894 for the California Midwinter International Exposition, the **Japanese Tea Garden ★★★** (*$4; 8am to 5:30pm; ☎ 752-*

1171) was the result of a long, close collaboration between Australian George Turman Marsh and Japanese Makato Hagiwara. With the help of his family, Hagiwara took care of the garden until 1942, the year during the Second World War when all citizens of Japanese descent were forced to move to relocation centres. When the war ended, the Hagiwaras were unable to get their gardening jobs back. It was not until 1975 that the city finally recognized its failings and thanked this honourable family by erecting a 10ft-high (3m) bronze statue of Buddha, as recognition for its services. Note that this is the highest bronze Buddha outside Asia.

The Japanese Tea Garden is decorated with bonsai trees, ponds and a pagoda where visitors are served tea by Japanese women draped in brightly coloured kimonos. If you visit this magnificent Oriental garden in late March, you will enjoy a lovely spectacle of colours as the blooming cherry trees beautify this enchanting landscape.

Those who have extra time and aren't too tired can take their exploring farther west, eventually reaching Stow Lake.

Stow Lake ★ ★ is a charming artificial lake crossed by quaint little bridges and surrounded by greenery. Those who wish to do so can rent boats and sail its calm waters. At the centre of the lake is an islet where you can have a picnic and admire the scenery. There is also a Chinese pavilion.

Farther along, you will come to the Buffalo Paddock.

Some visitors might be surprised to see bisons at the **Buffalo Paddock** ★ *(near 38th St.)* in Golden Gate Park. Have no fear: they are fenced in. The enclosure was created to protect this endangered species.

Finally, at the northwestern tip of Golden Gate Park, near the ocean, perseverant visitors will be able to admire the Dutch Windmill.

The **Dutch Windmill** ★ was built between 1873 and 1902 to supply water to irrigate the park. When electricity was introduced to Golden Gate Park some 10 years later, the windmill became obsolete. It was renovated a few times but without much success. In spring, the tulips that surround it make for a lovely show.

49 Mile Scenic Drive

If you're travelling by car or bicycle, an original and somewhat quick way to discover San Francisco's attractions is to follow the 49 Mile Scenic Drive. This 49mi (79km) tourist road runs through the city's most picturesque and charming neighbourhoods. It is identified by easily recognizable signs: just look for the white seagull.

Tour N: Richmond

In this district, two blocks separate a Chinese restaurant from an Irish pub, and Eastern Europe is only 5min away from Greece and Russia. In this highly multicultural district that stretches between Golden Gate Park and the Presidio, the proportion of Chinese residents is so high that the area is known as San Francisco's other Chinatown.

This neighbourhood covers a large area, but the attractions are relatively rare and somewhat dispersed. In fact, they are mostly found in the westernmost section, near the ocean, in Lincoln Park; the tour actually begins at the Lincoln Park Golf Club, which encompasses the California Palace of the Legion of Honor.

Lincoln Park is a lush golf club with superb views of the Golden Gate Bridge. It includes a magnificent museum, the **California Palace of the Legion of Honor** ★ ★ ★ *($8; Tue to Sun 9:30am to 5pm;* ☎*863-3330).* Built spectacularly on a hill overlooking the Golden Gate Bridge (weather permitting), this museum features a remarkable collection of European art in a building that was modelled on the Palais de la Légion d'Honneur in Paris. Here you will find the largest collection of works by Rodin outside Paris, which is the museum's main attraction. In fact, before you even purchase your ticket, a reproduction of his famous *The Thinker* will give you a taste of what's to come. Lovers of European art (from the 14th to

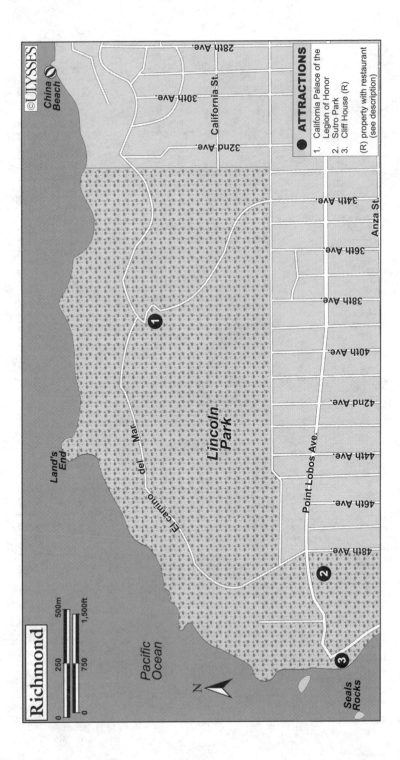

Richmond

Pacific Ocean

Land's End

El camino del Mar

Lincoln Park

Point Lobos Ave.

Anza St.

Seals Rocks

China Beach

28th Ave.

30th Ave.

California St.

32nd Ave.

34th Ave.

36th Ave.

38th Ave.

40th Ave.

42nd Ave.

44th Ave.

46th Ave.

48th Ave.

N

0   250   500m

0   750   1,500ft

© ULYSSES

● ATTRACTIONS

1. California Palace of the Legion of Honor
2. Sutro Park
3. Cliff House (R)

(R) property with restaurant (see description)

San Francisco and Surroundings

the 20th centuries), especially those who love the works of Rembrandt, Matisse, Monet, Picasso and Rubens, will be overjoyed. There are also European decorative arts, such as porcelain, sculpture and furniture. A restaurant in the basement allows visitors to enjoy a snack.

The next attraction is at the westernmost section of Richmond, near the ocean. We recommend you take a taxi to get to Sutro Park.

Sutro Park is a lovely green space where eucalyptus and cypress trees abound. The park was created in the late 19th century by philanthropist and former mayor Adolph Sutro. The Sutro Baths, now in ruins, used to form an ensemble of six pools. Around 1880,

after striking it rich thanks to Comstock's silver mines in Nevada, Adolph Sutro bought the land to create the park and the public baths for all social classes to enjoy. Cliff House, the house that stands on the edge of the sea, was also renovated by Sutro.

Built around 1863, **Cliff House** ★ refuses to disappear, having suffered through many years of lightning, earthquakes and fires. Rebuilt and transformed three times, it was bought in 1881 by Sutro, who refurbished it and incorporated it to the park. Today, it is unfortunately not as authentic and beautiful as it used to be, but it is still popular with tourists who take advantage of its lovely views and admire the waves crashing upon

Ocean Beach, as well as the sea lions lounging on the steep cliffs around the beach. Ocean Beach is not fit for swimming, but it is a pleasant place for a stroll. Cliff House features an archaic museum, the **Musée Mécanique** ★ *(Mon to Fri 11am to 7pm, Sat and Sun 10am to 8pm; ☎386-1170)*, where you will find a delightful collection of coin-operated relics.

Tour O: South of Market (SoMa)

SoMa, which stands for "South of Market," does, in fact, lie directly south of Market Street. In addition to the Convention Center, the SFMOMA, the Yerba Buena Gardens, the

The Cable Car

One beautiful summer afternoon, British engineer Andrew Smith Hallidie witnessed a terrible accident on the steep hills of San Francisco: a horse pulling a streetcar lost its balance and slid under the car, dragging along other horses and streetcars. Shocked, Hallidie decided he would the problem. He jotted down his ideas right then and there on a piece of paper. He then submitted his experimental project for a steel-cable urban transportation system to city officials. It was very well received and as soon as

1873, the first cable car made its appearance in San Francisco. The principle is quite simple. Indeed, there is no engine inside the cable car; instead, it is linked by a steel cable (hence the name "cable car") sliding between the tracks to a central engine. The cable-car conductor is called the gripman. With a grip (a type of pliers), the gripman responsible for tightening the cable to stop the car and letting it go to make it run. Obviously, this requires him to be quite strong and in excellent physical shape. In 1947,

city authorities decided to replace the cable cars, which they thought had become obsolete, with modern and more efficient buses. But in a gesture of solidarity, the citizens of San Francisco demonstrated against the change, and thanks to them, cable cars are still part of the San Francisco landscape, attracting many tourists each year. The cable cars were declared a National Historic Landmark in 1964. These relics from the past travel at a maximum speed of 9mi/hr (15km/h).

Metreon and the Pacific Bell Park, which all directly contributed to this area's revival, there are also a good number of trendy restaurants and nightclubs here.

The district still shows traces of its industrial past but has gradually managed to become a major location for multimedia businesses, which abound near South Park. In this expanding neighbourhood, some cohabitation problems have arisen due to its rapid economic development: indeed, the appearance of bars and nightclubs has contributed to a noisy nightlife that has some residents slightly annoyed.

The tour begins at Yerba Buena Gardens. Most of the attractions are around this area.

Inaugurated in 1993, the **Yerba Buena Gardens** ★★★ *(701 Mission St., bordered by Third, Fourth and Folsom streets.; ☎978-2787)* are the result of many years of hard work that began around 1955. The next 30 years were punctuated by differing opinions, indecision and both external and internal conflicts. It was a long time coming but the result speaks for itself: covering an area of approximately 99 acres (40ha), this multidisciplinary art centre houses exhibit rooms where contemporary and iconoclastic artists can display their talent by means of multimedia technologies. The establishment is surrounded by lush gardens and a lovely esplanade where you will find a waterfall and a memorial to Martin Luther King.

The Yerba Buena Gardens are also home to the Zeum and the Metreon.

Located in a lovely open area surrounded by greenery, the **Zeum** ★ *($7; www.zeum.org)* is a centre for new technology aimed at children.

The Yerba Buena Gardens are also linked to the **Metreon** ★ *(101 Fourth St., www. metreon.com)*, a new shrine to entertainment and consumption. Sony Entertainment spent a mere $85 million to make it the ideal place for movie buffs and window-shoppers. Many elegant boutiques, including the only store specialized in Microsoft products in the world, offer a wide array of goods that will certainly please visitors who like to spend. Aside from 15 theatres screening the latest blockbusters, the movie experience is taken to new levels thanks to the Imax cinema and its breathtaking images.

Head east of the Yerba Buena Gardens.

Founded in 1871, inaugurated in 1935 and moved in 1995 to a venue designed by architect Mario Botta, the **San Francisco Museum of Modern Art (SFMOMA)** ★★★ *($9; Fri to Tue 11am to 6pm, Thu 11am to 8pm; 151 Third St., ☎357-4000)* is attempting to revitalize the SoMa. After working with Le Corbusier, Louis Kahn and Carlo Scarpa, Mario Botta not only completed his first project in the United States but also his first museum. This building, conceived to showcase modern art, has a bold silhouette and geometric features, covers 226,044 sq ft (21,000m²) and cost some $60 million. Its permanent collection features almost 20,000 pieces, including approximately 10,000 photographs, all displayed in rooms set around a spectacular atrium. The main floor focuses on works by Warhol, Magritte, Matisse and Klee, the second floor is dedicated to photographs, and the other floors display temporary exhibits by famous and not-so-famous artists.

Museum of Modern Art

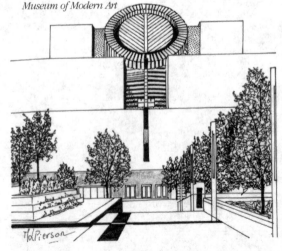

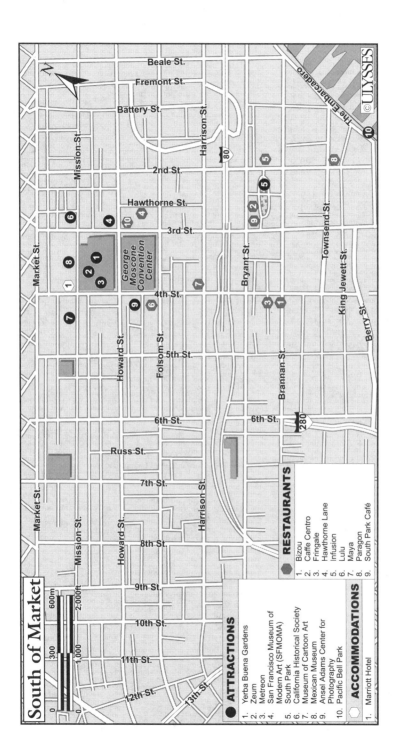

South of Market

Beale St.
Fremont St.
Battery St.

Mission St.

Harrison St.

2nd St.

Hawthorne St.

3rd St.

Market St.

George
Moscone
Convention
Center

Bryant St.

4th St.

5th St.

Howard St.

Folsom St.

Brannan St.

Townsend St.

King Jewett St.

Berry St.

6th St.

6th St.

Russ St.

7th St.

Harrison St.

Howard St.

8th St.

Mission St.

9th St.

Market St.

10th St.

11th St.

12th St.

13th St.

80

280

The Embarcadero

© ULYSSES

0   300   600m
0   1,000   2,000ft

● **ATTRACTIONS**

1. Yerba Buena Gardens
2. Zeum
3. Metreon
4. San Francisco Museum of
   Modern Art (SFMOMA)
5. South Park
6. California Historical Society
7. Museum of Cartoon Art
8. Mexican Museum
9. Ansel Adams Center for
   Photography
10. Pacific Bell Park

○ **ACCOMMODATIONS**

1. Marriott Hotel

⬡ **RESTAURANTS**

1. Bizou
2. Caffe Centro
3. Fringale
4. Hawthorne Lane
5. Infusion
6. Lulu
7. Maya
8. Paragon
9. South Park Café

South Park ★★ *(Third St. between Bryant St. and Brannan St.)* is a small, charming park that has nothing to do with the off-the-wall television comedy of the same name. Flanked by a few good restaurants, it attracts pedestrians who like to enjoy the sun or grab a bite in the neighbouring snack bars. This area is home to so many multimedia businesses that the place is now known as "Multimedia Gulch."

The following attractions are located north of the Yerba Buena Gardens.

The **California Historical Society** ★ *($2; Tue to Sat 11am to 5pm; 678 Mission St. near Third St., ☎357-1848)* retraces the major events of the city's rich and tumultuous history, as well as that of California in general, with didactic material and a wide array of old photographs.

The **Museum of Cartoon Art** ★★ *(814 Mission St. at Fourth St.)* is a light-hearted museum dedicated to cartoons. Its exhibit rooms display an extraordinary collection of comic strips dating from the 18th century until today.

The **Mexican Museum** ★ *(Mission St. at Third St.)* just moved from Fort Mason to South of Market. It is a perfect opportunity for visitors to initiate themselves to Mexican culture and discover the works of such talented artists as Diego Rivera.

Finally, continue exploring south of Yerba Buena Gardens.

Those who are interested in photography won't want to miss the works of famous photographer Ansel Adams, as well as

other talented artists, at the **Ansel Adams Center for Photography** ★★ *($5; Mon to Fri 11am to 5pm; 250 Fourth St., between Howard St. and Folsom St., ☎495-7000).*

The **Pacific Bell Park** ★, the San Francisco Giants' new stadium, is always filled with baseball fans who come to cheer their favourite team.

Tour P: Castro

Roughly bordered by 14th Street to the north, 22nd Street to the south, Douglas Street to the west and Dolores Street to the east, this neighbourhood, whose main artery is **Castro Street** ★, is filled with café-terraces, bookstores and small shops and bars where the gay flag assertively displays its rainbow colours. Every year, a gay-rights parade begins at Castro Street and winds its way to city hall to honour the memory of Harvey Milk, who was cowardly murdered by a homophobic man named Dan White.

There isn't much to see in Castro. You can stroll at your leisure, stop by a café or terrace and simply discover the district on your own. Those who wish to learn more about gay history in San Francisco should not miss the guided tour offered by **Cruisin' the Castro** *(375 Lexington St., ☎550-8110, trvrbailey@aol.com).*

One of the best places to begin your tour is at the corner of Castro Street and Market Street.

Facing the Castro Street subway station, **Harvey Milk Plaza** *(Castro St. at Market*

St.) displays a commemorative plaque in honour of Harvey Milk.

A little farther south, the **Castro Theater** ★★ *(429 Castro St.)* is easily recognizable thanks to its lovely neocolonial-style facade. Built in 1922, this superb hall features 1,450 seats and screens classic, silent, art and essay films. The San Francisco International Film Festival is held here, as is the Gay and Lesbian Film Festival, in June.

The **Different Light Bookstore** *(489 Castro St. between Market St. and 18th St., ☎431-0892, adl@adlbooks.com)* is a key establishment for gay culture in the city, offering a great selection of gay, lesbian and bisexual literature. Book signings are often held here as well.

Twin Peaks is located southwest of Castro. It is said that the Spanish named these two mountains *Los pechos de la chola,* meaning "the Indian woman's breasts." At the top of these twin mountains, a lookout offers an amazing view of the city.

Noe Valley, just south of Castro, is a quiet neighbourhood whose commercial activity is centred around 24th Street, which boasts a number of café-terraces, casual restaurants and somewhat eccentric shops. This area is nicknamed Nowhere Valley by its residents who wish to hold on to their privacy and avoid the attention of the tourism industry.

Tour Q: Mission

South of the downtown area, Mission presents

itself as a somewhat proletarian neighbourhood, with **Mission Street** at its heart. Because of its strong Hispanic presence, Mission is also known as *El barrio* ("the neighbourhood" in Spanish). From the stores and houses that make up the urban fabric of this area, you can often hear the sounds of Latin-American folk music.

This area does not feature many attractions, and most visitors come here to admire its many murals or to visit Mission Dolores. Those who are curious about the painted murals should stop by the **Precita Eyes Mural Arts Center** *(2981 24th St. near Harrison St., ☎285-2287, www. precitaeyes.org)*, an arts centre dedicated to muralists, which also organizes neighbourhood tours.

The Mission tour begins at Mission Dolores.

Built in 1776, **Mission Dolores** ★ *($2; 9am to 4:30pm; Dolores St. at 16th St., ☎621-8203)* is not only the oldest building in town but also one of the oldest sanctuaries in California. This modest former mission features 3ft-thick (1m) adobe walls that can resist the devastating earthquakes that regularly hit this region. A splendid baroque retable imported from Mexico beautifully decorates the altar. There is also a small religious museum and a cemetery for European pioneers and Native Americans.

Leaving the Mission, turn right on Dolores Street and walk to the corner of 18th Street.

Mission Dolores Park *(Dolores St. at 18th St.)* is popular with residents, who come here with their children or dogs. There are also tennis courts and a small play area.

Turn right on 18th Street and walk to Valencia Street. Turn left and stop between 13th Street and 14th Street.

The **Levi Strauss Factory** ★ *(open house Wed at 10:30am and 1pm; 250 Valencia St., ☎210-0110)* is one of the oldest jeans manufacturers in the world, and is worth a detour.

Tour R: The San Francisco Area

Treasure Island ★ is an artificial island that was

Levi Strauss

A Jewish immigrant from Bavaria, Levi Strauss landed in San Francisco in 1947 with a batch of serge—a durable, waterproof fabric used to cover merchandise. Exported from the port of Genoa, this fabric from Nîmes, France was said to have been used for the sails of the caravels in which Christopher Columbus set off to conquer the Americas. Finding no buyers for his fabric, Levi Strauss decided to make a pair of pants out of the material. The result was hardly fancy, but very sturdy,

with seams reinforced by rivets. As for all successful entrepreneurs who succeed, Lady Luck smiled on Levi Strauss. In 1849, the gold rush hit and miners were in need of extremely durable clothing. The whiz-kid's pants arrived at just the right moment and were an instant hit with prospectors. It was the beginning of the great business of the "blue Genoas," which became known as blue jeans, a North American symbol. The Denim brand sustained the supply of *serge de Nîmes* (from which it is

said to derive its name). In 1850, Levi Strauss founded his first manufacturing plant, which was a phenomenal success. From a utilitarian item of clothing in its infancy, jeans gradually became very popular with the masses, to the point that they have now become a universal garment. Strauss undoubtedly had no idea his pants would one day gain the favour of the ready-to-wear industry, movie stars and just about everybody else.

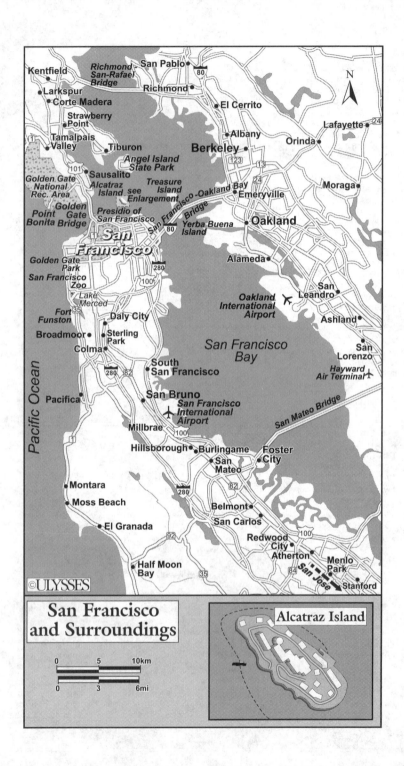

Kentfield
Richmond San-Rafael Bridge
San Pablo
80
Larkspur
Corte Madera
Richmond
El Cerrito
Strawberry Point
Lafayette 24
Tamalpais Valley
Tiburon
Albany
Berkeley
Orinda
Angel Island State Park
123
13
101
Sausalito
Golden Gate National Rec. Area
Alcatraz Island
Treasure Island
see Enlargement
24
Bay
Moraga
Emeryville
Golden Gate Bonita Bridge
Presidio of San Francisco
San Francisco-Oakland Bay Bridge
80
Oakland
San Francisco
Yerba Buena Island
Golden Gate Park
280
Alameda
San Francisco Zoo
100
Oakland International Airport
San Leandro
Lake Merced
35
Ashland
Fort Funston
Daly City
San Lorenzo
Broadmoor
Sterling Park
San Francisco Bay
Colma
280 82
South San Francisco
Hayward Air Terminal
Pacifica
San Bruno
San Francisco International Airport
San Mateo Bridge
Millbrae
100
Hillsborough
Burlingame
Foster City
San Mateo
Montara
280
Moss Beach
82
Belmont
El Granada
San Carlos
92
Redwood City
100
Atherton
Menlo Park
Half Moon Bay
84
San Jose
Stanford
35

©ULYSSES

Pacific Ocean

N

San Francisco and Surroundings

0   5   10km
0   3   6mi

Alcatraz Island

created for the international fair of 1939. Today it is used by the Navy.

Angel Island ★ is easily accessible by boat from the San Francisco pier. This haven of peace and greenery features hiking trails and bike paths, and visitors can also rent kayaks.

A family destination that is usually popular with kids, the **San Francisco Zoo ★** (*Sloat Blvd. at 45th Ave., ☎ 753-7080, www.sfzoo.com*), is neither as large nor as famous as the San Diego Zoo but it does feature one of the largest gorilla populations in the world. This zoo is home to more than 250 animal species.

★★
**Sausalito
(Marin County)**

The lovely village of Sausalito ("willow" in Spanish) is named after the majestic forests that were discovered by Spanish explorers. Today, beautiful Victorian homes flank the hills that plunge into the sea. This small village is easily accessible by the Embarcadero ferry and many suburban residents take the Sausalito ferry to go to work in San Francisco. Here, the commercial activity is centred around its main street, Bridgeway, which is filled with art galleries of all kinds. The city is also home to one of the region's best restaurants, Ondine (see p 449).

Tour S: East Bay

The east side of San Francisco Bay has seen the development of two completely different cities that both play an important role: collegial Berkeley and industrial Oakland.

★★
Berkeley

A city whose name is synonymous with students protesting on the campus that shares its name, Berkeley only developed after the 1906 earthquake. Indeed, this terrible natural catastrophe provoked the exodus of many San Francisco residents who chose to settle across the bay. Today, Berkeley is home to more than 100,000 people who have become much more middle-class since the 1960s. There are also many green spaces, bookstores and cafés, as well as noteworthy restaurants, in particular the one

where "California cuisine" was invented, Chez Panisse (see p 450).

A rare stronghold of the left-wing movement, centre of intellectual protests and unique iconoclastic campus, the Berkeley campus owes its fame to its nonconformist students, as well as the excellence of its graduates.

Although the **University of California, Berkeley ★★** has existed since 1868 thanks to famous landscape architect Frederic Law Olmsted (1822-1903; creator of New York's Central Park and Montréal's Mount Royal), it became a household name in the 1960s when the left wing affirmed itself and generated such protests as the Free Speech Movement. At the same time, the approach of the police,

The Names Project–
AIDS Memorial Quilt

The Names Project Foundation is a non-profit organization whose goal is to promote AIDS awareness and remember the victims of the disease. The idea for this project sprouted in the mind of a gay militant from San Francisco, Cleve Jones, who in 1987 began working on a quilt in honour of his best friend. Since then, it has evolved into a huge quilt made of approximately 30,000 patches, each measuring 35in by 70in (90cm by 180cm), and

each dedicated to someone who died of AIDS. The quilt is so large it would cover 11 football fields. Created as a solemn and moving tribute to AIDS victims, it is known as the Names Project–AIDS Memorial Quilt. Long established on Market Street, in the Castro district, the organization is now looking for a new home.

Its temporary offices are located at:
310 Townsend St., Suite 310
☎ *882-5500*
www.aidsquilt.org

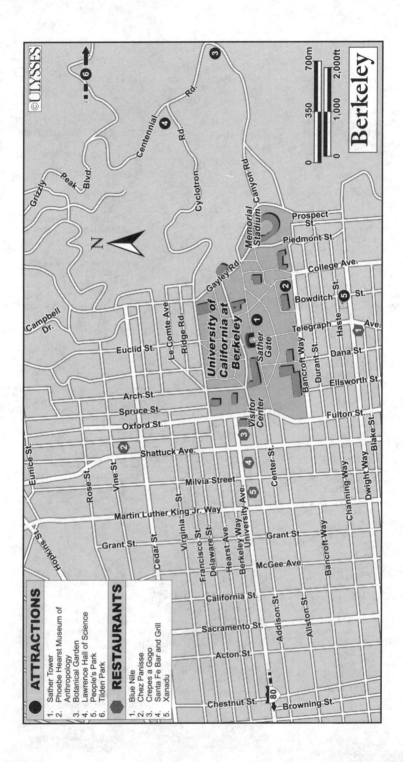

Berkeley

© ULYSSES

ATTRACTIONS

1. Sather Tower
2. Phoebe Hearst Museum of Anthropology
3. Botanical Garden
4. Lawrence Hall of Science
5. People's Park
6. Tilden Park

RESTAURANTS

1. Blue Nile
2. Chez Panisse
3. Crepes a Gogo
4. Santa Fe Bar and Grill
5. Xanadu

University of California at Berkeley

Memorial Stadium

Sather Gate

Visitor Center

Prospect St.
Piedmont St.
College Ave.
Bowditch St.
Haste St.
Telegraph Ave.
Dana St.
Ellsworth St.
Fulton St.

Gayley Rd.
Le Comte Ave.
Ridge Rd.
Euclid St.
Arch St.
Spruce St.
Oxford St.
Shattuck Ave.
Milvia Street
Martin Luther King Jr. Way
Grant St.
Grant St.
McGee Ave.
California St.
Sacramento St.
Acton St.
Chestnut St.
Browning St.

Campbell Dr.
Eunice St.
Rose St.
Vine St.
Cedar St.
Virginia St.
Francisco St.
Delaware St.
Hearst Ave.
Berkeley Way
University Ave.
Center St.
Channing Way
Dwight Way
Blake St.
Bancroft Way
Addison St.
Allston St.
Hodgkin St.

Grizzly Peak Blvd.
Centennial Rd.
Cyclotron Rd.
Canyon Rd.
Bancroft Way
Durant St.

80

700m
1,000
2,000ft
350
0

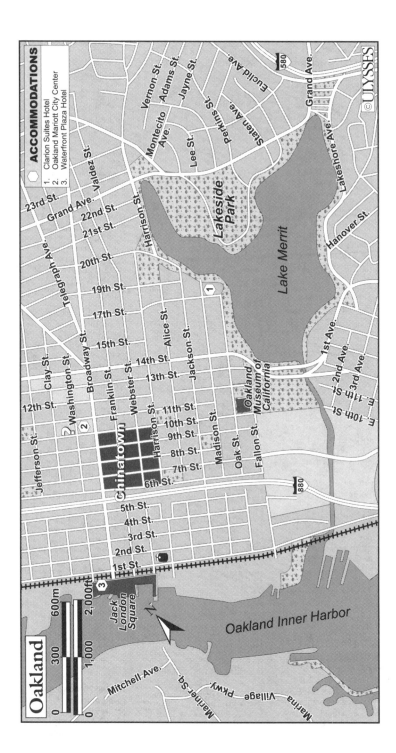

Oakland

ACCOMMODATIONS

1. Clarion Suites Hotel
2. Oakland Mariott City Center
3. Waterfront Plaza Hotel

Lake Merrit

Lakeside Park

Oakland Inner Harbor

Jack London Square

Chinatown

Oakland Museum of California

580

880

23rd St.
Grand Ave.
22nd St.
21st St.
20th St.
19th St.
17th St.
15th St.
14th St.
13th St.
12th St.
11th St.
10th St.
9th St.
8th St.
7th St.
6th St.
5th St.
4th St.
3rd St.
2nd St.
1st St.

Valdez St.
Harrison St.
Telegraph Ave.
Clay St.
Washington St.
Broadway St.
Franklin St.
Webster St.
Harrison St.
Jackson St.
Alice St.
Madison St.
Oak St.
Fallon St.
Jefferson St.

Vernon St.
Adams St.
Jayne St.
Montecito Ave.
Lee St.
Perkins St.
Staten Ave.
Euclid Ave.
Grand Ave.
Lakeshore Ave.
Hanover St.
1st Ave.
2nd Ave.
3rd Ave.
E. 10th St.
E. 11th St.

Mitchell Ave.
Mariner Sq.
Village Pkwy.
Marina

300 600m
0
1,000 2,000ft
0

who used force on students pretesting against the Vietnam War, yelling "Stop the draft!" cast a shadow on its reputation and solidified the activists' goals. Today, there is still a hint of revolution in the air, but there is a world of difference between yesterday's resistance and today's more peaceful approach.

If you have the time, take the free guided tour offered by the student staff at the **Visitor Center** *(101 University Hall or 2200 University Ave. at Oxford St.)*

The university has a student population of about 30,000, constantly coming and going in the halls and classrooms.

Telegraph Avenue ★ is directly linked to the many demonstrations that were held in the 1960s. This historic site has lost most of its anti-establishment "mood," but you will still find many bookstores, cafés and stores of that kind here, frequented by a colourful crowd of students, aging hippies, wandering musicians and the occasional "visionary."

Inspired by the clock tower of St. Mark's Square in Venice, the **Sather Tower** ★ *($2; Mon to Fri 10am to 4pm, Sat and Sun 10am to 5pm)* is 311ft (95m) high and virtually stands in the middle of the campus. An elevator brings visitors to a lookout where they can enjoy a lovely view.

The **P.A. Hearst Museum of Anthropology** ★★ *($2; Kroeber Hall; Wed to Sat 10am to 4pm, Sun 10am to 9pm)* showcases temporary exhibits on American history. The collection includes more than 625,000 pieces.

Located on the green hills behind the campus, **the Botanical Garden** ★★★ *($3; every day 9am to 4:45pm)* will please those who are interested in the plant world. The garden features many trails amidst a wide variety of species from all over the world.

The **Lawrence Hall of Science** ★ *(Centennial Dr.)* is a small museum offering a few exhibits that make it easy to learn about science, thanks to the use of multimedia. Star-gazers will want to check out the planetarium.

The following attractions are located beyond the campus.

A popular place for demonstrations, **People's Park** ★ *(bordered by Bowditch, Haste and Dwight streets)* is located three streets south of the campus, near Telegraph Avenue. In May 1969, left-wing demonstrators decided to occupy the park peacefully, but the quick-acting police squad provoked violent riots and one protestor died. A few years ago, a homeless person who lived in the park burst into the university rector's office with a machete and was shot by police. Today, many homeless people still sleep here.

Farther east from downtown, **Tilden Park** ★★ is a small green space that will please children and adults alike. Whether you choose to hop on the little steam train that travels through the sequoia trees or enjoy a few spins on the carousel, a good time is guaranteed for all. You will also find many hiking trails and bike paths, as well as a botanical garden filled with various plant species.

Oakland

Linked to San Francisco by the Bay Bridge, Oakland was named for the oak plantations that abound in the area. The city experienced an economic boom when the transcontinental railroad first appeared, which prompted a good number of the African-Americans who were building it to settle here. Today, approximately 40% of the population is African-American. The Bay Bridge was completed in 1936, finally connecting Oakland to San Francisco. The population grew once again during the Second World War when many workers found employment in its army factories and shipyards. The town attracted the world's attention in the 1960s when the Black Panthers held demonstrations here.

An industrial town where tourism does not flourish like it does in San Francisco, Oakland features one of the largest container ports in the country. The city is a cultural melting pot that is home to African-Americans, Chinese, Portuguese, Mexicans and Italians. Oakland has few tourist attractions.

Lake Merrit ★ truly stands out in these rather uninspiring surroundings. This precious lake is bordered by a few green spaces, forming the "green lung" of this industrial town, and also features a bike path that is used by cyclists and joggers alike.

The Oakland Museum of California ★★ *(1000 Oak St., ☎(510)238-3818, www.museumca.org)* houses the most important

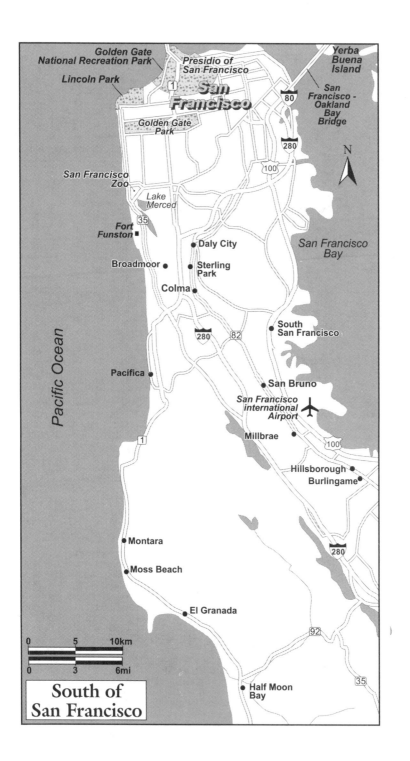

**South of
San Francisco**

The Black Panthers

With regards to emancipation movements like feminism and anti-Vietnam War demonstrations, the 1960s were a time of progress and advancement. A perfect example of this type of movement one that forcefully demanded social change, was the Black Panthers. The Black Panthers advocated human rights and the emancipation of African-Americans by using guns and adopting an intimidating attitude.

Founded in Oakland in 1966 by Huey P. Newton and Bobby Seale, the Party for Self-Defense later became the Black Panther Party. Two years later, in 1968, factions of the Black Panthers appeared in Brooklyn, Harlem and Manhattan. The movement rapidly grew and gained many partisans all over the United States. This enthusiasm scared the U.S. government, who decided to put a stop to it. A number of strong-arm raids by the federal police had a deterrent effect. As time went on, internal dissension drained the group's energy and finally brought it to and end.

collection of California-related paintings, sculptures and photographs from the early 19th century until today.

Set up on the very spot Jack London used to frequent, **Jack London Square** is not particularly interesting. Facing the sea and surrounded by restaurants, hotels and souvenir shops, it is, in fact, a tourist trap with little to offer.

Tour T: South of San Francisco

Route 1, also called the **Pacific Coast Highway**, runs along the Pacific coast and its isolated beaches, which are usually deserted because of the cold water.

Built in 1875, the **Point Montara Lighthouse ★**, overlooking the ocean from a cliff, was once a major reference point for sailors. The lighthouse has since been transformed into a youth hostel. The panorama is quite awe-inspiring, allowing visitors to admire phenomenal waves crashing upon steep cliffs.

A small village with many fishing boats, **Half Moon Bay ★** was named after the crescent bay it was built on. Located approximately 37mi (60km) from San Francisco, this village is the only one between San Francisco and Santa Cruz that is of any importance.

On Main Street, you will find Victorian homes, cafés and restaurants.

Outdoor Activities

San Francisco has more than its fair share of outdoor activities, inviting parks and idyllic gardens to satisfy nature-lovers.

Indeed, the city and its surroundings offer all kinds of opportunities to indulge in your passion for sports and fitness activities.

Parks

Golden Gate Park
bordered by Fulton St., Stanyan St., Lincoln Way and Great Hwy.
Considered the Central Park of the U.S. West Coast, Golden Gate Park is truly the "green lung" of the city. This park is one of San Francisco's largest and is great for all kinds of activities; it features tennis courts, bike paths, trails, lakes, in-line skating areas, as well as historic buildings.

Alamo Square
bordered by Fulton St., Scott St., Hayes St. and Steiner St.
Alamo Square is a lovely park that features a splendid row of six Victorian houses, nicknamed "Postcard Row." You probably guessed it: this is the most photographed row of Victorian homes in the city.

South Park
Third St. between Bryant St. and Brannan St.
A great little oasis of greenery, South Park is a

small, lovely park that has nothing to do with the biting television comedy of the same name. Bordered by a few good restaurants, it often attracts walkers taking advantage of a sunny day to enjoy an outdoor snack.

Washington Square
bordered by Union St., Powell St., Filbert St. and Stockton St.

Honouring the memory of the first president of the United States, George Washington, Washington Square's main feature is a religious structure, the St. Peter and St. Paul church. In the middle of the park stands a bronze statue of Benjamin Franklin. It is not rare to see Chinese people practicing tai chi here.

Presidio
A former military garrison founded by the Spanish in 1776, the Presidio was declared a national park in 1994. Nature-lovers will enjoy the many trails that run through the park's bucolic hills.

Tilden Park
Berkeley

Covering an area of 2,077 acres (840ha) Tilden Park is filled with attractions to satisfy just about everyone. Children can enjoy pony rides or a spin on the carousel. Adults will prefer walking through the botanical garden, enjoying a peaceful picnic near Anza Lake or taking a bike ride. This park has more than 30mi (48km) of trails. From Berkeley, a bus leaves the Bart station on a regularly basis.

Beaches

The beaches of San Francisco and its bay are not ideal for swimming. Indeed, there aren't many opportunities to swim here since, even in the middle of summer, the temperature rarely rises above 14°C (57°F) and the undertow is quite powerful. The beaches are usually reserved for walking and picnicking. But for hard-core swimmers, there are a few exceptions among the beaches listed below.

Ocean Beach *(near Cliff House)* is *not* fit for swimming; it could even be dangerous to do so. However, many visitors enjoy taking walks here and admiring the ocean.

Lands End Beach is bordered by the Lands End Trail (see p 431). This is not the best place to swim, but the beach is dotted with picnic tables and is a great place for a stroll.

Located between the Presidio and Lands End Beach, small **China Beach** will suit swimmers who are not afraid of cold water.

For its part, **Baker Beach** also offers picnic tables. This is a popular spot for family outings or for those who want to walk their dog and breathe in the sea air. The undertow here is quite powerful.

Cycling

San Francisco by bicycle? This city has obviously not been designed for cyclists, but if you've got strong calves and aren't afraid of traffic, cycling can be a good way to discover its splendid neighbourhoods and panoramas. You will encounter some infernal hills, but try to follow a zigzag route so as to reduce the steepness of your trek as much as possible. You will also notice that the city has made some efforts to create areas for cyclists.

Every Sunday at **Golden Gate Park**, a section of John F. Kennedy Drive is closed to vehicles and reserved for cyclists, in-line skaters and walkers.

Cycling enthusiasts who are looking for a bit of an escape should travel along the Marina Green and cross the Golden Gate Bridge to reach **Marin County**. Those who would rather rest their tired legs will prefer to jump aboard the ferry (with their bikes) to go to **Sausalito** or **Angel Island**.

Formerly known as Ellis Island, **Angel Island** was once a cloistered enclave for Asian immigrants whose fate was undecided. Today, it is a quiet island where visitors can enjoy cycling, hiking and even sea kayaking. You can reach it by taking the ferry at Pier 41 or Tiburon.

There is also a lovely **bike path** running along Golden Gate Park up to Cliff House.

Bike Rentals

Blazing Bikes
1095 Columbus Ave.
corner Francisco St.
☎*202-8888*
or
Pier 41
www.blazingsaddles.com
Blazing Bikes rents bicycles and organizes excursions of varying levels of difficulty from Pier 41 to Tiburon or Sausalito. Cyclists who are interested in a 23mi (37km), 5hr trek can take part in the excur-

sion that crosses the Golden Gate Bridge and explores the Muir Woods National Monument. Mountain-biking enthusiasts are not forgotten, as this place also offers trips to Mount Tamalpais.

Golf

San Francisco's golf courses will undoubtedly meet the expectations of both beginners and pros, even the most experienced.

Lincoln Park Golf
34th Ave., corner Clement St.
☎221-9911
Surrounding the Legion of Honor and offering spectacular views, Lincoln Park Golf is an 18-hole course that can be covered in a relatively short amount of time.

Presidio Golf Club
300 Finley Rd., Arguello Gate, Presidio
☎561-4653
www.presidiogolf.com
A posh historic site located south of the Golden Gate Bridge, the Presidio Golf Club was once a private club for high society. This 18-hole golf course became public in 1995 when the Presidio was declared a national park.

Harding Park Golf
Harding Rd., corner Skyline Blvd.
☎664-4690
Harding Park Golf is a lovely 27-hole course with many trees.

Tilden Park Golf Club
Grizzly Peak Rd., corner Shasta Rd., Berkeley
☎(510) 848-7373
Located on the other side of the bay, the Tilden Park Golf Club offers 18 holes that will please all golfers.

Half Moon Bay Golf Club
2000 Fairway Dr., Half Moon Bay
☎(650) 726-4438
South of San Francisco, the Half Moon Bay Golf Club has 36 holes.

Fishing

Offering fishing enthusiasts a blend of fresh and salt water, the San Francisco bay is the ideal place to enjoy the pleasures of this sport. Along the Fisherman's Wharf pier, many boats offer deep-sea fishing excursions.

Berkeley Marina Sport Center
225 University Ave., Berkeley
☎(510) 849-2727
On the other side of the bay, the Berkeley Marina Sport Center also organizes deep-sea fishing trips.

Cruises

Participating in a guided cruise is another pleasant (and affordable) way to discover San Francisco and its beautiful bay.

Here are two companies that offer mini-cruises.

The Blue and Gold Fleet
Pier 41
☎705-5555
www.blueandgoldfleet.com
The Blue and Gold Fleet offers visits to Alcatraz Island and the bay. All excursions to Alcatraz ($20; approximately 2.5hrs) leave from Pier 41. Note that only 300 people can visit Alcatraz at a time. It is highly recommended to reserve tickets in advance (a few days, even a few weeks ahead, according to the tourist season, which

lasts from June to October).

The Red and White Fleet
Pier 43-1/2
☎673-2900
⇄447-2794
www.redandwhite.com
The Red and White Fleet also organizes guided visits to the San Francisco Bay and Alcatraz Island ($20; approximately 2.5hrs).

Kayaking

California Canoe & Kayak
409 Water St., Jack London Square, Oakland
☎(510) 893-7833
⇄(510) 893-2617
www.calkayak.com
For almost 30 years now, California Canoe & Kayak has been offering beginner and advanced kayaking excursions.

Whale-Watching

Oceanic Society Expeditions
Ft. Mason Ctr., Building E
☎474-3385
Oceanic Society Expeditions offer whale-watching excursions. The best time to observe these sea mammals is from October to December.

In-line Skating

Although in-line skating has rapidly become the favourite sport of many, the streets of San Francisco are not exactly ideal for this activity. However, some areas have been specifically designed for skaters. Here are some examples.

Whether you wish to breath in some fresh air, burn some calories or simply enjoy a leisurely excursion, both beginner and expert in-line skaters will want to hit the pavement of **Golden Gate Park** (see p 428).

The **Marina Green** is bordered by a bike path shared by cyclists, joggers and in-line skaters.

In-line Skate Rentals

Marina Skate and Snowboard
2271 Chestnut St.
☎567-8400
Marina Skate and Snowboard sells and rents equipment for in-line skating and snowboarding. They also offer in-line-skating lessons.

Jogging

Jogging may very well be the only sport you can practice with a minimum of equipment! However, be sure to wear shoes that absorb shock and prevent knee and back injuries. The paved trails between the bay and the Marina Green are great for jogging.

Golden Gate Park also features lovely paths to enjoy this activity.

Hiking

Experienced hikers won't want to miss the **Lands End Trail**. This trail begins near Camino del Mar, in Lincoln Park, snakes through the hills and a cypress forest and ends at the Cliff House parking lot. The vistas from this trail are absolutely breathtaking.

Sailing and Windsurfing

ABK Windsurfing School
101 Casa Buena Dr., Suite F
Corte Madera
☎927-8835
≈927-7634
info@abksports.com
The ABK Windsurfing School has been offering courses for more than 15 years. The instructors here are extremely competent and friendly.

Hawaiian Chieftain Sailing Charters
3020 Bridgeway, Suite 266,
Sausalito
CA 94965
☎331-3214
www.hawaiianchieftain.com
Hawaiian Chieftain Sailing Charters owns a boat modelled after a 103ft, 1790 sailboat, but with a cutting-edge, 20th-century design. It only fits 47 passengers. This excursion offers beautiful views of the San Francisco Bay.

Accommodations

San Francisco's hotel scene offers something for everyone—from no-frills boarding houses with shared bathrooms and charming Victorian-style bed and breakfasts, to standard establishments, well-known chain hotels and ostentatious luxury accommodations exuding splendour and opulence.

What's more, the plethora of motels along the highways (outside of town) provides travellers with rooms at affordable rates, among the cheapest in the country. Keep in mind, however, that the city's hotel industry is riding high. Indeed, San Francisco is not the place for those who are short on cash, and decent hotels with rooms for less than $100 a night are few and far between.

The bed-and-breakfast formula is very popular in San Francisco. This type of establishment is often found in lovely, harmoniously decorated Victorian houses that generally offer fewer than 10 rooms (usually non-smoking).

San Francisco Reservations
360 22nd St., Suite 300, Oakland
CA 94612
☎*(510) 628-4450*
☎*800-677-1500*
≈*(510) 628-9025*
sfr@hotelres.com
San Francisco Reservations provides information about many area hotels and takes care of confirming your reservations.

The *www.hotelres.com* Web site specializes in San Francisco hotel reservations.

Where to Stay

As San Francisco is divided into different districts, it's important to decide which neighbourhood you wish to stay in. Most hotels are located around Union Square, but the city's top-notch public-transportation system (BART) makes it fairly easy to get from one district to another.

Union Square

Hostel at Union Square (AYH)
$
312 Mason St., between Geary St. and O'Farrell St., CA 94102
☎ *788-5604*
= *788-3023*
A bivouac prized by cash-strapped wayfarers, Hostel at Union Square (AYH) rents out shared rooms offering basic, bare-bones comfort. There is, however, a common room in which travellers can swap travel stories and watch videos.

Adelaide Inn
$$-$$$
5 Isadora Duncan Court, between Post St. and Geary St., CA 94102
☎ *441-2261*
= *441-0161*
Tucked away at the end of a dead-end street, the Adelaide Inn features quiet rooms offering basic comfort and shabby furnishings, but at low prices. Perfect for budget travellers oblivious to their lodgings' interior decor.

Halcyon
$$-$$$
K
649 Jones St., between Post St. and Geary St., CA 94102
☎ *929-8033 or 800-627-2396*
reservations@halcyonsf.com
Formerly known as Brady Acres, the Halcyon Hotel is just the place for those planning on an extended stay. The 25 rooms of various sizes come with a kitchenette with micro-wave oven, coffee maker, toaster and fridge. The establishment is located three blocks west of

Union Square, right near the Powell Street cable-car line.

Petite Auberge
$$$ bkfst incl.
®
863 Bush St., between Taylor St. and Mason St., CA 94108
☎ *928-6000 or 800-365-3004*
= *673-7214*
www.foursisters.com
As its name suggests, the Petite Auberge looks like a small French inn, with a decor featuring a bunch of small teddy bears. Of various sizes, the 26 non-smoking rooms with flowered wallpaper feature a wooden armoire and a cute teddy bear resting comfortably on each bed. Honeymooners who choose to stay here will no doubt opt for the suite with a whirlpool bath; what's more, they'll be treated to a bottle of champagne, chocolates and still more teddy bears.

White Swan Inn
$$$ bkfst incl.
845 Bush St., between Taylor St. and Mason St., CA 94108
☎ *775-1755 or 800-999-9570*
= *775-5717*
www.foursisters.com
A notch in comfort above its sister establishment, the Petite Auberge, the White Swan Inn is a cozy place that exudes British—rather than French—charm and ambiance. Little teddy

bears are just as prevalent here and found in equal abundance in each of the 26 rooms of various sizes, stylishly appointed with dark-wood furnishings. Guests graciously receive the morning paper at their door and are served afternoon tea with homemade biscuits.

King George Hotel
$$$
334 Mason St., CA 94102
☎ *781-5050*
= *391-6976*
A mere glance at the King George Hotel's slender Victorian facade conveys that this establishment is steeped in an English atmosphere. The rooms are comfortable, if lacklustre, but rented out at "reasonable" rates considering its proximity to Union Square. Courteous staff.

Hotel Diva
$$$-$$$$ bkfst incl.
ℜ
440 Geary St., CA 94104
☎ *885-0200 or 800-553-1900*
= *885-3268*
www.hoteldiva.com
A member of the Personality Hotels on Union Square group, Diva offers 111 ultra-modern, cool-looking rooms that are dead ringers for those of a hip SoHo hotel in Manhattan. What's more, each features a laptop-computer data port. A small business centre is available to those without a laptop. Room service is provided by the kitchen of the adjacent restaurant, California Pizza Kitchen. Warm welcome.

Hotel Monaco
$$$$
ℜ, △, ®
501 Geary St., CA 94102
☎ *292-0100 or 800-214-4220*
= *292-0111*
www.monaco-sf.com
One of the city's new trendy addresses, Hotel Monaco features a magnifi-

cent marble staircase that leads to a series of colourful, rather small but lovely rooms, painstakingly decorated with an Oriental touch. Among the facilities that will undoubtedly please guests are the sauna and whirlpool, as well as a wonderful restaurant, the Grand Cafe (see p 441).

Hotel Union Square
$$$$ bkfst incl.
114 Powell St., CA 94102
☎397-3000 or 800-553-1900
⇌885-3268
www.personalityhotels.com
Hotel Union Square is also a member of Personality Hotels on Union Square, but offers a quintessential San Franciscan atmosphere. Some of the hotel's brick walls still bear the blackened marks of the fire that followed the 1906 earthquake. It's also said that Dashiell Hammett wrote part of his detective novel *The Maltese Falcon* in one of the hotel's rooms.

Kensington Park
$$$$-$$$$$
ℜ
450 Post St., CA 94102
☎788-6400
⇌399-9484
www.personalityhotels.com
Another very British, conservative establishment, Kensington Park is right near Union Square. The 87 Queen Anne–style rooms offer views of Union Square or Nob Hill. Moreover, guests are offered complimentary tea and sherry while treated to classical music that is played by a pianist who tickles the ivories while chatting about life's ups and downs. The hotel will also delight gourmets, as it is home to the top-notch Farallon restaurant (see p 441).

 Hotel Triton
$$$$-$$$$$
342 Grant Ave., corner Bush St. CA 94108
☎394-0500
⇌394-0555
www.hotel-tritonsf.com
Fans of unconventional hotels with atypical decor must make a mental note of the Triton, ideally located at the gates to Chinatown. The resolutely avant-garde, contemporary lobby features whimsical Art Deco–style furnishings with rich, jewel-like colours. The decor of the rooms is along the same lines, and environmentally minded guests can opt for one of the Eco Rooms, which offer filtered water and biodegradable hair and skin products. Those who want to treat themselves can stay in one of the different, evocatively themed suites, like the Jerry Garcia Suite.

Prescott Hotel
$$$$$ bkfst incl.
ℜ
545 Post St., CA 94102
☎563-0303 or 800-283-7322
⇌563-6831
www.prescotthotel.com
Just two blocks from Union Square, the chic Prescott Hotel houses 164 elegantly appointed rooms, offering each guest a refined setting. Those who wish to eat in their room can choose among the dishes featured on the menu of the establishment's famous restaurant, Postrio—and this, without having to beg the maitre d' for last-minute reservations. In short, the comfort, location and services offered by this top-of-the-line hotel as well as the extreme friendliness of the staff encourages a fair share of well-off visitors to make this their home away from home whenever they're in San Francisco.

Clift Hotel
$$$$$
ℜ
495 Geary St., corner Taylor St. CA 94102
☎800-652-5438
☎/⇌931-7417
www.Clifthotel.com
Two blocks from Union Square stands the Clift Hotel, owned by none other than Ian Schrager, the king of cool, ultra-hip, high-profile hotels. Schrager also operates the Paramount in Manhattan and the Delano in South Beach, two renowned establishments designed by Philippe Starck. Rumours are flying thick and fast that Starck will once again let his unbridled imagination run wild to give the Clift Hotel a makeover. In the meantime, the reception area exudes classical elegance, with decorated woodwork gleaming in the glow of chandeliers. The fabulous and aptly named Redwood Room (see p 453) is unquestionably one of the hotel's notable assets, displaying quintessential Art Deco splendour. All rooms feature a minibar, an in-room safe and a modem data-port connection.

 Pan Pacific Hotel
$$$$$
ℜ
500 Post St., corner Mason St. CA 94102
☎771-8600 or 800-533-6465
⇌398-0267
Located a few blocks west of Union Square, the Pan Pacific embodies all the services and facilities business and leisure travellers have the right to expect of a luxury hotel. Take one of the panoramic elevators to the hotel's reception area, graced with a beautiful contemporary fountain sculpture artistically displayed alongside a fireplace, to reach the entrance to a top-notch gour-

met restaurant, the Pacific (see p 441). The large, elegantly decorated rooms are equipped with a minibar, fax machine, data-port modem connection and in-room safe, as well as bathrooms that are both spacious and well ventilated. Gracious staff.

Westin St. Francis
$$$$$
ℜ
355 Powell St., CA 94102
☎*397-7000*
≈*774-0124*

A San Francisco landmark since 1904, the Westin St. Francis is now considered one of the city's great historic places, both for its architecture from days gone by and for the number of notorious people it has hosted over the years. However, much like many other buildings erected here in the early 20th century, the hotel was unfortunately badly damaged by the fire caused by the 1906 earthquake. It has since been admirably well restored and now ostentatiously occupies the whole west side of Union Square. In 1972, panoramic elevators were added to the hotel, providing guests with heart-stopping climbs and striking bird's-eye views of San Francisco's spectacular urban landscape. Crowned heads of state and transient celebrities never fail to stop here. The 1,189 rooms unfortunately prove to be somewhat lacking with regard to current standards of quality, but are comfortable and well equipped nonetheless.

Chinatown

Grant Plaza Hotel
$$-$$$
465 Grant Ave., CA 94108
☎*434-3883 or 800-472-6899*
≈*434-3886*

Located right in the middle of Chinatown, the Grant Plaza Hotel is a decent establishment, suitably comfortable and genuine, but lacking in any extras. Perfect for those who plan on exploring the city and not spending their days inside.

The Financial District and the Embarcadero

Mandarin Oriental
$$$$$ bkfst incl.
ℜ, ☺
222 Sansome St., CA 94104
☎*276-9888*
≈*433-0289*
www.mandarin-oriental.com

Occupying the 11 top floors of the California Center (one of the tallest skyscrapers in San Francisco), the Mandarin Oriental is just the place for those unafraid of heights and with a high-limit credit card. This deluxe establishment has a mere 60 rooms simply decorated in the Oriental style, but lacking in absolutely nothing: minibar, cable TV, voice mail, modem hookup and even silk slippers. But the rooms' main asset is the stunning, sweeping views they offer of the city and the bay. What's more, they feature gleaming bathrooms whose windows allow guests to admire the skyline while brushing their teeth. The on-site business centre will meet the needs of business trav-

ellers. There is also a fitness centre on the premises.

Hyatt Regency
$$$$$
ℜ, ☺
5 Embarcadero Center, CA 94111
☎*398-2567*
≈*398-1234*
www.hyatt.com

The Hyatt Regency is more than a mere link in this international chain. The spacious, comfortable and well-equipped rooms truly conform to the quality standards of high-class hotels, but the establishment indisputably stands out for its magnificent 17-storey atrium embellished with a profusion of plants and trees. Standing in the middle of this "garden," you eyes will be inexorably drawn to the shafts of the panoramic elevators that lead not only to the rooms, but to a revolving rooftop restaurant, the Equinox (see p 443), which makes a full rotation every 40min. A fitness room is available to those looking to tone up.

Sheraton Palace Hotel
$$$$$
☺, ℜ, ≈
2 New Montgomery St.
corner Market St., CA 94105
☎*512-1111 or 800-325-3535*
≈*543-0671*

At the Sheraton Palace, the word "palace" takes on its full meaning. Inaugurated with great fanfare in 1875, the hotel was once on the list of establishments to which were fixed qualifiers such as "sumptuous, gleaming, chic, opulent and ostentatious." Unfortunately, it was razed during the fire provoked by the 1906 quake, though quickly rebuilt in a more sober, classic style. Between 1989 and 1991, the owners poured $150 million into the place so that it could continue to compete with the heavyweights of the industry. Among the celebrities who have stayed here are writer Oscar Wilde and actress Sarah Bernhardt. Although decorated without any great originality and seemingly soulless, the 550-odd well-equipped rooms will suit business people to a tee. Still, be sure to dine at the extraordinary Garden Court restaurant (see p 442), crowned with a magnificent stained-glass dome. An indoor swimming pool, rooms equipped for people with disablities, a business centre and exercise room complete the facilities.

North Beach

Green Tortoise Hostel
$ bkfst incl.
494 Broadway, corner Kearny St.
CA 94133
☎ *834-1000*
www.greentortoise.com/
sanfrancisco.hostel.2.html
hostel@greentortoise.com
Well situated, safe and cheap, the Green Tortoise is a popular stopping place among budget travellers. The hostel also serves as a travel agency and organizes tours in and around the city.

Hotel Bohème
$$-$$$
444 Columbus Ave., between Vallejo St. and Green St., CA 94133
☎ *433-9111*
= *362-6292*
www.hotelboheme.com
Like the beatniks of the 1950s who refused to conform to the rigid standards of the time, Hotel Bohème is the antithesis of major international-chain hotels that primarily cater to business travellers. Well located near Washington Square, the place offers some 15 non-smoking rooms that are well furnished but steeped in the

somewhat passé bohemian atmosphere of a bygone era.

Nob Hill

Nob Hill Lambourne
$$$$$ bkfst incl.
⊚, ℜ
725 Pine St., between Powell St. and Stockton St., CA 94108
☎ *433-2287 or 800-274-8466*
= *433-0975*
Making the Nob Hill Lambourne a home away from home is a judicious choice for business people looking to get pampered. The rooms are equipped with all the usual gadgets, including an in-room safe, fax machine, modem hookup, VCR, minibar and voice-mail service. Some rooms also feature a whirlpool bath.

The Huntington Hotel
$$$$$
ℜ
1075 California St., CA 94108
☎ *474-5400 or 800-227-4683*
= *474-6227*
Formerly a 1920s' apartment complex, the Huntington Hotel gradually changed its vocation to become the luxury family-owned and operated establishment it is today. The rooms feature windows that actually open (a rare treat in San Francisco!), providing gorgeous panoramic views of the city and its surrounding area. The suites are a haven for high-ranking dignitaries and public figures, prized by all those who seek a little privacy and anonymity in the heart of the city. The hotel's excellent The Big Four restaurant (see p 444) will satisfy business people looking to woo clients while treating themselves to a good meal.

Fairmont Hotel
$$$$$
ℜ
950 Mason St., corner California St.
CA 94108
☎ *772-5000 or 800-527-4727*
= *772-5086*
sanfrancisco@fairmont.com
The Fairmont Hotel's sumptuous, polished lobby rarely fails to impress. Indeed, your gaze will immediately fall on the gleaming floor, then on the dizzying columns and exquisitely decorated ceiling. In early 2000, the rooms were given a major facelift in order to rival the lobby in splendour.

Renaissance Stanford Court Hotel
$$$$$
ℜ
905 California St., corner Powell St.
CA 94108
☎ *989-3500*
= *391-0513*
sales@stanfordcourt.net
The Renaissance Stanford Court Hotel also boasts a splendid lobby. You can contemplate fine antiques and a trickling fountain crowned by a spectacular Tiffany-style glass dome. The establishment houses 393 charming, well-appointed rooms, and offers complimentary car service to downtown.

Ritz-Carlton
$$$$$
ℜ, ≈, △
600 Stockton St., corner California St., CA 94108
☎ *296-7465*
= *296-8261*
The Ritz-Carlton's magnificent neoclassical facade is more like that of a huge museum than a hotel, however prestigious and renowned. Moreover, once inside, visitors will be further amazed by the lobby's museum-quality paintings, antiques and works of art. The spacious and comfortable rooms afford great

views of the city. The hotel also offers a wide range of services that will undoubtedly please its "dear clients," including an indoor swimming pool, a fitness centre, sauna, gourmet restaurant and business centre. Last but not least, the faultlessly amiable and gracious staff provides guests with the highest level of personal service.

Fisherman's Wharf

 San Remo
$$-$$$
sb
2337 Mason St., corner Chestnut St.
CA 94133
☎776-8688 or 800-352-7366
≈776-2811
Unquestionably offering one of the best deals in town, the San Remo will please those keeping a tight rein on their travel budget but still in search of comfortable accommodations. The rooms are a little small, but clean and well kept. The only drawback is the shared bathrooms, though they are spotless and equipped with all the conveniences you may require.

Marriott
$$$
☺, ℜ
1250 Columbus Ave.
CA 94133
☎775-7555
≈474-2099
The Marriott belongs to the world-famous chain of the same name. The 285 pleasantly decorated rooms come with a minibar, coffee maker, iron and ironing board. A fitness centre is available for those looking to stay in shape.

The Marina

Hostelling International–San Francisco–Fisherman's Wharf (AYH)
$
K
Fort Mason, Building 240
CA 94123-1303
☎771-7277
≈771-1468
This hostel is the perfect stop for wayfarers seeking a quiet room with a lovely view of the Golden Gate Bridge (weather permitting). Guests who wish to prepare their own meals have access to a kitchen.

Edward II Inn
$$-$$$$ bkfst incl.
3155 Scott St., corner Lombard St.
CA 94123
☎922-3000 or 800-473-2846
≈931-5784
edwardII@gateway.net
Located a few minutes' walking distance from San Francisco Bay, the Edward II Inn offers small, simple, no-frills rooms as well as more spacious, tastefully appointed suites spread out over three floors.

Motel Capri
$$-$$$
2015 Greenwich St.
corner Buchanan St., CA 94123
☎346-4667
≈346-3256
Motel Capri offers low-priced rooms devoid of all

but the necessary comforts, but perfectly suitable for travellers only planning a short stay.

Pacific Heights

Jackson Court
$$$-$$$$
2198 Jackson St., corner Buchanan St.
CA 94115
☎929-7670
≈929-1405
Located in a slightly remote district in relation to Union Square, the Jackson Court is a 19th-century mansion converted into an enchanting bed and breakfast that plainly advertizes itself as a smoke-free establishment. The place only rents out 10 quiet rooms, pervaded with faded, old-world charm that will doubtless please travellers inclined to be nostalgic for a distant, bygone era.

Japantown

Hotel Majestic
$$
1500 Sutter St., corner Gough St.
CA 94109
☎441-1100 or 800-869-8966
≈673-7331
When it first opened in the early 20th century, Hotel Majestic ranked among the city's most beautiful hotels. Although the place has certainly lost some its former prestige, it offers a perfect romantic hideaway in its rooms furnished with tastefully chosen and arranged antiques. Moreover, most rooms have a fireplace.

The Civic Center, the Tenderloin and Hayes Valley

Aida Hotel
$$
pb/sb
1087 Market St., CA 94102
☎*863-4141*
Located right in front of a central-route bus stop, but in a somewhat sketchy neighbourhood, the Aida Hotel is an inexpensive option with fairly spacious but very sparsely decorated rooms. Perfect for budget-conscious travellers.

Renoir Hotel
$$-$$$
ℜ
45 McAllister St., corner Market St. CA 94102
☎*626-5200 or 800-576-3388*
≈*626-5581*
www.renoirhotel.com
Located at the corner of McAllister and Market streets, the Renoir Hotel seems a haven of peace or an enclave in the middle of this disreputable district. What's more, rates here are more affordable than around Union Square. The atmosphere that pervades the place is miles away from that of an international chain hotel. Featuring a reproduction of a painting by the hotel's famous namesake hanging above each bed, the Victorian-style rooms are large and comfortable, though modestly and archaically decorated. Then again, they draw a young, globetrotting or hard-up clientele. The lobby is flanked by a great little Victorian-looking dining room. The fairly young staff is affable.

Abigail Hotel
$$$ bkfst incl.
ℜ
246 McAllister St., between Hyde St. and Larkin St., CA 94102
☎*861-9728 or 800-243-6510*
≈*861-5848*
Located a stone's throw from city hall and the opera, ballet and symphony, the Abigail exudes old-fashioned charm, but offers comfortable, simply decorated rooms. The hotel also houses one of the best vegetarian restaurants in town, the Millennium (see p 446).

🌴 Phoenix Hotel
$$$
ℜ
601 Eddy St., corner Larkin St. CA 94109
☎*776-1380*
≈*885-3109*
Once a simple, slightly dreary motel, the now-hip and funky Phoenix Hotel is definitely a favourite with theatre and rock'n'roll stars. Arranged in a half circle around a palm-tree-lined swimming pool, the meticulous, comfortable rooms sport tropical colours and bamboo furnishings. The suites are generally occupied by celebrities with well-padded wallets. The hotel is also home to the ultra-trendy Backflip bar.

🌴 Inn at The Opera
$$$
ℜ
333 Fulton St., CA 94102
☎*863-8400 or 800-325-2708*
≈*861-0821*
The former haunt of baritones and tenors, the Inn at The Opera is strategically located a short distance from the city's performing-arts venues. These days, though some rooms still shelter opera singers, the clientele is varied. The 48 rooms, stocked with a minibar, microwave oven and queen-size bed, provide all the creature comforts sought by travellers.

Hotel Metropolis
$$$-$$$$ bkfst incl.
25 Mason St., CA 94102
☎*775-4600 or 800-553-1900*
≈*885-3268*
www.hotelmetropolis.com
The Metropolis's front door is hard to locate as it isn't right on Mason Street, but rather at the back, past the parking lot. The decor of the 10-storey hotel's 105 rooms is inspired by the elements: water, earth, wind and fire. There's even a small feng-shui room catering to Zen-Buddhist guests.

Haight-Ashbury

The Upper Haight

🌴 The Red Victorian
$$-$$$ bkfst incl.
pb/sb
1665 Haight St., CA 94117
☎*864-1978*
≈*863-3293*
www.redvic.com
For all those with still-fresh memories of the "summer of love," the Red Victorian is a near-symbolic place in the former hippy district. Both a colourful bed and breakfast and contemporary-art gallery, the establishment is located near Golden Gate Park and offers 18 mismatched, vividly themed rooms (most of which don't have a private bathroom) that are sure to please flower children and those looking to relive the San Francisco Sound's heyday.

The Lower Haight

Archbishop's Mansion
$$$-$$$$ bkfst incl.
1000 Fulton St., CA 94117
☎ *563-7872 or 800-543-5820*
⇌ *885-3193*
www.archbishopsmansion.com
Located northeast of Alamo Square, Archbishop's Mansion is unquestionably one of the city's most inviting and charming bed and breakfasts. The 15 rooms of varying sizes exude a warm cachet created by tasteful antiques carefully scattered about. Moreover, you can even have breakfast in the privacy of your own room.

Alamo Square Inn
$$$$ bkfst incl.
719 Scott St., CA 94117
☎ *922-2055 or 800-345-9888*
⇌ *931-1304*
www.alamoinn.com
Bordering the northwest side of Alamo Square, this inn is made up of two adjoining (Queen Anne– and Tudor–style) Victorian houses, the sum total now transformed into a bed and breakfast. Guests are graciously offered complimentary wine in the afternoon.

South of Market (SoMa)

Globe Hostel/Inter-Club
$
pb/sb
10 Hallam Place, corner Folsom St. CA 94103
☎ *431-0540*
⇌ *431-3286*
A no-frills "crash pad" located in the very heart of the city's night time action, the Globe Hostel/Inter-Club rents out (shared) rooms with Spartan comfort. Private rooms are also available for about twice the price. Among the perks offered to guests are

a pool table and laundry service.

San Francisco Marriott
$$$$
ℜ, ≈, ◔, ⊛
55 Fourth St., between Market St. and Mission St., CA 94103
☎ *896-1600 or 800-228-9290*
⇌ *567-0391*
www.marriott.com
Ideally situated a stone's throw from the Convention Center, the San Francisco Marriott Hotel is hardly a unanimous favourite with architects. When construction work was completed in 1989, spiteful tongues delighted in comparing the hotel to a common parking meter or a broken-down jukebox. Be that as it may, this 39-storey mammoth of the hotel industry houses some 1,500 spacious, well-equipped rooms with beautiful city views. Guests have access to an indoor swimming pool, whirlpool and fitness centre. Rooms specially designed for travellers with disabilities are also available.

Castro

Black Stallion
$$-$$$ bkfst incl.
635 Castro St., corner 19th St. CA 94114
☎ *863-0131*
Set up in a Victorian house, the Black Stallion is a bed and breakfast that wins the favour of the gay "Levi's & leather" crowd. The rooms are simply decorated, but comfortable.

Willow Inn
$$-$$$ bkfst incl.
710 14th St., corner Market St. CA 94114
☎ *431-4770*
⇌ *431-5295*
www.willowssf.com
The Willow Inn is very conveniently located near

public-transportation routes. The hotel occupies a venerable Edwardian house dating from 1903, and each room is furnished with antiques and stocked with bathrobes. A hearty breakfast helps you start the day off on the right foot.

The Parker House
$$$-$$$$ bkfst incl.
520 Church St., CA 94114
☎ *621-3222*
⇌ *621-4139*
A charming Edwardian house located in the very heart of the Castro district, the Parker House features 10 inviting and well-equipped rooms. The place also offers a business centre and free parking.

Mission

Dolores Park Inn
$$-$$$
3641 17th St., CA 94114
☎ /⇌ *621-0482*
Conveniently located near the bars and Dolores Park, this inn stands on a fairly quiet street. Individually decorated and attractive, the establishment offers antique-laden rooms.

The San Francisco Area

Near the Airport

Embassy Suites San Francisco
$$$$
◔, ℜ, ≈
150 Anza Blvd., Burlingame CA 94010
☎ *(650) 342-4600*
☎ *800-362-2779*
sales@embassysfo.com
Located a few kilometres south of San Francisco International Airport, the Embassy Suites San Francisco features rooms set out around an attractive nine-storey atrium with waterfalls trickling in a

tropical environment. You'll want to take advantage of the indoor swimming pool, sauna or whirlpool before catching your flight.

Sausalito (Marin County)

Casa Madrona
$$$$ bkfst incl.
ℜ
801 Bridgeway, CA 94965
☎*(415) 332-0502*
☎*800-567-9524*
≈*(415) 332-2537*
www.casam.com
Perched on a sloping hill, Casa Madrona is a luxury hotel housed in a venerable Victorian home built in 1885. The place offers 30 rooms, most of which afford magnificent views of San Francisco Bay. Some also feature a fireplace.

Inn Above Tide
$$$$ bkfst incl.
30 El Portal, CA 94965
☎*(415) 332-9535*
≈*(415) 332-6714*
The Inn Above Tide is one of the most luxurious hotels in the area. Located steps away from the ferry dock (a 25min crossing to San Francisco), this hotel will please those in search of quiet, comfortable accommodations. All rooms offer striking views of San Francisco Bay and most have a balcony and fireplace. The rooms are also spacious and attractive, providing all the necessary comfort for a pleasant stay. Moreover, they also feature a laptop data-port connection. The multilingual staff speaks French, German and Spanish in addition to English. A small gem by the bay, the Inn Above Tide offers its guests a California-wine reception every night.

Hotel Sausalito
$$$$
16 El Portal, CA 94965
☎*(415) 332-0700*
≈*(415) 332-8788*
Inaugurated in 1915 and renovated in 1996, Hotel Sausalito is located close to the ferry boarding dock. The establishment offers 16 warmly coloured rooms distributed over two floors.

East Bay

Berkeley

Berkeley & Oakland Bed and Breakfast Network
☎*(510) 547-6380*
www.bbonline.com/ca/berkeley-oakland
The Berkeley & Oakland Bed and Breakfast Network is an association encompassing several establishments of this type, most of which are nonsmoking.

University of California at Berkeley
Department of Housing and Services
2401 Bowditch St., Berkeley, CA 94720
☎*510-642-4108*
www.housing.berkeley.edu
In the summer, out-of-towners can rent a room in the residence halls of the University of California at Berkeley.

YMCA
$
2601 Allston Way, corner Milvia St. CA 94720
☎*(510) 848-6800*
While the YMCA certainly isn't the most comfortable place in town, it offers cheap accommodations that will satisfy the needs of budget travellers. The (shared) rooms are safe and relatively clean.

Berkeley Travelodge
$-$$
1820 University Ave., CA 94703
The Berkeley Travelodge is affordable and well situated near the BART station (about 20min from downtown San Francisco). The rooms, while hardly spectacular, provide all the necessary comfort.

Rose Garden Inn
$$$-$$$$ bkfst incl.
2740 Telegraph Ave., CA 94705
☎*(510) 549-2145*
☎*800-992-9005*
≈*(510) 549-1085*
info@rosegardeninn.com
The Rose Garden Inn is an inviting bed and breakfast.

Oakland

Oakland Marriot City Center
$$$-$$$$
≈, ☉, ℜ
1001 Broadway, CA 94607
☎*(510) 451-4000*
≈*(510) 835-3466*
www.marriott.com
Linked to the Oakland Convention Center, the 21-storey Oakland Marriot City Center offers 479 rooms fitted with double-glazed windows to stifle street noise. A fitness centre, whirlpool and outdoor swimming pool complete the facilities. The hotel is also located right near the BART (which takes you to San Francisco in 15min).

Clarion Suites Hotel
$$$$
K
1800 Madison St., CA 94612
☎*(510) 832-2300*
≈*(510) 832-7150*
Located on Lake Merritt, the six-storey Art Deco–style Clarion Suites Hotel offers 50 suites with kitchenette and laptop modem hookup.

Waterfront Plaza Hotel
$$$$-$$$$$
≈, ℜ, ⊘, ⌂
10 Washington St., Jack London
Square, CA 94607
☎*(510) 836-3800*
☎*800-729-3638*
⇝*(510) 729-3668*
The Waterfront Plaza Hotel
ranks among the city's
high-end establishments,
with rooms that provide all
the creature comforts worthy of this category. A
sauna, fitness centre,
swimming pool and busi-
ness centre round out the
facilities. The hotel is strategically located near the
San Francisco-bound ferry-
boarding dock and down-
town Oakland.

South of San Francisco

Montara

Pigeon Point Lighthouse
$
K
210 Pigeon Point Rd., corner Hwy. 1
CA 94060
☎*(650) 879-0633*
☎*800-909-4776*
Located about 6mi (10km)
south of Pescadero, the
Pigeon Point Lighthouse is
a favourite with budget
travellers. In addition to
inexpensive shared rooms,
the place features a hot
tub set up in the former
semaphore. Those who
wish to stay here anytime
between January and Sep-
tember are strongly ad-
vised to make reservations.
Access to the kitchen.

Point Montara Lighthouse
$
K
16th St., corner Hwy. 1
P.O. Box 737, Montara
CA 94037-9999
☎*(650) 728-7177*
☎*800-909-4776*
Located about 4mi (6km)
north of Half Moon Bay,
the Point Montara Light-

house rents out low-priced
(shared) rooms. Private
rooms are also available at
a slightly higher rate. The
establishment offers guests
access to the kitchen and
luggage-storage facilities.
Laundry service.

Half Moon Bay

Old Thyme Inn
$$-$$$ bkfst incl.
779 Main St., CA 94019-1924
☎*(650) 726-1616*
☎*800-720-4277*
⇝*(650) 726-6394*
www.oldthymeinn.com
The Old Thyme Inn is a
venerable 1898 Victorian
house that has been
turned into a charming
little bed and breakfast.
Some rooms feature a
fireplace and whirlpool
bath.

Mill Rose Inn Bed and Breakfast
$$$-$$$$ bkfst incl.
615 Mill St., CA 94019-1726
☎*(650) 726-8750*
☎*800-900-7673*
⇝*(650) 726-3031*
www.millroseinn.com
For a peaceful, romantic
stay, check into the Mill
Rose Inn Bed and Break-
fast, set amidst perfectly
bucolic gardens. The es-
tablishment features rooms
graced with antiques and
floral arrangements. Visi-
tors who can afford to
loosen their purse strings
can opt for a room with
whirlpool bath. Compli-
mentary wine and cheese
offered every afternoon.

Half Moon Bay Lodge
$$$$ bkfst incl.
2400 Hwy. 1, CA 94019
☎*(650) 726-9000*
☎*800-368-2468*
⇝*(650) 726-7951*
www.woodsidehotels.com
Located south of Half
Moon Bay, the Half Moon
Bay Lodge offers 80 spa-
cious, opulent rooms en-
hanced with luxury fea-
tures. Several rooms also

feature a fireplace. The
hotel, made up of
hacienda-like orange-
roofed buildings, offers all
the services worthy of a
major hotel, including a
swimming pool, sauna and
exercise room.

Restaurants

Few cities offer such a
large variety of delectable
food specialties as San
Francisco.

Whether you are on the
lookout for Californian
fusion cuisine or purely
exotic (Chinese, Italian,
Ethiopian, Indian, Thai,
Vietnamese, French, Medi-
terranean, Japanese, Mexi-
can) dishes, or a more
typical, delicious, juicy
steak or reassuring comfort
food, you will no doubt
find something to delight
your taste buds in San
Francisco—guaranteed.
Here, master chefs elo-
quently express their art
by striking a subtle bal-
ance of spices in order to
create a wide range of
well-prepared and mouth-
watering dishes.

Union Square

Café de la Presse
$
352 Grant Ave.
☎*398-2680*
Located next to the gates
to Chinatown, the Café de
la Presse serves pasta, fish,
spirits, beer and coffee.
Breakfast portions are
generous. The restaurant
offers a vast selection of
international newspapers
and magazines. If you are
looking for something
upscale, a restaurant is
located adjacent to the
café (*$$; 469 Bush St.,* ☎*249-*

San Francisco and Surroundings

0900). It features a more generous menu and offers conserve of duck, crab ravioli, *croque-monsieurs* and *croque-madames*.

Café Claude
$$
7 Claude Lane, between Grant Ave. and Kearny St.
☎392-3515
www.cafeclaude.com
Located in a small lane near the gates to Chinatown, the Café Claude is the meeting place of expatriate Europeans. It features a bistro-like setting and its typically French menu offers a variety of mouth-watering dishes, ranging from merguez sausages to rib steak. Jazz musicians provide pleasant entertainment and enhance the dining experience.

Wolfgang Puck Café
$$
170 O'Farrell St., corner Stockton St.
The Wolfgang Puck Café is the latest venture of the renowned chef. Visitors who have a weakness for California cuisine and who want to satisfy hunger pangs between shopping purchases should head for this café, located in Macy's basement. Its luxury cafeteria style allows customers to get a quick meal, as they first make their choice at the counter and then pay at the cash.

Jeanne d'Arc
$$-$$$
715 Bush St., corner Mason St.
☎421-3154
Located in the basement of the Cornell Hotel de France is one of San Francisco's most original and least known dining rooms, the Jeanne d'Arc. The restaurant really wears its name well—you could swear you were dining in a theme museum devoted to the era of Joan of Arc, as you are lulled by French music. The obvi-ously French-inspired cuisine is delicious.

Compass Rose
$$-$$$
355 Powell St., between Post St. and Geary St.
☎774-0167
Located inside the famous Westin St. Francis, the Compass Rose seems frozen in 1904. In a magnificent by panelled dining room, which will impress you immediately, customers enjoy dishes featuring a medley of flavours such as the beef medallion or smoked salmon sandwich, and sip goblets of bubbling champagne.

Farallon
$$$
450 Post St., between Mason St. and Powell St.
☎956-6969
www.farallonrestaurant.com
Once you open the doors to fascinating Farallon, you will forget your idea of the traditional, banal sea-inspired decor. The fabulous dining room, designed by Pat Kuleto, seems to be right out of the imagination of Jacques Cousteau in an altered state of consciousness, featuring, among other things, medusa-shaped mood-setting lamps that skillfully provide illumination. The owners put so much effort into designing and creating a spectacular decor that it's easy to forget you've come here to eat. The menu lives up to the decor and offers a variety of extraordinarily fresh fish and shellfish dishes that are always well seasoned and exquisitely presented.

Postrio
$$$
545 Post St.
☎776-7825
www.postrio.com
Situated on three floors, Postrio is owned by re-nowned chef Wolfgang Puck. Foodies who do not have a reservation usually have to wait at the bar before climbing a some-what dazzling staircase to a spacious, convivial dining room that is often jam-packed. The open kitchen lets you watch the hat-clad chefs cook up a storm. The menu features Californian dishes, which combine French and Asian flavours. Desserts are simply succulent. Service is pleasant and friendly.

Grand Café
$$-$$$
501 Geary St., corner Taylor St.
☎292-0101
You will better understand the meaning of the Grand Café's name once you walk through the door. The dining room is set in a former ballroom, which has preserved the breath-taking columns that support the extremely high ceilings, and Art Deco chandeliers adorn the room. The menu offers a variety of dishes such as a meat lover's plate, chicken fricassee, vegetable cassoulet and crispy pizza.

Pacific
$$$-$$$$
500 Post St., corner Mason St., third floor
☎929-2087
An underrated pearl of gourmet cuisine, the restaurant of the chic Pan Pacific Hotel (see p 433) is succinctly named Pacific. However, there is nothing succinct about its dishes, which are prepared by chef Erik Oberholzer. The delicious Californian menu offers a good choice of dishes inspired by a medley of cuisines from the Americas, Europe and Asia. Those who wish to indulge in a feast can choose the four-course sampling menu. The wine list features a lovely selection of vintages that were

chosen to accompany the menu's savours and flavours.

Masa
$$$$
648 Bush St., corner Powell St.
☎989-7154
The French restaurant Masa is another prized establishment on San Francisco's gourmet tour and has enjoyed an excellent reputation for years. After having been awarded several awards of excellence, former chef Julian Serrano left Masa's kitchen to take on new challenges in Las Vegas. However, Chad Callahan, who assisted Serrano for nearly 10 years, has brilliantly taken charge by carrying on as head chef in the tradition of his predecessor. The sampling menu lets you dig into a great selection of dishes. Desserts are a must.

Chinatown

Lotus Garden
$$
532 Grant Ave., between Pine St. and California St.
☎397-0078
The Lotus Garden is a small exotic place that prepares mouth-watering Chinese creations at pretty reasonable prices.

Far East Café
$$
631 Grant Ave.
☎982-3245
Located a stone's throw from St. Mary's Cathedral, the Far East Café is housed in a lovely, well-ventilated room and is decorated in the Chinese tradition with a lot of dark wood. As you would expect, the restaurant's cuisine centres on Chinese specialties.

R&G Lounge
$$-$$$
631 Kearny St.
☎982-7877
The R&G Lounge is another restaurant whose menu draws its inspiration from Chinese cuisine. The main floor's decor is nothing exciting, but if you are looking for a good, flavourful meal in a more refined setting, head upstairs.

The Financial District and the Embarcadero

Tadich Grill
$$-$$$
240 California St., corner Battery St.
☎391-1849
The Tadich Grill opened its doors in 1849 during the gold rush era. The restaurant has certainly changed its look since then, but the kitchen still serves up delicious grilled fish dishes. Regulars still gather at its long bar to relax after a hard day's work. Art Deco murals and panelled walls add to the restaurant's warm and convivial ambiance.

Yank Sing
$$$
427 Battery St., corner Clay St.
☎781-1111
This restaurant, which is unanimously considered one of the city's best restaurants for *dim sum* and whose reputation is well established, serves some 60 small dishes on carts that go around the room. The busy dining room always seems to be packed.

Zaré
$$$
568 Sacramento St.
☎291-9145
Zaré is currently one of the city's most acclaimed restaurants. It's set in an intimate dining room with a bronze ceiling that is adorned with velvet curtains and flickering candles to soften its corners. Soft cushions on wooden seats help customers get comfortable as they savour braised osso bucco, curry salmon or other delicious creations that are beautifully presented and inspired by the Mediterranean. Service is flawless and the wine list offers a good selection.

Garden Court
$$$
2 New Montgomery St., corner Market St.
☎512-111
Crowned with a magnificent and spectacular dome that is ornamented with stained glass, the Garden Court without a doubt features one of the city's most stunning dining rooms. This is the perfect place to satisfy your hunger in a restaurant loaded with ambiance.

Bix
$$$
56 Gold St., corner Sansome St.
☎433-6300
Trendy and sophisticated Bix draws a chic crowd. This huge restaurant-bar is adorned with Art Deco paintings. Jazz and blues music, and the brick walls and skylight make for a pleasant setting that is great for intimate conversations. This ravishing, cozy decor only adds to the pleasure of enjoying the restaurant's refined California cuisine.

Carnelian Room

$$$

555 California St., corner Kearny St.
52nd floor

☎433-7500

Let it be said straight off the bat that the Carnelian Room's best attraction is its magnificent view. Located on the 52nd floor, it lays claim to being the city's highest restaurant. Men in designer suits and women adorned with shiny jewellery mingle in the discreet and refined decor. The restaurant has an excellent wine list.

Rubicon

$$$$

558 Sacramento St.

☎434-4100

Named after the river crossed by Julius Caesar, the Rubicon offers nothing exciting, even though it is owned by Hollywood big boys. No, not Arnold, Bruce and Sly, but Robin Williams, Francis Ford Copolla and Robert de Niro. The main level features a bar and a warm dining room, where wood and a brick wall dominate the decor. Both, however, are somewhat noisy. For a more intimate and quiet dinner, go upstairs. The menu includes modern California cuisine, as well as a vegetarian menu. Bacchanalian types will be delighted by the restaurant's excellent wine list.

Aqua

$$$$

252 California St.

☎956-9662

Considered (with good reason) one of the city's best restaurants for several years, Aqua no longer needs an introduction. Michael Nima's refined restaurant lives up to its reputation thanks to its Californian culinary delights, which mostly feature fish and shellfish. The elegant decor features lovely floral arrangements

and enormous mirrors that make the room seem bigger. Have a seat at the bar while you wait for your table, and watch the "beautiful people." The great courtesy of the staff combined with the extremely flavourful dishes make for an unforgettable dining experience, which will be even more memorable thanks to the restaurant's excellent wine cellar.

🦐 Tommy Toy

$$$$

655 Montgomery St.

☎397-4888

Located right next to the Transamerica Pyramid, Tommy Toy is a marvellous Chinese restaurant that subtlely fusions French influences. It is a gourmet stop any respectful foodie will appreciate. Tommy Toy is the place to spend a romantic evening in a setting where the chandeliers, soft lighting, old photographs, gleaming cutlery and courteous staff create a unique ambiance worthy of an upscale restaurant. The extremely varied sampling menu is a feast fit for kings and queens, and all of it is topped off by a great wine list.

Equinox

$$$$

5 Embarcadero Center

☎398-2567

The Equinox is a breathtaking gourmet stop located atop the Hyatt Regency Hotel. The menu does not feature any unusual dishes, and guests come especially for its extremely enviable panorama of the city. The decor changes from hour to hour, as the restaurant completes a full rotation every 45min.

Boulevard

$$$-$$$$

1 Mission St., corner Steuart St.

☎543-6084

A pillar of the city's restaurant industry, Boulevard is the fruit of the partnership between chef Nancy Oakes and designer Pat Kuleto. The interior is split into three dining rooms and is reminiscent of Edwardian-era decor with its Art Nouveau paintings. The food is synonymous with a medley of American cuisine. You have the option of dining with a view of the Bay Bridge or of the hat-clad chefs cooking up a storm in the open kitchen.

🦐 Shanghai 1930

$$$$

133 Steuart St.

☎896-5600

Those who wish to experience the delights of Asian cuisine should head to an inescapable stop on the city's gourmet circuit, Shanghai 1930. Under the direction of chef Xu, the kitchen team prepares dishes that are a cross of various influences. Go for the house specialties (easily recognizable by the stars). The Chinese food is simply brilliant. The wine list offers great vintages and the sumptuous desserts will take you on a delicious voyage. Jazz musicians add to the classic ambiance on weekends.

North Beach

Mona Lisa

$-$$

353 Columbus Ave.

☎989-4917

www.citysearch.com_sfo_monalisa

A beacon of North Beach, Mona Lisa is a great place to have a feast in pure Italian style, especially between 5pm and 7pm, when you are free to choose from 58 pasta dishes, all priced less than $10. Those who would prefer something from the *à la carte* menu can set their heart on the veal or the fish.

Café Niebaum-Coppola
$$
916 Kearny St.
☎291-1700

Owned by renowned producer Francis Ford Coppola, the Café Niebaum-Coppola is at once a café, restaurant, wine bar and store. The menu includes fresh and voluptuous pasta, crispy pizza and hearty sandwiches. Guys in designer suits mingle among elegantly dressed women. Obviously, vintages of the Niebaum-Coppola wineries in the Napa Valley dominate the wine list.

The Stinking Rose
$$
325 Columbus Ave.
☎781-7673
www.thestinkingrose.com

Best be on your way if you don't like garlic, because all dishes (including desserts!) at the Stinking Rose Italian restaurant are made with garlic. Numerous garlic bulbs dangle throughout the restaurant and only add to the spicy hot atmosphere that reigns in the four dining rooms, which are often filled to capacity with curious tourists and locals.

PJ Mulhern's
$$$
570 Green St., near Columbus Ave.
☎217-7000

New to North Beach, PJ Mulhern's is already claiming its spot among the neighbourhood's best restaurants. Its elegant, panelled setting evokes an ambiance reminiscent of a charming Parisian brasserie. The chef creates

Californian-style American dishes such as the tender medallion of Atlantic salmon or the juicy, spicy, medium steak, which are savoured by guests seated on rich-coloured mahogany chairs. Service is efficient and unpretentious.

Rose Pistola
$$$
532 Columbus Ave.,
between Green and Union sts.
☎399-0499

A stone's throw from Washington Square, the Rose Pistola is a trendy restaurant that offers its customers a savoury and generous Italian menu. The dining room, which features a gleaming tiled floor and wooden tables, is constantly filled with guests who are served by bustling, considerate staff. The crispy pizzas have generous toppings and pasta is served with all types of sauces. A vast terrace also offers lovely views of the commercial activity of Columbus Avenue.

Nob Hill

The Big Four
$$$
1075 California St., corner Taylor St.
☎474-5400

The Big Four's name might not be all that grand, but it perfectly evokes the nickname once given to the West's four railroad magnates. The chef has been cooking up a storm at the renowned restaurant for 25 years and concocts a range of specialties such as wild mushroom risotto, Provençale-style salmon and grain-fed ostrich steak. The setting, which is dominated by wood and bathed in soft lighting enhanced by the glow of the fireplace, is perfect for

intimate conversations or important business dinners.

Harris'
$$$
2100 Van Ness, corner Pacific Ave.
☎673-1888

Harris' is a temple devoted to red meat and serves generous portions of tender, juicy steak. The refined decor, unpretentious service and jazz music playing in the background create the perfect ambiance to enjoy a delicious meal. The menu also features fish and shellfish. To wash it all down, Harris' offers an excellent selection of Californian wines. The pieces of dried meat at the door will no doubt send vegetarians scurrying on their way.

Fisherman's Wharf

Buena Vista Café
$$
2765 Hyde St., corner Beach St.
☎474-5044

The Buena Vista is not a café, but a restaurant-bar that prides itself for having invented Irish coffee. The menu offers no surprises but will satisfy the appetite of those who want to eat something salty and solid as they drink their Irish coffee or cold beer.

Rainforest Café
$$
Jefferson St., corner Mason St.
☎440-5610

Parents looking for a family restaurant where the decor and menu deserve high marks should head to the Rainforest Café. The café is part of an ecological-theme restaurant chain that features a setting and decor inspired by the lush environment of tropical rainforests. Kids will definitely love the giant aquariums full of colourful fish, the growling mechanical animals, the waterfalls and the shrill howls emanating from loudspeakers that are hidden amongst the trees' foliage. You don't come to the Rainforest Café for the dining experience, but the setting will no doubt enthuse families that want to please their kids.

McCormick & Kuleto's
$$-$$$
900 North Point St.
☎929-1730
McCormick & Kuleto's serves remarkably fresh fish and shellfish, prepared in 30 different ways. The ceiling is decorated with fake tortoise shells, but guests will particularly feast their eyes on the lovely views of the port in the background. While you wait for your table, you can have a drink at the mahogany bar. Service is friendly.

Franciscan
$$$
Pier 43 1-2
☎362-7733
www.franciscanrestaurant.com
The Franciscan is a refreshing addition to the ultra-touristy atmosphere of the Fisherman's Wharf district and enjoys a favourable location near the water. The huge dining room is split on three levels and can seat 300 people. Not only do you not feel cramped, but each guest has a splendid view of the water. The solid, predictable menu is especially focussed on seafood and offers fish and chips, fresh oysters, crab and pasta with shrimp.

The Marina and Cow Hollow

East Side
$$
3154 Fillmore St., corner Greenwich St.
☎885-4000
www.eastsidewest.com
East Side is the neighbourhood's new cool restaurant. Its raw-bar delights guests who have come to enjoy fresh oysters or a well garnished ceviche. Its terrace is the perfect spot for a favourite local activity: people-watching.

PlumpJack Café
$$-$$$
3127 Fillmore St.
☎563-4755
Chefs at the PlumpJack Café prepare imaginative seasonal California cuisine. The restaurant also offers a great wine list at very reasonable prices. A variety of vintages are also served by the glass.

Greens
$-$$$$
Fort Mason Center, Building A,
☎771-6222
For over 25 years, Greens has redefined the quality standards of vegetarian cuisine by offering an imaginative, mouth-watering, healthy menu that is full of subtle flavours: tomato and lentil soup with spinach and sprinkled with Parmesan cheese, Sri Lankan curry, grilled mushroom brochettes with red onions and zucchini, as well as marinated tofu served on a bed of almond couscous. Try to get a table with a view of the bay. Reservations are strongly recommended. The wine list is remarkable. Greens also has a fast-food counter ($) for those who prefer to eat outdoors.

The Civic Center, the Tenderloin and Hayes Valley

Café do Brasil
$-$$
1106 Market St., corner McAllister St.
☎626-6432
At the Café do Brasil, the sunny Brazilian cuisine will satisfy your appetite every time. The restaurant is decorated with the colours of the Brazilian flag. Staff is friendly and the ambiance is relaxed. Good quality/price ratio.

Caffe delle Stelle
$$
359 Hayes St., corner Gough St.
☎252-1100
Caffe delle Stelle is a cheerful Italian trattoria located in a room whose large windows let in light that reflects off its yellow walls. The menu features appetizers such as carpaccio and bruschetta, and includes fresh pasta, osso buco and the catch of the day. The wine list is very respectable. The place is often packed, as regulars come to enjoy one of the city's best quality/price ratios.

Zuni Café
$$-$$$
1658 Market St., corner Franklin St.
☎522-2522
The Zuni Café continues to gain popularity among both food critics and trendsetters, thanks to its mainly Mediterranean menu that features crispy wood-oven baked pizza, as well as its big, generously garnished hamburgers and its assortment of fish and shellfish at the raw bar. The restaurant's huge windows open onto

Market Street, to the delight of guests who love to see and be seen.

 Millennium
$$-$$$
246 McAllister St.
☎487-9800
www.millenniumrestaurant.com

Millennium is the Abigail Hotel's fabulous vegetarian restaurant. Guests are seated in a small, cozy dining room located next to the hotel's reception where they savour sumptuously prepared, health-conscious meals. You won't find tasteless soya-sprout salads or cucumber sandwiches here. In fact, practically no dairy products are used as ingredients. The result is a set of audacious culinary creations that will please vegetarians and indomitable meat lovers alike. The wine list complements the menu well. Service is courteous and considerate.

 Jardinière
$$$
300 Grove St., corner Franklin St.
☎861-5555

Customers of renowned chef Traci Des Jardins's restaurant, who consist of loyal regulars, continue to flock to Jardinière to enjoy California-style French cuisine under an imposing, arched ceiling. The restaurant is a popular stop before going to an opera or ballet, and is only located a block from city hall. The wine list admirably complements the menu.

Stars
$$$
55 Golden Gate St.,
corner Van Ness Ave.
☎861-stars

Talented chef Jeremiah Tower (a precursor of California cuisine) is unfortunately no longer at the helm of Stars's kitchen. The bar, however, is still

the city's longest and the quality and freshness of the food served continues to draw its inspiration from Californian products with Mediterranean influences. Stars has a bistro-like feel to it.

Absinthe
$$$
398 Hayes St., corner Gough St.
☎255-2385
www.absinthe.com

Absinthe is reminiscent of a charming Parisian *brasserie* (restaurant-bar), and is decorated with stylized mirrors, open wood trim and velvet seats. The menu includes *croque monsieur*, fresh oysters and fresh pasta. Cold beer and a good selection of explosive cocktails such as Death in the Afternoon (a mix of champagne and Pernod) quench the thirst of guests.

Haight-Ashbury

Upper Haight

Cha cha cha
$-$$
Haight St., corner Shrader St.
☎ 386-5758

If you are looking for an informal and laid-back place to have dinner with friends, try Cha cha cha. Spicy Caribbean cuisine holds a place of honour and the house sangria is refreshingly cold. The restaurant attracts a young and colourful crowd.

Magnolia Pub Brewery
$-$$
1398 Haight St., corner Masonic St.
☎864-7568
www.magnoliapub.com

The Magnolia Pub Brewery offers customers a delicious and varied assortment of house beers brewed right on the premises. It serves up light or heavy, greasy and salty meals such as spinach

salad, fried, crispy calamari or spicy Italian sausage sandwiches covered with provolone cheese.

 Eos
$$$
901 Cole St., corner Carl St.
☎566-3063
www.eossf.com

Eos is without a doubt *the* best restaurant in the neighbourhood. If you can't get a table, head to the wine bar adjacent to the restaurant. The chef cooks up delicious, creative food that combines Asian and Mediterranean flavours. The wine list features over 400 wines, 40 of which are served by the glass.

Lower Haight

Squat & Gobble Café and Crepery
$
237 Fillmore St., corner Haight St.
☎487-0551

The Squat & Gobble Café and Crepery's laid-back and casual atmosphere attracts idealist bachelors and penniless artists, who blend into the colourful crowd. The menu offers a delicious assortment of savoury and sweet crepes, as well as sandwiches, soups, omelettes and salads.

 Indian Oven
$$-$$$
233 Fillmore St.,
between Haight St. and Waller St.
☎626-1628

Next door to the Squat & Gobble Café and Crepery stands Indian Oven, which is located in a Victorian residence whose dining room is decorated with a few paintings reminiscent of India. The menu offers delicious dishes such as tandouri chicken, masala fish or curried lamb, which are all accompanied by the inseparable naan or chapati.

Thep Phanom
$$-$$$
400 Waller St., corner Fillmore St.
☎431-2526
Year after year, the Thep Phanom Thai restaurant is showered with praise by the city's food critics and foodies. Enjoy the salmon topped with a curry sauce or minced-garlic chicken. The lovely, painted-wood trim creates a cozy, pleasant ambiance.

Richmond

Cliff House
$$
1090 Point Lobos
☎386-3330
Cliff House serves up respectable California cuisine that can be savoured in one of its two dining rooms. Its main asset, however, is its spectacular view of the Pacific Ocean.

Alain Rondelli
$$$
211 Clement St., corner Second St.
☎387-0408
Owner Alain Rondelli studied in France before transposing a small part of French heritage to San Francisco. Tables are beautifully set, service is courteous and dishes are impeccably presented.

Nasturtium
$$-$$$
4134 Geary St.,
between Fourth St. and Fifth St..
☎387-1090
www.nasturtium.com
Located in a district that is dominated by Chinese restaurants and Irish pubs, Nasturium got off on the right foot in the new millennium by opening its doors at the very end of 1999. Its chef concocts a variety of eclectic French and Californian-inspired specialities. The menu features lovely and well-seasoned dishes such as

Ahi Tuna Tar Tar, foie gras or lobster-stuffed ravioli with wild mushrooms and covered with goat cheese and a brown-butter sauce. The decor will help you relax and unwind. To let yourself indulge in gourmet excess, there is always the delicious, not-to-be-missed *crème brûlée*. If you have a sweet tooth though, we strongly urge you to go for the irresistible chocolate and nougat *semifreddo* with espresso caramel, accompanied by a good glass of port. The friendly staff is extremely kind.

South of Market (SoMa)

Caffe Centro
$
102 South Park
☎882-1500
www.caffecentro.com
Caffe Centro is a small local eatery without the bells and whistles, that serves up grilled-chicken sandwiches, spinach salad, croissants, lasagna and coffee. If the weather is pleasant, you can also order your meal at the counter and eat in the neighbouring park.

South Park Café
$-$$
108 South Park
☎495-7275
A little more upscale, the South Park Café is reminiscent of a small French bistro. Smaller, more intimate and more expensive than its neighbour, it attracts regulars who come to enjoy the French-inspired fixed-price menu. An *à la carte* menu is also available. A small terrace lets you watch the activities in the park.

Infusion
$$$
555 Second St.
☎543-2282
Infusion gets its name from the assortment of vodkas at the restaurant's bar that are infused with fruit or vegetables. The menu offers filet mignon covered with a tequila sauce, pork cutlets with an apple barbeque sauce, vegetarian lasagna, eggplant sandwiches with goat cheese or a good ol' hamburger with fries. The clientele is trendy.

Paragon
$$$
701 Second St., corner Townsend St.
☎537-9020
Strategically located next to the new Pacific Bell Park baseball stadium, Paragon is the district's latest trendy and lively restaurant that resembles a modern American version of a Parisian brasserie. The contemporary and industrial setting is an astute mix of metal, wood and leather seats in a dining room where the ceiling is just a little over 9ft (3m) high. The food is an excellent Californian repertoire that incorporates French influences and produces impeccably fresh dishes. The menu includes such offerings as steak tartar, home-made garlic sausage with linguini, fresh oysters and lobster. An intelligent selection of wine is also available, so don't be afraid to take the servers' sound advice on selecting a vintage that will admirably complement your meal.

Thirsty Bear
$$-$$$
661 Howard St.,
between Second St. and Third St.
☎974-0905
Don't let yourself be turned off by Thirsty Bear's somewhat odd-sounding name. The huge

Spanish restaurant resembles a gigantic industrial loft, at the heart of which tower stainless steel vats that hold the restaurant's own fermenting beer. Some 30 tapas, paella and fried calamari dominate the menu, and billiard tables are found upstairs. Cheerful atmosphere and spruce-looking crowd.

Maya
$$-$$$
303 Second St., corner Harrison St.
☎543-2928

In a city where Mexican cuisine is usually summed up by inexpensive local eateries, which are a little run-down and serve overly spicy burritos and greasy tacos, Maya is a delicious change of pace. Guests are seated on hand-crafted wooden chairs in the spacious dining room, where they enjoy shrimp quesadillas, Toltec-style salmon, well-seasoned guacamole and pork cutlets covered in a pumpkin sauce. Salads are marvellously dressed with subtle vinaigrettes. You can wash down your meal with some good tequila or mescal.

Lulu
$$-$$$
816 Folson St., corner Fourth St.
☎495-5775
www.restaurantlulu.com

For a stop in the land of Rimbaud, Lulu offers a diverse menu inspired by the south of France, including duck specialties, bouillabaisse and rabbit. A specific dish is added to the menu each night. Lulu also serves crispy pizzas.

Fringale
$$-$$$
570 Fourth St., corner Brannan St.
☎543-0573

Around a decade ago, Fringale was one of the first restaurants in San Francisco to replicate the simple Parisian bistro model. The kitchen serves up eclectic French dishes with a touch of California, of course, in a minimalist setting. The French staff will be happy to guide you through your choice of wine to accompany your meal. For dessert, the fruit clafoutis will please those with a sweet tooth.

Bizou
$$-$$$
Fourth St., corner Brannan St.
☎543-2222

Bizou is a warm bistro that pays homage to French cuisine. The restaurant features a curved wooden bar and is adorned with glass bay windows that filter light onto its orange walls. The menu includes cassoulet, braised rabbit and the pasta dish of the day.

Hawthorne Lane
$$$$
22 Hawthorne Lane
☎777-9779
www.hawthornelane.com

After having spent many years working in Postrio's kitchen, chefs Annie and David Gingras decided to strike out on their own and open the splendid Hawthorne Lane. San Francisco's foodies and visitors alike never seem to tire of this warm restaurant, where they can indulge in a medley of California cuisine, and wash down their meal with an excellent vintage from the extensive wine list. Staff is stylish and pleasant.

Castro

Squat & Gobble Café and Crepery
$
3600 16th St., corner Market St.
☎552-2125

The Squat & Gobble Café and Crepery in the Castro district is smaller and more modern than the one in Lower Haight, but offers Mission district customers the same inexpensive and delectable menu for which it is known.

Luna Piena Restaurant
$$-$$$
558 Castro St., corner 18th St.
☎621-2566

The Luna Piena Restaurant prepares delicious, eclectic Italian cuisine. We recommend you ask for a table on the rear terrace (covered and heated on cloudy, chilly days with gas burners like in Paris or Montreal), which is a real oasis for relaxation and for savouring a succulent meal in complete peace.

2223
$$-$$$
2223 Market St.,
between Noe St. and Sanchez St.
☎431-0692

Simply called 2223, this restaurant-bar is located precisely at 2223 Market Street. It's the loud, trendy and somewhat straight-laced meeting place of gays, lesbians and people with mixed sexual orientations. The restaurant serves eclectic California cuisine in a refined decor that nevertheless features comfortable seats. Lively conversations can be enjoyed in a rhythmic and spirited atmosphere.

Mission

Dolores Park Café
$
501 Dolores St., corner 18th St.
☎621-2936

The Dolores Park Café is a small convivial and extremely bright café that attracts regulars. Salads, bagels and sandwiches line up next to freshly squeezed vitamin-enriched drinks and the usual assortment of strong coffees.

Napa Valley, a narrow mosaic of vineyards dotted with windmills, barns, wineries and magnificent stone buildings, covers more than 34mi (55km) and is a feast for the senses.
- *Claude Hervé-Bazin*

The Carson Mansion in Eureka was built in 1886 and is said to be the most photographed Victorian home in the United States. Indeed, the old town and downtown area are filled with magnificently restored Victorian houses.
- *Don Leonard*

The result of glaciers, volcanoes, fire and water, Mono Lake is one of California's most striking natural attractions. At an altitude of more than 8,858ft (2,700m), this immense, alkaline, saltwater lake is actually the remains of a prehistoric sea that is some 760,000 years old.
- *Claude Hervé-Bazin*

The Ahwahneechee named the Bridalveil Falls in Yosemite Valley Pohomo, or "spirit of the blowing wind." Surrounded by imposing rock walls, the falls don't seem exceptionally high, but actually reach 607ft (185m), the equivalent of a 62-storey building.
- *Claude Hervé-Bazin*

Each of the slopes in California's main mountain range, the Sierra Nevada, has a unique personality; to the west, they descend gently for many miles, while to the east, they are dramatically steep. The rocky, jagged walls of the snowy summits create a spectacular alpine landscape.
- *Claude Hervé-Bazin*

Known as one of the oldest and most imposing living entities on the planet, the sequoia tree has survived many millions of years. In ancient times, a number of species of this large tree covered the earth's vast forests.
- *Patrick Escudero*

Bodie State Historic Park, near Bridgeport, is one of California's best-preserved ghost towns.
- *Claude Hervé-Bazin*

Lighthouses, perched atop green hills along the coast, are part of the typical scenery in Northern California.
- *Carrie Grant*

Ti Couz
$-$$
3108 16th St., corner Valencia St.
☎252-7373
Breton crepes are honoured at Ti Couz. Opt for the bowl of cider that marvellously complements the variety of crepes on the menu, which also features fresh salads.

Flying Saucer
$$$
1000 Guerrero St., corner 22nd St.
☎641-9955
Under the direction of chef Albert Tjordman, the charming and stylish Flying Saucer restaurant offers explosive Californian gourmet dishes that are marvellously presented. You eat elbow to elbow, but that doesn't seem to bother the visibly delighted customers.

The Slanted Door
$$$
584 Valencia St., corner 17th St.
☎861-8032
One of the city's most popular restaurants, The Slanted Door serves authentic and delectable Vietnamese dishes. Its menu changes regularly and includes green papaya salad, *satay* and crispy rolls, all of which are beautifully presented. The prompt and efficient staff slips between the tables of the cramped dining room, which always seems packed.

The San Francisco Area

Sausalito (Marin County)

Sushi Ran
$$
107 Caledonia St.
☎(415) 332-3620
Those who love Japanese cuisine must head to Sushi Ran. Guests savour sushi, sashimi and teriyaki in a quaint dining room that is furnished with warm wooden tables.

Ondine
$$$$
558 Bridgeway St.
☎(415) 331-1133
Undoubtably one of the region's best restaurants, Ondine prepares delectable mixed dishes that admirably combine French and Californian traditions, presented in a quasi-artistic fashion. The menu is a brilliant example of upscale gourmet dining and features smoked salmon sushi terrine, foie gras and scampi, a seafood trio or Maine lobster with Asian vegetables and spaghettini. Guests with a sweet tooth should know that desserts are simply sumptuous. Wine lovers will certainly not be disappointed by the long list of quality wines available. The large windows offer privileged views of San Francisco Bay. Service is extremely courteous and efficient and definitely makes customers want to return.

Corte Madera

Those who want to curb their hunger at Corte Madera can stop at The Village at Corte Madera shopping centre just long enough to catch their breath before continuing on their way.

Dragon Fly Café & Jazz Bar
1546 Redwood Hwy.,
The Village at Corte Madera
☎(415) 927-8889
Located in the Corte Madera shopping centre, 10min north of Sausalito by car, the Dragon Fly Café & Jazz Bar prepares good California cuisine combined with Asian flavours. The sober, yet elegant decor is dominated by two dragon flies that adorn the wall at the back of the restaurant. For dessert, we strongly recommend the delectable vanilla and almond *crème brûlée*. Jazz shows are feature for customers' entertainment.

East Bay

Berkeley

Blue Nile
$
2525 Telegraph Ave.,
south of Dwight St.
☎540-6777
The Blue Nile is a modest little Ethiopian restaurant that serves up flavourful dishes at good prices.

Crepes a Go Go
$
2125 University Ave., corner Shattuck
☎(510)-841-7722
Crepes a Go Go is worshipped by penniless university students and prepares tasty, salty or sweet crepes at quite reasonable prices.

Santa Fe Bar & Grill
$$-$$$
1310 University Ave.
☎(510) 841-1110
The Santa Fe Bar & Grill is located in an old 1904 train station. The chef prepares regional California cuisine that is fusioned with Mediterranean flavours and only uses the freshest, pesticide-free ingredients. Jazz musicians perform nightly. Lunchtime offers a fixed-price menu at extremely reasonable prices.

Xanadu
$$$-$$$$
700 University Ave.
☎(510) 548-7880
Xanadu is a classy Asian restaurant where the dark woodwork and shiny chandeliers help create a mood that is perfect for

dining. The Pan Asian Cuisine menu combines Asian and American flavours by using the freshest ingredients.

Chez Panisse
$$$-$$$$
1517 Shattuck Ave.
☎548-5525

Unanimously considered as the figurehead of California cuisine, Alice Waters has been at the helm of Chez Panisse for more than a quarter of a century, thanks to her influential culinary creations. The dining room is almost always packed and reservations are strongly recommended.

Oakland

Bay Wolf
$$$
3853 Piedmont Ave.
☎655-6004

According to many, Bay Wolf always claims its spot among the city's best restaurants. The kitchen draws its inspiration from the repertoire of Mediterranean dishes. Service is courteous and attentive.

South of San Francisco

Half Moon Bay

2 Fools
$-$$
408 Main St.,
☎712-1222

Head to 2 Fools to enjoy home-made no-frills food in a cheery, relaxed setting. You'll be given some wax crayons to kill the time by scribbling on your paper placemat while you wait for your meal. Service is pleasant and attentive, and dishes are always undeniably fresh.

Pasta Moon
$$-$$$
315 Main St.
☎726-5125

Pasta Moon's specialty is Italian food and it is without a doubt one of the city's best restaurants. It offers a catering service and bakes its own bread, as well. The menu also features pasta medleys and fish, and often changes depending on availability, but always succeeds in offering a dish you will enjoy. The home-made desserts literally melt in your mouth. Service is professional, attentive and unpretentious.

Entertainment

Among the plethora of bars, dance clubs, theatre, dance and concert venues that pull out all the stops to attract patrons, visitors are sure to find a place to suit their taste and personality. Indeed, San Francisco definitely has no shortage of nightspots and diversions of all kinds: from "suit bars," neighbourhood watering holes and comedy clubs to blues and jazz showrooms, stylish nightclubs and student hangouts, this city has it all.

The *San Francisco Weekly* and *Bay Guardian* weeklies exhaustively cover dance, music, theatre, dining and many of the city's cultural, social and artistic events on a weekly basis. These papers are free and available in a number of popular hangouts, including bars, restaurants and a handful of shops.

Published monthly, *Where* magazine is another good source of information on

music shows of all kinds. It also features listings of new restaurants, bars, nightclubs and concert venues, as well as the movie schedules of the main cinemas.

Tix Bay Area *(Stockton St., between Geary and Post sts., Union Square, ☎433-7827)* offers bargain hunters discounts of up to 50% on regular ticket prices for dance, opera or theatre performances. Note, however, that these tickets are generally only valid for same-day productions.

Bass *(☎510-762-2277)* is an info line that provides comprehensive listings of concerts and sporting events taking place in the San Francisco Bay area.

Theatres and Concert Halls

Concert Venues

Classical Music

San Francisco Symphony Orchestra
201 Van Ness Ave., corner Grove St.
☎864-6000

Sheer pleasure for those with a sensitive ear for classical music, the San Francisco Symphony Orchestra performs regularly at Davies Hall from September to late May.

Opera

San Francisco Opera
301 Van Ness Ave., corner Grove St.
☎864-3330

Those who prefer combining visual and auditory pleasure may want to spend an evening with the San Francisco Opera. Tenors and baritones sing their hearts out at the War

Woody Guthrie

Born in Oklahoma in 1912, folk singer Woody Guthrie lost his sister in a disastrous fire, saw his father severely injured in another fire and, to cap it all, lost his mother to a chronic illness—all this before even reaching adulthood. When local farmers were ruined by the Great Depression, he left with other Dust-Bowl migrants. Undoubtedly devastated by bitterness, he wandered the country like a lone troubadour with his guitar and harmonica, riding the rails, singing odes to working-class people and songs championing left-wing causes. Primarily renowned for his great Dust-Bowl ballad *Tom Joad*, Guthrie inspired some beat-generation writers and was a major influence on none other than Bob Dylan.

Memorial Opera House from early September to late December.

San Francisco Pocket Opera
44 Page St., Suite 200
☎575-1102
The San Francisco Pocket Opera will interest opera buffs looking for something a little different. In a more intimate hall, the cultural elite is sure to spend a wonderful evening with this renowned company.

Rock

The Fillmore
1850 Geary Blvd., corner Fillmore St.
☎346-6000
www.thefillmore.com
The legendary concert venue that hosted the *crème de la crème* of the 1960s music scene, the Fillmore still draws big-name rock acts.

Bottom of the Hill
1233 17th St., corner Missouri St., Potrero Hill
☎621-4455
Set up in an old Victorian house, this great live-music venue features top-notch, booming speakers. Just the place for rock purists.

Purple Onion
140 Columbus Ave., between Pacific and Jackson sts., North Beach
☎398-8415
Located in the heart of the North Beach night-time action, this landmark has hosted a stream of bands and underground acts with punk-rock leanings over the years. The place itself has seen better days, but the beer is cold and the crowd pretty sizzling, even feverish, some nights.

Jazz and Blues Bars

Biscuits and Blues
401 Mason St., corner Geary St., Union Square
☎292-2583
Wayfarers and blues devotees religiously flock to Biscuits and Blues. Located near Union Square, this show bar consistently books gifted acts. The kitchen is open for those with a hankering for some food after a few beers.

Boom Boom Room
1601 Fillmore St., corner Geary Blvd.
☎673-8053
Located across from The Fillmore (see above), the Boom Boom Room is

owned by none other than John Lee Hooker. Whatever the season, the quality acts that perform here draw a crowd of regulars and hard-core blues enthusiasts. John Lee Hooker himself even takes the stage on occasion. The southern-flavoured music is heavy and incisive, and the beer is nice and frosty.

Jazz at Pearl's
256 Columbus Ave., North Beach
☎291-8255
Jazz at Pearl's brings together a group of top-notch musicians steeped in jazz or blues for a perfectly low-key vibe. You can also enjoy a meal while revelling in all that cool, sweet jazz.

Slim's
333 11th St., between Folsom and Harrison sts., South of Market
☎522-0333
Jazz is the rallying point for aficionados and regulars alike at Slim's. This is just the place to sip a glass of port in good company while enjoying a relaxing evening listening to great bands.

Elbo Room
647 Valencia St., between 17th and 18th sts., the Mission
☎552-7788
At the Elbo Room, young bohemians generally first make their way to the cozy, street-level bar to drink with friends before heading upstairs for live jazz fuelled by Latin rhythms.

Club Deluxe
1509 Haight St., Haight-Ashbury
☎552-6949
An über-trendy place, Club Deluxe showcases jazz and swing combos. Turning the heads of hipster swingers, the waitresses seem to have stepped right out of a fashion magazine. Guys and dolls looking for company or love exchange

furtive glances in the suitably dimly lit space.

Dance

San Francisco Ballet
301 Van Ness Ave., corner Grove St.
☎865-2000
The fabulous San Francisco Ballet classical-dance troupe, the oldest ballet company in the United States, also graces the stage at the War Memorial Opera House. The repertory season runs from February to late June.

Theatre

Beach Blanket Babylon
678 Green St., Club Fugazi
☎421-4222
A veritable San Francisco institution, Beach Blanket Babylon, a satyrical musical revue featuring actors in extravagant costumes, has been delighting audiences for more than 20 years. Minors (under 21 years of age) are only admitted to the weekly Sunday matinees.

Below is a cursory rundown of the city's main theatres.

American Conservatory Theater
415 Geary St.
☎749-2228
Unquestionably one of San Francisco's leading theatre troupes, the American Conservatory Theater has earned a solid reputation in the American art world over the last 30-odd years. For that matter, ACT prides itself on having moulded such renowned actors as Denzel Washington and Annette Bening. Theatregoers can attend one of its performances at the splendid Geary Theater, built in 1909 and designated a national historic landmark.

Curran Theater
445 Geary St.,
between Mason and Taylor sts.
☎512-7770
The Curran Theater is a gorgeous 1,665-seat theatre hall that hosts several Broadway plays a year. A wealth of quality dramas are staged here year-round, including past productions like *The Phantom of the Opera*, which enjoyed an extended, sold-out run.

Golden Gate Theater
One Taylor St., corner Golden Gate St.
☎551-2000
A good selection of Broadway plays is also offered at the Golden Gate Theater.

Comedy Clubs

Punch Line
444 Battery St., corner Clay St.
☎397-7573
The Punch Line is the mecca of San Francisco comedy clubs. A good number of big-name stand-up comics, including the likes of Robin Williams and Ellen DeGeneres, have often entertained audiences here.

Finocchio's
506 Broadway St.
☎982-9388
Finocchio's spotlights female impersonators who mimic the likes of Whoopie Goldberg and Madonna.

Cobb's Comedy Club
2801 Leavenworth St., corner Beach St., Fisherman's Wharf
☎928-4320
Located in the Cannery, Cobb's Comedy Club is another good venue for those looking to get their funny bone tickled. The place welcomes its fair share of comics who regale the audience with biting humour.

Shanghai

In the tumultuous gold-rush era, the ships that put into port in San Francisco on their way to Shanghai sought sailors to supplement their crew. Unscrupulous, sinister-looking seamen from these crews often hit the local bars in small groups to recruit other sea dogs against their will. After finding a potential candidate, they would slyly get him filthy drunk (or, if need be, simply knock him senseless), then toss him into the hold of the ship, which had already suddenly set sail for Asia before the poor wretch could even regain consciousness.

Cinema

A Few Movie Theatres

Castro Theater
429 Castro St., the Castro
☎621-6120
A fabulous movie house dating from 1922, the Castro Theater screens foreign and alternative films.

Metreon
101 Fourth St., South of Market
www.metreon.com
The Sony Entertainment–owned 15-screen Metreon multiplex presents the latest Hollywood blockbusters. An IMAX theatre is also on site.

Bars and Dance Clubs

Union Square

Café Claude
7 Claude Lane, between Grant Ave. and Kearny St.
☎392-3515
www.cafeclaude.com
If you feel like catching a great jazz show while treating yourself to a good dinner, book a table at Café Claude. Tucked away in a small alley, right near the gates to Chinatown, the place looks like a small, cheerful French bistro.

Lefty O'Doul's
333 Geary St.
☎982-8900
At Lefty O'Doul's, sports fans huddle around a cold beer while watching televised games and cheering on their favourite team. The kitchen is open for those who've worked up an appetite watching others exert themselves.

Redwood Room
495 Geary St., corner Taylor St.
☎931-7417
The aptly named Redwood Room is the Clift Hotel's magnificent bar. Sipping a gin-and-tonic or a martini beneath Art Deco–style lamps suspended from the high ceilings and surrounded by reproductions of Gustav Klimt paintings, gives patrons the impression of drinking in a swanky retro establishment. Just the place for playing the *nouveau riche* dilettante. Remember to dress the part.

The Financial District and the Embarcadero

Bix
56 Gold St., corner Sansome St.
Financial District
☎433-6300
Bix is a wonderful "supper club" whose swanky decor wouldn't be out of place in a big-budget spy movie. Adorned with Art Deco paintings and brick walls, the place is pervaded with ultra-stylish hipsters and jazz and blues background music. Those feeling peckish can chow down on California cuisine.

Carnelian Room
California St., 52nd floor, Financial District
☎433-7500
Located on the 52nd floor of the Bank of America building, the Carnelian Room is an elegant bar-restaurant with a breathtaking view of the San Francisco skyline. After a few glasses of wine or port, those who don't suffer from vertigo will enjoy a hard-to-beat atmosphere that will make an evening here an unforgettable experience.

Chalkers
101 Spear St., One Rincon Center, the Embarcadero
☎512-0450
To shoot some pool in a classy, relaxed setting, venture into Chalkers. An after-work crowd of young executives readily gathers here to unwind with a leisurely game of pool. The place offers over 20 cherrywood pool tables.

Cypress Club
550 Jackson St., corner Montgomery St., Financial District
☎296-8555
A fabulous restaurant-bar that resembles a venerable jazz club caught in a 1920s time warp, the chi-chi Cypress Club is adorned with gleaming, bulbous

columns and velvet curtains. Add to that subdued lighting and a typically Californian menu, and you have the perfect recipe for a classy evening.

Equinox
5 Embarcadero Center, the Embarcadero
☎398-2567
Once inside the Hyatt Regency Hotel, take one of the panoramic elevators to the revolving rooftop Equinox bar-restaurant. Cozy up to the bar and take in a 360° view of the city as the establishment completes a full rotation every 40min.

Gordon Biersh
2 Harrison St., corner Spear St., the Embarcadero
☎243-8246
Gordon Biersh serves up a good selection of homemade beer. This brew pub is the stronghold of thirtysomethings who come in for a drink after the day's grind. Weather permitting, you can enjoy fine views of the water and the Bay Bridge.

Harry Denton's
161 Steuart St., corner Embarcadero
☎882-1333
Harry Denton's is primarily frequented by those who want, and are even anxious, to see and be seen. Up-and-coming young executives, power suits and young, unescorted women looking for company or a fling strut their best stuff here.

North Beach

Bubble Lounge
714 Montgomery St.
corner Columbus Ave.
At the Bubble Lounge, bottles of champagne are popped and the precious liquid poured into slender flutes. Patrons sip bubbly while comfortably ensconced in velvet couches, sharing eloquent smiles

San Francisco and Surroundings

with other "beautiful people."

Cafe Niebaum-Coppola
916 Kearny St., corner Columbus Ave.

☎291-1700

Cafe Niebaum-Coppola is a low-key wine bar and restaurant where *vinos* from the Napa Valley Niebaum-Coppola winery occupy the place of honour. Populated with stylish wine connoisseurs in well-cut suits and dresses.

San Francisco Brewing Company
155 Columbus Ave.

☎434-3344

Located in the heart of North Beach, the San Francisco Brewing Company prides itself on being the city's first brew pub. The tavern first opened its doors in 1907 as the Andromeda Saloon, during the wild Barbary Coast era. Today, the place is graced with a warm mahogany bar that offers great home-brewed suds and displays a magnificent, handcrafted, copper brew kettle. Beer drinkers can also quench their thirst while eating their fill of fried calamari, quesadillas, nachos or sandwiches. Live swing, jazz or blues shows often liven up the evenings.

Tosca Cafe
242 Columbus Ave., corner Broadway

☎986-9651

The venerable Tosca Cafe has been a San Francisco standby since the early 20th century. This warm, wood-panelled bar serves a good assortment of beer, wine and coffee, accompanied by the sound of opera emanating from a vintage jukebox. Apparently, there's even a secret room behind the bar where a coterie of film types go to drink and chat undisturbed.

Vesuvio Café
255 Columbus Ave., corner Broadway

☎362-3370

Located right next to the City Lights Bookstore, the Vesuvio Café is a former Beat hangout. The bar's walls are plastered with beatnik-era memorabilia such as poems and newspaper clippings. A must for nostalgic folks who want to drink to Jack Kerouac and his cronies.

Nob Hill

Tonga Room
950 Mason St.

☎772-5278

The Fairmont Hotel houses a *tiki* bar that's sure to raise a few quizzical eyebrows. In a colourful, faux-Polynesian setting, sybarites sip explosive tropical cocktails garnished with the requisite umbrellas. A well-dressed, money-loving crowd of exhibitionists.

Fisherman's Wharf

Buena Vista Café
2765 Hyde St., corner Beach St.

☎474-5044

Ordering an Irish Coffee is a must at the Buena Vista Café, which actually takes credit for having invented the drink. Purists can always go for a cold beer.

The Civic Center, the Tenderloin and Hayes Valley

Backflip
601 Eddy St., corner Larkin St., the Tenderloin

☎771-3547

Walking into Backflip can be a little disorienting due to the faint blue light that floods the atmosphere. Adjacent to the Phoenix Hotel, this bar has a true-blue aquatic decor that would make Aquaman,

Captain Nemo or Marine Boy feel right at home. The club is awash in water, which runs down the wall behind the row of bottles adorning the minimalist, circular bar. It then goes on to form a small waterfall under the gangway leading from the tiny dance floor to the lounge section, where you can sit on blue-vinyl banquettes to munch on an appetizer, while feeling like you've been parachuted into a *Jetsons* episode! Those who can't resist the urge to smoke—prohibited in San Francisco bars and nightclubs—can light up by the Phoenix Hotel's pool. Scenesters here are treated to laid-back grooves, closer to trip-hop than ambient rave-style music.

Edinburgh Castle
950 Geary St., the Tenderloin

☎885-4074

A Scottish pub with a lively atmosphere, Edinburgh Castle offers a good range of whiskeys and imported beers, as well as a few good American microbrews. The place also features pool tables, dart boards and, of course, serves fish and chips.

Place Pigalle
520 Hayes St., between Laguna and Octavia sts., Hayes Valley

☎552-2671

A neighbourhood bar with fine Parisian nuances, Place Pigalle draws its fair share of French expats and those looking for a mellow place in which to enjoy a glass of wine with proper decorum. The stylishly hip clientele practises the art of cruising, exchanging knowing smiles with fellow lounge lizards. Happy Hour every day from 4pm to 7pm.

Haight-Ashbury

Eos Wine Bar
901 Cole St., corner Carl St.,
the Upper Haight
☎ 566-3063
www.eossf.com
A must for wine-lovers, the Eos Wine Bar offers about 400 kinds of *vino* as well as more than 40 selections sold by the glass. A choice place to enjoy an aperitif while chatting about life's ups and downs before sitting down to eat in the adjoining restaurant (see p 446).

South of Market (SoMa)

Most dance clubs are located in the South of Market area (SoMa). Not so long ago, even the locals shunned the deserted streets and dark alleys of this down-and-out district. Revitalized by the scores of dot-com companies that set up shop here, it's now one of the hippest neighbourhoods in town.

1015 Folsom
cover charge
1015 Folsom St., between Sixth and Seventh sts.
☎ 431-0700
Despite its pithy, uninspired name, this hopping dance club draws a rather well-turned-out crowd of regulars. In fact, the beefy bouncer pays particular attention to the dress code. DJs spin a wide variety of beat-heavy styles.

AsiaF
201 Ninth St., corner Howard St.
☎ 255-2742
After enjoying a meal topped off with a drag queen show, some of you may feel like moving on to the adjoining nightclub. The place features a large dance floor surrounded by mirrors for those who like to watch themselves strut-

ting their own stuff. Gay, lesbian and "straight" crowd.

Café du Nord
2170 Market St.
☎ 861-5016
Café du Nord is a venerable bar-restaurant that showcases a wide-ranging assortment of live music, including jazz, blues and rock. The ambiance is warm and the crowd eclectic. Good choice of whiskey.

Club Townsend
177 Townsend St., between Second and Third sts.
☎ 974-6020
Club Townsend draws night owls who come to shake their groove "thang" to pumping beats. Different theme nights such as "fag night" attract drag queens and other colourful, fun-loving folks. The first Friday of every month is generally "dyke night."

DNA Lounge
375 11th St., corner Harrison St.
☎ 626-1409
The DNA Lounge still ranks among the city's hottest nightclubs. The club draws a bevy of wannabes, "soon-to-bes" and "never-will-bes," readily strutting their stuff to the frenzied beats spun by the DJ on the decks. Live music is sometimes featured.

Fourth Street Bar and Deli
55 Fourth St.
Located right across from the Metreon, in an annex of the Marriott Hotel, the Fourth Street Bar and Deli is a typical sports bar, complete with big-screen TVs and various team pennants adorning the walls. This is just the place to drink a pitcher of beer while munching on deli-style food and watching a game via satellite.

Paradise Lounge
1501 Folsom St.,
corner 11th St.
☎ 861-6906
A dazzling nightclub, the Paradise Lounge has something for everyone. In one room, DJs spin beat-laden tracks while, in another, bands perform. There are even billiard tables upstairs on which to play a leisurely game of pool. What's more, the place also has a room set aside for spoken-word (poetry/performance) evenings.

Paragon
701 Second St.,
corner Townsend St.
☎ 537-9020
Located near the new Pac Bell Park, the Paragon offers demanding baseball fans an alternative worth considering. A former Marina district sports bar patronized by well-off yuppies, this new "bar-restaurant" now claims to capture the atmosphere of a genuine, if distinctly American-looking, French brasserie. The imposing bar seemingly draws a large contingent of the same free-spending, fashion-conscious crowd.

Sound Factory
525 Harrison St., corner First St.
☎ 243-9646
A popular night spot for club kids born to dance, the Sound Factory features three dance floors and a wide range of eclectic beats that give its clients total freedom to cut loose and exchange yearning glances.

Thirsty Bear
661 Howard St., between Second and Third sts.
☎ 974-0905
You won't find any big scruffy or parched bears at the Thirsty Bear. What's more, if after a certain hour you're looking for a

quiet spot for a bite to eat or a drink, just keep on walking. Indeed, the more the night wears on, the louder the music mingled with the drone of conversation gets, adding to the lively, festive atmosphere akin to that of a modern tavern where patrons can eat tapas or play a leisurely game of pool.

Twenty Tank Brewery
316 11th St.
☎255-9455
Offering a large selection of home-brewed beer, the Twenty Tank Brewery is a good place to start off the night before moving on to nightclubs with warmer atmospheres. Some fond memories are revived by golden oldies.

V/SF
278 11th St., corner Folsom St.
☎621-4863
V/SF has made a name for itself as one of the city's hip dance clubs. Crazed clubbers come to shake their booties to frenzied, pounding techno beats and exhilarating electronica. Mixed, young and wild crowd.

Castro

Bar on Castro
456 Castro St.
between 17th and 18th sts.
☎626-7220
A resolutely male crowd regularly patronizes the Bar on Castro. An attractive and stylish clientele gathers here to cruise and guzzle cold beer.

Harvey's
500 Castro St., corner 18th St.
☎431-4278
Harvey's bar honours the memory of assassinated city supervisor Harvey Milk. A mixed crowd gathers here to drink while gazing out the picture windows to watch passersby strolling along

the street. Unaccompanied clients can always drink their beer while watching TV on one of the wall-mounted sets.

The Café
2367 Market St.
www.cafesf.com
The Café isn't a coffee shop, but a dance club where a mixed, high-spirited, mainly gay crowd whoops it up amidst the general jubilation. There are a few pool tables, but be sure to get here early because playing is forbidden after 9pm as the place simply gets too crowded. The club also features an outdoor terrace where smokers can light up without breaking the law.

The Eagle
398 12th St., corner Harrison St.
☎626-0880
A hot spot for the "Levi's & leather" set, the sparsely decorated Eagle tavern is just the place for having a drink with friends. The bar features a terrace where smokers can light up with impunity.

Twin Peaks
401 Castro St., corner Market St.
☎864-9470
A bar with a laid-back vibe, Twin Peaks is in no way linked to David Lynch's cult TV series. The place features mismatched armchairs, but the wall behind the bar is graced with gorgeous decorative woodwork. A mature male crowd comes to quietly chat with friends over a cold beer.

Mission

Dylan's
2301 Folsom St., corner 19th St.
☎641-1416
Named after Dylan Thomas, Dylan's is a fine little pub. Artists in search of inspiration as well as regulars congregate at the

bar to raise a pint to the Welsh poet's memory.

Lexington Club
3464 19th St.
between Valencia and Mission sts.
☎863-2052
The Lexington Club is *the* lesbian bar in town. Women come here to dance, chat, play pool, have a drink, check each other out and swap phone numbers. The jukebox plays hits from the 1970s and 1980s.

The San Francisco Area

Sausalito (Marin County)

No Name Bar
757 Bridgeway St.
☎332-1392
Clint Eastwood's former haunt is a warm bar that regularly showcases live jazz.

East Bay

Berkeley

Bison Brewing Co.
2598 Telegraph Ave.
☎(510) 841-7734
If you can't resist the urge to try a chocolate- or coriander-flavoured beer, head to the Bison Brewing Co. and order a Chocolate Stout or a Coriander Rye. Of course, the bar also offers more traditional home-brewed beers for the less adventurous. You can also fill up on mussels, pizza or "tacodillas" (a cross between a taco and a quesadilla).

Jupiter
2181 Shattuck Ave.
☎(510) 843-8277
Housed in a former 1890s livery stable, Jupiter is a brew pub decorated in the Gothic style, complete with a copper-plated bar. A top-notch selection of

home-brewed and imported beers is offered, and jazz combos occasionally liven up evenings. Patrons can also enjoy *focaccia* sandwiches, wood-fired pizzas or a game on the vintage pinball machine.

Triple Rock Brewery & Alehouse
1920 Shattuck Ave.
☎(510) 843-2739
The Triple Rock Brewery & Alehouse prides itself on being the fifth brew pub to open its doors in the United States, offering an outstanding choice of strong and light beers. The kitchen dishes up nachos, chili and homemade soup for those feeling peckish. Weather permitting, you can sip your beer on the rooftop terrace while admiring the view.

Oakland

Ben and Nick's
662 College Ave.
☎(510) 923-0327
Ben and Nick's is a friendly, unpretentious brew pub. Hungry patrons can also chow down on chicken wings and juicy burgers.

Eli's Mile High Club
3629 Martin Luther King Jr. Blvd.
☎(510) 655-6661
Located off the beaten track, Eli's Mile High Club draws a crowd of regulars and wayfarers with a soft spot for heavy, incisive, haunting blues. The decor is basic and the beer is cold.

Kimball's East
5800 Shellmound, Emeryville
☎(510) 658-2555
Located northwest of town, Kimball's East is renowned for showcasing top-notch blues and jazz acts.

Fifth Amendment
3255 Lakeshore Ave.
☎(510) 832-3242
The Fifth Amendment is another good spot that will live up to the expectations of blues and jazz aficionados. The facade isn't much to look at, but the clientele is surprisingly dapper.

Spectator Sports

Baseball

Between the months of April and August, the **San Francisco Giants** go to bat at Pacific Bell Park (**☎467-8000**), the first privately financed major-league ballpark since Dodgers Stadium in 1962. The right-field fence is so close to the water that a mini-scoreboard displays the number of home runs sent into the bay.

Fans of the **Oakland A's** (**☎569-2121**) only have to ride the BART across the Bay Bridge to cheer on their favourite team at the Oakland Coliseum.

Ice Hockey

If you're visiting the area sometime between October and April, note that the **San Jose Sharks** play their local games at the San Jose Arena (**☎408-287-7070**), located less than an hour's drive from San Francisco.

From October to April, the **San Francisco Spiders** slug it out with their rivals at the Cow Palace (**☎656-3000**). The Spiders are part of the International Hockey League (IHL) and generally offer high-calibre hockey action.

Football

From September to November, the **San Francisco 49ers** face their adversaries at 3Com Park, better known under its former name Candlestick Park (**☎467-8400**).

On the other side of the bay, the **Oakland Raiders**, who once moved to Los Angeles only to return to Oakland, also have the home-field advantage at the Oakland Coliseum (**☎569-2121**).

Basketball

Between November and April, the **Golden State Warriors** take on their rivals at the Oakland Coliseum (**☎510-639-7700**).

Shopping

Most stores and boutiques are located in the Union Square district. In fact, those who love to shop and have money to burn will be in shopping heaven, as they clean out the chic boutiques located on and around Union Square. Neiman Marcus, Saks Fifth Avenue, Versace and Macy's are a few of the A-list stores worth mentioning.

Department Stores

Macy's in Union Square
170 O'Farrell St., corner Stockton St., Union Square
☎397-3333
Macy's is one of the world's biggest stores with seven floors featuring, among other things, personalized clothing lines, cosmetics, as well as

comfortable lingerie. The store also houses the Rainforest Café (see p 444) on the eighth floor and the Wolfgang Puck Café (see p 441) in the basement, for those who want a snack between purchases.

Neiman Marcus
150 Stockton St., corner Geary St., Union Square
☎362-3900
Neiman Marcus has not been the most popular store among locals since it replaced the defunct City of Paris (once considered the city's most stylish department store) at the start of the 20th century, to the great displeasure of many residents. It has, however, preserved the beautiful glass rotunda and carries selected designer fashions such as Prada, Gucci, Armani, Chanel and Dior. You will also find a fabulous Baccarat crystalware collection, if you are thinking of replacing your own fine glassware.

Saks Fifth Avenue
384 Post St., Union Square
☎986-4300
A New York institution, the swank Saks Fifth Avenue also stands northwest of Union Square in San Francisco, and offers a vast array of attire for both mother and daughter. Men are not left out, however, as the store also has a few sections to answer their needs.

Saks Fifth Avenue Men's
220 Post St., corner Stockton St., Union Square
☎986-4300
Men seeking designer threads by Giorgio Armani or Ralph Lauren in a shiny decor reminiscent of Art Deco should head to Saks Fifth Avenue Men's, located a stone's throw from the main store on the same street.

Shopping Centres

The Cannery
2801 Leavenworth St., between Jefferson St. and Beach St., Fisherman's Wharf
Once a fruit canning plant, The Cannery was transformed into a three-storey commercial building on a quaint central square with neighbouring restaurants and boutiques.

Ghirardelli Square
North Point St., between Larlin St. and Polk St., Fisherman's Wharf
Ghirardelli Square is a former chocolate factory whose time-worn premises were transformed into a shopping centre. By offering a wide range of services to the public, this shopping centre strives to attract and seduce as many shoppers as possible, who come from all over.

San Francisco Shopping Center
Market St., corner Fifth Ave., Union Square
Even if you don't buy anything at the San Francisco Shopping Center, it's worth a visit, if only to take one of its spiral staircases, which provide greater space for shoppers at the heart of a lovely oval atrium.

Metreon
101 Fourth St., South of Market
www.metreon.com
Owned by Sony Entertainment, the Metreon is the latest addition to San Francisco's shopping and entertainment scene. This huge shopping centre features such shops as The Discovery Channel Store, Sony Style Store, Sony PlayStation Store and the only Microsoft store in the world (there isn't even one in Seattle). Aside from these specialized stores, the shopping centre also holds 15 movie theatres and an IMAX theatre.

Crocker Galleria
50 Post St., Financial District
Adorned with a magnificent glass dome, the Crocker Galleria is modelled after Milan's Galleria Vittorio Emmanuel II. Several renowned ready-to-wear designers such as Gianni Versace, Polo Ralph Lauren, Cesare Paciotti and Nicole Miller, have stores here. Shoppers can also satisfy their hunger pangs at one of the shopping centre's many small cafés and restaurants.

Clothing

Clothing and Fashion Accessories

Kenneth Cole
166 Grant Ave., Union Square
☎981-2653
or
2078 Union St., Cow Hollow
☎346-216
or
865 Market St., Union Square
☎227-4536
Fans of Kenneth Cole will certainly want to stop and take a look inside his huge San Francisco store, which carries his KC clothing line.

Diesel
101 Post St., Union Square
☎982-7077
If you want stylish threads, Italy's Diesel line carries a vast array of clothes on three floors that will satisfy the most unconventional tastes of men, women and children.

Banana Republic
256 Grant Ave., corner Sutter St., Union Square
☎788-3087
Banana Republic is enjoying exceptional growth and the sportswear com-

pany has one of its biggest stores in San Francisco. You will find pants, turtle-necks, shoes, numerous jackets and even a few accessories.

Bella Donna

539 Hayes St., Hayes Valley
☎861-7180
or
1528 Grant Ave., Union Square
☎861-7182
In the fashion and ready-to-wear world, Bella Donna is a name that stands for certain refined aesthetic values. The store also offers an excellent array of hats and wedding gowns.

Betsy Johnson

160 Geary St., Union Square
☎398-2516
or
2033 Fillmore St., Pacific Heights
☎567-272
Known in fashion's high circles for the quality of her innovative clothes, Betsy Johnson's boutiques will rise to the expecta-tions and meet the needs of customers looking for a touch of unconventional-ity.

Chanel Boutique

155 Maiden Lane, Union Square
☎981-1550
A symbol of femininity, the Chanel Boutique offers customers spicy and colourful fragrances, pre-sented in lovely bottles that are exclusive to this renowned line of perfume. The store also sells shoes, jewellery and other stylish accessories.

Gucci

200 Stockton St., Union Square
☎392-2808
In the selective world of this flamboyant Italian fashion house, the Gucci store offers stylish clothes and accessories to add a little flair to your ward-robe.

Retro Clothing

Buffalo Exchange

1555 Haight St., Haight-Ashbury
☎431-7733
or
1800 Polk St.
☎346-5726
Buffalo Exchange is a retro-clothing store featur-ing styles and fashions from the 1950s. You will find loud shirts, old Levi's and a good selection of more or less outdated garb.

Women's Lingerie

Victoria's Secret

335 Powell St.
☎433-9671
or
2061 Chestnut St., Marina
☎923-9750
or
865 Market St., Union Square
☎882-0864
Victoria's Secret is no lon-ger a secret to anyone: everybody knows it carries a beautiful range of ladies' undergarments that will please women as much as men.

Children's Clothing

Mudpie

2220 Chestnut St., Marina
☎474-8395
or
1694 Union St., Cow Hollow
☎771-9262
Popular with parents with money to burn, Mudpie is renowned for its quality designer products that will make your kids shine. Good toy selection.

Kids Only

1608 Haight St., Haight-Ashbury
☎552-5445
Though less posh than Mudpies, Kids Only carries children's clothing and toys.

Hats

Mrs. Dewson's Hats

2050 Fillmore St.
☎346-1600
If you are seeking to add an eclectic element to your wardrobe, head to Mrs. Dewson's Hats to pick up a panama or another styl-ish hat.

Hats on Post

210 Post St., Union Square
☎392-3737
Hats are also the main attraction at Hats on Post. This is a great place to buy original and unusual hats.

Shoes

Frank More Shoes

105 Grant Ave., Union Square
☎732-7245
If you are looking for quality shoes, drop by Frank More, which carries the big names in shoes.

Rockport

165 Post St., Union Square
☎951-4801
Rockport carries a wide range of its well-known and extremely comfortable walking shoes. Ideal for tackling the city's steep hills.

Birkenstock

42 Stockton St.
☎989-2475
Those who prefer comfort-able sandals will opt for classic Birkenstocks.

Sporting Goods

The North Face

1325 Howard St., South of Market
☎626-6444
The North Face is ex-tremely popular with outdoor enthusiasts and the store sells a whole range of backpacks, hiking shoes and quality parkas. Service is courteous and advice is most often sound.

Patagonia
770 Northpoint St.,
Fisherman's Wharf
☎*771-2050*
Synonymous with quality
outerwear, Patagonia rises
to the expectations of
mountain dwellers and
outdoor lovers thanks to
an excellent array of items
and clothing that let them
practise all outdoor activities in any weather.

Nike Town
278 Post St.
☎*392-NIKE*
Housed on three floors in
a huge, modern building,
Nike Town welcomes you
to its temple consecrated
to the glory of sport. Large
screens constantly feature
the exploits of certain athletes, who are obviously
wearing Nike products.
This presentation, which
apparently serves to pro-
mote and glorify sport in
general, specifically aims
to get you to take out your
wallet and buy the prod-
ucts modelled by the elite
athletes, who seem so
proud to be wearing Nike.

Toys

F.A.O. Schwarz
48 Stockton St., Union Square
☎*394-8700*
A real Ali Baba cave for
mischievous boys and
girls, F.A.O. Schwarz is a
source of wonder like no
other for kids. Children
can rove around several
floors of toys that will
spark their imaginations
and live up to their wildest
dreams.

Disney Store
400 Post St., Union Square
☎*391-6866*
As the supplier of the vast
array of "Wonderful World
of Disney" products, the
Disney Store offers kids all
the knick-knacks they see
in cartoons and in their
dreams, ranging from

Mickey Mouse T-shirts to
Donald Duck coffee mugs.

Wine, Beer and Spirits

PlumpJack Wine Store
3201 Fillmore St., Pacific Heights
☎*346-9870*
The PlumpJack Wine Store
carries great Californian,
European and Australian
vintages.

Napa Valley Winery Exchange
415 Taylor St.
☎*771-2887*
The Napa Valley Winery
Exchange specializes in
California wines.

Wine Club
953 Harrison St., between Fifth St.
and Sixth St., South of Market
☎*512-9086*
A quick glance at the Wine
Club's window does not
do the store justice. The
Wine Club is a place to
keep in mind for wine at
absolutely unbeatable
prices.

Florists

Ixia
2331 Market St., corner Castro St.,
Castro
☎*431-3134*

Podesta Baldocchi
508 Fourth Ave.
☎*346-1300*
Ixia and Podesta Baldocchi
are two excellent stops for
those looking for colourful
flower arrangements or
flamboyant bouquets.

Bookshops

City Lights Bookstore
261 Broadway, Columbus
☎*362-8193*
www.citylights.com
The City Lights Bookstore
is the mecca of counterculture and was the first
bookstore in North Amer-

ica to sell pocket books. It
still sells books at the opposite end of political cor-
rectness. Catering to the
general public, it also has
a beatnik literature section.
This is the perfect book-
store to browse for hours
and uncover a classic, out-
of-print book lying unno-
ticed on a shelf.

Borders Books and Music
400 Post St., corner Powell St.,
Union Square
☎*399-1633*
www.borders.com
The Borders Books and
Music mega-chain invites
customers to browse its
four floors that are stocked
with over 100,000 books.
This huge store also fea-
tures a large selection of
CDs and DVDs. Customers
can leaf through books in
peace as they sip a deli-
cious coffee in the store's
café and enjoy the view of
Union Square.

A Different Light
489 Castro St. between 17th St. and
18th St., Castro
☎*431-0891 or 800-343-4002*
A Different Light is a
branch of a bookstore that
specializes in gay, lesbian
and bisexual literature.

San Francisco Museum of Modern Art Bookstore
151 Third St.,
between Mission St. and Howard St.
☎*357-4035*
After visiting the Museum
of Modern Art, why not
stop at its souvenir shop
and pick up an art book to
bring home? The book-
store also offers a lovely
collection of children's
books.

Rizzoli
117 Post St., Union Square
☎*984-0225*
Rizzoli is renowned for its
cookbooks and interior
decorating books. Custom-
ers can also enjoy a full-
flavoured, strong espresso
at its small café.

Comix Experience

305 Divisidero St., Haight-Ashbury
☎ 863-9258

If you have a weakness for comics, head to the Comix Experience, a small store that sells all kinds of comics.

San Francisco Mystery Bookstore

4175 24th St., between Castro St. and Diamond St., Noe Valley
☎ 282-7444
www.mysterynet.com/sfmb

Whodunnit and mystery fans should know that the venerable San Francisco Mystery Bookstore has been the *crème de la crème* in this genre for over 25 years.

Café de la Presse

352 Grant Ave. Union Square

Located at the gates to Chinatown, the Café de la Presse is a small café that specializes in carrying a vast array of European magazines and newspapers.

Travel Bookshops

Rand McNally

595 Market St., Union Square
☎ 777-3131

Rand McNally wins hands-down for the store offering the biggest selection of road maps. It has a good selection of road and city maps, as well as travel accessories. The store also sells a few travel guides.

Get Lost Travel Books Maps & Gear

1825 Market St., Union Square
☎ 437-0529

Get Lost Travel Books Maps & Gear carries a good selection of travel guides and maps.

Music

Virgin Megastore

2 Stockton St., corner Market St.
☎ 397-4525

Those looking for a CD, audiocassette, DVD or videocassette at competitive prices will no doubt find what they are looking for and much more at the Virgin Megastore. Several listening stations are also available for those who prefer listening to CDs before buying them.

Recycled Records

1377 Haight St., corner Masonic Ave., Haight-Ashbury
☎ 626-4075

Recycled Records is the obvious place to go for old retro music LPs protected between record sleeves.

Musical Instruments

Music Center

1540 Haight St., Haight-Ashbury
☎ 863-7327
www.haight-ashbury-music.com

The Music Center is the place to go to buy guitars, or new or used amplifiers. You can also purchase bass guitars and guitar strings.

Drum World

5016 Mission St., Mission
☎ 334-7559

As its name indicates, Drum World offers a good selection of drums and cymbals.

Computers

Microsoft Store

101 Fourth St., South of Market
www. metreon.com

The Microsoft Store, which is the only store in the world devoted to the exclusive sale of Bill Gates's products, will definitely answer the needs of Windows users. The store also has a few computers equipped with

Microsoft's latest operating system on display for customers. You can also surf the net or open your own e-mail account for free.

Computer Ware

343 Sansome St., Financial District
☎ 362-3010
www.macsource.com

Fans of Macintosh products will find software or video games that are compatible with their Imac or Power MacG4 (with double processor) at Computer Ware.

Art Galleries

The stretch of Bridgeway Street that runs along the Viña del Mar Park features a good number of art galleries. Caledonia Street is also bordered by a few interesting shops.

Miscellaneous

Discovery Channel Store

101 Fourth St., South of Market
☎ 442-0706

As you have no doubt guessed, the Discovery Channel Store sells a range of products that stem from the eponymous television chain, including videos, CD-ROMs, books, games and telescopes.

Good Vibrations

1210 Valencia St., corner 23rd St., Mission
☎ 974-8980
2504 San Pablo Ave., corner Dwight St., Berkeley
☎ (510)841-8987

Open since 1977, Good Vibrations is not a shabby sex-shop run by disturbing-looking characters with lustful eyes. This non-conformist sex-shop caters mainly to women and provides information on a healthy sex life. Good selection of "toys," books and videos to spice up your sex life.

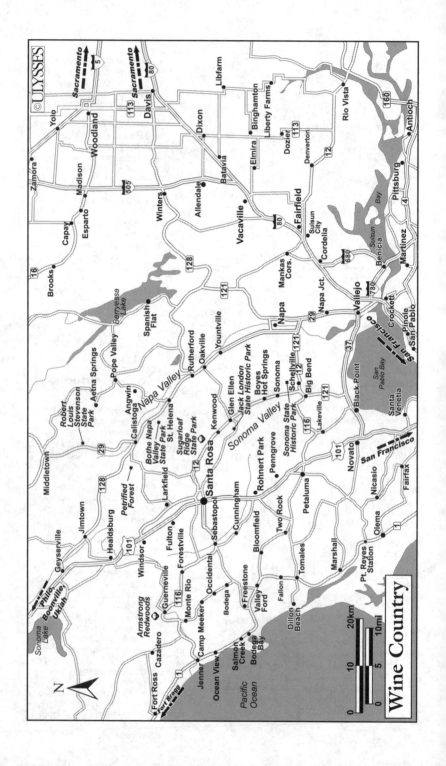

Wine Country

Wine Country

The parallel valleys of Sonoma and Napa have become so renowned as the home of fine wines and wineries that they attract millions of visitors annually from all over the world.

Despite their great fame, Sonoma and Napa counties (about an hour's drive north of San Francisco) actually only account for a small percentage of the total production of California's wine industry.

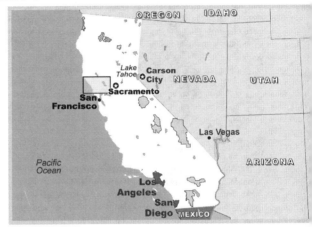

This industry had its humble beginning in 1823 when the first grapes were planted by Franciscan padres associated with the Mission San Francisco Solano de Sonoma, the northernmost and final mission to be established in California. However the foundation for the industry's modern-day success rested on the outstanding contributions of a Hungarian emigre, Count Agoston Haraszthy.

Indeed, viticulture reigns over all 17mi (27.4km) of Sonoma Valley, on or near Route 12, beginning with the history-rich, small town of Sonoma and extending northward to the busy urban county seat of Santa Rosa. Yet there is much to savour in this area besides a delicious Chardonnay or Cabernay Sauvignon. Is it any surprise to find that wherever fine wines prevail, so too do fine dining establishments and overnight accommodations? And for those wishing to offset the effects of all that tempting wine and food—as well as for those who don't overindulge in the first place—opportunities to hike, fish, camp and bike are plentiful. On the other hand, those with a literary appetite will likely find satisfaction exploring Glen Ellen's Jack London State Park with its museum full of mementos from the life of the celebrated adventurer-author of the novels *The Call of the Wild* and *The Iron Heel*. In nearby Santa Rosa, the achievements of great horticulturalist Luther Burbank, who developed or improved upon 800 botanical hybrids, will intrigue plant enthusiasts who stop to investigate the Luther Burbank Home and Gardens.

Moving east to the more famous, if less scenically varied Napa Valley, travellers primarily interested in what the world of wine has to offer need but stay on one road, Route

29, for 35mi (56km), and they'll have access to almost 300 wineries! This trip from south to north (keep in mind that a parallel route a couple of miles to the east called the Silverado Trail always provides a ready escape from the ardors of the beaten path) begins in Napa, passes through Yountville, Rutherford, Oakville, Saint Helena and winds up in Calistoga, a town best-known for its bottled water, hot springs, spas and mud baths. Along the way, many charming bed and breakfasts and gourmet restaurants alternate with well-known winery names like Beringer and Robert Mondavi.

Like Sonoma Valley, Napa Valley features a number of beautiful state parks devoted to outdoor recreation, as well as one devoted to a literary celebrity—Robert Louis Stevenson. This Scottish author is also honoured with a museum in Saint Helena. By heading 8mi (13km) north of Calistoga, you will reach the undeveloped Robert Louis Stevenson State Park, where the author of *Trea-*

sure Island and *The Strange Case of Dr. Jekyll and Mr. Hyde* honeymooned in 1880. A splendid way to cap off a tour of the wine country is to climb the park's extinct volcano, Mount Saint Helena, to enjoy the panoramic views as far south as San Francisco and, on a clear day, as far northeast as Mount Shasta.

For those who are interested in exploring wine country but seek to avoid the Sonoma and Napa valley crowds, Sonoma County's three valleys of the Russian River—The Alexander, The Dry Creek and the Russian River—provide a relaxing alternative. Extending west from Guerneville to Healdsburg and then north to Ukiah, the Russian River region is home to more than 75 wineries, ranging from small family-owned operations to reputable corporate giants. Travellers hoping to take advantage of the region's outdoor recreational possibilities will find many places to hike, camp, swim, fish, canoe, raft, sunbathe and picnic to their heart's content. Family and gay-friendly, Guerneville is the major gay resort in Northern California. Russian River country will please just about everyone with its

vast array of laid-back vacation opportunities.

Finding Your Way Around

By Car

Napa Valley

Though not very interesting, the quickest route to Napa Valley is Route 80. From San Francisco, this highway heads northeast until Vallejo where it joins Route 37 and then Route 29—the principal axis route of the valley.

Another option is to take Route 101 north. It also meets up with Route 37, which encircles the San Pablo Bay before crossing Route 29.

Sonoma Valley

The most scenic drive, however, is along Highway 121 up to Highway 37. This country road, which is also connected to Route 29, nicely foreshadows wine country, since the hills are covered with vineyards, ranches and sheep pastures. Highway 121 crosses, among others, Highway 12, which leads to the Sonoma Valley.

The Russian River Region

The Russian River region is crossed by busy Highway 101, providing those in a hurry with easy access to the wineries that border it. We highly recommend that you venture off Highway 101, however, in order to explore Highway 116, the

Bohemian Highway, Westside Road and other side roads. If your destination is Guerneville, take Highway 116.

By Bus

Greyhound Bus Lines
☎800-231-2222
Greyhound has frequent service to the Napa and Sonoma Valleys. Buses also stop at Healdsburg, and Geyserville in addition to other northern spots.

Public Transportation

There is no public transportation in Napa.

Sonoma County Transit
☎(707) 576-7433
The Sonoma County Transit covers the region between Sonoma and Santa Rosa, stopping in Glen Ellen and Kenwood. From Santa Rosa it goes to Windsor, Healdsburg and Geyserville as well as servicing other communities that are located between these two latter destinations.

By Limousine/Taxi

Sonoma Valley

Sonoma Airporter
524B W. Napa St.
Sonoma
☎(707) 938-4246
☎800-611-4246
This is a very handy service for those who want to travel around in Wine Country without renting a car, since it provides transportation between San Francisco International Airport and Sonoma Valley.

Practical Information

The area code is **707** unless otherwise indicated.

Emergencies

Napa Valley

Urgent Care Center
every day noon to 9pm, no appointment necessary
(two blocks east of the Trancas Ave. and Hwy. 29 intersection, one block from the Queen of the Valley Hospital)
3230 Beard Rd., Napa
94558
☎254-7778
If, God forbid, you have a medical emergency to deal with while you're in Wine Country, this is a good bet because it offers fairly prompt service and is cheaper than going to an emergency room.

Tourist Information

Napa Valley

Napa Valley Conference and Visitors Bureau
1310 Napa Town Center
94559
☎226-7459
≈255-2066
www.napavalley.com
info@napavalley.org

Sonoma Valley

Sonoma County Wine and Visitor's Center
5000 Roberts Lake Rd.
Rohnert Park 94928
☎586-3795
☎800-939-7666
www.sonomawine.com
info@sonomawine.com

Sonoma Tourism and Visitor's Bureau
453 First St. E.
Sonoma
☎996-1090

Russian River Region Visitor's Information Center
14034 Armstrong Woods Rd.
Guerneville
☎869-9212

Banks

Sonoma Valley Bank
Mon to Fri 9am to 5pm, Sat 10am to 2pm
202 W. Napa St.
☎935-3200

Exploring

★★★

Napa Valley

A narrow valley that forms a quilt of assorted vine patches dotted with windmills, wooden barns and gorgeous stone wineries, the 35mi (56.3km) expanse of Napa Valley is a feast for all the senses. Socially, it's dominated by movie stars dressed incognito, auspicious and closet millionaires, authentic and affected connoisseurs and, of course, tourists.

To avoid traffic jams, it is probably a good idea to visit the valley during the week and, if possible, outside of the summer months. When possible, cross over to the Silverado Trail and do some of your exploring there. Most people like to take Highway 29 to Calistoga and then to take the Silverado Trail back to Napa, but there is always the option of crossing over

Wine Country

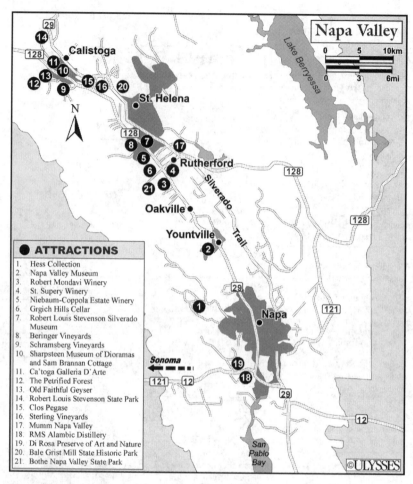

Napa Valley

0   5   10km
0   3   6mi

● ATTRACTIONS

1. Hess Collection
2. Napa Valley Museum
3. Robert Mondavi Winery
4. St. Supery Winery
5. Niebaum-Coppola Estate Winery
6. Grgich Hills Cellar
7. Robert Louis Stevenson Silverado Museum
8. Beringer Vineyards
9. Schramsberg Vineyards
10. Sharpsteen Museum of Dioramas and Sam Brannan Cottage
11. Ca'toga Galleria D'Arte
12. The Petrified Forest
13. Old Faithful Geyser
14. Robert Louis Stevenson State Park
15. Clos Pegase
16. Sterling Vineyards
17. Mumm Napa Valley
18. RMS Alambic Distillery
19. Di Rosa Preserve of Art and Nature
20. Bale Grist Mill State Historic Park
21. Bothe Napa Valley State Park

©ULYSSES

at other junctures. The **Napa Valley Wine Train** (see p 486) will take you pretty far up alongside Highway 29, providing escape from the traffic on the highway itself. You can then restrict your car exploration to the less congested Silverado Trail. No matter which route you decide on, you are in for a treat!

Napa and Surroundings

The town of Napa is mainly a residential area for those that live year-round in the valley and thus not traditionally considered a hub of cultural and gastronomical activity. This may soon change, however. Not only is the downtown core of Napa undergoing a facelift to provide a more interesting tourist infrastructure, an exciting new addition to the town is scheduled to open in the fall of 2001. On June 1, 1999, plans got underway for **The American Center for Wine, Food and the Arts** *(will be located on First St. between Soscol St. and Silverado Trail, 257-3606;* *www.theamericancenter.org)*, the brain-child of re-nowned wine-maker Rob-ert Mondavi. This grand cultural institution is in-tended to be the first fo-rum of its kind to salute the United States' unique contributions to wine, food and the arts. The plan calls for an 80,000 sq ft (7,432m²) two-storey pavil-ion that will be equipped with more than 13,000 sq ft (1,208m²) of galleries featuring interactive exhib-its (including a Gallery of the Senses), displays and working kitchens; 3.5 acres (1.4ha) of working and

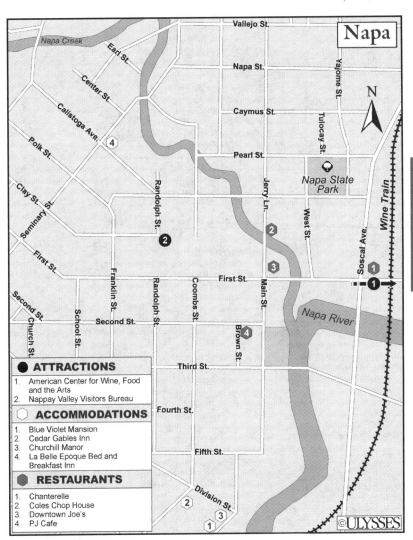

Napa

N

● ATTRACTIONS

1. American Center for Wine, Food and the Arts
2. Nappay Valley Visitors Bureau

⬡ ACCOMMODATIONS

1. Blue Violet Mansion
2. Cedar Gables Inn
3. Churchill Manor
4. La Belle Epoque Bed and Breakfast Inn

● RESTAURANTS

1. Chanterelle
2. Coles Chop House
3. Downtown Joe's
4. PJ Cafe

Wine Country

decorative gardens; an outdoor concert terrace for live music and theater performances; and a lively array of public programs for all ages, including seminars, lectures, culinary demonstrations, wine-tastings and workshops. This is definitely something to consider if you're planning a trip around this time.

Not exactly on Highway 29, but well worth a detour just before you venture up that way, is the **Hess Collection** ★★ *(every day 10am to 4pm except major holidays; 4411 Redwood Rd. Napa; ☎255-1144, www.hesscollection.com)*. In keeping with the predominant Napa tendency to fuse wine and art, the collection here is a mixture of 130 contemporary European and U.S. artworks, with the newest releases of Hess Collection and Hess

Select cabernets and chardonnays. Donald Hess, winery founder and art collector, has a preference for wines made with American Canyon and Mayacamas mountain grapes as well as for thought-provoking art made by U.S. Pop artist Robert Rauschenberg and various contemporary installation artists from both sides of the Atlantic. Three dollars will buy you a taste of a magnificent cabernet sauvignon and a few other choice wines.

Highway 29

Yountville

Once you're on Highway 29, the first mandatory stop is what has become known as the gastronomical capital of Napa Valley, Yountville. Before stopping for lunch or dinner (see p 487), however, why not check out the **Napa Valley Museum** ★ *($4.50; Wed to Mon 10am to 5pm; 55 President's Circle, ☎944-0500, www. napavalleymuseum.org)* In addition to hosting some very interesting travelling exhibitions, this small modernist museum features a permanent interactive wine exhibit, though it can't really compete with the one at the St. Supéry Winery in Rutherford (see p 468).

Oakville

If you're interested in visiting a large, commercial winery with one of the more informative winemaking tours in the valley, stop at the **Robert Mondavi Winery** ★ *(7801 St. Helena Hwy.; ☎226-1395)* in Oakville. What's more, participation in the free 1hr tour that is given between 10am and 4pm entitles you to a free wine tasting. In-depth tours lasting from 3 to 4hrs are also available by appointment for those who want to become experts overnight.

Rutherford

More a conglomeration of wineries and restaurants than a town, Rutherford has at least three sites that

are worth checking out in addition to some very fine restaurants, The Auberge de Soleil and La Toque (see p 483 and 487).

What makes the **St. Supéry Winery** ★★★ *($3 tasting fee; free self-guided tour; every day 9:30am to 4:30pm; 8440 St. Helena Hwy., ☎963-4507, www.stsupery.com)* special is the original way in which it portrays the many facets of wine. Displays featuring life-sized grapevine replicas, explanations of wine colours, topographical maps demonstrating Napa's ideal climate for grape growing and "smell-a-vision" samples of wine aromas are among the best in all of Wine Country.

An attractive winery run by Francis Ford Coppola and his wife Eleonor, the **Niebaum-Coppola Estate Winery** ★ *(1991 St. Helena Hwy.; ☎963-9099; www.niebaum-coppola.com)* houses a display of artifacts from *The Godfather*, costumes from *Dracula* and movie stills from the great film director's career, as well as an exhibit explaining the history of the Niebaum Estate. Famous for its cabernet sauvignon and its Rubicon wines, the estate was once used as collateral to finance the making of *Apocalypse Now* and then saved by the success of *The Godfather III*. How about buying some Coppola Mammarella organic pasta sauce or merlot vinaigrette in the gift shop while you're at it?

A smaller winery with no gimmicks, **The Grgich Hills Cellar** ★ *(tasting free on weekdays, $3 on weekends, every day 9:30am to 4:30pm; 1829 St. Helena Hwy.; ☎963-2411)* offers up some of the best wine around for tasting in its humble cellar.

Tours are possible by appointment only.

St. Helena

A charming Victorian false-front town that originally served local farmers, St. Helena has a main street that definitely merits an attentive stroll. Don't miss the old-fashioned movie theatre, the brick-and-stone IOOF Building and the ornate Ritchie Building.

If you're a literature buff, make sure you take in the **Robert Louis Stevenson Silverado Museum** *(every day noon to 4pm, closed Mon; 1490 Library Lane, ☎963-3757)* before you hit the main drag. This fine museum houses various manuscripts, letters, photographs and personal effects from the life of the globetrotting Victorian author, Robert Louis Stevenson. (See box)

The oldest continuously operating winery in Napa Valley and one of our personal favourites is **Beringer Vineyards** ★★★ *(2000 Main St.; ☎963-7115; www.beringer.com)*. The spectacular centrepiece to this winery, founded in 1876 by brothers Frederick and Jacob Beringer, is the Rhine House, a 17-room Tudor-style mansion built to be Frederick's private residence. Patterned after the Beringer home on the Rhine River in Mainz, Germany, the Rhine House features Belgian-style Art-Nouveau stained-glass windows with specific themes pertaining to the rooms they illuminate. Also noteworthy is the locally quarried rhyolite, a slate gabled roof and hand-carved German white oak. The house now serves as the Beringer hospitality centre. The tour of the the cellar tunnels—

Robert Louis Stevenson

Dipping into Robert Louis Stevenson's short book, *The Silverado Squatters*, the reader encounters early on the delicious comparison of wine to "bottled poetry." Stevenson is talking about the prospects for California wine, Napa Valley in particular, which was then (1880) in what he called "the experimental stage." He was right in his prediction of the success of these wines that would irventiably follow as evidenced in his statement that "the smack of California earth shall linger on the palate of your grandson." The man whose literary fame rests on such works as *Treasure Island*, *A Child's Garden of Verses*, and *The Strange Case of Dr. Jekyll and Mr Hyde* spent his honeymoon on the slopes of Mount Saint Helena, several miles north of Calistoga. His

bride was Fanny Osborne, a U.S. divorcee and mother, whom he had met four years before at an artist's colony in Grez, France and had followed to California. Always physically fragile, the young writer, impoverished and ill, lived in Monterey, San Francisco and Oakland while he waited for her divorce.

During their several months as squatters camping out in a broken-down shack next to the abandoned Silverado Mine, enjoying the restorative climate, Robert regained his health sufficiently to be able to return to his native Scotland with his new wife. Today, there is nothing left of their rugged, make-shift Silverado home in what has become the undeveloped Robert Louis

Stevenson State Park. However, anyone interested in finding out more about Robert Louis Stevenson can pore over more than 8,000 items in the Silverado Museum of Calistoga, a silver mine of Stevensoniana. It is a great pity that this gifted writer and California wine enthusiast did not live past the age of forty-four (1850-1894).

The following quotation attests to Stevenson's passion for this local elixer... *"I tasted every variety and share of Schramberger (this winery continues to operate today) red and white Schramberger, burgundy Schramberger, Schramberger Hock, Schramberger golden chasselas, the latter with a notable bouquet, and I fear to think how many more."*

Wine Country

literally chiselled from underground stone by Chinese labourers—is capped off with wine-tasting in the former Gentlemen's Quarters of the Rhine House. In our opinion this is the best tasting given in Wine Country. If you can afford it, pick up a bottle of the 1986 Private Reserve Cabernet Sauvignon or the 1994 Private Reserve Chardonnay, both of which have received honours as the *Wine Spectator* Wine of the Year.

★
Calistoga

How would you like to taste a sparkling wine that is served to diplomats and VIPs when they are visiting the White House? If you have been smart enough to phone in advance for an appointment, you will get your chance as you approach Calistoga. **Schramsberg Vineyards** *(Schramsberg Rd.,* ☎*942-4558 for appointment; www.schramsbrg.com)* was

originally made famous as the place where Robert Louis Stevenson tasted 18 different wines during his *Silverado Squatter* days. Nowadays, the specialty at this California Historical Landmark winery is sparkling wine made according to the *methode champenoise*. Check out the photographs of various Heads of State, including former U.S. President Bill Clinton, French Prime Minister Jacques Chirac and Canadian Prime Minister Jean Chretien as you savour

Sam Brannan

After a voyage of several months from New York City around the Horn, a ship anchored in July 1846 at the village of Yerba Buena, California. The 238 Mormons—men, women, and children—aboard were seeking refuge from religious persecution. The group was led by a 26-year old Mormon printer and entrepreneur named Sam Brannan. A few months later, Yerba Buena changed its name to San Francisco and Brannan began printing the first newspaper in California, the *California Star*. This ambitious, clever man had thus launched a career that would make him California's first millionaire. Yet, interestingly enough, he became rich not by mining gold but by catering to the needs of those who did.

In early April 1848, a few months after the major discovery of gold had been made at Sutter's Mill in Coloma, Sam Brannan visited the area and even found some gold. In very short order he established stores at Sutter's Fort, at the Sacramento landing, 3mi (4.8km) below the fort, and at Sutter's Mill itself. The supplies and equipment he sold to understocked miners (such as tents, whiskey, boots, blankets and clothing) regularly earned him a profit of from 300 to 400%! In an effort to encourage emigration and, of course, therefore

increase business, Brannan had 2,000 copies of the *California Star*'s April 1, 1848, "Great Express Extras" mule-trained to Missouri. Its enticing message proclaimed "The Great Sacramento Valley has a mine of gold... From all accounts it is immensely rich and already we learn, the gold collected from it, collected at random and without trouble, has become an article of trade." On his return to San Francisco from Coloma on Friday May 12, 1848, Brannan created wild, widespread anticipation and excitement. He walked up Montgomery Street in San Francisco, a crowd following him, holding aloft a bottle containing gold flakes, grains and dust, and shouting "Gold! Gold! Gold from the American River!"

In Sacramento, where Brannan made a fair amount of money as the owner of the city's most prestigious hotel, the City Hotel, he made even more money as the result of his acumen in real-estate dealings. Understanding that the landing on the banks of the Sacramento River' rather than Sutter's Fort, would be a better location for a new commercial center, he convinced Sutter's oldest son to survey the area so that lots could be sold. And then he schemed to secure title to 500 prime waterfront lots in the city-

to-be. It can hardly come as a surprise then when Brigham Young, leader of the Mormon Church, tried to get back the tithing money that had initially underwritten this fabulously successful businessman's financial ventures. Brannan is reputed to have replied that he would return it when he received a receipt signed by the Lord!

Heavy drinking helped bring about Brannan's death as a pauper in San Diego County in 1889. Long before that, however, he called attention to himself as a public figure in a way that had nothing to do with making money. On June 9, 1887 in the city of San Francisco, where corruption was wide-spread at city hall (for example, judges and juries were often bribed) and great fires were commonplace (the fire of May 4, 1851 destroyed the whole business district, very likely the result of arson by organized gangs of robbers), a group of businessmen petitioned Sam to lead the Committee of Vigilance. The next day a man caught with a stolen safe was tried, pronounced guilty and hanged. His corpse remained suspended in mid-air for hours by men holding on to the rope, enforcing Brannan's command, "Every lover of liberty and good order, lay hold."

your glass of champagne. Beautiful gardens and a charming pond with a rather jubilant bronze frog holding a champagne glass are a couple of the other attractive features of this hillside winery.

Calistoga is probably the most interesting town in Napa Valley. Founded in 1859 by opportunistic entrepreneur Sam Brannan, who saw a potential fortune in its hot springs and underground reservoirs, Calistoga quickly became a renowned health resort. Today, the tradition continues as spas compete with each other for the bodies of stress-weary travellers who have already partaken of some of the divine elixir to be found on the various paths leading to Calistoga. If you would like to try out one of these spas, browse through our review of the pickings on p 481.

Of course, there are other things in town besides spas. **The Sharpsteen Museum of Dioramas and Sam Brannan Cottage** ★ *(Summer: 10am to 4pm; Winter: noon to 4pm; 1311 Washington St.; ☎942-5911, www.napanet. net/vi/sharpsteen)* showcases some impeccably crafted dioramas put together under the direction of Ben Sharpsteen, whose career with Walt Disney spanned 30 years. The most extraordinary display, which took three years to mount, depicts the Calistoga Hot Springs Resort when it was a popular hangout for wealthy San Franciscans. Another model, animated by a mechanized miniature locomotive, illustrates how Calistoga's Railroad Depot and picturesque Chinatown looked in the late 1800s. Two larger, almost life-size dioramas enchant

visitors with a stereoscopic vision of a 19th-century combination General Store and Post Office and an incredibly genuine barn scene from the same era. Apart from the dioramas, the Horseless Carriage Exhibit, which features some original paintings by Sharpsteen and the only remaining stagecoach from the Calistoga and Clear Lake Stage Line fleet, merits some attention. Lastly, the Sam Brannan Cottage, which is now attached to the museum, will give you an idea of what a guest cottage looked like in Calistoga's heyday.

A fascinating, recent addition to downtown Calistoga, the **Ca'toga Galleria D'Arte** ★★★ *(Wed to Sun 11am to 6pm; Fri and Sat 11am to 8pm; 1206 Cedar St.; ☎942-3900; ≈942-3939; www.catoga.co, galleria@catoga.com)* is a Palladian barrel-vaulted art gallery designed in the grand Renaissance style. Owner and *"Maestro d'Arte"* Carlo Marchiori has an international reputation as a mural painter and has completed projects for such prestigious organizations as The National Ballet of Canada, DisneySea Tokyo, The Smithsonian Institute in Washington, and the Cannes International Film Festival. He has been commissioned to work for such renowned individuals as Donald Trump and the late Pierre Elliot Trudeau.

You could say that the theme of this gallery is the sun, the stars and the moon. While the ceiling shows a mural representing the 48 Ptolemaic constellations and the 12 signs of the zodiac, the terazzo floor is a chart of the universe as conceived before Copernicus. Thus, you'll

have a chance to walk on the sun, the phases of the moon and the earth—the latter of which is inscribed with the Latin *"Hic es"* (you are here). Carlos Marchiori's own work fills the middle space: ceramics, watercolours, wood sculptures, furniture and garden accessories —all thoroughly unique and metaphysical. If you're lucky enough to be passing through Napa Valley on a pre-selected weekend in the early summer, Marchiori's home, a replica of a Venetian villa decorated throughout with fresco murals, is open for tours and is well worth a visit.

Though somewhat hokey, if you're travelling with children you might want to visit **The Petrified Forest** *(every day 10am to 6pm; 10am to 5pm in winter; 4100 Petrified Forest Rd., ☎942-6667)* and **Old Faithful Geyser** *(every day 9am to 5pm; 1299 Tubbs Lane, ☎942-6463; www.oldfaithfulgeyser. com)* while you're in Calistoga.

As you leave Calistoga, before heading down the Silverado Trail, take a 5mi (8km) detour to the **Robert Louis Stevenson State Park** and **Mount St. Helena** (see p 479) by way of Lincoln Avenue through to the continuation of Highway 29.

The Silverado Trail

Heading back towards Napa from Calistoga, on the Silverado Trail, veer left at Dunaweal Lane in order to visit two wineries that are interesting for different reasons. First you will encounter the postmodern **Clos Pegase** *(1060 Dunaweal Lane, ☎942-4981, www.clospegase.*

Wine Country

com). This winery features a tasting room with Honduran mahogany and antique glass highlights, a sculpture garden, a very fine art collection and a tank room with a large viewing window; this latter lets you gaze onto the mysterious production of some of the Dionysian liquids that are teasing your palette. **Sterling Vineyards** *($6; every day 10:30am to 4:30pm; 1111 Dunaweal Lane, ☎942-3344, www. sterlingvineyards.com),* on the other hand, is a white Greek monastery-style winery on a hillside with beautiful stained-glass windows and 18th-century church bells. The only way to get to the winery is via a **sky tram**, which gives visitors a stunning view of Napa Valley.

Continuing down the Silverado Trail just after Rutherford Cross, make sure to stop at **Mumm Napa Valley** ★ *(every day 10:30am to 6pm, tours every hour between 11am and 4pm; 8445 Silverado Trail, Rutherford, ☎942-3434 or 800-686-6272, www. mumm.com),* a winery (for sparkling wine) which offers fabulous tours and a permanent exhibit of some rare historic Ansel Adams photographs entitled "The Story of a Winery." Sitting down to taste a glass of champagne after the tour, you'll certainly agree with the declaration of Mumm Napa's Alan Packman that "Champagne is like a banjo: you can't play a sad song on a banjo; you can't drink champagne and be unhappy."

Los Carneros

To get to Sonoma Valley from Napa Valley why not take the natural link, Los Carneros? By travelling on either Highway 121 or Old Sonoma Road out of Napa, you'll inevitably find yourself at Highway 12. When you get to Cuttings Wharf Road, turn left and stop when you arrive at the **RMS (Remy Martin Signature) Alambic Distillery** ★ *(every day 10am to 4:30pm; 250 Cuttings Wharf Rd.; ☎253-9055, www.rmsbrandy.com).* Here, it is not wine, but brandy that rules. And fine brandy it is! One of the highlights of the very aesthetic tour is actually intended for the nose: a building full of barrels emitting the seductive aroma of fine brandy as it ages. The tours begin and end in an attractive visitors centre that is equipped with a model of an alambic brandy still fashioned by George Lucas of *Star Wars* fame.

Not far from the RMS distillery, but located on the other side of Highway 12, is the **di Rosa Preserve of Art and Nature** ★★ *($10; call ahead, guided tours by appointment only; closed on Sat afternoons, Sun and public holidays; 5200 Carneros Hwy, ☎226-5991).* Over 1,000 works from an outstanding private collection of San Franciscan contemporary art are displayed here in various galleries, a historical residence and a number of luxuriously open spaces. Please note that smoking, food and drinks are prohibited everywhere and that all large parcels and packs must be left in your car.

Sonoma Valley

While Napa Valley may be California Wine Country's most prestigeous region, Sonoma Valley is certainly its historical nucleus. After all, it was here that the Franciscan padres first planted grapes for their mission, later followed by the more entrepreneurial Colonel Agostin Haraszthy in the 1850s.

★★★
Sonoma

For a good introduction to Sonoma Valley, head to the **Sonoma Valley Visitors Bureau** (see p 465) in the heart of the town of Sonoma. The Plaza, as this historic part of town is referred to, has been Sonoma's downtown since 1835. However, it was left relatively unsettled until the fateful Bear Flag Rebellion in 1846, when a group of renegade settlers fashioned a flag from some women's petticoats and declared Sonoma the capital of the Bear Republic. The U.S. Government declared the land U.S. territory a month later and placed the official state flag on the homemade one created here.

A lovely park square framed by First Street East, First Street West, Spain Street and Napa Street, the Plaza is lined with old stone buildings, false-front stores and Spanish adobe structures, the most famous of which is the **Mission San Francisco Solano** *(First St. E. and E. Spain St., ☎938-1519)* California's most northernmost and final mission. The Sonoma Mission features a colourful chapel adorned with carved wooden sculptures and a multitude of paintings depicting other California missions. It is part of the **Sonoma State Historic Park** *($3 for a tour of all the buildings; every day 10am to 5pm; ☎938-1406,*

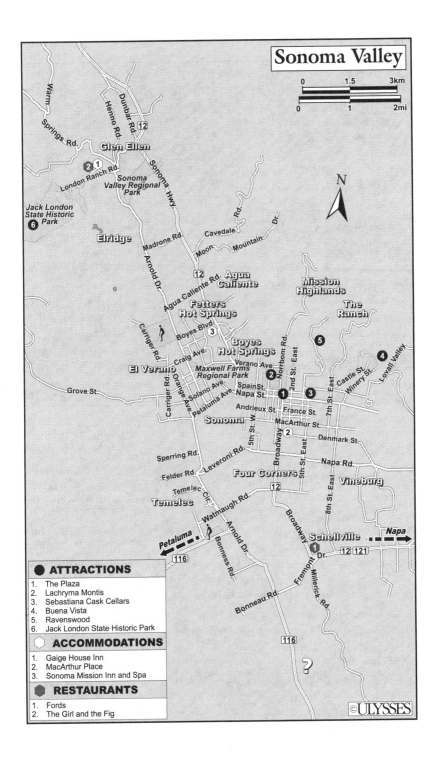

Sonoma Valley

0   1.5   3km
0   1   2mi

N

Warm

Springs Rd.

Dunbar Rd.

Henno Rd.

12

Glen Ellen

2 1

London Ranch Rd.

Sonoma Valley Regional Park

Sonoma Hwy.

Jack London State Historic Park
6 Park

Elridge

Madrone Rd.

Cavedale

Moon

Mountain

Dr.

Arnold Dr.

12 Agua Caliente Rd. Agua Caliente

Mission Highlands

The Ranch

Fetters Hot Springs

Carriger Rd.

Boyes Blvd.

3

Boyes Hot Springs

Verano Ave.

Norrbom Rd.

2nd St. East

5

4

Castle St.

Winery St.

Lovall Valley

El Verano

Craig Ave.

Carriger Rd.

Orange Ave.

Maxwell Farms Regional Park

Spain St.

Solano Ave.

Petaluma Ave.

Napa St.

2

1

3

7th St. East

Grove St.

Andrieux St.

France St.

MacArthur St.

Sonoma

5th St. W.

Broadway

2

Denmark St.

5th St. East

Sperring Rd.

Leveroni Rd.

Napa Rd.

Felder Rd.

Four Corners

12

8th St. East

Vineburg

Temelec Cir.

Temelec

Watmaugh Rd.

Arnold Dr.

Bonness Rd.

Petaluma

Broadway

Schellville

Napa

1

116

Fremont Dr.

12 121

Millerick Rd.

Bonneau Rd.

116

?

● ATTRACTIONS

1. The Plaza
2. Lachryma Montis
3. Sebastiana Cask Cellars
4. Buena Vista
5. Ravenswood
6. Jack London State Historic Park

◻ ACCOMMODATIONS

1. Gaige House Inn
2. MacArthur Place
3. Sonoma Mission Inn and Spa

◆ RESTAURANTS

1. Fords
2. The Girl and the Fig

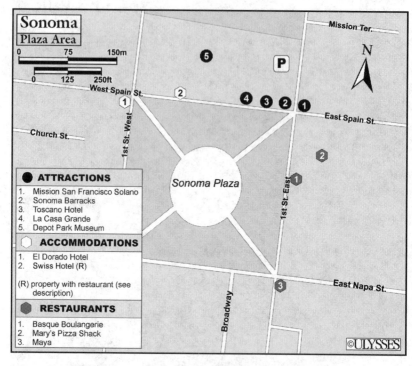

Sonoma Plaza Area

0   75   150m
0   125   250ft

Mission Ter.

West Spain St.

Church St.

1st St. West

East Spain St.

Sonoma Plaza

1st St. East

East Napa St.

Broadway

● **ATTRACTIONS**
1. Mission San Francisco Solano
2. Sonoma Barracks
3. Toscano Hotel
4. La Casa Grande
5. Depot Park Museum

⬡ **ACCOMMODATIONS**
1. El Dorado Hotel
2. Swiss Hotel (R)

(R) property with restaurant (see description)

⬢ **RESTAURANTS**
1. Basque Boulangerie
2. Mary's Pizza Shack
3. Maya

©ULYSSES

www.napanet.net/~sshpa), a complex of historical buildings that includes the Sonoma Barracks, the Toscano Hotel, La Casa Grande, Lachryma Montis, the Depot Park Museum and some of the older buildings that frame the Plaza. The **Sonoma Barracks** is a two-storey adobe building that was constructed to accommodate the troops of General Vallejo in 1836 and harbours a museum that highlights some early moments in California's history. The more up-scale **Toscano Hotel** *(Sat to Sun 1pm to 4pm, Mon 11am to 1pm, closed Mon in winter)*, originally a general store and library in 1852, was converted in 1886 to a hotel for Italian workers. **La Casa Grande** is actually a humble servant's quarters, the only part still remaining of General Vallejo's first adobe home.

If you would like to get a panoramic view of the Sonoma of the late 19th century or better understand the Bear Flag Rebellion, walk slightly north from the Plaza on First Street West and step into the **Depot Park Museum** *(Wed to Sun 1pm to 4:30pm; 270 First St. W., ☎938-1519)*.

At the very outskirts of Sonoma and easily accessible by bike is General Vallejo's final residence, **Lachryma Montis** *(end of Third St. W)*. This is the Yankee-style Victorian home General Vallejo had built in 1851 once his domain was taken over by the Americans. It was while living here that Mariano Vallejo re-made his image, serving in the U.S. government, writing a five-volume history of early California and trying his hand at wine-making.

One of the more interesting parts of the estate is the cookhouse and living quarters of the Chinese cook.

There are at least three wineries located in and around the town of Sonoma that merit a visit. Right in town, on Fourth Street East at the end of East Spain Street, is **Sebastiani Cask Cellars** *(free shuttle from the Plaza; every day 10am to 5pm; 389 Fourth St. E., ☎938-5532)*. This historical stone winery features a display of antique winemaking equipment and an impressive collection of hand-carved wine casks. For those who want to bring some local fruit, cheese and sourdough bread, a neighbouring picnic area allows you to catch some rays while savouring some fabulous wine along with your lunch.

Jack London

By the year 1905, when Jack London purchased the Hill Ranch near Glen Ellen, California, the 29 year old author/adventurer had become the first novelist to earn a $1,000,000. He was internationally famous for such novels as *Call of the Wild* and *The Sea Wolf.* Only eleven years later, at age 40, he would die of uremic poisoning on his beloved ranch, having written 50 books in 17 years. As he put it, "I am a believer in regular work and never wait for an inspiration." That same intense work ethic fuelled his major non-literary activities as well, including overseeing the building of his custom-made sailing vessel *The Snark* and of his dream dwelling the Wolf House, and attending to the everyday requirements of operating Beauty Ranch, which eventually expanded to 1,400 acres (567ha).

Anyone visiting Jack London State Historic Park today can easily see just by looking at the ruins of the Wolf House, with its 26 rooms and nine fireplaces, which Jack London hoped would stand for a thousand years, how grand his ambitions were and how dedicated he was to fulfilling them. Tragically, in August of 1913, a month before London and his wife Charmian were to move in, the 15,000 sq ft (1,394m²) house built of unpeeled redwood logs, lava rocks, and Spanish tile burnt to the ground.

In that same year of 1913, continuing to write, he published the novel *The Valley of the Moon,* and *John Barleycorn* a semi-autobiographical work on alcoholism, and the next year saw duty as a war correspondent for Colliers during the Mexican Revolution. But his principal focus during the final three years of his life was living close to the earth at the Beauty Ranch and taking in the challenges of learning how to farm scientifically. With a maximum of agricultural productivity as his goal, Jack London had workers construct cement-block silos over 40ft (12m) tall to store fodder, and paid Italian stone masons to make a manure pit so that fields could later be fertilized. He also had his steepest fields terraced so as to hold moisture and decrease erosion, and designed an extraordinary piggery called Pig Palace. Seventeen pens in a circle surrounded a central feedhouse, making it possible for each of the family of pigs to have its own living space. London's planting of fruit, grain and vegetable crops together with his raising of horses, pigs, cattle and other animals—in addition to his voluminous writings— assured that he would be survived by the fruit of his agricultural and literary labours even as he himself bowed out of this life early, declaring "*I would rather be ashes than dust! I would rather that my spark should burn out in a brilliant blaze than it should be stifled by dry rot.*"

By all means, don't miss the opportunity to see the place where it all began! If you take East Napa Street to Old Winery Road, following the latter to its very end, you surely won't be disappointed by a vist to **Buena Vista** ★★ *(every day 10:30am to 5pm; self-guided tour; 18000 Old Winery Rd., ☎800-926-1266, www.buenavistawinery.com).* Though the actual wine making now takes place in the Carneros region, the vintages are sampled here in the old stone winery where Count Agoston Haraszthy originally made the wine from the over 100,000 vines that he imported from Europe. A creekside picnic area is an ideal place for lunch.

A winery with the motto "no wimpy wines" possesses a rare sense of humour about itself alongside the customary serious commitment to produce fine wine. If you are in the mood for a small yet elegant winery that perfectly lives up to this description, take Gehricke Road north of Sonoma, to the **Ravenswood** *(every day 10am to 4:30pm; 18701 Gehricke Rd., ☎938-1960)*. In the summer come and enjoy a weekend barbeque and winetasting.

Glen Ellen

If Robert Louis Stevenson is Napa Valley's literary figure, then Jack London is the definitely his Sonoma Valley counterpart.. A visit to Glen Ellen cannot be considered complete without a trip to the **Jack London State Historic Park ★★★** *($6 per car; every day 9:30am to sunset; 2400 London Ranch Rd., ☎938-5216)*. The commonly used romantic expression for this area, "the valley of the moon" was coined by London himself, who built an elaborate 26-room stone mansion here called the **Wolf House**. Unfortunately, the dream house of Jack and his wife Charmian was mysteriously burned to the ground only days before they were to move in. Its tragic ruins are one of the sites open for contemplation inside the park, along with the more cheerful **House of Happy Walls** *(every day 10am to 5pm)*, which pays tribute to London and was lovingly built and decorated by Charmian after her husband's early death at the age of 51. Now a museum, the House of Happy Walls displays original manuscripts and first editions of London's 51 books, along

with the original artwork for his stories, interesting and exotic souvenirs from his world travels and a replica of his study. His resignation letter from the communist party and some other tidbits of correspondence are also laid open for inspection. What's more, visitors can also visit London's simple stone gravestone near the cottage where he spent the last five years of his life.

Northern Wine Country and the Russian River Valley

As you head north out of Sonoma Valley on Highway 12, you will quickly hit Highway 101 and Santa Rosa, the largest city in Wine Country and its commercial centre. Once you have toured the few attractions in Santa Rosa, we strongly recommend that you head by back to the countryside looping over to Sebastopol and Freestone on Highway 12 and then taking the Bohemian Highway up through Occidental and Monte Rio. Once you hit the Russian River, follow its contours by veering towards Guerneville on Highway 116. When leaving Guerneville, make sure that you take the scenic Westside Road to Healdsburg.

★
Santa Rosa

A modern commercial centre set in the midst of incredible natural beauty, Santa Rosa can't really compete with its neighbouring towns for the attention of travellers. There are, however, a few attractions that make it

worth the trip. One of these focuses on Santa Rosa's most renowned citizen, Luther Burbank, the innovative horticulturalist. The **Luther Burbank Home & Gardens** *(Gardens are free and always open; the Victorian home is open Tue to Sat, Apr to Oct; corner of Santa Rosa and Sonoma avenues; ☎524-5445)* showcases some of the plant inventions that Burbanks became famous for including: the Santa Rosa plum, the Shasta daisy and many other hybrids. Another worthwhile stop is the kid-friendly **Sonoma County Museum** *($3, Wed to Sun, 425 Seventh St., ☎579-1500, www.pressdemo.com/ scmuseum)* housed in in a former post office. This institution is dedicated to providing visitors with a historical and cultural perspective of Sonoma County and has an interesting collection of early California art and another of metal sculpture and jewellery, in addition to its temporary exhibits. If you're a Charles Schulz fan, don't miss the opportunity to see an impressive collection of Peanuts paraphenalia at **Snoopy's Gallery** *(free admission; every day 10am to 6pm;1667 W. Steele Lane, ☎546-3385)*. Other sites of interest are the 19th-century mansions along Macdonald Avenue, the Farmer's Market, **The Church Built From One Tree** and the **Historic Railroad Square**.

Sebastopol to Guerneville

Sebastopol

Referred to as the Gold Ridge region, Sebastopol is famous for its numerous orchards, particularly those that bear Gravenstein

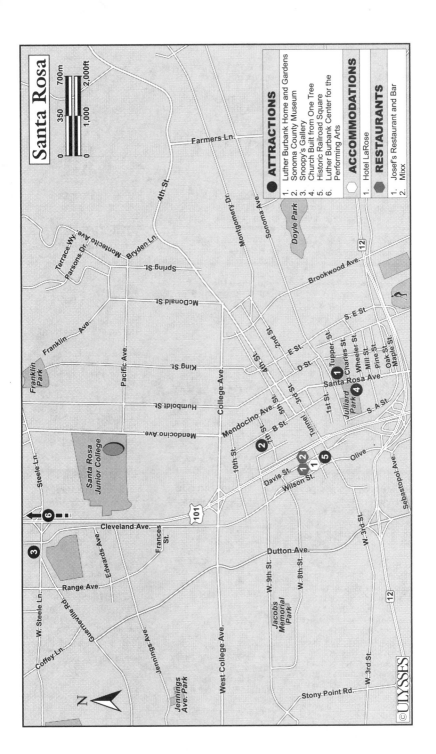

Santa Rosa

ATTRACTIONS
1. Luther Burbank Home and Gardens
2. Sonoma County Museum
3. Snoopy's Gallery
4. Church Built from One Tree
5. Historic Railroad Square
6. Luther Burbank Center for the Performing Arts

ACCOMMODATIONS
1. Hotel LaRose

RESTAURANTS
1. Josef's Restaurant and Bar
2. Mixx

© ULYSSES

apples. One of the more enjoyable ways to explore this area is to stop at a local farm to pick some apples, grapes, pears, cherries or peaches. The *Sonoma County Farm Trails Guide (www.farmtrails.org)* shows you where to find these farms and can be picked up in Sonoma or at the **Sebastopol Chamber of Commerce** *(265 S. Main St., ☎823-3032, www.sebastopol.org)*.

If you're in the mood for a bit of a twist on the ubiqitous winery visit, pull into the **California Cider Company and the Ace in the Hole Pub ★** *(3100 Gravenstein Hwy. N., ☎829-1ACE)*, where you can enjoy a swig of their experimental hard cider in a new cider-tasting room. A delicious apple cider combining Russian Gravenstein apples with Sonoma County wildflower honey is what built the reputation of this company, but their award-winning Ace Pear Cider and two other Ace beverages also come highly recommended.

Head west on the Bodega Highway (the continuation of Highway 12) and you'll hit the small town of Freestone where you can indulge in a Japanese enzyme bath (see p 481), then take the turn off towards Occidental on the Bohemian Highway. Occidental is a charming historical town hidden in the middle of the forest that the somewhat-radical locals try to keep a secret. This is a great place to stop for lunch (see p 489). As you continue on the Bohemian Highway past Camp Meeker and Monte Rio, it might occur to you that this "Highway" is named for the carefree, off-beat people and sites that are found in the

towns that dot it. Maybe, maybe not—but who cares, you've arrived at the Russian River! Take the Monte Rio Bridge over the river to River Road and follow its sinewy curves to Guerneville, the heart of Gay Wine Country.

Guerneville

A favoured resort area for San Francisco's gay community that is popular with families as well, Guerneville offers visitors a wealth of outdoor activities (see p 479) in addition to some wonderful wine and food. Hiking, fishing, horseback riding and swimming are the most popular sports here and the town abounds with resorts that make these activities very accessible to guests (see p 485).

The River Road will take you out of Guerneville, past the **Korbel Champagne Cellars** *(13250 River Rd., ☎824-7000)* and on towards the Westside/River Road fork. Take the Westside Road into Healdsburg.

Healdsburg to Geyserville

With its Spanish-style plaza bordered with shops, a bed and breakfast inn, art galleries, wine-tasting rooms, restaurants and attractive Victorian buildings, Healdsburg is a charming, less-developed miniature version of Sonoma. And like Sonoma, it has its fair share of nearby wineries. Because it is located close to the Russian River, it is also an ideal place to stay if you would like to combine refined creature comforts with plenty of outdoor fun.

If you head north on Highway 128, you will discover another town, Geyserville, that offers interesting accommodations within the Alexander Valley region (see p 485).

Parks

Bale Grist Mill State Historic Park

You can either drive to the quaint Bale Grist Mill State Historic Park *(off Hwy. 29, ☎942-4575)* as you leave Saint Helena, or hike in on the 1mi (1.6km) History Trail from Bothe-Napa Valley State Park. Built in 1846 by English-born surgeon Dr. Edward Bale, the flour mill possesses an imposing wooden 36ft (11m) overshot wheel outside and massive grindstones inside. This small park is a pleasant place to picnic.

Bothe Napa Valley State Park

Four miles (6.4km) north of Saint Helena on Highway 29, the Bothe-Napa Valley State Park provides rare camping and hiking opportunities in the midst of Wine Country. By hiking the 10mi (16km) of trails amongst the redwoods or camping at one of 40 tent/RV sites or nine walk-in sites, (see p 482) the winery crowds will quickly fade from your mind.

Robert Louis Stevenson State Park

When the Scottish writer Robert Louis Stevenson honeymooned with his bride Fanny at the abandoned Silverado mine site on the slopes of Mount St. Helena, his always-fragile health benefitted from the restorative air. At the northern end of Napa Valley, undeveloped Robert Louis Stevenson State Park *(situated about 8mi or 12.9km north of Calistoga on Hwy. 29, ☎942-4575)* features a 5mi (8km) hike to the summit of 4,343ft (1,324m) Mount Saint Helena, which will give climbers magnificent views that extend, on clear days, all the way from the Sierra Nevada to the San Francisco Bay area.

Sugarloaf Ridge— Bald Mountain

Seven miles (11km) east of Highway 12, Adobe Canyon Road leads to the 2,700 acre (1,093ha) Sugarloaf Ridge State Park *(☎833-5712)*. Some 25mi (40km) of hiking trails in combination with about 50 campsites guarantees refuge from the hoardes of wine enthusiasts. From atop 2,729ft (832m) Bald Mountain, the Sierra Nevada and the Golden Gate will be visible if the skies are clear.

Armstrong Redwoods State Reserve *(☎869-2958)*

Those who love redwood groves will delight in this reserve. Two miles (3.2km) north of Guerneville on Armstrong Woods Road, this park is the perfect place to take a leisurely stroll through an 800-acre (324ha) concentration of ancient redwood giants. Picnicking and camping facilities are also available.

Outdoor Activities

Cycling

Napa Valley Bike Tours
4080 Byway E.
Napa, CA 94558
☎255-3377
☎800-707-BIKE (U.S. and Canada)
www.napavalleybiketours.com
If you would like to take an organized cycling tour of Napa Valley with a reputable company, this is your best choice. The most popular tour is the 20mi (32.2km) full-day tour that features stops at three wineries, a fully catered picnic and a support van that can carry any wine or gifts that you purchase along the way. The price is $85 and includes a T-shirt and water bottle as well as the bicycle and helmet rental.

Getaway Adventures
1117 Lincoln Ave.
Calistoga
☎942-0332
www.getawayadventures.com
For more independent exploration, stop off at Getaway Adventures to rent a bike and take off on your own!

Sonoma Valley Cyclery
every day, year-round
20093 Broadway
☎935-3377

In the Russian River Region, your best bet can be found on the Plaza in Healdsburg:

Spoke Folk Cyclery
249 Center St.
Healdsburg
☎433-7171
www.spokefolk.com

Hot-Air Ballooning

Napa Valley Balloons
P.O. Box 2860
Yountville 94599
☎(707) 944-0228
☎800-253-2224
One of the more interesting ways to see the valley is from the heights of a hot-air balloon. There are now several companies that offer this service, but Napa Valley Balloons is the oldest and largest. It is also considered one of the safest and is FAA certified.

Flying

The Wine Plane
$100 to $150/pers.
P.O. Box 4074
Napa 94558
☎(707) 747-5533
☎888-779-6600
www.wineplane.com
info@wineplane.com
Jim Higgins, a FAA-certified pilot, and his wife Kim offer a unique alternative to the Napa Valley hot-air balloon experience by offering actual plane excursions. Using modern

FAA-certified and commercially inspected aircraft, they provide private, themed flights for parties of two or three. These outings include a choice of in-flight wine and music and prime seating by panoramic windows. A round-trip BMW livery service from your hotel to your favourite winery is also included in the price.

Kayaking and Canoeing

Burke's Canoe Trips
Box 602, 8600 River Rd.
Forestville
☎*887-1222*
Located on River Road after the Westside/River intersection (as you are coming from Guerneville), Burke's provides canoes to those who want to explore the magnificent scenery and wildlife of the Russian River for only $35 per canoe, per day.

W.C. "Bob" Trowbridge Canoe Trips
20 Healdsburg Ave.
Healdsburg
☎*433-7247*
☎*800-640-1386*
A Healdsburg-based outfitter that provides both canoe and kayak rentals along with accompanying tour documentation, W.C. "Bob" Trowbridge offers one-day trips in Grumman canoes starting at $29 for 5mi (8km) and kayak trips for $22.

King's Sport and Tackle Shop (see description below) also rents kayaks.

Fishing

King's Sport and Tackle Shop
every day (special early morning hours during steelhead and salmon season)
16258 Main St., Box 347
Guerneville, CA 95446
☎*869-2156*
Whether it be catfishing in April, striped bass fishing in the summer, chinook and coho salmon fishing in the fall, or steelhead fishing in the winter, this is the place to go if you intend to fish in the Russian River. The very knowledgeable fishing staff can book you a fishing trip, hook you up with a local river guide service, or simply provide you with an informational sheet about the river, which includes seasonal catches, best bait, lures and up-to-date river and ocean conditions. Kiwi Kayaks can also be rented here.

Golf

Chardonnay Golf Club
2555 Jameson Canyon Rd.
P.O. Box 3779
Napa
☎*800-788-0136*
☎*257-1900*
tee-time reservations: ext. 2263
www.chardonnaygolfclub .com
A stunning golf course surrounded by Merlot and Chardonnay vineyards and endowed with two championship courses, Chardonnay Golf Club is ideal for those who want to mix

their passions for wine and golf. The Vineyards Course, an 18-hole, par 72 course is open to the public, while The Club Shakespeare Course, also 18-holes and par 72, is open to members only.

Northwoods Golf Course
open seasonally, call for hours
19400 Hwy. 116 Rd.
Monte Rio
☎*865-2454 for reservations*
☎*865-1116 for hours*
An entirely different course, but equally stunning, the 9-hole, par 36 Northwoods Golf Course is set in a redwood forest. It was designed by the famous golf architect Alistair MacKenzie.

Horseback Riding

Sonoma Valley Company and Napa Valley Trail Rides
PO Box 877
Glen Ellen CA 95442
☎*996-8566*
www.thegrid.net/trailrides
This outfitter services both the Sonoma and Napa valleys, providing a range of options in three of their parks. One of the more attractive options is the Sunset and Full Moon Ride that is offered between 5pm and 7pm in both Sugar Loaf Ridge and Bothe-Napa Valley state parks at a cost of $45 per person. Please note that the park admission is an additional $5 to $6 and that tipping the guide is appreciated.
Year-round: **Sugarloaf Ridge State Park** (Kenwood)
May to October: **Jack London State Historic Park** (Glen Ellen)
May to October: **Bothe-Napa Valley State Park** (Calistoga)

Armstrong Woods PackTrips
phone between 7am and 10pm for reservations
P.O. Box 970
Guerneville, CA 95446
☎*887-2939*
www.metro.net/ayers
Located 1mi (1.6km) into Armstrong Redwoods State Reserve, this outfitter provides visitors with the opportunity to ride fine American Quarter horses through giant, old-growth redwood forest. Various options are offered beginning at $40 for a 1.5hr afternoon trail ride and extending up to $450 for a three-day pack trip.

Swimming

Indian Springs Resorts and Spa
Calistoga
☎*942-4913*
Don't miss a chance to swim in a wonderful Olympic-size pool supplied with mineral water from three thermal geysers, located on traditional Wappo sweat-lodge territory. 100% Volcanic ash baths.

Russian River

In the Russian River Region the best swimming spots are: Memorial Beach in the town of Healdsburg, Monte Rio Beach in Monte Rio, and of course, Johnson's Beach in the town of Guerneville.

Spas

Lincoln Avenue Spa
1339 Lincoln Ave.
Calistoga
☎*942-5296*
www.napavalley.com/las
The Lincoln Avenue Spa has the reputation of being the most elegant spa in Calistoga. Featured here are herbal body mud treatments, herbal blanket wraps, therapeutic massage, herbal facials and foot reflexology. Visits without reservations are also welcome, which is not the case with all of the spas in Calistoga.

Calistoga Village Inn and Spa
see p 482 for accommodation information
☎*942-0991*
www.greatspa.com
This popular and accessible spa is renowned for its mud baths, salt scrubs and mineral pools.

Cedar Street Spa
1107 Cedar St.
Calistoga
☎*942-2947*
www.cedarstreetspa.com
If a good massage is what you're really interested in, this is the place.

Lavender Hill Spa
☎*800-582-4772*
www.lavenderhillspa.com
This small specialty spa distinguishes itself from the others by its volcanic ash bath, seaweed bath, herbal blanket wrap, aromatherapy mineral salt bath, aromatherapy facial and hot-rocks massage.

Mount View Hotel & Spa
1015 Foothill Blvd.
Calistoga
One of the better small resort spas, Mount View is famous for Moor and Fango Mud baths (see p 483).

Dr Jami's Angel Wrap Spa
☎*942-8740*
www.angelwrapspa.com
Attracting many weight-conscious clients with its slenderizing body wrap, Dr Jami's also offers Ayurvedic, Thai, Essential Oil and Swedish massages.

The Spa at MacArthur Place
☎*933-3193*
In Sonoma, an ideal spot to enjoy a spa on a business trip is at MacArthur Place (see p 484). Offering activities as diverse as yoga, cycling and hiking programs, Ayurveda rejuvenation therapy, aromatherapy, phytotherapy, acupressure massage and aloe/tea-tree body mask treatments, the spa complements the many convention and conference facilities found here.

Osmosis Enzyme Bath and Massage
209 Bohemian Hwy.
Freestone
☎*823-8231*
www.osmosis.com
Touted as the only place in North America where you can indulge in a genuine Japanese enzyme bath (cedar fiber, rice bran and over 600 active enzymes), Osmosis is found in the laid-back and alternative Russian River Region.

Accommodations

General Pointers for Accommodations in the Napa Valley:

- There is 12% bed tax.
- Contrary to many European bed and breakfasts, most of these types of establishments in Napa Valley are meant for couples only and are not ideal for kids or friends who want to share a room without sharing a bed. If you are travelling as a family or platonically and don't want to stay in a chain hotel, we suggest that you look into staying at a small hotel, cabin or campsite.

Wine Country

- Check-in for most bed and breakfasts is usually between 3pm and 6pm.
- Because of concerns about water conservation in California, you will often notice that there are low pressure levels in the toilets.

Napa Valley

Napa

The Churchill Manor
$$-$$$ bkfst incl.
≡, *pb/sb*
485 Brown St., Napa 94559
☎*253-7733*
Now a 10-room bed and breakfast, this 1889 manor with a wrap-around veranda is located on a beautiful piece of land in Victorian Napa. Because it is well-located and reasonably priced, it has deservedly become one of the more popular bed and breakfast establishments.

Cedar Gables Inn
$$$ bkfst incl.
≡, ⊛
486 Coombs St., Napa 94559
☎*224-7969*
☎*800-309-7969*
www.cedargablesinn.com
Another property dating from the 1890s is the Cedar Gables Inn, designed in Old English style by British architect Ernest Coxhead. Offering visitors uniquely shaped rooms with eccentric little Victorian touches and names to match (like the Maid's Quarters, Edward's Study, Miss Dorothy's Room) this inn is ideal for those who nourish fantasies of romance in the midst of cozy British-style refinement. Other fine touches are the complimentary port and chocolates, the evening wine and cheese in the firelit den, the period antiques and the redwood staircases. Some of the

rooms even come equipped with two-person whirlpools and gas-fired coal burning fireplaces. A delicious gourmet breakfast in also served in a tastefully decorated sunroom.

Blue Violet Mansion
$$$-$$$$ bkfst incl.
⌂, ≡, ⊛, ℜ
443 Brown St., Napa 94559
☎*800-959-2583*
www.bluevioletmansion.com
This 1886 Queen Anne mansion has enjoyed the honour of winning the 1996 Gold Award for best bed and breakfast in North America! As it was originally built for a leather tanner, embossed leather adorns the walls on the main staircase. The most striking aspects of this property, however, are its theme floor devoted to Camelot and its hand-painted salon. A seven-course dinner is served each evening in the salon and is often accompanied with quality live music on Saturdays. Make sure that you are in good company and not pressed for time since it can take 3hrs to get through the meal!

La Belle Epoque Bed and Breakfast Inn
$$$ bkfst incl.
☎, ≡
Six rooms
1386 Calistoga Ave., Napa 94559
☎*257-2161*
☎*800-238-8070*
A smaller Queen Anne style Victorian Inn, La Belle Epoque is remarkable for its magnificent collection of period antiques, oriental carpets, stained glass windows, wine cellar, gourmet breakfasts and—yes—its incredible bed linens. A secretarial desk equipped with photocopier, fax and modem are also available if you happen to be travelling with a workaholic. Try

not to leave here without tasting the poached pears or the grand-marnier french toast.

St. Helena

Bothe Napa Valley State Park Camping
$
3601 St. Helena Hwy.
☎*942-4575*
This park offers 50 developed campsites, restrooms, showers, hiking trails on 1,800 acres (728ha) and horseback riding. It is undoubtedly the most enjoyable place to camp in the Napa Valley.

Calistoga

Calistoga Inn and Brewery
$-$$
☎, *sb*, ℜ
1250 Lincoln Ave., Calistoga 94515
☎*942-4101*
≈*942-4914*
www.napabeer.com
Budget accommodations are few and far between in Napa Valley, but luckily there is a conveniently located inn where you can get an inexpensive "European-style"room (i.e. small and with shared bathroom facilities). The rooms at the Calistoga Inn are worn but well-kept and come equipped with private sinks. They are located above a popular restaurant and brewery (see p 486) though, so don't expect peace and quiet.

Calistoga Village Inn & Spa
$$-$$$
⌂, ≡, ≈, ⇄, *tv*
1880 Lincoln Ave., Calistoga 94515
☎*942-0991*
≈*707-942-5306*
www.greatspa.com
If you want the live-in spa experience without all of the expensive frills, Calistoga Village Inn & Spa can give it to you at a reasonnable price. Located

within walking distance from Calistoga village, yet looking out onto some of the gorgeous hillside vineyards across Silverado Trail, this property offers basic rooms that each have sliding doors leading to an outdoor patio.

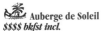 Cottage Grove Inn
$$$-$$$$
☎, ≡, *tv*, ⊛
1711 Lincoln Ave., Calistoga 94515
☎*800-799-2284*
☎*942-8400*
⇌*707-942-2653*
www.cottagegrove.com
This charming little complex of resort cottages located in a historic elm grove in the heart of Calistoga's spa district is one of the best places to stay in the Napa Valley if you want both privacy and convenience. Each cottage is decorated with colourful and original local art work and has a wood-burning fireplace, deep jacuzzi for two, stereo system, tv/vcr and fridge. A private, complimentary breakfast and afternoon wine are included as well.

Mount View Hotel and Spa
$$$-$$$$ bkfst incl.
△, ≡, ≈, *tv*, *sb*, ⊛
20 guestrooms, nine suites and three cottages
1457 Lincoln Ave., Calistoga 94515
hotel:
☎*942-6877*
☎*800-816-6877*
www.mountviewhotel.com
If you're looking to stay in a quaint, small-town hotel with a spa on the premises, this historical Victorian landmark with contemporary flourishes is one of your best bets. The full-service in-house European spa is famous for its Moor and Fango mud baths. Spa treatments can be easily preceded or followed by a dip in the large outdoor pool

that is surrounded by palm trees and fountains.

La Chaumiere
$$-$$$ bkfst incl.
△, ≡, ⊛
1301 Cedar St., Calistoga 94515
☎*942-6877 or*
☎*800-474-6800*
www.lachaumiere.com
How about lounging around in a redwood treehouse hot tub in the backyard of a French cottage-style bed and breakfast? This charming establishment is within walking distance to the village of Calistoga and offers visitors private baths, complimentary wine with hors d'oeuvres and a full breakfast.

Rutherford

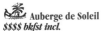 Auberge de Soleil
$$$$ bkfst incl.
△, ≡, ≈, ⊛, ℜ
13 cottages
180 Rutherford Hill Rd.
☎*963-1211*
☎*800-348-5406*
⇌*963-8764*
www.aubergedusoleil.com
If Victorian clutter is not your cup of tea, why not stay in one of the sun-filled French Mediterranean-style cottages at the Auberge du Soleil? Decorated in a Californian and Southwestern theme and featuring Mexican tile, on the floor each hillside cottage has a private terrace with a view onto the valley. An excellent in-house restaurant (see p 487) and an onsite pool make this one of the

most luxurious cottage complexes in Wine Country.

Rancho Caymus Inn
$$$$
☎, ≡, *tv*, ⊛, ℜ
26 rooms
1140 Rutherford Rd.
☎*963-1777*
☎*800-845-1777*
⇌*963-5387*
www.ranchocaymus.com
This Spanish colonial-style inn exudes a cozyness that will enchant those who are fond of wood and adobe. Split-level rooms with queen-size carved wooden beds and adobe beehive fireplaces open out onto a lush interior courtyard, studded with gorgeous flowers and an earth-toned colonnade. What's more, a five-star dining experience can be had at the inn's restaurant, La Toque (see p 487).

Sonoma Valley

Sonoma

El Dorado Hotel
$$-$$$ bkfst incl.
☎, ≡, ≈, *tv*, ℜ
27 rooms
405 First St. W., Sonoma 95476
☎*996-3030*
⇌*996-3148*
☎*800-289-3031*
www.hoteleldorado.com
Conveniently located on the Plaza, El Dorado is one of the better values in downtown Sonoma. French windows open out onto terraces laced with wisteria, while inside the rooms feature four-poster beds covered in goose-down linens and mexican tile floors. Also noteworthy are the Ristorante Piatti, a heated pool, the garden patio with a fig tree and a complimentary continental breakfast.

Wine Country

Swiss Hotel
$$
≡, ℜ
18 West Spain St, Sonoma
☎938-2884
≈707-938-3298
If history is your main
interest, be sure to stay in
one of the oldest adobes
on the Sonoma Plaza: The
Swiss Hotel. This establish-
ment features five hostelry-
style rooms with private
baths and refrigerators. An
absolutely charming res-
taurant and bar are found
on the main floor (see
p 488).

MacArthur Place
$$$-$$$$ bkfst incl.
△, ≡, ≈, ≈, tv, ⊛, ℜ
29 East MacArthur St.
Sonoma 96476
☎800-722-1866
≈933-9833
www.macarthurplace.com
If you're travelling to Wine
Country on business, this
restored manor house and
barn is an excellent
choice. It has recently un-
dergone extensive expan-
sion, offering 29 additional
suites with wood-burning
fireplaces and a library in
addition to its six cottages
and 10 rooms. A very
good steakhouse, Saddles,
is located on the premises
along with a conference
center and one of the
better spas in Wine Coun-
try.

Boyes Hot Springs

Sonoma Mission Inn and Spa
$$$$-$$$$ bkfst incl.
△, ≡, ≈, ≈, tv, ⊛, ℜ
18140 Hwy 12
☎938-9000
☎800-862-4945
≈938-4250
www.sonomamissioninn.com
If you are seeking a large,
full-service resort with a
famous on-site spa, an 18-
hole championship golf
course, two swimming
pools and a staff that in-
cludes first rate hiking,
biking and martial- arts

guides, look no further.
There is probably no es-
tablishment in this cate-
gory in all of Wine Coun-
try that can compete with
the Sonoma Mission Inn
and Spa. This pale pink
Mission Revival-style hotel
is decorated in soothing
earth-tone rooms within a
complex that is a world
unto itself.

Glen Ellen

 **Gaige House Inn**
$$$$-$$$$$ bkfst incl.
☎, ≡, ≈, ≈, tv, ⊛
13540 Arnold Dr., Glen Ellen 95442
☎935-0237
≈935-6411
www.gaige.com
What happens when a
talented Feng Shui consul-
tant gets together with a
couple of sharp innkeep-
ers? The answer is the
Gaige House Inn. Enlight-
ened would not be too
strong a word to describe
this inn, which has been
thought out down to the
tiniest detail. Intelligence
exudes from the living
room animated by a fire-
place and containing ex-
tremely interesting reading
material, as well as from
the hall with its refined
Asian prints, and from the
dining area where foun-
tains and orchid flower
arrangements are comple-
mented by exquisite music
pouring out of the well
placed speakers. Of
course, the rooms them-
selves are equally remark-
able with their outstanding
botanical prints, refined
designer linen, pristine
whirlpool tubs, gas-burn-
ing fireplaces and single
orchids strategically placed
throughout. A heated pool,
full-service concierge, 24hr
cookie supply and delecta-
ble gourmet breakfast add
the finishing touches to
this masterpiece of
innkeeping.

Northern Wine Country and the Russian River Valley

Santa Rosa

Hotel La Rose
$$$ bkfst incl.
☎, ≡, tv, ℜ
308 Wilson St.
☎579-3200
☎800-527-6738
≈579-3247
www.hotellarose.com
The Hotel La Rose is probably the most interesting
hotel in Santa Rosa, found
in the heart of the Historic
Railroad Square. Built in
stone at the same time as
the depot (1907), it has
been listed in the National
Register of Historic Places.
Particularly intriguing are
the sloped attic rooms
with skylights and brass
beds.

Sebastopol

Vine Hill Bed & Breakfast
$$$ bkfst incl.
≡, ≈
3949 Vine Hill Rd.,
Sebastopol 95472
☎823-8832
www.vine-hill-inn.com
What better way to experi-
ence Sebastopol than in a
renovated 1897 farmhouse?
Surrounded by organic
gardens, vineyards and a
forested area inhabited by
songbirds and quails, the
Vine Hill Bed & Breakfast
also offers private baths
and a swimming pool with
a deck and jacuzzi whirl-
pool.

Guerneville

Fifes Resort
$-$$$
≈, tv, pb/sb
16467 River Rd.
☎*869-0656 or 800-734-3371*
↝*869-0658*
www.fifes.com
info@fifes.com
For a large, reasonably priced gay resort with everything from budget campsites to moderate cabins, you might want to give Fife's a try. Outdoor activities like beach volleyball and swimming, as well as indoor activities like working out in the gym and dancing the night away in the dance club are the highlights here. The accommodations are little more than a bed to sleep on when you're exhausted from all of your partying.

Riverlane Resort
$$
△, ≡, ≈, pb/sb, ⊛
Box 313
First and Church St.
☎*869-2323*
☎*800-201-2324*
Finally a place for the whole family! The Riverlane Resort rents out housekeeping cabins for one to eight people and has its own private beach on the river with a well-known fishing hole. There is also a swimming pool and spa. Unfortunately, you'll have to leave your pets at home. Reservations are highly recommended.

🦂 Fern Grove Cottages
$$-$$$
≈, pb/sb
16650 River Rd., Guerneville, 95446
☎*869-8105 for reservations*
Another good place for couples or families (with well-behaved pets) is this complex of antique pine cottages which come equipped with one or two bedrooms, all with fireplaces. A large swimming pool and 8 acres (3.2ha) of terrain amid 100ft (30.5m) redwoods make for an enjoyable setting. Downtown Guerneville amenities are only a 0.25mi (0.4km) away.

Ridenhour Ranch House Inn
$$$, bkfst incl.
≡
eight rooms
12850 River Rd., Guerneville 95446
5mi (8km) east of Guerneville
☎*887-1033*
This former 900 acre (364ha) ranch with its orchards of Gravenstein apple, persimmon, plum, pear and fig trees has been converted into a cozy inn. Landcaped grounds with redwoods and oak trees combined with the secluded river beaches only a short walk away give visitors plenty of opportunity to peacefully enjoy the wonders of nature. Hopping into the hot tub and tasting local wines by the fire in the living room are a great way to cap off your day.

Russian River Resort
$$$-$$$$ bkfst incl.
△, ≡, ≈, tv, ⊛
16390 Fourth St.
☎*869-0691*
☎*800-417-3767*
↝*869-0698*
www.russianriverresort.com
A more upscale gay resort that is organized around a large hot tub attracting both clothed and unclothed guests, the Russian River Resort offers up-to-date rooms with private baths and cable television. Several of the rooms are equipped with wood-burning fireplaces as well.

Geyserville

Hope-Bosworth House
Hope-Merril House
$$$ bkfst incl.
≡, tv, ⊛
21238 and 21253 Geyserville Ave.
P.O. Box 42, Geyserville 95441
☎*857-3356*
☎*800-825-4BED*
↝*857-HOPE*
These two Victorian homes, facing each other on Geyserville Avenue, were lovingly restored in the early 1980s by Bob amd Rosalie Hope, so that people like us could enjoy them as inns. Although every detail of the Victorian decor has been carefully and tastefully chosen, the focus here is comfort and cordiality. There are three rooms with whirlpool baths and three others that have fireplaces. If privacy is important to you, a self-sufficient suite is also available.

🦂 Isis Oasis
$-$$ bkfst incl.
△, ≈, pb/sb, ⊛, ℜ
20889 Geyserville Ave.
☎*857-4747*
☎*800-679-7387*
↝*857-3287*
www.isisoasis.org
New agers, take note: this is the place for you! This 10-acre (4ha) esoteric campsite just outside of small town Geyserville offers lodging in a tower, a three-room cottage, a geodisic dome or a bohemian lodge. The entrance is marked by an Egyptian chapel dedicated to Isis; as you drive further onto the site, stopping at the dining and entertainment quarters, you will be greeted by a grey-haired woman with feline-looking eyes, who will introduce you to her exotic menagerie. As is the case with bohemian pads, the furniture is old and the housekeeping may leave something to be desired, but this may be

exactly want you want! A hot tub, sauna and swimming pool are available. You can also partake of the tarot readings and new age events focussing on the study and celebration of goddesses, that are offered at this one-of-a-kind campsite.

Restaurants

Napa Valley

Napa

Chanterelle
$-$$
804 First St.
A good spot for a creative lunch, Chanterelle serves up delicious sandwiches that come with soup, salad, potato chips, onion rings or french fries. Our favourites were the goat cheese and grilled pear sandwich, and the turkey, avocado, smoked cheddar and cranberry sauce sandwich, accompanied by house potato chips with blue cheese.

PJs Cafe
$-$$
1001 Second St.
☎224-0607
Travelling in a renowned gastronomical region when you have specific dietary restrictions can be hell. If you are such a person, PJs will be welcome indeed. Because of its special interest in lifestyle diets, PJs makes desserts without eggs, oil or animal products and provides entrees with low amounts of fats, oils, dairy products, eggs, salt and sugar. You can't go wrong with the vegetable minestrone soup, the blackbean soup, the fettucini and brie, the

wholewheat calzones, the stir fry veggies or the White Pizza.

Downtown Joe's Restaurant & Brewery
$$
8:30am to 2am
Happy hour: 4pm to 6pm
902 Main St.
☎258-2337
www.dowtownjoes.com
If you are looking for an entertaining evening out that includes good drink and grub, you will be in like-minded company at Joe's. Beer specialties include Ace High Cream Ale, Tail Waggin' Ale, Past Due Dark Ale and the local favourite, Golden Thistle Bitter Ale. Of course, good wines can be found as well, but you may have already had your fill during the day. As for food, the toasted ravioli, brewhouse sandwich and rotating fish and pasta of the day are wise choices. They can be accompanied by homemade ginger ale or a delicious, homemade rootbeer float. As a live music venue, Joe's is one of the most popular in Wine Country. Live music is featured Thursdays, Fridays and Saturdays.

Cole's Chop House
$$$-$$$$
Tue to Sat 5pm to 10pm
Sun 5pm to 9pm
1122 Main St.
☎224-6328
≈254-9692
Veal chops, beef chops, lamb chops and pork chops—eating chops has never been so good! Located in a historical building in downtown Napa, Cole's owes it success to an award-winning chef, Greg Cole, who dishes out the best chops and steaks you are likely to find anywhere. If you have room for dessert, you must try the Scotch whiskey bread

pudding or the vanilla bean creme brulee.

Napa Valley Wine Train
$$$-$$$$
1275 McKinstry St.
☎(707) 253-2111
☎800-427-4124
Now an established part of Wine Country, the Wine Train is, in effect, a 1915 vintage Pullman dining car that chugs alongside Highway 29 while serving gourmet meals accompanied by some of the finest wines in Napa Valley. You can choose from lunch, dinner or a brunch that is served on Saturdays, Sundays and holidays. The 36-mi (60km) round-trip between Napa and St. Helena takes about 3hrs. Prices range as follows: $25, $57, $63, or $70. The train departs from McKinstry Street near First Street.

Calistoga

Calistoga Inn, Restaurant and Brewery
$-$$
1250 Lincoln Ave.
☎942-4101
≈942-4914
calistoga@napabeer.com
Come rub elbows with Robert Redford at this laid-back local restaurant that offers moderately priced California cuisine with some of the best homemade ale around.

Smokehouse Cafe
$-$$
1458 Lincoln Ave.
☎942-6060
How about on old-fashioned Southern barbeque served in a fun decor? Stop off at the old Depot in Calistoga and follow your nose to the place where meat, salmon and sausages are smoked on the spot.

Yountville

 The Diner
$
6476 Washington St.
☎944-2626
Yes, there is a place to eat in Yountville that will not completely empty your wallet! Why not stop by for a lunch of down-to-earth Mexican burritos or quesadillas?

Mustards Grill
$$-$$$
7399 St. Helena Hwy.
☎944-2424
In the mood for seafood cooked on a wood-burning grill? At this contemporary restaurant you will be able to choose from such things as salmon, shark, sea bass and spearfish. Grilled porkchops and smoked duck are also available for those who aren't in the mood for seafood.

Domaine Chandon
$$$-$$$$
1 California Dr.
☎944-2892
⇌944-1123
www.chandon.com
Located within a winery that specializes in sparkling wine, this award-winning restaurant is the place to stop for a gourmet lunch. Highlighted are entrees such as mequite-grilled asparagus salad and tuna peppersteak with mustard sauce.

The French Laundry
$$$$-$$$$$
6640 Washington St.
☎944-2380
It is because of restaurants like this one that Yountville is considered the gastronomical capital of Napa Valley. A fusion of Californian and French cuisine offered through a fixed-price menu that changes nightly, the food is fabulous and can be served with wine chosen

from the best producers in the valley. Do not even think of arriving without a reservation.

Rutherford

La Toque
$$$$-$$$$$
1140 Rutherford Rd.
☎963-9770
For an unforgettable lesson in wine pairing, you must come to La Toque. A new addition to Rutherford, this restaurant (along with the Auberge de Soleil) may put Rutherford ahead of Yountville as gastronomical capital of the valley. Chef Ken Frank oversees the creation of varying fixed-price menus composed of seven delectable courses that are carefully paired with a selection of California and International wines. The service is artfully rendered by authentic *sommiers* who, while uncorking one of the seven bottles of wine that is designed to go with your seven courses, deliver wry and eloquent explanations of what is supposed to happen in your mouth when it experiences, for example, the pairing of a 1997 El Molino Chardonnay wine from Rutherford with a "Corn Flan in a Savory Lobster Broth with Spring Vegetables." The atmosphere is casually elegant, which is typical of most fine dining establishments in Northern California.

Auberge de Soleil
$$$$$
180 Rutherford Hill Rd.
☎967-3111
⇌963-8764
www.aubergedusoleil.com
As mentioned above, Rutherford gives Yountville some very serious gastronomical competition with this creme-de-

la-creme establishment. As remarkable for its breathtaking architecture as it is for its stupendous cuisine, Auberge du Soleil is a must for the true connaisseur who has no fear of fat. Though you can order lighter items like oak-barrel roasted salmon, thyme-roasted pheasant, and grilled asparagus and wild mushroom lasagna, it is treats like the Seven Sparkling Sins appetizer (including foie gras, truffled quail eggs and caviar) that are the most tempting.

Sonoma Valley

Fords
$
22900 Broadway
(5mi or 8km south of Sonoma at the juncture of Hwy. 12 and Hwy. 121)
Occupying the same spot since 1929, Ford's Café provides a startling contrast to the upscale restaurants which dominate the wine country. Starting at the dark hour of 5am, local working class people pile into this venerable roadhouse to begin their day with coffee and a hearty breakfast. If you are not particularly hungry, you might settle for "the Travelin' Man" (one slice of french toast served with one egg and a strip of bacon), but if you want a gargantuan send-off for the day, try "Going Fishing." The friendly waitresses scurrying about the tables covered with red-checked cloths against walls chock-full of intriguing old road signs, posters, jokes and photographs, will assure you a pleasant, truly casual dining experience.

Wine Country

Sonoma

Basque Boulangerie
$
460 First St. E.
☎935-7687

This is about as fine a small bakery as you will find outside of a big city. It is frequently jam-packed in the morning, simply because its baked goods, from muffins to turnovers to loaves of Northern California's sour dough French bread, are so delicious. Sit down inside the café or outside at tables on the sidewalk for a continental breakfast, or come for light lunch and have a bowl of soup accompanied by a croque monsieur. You will invariably be in the company of animated customers from interestingly diverse walks of life.

Mary's Pizza Shack
452 First St. E.
☎938-8300

If you are in the mood for some tasty local pizza and beer, stop at Mary's, a simple hangout hidden behind the shops on the east side of the Plaza.

Maya Restaurant
101 East Napa St., Sonoma 95476
☎935-3500

A colourful new restaurant found right on the Plaza, Maya specializes in recipes from the Yucatan.

The Swiss Hotel
$$$
18 West Spain St.
☎938-2884

As appealing for its cozy, historical ambience as for its delectable northern Italian fare, the restaurant in the Swiss Hotel is an ideal place to dine after sunset when the tables are lit by candles and the traffic on the Plaza has come to a halt.

Glen Ellen

The Girl and the Fig
$$$-$$$$
13690 Arnold Dr.
☎938-3634

This cheerful, eclectic country eatery prides itself on its fusion of southern French and California cuisine. Sondra Bernstein—"the girl" who opened the restaurant in 1997—has made "the fig" the star of many of the dishes served here (the grilled fig salad is to die for), though other sophisticated-yet-rustic items are given a fair chance as well. A very unusual wine list is composed of many lesser-known Rhone varietals from California and France; this is combined with the imaginative menu, Mediterranean art work and ochre-painted wooden chairs—none of which resembles another—which makes eating here a one-of-a-kind experience.

Petaluma

Original Marvins Restaurant
$
317 Petaluma Blvd.
South Petaluma
☎765-2808

Here is your chance to savour a hearty omelette in the "egg capital of the world!" If you drive just south of Sonoma, you will find Petaluma, the aforementioned capital. Located in a historical creamery building, this eatery is renowned for its fresh eggs and homemade sausages.

JM Rosen's Bakery and Waterfront Grill
$-$$
54 E. Washington St.
☎773-9644 to order a cheese-cake
☎773-3200 to make reservations for the grill

Is it so surprising to find an award-winning cheese-cake bakery in the dairy heartland of Wine Country? Since opening in 1976, sisters Jan and Michele Rosen have extended their bakery to include a popular grill that is perfect for a casual lunch or dinner.

Northern Wine Country and the Russian River Valley

Santa Rosa

Josef's Restaurant and Bar
$$$-$$$$
reservations advised
308 Wilson St.
☎571-8664

Located in the charming Hotel La Rose in the Historic Railroad Square of Santa Rosa, this restaurant owes it success to a jovial Swiss-trained chef, Josef Keller. Fresh local ingredients are used as a base for a French-inspired menu, which is complimented with rare and special vintage wines from Josef's cellar. The lobster bisque is out of this world.

Mixx
$$$
closed Sun.
135 Fourth St.
☎573-1344

For eclectic, award-winning California cuisine served in an innovative and homey decor, Mixx is difficult to beat. Make sure that you leave some room for dessert as it would almost be a sin to leave without at least trying one of these tempting creations.

Occidental

Bohemian Cafe
$-$$$
lunch Wed to Sun, every day for dinner
3688 Bohemian Hwy.
☎874-3931
Though the floors and the furniture are a bit worn, the gourmet lunches here are reasonably priced and delicious. As good a place as any if you would like to absorb some of the Russian River's easy going culture by eavesdropping on conversations about such things as what is included in the local mud and enzyme baths.

Negri's Original Occidental
$-$$$
3700 Bohemian Hwy.
☎823-5301
This old-fashioned Italian trattoria is an Occidental landmark. The food is tasty and the price is fair. A great place for family or group dining.

Sebastopol

 Screamin' Mimi's
$
6902 Sebastopol Ave.
☎823-5902
Winner of countless awards for its ice cream, Screamin' Mimi's scoopings include: the Screamin' Mimi (sundae made entirely from homemade ice cream, brownies and hot fudge), Affogato (homemade ice cream topped with whipped cream and a freshly brewed double shot of Illy espresso), and pomegranate, chai and watermelon sorbets. You'd be crazy to miss out on this!

Papas and Pollo
$-$$
every day 11am to 9pm
915 Gravenstein Hwy. S.
☎829-9037
Those of you who would like to be introduced or re-familiarized with southwestern mesquite barbeque should find your way to Papas and Pollo. House specialties are mesquite-grilled tofu, fish, beef and chicken tacos and a fabulous "guilt-free burrito" made with artichoke hearts, diced baked potatoes and organic salad mix. Premium micro-brews and mineral water round off the healthy and reasonably priced meals.

 Pasta Bella
$-$$$
796 Gravenstein Hwy. S.
☎824-8191
This simply decorated restaurant is blessed with a Zen-trained chef, Ryn Wood, who has fused Italian and Californian cuisine to create dishes that she has named after her friends. For instance, Lorelei is a salad made up of fuji apples, carmalized walnuts, wild greens and gorgonzola cheese with a champagne citrus vinaigrette. Lisa Shiffman, on the other hand, is linguini topped with grilled chicken, fresh roma tomatoes and a divine prosciutto-sage cream sauce. Good beer and wine make the perfect companions for these dishes.

Healdsburg

Bistro Ralph
$$-$$$
every day Mon to Fri
109 Plaza St.
☎433-1380
A casually elegant bistro right on the plaza in Healdsburg, Bistro Ralph offers tasty food and a great wine bar.

Entertainment

Napa Valley

Napa

Downtown Joe's Restaurant & Brewery
(see p 486)

Smokehouse Cafe
(see p 486)
For live music (jazz, blues and country and western) in Calistoga on Friday, Saturday or Sunday night, stop by the Smokehouse Cafe.

Petaluma

Kodiak Jack's Honky Tonk & Saloon
256 Petaluma Blvd. N.
For those needing a break from high culture in Wine Country, Kodiak Jack's may be the perfect remedy. This popular country and western nightclub and saloon features nightly lessons (7pm to 9pm) in such dances as the Two Step, Line Dancing or West Coast Swing. A computerized bucking bull named Kodiak is another option for those with cowboy or cowgirl fetishes. Because the place is huge, cramped dancing is not a problem. Live country and western music can be enjoyed here as well.

Wine Country

Northern Wine Country and the Russian River Valley

Cotati

Buffalo Billiards
every day 10am to midnight
8492 Gravenstein Hwy.
☎ *794-7338*
☎ *800-400-4CUE*
This is the largest and most famous pool hall in Northern California. This place is sure to please if you would like to get lessons from one of the professional instructors, watch some great matches, or simply check out the American West/Buffalo-themed showroom, with all kinds of accessories and antique pool and billiard tables.

Santa Rosa

Luther Burbank Center for the Performing Arts
50 Mark West Springs Rd.
☎ *546-3600 (Box Office)*
www.lbc.net
www.basstickets.com
To see world-class performances of classical, folk, swing music and comedy while you are visiting Wine Country, check out the LBC Web site and reserve in advance.

Sebastopol

Jaspar O'Farrells
every day 10am to 2am
6957 Sebastopol Ave.
☎ *823-1389*
To enjoy traditional "pub fare" amid a dynamic selection of live music (blues, zydeco, cajun, reggae, rock 'n' roll) in the Russian River region, spend a night at Jaspar O'Farrells. Celtic and Irish music are often featured

on Sundays. U.S. and European Beers, along with the obvious California Wines can be enjoyed in the 1890s bar, whose high ceilings are speckled with European flags.

Guerneville

Main Street Station Pizza & Jazz Club
16280 Main St.
☎ *869-0501*
This fun family-run Guerneville hangout is many things: a gourmet pizza house, a jazz club and an occasional comedy club. The light and crunchy pizza dough is topped by a visual artist, making it almost too beautiful to eat. If you're lucky, you'll be in town when the Russian River Jazz Ensemble is playing or when it is stand-up comedy night.

Shopping

Napa Valley

Oakville

Oakville Grocery
7856 St. Helena Hwy.
☎ *944-8802*
www.oakvillegrocery.com
This is no ordinary grocery store! We encourage you to walk in for some picnic fixings so you can see what we mean.

St. Helena

Hurd Beeswax Candles
3020 N. St. Helena Hwy.
☎ *(707) 963-7211*
☎ *800-977-7211*
The historical Freemark Abbey is filled with some

very fine candles that visitors can take home as gifts or souvenirs, thanks to Hurd. All of the candles are crafted on the premises with sheets of pure beeswax. This means that they can hold more delicate and transparent designs than molded candles. The workshop/store with its accompanying demonstration beehive displays exquisite items, such as a beautiful iris-shaped candle with all of the delicacy of the actual flower.

Calistoga

Depot RR Station
1458 Lincoln Ave.
Some of the most enjoyable shopping in Napa Valley can be had at the oldest railroad depot remaining in California. Wander through the six restored Pullman Railroad cars, which have been converted into shops like the American Indian Trading Co., the Calistoga Wine Stop, Le Artisan and the Treasures of Tibet.

Sonoma Valley

One of the preferred places to shop in the Sonoma Valley is along the Plaza, with its whimsical art and print shops, its expensive children's-wear boutiques and its fabulous independent bookstore:

Readers Books
130 E. Napa St.
☎ *939-1779*
www.readersbooks.com
Some of the most interesting shopping, however, is to be had at the outside stands that occasionally line the Plaza park, especially the Farmer's Market.

Kenwood

Jonathan's Farmhouse
9255 Sonoma Hwy.
☎833-6532
☎888-833-6577
jonfarm@aol.com
This unusual roadside
venue is new to Sonoma
Valley and is a goldmine
for those of you looking
for a unique gift to bring
home from your trip.
Whether it be a cheap little
knick-knack like a wood-
carved refrigerator magnet,
an innovative windmill for
your garden or a more
expensive item like a fish
plaque that breaks out into
song when you walk past
it, you're guaranteed to
walk out with a smile.

Petaluma

Marin French Cheese Factory
7500 Red Hill Rd.
☎762-6001
☎800-292-6001
Lovers of Camembert
cheese must stop here and

buy the famous Rouge et
Noir Camembert that is
produced on the spot.

Northern Wine Country and the Russian River Valley

Santa Rosa

Sawyer's News
733 Fourth St.
☎542-1311
With a selection of over
2,000 magazines and
newspapers, Sawyer's is
the largest newstand north
of San Francisco. Added
attractions are an interesting picture window gallery
and great espresso coffee
served on the premises.

Guerneville

The Hubcap Cafe and Deli
8am to 7pm
16337 Main St.
☎869-2393
For picnic fixings in the
Russian River Region,

don't forget to pack some
of Brenda's beer and
garlic-roasted pot roast!
While you're waiting you
can check out the impres-
sive vintage hubcap and
license plate display.

River Reader Bookstore
*every day 10am to 6pm in
winter*
*Sun to Thu 10am to 6pm, Fri
and Sat 10am to 8pm*
16355 Main St.
☎869-2240
This is an interesting bookstore located only two
blocks from a public
beach on the Russian
River. With a good selec-
tion of general fiction,
gay/lesbian subjects, spirituality and some great children's books, stopping
here is mandatory if you
want to read a good book
on the beach. For those
who are interested, there
are also regular author
readings and a children's
storytelling hour.

Beringer Vineyards

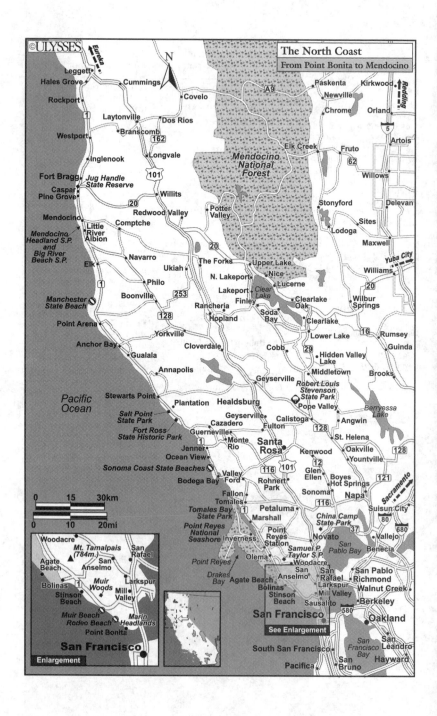

The North Coast
From Point Bonita to Mendocino

©ULYSSES

Eureka

N

Leggett
Hales Grove
Rockport
Cummings
Covelo
Laytonville
Dos Rios
Westport
Branscomb
162
Inglenook
Longvale
Fort Bragg
Jug Handle
State Reserve
101
Caspar
Pine Grove
Willits
Mendocino
20
Redwood Valley
Potter Valley
Comptche
Little River
Albion
Navarro
20
Elk
Ukiah
The Forks
Philo
N. Lakeport
Boonville
253
Lakeport
Rancheria
Manchester
State Beach
128
Finley
Hopland
Point Arena
Yorkville
Anchor Bay
Cloverdale
Gualala
Annapolis
Geyserville
Stewarts Point
Plantation
Healdsburg
Salt Point
State Park
Geyserville
Fort Ross
State Historic Park
Cazadero
Guerneville
Monte Rio
Jenner
Ocean View
Sonoma Coast State Beaches
Valley Ford
Bodega Bay
Rohnert Park
Fallon
Tomales
Tomales Bay
State Park
Marshall
Point Reyes
National
Seashore
Inverness
Point Reyes
Station
Drakes Bay
Olema
Agate Beach
Bolinas
Stinson Beach
Sausalito

Paskenta
Newville
Kirkwood
Chrome
Orland
Redding
A9
5
Elk Creek
Fruto
Artois
62
Willows
Mendocino
National
Forest
Stonyford
Delevan
Sites
Lodoga
Maxwell
Yuba City
Upper Lake
Nice
Williams
Lucerne
20
Clear Lake
Clearlake Oak
Wilbur Springs
Soda Bay
Clearlake
16
Lower Lake
Rumsey
Cobb
Hidden Valley Lake
Guinda
29
Middletown
Brooks
Robert Louis
Stevenson
State Park
Pope Valley
Berryessa Lake
Calistoga
Angwin
128
St. Helena
Santa
Rosa
Kenwood
Oakville
Yountville
12
128
Glen Ellen
Boyes Hot Springs
121
Sonoma
Napa
Suisun City
116
Petaluma
China Camp
State Park
37
80
Samuel P.
Taylor S.P.
Novato
Vallejo
680
Woodacre
San Pablo Bay
Benicia
San Anselmo
San Rafael
San Pablo
Larkspur
Richmond
Mill Valley
Walnut Creek
Berkeley
580
San Francisco
See Enlargement
Oakland
San Leandro
South San Francisco
San Francisco Bay
Hayward
Pacifica
San Bruno

Pacific
Ocean

Mendocino
Headland S.P.
and
Big River
Beach S.P.

0   15   30km
0   10   20mi

Woodacre
Mt. Tamalpais
(784m.)
Agate Beach
San Rafael
San Anselmo
Bolinas
Muir Woods
Larkspur
Mill Valley
Stinson Beach
Muir Beach
Rodeo Beach
Marin Headlands
Point Bonita

San Francisco
Enlargement

The North Coast

D riving north across the Golden Gate Bridge over the swirling waters of San Francisco Bay, then following the coastline for the approximately 400mi (644km) that it takes to reach the Oregon Border, you will pass through a spectacular, often wild realm of beauty.

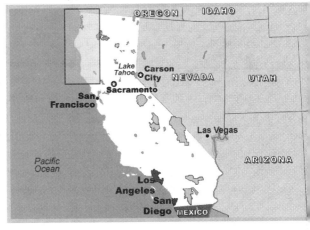

S tarting in Marin County and making your way north through the counties of Sonoma, Mendocino, Humboldt, you will be surrounded on all sides by a type of tree that grows almost nowhere else in the world, namely *Sequoia sempirvirens* commonly known as redwood. These trees, blessed by natural resistance to fire and water, insects and fungi, regularly grow taller than any other living thing. They can reach heights of well over 300ft (91.4m) and live to be more than 2,000 years old. Fittingly, within sight of majestic redwoods, gigantic mammals known as grey whales, 35 to 50ft (10.6 to 15.2m) in length and weighing up to 40 tons (41 tonnes), traverse the waters of the

Pacific Ocean all along the Northern California Coast between mid-December and mid-May as part of their annual 6,000mi (9,656km) migration. When your attention is not drawn to redwoods or whales—if the ubiquitous fog of the coast permits— you'll have a field day even if you only have a modest interest in birdwatching, since it's easy to sight an immense variety of species, including cormorants, egrets, godwits, pelicans, mallards, widgeons, great blue herons, ravens, turkey vultures and red-tailed hawks. If you prefer to direct your eyes down-

ward on this coastline so conspicuously lacking in sandy beaches (and water warm enough for humans to swim in!), you will have little trouble finding tide pools in which to study octopi, jellyfish, sponges, sand dollars, starfish, mussels, crabs, squid, sea anemones and clams.

A part from its manifold scenic wonders (and we haven't even mentioned Marin County's commanding Mount Tamalpais or, along the remote so-called Lost Coast, the rugged King Mountain Range—subject to 100in or 254cm of annual rainfall), several historically and culturally important communities, albeit widely separated from each other, deserve close attention. For example, near the beginning of the 160mi (257km) stretch of Highway 1 between Bodega Bay and Leggett sits Fort Ross, a reconstruction of a settlement built in 1812 by the Russians to serve as a headquarters for their sea-otter trade. Seventy-five miles (121km) farther up the coast, the small town of Mendocino has long enjoyed fame for its handsome New England-style architecture, the legacy of its 19th century founders who were mariners from Maine. It is also renowned and as a marketplace for artwork and crafts off all kinds. If you're looking for an entire town of well-preserved Victorian homes, Ferndale, 20mi (32km) south of Eureka, is sure to please you. Eureka itself is also a place well worth exploring once you get off the tiresome main thoroughfare, Highway 101. Among its principal attractions is Humboldt Bay, the first major harbour north of San Francisco. Although the mining and lumber industries have long since ceased to dominate the local economy, fishing continues to thrive here, as the hustle and bustle of Fisherman's Wharf can attest to. A trip to Clarke Memorial Museum could well serve as an appropriate finale to a visit to Eureka because of

its first-rate collection of Native American artifacts. This unique collection suggests what life in this part of the northern California coast was like before Europeans settled it—an idea that, despite all of the adulterations of civilization, is possible to arrive at today, because so much true paradise still remains.

Finding Your Way Around

By Plane

The **Eureka-Arcata Airport,** located in McKinleyville, receives local flights from the San Francisco Airport. You can use either **United Express** or **Horizon Air** to get here.

By Car

The main highway is the winding Highway 1. Though taking this route will not win you any speed records, it is definitely the way to go if you want to stay alert at the wheel while taking in a panoramic view of the Pacific Ocean, as well as the enchanting flora and fauna that inhabit its dramatic cliffs and boulders.

Almost parallel to Highway 1 is Highway 101, which traverses the coast's interior. If you're in a hurry to get somewhere and not particularly interested in taking in the scenery on the way, then this is the better choice.

If you're planning to drive in the mountains at all, we strongly advise that you call the **Road Conditions Hotline** (☎*800-427-ROAD*) first. Believe it or not, many northern California roads are blocked by snow right up into the month of May!

Car Rentals

San Francisco is really the place to rent your car. Not only is it usually cheaper, but your choice is substantially greater. The San Francisco Airport has one of the largest car rental facilities in the world and is very well organized for car rental returns.

If you choose to fly to the Eureka-Arcata Airport rather than to drive up the coast, there are several choices of car rentals at the airport:

Avis
☎*(707) 839-1576*
☎*800-331-1212*

Hertz
☎*(707) 839-2172*
☎*800-654-3131*

National Interrent
☎*(707) 839-3229*
☎*800-227-7368*

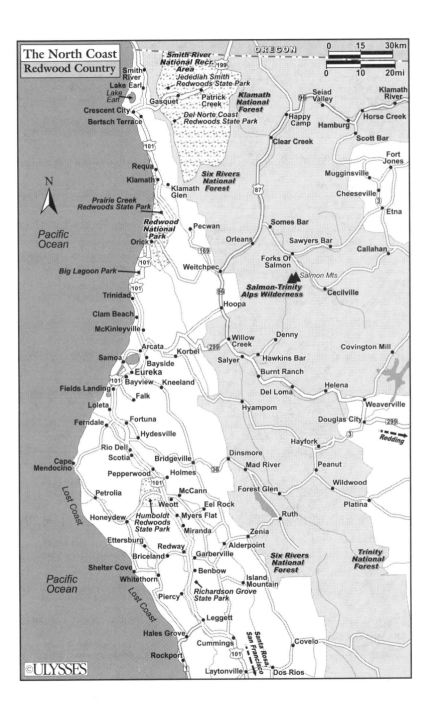

The North Coast
Redwood Country

OREGON

0   15   30km

0   10   20mi

Smith River National Recr. Area

Jedediah Smith Redwoods State Park

199

Smith River

Lake Earl
Lake Earl

Gasquet

Patrick Creek

Klamath National Forest

96

Seiad Valley

Klamath River

Crescent City

Bertsch Terrace

Del Norte Coast Redwoods State Park

Happy Camp

Hamburg

Horse Creek

Scott Bar

101

Clear Creek

Fort Jones

Requa

Klamath

Klamath Glen

Six Rivers National Forest

Mugginsville

Cheeseville

3

Etna

87

Prairie Creek Redwoods State Park

Pacific Ocean

Redwood National Park

Pecwan

Somes Bar

Orick

169

Orleans

Sawyers Bar

Callahan

Big Lagoon Park

101

Weitchpec

Forks Of Salmon

Salmon Mts.

Cecilville

101

96

Salmon-Trinity Alps Wilderness

Trinidad

Hoopa

Clam Beach

McKinleyville

Willow Creek

Denny

Covington Mill

Arcata

Korbel

299

Samoa

Bayside

Salyer

Hawkins Bar

Eureka

Bayview

Kneeland

Burnt Ranch

Helena

101

Del Loma

Weaverville

Fields Landing

Falk

Loleta

Hyampom

Douglas City

299

Fortuna

Ferndale

Hydesville

Hayfork

3

Redding

Rio Dell

Dinsmore

Scotia

Bridgeville

Mad River

Peanut

Cape Mendocino

Pepperwood

Holmes

36

Wildwood

Petrolia

McCann

Forest Glen

Platina

101

Lost Coast

Weott

Eel Rock

Honeydew

Humboldt Redwoods State Park

Myers Flat

Ruth

Miranda

Zenia

Ettersburg

Redway

Alderpoint

Six Rivers National Forest

Trinity National Forest

Briceland

Garberville

Shelter Cove

Benbow

Pacific Ocean

Whitethorn

Island Mountain

Lost Coast

Piercy

Richardson Grove State Park

Leggett

Hales Grove

Santa Rosa
San Francisco

Covelo

Cummings

101

Rockport

©ULYSSES

Laytonville

Dos Rios

N

By Bus

Greyhound Bus Lines
☎*(415) 444-0370*
☎*800-231-2222*
Greyhound has a route
that services Highway 101
all the way from San
Francisco to Oregon.

Public Transportation

Golden Gate Transit
☎*(415)332-6600*
If you want to get to Point
Reyes Nation Seashore, the
Golden Gate Transit has
weekend departures to get
you there.

Mendocino Transit Authority
241 Plant Rd.
Ukiah, CA 95482
This company offers pub-
lic transportation between
Mendocino, Fort Bragg
and Santa Rosa. If you
want to explore some of
Highway 1 between Bo-
dega Bay and Point Arena
using public transporta-
tion, this is the way to do
it. But because there is
only one departure per
day, make sure you get to
the station on time! A
connection with the Santa
Rosa Airporter for service
to and from the San Fran-
cisco/Oakland Airports is
also conveniently offered.

Mendocino Stage
☎*(707) 964-0167*
In addition to providing
service to Gualala, Point
Arena, Mendocino and
Fort Bragg, this will take
you to the interior as far as
Ukiah.

Humboldt Transit System
Mon to Fri
☎*(707) 444-0826*
This company offers con-
nections from the Eureka-
Arcata Airport to down-
town Eureka or Arcata, in
addition to local service in
Eureka and Arcata.

By Train

Skunk Train
summer months only
Reservations recommended
Tickets are available at the
train depots in Willits and
Fort Bragg
(from Fort Bragg to Willits)
foot of Laurel St., on the west side of
North Main St.
Fort Bragg, CA
☎*(707) 964-6371 (Fort Bragg)*
☎*(707) 459-5248 (Willits)*
☎*800-77S-KUNK*
Currently run by California
Western Railroad, this
route was originally used
for logging in 1885. Be-
cause the original gas
engines in the bright
yellow cars gave off nox-
ious fumes they were
nicknamed skunks—hence
the name Skunk Train.
Today the train runs on
diesel and slithers through
40mi (64.3km) of moun-
tains, redwood forests,
meadows, rivers and
tunnels along the Noyo
River. The round trip takes
about 7.5hrs, though other
options are available if you
make arrangements in
advance.

By Ferry

Golden Gate Transit Ferry
☎*(415) 923-2000 (San Fran-*
cisco County)
☎*(415) 455-2000 (Marin*
County)
☎*(707) 541-2000 (Sonoma*
County)
www.transitinfo.org/GGT/

TiburonAngel Island State Park Ferry
pier on Main St in Tiburon
☎*(415) 435 1915*

By Boat

Humboldt Bay Harbour Cruise
Sails daily from May to Oct at
1pm, 2:30pm and 4pm
MV Madaket
foot of C St.
Eureka, CA
☎*(707) 4451910*

Practical Information

The area code is **707** unless
otherwise indicated.

Road Conditions
☎*800-427-7623*

Weather Information
☎*443-7062*

Fish and Game
☎*964-9078*

Tourist Information

Marin and Sonoma Counties

West Marin Chamber of Commerce
☎*(415) 663-9232*
www.pointreyes.org

Mendocino County

Fort Bragg-Mendocino Chamber of Commerce
332 North Main St.
Fort Bragg, CA 95437
☎*961-6300*
www.mendocinocoast.com

Humboldt County

Eureka-Humboldt County Convention and Visitors Bureau
Mon to Fri 9am to noon and
1pm to 5pm
1034 Second St. at the corner of L St.
Eureka, CA
☎*443-5097 or 800-346-3482*

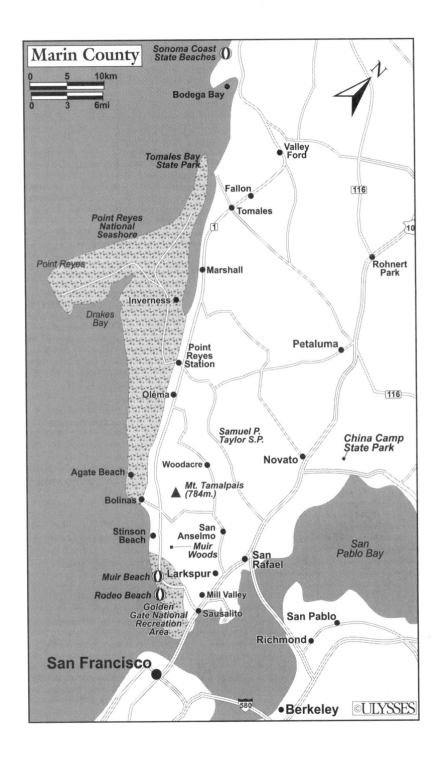

Marin County

Sonoma Coast
State Beaches

0   5   10km
0   3   6mi

N

Bodega Bay

Valley
Ford

Tomales Bay
State Park

116

Fallon

Tomales

Point Reyes
National
Seashore

1

10

Point Reyes

Marshall

Rohnert
Park

Inverness

Drakes
Bay

Petaluma

Point
Reyes
Station

116

Olema

Samuel P.
Taylor S.P.

China Camp
State Park

Woodacre

Novato

Agate Beach

Mt. Tamalpais
(784m.)

Bolinas

Stinson
Beach

San
Anselmo

Muir
Woods

San
Rafael

San
Pablo Bay

Muir Beach

Larkspur

Rodeo Beach

Mill Valley

Golden
Gate National
Recreation
Area

Sausalito

San Pablo

Richmond

San Francisco

580

Berkeley

©ULYSSES

Telecommunications

Radio

Marin and Sonoma Counties

The Coast KOZT
FM 95.3 (coast)
FM 95.9 (inland)
Local news in the morning, weather, current events and local music programming.

Humboldt and Mendocino Counties

KMUD Community Radio
91.1 FM (South Humboldt)
88.3 FM (EurekaArcata)
88.9 FM (north of Mendocino)

Exploring

Inland Marin County

If instead of concentrating strictly a coastal Marin County, you decide to explore destinations east and north on Highway 101, a good starting point is **Angel Island State Park** *(Headquarters: 1455 East Francis Blvd. San Rafael 94501, ☎415-435-1915).* To get there, board a ferry in San Francisco, Tiburon or Vallejo. This 740-acre (299ha) island used to be called the Ellis Island of the West because for decades Asian immigrants to the U.S. were processed here. The **Immigration Station Museum** details this history. Nearby stands the largest remaining collection of wooden **Civil War Buildings**, all on the site of 1863 Camp Reynolds, built to protect

Union troops against a Confederate invasion which never materialized. Also nearby sits **Fort McDowell**, a World War II military embarkation centre. Hike to the top of the island's 781ft (238m) high Mount Livermore for marvellous views of the Bay Area.

San Rafael

San Rafael is Marin's county seat, its largest city and its cultural centre. San Rafael's historical downtown mansion district includes a replica of the **Mission San Rafael** *(every day 11am to 4pm; 1104 Fifth Ave.),* the second-most-northern California mission. Of special architectural interest is Frank Lloyd Wright's last major creation, the **Marin Civic Center** *(just off of Hwy. 101; weekdays 8am to 5pm, except legal holidays; ☎415- 499-7407; ♿; docent-led tours available with advance notice),* a structure that gives the impression that Wright was trying to simulate the rolling hills around it. The surrounding 140 acres (56.7ha) serve as the site for the annual county fair in July. Apart from housing the county's administrative offices, the Civic Center regularly hosts the Marin Symphony, the Marin Ballet

Heron

and the Marin Opera, among many other cultural events. Not to be missed is the **Marin County Farmer's Market** *(year-round on Thu mornings, Sun 9am to 2pm, May to Oct)*—considered by locals to be the best farmer's market in the county. Driving several miles east of San Rafael on San Pedro Road will allow you an altogether different cultural experience, namely, the kind of life Chinese immigrant fishers led in the late 1800s. This partially restored Chinese fishing camp, once one of many near San Francisco, is the last such village in existence. In the vicinity of its museum, **The China Camp State Historic Park**, *($5; every day sunrise to sunset; museum open daily in the summer —Memorial Day to Labour Day—and on weekends for the rest of the year, from Hwy. 101, take the San Pedro road exit and continue past the Civic Center; follow the signs, Hwy 1, Box 244, San Rafael, 94901, ☎415-456-0766)* has rebuilt piers and a 1900 general store. Here you can still find one last inhabitant and practitioner of shrimp-fishing art as practiced in the time of his grandfather, father and uncle. Frank Quan provides a rare living window on the history of his shrimp fishing forbears.

Vallejo

Marine World/Africa USA *($25, parking extra; Marine World Parkway Vallejo 94589, ☎424-5605)* If you're travelling with children and would like to include a theme park in your itinerary, stop at Marine World/ Africa USA on your way to the North Coast or to Wine Country.

Featured here are trained animal performances by sea lions, dolphins, tigers, elephants and orangutans. You can also get close to some exotic birds and walk through a greenhouse that shelters tropical butterflies.

At the northernmost end of Marin County on Highway 101, Novato's pleasant downtown Grant Avenue district welcomes you to look over its various business establishments and 1896 City Hall, which was once a church. But when in Novato, visitors should, above all else, stop in at the **Novato History Museum** *(free admission; Thu and Sat 10am to 4pm; 815 De Long Ave., ☎415-897-4320)* and the **Marin Museum of the American Indian** in Miwok Park *(free admission; Tue to Sat 10am to 4pm, Sun noon to 4pm, closed in Dec; 2200 Novato Blvd., ☎415-897-4064)*. Through its displays of photographs and various artifacts, the Novato History Museum does a good job of revealing Novato's pioneer past—everything from its apple-orchard greatness in the late 19th century to its Second World War importance as home of the Hamilton Air Force Base *(☎928-1975)*. Highlighting the Coast Miwok and Pomo cultures, the small, handsomely arranged Marin Museum of the American Indian also mounts exhibits and sponsors activities featuring the cultures of a wide range of North American indigenous peoples. Perfectly reinforcing the museum's mission, a summer camp for six to 10 year olds called Camp Coyote, in several five-day sessions, provides hands-on education in Native American culture.

The Marin Coast

Extending north all the way from Fort Funston in San Francisco to Point Reyes National Seashore, the **Golden Gate National Recreation Area (GGNRA)** covers some 70,000 acres (28,329ha) and draws more visitors annually (almost 20 million) than any other national park. The jewel in its crown is the **Marin Headlands**, ranging in topography from steep cliffs to inland valleys to those characteristically Californian loping grass-covered hills. The Headlands offer numerous hiking and backpacking opportunities (see p 515).

One of the parks contained within the GGNRA is the popular **Muir Woods National Monument ★ ★**, named after the celebrated naturalist John Muir *(☎838-1914)*. Only 12mi (19.3km) north of the Golden Gate Bridge via Highway 101 and 1, Muir Woods contains the last remaining old growth redwoods in the Bay Area. It is also home to some of the less well-known Chinese dawn redwoods and albino redwoods. To properly savour the grandeur of these old, mighty coastal redwoods, you should get well away from the parking lot with its tour bus crowd and walk at least the mile of the paved trail next to Redwood Creek, if not some of the additional 5mi (8km) of unpaved trails. Muir Woods had the single, appropriate honour of hosting a ceremony following the signing in April, 1945 of the United Nations Charter by delegates from 50 nations.

West of Muir Woods lies **Muir Beach**, which affords the weary and not-so-

weary traveller a pleasant sandy beach and good seaward views, but no swimming. **Stinson Beach**, on the other hand, just a few miles north on Highway 1, provides 4mi (6.4km) of beach ideal for summer swimming, sunbathing and surfing (see p 515). The town of Stinson Beach is an attractive little community perfect for a pre-beach or post-beach stroll.

From Stinson Beach, take Panoramic Highway west, then Ridge crest to get to the 6,218-acre (2,516ha) **Mount Tamalpais State Park** and access to Mount Tamalpais. A road popular with cyclists ascends to the top. This park is a hiker's dream with its 200mi (322km) of trails (see p 514). The East Summit of Mount Tamalpais (elevation 2,571ft or 783m) will reward climbers with views of the whole Bay Area and, on a clear day, of the Farallon Islands 30mi (48.2km) to sea, and of the Sierra Nevada a full 200mi (322km) east. If you're are looking for another memorable experience in the park, stay overnight in one of the ten cabins in **Steep Ravine** overlooking the Pacific Ocean. If you return to Stinson Beach and head north on Highway 1 to Bolinas Lagoon, you'll be able to fully satisfy your ornithological appetites (see p 519).

Furthermore, 3.5mi (5.6km) up the road, from early March to early July, you can observe, from above, great blue herons and great and snowy egrets courting and raising their offspring. When you finally succeed in making your way into the town of Bolinas, in spite of the absence of directional signs (the work of people

The North Coast

The Coastal Redwoods

Long ago, the ancestors of today's redwoods grew all over the Northern Hemisphere. Today, they flourish only along the Pacific coast of California and Southwestern Oregon in a narrow band 5 to 35mi (8 to 56km) wide and 450mi (724km) long, extending north from the Santa Lucia Mountains of Monterey County, California to the Cletco River, Oregon and on the western slopes of California's Sierra Nevada Mountains. The inland species (*sequoia gigantea*) should not be confused with the generally taller, narrower and shorter-living coastal species (*sequoia sempervirens*—"always green"). This latter titan lives comfortably today on average from 500 to 700 years on alluvial terraces and low-level slopes; that is from sea-level to around 3,100ft (around 945m). The oldest-known coastal redwood, now long dead, lived more than 2200 years; the tallest (as documented by the National Geographic Society in 1963) fell just short of 368ft (112m) in height.

Another difference between the two species, and a crucial one at that, is that the coastal redwood can reproduce not just by germinating from seeds, but also by sprouting from dormant bud collars or burls, wart-like tissue growths usually near the base of the tree. From each of a tree's thousands of thimble-sized cones, about 60 winged seeds, approximately the size of tomato seeds, fall to the ground. Fungal attack, insufficient sunlight, and lack of water reduce the chances of a seed becoming a mature tree to less than one in a million. But if a seedling lasts its first summer, its chances of survival are much improved because the bud collar at its base can grow. Bud tissue on a developing tree will emerge from dormancy if the stem is cut, eaten (by deer, for example), broken by stong winds, or burnt by fire, giving off sprouts which are nourished by the root system of the parent tree. The dominant sprouts soon form what is known as a "fairy ring," a circle of newly cloned trees around the parent.

Adult coastal redwoods are equipped with remarkable built-in protection against enemies. Their thick, moist bark resists fire; the tannin in their bark drives away insects; their imperviousness to disease underscores their apparent lack of anything analogous to human aging. And yet, even in a climate that they thrive in, one that is blessed with warmth (never freezing temperatures), moisture (high annual rainfall abetted by summer coastal fog), these trees do meet with disaster. For example, their roots may be suffocated if a major flood deposits too much silt. More often what causes a tree to die is its toppling by winds. Such wind throw occurs because, despite its immense height, the coastal redwood has a taproot and a fairly shallow lateral root system.

This tree's extreme height has a further surprising consequence: a mature tree is home to three distinct climatic zones, at the level of the base, at the level of the stem and at the level of the crown. Whereas at ground level the tree is experiencing shade, coolness and wetness, at its very top it can be subjected to wind and dryness. This diversity accounts for its two different kinds of needles. While most needles on the tree are broad and flat so as to be able to capture a maximum of sunlight, those close to the top have smaller, more tightly positioned scale-like spikes to minimize evaporation.

All the above information notwithstanding, there is no rational way to account for the stupendous impact these redwoods can have on an observer. Whether lying on the ground fallen or reaching straight up into the heavens, however, the *sequoi sempervirens* dwells near the seacoast with an everpresent majesty that discourages human chatter in favour of awed silence. A grove of redwoods is often aptly compared to a cathedral. Especially if the sun is shining down through the canopy of these soaring giants, it is hard not to feel a natural spirituality which could turn even an otherwise-irreligious person into something of a worshipper.

who want to keep Bolinas to themselves), you'll enjoy a long-established Bohemian enclave and its beautiful Agate Beach.

Another park enveloped by the GGNRA, located 15mi (24.1km) west of San Rafael on Sir Francis Drake Boulevard and just east of Point Reyes National Seashore, is the 2,600-acre (1,052ha) **Samuel P. Taylor State Park**. Here, there are hiking and equestrian trails galore as well as paved biking paths and picnicking, swimming and camping facilities amidst a combination of old-growth and young redwoods.

★★★
Point Reyes National Seashore

Point Reyes is aptly named: the natural beauty of this spectacular convergence of land, sea, and sky is nothing short of majestic. The actual history of its name is more mundane: on January 6th 1603, Spanish explorer Don Vizcaino, sailing past the steep headlands just outside Drake's Bay, came up with the name *La Punta de Los Tres Reyes*—the point of the three kings—because it happened to be the Feast of the Three Kings' Day. Today's adventurer, whether coming from the north or south via High-

way 1, and presumably travelling with a car, will find the **Bear Valley Visitor Center** (☎*415-663-1092, www.nps.gov/pore*), Point Reyes National Seashore Park Headquarters. Only a minute's drive from Olema, this is an excellent place from which to launch your explorations. Effortlessly, you can begin on a highly dramatic geological note by realizing that, as you enter the park, you're riding directly over the celebrated and feared San Andreas Fault, part of a 600mi (966km) long zone of faults. When the catastrophic San Francisco Earthquake of 1906 occurred, this fault was responsible for moving Point Reyes Peninsula a full 21ft (6.2m) northwestward. The explanation lies in plate tectonics; that is, the grinding together of the always slowly moving Pacific Plate and the North American Plate produced such great pressure that the Earth's surface moved.

From the principal visitor's center (the other two are the **Kenneth C. Patrick Visitor Center** on Drake's Beach and **Point Reyes Lighthouse Visitor Center**), take Bear Valley Road north a couple of miles until it joins Sir Francis Drake Boulevard. Then, proceed north to Anchor Bay and, soon after, Inverness, in either

of which towns you can stop to eat or stock up on whatever supplies you need. About 5mi (8km) west of Inverness, take an upward road to **Johnson's Oyster Company** on Drake's estero (estuary) and treat yourself by purchasing freshly caught oysters.

What next arrests the eye a few miles farther down Sir Francis Drake Boulevard borders on the surreal. Like ship-less, sailless masts, one giant antenna after another rises up from the flat terrain facing out across the Pacific Ocean. What you're looking at is AT&T's high-seas radio-telephone station KMI. This station makes it possible for ships at sea or aircraft to communicate with telephones on land. Inasmuch as Point Reyes is the best receiving station on the West Coast, these antennas receive transmissions from all over the Pacific Ocean. Weather and safety matters are KMI's top broadcasting priorities.

The antennas in front of you also make communication possible between commercial ships and land-to-land networks through MCI Radio Station KPH. Located first at the Palace Hotel in San Francisco in 1904 and 10 years later moved to the Marconi property on Tamales Bay, KPH is both one of the

The North Coast

Sea lion

If you choose to walk down the 308 steps to the lighthouse—dressed, of course, in anticipation of a possible sudden onset of cold weather—you're more likely to see grey whales migrating to their summer home off Baja, California. Warm, salty water makes this a good

the Miwok people were the sole inhabitants of remarkable Point Reyes. Its forests, chapparal, seacoast and grasslands provided the indispensable sustenance of deer and elk, acorns and berries, salmon and shellfish. These hundreds of years later, the Point Reyes National Seashore's more than 70,000 acres (28,329ha) provide today's visitors with the equally indispensable food of wild natural beauty.

Fort Ross

What brought 25 Russians and 80 Alaskans south to Spanish-owned northern California in March of 1812 to begin settling a place that would become known as Fort Ross was the need to hunt sea otter and to grow food to feed hungry settlers along the Alaskan coast. On August 13 1812, the Fort was formally dedicated, "Ross" being an abbreviated name for Russia during Czarist days. As the result of massive restoration and reconstruction efforts by the California Department of Parks and Recreation, today the Fort closely resembles what it was during the Russians' tenure here until they abandoned the fog-prone settlement in 1841.

oldest sets of radio call letters in the United States and the finest receiving station in the western part of the country.

In springtime especially, a comforting antidote to the electronic devices that thrust up out of the earth is the profusion of wildflowers blooming all around, 80 species of which have been documented at **Chimney Rock**, the eastern tip of Point Reyes. The windswept landscape here is covered with purple Douglas iris and rosy hollyhock. Near the lighthouse, on the western tip of the Point Reyes promontory, Indian paintbrush and California buttercups are likely to abound. Hiking down to land's end makes you acutely aware of beautiful but dangerous steep cliffs (never climb on the cliffs because they crumble easily) descending to the ocean's edge. One hundred and forty or so days of the year, however, fog largely obliterates such dramatic scenes.

place for mother whales to give birth because young calves lack the fat to confer enough buoyancy to learn how to swim and enough insulation to keep them warm in the Arctic waters of the North Pacific. Whether or not whales present themselves for viewing, pocket beaches between cliffs will often reveal sea lions and seals lying on the sand in seemingly ultimate postures of relaxation. Meanwhile, above and around the cliffs, meanwhile, many species of seabirds fill the skies. The park as a whole attracts more than 400 species of birds. **Abbots Lagoon** (see p 519) and **Tomales Point** favour raptors while Tomales Bay and Olema Marsh see many kinds of egrets, waterfowl and shorebirds.

Long before Sir Francis Drake, in the service of Queen Elizabeth I of England, came ashore off his ship the *Golden Hind* in the summer of 1579 (in the vicinity of what is now known as Drake's Estero),

Drive 11mi (17.7km) north of Jenner on Highway 1 to arrive at a well-done recreation of an interesting piece of California history. What first meets the eye is a huge rectangular stockade with blockhouses at the north and south corners, bristling with cannons ready to defend and protect those within. Principal structures—all of them are and were made of redwood—within the stockade include the two-storey house of the manager, the most important of whom was the first and very able Ivan Kuskof. The structures also include the officials' quarters, barracks for the Russian employees of the Russian-American Company and a variety of storehouses. In the centre, a well supplied the colony with water. The Russian Orthodox chapel, added in 1824, is a particularly striking building. In the days of the Russian presence here, company laborers, native Alaskans, and local Native Americans, the Kashaya Pomo, built dwellings outside the stockade.

As early as 1820, the hunters of sea otter, who were for the most part Kodiak islanders, had so reduced the otter population that the principal activities of Fort Ross became agriculture and the raising of livestock, though never on a profitable basis. By 1841, the Russian-American Company had given up on the Ross Colony, first trying, to no avail, interest the Mexican government in buying it. Then, in December 1841, they worked out a deal with John Sutter of Sutter's Fort in the Sacramento Valley, to whom the purchased movables such as hardware, arms and ammunition, and herds of cattle and sheep were transported.

As of 1992, the State of California has acquired a total of 3,277 acres (1,326ha) in and around Fort Ross. Thus, visitors can explore such diverse attractions as the old Russian orchard, 20 primitive campgrounds, ocean access and several redwood groves which, logged more than 100 years ago by the Russians, are now the oldest second-growth redwoods in the world. A visitor centre features interpretive exhibits and publications that place Fort Ross in the context of western U.S. history.

Sonoma Coast: Bodega to Jenner

If you're a movie enthusiast and, more particularly, a fan of Alfred Hitchcock's films, you'll probably want to see **Bodega's Potter School** (1863) and **Saint Teresa's Church** (1860). These are two of the locations featured in Hitchcock's celebrated opus *The Birds*. Five miles (8km) north on Highway 1, Bodega Bay is the southernmost town on the Sonoma Coast. The area provided an additional ready-made setting for the movie with its flocks of harbour birds. It is, naturally, a fine place to birdwatch; it's also a great place from which to embark on deep-sea sport fishing. Three hundred or so commercial fishing boats bobbing in Bodega Bay's harbour make the April **Fisherman's Festival** and **Blessing of the Fleet** a sight to behold.

Just to the north, Bodega Head affords Bodega Bay dramatic protection from the wild ocean waters. Nearby, the University of California's marine biology research center, **Bodega Bay Marine Station**, warrants a stop. If you're in an ambling mood, you can walk the paths in the vicinity of the head or the trails (there are 5mi or 8km of them) through the Bodega Dunes. On the south side of the bay at **Doran County Park**, you'll be able to swim at protected beaches or even go clamming.

The 13mi (21km) from Bodega Bay to Jenner alongside Highway 1 constitute one of the most accessible stretches of northern California coastline. Within that short distance, seventeen public beaches, the **Sonoma Coast State Beaches**, assure you of all sorts of opportunities for fishing, picnicking, whale-watching, beach-combing, tide-pooling and camping. Unfortunately, the very cold water, the undertow, the

Bodega Church

heavy surf and the occasional but potentially lethal "sleeper" or "rogue" wave rule out swimming.

Perched high above the sea on dramatic cliffs, the village of Jenner is an inviting resort town marked by the meeting place of the Russian River and the Pacific Ocean at **Goat Rock Beach**. At the mouth of the river, a colony of more than 200 harbour seals lives on a sand bar. Unlike sea lions, which can propel themselves forward on flippers, seals must wriggle their way about—but don't put them to the test by approaching them too closely because to maintain their body temperature on land, they shouldn't move. Behind Goat Rock, Penny Island affords bird watchers a chance to spot many different kinds of migratory and native species. If you approach this island by rubber raft, kayak, canoe or rowboat, you may see river otters as well.

Mendocino Coast

Fort Bragg

Once a thriving lumber centre, Fort Bragg, 8mi (13km) north of Mendocino on Highway 1, is today a busy and diverse city that holds its own in terms of touristic interest next to any other northern California coastal city. Of major economic and social importance to Fort Bragg is the **Noyo Harbour**, at the south end of town. It is the home of a commercial fishing fleet, which includes trollers and dragboats, and its concomittant fish markets, processing plants, and bait and tackle shops. As the largest port between San Francisco and Eureka, the

harbour is an extremely busy place where you'll nevertheless see harbour seals and sea lions lying languorously on docks or floating in the water. Sport fishers have come to the right place to indulge themselves from aboard charter boats or private vessels. During migration season, from December through April, you might want to go on a grey whale-watching excursion. Or perhaps you prefer rock fishing, surf fishing, jigging for herring or diving for abalone (when the tides and season are right). If you happen to be around in July, join in the fun at the annual **World's Largest Salmon Barbecue**.

Anyone interested in a first-rate micro-brewery, noted for its Red Seal Ale, ought to take a free tour of the **North Coast Brewing Company** (see p 526). The pleasantly penetrating aroma surrounding it makes it impossible for the nose to miss! From May to October on Wednesday afternoons, you can inspect the fresh produce at the **Farmer's Market** in front of City Hall.

If you wish to partake of the art scene, begin at the **Fort Bragg Center for the Arts** in the historic White House (*321 North Main St.*). Started in 1989 as part of the city's centennial observance, this centre goes out of its way to encourage youngsters to make art. Live theatre, opera and classical music receive their due through the **Wavehouse Repertory Theatre**, the **Gloriana Opera Company** and the **Symphony of the Redwoods**, respectively.

A must for those who want to learn about Fort Bragg's past is the 1892

Victorian Guest House Museum (*342 North Main St.*), made entirely of redwood. In this house, built for C.R. Johnson, the Union Lumber Company's founder and first mayor of Fort Bragg, artifacts, photos and exhibits illuminate the town's history. Long before Europeans took over, Pomo Indians dwelt on these shores. In 1857, a year after they were placed on a 25,000-acre (10,117ha) reservation by the Bureau of Indian Affairs, a fort was built to preserve order, a part of which still stands slightly north of City Hall. Several yards away, Fort Bragg's **Depot** exhibits a collection of impressively refurbished logging steam engines and steam donkeys (a complicated-looking log hauler), the mainstays of the lumber industry in its prime. The Depot also serves as the western terminus of the famed **Skunk Train**, which winds its way 40mi (64km) over trestles through redwoods alongside the Noyo River to Willits and back.

If you want to stay closer to home to enjoy natural beauty, nearby beaches are good for beach-combing, picnicking and surfing. **Glass Beach**, accessible from the end of Elm Street by walking down a path to the ocean, will likely reward efforts to sift the sand for—you guessed it—wave-worn glass. To conclude the day on a high note, spend some time 2mi (3.2km) south of Fort Bragg at the **Mendocino Coast Botanical Gardens** (*18220 North Hwy. 1 on the west side of Hwy. 1, 2mi or 3.2km south of Fort Bragg, 7mi or 11.2km north of Mendocino Village*). Comprised of acres of trees, shrubs and flowers, the

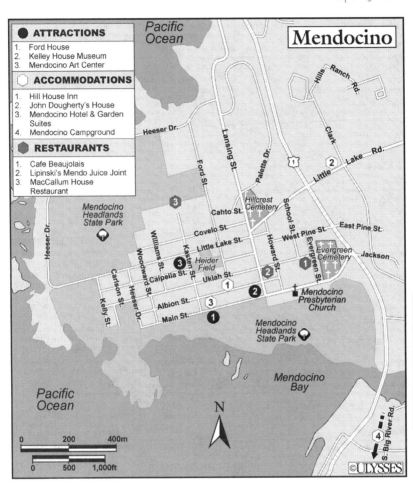

Mendocino

ATTRACTIONS
1. Ford House
2. Kelley House Museum
3. Mendocino Art Center

ACCOMMODATIONS
1. Hill House Inn
2. John Dougherty's House
3. Mendocino Hotel & Garden Suites
4. Mendocino Campground

RESTAURANTS
1. Cafe Beaujolais
2. Lipinski's Mendo Juice Joint
3. MacCallum House Restaurant

gardens' springtime rhododendrons, irises and fuchsias might just overwhelm you as you stroll toward the sea.

★★★
Mendocino

Around 150mi (241km) north of San Francisco on Highway 1 lies Mendocino, an extremely sophisticated small town with a large number of artistically minded souls. Balancing all that cultivation and also nourishing it are several parks close by

(all off Hwy. 1). Journey to them to take a look or, better still, hike through and come close to at least some of their special features. Three miles (4.8km) south of Mendocino, **Van Damme State Park** offers a sheltered beach front which draws abalone divers. Across the road, there is a fern canyon trail and that curious botanical phenomenon, a pygmy forest, which is a naturally occurring bonsai-like thicket. Going north of Mendocino, 3mi (4.8km) past Fort Bragg, **Mackerricher State Park**'s

Laguna Point is a great place to watch harbour seals pupping in April and May while adults bask in the sun on the rocks, not to mention the excellent opportunities for whale-watching during migration season.

Taking a walk with a self-guiding brochure on **Ecological Staircase Trail** in **Jughandle State Reserve**, 1mi (1.6km) north of Caspar, will provide a lesson in evolutionary geology as you view a series of five terraces, 100ft (30m) higher and 100,000 years older than each one below. Ocean water rushing through a a collapsed sea cave called the Devil's Punch Bowl is a distinguishing feature of **Russian Gulch State Park**, just 2mi (3.2km) north of Mendocino. It is also popular with abalone divers. Finally, surrounding the village of Mendocino on three sides is the **Mendocino Headlands State Park** ★ *(day use only)* brought into existence in the 1970s by concerned citizens who wanted to protect a natural buffer-zone of bluffs covered with grass and wildflowers, dramatic cliff faces and quiet beaches from the inroads of developers. **Ford House** (1854) *(free admission; every day 10am to 5pm; Main St.,* ☎*937-5397)* serves as a visitor's centre for the Mendocino Headlands State Park. Its museum houses a miniature version of Mendocino in 1890, Pomo Indian artifacts, and exhibits on redwood logging and natural history. One street over (Albion), the 1861 **Kelley House Museum** *(free admission; Fri to Mon 1pm to 4pm or call for an appointment; 45007 Albion St.,* ☎*937-5397)* displays interpretive material on the distinctly Victorian architecture of the town, as well as on its logging and shipping past. The Kelley House, along with the Presbyterian Church that looks out over Mendocino Bay with its front door around back, strongly attests to why the entire town of Mendocino has been designated a Historic Preservation District. The latter structure, designed by the same architect who designed the State Capitol building in Sacramento, was built in 1867 and is still in use. On a stroll through the town, you'll encounter many other buildings that under-

line the elegant historicity of Mendocino, one such being the Mendocino Hotel on Main Street, built in 1878.

Nothing visible in Mendocino today indicates that, in 1959, it was in bad economical shape and in need of an institution like the Mendocino Art Center to act as a guardian of its beauty and a stimulus in the formation of an art colony which, in turn, led to the rejuvenation of the local economy. In fact, numerous art galleries thrive in what has become a paradise for art collectors. Not surprisingly, fine overnight accommodations and dining establishments are also available here. Entertainment in the form of year-round theater productions by **The Mendocino Theater Company**, the summer's annual **Mendocino Music Festival** (from classical to jazz), and the annual **Mendocino Whale Festival**, held in March, cannot but enrich a vacation stay in this much-loved community.

★★★
Avenue of the Giants and Scotia

The 53,000-acre (21,449ha) **Humboldt Redwoods State Park** ★★ (the largest state park in northern California), with its 17,000 acres (6,880ha) of old-growth coastal redwoods, includes the splendid sylvan corridor called the Avenue of the Giants. Grove after grove, these trees grow so high that they are the tallest living things on Earth—truly giants.

About 6mi (9.7km) north of Garberville, the **Avenue of the Giants**, originally the old stage coach and wagon road, runs 33mi

(53.1km) alongside Highway 101 and along the Eel River. Thus begins a magnificent journey past trees the likes of which made John Steinbeck write: "*The redwoods once seen, leave a mark or create a vision that stays with you always... from them comes silence and awe. The most irreverent of men, in the presence of the redwoods, goes under a spell of wonder and respect.*"

Stopping by the Visitor Center & Interpretive Association and/or the State Park Headquarters, both near Weott, will help you answer questions on just about anything pertaining to the park and, maybe most importantly, to practical matters like where to camp, hike, swim, bike, picnic, raft, kayak or fish. The many different kinds of campgrounds and the fishing and boating potential on the Eel River (after the sometimes dangerous spring rainfall) will greatly increase the chances that whatever your particular outdoor requirements may be, they will be met. And if camping is not to your liking, Garberville will be able to provide an adequate choice of indoor accommodation.

About two thirds of the way up the Avenue, extending 5mi (8km) west of Highway 101, stands the 13,000-acre (5,261ha) **Rockefeller Forest** (a gift from the J.D. Rockefeller family), known for some of the most valuable virgin trees remaining on the north coast. To the east, the **Founders Grove** gives you a chance to walk a Nature Loop Trail in 20 or 30min and perhaps forge an intimate bond with the wondrous trees. The Founders Tree's measurements alone should suffice to account for why a human might marvel at it: it rises 346ft (105m) straight up; its diameter is 12.7ft (4m); its circumference is 40ft (12m); and the distance from the ground to its lowest limb is some 190ft (58m)! The foresighted men to whom The Founders Grove is dedicated, established the **Save-the-Redwoods League** in 1918 because they rightly feared that, unprotected, virtually all such majestic redwoods would succumb to the greed of the timber industry.

Just a few minutes north of the end of the Avenue of the Giants, off Highway 101 on the scenic Eel River, the town of **Scotia** ★ ★, so named because many of its original residents came from Nova Scotia, is a rarity in America today: it is a town owned by one company, the Pacific Lumber Company. Its **redwood sawmill**, the largest in the world, gives off the sweet aroma of freshly cut redwood, an unusual form of invitation to take a self-guided tour to discover how the mill transforms logs into lumber. If you wander about until you come upon retired PLC Locomotive #9, you will be within sight of the company's museum *(every day in summer)*. This redwood imitation of a columned Greek temple sheds light on logging and the products of lumber.

The handsome **Scotia Inn** *(corner of Mill and Main)*, a redwood hostelry, first built in 1886 as a home for officials of the PLC and soon after expanded to house travellers and lumberjacks, deserves at least a good look. So too does the fish pond, six blocks south of the museum, where the PLC annually

rears 15,000 to 20,000 steel-head. And also deserving of attention is the company's **Demonstration Forest** 4.5mi (7.2km) south on Highway 1. A self-guided walking tour (possible during summer only) will show you how a forest harvested nearly 60 years ago grows back.

Where else but in tranquil Scotia would one find charming yellow traffic signs at several intersections marking duck crossings? From this orderly town's immaculate appearance, what visitor would ever guess that the entire business district and many homes (though not the mill), almost entirely constructed of redwood, were destroyed by fires caused by the earthquake in April 1992?

★ ★
Eureka and Arcata

Eureka, the largest city (pop. 27,000) on the California coast between San Francisco and the Oregon Border, with the largest landlocked bay between San Francisco and Puget Sound, is the cultural, economic and geographical centre of Humboldt County. In Greek, Eureka means "I have found it," and that is most appropriate for the traveller who realizes what he or she has discovered by visiting this exciting little city.

To start with, Eureka can boast that it has the highest per capita proportion of Victorian houses in the United States. And what remarkable houses they are is in ample evidence when passing such intricately adorned edifices as **The Carson House**, built between 1884 and 1886, reputedly the most photographed Victorian house in the country, or "**The Pink Lady**" just across the street. Old Town and Downtown practically overflow with handsomely restored Victorian buildings.

Eureka can also brag about its standing as one of the finest small art towns in the country. To begin to verify this, you might inspect the **Morris Graves Museum of Art**, located in the restored Carnegie Library *(corner of O St. and Third St.)*. Then walk the city streets with a tour map (available at the Chamber of Commerce) that shows the location of many wall murals painted by local artists. Folk art aficionados will want to stop by the **Roman Gabriel Sculpture Garden** *(on Second St., between D and E St.)*. Music receives special

The Carson House

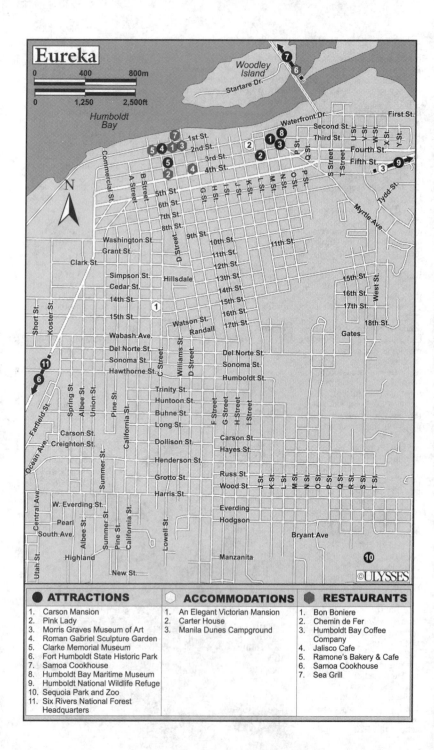

Eureka

0   400   800m

0   1,250   2,500ft

Humboldt Bay

Woodley Island

Startare Dr.

Waterfront Dr.

First St.
Second St.
Third St.
Fourth St.
Fifth St.

Commercial St.

1st St.
2nd St.
3rd St.
4th St.
5th St.
6th St.
7th St.
8th St.
9th St.
10th St.
11th St.
12th St.
13th St.
14th St.
15th St.
16th St.
17th St.
18th St.

Myrtle Ave.

Tydd St.

B Street
A Street
H St.
G St.
I St.
J St.
K St.
L St.
M St.
N St.
O St.
P St.
Q St.
S Street
T Street
U St.
V St.
W St.
X St.
Y St.
West St.

Washington St.
Grant St.
Clark St.
Simpson St.
Cedar St.
14th St.
15th St.

Hillsdale

Wabash Ave.
Del Norte St.
Sonoma St.
Hawthorne St.

Watson St.
Randall

Del Norte St.
Sonoma St.
Humboldt St.

Short St.
Koster St.

Fairfield St.
Ocean Ave.

Spring St.
Albee St.
Union St.
Pine St.
California St.
Summer St.

Carson St.
Creighton St.

C Street
Williams St.
D Street
F Street
G Street
H Street
I Street

Trinity St.
Huntoon St.
Buhne St.
Long St.
Dollison St.
Henderson St.
Grotto St.
Harris St.

Carson St.
Hayes St.
Russ St.
Wood St.

J St.
K St.
L St.
M St.
N St.
O St.
P St.
Q St.
R St.
S St.
T St.

Central Ave.
W. Everding St.
Pearl
South Ave.
Highland
New St.

Utah St.
Albee St.
Summer St.
Pine St.
California St.
Lowell St.

Everding
Hodgson

Bryant Ave.

Manzanita

Gates

©ULYSSES

⬤ ATTRACTIONS

1. Carson Mansion
2. Pink Lady
3. Morris Graves Museum of Art
4. Roman Gabriel Sculpture Garden
5. Clarke Memorial Museum
6. Fort Humboldt State Historic Park
7. Samoa Cookhouse
8. Humboldt Bay Maritime Museum
9. Humboldt National Wildlife Refuge
10. Sequoia Park and Zoo
11. Six Rivers National Forest Headquarters

⬡ ACCOMMODATIONS

1. An Elegant Victorian Mansion
2. Carter House
3. Manila Dunes Campground

⬡ RESTAURANTS

1. Bon Boniere
2. Chemin de Fer
3. Humboldt Bay Coffee Company
4. Jalisco Cafe
5. Ramone's Bakery & Cafe
6. Samoa Cookhouse
7. Sea Grill

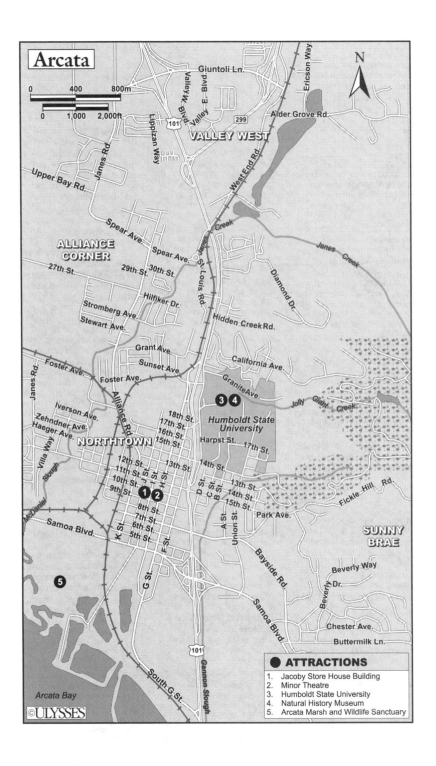

Arcata

N

VALLEY WEST

ALLIANCE CORNER

NORTHTOWN

Humboldt State University

SUNNY BRAE

Arcata Bay

©ULYSSES

● **ATTRACTIONS**
1. Jacoby Store House Building
2. Minor Theatre
3. Humboldt State University
4. Natural History Museum
5. Arcata Marsh and Wildlife Sanctuary

attention at the annual **Redwood Coast Dixieland Jazz Festival** and the annual **Blues by the Bay** concerts. Theatre flourishes in productions stages by at least nine amateur and professional companies.

History buffs will have a field day in Eureka. **The Clarke Memorial Museum** *(free admission; Tue to Sat from noon to 4pm, closed in Jan; 240 E St., ☎443-1947)*, its building once a bank, deserves singling out because it contains a distinguished collection of Yurok, Hupa and Karuk basketry and dance regalia, as well as large collections of photographs, weapons and Victoriana. **Fort Humboldt State Historic Park** *(free admission; every day 9am to 5pm; 3431 Fort Ave., ☎445-6567)*, where a disgruntled, hard-working president-to-be named Ulysses S. Grant spent several months in 1854, combines restored military post buildings, a Native American military museum and an extensive outdoor exhibit of historic logging equipment. This last includes steam donkeys, huge machines that hauled logs over skid roads while dragging themselves through the woods, and two of the kinds of locomotives which eventually made steam donkeys obsolete. Across the Samoa Bridge from Eureka, the **Samoa Cookhouse** (see p 526), dating from 1885, also displays logging equipment in addition to lumber camp culinary paraphernalia. One more museum worth mentioning is the **Humboldt Bay Maritime Museum** *(free admission; every day 11am to pm; 1410 Second St., ☎444-9440)*, which features photos, models, and artifacts that recounts the life and

work of Eurekans who went to sea.

Just south of town, the **Humboldt National Wildlife Refuge** *(☎733-5406)* gives excellent vantage points for birders, what with its extremely diverse habitats—sand-spits, diked seasonal wetlands, eel grass beds, mud-flats, uplands, salt marsh, brackish marsh and fresh watermarsh—that are stopovers on the Pacific Flyway for more than 200 species. Black brant (geese) receive special monitoring attention from refuge biologists. **Sequoia Park and Zoo** *(free admission; May to Sep, Tue to Sun from 10am to 7pm, closes at 5pm between Oct and Apr; 3414 W St., ☎445-1910)*, on Eureka's south side, give visitors a chance to visit old-growth redwoods, a walk-in aviary and a variety of other animals.

Practically next door (by car) to Eureka, north on Highway 101, sits tiny **Arcata**, a town that Bret Harte, later a celebrated short-story writer about gold mining community life, was driven out of in the late 1850s by angry locals because of his editorial in *The Northern Californian* condemning the settlers' massacre of Wiyot villagers. Arcata is dominated by its plaza and its University. The plaza, predictably surrounded by coffee shops and bookstores, has at its centre a 1906 **statue of President William McKinley** flanked by palm trees and, at diagonally opposite corners, old **Hotel Arcata** (1915) and the **Jacoby Store House Building**. This last, now handsomely restored (originally completed in 1857), was made out of bricks and wood as merchant Augustus Jacoby's answer to the threat

of fire. The **Plaza's Minor Theatre**, constructed in 1914, is supposedly the oldest movie theatre still operating in the U.S.

Humboldt State University, the only university on the north coast, perches on a hill overlooking the bay and Arcata's many restored Victorian homes. Its **Natural History Museum** (*10am to 4pm, Tue to Sat; 1315 G St., ☎826-4479*) houses a first-rate fossil collection. No less important to investigate is the **Arcata Marsh and Wildlife Sanctuary** at the foot of F Street. Here, 154 acres (62.3ha) of restored marshland offer a splendid chance to see egrets, marsh wrens, kingfishers, among many species of birds—and to see, in operation, a natural filtration system which deals effectively with the solid waste from the city's main sewage plant. Slightly east of Arcata, the 213-acre (86ha) **Lanphene-Christensen Dune Preserve** hosts an extraordinary intermingling of southern and northern dune vegetation within an ecosystem so fragile that a person can explore it only in the company of a Friends of the Dunes tour guide.

To round out a visit to Arcata, why not drive a few miles east on Highway 299 to Blue Lake to learn what the **Dell Arte School of Physical Theatre** (the only *commedia dell'arte* training centre in the U.S.) is up to? During the summer, you can sit in the stands of the Arcata ballpark at Eighth and F streets and cheer on the semi-professional baseball team **The Crabs** (see p 528). Should you be around in late May, you can attend the zaniest of zany races, **The World Championship Great Arcata to Ferndale**

The Oregon Caves

In 1874, while hunting a bear being pursued by his dog Bruno, Elijah Davidson found himself following his dog into a hole in a mountainside and then becoming completely enveloped by darkness when he ran out of matches. Luckily, wading through a cold stream he made his way out, as did the dog shortly afterward. The cave received official status in 1909 when President William Howard Taft designated a parcel of 480 acres (194ha) as Oregon Caves National Monument. Today's traveller in Northern California has only to drive a total of 76mi (122km). northeast from Crescent City on U.S. Highway 1999 and Oregon Highway 46 from Cave Junction, to explore the Oregon Caves in all their spectacular, otherworldly beauty. (Please note that children under six must pass a safety test and be at least 42in or 107cm tall.)

The mineralized ground water seeping drop by drop into the cave precipitates its calcite into such fantastic formations as flowstone, moonmilk and cave popcorn. The more familiar stalagmites and stalagtites also adorn the limestone and marble caverns you will pass on the 0.5mi (0.8km) (there are 3.5mi or 5.6km of tour tunnels in all) tour conducted by a private company called the Oregon Lanes Company. You climb the more than 500 stairs in temperatures that are around 40° (4°C) year-round, and walk over sometimes wet and slippery terrain. During your trek a tour guide offers commentary on everything from the cave's geology—there are two different kinds of each of the three basic rock types: igneous, sedimentary and metamorphic—to its animal inhabitants, which include Townsend's big-eared bats and legions of daddy longlegs. The guide will also be ready to assist you in differentiating scalping ledges from merely haircutting ledges.

What is not so readily apparent is that since 1985 the National Park Service has been trying to undo the damage done in the 1930s by workers who covered formations with rubble created by blasting open new tunnels and widening existing ones. The debris from these operations changed the cave's air-flow patterns, which in turn led to wide fluctuations in temperature, even to the cracking of rock layers by freezing water. In addition lights installed by the workers stimulated algae to grow, coating the cave green and dissolving some formations! Rectifying this damage has required removing over 1,000 tons (1,016 tonnes) of rubble, placing airlocks in artificial tunnels to restore the pattern of natural airflow, and inhibiting algae growth by spraying it with bleach. However, these efforts have paid off, and matters are greatly improved.

In order to enjoy visiting the cave and/or go hiking on nearby trails in the Siskyou National Forest, you can stay at the 1934–style Oregon Caves Lodge, Oregon. Although there is no camping in the park itself, you can camp at the Grayback and Cave Creek Campgrounds *(on Oregon Hwy. 46),* run by the Forest Service, or at private campgrounds.

For more information contact:
Oregon Caves Company
P.O. Box 128, Cave Junction
Oregon 97523
☎*(541) 592-6654*
www.oregoncaves.com.

The North Coast

Cross-Country Kinetic Sculpture Race (see below).

The Lost Coast

After passing through Fort Bragg, you'll notice that at one point Highway 1 ends abruptly and joins Highway 101. This section of the coast is apparently too wild and dramatic to be tamed by such civilizing interventions as highways, and is thus quite appealing to rugged outdoors-types who want to get as far away from civilization as possible.

The southern and most fascinating part of the Lost Coast is currently protected as **The King Range National Conservation Area** and **The Sinkyone Wilderness State Park**.

Among one of the most rainy regions on the coast, **King Range** receives about 100in (254cm) of yearly rainfall, most of it between October and April. Virgin and wild, the 35mi (56km) of varied and rugged coastline offer up magnificent vistas because of a succession of steep mountain ridges that plunge into the sea. The highest of these is King's Peak at 4,087ft (1,246m). A superb hiking trail appropriately called **The Lost Coast Trail** will give you a chance to explore an abandoned light house and some ruins from ship wrecks. (see p 512) The best place to obtain information is at **BLM office** in Arcata:

Bureau of Land Management
Arcata Field Office
1695 Heindon Rd.
Arcata, CA 95521-4573
caweb330@ca.blm.gov

The 7,367 acres (2,981ha) of **Sinkyone Wilderness State Park**, replete with black-sand beaches and coastal terraces inhabited by over 300 species of birds, Roosevelt elk and a wealth of marine life, is probably the best place to camp. There are several campsites in protected areas with access to streams and beaches. (see p 515).

Shelter Cove, a seaside resort and retirement community, is about the only town around offering any infrastructure to speak of. You get here via a paved 23mi (37km) access road that departs from Garberville. Give yourself at least 1hr to drive this stretch.

★★★
Ferndale

Set in the coastal hills and close to the Eel River, the town of Ferndale in its entirety is a State Historical Landmark and its Main Street is on the National Register of Historic Places. In the late 1800s, its many fine Victorian houses, paid for by prosperous dairy farmers, came to be known as "butterfat palaces." A walking tour of Ferndale reveals that most of the historical commercial buildings occupy a three-block stretch of Main Street. A short distance away, on Berding Street, the **Gingerbread Mansion Inn** stands in unrivalled elaborateness of fancy woodwork and flamboyance of colour scheme.

Small as it is, Ferndale residents are all the more proud to be able to point out the **Arts Cooperative** on Main Street, which exhibits the work of local artists, the year-round **Ferndale Repertory Theatre** (see p 527) and **Russ Park**, the 105 acres (42.4ha) of which are a pleasant place to hike, ride the trails on horseback, or birdwatch. The adjacent **Ferndale Cemetery** is an especially well-appointed resting place for departed pioneers with a view of the ocean to the west. At the corner of Third Street and Shaw Avenue, the **Ferndale Museum** includes an old-time barbershop, an old switchboard and telephones, a complete blacksmith shop, a barbed-wire collection and the equipment or machinery used in such diverse occupations as fishing, camping, farming, dairying, ranching and logging.

All manner of activity in usually peaceful Ferndale came to a halt on April 25 and 26, 1992, as the troublesome San Andreas Fault went about its disruptive work. Within 45 seconds that Saturday, an earthquake close to seven on the Richter Scale sent many structures a-tumbling. The next day, 2hrs apart from each other, two quakes of only slightly less magnitude completed nature's demolition job.

Ferndale, however, made a complete recovery and has continued to play an important part in the annual May competition memorated in its **Main Street Kinetic Sculpture Race Museum** *(free admission; every day 10am to 5pm; 580 Main St., ☎ 786-9259)*. Started in 1969 by Hobart Brown and Jack Mays, this 38mi (61km) race over sand, water and mud begins in Arcata and ends in Ferndale. The wildly inventive competition (with vehicles bearing names like the Pencil-head Express, the Hammerhead Cadillac and the Chicken and Egg Mobile) requires amphibious people-powered contraptions that are, under the appropriate circumstances, ready to cheat. True to the race's commitment to zaniness, an *Aurea Mediocritas* prize is bestowed upon the vehicle closest to the exact middle of its rivals (see p 528). If such happy madness prompts a quick exit, head either south on Mattole Road into the rugged so-called "Lost Coast," or northeast to the charming cheese factory town of Loleta.

★
Trinidad

If you're looking for a quiet village surrounded by exceptional scenic beauty along the northern California coast, then Trinidad should be your destination. About 285mi (458km) north of San Francisco, or 25mi (40km) north of Eureka and 80mi (129km) south of the Oregon border, Trinidad's 400 or so year-round residents have it good indeed. The first European to discover the bay's dramatic rocky splendour was a Portuguese sea captain in 1595. Of course, the Tsurai were living on this lovely stretch of coast long before that.

Today's working fishing pier harkens back to the 1850s and the need to supply gold-rush miners along the Klamath, Trinity and Salmon rivers. A small fleet of commercial fishers and assorted sport-fishing boats now account for a busy pier and tackle shops up and down Trinidad Bay. **Trinidad Head Lighthouse** has been in service since 1871, although its light and foghorn have long since been automated. The nearby intown **Trinidad State Beach** (a sandy one) benefits from its location in a protected cove. Adjacent to it, **Humboldt State University's**

Marine Laboratory *(every day Mon to Fri 8am to 4pm, Sat and Sun 10am to 4pm; Edwards and Ewing sts.,* ☎*826-3671)* has a small aquarium open to the public. Up on Main Street, the **Trinidad Memorial Lighthouse,** with its gigantic fog bell, honours fishers who lost their lives at sea. Close by you'll be able to find smokehouses where you can purchase delicious local salmon and albacore tuna.

Either side of Trinidad, whether 2mi (3.2km) to the south at **Luffenholtz Beach**, a surfer's paradise, or 5mi (8km) to the north at **Patrick's Point State Park** (☎*677-3570)*, is decidedly worthy of a visit. Patrick's Point provides many hiking trails and three campgrounds with a total of 123 campsites. **The Rim Trail**, dangerously close to the cliffside, penetrates a coastal scrub habitat, whereas the **Octopus Grove Trail** leads to Sitka spruces which, having taken root on rotten logs, end up with their gnarled roots hanging in mid-air once the decomposing wood falls away. Another trail that leads to a delight of nature is the **Agate Trail** down to **Agate Beach**, where, yes, many of the semi-precious stones called agates are buried in the sand. **Ceremonial Rock**, **Lookout Rock** and **Wedding Rock** are not to be missed for the excellent observation posts they provide for viewing the Pacific Ocean and for whale-watching (November to May). Walk around **Sumeg**, a recently constructed Yurok village at **Patrick's Point State Park**, to get an idea of how the Yuroks once lived. Think about how much work must have gone into hollowing out large redwood logs by

repeated applications of fire and repeated scrapings of burnt wood in order to make traditional canoes on site. Finally, imagine how the Yuroks, who once used these grounds as a seasonal fishing village, led their daily lives in some of the structures that you'll see as you meander through Sumeg: traditional family houses, a sweat house and dance pits. Modern day members of the Yurok tribe make use of this village to stage ceremonial dances which are open to the public.

Parks and Beaches

Parks

Of the 265 California state parks, over 50 are located in the north coast region alone. If you add to the register the seven national parks situated in this region, it's easy to understand why this is a nature lover's paradise.

Golden Gate National Recreation Area

Extending north all the way from Fort Funston in San Francisco to Point Reyes National Seashore, the Golden Gate National Recreation Area (GGNRA), covering some 70,000 acres (28,329ha), draws more visitors annually (almost 20 million) than any other national park. The jewel in its crown is the **Marin Headlands**, ranging in topography from steep cliffs to inland valleys to those characteristically Californian loping grass-covered hills. The Headlands offer numerous hiking and backpacking opportunities (see p 515).

Muir Woods National Monument

One of the parks enveloped by the GGNRA is the popular Muir Woods National Monument, named after the celebrated naturalist John Muir (1838-1914). Only 12mi (19.3km) north of the Golden Gate Bridge via Highway 101 and 1, Muir Woods contains the last remaining old-growth redwoods in the Bay Area and some of the less well-known Chinese dawn redwoods and albino redwoods. To savour properly the grandeur of the tall, old, mighty coastal redwoods, you should get well away from the parking lot with its tour-bus crowd and walk at least the mile of the paved trail next to Redwood Creek, if not some of the additional 5mi (8km) of unpaved trails. Muir Woods had the single, appropriate honour of hosting a ceremony following the signing in April of 1945 of the United Nations Charter by delegates from 50 nations.

Mount Tamalpais State Park

The 6,218-acre (2,516ha) Mount Tamalpais State Park is a hiker's dream with its 200mi (322km) of trails. The east summit of Mount Tamalpais (elevation 2,571ft or 784m) will reward the climber with views of the whole Bay Area and, on a clear day, of the Farallon Islands 30mi (48.3km) out to sea, and of the Sierra Nevada a full 200mi (322km) east.

Samuel P. Taylor State Park

Another park enveloped by the GGNRA, this one 15mi (24km) west of San Rafael on Sir Francis Drake Boulevard and just east of Point Reyes

Condor

National Seashore, is the 2,600-acre (1,052ha) Samuel P. Taylor State Park. Here there are hiking and equestrian trails galore as well as a paved biking path and picnicking, swimming and camping facilities amidst a combination of old-growth and young redwoods.

Angel Island State Park

To get to Angel Island State Park (*Headquarters: 1455 East Francis Blvd., San Rafael 94501, ☎415-435-1915*), board a ferry in San Francisco, Tiburon or Vallejo. This 740-acre (299ha) island used to be called the Ellis Island of the West because for decades Asian immigrants to the country were processed here. (See p 498.)

Point Reyes National Seashore

Point Reyes is aptly named: the natural beauty of this spectacular convergence of land, sea, and sky is nothing short of majestic. (See p 501.)

Van Damme State Park

Three miles (4.8km) south of Mendocino, Van Damme State Park offers a sheltered beach front which draws abalone divers and, across the road, a fern canyon trail and that curious botanical phenomenon, a pygmy forest, which is a naturally occurring bonsai-like thicket.

MacKerricher State Park

Going north of Mendocino, 3mi (4.8km) past Fort Bragg, Mackerricher State Park's Laguna Point is a fine place to watch harbour seals pupping in April and May while adults bask in the sun on the rocks. There are also excellent opportunities here for whale-watching during migration season.

Jughandle State Reserve

Taking a walk with a selfguiding brochure on **Ecological Staircase Trail** in Jughandle State Reserve, 1mi (1.6km) north of Caspar, will provide a lesson in evolutionary geology as the visitor views a series of five terraces, 100ft (30.5m) higher and 100,000 years older than each one below.

Russian Gulch State Park

Ocean water rushing through a a collapsed sea cave called the Devil's Punch Bowl is a distinguishing feature of Russian Gulch State Park, just 2mi (3.2km) north of

Mendocino. It is also popular with abalone divers.

Mendocino Headlands State Park

Surrounding the village of Mendocino on three sides is the Mendocino Headlands State Park *(day use only)*, brought into existence in the 1970s by concerned citizens who wanted to protect a natural buffer-zone of bluffs covered with grass and wildflowers, dramatic cliff faces and quiet beaches from the inroads of developers.

Humboldt Redwoods State Park

The 53,000 acre (21,449ha) Humboldt Redwoods State Park (the largest state park in northern California), with its 17,000 acres (6,880ha) of old-growth coastal redwoods, includes the splendid sylvan corridor called the **Avenue of the Giants**. Grove after grove, these trees grow so high that they are the tallest living things on Earth—truly giants. (See p 500.)

Humboldt National Wildlife Refuge

Just south of town, the Humboldt National Wildlife Refuge gives excellent vantage points for birders, what with its extremely diverse habitats—sandspits, diked seasonal wetlands, eel grass beds, mud-flats, uplands, salt marsh, brackish marsh, and fresh water-marsh—stopovers on the Pacific Flyway for more than 200 species. Black brant (geese) receive special monitoring attention from refuge biologists.

King Range National Conservation Area and Sinkyone Wilderness State Park

The southern and most fascinating part of the Lost Coast is currently protected as King Range National Conservation Area and Sinkyone Wilderness State Park. (See p 512)

Beaches

Muir Beach and Stinson Beach

West of Muir Woods lies Muir Beach, which affords the weary and not-so-weary traveller a pleasant sandy beach and good seaward views, but no swimming. Stinson Beach, on the other hand, just a few miles north on Highway 1, provides 4mi (6.4km) of ideal beach for summer swimming, sunbathing and surfing (see p 517).

Sonoma Coast State Beaches

The 13mi (20.9km) from Bodega Bay to Jenner alongside Highway 1 constitute one of the most accessible stretches of northern California coastline. Seventeen public beaches, the Sonoma Coast State Beaches, within that short distance assure you of all sorts of opportunities for fishing, picnicking, whale-watching, beach-combing, tidepooling and camping, but do not to go swimming: the very cold water, undertow, heavy surf and occasional but potentially lethal "sleeper" or "rogue" wave rule this.

Outdoor Activities

Hiking

Golden Gate National Recreation Area

Fort Funston Sunset Trail *(take Hwy. 1 south after the Golden Gate Bridge to Sloat Blvd., take Sloat Blvd. west 1mi or 1.6km to Skyline Blvd. or Hwy. 35 and then turn left; the park entrance is 1.5mi or 2.4km on the right side of the road)*. This trail, which begins at the summit of a bluff that is a kind of mecca for whale-watchers, bird-watchers, wildflower aficionados and beach combers, is a little over 3mi (4.8km) in length. The route is paved—and thus wheelchair and stroller accessible—until you get to the dunes halfway through the trail. Dogs are allowed, provided they're on a leash.

Tennessee Valley Trail *(take the Hwy. 1/Stinson Beach exit at the Hwy. 1 and Hwy. 101 intersection in Mill Valley; go under the freeway and follow the Shoreline Hwy. about 0.5mi or 0.8km to Tennessee Valley Rd.; turn left here and drive to the end—about 2mi or 3.2km)* This 4mi (6.4km) trail is nestled in a valley that is set amid the huge cliffs surrounding Tennessee Cove, which harbours one of the few accessible beaches along the Marin Headlands coastline. No dogs are allowed.

The North Coast

Audubon Canyon Ranch

Rawlings/Griffin Loop Trail
(see p 519)

Point Reyes National Seashore

Coast Trail (from Palomarin to Bass Lake)
(from the intersection of Hwy. 1 and Hwy. 101 in Mill Valley, take Hwy. 1 north for about 13mi or 20.9km until you reach Olema-Bolinas Rd.—the first left at the northern end of the Bolinas Lagoon—when you get to a stop sign about 0.5mi or 0.8km down the road, turn right and go 4mi or 6.4km until you get to the trail-head at the end of the dirt road). For a more challenging hike, try taking this old farm road that leads you through coastal flora set on the dramatic bluffs overlooking the Pacific Ocean. If you don't give up and turn back, it will also take you to what is referred to as the "lakes district" of Point Reyes. On a warm afternoon, if you have your swim suit along, you can swim in the 10-acre (4ha), beautifully located Bass Lake. The total length of the trail is a little over 5mi (8km), so give yourself a good 3hrs to cover it. No dogs are permitted.

Tomales Bay State Park

Indian Beach Loop
(from CA Hwy. 1 turn left at Bear Valley Rd. just after Olema. Once you get to Sir Francis Drake Blvd., turn left and drive to Pierce Point Rd.—around 7mi or 11km— turn right here and drive 2mi or 3.2km until you get to the park entrance; to get to the trail-head, turn in the direction of the bay; the parking for Heart's Desire Beach will

be on your right). If you want the thrill of hiking right on the San Andreas Fault, there is no better spot than Tomales Bay. Among the sites to take in on this trail are pastoral ranch land, forests of oak, bay and madrone trees and reconstructed Miwok dwellings on Indian Beach.

Jughandle State Reserve

The Ecological Staircase Trail
(see p 514)

Van Damme State Park

Fern Canyon Trail (see p 505)

Humboldt Redwoods State Park

The Founder's Grove Nature Trail (see p 506)

Redwood National Park

Miner's Ridge Trail in Prairie Creek Redwoods SP
(trailhead starts at the Prairie Creek Visitor Center at the end of Godwood Trail). This 4mi (6.4km) trail, originally a supply route for pack horses to a miner's camp in Fern Canyon, traverses redwood, sitka spruce and douglas fir forests on its way to a magnificent lookout over the Pacific Ocean. If you're interested in hiking to a dramatic campsite, this trail is definitely for you, since it leads directly to **Gold Bluff Beach Campground**. To make the trail into a loop, return via the **James Irvine Trail**.

Redwood Creek Trail
Tall Trees Trail
Emerald Ridge Trail
(to reach the trailhead of the Redwood Creek Trail, take Bald Hills Rd. from Hwy. 101 for 2mi or 3.2km north of Orick; the parking area for this trail is on your first right)
This trail, along with the trails it is linked to, is well worth a detour. Whether you're interested in photographing wildlife, swimming, crossing streams or viewing some of the tallest trees in the world, this network of trails will more than please you. Backcountry camping permits for this wild area are available at the Redwood Information Center. Some warnings however: do not drink unboiled water from Redwood Creek as it is contaminated by cattle upstream, and only cross streams during low-water flows.

Revelation Trail
(just south of the Prairie Creek Visitor Center)
Here is a trail that caters to both people in wheelchairs and those with visual impairments. There are wooden and rope handrails running the full length of the trail along with many touchable features that are described on signs and in a cassette guide available at the Visitor Center.

Golf

Bodega Harbour Golf Links
Box 368, 21301 Heron Dr.
Bodega Bay
☎875-3538
Located 65mi (105km) north of San Francisco at Bodega Harbour is one of the best coastal golf courses in the United States. The designer, Rob-

ert Trent Jones Jr., has arranged the 6,220yd (5,688m). championship course in such a way as to ensure that there are panoramic ocean views from all 18 of the tees. A smaller 5,630yd (5,148m) course offers less challenge-hungry golfers an attractive alternative to the championship course. After a vigorous day of driving and putting, relax with a drink in the spectacular ocean-view lounge.

Horseback Riding

Point Reyes National Seashore

Five Brooks Ranch Horse Rental
8001 Hwy. 1, Olema
☎(415) 663-1570
www.fivebrooks.com
This public riding stable, located within Point Reyes National Seashore at the Five Brooks Trail-head, offers rides that take anywhere from 1 to 6hrs. The Glen Trail Ride *(3.5hrs/$80)* and the Wildcat Beach Ride *(6hrs/$110)* are unforgettable trips.

Sonoma Coast

Chanslor Horse Stables
every day 8:30am to 6pm
Bodega Bay
☎875-3333
www.chanslor.com
This outfitter caters to those who wish to explore the beaches or the rolling hillsides of the Sonoma Coast on horseback. Various thematic trail rides are offered and directed by knowledgable guides. Prices vary with the length of the trail, ranging from $25 to $60. Lessons are also offered at $50 per hour.

Redwood National Park

Tall Tree Outfitters
Tall Trees Arena
124580 Hwy 101
P.O. Box 12, Orick
☎488-5765 or 465-4227
This outfitter services trails beginning from the Orick rodeo grounds and passing through clear-cut and old-growth forest on the west side of Redwood Creek. There are three trails of varying length offered:

half day
6.5mi (10.5km)

one day
18.5mi (29.8km)

three days
31mi (49.9km)

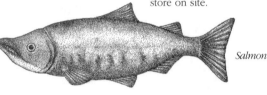

Salmon

Fishing

Russian River Region Inc. publishes a series of very handy fishing and access maps for the Sonoma Coast. These maps provide information on what to catch and where, in addition to giving helpful hints about fishing regulations. It may well be worth your while to obtain one of these in advance by inquiring at:

Russian River Region Inc.
P.O. Box 255MAP
Guerneville, CA 95446
☎800-253-8800

Bodega Bay Sport Fishing Center
Charters gather between 5:30am and 6:30am and leave at 7am.
1500 Bay Flat Rd.
☎875-3495
For sport-fishing and whale-watching charters operated by local experts, this place can't be beat. Owner Rick Power ensures that all departures are staffed with helpful and knowledgable deck hands that can assist both sightseers in their quest to see a California grey whale or elephant seal, and fishers to catch fish along the Cordell Banks (one of the richest marine ecosystems on the West Coast). A good selection of bait and gear, along with fishing licenses and local tips, are available in the general store on site.

King Salmon Charters
3458 Utah St.
☎442-3474
High-sea excursions in 36ft (11m) fibreglass boats for salmon, white tuna and fletan.

Surfing

Northern Light Surf Shop
17191 Bodega Hwy., Box 138
Bodega
☎876-3032
This is the store for hardcore surfers who are looking for high-caliber surf gear, board and wetsuit rentals or custom-designed boards made by a locally renowned shaper.

Surf Shack Bike, Board and Kayak Rentals
1400 Hwy. 1 in the Pelican Plaza
Bodega Bay
☎*875-3944*
The Surf Shack is a family-run enterprise that is a kind of unofficial surfing headquarters for Sonoma County. Along with a good selection of surf-wear, surf-boards, surf-accessories, sun-wear and reasonably priced surfing literature and videos, they also rent bikes and kayaks at $5/hr or $23/day. An added bonus is a Special Surf and Weather Report offered by phone 24hrs a day. For news about the latest surf contests and family-friendly parties, or for inexpensive surf lessons, this is the spot.

Kayaking

Marin Coast

Blue Water Kayaking
$25/2hrs/person
$35/2hrs/2 people
full-day rates also available.
year-round
at the Golden Hinde Inn & Marina in Tomales Bay
☎*(415)566-9260*
www.bwkayak.com
This outfitter provides guided natural-history tours by kayak in the Tomales Bay area in addition to basic rentals.

Sonoma Coast

Gold Coast Coffee & Kayaks
$10/hr and $25 sunset specials
Box 100, Jenner
or
Steelhead Blvd., Duncans Mills
☎*865-1441*
Famous for their coffee, which they've been roasting at their Duncan Mills address for 10 years (try the organically grown Cyclops if you need to

have your eyes opened for challenging driving or kayaking), this place rents new Aquaterra kayaks to explore the lower Russian River.

Dive Crazy Adventures at Schooner's Landing Campground
☎*937-3079*
divecrazy@humboldt.net
www.divecrazy.com
On the Mendocino Coast, an excellent outfitter exists in Albion, a town a bit south from Mendocino Village that sits at the intersection of the Pacific Ocean and the Albion River. Dive Crazy rents kayaks and canoes in addition to providing scuba/skin-diving lessons and operating fishing and diving charters.

Rafting

Aurora River Adventures
P.O. Box 938
Willow Creek
East of Arcata on Trinity Scenic Byway
☎*(530) 562-8475*
☎*800-562-8475*
Offering one and two-day rafting trips on the Salmon, Smith, Eel and Trinity rivers in French, English or Spanish, Aurora River Adventures is one of the more reliable outfitters for rafting in Northern California. Excursions cater to all ages and levels of experience.

Cycling

Unless you're a very experienced cyclist, it is not recommended that you to attempt to cycle along Highway 1. Because the

narrow route has many dramatic turns and the occasional logging truck or camper is limited in manouvering flexibility on the road, anyone but the extremely daring should load their bike on the car or bus while on the main thoroughfare or rent a bike at specific locations along the coast that offer safer trails for cyclists.

Point Reyes National Seashore, with its numerous bike paths, is a good place to begin. The **Bear Valley Trail** is one of the better paths and has rentals at the trail-head:

Trail Head Rentals
closed Wed
88 Bear Valley Rd.
Olema
☎*(415) 663-1958*

Catch a Canoe and Bicycle Too!
Coast Hwy. 1 at the Compthce-Ukiah intersection
☎*937-0273*
☎*800-320-BIKE*
Further upshore, the Mendocino Coast also has an interesting network of bike paths. A good starting point is Catch a Canoe and Bicycle Too! at the Stanford Inn in Mendocino. In addition to renting Canoes and Kayaks, this outdoors store rents high quality mountain bikes and can provide you with excellent advise as to where you can find the path that is best for you on the Mendocino Coast.

If cycling amid some of the tallest trees in the world excites you, then try out the paths in the **Redwood National Forest.** One of the more interesting ones is the **Holter Ridge Bike Trail.** This 11.5mi (18.5km) trail, a former logging road, passes along Lost Man Creek Trail and Bald Mills Road through spectacular old-growth and second-growth forests. Bring your lunch and eat nearby at the Redwood Creek Overlook picnic area.

Whale-Watching

Not far from San Francisco in Marin County the **Fort Funston Sunset Trail** (see p 515) provides good views for whale-watchers.

On the Sonoma Coast, one of the better whale-watching outfitters is **Bodega Bay Sport Fishing.** (see p 517)

For whale-watching on the Mendocino coast, rendezvous at **Anchor Charter Boats** in Fort Bragg (☎ *707-964-4550; www. anchorcharterboats.com).*

Bird-Watching

Golden Gate Recreation Area

Fort Funston Sunset Trail (see p 515)

Audubon Canyon Ranch

Rawlings/Griffin Loop Trail *(Mar to Jul, appointment required; take the Hwy. 1/Stinson Beach exit at the Hwy. 1 and Hwy. 101 intersection in Mill Valley; follow Hwy. 1 about 12mi or 19km until you get to the Audubon Canyon Ranch.)* What better way to view birds than to look down into their treetop nests? At the Audubon Canyon Ranch, after hiking up into the forest of Pilcher's Can-

yon, this is exactly what you do in order to observe snowy egrets and great blue herons. Although the hike is a bit grueling, the trail is in good shape and well-shaded.

Point Reyes National Seashore

Abbots Lagoon Trail *(From Hwy. 1 turn left at Bear Valley Rd. just after Olema; once you get to Sir Francis Drake Blvd., turn left and drive to Pierce Point Rd., around 7mi or 11.3km; turn right here and drive 5mi or 8km; Abbots Lagoon will be on your left)* Because Abbots Lagoon is a prime nesting spot for many birds, most notably the snowy plover, this is a fantastic spot to bird-watch. Make sure to bring warm clothes though, because it can be quite windy in the afternoon. No dogs are permitted.

Accommodations

For general camping information contact:

National Park Campground ☎ *877-444-6777* ☎ *800-280-CAMP*

State Park Campground ☎ *800-444-7275*

National Forest Campgrounds Camping in these campgrounds is managed on a first come, first served basis. Maps of the various locations are issued at district offices for a small fee.

Olema

Olema Inn *$$$-$$$$* ℜ, *no smoking* 10000 Sir Francis Drake Blvd. at Hwy. 1, P.O. Box 37 Olema, CA 94950 ☎ *(415) 663-9559* ☎ *800-532-9252* *www.olemainn.com* Recently taken over by a young couple with an exquisite sense of the seacoast aesthetic, this inn originally opened in 1876 as a gathering place for rowdy loggers, ranchers and farmers. Though some of the rooms lack appropriate sitting space and the cabinets on some of the antique furnishings don't close all the way, the bathrooms are equipped with brand-new fixtures and the beds are very comfortable. Of particular note is the excellent restaurant and bar on the first floor. With a little more attention to detail and service this establishment could be among the best in the Point Reyes Seashore area.

Inverness

Motel Inverness and The Dacha *$$$-$$$$$* ≡, ℝ, *tv, no smoking* 12718 Sir Francis Drake Blvd. Inverness, CA 94937 ☎ *(415) 669-1081* ⌨ *(415) 669-1906* *www.coastaltraveler.co/motelinverness* Located along the shoreline of Tomales Bay and surrounded by three wildlife refuges, the Motel Inverness offers reasonably priced and comfortable rooms. What's more it has a large, cozy lounge with a 17ft (5.2m) fireplace crafted from Yosemite slate and granite, as well as a championship pool table.

Part of the Inverness Motel, but down the beach 1mi (1.6km), is an unusual Russian Orthodox three-bedroom cottage called The Dacha. This ornately crafted redwood and cedar building has stained-glass windows, 12 copper and wooden cupolas, a complete kitchen and living room and a wraparound stilted deck that suspends the house above the waters of Tomales Bay. On weekends, a two-night minimum stay is required. This is worth stopping to look at, even if you don't stay here.

Bodega Bay

 Anchor Bay Campground
$
P.O. Box 1529, 7mi (11.3km) north of Gualala on Hwy. 1
Gualala CA 95445
☎884-4222
www.abcamp.com
Because of its ideal location and excellent neighbouring infrastructure, the Anchor Bay Campground is a prime camping spot on the Sonoma Coast. In addition to providing coast access and fishing to its users, great laundry facilities, food shopping and a bus stop are within walking distance from the campground entrance.

Chanslor Guest Ranch
$$ bkfst incl.
≡, ℝ, *tv*
Box 1510, 2660 Hwy. 1
Bodega Bay, CA 94923
☎(707) 875-2721
Just north of Bodega Bay is a horse-lovers paradise. The Chanslor Guest Ranch contains a complex consisting of a main **Ranch House** (three rooms with private bath), a **Loft Suite**

(for one or two couples) and a **Bunk House** (Two main bedrooms with a third opened for groups, two bathrooms, a large fully equipped kitchen, separate eating alcove and furnished living room) and a historic 700-acre (283ha) working horse, sheep and cattle ranch that has been in operation since the 1850s. **The Chanslor Horse Stables** (see p 517) are located on site, allowing visitors easy access to magnificent trail rides along the beach or on the ranch amid wildlife and coastal scenery. Hiking, rock climbing and fishing are also possible.

Gualala Country Inn
$$ bkfst incl.
≡, ℝ, *tv*
P.O. Box 697, Gualala, CA 95445
☎884-4343
☎800-564-4466
≈(707) 884-1018
www.gualala.com
countryinn@gualala.com
This motel-style inn is an unpretentious and comfortable alternative to staying at a bed and breakfast where you don't always have the privacy you may crave. The large rooms are decorated by local craftspeople and decked out with beds covered with cozy quilts. A hearty (and complimentary) continental breakfast is served in a beautiful lounge decorated with interesting local antiques.

Bodega Estero Bed and Breakfast
$$$ bkfst incl.
four rooms
Box 362, 17699 Hwy. 1
Bodega, CA 94922
☎876-3300
☎800-422-6321
If you want to stay at an environmentally innovative and responsible bed and breakfast on the coast, the Bodega Estero Bed and

Breakfast is a good choice. Inn keepers Edgar Furlong and Michael O'Brien have opened their geodesic dome and modern-day farm to the conscientious visitor, adding to the mix their award-winning spinning craftsmanship and culinary talents. Set amid rolling hills blanketed with wildflowers, fruit and eucalyptus trees, and inhabited by sheep, llamas, goats, chickens and exotic birds, a stay here would be difficult to forget.

Old Milano Hotel
$$$-$$$$ bkfst incl.
≡, ℝ
38300 Hwy. 1, Gualala, CA 95445
☎ 884-3256
www.oldmilanohotel.com
One mile (1.6km) north of Gualala on a cliff offering a dramatic view of Castle Rock, is an eight-room bed and breakfast hotel that is on the National Register of Historic Landmarks. With fine five-course gastronomy accompanied with award-winning wines served in-house, and unique and romantic rooms overlooking spectacular scenery, the Old Milano Hotel is hard to beat for colourful elegance.

The Inn at the Tides
$$$$-$$$$$ bkfst incl.
≡, ℝ, ⊛, ℝ, ≈, ⊘, *tv*, △
800 Coast Hwy. 1
Bodega Bay, CA 94923
☎875-2751
☎800-541-7788
www.innatthetides.com
For those of you who prefer larger establishments with all of the amenities, the 12 lodges of the Inn at the Tides may be just what you're looking for. Situated on the slope of Bodega Bay coast, the lodges house a total of 86 light, airy rooms and suites equipped with large bay-view windows and skylights. The contemporary earth-tone decor is sooth-

ing. A good seafood restaurant (Tides Wharf, see p 525) with a spectacular view of the ocean is right across the street.

Jenner Inn and Cottages
$$$$ bkfst incl.
reservations recommended
≡, ℜ, ⊛, ℝ, *tv*
Hwy. 1, Box 69, Jenner
☎865-2377
☎800-732-2377
www.jennerinn.com
Situated at that magical place where the Russian River meets the Pacific Ocean, Jenner Inn and Cottages is composed of a main lodge and eight early village homes, some of which are private cottages and others that contain bed-and-breakfast rooms and suites with fireplaces, spas and private decks. The main redwood lodge has 21 rooms the majority of which open onto the water, and a game parlour that serves complimentary tea.

Mendocino

Mendocino Campground
$
1/4 mile (0.4km) south of Mendocino Village, corner of Hwy. 1 and Comptche-Ukiah Road
☎937-3130
If you want remarkable coastal views and access to the forest without paying for the somewhat pricey accommodations in the village, try camping here.

John Dougherty House
$$$ bkfst incl.
six rooms
≡
571 Ukiah St.
PO Box 817, Mendocino 95460
☎937-5266
☎800-486-2104
jdhbmw@mcn.org
This 1867 saltbox building, located in the Historic Preservation District of

Mendocino Village, has many assets: great ocean views, early U.S. antiques, wood-burning fireplaces and a wonderful English garden.

Mendocino Hotel & Garden Suites
$$$ bkfst incl.
≡, ℜ, ⊛, *tv*
51 rooms and suites
45080 Main St.
Mendocino, CA 95460
☎937-0511
☎800-548-0513
reservations@mendocinohotel. com
www.mendocinohotel.com
Considered by some as the best small hotel in Northern California, this charming, full-service, historic Victorian hotel offers an experience as well as a bed. Authentically and tastefully decorated in a manner suited to 1878 (the year the hotel opened), guests benefit from a relaxing Garden Room, an intimate and elegant Victorian Dining Room and a cozy lounge featuring a beautifully carved antique bar where locals and visitors mingle and exchange tall tales. The European-style rooms (shared bath facilities) at $85 a night enable those without the budget for luxury to steal a few nights of it guilt-free.

The Hill House Inn
$$$ bkfst incl.
≡, ℜ, ⊛, ℝ, ⊘, *tv*
44 rooms
10701 Palette Dr.
Mendocino, CA 95460
☎937-0554
☎800-422-0554
≂937-1123
www.hillhouseinn.com
Nestled on a bluff overlooking the dramatic North Coast in the quiet outskirts of Mendocino Village, this New England-style inn is a good choice for those who don't want to be in the middle of the hustle and bustle of Mendocino in

high tourist season. The rooms feature brass beds and decks with striking views of the ocean and countryside. Though the inn is out of the main action, Mendocino Village is within easy walking distance. There are also good dining facilities right on the premises, which are particularly popular at sunset.

Fort Bragg

The Lodge at Noyo River
$$$$ bkfst incl.
≡, ℜ, ⊛, ≈, ⊘, *tv*
500 Casa Del Noyo Dr.
Ft. Bragg, CA 95437
☎964-8045
☎800-628-1126
www.mcn.org/a/noyoriver/
Built of heartwood fir and redwood by Scandinavian shipbuilders in 1868, this 16-unit lodge sits on 2 acres (0.8ha) of cypress-ringed bluff overlooking the spectacular Noyo Harbour and fishing village. Considered by some to be the best value on North Coast, and by others as one of the best places to be visited by a ghost, the Lodge offers sunrooms, large soaking tubs, fireplaces and private decks in many of its rooms (all non-smoking).

The Lost Coast

To register for a campsite or get trail maps on the Lost Coast:

Needle Rock Ranch House
$
☎986-7711
For those concerned about rain, there are two unfurnished bedrooms in the Ranch House that can serve as indoor camping spots. Call up to nine weeks ahead to reserve.

The North Coast

Jedediah Strong Smith

Those who thoroughly explore the northwesternmost county of California, Del Norte, will encounter the name Smith everywhere: the town of Smith River, Smith River National Recreation Area, Smith River National Scenic Byway, the Smith River itself, and the Jedediah Smith Redwoods State Park. Who was this Smith after whom so much is named in this farflung corner of the state?

Jedediah Strong Smith (1799-1831) was arguably as important as Lewis and Clark to the opening up of the American West—and yet, whereas even the most casual student of U.S. history is familiar with the exploits of Lewis and Clark, few know more than the name of Smith. Born in Bainbridge, New York on January 6, 1799, one of 14 children of poor parents who were transplanted New Englanders, Jedediah first learned about and became fascinated by the life of trappers and traders as a teenager clerking on a Lake Erie vessel. By the time that he was killed, at age 32, by Comanches on the Cimarron River in southwestern Kansas while making his trapping and trading way to Sante Fe, New Mexico, he had earned a place in the elite ranks of such great mountain men as Jim Bridger (1804-1881).

Smith began his fur-trapping career in 1822 on the Upper Missouri River while working for the Ashley Fur Company of Saint Louis. The following year he helped defend against an attack on Ashley's second party of explorers by the Arikara Indians. He then led a group to the Black Hills, where he survived a vicious mauling by a grizzly bear, almost losing an ear. On that particular trip, he rediscovered the South Pass, a relatively easy way to cross the Continental Divide in southwestern Wyoming. In 1826, starting from just south of the Utah-Idaho border, he set out for Utah Lake via the Great Salt Lake and then, following the Serier River, the Virgin River and the Colorado River, worked his way southwest to Mission San Gabriel (near Los Angeles), thus becoming the first American to complete a journey overland to California.

Unwilling to heed the (Mexican) governer of San Diego's instructions to return the dangerous way he had come, he instead led his men into the San Joaquin Valley looking for a way to cross the Sierra Nevada Mountains. With only two other men, having left the rest behind in the valley

of the Stanislaus, Smith broke through the Sierra Nevada at what is now Ebbett's Pass on May 20, 1827. His journal entries for June 24 and June 25, 1927, graphically describe the torturous trek across the Nevada desert back to Salt Lake City (a first):

...we pushed forward, walking as we had been for a long time... burning with thirst... When morning came it saw us in the same unhappy situation pursuing our journey over the desolate waste now gleaming in the sun and more insupportably tormenting than it had been during the night... At 10 o'clock Robert Evans laid down... being able to proceed no further. We could do no good by remaining to die with him and we were not able to help him along...

In July of 1827, when Smith, along with 19 men, made the return journey to California, the Mohave Indians, who had been hospitable the first time around, set upon and killed 10 of his men as they were crossing the Colorado River (near Needles, California). After he reached San Gabriel, he was thrown in jail for weeks and saved from being sent to Mexico as a prisoner only by the intercession of two U.S. sea captains.

Moreover, a bond of $30,000 had been posted to guarantee that within months he would no longer be in California.

Going up the Sacramento Valley, Smith was unable to locate a pass through the Sierras. This meant that he and his men had to struggle up the coast through winter rain, traversing the heavily forested Coastal Mountains (another first) and hard-to-negotiate canyons of Northern California and Southern Oregon. As if he had not already met with enough disaster in his young life, on July 14, 1828, near Oregon's Umpqua River, Kelawatset Indians killed 16 of his 20 men and stole everything they owned. The remaining four managed to escape and reach Fort Vancouver on the Columbia River before returning to the East.

And this is by no means a complete account of the trailblazing travels of Jedediah Strong Smith. The accomplishments of this devoutly Christian, fairly well-educated man who departed radically from the stereotype of a hell-raising ruffian frontiersman, clearly deserve far greater recognition than they have thus far received from the general public.

Ferndale

🌿 The Gingerbread Mansion Inn
$$$-$$$$ bkfst incl.
≡, ☀
400 Berding St.
Ferndale
☎786-4000
☎800-952-4136
kenn@Humboldt1.com
www.gingerbreadmansion.com
For an unforgettable stay in a bed and breakfast that could easily be considered a work of art as well as a fine place to sleep, eat and play games in the parlour, this unique property is the place. Claw-foot bathtubs raised on platforms and framed by elaborate white gates are found in most of the rooms, as are astounding *trompe d'oeil* murals by locally renowned Peri Sue Pfenniger. The Veneto Room is particularly striking in both of these respects, offering visitors the opportunity to bathe amid panoramic vistas of Venetian country side that are seamlessly linked to the local landscape of Ferndale. The Empire Suite is for lovers of luxury, featuring a bed with ornate ionic columns, an intimate reading corner and a whirlpool bath. Amateurs of fancy English gardens will be at odds to find a better place to rest their travel-weary souls.

The Victorian Inn
$$$-$$$$ bkfst incl.
≡, ℜ, ☀
12 rooms
400 Ocean Ave.
P.O. Box 96, Ferndale, CA 95536
☎864-4949
☎888-589-1808
⌐(707) 786-4558
innkeeper@avictorianinn.com
www.avictorianinn.com
If you're looking for accommodation in central Ferndale, then the Victorian Inn, built in 1890 entirely from Humboldt County redwood, would be your best choice. This magnificently detailed Victorian property has 16 and 14ft (4.9 and 4.3m) ceilings throughout, and the rooms are equipped with vintage fixtures and furnishings. Some of the rooms also have claw-foot baths and cozy fireplaces.

Garberville

Benbow Inn
$$$
≡, ℜ
445 Lake Benbow Dr.
Garberville, CA 95542
☎923-2124
☎800-355-3301
www.benbowinn.com
benbow@benbowinn.com
Another National Historic Landmark, the Benbow Inn is probably the place with the most character in Garberville, which is otherwise full of motels. A very fine restaurant serves up innovative meals made with fresh, seasonal ingredients and complimentary English tea and scones are served at 3pm daily in the lounge. A spacious patio overlooks the Benbow Lake and some fine English gardens. If the Lost Coast is of interest to you, organized excursions depart from here as well.

Eureka

Manila Dunes Campground
$
on the Samoa Peninsula between
Humboldt Bay and the Ocean
☎445-3309
☎444-3803
Famous for its guided
Saturday nature walks and
prime seating for the
Kinetic Sculpture Race, this
spot is ideal for those who
want a bit of infrastructure
(hall and meeting room)
while maintaining easy
access to the beach, the
dunes and the forest.

Patrick Creek Lodge and Historical Inn
$-$$$ bkfst incl.
≡, ℜ, ℝ, tv, no pets, no smoking.
$50 deposit upon reservation,
cancellation fee of $25 for
reservations not cancelled
prior to 48hrs
8mi (13km) east of the village of
Gasquet
13950 Hwy. 199, Gasquet, CA 95543
☎457-3323
Located in the heart of the
Six Rivers National Forest,
at the edge of the Smith
River, this a good choice
for those who are looking
for a comfortable, laid-
back place to sleep and
eat after spending most of
the day outdoors. Simply
furnished single and dou-
ble rooms are offered in
the lodge, while a self-
contained, furnished two-
bedroom cabin will give
those travelling with others
even better value for their
money. This inn was
originally built by an Irish
gold miner as a stage
station for those caught in
gold rush traffic. Its reputa-
tion as a hospitality estab-
lishment, however, is due
to a French-Canadian
immigrant known locally
as Grandma Raymond,
whose fine cooking at-
tracted bachelors and
others from

miles around between
1910 and 1925. Today, the
culinary tradition continue
with the superb evening
meals and an excellent
Champagne Brunch that is
offered on Sundays be-
tween 10am and 2pm.

Trinidad Bay Bed and Breakfast
$$ bkfst incl.
Trinity and Edwards St.
☎677-0840
For an intimate seaside
experience in a traditional
fishing village, stay at this
recently renovated bed
and breakfast that looks
right out onto Trinity Bay.
The dock and lighthouse
are within easy walking
distance and the amenities
of the village are a stone's
throw away.

An Elegant Victorian Mansion
$$$ bkfst incl.
≡, tv, non-smoking
1406 C St., Eureka, CA 95501
☎444-3144
An innovative way to truly
experience history awaits
those who choose to stay
at this National Historical
Landmark property in the
heart of Victorian Eureka.
Not only do innkeepers
Doug and Lily wear Victo-
rian attire but Doug drives
an antique Ford, Lily occa-
sionally puts on the pho-
nograph in the music
parlour and an old pull-
string toilet can be used by
guests wishing to experi-
ence history more inti-
mately. Our favourite
room was the Van Gogh
Room with its brightly
coloured, incredibly de-
tailed walls, floors and
ceilings; its vintage edition
of *Lust for Life* at the secre-
tary desk and its Salvador
Dali print of Van Gogh
after the fateful ear-splic-
ing incident. But the other
four rooms also have a lot
of character. Lily serves a

wonderful breakfast that
suits both light and hearty
eaters. Those of you who
speak French will be
pleased to know that you
can speak it here and actu-
ally be understood.

The Carter House
$$$ bkfst incl.
≡, ℜ, ℝ, tv
301 L St., Eureka, CA 95501
☎800-404-1390
⇆444-8067
reserve@carterhouse.com
Mark and Christi Carter,
the owners of this com-
plex of four Victorians in
the heart of Old Eureka,
have made hospitality their
life calling. Though the
Carter House, the Carter
Hotel, the Carter Cottage
and the Bell Cottage cater
to clients with varying
needs, they have the com-
mon bond of original local
artwork, fine period fur-
nishings and access to the
services of one of North-
ern California's finest restaurants with an award-
winning wine list.

Restaurants

Novato

La Hacienda Taqueria
$
1401 Grant Ave.
☎(415) 897-5514
If you're heading into wine
country and would like to
experience a good down-
to-earth contrast to some
of the culinary pretensions
you're about to encounter,
stop here for a Macho
Burrito and a Corona. This
white-brick adobe restau-
rant is where the Mexican
gardeners eat. A serving of
authentic house nachos
precedes your meal.

Olema

The Olema Farmhouse
$$
Located in a historical building in the heart of Olema, this down-to-earth eatery will please those with an interest in Americana, friendly service and delicious home-cooked meals.

Inverness

 Debra's Bakery
$
12301 Sir Francis Drake Blvd.
☎*(415) 663-9496*
Debras is the perfect place to stop for authentic European breakfast pastries and rich coffee in a relaxed atmosphere.

Lipinski's Mendo Juice Joint
$
Mon to Thu: 6:30am to 7pm
Fri and Sat: 6:30am to 11pm
Sun: 6:30am to 9pm
On Ukiah east of Lansing
Mendocino
☎*937-4033*
New to Mendocino, and sharing a building with the local environmental awareness group, Lipinski's serves great home-squeezed organic juices (try the carrot-apple-ginger, the Body Cleanser or, if necessary, the Hangover Helper), wheat-grass drinks, smoothies (the Buddha Boost is particularly tasty and nourishing), old-fashioned sodas made with spritzer and syrup as well as socially and environmentally conscious coffees. Though the food selection is simpler, high-quality seasonal scones and muffins, buttermilk waffles and a steamed western omelette are great for the morning and the Mendocino Ploughman sandwich is to die for. Board games and a good

selection of magazines are also available. For an unpretentious and progressive atmosphere with occasional live entertainment *(Fri to Sat)* in Mendocino, this is a wise choice.

North Coast Brewing Tap Room & Grill
$-$$
444 Main St., Fort Bragg
☎*964-3400*
www.ncoastbrewing.com
Voted one of the 10 best breweries in the world by the beverage-testing institute in 1998 (the year it opened!) the North Coast Brewing Tap & Grill also serves scrumptious food—particularly seafood. Try the famous Red Seal Ale or if you are a fan of stout beers, Old Rasputin.

Sizzling Tandoor
$$
9960 Hwy. 1, Jenner
☎*865-0625*
Providing a choice between a pastoral outdoor patio setting or one in an ornate dining room with panoramic windows, Sizzling Tandoor serves award-winning Tandoori cooking seemingly in the middle of nowhere! Coming highly recommended are the great Mulligatawny soup, the Tandoori mixed grill, and the Masala tea. California home brews and wines are available as well.

River's End
$$-$$$
reservations strongly recommended
Hwy. 1, Jenner
☎*865-2484*
info@riverend.com
www.riverend.com
In that magical setting at the confluence of the Russian River and the Pacific Ocean, the River's End is considered by many to be the best restaurant for your money on the North Coast. In addition to offering over

100 selections of Sonoma County and Russian River wines, the chefs of this establishment continue to offer the same kind of creative menus that their forbear Wolfgang Gramatzki did. Some of the house specialties to keep in mind: Bahmie Goreng (chicken, shrimp, scallop, beef and Indonesian vegetable noodles with famous house peach chutney), boneless quail and venison medallions.

MacCallum House Restaurant
$$$
Albion St., Mendocino
☎*937-5763*
Located in the heart of Mendocino Village and in business since 1882, the MacCallum House Restaurant enjoys a well-merited reputation as one of the best places to eat in Mendocino. Chef Alan Kantor works in cooperation with local organic farmers, wine producers, fishers and sheep, duck, cow and chicken raisers to present Mendocino diners with a creative, tasty cuisine that is also socially responsible. The McCormack/Anderson Ranches Lamb Loin Chops and the Pecan-Crusted North Coast Rock Cod are scrumptious. The MacCallum House Cafe offers abridged versions of certain items on the evening menu such as the Liberty Farms Duck Hash Wrap and the Pacific Rim Oysters. Home-made ice cream or tangerine souffle is the perfect way to finish off your meal.

Tides Wharf Restaurant
$$$
every day 7:30am to 10pm
835 Coast Hwy. 1
Bodega Bay
☎*875-3652*
For its view onto Bodega Bay, the Tides Wharf is unbeatable! Chosen by Alfred Hitchcock as part of

The North Coast

the film set for "The Birds," this restaurant is also a great place to watch fishers unload the fresh ingredients for your delectable seafood meal.

Top of the Cliff
$$$
reservations strongly recommended
lunch from 11:30am to 2:30pm
dinner from 5:30pm
P.O. Box 1068, 39140 S. Hwy. 1
in Seacliff Shopping Center
Gualala
☎ *884-1539*

In addition to having a reputation for making some of the best soup around, this establishment is famous for their Newfoundland deep-dish pot of fresh seafood and assorted shell fish in mussel broth topped with pastry. Also worth a try are the coppa, portabella mushrooms and sundried tomatoes in Madera cream sauce and the oven-baked Canadian halibut stuffed with crab and brie. A fantastic selection of California wines is available to complement your meal.

Cafe Beaujolais
$$$$
961 Ukiah St., Mendocino
☎ *937-1955*

This is the most famous of Mendocino's restaurants primarily because of the famous people who come here to eat. Excellent and creative cuisine are also to be had in this tiny Victorian farmhouse at the side of the village. The menu constantly fluctuates as they do at most prima donna restaurants like this. Reservations are strongly recommended.

Eggheads Restaurant
$
7am to 2pm
326 N. Main St.
Fort Bragg
☎ *964-5005*

This is the place that locals swear by for breakfast or

lunch. For breakfast, which can go on all day if you wish, you have over 49 crepes and omelettes, specialty pancakes, waffles and french toast to choose from. Innovative sandwiches and salads are offered for lunch.

Ukiah

🌴 Ruen Tong
$-$$
reservations suggested
801 N. State St.
☎ *462-0238*

For some of the best Thai food in Northern California, you must stop off at this unpretentious Victorian house with an authentic Thai decor. Not only will your taste buds rejoice and your spirit be enchanted, but your wallet will keep its original shape!

Eureka

Bon Boniere
$
215 F St., Old Town Eureka
founded in 1898
Ice cream, ice cream... anyone want ice cream? Here is an old-fashioned parlour with locally-made ice cream in a fun Victorian decor with hairpin chairs and a marble floor.

The Galaxy Milkway Espresso & Juice Bar
$
Sat to Thu 10am to 8pm
Fri 10am to 10pm
summer:
every day 10am to 10pm
the Espresso and Juice Bar opens at 5:30am
849 Redwood Drive
Garberville
☎ *923-2664*

For gourmet fast food on your way through the majestic redwoods, stop here for a Galaxy Burger, Shelter Cove Fish and Chips, homemade soups,

salads and sandwiches or a number of vegetarian specialties. Bon Boniere ice cream and Humboldt Bay Coffee Co. coffee are also available along with fresh juices and smoothies.

Humboldt Bay Coffee Company
$
211 F St., Old Town Eureka
☎ *444-3969*

Ramone's Bakery & Cafe
$
209 E St.
☎ *442-6082*

There is a serious rivalry between Ramone's and the Humboldt Bay Coffee Company that is difficult to settle. We recommend that you walk down to Old Eureka and take in both, inhaling the aroma of the full-bodied coffee seeping out onto the street from both establishments. Perhaps then you will be able to determine the one that feels right for your palette.

Samoa Cookhouse
$-$$
7am to 10pm
take Samoa Bridge to end, turn left on Samoa Rd., take first left
☎ *442-1659*
www.humboldtdining.com/cookhouse

Founded in 1885, this is the last surviving logging-camp cookhouse in the West. Red and white checkered tablecloths cover the long communal tables that are framed by mismatched chairs. Friendly servers dish out simple, hearty meals lumber-jack-style (fixed menu of soup, salad, main dish and dessert served with lots of fresh bread and accoutrements). They even ask you if you want seconds. There are special prices for older children and those four and under eat free. Not to be missed are the old logging relics and photographs that line the walls and aisles. Out in the parking lot, a tacky Christmas gift shop blasts Christmas musak in the heat of the summer, and is best to avoid unless you are into kitsch.

Jalisco Cafe
$$
10am to 10pm
1718 Fourth St., Eureka, CA
☎*445-9324*
If you're in the mood for some mouth-watering Mexican food that is praised to the sky by locals, the Jalisco Cafe is the place to go. You can enjoy a number of house specialties: Chicken Mole, Camarones al Diablo, Mexican-style fish Tofu en Mole or veggie enchiladas (to name a few) in a setting recalling turn-of-the-century Jalisco, Mexico. A hearty lunch buffet is also offered for those who have difficulty making up their minds.

Rolf's Park Cafe
$$
at the entrance to Gold Bluff Beach and Fern Canyon, Orick, CA
☎*488-3841*
Though it may not be everybody's thing to chew on Elk Steak while admiring the Elk herds from a solarium window, Rolf's is well worth the stop for unsentimental meat eaters. In addition to offering the somewhat exotic meats of Buffalo, Boar and Elk, some authentic German dishes and seafood are served here. Contemporary German music hums within the redwood walls and a cheerful woman with a German accent is happy to serve you some great California wine as well.

The Sea Grill
$$
closed Sun
316 E St., Old Town Eureka
☎*443-7187*
Located in a charming Victorian building in old town, this restaurant has been voted the best seafood restaurant in Humboldt County by the locals and it is not hard to see why. We recommend that you begin your meal with the award-winning seafood chowder or the comprehensive salad bar. Where you go from there is really up to you: oysters, clams, mussels, salmon and halibut (just to name a few) can be prepared in just about every way imaginable and some very fine sauces can be chosen to accompany them. For those seafood fans who are dining with beef lovers, the Harris Ranch aged filet mignon and New York charbroiled steaks are nothing to be snuffed at either.

Chemin de Fer
$$-$$$
lunch: Thu to Sat 11:30am to 2pm; dinner: Tue to Thu & Sun 5:30pm to 9pm Fri and Sat 5:30 to 9:30pm
518 F St.
☎*441-9292*
www.humboldtdining.com/ chemin
With a menu changing daily according to the fresh ingredients available, the Chemin de Fer is one of Eureka's best restaurants. Lunch classics include a Caesar Salad with anchovies and Fresh Garlic and a Basmati Risotto with Apricots and Blue Cheese.

The dinner is a fixed-price menu and includes a selection of a first and second course. The restaurant is small and intimate, thriving mainly from word-of-mouth recommendations.

Entertainment

Bars and Nightlife

Caspar Inn and Blues Cafe
every day
on Caspar Street off of Hwy. 1 between Mendocino and Fort Bragg
☎*(707) 964-5565*
www.casparinn.com
The local hot-spot for live music and dancing since 1912 is found in the charming village of Caspar. On your way there or back (depending on what offers more daylight), don't miss the synagogue and Jewish cemetery.

Theatre, Music and the Arts

Rafael Film Center
$7.50
1118 Fourth St. (between A and B Sts.) San Rafael
☎*(415) 454-1222*
www.finc.org
Though it has only existed for a year, the Rafael film center, which is part of the Film Institute of Northern California, is a mecca for buffs of experimental, foreign, classic and art films.

Ferndale Repertory Theatre
Fri and Sat 7:30pm Thu 8pm
447 Main St.
P.O. Box 892, Ferndale
☎*786-5483*
If you'd like to see some quality live-theatre performances while you're tour-

The North Coast

ing the North Coast, make sure you book something here.

Dell' Arte International School of Physical Theatre

Performances at:
131 H St.
Blue Lake, CA 95525
☎668-5663
and
Humboldt State University
If you enjoy comedia dell' arte and are lucky, you'll find yourself somewhere close to Arcata when the School of Physical Theatre gives a performance.

Festivals

Annual Mad River Festival

Blue Lake
Hosted by Dell' Arte

March

Mendocino Whale Festival

Redwood Coast Dixieland Jazz Festival

late Mar
Eureka
☎445-3378
Three-day festival.

April

Rhododendron Festival

Eureka
Call Eureka Chamber of Commerce at:
☎442-3728
With a grove of the tallest rhododendrons in the world close by, it's surprising to find a festival celebrating this flower in Eureka. The centrepiece of the festival is the parade featuring dozens of floats decorated with rhododen-

dron blooms and other flowers.

May

World Championship Great Arcata to Ferndale Cross Country Kinetic Sculpture Race

late May
Started in 1969 by two Ferndale sculptors, this curious race features elaborate, homemade machines that are powered by people who must traverse paved roads, sand dunes, mud and water with them. The 35mi (56.3km) race lasts three days, beginning at Arcata's Plaza and ending at the Ferndale Fairgrounds. The first one across the finish line is not necessarily the winner, as bonus time is allotted for contestants who do not have to push their vehicle at any time in the race and cheating and bribery are permitted as long as they are done with the right flair.

The race is preceded by a Kinetic Kickoff Party and the Rutabaga Queen Contest. The best viewing spots are: the Arcata Plaza; the Manila Dunes; Old Town Eureka and the Ferndale Fairgrounds.
☎923-9613
☎786-9259

Westport's Annual Great Rubber Ducky Race and Tritip Steak Barbecue

mid-May
at Wages Creek Campground
Yes, you read it right! Whether you want to be a simple observer or a passionate-participant, several rubber-duck races

and a rubber-duck beauty contest are waiting for you in Westport.

August

Reggae on the River

at French's Camp
9mi (14.5km) south of Garberville on Hwy 101, next to the Eel River
Reggae hotline:
☎923-4583
www.reggaeontheriver.com
This is the West Coast's largest outdoor reggae festival and reputedly one of the best in the world.

Spectator Sports

Humboldt Crabs Baseball

Arcata Ballpark
Ninth and F sts.
Arcata's semi-pro baseball team plays all summer long. Most games are in the evening, but there are some in the afternoon as well.

Shopping

Stinson Beach Books

10:30pm to 5pm
3455 Shoreline Hwy.
Stinson Beach
☎(415) 868-0700
This is a good place to stop for local hiking books, nature books, maps and cards as you begin your tour of the North Coast.

Anchor Bay Store Village Market & Wineworld

8am to 8pm
35501 Shoreline Hwy. 1
Anchor Bay
☎884-4245
www.anchorbaystore.com
Having been in business for over 80 years, the Anchor Bay Store is much more than your ordinary grocery store. In addition to finding a carefully se-

lected variety of organic and natural local products, you will discover a host of imported multicultural foods, picnic supplies, a fantastic selection of micro-brews, and the largest selection of premium wines on the coast. Whatever it is that you're looking for, you're likely to find it here.

Candy and Kites
seasonally from 11am to 5pm
1415 Hwy. 1, Bodega Bay
☎875-3777
One of the most entertaining activities for families on the windy North Coast is flying kites. For a very good selection of kites: including eight different types of stunt kites (illuminated kites and lighted kites), Candy and Kites is the place to go. Prices range from under a dollar to over a hundred and kite-flying videos are available for viewing as well. Premium, novelty and saltwater taffy candies are also sold here.

The Crab Pot Fish Market
1750 Hwy. 1
just north of Bodega Bay
☎875-9970
As you are driving through Bodega Bay on Highway 1, you'll see a small orange-and-white shack on the side of the road, surrounded by a hodgepodge of antiques and fishing paraphernalia. Stop here if you want to purchase some of the best smoked Pacific Coast fish products. Fresh crab, smoked salmon, tuna, kippered cod and salmon, oysters, prawns, clams, scallops, abalone and lobster tails are some of the things that you can expect to find here, along with beer, wine and non-alcoholic beverages.

The Ren Brown Collection
10am to 5pm Thu to Mon and by appointment
Box 156, 1781 Hwy. 1
Bodega Bay
☎875-2922
☎800-585-2921
Right on Highway 1 at northern end of Bodega Bay, your attention may be caught by a barn with a bit of a Japanese look. If you stop and get out, an incredible variety of Japanese and local contemporary art are ready for your perusal. The Ren Brown Collection is locally renowned for its rotating exhibits, Japanese garden, and a wide selection of original Japanese etchings, wood-block prints and serigraphs in addition to sculpture and painting by local artists. Jewellery, ceramics and Japanese antiques are also available.

Loleta Cheese Factory
Mon to Fri 9am to 5pm
Sat 9am to 4pm
Sun noon to 4pm
252 Loleta Drive, Loleta
☎733-5470
☎800-995-0453
So you've got your smoked fish, your fruits, your wine, your bread... now all you need is some award-winning cheese to round off the fixin's. A small family-run business just a few minutes off Highway 101 in the dairy community of Loleta, the Cheese Factory is here to help you out. Creamy Monterey Jack and Smoked Salmon Cheddar are just two of the highly recommended cheeses you'll find here. It is also possible to watch the actual manufacturing of the cheeses through a picture window and to enjoy samples in a tasting room.

Corners of the Mouth
9am to 7pm
P.O. Box 367, Mendocino
☎937-5345
As interesting for the building (an old redwood church with a large circular stained-glass window) as for the contents, this cooperative natural food store in Mendocino will provide you with everything from organic produce and homemade picnic fixings to beautiful postcards and fun pins with messages like: "Just smile and say: Yes Mistress."

Lark in the Morning
Old Carriage House
10460 Kasten St., next to Zimmer Gallery
Mendocino
☎937-LARK(5275)
For mail orders:
P.O. Box 799, Fort Bragg, CA 95437
☎964-5569
This is one of the most unique and eclectic musical instrument stores anywhere. Here's a sampling of some of the pickings: Phoenix Hurdy Gurdys, King Davids' Lyres, Japanese Tai Drums, Sweet Potato Ocarinas, Celtic Song Stones, Highland Bagpipes, Cajun Accordions, Mockingbird Calls, Shofars, McSpadden Dulcimers... just to name a few! There is also a wide selection of books and videos to go with these instruments. Make sure you pick up one of their catalogues.

Carol Hall's Hot Pepper Jelly Co.
10am to 5:30pm
330 N. Main St.
Fort Bragg
☎962-1422
☎800-892-4823
Award-winning Mango jelly with prange brandy and Ollallie-berry jelly with Cabernet Sauvignon, as well as a selection of other fun and tasteful gifts are sold here.

The North Coast

Fiddles and Cameras
400 N. Main St.
Fort Bragg
☎*964-7370 (photo)*
☎*964-9203 (music)*
An ordinary-looking store on the outside, but a very unusual one on the inside, Fiddles and Cameras offers a wide range of products and services related to playing musical instruments and taking photographs. Binoculars can also be purchased here.

Many Hands Gallery
438 Second St.
Old Town Eureka
☎*445-0455*
For eclectic shopping in the heart of Old Eureka, head for the Many, Hands Gallery. Here, you'll find everything from Celtic jewellery to wind gauges to Yurok, Karuk and Hupa baskets, to Victorian mosaic art tiles to ship models, to wheat-weavings, to reproduction swords and thimbles. There are also books to go with all of these items. Incredible!

Moon's Play and Learn
3022 Broadway, Eureka, CA
☎*442-5761*
This is the largest toy store north of San Francisco. So why not take some time out to pick up a kinetic yard art kit, repair your yo-yo or to get a unique, educational gift for one of your favourite kids?

Northern Mountain Supply
every day
corner of Fifth and Commercial sts.
Hwy. 101 northbound in Eureka
☎*445-1711*
☎*800-878-3583*
As the biggest outdoor-gear store on the North Coast, Northern Mountain Supply has a great selection of camping, backpacking and climbing equipment. You can also rent canoes and camping equipment here!

Sports Exchange
Eureka
☎*444-3644*
If you want to pick up some used camping, golfing or other outdoor gear, come to the Sports Exchange. They will even buy it back if you take good care of it.

Wildberries Marketplace
every day 7am to 10pm
G or H St. at 13th St.
A full-service grocery store with organic products along with the more conventional ones, Wild-berries Marketplace also has an award-winning deli and juice bar.

Northtown Books
957 H St., Arcata
☎*822-2834*
www.northtownbooks.com
Independent bookstore lovers, here's a place for you! With an up-to-date selection of contemporary literature and intelligent books in general, Northtown Books is the ideal spot to pick up some inspiring bedside reading.

The Humboldt Woodworkers Guild
If you're interested in purchasing fine-crafted furniture made from redwood and other woods found in Humboldt County, you can shop online at *www.woodguild.com*. Each artisan that is a member of this important guild has an online portfolio.

Seals

Northeastern California

U nlike certain areas of Southern California, where paradise seems instantly accessible when you step off the plane, this

most-remote area of Northern California plays "hard to get", opting to save its mysterious, primeval beauty for those pioneering souls who prefer to sweat a little for their piece of Eden.

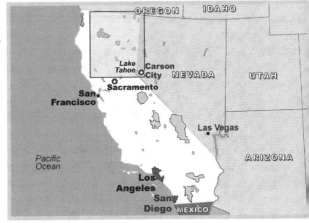

H owever, gazing down from the heights of the revered volcano of Mount Shasta across to the lava badlands of Lassen Volcanic National Park or the Lava Beds National Monument, images of the inferno may come more readily to mind. Especially since the tule fog that hovers above the Lava Beds is believed locally to be haunted by the spirits of the Modoc people who were starved into surrendering inside "Captain Jack's Stronghold" while defending their ancestral homelands against Confederate soldiers who sought

to claim the area for land-hungry settlers.

A remote land of paradoxes, the touristic region of the Shasta Cascade has much to offer those adventurers with a keen interest in wildlife and geology. With a total of six wildlife refuges that provide habitats to such exotic fauna as mountain lions, bald eagles, peregrine falcons, and black-tailed mule deer, the region is also considered by many to be a kind of open-air botanical sanctuary where many rare and

endemic species find reprieve from the environmental threats posed by deforestation and other forms of land development.

B eginning in the Marble Mountains and Trinity Alps Wilderness areas that belong to the Klamath Mountains, rugged outdoor types will be treated to a wonderland of glacial landforms: jagged glacier-carved promontories, concave scoured-out valleys, precipitous canyons, enchanting waterfalls, sapphire and vermilion alpine lakes and moraines. During the short summer season, world-class trout- and salmon-fishing, kayaking, white-water rafting and mountain-biking are just a few of the activities that the area is known for. And in the winter—who knows?—you may even steal a glimpse of Bigfoot.

Nearing Mount Shasta— the highest point in this most southern tip of the Cascades—the marvels of Castle Crags, Shasta Lake, the Shasta Dam and, of course, Mount Shasta itself will summon your attention. The world-famous Central Valley Project, a masterpiece in irrigation engineering, originates here.

We move onward to Lassen Volcanic National Park, home to the world's largest plug volcano, where you can learn everything that you always wanted to know about volcanos but were afraid to ask. Welcome to the world of hot springs,

fumaroles, steam vents, boiling mud pots, cinder cone, lava tunnels and indian-well caves. This area is also rich in Native American heritage since the Atsugewi, Maidu, Yana and Yahi peoples all shared this land at one time. The story of Ishi, the last survivor of the Yahi people, is legendary in these parts. When he was discovered outside of an Oroville slaughter-house in 1911, Ishi was emaciated and speaking an incomprehensible tongue.

Finally, we arrive in Modoc County, which was at one time the setting for the most expensive war ever waged against indigenous peoples by the U.S. government. In addition to roaming the solemn site of Captain Jack's Stronghold—a virtual labyrinth and fortress in hardened lava—one can witness a number of indian-well caves graced with ancient petroglyphs. Because the area is also a major resting spot for migratory shorebirds and waterfowl, such as Canada

geese and the exotic wood duck, it is also ideal for bird-watching.

★ ★

Lake Tahoe

More often associated with Nevada than California because of the illustrious casino resorts on its east shore (the Nevada side), the resorts to the west of Lake Tahoe offer world-class skiing opportunities that were highly publicized during the 1960 Winter Olympics in Squaw Valley. In fact, almost 40 years after its Olympic glory, California has (at least on one occassion in 1998) surpassed Colorado as the top U.S. destination for a ski vacation primarily because of the resorts around Lake Tahoe.

The famous body of water at the heart of this region is a sapphire-blue alpine lake so clear that you can supposedly see objects suspended 75ft (22.9m) below the surface. It is oval in shape and 22mi (33.8km) long, 12mi (19.3km) wide and an average of 989ft (301m) deep—so deep, in fact, that it never freezes.

The lakefront was occupied primarily by the Washoe people until it was "discovered" by Kit Carson and John C. Fremont in 1844. Though it missed most of the gold-rush traffic, it was very popular with silver miners and loggers. It became a resort area for the wealthy at the turn of the 20th century, and in the 1930s, the middle classes moved in. When the 1960 Winter Olympics were held in Squaw Valley, Tahoe became world-famous and sweeping commercial

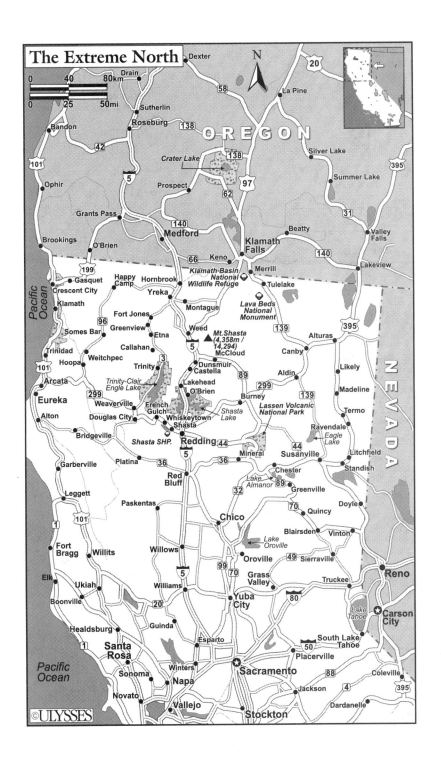

The Extreme North

development began. If you want to avoid crowds and traffic congestion, the best time to visit is late spring or fall.

Finding Your Way Around

By Car

The Klamath Mountains

Highway 299 (Arcata to Redding), Highway 96 (along the Klamath River between Willow Creek and Yreka) and Highway 3 (Weaverville to Yreka) are the major arteries through the Klamath Mountain area. There are a number of well-maintained scenic roads as well, such as the Pacific Crest National Scenic Trail, Coffee Creek Road, Canyon Creek Road and Hobo Gulch Road.

The Shasta Cascade, the Modoc Plateau and Ski Country

Highway 5 will take you from Sacramento through to Red Bluff, Anderson and Redding before leading you to Dunsmuir and Mt. Shasta. Highway 89 turns off from the city of Mt. Shasta to get you to McCloud and Burney Falls before giving you the opportunity to explore the Lassen Volcanic Park area via Highway 44. If you take Highway 97 from Weed and then take Highway 161 along the California/Oregon border, you will end up at the Klamath Basin Wildlife Reserves

and Lava Beds National Monument. Highway 139 will take you down to Highway 299 which in turn leads to Alturas. The main artery in cowboy country and the Lake Tahoe area is Highway 395, with side trips to Quincy and Oroville being accessible via Highway 70. Highway 80 will get you back to Sacramento.

Road Conditions

It is advisable to inquire about road conditions before heading anywhere in this region, since roads can be blocked by snow right up until May and sometimes until July in Lassen Volcanic Park. The number to call for information is: ☎800-427-7623.

By Bus

Greyhound Bus Lines
☎800-231-222
Greyhound offers service to Redding, Dunsmuir, Mount Shasta, Yreka and Lake Tahoe.

By Train

Amtrak
☎800-872-7245
You can get to Redding and Dunsmuir daily with Amtrak. There is also service to Truckee in the Lake Tahoe area.

Public Transportation

Trinity Transit Bus Company
☎(916) 623-5438
This company offers round trips daily between Weaverville, Lewiston and Hayfork.

North Lake Tahoe and Truckee Area Transit
☎530-581-8341
☎800-441-4423
www.laketahoetransit.com
For shuttles, buses and trolleys in the North Lake Tahoe area contact this organization.

South Tahoe Area Ground Express
☎530-573-2080
In the South Lake Tahoe area or in Tahoe City you can contact this company.

Practical Information

Area Code

The area code is *530* unless otherwise indicated.

Tourist Information

The Shasta Cascade and the Modoc Plateau

Shasta Cascade Wonderland Association
1699 Rte. 273
Anderson
☎365-7500
☎800-474-2782
scwa@shastacascade.org
www.shastacascade.org

Upper Sacramento Valley

Lake Oroville Visitors Center
every day except Thanksgiving, Christmas and New Year's Day
☎538-2219
www.dwr.water.ca.gov

Ski Country

Truckee Donner Visitor Center
inside the train depot
☎587-0476

Exploring

The Trinity Alps, Marble Mountains and Russian Wilderness Areas

The kind of cultural attractions that we're accustomed to as 21st-century urbanites are few and far between in the sparsely populated high alpine wilderness areas in and around the Klamath Mountains. In this neck of the woods, cows direct the traffic and stoplights are not yet necessary. The rugged mountain peaks, which are between 7,000 and 9,000ft (2,134 and 2,743m) high, are almost completely covered in National Forest Land and have been sculpted by glaciers rather than artists. The only hints of civilization lie in the decaying mining towns that dot the long stretches of sinewy roads that are bordered by dangerous drop-offs on at least one side. Six of the most unspoiled rivers in the U.S. originate here: the Klamath, Trinity, Smith, Mad, Eel and Van Duzen. The purity of their waters makes them an extremely important habitat for fish—namely steelhead and salmon, though mining nearly decimated the fish population and now logging is doing its damage as well. It would be difficult to find a better place to fish, hike, stargaze, or ride

the rapids. Please refer to the "Outdoors" and "Parks" section to peruse the variety of options available.

As you make your way to the Shasta Cascade region heading south from Siskiyou County, an interesting glimpse of the culture of the Hupa, Yurok and Karok peoples can be found inside the **Hoopa Valley Indian Reservation**, the largest Native American reservation in California.

The **Hoopa Tribal Museum** *(free admission; Mon to Fri 8am to 4pm and Sat in the summer; next to the Lucky Bear Casino in the Hoopa Shopping Center,* ☎*916-625-4048)* is the only indigenous-owned museum in California and features redwood dugout canoes along with some authentic artifacts from the Hupa, Yurok and Karok tribes. Tours to visit sacred sites can also be arranged here. If for some reason the museum is closed during opening hours, walk into the neighbouring Lucky Bear Casino and ask them to check up on it for you. Perhaps a cheerful woman named Cyndi will be there to help you. The greeting we got was: "If we knew you were coming we'd've baked an eel."

If you continue south on Highway 299 you'll eventually end up in **Weaverville**, an old gold-rush town nestled at the base of the Trinity Alps. As you stroll around on Main Street you'll come across a number of historical buildings dating from the 1850s. Make sure you take in the **Weaverville Drug Store**, **Morris Hardware**, the **Trinity County Courthouse** and the **Highland Art Center**.

There are two museums conveniently placed next to each other that also merit some attention. The **J.J. Jackson Memorial Museum** *(free admission; May 1 to Oct 31 10am to 5pm, Apr and Nov noon to 4pm, winter Tue noon to 4pm; located next to the Joss House,* ☎*916-623-5211)* features a replica of a miner's cabin, a steam-powered stamp mill, a restored blacksmith shop and a slew of fascinating Chinese and Native American artifacts. Particularly attention-grabbing are the various remnants of the Tong War.

A testimony to the vital Chinese gold-rush culture that once prevailed in Weaverville, the **Weaverville Joss House State Historic Park** *(year-round, tours every 30min in summer, every hour in winter,* ☎*916-623-5284)* is the site of the oldest Taoist temple in continous operation in California. Constructed in 1852 and rebuilt in 1874 after being destroyed by fire, the temple houses many artifacts that were imported from China near the turn of the 20th century. The altar itself is more than 3,000 years old.

The Shasta Cascade

A good place to begin a tour of the Shasta Cascade region is the excellent Visitors Information Center in Anderson, a small town just south of Redding. (See Shasta Cascade Wonderland Association, p 534).

Unless you need to stock up on groceries or camping supplies, we would strongly advise that you take Highway 5 right through Redding, as it is a bit of a throwback to 1950s tourism with its motel strips and fairly

Northeastern California

A Cowboy's Life in Northern California

Modoc County, in the southern portion of the Modoc Mountain Range and the Modoc National Forest, a few miles from the Nevada border, has a population of only 10,000 inhabitants. The people living here are greatly outnumbered by cows, but a cowboy in these parts must face a grim reality: cattle ranching as a way of life is dying. Here's a man who has spent all of his adult life with a horse underneath him and cows in front of him, trying to cope with federal government actions, such as the closing of many roads in federally owned property—and most of the county is federally owned—which are necessary for bringing in fire equipment, hunting, putting down salt for cattle and deer, and maintaining fences. The high desert country in the vicinity of the South Fork of the Pit River has been a fine home to this cowboy, but if cattle ranching is doomed, how can his children find meaningful employment on home ground? He hardly needs to be reminded that if a man were fool enough to complain to him, "Look at all that cow manure on my car," he would immediately fire back, "it pays for the car, so shut up." It is extremely painful for him even to contemplate leaving a region richly blessed by wildlife,

including mountain lions, bald and golden eagles and white pelicans, high peaks and dense forests and clear lakes—and deliciously unpolluted air to breathe.

To understand what's at the heart of the Northern California cowboy's threatened way of life, a visitor would do well to witness what goes on in conjunction with both main cattle drives of the year, one occuring in spring time, from mid-April to the beginning of May, the other from the end of September to mid-October. As the hard work of cattle ranching is going on, participants and onlookers alike are also enjoying a social event.

Once the mother cows and the close-following calves are brought to a suitable field, watchful cowboys on horseback and their equally watchful canine helpers, border collies, round up all the animals and drive them in the direction of a three-sided, fenced-in enclosure. Once all the animals are so confined, several horsemen—including the occassional horsewoman, who is no less skilled than her male counterparts—block off the open end, simply sitting quietly astride their mounts for a few minutes to encourage the bellowing creatures, milling

about in fear and sometimes even in panic, to calm down. This accomplished, the team of riders, assisted by men and women on foot, go to work as one smoothly coordinated ensemble to brand, castrate and innoculate the calves one by one. The average time it takes per calf to perform all three operations is a mere minute and a half.

First one cowboy on horseback almost effortlessly lassoes a squealing calf around the neck, followed by a second cowboy, on the far side of the animal, doing the same to one of the hind legs. As the two horsemen ride a few feet in opposite directions, within seconds two men on the ground wrestle the calf into a more or less supine position, the cowboy near the head of the animal removing the rope from the neck and placing it around the front hooves, the cowboy at the animal's hind end placing the second rope over the calf's rear hooves. In rapid succession, one cowboy applies a red-hot branding iron, more to the calf's hair than its actual skin; another castrates the animal swiftly and cleanly with an emasculating device which minimizes blood loss (since the testicles, known as prairie oysters, are regarded as delicacies, they are saved for later cooking andconsumption); another deftly cuts a piece out of one ear for purposes of identification; and yet another, using large, spring-loaded syringes innoculates the calf against a host of diseases cows are susceptible to. Hard as it may be for the uninitiated to believe, all of this activity happens with an astonishing degree of controlled strength and skillful ease. Beautiful it is to watch, for instance, how these cowboys ride their horses so gracefully that the horses appear to be powerful extensions of the men. On horseback, riding through a field of yellow spring flowers, the Modoc County cowboy may notice a formidable cluster of blue-black storm clouds overhead; and if he is something of a poet, as he may very well be, he will view the impending storm as a sign of dark things to come.

predictable parks and museums. After all, the real attraction of this area is the wilderness itself.

If houseboating is something that you'd like to try, you might want to stop at Shasta Lake for the night—after you've visited the Shasta Dam, that is. The **Shasta Dam ★** *(Shasta Dam Visitors Center:* ☎275-1554) is the second-highest dam in the U.S. and is actually three times higher than Niagara Falls at 620ft (189m). Built to secure an abundant supply of water to California's fertile Central Valley, this dam is considered a masterpiece in irrigation engineering. Shasta Lake has been created by this dam and is thus the largest artificial lake in California. If you are travelling with children, the **Lake Shasta Caverns** *($15; tour lasts approx. 2hrs; take Shasta Cavern Rd. exit for Hwy. 5 and follow the panels,* ☎238-2341 or 800-795-2283) has daily tours of these limestone and marble caves. A boat ride across Lake Shasta is included, and a sweater is a must.

As you leave Shasta Lake heading on Highway 5 toward Mount Shasta, you'll regret it if you don't turn off at **Castle Crags State Park**. (see p 543)

There are basically four choices for a homebase around which you can organize your exploration of the Mount Shasta region: Dunsmuir, McCloud, Mount Shasta (City) and Weed.

Dunsmuir

A town built by the Southern Pacific Railroad, Dunsmuir actually began as a railroad camp. It contains a nice city park and couple of waterfalls, but will prove most interesting for those with a train fetish. See the **Railroad Park Caboose Motel** (see p 546).

Mount Shasta (City)

A humble settlement at the base of a majestic mountain, Mount Shasta was at one time a mecca for awestruck Shasta, Karuk, Klamath, Modoc, Wintu and Pit tribes before they were so rudely pushed aside by hordes of irreverant gold miners. Once the greed for gold died down, a booming lumber industry took hold in the surrounding area and the town quickly became a party town for lumberjacks who were attracted to the mysterious availability of liquor during prohibition. A New Age colony now determines much of the community's culture and attempts are being made to recultivate some of the original respect and awe for the dormant volcano that towers above the town. An abundance of wild strawberries found here inspired the original name of Strawberry Valley. This was replaced by Sisson in the early lumberjack years, but then changed to Mount Shasta in the 1920s. If you're curious about the mythology of Mt. Shasta or the counter-culture community that is now transforming it into another mecca, drop into either **Village Books** *(320 N. Mt. Shasta Blvd.,* ☎926-3041) or the **Golden Bough Bookstore** *(219 N. Mt. Shasta Blvd.,* ☎926-3228, *www.goldenboughbooks.com)* and scour the shelves and bulletin boards.

McCloud

If you would prefer to be based in a charming historic lumber village with well-preserved original architecture and cozy upscale hospitality, then McCloud is your best bet.

Renowned as a skiing and square-dancing centre, McCloud also harbours an unusual **Irish Catholic Church** made from redwood, a restored historic train depot, and an old-fashioned candy store, general store and soda fountain. The popular **Shasta Sunset Dinner Train** (see p 549) also departs from here.

Weed

Another historic lumber town, but one with a working-class aura, Weed offers some spectacular views of Mount Shasta. It is also one of the windiest towns that you may ever encounter. The town was founded in the late 1880s by Abner Weed, a man who had dreams of powering a lumber mill by harnessing the wind created by the mountain.

Although there are a couple of small attractions right in town—the **Black Butte Saloon** (*Fri to Sun 11am to 3pm; ☎916-938-2352*) and the **Lumber Town Museum** (*free admission; Jun to Sep; 303 Gilman Ave., ☎916-938-5050*), for instance—the major sites are outside the town limits. The Stewart Mineral Springs and Living Memorial Sculpture Garden are definitely both worth visiting. Founded in 1875 by Henry Stewart, who claimed that he was saved from death by its healing powers, **Stewart Mineral Springs** (*$15/day; 2222 Stewart Springs Dr., ☎938-2222*) is a spa/resort for the person of modest means. How about stopping for awhile to rid your body of toxins and stress in a claw-foot tub filled with soothing mineral water, or sitting in a Native American sweat lodge? If you'd like to spend the

night, very reasonably priced and varied accommodations (including teepees) are available onsite.

Heading towards the high desert on Highway 97, you will pass the **Living Memorial Sculpture Garden ★★** (*1mi or 1.6km north of Hwy. 12, ☎938-2218*), a solemn and moving memorial to those who have died or suffered as a result of war. Conceived by a local Vietnam veteran and sculptor, Dennis Smith, this complex of 10 gigantic sculptures strategically placed at various spots on a plateau laced with Ponderosa pine and manzanita is nothing short of awe-inspiring. Sublime panoramas of Mt. Shasta and the High Desert encircle the site and the seemingly endless sky is eerily still except for the occasional eagle hovering above.

The Modoc Plateau

If you have never experienced the high desert, you owe it to yourself to come here. Pure sage-scented air, vast expanses of a slightly otherworldly terrain composed in blacks, greys, and earth-tone reds, and a sky speckled with birds of prey and migrating waterfowl—this is what you can expect when you arrive in the Modoc Plateau.

The two most stunning areas on the plateau sit side by side in the top Northeastern corner of California: the **Lava Beds National Monument ★★★** and the **Klamath Basin Wildlife Refuges ★★★**. Take Highway 97 to Highway 161 and then Highway 161 to Hill Road for

the most dramatic entrance to this area. Highway 161 goes right along the Oregon/California border and passes directly through parts of the Wildlife Refuges. (For information on the Klamath Basin Wildlife Refuges, refer to the "Outdoor Activities" section, p 545) Turning down Hill Road will bring you to the northern limits of **Lava Beds National Monument**. Although this is not the conventional way to enter the Lava Beds, it has its merits since it allows you to tour the historic site of **Captain Jack's Stronghold** (see box), as well as do some wildlife and petroglyph viewing before you make your way to the **Visitors Center** (*☎916-667-2282*) to pick up your hard hats, flashlights and maps for some intense lava-tube exploration. In order to get to **Petroglyph Point**, the **Wildlife Overlooks** and the Stronghold, take Hill Road until you reach the fork and then turn left. We recommend that you go all the way to the end, visiting Petroglyph Point first and then make your way back, stopping at the East and West Wildlife Overlooks at the border of **Tule Lake**. There is an information kiosk at the turn-off to Petroglyph Point if you feel you need additional directions. Pamphlets for a self-guided tour of Petroglyph Point are available at the trailhead. They explain the history and meaning of this site from the Modoc perspective and suggest the best vantage points from which to see the birds' nests and the petroglyphs.

The Wildlife Outlooks offer panoramic views of what was the source of life for the Modocs for thousands of years: Tule Lake with its fish, waterfowl

Captain Jack and the Modocs

The Klamath Basin was home to the Modoc Indians for many peaceful centuries until the 1850s when padres and settlers began to encroach upon their territory and their time-honoured way of life. Although in October 1864, the Bureau of Indian Affairs administrators succeeded in convincing the Modocs to go north and join their neighbours, the Klamaths, on the Klamath Reservation, the Modocs soon found the arrangement unacceptable. Under the leadership of Kientpoos, Captain Jack, they returned to their traditional home on the Lost River near the Oregon-California border. The settlers strongly disapproved of this move and prevailed upon the First Calvary from Fort Klamath, Oregon, to order Captain Jack's men to disarm and resume life on the reservation.

On the morning of November 29, 1872, a fight broke out, leaving one soldier dead and seven wounded. Captain Jack's Modocs gathered in what came to be known as the Stronghold, a natural fortress about 150yds (137m) in diameter located in the rough

lava beds. On that same morning, another band of Modocs, fighting under Hooker Jim, were attacked by volunteers, who killed several of them. In retreat, Hooker Jim avenged these deaths by killing 12 male ranchers in the vicinity. Despite his disapproval of this slaughter, Captain Jack allowed Hooker Jim and his group to join him in the Stronghold, and awaited further confrontation with the Army. That came on January 17, 1873, when the Army attacked simultaneously from the east and west. A thick fog and the rugged terrain contributed to 37 casualties for the Army, and none for the Modocs.

As the Army called for reinforcements, President Ulysses S. Grant convened a peace commission made up of five non-Native Americans including General E.R.S. Canby. The talks stalled over the Army's unwillingness to give the Modocs their own reservation and Captain Jack's refusal to hand over Hooker Jim and those who assisted him in killing the settlers. Fearful that Captain Jack might cave in to the Army, Hooker Jim and his followers manipulated him into agreeing to

assissinate General Canby—even though Jack must have known that he was thereby signing his own death warrant. Three days after General Canby, along with Reverend Eleazor Thomas, was indeed killed on April 15, 1873, the much beefed-up Army made an all-out assault on the Modocs backed up by mortars and howitzers. Fighting for two days forced the Modocs, who were cut off from their water-supply, to retreat south, pursued by the Army. By late May and after much bloodshed, the Army had captured most of the Modocs. Captain Jack surrendered on June 1, 1873; he and three other Modoc leaders were hanged on October 3, 1873.

And thus the only Native-American war fought in California ended with the destruction of a way of life (the survivors were banished to an Oklahoma reservation). It should never be forgotten, though, that over a period of nearly five months, a mere 50 or so Modoc warriors bravely fought it out with a force eventually 20 times larger.

Northeastern California

and, of course, its tule grass. A well-illustrated and thorough booklet on the historic trail to Captain Jack's Stronghold is also available at the trailhead for $0.25. (Please return your copy if you don't want to actually buy it.) To get to the Visitor's Center once you've explored this solemn trail, head back to Hill Road and take the road that you didn't take the last time. It will take you awhile to get there, but you probably won't notice since the landscape on the way is so unusual. The Lava Beds themselves are made up of several kinds of volcanic landforms, the most predominant being lava tube caves. There are over 400 of these tube caves, many of them concentrated around a road loop behind the Visitors Center. With names like Mushpot, Indian Well, Catacombs, Labyrinth and Paradise Alley, you can imagine what is in store for you once you equip yourself with the appropriate tools. Make sure to wear sturdy shoes and pants since you'll be required to crawl and duck walk in some of the caves. **Never** explore the caves alone.

If you leave the Lava Beds by Highway 10, you'll pass through a small town called Tionesta just before hitting Highway 139. Take Highway 139 to Highway 299 and swing left towards Alturas.

Alturas

Alturas is the county seat of Modoc County and also its cultural center. And in case you haven't already

guessed, culture, in these parts, centers around the rituals of the rodeo and cattle drive. Indeed, now that you've contemplated the plight of the "Indians" that inhabited this region, it is now time to focus some attention on the "cowboys" that replaced them. For a historical overview of these "cowboys and Indians," drop into the **Modoc County Museum** *(May to Oct, Tue to Sat 10am to 4pm; 600 S. Main St.,* ☎*233-6328)* and peruse its intriguing collection and Modoc County history books. This may be a good place to overnight before you take the long road back to civilization.

If you head south from Alturas on Highway 395, trying not to blink too often, you may just catch a glimpse of a watering hole called **Likely** after travelling through the **Modoc National Wildlife Refuge**. If you're feeling particularly adventurous and want to witness some spectacular scenery that is truly off of the beaten path, take Jess Valley Road in Likely to the South Warner Wilderness. Here is the lower part of that valley oasis that some of the pilgrims on the Oregon trail came across after passing through rugged

high desert terrain spotted with huge alkali lakes. And *here* is some authentic cowboy country. (see box).

Highway 395, between the small town of Madeline and its juncture with Highway 139 just south of Susanville, traverses a long stretch of "the middle of nowhere." If you're interested in spending the next day participating in watersports and camping, we advise that you take Route 313 from the small town of Termo and head towards Eagle Lake on Highway 139 South—or if you're not in a hurry, pass through dramatic scenery punctuated with railroad development that seems to defy the realm of the possible on your way to Bucks Lake, close to Quincy. If you're craving something with more creature comforts but would still like to indulge in watersports—or at least be close to the water—head towards the thoughtfully developed old gold-rush town named Oroville.

Upper Sacramento Valley

Quincy

Nestled in a valley in the High Sierra, Quincy is a charming, historic watering-hole town that served miners, then railroad workers, then lumberjacks. It now predominantly serves tourists. It is the county seat of Plumas County and thus harbours the rather impressive **Plumas County Courthouse** and **Plumas County Museum**

($1; May to Sep, Mon to Fri 8am to 5pm, weekends and holidays 10am to 4pm; 500 Jackson St., ☎283-6320), located about a block away from the court house. If you'd like to take a walk or heritage driving tour, make sure you pick up the complimentary pamphlet given out by the **Plumas County Visitors Bureau** *(8am to 5pm; Hwy. 70, 0.5mi or 0.8km to the west of Quincy, ☎283-6345 or 800-326-2247)*. Head west on Bucks Lake Road for about 20min and you'll reach Buck's Lake, a crystalline mountain lake surrounded by an enchanting pine forest, and a great place to engage in outdoor activities in the summer and winter (though the road is often blocked by snow in the winter—entrance only by cross-country skis or snowshoes).

Oroville

Originating as a gold-rush town with the second largest Chinese community outside of San Francisco, Oroville is now more renowned for its lake. Like Lake Shasta, **Lake Oroville** is the result of a fairly impressive dam that is located 9mi (14.5km) north of the town of Oroville. Before exploring the lake area, make sure you stop at the excellent **Lake Oroville Visitor Center** *(every day 9am to 5pm; 917 Kelly Ridge Rd., ☎538-2219)*. In addition to taking in some interesting exhibits, you can pick up brochures that suggest hiking, biking and driving tours. We highly recommend the **Bald Rock Trail**.

An absolute must-see while you're in Oroville, the **Chinese Temple ★ ★ ★** *($2; Thu to Mon 11am to 4:30pm, Tue to Wed 1pm to 4pm, closed Dec 15 to Jan 31;*

1500 Broderick St., ☎538-2497 or 888-OROVILLE) was built in 1863 to serve 10,000 Chinese people who lived here. There are three chapels for each of the major ways of life in China. The main chapel **Liet Sheng Kong-Temple** is Taoist and therefore dedicated to an assortment of deities. It is surrounded by a well-kept **Taoist Garden** whose plants originate in China. The Confucianist **Chan Room** is an excellent example of Chinese ancestor worship. Finally, the **Moon Temple** is the Buddhist chapel. Other parts of the complex well worth visiting are as follows: the **Council Room,** where workers attended to civil and cultural needs such as banking, letter writing and arranging for the burial of their dead; the **Chinese Dwelling**, which allows a glimpse into the life of a typical Chinese miner in the 1800s; and the dazzling **Tapestry and Display Halls** with their collection of embroidered tapestries, parade parasols, Chinese folk art, pottery, Chinese and U.S. costumes and three-dimensional shadow puppets that were used in the Oroville Chinese Opera Theatre. The docent that leads the guided tour through the grounds is extremely well-educated and it wouldn't be an exaggeration to say that the collection contains items that couls easily be the envy of the Smithsonian.

Included with your admission to the Chinese Temple is entry to the neighbouring **C.F. Lott Historic Home** *($2; 1067 Montgomery St.)*, which is listed on the National Register of Historic Places. This is a good place to learn about the early pioneers of the area and to acquaint yourself with the story of Ishi, the

last survivor of the Yahi people. (see box).

Ski Country

Probably the better known part of the wild Northeastern corner of California is the area in and around Lake Tahoe. This part of the state is referred to by many as Ski Country because of its claim to fame as host to the 1960 Winter Olympics and because of the excellent opportunities it affords winter-sports enthusiasts from the world over.

Truckee

The gateway to ski country is definitely Truckee, a historic mining and railroad town named after a Paiute chief who assisted John Fremont in getting from Los Angeles to Montana just before the gold rush. The town began to develop in 1863 and was soon famous for its saloons, gambling halls and whorehouses. It served as a strategic point during the establishment of the first transcontinental railroad, since workers built the tracks east and west from here. You can begin your visit of Truckee and neighbouring Donner Lake by dropping into the Visitor Center, which is located in the historic train depot right off of Commercial Row. Truckee is a great place to get yourself oriented and equipped with train, shuttle and bus schedules, as well as camping and outdoors equipment, and anything else you may need for your stay in the area. It also offers some great accommodation and can thus serve as a homebase for your exploration of the region.

Northeastern California

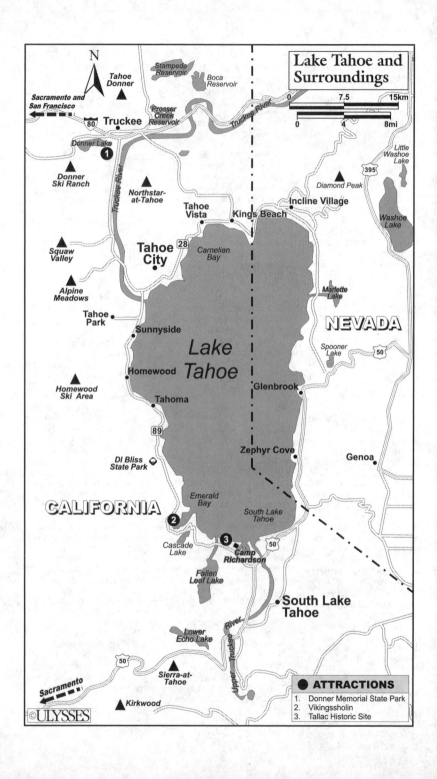

Donner Memorial State Park

For a lesson in the potential hazards of the region, begin at the **Emigrant Trail Museum ★** *($2 or free with the $5 park admission; every day 9am to 4pm;* ☎582-7894) in Donner Memorial State Park. The museum recounts the horrendous trials of the Donner Party, whose attempted journey through this part of the country in 1846 ended in disaster.

Tahoe City

Tahoe City, situated at the junction of Highway 89 and Highway 28, is the largest community on Lake Tahoe's northern shore. There is no real downtown to speak of, so unless you're planning to stay at one of the better-known northern resorts such as Royal Gorge (see p 544), we strongly recommend that you stay near or in one of the charming villages or resorts that border the Southwestern side of the lake, or make your homebase in Truckee.

★★★ Emerald Bay

Lake Tahoe's only island is harboured in the truly emerald waters of Emerald Bay. This is one of the most photographed areas in the United States because of its astounding views.

At the south of Emerald Bay is **Vikingsholm ★★** *(Jun to Sep, every day 10am to 4pm, Oct to May weekends only;* ☎525-7277), a Scandinavian-style mansion decorated with Viking furniture and carved wooden ceilings.

For a taste of what Lake Tahoe was like in the swinging 1920s, drop by the ruins of three of the estates of the rich and the famous, which now comprise the **Tallac Historic Site** *(Emerald Bay Rd. at the junction of Hwy. 5 and Hwy. 89,* ☎541-5227) just outside of South Lake Tahoe.

Parks and Beaches

Beaches

Whiskeytown-Shasta-Trinity National Recreation Area

www.nps.gov/whis

Whiskeytown Lake
With 3,220 acres (1,303ha) of water, it's easy to understand why swimming, fishing, canoeing and sailing are popular at Whiskeytown Lake. The most popular beaches with nearby camping are at Brandy Creek and Oak Bottom.

Shasta Lake *(www.r5.fs.fed.us/shastatrinity)*
The largest artificial lake in Northern California has 130mi (209km) of shoreline and consistently warm water (85F° or 29.4C°), which makes it ideal for houseboating, swimming, waterskiing and fishing.

Trinity Lake
A less-developed lake with 150mi (241km) of shoreline at the foot of the Trinity Alps, Trinity Lake is a better choice if you want to swim, sail, waterski, houseboat, or fish in some privacy.

Lake Tahoe

Your best bet for swimming in Lake Tahoe is off of one of its southwestern shores between Tahoe City and Emerald Bay. **Lester Beach** (or **DL Bliss Beach**) *($5 parking)* is one of the better beaches on the lake and is located in beautiful DL Bliss State Park. However, try to arrive before 10am if you'd like a parking spot.

Parks

Castle Crags State Park *($5/vehicle; just off Castle Creek Rd., Castella,* ☎235-2684). As you drive towards Mount Shasta from Redding on Highway 5, you'll be directed to Castle Crags, a grouping of ancient granite spires that shoot up from 2,000 to 6,544ft (610 to 1,995m) in the air. If you venture through the more than 28mi (45km) of hiking trails (including 7mi or 11.3km of the famous Pacific Crest Trail), you'll also discover formations similar to the ones in Yosemite National Park, such as the Castle Dome, which strongly resembles the Half Dome that was made famous in a photograph by Ansel Adams.

Lassen Volcanic National Park ★★ *(federal fee; year-round but limited road access in the winter; 48mi or 77km east of Redding,* ☎530-595-4444, *www.nps.gov/lavo)* houses the southernmost volcano in the Cascade Range and is part of a lava plateau that includes Lava Beds National Monument and Crater Lake National Park. Established in 1916 as a kind of protected study ground for active volcanism, it harbours a dazzling array of **volcanic**

landscapes in addition to other natural wonders. The over 150mi (241km) of hiking trails (17 of which are part of the Pacific Coast Trail) take you through lava flows, steaming sulphur vents, hot springs, cinder cones, craters, forests, meadows, lakes and streams, all of which are inhabited by over 700 flowering plant species, 58 mammal species and 200 bird species. Self-guided interpretive trails and the historic Nobles pioneer trail are other highlights. The only drawback is the difficulty in actually getting into the park, since the access road can be covered in snow right up until the middle of summer. Call for road conditions before you come (see p 534).

Modoc National Forest
Also known as the South Warner Wilderness Area, Modoc National Forest is equipped with 77mi (124km) of hiking trails that are accessible from July to mid-October. For more information, stop by the Modoc National Forest Supervisor's Headquarters in Alturas.

Outdoor Activities

Snowplay

Snowplay is something that snow lovers practise in designated areas known as snowparks. It's very popular, particularly with families. Activities range from snowbiking and snowscooting, to ski-foxing to inner-tubing to "zorbing"—just to mention

a few of the many choices. A snowbike is basically very similar to bicycle, except that there are steerable skis instead of tires. Balance is maintained by short skis that are attached to the skier's feet. The snowscooter is a scooter on skis, while the ski fox is a somewhat unusual contraption that looks like a chair mounted on a ski. The most cutting-edge snow toy is the "Zorb," a gigantic inflatable ball that you strap yourself into so that you can literally roll down a bob-sled-like course made of steep walls of snow.

Snowshoeing

Snowshoes have come a long way from their rawhide and wood beginnings. With the high-tech application of titanium, aluminum and nylon to the fabrication of snowshoes, snowshoeing has become a prestigious and popular winter sport in the U.S. As a winter resort area, the High Sierra has some fabulous places to practice this sport.

Cross-Country Skiing and Cross-Country Skating

Royal Gorge Cross-Country Skiing Resort
This is the largest groomed cross-country track system in North America (205mi or 330km), with 9,000 acres (3,642ha) of skiing terrain, 90 trails, 10 warming huts and four trailside cafes.

The trails are excellent and frequently groomed. Inn-to-inn trails and an on-site ski school will please skiers of all ages. (see p 548)

Sorensen's Resort and Hope Valley (see p548)

Donner Lake Sno-Park
☎ *582-7892*

Dogsledding

If you're interested in navigating some of the Northern California winter landscape (Mount Shasta, the Trinity Alps and the Marble Mountains) on a dogsled, book yourself an excursion with:

Dogsled Express
$85/singles
$135/two
$250/multiple passenger two-sled trip
winter camping can be arranged here as well
P.O. Box 15
Etna, CA 96027
☎ *(916) 467-5627*

Bird-Watching

Ash Creek Wildlife Area
The 3,000 acres (1,214ha) of wetlands known as the Big Swamp offer great opportunities for wildlife (deer and antelope) observation and bird-watching.

Klamath Basin National Wildlife Refuges
$3/vehicle
Visitors Center: Mon to Fri 8am to 4:30pm, weekends and holidays until 4pm on Hill Rd.
☎*667-2231*
www.klamathnwr.org
Klamath Basin National Wildlife Refuges is a complex of six refuges created to conserve the disappearing wetlands of Northern California and Southern Oregon that are made up of freshwater marshes, sagebrush and juniper grasslands, coniferous forest, open water and grassy meadows. Tule Lake and Clear Lake are entirely in California, while the Lower Klamath refuge is shared by the two states. Unfortunately, Clear Lake is closed to the public but the **Tule** and **Lower Klamath** refuges are open during the day. Because these refuges provide a perfect habitat for birds migrating along the Pacific Flyway, nearly three-quarters of all of the birds on this flyway stop here to nest and mate. In the spring and fall it's particularly dramatic as hundreds of thousands of birds, (including northern pintails, white-fronted geese and American widgeon) fill the skies and the wetlands. But the summer and winter seasons have their appeal as well: the summer is the time for American white pelican, double-crested cormoran and herons; and the winter is the season for ducks, Canada geese and the largest concentration of bald eagles in the contiguous United States. Self-guided driving tours are mapped out in a pamplet that you can pick up at the visitors center. The Tule Lake Refuge even offers self-guided canoe trails (*Jul 1 to Sep 30*), but you need to bring your own canoe.

Modoc National Wildlife Refuge
☎*233-3572*
Driving south from Alturas on Highway 395 will automatically take you through this wildlife refuge. Make sure you have your binoculars handy!

Mountain-Biking

Mount Shasta Ski Park
late Jun to early Sep
off Hwy. 89 just before McCloud
☎*926-8610*
One of the most popular places to mountain bike is down Mount Shasta. In the summertime, take the lift up and your bike down.

Fishing

This entire region is a fisher's paradise. Because the fish population is so precious, a catch-and-release policy is in effect in many places, so make sure you inquire about conditions before you cast your line.

Here are some choice fishing spots and their catch:

Whiskeytown Lake
Bass, kokanee, salmon, trout.

Shasta Lake
Bass, trout, bluegill, sturgeon.

Trinity Lake
Trout and smallmouth bass.

Trinity River
Chinook and Cahoe salmon, steelhead and German trout.

Orleans
Steelhead and trout.

Horseback Riding

For a unique horseback-riding experience, head east from Redding in the direction of Lassen Volcanic National Park on Highway 44 until you come across a tiny town called Shingletown. Turning right on a road leading to Manton will take you to **The Wild Horse Sanctuary**, a natural wild-horse-sanctuary refuge where you can ride tamed horses in order to track wild ones. This unique place offers horse lovers two- and three-day pack trips that begin and end around a campfire at a base camp made up of sleeping cabins and a communal cookhouse with bathroom and shower facilities. All riders must be in good physical condition. A weight limit of 205lbs (92.9kg) and a minimum age of 14 years apply. (*$235/person for two-day pack trip, $335/person for three-day pack trip*).

For reservations:
Wild Horse Sanctuary
P.O. Box 30
Shingletown, CA 96088
☎*222-5728*

Another option is to get a local horse from one of the ranchers around Alturas and ride it on the horse trails in cowboy country. The **Alturas Chamber of Commerce** (☎*233-4434*) will provide a horse-trails map and connect you with someone who can provide a horse. We recommend getting a horse from someone in Likely and heading up to the **Soup Spring Trail** at the edge of the South Warner Wilderness. A nearby bed and breakfast provides horse parking if you're not interested in using the corrals at the **Soup Spring Campground**. (see Mill Creek Lodge, p 547) For information on this and other horse trails, contact the **Warner Mountain Ranger** (☎279-6116).

Accommodations

Whiskeytown Lake
$
Oak Bottom
☎800-365-2267
If you're interested in pitching a tent on or near the beach on Whiskeytown Lake, try doing it here.

Trinity Lake
$
☎623-2121
⇌623-6010
The forest service has campgrounds (10 units) here—some of which are located right on the beach.

Lava Beds National Monument and Modoc National Forest
$
first come, first served
two vehicle/10 people max/site
These 43 sites are suited for a variety of camping possibilities: tents, pick-up campers, small trailers and motor homes. Each site is equipped with a picnic table, fire pit and cooking grill. The campground has water and flush toilets. Please note that there are no showers, hookups, dumpstations, stores, gas stations, or snackbars. Firewood for wood fires is available onsite.

Eagle Lake

Eagle Lake District Campgrounds and Marina
P.O. Box 1771
Susanville, CA 96130
campground: ☎825-3212
marina: ☎825-3454
winter: ☎257-6952
www.psln.com/camping
The five campgrounds on Eagle Lake include access to boats, a grocery store, jet-skis, fishing supplies and licenses, bike rentals, laundry and showers.

Orleans

 Sandy Bar Ranch
$$
P.O. Box 347
Ishi Pishi Rd.
Orleans, CA 95556
☎627-3379
sandybar@pcweb.net
For those of you looking for an environmentally responsible "easy camping" experience at a fantastic price, check out the Sandy Bar Ranch. A total of six simply furnished cabins are offered at the edge of the wild Klamath River, with private decks and an impressive selection of kitchen utensils. The cooperative owners of this property also allow visitors to select produce from their organic gardens to complement other camping fixin's. If you don't already have sophisticated recycling habits, you'll definitely learn them here. A bonfire site, sand

volleyball court, and an extensive private beach and hiking area are some other great advantages to be had by staying here. Great kayaking, rafting and fishing are also very close by. The drive into the site is on a very narrow road that overlooks a steep drop, but try not to get intimidated by this because what is on the other side is well worth the risk.

Weaverville

Weaverville Hotel
$$
pb/sb, ℜ
seven rooms
201 Main St.
☎623-3121
This charming establishment has been open since 1861 and still offers a good value if you are seeking creature comforts without lots of frills.

Dunsmuir

Railroad Park Caboose Motel
$$
☎, ≡, ⇌, tv, ℜ
100 Railroad Park Rd.
☎235-4440
⇌235-4470
Does somebody you know fantasize about trains? Perhaps you could arrange an unforgettable stay in one of the 23 cabooses that have been converted into sleeping quarters at the Railroad Park in Dunsmuir. These cabooses are spacious with large, comfortable beds and cozy pine panelling, and some offer good views of Castle Crags State Park. A caboose restaurant serves slightly overpriced traditional U.S. fare, but you might decide that the novelty is worth it.

McCloud

 McCloud Hotel
$$$-$$$$ bkfst incl
☎, ≡, ⊛
17 rooms
408 Main St.
☎*964-2822*
⇌*964-2844*
mchotel@snowcrest.net
www.mccloudhotel.com
This attractive yellow, New England-style mansion is one of the finest examples of historical inn restoration in this region of California. Originally a rooming-house for loggers in 1916, it was abandoned until quite recently, when it caught the eye of a couple from the San Francisco Bay area who had dreams of opening a bed and breakfast inn. Painstakingly and authentically restored by family and community efforts (see the touching album that documents the process in the lobby), the hotel now offers cozy hospitality in the form of spacious, tastefully decorated rooms and delicious in-room breakfasts. The wisteria-lined front porch offers a splendid view of Mount Shasta.

Alturas

Niles Hotel
$-$$$ bkfst incl
≡, sb
304 S. Main St.
☎*233-3261*
This historic-landmark property is definitely the place to stay if you'd like a taste of Wild West Alturas. Recently rejuvenated, two of its greatest assets are a restaurant that serves up prime rib that is out of this world (see p 549) and a lively saloon. The hotel is also close to the intriguing Modoc County Museum.

Mill Creek Lodge
$$-$$$ bkfst incl
≡, sb
13mi (20.9km) from Likely, 33mi (53.1km) from Alturas
P.O. Box 65
Likely 96116
☎*233-4934*
Dixie and Duane McGarva have recently opened the doors of their custom-built rustic cedar home in the heart of cowboy country to passers-by (with or without horses) who want a taste of the "real thing." Located near the Warner Mountain Wilderness, the veranda of the house is equipped with a rocking chair made from horse-shoes—perfect to wile away some time contemplating the cattle ranches of the picturesque Jess Valley. The sleeping arrangements (two bedrooms on a second-floor loft with a shared bath) are perfect for four couples travelling together or for a couple on their own who don't mind sharing a bathroom with another party. As for meals, a delicious western breakfast is definitely included, but arrangements for other meals can be made as well. Don't miss out on Dixie's wild plum jam or Duane's western photography studio! If you're planning to arrive with a horse, make sure to give advance warning.

Spanish Springs Ranch
$$-$$$$$ bkfst incl.
Hwy. 395
Ravendale
☎*234-2150*
☎*800-560-1900*
spanishs@spanishsprings.com
www.spanishsprings.com
If you're looking for a more intense (and more expensive) cowboy experience, you might want to check out the local dude ranch. Spanish Springs organizes week-long cattle and horse drives on its 70,000-acre (28,329ha) grounds, where you have the choice of pitching a tent, staying in a cabin, suite, duplex, or even renting a 19th-century home-on-the-range.

Truckee

Richardson House
$$$-$$$ bkfst incl.
pb/sb, wc
eight rooms, six w/pb
10154 High St.
Truckee 96161
☎*888-229-0365*
☎*587-5388*
⇌*530-587-0927*
www.richardsonhouse.com
A bed and breakfast reminiscent of the Victorian Old West, the Richardson House sits atop a hill that overlooks historic Truckee on one side, and an Aspen grove and distant Sierra mountain peaks on the other. If you're in a romantic frame of mind, ask for the room with the clawfoot tub for two.

The Truckee Hotel
$$-$$$ bkfst incl
pb/sb, ℜ
36 rooms, eight w/pb and clawfoot tubs
right at Commercial Row
10007 Bridge St.
Truckee 96161
☎*800-659-6921*
History buffs in the Tahoe region need look no further! Opened in 1881 as a stage coach stop, the Truckee Hotel served as a rooming house for successive waves of railroad workers, ice harvesters and lumberjacks before becoming the hotel it is today. What's more, in 1994 the Truckee Hotel was the proud recipient of a prestigious award for historic restoration. The Victorian parlour and marble fireplace provide a cozy and relaxing atmosphere that is enhanced by

excellent service in other parts of the hotel. Ski racks and lockers are provided, and the Historic Emigrant Trail is just out the door. A fine in-house restaurant, The Passage, offers delicious meals along with a bar and live entertainment on the weekends.

Hope Valley

🏕️ **Sorensen's and Hope Valley Resort**
$-$$$$$
ℜ
14255 Hwy. 88 (east of the Hwy 88/89 junction), Hope Valley 96120
☎*(916) 694-2203*
☎*800-423-9949*
www.sorensensresort.com
Located in an undeveloped pocket of pine and aspen forest in the Alpine Sierra, south of Lake Tahoe, this exceptionally well-managed, four-season resort offers fantastic variety and value. Accommodations range from simple campsites to cozy cabins with wood-burning stoves, Mexican tiles, rockers and wall-to-wall pine interiors. A comfortable dining hall serves breakfast, lunch and dinner, and provides tasty hot beverages throughout the day.

Sequoia

Though most reputed as a cross-country ski resort, Sorensen's is also a great place for hiking. Visit their Web site for information on the activities and events scheduled to take place when you're passing through.

Lake Tahoe

Donner Spitz Hutte
$-$$ bkfst incl
sb
P.O. Box 8,
Norden 95724
☎*426-9108*
≈*426-3063*
If you're on a tight budget and your primary interest is skiing, try out this "bunk and breakfast" run by Alpine Skills International. Located at the top of the Donner Pass and right on the Sierra Crest, it feels secluded but is still only minutes away from great nordic, alpine and cross-country skiing. Mini-dorms with sleeping-bag bunks that sleep six to eight people are the main form of accommodation, but there are a limited number of private rooms as well. Breakfast is included and if you're here on a weekend or holiday you can participate in one of the generous community dinners. Other features are plowed parking and plentiful supplies of wine, espresso coffee, and domestic and imported beer.

Historic Camp Richardson Resort
$-$$$$
ℜ
P.O. Box 9028
South Lake Tahoe 96158
☎*541-1801 or 800-544-1801*
≈*541-1802*
www.camprichardson.com
Adjacent to the Tallac Historic Site and South Lake Tahoe, the year-round Camp Richardson Resort offers just about every type of accommodation and outdoor activity imaginable at a very reasonable price. Whether you're seeking a charming, historic hotel room, a lakefront cabin with a fully equipped kitchen, a beachside motel room or a place to pitch your tent or to park your RV, you'll find it along this 150-acre (60.7ha) terrain. In the winter, activities include cross-country skiing, snowshoeing, sleigh rides, sledding and lift packages for downhill skiing. In the summer, a full-service marina provides boat and kayak rentals. A mountain sports store and service facility offers horseback riding, mountain bike rentals, hiking and rock climbing. Lessons and tours can be arranged as well. The Beacon Bar & Grill offers decent food and is located right on the lake.

Royal Gorge Cross Country Ski Resort
$$-$$$$
sb/pb, ℜ, (all inclusive)
9411 Hillside Dr.
P.O. Box 1100
Soda Springs 95728
☎*426-3871 or 800-500-3871*
≈*426-9221*
www.royalgorge.com
How about waking up with the largest cross-country skiing network in the United States at your doorstep? If you stay at one of the lodges or cabins at Royal Gorge, this is what you can expect. A 60-room former hunter's lodge has been converted into what is known today as the Wilderness Lodge. This establishment is also blessed with a chef with a predilection for French cuisine served by candlelight. The spacious cabins are secluded and equipped with sauna-like bathroom facilities, woodstoves and wall-to-wall pine.

Restaurants

Weaverville

Pacific Brewery Cafe
$-$$
401 S. Main St.
☎*623-3000*
To eat a home-cooked meal while seated amid items that you might find in a local auction (old lamps, rifles, gold pans, street signs, etc.), drop into this former brewery for breakfast or lunch.

Mount Shasta

The Black Bear Diner
$
24hrs
401 W. Lake St.
☎*926-4669*
If you're travelling with little ones that like bears and hamburgers, or if you're the type that is predisposed to hamburger cravings in the middle of the night, you might keep this themed diner in mind.

Willy's Bavarian Kitchen
$-$$
107 Chestnut St.
☎*926-3636*
Being in the mountains might just put you in the mood for some hearty Bavarian wienerschnitzel or sauerbraten with spaetzle. If so, head for the wooden booths at Willy's. Vegetarians will be pleased to know that they can eat well.

Shasta Sunset Dinner Train
$$$$
Sat (except Jan), Fri (May to Oct), Thu (Jul to Sep)
☎*964-2142*
www.mctrain.com
If you have the money to spare on a four-course

gourmet meal served on a deluxe train that circles Mt. Shasta at sunset, the 3hr experience offered at the train depot in McCloud is well worth it.

Alturas

Niles Hotel Restaurant
$$$
304 S. Main St.
☎*233-3261*
www.nileshotel.com
Serving prime rib that is famous all over the county, this establishment is also a beautifully restored museum devoted to the Wild West. Hundreds of vintage photographs adorn the walls and eye-catching antiques are displayed throughout, making it difficult to stay seated.

Susanville

Grand Cafe
$
730 Main St.
☎*257-4713*
In a town that seems to stubbornly refuse to change with the times, you'll be at odds to find a more interesting time-warp experience than the one to be had at the Grand Cafe. A 30ft (9m) long formica counter with wooden swivel chairs is where regulars have been meeting for the past 75 years to catch up on all the local gossip while sipping coffee with breakfast, or soup at lunch.

Tahoe City

Wolfdale's Cuisine Unique
$$$-$$$$
640 N. Lake Blvd.
☎*583-5700*
www.wolfdales.com
Wolfdale's is the place to go on the northern shore of Lake Tahoe for gour-

met dining in the evening. The menu changes according to what is fresh, but is often based on locally caught seafood and game, and is complimented by a comprehensive wine list.

South Lake Tahoe

Alpen Sierra
$
822 Emerald Bay Rd.
☎*541-7449*
www.alpensierra.com
The best hot and iced mountain-roasted coffee around can be found here. Alpen also serves great teas (especially Chai tea and various Jet teas—fruits, green tea, ginkgo biloba and panax ginseng) and blended drinks (try the Mount Tallac: green tea chai blended with ice cream and white chocolate). Vegans take note: you can even add Rice Dream or Soy Milk in your coffee or tea for a small fee.

Evan's American Gourmet Cafe
$$$-$$$$
536 Emerald Bay Rd.
☎*542-1990*
www.evanstahoe.com
Housed in a charming South Lake Tahoe cottage, Evan's American Gourmet Cafe combines an eclectic and constantly fluctuating menu with a softly lit, artistically enhanced atmosphere. Make sure you leave some room for dessert. Call in advance to inquire about the daily menu and to make a dinner reservation.

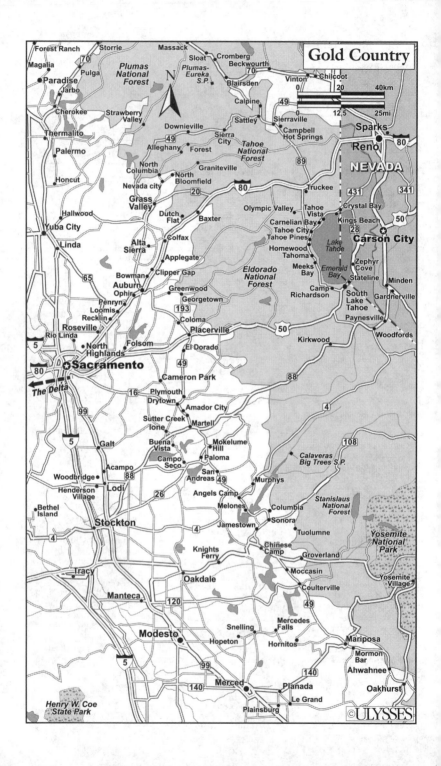

Sacramento, the Delta and Gold Country

A side from the hearty and colourful products of rich farmlands and a beautiful conglomeration of rivers and lakes, the city of Sacramento, the Delta Region and nearby Gold Country have a great deal of history to offer the inquisitive traveller.

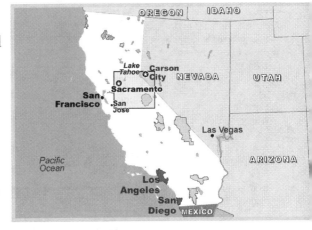

After all, it is here that the official U.S. experience of California began. If all California license plates end with the nostalgic epithet "The Golden State" it is due to what happened in and around the state capital of Sacramento in the middle of the 19th century.

It was not literal gold that John Sutter was dreaming of when, in 1839, he established a fort near the present-day site of Sacramento in order to protect immense stretches of some of the world's most fertile land from the greed of other colonists and Native American reprisal. No, his intention was to build a new empire of the interior, New

Helvetia, and finance it from profits derived from the labour of Native American slaves, who were coerced into cultivating a succession of golden harvests from the sacred grounds of their ancestors.

It *was* literal gold, however, that spelled the downfall of Sutter when it was discovered by one of his labourers, John Marshall, in 1848. Of course, it wasn't long before New Helvetia was invaded by hordes of migrant workers, prodigal farmers and out-

right opportunists who had absolutely no interest in agriculture— not at first, at least—and whose riding passion was gold, gold, gold.

By 1852 most of Sutter's own labourers joined forces with the roughly 150,000 others who had overcome sometimes life-threatening obstacles in order to try their luck at mining. As luck was often slow in coming— sometimes very slow, indeed—the buildings of Sutter's empire-to-be quickly became kindling for the campfires of the die-hard dreamers struggling to keep warm during the chilly Northern California winters. Sutter ended up going bankrupt.

Politicians often ride on the coattails of opportunity. Thus, it is not surprising that California achieved official statehood in 1850—only 2 years after the initial flakes of gold were found. A state capital was fashioned from the boom-town and supply centre of Sacramento in 1854, giving the "Big Four" train moguls a political base from which to launch plans for the first state railroad—eventually to become the first transcontinental railroad. Other transportation and communication infrastructures were soon to follow. For example, the first transcontinental telegraph message was sent from Sacramento in 1863 from the western end of the Pony Express.

At the turn of the 21st century, Sacramento is the little, somewhat conservative sister of the larger California metropoli of San Francisco, Los Angeles and San Diego. Despite this, it retains a more historical character and serves as a good point of departure to explore the remains of the ghost and boom-towns along the famous gold-trail of Route 49. You can also indulge in cheery, nourishing picnics featuring some of the best tomatoes, asparagus, cherries, grapes and almonds in the world.

Finding Your Way Around

By Plane

Sacramento International Airport
6900 Airport Blvd.
Sacramento, CA 95837
☎*(916) 874-0700*
Because it is served by numerous airlines, you may choose to come here directly if you are not interested in passing through San Francisco. American Airlines, Delta Airlines, Northwest Airlines and Southwest Airlines are just some of the companies that fly into Sacramento.

By Car

From San Francisco, the fastest way to Sacramento is via Route 80. A much more scenic route, however, which allows exploration of what is referred to as the Delta, is via Route 160. If you are not pressed for time, we strongly recommend the latter.

As for Gold Country, it is basically found along Highway 49, which can be reached by following Highway 80 past Sacramento.

Car Rental

If you are coming in via San Francisco, take advantage of the excellent rental car facility at the airport.

However, if you wish to find something in Sacramento, most major rental companies are found at the Sacramento Metropolitan Airport:

Avis
☎*(916) 922-5601*
☎ *800-331-1212*

Budget
☎*(916) 922-7316*
☎*800-527-0700*

Hertz
☎*(916) 927-3882*
☎*800-654-3131*

By Bus

Baylink Coach-Ferry
☎*(707) 64-FERRY*
www.baylinkferry.com
Service between San Francisco and Sacramento.

Public Transportation

Sacramento Regional Transit
☎*(916) 321-2877*

By Boat

Exodus Boat Cruises
mid-May to mid-Oct
Sun only
115 Front St., Suite 9
Sacramento, CA 95814
☎*447-0266*
A great way to get to Sacramento from San Franciso via the scenic route of the Sacramento Delta is to travel the way everyone did before the invention of the automobile.

By Carriage

One of the best ways to tour the Calaveras Big Trees is in a carriage pulled by draft horses.

Big Trees Carriage Company
Rte. 2, Box 22
Angels Camp, CA
☎ *(209) 728-2602*
☎ *(209) 736-6821*

Road Conditions
☎ *(916) 445-7623*
☎ *800-427-7623*

Practical Information

The area code is **916** unless otherwise indicated.

Tourist Information

Placer County Visitor Information
13464 Lincoln Way
Auburn, CA
☎ *530-887-2111*
www. placer.ca.gov
oplacer@ quiknet.com

Sierra County Visitor's Bureau
☎ *800-200-4949*
www.sierracounty.org

Grass Valley/Nevada County Chamber of Commerce
248 Mill St.
Grass Valley, CA 95945
☎ *(530) 273-4667*
info@gvncchamber.org
www.gvncchamber.org

Calaveras Visitors Bureau
1211 S. Main St.
Angels Camp, CA
☎ *800-225-3764*
www.visitcalaveras.org

Telecommunications

The Press

The Sacramento Bee is the main daily for Sacramento.

The Mountain Messenger
(published in Downieville)
For good old-fashioned small-town culture, this oldest California weekly can't be beat. If you are around in late April, ask for the special Fish Wrap edition.

The Union Democrat
(published in Sonora)
Another one of the oldest newspapers in continous publication, this rag is known for its variety, depth and great community news. It also has some awards to brag about.

Radio

KVMR 89.5FM
Nevada City, CA
www.kvmr.org
Hungry for intelligent local and international news interspersed with music and poetry?
Tune in to KVMR when you are in the Sierra Foothills or the Sacramento Valley.

KKBN 93.5 FM
Twain-Harte, CA
www.cabinradio.com
Tune in to soft hits from the 70s to today, along with the CBS News.

Internet

Jack's Internet Cafe
everyday 6am to 11pm
115 S. Church St.
Grass Valley, CA
☎ *(530) 477-SURF*
Need to check your e-mail? How about stopping off in Grass Valley and doing it with a gourmet coffee at your side?

Emergencies

Sierra Doctors
7 days/week
275 Grass Valley Hwy.
Auburn, CA
☎ *(530) 885-0344*

Exploring

The Delta

The best way to Sacramento and Gold Country is via the drawbridge and waterway-lined Highway 160. If you are coming from San Francicso, you have a choice of taking Highway 80 until Highwayy 4 and then turning right, or taking Highway 80 until Highway 12 and then turning right.

If you're travelling with children, you might prefer the Highway 12 route as there are at least two attractions along it that are bound to please youngsters: the **Jelly Belly Candyland Tour** in Fairfield *(2400 N. Watney Way, ☎707-428-2838)* and the **Western Railway Museum** *(Jul to Aug, Wed to Sun, and on weekends for the rest of the year; 5848 Rte. 12, ☎707-374-2978)* between Susan City and Rio Vista.

As for the Highway 4 option, there are a few detours off of this Highway that are well worth the effort.

Port Costa is a quaint port town that has remained virtually untouched by what the city folks refer to as progress. Getting lost in and around this town, which is surrounded by rolling farmland and forest, is a bit like entering a pleasant time warp.

Located just a short drive southeast from Port Costa, the relaxed small town of **Martinez** is home to the **John Muir National Historic**

Sacramento, Delta and Gold Country

Site *(4202 Alhambra Ave, Martinez;* ☎*925-228-8192; www.nps.gov/jomv).* The 17-room Victorian home is the former residence of the renowned naturalist and founder of the Sierra Club.

Finally, if you cross the Carquinez Strait from Port Costa, you will find yourself in **Benicia**, the small town that once dreamed of being the State capitol. Check out the Senate chamber of the **Benicia Capitol** *(W. First and G sts., Benicia,* ☎ *707-745-3385, www.cal-parks.ca.gov)* and the **Benicia Camel Barn Museum** *(2060 Camel Rd., Benicia,* ☎ *707-745-5435),* a yellow sandstone building which once housed a herd of dromedary camels that had been imported by the U.S. Army to help open the southwestern desert to settlement.

Sitting on the outskirts of Antioch, the 3,900 acre (1,578ha) **Black Diamond Mines Regional Preserve** *(Somersville Rd., Antioch,* ☎*925-757-2620, www.ebparks.org)* at the foot of Mt. Diablo, features over 34mi (54.7km) of biking and hiking trails in addition to a 19th-century cemetery with tombstones engraved in Welsh.

The end of Highway 4 veers north and turns into Highway 160 just about at the same point where the San Joaquin and Sacramento rivers converge. Once you have crossed the San Joaquin River, you are in what is referred to as Bayou Country.

An absolute must-see as you coast along these misty, levee-dotted flat-lands is the rural, clapboard Chinatown called **Locke** ★★★

(pop 75). This National Historic Site lays claim to fame as the only rural community in the United States to be built by and for the Chinese. In the early 1900s Locke was a rough and tumble Chinese Wild West town replete with gambling parlours, brothels, speakeasies and opium dens. These days Locke is a weathered and unpretentious outdoor museum of leaning, two-storey tumble-downs, wooden sidewalks and billowing clotheslines. Make sure that you drop by the **Locke Museum** and **Al the Wops**, one of the most unusual restaurants that you will come across anywhere. (See p 578)

Sacramento

The Nisenan Maidu Native Americans held sway in the Sacramento Valley for thousands of years before the smallpox epidemic of 1833 cut a huge swath in their ranks by killing 20,000 of them. Six years later John Sutter, an émigré from Switzerland, settled near the confluence of the Sacramento and American rivers and went to work with the aid of Hawaiians and local Native peoples to build an agricultural community, the nucleus of which developed into a fort. And thus modern Sacramento's history began.

Historically speaking, it makes perfect sense to begin your visit to Sacramento at the **California State Indian Museum** ★ *($3; every day 10am to 5pm; 2631 K St.,*☎*916-324-0971, ≈916-322-5231).* Here, collections of indigenous baskets, dance regalia and

tools, mostly from the Northwest Coast, enable you to peer into the culture of a population which at one time totalled 300,000 in California. A special display devoted to the man known as Ishi, the last Yahi, presents what he revealed about himself to his anthro-pologist host in his final years (1911-1916). Walk a few feet over to 2701 L Street to experience what life was like in the compound called **Sutter's Fort** ★★ *($3; every day 10am to 5pm,* ☎*916-445-4422),* the first white settlement in the Sacramento area. The fort is enclosed in walls that are 2.5ft (0.8m) thick, 15 to 18ft (4.8 to 5.5m) high and 320ft (97.5m) long. Audio information will enlighten you on your self-guided tour of the fort's rooms that include a prison, blacksmith shop, bakery, carpenter shop, dining room and living quarters. As successful as he initially was in establishing his New Helvetia (New Switzerland) as an agricultural kingdom (by 1845 he owned 1,700 horses and mules, 4,000 cattle and 3,000 sheep on 48,000 acres or 19,426ha), unscrupulous characters like squatters and swindlers spawned by the gold rush, coupled with Sutter's ineptitude at business, led to his financial undoing and the demise of his domain by the end of 1849.

Walking or driving a dozen blocks west of Fort Sutter brings you to the **California State Capitol** ★★★ *(free admission; Mon to Fri 7pm to 6pm, Sat and Sun 8:30am to 5pm; 10th and L sts.,* ☎*916-324-0333),* which is, in and of itself, a marvellous museum of California

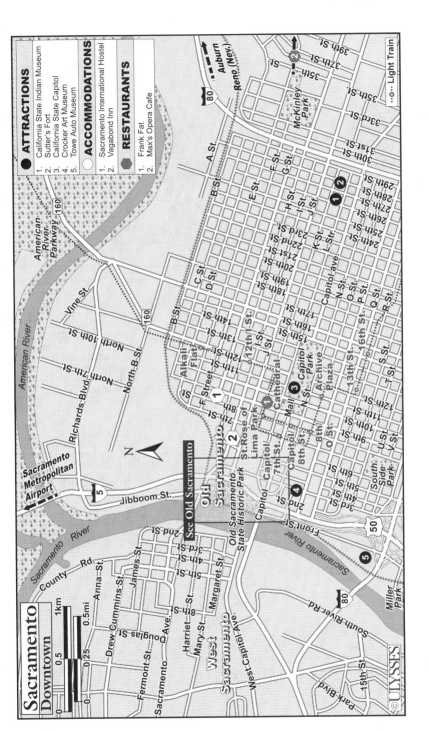

Sacramento Downtown

0   0.5   1km
0   0.25   0.5mi

© ULYSSES

ATTRACTIONS
1. California State Indian Museum
2. Sutter's Fort
3. California State Capitol
4. Crocker Art Museum
5. Towe Auto Museum

ACCOMMODATIONS
1. Sacramento International Hostel
2. Vagabond Inn

RESTAURANTS
1. Frank Fat
2. Max's Opera Cafe

.... Light Train

See Old Sacramento

Old Sacramento
State Historic Park

Sacramento Metropolitan Airport

American River

Sacramento River

American River Parkway

McKinley Park

Miller Park

South Side Park

Capitol Park

Rose of Lima Park

Archive Plaza

Capitol Mall

Reno, (Nev.)

Auburn

West Sacramento

California State Capitol

history. The first floor features the beautifully restored turn-of-the-century offices of the Governor, Attorney General, State Treasurer and Secretary of State. Looking up as you ascend the impeccably recreated staircases of Honduran mahogany and ash, on your way to the legislative chambers on the third floor, the craftsmanship that went into the restoration of the 120ft (36.6m) high rotunda is dazzlingly apparent. Galleries looking down on the Senate and Assembly Chambers allow visitors to closely observe the legislative-making centre of California, right down to the original desks made in 1869.

While you're in the vicinity, two stops are definitely in order. First, check out the **Wells Fargo History Museum** ★ *(free admission; Mon to Fri 10am to 5pm; 400 Capitol Mall, ☎916-440-4161)* where you can view all sorts of intriguing artifacts, among them a fully refurbished Concord Stagecoach. Your second stop should be at

the **Governor's Mansion State Historic Park** ★ *($3; every day 10am to 5pm; 1526 H St., ☎916-323-3047)* because you'll get a chance to tour the Victorian living quarters of 13 of California's governors from 1903 to 1967 and see furnishings reflective of their and their spouses' tastes.

Next on the agenda is probably the most important single building on Sacramento's artistic landscape, the **Crocker Art Museum** ★★★ *($4.50; Tue to Sun 10am to 5pm, Thu 10am to 9pm; 216 O St., ☎916-264-5423)*, the first public art museum in the west. Founded by the railroad tycoon Charles Crocker and his wife Margaret as an extension to their Victorian mansion, the museum has greatly expanded since 1873. It now houses, in addition to the original collection of principally European master drawings and paintings, 19th-century California paintings, contemporary California artwork and Asian ceramics. The museum now also plays host to

first-rate travelling exhibits such as, its recent photo sequence "Far From Home: The Latin Baseball Story" or the collection of 40-odd resonator guitars and related instruments, "Loud and Clear: Resonator Guitars and The Dopyera Brothers' Legacy to American Music."

The district known as Old Sacramento, eight city blocks on 28 acres (11.3ha) of riverfront, is the centre of the city's tourist activity. Numerous historic buildings alternating with shops, restaurants and museums will satisfy an extremely wide range of interests. One possible route to take would begin with the **Discovery Museum History Center** ★★ *($5; Memorial Day to Labour Day, every day 10am to 5pm; Labor Day to Memorial Day, Tue to Sun 10am to 5pm; 101 I St., ☎916-264-7057)*, a replica of the 1854 City Hall, that focuses on the gold rush. Next door, the still operational **Huntington 8 Hopkins Hardware** ★ *(free admission; 3 to 4 days each week, ☎916-323-7234)*, established in 1855, displays 19th century tools and hardware in a building called the Big Four in honour of Leland Stanford, Mark Hopkins, Collis P. Huntington and Charles Crocker, whose financial backing made it possible for the Transcontinental Railroad to be completed on Promontory Point, Utah on May 10, 1869. If railroad history is your passion, then you are in the right place, just a few paces from the finest railroad museum in the U.S., the **California State Railroad Museum** ★★★ *($6; every day 10am to 5pm; corner of Second and I sts., ☎916-445-6645)*. Do not rush through it. The sight

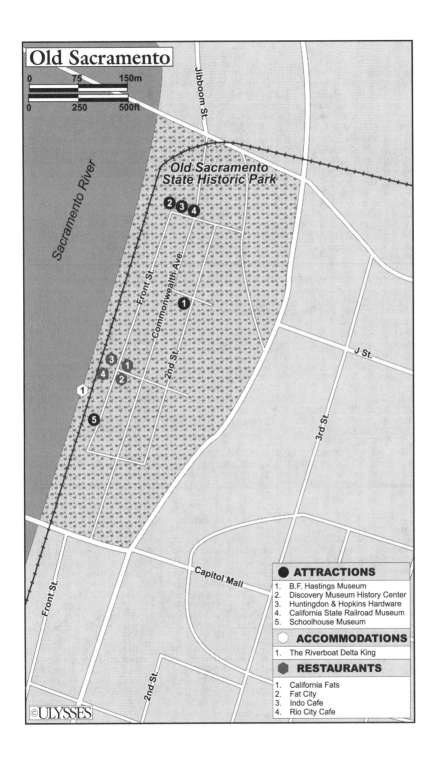

Old Sacramento

0   75   150m
0   250   500ft

Jibboom St.

Sacramento River

Old Sacramento
State Historic Park

Front St.

Commonwealth Ave.

2nd St.

J St.

3rd St.

Capitol Mall

Front St.

2nd St.

© ULYSSES

ATTRACTIONS
1. B.F. Hastings Museum
2. Discovery Museum History Center
3. Huntingdon & Hopkins Hardware
4. California State Railroad Museum
5. Schoolhouse Museum

ACCOMMODATIONS
1. The Riverboat Delta King

RESTAURANTS
1. California Fats
2. Fat City
3. Indo Cafe
4. Rio City Cafe

of all of these beautifully restored locomotives and railway cars, in a 100,000 sq ft (9,290m²) space, is nothing short of stunning. Don't miss climbing into the 1929 sleeping car *The Saint Hyacinthe* to experience simulated (even to the rocking motion!) nighttime travel. The reconstructed Central Pacific Passenger Depot, on Front Street between I and J streets, will give you a sense of what it was like to be on these premises back in their earliest days, the 1820s.

For one last destination in Old Sacramento, try the **Schoolhouse Museum ★** *(free admission; Mon to Sat 10am to 4pm, Sun noon to 4pm; Front and L sts)*. It is furnished with such items as McGuffey's readers and slates showing you the type of one-room school common in the Sacramento Valley in the late 1800s. Item #5 in a revealing "List of Instructions to the Teachers" drawn up in 1872 reads "After ten hours in the school the teacher should spend the remainder reading the Bible and other good books."

Not far from Old Sacramento, at 2200 Front Street, to be exact, the **Towe Auto Museum ★ ★** *($5; everyday 9am to 6pm, ☎916-442-6802)* will be a treat for anyone interested in the history of the automobile in America. More than 150 carefully restored antique vehicles await your inspection. Travel a few blocks east of the auto museum, to 10th and Broadway, and you'll arrive at a place where the residents have no further need for any mode of transportation, namely, the Sacramento Cemetery.

Founded in 1849, it is the final resting place for 20,000 pioneers. If you are history-minded, study the inscriptions chiselled in stone: they'll have much to tell you.

Gold Country

★★
Sierra City and Downieville

Wherever you begin to explore California gold rush country, you will most likely be on or near Highway 49, named after the fabled Forty-Niners, those thousands afflicted with gold fever who came to this part of California in 1849 to seek their fortune. The small Sierra Nevada town of Sierra City, at the highest altitude (4,100ft or 1,250m) of any community in the so-called Golden Chain of east-central California, not far from Reno and Lake Tahoe, is as good a place as any to start. It is reputedly the birthplace of that curious organization named E. Clampus Vitus, bogus latin for "from the handshake comes life." Mines in the Sierra Buttes, granite peaks which tower over the town, yielded staggeringly huge nuggets, some weighing over 1,000 ounces (28,350g)! And what arduous labour it took to extricate the gold and transport it down from heights of over 8,000ft (2,438m). Just a bit north of Sierra City, the grounds of the Kentucky mine, made over into the **Sierra County Historical Park**, will introduce the novice, through its museum and functioning stamp mill, to the kinds of mining equipment and machinery used during the almost 100 years the mine was

operated (from the late 1850s until 1953).

Thirteen miles (20.9km) west of Sierra City on Highway 49 is the remarkable town of **Downieville**, located at the confluence of the Yuba and Downie rivers. In 1850, about two years after gold deposits were first discovered here, the town had four bakeries, four butcher shops, and 15 hotels and gambling houses. Considerably quieter nowadays, Downieville is nonetheless regarded as the least changed of all of California's gold rush towns. Its narrow Main Street is lined with such historic buildings as the **Sierra County Museum**, once a Chinese store, opium den and gambling hall and the **Mountain Messenger Building**, named after California's oldest weekly newspaper, that has been published ever since 1853. Near where the rivers join, **Downieville Heritage Park** lets you inspect an assortment of mining equipment resting on the ground. A few feet away, next to the **Sierra County Courthouse**, the intact **Downieville gallows**, used only once in 1885 to hang a murderer, stands forbiddingly in the trees. If it's a grim piece of history you're after, look into the full story of the 1851 lynching of a woman named Juanita for the stabbing death of a miner who allegedly "pressed his attentions" upon her. But if you'd like to hear tales from the old days about driving a stagecoach or running mule-pack trains to the mines, look for an elderly gentleman sitting on a bench somewhere in town. If you're lucky, you'll find Gus Poggi, who will turn 90 in January of

2001, and get him to speak of his colourful past.

★★★
Nevada City

It was first named Deer Creek Dry Diggins in 1849, then Caldwell's Upper Store, then Nevada (Spanish for "snow-covered") and finally, Nevada City in order to avoid confusion after Nevada Territory was formed in 1861. The millions in gold that came out of this region, first through placer mining and later through hydraulic mining, underscored the city's importance—its natural role as the seat of Nevada County. Today Nevada City, 3mi (4.8km) north of Grass Valley, is easily one of the most authentic, attractive and sophisticated of the gold rush towns. Walking through its mostly steep, crazily arranged streets leads to building after building dating back to the 1850s and 1860s all of which are well preserved.

Gold rush statue

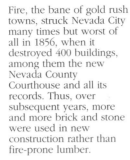

Fire, the bane of gold rush towns, struck Nevada City many times but worst of all in 1856, when it destroyed 400 buildings, among them the new Nevada County Courthouse and all its records. Thus, over subsequent years, more and more brick and stone were used in new construction rather than fire-prone lumber.

A good place to begin your walk is at one of the oldest buildings (1855) in Nevada City that today houses the **Chamber of Commerce** *(132 Main St.)* but was originally the home of the South Yuba Canal Company, a water system supplier for mining. Years later this company became one of the world's largest utility companies, the Pacific Gas & Electric Company. Next door is a brick two-storey building, Olt's Assay Office, through the doors of which passed some $27 million in gold, without even a single attempted robbery! Up the hill on Main Street, the gingerbread **Victorian Nevada Hose Company No. 1 Firehouse**, now turned into a museum, contains Maidu basketry, some Donner Party relics and the original Joss House altar of Grass Valley's Chinatown. Close by, the **Searles Library** *(215 Church St.)* is the repository of an interesting collection of Nevada County historical material. On gaslamp-lit Broad Street (401) stands the stone and brick **Nevada Theatre**, built in

1865, from whose the stage Mark Twain once lectured. The nearby elegantly furnished **National Hotel** has been open continuously since 1856. Its long bar downstairs in the saloon was shipped around the Horn (the southern tip of South America).

Other spots in Nevada City well worth visiting include the **Broad Street Pioneer Cemetery**, with its many graves inscribed with the names and dates of the town's earliest inhabitants, and the granite boulder on East Broad Street on which the Maidu clambered onto and reclined on so as to benefit from the combined healing powers of the rock and the sun. Several churches also merit a visit: **Saint Canice Catholic Church** (1864); **The Nevada City First Baptist Church** (1864); the **Trinity Episcopal Church** (1873); and the **Nevada City Methodist Church** (1864).

The cultural life of Nevada City is rich beyond belief for such a small town. Numerous theaters are devoted to live stage performance and/or film screenings, as well as to various kinds of music and dance productions. Fine bed and breakfasts, some of historic importance, and a number of good eating establishments guarantee that your stay in Nevada City will be thoroughly enjoyable.

★★★
Malakoff Diggins State Historic Park

For a totally unromantic picture of what gold mining can lead to, make a journey off Highway 49 either southwest from Downieville or northeast from Nevada City to the

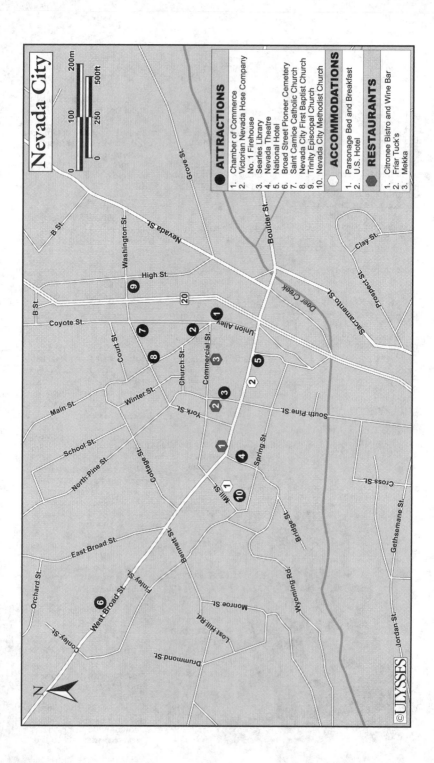

Nevada City

● ATTRACTIONS

1. Chamber of Commerce
2. Victorian Nevada Hose Company
3. No. 1 Firehouse
4. Searles Library
5. Nevada Theatre
6. National Hotel
7. Broad Street Pioneer Cemetery
8. Saint Camice Catholic Church
9. Nevada City First Baptist Church
10. Trinity Episcopal Church
11. Nevada City Methodist Church

⬡ ACCOMMODATIONS

1. Parsonage Bed and Breakfast
2. U.S. Hotel

⬢ RESTAURANTS

1. Citronee Bistro and Wine Bar
2. Friar Tuck's
3. Mekka

© ULYSSES

3,000-acre (1,214ha) Malakoff Diggins State Historic Park *(headquarters and museum; $5; ☎530-265-2740)*. Here you can see the horrendous price of the success of hydraulic mining, a method of extracting gold first practiced on a small scale in 1852 by one Antoine Chabot, but brought to diabolical and colossal perfection by the North Bloomfield Gravel Mining Company. This method of mining amounted to nothing more or less than blasting a hillside or mountainside with water through a large nozzle (known as a "monitor") under such great pressure that it could throw a 50 pound (22.7kg) boulder a large distance or kill a man or animal 200 or more feet (60m) away from the nozzle. Hillsides and mountainsides could not withstand such overwhelming force and came tumbling down. The sludge carrying the gold which was caught by sluices lining cuts or tunnels eventually piled up in a river or canyon.

Collecting and storing the water for this operation required an elaborate system of dams, lakes and reservoirs and the contribution of hundreds of miles of pipelines, ditches, tunnels and flumes. By November 15, 1874, the Malakoff Mine, the world's largest hydraulic mining undertaking, had completed the amazing feat of cutting an 8,000ft-long (2,438m) drainage tunnel through solid bedrock. This enabled the North Bloomfield Company to dump its mine tailings into the South Yuba River. The monstrous creation that resulted from mining the deep gravels (dry ancient

E Clampus Vitus

Plaques, plaques, plaques—historic sites throughout gold rush country receive recognition in the form of plaques because of the efforts of the Ancient and Honorable Order of E. Clampus Vitus. This organisations origins go back to 1850, when Joseph Zumualt "brought with him the secrets of the ancient and honorable order of E. Clampus Vitus and founded its first chapter." These origins are only credible if you can believe an inscription cut in stone on one of the main streets of Downieville—after all, it concludes with the exclamation *Credo Quo Absurdum*.

The brotherhood of E. Clampus Vitus was initially conceived as a mockery of the serious and secretive fraternal organizations of the day, but eventually made it its business to assist the widows and orphans of miners killed in the mines. However, above all else it now devotes itself to having a good time partying and carou-

sing while at the same time promoting an interest in California history.

One sentence on the wall of Comparative Ovations on Murphy's Main Street stands out as indicative of the quintessential spirit of the Clampers: "Every member held an office of equal indignity." Noble Grand Humbugs "presided" over meetings. The word presided is within quotation marks because if every member was of equal indignity then, of course, no one could assume authority over anyone else. In the gold rush days, the braying of "Hewgag" by the Clampers as they assembled does not sound the least bit out of character.

Can there be any doubt that a particularly uniformative and anonymous plaque in Georgetown is the work of a spoofer of spoofs? It reads "On this site in 1897, nothing happened." Yes, indeed—*Credo Quia Absurdum* (Believe what is absurd).

riverbeds) was the Malakoff Mine pit. At the peak of the company's frenzied activity, the pit became a crater about 7,000ft (2,134m) long, 3,000ft (914m) wide and

600ft (183m) deep (about 300ft or 91m deep today as a result of erosion).

The consequences for farming, not to mention fishing and navigating in the Sacramento and Yuba rivers, was devastating. For example, mine debris elevated the bottom of the Yuba to a level higher than the town and thus brought on very destructive flooding. Furthermore, the Sacramento River rose to the point that it flooded and seriously damaged the agricultural heart of the Central Valley. Farmers could not allow their land and livelihood to be endangered. Fortunately for them a Marysville property owner successfully filed suit agains the North Bloomfield Mining Company. A judge named Lorenzo Sawyer heard the case and handed down a landmark decision in January of 1884 that forbade further dumping of tailings into the Yuba River. The Sawyer decision, the first environmental legislation in the United States, put an end to hydraulic mining in California.

The ghost town that North Bloomfield inevitably became lies within the Malakoff Diggins State Historic Park. Several of the town's original buildings still stand, among them its oldest, the **E. Clampus Vitus Building**. But what will no doubt leave the most lasting impression on visitors is the spectacular work of art that time, nature and human beings have wrought here. A frightening beauty, manifest in strong rock and gravel colours and in bizarre landscape configurations, stuns the eye.

★★★
Empire Mine State Historic Park

Even those with only a slight interest in the history of mining will find the Empire Mine State Historic Park (*$3; everyday 9am to 6pm, winter 10am to 5pm, just off Hwy. 49; 10791 E. Empire St., Grass Valley, ☎530-273-8522*) fascinating. Next door to the visitor center, the Model Room provides a good idea of the vastness of the Empire State mine complex through its wonderfully executed large-scale model. Imagine a main shaft connected to 367mi (590km) of tunnels, shafts and drifts, some of the former 11,000ft (3,353m) on the incline, and reaches to a vertical depth of more than 5,000ft (1,524m)! You can't do much more than imagine this though because today the tunnels are, vertically, under 180 feet of water. The park does, however, feature an intact shaft opening, where wheeled carts called skips that carried men and ore used to speed up and down on the railroad tracks. Imagine also, if you can, mules (by World War I) with their sure-footedness and stamina pulling ore carts to the main shaft, from which the ore was hoisted to the surface. In October 1850, George D. Roberts stumbled upon a quartz ledge bearing gold that he called Ophir Hill (Old Testament Ophir was the source of gold for Solomon's Temple). There was no way he could have known it at the time, but this discovery was one of the deepest, richest and oldest hard rock gold mines of them all. By 1856, when the year the mine closed down for good, it had produced more than 5.8 million oz (164,430,000g) of gold, which at today's prices, would be worth more than $2 billion. The Empire Mine had more than its fair share of troubles, financial and otherwise, before 22-year old William Bourn Jr., son of the previous owner, came to the rescue. By 1879, after four difficult years of systematic probing into how to make the mine work safely and profitably, the Empire Mine moved into an extended period of continuous growth and profit.

Over the years, whether lean or prosperous, the mine was fortunate, thanks in large part to the expertise of men from Cornwall, England who had a 1000-year tradition of hardrock tin and copper mining behind them. Their immense contribution is confirmed by the reputed fact that they made up 85% of the population of Grass Valley by 1890.

Those responsible for reconstructing and/or maintaining the Empire Mine have clearly done everything they can to give visitors a sense of what the mine buildings, offices, workshops and equipment were like in their heyday. A good example of this is the Refinery Room, where amalgam, the result of washing stamp mill sand (a stamp mill is a huge ore-pulverizing devise) with quicksilver or mercury, which "captured the gold," was heated in a sealed retort, separating the gold from the amalgam. In 1910, a 40% more productive method was introduced that utilized sodium cyanide's ability to separate the gold from the sulfides, depositing it on zinc chips. The Machine Shop's machinery (for example, drills and lathes) was driven (after the retirement of uneconomic steam power in 1886) by energy produced by another important innovation: the Pelton Water Wheel. Lest you forget just how far technology had to come, the Empire Mine Park includes a blacksmith shop, revealing that in the earliest days, skilled workers had to make just about every piece of equipment on-site.

The Empire Mine's reputation for its deep concern for the safety of its employees and for its state-of-the-art operations attracted people from all over the world to study its *modus operandi*. One day, it just may attract a whole new crowd of mining people who know that there's still plenty of gold down below and who will devise new ways to extract it without going broke in the process! In the meanwhile, visitors to the park might want to end their day at the mine by stopping to look at the younger Bourn's cottage, a mansion, which compels you to admire its elegance and the surrounding property with its carefully attended lawns, rose gardens, fountains and reflecting pool. You can top it all off by biking along one of the many trails in the 750 acres (304ha) of forested countryside that belongs to the park.

Grass Valley

One October night in 1850, a Grass Valley miner named George McKnight, while chasing a runaway cow, stumbled over a rocky ledge on a hillside and accidentally broke off a piece. The moonlight reflecting off the rock told him that he had gold in his hands, which he soon confirmed back at his cabin after pulverizing the rock into fine sand with a hammer and then panning the sand. This discovery ignited a wild scramble for more gold on Gold Hill and initiated a boom in hardrock mining which eventually made Grass Valley the most famous and richest region in the entire Mother Lode, as well as the largest gold mining town in California. Many of the miners responsible for this success were from Cornwall, England. They came to be known by the moniker Cousin Jack, because whenever a mine needed an extra worker, a Cornish miner would always be able to call on "my cousin Jack." You would think that the explosive growth of Grass Valley would have been significantly checked by the fire of September 13, 1855, which in two hours, wiped out all 300 of its original buildings and devastated some 30 acres (12.1ha). But no, the town quickly rebuilt itself, this time mostly with brick and stone. In large part, these structures have survived to the present day. One such place that is especially worth a look is the elegant **Holbrooke Hotel** (*212 West Main St.*). Search the hotel's old account books and you'll find the illustrious names of Mark Twain and Presidents Grant, Harrison and Cleveland.

Two women left a lasting mark on Grass Valley history: Lola Montez and Lotta Crabtree. Dancer, actress and mistress to King Ludwig of Bavaria, Lola Montez scandalized the town of Grass Valley for a couple of years by performing the "Spider Dance" on stage and presiding over a European-style salon. Lotta Crabtree, the six-year old neighbour girl she gave song and dance lessons to, later achieved considerable fame as an actress and became the first woman millionare in the United States. A replica of the **Lola Montez Home** contains a small museum as well as the local Chamber of Commerce. Lotta Crabtree's original home stands a few feet away on Mill Street.

Today there is no trace of where Harvard professor and successor to William James, Josiah Royce (1855-1916) was born, but this Grass Valley native can lay claim to being one of the few great philosophers the United States has ever produced.

Housed in what was originally the North Star Mine Power House, is the **Nevada County Historical Museum** (*Allison Ranch Rd. off Hwy. 20*). This fine mining museum has the world's largest Pelton Wheel on display, 30ft (9.1m) in diameter and weighing 10 tons (10.2 tonnes), which generated the power needed to run various kinds of mining machinery. A half mile (0.8km) down the same road, the ruins of the foundations of the **North Star Sixty-Stamp Mill** silently attest to the gold mining grandeur that once reigned here. To obtain a fuller notion, however, of how a hardrock mine looked and functioned, take a complete tour of **The Empire Mine State Historic Park** (*10791 E. Empire St.*) and you'll be richly rewarded (see p 562).

Sacramento, Delta and Gold Country

Auburn

Thirty-odd miles (48km) southwest of Grass Valley on Highway 49, you will cross Interstate Highway 80 and arrive in Auburn. Situated at such an important crossroads means that today Auburn is a fully equipped modern city, just as it was a main trading and supply centre for Placer County during and after the gold rush days. (The Central Pacific Railway, after all, passed through Auburn on the way to Donner Pass.) On Washington Street, a huge 10-ton (10.2 tonnes) **statue** of Frenchman Claude Chana panning gold recalls the day in the spring of 1848 when this friend of James Marshall came up with three gold nuggets while panning in the north fork of the American River. Thereafter, Auburn became one of the major gold mining towns in Northern California.

Although it does not date back to the gold rush period, having been constructed between 1894 and 1898, the **Placer County Courthouse** *(101 Maple St.)*, sitting on a hill overlooking the "Old Town," is easily Auburn's most handsome architectural specimen and a perfect place from which to begin a stroll about town. On the first floor, inside the courthouse, the **Placer County Museum's** exhibits give an excellent introduction to life in Placer County in bygone mining days and to Indigenous culture through the Pate Collection and a Native American habitat with its own sound track. Down the hill in "Old Town," the **Auburn Hook & Ladder Company Firehouse** (1893) with its unusual bell tower has a volunteer fire department that is one of California's oldest, dating back to November 1852.

Almost next door, the **Wells Fargo Building** and the **Post Office Building** (California's oldest still in its original home) survived the horrendous fire of 1885. Three Chinese stores—the three brick buildings on the south side of Sacramento Street—are replacements for their wooden predecessors, which didn't survive that fire. Their basements served as gambling rooms, brothels and opium dens!

The **Traveler's Rest Hotel** (1851) *(291 Auburn-Folsom Rd.)* bought by German-born Benjamin Bernhard in 1868 as a home for his family, sits on a hill. It is fully refurnished in Victorian style to show how a middle class 19th century farm family might have lived. Still standing is the winery with it 2ft-thick (0.6m) rock walls built by the viticulturist Bernhard in 1874 on hotel property. It used to produce first-rate Zinfandel, sherry, port and grape brandy. The hotel and winery, together with a wine-processing building (1881) and a rebuilt carriage barn, constitute the **Bernhard Museum Complex** *(Tues to Fri 10:30am to 3pm, weekends noon to 4pm)*. Tours are led by the Placer County Museum Docent Guild.

A good way to finish your walking tour of Auburn is to stroll at a leisurely pace through the fine **Gold County Museum** *(Tue to Fri 10:30am to 3pm, weekends noon to 4pm; 1273 High St. on the Gold County Fairgrounds)*. Here you will find very informative exhibits on the gold rush and mining technology. A walk-through mine tunnel, a working stamp mill model and a replica of an early tent saloon, including a faro table, are sure to delight and instruct.

Georgetown — Coloma

If you find yourself in either Auburn of Placerville and would like to experiment with an interesting alternative to Highway 49, take Highway 193 to Georgetown. In its earliest days, this town was known as Growlersburg because its nuggets were supposed to be so large that they growled in a gold pan! Like so many gold rush towns, made up of tents and shacks to begin with, this town burnt down (1852) and had to be completely rebuilt. In so doing, Georgetown changed its location from a canyon to its present hillside site, using brick and stone and fire-proof iron doors in its reconstruction. Furthermore, it made its Main Street 100ft (30.5m) wide (which is why you see cars parked in the very middle of the street) and its side streets 60ft (18.3m) wide. Benefitting from its location well off the beaten track, Georgetown is refreshingly untouched by frantic tourism and therefore is a pleasant place to appreciate gold rush buildings at a leisurely pace.

On the contrary, when you arrive at Coloma, more or less halfway between Auburn and Placerville on Highway 49, you will, no doubt, have to contend with large crowds of visitors. It will be worth it, however, to perservere and familiarize yourself with the Coloma of today, which exists namely as

Marshall Gold Discovery State Historic Park. This is where it all began, that extraordinary phenomenon known as the gold rush that triggered the creation of the State of California and, in the process, afflicted tens of thousands of people with a fever for gold that, more often than not, dashed expectations and left many no better or—often worse—off than they were before. On the morning of January 24, 1848, James Marshall inadvertently set off the stampede for gold, while inspecting the tailrace of a sawmill in the Sierra Foothills which he and a crew of Mormons and Native Americans were in the process of building for John Sutter. Detecting glittering particles in the ice cold water, Marshall knew right away he had found gold. That Coloma's gold was almost completely mined within three years, or that Marshall and Sutter themselves ended up poor and despondent, did not really matter since the wild horses of history were off and running.

Unlike the populace of most other gold rush towns, Coloma's first residents lived in wooden frame houses, built out of lumber supplied by Sutter's sawmill, instead of in makeshift tents or shacks. This first important gold rush mining town sprang up so quickly that by the summer of 1848, thousands resided there and their currency became gold dust. The State Historic Park is an ambitious preservation and/or recreation of what Coloma was like when it was the hub of gold rush madness. The logical thing to investigate first is the operational replica of

Sutter's Mill near the South Fork of the American River, apparently a remarkably faithful rendering of the original mill. Various timbers and tools that were found at the original millsite are now exhibited across the highway at the Gold Museum, which doubles as a visitor centre. Its collections of Maidu artifacts, James Marshall mementos and historical displays will prove most informative.

On the outskirts of town, the **Pioneer Cemetery** *(Cold Springs Rd.)* contains the remains of about 500 of the earliest citizens of Coloma. Although the gravestones date back to 1850, there may be older graves once marked by wood which have disappeared. Up Monument Road, at the top of Marshall Hill, and looking down on what he set in motion, stands James Marshall, or more accurately, a 10'6" tall (3.2m) bronze **statue** of him mounted on a 31ft (9.4m) granite pedestal. Down a short walk from the monument, a reconstruction of **Marshall's Cabin** is furnished as it might have been when he lived there.

In town, many buildings deserve attention, but perhaps the most notable is **Frank Bekeart's Gunsmith Shop**, built out of bricks in 1855. His stock in trade includes: "Guns, Pistols, Powder Flasks, Shot Belts and Pouches, Game Bags, Bowie Knives and Pocket Cutlery." Only the **Man Lee** and **Wah Hop Stores** have survived from a once large Chinese settlement in Coloma. Constructed of native stone, these stores sold Chinese miners their traditional food and

clothing, in addition to other goods.

Rather than simply perusing buildings, a much less passive way of learning about the past at Marshall Gold Discovery State Park is to partake in what are called **Living History Activities**. The list of possibilities is impressive: quilting, blacksmithing, goatmilking, rag rug crocheting, cornhusk and muslin dollmaking, bonnetmaking, gold panning, butter churning, outdoor pioneer cooking and weaving and spinning. Witnessing these various activities will help put you in close touch with a bygone era.

Volcano

On the way into Volcano, off Highway 88 east of Jackson, stop at the **Chaw'se Indian Grinding Rock Historic Park**, perhaps to camp, but certainly to visit the **Chaw'se Regional Indian Museum**. In the meadow adjacent to the museum Miwok women used to crush acorns and other seeds, and you will see hundreds of huge grinding stones and petroglyphs. Here you will also see a reconstructed Native American village with a ceremonial roundhouse.

In Volcano itself, the first place to catch your eye will probably be the town's largest building, the three-storey brick **Saint George's Hotel**, built in 1863 for a fourth and final time after three total annihilations by fire. The **Volcano Schoolhouse**, the **Sing Kee Store** (1854) made of native stone with iron shutters, the **IOOF & Masonic Hall** (1856), the limestone facade of the **Kelley and Symonds Store** (1855), the **Clute Building**

(1855), the **General Store** (1854) and the **Methodist-Episcopal Church** (1852) are among the other structures that will together, transport you to the days of the gold rush. This time-travel is even more effective given that Volcano is not tarnished by the commercial clutter of the likes of convenience stores, motels and gas stations.

Volcano can brag about being the first town in California to attain a number of impressive achievements, such as: a lending library, the Miners' Library Association (1854); an astronomical observatory (the work of geologist George Madeira, who discovered a comet on the night of June 30, 1861); an amateur theatrical company, the Volcano Thespian Society; a private law school; the first publication, in 1855, of a philosophy text, *Horn's Examiner into the Laws of Nature*; and a literary debating society called the Volcano Lyceum.

Today, the gold is long gone and the town's population numbers not much more than 100, but the charm and authenticity of the place is strong enough that you may want to linger on and perhaps enjoy a picnic. Take time to wander through **Soldier's Memorial Park** in Soldiers Gulch (Volcano's original name) and you will understand why, on the basis of molten rock formations here, miners believed that they were standing within the crater of a defunct volcano. Examining a bronze cannon cast in Boston in 1837 will raise more questions than can be answered except

one—why is it in town? The answer is that it was supposed to deter southern sympathizers from making off with gold to assist the Confederacy during the Civil War. Apparently, the cannon did its job without firing a single shot! To end the day in style, you might want to attend a play at the **Cobblestone Theatre** or, in summer, across the street at the **Amphitheatre**.

Placerville

Placerville, pronounced as if it were spelled Plasserville, was first known as Dry Diggins (1848) because water was not available on-site for miners to separate gold from gravel and sand. By the time it had replaced Coloma as the seat of El Dorado County in 1854, Dry Diggins had earned the ominous name of Hangtown because of the 1849 oak tree lynching on Main Street of three men guilty of attempted robbery and suspected additional crimes. It received its third and present name as the result of having so many placer holes in its streets that it made them almost impassable.

By 1854, when it was incorporated, Placerville had grown so rapidly that its voting population was exceeded only by that of San Francisco and Sacramento. When the gold ran out, Placerville was certain to flourish for three reasons: 1) it was the gateway and hence the supply centre to the Overland Trail which led across the Sierras to mines both in the north and the south; 2) as of 1859, it was on the direct route to Nevada's Comstock Lode, the center of the "silver

rush"; and 3) as of 1860, it was a Pony Express stop.

As a breeding ground for highly successful entrepreneurship, Placerville was hard to beat. Two of the future four big Central Pacific Railroad magnates, Mark Hopkins and Collis P. Huntington, got their business start selling groceries and other supplies here. Butcher Philip Armour parlayed $6,000 worth of gold dust accumulated between 1852 and 1856 into his Chicago-based meat-packing empire. And between 1852 and 1858, John Studebaker made enough money building and selling wheelbarrows to miners at $10 a shot to launch a business making buggies and wagons in South Bend, Indiana, which eventually became the Studebaker Automobile Corporation.

Once you've accepted that there are no straight streets in Placerville because they very closely follow the original pathways the gold rush miners used on hills and through gulches, ravines and creeks, you'll be ready to visit some of its historic attractions here. While the **Boyles Building** *(248 Main St.)* operated as the town's post office, a man named Snowshoe Thompson became famous as the mailman who skied on 10ft (3m) skis over the Sierras to Nevada and back in five days with the mail and all sorts of other necessities, like medicine. The **Placerville Soda Works** *(594 Main St.)* has within its bowels rooms and tunnels to store ice and soda and, on the second storey, a bottling room. You can also check out the ruins of what was once the **Zeisz Brewery** *(658 Main St.)*.

Pony Express

In the 1850s, the Butterfield Overland Stage Company was the largest passenger and freight carrier on the U.S. plains. A rival freighting firm (which up to then hauled supplies in ox-drawn covered wagons) headed up by three men, Russell, Majors and Waddell, hoping to win a federal mail contract, started a new kind of speedy mail delivery service by pony rider relays called the Pony Express. The aim was to halve the time it usually took to get mail to California. On April 3, 1860, on the inaugural run, which began in Saint Joseph, Missouri, alternating riders completed the 1,800mi (2,897km) journey to Sacramento, California in a little over 10 days. It took plenty of courage and stamina to traverse the difficult geography of the deserts, valleys, hills and badlands. No wonder bonfires and parades greeted the final rider as he came by boat into San Francisco.

The trip from Saint Joseph to Sacramento via Salt Lake City required 500 fine horses, 190 waystations and 80 (40 in each direction) riders with an average age of 18. Parcels costing $5 a half ounce and telegrams costing $3.50 for 10 words were wrapped in oiled silk and then carried in a leather pouch at full gallop by riders expected to cover 75 to 100mi (121 to 161km) per run at an average 9mph (14km/h), day and night, and to change horses in a maximum of two minutes. In November 1860, news of Lincoln's election travelled from Fort Kearney, Nebraska to Fort Churchill, Nevada in the especially fast time of six days. Just imagine—all of the more than 200 Pony Express riders (the most famous among them Buffalo Bill and Wild Bill Hickok) received bibles from their employers and were forbidden to drink or smoke!

The winter of 1860-61 amounted to a critical test of the Pony Express's ability to survive. Added to the usual floods, Native American uprisings, wolves, panthers and mountain lions were the harsh conditions of winter itself. The mail deliveries did take several days longer, but they were delivered. However, the building of a trans-continental telegraph line constituted a far greater threat. Indeed, by October 24, 1861, the line had been completed; the short life of the Pony Express was over. Russell, Majors and Waddell not only never obtained the mail contract they sought, but also went bankrupt, losing $100,000 to $200,000. Within 18 months, technology rendered the Pony Express obsolete.

How the **Jane Stuart Building**, next to the City Hall, came to be is at least as interesting as the building itself. Stuart raised the money to build the place by selling a herd of horses she had driven across the plains. The 1898 **Steel Bell Tower** on Main Street tolled for fires and for other catastrophes, but also to summon the townspeople to special gatherings. Relocated to Thompson Way, the **Methodist Episcopal Church**, built in 1851, features local hand-hewn Ponderosa pine. An inverted ship's hull design distinguishes the interior of the 1865 **Episcopal Church of Our Saviour** (at the corner of Coloma and Conrad). At the **El Dorado County Historical Museum** on the El Dorado County Fairgrounds (100 Placerville Dr.), you can complete your survey of historic Placerville by taking in its gold rush general store, stage-coaches, trains, mining paraphernalia, a Studebacker wheelbarrow and Native American artifacts.

Jackson

First the county seat of Calaveras County in 1851 and then, three years later, of the newly formed Amador County, Jackson had two major mines on its northern perimeter, the Kennedy Mine and the Argonaut Mine. The former had its beginnings when a rich quartz vein was discovered in 1856 by an Irish immigrant named Andrew Kennedy. Eventually, this claim, along with others, grew to be one of the richest gold mines in North America. By the time it was closed because of wartime priorities in 1942, it had reached a record depth of 5,912ft (1,802m).

Long after the gold rush, in an attempt to comply with federal anti-debris legislation, the Kennedy Mine built a series of four tailing wheels, to carry the wastes that polluted rivers and streams and threatened farmland with flooding to an impounding basin half a mile from the mill. Two of the huge wheels, 58ft (17.7m) in diameter, still stand as evidence of 28 years (from 1914 to 1942) of serious efforts to prevent environmental damage.

The neighbouring Argonaut Mine also reached remarkable vertical depth (5,520ft or 1,682m) and produced great wealth. From its discovery in the mid 1850s by two black miners, until 1893, the mine was not worked to anywhere near its full potential. In August of 1922, it had the horrendous distinction of being the site of California's worst mining disaster when 47 men were trapped close to 5,000ft (1,524m) below the

surface and died of asphyxiation after fires and explosions devastated the mine.

Much earlier, between 1851 and 1855, Jackson entered the annals of history in another dubious way: 10 men were lynched from its Hanging Tree, the likeness of which apparently appears on the county seal. But to be fair to Jackson, you ought to turn your attention to its historical legacy apparent in the many interesting structures that line its streets. The **National Hotel**, for instance, has been around for close to 140 years of continuous operation, during which its saloon and bedrooms— one of them designated the "Bordello Suite"—have been frequented by many nationally well-known guests.

The nearby **Wells Fargo Club and Restaurant** is a curiosity in that it is made up of three distinct sections, runs for 150ft (45.7m) along Water Street, and was built over a period of nearly 50 years. The I.O.O.F building's third storey lays claim to being a most unusually tall third storey. For strikingly graceful architecture, your best bet in town is **Saint Patrick's Catholic Church** (1868) *(121 Court St.)*. Another church deserving of a visit is the **Saint Sara Serbian Orthodox Church** *(724 Main St.)*, created by the large contingent of Serbians living in Jackson in the 1890s.

When the worst fire in the town's history struck in 1862, an important piece of history would have gone up in smoke, had officials of the Amador County Courthouse not been able to bring the

county records across the street to the **Hubbard Fry Law Office** *(103 Court St.)*. The Ledger of August 29 conveys the horror succinctly: "*Within 20 minutes all our courthouse hill was wrapped in flames....The devouring flames swept like a whirlwind in every direction, and in less than three hours the whole town was either flames or ashes.*"

The **Amador County Museum**, in the two-storey brick Brown Home, constructed in 1859, is a fine museum. Since it is blessed with an abundance of relics from Jackson's gold rush past as well as different kinds of mining equipment on the grounds, you should not leave town before paying a visit.

Mokelumne Hill and San Andreas

Hurrying south down Highway 49 several miles from Jackson, you might miss the turnoff to Mokelumne Hill, and that would be a shame, since its block-long center is a pleasant place to dawdle for awhile. The richness of the earliest claims around what came to be known as Moke Hill led to a limit of 16 sq ft (1.5m²) per claim and one per man. Those limits in turn led to a "Chilean War" in 1849 and a "French War" in 1851, both jurisdictional disputes. The handsome **Hotel Leger**, dating back to the mid-1850s, is still in operation and, according to latest reports, is still a meeting place for the Ancient and Honorable Order of E. Clampus Vitus, which held some of its earliest (1851) meetings right here (see p 577).

At first inhabited almost exclusively by Mexicans

(1848-1851), **San Andreas** lured miners from all over the world after a prehistoric riverbed was discovered underneath the town in 1853. Thereafter, San Andreas enjoyed immense prosperity for many years. In fierce competition with Mokelumne Hill, San Andreas won out in the 1854 election for county seat of Calaveras County. Like Mokelumne Hill, San Andreas has but one block-long historically significant street. Undoubtedly, the most compelling place on the street to spend time in is the **Calaveras County Museum Complex** *(30 N. Main St.).* Mining artifacts on display include rocker boxes, gold pans and gold scales; the Chinese exhibit includes photos, tombstones, medicine bottles and herbs, a wooden gold pan, brass spoons and an incense burner. What may intrigue the history-minded visitor most about the premises, however, is their connection to the infamous bandit known as Black Bart.

Over a period of eight years, from 1875 to 1883, Black Bart, a masked bandit who always acted alone, robbed 28 stagecoaches. All that Black Bart left behind after a Russian River robbery he committed in August of 1877 was the following doggerel: *"I've labored long and hard for bread, /For honor and for riches,/ But on my corns too long you've tred,/ You fine-haired sons of bitches."* He signed this verse "Black Bart, the PO8" (poet). One year later, a masked man robbed a stagecoach travelling from Quincy to Oroville of $379 cash, a silver watch and a diamond ring once again

leaving behind some verses, signed as before, Black Bart, the PO8.

Despite hefty rewards for his capture, Black Bart continued as a highly successful bandit until November 3, 1883. In his haste to get away from his pursuers, the bandit left behind evidence (a handkerchief with a laundry mark) which was traced to a Charles E. Bolton in San Francisco. Brought back to San Andreas to stand trial in the Calaveras County Courthouse on November 17, Charles E. Bolton (alias Black Bart) spent three days awaiting trial in one of the five cells of the Calaveras County Jail. His cell has been preserved to look pretty much as it must have looked at the time. A final note on this most accomplished of Californian bandits: having served about four years of a six-year sentence in San Quentin, Charles E. Bolton was released and soon after vanished from sight forever.

★
Murphys

A few miles east of Angels Camp on Highway 4, the town of Murphys welcomes you with its charming Main Street lined with locust trees, along or near which you will come across plenty to keep you occupied. Founded in 1848 by brothers John and Daniel Murphy, Murphys was the location of some of the richest placers in Calaveras County. John Murphy's ability to get along with Native Americans literally paid off, as the San Andreas *Independent,* reminiscing about 1848, makes exceedingly clear: *"Only a few days previous to our*

arrival an Indian had found a five-pound lump of gold for which Murphy gave him a blanket." At the time he left camp for good, in December of 1849, John Murphy already possessed more gold than anyone else on the West Coast.

Among the buildings in town of special interest, **Murphys Hotel** *(457 Main St.)* is certainly pre-eminent. This fine-looking establishment, on the National Register of Historic Places, opened in August of 1856 as the Perry and Sperry Hotel, a good place to stay on the way to Calaveras Big Trees State Park. Rebuilt after a fire in 1859, the iron shutters and wrought-iron balconies are characteristic of Mother Lode architecture at its best. The list of illustrious guests who have spent at least a night here is long and most impressive: Horatio Alger Junior, John Jacob Astor, J.P. Morgan, Daniel Webster, John Crocker, President Ulysses S. Grant, William Randolph Hearst and Mark Twain to name a few. (see p 578) For a good laugh after perusing such a serious list, cross the street and study what E. Clampus Vitus has to say on its **Wall of Comparative Ovations**.

Other notable structures in Murphys include the **Bonnet/Compere Building** *(570 Main St.)* a store that once sold provisions to miners and is now a private home. Constructed of rhyolite blocks and limestone rubble in 1858 by Pierre Bonnet, it is a unique piece of architecture. Having survived Murphys' three major fires in 1859, 1874 and 1893, the Peter L. Traver Building, built in 1856 and now home to the

Old Timers Museum, merits special attention. Its tin roof filled with sand, iron shutters and stone walls have made it extremely resilient. Notable only for its claustrophobia-breeding small size and interior darkness is the Murphys one-cell jail or **pokey**. Supposedly, the first person incarcerated here was a man who helped build it. Finally, the two-room 40 by 60ft (12.2 by 18.3m) **Murphys Grammar School** can proudly call itself the oldest school in continuous use in California. It has counted among its students Dr. Albert Michelson, the first American to win a Nobel Prize for Physics (1907).

Traditionally, visitors to Murphys make sure to journey to the **Calaveras Big Trees State Park** several miles east on Highway 4. There, you can behold the largest living things in the world, giant sequoias, more commonly found farther south. When Augustus T. Dowd encountered one of these giants for the first time while chasing a wounded grizzly bear in the spring of 1852, he could hardly believe what he was seeing, a *tree* 24ft in diameter and over 300ft (91.4m) tall. Such wonder has surely been the common denominator of all those who have since made a pilgrimage to these magnificent redwoods.

Angel's Camp

For those acquainted with the work of the great American writer Mark Twain, Angel's Camp will probably be instantly redolent of a famous short story he wrote initially titled "Jim Smiley and His Jumping Frog" and later retitled "The Celebrated Jumping Frog of Calaveras County." On one of his regular visits to the saloon in Angel's Hotel, where he was primarily attracted to the billiards table, Mark Twain heard from a bartender the germ of the frog story, which would propel him into the world's literary spotlight. An offshoot of this 1865 story's influence is the frog-jumping contest held every May south of town at Frogtown, on the site of the Calaveras County Fairgrounds. If you're just passing through and don't have a frog or two in hand with which to participate, don't despair because you'll be able to rent one. No wonder the Utica Park in Angel's Camp features a statue of the incomparable humourist!

Mark Twain statue

Another famous writer with close ties to the region was Bret Harte, who at about the same time as Twain was spending his days around gold rush camps, was mining that difficult way of life for material to turn into fiction. In particular, the two short stories "The Luck of Roaring Camp" and "Outcasts of Poker Flat" secured for Harte a large reading audience and widespread literary celebrity.

Like so many other gold rush towns, Angels Camp enjoyed great placer mining success for only a relatively short time (1848-1853), then turned to mining gold-veined quartz. Five mines in the vicinity—the Stickle, the Utica, the Lightner, the Angels and the Sultana—yielded millions in gold from a quartz vein formed tens of millions of years beforehand. Production reached its peak in the 1880s and 90s with more than 200 stamp mills going full tilt. Evidence of the predominance of this hardrock mining can be found all around, nowhere more clearly than at two old mine sites right smack in the middle of town, the Utica Mine on Main Street and the practically adjacent Lightner Mine. Additional gold rush memorabilia is on display at the **Angel's Camp Museum** (*753 S. Main St.*). Near the museum grounds you can still see the ruins and foundations of the quartz mine. On these same grounds, near an overshot water wheel, a fine **Carriage Museum** houses a collection of vehicles and still more items pertaining to mining.

Mark Twain and the
Calaveras County Jumping Frog Contest

Every May at the Calaveras County Fairgrounds' Frogtown, contestants gather to determine which of their frogs can jump the farthest from a starting circle. Thousands of people watch as the frogs are prodded into leaping towards batrachian celebrity. How to account for such an unusual competition? The answer originates in the life and times of 29-year-old Samuel Clemens, best known to the world as Mark Twain, later to pen *The Adventures of Huckleberry Finn*.

In the winter of 1865, broke and unemployed as a newspaper reporter, and living in a cabin on Jackass Hill in the Mother Lode country, trying to eke out a subsistence by mining gold, Twain often frequented the Angel's Hotel Saloon in Angel's Camp. One day, he heard a bartender tell a story that Twain summarized in a notebook as follows: "Coleman with his jumping frog—bet a stranger $50—Stranger had no frog and C. got him one—In the mean time stranger filled C's frog full of shot and he couldn't jump. The stranger's frog won."
Encouraged by the great

U.S. humourist, Artemis Ward to write this story down, Twain did so, and then published it in *The New York Saturday Press* on November 18, 1865, under the title *Jim Smiley and His Jumping Frog*. Widely reprinted in newspapers, in May 1867 it became the centrepiece of Twain's first book, *The Celebrated Jumping Frog of Calaveras County and Other Sketches*. Hence it was that a well-known tall tale in the hands of Mark Twain launched him into an orbit of literary fame and fortune. He came to regard it as "the best humourous sketch that America has produced yet." Twain's remark immediately following this assessment—"I must read it in public some day, in order that people may know what there is in it"—hints at the distinguishing characteristics of this kind of literary work.

The story succeeds to the extent that the person telling it concentrates on the manner of narration rather than the content. Such a tale calls for a deadpan narrator who never lets on that what he is saying is laughably ridiculous and who meanders in the telling as a matter of course while

he takes advantage of a fine sense of timing and a good ear for ordinary speed rhythms. Even in so outwardly simple-seeming a piece of writing as *Jim Smiley and His Jumping Frog*, Twain as literary craftsman is heeding his famous dictum that the difference between the nearly right word and the right word is the difference between the lightning bug and lightning.

Lest the frog be forgotten in all this, Twain might well interject here that in keeping with his stated objective as a serious writer—to elicit laughter—the reader could do worse than to read through Mark Twain's retranslation back into English of the French translation (*Revue des Deux Mondes* of July 15, 1872) of the tale as he originally wrote it in English. As he concluded, "When I say, Well, I don't see no p'ints about that frog that's any better'n any other frog, is it kind, is it just, for this Frenchman to try to make it appear that I said, "Eh bien! I no saw not that that frog had nothing of better than each frog?"

Columbia

Columbia's downtown district looks as if it has declined to enter the 20th or the 21st century. Businesses of all sorts, often run by people dressed in period costumes and spread out over blocks and blocks, have a distinctly 1850s gold rush appearance, which means that red brick facades, fancy wrought-iron grillwork and heavy iron shutters greet you almost every step of the way. You're walking (no cars permitted in this part of town) around **Columbia State Historic Park ★★★**, which probably differs substantially from any other park you've set foot in. Many western films, including *High Noon*, not surprisingly, have been set in this outdoor gold rush museum. Created in 1945 by the State of California, this park is widely regarded as having the most extensive and best-restored collection of gold rush buildings in the world. If you want to transport yourself back to the rough-and-tumble world of yesteryear even more authentically, just conjure up a mental picture of the numerous bar fights, ladies of the night and the streets full of mud and manure!

It wasn't until a party headed by Dr. Thaddeus Hildreth found gold in a dry gulch in March of 1850 that Columbia, which came to be known as the Gem of the Southern Mines, even began to exist. A quintessential boomtown, Columbia expanded exponentially to a population of about 5,000, and by the end of 1852 had more than 100 businesses, 30 of them

saloons! However, it took the creation of the Tuolumne County Water Company as early as August of 1852 to provide a sufficient supply of water to guarantee that the abundant gold in the area could be mined. A town not inclined to do things in half measures, it pulled out all the stops when the first European woman came to live here in May of 1851. The townspeople happily went all out to welcome her with a huge parade, complete with a brass band, and escorted her the 4mi (6.4km) north from Sonora. Here, gas lighting also made its Californian debut in 1858. If you wish to stay overnight in Columbia to better absorb its ambiance, two historically important hostelries, the **City Hotel** (1857) and the **Hotel Fallon** (1860) are still in business. When, in 1885, the son of the latter's founder built a theatre and dance hall behind the hotel, he had iron springs installed underneath the dance floor so that it would bounce. The **Sierra Repertory Theatre** makes use of the 115-year-old theatre to stage year-round, award-winning professional productions.

A replica of the **Columbia Gazette Office** of 1853; **The Wells Fargo Office** of 1858 with its splendid gold scales (which were kept very busy weighing gold for 61 years); The **D.O. Mills Bank Building** of 1854 with its steps of Columbia marble (there were two marble quarries on the outskirts of town) and counters made of mahogany from Honduras; the **Charles Koch Barber Shop** with its bathing rooms with tubs (for dirty miners) in the back; two venerable **Firehouses** that contribute to the fun of the annual

Fireman's Muster in the first week of May; **John Duchon's Printing Office of 1857** where, upstairs, both the *Columbia Gazette* and the *Southern Miners Advertiser* were published, and downstairs, where a druggist dispensed medical concoctions, some of which are still on the shelves; the dentist's office with its fearsome implements from the anesthetic-less days; the rough cabin once occupied by a man named Franco; the brick **Saint Anne's Catholic Church** of 1856, which was entirely paid for by miners; the **Columbia School**, used continuously from 1860 to 1937, with its original desks and inkwells, old books, writing slates and maps and wood-burning stoves intact—all these buildings and many more truly fill Columbia State Historic Park to over-flowing. This is definitely the perfect place to become imbued with the particular past of the California gold rush.

Sonora

As might be expected, Sonora, seat of Tuolumne County, is so named because most of its first gold mines hailed from Sonora, Mexico. Explosive growth resulting from early mining success coupled with outright bigotry and avarice led to the disgraceful Foreign Miners Tax of 1850. This imposed a $20 per month levy that in the two months immediately after its enactment triggered much bloody violence and the economically devastating exodus of enough Mexicans, Chileans and Frenchmen to reduce the population of approxi-mately 5,000 by nearly half. None too soon, the

State abolished the tax in 1851. Regarding life in Sonora at around that time, Enos Christman of the *Sonora Herald* had this to say: "*Sonora has a population hailing from every hole and corner of the globe— Kanakas, Peruvians, Negroes, Spaniards, Mexicans, Chileans, Chinese, British convicts from New South Wales... Englishmen, Frenchmen, Paddies and not a small sprinkling of Yankees. We have more gamblers, more drunkards, more ugly, bad women, and larger lumps of gold, and more of them than any other place of similar dimensions within Uncle Sam's dominions.*" That last sentence appears to contain some fore-knowledge in that the Bonanza Mine, right in the centre of town, brought forth 990lbs (449kg) of gold in one week in 1879.

Travellers on the Gold Rush Trail will find much of interest in Sonora along its main thoroughfare, Washington Street. Look, for example, at the impressive **Opera Hall** of 1885 or the 1851 **Gunn House** *(286 S. Washington St.)* (now Gunn House Motor Hotel), Sonora's first residence and, on the lower floor, the office where the *Sonora Herald* was printed. Also be sure to check out the 1852 **City Hotel** *(Snell St. at Wyckhoff St.)* constructed of adobe brick and cut stone, or the 1860 **Saint James Episcopal Church** *(Snell St. at Wyckhoff St.)*, a handsome, red-coloured, wooden-frame structure with beautiful stained-glass windows. Still another gem is **Servente's** (1856) **Grocery Store** *(64 Washington St.)*, the front of which is cast. Also take a look at the 1857 **Sugg-Macdonald House** *(37 Theall*

St.), first owned by William Sugg, an African-American, whose descendants remained on the premises for over 120 years. And, finally, allot a substantial chunk of time to explore the **Tuolumne County Museum & History Center** *(158 W. Bradford Ave.)* For over 100 years (1857-1960), this centre was home to the Tuolumne County Jail. Now the museum has "cell by cell" exhibits which are sure to fascinate, and its pioneer gun collection and display of local gold specimens are particularly outstanding.

Chinese Camp

From what little is left today, there's no way of telling that Chinese Camp was once one of the largest Asian settlements in the U.S. Beginning with the arrival of 35 Cantonese miners in 1849, this settlement became officially known as Chinese Camp in 1854. Much more than their American counterparts, the Chinese labourers were willing to cope with the difficulty of mining without a handy water supply, and that probably helps to explain why the Chinese were not prevented from establishing a thriving community here. Partially obscured by overgrown Chinese "trees of heaven" (Ailanthus trees) and wild grass, the town, of course, gives no clue to that one raucous day in September of 1856 when two rival groups, the Yan-Wo Tong and the San-Yop Tong, fought it out for hours before coming to an honourable truce, but not before four men died.

Strolling through Chinese Camp after visiting the

Tuolumne County visitor's center, keep an eye out for the **Post Office Building** (1854) and, a few steps away, the **Rosenblohm Store**, built in 1851. You will see a variety of stone ruins scattered about. Cross Highway 49 and standing before you on a hill is **Saint Xavier's Catholic Church**. Think back to the days when the church's very first priest rode a mule on his circuit of the area's parishes.

Coulterville

About 30mi (48.2km) south of Sonora on Highway 49 lies Mariposa's second largest town, Coulterville, which is a state historic landmark in its entirety while its Main Street is on the National Register of Historic Places. What made Coulterville economically successful was twofold: its importance as a supply centre for the region and its location on top of a huge ledge of gold-bearing quartz. Its most famous and probably richest mine was the Mary Harrison. Underneath the town's old hanging tree, you will see the 8-ton (8.1 tonne) steam locomotive *Whistling Billy*, which conveyed ore from the Mary Harrison over 4mi (6.4km) of "the crookedest railway in the world" to a stamping mill at Black Creek. (To inspect the mine's ruins, drive 1mi or 1.6km south of town and 0.75mi or 1.2km west of Highway 49.)

Despite major conflagrations every 20 years from 1859 through 1899, Coulterville has no lack of historic buildings. To begin with, you might want to see what the **Northern Mariposa County History Center** and the adjacent remains of the

Coulter Hotel have to offer. From there move on to the 1860 adobe **Powder House**. Surprisingly, it is perfectly intact even though it stored explosives for mining. The **Sun Sun Wo Store** is the sole survivor of one of Gold Country's largest Chinatowns. Built in 1851, it was open continuously until 1926. Dirt heaped over the beamed ceiling helped insulate and also made the ceiling fire-resistant. Amazingly, the original shelves and counters are still in place. Out behind the store, the paucity of graves in the **Ching Cemetery site** reflects the Chinese belief that burial in foreign ground would give the soul no rest and that it was desirable to return the deceased's remains to China as soon as financially feasible.

Hands-down, the most striking of all the structures in Coulterville is the three-storey **Jeffery Hotel,** constructed with two storeys in 1851 as a saloon and fandango hotel. Why not conclude your little tour by walking through the batwing doors of the **Magnolia Saloon** next door to have a refreshing drink in a bar which has maintained the 1890s look right down to the last detail?

Mariposa

Once the private property of renowned explorer John Frémont because it fell within the boundaries of his 44,000 acre Mariposa Land Grant, Mariposa (Spanish for butterfly) is the southernmost large settlement to come into being as the result of the gold rush. Mariposa was blessed with an initial abundance of both placer and hardrock gold, but

didn't need to worry about its economic future since it was on the road to Yosemite.

The New England steeple atop **Saint Joseph's Catholic Church** (1863) compels your gaze toward this elegant church, which, along with its rectory and cemetery, is on the National Register of Historic Places. Immediately behind the church, high on a hill, you will find the **Mariposa Mine**, the first hardrock mine in California—and a most lucrative one at that. Above Bullion Street, the **Mariposa County Jail's** 2ft-thick (0.6m) granite block walls are a reminder of how daunting it must have been to be imprisoned there. Architecturally speaking, the **Mariposa County Courthouse** *(on Bullion between Ninth and 10th sts.)* made of hand-planed white pine with mortise and tenon joints and pine pegs (no nails) to hold it together, is the diametrical opposite of the jail. The 1866 addition of the clock tower and clock (the bell alone weighs 267lbs or 121kg) put the finishing touches of distinction on this 19th-century Greek Revival structure. It can boast that it has been in continuous operation longer than any other county courthouse west of the Rockies—ever since 1854.

The Schlageter Hotel (1867), the town's fanciest establishment for travellers, was graced by the overnight stay of two presidents, Grant and Garfield. For a comprehensive view of Mariposa County history, go to its **History Center** *(12th and Jessie sts.):* you can learn about those who first lived in the region, Native

Americans, and about its major gold rush figures. A complete old-time grocery store, moved from Hornitos, occupies the museum's first room. Interesting things to see outside include a mule-driven arrastra (a primitive ore-pulverizing device) and a stamp mill.

Outdoor Activities

Golf

The Ridge
☎ *(530) 888-PUTT*
www.RidgeGC.com
Designed by Robert Trent Jones II, this upscale golf course has been adapted to rock outcroppings and other natural landforms in order to provide golfers with one of the most challenging public courses in Gold Country.

Cycling

The American River Bike Trail, in the Folsom Lake State Recreation Area, goes along Folsom Lake, Lake Natoma, and the American River to Old Sacramento.

If you want to rent a bike to cycle the myriad mountain biking trails in the **Auburn Area State Recreation Area,** make sure to stop at the **Auburn Bike Works** *(227 Palm Ave. Auburn, CA* ☎*530-885-3861)* for rental bikes and bike repairs.

Downieville has a nationally recognized trail system for mountain biking that can be accessed via Lavessola Road.

Downieville Outfitters
101 Commercial St.
close to Hwy. 49 and Main St.
☎ *(530) 289-0155*
www.downievilleoutfitters.com
Biking around the foothills is easy thanks to this full service bicycle shop/outfitter. Not only will they rent you a bike, they'll arrange a shuttle to get you to the trail. Now that's service! Guided rides are also available.

Fishing

The Fish Hookers Sportfishing
1759 Circle Dr.
Isleton, CA
☎ *(916) 777-6498*
www.fishhookers.com
For striper, sturgeon, and catfish fishing in the Delta Region this outfitter can't be beat.

Whitewater Rafting

Whitewater Excitement, Inc.
P.O. Box 5992
Auburn, CA 95604
☎ *800-750-2386*
www.wwwinc.com
Servicing the middle, south and north forks of the American River, this outfitter enjoys one of the best reputations in California. One of the more exciting runs and the one most pertinent to Gold Country is the Middle Fork Run, with its "Tunnel Chute" that was blasted out by gold miners in the 1850s.

Canoeing and Hiking

Sierra Outdoor Center
440 Lincoln Way at Hwy. 49
Auburn, CA
☎ *(530) 885-1844*
www.sierraoc.com
If you're interested in a canoeing and hiking excursion with some local experts, the Sierra Outdoor Center organizes regular outings throughout the year. Check their Web site for dates and prices.

Calaveras Big Trees State Park
☎ *(209) 795-2334*
Two groves of giant sequoias in the midst of some 6,000 acres (2,428ha) of mountainous terrain straddling the Stanislaus River are the prize attractions of Calaveras Big Trees State Park. Drive 4mi (6.4km) northeast of Arnold on Highway 4 to arrive at the park entrance, adjacent to which are the North Grove Campground, visitor centre and ranger station. Walk the 1mi (0.6km) North Grove Big Trees Trail of the more primeval 3mi (4.8km) South Grove Trail to imbibe the magnificence of the inland redwood colossus *Sequoia gigantea*. If you need any further encouragement to visit Calaveras Big Trees State Park, keep in mind that it has miles of additional hiking trails and numerous campsites.

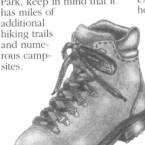

Accommodations

The Delta

B&W Resort Marina
$$
964 Brannan Island Rd.
Isleton, CA.
☎ 777-6161
⇄777-5199
www.bandwresort.com
Probably one of the best deals in the Delta Region, B&W offers well-maintained, wooden-framed efficiency cottages with simple, no frills interiors. Because it is set on the Mokelumne River, guests have access to a marina, a picnic area and a small beach in addition to the spacious grounds. Make sure you bring your own cutlery as the kitchenettes do not come with utensils. Also, take note that in July and August there is a one-week minimum stay policy.

Herman & Helen's Marina
$$-$$$$
⊛
Venice Island Ferry
Stockton, CA 95219
☎ *(209) 951-4634*
⇄ *(209) 951-6505*
hth@inreach.com
Probably the best way to explore the Delta is with a houseboat. This Value Certified Resort is one of the largest and oldest marinas on the Delta. Renting a houseboat here will give you access to the over 100 marinas and waterside resorts found along the 1,000mi (1,609km) of waterways that make up the Bayou, as well as some great waterskiing trails and

fishing holes. If you are into luxury houseboating, try out one of the two new luxury ODYSSEY houseboats complete with hot-tub and fireplace!

Tower Park Marina
$$
14900 W. Hwy. 12
Lodi, CA 95242
☎*(209) 368-3030*
www.h2orents.com
If you'd like to rent a houseboat for less than one week, H2O is the way to go! It will cost you roughly $450 for a six-person houseboat for two days and one night (plus a $500 deposit), but the longer you rent, the better deal you get. Special waterskiing, fishing and sports boats are also available for rental.

Sacramento

🚣 **Sacramento International Hostel**
$12-$14 for members, $3 extra for non-members
Children between 2 and 16 stay 1/2 price when accompanied by a parent
$
sb
900 H St.
Sacramento, CA 95814
☎*443-1691*
hisac@norcalhostels.org
Old Sacramento, great river recreation, some agreeable bike trails and the Amtrak and Greyhound Stations are all found within walking distance from this Victorian-style hostelry. This place offers the more adventurous traveller with either shared or private sleeping rooms, linen rental, a fully-equipped kitchen and dining area, a drawing room and parlour with an antique piano, a travel library and game room, a laundry room, lovely outdoor sitting areas

and bicycle storage and tools. Exceptional value for the money.

Vagabond Inn
$$ bkfst incl.
☎, ≡, tv
909 Third St.
Sacramento, CA 95814
☎*446-1481*
⇥448-0364
Conveniently located and well-maintained, the Vagabond Inn is suitable for those who want to be close to Old Town and have all of the creature comforts without paying a fortune for them. Additional values are: a free weekday newspaper, free incoming fax documents, free local calls and a free stay for children 18 and younger that share their parents' room.

The Riverboat Delta King
$$$$
☎, ≡, ≈, tv, ℜ
1000 Front St.
Old Sacramento, CA
☎*444-5464*
How about staying in a luxurious stationary riverboat instead of a hotel? The *Delta King* is, in fact, an authentic 285ft (86.8m) riverboat that was initially built in Scotland and finished in Stockton, California. The *King*, along with a twin boat called the *Queen*, was christened in 1927 as the initial riverboat that made the much-needed daily trajectory between San Francisco and Sacramento along the Sacramento River. After becoming redundant with the proliferation of automobile travel in the late 1930s, the *King* was drafted into the US Navy to shuttle between Canada and California and eventually sank in San Francisco Bay. In 1984, the King was rescued and completely renovated so that it could become, five years later, the unique

hotel and restaurant establishment that it is today. The award-winning restaurant, The Pilothouse, often hosts Murder Mystery Dinner Theatre.

Gold Country

Downieville

The Riverside Inn
$$ bkfst incl.
tv
206 Commercial St
Downieville, CA 95936
☎*(530) 289-1000*
Situated right on the Downie River, the Riverside Inn offers guests cozy cabin-like rooms with fully equipped kitchenettes and private balconies that overlook the river. Please be advised that although there is cable TV, there are no phones. This is a terrific place to stay if you want good value and privacy in the heart of a charming, historical gold rush town.

The Lure Resort
$-$$$$ bkfst incl.
△, ☎, ≡, ≈, ≡, tv, pb/sb, ⊛, ℜ
$$-$$$$
Hwy 49
Downieville, CA 95936
☎*(530) 289-3465*
☎*800-671-4084*
www.lureresort.com
Fishers and nature lovers, have we got a place for you! The Lure Resort is a complex of 16 cabins that range from rustic camping cabins with log bunk beds and no electricity to luxury vacation cabins with huge, well-equipped kitchens, cozy rock hearths and luxurious king- and queen-sized beds. Linens can also be rented here for $10. As the resort is located on 13 acres (5.3ha) of river-front terrain, it is a choice spot for trout fishing, private swimming holes and—yes—gold panning. If you are greeted by a woman named Mary at check-in,

ask her anything as she is a walking Chamber of Commerce!

Nevada City

The National Hotel
$$-$$$ bkfst incl.
☎, *pb/sb*, ℜ
211 Broad St.
Nevada City, CA 95959
☎*(530) 265-4551*
This National Historic Landmark, located in Nevada City's former red light district, is the oldest continuously operating hotel west of the Rocky Mountains. Featuring a lobby that houses a grand piano that jo urneyed around Cape Horn, the hotel also features a Victorian dining room that is softly lit with coal oil lamps. The rooms range from simple pensions with shared bathroom facilities to sumptuous suites with canopy or four-poster beds.

The US Hotel
$$-$$$ bkfst incl.
tv
233 B Broad St.
Nevada City, CA 95959
☎*(530) 265-7999*
☎*800-525-4525*
≈*(530) 265-7998*
ushotelc@aol.com
Under new ownership since December of 1999, this centrally located bed and breakfast is bound to please lovers of exposed brick walls and comfortable queen- or king-sized beds. Along with a full complimentary breakfast and afternoon wine and cheese, guests have access to a games parlour and library.

The Parsonage Bed & Breakfast
$$-$$$ bkfst incl
427 Broad St.
Nevada City, CA 95959
☎*(530) 265-9478*
≈*(530) 265-8147*
Set in the original parsonage of the Nevada City Methodist Church, this unique bed and breakfast really takes pains to bring you back in time. Each room is dedicated to a pioneer ancestor of the owner, replete with pictures and life stories, and is thus a virtual museum unto itself. The fine bed and table linens are line-dried and hand-pressed, transporting those with a keen sense of smell into ecstasy. A hearty country breakfast, which includes home-made muffins, croissants and jams is a fine way to begin a day of gallivanting around Nevada City.

Gamble Quail

Jackson

The National Hotel
$-$$ bkfst incl.
pb/sb, ℜ
2 Water St.
Jackson, CA 95642
☎*(209) 223-0500*
≈*(209) 223-4845*
nationalhotel@volcano.net
At first frequented by wealthy folks with mine holdings in Volcano, this hotel has greeted many a famous guest since then. Exuding history without resorting to expensive frills, this hotel offers a fun experience at great value if you are someone who is not particularly fussy about

having a private bathroom, a telephone and a television in your room. Rooms with private baths are available, however, for those who want to dish out the extra dough.The piano sing-a-longs and kerosene chandelier in the authentic saloon are worth coming for, even if you are lodging somewhere else.

Mokelumne Hill

Hotel Leger
$-$$$
pb/sb, ℜ
8304 Main St.
Mokelumne Hill, CA
☎*(209) 286-1401*
Located in what was once the heart of the rowdy French mining community, Hotel Leger is a 13-room Victorian hotel with an authentic gold rush era saloon. Today, this hotel exudes the same sleepy, backwater atmosphere of the small town that envelopes it—except on those weekends when live entertainment is featured in the saloon. Rooms range from small pensions with shared baths to larger, more luxurious quarters with private baths and fireplaces. An in-house restaurant is open Thursday through Saturday from 6pm to 9pm.

Amador City

The Mine House Inn
$$$-$$$$$ bkfst incl.
☎, *tv*, ℜ
14125 Hwy. 49
Amador City, CA
☎*(209) 267-5900*
☎*800-646-3473*
www.minehouseinn.com
A unique bed and breakfast establishment set in an old mining office, the Mine House Inn will particularly appeal to those who harbour a secret gold-vault fetish. This is your chance to sleep next to the

Sacramento, Delta and Gold Country

original vault that once guarded over $24 million in gold! Seven other rooms in the main brick office building with rocking chairs, authentic period decor and beautiful high headboards for queen, king and double beds have names like the Bookkeeping Room and the Director's Room. A neighbouring Super-intendent's House is the site of three luxury suites, including a special honeymoon suite. A third Victorian building is currently being renovated to house an on-site dining facility and a suite accessible to persons with handicaps. The breakfast here has received rave reviews from a host of happy guests for both its content and the way it is served. Don't forget to take a dip in the exquisitely set swimming pool!

Murphys

 Murphys Historic Hotel & Lounge
$$
☎, tv, ℜ
457 Main St.
Murphys, CA 95247
☎*(209) 728-3444*
☎*800-532-7684*
⇌*(209) 728-1590*
First opened in 1859, this historic hotel gained a reputation as the ideal place to stay while visiting the Calaveras Big Trees. After some rather prestigious guests like Ulysses S. Grant and Mark Twain stayed here on their way to the trees, the hotel itself became quite famous. Today, guests can choose to stay in the Ulysses S. Grant Historic Parlour Suite or in the neighbouring Mark Twain Room for a mere $80 a night. Motel rooms offering more privacy are available on the premises

for a slightly lower price, but they lack the historical charm of the rooms in the main building. A good breakfast attended by colourful locals is served in the restaurant downstairs.

Dunbar House Bed and Breakfast
$$$-$$$$$ bkfst incl.
4 rooms
☎
271 Jones St.
Murphys, CA 95247
☎*(209) 728-2897*
☎*800-692-6006*
www.dunbarhouse.com
Those searching for a taste of intimate luxury would be wise to book a sejour at this 1880 Italianate Victorian bed and breakfast, touted as the crown jewel of Gold Country. From the fabulous breakfasts served wherever you want to enjoy them, to the chocolate macadamia cookies served in the afternoon, to the claw-foot tubs, woodstoves, comfy beds and complimentary wine that awaits you when you retire into your room, you are in for a delightful treat.

Stanislaus National Forest

Dorrington Inn at Big Trees
$$$$$
6 cottages and 2 rooms
☎, tv
3450 Hwy. 4
P.O. Box 4446
Dorrington, CA 95223
www.dorringtoninm.com
Outdoorsy types who appreciate a cozy place to turn in for the evening are sure to find fulfillment in one of the six cottages at Dorrington Inn. Set in Stanislaus National Forest, close to the Big Trees, these alpine-style cottages with upstairs sleeping lofts, fireplaces and cable

televisions with VCRs, are perfect after a vigorous day of hiking around Gold Country and in the forest.

Restaurants

The Delta

Locke

Al the Wops
$
Main St., Locke
☎*(916) 374-2542*
An eccentric steak-house in the middle of the remains of a tumble-down Wild West Chinatown, Al the Wops is a mandatory stop even if you don't like steak. Upon opening the door, you are greeted by a bar decorated with baseball hats dangling from deer antlers, souvenir red G-string underwear and card chairs with faded Chinese calligraphy on the back. If you look straight up, wadded-up dollar bills dot the ceiling like used chewing gum under a student's desk. Once you step into the back, you realize that the cafeteria tables with peanut butter and jelly jar centerpieces are where you're supposed to enjoy your steak. And good steak it is! Come with cash, as credit cards are not accepted.

Sacramento

Indo Cafe
$
closed Mon
1100 Front St.
Old Sacramento, CA 95814
☎ 446-4008

For excellent Indonesian food at a very affordable price in the heart of Old Sacramento, be sure to stop here. The deli-style atmosphere is very basic and can be somewhat hectic, but if it's the food you've come for, you're in the right spot. Try the spiced lemon grass chicken with mixed vegetables and steamed rice, the *cap cay* (stir-fried chicken, beef and shrimp with mixed vegetables) or the *ketroprak* (cucumber, tofu and rice noodles with garlic and hot peanut sauce). Some fine Indonesian beverages are also offered here.

Max's Opera Cafe
$$-$$$
1735 Arden Way (in Market Sq.)
Sacramento
☎ 927-6297

Have you ever fantasized about finding yourself in the company of people who break out into song—*a la* Gene Kelley or Fred Astaire— instead of normal conversation? Well, at Max's Opera Cafe, this is what the servers do (after 6pm) as they hand you your seafood platter or dry-aged steak. It must be seen to be believed! Reservations are strongly recommended.

 Rio City Cafe
$$
1110 Front St.
Old Sacramento
☎ 442-8226
www.riocitycafe.net

Hugging the waterfront of the Sacramento River in the heart of Old Town, this restaurant has a lot going for it. In addition to offering outstanding, affordable cuisine made from fresh local ingredients, Rio City has an outstanding California wine list and friendly and efficient service. As an entree, try the chicken quesadillas with mango salsa or the chinese nachos— out of this world! A judicious lunch choice is the Thai beef salad or the smoked duck salad. House vanilla ice-cream is a delicious way to finish off your meal... if you still have room.!

Fat City
$$-$$$
1001 Front St.
Sacramento
☎ 446-6768

This is one of four restaurants opened by a Chinese man, Frank Fat, who immigrated to Sacramento in 1939. Don't expect Chinese food, though. Some house specialties, prepared by Lina Fat (one of Sacramento's premier chefs) and her team, are mouth-watering sirloin meat-loaf baked in a clay pot and salmon cooked in a mango, pineapple and cilantro sauce.

California Fats
$$-$$$
1015 Front St.
Sacramento
☎ 441-7966

Also part of the local Fats dynasty, California Fats offers diners some cosmopolitan California cuisine served in a decor of interesting memorabilia from the Chinese immigrant experience, as well as an unusual collection of early-American antiques. Some of the irresistible main courses, also overseen by Lina Fat, are lobster ravioli, charboiled ahi tuna and the drunk steak (New York sirloin marinated in brandy, garlic and ginger).

Frank Fats
$$-$$$
806 L St.
Sacramento
☎ 442-7092

This is *the* place to go for fine Chinese cuisine in Sacramento. You can rub elbows with Californian politicians while savouring dishes that originate in Beijing, Szechuan, Canton or Shanghai. Lunch is served from Monday to Friday only (as is common with all of the restaurants around the capitol), but you can enjoy dinner anytime. The decor is elegant.

Gold Country

Auburn

California Juice Co. & Cafe
$
944 Lincoln Way
Auburn
☎ (530) 889-8992

Famous for their tropical sunset smoothie (passion/guava juice, pineapple and banana) and their creative wraps, the California Juice Co. is a terrific place to stop for a light, healthy and delicious lunch. Vegetarians will salivate at the sheer fragrance of the veggie wrap, which includes jasmine rice, spinach leaves, portabella mushrooms, eggplant, tomato, onion and mint-basil dressing. Unfortunately for us, they are closed on Sundays.

Nevada City

Mekka
$
237 Commercial St.
Nevada City
☎(530) 478-1517
For an incredible selection of gourmet coffees, teas and desserts served in a casual cosmopolitan atmosphere that buzzes with intelligent conversation, do not miss Mekka. Several personalized seating areas have been created from comfy coaches and chairs, giving the impression of a collection of bohemian living rooms and parlours without walls. This is indeed a Mecca for certain kindred spirits who are either living or travelling in Gold Country.

Citronée Bistro and Wine Bar
$$-$$$
320 Broad St.
Nevada City
☎(530) 265-5697
A fusion of California and Mediterranean cuisine in an elegant yet casual atmosphere; this is Citronée. Enjoy some sea bass with wasabi mashed potatoes or better yet, some olive-oil-poached sword fish with Zinfandel sauce. There is, of course, a fine selection of California wines to accompany your meal.

Friar Tuck's
$$-$$$
111 N. Pine St.
Nevada City
☎(530) 265-9093
You'll have your choice of atmosphere to dine in when you eat at this popular fondue restaurant. Whether it be a cozy, intimate setting or a lively or historical one that you are looking for, you'll find it here along with some mouth-watering steak, shrimp and cheese fondues.

Grass Valley

Marshall's Pasties
$-$$
Mon to Sat, 9am to 6pm
203 Mill St.
Grass Valley
☎(530) 272-2844
Brought to the Mother Lode by "cousin Jacks" and "cousin Jennys," pasty was an integral part of the Cornish miner's lunch. At Marshall's you can still savour this Cornish working-class delicacy along with some fine California wine.

Downieville

The Double Shot
$
from 7am every day
☎(530) 289-0746
An early morning caffeine craving that requires sophisticated handling can easily be treated here.

The Downieville Diner
Main St.
Downieville, CA
☎(530) 289-3616
To experience the pulse of Downieville before encountering it with your feet or mountain bike, you must begin here. The waitresses at this cozy diner, decorated with old mining paraphernalia, can fill you in on the real opening hours of all of the local businesses while serving you biscuits fresh from the oven. House specialties include omelettes with names like "devil's post pile" (jack cheese, ortega chile, ham & avocado), country skillets such as the "Placer" (a bed of home-fries topped with mushrooms, green onions, jack cheese, avocado and two eggs), *Poker Flat griddle cakes, Secret Canyon biscuits and gravy,* and miscellaneous items like the *roadkill* (sautéed red potatoes, two cheeses, mushrooms, onions, tomatoes and green bell peppers).

Riverview Pizzeria
Main St. (at the junction of the Yuba and Downie rivers)
☎(530) 289-3540
Outstanding pizza and home-made ravioli are a couple of the things you can expect at the Riverview Pizzeria. Another is its incredible location at the confluence of two rivers.

Entertainment

Bars and Nightclubs

Sacramento

Fanny Ann's Saloon
1023 Second St.
Old Sacramento
☎441-0505
With one of the most fascinating decors of any establishment in Old Sacramento, this old-fashioned saloon merits, at the very least, a tour.

New Jamaica House
1704 Broadway St.
Sacramento
☎492-9336
For African and Caribbean dishes served alongside live Reggae music, head to the New Jamaica House on a Friday night. On Saturdays, a DJ playing a lively selection of Caribbean and African tunes encourages patrons to dance the night away.

Jazzmen's Art of Pasta
1107 Firehouse Alley
Old Sacramento
☎441-6726
Indoor and courtyard meals served with live jazz, blues or cabaret accompaniment down in the Old Town. Of particular note on the gastronomical side of this establishment is the award-winning imperial crab lasagna.

Sundown Casino
24 hrs
2217 Del Paso Blvd.
Sacramento
☎927-2481
What is great about this card room/casino is the free card lessons. Texas hold'em, seven card stud, six/ten/twenty limit lo-ball are just some of the games that you can learn here. If you have any worries about your safety, rest assured: the place is made very secure by some pretty intimidating guards.

Trino's Lounge
1443 Fulton Ave.
Sacramento
☎978-9000
If you are in Sacramento on a Thursday night and enjoy karaoke, drop by Trino's at 9:30pm and sing your heart out.

Theatre and Music

Sierra Repertory Theatre
P.O. Box 3030
Sonora, CA 95370
www.sierrarep.com
East Sonora Location:
13891 Hwy. 108
0.25mi (0.4km) east of The Junction Shopping Center
Columbia Location:
The Fallon House Theatre in Columbia State Historic Park
This award-winning repertory theatre stages everything from Shakespeare to Andrew Lloyd Webber to foot-stomping musicals like the Nunsense Jamboree. Check out their Web site to see what is playing during your visit.

Festivals & Special Events

Late May

Pacific Rim Street Festival
Old Sacramento
☎443-6223
A one-day celebration of the contribution of Asian culture to California. A fascinating variety of Asian foods, crafts, children's activities and cultural performances are highlighted.

Sacramento Jazz Jubilee
☎372-5277
www.sacjazz.com
This is a three-day festival, that claims the distinction of being the largest traditional jazz festival in

the world. Launched with a parade in the streets of Old Sacramento, this festival is followed by live jazz in over 40 venues throughout the greater Sacramento area.

Calaveras County Fair and Jumping Frog Jubilee
☎736-2561

June

The History Channel's Great Race
If you are interested at all in vintage cars, you owe it to yourself to show up at the Capitol Mall finish line of this timed, trans-continental rally-race that begins in Boston and ends in Sacramento. The best time to be here is between 11pm and 3pm. At the end of the race, a festival is held that features automobile booths that showcase the various models in the race along with other international vintage models.

Late July-Early August

Bear Valley Music Festival
☎754-2574
www.bearvalleymusic.org
Classical, jazz and pop music in Bear Valley Village—international solo artists, legendary entertainers and a 63-member orchestra in a tent that seats 1,200 people.

October

Calaveras Grape Stomp and Gold Rush Street Fair
☎728-9700

Spectator Sports

The Sacramento Kings Professional Basketball
Arco Arena, 1 Sports Parkway
just off Interstate 5
☎928-0000

Shopping

The Closet
1107 Front St., Old Sacramento
☎442-3446
There are dozens of antique shops in and around Sacramento, but one with a lot of character, and thus of interest to the antique collector and layperson alike, is The Closet. Because it is hidden in the bowels of a shopping complex in Old Sacramento, entering this store is in effect like entering an old, forgotten closet. In addition to old magazines, books, pocket watches, whiskey bottles, musical instruments, toys, signs and slot machines there are fascinating, time-worn people there to serve you as you purchase that one-of-a-kind item to take home. Jon will also pay you "top dollars" for any old things you might want to get rid of.

Produce Junction
1050 Front St. #190
Sacramento
☎443-1836
For some refreshing fresh-squeezed juices and home-made sorbets, stop here during your stroll through Old Sacramento.

Lazlo's Gourmet Smoked Fish
1100 Front St., #140
Old Sacramento
☎492-9089
If you are stocking up for a picnic and looking for some non-perishable protein, make sure you check out Lazlo's for some tasty smoked fish.

Gallery of the American West
121 K St., Old Sacramento
☎446-6662
www.gallerywest.com
Amid all the stores claiming to sell authentic Native American crafts, it is sometimes difficult to find one that actually has the genuine stuff. You won't go wrong if you head straight here. The only store in Sacramento to offer local indigenous jewellery and crafts in addition to fine Navajo pieces and work from other U.S. tribes, the Gallery of the American West is a true jackpot for anyone looking to purchase some bona-fide indigenous pieces.

49er Stage
☎289-1724
If you're the type to hide out in an obscure mountain town far away from the rat race, temporarily ditching your car, cell phone and cable television, this is a service that might interest you. By placing an order with Woody at the Downieville Grocery, you can order fresh produce, meats, office supplies, or laundry service from Reno and have them delivered twice a week to your rustic cabin. The trick is to know when Woody is in, since the opening hours to the grocery are as follows:

"open most days about 9 or 10, occasionally as early as 7, but some days as late as 12 or 1. We close about 5:30 or 6, occasionally about 4 or 5, but sometimes as late as 11 or 12. Somedays on afternoons we aren't here at all."

Probably your best bet is to ask the waitress at the Downieville Diner.

Mostly Clay and Fine Crafts
227 Broad St., Nevada City
☎(530) 265-3535
If you're hunting for a unique gift made by a local artisan, stop by this shop which features quilts, pottery, yard sculptures, candles, hand-made cards and paper and much more.

Crystal Rainbow Rock Shop
Sat and Sun only
10am to 5pm
310 Commercial St.,
Nevada City
☎(530) 265-3784
This little road-side shack offers great bargains on precious stones and items made with them.

Harmony Books
231 Broad St., Nevada City
☎(530) 265-9564
A wonderful independent bookstore in Nevada City, Harmony sells books and cards for those with discriminating tastes.

Hein & Co.
Used and Rare Books
204-A N. Main St., Jackson
☎(209) 223-9076
If you like perusing through a hodge-podge of old and unusual books, drop by Hein & Co. for awhile. If you have the time to linger, sit in their in-house café with an espresso and play a game of checkers.

Ironstone Winery and Vineyards Gift Shop
1896 Six Mile Rd., Murphys
☎(209) 728-1251
≈(209) 728-1275
Modelled after a 19th century gold stamp mill, Ironstone sells wine that can easily compete with any in Wine Country. The gift shop also sells unusual items made from quartz, crystalline and, of course, gold.

Index

Index

Index

Index

Index

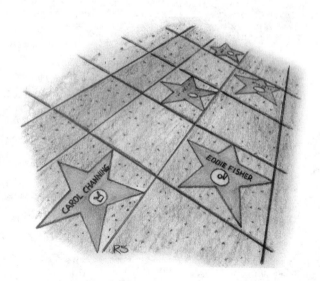

Travel Notes

Order Form

Ulysses Travel Guides

☐ Acapulco	$14.95 CAN / $9.95 US	☐ Louisiana	$29.95 CAN / $21.95 US
☐ Alberta's Best Hotels Restaurants	$14.95 CAN / $12.95 US	☐ Martinique	$24.95 CAN / $17.95 US
☐ Atlantic Canada	$24.95 CAN / $17.95 US	☐ Miami	$17.95 CAN / $12.95 US
☐ Beaches of Maine	$12.95 CAN / $9.95 US	☐ Montréal	$19.95 CAN / $14.95 US
☐ Belize	$16.95 CAN / $12.95 US	☐ New Orleans	$17.95 CAN / $12.95 US
☐ British Columbia's Best Hotels and Restaurants	$14.95 CAN / $9.95 US	☐ New York City	$19.95 CAN / $14.95 US
☐ Calgary	$17.95 CAN / $12.95 US	☐ Nicaragua	$24.95 CAN / $16.95 US
☐ Canada	$29.95 CAN / $21.95 US	☐ Ontario's Best Hotels and Restaurants	$16.95 CAN / $12.95US
☐ Cancun Cozumel	$17.95 CAN / $12.95 US	☐ Ontario	$27.95 CAN / $19.95US
☐ Cartagena (Colombia)	$12.95 CAN / $9.95 US	☐ Ottawa–Hull	$17.95 CAN / $12.95 US
☐ Chicago	$19.95 CAN / $14.95 US	☐ Panamá	$24.95 CAN / $17.95 US
☐ Chile	$27.95 CAN / $17.95 US	☐ Peru	$27.95 CAN / $19.95 US
☐ Colombia	$29.95 CAN / $21.95 US	☐ Phoenix	$16.95 CAN / $12.95 US
☐ Costa Rica	$27.95 CAN / $19.95 US	☐ Portugal	$24.95 CAN / $16.95 US
☐ Cuba	$24.95 CAN / $17.95 US	☐ Provence & the Côte d'Azur	$29.95 CAN / $21.95US
☐ Dominican Republic	$24.95 CAN / $17.95 US	☐ Puerto Plata–Sosua	$14.95 CAN / $9.95 US
☐ Ecuador and Galápagos Islands	$24.95 CAN / $17.95 US	☐ Puerto Rico	$24.95 CAN / $17.95 US
☐ El Salvador	$22.95 CAN / $14.95 US	☐ Puerto Vallarta	$14.95 CAN / $9.95 US
☐ Guadalajara	$17.95 CAN / $12.95 US	☐ Québec	$29.95 CAN / $21.95 US
☐ Guadeloupe	$24.95 CAN / $17.95 US	☐ Québec City	$17.95 CAN / $12.95 US
☐ Guatemala	$24.95 CAN / $17.95 US	☐ Québec and Ontario with Via	$9.95 CAN / $7.95 US
☐ Havana	$16.95 CAN / $12.95 US	☐ San Francisco	$17.95 CAN / $12.95 US
☐ Hawaii	$29.95 CAN / $21.95 US	☐ Seattle	$17.95 CAN / $12.95 US
☐ Honduras	$24.95 CAN / $17.95 US	☐ St. Martin and St. Barts	$16.95 CAN / $12.95 US
☐ Huatulco– Puerto Escondido	$17.95 CAN / $12.95 US	☐ Toronto	$18.95 CAN / $13.95 US
☐ Inns and Bed & Breakfasts in Québec	$14.95 CAN / $10.95 US	☐ Tunisia	$27.95 CAN / $19.95 US
☐ Islands of the Bahamas	$24.95 CAN / $17.95 US	☐ Vancouver	$17.95 CAN / $12.95 US
☐ Las Vegas	$17.95 / $12.95	☐ Washington D.C.	$18.95 CAN / $13.95 US
☐ Lisbon	$18.95 CAN / $13.95 US	☐ Western Canada	$29.95 CAN / $21.95 US
☐ Los Cabos and La Paz	$14.95 CAN / $7.99 US		

budget.zone

☐ Central America ...... $14.95 CAN
$10.95 US

☐ Western Canada ...... $14.95 CAN
$10.95 US

Ulysses Travel Journals

☐ Ulysses Travel Journal .. $9.95 CAN
(Blue, Red, Green, Yellow, Sextant)
$7.95 US

☐ Ulysses Travel Journal ... $14.95 CAN
(80 Days)
$9.95 US

Ulysses Green Escapes

☐ Cycling in France .... $22.95 CAN
$16.95 US
☐ Cycling in Ontario ...... $22.95 CAN
$16.95 US

☐ Hiking in the .... $19.95 CAN
Northeastern U.S.
$13.95 US
☐ Hiking in Québec .... $19.95 CAN
$13.95 US

Ulysses Conversation Guides

☐ French for Better Travel .. $9.95 CAN
$6.50 US

☐ Spanish for Better Travel .. $9.95 CAN
in Latin America
$6.50 US

Title	Qty	Price	Total
Name:		Subtotal	
		Shipping	$4 CAN $3 US
Address:		Subtotal	
		GST in Canada 7%	
		Total	

Tel: Fax:

E-mail:

Payment: ☐ Cheque ☐ Visa ☐ MasterCard

Card number_____ Expiry date_____

Signature_____

ULYSSES TRAVEL GUIDES

4176 St-Denis,
Montréal, Québec, H2W 2M5
☎(514) 843-9447
fax: (514) 843-9448

305 Madison Avenue,
Suite 1166,
New York, NY 10165
Toll-free: 1-877-542-7247

www.ulyssesguides.com
info@ulysses.ca

Theories of Nationalism

Theories of Nationalism

A Critical Introduction

Umut Özkırımlı

Foreword by Fred Halliday

First published 2000 by
MACMILLAN PRESS LTD
Houndmills, Basingstoke, Hampshire RG21 6XS
and London
Companies and representatives
throughout the world

ISBN 0–333–77711–5 hardcover
ISBN 0–333–77712–3 paperback

A catalogue record for his book is available
from the British Library.

This book is printed on paper suitable for recycling and
made from fully managed and sustained forest sources.

10   9   8   7   6   5   4   3   2   1
09 08 07 06 05 04 03 02 01 00

Printed in Hong Kong

 Published in the United States of America by
ST. MARTIN'S PRESS, INC.,
Scholarly and Reference Division
175 Fifth Avenue, New York, N.Y. 10010

ISBN 0–312–22941–0 (cloth)
ISBN 0–312–22942–9 (paper)

To my mother and father

Contents

Foreword

Anyone who sets out to provide a critical survey of theories of nationalism needs to be intrepid. The range of the material is immense, and rapidly developing. The various theories relate to a historical force that itself arouses great passion. At the same time theories of nationalism touch upon broader issues and trends in the social sciences – the sociology of knowledge, the impact of ideologies, the formation of communities and of movements, the role of the state, the very direction, or lack thereof, of modern history.

Umut Özkırımlı, a Turkish scholar, has succeeded in writing such a comparative and critical survey. His book provides a comprehensive, balanced and critical overview of current debates on nationalism: it represents a substantial resource for students and teachers of the subject, and for those who seek to relate debates on nationalism to other issues, analytic and normative, in contemporary intellectual life. In the course of such a survey, and not only in the final prospective chapters, Özkırımlı also suggests reflections on nationalism in general. This he does through the critique of other writings, and through the gentle but astute adjudication of contentious issues. This is at once an informed survey of a field of literature and, in its own right, an intervention in the subject.

The focus of this study is, quite properly, on the theories of nationalism that have emerged since the 1960s. Yet one may ask of theories of nationalism the question that those theories ask of nationalism itself – where they come from. Ernest Gellner asked of nations whether they have navels. Gellner's answer, a more relaxed and agnostic one than his association with a cogent modernism would suggest, is that some nations do have navels, some achieve them, and some have navels thrust upon them. Theories of nationalism clearly have navels. Primordialist theories have navels that relate them not so much to social theory as such, but to broader assumptions about the continuing existence of communities over centuries, something reflected in much history of nations, and in now fashionable writing in political theory on the prevalence of traditions, communities and civilizations. Liberal, Marxist, Durkheimian, and Weberian theories all derive their analytic strength, and their underlying sense of the direction of history, from broader, and anterior, social theories. The more recent trends to which Özkırımlı draws attention – feminism, social psychology and postmodernism – exemplify, once again, this derivation.

If it is one of the strengths of Özkırımlı's book that he allows these underlying assumptions of theory to be assessed, it is equally to be welcomed that, in his concluding chapter, he provides his own independent analysis of how the subject can move forward. Eschewing the aspiration to a general theory of nationalism, one that would encompass both ideology and movement, he focuses instead on what is general, a discourse of nationalism. At the same time, and drawing on the insights of gender and postmodernism, he stresses the lack of finality in nationalism: not only are there multiple definitions of nationalism available at any one time, but in response to social and political change, prevailing definitions of the nation change.

In stressing the constant redefinition of nationalist discourse, Özkırımlı also helps to set nationalism in proportion. He offers a way out of what may, in the eyes of nationalists and theorists of nationalism alike, appear to be an all-inclusive world, whereby all that is social and political in the contemporary world is encompassed by the nation, and the study of nationalism itself is divorced from other dimensions of analysis. Nationalism is one, but by no means the only one, of the forces that has shaped and continues to shape the modern world, and its development, like the theories that seek to explain it, has to be seen in this broader context.

It is one of the several contributions of this impressive book that it enables us, by comprehending the range of theories of nationalism, to see these debates in a wider, intellectual and historical context. We may recall Schiller's injunction in *On the Aesthetic Education of Man*: 'One is just as much a citizen of one's age as a citizen of one's state.' In writing this book and in assessing the different theories under review, Umut Özkırımlı has followed that injunction.

London School of Economics   FRED HALLIDAY

Acknowledgements

This book could not have been written without the help and advice of many people. First, I would like to thank Toktamış Ateş who supervised the PhD dissertation on which this book is based. His constant support has always been a source of great inspiration for me.

I owe special thanks to Fred Halliday for kindly accepting my invitation to write the Foreword and for generously sharing his knowledge and ideas with me. His comments and criticisms were extremely helpful in improving the book. Here, I would also like to add that I have benefited greatly from being his student. I am grateful to Gareth Winrow and Jeff Bowen for polishing up my English and for their helpful comments on various drafts of the manuscript. I would also like to express my warm thanks to my publisher Steven Kennedy and his anonymous reviewer for their perceptive criticisms. The book owes a great deal to them. As always, however, the responsibility for the views expressed herein is all mine.

Many thanks are due to Gülberk for her unrelenting love and support. And last but not least, I want to thank my mother and father who taught me, all throughout the years, the meaning of the word 'sacrifice'. It is to them that this book is dedicated.

İstanbul Bilyi University   UMUT ÖZKIRIMLI

1
Introduction

Thou knowest not how sweet is the *amor patriae*: if such would be expedient for the fatherland's protection or enlargement, it would seem neither burdensome and difficult nor a crime to thrust the axe into one's father's head, to crush one's brothers, to deliver from the womb of one's wife the premature child with the sword.

Coluccio Salutati (quoted in James 1996: 30)

No single political doctrine has played a more prominent role in shaping the face of the modern world than nationalism. Millions of people around the world have willingly laid down their lives for their 'fatherlands' and this almost ritualistic mass self-sacrifice continues unabated. Obviously, not everybody displays extremism on the level of Salutati. But as Elshtain remarks, that sort of extremism has been 'the norm in many of the great and horrible events of our century' (1991: 400).

Despite this pervasive influence, however, nationalism was not taken seriously by the social scientists until relatively recently. For much of the nineteenth and early twentieth century, it was seen as a passing phase, by liberals and Marxists alike, hence as 'intellectually unproblematic' (Halliday 1997a: 12). It was only in the 1920s and 1930s, with the pioneering works of historians like Carleton Hayes, Hans Kohn, Louis Snyder and E. H. Carr, that nationalism became a subject of sustained academic inquiry. Unlike their predecessors who were mainly interested in ethical issues, these historians took nationalism as a 'discrete subject of investigation' and made use of sociological factors in their accounts (Smith 1998: 17; Snyder 1997). The number and diversity of the studies of

1

nationalism increased in the following decades under the impact of the experience of decolonization and the 'proliferation' of new states in Asia and Africa. Subscribing to some version of the then ascendant 'nation-building' model, most of these studies saw nationalism as a concomitant of the modernization processes. The 1980s, on the other hand, mark a turning point in many respects. With the publication of John Armstrong's *Nations Before Nationalism* (1982), Benedict Anderson's *Imagined Communities* (1983), Ernest Gellner's *Nations and Nationalism* (1983), Eric Hobsbawm and Terence Ranger's *The Invention of Tradition* (1983) and Anthony D. Smith's *The Ethnic Origins of Nations* (1986), among others, the debate on nationalism completed its 'adolescence'. In this period, the theories grew more sophisticated and the 'lines of battle' became clearer. Nationalism, which had to wait until 1974 to have its first academic journal, finally had a stimulating, even polemical, literature.

There are, I think, two reasons for the belated development of a fully-fledged literature on nationalism. The first is the general indifference of social scientists to nationalism as a subject of investigation: nationalism was belittled by mainstream academic thinking until quite recently, and its full potential was not properly understood. Interestingly enough, this condescending attitude still prevails to a certain extent. One can observe its reflections in the studies of nationalism which take great pains to justify their 'right to exist': if we take a quick look at the articles and books written in the last few years, we can see that most of them begin by mentioning how important nationalism has become 'recently', that is after the collapse of communism, and by enumerating cases of ethnic conflict from this or that region of the world to support this argument. Even the examples cited are similar: Rwanda, Bosnia, Somalia, Eritrea and so on. This attitude is partly conditioned by the rigidity and conservatism of the established disciplines. A rigid conception of social science rules that political science should study the state or, say, democracy, party systems, equality, justice and power. International Relations should focus on the relations between states and analyse war or peace. Sociology should examine the society, for example the relations between individuals and various collectivities. According to orthodox conceptions which have dominated the established disciplines for many decades, nations and nationalism do not constitute a problem to be investigated: their existence is taken for granted.

This picture, however, is not an accurate representation of reality. Nationalism plays an important role in the creation of many states. In other cases, states have embraced nationalism later, to justify their right to exist in a world of nation-states. If democracy means 'rule by the people', then the people are almost always conceived as a nation. Equality or justice is usually required for the members of the nation, and elites compete for power in order to rule the 'nation'. On the other hand, both war and peace take place among 'nations', or more properly for the 'nations'. Finally, the society of the sociologist is more often than not a 'nation' whose members share a particular culture and live within definite borders. The culture that s/he explores is a 'national' or ethnic culture. In short, there is no area in the social sciences which has not felt, directly or indirectly, the spell of nationalism. Under these circumstances, it is quite surprising to encounter such indifference *vis-à-vis* nationalism. To understand this, we should consider the second reason.

The second reason that deferred scholarly intrusions into national phenomena was the tendency to equate nationalism with its extreme manifestations, that is with separatist movements that threatened the stability of existing states or with aggressive right-wing politics. Such a view confines nationalism to the periphery, treating it as the property of others, not of 'us' (Billig 1995: 5; Calhoun 1997). As Billig contends, ' "our" nationalism is not presented as nationalism, which is dangerously irrational, surplus and alien'; it is presented as 'patriotism', which is good and beneficial (1995: 55). In fact, this view is accepted consciously or unconsciously by all sides, namely by both those who do not take nationalism seriously as a subject of academic inquiry, and those who study it. Nothing illustrates this better than the 'standard introductions' I have alluded to earlier, which mention only protracted ethnic conflicts or wars as examples of nationalism. The same conviction lies behind the depictions of nationalism as a 'tide-like' phenomenon, that is emerging under crisis situations, then suddenly disappearing once normal conditions are restored. One particular manifestation of this is the 'return of the repressed' perspective which impels many commentators to suggest that we are faced with a new wave of nationalism after the collapse of Soviet type communism in 1989 (for example Ignatieff 1993: 2). Brubaker notes that there is a 'quasi-Freudian' flavour in these depictions:

> Lacking the rationally regulative ego of self-regulating civil society, the communist regimes repressed the primordial national id through a harshly punitive communist superego. With the collapse of the communist superego, the repressed ethnonational id returns in full force, wreaking vengeance, uncontrolled by the regulative ego. (1998: 285–6)

Brubaker argues convincingly that the policies pursued by communist regimes were anything but 'anti-national': 'The regime repressed *nationalism*, of course; but at the same time, it went further than any other state before or since in institutionalising territorial *nationhood* and ethnic *nationality* as fundamental social categories' (*ibid.*: 286). More generally, 'the claim that nationalism is returning implies that it has been away' (Billig 1995: 47). As Billig observes, the wars waged by democratic states are not labelled nationalist by those who subscribe to this view. Ignatieff, for instance, 'hardly mentions the Vietnam or Falklands Wars, let alone the various US sorties into Korea, Panama or Grenada', all of which occur 'during nationalism's so-called quiescent period' (*ibid.*).

This book will diverge from these more conventional accounts which take 'our' nationalism for granted, and will instead endorse an analytical framework developed by a number of scholars in recent years (Balibar 1990; Billig 1995; Brubaker 1996, 1998; Calhoun 1993, 1995, 1997). At the heart of this approach lies the belief that nationalism is not a latent force that manifests itself only under extraordinary conditions, a kind of natural disaster which strikes spontaneously and unpredictably. Nationalism is a discourse that constantly shapes our consciousness and the way we constitute the meaning of the world. It determines our collective identity by producing and reproducing us as 'nationals' (Billig 1995: 6). It is a form of seeing and interpreting that conditions our daily speech, behaviours and attitudes.

Obviously, this is a very general definition, one that might be criticized on the grounds that it does not explain too much or that it overlooks the differences between various types of nationalism. However, I will argue that this 'umbrella definition' is more useful than depictions based on a distinction between 'good' and 'bad' nationalisms or nationalism and patriotism. These definitions not only cause a 'terminological chaos' (Connor 1994: chapter 4), but also present us with the different versions of the same phenomenon as if they are separate phenomena – holding, for instance, that 'patriotism and nationalism represent two very different states of mind' (Billig 1995: 55). It is true that the Serbian militia in Kosovo or the ETA militants have different motives than ordinary French or American citizens, yet all these motives, despite their varying forms and intensity, belong to the same family. What unites them is the nationalist discourse: both the ETA militants who commit acts of terrorism and the French citizens who sing *La Marseillese* in football stadiums use the nationalist discourse to explain, justify, and hence legitimize their actions. The motives and the actions might take different forms, but they are all of the same kind. The definition I have offered above spots this commonality and shows that seemingly disparate emotions, beliefs and actions are all manifestations of the same phenomenon. The problem of overgeneralization, on the other hand, might be resolved by using additional sub-definitions or typologies.

To recapitulate, then, the tendency to equate nationalism with its extreme manifestations was the second reason that delayed the development of a diversified literature, because nationalism was the problem of those in the periphery, not 'ours': when they settled their territorial disputes and completed their nation-building processes, they would likewise reach the stage of 'good', harmless nationalism. This detached stance was accompanied by a certain dose of Eurocentrism. In the words of Löfgren:

> The old nations have images of operetta states and banana republics, and in these caricatures we see clearly the institutionalized patterns for what a proper nation is supposed to look like. Successfully accomplished national projects, such as that of the Swedish or the French, are quickly taken for granted. Unsuccessful examples, on the other hand, serve as examples of unrealistic ambitions or airy-fairy dreams, or merely comic attempts to imitate the old national giants. (1993: 166)

Needless to say, history did not unfold as expected by 'evolutionary determinists' who saw 'the rise of nations as part of the "movement of history", and a stage that was necessary . . . in the development of human history' (Smith 1991b: 353). Not only did the existing problems remain unresolved, but new ones cropped up incessantly. Moreover, the 'good', 'democratic' nationalisms of the developed countries could not thwart the emergence of ethnic discontent or separatist movements within their borders, as was the case in Québec, Northern Ireland or the Basque country.

Today, we witness that both reasons that delayed the development of a fully-fledged literature on nationalism are gradually disappearing. Despite the continuing intransigence of established disciplines who insist in seeing nationalism as an 'academic vogue' like postmodernism, destined to pass away as soon as another 'pastime' is found, nationalism is now one of the most explored subjects in social sciences. Almost every week, new books join the library shelves allotted to the burgeoning literature on nationalism. As Smith rightly observes, 'it has indeed become quite impossible to keep abreast of the tide of publications in the field' (1998: xi). *Canadian Review of Studies in Nationalism* is no longer the only academic journal in the field, and is accompanied by such journals as *Ethnic and Racial Studies, Nationalism and Ethnic Politics* and *Nations and Nationalism.*

As a result of these developments, specialization in the field has increased; new topics like identity, migration, diasporas, multiculturalism and genocide have been discovered; and nationalism has entered the curricula of many universities. A parallel interest can be observed in the media. Newspapers and television news are replete with the details of ethnic conflicts from various regions. Moreover, since the media plays an important role in shaping public opinion, people are on the whole more aware of the conflicts that involve their own countries.

On the other hand, it can also be asserted that the debate on nationalism has reached a more mature stage in recent years. Today, the questions and problems that bedevil the study of nationalism are well-known. The answers provided to these questions or the solution proposals are no longer uniform. In sum, we are faced with a much more diversified literature than 20 years ago: time, now, is ripe for a critical review of the theoretical debate on nationalism and for an assessment of the recent developments in the field.

Objectives

This book has three main objectives: first, to provide a systematic overview of some of the key theories of nationalism and to consider the main criticisms raised against them in a comparative perspective; secondly, to diagnose the deficiencies of the classical debate and to specify the theoretical problems we are still facing; and finally, to propose, in the light of these considerations and criticisms, an analytical framework that can be used in the study of nationalism. Before proceeding, however, certain points relating to the scope of the study should be clarified.

The first of these concerns my choice of period. Most of the theories/approaches reviewed in this study are formulated in the second half of the twentieth century, more specifically since the 1960s. In a way, this was inevitable: it is only in the last three or four decades that a fully-developed 'theoretical' debate on nationalism has emerged. Historians began to write the histories of particular nations or comparative studies of nationalism relatively early, but sociologists and political scientists remained silent on the subject until quite recently (Halliday 1997a, 1997b; Smith 1983). Ironically, however, there are not many studies reviewing the theories and approaches of this period in a systematic way – a notable exception being Smith's recent book *Nationalism and Modernism* (1998). My decision to write this book is also motivated by this astonishing lacuna.

The second point that needs to be clarified relates to my focus on a particular literature, namely the Anglo-Saxon literature. The reason for this is quite simple: most of the studies on nationalism are produced in the Anglo-Saxon world. Books and articles written elsewhere are translated into English, usually, though not always, in a short period of time. Under these circumstances, it is very difficult to talk about a 'meaningful' choice. A student of nationalism who wants to study the theories of nationalism has no alternative but to focus almost exclusively on the Western, particularly the Anglo-Saxon, literature. This is even valid in the case of the studies which criticize the Eurocentric nature of the mainstream literature on nationalism. The works of the Subaltern Studies Group are a good case in point. Scholars like Partha Chatterjee and Ranajit Guha attempted to reinterpret the history of South Asia from the vantage point of the subordinated (Eley and Suny 1996a), but, ironically enough, they have done this in the language of the colonizer, namely English. In short, whether we like it or not, and whether we call it 'cultural imperialism' or 'globalization', English has become a kind of *lingua franca* in most areas of social sciences. One last point that needs clarification concerns the choice of theories and writers to be included in the study. The first thing to be said is that such a choice cannot be totally objective. Hence, even though I took great pains to include all major theories and approaches, I cannot assert that my selection is perfect or impartial. Many scholars who have made important contributions to our understanding of nationalism are left out because of time and space limitations. Among these, Anthony Giddens (1985), Michael Mann (1995, 1996), Charles Tilly (1975, 1990), Partha Chatterjee (1986, 1990), Liah Greenfeld (1992) are the first that come to mind. The works of some of these scholars will be discussed briefly in Chapter 2 where I will provide an historical overview of the debate and Chapter 6 where I will focus on recent approaches. Suffice it to say at this point that all key sides of the theoretical debate on nationalism will be represented in this book with usually more than one theorist.

Structure of the Book

As I stated earlier, one of the objectives of this book is to offer a critical and comparative review of the main theories of nationalism, focusing mostly on the post-1960s literature. This does not mean, however, that the debates of earlier periods are irrelevant. Contemporary theorists of nationalism are heavily influenced by the assumptions and convictions of their predecessors. With this in mind, I will begin my survey by situating the contemporary debate historically and theoretically. I will identify four stages in the study of nationalism:

- The eighteenth and nineteenth centuries, when the idea of nationalism was born. Here, the contributions of thinkers like Kant, Herder, Fichte, Rousseau, Mill, Marx, Engels, Bauer and Renner, and historians like Michelet, Renan, von Treitschke and Lord Acton will be briefly discussed.

- 1918–45, when nationalism became a subject of academic inquiry. The works of Carleton Hayes, Hans Kohn and Louis Snyder will be considered in this context.
- 1945 to the late 1980s, when the sociologists and political scientists joined the debate and when, partly as a result of this, the debate became much more diversified. Here, the contributions of modernization theorists, for example Daniel Lerner, Karl W. Deutsch and early modernists will be discussed.
- From the late 1980s to the present, when attempts to transcend the classical debate (characteristic of the third stage) have been made.

In Chapter 2, I will also try to locate the main questions around which the debate on nationalism revolves.

The following four chapters will be devoted to the discussion of the main theoretical positions with regard to nationalism. In accordance with the chronological order and the general tendency in the field, I will start my discussion with the primordialist approach. After describing the different versions of primordialism, namely the 'naturalist', 'sociobiological' and 'culturalist' explanations, I will consider the main criticisms levelled against scholars who have subscribed to primordialism. This scheme of presentation will be largely preserved in the subsequent chapters.

Chapter 4 will be reserved for the modernists. In contrast to conventional accounts which treat the modernists as a unitary category, I will divide them into three groups in terms of the key factors they have identified in their accounts of nationalism. Hence, neo-Marxists like Tom Nairn and Michael Hechter who have stressed the importance of economic factors will be discussed under the heading 'economic transformation'; scholars like John Breuilly, Paul Brass and Eric Hobsbawm who have emphasized the role of politics and power struggles between contending elites will be considered under the heading 'political transformation'; finally, scholars like Ernest Gellner, Benedict Anderson and Miroslav Hroch who have given priority to cultural factors will be reviewed under the heading 'cultural transformation'. Needless to say, these are not mutually exclusive categories. As Breuilly has said, 'classifications are simply sets of interrelated definitions. Empirically, they are not right or wrong; rather they are either helpful or unhelpful' (1993a: 9). I will argue that the classification I am introducing here to present the modernist explanations is helpful, at least more helpful than accounts that treat the modernists as a monolithic category.

Chapter 5 will explore the ethno-symbolist position. I will first present the arguments of the two leading figures of this approach, John Armstrong and Anthony D. Smith, then consider the major criticisms raised against ethno-symbolist explanations.

Chapter 6 will be devoted to recent approaches. In this chapter, I will first try to substantiate the claim that we have entered a new stage in the debate on nationalism since the end of the 1980s. Briefly, I will argue that the Eurocentric, gender-blind character of the 'classical' debate on nationalism has been transcended by studies which have drawn our attention to such issues as the differential participation of women in nationalist projects, the daily reproduction of nationhood, the experience of nationalism in postcolonial societies, the specific contributions of the people on the national margins, that is the 'hybrids', to the construction of national identities and the like. Then I will discuss in some detail two well-received analyses of this type, namely Michael Billig's analysis of the daily reproduction of nationhood and Nira Yuval-Davis' study of the gendered dimension of nationalist projects.

In Chapter 7, I will first embark on a critical evaluation of the main theoretical positions. Then, in the light of these considerations, I will propose an analytical framework that might be used in the study of nationalism. This framework, based on a synthesis of ideas put forward by various scholars, will consist of five simple propositions:

Proposition 1.   There can be no 'general' theory of nationalism.
Proposition 2.   There is no 'one' nationalism; not only are there different types of nationalism, but different members of the national or ethnic collectivities promote different constructions of nationhood.
Proposition 3.   The common denominator of all these different movements, ideas, policies and projects is the nationalist discourse. In other words, what unites different nationalisms is the discourse and rhetoric of nationhood.
Proposition 4.   The nationalist discourse can only be effective if it is reproduced on a daily basis.

Proposition 5. Any study of national identity should acknowledge differences of ethnicity, gender, sexuality, class or place in the life-cycle that affect the construction and reconstruction of individual identities.

Further Reading

Despite the renewal of interest in the study of nations and nationalism, there have been very few attempts to provide a theoretical survey of the field. Two important exceptions are Smith (1983) [1971] and (1998). Smith's earlier book is the standard work of reference for the theories of the 1950s and 1960s, especially the model of 'nation-building'. His recent *Nationalism and Modernism*, on the other hand, constitutes a sequel to his first book and focuses on the theories and approaches of the last three decades. Though they do not provide a systematic overview of explanatory accounts of nationalism, the general studies by Calhoun (1997) and McCrone (1998) are very useful as guides in the field since they address many of the issues and debates around the subject.

The last ten years have also witnessed an outpouring of readers which contain articles or extracts from key texts on nationalism. Among these, the following are particularly helpful: Hutchinson and Smith (1994), Dahbour and Ishay (1995), Balakrishnan (1996b), Eley and Suny (1996b) and Woolf (1996).

Apart from these, the reader should also consult *The ASEN Bulletin*, issued by the Association of Ethnicity and Nationalism (based at the London School of Economics) for current publications.

2

Discourses and Debates on Nationalism

All fixed, fast-frozen relations, with their train of ancient and venerable prejudices and opinions, are swept away, all new ones become antiquated before they can ossify. All that is solid melts into air, all that is holy is profaned, and man is at last compelled to face with sober senses, his real conditions of life, and his relations with his kind . . .

Karl Marx–Friedrich Engels, *The Communist Manifesto*

Historical Overview

Nationalism, as an ideology and a social movement, has been very much in evidence since the end of the eighteenth century. In fact, it would not be an exaggeration to say that 'the history of Europe from 1789 to 1945 is synonymous with the history of the growth and development of modern nations' (Baycroft 1998: 3). Yet, as I stated in the introduction, nationalism did not become a subject of academic investigation until well into the first half of the twentieth century. Up to the First World War, interest in nationalism was largely ethical and philosophical. The scholars of this period, predominantly historians and social philosophers, were more concerned with 'the merits and defects' of the doctrine than with the origins and spread of national phenomena (Smith 1983: 257). The nation-state was treated as an alternative to the 'idiocy of rural life and precapitalist parochialism', hence as a progressive stage in the historical evolution of human societies (MacLaughlin 1987: 1). The corollary of this evolutionist view, shared by both the liberals

12

and the Marxists, was that nationalism would gradually wither away with the establishment of a peaceful international order (Halliday 1997d). In this context, the existence of nations was taken for granted. The social and political realities of the period did not leave room for alternative viewpoints: nationalism was the compelling norm and no one could remain indifferent to its emotional appeal. Not surprisingly, then, the scholars of this period were mostly guided by political concerns. In these early commentaries, Smith notes, there was 'no attempt to fashion a general theory applicable to all cases, or to resolve the antinomies of each issue in a coherent and systematic manner' (1998: 10).

This explains why the early works of Carleton Hayes and Hans Kohn are generally regarded as a turning point in the study of nationalism. Hayes and Kohn, 'the twin founding fathers' of the academic scholarship on nationalism in the words of Kemiläinen (1964), never questioned the fundamental assumptions of their predecessors. Yet, their analyses bequeathed important theoretical insights to succeeding generations. The next stage of the study of nationalism, which can be broadly dated from the end of the Second World War, was heavily influenced by the process of decolonization and the establishment of new states in the Third World (Snyder 1997: 233). From the 1960s onwards, the debate was no longer confined to historians. With the participation of sociologists and political scientists, the theoretical literature on nationalism became much more diversified. The debate shows no signs of abating to this day.

In the light of these considerations, a historical overview of the period after the First World War might seem more relevant for the purposes of this book. However, we need a wider historical perspective to make sense of the contemporary theoretical debate. There are mainly two reasons for this. First, despite its belated recognition as an object of study, nationalism as a political doctrine or ideology, that is 'a set of political principles that movements and individuals espouse', has a longer past (Halliday 1997d: 361; cf. Halliday 1997b). It is possible to trace the origins of the idea of nationalism back to German Romantics (eighteenth century), or even to the Enlightenment. Some scholars have indeed explained nationalism primarily as a political doctrine emanating from the musings of dislocated German intellectuals (most notably Kedourie 1994). Others, in a Durkheimian vein, have tended to see nationalism as a modern and secular surrogate for religion, emerging mostly in the painful period of transition to modernity (Smith 1998: Chapter 5). To make sense of these approaches, we need to explore the evolution of the idea of nationalism.

Secondly, and perhaps more importantly, starting the overview from the 1960s would obscure the degree to which contemporary theories are influenced by earlier reflection on nationalism. As I have stated earlier, the post-1960 debates were not born in a vacuum, and in that sense they have to be understood within the framework of the debates and discourses that preceded them, or as Anderson would probably say, out of which – as well as against which – they came into being (1991: 12). Examples that spring to mind include the influence of Gramsci on Tom Nairn, of Lenin on Michael Hechter, of Durkheim on Ernest Gellner and of Weber on Anthony D. Smith – among others. These examples clearly reveal that we need a broader historical perspective if we are to assess the current debates properly.

Taking these points into consideration, I will begin my overview with a discussion of the eighteenth and nineteenth centuries, when the doctrine of nationalism was first framed. My selection of thinkers and scholars will be necessarily incomplete since it is very difficult to determine exactly who – or in that respect which ideas – contributed to the genesis of the nationalist doctrine. This can also explain why scholars who explore the origins of the idea of nationalism highlight different thinkers in their accounts. In what follows, I will try to consider those thinkers whose role in the formation of the idea of nationalism is commonly acknowledged – by most, if not all, scholars. Needless to say, this does not mean that these are the only thinkers who have contributed to the idea of nationalism.

The study of nationalism is generally divided into three stages: before the First World War, 1918–45, and 1945 to the present (Snyder 1997: 231). In what follows I will largely conform to this classification, but with a minor qualification: I will argue that the period after 1945 should not be treated as a single stage. What lies behind this argument is the belief that some of the studies produced in the last decade signal a new stage in the study of nationalism, as they question – and refute – the fundamental premises upon which the 'classical' debate is based. Taking these attempts into account, I will treat the last decade as a separate stage in my historical overview. Obviously, it can be argued that it is too early to speak of a new stage or that most of these analyses are in fact partial and fragmentary (for such an argument see Smith 1998: 219). Against this view, I will stress the importance of these approaches and contend that the issues to which they draw our attention will gradually assert themselves within the academic community. The decision of *Nations and Nationalism*, one of the leading academic journals in the field, to publish a special issue on 'gender and nation' is a clear illustration of this trend.

I will thus identify four stages in the study – although the term 'study' may not be appropriate for the period before 1918 – of nationalism:

- The eighteenth and nineteenth centuries when the idea of nationalism was born;
- 1918–45 when nationalism became a subject of academic inquiry;
- 1945 to the late 1980s when the debate became more diversified with the participation of sociologists and political scientists;
- From the late 1980s to the present when attempts to transcend the 'classical' debate were made.

The Eighteenth and Nineteenth Centuries

The question of whether nationalism had its own 'grand thinkers' has always been a source of great controversy. Gellner's answer to this question is quite clear: 'these thinkers did not really make much difference. If one of them had fallen, others would have stepped into his place. No one was indispensable'. He concludes: 'we shall not learn too much about nationalism from the study of its own prophets' since they all suffered from a pervasive false consciousness (1983: 124–5). In a similar vein, Anderson argues that 'unlike most other isms, nationalism has never produced its own grand thinkers: no Hobbeses, Tocquevilles, Marxes or Webers' (1991: 5). Others, notably O'Leary, disagree with this view: 'It is strange not to classify Weber as a nationalist grand thinker, stranger still that Rousseau, Burke, John Stuart Mill and Friedrich

List are not seen as nationalist grand thinkers . . .' (1998: 87; *cf.* Minogue 1996). This discussion clearly shows that the problem lies in determining who can be considered as a 'nationalist thinker', and not in deciding whether those thinkers who have contributed to the nationalist doctrine are 'grand'.

Whatever the answer given to this question, the origins of the nationalist doctrine are generally traced back to German Romantic thought. But the thinkers of the period were heavily influenced by the ideas of their predecessors. Among these, the ideas of Immanuel Kant, considered by many as the epitome of cosmopolitan thought, were the most important. In fact, according to Kedourie, who explains nationalism in terms of a revolution in European philosophy, it all started with Kant (1994: chapter 2).

Immanuel Kant (1724–1804) was not of course a nationalist. Moreover, he cannot be held responsible for the ways in which his ideas were used. But the political consequences of the ethical and epistemological dualism he developed were far-reaching (Smith 1983: 31–2). At the heart of this dualism lies a separation between the external, that is phenomenal, world and man's inner world. According to Kant, the source of knowledge was the phenomenal world: our knowledge was based on sensations emanating from things-in-themselves. But the phenomenal world was a world of 'inexplicable contingencies' and 'iron necessities', and if our morality were also derived from this kind of knowledge 'then we could never be free but always the slave either of contingency or of blind personal laws' (Kedourie 1994: 14). Morality, then, had to be separated from knowledge, hence the phenomenal world: instead, it should be 'the outcome of obedience to a universal law which is to be found within ourselves'.

Kant held that man could only be free when he obeys the laws of morality which he finds within himself, and not in the external world. This was, according to Kedourie, a revolutionary definition of freedom. Kant equated virtue with free will. On the other hand, neither freedom nor virtue depended on God's commands. Hence the new formula: 'the good will, which is the free will, is also the autonomous will' (Kedourie 1994: 16). This was revolutionary because the formula made the individual the centre and the sovereign of the universe: self-determination was now the supreme good. Smith concludes that this makes republicanism the sole possible form of government, 'for only in a republic can the laws express the autonomous will of the citizens' (1983: 32).

Kant's new formula was not immune from philosophical difficulties. It was Kant's disciple Johann Gottlieb Fichte (1762–1814) who first attempted to solve the problems raised by his doctrine. As opposed to Kant who maintained that the external world is beyond our sensations and that things-in-themselves exist prior to – and independent of – the perceiving self, Fichte held that they are both the product of a universal consciousness and an Ego which embraces everything within itself. Such a theory eliminated Kant's 'inexplicable contingencies' or 'iron necessities' and made the external world – and hence knowledge which emanated from it – comprehensible. According to this view, the world is a coherent whole since it is a manifestation of the Ego (Smith 1983: 32): 'A world takes on reality and coherence because it is the product of a single consciousness, and its parts can exist at all and share in reality only by taking their place within this world' (Kedourie 1994: 29). This view was particularly relevant to politics because it implied that the whole is prior to, and more important than, all its parts: 'knowledge of the parts is illusory; no parts can be known by themselves, since they cannot exist on their own, outside a coherent and ordered whole' (*ibid.*). This was the origin of the famous – infamous? – 'organic theory of the state'. Kedourie sums this up succinctly:

> individuals, as such, are phantoms; they gain reality in so far as they have a place in a whole. Consequently, the freedom of the individual, which is his self-realization, lies in identifying himself with the whole . . . Complete freedom means total absorption in the whole . . . From this metaphysics the post-Kantians deduced a theory of the state . . . The state therefore is not a collection of individuals who have come together in order to protect their own particular interests; the state is higher than the individual and comes before him. It is only when he and the state are one that the individual realizes his freedom. (*Ibid.*: 30)

Another contribution to the doctrine of nationalism comes from 'historicism'. A brief review of the German thinker Johann Gottfried Herder (1744–1803) can help us understand the main arguments of this school of thought (Breuilly 1993a: 56–64). Herder's point of departure is quite simple: only language makes man human. The concept of 'pre-linguistic' man is meaningless for Herder since man is defined by his language capacity. Moreover, 'language can only be learnt in a community. It is synonymous with thought'. And 'every language is different from every other'. The implications of these views are not hard to guess: if language is thought and if it can only be learnt in a community, 'it follows that each community has its own mode of thought' (*ibid.*: 57). In fact, if each language is a different way of expressing universal values, then it is also the manifestation of unique values and ideas. Obviously, the same logic applies to customs, traditions, ceremonies and the like each of which can be considered as another sort of language. 'Community', then, is the sum total of these modes of expression. However, it is more than the mere collection of all these parts but has a unity of its own. Here, once again we encounter the 'organicist' thought. In order to understand a society, it is necessary to learn all the ways of the society in question. Understanding a society is like learning a language. According to the historicist, history is the major form such understanding took: it is the only way of apprehending the spirit of a community (*ibid.*).

In extolling the diversity of cultures, Herder's aim was to oppose the universalism of the Enlightenment. But according to Barnard, 'he had no wish to sacrifice diversity even if this meant a certain degree of tension or conflict, or some disorder and inefficiency, in the conduct of public affairs' (1983: 246). The political order he envisaged was inspired by the example of ancient Hebrews who were conscious of themselves as 'one people' despite their institutional and tribal fragmentation. In such a 'quasi-pluralist' order, individuals would be free to pursue their diverse interests and form a variety of autonomous institutions to serve these interests (*ibid.*: 246–7).

Historicist arguments were carried to the political arena with the help of other ideas. Breuilly contends that the most important of these is the idea of 'authenticity' (1993a: 59). What lies behind this idea is the need to determine what is 'natural' in a particular community and, by implication, what is 'unnatural'. Drawing on this idea, Herder objects to the conquest of one society by another, which he sees as a 'wild mixing together of different human species and nations under one spectre' (cited in Breuilly 1993a: 59). For him, societies are created by nature and nothing is more 'unnatural' than the disruption of the development of a particular society. Fichte joins Herder in the quest for authenticity, arguing that language mirrors the national soul, 'and to purge the language of alien impurities was to defend the national soul against subversion by foreign values'. He also applies these views to a concrete example and argues for the need to protect the German language from the impact of Latin, which he sees as a 'dead language'. As Breuilly notes, these views were taken up by the racist currents of the nineteenth century and linked to 'human nature' (*ibid.*: 60).

The political implications of all these ideas are not hard to guess: national communities are unique, *sui generis* formations. They might have forgotten their true natures or entered a period of recess, but this does not mean that they will not recover and reclaim their true, that is 'authentic', selves. The members of national collectivities should be able to determine their own future – self-determination is the supreme political good – and each nation, which is more than the sum total of all citizens, should establish its own state: 'the fatal equation of language, state and nation, which is the cornerstone of the German version of nationalism' was thus formulated (Smith 1983: 33).

Herder and Fichte were not the only representatives of German Romantic thought. The Lutheran theologian Friedrich Schleiermacher (1768–1834) who developed Kant's doctrines, his friend Friedrich Schlegel (1772–1829), Fichte's disciple F. W. Schelling (1775–1854), the publicist Adam Müller (1779–1805), the dramatist Friedrich Schiller (1759–1805), the publicist Ernst Moritz Arndt (1769–1860) and nationalist agitator Friedrich Jahn (1778–1852) were other important figures of this school of thought (for details see Kedourie 1994; Kohn 1950). However, the contributions of these thinkers are not generally considered to be as important as those of Herder and Fichte.

On the other hand, other ideas have also contributed to the formation of the nationalist doctrine. Chief among these was the principle of self-determination, that is 'the idea that a group of people have a certain set of shared interests and should be allowed to express their wishes on how these interests should best be promoted' (Halliday 1997d: 362), mostly associated with the French political thinker Jean-Jacques Rousseau (1712–78). Actually,

Kedourie does not consider Rousseau's contribution to be important, noting that he did not have a systematic theory of the state (1994: 32–3). Many scholars, however, disagree with Kedourie and maintain that Rousseau's writings played a crucial role in shaping the German Romantic thought (Dahbour and Ishay 1995; O'Leary 1996; Halliday 1997d).

For Rousseau, the biggest danger man faces when living in society is 'the possible tyranny of will by his fellowmen' (Barnard 1984: 245). To guard against this danger, men need to exchange their selfish will for the 'general will'. This can only be achieved if they cease to be natural men and become citizens instead. Natural men live for themselves, whereas men as citizens depend on the community of which they are a part. By becoming a citizen, man exchanges independence for dependence and autarky for participation and '[t]he best social institutions are those which make individuals most intensely conscious of their mutual interdependence' (*ibid.*: 245). In short, a political association makes sense only if it can protect men from the capriciousness of others: 'this it can solely bring about if it substitutes law for the individual, if it can generate a public will and arm it with a strength that is beyond the power of any individual will' (*ibid.*: 246).

While Rousseau emphasizes the distinction between man and citizen, he does not envisage conflictual relations between citizenship and patriotism. For Rousseau, Barnard argues, both 'citizen' and 'patriot' are conceivable only within the context of the nation-state: '[n]either citizen nor patriot could qualify as a cosmopolitan' (*ibid.*: 249). On the other hand, it is not easy to engender a simultaneous consciousness of patriotism and citizenship. It is only in the canton that 'citizenship is suffused with the passionate zeal animating the patriot'. A state that is as large as Poland, for example, cannot bring about this coincidence of citizenship and patriotism unless, perhaps, it is organized as a confederation of autonomous states (*ibid.*: 250).

At this stage, it needs to be pointed out that the sources of citizenship and patriotism are different for Rousseau. He defined patriotism as that 'fine and lively feeling which gives the force of self-love all the beauty of virtue, and lends it an energy which, without disfiguring it, makes it the most heroic of all passions' (cited in *ibid.*). Love of one's own country, Rousseau writes, is 'a hundred times more ardent and delightful than that of a mistress' (cited in Barnard 1983: 236). Unlike patriotism which is the work of spontaneous will, citizenship is the work of rational will. Rousseau claims that men do not unite simply because they resemble each other. In other words, cultural similarities are not sufficient to become a nation: individuals must see a point in sharing that culture. It follows that,

> what constitutes citizenship is not sentiments of affinity or love but reasoned agreement on what is and what is not in the common interest, and the will to abide by such an agreement. Citizenship, therefore, does not derive from patriotism; while patriotism is a spontaneous and unmediated given, citizenship is an artificial and mediated creation. (Barnard 1984: 252–3)

Rousseau believed that without some degree of political freedom, men have no way of knowing how to give expression to their own will. 'We cannot know what people might do or not do or say if they are enslaved'. (*ibid.*: 260) This stance was particularly clear in the case of the Jews. According to him, the Jews were destined to remain unable to escape the tyranny exercised against them until they had a free and just homeland to live in: 'not until they have "a free state of their own, with schools and universities, where they can speak and debate without risk", shall we be able to know what they have to say or wish to bring about' (*ibid.*).

This brings us to another, very important, source of influence on the development of the idea of nationalism, which was, of course, the French Revolution of 1789. It was, in fact, within the context of the French Revolution that the notion of the nation was put into practice in legal and political terms. For the revolutionaries of 1789, the nation was the only legitimate source of political power (Baycroft 1998: 5). Here the concept 'nation' expressed 'the idea of a shared, common, equal citizenship, the unity of the people': hence the motto of the French Revolution, *liberté, égalité, fraternité* (Halliday 1997d: 362). In this, the revolutionaries were inspired by a book by the abbé Emmanuel Joseph Sieyès entitled *What is the Third Estate?* In the ancien régime, the French parliament, the Estates-General, consisted of three parts: the First Estate, comprising the nobility; the Second Estate, embracing the clergy;

and the Third Estate, representing everyone else. Sieyès argued in his book that all members of the nation were citizens, hence equal before the law. He rejected 'the principle of class and special upper-class feudal privileges, and claimed that the first two estates did not even qualify as parts of the nation' (Baycroft 1998: 6). Halliday notes that this evolution in France was paralleled in the Americas, in the revolt against British rule in the North (1776–83) and in the uprising against Spanish rule in the South (1820–28). In both cases, the basis for the revolt was political, that is the rejection of rule from imperial centres in Europe (1997d: 362).

The translation of these various ideas into a fully-fledged ideology took some time. But the political doctrine we recognize today as nationalism was already in place by the early nineteenth century. On the other hand, scholarly interest in it was still largely ethical. We find two sorts of responses to nationalism in the nineteenth century. The first one, which I will call the 'partisan' for want of a better term, was the approach of scholars and thinkers who were sympathetic to nationalism and who used their works to justify or enhance particular nationalisms. The second was the 'critical' approach of those who have been sceptical of nationalism and who saw it as a temporary stage in the historical evolution of human societies (*cf.* Snyder 1997; Smith 1996a). This critical attitude was not confined to Marxists; some liberals too, notably Lord Acton, were wary of nationalism and its implications. The pioneering figures of the nascent fields of sociology and political science, such as Weber, Durkheim, Tönnies, Mosca and Pareto, did not disturb the pattern set by their predecessors and took their places within one of these two camps.

Before proceeding, however, two caveats must be added to this picture. First, this binary classification does not imply a complete separation between the two categories. There were a number of similarities between those who were sympathetic to nationalism and those who opposed it. Of these, perhaps the most important was that the scholars and thinkers of both camps took the existence of nations and nationalism for granted. None of them questioned the 'naturalness' of nationhood. Second, the labels I attached to these categories do not denote 'eternal' – or absolute – attributes. The attitudes *vis-à-vis* nationalism not only changed from one thinker to the next, but were also subject to fluctuations over time. Hence, the labels in question should be taken at their face value, that is as rough indicators of the main difference between the attitudes of these two groups of thinkers.

The 'partisan' camp was predominantly populated by historians. The role of historians in promoting particular national movements is widely recognized (Smith 1996a). Nationalist historians have often 'unearthed' (in most cases 'created') the evidence which will testify to their nation's perennial existence, or 'rediscovered' (in most cases 'invented') the customs, myths, symbols and rituals which will form the national culture (Hobsbawm and Ranger 1983). Here, I will briefly discuss the contributions of three such historians, namely Renan, Michelet and von Treitschke. Renan's views will be considered at the end of this section since he offered the most sophisticated analysis of his time and thus had a quite substantial impact on the thinking of succeeding generations.

The German historian Heinrich von Treitschke's (1834–96) nationalism was tinged with militarism and anti-semitism (Smith 1996a; James 1996; Guibernau 1996). According to him, the state is the supreme power: there is no authority above it. Rather, it is the state which formulates the laws and these are binding over all individuals that make up its population. The state exerts its power through war: 'The grandeur of history lies in the perpetual conflict of nations, and it is simply foolish to desire the suppression of their rivalry'. Thus, for him, war is political science *par excellence* (von Treitschke 1916, cited in Guibernau 1996: 8). Von Treitschke argued that the unity of the state should be based on nationality. However, nationality should not be understood in a restricted sense, that is as a legal bond. It should be complemented by blood-relationship – either real or imagined. Guibernau notes that von Treitschke rarely referred to nationalism in his writings (1996: 41). But he offers a definition of patriotism: 'genuine patriotism is the consciousness of co-operating with the body-politic, of being rooted in ancestral achievements and of transmitting them to descendants' (cited in Guibernau 1996: 10). These views led him to support the unification of Germany under Prussian leadership. He believed that there are two motor forces in history: 'the tendency of every state to amalgamate its population, in speech and manners, into one single unity, and the impulse of every vigorous nationality to construct a state of its own' (*ibid.*: 11). Given that only the large and powerful states counted for him as 'vigorous' nationalities, it is quite easy to understand why he saw Prussia as the 'unifying agent' of the German people. The best way to achieve a 'Greater Germany', then, was the incorporation of smaller states into Prussian territories.

The French historian Jules Michelet (1798–1874) on the other hand, saw the nation as the ultimate guarantee of individual freedom (Smith 1996a: 177–8). The Revolution of 1789 had signalled a new era, an era of fraternity, and in this new era there were neither poor nor rich, nobles nor plebeians. The disputes in the society had been solved; enemies had made peace. The new religion was that of patriotism and this religion was 'the worship of man, and the motive force of modern French and European history' (*ibid.*: 178). Michelet supported the nationalist movements in Italy, Poland and Ireland, all part of the Young Europe movement of Mazzini and saw them as 'fraternal sympathizers of France'.

The partisan camp did not consist of historians alone. The renowned English political theorist John Stuart Mill (1806–73) is a good case in point. Like his liberal nationalist predecessors, Mill fused the concept of republican citizenship with the principle of nationality which he defined in the following way:

> a portion of mankind may be said to constitute a Nationality if they are united among themselves by common sympathies which do not exist between them and any others – which make them cooperate with each other more willingly than with other people, desire to be under the same government, and desire that it should be government by themselves or a portion of themselves exclusively. (1996: 40)

Where the sentiment of nationality exists, Mill argued, 'there is a *prima facie* case for uniting all the members of the nationality under the same government, and a government to themselves apart. This is merely saying that the question of government ought to be decided by the governed' (*ibid.*: 41). Here we find, once again, the principle of self-determination to which Mill added the idea of representative government (Halliday 1997d: 362). For him, free institutions were next to impossible in a country made up of different nationalities: 'Among a people without fellow-feeling, especially if they read and speak different languages, the united public opinion, necessary to the working of representative government, cannot exist' (Mill 1996: 41–2). In short, the boundaries of governments should coincide in the main with those of nationalities if we are to have free institutions. These views enable us to move on to the 'critical' camp. The English historian and philosopher Lord Acton (1834–1902) who published an almost contemporaneous essay on the same theme (1862, reproduced in Balakrishnan 1996b) is a good starting point. Criticizing Mill, Lord Acton suggested that individual freedom was better maintained in a multinational state:

> If we take the establishment of liberty for the realization of moral duties to be the end of civil society, we must conclude that those states are substantially the most perfect which, like the British and Austrian Empires, include various nationalities without oppressing them. (1996: 36)

For Acton, to insist on national unity was to lead to revolution and despotism. The states in which 'no mixture of races has occurred are imperfect' and 'those in which its effects have disappeared are decrepit' (*ibid.*). It follows that 'a State which is incompetent to satisfy different races condemns itself; a State which labours to neutralize, to absorb or to expel them, destroys its own vitality'. Therefore, 'the theory of nationality . . . is a retrograde step in history' (*ibid.*).

The Marxists were indubitably the most important group within the critical camp. That nationalism has always created difficulties for the Marxist school is well-known, and these difficulties have been both political and theoretical (Kitching 1985; Munck 1986; Calhoun 1997). Is nationalism a form of 'false consciousness' which diverts the proletariat from the goal of international revolution? Or should we see the struggle of the proletariat with the bourgeoisie first as a national struggle? If so, then how do such national class struggles relate to the construction of international socialism (Kitching 1985: 99)? Besides these theoretical problems, Marxists were also faced with political exigencies. Communist parties had to change their positions *vis-à-vis* nationalism for tactical and strategic reasons. Sometimes nationalism was condemned (as in the case of nationalist movements against the Austro-Hungarian Empire), sometimes it was ardently supported (as in the case of anti-colonial nationalist movements).

Scholars offer different explanations for this ambivalent attitude and the ensuing lack of a Marxist theory of nationalism. For instance, Kitching argues that the Marxists, having their roots in Enlightenment rationalism, could not satisfactorily explain to themselves, let alone to others, 'how loyalty to a nation and particularly the placing of national identity above a class identity can be a rational thing to do'. For this reason, he contends, they have offered psychological explanations and saw nationalism as a manifestation of ideologically motivated 'irrational emotions' (Kitching 1985: 99). Calhoun notes that 'none of the other great social and political analysts has been as widely castigated for failure to grasp the importance of nationalism as Marx and Engels', and points to their overconfident internationalism for this failure (1997: 26). According to Calhoun, their greatest error was their assumption that people would respond to the material challenges of global economic integration simply as workers. However, 'workers suffered economic privations as heads of households, as members of communities, as religious people, as citizens – not just as workers' (*ibid.*: 27). Moreover, even when they thought of themselves as members of the working class, most workers continued to think of themselves first as members of particular occupations – as silk weavers, clockmakers and so on. In short, their responses to economic inequalities were shaped by their other identities as well, not only by their class loyalties. Guibernau, on the other hand, tries to account for Marx and Engels' failure to deal adequately with nationalism by pointing to their quest for a 'grand theory' capable of explaining all stages of societal evolution. For Marx, the central attribute of all social systems from Ancient Greece to present times was 'class struggle'. Accordingly, he explained the social, political and ideological aspects of societies by reference to economy, that is the mode and relations of production. In this context, Guibernau maintains, nationalism was a marginal phenomenon: 'Marx's emphasis upon the political sphere as "superstructure" led him to downplay both the nation-state and nationalism as major influences upon historical change' (1996: 42).

This 'classical' problem of Marxism has triggered a lively debate among the Marxists of the twentieth century. According to Poulantzas, for instance, the failure to theorize nationalism reveals all the impasses of traditional Marxism (Poulantzas 1980, cited in James 1996: 49). Poulantzas rejects the claim that the Marxists have underestimated nationalism by calling attention to the various debates that have taken place within the workers' movement. For him, the fact that no theory of nationalism could be formulated despite all these passionate debates shows clearly that there is no Marxist theory of the nation (James 1996: 49). Others disagree with him. One group of writers maintains that 'it is more important to recognize the strength of the [Marxist] theory of nationalism than worry about its imperfections (Blaut 1982, cited in James 1996: 50). Another group directly targets on the claim that there is no Marxist theory of the nation. Nimni (1991) for example rejects the idea that Marx and Engels' position *vis-à-vis* nationalism is conditioned by political exigencies, arguing that, despite their fragmentary nature, their writings on the nation have an underpinning coherence. Similarly, Munck criticizes attempts to deride the socialists who did try to come to grips with nationalism – namely Bauer, Ber Borochov, Connolly and Gramsci – and claims that they provide important insights into the nature of nationalism: 'It is now necessary to forge some kind of coherent Marxist approach to nationalism on the basis of these writers' (1986: 168). Neo-Marxists have also tried to overcome 'Marxism's great historical failure' by formulating a theory of their own (for example Hechter 1975; Nairn 1981; Hroch 1985). Some of these attempts will be discussed in Chapter 4.

For Marx (1818–83) and Engels (1820–95), who lived and worked through the age of nationalism, 'the modern nation was the direct result of a process whereby the capitalist mode of production superseded feudalism' (Nimni 1991: 18). It was the transition to a capitalist economy that forced the existing social formations in Western Europe to become more homogeneous and politically centralized. According to Nimni, this conceptualization of national formation was conditioned by their tendency to explain every significant social phenomenon in terms of an overall developmental logic, which led them to see nationalism as a necessary but temporary stage in the evolution of history (*ibid.*: 3–4).

It was in the context of this evolutionary logic that Marx and Engels revived the Hegelian distinction between 'historic' and 'non-historic' nations (Munck 1986: 9). Nimni notes that in their writings, the term nation was reserved for the permanent population of a nation-state, whereas an ethno-cultural community that had not achieved full national status, that is lacked a state of its own, was referred to as a nationality (1991: 23). They believed that nationalities will either become nations by acquiring a state of their own or remain as 'historyless peoples' (*Geschichtslosen Völker*). These non-historical nationalities were inherently reactionary, because they were unable to adapt to the capitalist mode of production. As their existence depended on the survival of the old order, they were necessarily regressive (*ibid.*).

In line with this general attitude, Marx and Engels supported the unification processes of what they considered to be historic nations, for example Germany and Italy, while rejecting those of small, non-historical nationalities – as in the case of the movements against the Austro-Hungarian and Russian empires. More generally, Marx and Engels thought that a common language and traditions, or geographical and historical homogeneity, were not sufficient to constitute a nation. 'Rather, a certain level of economic and social development was required, with a priority given to larger units' (Munck 1986: 11). According to Munck, this explains why they have objected to the ceding of Schleswig and Holstein to Denmark in 1848. For them, Germany was more revolutionary and progressive than the Scandinavian nations because of its higher level of capitalist development.

Marx and Engels did not change this stance during the revolutions of 1848. For them, only the great, historic nations of Germany, Poland, Hungary and Italy fulfilled the criteria for viable national states. Other, less dynamic nationalities, 'these residual fragments of peoples', were not worthy of working class support. Engels was particularly harsh towards Southern Slavs whom he described as 'peoples which have never had a history of their own . . . [who] are not viable and will never be able to achieve any kind of independence' (Marx and Engels 1976, cited in Munck 1986: 12).

Some commentators claim that Marx and Engels revised their attitudes on the nationality problem during the 1860s (Munck 1986; Guibernau 1996). Munck points to the Crimean War of 1853–56, where they supported the independence of the Slav peoples from the Ottoman Empire, to illustrate this change of attitude. The Irish case, he contends, is even a better example (1986: 15). Marx and Engels thought that England could not embark on a revolutionary path until the Irish question had been solved to the latter's advantage: 'The separation and independence of Ireland from England was not only a vital step for Irish development but was also essential for the British people since "A nation that oppresses another forges its own chains" ' (Nimni 1991: 33).

At this stage, it is important to stress that there is no universal agreement on the relevance of the Irish case. Munck considers it as a turning point in Marx and Engels' treatment of the national question and devotes a whole section to it in his book (1986: 15–20). Nimni, on the other hand, explains their support for Irish independence in terms of their general sympathy for the cause of historic nations. However, this support never extends to non-historical nations. In that sense, there is no contradiction or incoherence in their analytical logic. The Irish and Polish national movements deserved to be supported, because they were advancing the course of progress by establishing national states 'capable of developing a healthy contradiction between the proletariat and the bourgeoisie' (Nimni 1991: 33). The non-historical nations, on the other hand,

> either cannot develop a bourgeoisie, because they are peasant nations, or they cannot develop a state of their own, because they either live in a mixed area of residence or they are too small to create an internal market. Thus these nations must seek alliances with the defenders of the old order: the irresistible flow of progress requires either the voluntary assimilation or the annihilation of these national communities. (*Ibid.*)

A final point that needs to be underlined concerns Marx and Engels' commitment to internationalism. According to Munck, the founding fathers of Marxism never betrayed the internationalism of the *Communist Manifesto* where they wrote:

> National differences and antagonism between peoples are daily more and more vanishing, owing to the development of the bourgeoisie, to freedom of commerce, to the world market, to uniformity in the mode of communication and in the conditions of life corresponding thereto. (1976: 507)

Similarly, in his article on Friedrich List's *Das nationale System der politischen Ökonomie*, Marx commented:

The nationality of the worker is neither French, nor English, nor German, it is labour, free slavery, self-huckstering. His government is neither French, nor English, nor German, it is capital. His native air is neither French, nor English, nor German, it is factory air. The land belonging to him is neither French, nor English, nor German, it lies a few feet below the ground. (Marx and Engels 1975, cited in Guibernau 1996: 16)

Engels expressed similar views. He argued that the proletariat should only think in international terms because: 'the International recognises no country; it desires to unite, not dissolve. It is opposed to the cry for Nationality, because it tends to separate people from people, and is used by tyrants to create prejudices and antagonism' (cited in Guibernau 1996: 16).

On the other hand, certain sections in the *Communist Manifesto*, particularly those on the nature of the struggle of the proletariat, demonstrate a more complicated perspective:

Though not in substance, yet in form, the struggle of the proletariat with the bourgeoisie is at first a national struggle. The proletariat of each country must, of course, settle matters with its own bourgeoisie. (1976: 495)

or:

Since the proletariat must first of all acquire political supremacy, must rise to be the leading class of the nation, must constitute itself *the* nation, it is, so far, itself national, though not in the bourgeois sense of the word. (*Ibid.*: 502–3)

Some commentators claim that these phrases reflect their ambivalence on the national question. On the one hand, the workers are called upon to embark on a national struggle, that is against their own bourgeoisies; on the other hand, they are expected to remain loyal to the cause of international revolution. The question of how these two seemingly paradoxical objectives can be reconciled is left unanswered. According to other scholars however, notably Munck, the meaning of these phrases is far from being ambiguous. The workers should first become the leading class ('national class' in the first German edition) in their nation: only then can they work to diminish national antagonisms. In saying this, Munck concludes, Marx and Engels do not betray their internationalism (1986: 24; *cf.* Guibernau 1996: 18).

The most sophisticated account of nationalism within the Marxist tradition comes from Otto Bauer (1881–1938). Bauer's outstanding *Die Nationalitätenfrage und die Sozialdemokratie* (1907) has been variously described as 'the first substantial Marxist analysis of nation-states and nationalism' (Bottomore 1983, cited in James 1996: 48), 'the most important and convincing attempt among Marxists of the period to understand nationalism' (Breuilly 1993a: 40) and 'the first full-length study of nationalism from a historical standpoint' (Smith 1996a: 182). A brief overview of the historical and political context in which Bauer wrote his book will enable us to better evaluate his ideas, since they were primarily designed to meet the immediate needs of the Austrian Social Democrats who were trying to solve the problems their party – and in general the Austro-Hungarian empire – confronted (Smith 1996a: 181).

What dominated Austrian politics from 1897 onwards was the so-called 'nationalities question' (Breuilly 1993a: 40–1; Stargardt 1995). This problem took the form of ethnic antagonism between Czechs and Germans living in Bohemia. This antagonistic situation eventually led to the establishment of 'national socialist' political parties which tried to draw upon ethnic working class support. Other parties, notably the Austrian Social Democratic Party, were organized at a national level. The Austrian Social Democrats had explicitly recognized differences of nationality within their own ranks. According to Breuilly, this was particularly interesting in a party which claimed to subscribe to Marxism (1993a: 40). However, the attitude of the party changed when ethnic conflicts increased and began to threaten the labour movement. First, it recognized nationality differences on a territorial basis: a Czech worker could remain in the Czech sections of the party only if he was living in Czech-dominated areas. Later, recognition of nationality became more personal: now, the Czech worker could remain in Czech sections even when living in German areas as long as he so wished. This change of attitude shows clearly that the importance of national identity in the party's internal organization was gradually increasing. The same tendency could be observed in the party's political programme. The party first advocated the idea of realizing socialism under a unitary state; then moved to the defence of some form of federalism; finally, espoused 'a complex notion of political organisation and national autonomy' (Breuilly 1993a: 40). This shift in the party's programme reflected the fluctuations in the views of the leading figures of the movement, namely Karl Renner (1870–1950) and Otto Bauer.

Renner's solution to the problems emanating from differences of nationality was to separate the state and the nation (Stargardt 1995). He argued that economic and social issues as well as defence, justice and foreign policy should be delegated to the state. National functions, on the other hand, should be restricted to education and culture. The state should adopt federalism in its internal organization. Finally, national autonomy should be organized on the basis of the so-called 'personality principle', that is the sum total of individuals claiming a particular nationality. This principle became the hallmark of Austrian Social Democracy in the 1900s (*ibid.*: 90).

Bauer began his theoretical analysis by asking Renan's famous question: *Qu'est-ce qu'une nation?* The nation for him is 'a community of character that grows out of a community of destiny rather than from a mere similarity of destiny' (Bauer 1996: 52). Each nation has a character which, in turn, is defined as 'the totality of physical and mental characteristics that are peculiar to a nation'. The nations are far more contingent entities than nationalists' communities of language and shared culture. Moreover, 'the national character is changeable; in no way is the nation of our time linked with its ancestors of two or three millennia ago' (*ibid.*: 40–1). How did, then, this community of character come into being? For Bauer, the emergence of this community, the Herderian community of language, depended on various modernizing processes, including the breakdown of peasant subsistence farming and the following uprooting of the rural population by capitalism, the drawing of isolated rural areas into regional economic relationships so that dialects could become more homogeneous (*ibid.*: 43–5; Stargardt 1995: 97–8). There was also a second stage in which a 'cultural community' bridging the gap between the linguistic and national communities was created. Here, the focus was on the development of a 'high culture' and with it, a 'high language' above all spoken dialects. On the other hand, the most important factor in the transition from a cultural community to a nation was 'sentiment', a sense of the community's own shared destiny. For Bauer, commonality of destiny was at least as important as commonality of past, hence his definition of the nation as, above all, a 'community of fate'.

Bauer also found a way of bringing nation and class together. He argued that the national culture is shaped by the contribution of various classes. In a socialist society, conflicts among different nationalities would cease, because antagonistic relations were based upon class divisions. Once class divisions were removed, national distinctions would give rise to cooperation and coexistence. In other words, as long as national identity is not distorted by class divisions, the members of the nation would be able to participate in the national experience in a more intense manner. Bauer drew this conclusion by observing Czech–German relations in Austria–Hungary. 'It was essential to separate national (cultural and non-antagonistic) from class (economic and antagonistic) issues'. (Breuilly 1993a: 40) This could only be achieved by giving each nation a satisfying degree of autonomy, leaving conflict to focus around class divisions.

Before moving on to Renan, the last thinker I will review in this section, a few words on the contributions of the twin founding fathers of sociology, Émile Durkheim (1858–1917) and Max Weber (1864–1920), will be helpful. At the turn of the century, it was quite clear that the nation was not going to fade away in the foreseeable future. But, one generation after Marx and Engels, there were still no systematic studies of nationalism – or, in the words of James, 'anything approaching what we might call a theory of the nation' (1996: 83). Social theorists of the period did explore many of the issues neglected by earlier generations, including religion, but nationalism was generally ignored – with the partial exceptions of Georg Simmel who tried to make sense of the process of national integration, arguing that the French owe their national unity to their fight with Britain, and Gaetano Mosca who claimed that nationalism was replacing religion and becoming the chief factor of moral cohesion in Europe (James 1996: 86–7). Neither Durkheim nor Weber attempted to disturb this general 'reticence' on nationalism. Imbued with the geopolitics of their age, they were content to ally themselves with one of two camps (both writers were sympathetic to their respective nationalisms). However, their writings contained a number of themes that were to become central to the theories of the succeeding generations (Smith 1998: 13).

Durkheim's views on nationalism can be distilled from his writings on religion and the *conscience collective* (McCrone 1998: 18). Influenced by the events of the Third Republic (1870–1914), notably by the defeat by Prussia in 1870, the Paris Commune and the Dreyfus Affair, 'he did not approve of nationalism, denouncing it as an extreme and morbid form of patriotism' (*ibid.*). Smith argues that two aspects of Durkheim's work have been influential on contemporary theories of nationalism, more specifically, the modernist paradigm. The first was 'his analysis of religion as the core of moral community and his consequent belief that "there is something eternal in religion" . . . because all societies feel the need to reaffirm and renew themselves periodically through collective rites and ceremonies' (Smith 1998: 15). The second aspect was 'his analysis of the transition from "mechanical" to "organic" solidarity' (*ibid.*). Basically, Durkheim argued that traditions and the influence of the *conscience collective* decline, along with impulsive forces, such as affinity of blood, attachment to the same soil, ancestral worship and community of habits. Their place is taken by the division of labour and its complementarity of roles (*ibid.*). This aspect of his work was particularly influential on some modernist theories of nationalism, notably that of Ernest Gellner.

Weber, on the other hand, was 'both a cosmopolite and a contradictorily dispassionate nationalist' (James 1996: 89). According to Smith, the aspects of his work that proved most influential for subsequent theories included

> the importance of political memories, the role of intellectuals in preserving the 'irreplaceable culture values' of a nation, and the importance of nation-states in the rise of the special character of the modern West. (1998: 13)

Of these, the third aspect was the most important. For Weber, the nation was in essence a political concept. He defined it as 'a community of sentiment which would adequately manifest itself in a state of its own' (1948, cited in Smith 1998: 14). In other words, what distinguished nations from other communities was the quest for statehood. This particular conception of nationhood, Smith argues, 'has inspired a number of latterday theorists of nation-states to emphasise the political dimensions of nationalism and especially the role of the modern Western state' (*ibid.*).

The last scholar whose contribution will be discussed in this section is the French historian Ernest Renan (1823–92), who offered perhaps the most insightful analysis of this period. Some of the ideas contained in the famous lecture he delivered at Sorbonne in 1882, entitled *Qu'est-ce qu'une nation?* (1990), had a substantial impact on the theories of the succeeding generations and made him a figure of almost compulsory citation. Renan's formulations will therefore be a perfect stepping-stone to the studies of the twentieth century.

In this lecture, Renan rejected the popular conceptions that defined nations in terms of objective characteristics such as race, language or religion. He asked:

> How is it that Switzerland, which has three languages, two religions, and three or four races, is a nation, when Tuscany, which is so homogeneous, is not one? Why is Austria a state and not a nation? In what ways does the principle of nationality differ from that of races? (1990: 12)

For him, nations were not eternal entities. They had their beginnings and they will have an end. The nation is 'a soul, a spiritual principle':

> A nation is . . . a large-scale solidarity, constituted by the feeling of the sacrifices that one has made in the past and of those that one is prepared to make in the future. It presupposes a past; it is summarized, however, in the present by a tangible fact, namely, consent, the clearly expressed desire to continue a common life. A nation's existence is, if you will pardon the metaphor, a daily plebiscite, just as an individual's existence is a perpetual affirmation of life. (*Ibid.*: 19)

In short, race, language, material interest, religious affinities, geography and military necessity were not among the ingredients which constituted a nation; a common heroic past, great leaders and true glory were. Another, very important, ingredient was 'collective forgetting': 'forgetting, I would even go so far as to say historical error, is a crucial factor in the creation of a nation . . . No French citizen knows whether he is a Burgundian, an Alan, a Taifale, or a Visigoth, yet every French citizen has to have forgotten the massacre of Saint-Bartholomew' (*ibid.*: 11). What Renan wanted, then, was to affirm 'the primacy of politics and shared history in the genesis and character of nations' (Smith 1996a: 178).

These ideas take us to the twentieth century. The analyses of Renan and Bauer reflect the growing importance of nationalism as a political ideology and movement, and as a subject of academic investigation in its own right (*ibid.*: 182). The political repercussions of the doctrine of nationalism and the difficulties it gave birth to required more neutral analyses. In other words, nationalism had to be understood, not defended or criticized. The experiences of the First World War and its aftermath made this need all the more acute.

1918–45

The need for dispassionate analyses of nationalism was satisfied to a certain extent by 'the labours of sociologically inclined historians from the 1920s' (Smith 1998: 16). Snyder argues that the early writings of Carleton Hayes and Hans Kohn surpassed their predecessors in five distinct ways:

> They defined nationalism as a discrete subject of investigation, they treated nationalism as a positive fact rather than a compelling norm, they recognised that nationalism was in some sense a historical development, they used comparative analysis and they generally avoided biological analogies. (1997: 233)

On the other hand, there was also an important similarity between the studies of this period and that of the earlier generations. Historians like Carleton Hayes, Hans Kohn, Alfred Cobban, E. H. Carr and Louis Snyder were still taking the nation for granted, that is as a 'given'. This tacit presupposition inevitably limited the analytical effectiveness of their studies. Nevertheless, their writings opened a new era in the study of nationalism and acted as a constant source of inspiration for modern theorists.

We encounter two kinds of studies in the period between 1918–45. First, there were the histories of particular nationalisms. As Breuilly observes, these 'stories' tend to become absorbed into their subject: 'the very restriction to a "national" framework implies agreement with the nationalist argument that there is a nation' (1985: 65). Questions starting with 'why' are usually bypassed. A typical story of this kind begins with the traditional, pre-national state of affairs. The historian highlights the weaknesses of the pre-national institutions and criticizes the lack of political centralization. The story continues with the crumbling of traditional institutions in the face of modernizing forces. In the *dénouement*, the nationalists come and save the nation from vanishing by restoring the national unity (Breuilly 1996: 156–7). Breuilly argues that the narrative form explains nothing, as it is built on highly dubious assumptions. Moreover, narratives do not bring out the contingency of outcomes. These stories tend not to state the plain fact that things could have been otherwise (*ibid.*: 157–8). Smith also criticizes the narrative and chronological format of these studies and adds their European bias to the list of criticisms (1983: 257).

Secondly, there were the typologies. Most scholars of the period tried to construct classificatory schemes to order the varieties of nationalism into recurring types (Smith 1996a: 182). According to James, this reflected the urge to avoid the notorious problem of definition and the difficulty of formulating a theory of the nation (1996: 127).

Smith considers Hayes to be the first scholar to adopt a more neutral stance towards nationalism, one that seeks to distinguish the various types of nationalist ideology (1996a: 182). For Hayes,

> nationalism, the paramount devotion of human beings to fairly large nationalities and the conscious founding of a political 'nation' on linguistic and cultural nationality, was not widely preached and acted upon until the eighteenth century. (1955: 6)

Individuals had been patriotic about their city, locality, ruler or empire, but not about their nationality. The idea that 'nationalities are the fundamental units of human society and the most natural agencies for undertaking needful reforms and for promoting human progress' began to receive emphatic endorsement in Europe only in the eighteenth century (*ibid*.: 10). According to Hayes, modern nationalism manifested itself in six different forms (1955; for a concise summary see Snyder 1968: 48–53):

Humanitarian Nationalism

This was the earliest and for some time the only kind of formal nationalism. Expounded in the eighteenth century, the first doctrines of nationalism were infused with the spirit of the Enlightenment. They were based on natural law and presented as inevitable, therefore desirable steps in human progress. In object, they were all strictly humanitarian. Hayes holds that humanitarian nationalism had three main advocates: the Tory politician John Bolingbroke who espoused an aristocratic form of nationalism, Jean-Jacques Rousseau who promoted a democratic nationalism and finally, Johann Gottfried von Herder who was mainly interested in culture, not politics. As the eighteenth century neared its end, humanitarian nationalism underwent an important transformation. Democratic nationalism became 'Jacobin'; aristocratic nationalism became 'traditional'; and nationalism which was neither democratic, nor aristocratic became 'liberal'.

Jacobin Nationalism

This form of nationalism was based in theory on the humanitarian democratic nationalism of Rousseau, and was developed by revolutionary leaders for the purpose of safeguarding and extending the principles of the French revolution. Developing in the midst of foreign war and domestic rebellion, Jacobin nationalism acquired four characteristics: it became suspicious and quite intolerant of internal dissent; it eventually relied on force and militarism to attain its ends; it became fanatically religious; and it was characterized by missionary zeal. The Jacobins rendered their nationalism much more exclusive than that of their predecessors. Their tragedy was that 'they were idealists, fanatically so, in a wicked world' (Hayes 1955: 80). Hence, the more they fought, the more nationalist they grew. They bequeathed to the succeeding generations the idea of 'the nation in arms' and 'the nation in public schools'. Jacobin nationalism also set the pattern for twentieth-century nationalisms, in particular Italian fascism and German national socialism.

Traditional Nationalism

Certain intellectuals who opposed the French Revolution and Napoleon embraced a different form of nationalism. Their frame of reference was not 'reason' or 'revolution', but history and tradition. They detested everything that Jacobinism was supposed to stand for. Hence, while the latter was democratic and revolutionary, traditional nationalism was aristocratic and evolutionary. For the traditionalists, nationality and the state had just evolved. It was not necessary to discuss their origins. In that sense, the state was not a mere partnership to be made or dissolved at will. It was a combination between the living, the dead and those yet to be born. Its most illustrious exponents were Edmund Burke, Vicomte de Bonald and Friedrich von Schlegel. Traditional nationalism was the powerful motivating force of the revolts within France and in back of the growing popular resistance on the Continent, as exemplified in the nationalist awakenings in Germany, Holland, Portugal, Spain and even Russia.

Liberal Nationalism

Midway between Jacobin and traditional nationalism was liberal nationalism. It originated in England, 'that country of perpetual compromise and of acute national self-consciousness' (*ibid.*: 120), in the eighteenth century. Its leading spokesman was Jeremy Bentham who was intent on limiting the scope and functions of government in all spheres of life. For him, nationality was the proper basis for state and government. War, in this context, was peculiarly bad and should be eliminated. Bentham's liberal nationalism quickly spread from England to the Continent. His teachings were appropriated in Germany (Wilhelm von Humboldt, Baron vom Stein, Karl Theodor Welcker), France (François Guizot, Victor Hugo, Casimir-Périer) and in Italy (Guiseppe Mazzini). There were many differences in detail among these apostles with regard to the scope and implications of liberal nationalism. But they all assumed that each nationality should be a political unit under an independent constitutional government which would put an end to despotism, aristocracy and ecclesiastical influence and assure to every citizen the broadest practicable exercise of personal liberty. Liberal nationalism managed to survive the First World War. Yet it also suffered a transformation. 'Its liberalism waned as its nationalism waxed' because it had to compete now with a new form of nationalism (*ibid.*: 163).

Integral Nationalism

In the journal *L'Action Française*, Charles Maurras – the chief protagonist of this type of nationalism – defined integral nationalism as 'the exclusive pursuit of national policies, the absolute maintenance of national integrity and the steady increase of national power – for a nation declines when it loses its might' (cited in Hayes 1955: 165). Integral nationalism was hostile to the internationalism of humanitarians and liberals. It made the nation not a means to humanity, but an end in itself. It put national interests above those of the individual and those of humanity, refusing co-operation with other nations. On the other hand, in domestic affairs, integral nationalism was highly illiberal and tyrannical. It required all citizens to conform to a common standard of manners and morals, and to share the same unreasoning enthusiasm for it. It would subordinate all personal liberties to its own purpose and if the people should complain, it would abridge democracy in the name of 'national interest'. The philosophy of integral nationalism was derived from the writings of a varied and numerous group of theorists in the nineteenth and twentieth centuries, such as Auguste Comte, Hippolyte Adolpe Taine, Maurice Barrès and Charles Maurras. Integral nationalism flourished in the first half of the twentieth century, especially in countries like Italy and Germany. Its impact was also felt in countries like Hungary, Poland, Turkey and Yugoslavia.

Economic Nationalism

Superimposed upon these developing forms was continuing economic nationalism. Initially, political considerations lay behind this nationalism, but then a tendency developed to regard the state as an economic as well as a political unit. Tariffs were erected, economic self-sufficiency was praised. The resultant struggle for markets and raw materials came during the rise of integral nationalism. Economic nationalism merged with imperialism and became one of the driving forces of contemporary history.

Such is, in summary form, Hayes' typology. Snyder maintains that this classification is distinguished by two characteristics: 'it stresses a chronological, or vertical, approach, treating nationalism from its origins in modern form in the French Revolution; and its area is limited mainly to the European continent' (1968: 64). Smith criticizes this strong regional, that is Franco–English, bias. He also notes a more basic problem, namely the formulation of a typology based on purely ideological distinctions. He argues that such a typology is not 'easily amenable to sociological analysis, for different strands of the ideology may be found within a single movement, e.g. Traditional, Jacobin and Integral elements in Syrian Ba'athism' (1983: 196).

A much more influential typology was that of Hans Kohn. For him, nationalism was the fruit of a long historical process. He argues that 'modern nationalism originated in the seventeenth and eighteenth centuries in northwestern Europe and its American settlements. It became a general European movement in the nineteenth century' (1957: 3). The age of nationalism, he continues, brought a sense of conscious and growing differentiation: it has made 'the divisions of mankind more pronounced and has spread the consciousness of antagonistic aspirations to wider multitudes of men than ever before' (*ibid.*: 4). Kohn distinguished between two types of nationalism, namely 'Western' and 'Eastern' nationalisms, in terms of their origins and main characteristics (Kohn 1967: 329–31; Snyder 1968: 53–7; Smith 1983: 196; Smith 1996a: 182). In the Western world, for instance in England, France, the Netherlands, Switzerland, the United States and the British dominions, nationalism was the product of political and social factors. It was preceded by the formation of the national state or coincided with it. In Central and Eastern Europe and in Asia, on the other hand, nationalism arose later and at a more backward stage of social and political development. In conflict with the existing state pattern, it found its first expression in the cultural field and sought for its justification in the 'natural' fact of a community held together by traditional ties of kinship and status. The frontiers of the existing polity rarely coincided with that of the rising nationality.

Western nationalism was born out of the spirit of the Enlightenment. It was closely connected in its origin with the concepts of individual liberty and rational cosmopolitanism: thus, it was optimistic, pluralistic and rationalist. It was largely the expression of the political aspirations of the rising middle classes. Moreover, 'nationalism in the West stressed the political reality' (Snyder 1968: 55). The nation was regarded as a vital, existing, real thing. Political integration was sought around a rational goal.

Nationalism in the non-Western world rejected or belittled the spirit of the Enlightenment: instead, the authoritarian uniformity of state and faith was praised. Nationalism meant collective power and national unity, independence from foreign domination (rather than liberty at home) or the necessity for expansion by the superior nation. It reflected the aspirations of the lower aristocracy and the masses. Since it was not rooted in a political and social reality, it lacked self-assurance and this inferiority complex was often compensated by overconfidence. The dependence on the West, which remained for a long time the model, coupled with social backwardness, produced a much more emotional and authoritarian nationalism. The non-Western world was also detached from political reality. It became absorbed in a search for the ideal fatherland. Its nationalism was mostly concerned with myths and dreams of the future, without immediate connection with the present.

The two nationalisms had different conceptions of nation. The Western idea was that nations emerged as voluntary unions of citizens. Individuals expressed their will in contracts, covenants and plebiscites. Integration was achieved around a political idea and special emphasis was laid upon the universal similarities of nations. In the non-Western world, the nation was regarded as a political unit centering around the irrational, pre-civilized folk concept. Nationalism found its rallying point in the folk community, elevating it to the dignity of an ideal or a mystery. Here, emphasis was put on the diversity and self-sufficiency of nations.

As this brief summary reveals, Kohn was much more interested in the moral worth of different types of nationalism than in providing a descriptive classification of these types. Nevertheless,

Snyder maintains that Kohn's typology 'clarifies many inconsistencies and contradictions surrounding the meaning of nationalism'. It shows 'how the idea of nationalism could be communicated by cultural diffusion, while at the same time its meaning and form could take on characteristics directed by the aims and aspirations of the peoples concerned' (Snyder 1968: 56–7). On the other hand, the moralistic overtones of the classification leave Kohn vulnerable to the charge of Eurocentrism. Critics contend that 'the typology is far too favourable to the Western world, that he cleanses Western nationalism of tribal impurities, and that he disregards any manifestations of anti-democratic or non-Western nationalism in the West' (Snyder 1968: 57). Snyder holds that this criticism is unjust. For him, Kohn does not overlook the deleterious effects of nationalism in the West as well as in non-Western nations. His formula, Snyder argues, takes into account gradations of light and shadow: 'the open, pluralistic society is never perfect' (*ibid.*).

However, this was not the only criticism levelled against Kohn's typology. Smith raises a range of objections to this scheme: it is silent about Latin American and African experiences; its spatial distinction between 'East' and 'West' is not adequate since Spain, Belgium and Ireland, being at the time socially backward, belong to the 'Eastern' camp; some nationalisms like that of Turkish or Tanzanian elites blend 'voluntarist' and 'organic' elements in a single movement; too many levels of development, types of structure and cultural situations are included within each category (1983: 197). Nevertheless, Kohn's classification proved to be very long-lived and cast its shadow on the typologies of later periods.

Another contribution to the typologies of the period comes from Snyder himself. In his earlier work, Snyder opted for a chronological classification of nationalisms (1954; see also 1968: 48):

- *Integrative nationalism* (1815–71). In this period, nationalism was a unifying force. It helped consolidate states that had outgrown their feudal divisions and united others that had been split into various factions. The unifications of Germany and Italy were the products of this phase.
- *Disruptive nationalism* (1871–90). The success of nationalism in moulding the unification of Germany and Italy aroused the enthusiasm of subject nationalities in other countries. The

minorities in the Ottoman Empire, Austria–Hungary and other conglomerate states sought to break out of oppression.

- *Aggressive nationalism* (1900–45). The first half of the twentieth century witnessed the collision of opposing national interests and the explosive impact of two world wars. During this period, nationalism became identical with imperialism.
- *Contemporary nationalism* (1945–). This most recent form of nationalism asserted itself partly in colonial revolts against European imperialism. This period of colonial emancipation and nation-building saw the extension of nationalism into a global framework.

The historical taxonomy developed by Snyder is not immune from criticisms. Smith argues that it is unhistorical: for example, the Serbian, Greek and Belgian movements are early (in the 'integrative' phase) and of major importance: all three were 'disruptive' of the existing political systems. Conversely, the Japanese and Indian cases were 'integrative' although they appeared in the 'disruptive' period. Moreover, the dates chosen are arbitrary, being based largely on the German model (Smith 1983: 194; Smith 1996a: 184).

Noting that chronological conceptualization has little meaning for the 'new' nationalisms of the period since 1945, Snyder developed a continental or regional classification in his later work. This classification, he contended, is based on general area characteristics and should not be confused with such movements as Pan-Africanism, Pan-Arabism or Pan-Americanism (1968: 64–8):

- *Europe: Fissiparous nationalism.* In Europe, the new nationalism recapitulates the experience of the old and tends to remain fragmented, split and particularistic. It reflects the ideology of the small nations as the ultimate politico-economic units. Despite talks about a United States of Europe or about Europe being a 'third force', nationalism remains strong and unbending.
- *Africa: Black nationalism.* African nationalism emerged with an explosive impact and one state after another gained its independence. An important element in this process was the appearance of a dominant ethnic motif. This was the predictable response of peoples who have been subject to white imperialism for many decades. In form, African nationalism was

imitative of Western models, but deep inside, there was a racial core of hostility to white domination.

- *The Middle East: Politico-religious nationalism.* The experience of liberation, independence and nation-building in the Middle East was similar to that of Africa. Here, nationalism was affected by the area's close proximity to Western civilisations. The religious element always played a crucial role in it. The rise of Arab nationalism, the reconstruction of Israel and the appearance of state nationalism in Turkey and Egypt were conditioned by many factors, but in all these cases religious nationalism, tinged with political overtones, was a common denominator.

- *Asia: Anticolonial nationalism.* The developmental pattern of nationalism in Asia was mercurial and unpredictable. While varying from country to country, it is distinguished generally by an anti-Western tone. It is quite sensitive to domination from the outside. In Asian nationalism, the psychological motivations of anti-imperialism and anti-colonialism are more stronger than economic drives.

- *Latin America: Populist nationalism.* In Latin America, nationalism had a revolutionary tinge, 'reflecting generations of political change affected by rebellion against established but "temporary" authority' (Snyder 1968: 67). Democracy was utilized only in form: its spirit or deeper meaning did not prevail. Power was reserved for the strongest group, usually the military junta. This process, removed from that of British parliamentary rationalism, was a combination of 'Spanish pride, fickleness and fierce sense of independence'. The party in power often claimed exclusive monopoly of the national image. And the many variants of nationalism had in common the idea of opposing the 'Yankee domination'.

- *The United States: Melting-pot nationalism.* The United States was composed of people who were driven out of their homelands and came to a strange land, becoming in a relatively short period of time more alike than they were different. 'Their nationalism was an amalgam of spiritual idealism (libertarianism and egalitarianism) and materialism (business and industry)' (*ibid.*). Under the influence of the Puritan heritage, American nationalism took on a moralistic tone, a desire to convince the rest of the world that the American form of government was the best on earth and that all other peoples should imitate American virtues and ideals. When the United States took on the leadership role, the core of this nationalism was retained, while added to them were such characteristics as transition from provincialism to nationalism, retreat from autarchic isolationism and anti-communism.

* *The Soviet Union: Messianic nationalism.* The aim of communism in the Soviet Union was to destroy the archaic Czarist society cursed by capitalistic, bourgeois nationalism. Ironically, however, Soviet Russia revived Czarist messianic nationalism in another form. Earlier Czarist nationalism had confined itself to Russification of contiguous areas. The new Soviet nationalism, on the other hand, sought expansion not only in neighbouring countries, but in any weak area of the capitalist world. The Soviet urge for expansion took on the fervour of the Islamic *jihad* against unbelievers.

According to Smith, these general, necessarily overlapping, regional types only serve to point up the global diffusion of nationalism. Nevertheless, they act as a corrective to the Eurocentrism of earlier typologies (1996a: 184).

Another typology, largely forgotten in recent discussions of nationalism (Gellner 1995a: 20), was that of the renowned British historian E. H. Carr. Carr was more interested in delineating the various stages of European nationalism than the ethical value of it. For him, 'the nation is not a "natural" or "biological" group – in the sense, for example, of the family'. It is not a definable and clearly recognizable entity: 'It is confined to certain periods of history and to certain parts of the world' (Carr 1945: 39). Carr concedes that the modern nation has a place and function in the wider society. But, he continues, the claim of nationalism to make the nation 'the sole rightful sovereign repository of political power and the ultimate constituent unit of world organization' has to be challenged and rejected (*ibid.*).

According to Carr, 'the modern history of international relations divides into three partly overlapping periods, marked by widely differing views of the nation as a political entity' (*ibid.*: 1; see also Smith 1996a: 183). The first period began with the gradual dissolution of the medieval unity of empire and church and the establishment of the national state. It was terminated by the French Revolution and the Napoleonic wars. In this period, the nation was identified with the person of the sovereign. International relations were simply relations between kings and princes. Equally characteristic of the period was 'mercantilism', whose aim was not to promote the welfare of the community and its members, but to augment the power of the state – of which the sovereign was the embodiment.

The second period, Carr argues, 'was essentially the product of the French Revolution and, though its foundations were heavily undermined from 1870 onwards, lasted on till the catastrophe of 1914' (1945: 2). This was the most orderly and enviable period of international relations. Its success depended on balancing nationalism and internationalism, and on striking a compromise between political and economic power so that each can develop on its own lines. The diffusion of the idea of popular-democratic nationalism, first formulated by Rousseau, also played a role in this.

The third period, on the other hand, began to take shape at the end of the nineteenth century (after 1870) and reached its culmination between 1914 and 1939. This period was characterized by the catastrophic growth of nationalism and the bankruptcy of internationalism. The reestablishment of national political authority over the economic system – 'a necessary corollary of the socialization of the nation', in the words of Carr (*ibid.*: 27) – was crucial in bringing about this state of affairs.

Carr is not pessimistic about the future of international relations. He believes that the modern nation-state is under attack from within and from without, 'from the standpoint of idealism and from the standpoint of power':

> On the plane of morality, it is under attack from those who denounce its inherently totalitarian implications and proclaim that any international authority worth the name must interest itself in the rights and well-being not of nations but of men and women. On the plane of power, it is being sapped by modern technological developments which have made the nation obsolescent as the unit of military and economic organization and are rapidly concentrating effective decision and control in the hands of great multi-national units. (*Ibid.*: 38)

The future, Carr concludes, depends on the strength of each of these forces and on the nature of the balance that may be struck between them.

In passing, let us note that Carr's typology has been criticized by Smith for failing to allow for the possibility of a wave of anti-colonial nationalisms or renewed European and Third World secession nationalisms. This, according to Smith, reflects the moral and teleological basis of his analysis, as well as its Eurocentrism (1996a: 183). This brings us to the third stage of the theoretical debate on nationalism, heralded by the end of the Second World War.

1945 to the Late 1980s

The experience of decolonization, that is the dissolution of colonial empires and the establishment of new states in Asia and Africa, coupled with general developments in the social sciences, inaugurated the most intensive and prolific period of research on nationalism. The earlier studies of this period were produced under the sway of the modernization school, then ascendant within American social science. This was mainly caused by the incursion of American political scientists into the debate. Actually, political scientists like Apter, Coleman, Binder, Halpern, Pye and Emerson were more interested in the general problems of development than nationalism *per se*. However, the processes of nation-building were central to political and economic development, and it was not possible to study these processes without taking nationalism into account. Smith argues that the contributions of modernization theorists were crucial in that they helped to shift the study of the causes and consequences of nationalism away from its European setting on to a broader, global plane (1983: 258).

The point of departure of modernization theories was the classical sociological distinction between 'traditional' and 'modern' societies. Drawing on this distinction, scholars of the period posited three different stages in the modernization process: tradition, transition and modernity. In these accounts, modernization signified a breakdown of the traditional order and the establishment of a new type of society with new values and new relationships. Smith summarizes this line of argument aptly:

> To survive painful dislocation, societies must institutionalise new modes of fulfilling the principles and performing the functions

with which earlier structures can no longer cope. To merit the title, a new 'society' must reconstitute itself in the image of the old . . . Mechanisms of reintegration and stabilisation can ease and facilitate the transition; among them are collective ideologies like nationalism which spring up naturally in periods of social crisis, and appear meaningful and effective for the participants of the situation. (1983: 49–50)

Nationalism, then, has a clear 'function' in these accounts. It can provide identity in a time of rapid change; it can motivate people to work for further change; it can provide guidelines in such fields as the creation of a modern educational system and of a standard 'national' culture (Breuilly 1993a: 418–19). The archetype of such functionalist accounts was Daniel Lerner's *The Passing of a Traditional Society* (1958).

Lerner's book was based on the story of three characters from Balgat, a little village in Turkey, near the capital Ankara (Smith 1983: 89–95). These characters represented the different stages of the modernization process: the village Chief, contented, paternal, fatalistic was the epitome of traditional Turkish values; the Grocer, restless, unsatisfied, was the man of transition; and Tosun, Lerner's informant from the capital city was the man of modernity. The underlying logic was simple: 'all societies must pass from a face-to-face, traditional stage through an ambivalent, uncertain "transition" to reach finally the plateau of the modern, "participant" and national society and culture' (Smith 1983: 90). That there will be a transition to the Western model of society was undisputed: the only thing that mattered was 'pace'. Where did nationalism stand in this picture? Although nationalism only received a passing mention in Lerner's story, it was implicitly there as the ideology of 'Transitionals', to use Smith's term (*ibid.*: 94). It was a natural part of the transition process, an inevitable consequence.

Lerner's account was a typical example of a whole range of theories inspired by the modernization paradigm. All these accounts shared the basic assumption that nationalism was a concomitant of the period of transition, helping to alleviate the sufferings caused by that process. Predictably, functionalist theories of nationalism have been subject to many criticisms. The main objections to such accounts can be summarized as follows:

- Functionalist theories derive explanations from end-states. In these accounts, consequences precede causes and events are treated as wholly beyond the understanding of human agents (O'Leary 1996: 86). This inevitably limits the range of choices initially open to individuals who might respond rationally to their situation, hence redefine and modify it (Minogue 1996: 117; Smith 1983: 51). Smith argues that there are a large number of cases of traditional communities which failed to develop any form of protest when subjected to modernization. Most functionalist accounts, he continues, cannot cope with these exceptions (1983: 51). Moreover, Smith notes that most of the goals that are thought to be served by nationalism are logically and historically posterior to the emergence of a nationalist conceptual framework: thus, they cannot be invoked to explain it.

- Functionalist explanations are too holistic. The functions of nationalism, that is solidarity or modernization, are such large terms that one can hardly connect something as specific as nationalism to them. In the light of this observation, Breuilly asks the following question: 'Is one suggesting that without nationalism these things could not be achieved' (1993a: 419)?

- Functionalist theories cannot explain the variety of historical responses to modernization. Smith asks: 'Why was Pakistan's type of nationalism of the so-called neo-traditional kind, whereas Turkey's was secularist? Why the Bolshevik response in Russia, the Fascist in Italy, the socialist in Yugoslavia and Israel?' (1983: 53).

- There are a multitude of functions which it is suggested nationalism can serve. For some, Breuilly observes, it helps modernization; for others, it helps maintain traditional identities. There is no agreed interpretation: nationalism is associated with different functions in different contexts (1993a: 419).

- Functionalists tend to simplify and reify the ideal-types of 'tradition' and 'modernity'. The reality, however, is much more complex. Moreover, these types are modelled on Western valuations (Smith 1983: 50).

Another variant of the modernization theories is the so-called 'communications approach', generally associated with the idea of 'nation-building'. The most illustrious exponent of this approach was the American political scientist Karl W. Deutsch (1966). Deutsch begins by defining a 'people' as a large group of persons linked by complementary habits and facilities of communication. For Deutsch, '[m]embership in a people essentially consists in wide complementarity of social communication. It consists in the ability to communicate more effectively, and over a wider range of subjects, with members of one large group than with outsiders' (1966: 97). Drawing on these preliminary conceptual clarifications, he proposes a functional definition of nationality:

> In the political and social struggles of the modern age, *nationality*, then, means an alignment of large numbers of individuals from the middle and lower classes linked to regional centers and leading social groups by channels of social communication and economic intercourse, both indirectly from link to link and directly with the center. (*Ibid.*: 101)

In the age of nationalism, nationalities press to acquire a measure of effective control over the behaviour of their members. They strive to equip themselves with power, with some machinery of compulsion strong enough to make the enforcement of commands possible: 'Once a nationality has added this power to compel to its earlier cohesiveness and attachment to group symbols, it often considers itself a *nation* and is so considered by others' (*ibid.*: 104–5). This process is underpinned by a variety of functionally equivalent arrangements. More specifically, what set nation-building in motion were socio-demographic processes like urbanization, mobility, literacy and so on. The communications mechanisms had an important role to play in this scenario. They had to provide new roles, new horizons, strange experiences and imaginings to keep the process going smoothly (Smith 1983: 99).

The communications approach in general and Deutsch's model in particular had their share of criticisms:

- The crucial defect of this approach, Smith argues, is its omission of the particular context of beliefs, interpretations and interests within which the mass media operate. The mechanisms of communications were always those developed in the West and their effects outside the West were held to be identical to the Western results (1983: 99, 101).

- The conception of mass communication in these theories is uni-dimensional. Communication systems do not convey one single ideology, that is 'modernization', and the messages conveyed are not perceived in the same manner by the individuals that make up a community. In fact, Smith notes, 'exposure to mass communications systems does not automatically carry with it the desire for "modernity" and its benefits' (1983: 101).
- Breuilly remarks that intensified communications between individuals and groups can as often lead to an increase in internal conflict as to an increase in solidarity. Moreover, such conflict or solidarity may be expressed in terms other than nationalist ones. The structures of communication do not indicate what types of conflict and solidarity exist within a particular community and therefore cannot in itself predict what kinds of nationalism will develop (1993a: 406–7).

Deutsch's work gave a fresh impetus to the debate on nationalism. The 1960s saw the burgeoning of interdisciplinary interest in national phenomena, a sudden increase in the number of studies which treated nationalism as a subject in itself and, partly as a result of this, a diversification of theoretical perspectives. It was in this context that the pioneering works of the modernist approach, namely Kedourie's *Nationalism* and Ernest Gellner's *Thought and Change*, were published. Modernist explanations became the dominant orthodoxy in the field until the early 1980s.

Kedourie's conservative attack on nationalism was a milestone in the evolution of the theoretical debate. For him,

> nationalism is a doctrine invented in Europe at the beginning of the nineteenth century . . . Briefly, the doctrine holds that humanity is naturally divided into nations, that nations are known by certain characteristics which can be ascertained, and that the only legitimate type of government is national self-government. ([1960] 1994: 1)

As we have seen earlier, Kedourie traces the origins of this doctrine back to German Romantic thought. He explains it in terms of a revolution in European philosophy, showing how this revolution took place and which thinkers have contributed to it. He attaches a great weight in his account to the role played by Kant's epistemological dualism, the organic analogy developed by Fichte and his disciples, and historicism. But the story does not end here. The revolution in ideas, Kedourie holds, was accompanied by an upheaval in social life: 'at the time when the doctrine was being elaborated, Europe was in turmoil . . . Things which had not been thought possible were now seen to be indeed possible and feasible' (1994: 87). At this point, Kedourie draws our attention to the low social status of German romantics whose upward mobility was blocked at the time (Smith 1983: 33). The younger generation was spiritually restless, dissatisfied with things as they were, eager for change. This restlessness was partly caused by the legend of the French Revolution. But what really caused it was 'a breakdown in the transmission of political habits and religious beliefs from one generation to the next' (Kedourie 1994: 94). Kedourie's depiction of this situation is quite vivid:

> The sons rejected the fathers and their ways; but the rejection extended also to the very practices, traditions, and beliefs which had over the centuries moulded and fashioned these societies which suddenly seemed to the young so confining, so graceless, so devoid of spiritual comfort, and so unable to minister to the dignity and fulfilment of the individual. (*Ibid.*: 95)

According to Kedourie, this revolt against old ways can also explain the violent nature of many nationalist movements, because the latter, ostensibly directed against foreigners, were also the manifestation of a clash of generations: 'nationalist movements are children's crusades; their very names are manifestoes against old age: Young Italy, Young Egypt, the Young Turks' (*ibid.*: 96). Such movements satisfied an important need,

> [the need] to belong together in a coherent and stable community. Such a need is normally satisfied by the family, the neighbourhood, the religious community. In the last century and a half such institutions all over the world have had to bear the brunt of violent social and intellectual change, and it is no accident that nationalism was at its most intense where and when such institutions had little resilience and were ill-prepared to withstand the powerful attacks to which they became exposed. (*Ibid.*)

These frustrated, but passionate, young men turned to literature and philosophy which seemed to give way to a nobler world, 'a world more real and more exciting than the real world', failing to notice that philosophical speculation was incompatible with the civil order. However, there was no effective means to control the 'musings' of young men since they were not the fruit of conspiracy: 'They were inherent in the nature of things; they have emanated from the very spirit of the age' (*ibid.*: 100).

'This is a powerful and original thesis', Smith comments (1983: 34). But this originality did not make it immune to criticism. The major objections to Kedourie's account can be summarized as follows:

- Gellner disagrees with Kedourie on the question of Kant's contribution to the doctrine of nationalism. For him, 'Kant is the very last person whose vision could be credited with having contributed to nationalism'. In fact, 'if a connection exists between Kant and nationalism at all, then nationalism is a reaction against him, and not his offspring' (1983: 132, 134). Smith joins Gellner here and argues that even if Kedourie's interpretation of Kant is right, he forgets Kant's debt to Rousseau (1983: 35).
- As noted at the beginning of this section, Gellner argues, *contra* Kedourie, that we shall not learn too much about nationalism by the study of its own prophets (1983: 125). Similarly, Smith accuses Kedourie of 'intellectual determinism'. The social and political factors in Kedourie's account, for example the blocked mobility of the German intelligentsia, the breakdown of traditional ways, are overshadowed by the developments in the intellectual arena: social factors become contributory or intervening variables in what amounts to a single-factor explanation (1983: 37–8).
- Smith objects to Kedourie's use of the 'need to belong', arguing that this factor does not provide an answer to the following questions: 'why only at certain times and places it was the nation which replaced the family, the religious community, the village'; 'why does this need appear to affect some and not others in a given population'; 'how can we measure it in relation to other factors'? Without these answers, Smith concludes, the argument is 'a piece of circular psychologism' (1983: 35). A similar point is made by Breuilly who argues that 'identity needs' cover much more than nationalism. He notes that some of those who

have suffered from an identity crisis turned to other ideologies – of class, of religion; some accepted the changes that have taken place and sought simply to advance their interests as much as possible under the new conditions; some turned to drink; and about most we know nothing. He also remarks that nationalism has not received its strongest support from those groups which one would imagine to have been most damaged from an identity crisis (1993a: 417).

• Finally, Smith maintains, Kedourie's model does not explain how ideas have contributed to the breakdown of existing structures. He notes that rapid social change has occurred before the eighteenth century as well. Traditional institutions were always criticized, most of the time by the younger generations. Why, then, did nationalism appear so sporadically in earlier eras? What was unique about the recent onslaught on tradition (1983: 39–40)?

The 1970s have witnessed a new wave of interest in nationalism. The input of neo-Marxist scholars who emphasized the role of economic factors in their accounts was particularly important in that context. Significant contributions of the period include Michael Hechter's *Internal Colonialism: The Celtic Fringe in British National Development, 1536–1966* (1975) and Tom Nairn's *The Break-up of Britain* ([1977] 1981) amongst many others. The debate received a new twist in the 1980s. The works of John Armstrong (1982) and Anthony D. Smith (1986) laid the groundwork for an 'ethno-symbolist' critique of modernist theories. Ironically, the great classics of the modernist approach were also published in this period. Ernest Gellner's *Nations and Nationalism*, Benedict Anderson's *Imagined Communities* and Eric Hobsbawm and Terence Ranger's *The Invention of Tradition*, all published in 1983, set the scene for the ardent – sometimes even polemical – discussions of the last decade (all these theories will be discussed at length in Chapters 4 and 5). With these studies, the debate on nationalism reached its most mature stage.

From the Late 1980s to the Present

I have argued before that we have entered a new stage in the debate on nationalism since the end of the 1980s. This argument will be substantiated at length in Chapter 6 which is devoted to recent approaches. Here, I will briefly consider the following question: what separated the studies of the last decade from those of earlier periods? The answer is quite simple: some of the studies produced in this period tried to transcend the 'classical' debate – which covered most of the twentieth century and reached its heyday in the last three decades – by questioning the fundamental tenets upon which it is based and by adding new dimensions to the analysis of national phenomena. What underlay these attempts was the belief that the classical debate has become unnecessarily polarized around certain issues, such as the modernity of nations, and failed to address many problems the analysis of which might greatly enhance our understanding of nationalism. For example, mainstream scholars did not attempt to understand why nationhood is still so basic to modern politics and culture. They did offer various explanations of the 'origins' of nations, but they took 'our' nationhood – or, one might say, 'nationhood-in-the-present' – for granted. Not satisfied with such simplistic accounts, a number of recent studies tried to identify 'the factors that lead to the continual production and reproduction of nationalism as a central discursive formation in the modern world' (Calhoun 1997: 123; Billig 1995).

Moreover, the classical debate ignored the experiences of the so-called 'marginal' groups. Ethnic minorities, blacks, women, postcolonial societies could hardly find themselves a place in the mainstream literature. Again, a range of studies produced in the last decade tried to compensate for this decades-long neglect (see for example Chatterjee 1986; Bhabha 1990b; Yuval-Davis 1997).

Finally, the interaction between the studies of nationalism and research conducted in other fields, like diasporas, multiculturalism, identity, migration, citizenship, racism, increased. To this were added the insights gained from alternative epistemological approaches like feminism or postmodernism. These allowed for a richer understanding of the dialectic of national self-identification. In the light of these observations, I think, it can be fairly concluded that we have reached a new stage in the study of nationalism, in fact a stage which promises to be more prolific than the previous ones.

Main Questions, Fundamental Problems

The preceding discussion has suggested that the 'academic' debate on nationalism reached its most mature stage in the second half of the twentieth century. Many of the issues discussed in the literature took shape in that period. In this section, I will try to identify the main questions around which the contemporary theoretical debate revolves. These are:

- What is the nation? What is nationalism?
- What are the origins of nations and nationalisms? To what extent are they modern phenomena?
- What are the different types of nationalism?

It is important to note at the outset that these are not the only questions addressed by the scholars of nationalism. However, even a cursory glance at their writings will reveal that most of the other issues they explored derive from these three questions. In that sense, they can be regarded as 'primary' questions, that is questions that most – if not all – theorists address, as opposed to 'secondary', or derivative, questions that appear in particular studies. Some of these secondary questions will also be mentioned in the discussion that follows. It should also be stressed that the number of primary questions and the priority attached to any one of them varies. While some scholars argue that it is not possible to understand nationalism without first agreeing on basic definitions, others contend that the most important problem is the relationship of nationalism to the processes of modernization. Still others, on the other hand, set out to develop typologies, holding that a theory that will explain various forms of nationalism cannot be devised. These different viewpoints will also be explored below.

What is the Nation? What is Nationalism?

In a recent essay, Tilley argues that 'most arguments in the academia could be resolved if people would first take the time to define their terms' (1997: 497). Nowhere is this principle better demonstrated, she continues, than in the proliferating literature on ethnicity. The same could easily be argued in the case of nationalism.

In fact, this is probably the only point on which there is a general consensus among the scholars of national phenomena. How, then, can we account for this lack of agreement or, to put it differently, for the existence of a plethora of definitions, each stressing a different aspect of their subject-matter?

Walker Connor, an eminent scholar of nationalism who has written extensively on the problems of definition, answers this question by pointing to the widespread misuse of the key terms, in particular the 'interutilization' of the words 'state' and 'nation' (1994: 92). Actually, the origins of this confusion go back to the 1780s, when Jeremy Bentham invented the term 'international' for what we would now call 'interstate relations' (I owe special thanks to Fred Halliday for reminding me of this point). As Connor notes, the tendency to equate nation with state is not restricted to the academia. We can observe its reflections on the political scene, as the misnomers the 'League of Nations' or the 'United Nations' demonstrate (*ibid.*: 97).

What underlies this confusion is the ambiguity of the relationship between 'nation' and other, 'kindred', concepts such as ethnicity, ethnic group and so on. That nationhood is different from other objective criteria forming the basis of individual or collective identities such as class, region, gender, race or religious belief is commonly accepted. But the degree to which each of these elements contributes to the construction of national identities, hence to the definition of the nation, is a source of great controversy. The differences of opinion that exist on this subject are echoed in the competing definitions circulating in the literature. While some scholars emphasize 'objective' criteria like religion, language or race, others stress the importance of 'subjective' criteria such as self-awareness or solidarity in the definition of a nation. Most scholars employ a combination of the two. A similar disagreement exists between those who see the nation as a 'self-defined' (that is self-awareness) entity and those who see it as 'other-defined' (that is recognition by the international community).

The case of nationalism is no more promising. As Breuilly notes, nationalism can refer to ideas, to sentiments and to actions (1993a: 404). Each definition will have different implications for the study of nationalism: those who define it as an idea will focus on the writings and speeches of nationalist intellectuals or activists; those who see it as a sentiment will concentrate on the development of language or other shared ways of life and try to see how these 'folk ways' are taken up by the intelligentsia or the politicians; finally, those who treat nationalism as a movement will focus on political action and conflict (*ibid.*).

On the other hand, Kellas contends that nationalism is both an 'idea' and a 'form of behaviour' (1991: 3). Nationalism is a 'doctrine' for Kedourie (1994: 1), an 'ideological movement' for Smith (1991a: 51), a 'political principle' for Gellner (1983: 1) and a 'discursive formation' for Calhoun (1997: 3).

So far, I have argued that the study of nationalism has been severely impaired by the misuse of the key terms, which is in turn caused by the ambiguous relationship of the concepts of nation and nationalism to kindred concepts – such as ethnicity, ethnic group and so on. However, there are two more factors that exacerbate this situation.

The first is the 'idealist' thinking about nations and nationalism. Mainly advocated by nationalist ideologues, but also taken up by mainstream scholarship until the second half of the twentieth century, this way of thinking saw nations as natural and/or primordial entities. Those who espoused this view mostly shied away from defining the nation – which they took for granted – and embarked on devising typologies (Symmons-Symonolewicz 1985: 215). This approach has been subject to growing criticisms from the 1960s onwards and largely discredited by recent studies of ethnicity and nationalism.

The second factor is the close relationship between the concept of nation and politics. As Calhoun remarks, 'the notion of nation is so deeply imbricated in modern politics as to be "essentially contested", because any definition will legitimate some claims and delegitimate others' (1993: 215). Scientific knowledge, methodologies, definitions do not evolve in a socio-historical vacuum (MacLaughlin 1987). Scholars are inevitably affected by the political context in which they develop their ideas, hence the definitions they formulate reflect an intricate complex of interests and relationships. Breuilly sums this up brilliantly: 'the sheer universality and apparent power of nationalism has created a vast range of cases and vested interests which make it difficult to agree upon basic approaches to the subject' (1985: 65).

This brief discussion shows clearly that 'imprecise vocabulary' continues to sabotage our efforts to understand nationalism. Given the abundance of definitions and the lack of general agreement on any one of them, I have refrained from prioritizing any one definition in the course of this discussion. I have also tried to keep the number of examples at a minimum since many competing definitions of the concepts of nation and nationalism will be provided in the following chapters.

What are the Origins of Nations and Nationalisms? To what Extent are they Modern Phenomena?

The second key question addressed by the scholars concerns the origins and the nature of national phenomena. This question is the forebear of a large number of secondary questions: What is the relationship between nationalism and the processes of modernization? In other words, to what extent are nations and nationalisms the products of modern conditions such as capitalism, industrialization, urbanization and secularism? How did the rise of the modern state affect the emergence of nationalism? How do modern nations relate to pre-modern ethnic communities? Are nations just the lineal descendants of their medieval counterparts? Or are they the recent creations of a nationalist intelligentsia frustrated by the vagaries of the *ancien régime*? Is nationalism a kind of 'myth' invented and propagated by elites who then use it to mobilize the masses in support of their struggle to get or maintain power? Is it a kind of 'opium' diverting the masses from fulfilling their true selves?

One can multiply these questions. But the point is that all these secondary questions derive from the same basic dilemma: to what extent are nations and nationalisms modern phenomena? The attempts to resolve this dilemma have laid the foundations of arguably the most fundamental divide of the theoretical debate on nationalism, namely that between the 'primordialists' and the 'modernists'. Broadly speaking, those who think that nations are 'perennial' entities fall within the former category and those who believe in the modernity of nations and nationalism fall within the latter. This classification is widely accepted in today's literature. The labels attached to the categories may vary: some prefer the term 'essentialist' in place of 'primordialist'; others opt for the epithet 'instrumentalist' or 'constructivist' instead of 'modernist'.

But the description of the categories and the logic of classification remain the same. It should be pointed out that a third category has been added to this classification in recent years. This category consists of 'ethno-symbolists' who portray their position as a middle way between these two polar opposites. Very briefly, ethno-symbolists stress the durability of pre-modern ethnic ties and show how ethnic cultures set limits to elite attempts to forge the nation.

It is important to stress that not all scholars are content with the conventional classification. For example, Conversi (1995) introduces a five-tiered classification with the addition of 'homeostatic' and 'transactionalist' approaches to the categories I have mentioned above. On the other hand, there are also scholars who insist in keeping the twofold classification by merging the ethno-symbolists into the primordialists (see for example Breuilly 1996: 150). In the remainder of the book, I will follow the conventional threefold classification, mainly to represent the general tendency in the field. However, I will also review the criticisms levelled against this classification and introduce my own categorization in the concluding chapter.

What are the Different Types of Nationalism (if any)?

The final question concerns the varieties of nationalism. As we have seen earlier in this chapter, this was in fact the only question addressed by a whole generation of scholars, and the classificatory schemes developed by Kohn, Hayes and Snyder were discussed in that context. However, typologies are not peculiar to first-generation studies. Arguing that no single, universal theory of nationalism is possible, some scholars continue to espouse the view that the best way to deal with nationalism is to develop typologies (for example Hall 1993). In their view, nationalism is a chameleon-like phenomenon, capable of assuming a variety of ideological forms. It is not possible to account for all these variations in a single, 'grand' theory. However, this should not condemn us to complete particularism: 'to the contrary, middle ground can be cultivated by delineating various ideal types of nationalism' (Hall 1993: 1).

Predictably, typologies abound in the literature, even if we leave the earlier ones aside. Here, I will just enumerate a few examples: Smith follows Kohn's lead and draws a distinction between a

'Western' civic-territorial model of the nation which produces 'territorial' nationalisms and an 'Eastern' ethnic-genealogical model which produces 'ethnic' nationalisms (1991a: 79–84). Breuilly identifies three categories on the basis of the relationship between the nationalist movement and the state to which it either opposes or controls: 'separation', 'reform' and 'unification'. He then divides each of these categories into two sub-categories according to the nature of the political entity that is opposed, that is 'opposed to non-nation-states' and 'opposed to nation-states' (1993a: 9); Hall introduces a classification that consists of five categories on the basis of the characteristic logic and social underpinning of various forms of nationalism. The titles he chooses for his categories are rather singular: 'the logic of the asocial society', 'revolution from above', 'desire and fear blessed by opportunity', 'risorgimento nationalism', 'integral nationalism' (1993). Alter identifies three varieties, namely 'risorgimento', 'reform' and 'integral' nationalisms (1989). Finally, Sugar distinguishes four types of nationalism in Eastern Europe: 'bourgeois', 'aristocratic', 'popular' and 'bureaucratic' nationalisms.

This list can be doubled or even tripled. But such an exhaustive list would not be helpful at this stage. More examples will be given when discussing the particular theories. Suffice it to say that almost all scholars recognize the multifarious nature of nationalism, while some go one step further and argue that sorting the different types according to their intrinsic features is all that can be achieved theoretically.

Further Reading

There is a vast literature on nationalist ideology. The best source on the genesis of the idea of nationalism, however, is still Kedourie (1994), originally published in 1960. Kedourie's book suffers from an overemphasis on the role of intellectuals, especially the German Romantics, but is very useful for all that. For Rousseau's ideas on patriotism and citizenship see Barnard (1984); for a comparison of Rousseau and Herder see Barnard (1983). Historians' responses to nationalism are the subject of an insightful article by Smith (1996a) [1992]. For Mill's reflections on nationality see the short extract in Woolf (1996) [1861].

The relationship between Marxism and nationalism has been the subject of a heated debate for the last three or four decades. A survey of the controversy can be found in Munck (1986) and Nimni (1991). On Austrian Social Democrats see Stargardt (1995), who not only provides a review of their main ideas, but also presents a vivid description of the social and political context which shaped these ideas. The reader should also consult Bauer (1996) [1924], the first chapter of his classic *Die Nationalitätenfrage und die Sozialdemokratie*, for one of the earliest attempts to theorize nationalism within the Marxist camp. The famous lecture Renan delivered in 1882 can now be found in English: see Bhabha (1990b). For Durkheim and Weber see Guibernau (1996), chapter 1 and James (1996), chapter 4. A concise summary of the relevance of their ideas for the studies of subsequent periods is given in Smith (1998): 13–16.

As we have seen earlier, the first half of the twentieth century witnessed the rise of a number of general historical studies on nationalism. Of these, the following are still relevant: Hayes (1955) [1931], Kohn (1967) [1944] and Carr (1945).

For the modernization theories of the 1950s and 1960s, the work to consult is Smith (1983), originally published in 1971. Smith offers a comprehensive overview of the main theories of nation-building, together with a balanced criticism of them. Among primary sources, Deutsch (1966) [1953], regarded by many as the classic example of the communications approach, and Kedourie (1994) [1960], one of the pioneering works of the modernist paradigm, should be mentioned.

3
Primordialism

Our nationality is like our relations to women: too implicated in our moral nature to be changed honourably, and too accidental to be worth changing.

George Santayana (quoted in Gellner 1983)

What is Primordialism?

The earliest paradigm of nations and nationalism is the primordialist. To begin with, primordialism is an approach, not a theory. It is an 'umbrella' term used to describe scholars who hold that nationality is a 'natural' part of human beings, as natural as speech, sight or smell, and that nations have existed since time immemorial. In that respect, it is not different from the terms 'modernist' or 'ethno-symbolist', which are all used to classify various theories with regard to their common characteristics, thereby enabling researchers to compare them systematically.

The common denominator of the modernists is their conviction in the modernity of nations and nationalism; that of the ethno-symbolists is the stress they lay in their explanations on ethnic pasts and cultures; finally, that of the primordialists is their belief in the antiquity and naturalness of nations. Beyond these common denominators, the theories developed by the scholars of each category exhibit a bewildering diversity. Nevertheless, when we take a quick glance at the literature on nationalism, we notice that the primordialists are treated as a more homogeneous category than, say, the modernists. The shallowness of this view has been revealed by recent debates on ethnicity. The primordialists are not unlike the modernists or any other category in terms of the diversity they harbour. I will turn to these differences in a while, but let us first focus on the term 'primordialism' itself.

The term comes from the adjective 'primordial' which is defined in three ways: 'first in order of time, original, elemental'; 'first in order of appearance in the growth or development of an organism (biological meaning)'; and 'an elementary principle, first, primeval, transcending' (*The New International Webster's Comprehensive Dictionary of the English Language*, 1996 edn). It is generally thought that Edward Shils is the first one to have employed this term. In his famous 1957 article, Shils uses the term 'in reference to relationships within the family' (Eller and Coughlan 1993: 184). He argues that the strength of the attachments one feels for her/his family members does not stem from interaction, but from 'a certain ineffable significance . . . attributed to the tie of blood' (Shils 1957: 142). For Shils, these attachments could only be described as 'primordial'. Shils states that his conceptualization of primordial relations was influenced by several books on the sociology of religion, notably by A. D. Nock's *Conversion* and Martin P. Nilsson's *Greek Popular Religion*. Eller and Coughlan argue that this might also explain the mystical and spiritual language he uses to describe the attachments to family and kin (1993: 184). Clifford Geertz, another name identified with primordialism, uses a similar definition:

> By a primordial attachment is meant one that stems from the 'givens' – or, more precisely, as culture is inevitably involved in such matters, the assumed 'givens' – of social existence: immediate contiguity and kin connection mainly, but beyond them the givenness that stems from being born into a particular religious community, speaking a particular language, or even a dialect of a language, and following particular social practices. These congruities of blood, speech, custom, and so on, are seen to have an ineffable, and at times overpowering, coerciveness in and of themselves. (Geertz 1993: 259)

It needs to be stressed at the outset that we cannot consider primordialist accounts of nationalism independently from the debate on ethnicity. Primordialist arguments are first formulated to explain the origins and strength of ethnic identities. Thus, both Shils and Geertz use the term 'primordial' to describe the nature of ethnic attachments. This led some writers to suggest that there are in fact two separate debates, one over the antiquity of nations between the 'perennialists' and the 'modernists' and another over the nature of ethnic ties between the 'primordialists' and the 'instrumentalists' (Smith 1994: 376). This confusion inevitably reflects on the discussions of primordialism. In what follows, I will try to separate these debates as much as possible and try to show how, that is in which meanings, the term is imported from the literature on ethnicity.

I have already noted that the primordialists do not form a mono-lithic category. Thus, it is possible to identify three different ver-sions of primordialism. For the sake of a more systematic presentation, I will call them the 'naturalist', 'sociobiological' and 'culturalist' approaches. The classification I will use here is inspired by Smith's recent works (1994: 376–7; 1995: 31–3; 1998: chapter 7). Another classification is developed by Tilley (1997). She divides the primordialist approaches again into three cate-gories and calls them the 'biological', 'psychological' and 'cultural' approaches. However, Tilley's classification is designed for ethnic identities and based on different definitions than the ones adopted here.

The Naturalist Approach

This approach, which can be considered as the most extreme version of primordialism, asserts that national identities are a 'natural' part of all human beings, just like speech or sight: a man has a nationality as he has a nose and two ears (Gellner 1983: 6). The nation to which one belongs is predetermined, 'naturally fixed': in other words, one is born into a nation in the same way s/he is born into a family (Smith 1995: 31). The division of human-ity into different groups with different cultural characteristics is part of the natural order and these groups will tend to exclude others (Lieven 1997: 12). Those who subscribe to this view hold that nations have 'natural frontiers', hence, 'a specific origin and place in nature, as well as a peculiar character, mission and destiny' (Smith 1995: 32). As Smith notes, the naturalists do not make a distinction between nations and ethnic groups. Nationalism is an attribute of humanity in all ages (*ibid.*).

Not surprisingly, this is the view endorsed by most, if not all, nationalists. Since the nineteenth century, this 'ideological view of the past', to use Hutchinson's words (1994), has continued to shape the works of nationalist historians and the rhetoric of elites who were struggling to get or maintain state power. Thus, historians like Frantisek Palacky, Eoin MacNeill and Nicolae Iorga, all influential figures in their respective national movements, claimed that nations were primordial entities that 'were objectively identifiable through their distinctive way of life, their attachment to a territorial homeland, and their striving for political autonomy' (Hutchinson 1994: 3). According to them, the past was the story of the nation's perpetual struggle for self-realization.

There are a number of recurrent themes in every nationalist narrative. Let me briefly illustrate some of these themes with the help of an essay by the Turkish patriot Tekin Alp [Moise Cohen], taken from Kedourie's *Nationalism in Asia and Africa* (1971). First, there is the theme of the antiquity of the ('particular') nation:

. . . it was high time to make the whole world, and to begin with the Turks themselves, understand that Turkish history does not begin with Osman's tribe, but in fact twelve thousand years before Jesus Christ . . . The exploits of the Osmanlı Turks constitute merely one episode in the history of the Turkish nation which has founded several other empires. (*Ibid.*: 210)

Second, there is the theme of golden age:

Whilst the rest of humanity was living in caves, leading a most primitive life, the Turk had already in his motherland become civilized enough to know the use of wood and metal . . . At a time when the Turks had reached a high level of culture in their own motherland, the peoples of Europe were still in a savage state and lived in complete ignorance. (*Ibid.*: 216, 219)

Third, there is the theme of the superiority of the national culture:

'[i]f the Turks had not entered Muslim society, the civilization which we call Islamic would not have existed . . . It is because the

Turks who created this movement were superior to the other Muslim peoples from the point of view of culture and civilization. (*Ibid.*: 221)

Fourth, there is the theme of periods of recess, or in Gellner's words 'periods of somnolence' (1997: 93):

> . . . the Turks were agents of culture and progress, and . . . they have never ceased to be such except when subjugated by foreign cultures and moral forces. The civilized nations must not take into account this short period of decadence, when the Turkish people were acting out of character' (Kedourie 1971: 210).

Finally, there is the theme of the national hero, who comes and awakens the nation, ending this 'accidental' period of decadence:

> He [Kemal Atatürk] could not tolerate therefore this false conception of Turkish history which was current among some of the Turkish intellectuals . . . He has therefore taken it into his head to eliminate it by means of a revolutionary outburst which would subject it to the same fate as the other misconceptions from which the Turkish people have suffered for centuries. (*Ibid.*: 211)

As I have alluded to above, Smith distinguishes two separable claims within the naturalist version of primordialism. Some writers suggest that nations have existed since time immemorial without subscribing to the view that they result from any kind of 'primordial' ties (Smith 1984). Smith introduces the term 'perennialism' to cover this less radical version of primordialism. The term comes from the adjective 'perennial', which means 'continuing or enduring through the year or through many years' and 'growing continuously, surviving' (*The New International Webster's Comprehensive Dictionary of the English Language*, 1996 edn): hence the name 'perennialist' for those who see nations as historic entities which have developed over the centuries, with their intrinsic characteristics largely unchanged (Halliday 1997a; Smith 1984, 1995). Smith maintains that perennialists need not be primordialists since it is possible to concede the antiquity of ethnic and national ties without holding that they are 'natural'.

One of the core ideas of perennialism is that 'modern nations are the lineal descendants of their medieval counterparts' (Smith 1995: 53). According to this view, we might come across nations in the Middle Ages, even in the antiquity. Modernity, 'for all its technological or economic progress, has not affected the basic structures of human association'; on the contrary, it is the nation and nationalism which engenders modernity (*ibid.*). The perennialists concede that nations may experience periods of recess or decadence in the course of their historical journey: but 'bad fortune' cannot destroy the national 'essence'. All that is necessary is to 'rekindle the fires of nationalism', to reawaken the nation. Minogue uses the metaphor of the Sleeping Beauty to depict this view: the nation is the Sleeping Beauty who awaits a kiss to be revived, and the nationalists are the prince who will provide this 'magical' kiss (Smith 1995: 168).

Smith's distinction between primordialism and perennialism seems to be a useful one. There are, indeed, very few students of nationalism who continue to endorse the 'bedrock' primordialist position. In the words of Brubaker, 'no serious scholar today holds the view that is routinely attributed to primordialists in straw-man setups, namely that nations or ethnic groups are primordial, unchanging entities' (1996: 15). On the other hand, it is always possible to find scholars who believe in the antiquity of nations and nationalism.

The question of 'who can be considered as a perennialist in the literature on nationalism' has been the subject of much controversy. For example, Smith treats John Armstrong as a perennialist (Smith 1984), whereas Armstrong is regarded by many scholars as the pioneer of ethno-symbolism. This controversy stems partly from definitional problems, whose resolution depends on how we classify scholars who maintain that the formation of nations should be examined in *la longue durée*. If we decide that the latter approach is ethno-symbolism, then we should place scholars like Armstrong and Llobera in the same category as Smith. If, on the other hand, we conclude that such a perspective is perennialist, then we should consider Smith as a perennialist as well. There are in fact scholars who adopt this latter position (Breuilly 1996). Let me conclude this sub-section with the views of two scholars from the perennialist camp, Josep R. Llobera (1994) and Adrian Hastings (1997).

Perennialists do not identify a specific date of birth for nationalism. Thus, while Llobera traces the origins of nations back to the Middle Ages (1994: 219–21), Hastings argues that national consciousness has been shaped in England – the first nation according to him – between the fourteenth and sixteenth centuries (1997: 5). More specifically, Llobera holds that only if we adopt a very restricted definition of nationalism can we conclude that it is a recent phenomenon and claims that a rudimentary sense of national identity existed already in the medieval period (1994: 220). Hastings, on the other hand, argues that it is possible to identify English nationalism of a sort in the fourteenth century, especially in the long wars with France and contends that this nationalism has completed its development in the sixteenth and seventeenth centuries (1997: 5). These examples reveal clearly that for perennialist writers the origins of both nations and nationalism stretch back to the medieval period – that is, well beyond the modern ages. The 'essence' which differentiates any particular nation from others manages to remain intact despite all vicissitudes of history. To focus exclusively on the modern period, that is on the last two centuries, in order to understand the processes of nation formation is in this context 'a recipe for sociological disaster' (Llobera 1994: 3).

The Sociobiological Approach

The sociobiological approach to nationalism has gained new momentum in recent years with the works of a range of scholars who have applied the findings of the new field of sociobiology to the study of ethnic ties. The basic question asked by sociobiology is: 'why are animals social, that is, why do they cooperate?' (van den Berghe 1978: 402). According to Pierre van den Berghe, the leading exponent of this approach in the literature on nationalism, the answer to this question was long intuitively known: 'animals are social to the extent that cooperation is mutually beneficial'. What sociobiology does, van den Berghe argues, is to supply the main genetic mechanism for animal sociality, namely kin selection to increase inclusive fitness:

> an animal can duplicate its genes directly through its own reproduction, or indirectly through the reproduction of relatives with

which it shares specific proportions of genes. Animals, therefore, can be expected to behave cooperatively, and thereby enhance each other's fitness to the extent that they are genetically related. This is what is meant by kin selection. (*Ibid.*: 402)

Van den Berghe claims that kin selection, or mating with relatives, is a powerful cement of sociality in humans too. In fact, both ethnicity and race are extensions of the idiom of kinship: 'therefore, ethnic and race sentiments are to be understood as an extended and attenuated form of kin selection' (*ibid.*: 403). That the extended kinship is sometimes putative rather than real is not important. Just as in the smaller kin units, the kinship is often real enough 'to become the basis of these powerful sentiments we call nationalism, tribalism, racism, and ethnocentrism' (*ibid.*: 404). If that is the case, then how do we recognize our 'kin'? According to van den Berghe, 'only a few of the world's societies use primarily morphological phenotypes to define themselves'. It follows that cultural criteria of group membership are more salient than physical ones, if the latter is used at all. In a way, this is inevitable because neighbouring populations resemble each other in terms of their genetic composition. Eye color in Europe, van den Berghe notes, is a good case in point. The further north one goes, the higher the proportion of lightly pigmented eyes. 'Yet, at no point in the journey is there a noticeable discontinuity'. The criteria for identifying kinsmen, on the other hand, should discriminate more reliably between groups than within groups. In other words, 'the criterion chosen must show more *inter*group than *intra*-group variance'. Cultural criteria, like differences of accent, body adornment and the like, meet this requirement far more reliably than physical ones (*ibid.*: 406–7).

Noting that kin selection does not explain all of human sociality, van den Berghe identifies two additional mechanisms: reciprocity and coercion. 'Reciprocity is cooperation for mutual benefit, and with expectation of return, and it can operate between kin or between non-kin. Coercion is the use of force for one-sided benefit'. All human societies continue to be organized on the basis of all three principles of sociality. But, van den Berghe adds, 'the larger and the more complex a society becomes, the greater the importance of reciprocity'. (*ibid.*: 403) Moreover, while kin selection – real or putative – is more dominant in intra-group relations, coercion becomes the rule in inter-ethnic (or inter-racial) relationships. Ethnic groups may occasionally enter into a symbiotic, mutually beneficial relationship (reciprocity) but this is usually short-lived: relations between different groups are more often than not antagonistic (*ibid.*: 409).

The Culturalist Approach

This approach, which might also be called 'cultural primordialism', is generally associated with the works of Edward Shils and Clifford Geertz. Eller and Coughlan argue that the concept of primordialism used in the works of these writers contains three main ideas:

1. Primordial identities or attachments are 'given', *a priori*, underived, prior to all experience and interaction – in fact, all interaction is carried out *within* primordial realities. Primordial attachments are 'natural', even 'spiritual', rather than sociological . . . [T]hey have no social source. Accordingly, those things called primordial presumably have long histories.
2. Primordial sentiments are 'ineffable', overpowering, and coercive . . . If an individual is a member of a group, he or she *necessarily* feels certain attachments to that group and its practices (especially language and culture).
3. Primordialism is essentially a question of emotion and affect (1993: 187).

These arguments have revealed a misinterpretation – caused by a careless reading of Geertz and Shils – which went largely unnoticed for many years and led to a highly polemical discussion (see for example Grosby 1994; Tilley 1997). As might be recalled, Geertz cites the congruities of blood, language, religion and particular social practices among the objects of ethnic attachments. Contrary to Eller and Coughlan's formulations, however, Geertz never suggests that these objects are themselves 'given' or primordial: rather, they are 'assumed' to be given by individuals. What attributes the quality of being 'natural' or mystical to the 'givens of social existence' are the perceptions of those who believe in them. In the words of Smith,

Geertz is underlining the power of what we might term a 'participants' primordialism'; he is not saying that the world is constituted by an objective primordial reality, only that many of us believe in primordial objects and feel their power. (1998: 158)

As Tilley forcefully argues, Geertz's approach to culture can in fact be considered as 'constructivist'. Nothing illustrates this better than these words she takes from *The Interpretation of Cultures*:

Believing with Max Weber, that man is an animal suspended in webs of significance he himself has spun, I take culture to be those webs, and the analysis of it to be therefore not an experimental science in search of law but an interpretative one in search of meaning. (1993: 5)

The same goes for Shils. Eller and Coughlan infer from Shils' 1957 essay that he believes in the sacredness of primordial attachments. The evidence, they contend, is provided by his following assertion: 'the primordial property . . . could have had sacredness attributed to it' (Shils 1957: 142). But, like Geertz, Shils did not attribute sacredness to these attachments (Tilley 1997). Instead, he noted that the attachment derives his strength from 'a certain ineffable significance . . . *attributed* to the tie of blood' (Shils 1957: 142, emphasis added). Ironically enough, Eller and Coughlan refer to these words as well, before reaching their final verdict on Shils. Here, it should be noted that Eller and Coughlan are not the only ones who have fallen prey to this misconception; many scholars have taken their share of the confusion (see for example Brass 1991).

Cultural primordialism in a Geertzian way, then, may be defined as an approach which focuses on the webs of meaning spun by the individuals themselves. As Tilley explains convincingly, Geertz is in fact 'making use of the term "primordial" more in its sense of "first in a series" . . . in order to highlight the ways in which foundation concepts provide the basis for other ideas, values, customs or ideologies held by the individual' (1997: 502).

Such a definition enables me to advance a somewhat controversial claim, namely that some scholars who advance a 'subjective' definition of the nation might also be considered as cultural primordialists. One example might be Walker Connor who defines the nation as 'a group of people who *feel* that they are ancestrally related.' Connor continues: 'It is the largest group that can command a person's loyalty because of *felt* kinship ties; it is, from this perspective, the fully extended family' (Connor 1994: 202, emphases added). Now, Connor is seen by many scholars as a modernist (for example Hutchinson 1994). In a way this is true, since he explicitly rejects the claim that nations have existed in the Middle Ages (Connor 1994: 210–27), but this does not contradict with the definition of 'cultural primordialism' I have proposed above. Such a definition does not specify any date for the emergence of nations and/or nationalism – neither did Geertz. It only states that individuals do feel attached to certain elements of their culture, assuming that they are 'given', 'sacred' and 'underived'. The approach, then, deals with perceptions and beliefs. This is also what Connor chooses to stress as the above quotation demonstrates. In the same essay, he suggests that what influences attitudes and behaviour is not 'what is' but 'what people perceive as is' (1994: 197). This, I think, makes him a cultural primordialist in the sense I have specified above.

Let me briefly recapitulate what I have said so far before moving on to the criticisms raised against primordialist explanations. Apart from the *naturalist approach* characterizing the writings of nationalists, primordialism appears in three different forms in the literature on nationalism. *Perennialists* argue that nations have always existed and that modern nations are nothing but the extensions of their medieval counterparts. *Sociobiologists* seek the origins of ethnic and national ties in genetic mechanisms and instincts, treating the nation as an extension of the idiom of kinship, or a kind of superfamily. Finally, *cultural primordialists* focus on the perceptions and beliefs of the individuals. What generates the strong attachments people feel for the 'givens of social existence', the culturalists contend, is a belief in their 'sacredness'.

A Critique of Primordialism

Several objections have been raised against the primordialist approach. For the sake of clarity, I will mainly focus on the general criticisms, only mentioning the particular charges brought against the different versions of primordialism when necessary. This will also enable me to avoid the risk of ending up with an exhausting list. The criticisms I will discuss relate to five aspects of primordialist explanations: the nature of ethnic and national ties, the origins of ethnic and national ties, the relationship of ethnic and national bonds with other types of personal attachments, the question of emotion and affect, the date of the emergence of nations.

The Nature of Ethnic and National Ties

One common denominator of the primordialists – with the exception of culturalists – is their belief in the 'givenness' of ethnic and national ties. If the strong attachments generated by language, religion, kinship and the like are given by nature, then they are also fixed, or static. They are transmitted from one generation to the next with their 'essential' characteristics unchanged. In other words, what we witness today is merely a reassertion of the national essence. This view is challenged in recent years by an ever-growing number of studies on ethnicity. These studies stress the role of individual choice in the construction of ethnic identities, claiming that 'far from being self-perpetuating, they require creative effort and investment' (Hoben and Hefner 1990, cited in Eller and Coughlan 1993: 188). They are redefined and reconstructed in each generation as groups react to changing conditions. It follows that the content and boundaries of ethnic identities are fluid, not fixed. Eller and Coughlan, following Nagel, suggest that the recent studies provide a compelling case for seeing ethnicity as 'a socially constructed, variable definition of self and other, whose existence and meaning is continuously negotiated, revised and revitalized' (Nagel 1991, cited in Eller and Coughlan 1993: 188).

A similar argument comes from Brass, who espouses an 'instrumental' approach to ethnicity (1991: 70–2). For him, some primordial attachments are clearly variable. To begin with, Brass contends, many people speak more than one language, dialect or code in multilingual developing societies. Many illiterate people in these countries, far from being attached to their mother tongues, will not even know its name when asked. In some cases, members of different ethnic groups will choose to change their language in order to provide better opportunities for their children or to differentiate themselves further from other ethnic groups. Finally, Brass argues, many people never think about their language anyway, nor do they attach to it any emotional significance. The situation is not different for other sources of ethnic and national attachments. Religions too have been subject to many changes over the centuries. Brass holds that 'shifts in religious practices brought about under the influence of religious reformers are common occurrences in pre-modern, modernizing, and even in postindustrial societies' (*ibid.*: 71). Moreover, some people in cosmopolitan settings have engaged themselves in alternative spiritual quests. As for the place of birth, it can be conceded that one's homeland is still important for some people; but, Brass remarks, many people have migrated by choice from their native places and a considerable proportion of them have chosen to assimilate to their new society and have lost any sense of identification with their homelands. More importantly, a person's attachment to her/his region or homeland rarely becomes politically significant unless there is some degree of perceived discrimination against the region or its people in the larger society. Besides, even the fact of one's place of birth is subject to variation since a region may be defined in many ways. When it comes to kinship connections, Brass claims that 'the range of genuine kin relationships is usually too small to be of political significance' (*ibid.*). 'Fictive' kin relationships may extend the range of ethnic groups but the fact that they are fictive presumes their variability by definition. Moreover, the meaning of such fictive relationships will naturally vary from person to person since the 'imagined' character of the attachment will be dominant in these relationships.

On the other hand, Smith argues that 'ethnic ties like other social bonds are subject to economic, social and political forces, and therefore fluctuate and change according to circumstances' (1995: 33). Intermarriages, migrations, external conquests and the importation of labour have made it very unlikely for many ethnic groups to preserve 'the cultural homogeneity and pure "essence" posited by most primordialists' (*ibid.*).

Some primordialists concede that the boundaries and content of ethnic identities may change in time. But they insist that the 'essence' of the ethnic culture, for example its origin myths and symbols, persists through time. According to Brass, even this bedrock position poses a number of problems. He claims that except for certain ethnic groups which have rich cultural heritages like the Jews, many movements create their cultures 'after-the-fact'. These movements were not any less successful in generating cohesion and solidarity than those of the groups with a richer cultural heritage. He cites the 'mushroom growth' of ethnic political movements in the United States to illustrate this point (1991: 72–3). Eller and Coughlan argue the same for the new ethnic groups appearing under colonial rule. They note that in many parts of the world, especially in Africa, 'new ethnic identities and groups are being created which claim, and receive from some researchers, primordial status. These new primordials (a shocking contradiction in terms) are "made", not "given"' (1993: 188). In most of these cases, the appropriate cultural givens were lacking, so they were often constructed (Kasfir 1979, cited in Eller and Coughlan 1993: 188).

In short, then, the assumption that primordial attachments and the cultural sources that generate them are 'given' does not square with facts. It should be stressed that this criticism is not the preserve of instrumentalist scholars: as we have seen, ethno-symbolists, notably Smith, express similar concerns.

The Origins of Ethnic and National Ties

Another fundamental claim of the primordialists (with the exception of cultural primordialists) is that ethnic and national attachments are 'underived', hence prior to all social interaction. This automatically creates a mystical aura around them: primordial sentiments are ineffable, that is 'incapable of being expressed in words', thus unanalysable. Eller and Coughlan claim that 'primordialism has tended to treat the identification of "primordial" attachments as the successful and inevitable end of analysis' (1993: 189).

Brass disagrees with this primordialist assertion. He argues that the knowledge of ethnic cultures does not enable us to predict either which ethnic groups will develop a successful political movement or the form this movement will assume. He cites the creations of Israel and Pakistan as examples. According to Brass, a knowledge of orthodox Judaism or traditional Islam in India would have suggested that the least likely possibilities would have been the rise of a Zionist movement or the movement for the creation of Pakistan since the traditional religious authorities in both cases were opposed to a secular state (1991: 73). A similar point is raised by Breuilly who argues that the use of ethnic cultures in a nationalist manner will transform their meanings. He suggests that 'it is the way in which nationalism constructs identities anew, even if that construction involves appeals to history and culture and sees itself as discovery rather than construction, to which one must pay attention' (1993a: 406).

Zubaida joins Brass and Breuilly by arguing that there is no systematic way of designating a nation (1978: 53). He raises the question 'why does India constitute a "nation" while the old Ottoman Empire, arguably with greater homogeneity than modern India, did not?'. The answer, he maintains, lies in historical conjunctures: 'There is no systematic way in which any social theoretical discourse can justify the state of nationhood in the one case and deny it in the other' (*ibid.*).

Gellner approaches this problem in his own remarkable way (1996b; 1997: chapter 15). For him, the crucial question is: 'do nations have navels?' The analogy here is with the philosophical argument about the creation of mankind (McCrone 1998: 15). If Adam was created by God at a certain date, then he did not have a navel, because he did not go through the process by which people acquire navels. The same goes with nations, says Gellner. The ethnic, the cultural national community is rather like the navel. 'Some nations have it and some don't and in any case it's inessential' (1996b: 367). If modernism tells half the story, that for him is good enough, because 'the additional bits of the story in the other half are redundant' (*ibid.*: 370). He refers to the Estonians to illustrate his argument. The Estonians, he argues, are a clear example of highly successful navel-free nationalism (1997: 96–7):

> At the beginning of the nineteenth century they didn't even have a name for themselves. They were just referred to as people who lived on the land as opposed to German or Swedish burghers and aristocrats and Russian administrators. They had no ethnonym. They were just a category without any ethnic self-consciousness. Since then they've been brilliantly successful in creating a vibrant culture . . . It's a very vital and vibrant culture, but it was created by the kind of modernist process which I then generalise for nationalism and nations in general. (1996b: 367–8)

Let us note in passing that this criticism is valid in the case of socio-biological explanations as well. These accounts, based on such presumably 'universal' factors as blood ties, kinship relationships, are not able to explain why only a small proportion of ethnic groups become aware of their common identity, while others disappear in the mists of history. If we accept that ethnic groups are extensions of the idiom of kinship, that is superfamilies, then this has to be valid in the case of all ethnic groups. But as some scholars have underlined, for every successful nationalist movement there are *n* unsuccessful ones (Gellner 1983: 44–5; Halliday 1997a: 16). Why do some groups effectively establish their own political roof, while others fail? Sociobiological explanations are silent on this issue. Moreover, Smith notes, the mechanisms proposed by sociobiologists do not explain 'why the quest for individual reproductive success should move beyond the extended family to much wider cultural units like *ethnies*' (1995: 33).

The Relationship of Ethnic and National Bonds with Other Types of Personal Attachments

Another objection raised against the primordialists concerns their tendency to give priority to ethnic and national identities among other forms of identity. Smith argues that 'human beings live in a multiplicity of social groups, some of which are more significant and salient than others at various times' (1995: 33). Individuals have multiple identities and roles – familial, territorial, class, religious, ethnic and gender (Smith 1991a: 4). These categories sometimes overlap and/or complement each other; at other times, they clash. It is not possible to predict which identity will be dominant at a particular point in time. The salience of each category changes according to circumstances.

The Question of Emotion and Affect

Primordialism is about emotions and affect. Even the terminology used reflects this: attachment, bond, tie, sentiment. The affect dimension makes primordial identities qualitatively different from other kinds of identities, such as those of class (Eller and Coughlan 1993: 187).

Eller and Coughlan, while recognizing the important role emotions play in human social life, object to their mystification. They argue that the mystification of the primordial has led to a fallacy, namely the desocializing of the phenomenon. It is suggested that these emotional ties are not born in social interaction, but are just there, 'implicit in the relationship (kin or ethnic) itself' (1993: 192). According to Eller and Coughlan, the source of this fallacy 'is the failure of sociology and anthropology to deal intelligibly with emotion' (*ibid.*). To illustrate this, they refer to Durkheim's observations on religion. The crucial question, they contend, is 'how are sentiments (religious or ethnic) induced in people?' The answer is the same for both: in rituals. Rituals

> magically work their effect on participants, making some sensations stronger, producing others at that very moment. There is little or no awareness of the day-to-day activities which might produce or reproduce sentiment or knowledge, religious or otherwise. (*Ibid.*: 193)

It seems difficult to disagree with Eller and Coughlan's assertions. However, it must be stressed once again that Geertz, who is their main target, does not deserve these criticisms. On the contrary, the way out of this impasse is hidden in Geertz's writings. As Tilley forcefully argues:

> the 'primordial' elements of culture are not affect but the cognitive framework which shapes and informs affect . . . Certain assumptions or knowledge systems set the stage for affect, and to the extent that such knowledge systems form a kind of cognitive substratum not only for affect but for most conscious thought, they might be said to be 'primordial'. (1997: 503)

The Date of the Emergence of Nations

A final criticism concerns the perennialists' belief in the antiquity of nations and nationalism. Zubaida (1978) refutes this claim from a modernist viewpoint in an article written more than 20 years ago. According to Zubaida, the most serious problem the nationalists face is the historical novelty of both the concept of nation and the forms of political units now called nation-states. Many of the states and empires in history ruled over diverse populations. Neither the state personnel, nor the subject population were ethnically homogeneous. The rulers more often than not had a different ethnicity than the population they ruled over. Moreover, 'shared ethnicity between ruler and ruled did not always constitute grounds for favour or mutual support' (1978: 54). In other words, ethnicity was not as important as it is today (see also Breuilly 1993a: 406). Zubaida turns to the Ottoman Empire to illustrate his arguments. He notes that the state and military apparatus of the Ottoman Empire was not exclusively Turkish – it included various Caucasian ethnicities, Albanians and Kurds, and the Turkish-speaking populations were not favoured over others. In short, 'within this form of political organisation, the units of identity and solidarity were by no means always those of ethnicity, common language, culture, etc., but varied and overlapped in different times and places' (*ibid.*). Even wars and conflicts were different from the ones we witness today. The contending sides were not ethnically homogeneous; members of the same ethnic groups were fighting each other in the service of different lords. According to Zubaida, nationalists, for the sake of establishing historical continuity, 'evade these obstacles, or explain them away as manifestations of past national oppressions and dispersions' (*ibid.*: 55). Breuilly makes the same point by arguing that being a German in eighteenth-century Germany did not have the same meaning as to be a German today. Two centuries ago Germanness was only *an* identity among others – social estate, confession and so on. (1993a: 406).

Another attempt to counter the arguments put forward by perennialists comes from Smith (1991a: 45–51). The fact that Smith is an ethno-symbolist, hence more sensitive to ethnic pasts and cultures than the modernists, makes this attempt even more interesting. He begins his critique by asking the following question: 'Were there nations and nationalism in antiquity?'

Smith tries to answer this question by observing some pre-modern civilizations. Ancient Egypt is his first stop. Smith argues that while ancient Egyptians constituted what he calls an *ethnie*, that is ethnic community, with a corresponding ethnocentrism, they were far from being a nation in the contemporary sense of the word (1991a: 45). Its economy was divided into regions and districts; the production was directed to self-subsistence, not interregional trade. Legally, there was no idea of citizenship, hence no conception of rights and duties. Education was class-divided and far from being centralized. Finally, while there were common myths and memories that differentiated the Egyptians from other peoples, these operated largely through religious institutions and 'were unable to compensate for the regionalism that so often undermined the unity of the Egyptian state'. (*ibid.*: 46) In sum, it is more correct to call ancient Egypt an ethnic state than a nation. Smith also argues that it is not possible to speak of an Egyptian nationalism since nationalism can be defined as an ideology – and a movement – which presupposes 'a world of nations, each with its own character, and a primary allegiance to the nation as the sole source of political power and the basis of world order' (*ibid.*: 46–7). It was difficult to find such movements even in the medieval world, let alone in ancient Egypt.

Smith then turns to ancient Greeks and Jews. In the case of ancient Greece, Smith points to the fact that unity was more cultural than political. In fact, even in the cultural sphere the picture was more complex as religious rituals and artistic forms varied from one city-state to the next. So again, Smith claims, it is more appropriate to speak of a Greek ethnocentrism. As for the Jews, it can be suggested that they were displaying more unity than the two previous examples. But here, religion made things more difficult since there was 'near-identity in Jewish thought and practice of what we consider to be separate [phenomena], namely the religious community and the nation with religious messianism and nationalism' (*ibid.*: 48).

What complicates matters further in all these cases and in general for any attempt to see whether there were nations and nationalism in antiquity is lack of evidence, even from the small ruling strata (Smith 1991a: 47). In the words of Connor,

Such vast disagreement among eminent authorities [on the question of when nations have emerged] has been made possible by the near absence of conclusive evidence. Nationalism is a mass phenomenon. The fact that members of the ruling elite or intelligentsia manifest national sentiment is not sufficient to establish that national consciousness has permeated the value systems of the masses. And the masses, until recent times totally or semi-illiterate, furnished few hints concerning their view of group-self. (1994: 212)

These and other criticisms led to a marginalization of the extreme versions of primordialism in the literature on nationalism. Some scholars even suggested that the sociological usage of primordialism should be abandoned altogether 'because of its lack of empirical support and its inherent social passivity and anti-intellectualism' (Eller and Coughlan 1993: 200). Obviously, these views are not shared by everybody. Brass, for instance, while sharply criticizing some of the arguments advanced by primordialists, concedes that the primordialist perspective is relevant to our understanding of ethnic groups with long and rich cultural heritages (1991: 74). He admits that such heritages provide an effective means of political mobilization. Similarly, Smith defends the concept by arguing that it enables us to understand the enduring power and hold of ethnic ties (1995: 34).

I would suggest that the real importance of the concept lies elsewhere. Primordialism, as defined by Geertz and elaborated by Tilley, that is in the sense of webs of meaning spun by individuals and the strong emotions these meanings generate, enables us to explore how these meanings are produced and reproduced, and how these 'knowledge systems suggest themselves as "givens", prior to individual thought and action' (Tilley 1997: 503). The concept underlines the importance of perceptions and beliefs in guiding human action. In this context, it seems quite unreasonable to follow Eller and Coughlan's suggestion and remove the term from the sociological lexicon.

Further Reading

Any bookshop will contain a plethora of nationalist histories stressing the primordial roots of particular nations. A useful introduction in this respect is a collection of essays edited by Kedourie (1971). Compiled from the writings of various nationalists, the book illustrates many of the themes that recur in nationalist narratives. For a sociobiological account of nationalism see van den Berghe (1978). For cultural primordialism see the famous articles by Shils (1957) and Geertz (1993)

[1973], chapter 10. For a critique of primordialism from an instrumentalist standpoint see Brass (1991). A comparison of primordialism with instrumentalism and constructivism is provided in Tilley (1997). For a controversial discussion of Shils and Geertz see Eller and Coughlan (1993).

4
Modernism

Man is an animal suspended in webs of significance he himself
has spun.

Clifford Geertz, *The Interpretation of Cultures*

What is Modernism?

Modernism emerged as a reaction to the primordialism of the
older generations who tacitly accepted the basic assumptions of the
nationalist ideology. According to Smith, classical modernism
achieved its canonical formulation in the 1960s, above all in the
model of 'nation-building' which had a wide appeal in the social
sciences in the wake of the movement of decolonization in Asia
and Africa (1998: 3). This was followed by a variety of models and
theories, all of which regarded nations as historically formed constructs. Modernist explanations soon became the dominant orthodoxy in the field. Despite sustained criticisms by ethno-symbolists
since the early 1980s, many scholars today still subscribe to some
form of modernism.

The common denominator of all these studies is a belief in the
modernity of nations and nationalism. According to this perspective, both appeared in the last two centuries, that is in the wake of
the French Revolution, and they are the products of specifically
modern processes like capitalism, industrialism, the emergence of
the bureaucratic state, urbanization and secularism (Smith 1994:
377; 1995: 29). In fact, they become a sociological necessity only
in the modern world: there was no room for nations or national-

ism in the pre-modern era. In short, 'nationalism comes before nations. Nations do not make states and nationalisms but the other way round' (Hobsbawm 1990: 10).

Apart from this basic belief, modernists have very little in common. They all stress different factors in their accounts of nationalism. With this in mind, I will refrain from treating modernist scholars as a 'monolithic' category, and I will divide them into three categories in terms of the key factors – economic, political and social/cultural – they have identified. At first glance, this classification may seem overly simplistic: it might be argued that none of these theorists rely on a single factor in their accounts of nationalism. Nevertheless, most of the theories we will discuss below, whatever their degree of sophistication, emphasize one set of factors at the expense of others. In fact, this is what lies behind the major charge brought against modernist interpretations, namely the charge of 'reductionism' (Smith 1983; Calhoun 1997). Moreover, the classification I am introducing here does not consist of 'mutually exclusive' categories. Scholars are classified on the basis of the factor they 'prioritize' in explaining nationalism. This does not imply that they have identified a single factor in their theories, but that they have attached a 'greater weight' to one set of factors as opposed to others.

Economic Transformation

I will begin my critical review with neo-Marxist scholars who stress economic factors in their theories. The late 1960s and 1970s were very crucial in Marxist thinking about nationalism for a variety of reasons. The orthodox Marxist position was beginning to be challenged with the emergence of anti-colonial nationalist movements in many parts of the Third World. The majority of left-wing intellectuals were sympathetic to these movements and some were even actively involved in them. It was increasingly avowed that the fight against 'neo-imperialism', 'economic imperialism' or 'international capital' was first a national one (Zubaida 1978: 65–6).

Another development that induced many Marxists to 'come to terms' with their creed was the recent 'ethnic revival' in Europe and North America. The proliferation of 'fissiparous' nationalist movements, based on seemingly primordial attachments which were thought to be long-forgotten by liberals and Marxists alike, was now threatening the unity of the established nation-states of the Western world (James 1996: 105–7). Traditional Marxism was ill-prepared to cope with these developments. It was in such a context that attempts to reform the orthodox credo came to the fore. The new generation of Marxists, who were not intent on 'dismantling the old edifice' in James' words, attached a greater weight to the role of culture, ideology and language in their analyses (*ibid.*: 107). The New Left had a much more ambivalent attitude *vis-à-vis* nationalism. Probably the most important statement of such a position was Tom Nairn's *The Break-up of Britain* (1981).

Tom Nairn and 'Uneven Development'

The Scottish Marxist intellectual Tom Nairn taught social science and philosophy at Birmingham University and Hornsey College of Art. He was sacked from the latter in 1968 for participating in the student rebellions of the same year. He returned to academic life in 1993–94, and since then he has been teaching nationalism at Edinburgh University.

Nairn was heavily influenced by Gramsci's writings. He had read Gramsci in 1957–58 when he was studying at the Scuola Normale Superiore of Pisa. In 1963, he published a Gramscian analysis of English class history entitled 'La nemesi borghese' in *Il Contemporaneo* (Forgacs 1989: 75). This analysis was to underlie a series of articles on the British state and the labour movement, published mainly in the *New Left Review* whose editorial board he joined in 1962. Together with similar essays by Perry Anderson, another influential figure of the New Left, these became known as 'Nairn–Anderson theses' and led to a major debate with Edward Thompson in the 1960s. In 1975, he published a book-length polemic against the British Left's opposition to the Common Market. This was the harbinger of a long-term engagement with issues of nationalism, which resulted in *The Break-up of Britain: Crisis and Neo-Nationalism* (1981), originally published in 1977 (Eley and Suny 1996b: 78).

Though he never abandoned Marxism, Nairn is quite sympathetic to the claims of the Scottish National Party (SNP). For him, this reflects 'the dilemma of an insecure national identity' (1981:

397). Gellner, who thinks that Nairn's theory of nationalism is substantially correct but is puzzled as to how Nairn could think his theory was at all compatible with Marxism, interprets this dilemma in a different way. The passage, reflecting Gellner's exceptionally witty style, is worth quoting in full:

> The Christians have passed through at least three stages: the first, when they really believed what they said, when the actual message and its promise of salvation was what attracted them to it, and when the historic continuity with earlier believers was an irrelevancy; the second, when they had to struggle to retain their faith in the face of increasingly pressing grounds for unbelief, and many fell by the wayside; and the third, that of modernist theology, when the 'belief' has acquired negligible (or sliding-scale) content, when the claim to continuity with their purely nominal predecessors becomes the only real psychic reward and significance of adherence, and it is doctrine which is played down as irrelevancy. Marxists seem doomed to pass through the same stages of development. When they reach the third stage (some already have), their views also will be of no intellectual interest. Tom Nairn is still in the second stage . . . His struggles with or for faith are still passionate, troubled and sincere, which is what gives the book some of its interest. (1979: 265–6)

Nairn's stated aim in *The Break-up of Britain* is not to provide a theory of nationalism, but to present 'the scantiest outline' of how this might be done. He begins with the following contention: 'the theory of nationalism represents Marxism's great historical failure' (1981: 329). This failure, which can be observed either in theory or in political practice, was inevitable. Moreover, it was not peculiar to Marxists: nobody could or did provide a theory of nationalism at that period simply because the time was not yet ripe for it. However, Nairn maintains, nationalism can be understood in materialist terms. The primary task of the theorist is to find the right explanatory framework within which nationalism can be properly evaluated.

According to Nairn, the roots of nationalism should not be sought in the internal dynamics of individual societies, but in the general process of historical development since the end of the eighteenth century. Thus, the only explanatory framework which is of any utility is that of 'world history' as a whole. Nationalism, in this sense, is 'determined by certain features of the world political economy, in the era between the French and Industrial Revolutions and the present day' (1981: 332). Here, we can see that Nairn's views on the subject have been greatly influenced by the 'dependency school', especially the work of André Gunder Frank, Samir Amin and Immanuel Wallerstein on the international system of capitalist exploitation (Zubaida 1978: 66).

On the other hand, the origins of nationalism are not located in the process of development of the world political economy as such – in other words, nationalism is not simply an inevitable concomitant of industrialization – but the 'uneven development' of history since the eighteenth century. For many centuries, it was believed that the opposite would indeed be the case, that is that material civilization would develop evenly and progressively. According to this view, characteristic of the Enlightenment thought, Western European states have initiated the capitalist development process and accumulated the necessary capital for perpetuating this process for a long period of time. The idea of 'even development' maintained that 'this advance could be straightforwardly followed, and the institutions responsible for it copied – hence the periphery, the world's countryside, would catch up with the leaders in due time' (Nairn 1981: 337). But history did not unfold as expected by Western Philosophers. Capitalist development was not experienced 'evenly'.

Instead, the impact of the leading countries was experienced as domination and invasion. This was in a way inevitable because the gap between the core and the periphery was too great and 'the new developmental forces were not in the hands of a beneficent, disinterested elite concerned with Humanity's advance' (*ibid.*: 338). The peoples of backward countries learned quickly that '[p]rogress in the abstract meant domination in the concrete, by powers which they could not help apprehending as foreign or alien'. However, popular expectations were not thwarted by the recognition of this fact. Since these expectations were always racing ahead of material progress itself, 'the peripheric elites had no option but to try and satisfy these demands by taking things into their own hands' (*ibid.*: 339). For Nairn, 'taking things into one's own hands' denotes a great deal of the substance of nationalism. The elites had to persuade the masses to take the short cut. They had to contest the concrete form assumed by progress as they were setting out to progress themselves. They wanted factories, schools and parliaments, so they had to copy the leaders somehow; but they had to do this in a way which rejected the direct intervention of these countries. 'This meant the conscious formation of a militant, inter-class community rendered strongly (if mythically) aware of its own separate identity *vis-à-vis* the outside forces of domination' (*ibid.*: 340). There was no other way of doing it. 'Mobilization had to be in terms of what was there; and the whole point of the dilemma was that there was nothing there'. Or more exactly, there was only the people with its speech, folklore, skin colour and so on. Under these circumstances, 'the new middle-class intelligentsia of nationalism had to invite the masses into history; and the invitation-card had to be written in a language they understood' (*ibid.*).

In short, the socio-historical cost of the rapid implantation of capitalism into world society was 'nationalism'. However, that was not the whole story. Of course, it was possible to end the story here and deduce from all this a theory of anti-imperialism whereby nationalism could be seen in a positive moral light, that is as the motor force of peripheric struggles against the imperialist forces of the West. But the story was dialectical. The process did not end with the emergence of nationalism in the peripheral countries under the impact of uneven development; once successful, nationalism reacted upon the core countries and they too fell under its spell. These countries did not invent nationalism; they did not need to since they were in front and 'possessed the things nationalism is really about' (*ibid.*: 344). But once the nation-state had been transformed into a compelling norm, or the 'new climate of world politics', the core countries were bound to become nationalist. In short, ' "uneven development" is not just the hard-luck tale of poor countries' (*ibid.*). The 'founder-members' and the '*parvenus*' were forcing each other to change continuously. In the long term, core area nationalism was as inevitable as peripheric nationalism.

This picture, Nairn contends, shows clearly that it is not meaningful to make a distinction between 'good' and 'bad' nationalisms. All nationalisms contain the seeds of both progress and regress. In fact, this ambiguity is its historical *raison d'être*:

It is through nationalism that societies try to propel themselves forward to certain kinds of goal (industrialization, prosperity, equality with other peoples, etc.) *by a certain sort of regression* – by looking inwards, drawing more deeply upon their indigenous resources, resurrecting past folk heroes and myths about themselves and so on. (*Ibid.*: 348)

It follows that the substance of nationalism is always morally and politically ambiguous. Nationalism can in this sense be pictured as the old Roman god Janus, who stood above gateways with one face looking forward and one backwards. Nationalism is standing over the passage to modernity: 'As human kind is forced through its strait doorway, it must look desperately back into the past, to gather strength wherever it can be found for the ordeal of "development"' (*ibid.*: 349).

Orthodox Marxism's greatest failure was the conviction that class is always more important in history than national differences. But, Nairn claims, the uneven – imperialist – spread of capitalism has insured that the fundamental contradiction was not that of class struggle, but that of nationality (Zubaida 1978: 68). 'As capitalism spread, and smashed the ancient social formations surrounding it, these always tended to fall apart along the fault-lines contained inside them. It is a matter of elementary truth that these lines of fissure were nearly always ones of nationality' (Nairn 1981: 353).

Now the time was ripe for the formulation of a Marxist theory of nationalism. Marxism should get rid of its Enlightenment foundations and become an 'authentic world-theory', that is a theory that focuses on the social development of the whole world. The 'enigma of nationalism' had displayed Marxism's Eurocentric nature. However, it could not see – and overcome – these theoretical limitations until they had been undermined in practice. The events of the 1960s and 1970s were crucial in that respect since they enabled Marxism to come to terms with its own failures. It was finally possible to separate out the durable – the 'scientific' historical materialism – from the ideology, 'the grain from the husks represented by the defeat of Western Philosophy' (*ibid.*: 363).

Such were Nairn's basic arguments, as articulated in *The Break-up of Britain*. Nairn perseveres with the general thrust of this account in his subsequent writings – developing, however, a much more sympathetic attitude towards 'primordialism' (1997, 1998). Let me now turn to the major criticisms raised against Nairn's theory. These can be summarized as follows: Nairn's theory does not fit the facts; it perpetuates the classical Marxist distinction between 'historic' and 'historyless' nations; it is 'essentialist'; it does not provide an adequate account of the origins of nations and nationalism; it is 'reductionist'; finally, it pretends that nationalisms are always successful.

Nairn's Theory Does Not Fit the Facts

Breuilly argues that Nairn's theory, although plausible in the abstract, does not fit the facts. He holds that Nairn inverts the actual sequence of events by placing the origins of nationalism within the less developed countries. For Breuilly, nationalism originates in Europe before the establishment of colonial empires in overseas areas. Hence, anti-colonial nationalisms, which can be seen as a reaction to imperialism, postdate European nationalisms. Moreover, it is not possible to account for the first nationalist movements in terms of economic exploitation or backwardness. Breuilly cites the example of Magyar nationalism in the Habsburg Empire to support this assertion. He notes that the Magyars, who developed the first strong nationalist movement in the Habsburg Empire, were not a backward or exploited group; to the contrary, they had a number of privileges. Breuilly argues that Magyar nationalism was a reaction to the oppressive control exercized by Vienna. There were other nationalist movements as well, especially among the non-Magyar groups exploited by Magyars, but, Breuilly insists, this was a later development (1993a: 412–3). Similarly, Smith argues that locating the origins of nationalism in the periphery constitutes a historical error since the first nationalist sentiments and movements occurred in the 'core' areas of England, France, Holland, Spain and so on. (1983: xvii).

Orridge multiplies the number of examples. He remarks that Catalonia and the Basque country, where there are strong nationalist movements, were and are the most developed regions of Spain. Similarly, Bohemia, 'the heartland of nineteenth century Czech nationalism' in Orridge's words, was the most developed part of the Habsburg Empire. Finally, Belgium was highly industrialized at the time it separated from the Netherlands in the 1830s (Orridge 1981b: 181–2). As Orridge reminds us, Nairn tries to avoid these criticisms by arguing that 'uneven development' can sometimes operate in reverse and produce highly developed peripheries within backward states. However, Orridge notes, there are also 'instances of nationalism not accompanied by any great differences in developmental level from their surroundings' (*ibid.*: 182). Thus, there was no significant difference – as far as their developmental level is concerned – between Norway and Sweden or Finland and Russia, when the smaller countries developed their nationalisms. Similarly, when the Balkan nations won their independence in the course of the nineteenth century, they were not more developed or backward than the core region of the Ottoman Empire. Orridge maintains that it is more difficult to accommodate these cases within Nairn's theory (*ibid.*).

A further difficulty with Nairn's account is that there are instances of 'uneven development' without strong nationalist movements. Orridge asks why there is no counterpart to the nationalisms of Scotland and Wales in Northern England or Southern Italy (*ibid.*). Breuilly goes one step further and argues that it is difficult to correlate the strength and intensity of a nationalist movement with the degree of economic exploitation and backwardness. He notes that nationalisms have often developed fastest in the least exploited or backward areas and that there were no significant nationalist movements in areas where the most naked forms of exploitation took place (1993a: 413).

Nairn Perpetuates the Classical Marxist Distinction between 'Historic' and 'Historyless' Nations

Nairn tends to treat the original formation of the 'historic' nations like France and England as a historical given (James 1996: 111). In other words, he does not question the origins of 'core' nations: he just notes that they owe their nationalisms to a dialectical process whereby peripheric nationalisms react upon them, forcing them to become nationalist. He remains silent as to how these nations have come into being in the first place. This tendency manifests itself clearly in his attitude towards Scotland, his 'homeland'. As Benedict Anderson – another *New Left Review* writer – notes, Nairn treats 'his "Scotland" as an unproblematic, primordial given' (1991: 89). But Scotland presents an anomaly for Nairn's theory because Scottish nationalism develops at a relatively later date (Tiryakian 1995: 221). Nairn explains this by pointing to the fact that Scotland had been incorporated into the British state before the great period of industrialization. Therefore, it did not experience economic exploitation until very recently (Nairn 1974).

Nairn's Theory is 'Essentialist'

Nairn's tendency to treat the existence of 'historic' nations as a given brings us to the third criticism levelled against his theory, namely that of essentialism. Zubaida rightly asks how, without assuming the existence of essential nations, could 'nationality' constitute the 'fault-lines' of fissure contained within the ancient social formations (1978: 69; see the relevant quotation from Nairn above). Nairn seems to confirm this observation when he claims that England was 'a country of ancient and settled nationality' (1981: 262) or that 'nationalism, *unlike nationality or ethnic variety*, cannot be considered a "natural" phenomenon' (*ibid.*: 99, emphasis added). Clearly, then, nationality or ethnic variety are 'natural' phenomena for Nairn.

Drawing on these examples, Zubaida argues that Nairn falls prey to the fundamental assumptions of the nationalist discourse. Nairn considers nations to be 'historical super-subjects' which 'mobilize', 'aspire', 'propel themselves forward' and so on. However, Zubaida notes, 'there must be a way of systematically determining "a nation" for the fault-lines to be considered to be those of nationality' (1978: 69). MacLaughlin joins Zubaida by arguing that Nairn accords a higher degree of historical agency and explanatory power to factors such as ethnicity and nationalist ideology than would appear to be justified by the evidence (1987: 14).

This point leads Orridge to question the relationship between 'uneven development' and pre-existing ethnic identities. He raises the following question: 'Does uneven development alone create the sense of separateness or does it need a strong pre-existing sense of distinctiveness to work on' (1981b: 188)? Orridge claims that Nairn is not very clear about this point and goes on to argue that no modern European nationality has been distinguished from its environment by uneven development alone. According to

Orridge, uneven development should be joined by other distinguishing features such as religion or language for discontent to take the form of nationalism. This can also explain why there are no nationalist movements in Northern England or Southern Italy (*ibid.*: 188–9). This ethno-symbolist (primordialist?) criticism is also expressed by Llobera who argues that the effects of capitalism were felt at a time when national identities were already there (1994: 215). Nairn stands much closer to 'essentialism' in his recent writings. Thus, in a talk given to students at Edinburgh in early 1997, Nairn stressed the need for a new paradigm which will combine sociology and biology to study nationalism. This new paradigm – what he calls a 'life science' – 'depends . . . on establishing a more plausible link between biology and kinship on one hand, and the world of political nation-states and resurgent nationality on the other' (1997: 13). Elsewhere, he asserts that 'the kind of remaking which features in modern nationalism is not creation *ex nihilo*, but a reformulation constrained by determinate parameters of [a particular] past' (1998: 121). Clearly, Nairn has not made much progress as far as 'essentialism' is concerned. It seems that Scottish nationalism has triumphed over Marxism!

Nairn's Theory Does Not Provide an Adequate Account of
the Origins and Spread of Nationalism

According to Orridge, Nairn's theory explains why there should be a developmental difference between core and peripheral areas and why those at the periphery should object to this state of affairs, but it does not explain why this reaction takes the form of nationalism. The peripheral elites may well choose to reform their traditional institutions instead of creating new ones. Nationalism, Orridge argues, is not simply a reaction against subjection and superiority: 'it is an attempt to construct a particular kind of political order and has its own subjective content' (1981b: 183). For him, what underlies this failure is the absence of a theory of the nation-state in Nairn's writings. Obviously, it might not be necessary for a theory of nationalism to explain the emergence of nation-states, but it must surely explain 'why, once in existence, this form of political organization has proved so attractive' (*ibid.*: 184).

In short, uneven development may tell us that the world is divided into smaller units, but it does not explain why these units take the form of nation-states.

Nairn's Theory is 'Reductionist'

A common objection raised against all neo-Marxist and most modernist theories of nationalism concerns their 'reductionism'. At the heart of this objection lies the belief that nationalism is too complex to be explained in terms of a single factor. Thus, Smith argues that Nairn's formula is too simple and crude to encompass the variety and timing of nationalisms. Moreover, 'we cannot simply reduce ethnic "sentiments" to "real" class interests, if only because sentiments are equally "real" and nationalism involves a good deal more than sentiments' (1983: xvii–xviii; see also Orridge 1981b: 190).

Nairn's Nationalisms are Always Successful

This criticism comes from Zubaida. In Nairn's account, the masses are always mobilized by nationalism as it offers them 'something real and important – something that class consciousness could never have furnished' (1981: 22). For Zubaida, this constitutes another aspect of Nairn's participation in the nationalist myths. Zubaida argues that nationalist movements are highly variable in terms of their contents and goals. The nature of the relationship between nationalist leaders and mass support cannot be assumed, but has to be shown in relation to each particular case (1978: 69–70).

Michael Hechter and 'Internal Colonialism'

Michael Hechter's *Internal Colonialism: The Celtic Fringe in British National Development, 1536–1966* (1975) was another influential contribution to the growing literature on nationalism from the neo-Marxist camp. Hechter's book was particularly important in two respects. First, it introduced Lenin's concept of 'internal colonialism' to the study of nationalism. Before that, the concept was used in other contexts, notably by Gramsci to discuss the Italian

Mezzogiorno and, more recently, by Latin American sociologists to describe the Amerindian regions of their societies (Hechter 1975: 9). Second, unlike many of his predecessors – a notable exception is Deutsch (1966) – Hechter made sustained use of quantitative data and multivariate statistical analysis to support his thesis. The book led to a variety of studies on both sides of the Atlantic either challenging it or following in its footsteps (Tiryakian 1985: 6). Hechter later revised his original assumptions in response to the criticisms questioning the factual adequacy of his theory (1985). More recently, he moved to a 'rational choice' analysis of the changing fortunes of ethnoregional political parties, which in turn led him 'to raise microsociological questions about the nature of group solidarity' (Tiryakian 1985: 6; Hechter and Levi 1979). Hechter currently teaches sociology at the University of Arizona.

Hechter's point of departure was the problems of ethnic conflict and assimilation which preoccupied American politics since the 1960s. Broadly speaking, there were two alternative ways of solving these problems in the scholarly literature on intergroup relations: 'assimilationism' and 'nationalism'. Hechter notes that the majority of academics endorsed the assimilationist position at that time. Briefly, assimilationists held that ethnic/racial minorities were poor and frustrated because they were isolated from the national culture. The norms and values of ghetto communities were dysfunctional in the wider society. This implied a solution: if the governments were to invest the necessary resources to educate and socialize the ghetto children, then the problems of maladjustment and the so-called 'culture of poverty' would cease (1975: xiv–xv).

According to Hechter, a particular model of national development underlies the assimilationist perspective. He calls this the 'diffusion model of development'. This model identifies three stages in the process of national development. The first stage is pre-industrial. At this stage, there is no relationship between the core and the periphery: they exist in virtual isolation from one another. Moreover, there are fundamental differences in their economic, cultural and political institutions. Increased contact between the core and peripheral regions leads to the second stage of national development. The second stage was generally associated with the process of industrialization. 'As a rule, the diffusionist view holds that from interaction will come commonality'

(1975: 7). It was believed that the institutions of the developing core will, after some time, 'diffuse' into the periphery. The cultural forms of the periphery, evolved in complete isolation from the rest of the world, will renew, or in Hechter's words 'up-date' themselves as a result of increased contact with the modernizing core. True, massive social dislocation brought about by industrialization and expansion of regional interaction might initially lead to an increased sense of cultural separateness in the periphery, inducing those who suffer from this process of rapid change to cling to their familiar cultural patterns. However, this 'traditional behaviour' is temporary: it will tend to decline as industrialization promotes the general welfare and reduces the initial regional differences. The model posits that the core and peripheral regions will become culturally homogeneous in the long run as the economic, political and cultural bases of ethnic differentiations will disappear. In the third and final stage, regional wealth will become equal; cultural differences will no longer be socially meaningful; and political processes will be conducted within a framework of national parties (*ibid.*: 7–8).

Hechter argues that this is an 'over-optimistic' model of social change. For him, the model which seems to be more realistic is what he calls the 'internal colonial model'. This model holds that an altogether different relationship will ensue from increased core–periphery contact. The core will dominate the periphery politically and exploit it economically. With the exception of a small number of cases, industrialization and increased regional contact will not lead to national development (*ibid.*: 8–9).

The main assumptions of this model can be summarized as follows. The uneven wave of modernization over state territories creates two kinds of groups: 'advanced' and 'less advanced' groups. As a result of this initial fortuitous advantage, resources and power are distributed unequally between the two groups. The more powerful group, or the core, tries to 'stabilize and monopolize its advantages though policies aiming at the institutionalization of the existing stratification system' (*ibid.*: 9). The economy of the core is characterized by a diversified industrial structure, whereas the peripheral economy is dependent and complementary to that of the core:

Peripheral industrialization, if it occurs at all, is highly specialized and geared for export. The peripheral economy is, therefore, relatively sensitive to price fluctuations in the international market. Decisions about investment, credit, and wages tend to be made in the core. As a consequence of economic dependence, wealth in the periphery lags behind the core. (*Ibid.*: 9–10)

On the other hand, the advanced group regulates the allocation of social roles in such a way that the more prestigious roles are reserved for its members. Conversely, the members of the less advanced group are denied access to these roles. Hechter calls this stratification system the 'cultural division of labour'. This system may be enforced *de jure*, when the state actively intervenes to deny certain roles to the members of the disadvantaged collectivity. Alternatively, it may be preserved *de facto*, through discriminatory policies, that is by providing differential access to institutions conferring status in the society, such as educational, religious or military institutions (*ibid.*: 39–40). The cultural division of labour leads individuals to identify themselves with their groups and contributes to the development of distinctive ethnic identification. 'Social actors come to define themselves and others according to the range of roles each may be expected to play. They are aided in this categorization by the presence of visible signs' (*ibid.*: 9). Such visible signs increase group solidarity and unite them around a certain commonality of definitions.

Drawing on Marxism, Hechter identifies two further conditions for the emergence of group solidarity. First, there must be substantial economic inequalities between individuals such that these individuals may come to see this inequality as part of a pattern of collective oppression. But this in itself is not sufficient for the development of collective solidarity since there must also be 'an accompanying social awareness and definition of the situation as being unjust and illegitimate', hence the second condition: there must be adequate communication among members of the oppressed group (*ibid.*: 42). These general observations can be summed up by three propositions:

1.   The greater the economic inequalities between collectivities, the greater the probability that the less advantaged collectivity will be status solidary, and hence, will resist political integration.
2.   The greater the frequency of intra-collectivity communication, the greater the status solidarity of the peripheral collectivity.

3. The greater the intergroup differences of culture, particularly in so far as identifiability is concerned, the greater the probability that the culturally distinct peripheral collectivity will be status solidary (*Ibid.*: 43).

In short, when objective cultural differences are superimposed upon economic inequalities, leading to a cultural division of labour, and when an adequate degree of intra-group communication exists, the chances for successful political integration of the peripheral collectivity into the national society are minimized (*ibid.*). The members of the disadvantaged group may start to assert that their culture is equal or superior to that of the advantaged group, claim the separateness of their nation and seek independence (*ibid.*: 10).

The picture drawn by the model of internal colonialism is in many ways similar to that of the overseas colonial situation. The peripheral/colonial economy is forced into complementary development to that of the core/metropolis and therefore becomes dependent on international markets. The movement of labour in the periphery/colony is determined by the decisions made in the core/metropolis. This economic dependence is reinforced through political and military measures. There is a lower standard of living in the periphery/colony and a stronger sense of deprivation. Discrimination on the basis of language, religion or other cultural forms are routine, daily occurrences (*ibid.*: 31–4).

Hechter maintains that the internal colonial model provides a much more adequate explanation of the process of national development than the diffusion model. It accounts for the persistence of backwardness in the midst of industrial society and the volatility of political integration. Moreover, by linking economic and occupational differences between groups to their cultural differences, it suggests an explanation for the resilience of peripheral cultures (*ibid.*: 34).

The model of internal colonialism developed by Hechter has been subject to a number of criticisms – some of which will be reviewed below (Page 1978; Brand 1985; Kellas 1991). The most important objection to the theory concerned its factual (in)adequacy: certain cases did not seem to fit the model. In particular, Scotland constituted a real anomaly for Hechter's account since the Scots were not relegated to inferior social positions in Britain, and Scotland has been as industrialized as Britain from the eighteenth century onwards (Kellas 1991: 40). In the light of these criticisms, Hechter made an important amendment to his theory (1985). The inspiration for the amendment came from American Jews. As might be recalled, Hechter argued in his original theory that economic inequalities increase group solidarity. On the other hand, the Jews in America also had high solidarity, but 'in no sense could they be regarded as materially disadvantaged' (1985: 21). Hechter explains this anomaly by pointing to the high degree of 'occupational specialization' among the Jews. The clustering of Jews in specific occupational niches contributed to group solidarity by promoting status equality and a commonality of economic interests within group boundaries. Drawing on this observation, Hechter concludes that the cultural division of labour had at least two separate and independent dimensions: 'a hierarchical dimension, in which the various groups were vertically distributed in the occupational structure, and a segmental one, in which the groups were occupationally specialized at any level of the structure' (*ibid.*: 21).

Hechter holds that this second dimension enables us to make sense of the Scottish case. Scotland did not experience internal colonialism to any great degree, but instead had a high level of 'institutional autonomy'. According to The Act of Union signed in 1707 between England and Scotland, the latter had the right to establish its own educational, legal and ecclesiastical institutions. Hechter argues that this institutional autonomy created a potential basis for the development of a 'segmental' cultural division of labour. The Scots were clustered in the specific occupational niches created by Scotland's institutional autonomy. Let alone being discriminated against for their cultural distinctiveness, they often owed their very jobs to the existence of this distinctiveness. Moreover, these jobs were not less prestigious than the ones found in England. The existence of these institutions helped those in the periphery to identify with their culture and provided a strong incentive for the reproduction of this culture through history (*ibid.*: 21–2).

As I have mentioned above, this model has been criticized on many grounds. If we leave the methodological ones aside (Page 1978: 303–15), these criticisms converge on two aspects of Hechter's account: its factual inadequacy and its reductionism.

Hechter's Model of 'Internal Colonialism' Does Not Fit the Facts

The most obvious examples are Catalonia and Scotland. Catalonia has never been an internal colony. On the contrary, it was – and still is – the strongest regional economy in Spain. Brand notes that Catalonia was the only industrial economy in Spain when nationalism acquired mass support, 'second only to Britain in its productive capacity and technical superiority in the textile industry' (1985: 277). Scotland, on the other hand, was a case of 'overdevelopment': 'The Scots had long been innovators in the British context – in education, finance, technology, and the physical and social sciences' (Hechter 1985: 20). We have already discussed Hechter's attempt to amend his theory by adding a second dimension to the cultural division of labour, namely 'segmental' dimension, whereby the members of the disadvantaged groups cluster in specific occupational niches. In the Scottish case, this segmental division of labour operates through the mechanism of 'institutional autonomy': the Scots, finding jobs in specifically Scottish institutions, developed a higher degree of group solidarity than would be predicted by the original theory.

However, this amendment does not save Hechter's theory. Brand argues that the initial version was tied into a wider Marxist model of society. But the new version bears no relation to the original theory put forward by Lenin. Hence, Brand concludes, 'it makes no sense to call this "internal colonialism"' (1985: 279). More importantly, the conditions of segmentation, adduced specifically to cope with exceptional cases such as Scotland or Catalonia, did not exist in these countries.

First, the proportion of Scots working in the institutions created by the Settlement of 1707 was very small. Secondly, 'even if we allow that their centrality outweighs their small size, there is very little evidence that they were important in the early regionalist and nationalist organizations' (Brand 1985: 281). Brand notes that these specifically Scottish institutions have not been sympathetic to nationalism. For instance, The Church of Scotland only started to support Home Rule after the Second World War and by this time, it was a rapidly waning force in Scottish society. Finally, a considerable number of Scots were employed in the colonial and administrative services of the British empire (Smith 1983: xvi). The case of Catalonia was not more promising. As mentioned above, Catalonia was a highly industrialized region. However, 'the industrial workers of Catalonia, especially those of Barcelona, were the most difficult to recruit for the Catalan cause' (Brand 1985: 282). On the other hand, Brand notes that the occupational breakdown of the population in Scotland does not have the feature which Hechter identified among American Jews. A large proportion of Scots were engaged in agriculture. For occupational clustering to produce greater group solidarity, there must be sufficient communication among the members of the group in question. However, of all occupations, agricultural workers are the most difficult to organize. Brand holds that much of this has to do with sheer geography since two hundred men in the factory can be contacted in half an hour, whereas this may take three weeks in the countryside (1985: 280). But the heart of the matter lies elsewhere. It may be conceded that individuals concentrated in particular occupations will meet regularly and share opinions. From this interaction, a point of view will probably emerge. However, 'this does not answer the question as to why a nationalist point of view specifically should grow up' (Brand 1985: 282).

Hechter's Model is Reductionist

Despite the amendment to the earlier model, Hechter's theory continues to explain cultural cleavages and ethnic sentiments by purely economic and spatial characteristics. Such an account reduces nationalism to discontent caused by regional economic inequalities and exploitation. We have only to consider the cases of ethnic revival among the scattered Armenians, Jews, Blacks and Gypsies to realize the shallowness of this view. According to Smith, economic exploitation can only exacerbate a pre-existing sense of ethnic grievance (1983: xvi; cf. Orridge 1981b: 188–9).

Moreover, Smith contends, explaining nationalism by a single factor, that is 'internal colonialism', inevitably limits the utility of the model. As such the model cannot explain why there has been cases of national revival in areas where the impact of capitalism, let alone industrialization, has been minimal (Eritreans); why there has been a long time-interval between the onset of industrialization and nationalist revival within the Western states; and why there has been no ethnic revival or a strong nationalist movement in economically backward areas like Northern England or Southern Italy (1983: xvi).

Political Transformation

Another variant of modernism has been propounded by scholars who focus on the transformations in the nature of politics, for example the rise of the modern bureaucratic state, or the extension of suffrage, to explain nationalism. Here, I will discuss the contributions of three scholars who espoused this standpoint, namely John Breuilly, Paul R. Brass and Eric J. Hobsbawm. As criticisms levelled against these theories tend to converge on a number of assumptions shared by all three scholars, I will review them at the end of the section.

John Breuilly and Nationalism as a Form of Politics

John Breuilly's *Nationalism and the State* has become established as one of the key general works on nationalism since its initial publication in 1982. Breuilly's massive historical survey differs from the historical studies of earlier periods, which were mainly chronological narratives of particular nationalisms, by its insistence in combining historical perspectives with theoretical analysis. Through the comparative analysis of a wide variety of examples, Breuilly introduces a new conception of nationalism, that is nationalism as a form of politics, and constructs an original typology of nationalist movements. The breadth of his book (he reviews more than 30 individual cases of nationalism from different continents and historical periods) is even appreciated by critical reviewers, who concede that the book is a 'valuable and useful' source of information (Symmons-Symonolewicz 1985b: 359). Breuilly currently teaches history at the University of Birmingham.

It should be stressed at the outset that Breuilly's historical analysis does not amount to a 'theory of nationalism'. His aim, declared in the introduction, is to outline and apply a general procedure for the study of nationalism (1993a: 1). He states clearly that he is sceptical of 'grand' theories or studies which develop a general argument, using examples only in an illustrative fashion. He believes that such examples are unrepresentative and removed from their historical context. For him, a general framework of analysis is only acceptable if it permits an effective analysis of particular cases. Breuilly argues that this requires two procedures. First, it is necessary to develop a typology of nationalism since nationalisms are too varied to be explained by a single method of investigation. Thus, any study should begin by identifying various types of nationalism which can be considered separately. Second, each type should be investigated by the method of comparative history (*ibid.*: 2). In the light of these observations, Breuilly first develops a typology of nationalism, then selects a few cases from each category and analyses them at length, using the same methods and concepts. This procedure, he argues, enables him to compare and contrast these various types systematically.

Breuilly uses nationalism to refer to 'political movements seeking or exercising state power and justifying such action with nationalist arguments'. A nationalist argument in turn is a political doctrine built upon three basic assertions:

1. There exists a nation with an explicit and peculiar character.
2. The interests and values of this nation take priority over all other interests and values.
3. The nation must be as independent as possible. This usually requires at least the attainment of political sovereignty. (*Ibid.*: 2).

Breuilly notes that nationalism has been variously explained in the literature by reference to ideas, class interest, economic modernization, psychological needs or culture. But for him, although particular nationalisms can be illuminated with respect to this or that class, idea or cultural achievement, none of these factors can help us understand nationalism generally. He contends that all these approaches overlook a crucial point, namely that nationalism is above all about politics and politics is about power. 'Power, in the modern world, is principally about control of the state'. Our central task therefore is 'to relate nationalism to the objectives of obtaining and using state power. We need to understand why nationalism has played a major role in the pursuit of those objectives' (*ibid.*: 1). In other words, we need to find out what it is about modern politics that makes nationalism so important. Only then might we go on to consider the contributions of other factors such as class, economic interests or culture. It follows that the first step in formulating an analytical framework to study nationalism is to consider it as a form of politics. Breuilly argues that such an approach will also enable us to assess the importance of the subject, since it is possible to ask how much support nationalist movements are able to tap within their society, whereas it is very difficult to estimate the significance of ideas or sentiments (1996: 163). The next step consists of relating nationalism to the process of modernization. Breuilly conceives of modernization as involving a fundamental change in the 'generic division of labour'. The most important stage of this change is the transition from a 'corporate' to a 'functional' division of labour. The former exists in a society where a collection of functions are performed by particular institutions, usually on behalf of some distinct group. Breuilly refers to guilds as an example of such institutions. An ideal-typical guild will perform economic functions (regulating production and distribution of goods and services); cultural functions (education of apprentices, organizing recreational or ceremonial activities for the members of the guild); and political functions (running courts which impose sanctions upon unruly behaviour, sending members to town governments). In such an order, churches, lordships, peasant communes and even the monarchs are multifunctional. Breuilly argues that this order was increasingly criticized from the eighteenth century onwards and was crumbling in many parts of Western and Central Europe. The new order was based on a different division of labour, with each major social function carried out by a particular institution. Economic functions were handed over to individuals or firms competing in a free market; churches became free associations of believers; and political power was delegated to specialized bureaucracies controlled by elected parliaments or enlightened despots (*ibid.*: 163–4).

Historically, this transformation was not smooth. It developed at different paces and in different ways. The linking of this transformation to nationalist politics constitutes the third step of Breuilly's general framework. He argues that this requires focusing on one aspect of the transformation, namely the development of the modern state (*ibid.*: 164).

According to Breuilly, the modern state originally developed in a liberal form. Thus, 'public' powers were handed over to specialized state institutions (parliaments, bureaucracies) and many 'private' powers were left under the control of non-political institutions (free markets, private firms, families and so on). This involved a double transformation: 'institutions such as the monarchy lost "private" powers . . . other institutions such as churches, guilds, and lordships lost their "public" powers to government' (1993b: 22). In this way, Breuilly continues, the distinction between the state as 'public' and civil society as 'private' became clearer.

On the other hand, with the breakdown of corporate division of labour, there was now a new emphasis upon people as individuals rather than as members of particular groups. Under such circumstances, the main problem was how to establish the state–society connection, or to put it differently, how to reconcile the public interests of citizens and the private interests of selfish individuals. It was precisely at this juncture that nationalist ideas came on the scene. Breuilly holds that the answers provided to this critical question took two major forms and nationalism played a crucial role in both (1996: 165; 1993b: 23).

The first answer was 'political' and rested on the idea of citizenship. In this case, Breuilly observes, the society of individuals was simultaneously defined as a polity of citizens. According to this view, commitment to the state could only be generated by participating in democratic and liberal institutions. The 'nation' was simply the body of citizens and only the political rights of the citizens – not their cultural identities – mattered. Breuilly claims that such a conception of nationality underlayed the programmes of eighteenth century patriots. In its most extreme form, it equated freedom with the implementation of the 'general will' (1996: 165).

The second answer, on the other hand, was 'cultural': it consisted of stressing the collective character of society. This was initially formulated by political elites confronted both by an intellectual problem (how did one legitimize state action?) and by a political problem (how could one secure the support of the masses?). Subsequently, this solution was standardized and became the major way of providing an identity to members of different social groups (*ibid.*).

Breuilly maintains that liberalism's inability to cope with collective or community interests was very crucial in this context. More-over, many groups were not attracted to liberalism, 'the first major political doctrine of modernity' in Breuilly's words, since the system it gave birth to was largely based on socially structured inequality. According to Breuilly, such groups were easy prey for nationalist ideologues. But the picture was not that simple. What complicated matters further was the 'modern' need to develop political languages and movements which could appeal to a wide range of groups. This could best be done by nationalism which has been a 'sleight-of-hand ideology' connecting the two solutions, that is the nation as a body of citizens and as a cultural collectivity, together (*ibid.*: 166; 1993b: 23–4).

Breuilly argues that the general picture sketched so far does not enable us to analyse particular nationalist movements, mainly because, being politically neutral, nationalism has assumed a bewildering variety of forms. To investigate all these different forms, a typology and auxiliary concepts which draw our attention to the different functions performed by nationalist politics are required (1996: 166). Breuilly concentrates on two aspects of nationalist movements when developing his typology. The first of these concerns the relationship between the movement and the state to which it either opposes or controls. In a world where the basic source of political legitimacy was not yet the nation, such movements were necessarily oppositional:

> it was only at a later stage that governments, either formed by the success of nationalist oppositions or taking on board the ideas of those oppositions, would themselves make nationalist arguments the basis of their claims to legitimacy. (*Ibid.*)

The second aspect concerned the goals of nationalist movements: hence, a nationalist opposition can strive to break away from the present state (separation), to reform it in a nationalist direction (reform) or to unite it with other states (unification) (1993a: 9). In addition to these two aspects, Breuilly notes, the state which is opposed may or may not define itself as a nation-state. The typology should mirror this distinction as well since this will have certain implications for the nature of the conflict between the state and the relevant nationalist movement. Having made these specifications, Breuilly introduces his typology (*ibid.*):

	Opposed to non-nation states	Opposed to nation-states
Separation	Magyar, Greek, Nigerian	Basque, Ibo
Reform	Turkish, Japanese	Fascism, Nazism
Unification	German, Italian	Arab, Pan-African

Finally, Breuilly identifies three different functions performed by nationalist ideas: 'coordination', 'mobilization' and 'legitimacy'. By coordination he means that 'nationalist ideas are used to promote the idea of common interests amongst a number of elites which otherwise have rather distinct interests in opposing the existing state'. By mobilization he means 'the use of nationalist ideas to generate support for the political movement from broad groups hitherto excluded from the political process'. And by legitimacy he means 'the use of nationalist ideas to justify the goals of the political movement both to the state it opposes and also to powerful external agents, such as foreign states and their public opinions' (1996: 166–7).

Having outlined this framework, Breuilly examines the development of nationalism in a number of cases. As I have alluded to above, he covers a wide range of nationalist movements from Europe to the Arab world, from Africa to the Indian sub-continent and a large time span, that is from the eighteenth century to 1989. Since a review of his findings will be beyond the scope of this book, I will now turn to Brass' analysis of nation-formation.

Paul R. Brass and Instrumentalism

Professor of Political Science and South Asian Studies at the University of Washington-Seattle, Paul R. Brass is best known in the literature on nationalism for his studies stressing the 'instrumental' nature of ethnicity. Broadly speaking, instrumentalists hold that ethnic and national identities are convenient tools at the hands of competing elite groups for generating mass support in the universal struggle for wealth, power and prestige (Smith 1986: 9). In stark contrast to primordialists who treat ethnicity as a 'given' of the human condition, they argue that ethnic and national attachments are continually redefined and reconstructed in response to changing conditions and the manipulations of political elites. It follows that

> the study of ethnicity and nationality is in large part the study of politically induced cultural change. More precisely, it is the study of the process by which elites and counter-elites within ethnic groups select aspects of the group's culture, attach new value and meaning to them, and use them as symbols to mobilize the group, to defend its interests, and to compete with other groups. (Brass 1979: 40–1)

These views led Brass to a fierce debate with Francis Robinson about the role of political elites in the process culminating in the formation of two separate nation-states in the Indian sub-continent, India and Pakistan. Leaving this highly polemical exchange to the section on criticisms, I will now turn to Brass' account of nationalism, which can be considered as the 'quintessential' illustration of the instrumentalist position.

Brass' theoretical framework is built upon a few basic assumptions. The first concerns the variability of ethnic identities. Brass holds that there is nothing inevitable about the rise of ethnic identities and their transformation into nationalism. To the contrary, the politicization of cultural identities is only possible under specific conditions which need to be identified and analysed carefully. Secondly, ethnic conflicts do not arise from cultural differences, but from the broader political and economic environment which also shapes the nature of the competition between elite groups. Thirdly, this competition will also influence the definition of the relevant ethnic groups and their persistence. This is because the cultural forms, values and practices of ethnic groups become political resources for elites in their struggle for power and prestige. They are transformed into symbols which can facilitate the creation of a political identity and the generation of greater support; thus, their meanings and contents are dependent on political circumstances. Finally, all these assumptions show that the process of ethnic identity formation and its transformation into nationalism is reversible. Depending on political and economic circumstances, elites may choose to downplay ethnic differences and seek cooperation with other groups or state authorities (Brass 1991: 13–16).

Having laid down his basic assumptions, Brass sets out to develop a general framework of analysis that focuses on processes of identity-formation and identity-change. He begins by defining what he calls an 'ethnic category'. In the words of Brass,

any group of people dissimilar from other peoples in terms of objective cultural criteria and containing within its membership, either in principle or in practice, the elements for a complete division of labour and for reproduction forms an ethnic category. (*Ibid.*: 19)

However, Brass is quick to stress that these 'objective cultural criteria' are not fixed: on the contrary, they are susceptible to change and variation. Moreover, he adds, in pre-modern societies where the process of ethnic transformation (into nationalism) has not yet begun or in postindustrial societies where a great deal of cultural assimilation has taken place, the boundaries separating various ethnic categories are not so clear.

The boundaries in question become clearer and sharper in the process of ethnic transformation. In this process, which should be distinguished from the mere persistence of ethnic differences in a population,

cultural markers are selected and used as a basis for differentiating the group from other groups, as a focus for enhancing the internal solidarity of the group, as a claim for a particular social status, and, if the ethnic group becomes politicized, as justification for a demand for either group rights in an existing political system or for recognition as a separate nation. (1991: 63)

Brass notes that the existence of objective cultural markers – here, read ethnic differences – in a given population is a necessary, but not a sufficient condition for the process of ethnic transformation to begin.

Another necessary, but still not sufficient condition, is the presence of elite competition for the leadership of an ethnic group or for control over various tangible and/or intangible resources. According to Brass, competition for local control may take four different forms: those between local land controllers and alien authorities, between competing religious elites, between local religious elites and collaborationist native aristocracies, and between native religious elites and alien aristocracies. Another general type of competition arises from the uneven processes of modernization and takes the form of competition for jobs in the government, industry and universities (*ibid.*).

However, as stressed above, neither the existence of ethnic differences nor elite competition are sufficient conditions for the inception of the process of ethnic transformation. The sufficient conditions, Brass argues, are

> the existence of the means to communicate the selected symbols of identity to other social classes within the ethnic group, the existence of a socially mobilized population to whom the symbols may be communicated, and the absence of intense class cleavage or other difficulties in communication between elites and other social groups and classes. (*Ibid.*)

Brass cites growth in literacy rates, the development of media of mass communication, particularly newspapers, the standardization of local languages, the existence of books in local languages and the availability of schools where the medium of instruction is the native language among the factors necessary to promote such interclass communication. Referring to Deutsch, he contends that the growth of communication facilities should be complemented by the emergence of new groups in the society who are 'available' for more intense communication and who demand education and new jobs in the modern sectors of the economy. In short, demand is as important as supply.

Brass notes in passing that a high degree of communal mobilization will be achieved most easily in two types of situations: (a) where there is a local religious elite controlling the temples, shrines or churches and the lands attached to them as well as a network of religious schools; and (b) where the local language has been recognized by the state authorities as a legitimate medium of education and administration, thereby providing the native intelligentsia the means to satisfy the new social groups aspiring to education and job opportunities (*ibid.*: 63–4).

According to Brass, the necessary and sufficient conditions for ethnic transformation are also the preconditions for the development of a successful nationalist movement. He claims that nationalism as an elite phenomenon may arise at any time, even in the early stages of ethnic transformation. However, for it to acquire a mass base, it should go beyond mere elite competition:

> The mass base for nationalism may be created when widespread intraclass competition occurs brought about by the movement of large numbers of people from either a previously overwhelmingly rural group or from a disadvantaged group into economic sectors occupied predominantly by other ethnic groups. If such a movement is resisted by the dominant group, supported openly or tacitly by state authorities, then the aspirant group will be easily mobilized by nationalist appeals that challenge the existing economic structure and the cultural values associated with it. (*Ibid.*: 65)

On the other hand, if the dominant group perceives the aspirations of the disadvantaged group as a threat to its status, then it may develop a nationalist movement of its own. Brass argues that uneven distribution of ethnic groups in urban and rural areas may exacerbate the situation since this will lead to a fierce competition over scarce resources and/or for control of the state structure.

While the mass base of nationalism is provided by ethnic competition for economic opportunities, or what Brass calls 'sectorally-based competition for control over state power', the demands that are articulated and the success of a nationalist movement depend on political factors. Brass cites three such factors: the existence of and the strategies pursued by nationalist political organizations, the nature of government response to ethnic group demands, and the general political context (*ibid.*).

Political Organization

According to Brass, nationalism is by definition a political movement. Thus, it requires healthy organization, skilled leadership and resources to compete effectively in the system. Brass puts forward five propositions with regard to political organizations. First, organizations that control community resources are likely to be more effective than those that do not. Secondly, organizations that succeed in identifying themselves with the community as a whole are likely to be more effective than those that 'merely' represent the community or those pursuing their own interests. Thirdly, effective nationalist organizations must be able to shape the identity of the groups they lead. Fourthly, they must be able to provide continuity and to withstand changes in leadership. Finally, for a nationalist movement to be successful, one political organization must be dominant in representing the interests of the ethnic group against its rivals (*ibid.*: 48–9).

Government Policies

Brass maintains that institutional mechanisms in a given polity and the responses of governments to ethnic demands may be very crucial in determining a particular group's capacity to survive, its self-definition and its ultimate goals. The strategies adopted by governments to prevent the 'rekindling of ethnic fires' display a great diversity. They range from the most extreme forms of repression (genocide, deportation) to policies designed to undermine the mass base of ethnic groups (assimilation through schooling, integration of ethnic group leaders into the system). Alternatively, governments may attempt to satisfy ethnic demands by following explicitly pluralist policies. These may include the establishment of political structures such as federalism or some special concessions such as the right to receive education in the native language (*ibid.*: 50).

Political Context

The third factor that may influence the success of nationalist movements is the general political context. According to Brass, three aspects of the political context are particularly important: 'the possibilities for realignment of political and social forces and organizations, the willingness of elites from dominant ethnic groups to share power with aspirant ethnic group leaders, and the potential availability of alternative political arenas' (1991: 55).

Brass notes that the need for political realignment may not arise in early modernizing societies where the first groups to organize politically are ethnic groups, or where the leading organizations articulate local nationalisms. Such a need arises when existing political organizations are not able to cope with social changes that erode their support bases or in times of revolutionary upheaval.

Brass argues that a general political realignment will lead to the establishment of new nationalist organizations and present them with new opportunities to secure mass support.

On the other hand, the willingness of elites from dominant ethnic groups to share political power determines the way ethnic conflicts are resolved: '[w]here that willingness does not exist, the society in question is headed for conflict, even civil war and secessionism. However, where such willingness does exist, the prospects for pluralist solutions to ethnic group conflicts are good' (*ibid.*: 57–8).

The third crucial aspect of the general political context is the availability of alternative political arenas and the price to be paid by ethnic groups for shifting to such arenas. Brass contends that unitary states containing geographically concentrated minorities will definitely face at some point demands for administrative and/or political decentralization, if the political needs of these minorities are not adequately satisfied by the state authorities. Under such circumstances, governments may opt for the reorganization of old political arenas or the construction of new ones to satisfy ethnic demands. According to Brass, the use of these strategies work best under the following conditions:

- where there is a relatively open system of political bargaining and competition;
- where there is a rational distribution of power between the federal and local units so that the capture of power at one level by one ethnic group does not close all significant avenues to power;
- where there is more than two or three ethnic groups;
- where ethnic conflicts do not overlap with ideological disagreements between unitarists and federalists; and
- where external powers are not willing to intervene (*ibid.*: 60–1).

Brass claims that where any of these conditions are lacking, pluralist (or federalist) solutions may fail and civil war or secession may ensue. However, Brass adds, secessionism is a high-cost strategy which most political elites will not adopt unless all other alternatives are exhausted and there is a reasonable prospect of external intervention in their favour (*ibid.*: 61). As a result of this, secession has been the least adopted strategy of ethnic conflict resolution in the period following the Second World War (see also Mayall 1990).

It is hard to do justice to this sophisticated theory in a few pages. Suffice it to say that for Brass, or in that respect for any 'instrumentalist', elite competition and manipulation provide the key to an understanding of nationalism.

Eric J. Hobsbawm and the 'Invention of Tradition'

The distinguished Marxist historian Eric J. Hobsbawm is another scholar who stressed the role of political transformations in his analysis of nationalism. Born in the year of the Bolshevik Revolution, Hobsbawm grew up in Vienna as the threat of Nazism moved across central Europe. Living through state-fascism's destruction, he has become 'the most outspoken critic of the "new nationalisms" of Europe, arguing that the Mazzinian age in which nationalism was integrative and emancipatory has long passed' (Anderson 1996: 13). It should also be noted that Hobsbawm's theory of nationalism is part of his broader project of writing the history of modernity: hence his account of nationalism as an outgrowth of the industrial revolution and the political upheavals of the last two centuries. Hobsbawm assembled his theses in *The Invention of Tradition* (1983) which he co-edited with Terence Ranger and, more recently, in *Nations and Nationalism since 1780: Programme, Myth, Reality* (1990) which consists of the Wiles Lectures he delivered at the Queen's University of Belfast in 1985.

According to Hobsbawm, both nations and nationalism are products of 'social engineering'. What deserves particular attention in this process is the case of 'invented traditions' by which he means

a set of practices, normally governed by overtly or tacitly accepted rules and of a ritual or symbolic nature, which seek to inculcate certain values and norms of behaviour by repetition, which automatically implies continuity with the past. (1983: 1)

Hobsbawm argues that 'the nation' and its associated phenomena are the most pervasive of such invented traditions. Despite their historical novelty, they establish continuity with a suitable past and 'use history as a legitimator of action and cement of group cohesion' (*ibid.*: 12). For him, this continuity is largely factitious. Invented traditions are 'responses to novel situations which take the form of reference to old situations' (*ibid.*: 2). Hobsbawm cites the deliberate choice of the Gothic style for the rebuilt British parliament in the nineteenth century to illustrate this point.

Hobsbawm distinguishes between two processes of invention, namely the adaptation of old traditions and institutions to new situations, and the deliberate invention of 'new' traditions for quite novel purposes. The former can be found in all societies, including the so-called 'traditional' ones as was the case with the Catholic Church faced with new ideological and political challenges or professional armies faced with conscription. The latter, however, occurs only in periods of rapid social change when the need to create order and unity becomes paramount. This explains the importance of the idea of 'national community' which can secure cohesion in the face of fragmentation and disintegration caused by rapid industrialization (Hobsbawm and Ranger 1983: chapter 7; Smith 1991b: 355).

According to Hobsbawm, the period from 1870 to 1914 can be considered as the apogee of invented traditions. This period coincides with the emergence of mass politics. The incursion of hitherto excluded sections of the society into politics created unprecedented problems for the rulers who found it increasingly difficult to maintain the obedience, loyalty and cooperation of their subjects – now defined as citizens whose political activities were recognized as something to be taken into account, if only in the form of elections (Hobsbawm and Ranger 1983: 264–5). The 'invention of tradition' was the main strategy adopted by the ruling elites to counter the threat posed by mass democracy. Hobsbawm singles out three major innovations of the period as particularly relevant: the development of primary education; the invention of public ceremonies (like the Bastille Day); and the mass production of public monuments (*ibid.*: 270–1). As a result of these processes, 'nationalism became a substitute for social cohesion through a national church, a royal family or other cohesive traditions, or collective group self-presentations, a new secular religion' (*ibid.*: 303). And since

so much of what subjectively makes up the modern 'nation' consists of such constructs and is associated with appropriate and,
in general, fairly recent symbols or suitably tailored discourse
(such as 'national' history), the national phenomenon cannot
be adequately investigated without careful attention to the
'invention of tradition'. (*Ibid.*: 14)

In the light of these observations, Hobsbawm concurs with
Gellner's definition of nationalism in his later work; that is, 'a principle which holds that the political and national unit should be
congruent' (1990: 9; Gellner 1983: 1). For him, this principle also
implies that the political duties of citizens to the nation override
all other obligations. This is what distinguishes modern nationalism from earlier forms of group identification which are less
demanding. Such a conception of nationalism overrules 'primordialist' understandings of the nation which treat it as a 'given' and
unchanging category. Hobsbawm argues that nations belong to a
particular, historically recent, period. It does not make sense to
speak of nations before the rise of the modern territorial state;
these two are closely related to each other (1990: 9–10). Here,
Hobsbawm once again refers to Gellner:

Nations as a natural, God-given way of classifying men, as an
inherent though long-delayed political destiny, are a myth;
nationalism, which sometimes takes pre-existing cultures and
turns them into nations, sometimes invents them, and often
obliterates pre-existing cultures: *that* is a reality, and in general
an inescapable one. (Gellner 1983: 48–9)

In short, 'nations do not make states and nationalisms but the
other way round' (Hobsbawm 1990: 10).

On the other hand, Hobsbawm holds that the origins of nationalism should be sought at the point of intersection of politics,
technology and social transformation. Nations are not only the
products of the quest for a territorial state: they can come into
being in the context of a particular stage of technological and economic development. For instance, national languages cannot
emerge as such before the invention of printing and the spread of
literacy to large sections of the society, hence mass schooling

(*ibid.*). According to Hobsbawm, this shows that nations and nationalism are dual phenomena,

> constructed essentially from above, but which cannot be understood unless also analysed from below, that is in terms of the assumptions, hopes, needs, longings and interests of ordinary people, which are not necessarily national and still less nationalist. (*Ibid.*)

Hobsbawm finds Gellner's account wanting in that respect since it does not pay adequate attention to the view from below. Obviously, the views and needs of ordinary people are not easy to discover. But, Hobsbawm continues, it is possible to reach preliminary conclusions from the writings of social historians. He suggests three such conclusions. First, official ideologies of states and movements are not reliable guides as to what ordinary people – even the most loyal citizens – think. Second, we cannot assume that for most people national identification is always or ever superior to other forms of identification which constitute the social being. And thirdly, national identification and what it means to each individual can shift in time, even in the course of short periods (*ibid.*: 10–11).

Broadly speaking, Hobsbawm identifies three stages in the historical evolution of nationalism. The first stage covers the period from the French Revolution to 1918 when nationalism was born and gained rapid ground. Hobsbawm makes a distinction between two kinds of nationalism in this stage: the first, which transformed the map of Europe between 1830 and 1870, was the democratic nationalism of the 'great nations' stemming from the ideals of the French Revolution; and the second, which came to the fore from 1870 onwards, was the reactionary nationalisms of the 'small nations', mostly against the policies of the Ottoman, Habsburg and Tsarist empires (1990: chapter 1; Smith 1995: 11).

Hobsbawm's second stage covers the period from 1918 to 1950. For him, this period was the 'apogee of nationalism', not because of the rise of fascism, but the upsurge of national sentiment on the left – as exemplified in the course of the Spanish Civil War. Hobsbawm claims that nationalism acquired a strong association with the left during the anti-fascist period, 'an association which was subsequently reinforced by the experience of anti-imperial strug-

gle in colonial countries' (1990: 148). For him, militant nationalism was nothing more than the manifestation of despair, the utopia
of 'those who had lost the old utopias of the age of Enlightenment'
(*ibid.*: 144).

The late twentieth century constitutes Hobsbawm's last stage. He
argues that the nationalisms of this period were functionally different from those of the earlier periods. Nationalisms of the nineteenth and early twentieth centuries were 'unificatory as well as
emancipatory' and they were a 'central fact of historical transformation'. However, nationalism in the late twentieth century was no
longer 'a major vector of historical development' (*ibid.*: 163). They
are

> essentially negative, or rather divisive . . . In one sense they may
> be regarded as the successors to, sometimes the heirs of, the
> small-nationality movements directed against the Habsburg,
> Tsarist and Ottoman empires . . . Time and again they seem to
> be reactions of weakness and fear, attempts to erect barricades
> to keep at bay the forces of the modern world. (*ibid.*: 164)

Hobsbawm cites Québec, Welsh and Estonian nationalisms to illustrate this claim and argues that 'in spite of its evident prominence,
nationalism is historically less important'. After all, the fact that historians are now making rapid progress in analysing nationalism
means that the phenomenon is past its peak. He concludes: 'The
owl of Minerva which brings wisdom, said Hegel, flies out at dusk.
It is a good sign that it is now circling round nations and nationalism' (*ibid.*: 181, 183).

*   *   *

So far, I have tried to summarize the theories/approaches of three
scholars who focus on the role of political transformations to
explain nationalism. A brief recapitulation of their main arguments will be helpful here in terms of setting the scene for criticisms. Breuilly treats nationalism primarily as a form of politics and
tries to make sense of it in the context of the development of the
modern state. Pouring scorn on 'general theories', he develops a
typology of nationalism and explores each type by the method of
comparative history. Brass, on the other hand, provides an 'instrumentalist' account of nationalism which stresses the role of elite
competition in the genesis of ethnic and national identities. He

holds that the cultural forms, values and practices of ethnic groups become political resources for elites who are engaged in an endless struggle for power and/or economic advantage. Hence, the study of ethnicity and nationality should be the study of 'politically-induced cultural change'. Finally, Hobsbawm regards the nation and its associated phenomena as products of 'social engineering', more specifically as traditions invented by ruling elites who felt threatened by the incursion of the masses into politics. Their aim was to secure the obedience and loyalty of their subjects, now redefined as citizens, in an age when other forms of legitimacy like religion or dynasty were rapidly losing ground. By establishing continuity with a suitable historical past, they smoothed the transition to a new kind of society.

For the sake of a more systematic presentation, I will divide the criticisms raised against political explanations into two categories. The first category will be devoted to 'general' criticisms which concentrate on the assumptions common to all three accounts. I will identify four such criticisms: theories of 'political transformation' are misleading so far as the date of first nations is concerned; they fail to account for the persistence of pre-modern ethnic ties; they cannot explain why so many people are prepared to die for their nations; and finally, they put too much emphasis on one set of factors at the expense of others. The second category on the other hand, will be reserved for more 'specific' criticisms, that is criticisms levelled against particular aspects of each theory. Three such criticisms will be singled out: state-building should not be equated with nation-building; instrumentalists exaggerate the part played by elites in shaping national identities; and Hobsbawm fails in his predictions about the future of nationalism. Let me now discuss each of these criticisms in more detail.

General Criticisms

Theories of 'Political Transformation' are Misleading so far as the Date of First Nations is Concerned

Mostly articulated by ethno-symbolists, this 'counter-argument' suggests that the first examples of nationalism can be found much earlier than the eighteenth century. For example Smith, while conceding that nationalism as an ideology and a movement is a fairly

recent phenomenon, argues that the origins of national sentiments can be traced back to the fifteenth and sixteenth centuries
in many states of Western Europe. According to Smith, the small
clerical and bureaucratic classes of France, England, Spain and
Sweden began to feel a strong attachment to their nation – which
they conceived as a territorial-cultural community – from the fifteenth century onwards. And a wider 'middle-class' nationalism
was already in place by the sixteenth century, especially in England
and the Netherlands (1995: 38). Similarly, Greenfeld locates the
emergence of national sentiment in England in the first third of
the sixteenth century (1992: 42). Hastings goes one step further
and contends that 'English nationalism of a sort was present
already in the fourteenth century in the long wars with France'
(1997: 5). However, he admits that the most intense phase of that
nationalism should be located in the late sixteenth century.

Such Theories Fail to Account for the Persistence of Pre-modern Ethnic Ties

Ethno-symbolists also argue that political modernists cannot
explain the continuing relevance of pre-modern ethnic attachments. Holding that traditional structures have been eroded by the
revolutions of modernity, the modernists fail to notice that the
impact of these revolutions has been more marked in certain areas
than others and has penetrated some strata of the population more
profoundly than others. Smith argues that religion and ethnicity
in particular have resisted assimilation to the 'dominant and
secular ethos of modernity' (1995: 40–1). For him, theories which
do not take the durability of ethnic ties into consideration cannot
answer the following questions: 'Can such manipulations hope to
succeed beyond the immediate moment? Why should one
invented version of the past be more persuasive than others? Why
appeal to the past at all, once the chain of tradition is seen to be
beyond repair?' (1991b: 357).

Drawing on these observations, Smith objects to Hobsbawm's
notion of 'invented traditions' and claims that these turn out to be
more akin to 'reconstruction' or 'rediscovery' of aspects of the
ethnic past. He notes that although the past can be interpreted in
different ways, it is not any past, but rather the 'past of that particular community, with its distinctive patterns of events, person-

ages and milieux'. This past acts as a constraint on the manipulations of elites, hence on invention (*ibid.*: 358). 'New' traditions will be accepted by the masses in so far as they can be shown to be continuous with the living past. Lieven makes a similar point, arguing that from a practical, non-academic point of view 'it is of secondary importance where nationalist ideas . . . came from, how "genuine" or "artificial" they may be, or how recently they were generated'. The real test is: do they work? In other words, do they succeed in mobilizing the people to which they appeal? Do they make them willing to fight and die? (1997: 16).

These Theories Cannot Explain Why So Many People are Prepared to Die for Their Nations

Another criticism voiced by ethno-symbolist writers concerns the instrumentalism of these theories. For them, such accounts are unable to explain why millions of women and men have sacrificed their lives for their nations. Smith argues that this failure stems from the 'top-down' method employed by most modernist theorists: 'They concentrate, for the most part, on elite manipulation of "the masses" rather than on the dynamics of mass mobilisation *per se*' (1995: 40). As a result of this, they do not pay enough attention to the needs, interests, hopes and longings of ordinary people. They fail to notice that these needs and interests are differentiated by class, gender, religion and ethnicity (*ibid.*). This also applies to Hobsbawm who criticizes Gellner for ignoring 'the view from below'. Koelble notes that Hobsbawm 'does not himself provide much of an analysis of the effects of modernization on the lower classes' (1995: 78). As I have alluded to earlier, for ethno-symbolist writers the answer lies in the subjective 'ethno-history' which continues to shape our identity and helps to determine our collective goals and destinies. Thus, they prefer to focus on the ways in which these groups have been mobilized by their own cultural and political traditions, their memories, myths and symbols (Smith 1991b: 358).

Strikingly enough, Breuilly expresses a similar complaint about the instrumentalist approach. He argues that this approach cannot explain why – and how – nationalism convinces those who have no interest – or those who actually go against their own interests – in supporting it (1993b: 21). Actually, all these criticisms revolve around one simple question: how does nationalism succeed in persuading so many people to lay down their lives for their country? To put it differently, how do we explain the emotional appeal or the 'charm' of nationalism?

These Theories Put Too Much Emphasis on One Set of Factors at the Expense of Others

This final criticism concerns the modernists' portrayal of recent history. Some ethno-symbolist writers argue that the modernists depict the last two centuries as shaped by a single decisive transition. Political revolutions, industrial take-off and the decline of religious authority were the main features of this transition. Hutchinson calls this the 'revolutionary' model of modernization (1994: 23). For scholars who espouse some version of the revolutionary model, nationalism is one of the by-products – albeit an important one – of this momentous transition to modernity. Hutchinson contends that this model cannot explain the much more evolutionary formation of national states in Western Europe. According to him, this process needs to be examined in *la longue durée*, that is by focusing on a much larger time span. In other words, post-eighteenth century nationalism can only be understood within the framework of 'a wider theory of ethnic formation that refers to the factors that may be common to the premodern and modern periods' (*ibid.*: 24; see also Llobera 1994).

Smith puts this in a different way. He argues that modernist approaches underestimate the significance of local cultural and social contexts. For him, what determines the intensity, character and scope of nationalism is the interaction between the tidal wave of modernization and these local variations. He accepts that modernity played its part in generating Aboriginal nationalisms in Australia just as it had done in France and Russia; but this does not tell us much about the timing, scope and character of these completely different nationalisms (1995: 42).

Specific Criticisms

State-building Should Not be Equated with Nation-building

Smith holds that state-building is not to be confused with the forging of a national identity among culturally homogeneous populations, because the establishment of incorporating state institutions is no guarantee that the population will identify with these institutions and the national myth they promote. On the contrary, the formulation of an assimilative myth by the ruling elites may alienate those groups who refuse to identify with it (Smith 1995: 38). He refers to the experiences of the new states of Asia and Africa to illustrate this point and argues that in many cases 'there has been not the fusion of *ethnies* through a territorial national identity but the persistence of deep cleavages and ethnic antagonisms that threaten the very existence of the state' (*ibid.*: 39). In other cases, attempts by state authorities to create a homogeneous national identity were perceived as repression, even 'ethnocide' or genocide by the victimized groups who in turn resorted to mass resistance, if not outright revolt, to counter them. In short, then, the role of the modern state in the genesis of nationalism should not be exaggerated. There are other forces which may predispose populations to nationalist programmes (*ibid.*).

Instrumentalists Exaggerate the Part Played by Elites in Shaping National Identities

This criticism led to a memorable exchange between Francis Robinson and Paul R. Brass on the relative weight to be attached to Islamic values and to elite manipulation in the process leading up to the formation of two separate states in the Indian subcontinent (Brass 1977, 1979; Robinson 1977, 1979). Accusing Brass for exaggerating the role of elite manipulation in this process, Robinson holds that the values and religio-political ideas of Islam, especially those that stress the existence of a Muslim community, limited the range of actions open to Muslim elite groups. These ideas formed 'their own apprehensions of what was possible and of what they ought to be trying to achieve' and thus acted as a constraining factor on Hindu–Muslim cooperation (1979: 106).

For Robinson, the religious differences between Muslims and Hindus in the nineteenth century were too great to allow peaceful coexistence: in a way, they were predisposed to live as separate national groups. Brass does not ignore these differences, or more generally pre-existing cultural values that may influence the ability of elites to manipulate particular symbols. But for him, the crucial question is:

given the existence in a multi-ethnic society of an array of cultural distinctions among peoples and of actual and potential cultural conflicts among them, what factors are critical in determining which of those distinctions, if any, will be used to build political identities? (1991: 77)

Here, Brass turns to the role of political elites, the balance between rates of social mobilization and assimilation between ethnic groups, the building of political organizations to promote group identities and the influence of government policies. Clearly, the answer to this question has broader theoretical implications with regard to the most fundamental divide of the literature on nationalism, namely that between the 'primordialists' and 'instrumentalists'. Both writers agree that these are extreme positions and that the answer lies between the two (Brass 1991: chapter 3; Robinson 1979: 107). As the above discussion shows, Brass veers towards the instrumentalist position, whereas Robinson insists that 'the balance of the argument should shift more towards the position of the primordialists' (1979: 107).

Hobsbawm Fails in his Predictions about the Future of Nationalism

We have seen that for Hobsbawm nationalism no longer constitutes the major vector of historical development: it has rapidly lost ground in the late twentieth century *vis-à-vis* the forces of globalization. The fragments of ethnic and linguistic nationalisms we witness today are no more than ephemeral reactions of weakness and fear of those who feel threatened by the processes of modernization (1990: chapter 6). Some scholars argued that this was a rather 'naive' prediction as the events of the last decade, especially the post-1989 'nationality boom', have revealed. Tiryakian, for example, asserts that 'the keenest historian was no more prescient about the impending implosion of the Soviet Empire than anybody else' (1995: 213).

Smith makes the same point with the help of examples. He argues that nationalism continues to flourish, if in sometimes less violent forms, in some of the most advanced industrial societies such as France, Canada, Spain and the United States (1995: 42–3). There is also the recent problem of xenophobia and ethnic violence against immigrants, *Gastarbeiter* and asylum-seekers. Smith remarks that this takes both popular and official forms. Given the continuing power of ethnicity, he concludes, 'it would be folly to predict an early supersession of nationalism and an imminent transcendence of the nation' (*ibid.*: 160).

Social/Cultural Transformation

The last group of theories I will consider in this chapter stresses the importance of social/cultural transformations in understanding national phenomena. The influential analyses of Ernest Gellner and Benedict Anderson will be reviewed in this section. The chapter will then conclude with an assessment of Hroch's account of the rise of national movements among the 'small nations' of Central/Eastern Europe.

Ernest Gellner and 'High Cultures'

Tom Nairn once made the important point that 'personal biography and life experience have been a major determinant of what and how nationalism gets studied' (cited in McCrone 1998: 172). Nothing illustrates this better than the work of the Czech polymath Ernest Gellner. The circumstances of Gellner's life made it utterly impossible for him to neglect nationalism (Hall 1998: 1; see also Hall and Jarvie 1996a; Gellner 1997; McCrone 1998). Born in Paris in 1925, he grew up in Prague which was then a multicultural and highly cosmopolitan city. Both his parents were lower middle class Bohemians of Jewish background, who shifted their allegiance from the German to the Czech community (Hall 1998: 1). Gellner himself spoke German with his parents, Czech with his sister and friends, and learned English after he was sent to the Prague English Grammar School.

In the late 1930s, when the Nazi threat became obvious, the family fled the country, crossing Germany by train: 'not all their relatives managed to escape in time' (Gellner 1997: viii). Later, he joined the Czech brigade who fought as part of the British army and saw active service in northern Europe in 1944 and 1945. As a member of the brigade, he took part in the victory parades in

Pilsen and Prague in May 1945. These experiences led Gellner to theorize nationalism. We might note in passing that much theorizing on nationalism has been done by scholars from similar backgrounds, that is coming from cosmopolitan urban settings destroyed by the rise of nationalism – like Hans Kohn, Karl W. Deutsch, Miroslav Hroch, Eric J. Hobsbawm and Elie Kedourie.

Gellner's theory is generally considered as the most important attempt to make sense of nationalism. The originality of his analysis is conceded even by his most staunch critics. Thus, the Marxist Tom Nairn calls Gellner's 1964 essay 'the most important and influential recent study in English' (1981: 96). Another critic, Gavin Kitching, praises Gellner's 'trenchant clarity' in *Nations and Nationalism* (1985: 98). Finally, Anthony D. Smith, who wrote his PhD dissertation under the auspices of Gellner in 1966, considers his theory to be 'one of the most complex and original attempts to come to grips with the ubiquitous phenomenon of nationalism' (1983: 109).

The originality of Gellner's analysis lies in its broad theoretical sweep. The theses he advanced in the seventh chapter of *Thought and Change* (1964) surpassed those of its predecessors in terms of both scope and detail. However, the sweep of his analysis also made him the target of a large number of criticisms. It is indeed true that Gellner was not modest when presenting his model:

A theoretical model is available which, starting from generalizations which are eminently plausible and not seriously contested, in conjunction with available data concerning the transformation of society in the nineteenth century, does explain the phenomenon in question. (1996a: 98)

After providing a brief summary of his model, he continues:

The argument . . . seems to me virtually Euclidean in its cogency. It seems to me impossible to be presented with these connections clearly and not to assent to them . . . As a matter of regrettable fact, an astonishing number of people have failed to accept the theory even when presented with it. (*Ibid.*: 110–11)

Gellner's analysis (in particular the original version formulated in *Thought and Change*) set the terms of the debate in subsequent years and provoked a large body of work critically evaluating his contribution to the study of nationalism (see for example Hall and Jarvie 1996b; Hall 1998). In the meantime, Gellner continued to refine his model and to defend it in the face of ever-growing criticisms. He divided his last years between Cambridge and Prague where he set up a Center for the Study of Nationalism – in the former Prague College of the Central European University. He passed away prematurely on 5 November 1995, one month before a conference organized by the Central European University to mark the occasion of his seventieth birthday. Gellner's 'last words' on nationalism are compiled in a small volume which saw the light of day in 1997.

Gellner's theory of nationalism can be better understood within the context of a long-lasting sociological tradition whose origins go back to Durkheim and Weber. The cardinal feature of this tradition is a basic distinction between 'traditional' and 'modern' societies. Following in the footsteps of the founding fathers of sociology, Gellner posited three stages in human history: the hunter-gatherer, the agro-literate and the industrial. This distinction forms the basis of Gellner's explanation which he presents as an alternative to 'false theories of nationalism'. He identifies four such theories:

1.   the nationalist theory which sees nationalism as a natural, self-evident and self-generating phenomenon;
2.   Kedourie's theory which treats it as 'an artificial consequence of ideas which did not need ever to be formulated, and appeared by a regrettable accident';
3.   'The Wrong Address Theory' favoured by Marxists which holds that the 'awakening message was intended for *classes*, but by some terrible postal error was delivered to *nations*'; and
4.   'Dark Gods Theory' shared by both lovers and haters of nationalism which regards it as 'the re-emergence of the atavistic forces of blood or territory' (1983: 129–30).

For Gellner, on the other hand, 'nationalism is primarily a political principle which holds that the political and the national unit should be congruent' (*ibid.*: 1). It is also a fundamental feature of the modern world since in most of human history political units were not organized along nationalist principles. The boundaries of city-states, feudal entities or dynastic empires rarely coincided with those of nations. In pre-modern times, the nationality of the rulers was not important for the ruled. What counted for them was whether the rulers were more just and merciful than their predecessors (1964: 153). Nationalism became a sociological necessity only in the modern world. And the task of a theory of nationalism is to explain how and why did this happen (1983: 6; 1996a: 98).

Gellner tries to account for the absence of nations and nationalisms in pre-modern ages by referring to the relationship between power and culture. He does not dwell too much on the first, hunter-gatherer, phase as there are no states at this stage, hence no room for nationalism which intends to endow the national culture with a political roof. Agro-literate societies, on the other hand, are characterized by a complex system of fairly stable statuses: 'the possession of a status, and access to its rights and privileges, is by far the most important consideration for a member of such a society. A man is his rank' (1996a: 100–1). In such a society, power and culture, two potential partners destined for each other according to nationalist theory, do not have much inclination to come together: the ruling class, consisting of warriors, priests, clerics, administrators and burghers, uses culture to differentiate itself from the large majority of direct agricultural producers who are confined to small local communities where culture is almost invisible (1983: 9–10, 12). Communication in these self-enclosed units is 'contextual', in contrast to the 'context-free' communication of the literate strata. Thus, this kind of society is marked by 'a discrepancy, and sometimes conflict, between a high and a low culture' (1996a: 102). There is no incentive for rulers to impose cultural homogeneity on their subjects: on the contrary, they derive benefit from diversity. The only class that might have an interest in imposing certain shared cultural norms is the clerisy, but they do not have the necessary means for incorporating the masses in a high culture (1983: 11). The overall conclusion for Gellner is quite simple: since there is no cultural homogenization in agro-literate societies, there can be no nations.

Gellner postulates an altogether different relationship between power and culture in industrial societies. Now, 'a high culture pervades the whole of society, defines it, and needs to be sustained by the polity' (1983: 18). Shared culture is not essential to the preservation of social order in agro-literate societies since status, that is an individual's place in the system of social roles, is ascriptive. In such societies, culture merely underlines structure and reinforces existing loyalties. Conversely, culture plays a more active role in industrial societies which are characterized by high levels of social mobility – and in which roles are no longer ascribed. The nature of work is quite different from that of agro-literate societies:

> Physical work in any pure form has all but disappeared. What is still called manual labour does not involve swinging a pick-axe or heaving soil with a spade . . . it generally involves controlling, managing and maintaining a machine with a fairly sophisticated control mechanism. (1996a: 106)

This has profound implications for culture in that the system can no longer tolerate the dependence of meaning on 'local dialectical idiosyncrasy', hence the need for impersonal, context-free communication and a high level of cultural standardization. For the first time in history, culture becomes important in its own right: it 'does not so much underline structure: rather it replaces it' (Gellner 1964: 155; see also O'Leary 1996).

There is, however, another factor making for the standardization of culture. Industrial society is based on the idea of 'perpetual growth' and this can only be sustained by a continuous transformation of the occupational structure: 'this society simply cannot constitute a stable system of ascribed roles, as it did in the agrarian age . . . Moreover, the high level of technical skill required for at least a significant proportion of posts . . . means that these posts have to be filled "meritocratically"' (Gellner 1996a: 108). The immediate upshot of this is 'a certain kind of egalitarianism'. The society is egalitarian because it is mobile and in a way, it has to be mobile. The inequalities that continue to exist tend to be camouflaged rather than flouted.

On the other hand, the industrial society is also a highly-specialized society. However, the distance between its various specialisms is far less great. This explains why we have 'generic training' before any specialized training on and for the job:

> A modern society is, in this respect, like a modern army, only more so. It provides a very prolonged and fairly thorough training for all its recruits, insisting on certain shared qualifications:

literacy, numeracy, basic work habits and social skills . . . The assumption is that anyone who has completed the generic training common to the entire population can be re-trained for most other jobs without too much difficulty. (1983: 27–8)

This system of education is quite different from the one-to-one or on-the-job principle found in pre-modern societies: 'men are no longer formed at their mother's knee, but rather in the *école maternelle*' (1996a: 109). A very important stratum in agro-literate societies was that of the clerks who can transmit literacy. In industrial society where exo-education becomes the norm, every man is a clerk: they are and must be 'mobile, and ready to shift from one activity to another, and must possess the generic training which enables them to follow the manuals and instructions of a new activity or occupation' (1983: 35). It follows that

the employability, dignity, security and self-respect of individuals . . . now hinges on their *education* . . . A man's education is by far his most precious investment, and in effect confers identity on him. Modern man is not loyal to a monarch or a land or a faith, whatever he may say, but to a culture. (*Ibid.*: 36)

Obviously, this educational infrastructure is large and exceedingly expensive. The only agency capable of sustaining and supervising such a vast system is the central state:

Given the competition of various states for overlapping catchment areas, the only way a given culture can protect itself against another one, which already has its particular protector-state, is to acquire one of its own, if it does not already possess one. Just as every girl should have a husband, preferably her own, so every culture must have its state, preferably its own. (1996a: 110)

This is what brings state and culture together: 'The imperative of exo-socialization is the main clue to why state and culture *must* now be linked, whereas in the past their connection was thin, fortuitous, varied, loose, and often minimal. Now it is unavoidable. That is what nationalism is about' (1983: 38).

In short, nationalism is a product of industrial social organization. This explains both its weakness and its strength. It is weak in the sense that the number of potential nations far exceeds the number of those that actually make the claim. Most cultures enter the age of nationalism without even the 'feeblest effort' to benefit from it themselves (*ibid.*: 47). They prefer to remain as 'wild' cultures, producing and reproducing themselves spontaneously, without conscious design, supervision or special nutrition. By contrast, the cultures that characterize the modern era are 'cultivated' or 'garden' cultures which are usually sustained by literacy and specialized personnel and would perish if deprived of their distinctive nourishment (*ibid.*: 50; see also Smith 1996d: 132–3).

On the other hand, nationalism is strong because 'it determines the norm for the legitimacy of political units in the modern world' (Gellner 1983: 49). The modern world can be depicted as a kind of 'giant aquarium' or 'breathing chamber' designed to preserve superficial cultural differences. The atmosphere and water in these chambers are specifically tailored to the needs of a new species, the industrial man, which cannot survive in the nature-given atmosphere. But the maintenance of this life-preserving air or liquid is not automatic: 'it requires a special plant. The name for this plant is a national educational and communications system' (*ibid.*: 51–2).

That is what underlies Gellner's contention that 'nations can be defined only in terms of the age of nationalism'. Nations can emerge 'when general social conditions make for standardized, homogeneous, centrally sustained high cultures, pervading entire populations and not just elite minorities'. Hence, 'it is nationalism which engenders nations, and not the other way round' (*ibid.*: 55; see also Smith 1996d: 132):

> Nationalism is, essentially, the general imposition of a high culture on society, where previously low cultures had taken up the lives of the majority, and in some cases of the totality, of the population . . . It is the establishment of an anonymous, impersonal society, with mutually substitutable atomized individuals, held together above all by a shared culture of this kind. (*ibid.*: 57)

How do the small local groups become conscious of their own 'wild' culture and why do they seek to turn it into a 'garden' culture? Gellner's answer to this question is simple: labour migration and bureaucratic employment disclosed 'the difference between dealing with a co-national, one understanding and sympathizing with their culture, and someone hostile to it. This very concrete experience taught them to be aware of their culture, and to love it (or, indeed, to wish to be rid of it)' (*ibid.*: 61) Thus, in conditions of high social mobility, 'the culture in which one has been *taught* to communicate becomes the core of one's identity' (*ibid.*).

This is also one of the two important principles of fission in industrial society. Gellner calls this 'the principle of barriers to communication', barriers based on pre-industrial cultures. The other principle is what he terms 'entropy-resistant traits' like skin colour, deeply engrained religious and cultural habits which tend not to become, even with the passage of time, evenly dispersed throughout the entire society (*ibid.*: 64). Gellner holds that in the later stages of industrial development, when 'the period of acute misery, disorganization, near-starvation, total alienation of the lower strata is over', it is the persistent 'counter-entropic' traits (whether they be genetic or cultural) which become the source of conflict. In the words of Gellner, 'resentment is now engendered less by some objectively intolerable condition . . . it is now brought about above all by the non-random social distribution of some visible and habitually noticed trait' (*ibid.*: 74–5). This conflict may give rise to new nations organized around either a high or a previously low culture.

I have tried to offer a relatively full account of Gellner's theory by concentrating mostly on *Nations and Nationalism*, referring to the earlier chapter in *Thought and Change* and other writings only where appropriate. Gellner later reworked his theory and made some important refinements to it. One such refinement concerns the transition from an agrarian to a full-grown industrial society. Observing that the original version of his theory remained silent on this issue, Gellner postulated five stages on the path from a world of non-ethnic empires and micro-units to one of homogeneous nation-states (1995a, 1996a):

1. *Baseline.* At this stage, ethnicity is not yet important and the idea of a link between it and political legitimacy is entirely absent.

2. *Nationalist Irredentism.* The political boundaries and structures of this stage are inherited from the previous era, but ethnicity – or nationalism – as a political principle begins to operate. The old borders and structures are under pressure from nationalist agitation.

3. *National Irredentism triumphant and self-defeating.* At this stage, multi-ethnic empires collapse and the dynastic-religious principle of political legitimation is replaced by nationalism. New states emerge as a result of nationalist agitation. But, Gellner contends, this state of affairs is self-defeating since these new states are just as 'minority-haunted' as the larger ones they replaced.

4. *Nacht und Nebel.* This is an expression used by the Nazis to depict some of their secret operations in the course of the Second World War. At this stage, all moral standards are suspended and the principle of nationalism, which demands homogeneous national units, is implemented with a new ruthlessness. Mass murder and forcible transplantation of population replace more benign methods such as assimilation.

5. *Post-industrial stage.* This is the post-1945 period. High level of satiation of the nationalist principle, accompanied by general affluence and cultural convergence, leads to a diminution, though not the disappearance, of the virulence of nationalism (1996a: 111–12).

For Gellner, these five stages represent a plausible account of the transition from a non-nationalist order to a nationalist one. However, this schema is not universally applicable, even in Europe. He observes that the stages he postulated played themselves out in different ways in various time zones. He identifies four such zones in Europe:

• Going from West to East, there is first the Atlantic sea-coast. Here, from pre-modern times, there were strong dynastic states. The political units based on Lisbon, London, Paris and Madrid corresponded roughly to homogeneous cultural-linguistic areas. Thus, when the age of nationalism came, relatively little redrawing of frontiers was required. In this zone, one hardly finds 'ethnographic nationalism', that is 'the study, codification, idealization of peasant cultures in the interest of forging a new national culture' (1995a: 29). The problem was rather that of turning peasants into citizens, not so much that of inventing a new culture on the basis of peasant idiosyncrasy (*ibid*.: 29; 1996a: 127–8).

- The second time zone corresponds to the territory of the erstwhile Holy Roman Empire. This area was dominated by two well-endowed high cultures which existed since the Renaissance and the Reformation, namely the German and Italian cultures. Thus, those who tried to create a German literature in the late eighteenth century were merely consolidating an existing culture – and not creating a new one. In terms of literacy and self-awareness, the Germans were not inferior to the French and a similar relationship existed between the Italians and the Austrians. All that was required here was to endow the existing high culture with its political roof (1995a: 29–30; 1996a: 128–9).

- Things were more complicated in the third time zone further east. This was the only area where all five stages played themselves out to the full. Here, there were neither well-defined high cultures, nor states to cover and protect them. The area was characterized by old non-national empires and a multiplicity of folk cultures. Thus, for the marriage between culture and polity required by nationalism to take place, both partners had to be created. This made the task of the nationalists more difficult and 'hence, often, its execution more brutal' (1995a: 30; 1996a: 129).

- Finally, there is the fourth time zone. Gellner maintains that this zone shared the trajectory of the previous one until 1918 or the early 1920s. But, then, the destinies of the two zones diverged. While two of the three empires covering the fourth zone, the Habsburg and Ottoman empires, disintegrated, the third one was dramatically revived under a new management and in the name of a new, inspiring ideology. Gellner notes that the victorious advance of the Red Army in 1945 and the incorporation of a considerable portion of zone three into zone four complicated matters still further. The new regime was able to repress nationalism at the cost of destroying civil society. Hence, when the system was dismantled, nationalism emerged with all its vigour, but few of its rivals. Having been artificially frozen at the end of the second stage, the fourth time zone can resume its normal course at stage three (irredentist nationalism), four (massacres or population transfers) or five (diminution of ethnic conflict). Which of these options will prevail – that is the crucial question facing the territories of the former Soviet Union (1995a: 30–1; 1996a: 129–32).

As I have mentioned earlier, the theoretical sweep of his model and the assertive tone with which he presented it made Gellner the target of a great deal of criticism. Here, I will confine myself to the standard criticisms raised against his theory, which can be summarized as follows: Gellner's model is too functionalist; he misreads the relationship between industrialization and nationalism; he fails to account for the resurgence of ethnic and nationalist sentiments within advanced industrialized societies; his model cannot explain the passions generated by nationalism; the processes underlying his explanation are too general and vacuous.

Gellner's Theory is Too Functionalist

Many scholars reject the stark functionalism of Gellner's theory. It is indeed true that Gellner tries to account for nationalism on the basis of the consequences it generates. More specifically, 'nationalism is "explained" by reference to an historical outcome (the emergence of Industrial Society) which chronologically follows it' (Kitching 1985: 102). For Gellner, nationalism is required by industrial society which could not 'function' without it: thus, nationalism is beneficial for modernizing states. In such a picture, nationalism is unintended by the actors producing modernization as they are unaware of the causal relationship between these two processes (O'Leary 1996: 85). O'Leary contends that

> Gellner's argument displays all the vices of functionalist reasoning – in which events and processes occur which are implausibly treated as wholly beyond the understanding of human agents, in which consequences precede causes, and in which suspicions arise that supra-individual and holistic entities are being tacitly invoked to do explanatory work. (*Ibid.*: 86)

Breuilly, on the other hand, notes that there are a multitude of functions which it is suggested nationalism can serve. For some, nationalism facilitates the process of modernization; for others, it helps the preservation of traditional identities and structures. For some, it is a function of class interest; for others, of identity need. Since there is no universally accepted interpretation, it makes no sense to explain nationalism in terms of the 'function' it serves (Breuilly 1993a: 419).

Minogue goes one step further and argues that functional explanations patronize in the sense of treating the researcher/theorist as a kind of omniscient being. Such explanations imply that what people are doing is actually different from what they believe they are doing and the theorist is in a position to perceive the reality. Hence, nationalists may think that they are liberating the nation, but Gellner knows that what they are really doing is in fact facilitating the transition to an industrial society. The olympian theorist spots the real causes of what is happening and reveals them to the readers (Minogue 1996: 117). Minogue also criticizes Gellner – and functional explanations in general – for underestimating the full conditions of human agency. He maintains that individuals respond rationally to the situations in which they find themselves in the light of the understanding they have of it. According to Minogue, 'different ideas, like the fluttering of the famous butterfly's wing that produces tempest on the other side of the globe, can lead to quite unpredictable consequences' (*ibid.*: 118). Discarding these ideas may doom a theory to extrapolation.

Gellner's functionalism does not manifest itself only in his portrayal of the relationship between nationalism and industrialization. His account of the rise of mass education displays similar functionalist overtones. The theory postulates that the new educational system based on generic training is a product of the new societal conditions. But again a process – here, the emergence of standardized educational systems – is explained by reference to a function which it is purported to play. Breuilly asks: 'education may eventually function in this way but does that explain its development' (1985: 68)? His answer is negative: 'unless one specifies either a deliberate intention on the part of key groups to produce this result or some feed-back mechanism which will "select" generic training patterns of education against other patterns, this cannot count as an explanation' (*ibid.*).

In addition to these theoretical complications, Gellner's functionalism also creates some factual difficulties. This brings us to the second criticism.

Gellner Misreads the Relationship between Industrialization and Nationalism

This is probably the most common charge brought against Gellner's theory. Many scholars cast doubt on Gellner's assumptions by pointing to a series of 'counter-examples'. First, it is argued that many nationalist movements flourished in societies which had not yet undergone industrialization. For instance, Kedourie asserts that nationalism as a doctrine was articulated in German-speaking lands in which there was as yet hardly any industrialization (1994: 143). Kitching makes a similar point for Britain, claiming that the emergence of nationalism in the British Isles precedes even early industrialism by 150–200 years (1985: 106). Minogue suggests the opposite by contending that Britain industrialized without having nationalism at all, and concludes that nationalism is not a necessary condition of industrial society (1996: 121). Kedourie concurs with Minogue and argues that the areas where industrialism first appeared and made the greatest progress, that is Great Britain and the United States, are precisely those areas where nationalism is unknown (1994: 143). However, this disagreement does not save Gellner's theory. Counter-examples abound. Areas like Greece, the Balkans and parts of the Ottoman Empire fell prey to nationalist ideology when they were innocent of industrialization (Kedourie 1994: 143).

Breuilly notes that one can find broadly shared national sentiments in parts of the world which have still not reached this stage. According to him, commercial agriculture, mass education and modern systems of communication can all produce the effects Gellner relates to industrialism. Thus, he concludes, there are other means of diffusing a national culture in non-industrial societies (1996: 162). Anti-imperialist or post-colonial nationalisms are another case in point. Gandhi's nationalism, for example, was quite explicitly hostile to industrialism. In Russia, a regime deeply hostile to nationalism took over the empire in 1917 and proceeded to supply just the conditions Gellner takes to be necessary to an industrial society (Minogue 1996: 120). A final difficulty is created by Nazi Germany, Italy in the Fascist era, and Japan in the 1920s and 1930s which produced the most frenzied nationalist movements despite their high level of industrialization (Kedourie 1994: 143). To sum up, nationalism preceded industrialization in many places; and in still others, nationalism was not a concomitant of the process of industrialization.

It is worth noting that Gellner tries to counter these criticisms by arguing that 'industrialism casts a long shadow' before its actual reality and that at any rate it was only the intellectuals who were nationalists (BBC radio discussion with Kedourie, cited in Minogue 1996: 120). On the other hand, he explicitly admits that Balkan nationalism constitutes a problem for his theory (1996c: 630).

Gellner's Theory Fails to Account for the Resurgence of Ethnic and Nationalist Sentiments within Advanced Industrialized Societies

As might be recalled, one of Gellner's core arguments was that the late industrial society is going to be one in which nationalism persists, but in a muted, less virulent form (1983: 122). This argument was an inevitable consequence of the industrialism/nationalism link he postulated in his theory. Kellas questions the validity of this assumption by pointing to the contemporary nationalist movements that have erupted in long-industrialized countries such as Britain, Spain and Belgium (1991: 44). Similarly, Hutchinson argues that Gellner's theory cannot explain the revival of 'ferocious terrorist nationalisms' within the heartlands of Europe, for instance among the relatively prosperous Basques and Catalans in Spain (1994: 22). On the other hand, Smith makes the same point by invoking the popular reaction to the Maastricht Treaty in countries like France, Britain and Denmark. According to him, the popular doubts and resistance we have witnessed in these countries suggest that we should not overlook the continuing importance of national traditions and experiences (1996d: 141).

Gellner's Model Cannot Explain the Passions Generated by Nationalism

As Gellner himself notes, this point has been raised by various critics from opposed ends of the ideological spectrum (1996c:

625). For instance, Perry Anderson, a leading figure of the New Left, contends that Gellner's theory cannot explain the emotional power of nationalism and adds: '[w]here Weber was so bewitched by its spell that he was never able to theorize nationalism, Gellner had theorized nationalism without detecting the spell' (1992: 205). O'Leary and Minogue, who have nothing to do with Marxism, make much the same point: while O'Leary accuses Gellner for relying on 'culturally and materially reductionist accounts of the political motivations which produce nationalism', Minogue is critical of his neglect of the power of identity (O'Leary 1996: 100; Minogue 1996: 126).

As we saw earlier, this point also forms one of the core arguments of the ethno-symbolist critique of modernist theories. Smith, the leading exponent of the ethno-symbolist approach, begins by asking the following question: why should people ardently identify with an invented high culture and be willing to lay down their lives for it (1996d: 134)? Gellner seeks the answer in modern systems of mass education. However, Smith notes, the ardour of the early nationalists, those who create the nation in the first place, cannot be the product of a national mass education system which has not at that date come into being (1996d: 135). It is not possible to establish a 'national' educational system without first determining who the 'nation' is. Who will receive the education? In which language? To explain the nationalism of those who propose answers to these questions, that is those who 'construct' the nation, by mass education is to fall, once again, into the trap of functionalism. According to Smith, the solution to this problem lies in pre-existing ethnic cultures, the elements of which (its myths, symbols and traditions) have been incorporated into the nascent national cultures.

Gellner rejects these charges by arguing that they are based on a misreading of his theory. He stresses that the model does not explain nationalism by the use it has in legitimating modernization, but by the fact that 'individuals find themselves in very stressful situations, unless the nationalist requirement of congruence between a man's culture and that of its environment is satisfied' (1996c: 626). He contends that without such a congruence, life would be hell: hence the deep passion which is thought to be absent from the theory. The passion, he continues, is not a means to an end, 'it is a reaction to an intolerable situation' (*ibid.*). It is best to end this sub-section with Gellner's reply to Anderson:

Perry gets it absolutely wrong: I *am* deeply sensitive to the spell of nationalism. I can play about thirty Bohemian folk songs (or songs presented as such in my youth) on my mouth organ. My oldest friend, whom I have known since the age of three or four and who is Czech and a patriot, cannot bear to hear me play them because he says I do it in such a schmaltzy way, 'crying into the mouth organ'. I do not think I could have written the book on nationalism which I did write, were I not capable of crying, with the help of a little alcohol, over folk songs, which happen to be my favourite form of music. (*ibid.*: 624–5)

The Processes Underlying his Explanation are Too General and Vacuous

According to Zubaida, all general theories of nationalism assume a 'sociological homogeneity', that is that there are common social structures and processes which underlie the ideological/political phenomena (1978: 56). He notes that all these theories share a basic structure despite their conceptual and terminological variations. To illustrate this structure, he focuses on Gellner's theory which can be regarded as the clearest example of such theories. The main elements of the narrative are: a world historical process (modernization/industrialization); traditional societies which this process hits at a differential pace, leading to differences in the degree of development and resulting in the breakdown of traditional ties and structures; particular social groups (intelligentsia and proletariat for Gellner) taking up the double fight against tradition and against external enemies. The story ends with the establishment of national states. That is followed by the struggle to replace traditional loyalties with national ones among the population at large. For Gellner, this is generated by an educational system which produces citizens with the needed qualifications (*ibid.*: 57).

According to Zubaida, the reality is much more complex. He argues that the sociological explanations of nationalist movements are based on processes and groups which are not generalizable or comparable between the various social contexts. For instance, the term 'industry' does not have the same meaning everywhere: it covers a wide range of forms of production, in scale from small workshops to nuclear power stations. Moreover, the consequences of industrial development are not uniform: factors like capital intensivity, the stratification or segmentation of labour markets, the source, nature and duration of capital investment, the relationship of industry to the agricultural sector may influence the outcome of industrialization and lead to very different socioeconomic configurations. In short, industrialization may not lead to nationalism in all these societies. Gellner's theory – or in that respect any general theory of nationalism – overlooks regional and historical variations (1978: 58–9). In his review of Gellner's *Nations and Nationalism*, Breuilly makes a similar point by arguing that a more differentiated model is needed to explain nationalism (1985: 70).

Benedict Anderson and 'Imagined Communities'

The year 1983 saw the publication of yet another very influential book on nationalism – along with Gellner's *Nations and Nationalism* and Hobsbawm and Ranger's *The Invention of Tradition* – namely *Imagined Communities: Reflections on the Origin and Spread of Nationalism*. Its author, Benedict R. O'G. Anderson, was a Southeast Asia specialist who had done extensive fieldwork in Indonesia, Siam and the Philippines. The initial impetus for writing this book, Anderson later recalls, came from 'the triangular Third Indochina War that broke out in 1978–79 between China, Vietnam, and Cambodia' (1998: 20). More generally, Anderson was intrigued by the fact that 'since World War II every successful revolution has defined itself in *national* terms' and sought to explain how this state of affairs came into being, focusing mainly, but not exclusively, on the cultural sources of nationalism – particularly the transformations of consciousness that made presently existing nations thinkable (Eley and Suny 1996b: 242).

Anderson's point of departure is that nationality and nationalism are cultural artefacts of a particular kind. In order to understand them properly, we need to find out how they have come into being, in what ways their meanings have changed over time and why they command such profound emotional legitimacy. Anderson argues that nationalism emerged towards the end of the eighteenth century as a result of the 'spontaneous distillation of a complex "crossing" of discrete historical forces' and once created, they became models which could be used in a great variety of social terrains, by a correspondingly wide variety of ideologies (1991[1983]: 4). For him, a persuasive explanation of nationalism should not confine itself to specifying the cultural and political factors which facilitate the growth of nations. The real challenge lies in showing why and how these particular cultural artefacts have aroused such deep attachments. In other words, the crucial question is: 'what makes the shrunken imaginings of recent history (scarcely more than two centuries) generate such colossal sacrifices' (*ibid*.: 7)? Before addressing this question, however, he considers the concept of 'nation' and tries to offer a workable definition.

For Anderson, the terminological confusion surrounding the concept of nation is partly caused by the tendency to treat it as an ideological construct. Things would be easier if it is seen as belonging to the same family as 'kinship' or 'religion'; hence his definition of the nation as 'an imagined political community – and imagined as both inherently limited and sovereign'. It is imagined because 'the members of even the smallest nation will never know most of their fellow-members, meet them, or even hear of them, yet in the minds of each lives the image of their communion'. It is imagined as limited because each nation has finite boundaries beyond which lie other nations. It is imagined as sovereign because it is born in the age of Enlightenment and Revolution, when the legitimacy of divinely-ordained, hierarchical dynastic realm was rapidly waning: the nations were dreaming of being free, and if under God, then at least directly so. Finally, it is imagined as a community because, 'regardless of the actual inequality and exploitation that may prevail in each, the nation is always conceived as a deep, horizontal comradeship'. According to Anderson, it is ultimately this sense of fraternity which makes it possible for so many millions of people to willingly lay down their lives for their nation (*ibid*.: 6–7).

Here, it is worth stressing that for Anderson, 'imagining' does not imply 'falsity'. He makes this point quite forcefully when he accuses Gellner for assimilating 'invention' to 'fabrication' and 'falsity', rather than to 'imagining' and 'creation' with the intention of showing that nationalism masquerades under false pretences. Such a view implies that there are 'real' communities which can be advantageously compared to nations. In fact, however, all communities larger than small villages of face-to-face contact (perhaps even these) are imagined. Communities, Anderson concludes, should not be distinguished by their falsity/genuineness, but by the style in which they are imagined (*ibid.*: 6).

Anderson then turns to the conditions which give rise to such imagined communities. He begins with the cultural roots of nationalism, arguing that 'nationalism has to be understood by aligning it, not with self-consciously held political ideologies, but with the large cultural systems that preceded it, out of which – as well as against which – it came into being' (*ibid.*: 12). He cites two such systems as relevant, the religious community and the dynastic realm. Both of these systems held sway over much of Europe until the sixteenth century. Their gradual decline, which began in the seventeenth century, provided the historical and geographical space necessary for the rise of nations.

The decline of the 'great religiously imagined communities' was particularly important in this context. Anderson emphasizes two reasons for this decline. The first was the effect of the explorations of the non-European world which widened the general cultural and geographical horizon, and showed the Europeans that alternative forms of human life were also possible. The second reason was the gradual decay of the sacred language itself. Latin was the dominant language of a pan-European high intelligentsia; in fact, it was the only language taught in medieval Western Europe. But by the sixteenth century all this was changing fast. More and more books were coming out in the vernacular languages and publishing was ceasing to be an international enterprise (1991: 12–19).

What was the significance of all these developments for the emergence of the idea of nation? The answer lies, Anderson argues, in the crucial role played by traditional religions in human life. First and foremost, they soothed the sufferings resulting from the contingency of life ('Why is my best friend paralysed? Why is my daughter retarded?') by explaining them away as 'destiny'. At a more spiritual level, on the other hand, they provided salvation from the arbitrariness of fatality by turning it into continuity (life after death), by establishing a link between the dead and the yet unborn. Predictably, the ebbing of religious world-views did not lead to a corresponding decline in human suffering. In fact, now, fatality was more arbitrary than ever. 'What then was required was a secular transformation of fatality into continuity, contingency into meaning'. Nothing was better suited to this end than the idea of nation which always looms out of an immemorial past, and more importantly, glides into a limitless future: '[i]t is the magic of nationalism to turn chance into destiny' (*ibid.*: 11, 12).

It would be too simplistic, however, to suggest that nations grew out of and replaced religious communities and dynastic realms. Beneath the dissolution of these sacred communities, a much more fundamental transformation was taking place in the modes of apprehending the world. This change concerns the medieval Christian conception of time which is based on the idea of simultaneity. According to such a conception, events are situated simultaneously in the present, past and future. The past prefigures the future, so that the latter 'fulfils' what is announced and promised in the former. The occurrences of the past and the future are linked neither temporally nor causally, but by Divine Providence which alone can devise such a plan of history. In such a view of things, Anderson notes, 'the word "meanwhile" cannot be of real significance' (*ibid.*: 24). This conception of 'simultaneity-along-time' was replaced by the idea of 'homogeneous empty time', a term Anderson borrows from Walter Benjamin. Simultaneity is now understood as being transverse, cross-time, marked by temporal coincidence and measured by clock and calendar. The new conception of time made it possible to 'imagine' the nation as a 'sociological organism' moving steadily down (or up) history (*ibid.*: 26). To illustrate this point, Anderson examines two popular forms of imagining, the novel and the newspaper.

He first considers a simple novel-plot consisting of four characters: a man (A) has a wife (B) and a mistress (C), who in turn has a lover (D). Assuming that (C) has played her cards right and that (A) and (D) never meet, what actually links these two characters? First, that they live in 'societies' (Lübeck, Los Angeles): '[t]hese societies are sociological entities of such firm and stable reality that their members (A and D) can even be described as passing each other on the street, without ever becoming acquainted, and still be connected' (*ibid.*: 25). Second, that they are connected in the minds of the readers. Only the readers could know what (A) and (D) are doing at a particular moment in time. According to Anderson, that all these acts are performed at the same clocked, calendrical time, but by actors who may be largely unaware of one another, shows the novelty of this imagined world conjured up by the author in his readers' mind. (*Ibid.*: 26)

This has profound implications for the idea of nation. An American would probably never meet, or even know the names of more than a handful of his fellow-Americans. He would have no idea of what they are doing at any one time. Yet he has complete confidence in their existence and their 'steady, anonymous, simultaneous activity' (*ibid.*).

A similar link is established by the newspaper which embodies a profound fictiveness. If we take a quick glance at the front page of any newspaper, we will discover a number of, seemingly independent, stories. Anderson asks: what connects them to each other? First, calendrical coincidence. The date at the top of the newspaper provides the essential connection: 'Within that time, "the world" ambles sturdily ahead'. If, for example, Mali disappears from the front pages of newspapers, we do not think that Mali has disappeared altogether. 'The novelistic format of the newspaper assures them that somewhere out there the "character" Mali moves along quietly, awaiting its next appearance in the plot' (*ibid.*: 33).

The second connection is provided by the simultaneous mass consumption of newspapers. In that sense, the newspaper can be considered as an 'extreme form of the book', a 'book sold on a colossal scale' or 'one-day best-sellers' (*ibid.*: 33–4). We know that a particular edition will be read between this and that hour, only on this day, not that. This is, in a way, a mass ceremony, a ceremony performed in silent privacy, '[y]et each communicant is well aware that the ceremony he performs is being replicated simultaneously by thousands (or millions) of others whose existence he is confident, yet of whose identity he has not the slightest notion' (*ibid.*: 35). It is difficult to envision a more vivid figure for the secular, historically clocked imagined community. Moreover, observing that the exact replicas of his own newspaper are consumed by his neighbours, in the subway or barbershop, the reader is continually reassured that the imagined world is rooted in everyday life: 'fiction seeps quietly and continuously into reality, creating that remarkable confidence of community in anonymity which is the hallmark of modern nations' (*ibid.*: 36).

To recapitulate, the cultural origins of the modern nation could be located historically at the junction of three developments: a change in the conceptions of time, the decline of religious communities and of dynastic realms. But the picture is not complete yet. The missing ingredient is provided by commercial book-publishing on a wide scale, or what Anderson calls 'print-capitalism'. This made it possible, more than anything else, for rapidly growing numbers of people to think of themselves in profoundly new ways.

The initial market for capitalist book-publishing was the thin stratum of Latin-readers. This market, Anderson notes, was saturated in 150 years. However, capitalism needed markets, hence profit. The inherent logic of capitalism forced the publishers, once the elite Latin market was saturated, to produce cheap editions in the vernaculars with the aim of reaching the monoglot masses. This process was precipitated by three factors. The first was a change in the character of Latin. Thanks to the Humanists, the literary works of pre-Christian antiquity were discovered and spread to the market. This generated a new interest in the sophisticated writing style of the ancients which further removed Latin from ecclesiastical and everyday life. Second was the impact of the Reformation, which owed much of its success to print-capitalism. The coalition between Protestantism and print-capitalism quickly created large reading publics and mobilized them for political/religious purposes. Third was the adoption of some vernaculars as administrative languages. Anderson remarks that the rise of administrative vernaculars predated both print and the Reformation, hence must be regarded as an independent factor. Together, these three factors led to the dethronement of Latin and created large reading publics in the vernaculars (*ibid.*: 38–43).

Anderson argues that these print-languages laid the bases for national consciousnesses in three ways. First, they created 'unified fields of exchange and communication below Latin and above the spoken vernaculars'. Second, print-capitalism gave a new fixity to language which helped to build the image of antiquity so central to the idea of the nation. And third, print-capitalism created languages-of-power of a kind different from the earlier administrative vernaculars. In short, what made the new communities imaginable was 'a half-fortuitous, but explosive, interaction between a system of production and productive relations (capitalism), a technology of communications (print), and the fatality of human diversity' (*ibid.*: 42–4).

Having specified the general causal factors underlying the rise of nations, Anderson turns to particular historical/cultural contexts with the aim of exploring the 'modular' development of nationalism. He begins by considering Latin America. This section contains one of the most interesting – and controversial – arguments of the book, namely that the *creole* communities of the Americas developed their national consciousnesses well before most of Europe. According to Anderson, two aspects of Latin American nationalisms separated them from their counterparts in Europe. First, language did not play an important role in their formation since the colonies shared a common language with their respective imperial metropoles. Second, the colonial national movements were led by creole elites and not by the intelligentsia. On the other hand, the factors that incited these movements were not limited to the tightening of Madrid's control and the spread of the liberalizing ideas of the Enlightenment. Each of the South American Republics had been an administrative unit between the sixteenth and eighteenth centuries. This led them to develop a 'firmer reality' over time, a process precipitated by 'administrative pilgrimages', or what Anderson calls the 'journey between times, statuses and places'. Creole functionaries met their colleagues ('fellow-pilgrims') from places and families they have scarcely heard of in the course of these pilgrimages and, in experiencing them as travelling-companions, developed a consciousness of connectedness (why are *we . . . here . . . together?*) (*ibid.*: 50–6).

The close of the era of successful national movements in the Americas, Anderson argues, coincided with the onset of the age of nationalism in Europe. The earlier examples of European nationalisms were different from their predecessors in two respects: national print-languages were an important issue in their formation and they had 'models' they could aspire to from early on. Anderson cites two developments which speeded up the rise of classic linguistic nationalisms. The first was the discovery of distant 'grandiose' civilizations, such as the Chinese, Japanese, Indian, Aztec or Incan, which allowed Europeans to think of their civilizations as only one among many, and not necessarily the Chosen or the best (*ibid.*: 69–70).

The second was a change in European ideas about language.

Anderson observes that the scientific comparative study of languages got under way from the late eighteenth century onwards. In this period, vernaculars were revived; dictionaries and grammar books were produced. This had profound implications for the old, sacred languages which were now considered to be on an equal footing with their vernacular rivals. The most visible manifestation of this egalitarianism was 'bilingual dictionaries', for 'whatever the political realities outside, within the covers of the Czech–German/ German-Czech dictionary the paired language had a common status' (*ibid.*: 71). Obviously, this 'lexicographic revolution' was not experienced in a vacuum. The dictionaries or grammar books were produced for the print-market, hence consuming publics. The general increase in literacy rates, together with a parallel growth in commerce, industry and communications, created new impulses for vernacular linguistic unification. This, in turn, made the task of nationalism easier.

On the other hand, these developments created increasing political problems for many dynasties in the course of the nineteenth century because the legitimacy of most of them had nothing to do with 'nationalness'. The ruling dynastic families and the aristocrats were threatened with marginalization or exclusion from the nascent 'imagined communities'. This led to 'official nationalisms', a term Anderson borrows from Seton-Watson, which was

a means for combining naturalization with retention of dynastic power, in particular over the huge polyglot domains accumulated since the Middle Ages, or, to put it another way, for stretching the short, tight, skin of the nation over the gigantic body of the empire. (*Ibid.*: 86)

Anderson stresses that official nationalisms developed after, and in reaction to, the popular national movements proliferating in Europe since the 1820s. Thus, they were historically 'impossible' until after the appearance of the latter. Moreover, these nationalisms were not confined to Europe. Similar policies were pursued in the vast Asian and African territories subjected in the course of the nineteenth century. They were also picked up and imitated by indigenous ruling elites in areas which escaped subjection (*ibid.*: 109–10).

This brings Anderson to his final stop, namely anti-colonial nationalisms in Asia and Africa. This 'last wave' of nationalisms, he contends, was largely inspired by the example of earlier movements in Europe and the Americas. A key part was played in this process by official nationalisms which transplanted their policies of 'Russification' to their extra-European colonies. Anderson claims that this ideological tendency meshed with practical exigencies as the late nineteenth century empires were too large and too far-flung to be ruled by a handful of nationals. Moreover, the state was rapidly multiplying its functions in both the metropoles and the colonies. What, then, was required was well-educated subordinate cadres for state and corporate bureaucracies. These were generated by the new school systems, which in turn led to new pilgrimages, this time not only administrative, but also educational.

On the other hand, the logic of colonialism meant that the natives were invited to schools and offices, but not to boardrooms. Result: 'lonely, bilingual intelligentsias unattached to sturdy local bourgeoisies' which became the key spokesmen for colonial nationalisms (*ibid*.: 140). As bilingual intelligentsias, they had access to models of nation and nationalism, 'distilled from the turbulent, chaotic experiences of more than a century of American and European history'. These models could be copied, adapted and improved upon. Finally, the improved technologies of communication enabled these intelligentsias to propagate their messages not only to illiterate masses, but also to literate masses reading different languages (*ibid*.). In the conditions of the twentieth century, nation-building was much easier than before.

It is hard to do justice to Anderson's sophisticated analysis in a few pages. Suffice it to say that it constitutes one of the most original accounts of nationalism to date. Before proceeding, it needs to be noted that Anderson's theory has not been immune to the general criticisms raised against modernist explanations of nationalism. I will not repeat them here since they were discussed in detail in previous sections. Apart from these general points, it is possible to identify five specific objections to Anderson's account: it is culturally reductionist; his arguments concerning the relationship between nationalism and religion do not work for certain cases; his thesis that nationalism is born in the Americas runs counter to available evidence; his examples of official nationalism are not correct; he misinterprets the rise of anti-colonial-nationalisms.

Anderson's Account is Culturally Reductionist

Anderson's emphasis on the way in which nations as 'imagined communities' come to be constructed through cultural representations led some scholars to accuse him of 'cultural reductionism'. Breuilly, for instance, criticizes Anderson for underestimating the political dimension of nationalism, and more specifically, for exaggerating the importance of cultural nationalism in nineteenth century Europe (1985: 71–2). According to Breuilly, Anderson's theses, while plausible in eighteenth century America, falter when he moves to Europe: he cannot tackle the thorny problem of the lack of congruence between 'cultural' and 'political' nationalism in certain cases (*ibid.*). To illustrate this point, Breuilly points to the 'political' unification of Germany which was not accompanied by a 'cultural' unification. The political dimension plays a more significant role even in the case of the liberation movements that developed in eighteenth century America, for which Anderson's argument works better. Most of these movements, Breuilly notes, worked within the territorial framework set down by the colonial system.

In general, Breuilly concurs with Anderson that the cultural dimension is important for understanding nationalism, but adds that this dimension can only explain why certain small groups might be disposed to imagine themselves as a nation and act politically on the basis of this assumption. Anderson's theory, he continues, cannot provide an answer to the question of 'why are those groups important': in other words, 'why does anyone either above (in power) or below (in the society claimed to be national) take these arguments seriously' (*ibid.*: 73). Breuilly contends that Gellner's theory is more satisfactory in this respect since it tries to pinpoint some basic changes in the social structure which might underpin the type of cultural processes Anderson considers. He concludes by claiming that a closer examination of the links between the modern state and nationalism might provide a solution to this problem.

Balakrishnan makes a similar point when he argues that the cultural affinities generated and shaped by print-capitalism do not seem sufficient to explain the colossal sacrifices that peoples are at times willing to make for their nation. It is easier to understand the sacrifices people make for their religion since 'weightier issues than mere life on this earth hang in the balance' (1996a: 208). It is harder to see how societies operating in a vernacular could ever inspire the same pathos. At this stage, Balakrishnan points to the impact of wars in shaping national consciousness and blames Anderson for neglecting the role of domination and force in history (*ibid.*: 208–11). Smith agrees with Balakrishnan and calls attention to the needs of the 'state-at-war' which antedate both print and expanding capitalism in Western Europe (1991b: 363).

Anderson's Arguments Concerning the Relationship between Nationalism and Religion Do Not Work for Certain Cases

Kellas claims that religion is not always replaced by nationalism: he refers to the examples of Ireland, Poland, Armenia, Israel and Iran, where religious institutions have reinforced nationalism, to support this argument. There are also cases where nationalism and religion thrive together. Therefore, it is difficult to relate the rise of nationalism to the decline of religion (1991: 48).

Greenfeld goes one step further and argues that '[n]ationalism emerged in a time of ardent religious sentiment, when questions of religious identity grew more, rather than less acute, and faith became more significant – the time of the Reformation' (1993: 49). According to Greenfeld, nationalism was able to develop and become established with the support of religion. Even at later stages, when it replaced it as the governing passion, it incorporated religion as a part of the national consciousness in many cases.

The same point is raised by Smith who observes that religious nationalism, 'or the superimposition (or uneasy coexistence) of mass religion on nationalism', has made a remarkable come back in the Islamic world, the Indian sub-continent and in parts of Europe and the Soviet Union. For Smith, this is hardly surprising since world religions have often served as repositories of popular myths, symbols and memories which often form the basis of modern nations (1991b: 364).

His Thesis that Nationalism is Born in the Americas Runs Counter to Available Evidence

As noted above, Anderson's contention that the national liberation movements in the Americas constitute the earliest examples of modern nationalism has been the subject of much controversy. The first examples of nationalism have been identified variously as appearing in England (Greenfeld 1992; Hastings 1997), France (Alter 1989), Germany (Kedourie 1994). Anderson, on the other hand, asserts that 'it is an astonishing sign of the depth of Eurocentrism that so many European scholars persist, in the face of all the evidence, in regarding nationalism as a European invention' (1991: 191, note 9). Anderson's argument about nationalism's 'place of birth' has not been attacked directly until recently. This silence ended in 1997, when Hastings stated that Anderson does not explain why the first wave of nation-making was the American. According to Hastings, Anderson offers no explanation 'as to why the growth in books did not have in the sixteenth century the effect he postulates for the late eighteenth' (1997: 11).

Anderson's Examples of Official Nationalism are Not Correct

This criticism comes from Breuilly, who argues that Anderson brackets some genuine cases of official nationalism (Russia, Siam) with cases that should be understood in quite different ways (1985: 72). He cites Magyar nationalism as an example. According to Breuilly, Magyar nationalism cannot be understood as an aristocratic response to nationalist threats from subordinate groups. In fact, Breuilly continues, the chronological sequence is the other way around: it was the development of Magyar nationalism which helped promote nationalist movements among subordinate groups. Breuilly notes that these movements did take on the character of an 'official nationalism' only at a later stage.

More complicated was the case of what Anderson calls a policy of official English nationalism in India. Breuilly admits that a policy of Anglicizing was pursued in India and that this was marked by assumptions of cultural superiority; but, he contends, this policy was never conceived of along national lines. This was similar to the Habsburg policy of adopting German as the official language of government which had nothing to do with nationalism, but rather with choosing the most suitable vehicle for the exercise of rational government. The real problem was (and this was underlined by Anderson as well) 'that the transfer of certain English . . . qualities to Indians was not envisaged as being synonymous with the transfer of "Englishness", and this led to cruel disillusionment amongst some Indians' (*ibid.*). Breuilly concludes by noting that the British government never tried to convince the Indians that they shared a common national identity with those in power. Thus, we cannot speak of a policy of 'official nationalism' in this case.

Anderson Misinterprets the Rise of Anti-colonial Nationalisms

This last objection is raised by Chatterjee. Drawing on Anderson's definition of the nation, Chatterjee asks:

> If nationalisms in the rest of the world have to choose their imagined community from certain 'modular' forms already made available to them by Europe and the Americas, what do they have left to imagine? History, it would seem, has decreed that we in the postcolonial world shall only be perpetual consumers of modernity. Europe and the Americas, the only true subjects of history, have thought out on our behalf not only the script of colonial enlightenment and exploitation, but also that of our anti-colonial resistance and postcolonial misery. Even our imaginations must remain forever colonized. (1996: 216)

Chatterjee rejects such an interpretation on the basis of the evidence provided by anti-colonial nationalisms. He holds that 'the most powerful as well as the most creative results of the nationalist imagination in Asia and Africa are posited not on an identity but rather on a *difference* with the "modular" forms of the national society propagated by the modern West' (*ibid.*). According to Chatterjee, this common error arises from taking the claims of nationalism to be a political movement much too literally and seriously. However, he claims, 'as history, nationalism's autobiography is fundamentally flawed' (*ibid.*: 217).

His own interpretation rests on the argument that anti-colonial nationalism creates its own domain of sovereignty within colonial society well before it begins its battle with the colonizer. It does this by dividing the social institutions and practices into two domains: the material and the spiritual. The material is the domain of the economy, statecraft, science and technology where the West is superior. In this domain, therefore, the superiority of the West has to be acknowledged and its success replicated. The spiritual domain, on the other hand, bears the essential marks of the nation's cultural identity. In this domain, the distinctness of one's culture needs to be preserved. As a result of this division, 'nationalism declares the domain of the spiritual its sovereign territory and refuses to allow the colonial power to intervene in that domain'. This does not mean that the spiritual domain is left unchanged. On the contrary, here nationalism launches its most creative and historically significant project: 'to fashion a "modern" national culture that is nevertheless not Western'. If the nation is an 'imagined community', then this is exactly where imagination works. The dynamics of this process, according to Chatterjee, are missed by conventional histories of nationalism (hence by Anderson) in which the story begins with the contest for political power (*ibid.*: 217–18).

Miroslav Hroch and the Three Phases of Nationalism

The last theoretical model I will discuss in this section is that of the Czech historian Miroslav Hroch. His work, compiled in *Die Vorkämpfer der nationalen Bewegungen bei den kleinen Völkern Europas: Eine vergleichende Analyse zur gesellschaftlichen Schichtung der patriotischen Gruppen* (Prague 1968) and *Obrození malých evropských národu. I: Národy severní a vychodní Evropy* [The Revival of the Small European Nations. I: The Nations of Northern and Eastern Europe] (Prague 1971), was pioneering in many respects. Hroch was the first scholar who undertook the quantitative social-historical analysis of nationalist movements in a systematic comparative framework. Second, he related nation-forming to the larger processes of social transformation, especially those associated with the spread of capitalism, but did so by avoiding economic reductionism, focusing on the effects of social and geographical mobility, more intense communication, the spread of literacy and generational change as mediating factors. Finally, he provided 'a socially and culturally grounded model of political development' (Eley and Suny 1996b: 59).

Strikingly enough, Hroch's pathbreaking studies were not translated into English until 1985. Until then, his findings were made accessible to a wider audience through the writings of Eric Hobsbawm (1972) and Tom Nairn (1974) who both treated Hroch's work as an excellent piece of comparative analysis. In a similar vein, Gellner commented that the publication of *Social Pre-conditions of National Revival in Europe* (1985) made it difficult for him to open his mouth for fear of making some mistake (cited in Hall 1998: 6). As Eley and Suny remark, his work still remains relatively little emulated and this is what makes it so 'important and exciting' (1996a: 16).

Hroch's point of departure is an empirical observation: at the beginning of the nineteenth century, there were eight 'state-nations' in Europe with a more or less developed literary language, a high culture and ethnically homogeneous ruling elites (including the aristocracy and an emerging commercial and industrial bourgeoisie). These eight state-nations – England, France, Spain, Sweden, Denmark, Portugal, the Netherlands and later Russia – were the products of a long process of nation-building that had started in the Middle Ages. There were also two emerging nations with a developed culture and an ethnically homogeneous elite, but without a political roof: the Germans and the Italians (Hroch 1993, 1995, 1996).

At the same time, there were more than 30 'non-dominant ethnic groups' scattered around the territories of multi-ethnic empires and some of the above-mentioned states. These groups lacked their own state, an indigenous ruling elite and a continuous cultural tradition in their own literary language. They usually occupied a compact territory, but were dominated by an 'exogenous', that is belonging to a different ethnic group, ruling class (Hroch 1995; 1996). Hroch notes that although these groups have come to be identified with Eastern and Southeastern Europe, there were many similar communities in Western Europe too (1993: 5). Sooner or later, some members of these groups became aware of their own ethnicity and started to conceive of themselves as a potential nation. Comparing their situation with that of the established nations, they detected certain deficits, which the future nation lacked, and began efforts to overcome them, seeking the support of their compatriots. Hroch observes that this national agitation started very early in some cases, that is around 1800 (the Greeks, Czechs, Norwegians, Irish), one generation later in others (the Finns, Croats, Slovenes, Flemish, Welsh), or even as late as the second half of the nineteenth century (Latvians, Estonians, Catalans, Basques) (1996: 37).

Hroch calls these 'organized endeavours to achieve all the attrib-

utes of a fully-fledged nation' a national movement. He argues that
the tendency to speak of them as 'nationalist' leads to serious confusion since nationalism *stricto sensu* is something else, namely that
'outlook which gives an absolute priority to the values of the nation
over all other values and interests' (1993: 6). In that sense, nationalism was only one of many forms of national consciousness to
emerge in the course of these movements. The term 'nationalist'
could be applied to such representative figures as the Norwegian
poet Wergeland who tried to create a language for his country or
the Polish writer Mickiewicz who longed for the liberation of his
homeland, but it cannot be suggested that all the participants of
these movements were 'nationalist' as such. Nationalism did of
course become a significant force in these areas, Hroch admits, but
as in the West, this was a later development. The programmes of
the classic national movements were of a different type. According
to Hroch, they included three groups of demands:

1. The development or improvement of a national culture based
    on the local language which had to be used in education,
    administration and economic life.
2. The creation of a complete social structure, including their
    'own' educated elites and entrepreneurial classes.
3. The achievement of equal civil rights and of some degree of
    political self-administration (1995: 66–7).

The timing and relative priority of these three sets of demands
varied but the trajectory of any national movement was only completed when all were fulfilled (1993: 6).

On the other hand, Hroch distinguishes three structural phases
between the starting-point of any national movement and its successful completion. During the initial period, which he calls Phase
A, activists committed themselves to scholarly inquiry into the linguistic, historical and cultural attributes of their ethnic group.
They did not attempt to mount a patriotic agitation or formulate
any political goals at this stage, in part because they were isolated
and in part they did not believe it would serve any purpose (1985:
23). In the second period, Phase B, a new range of activists
emerged who intended to win over as many of their ethnic group
as possible to the project of creating a nation. Hroch notes that

these activists were not very successful initially, but their efforts found a growing reception in time. When the national consciousness became the concern of the majority of the population, a mass movement was formed, which Hroch terms Phase C. It was only at this stage that a full social structure could be formed (1993: 7; 1995: 67). Hroch stresses that the transition from one phase to the next did not occur at one stroke: 'between the manifestations of scholarly interest, on the one hand, and the mass diffusion of patriotic attitudes, on the other, there lies an epoch characterized by active patriotic agitation: the fermentation-process of national consciousness' (1985: 23).

This periodization, Hroch continues, permits meaningful comparisons between national movements. For him, the most important criterion for any typology of national movements is the relationship between the transition to Phase B and then to Phase C on the one hand, and the transition to a constitutional society on the other. Combining these two series of changes, he identifies four types of national movements in Europe:

1. In the first type, national agitation began under the old regime of absolutism, but it reached the masses in a time of revolutionary changes. The leaders of Phase B formulated their national programmes in conditions of political upheaval. Hroch cites the case of Czech agitation in Bohemia and the Hungarian and Norwegian movements to illustrate this type. All these movements entered Phase B around 1800. The Norwegians obtained their independence (and a liberal constitution) in 1814; the Czech and Magyar national programmes were developed in the course of the revolutions of 1848.

2. In the second type, national agitation again started under the old regime, but the transition to Phase C was delayed until after a constitutional revolution. This shift resulted either from uneven economic development, as in Lithuania, Latvia, Slovenia or Croatia; or from foreign oppression, as in Slovakia or the Ukraine. Hroch maintains that Phase B started in Croatia in the 1830s, in Slovenia in the 1840s, in Latvia in the late 1850s and in Lithuania not before the 1870s. This delayed the transition to Phase C to the 1880s in Croatia, the 1890s in Slovenia and the revolution of 1905 in Latvia and Lithuania.

He argues that the policies of Magyarization held back the transition to Phase C in Slovakia until after 1867, as did forcible Russification in the Ukraine.

3. In the third type, a mass movement was already formed under the old regime, thus, before the establishment of a constitutional order. This model was confined to the territories of the Ottoman Empire in Europe – Serbia, Greece and Bulgaria.

4. In the final type, national agitation began under constitutional conditions in a more developed capitalist setting; this pattern was characteristic of Western Europe. In some of these cases the transition to Phase C was experienced quite early, as in the Basque lands and Catalonia, while in others it did so after a very long Phase B, as in Flanders, or not at all as in Wales, Scotland or Brittany (for these types see 1985: chapter 7; 1993: 7–8).

Hroch maintains that these patterns do not enable us to understand the origins and outcomes of various national movements as they are based on generalizations. Any satisfactory account has to be 'multi-causal' and establish the links between the structural phases we have identified above. In the light of these considerations, Hroch tries to provide answers to the following questions: how did the experiences (and structures) of the past affect the modern nation-building process? How and why did the scholarly interest of a small number of intellectuals transform into political programmes underpinned by strong emotional attachments? What accounts for the success of some of these movements and the failure of others? He begins by considering the 'antecedents to nation-building'.

According to Hroch, the experiences of the past, or what he calls 'the prelude to modern nation-building' (that is earlier attempts at nation-building), were not only important for the 'state-nations' of the West, but also for the non-dominant ethnic groups of Central and Eastern Europe. The legacy of the past embodied three significant resources that might facilitate the emergence of a national movement. The first of these were 'the relics of an earlier political autonomy'. The properties or privileges granted under the old regime often led to tensions between the estates and the 'new' absolutism, which in turn provided triggers for later national movements. Hroch points to the resistance of Hungarian,

Bohemian and Croatian estates to Josephine centralism to illustrate his argument. A second resource was 'the memory of former independence or statehood'. This could also play a stimulating role as the cases of Czech, Lithuanian, Bulgarian and Catalan movements demonstrate. Finally, the existence of 'a medieval written language' was crucial as this could make the development of a modern literary language easier. Hroch notes that the absence of this resource was much exaggerated in the nineteenth century, leading to a distinction between 'historical' and 'unhistorical' peoples. In fact, its salience was limited to the tempo at which the historical consciousness of the nation developed (1993: 8–9; 1995: 69).

Whatever the legacy of the past, the modern nation-building process always started with the collection of information about the history, language and customs of the non-dominant ethnic group. The ethnic archeologists of Phase A excavated the group's past and paved the way for the subsequent formation of a national identity. But, Hroch argues, their efforts cannot be called an organized political or social movement since they articulated no national demands as yet. The transformation of their intellectual activity into a movement seeking cultural and political changes was a product of Phase B. Hroch distinguishes three developments that precipitated this transformation:

1. a social and/or political crisis of the old order, accompanied by new tensions and horizons;
2. the emergence of discontent among significant elements of the population;
3. loss of faith in traditional moral systems, above all a decline in religious legitimacy, even if this only affected small numbers of intellectuals (1993: 10).

On the other hand, the initiation of national agitation (Phase B) by a group of activists did not guarantee the emergence of a mass movement. Mass support and the successful attainment of the ultimate goal, that is the forging of a modern nation, depended in turn on four conditions:

1. a crisis of legitimacy, linked to social, moral and cultural strains;

2. a basic volume of vertical social mobility (some educated people must come from the non-dominant ethnic group);
3. a fairly high level of social communication, including literacy, schooling and market relations;
4. nationally relevant conflicts of interest (*ibid.*: 12).

Hroch takes the second and the third conditions from Deutsch. He accepts that a high level of social mobility and communication facilitates the emergence of a national movement. However, his endorsement is not unqualified. He notes that these conditions do not work in at least two cases. First, he points to the case of the district of Polesie in interwar Poland where there was minimal social mobility, very weak contacts with the market and scant literacy. The same pattern prevailed in Eastern Lithuania, West Prussia, Lower Lusatia and various Balkan regions. In all these cases, the response to national agitation was quite ardent. On the other hand, in Wales, Belgium, Brittany and Schleswig, high levels of social mobility and communication were not sufficient to generate mass support for the respective national movements (1993: 11).

Drawing on these observations, Hroch argues that there must be another factor that helped the transition to Phase C. This is what he terms 'a nationally relevant conflict of interest', that is 'a social tension or collision that could be mapped onto linguistic (and sometimes also religious) divisions'. According to Hroch, the best example of such a conflict in the nineteenth century was the tension between new university graduates coming from a non-dominant ethnic group and a closed elite from the ruling nation that kept a hereditary grip on leading positions in state and society. There were also clashes between peasants from the non-dominant group and landlords from the dominant one, between craftsmen from the former and large traders from the latter. Hroch stresses that these conflicts of interest cannot be reduced to class conflicts since the national movements always recruited supporters from several classes (*ibid.*: 11–12).

Finally, Hroch asks the following question: 'why were social conflicts of this kind articulated in national terms more successfully in some parts of Europe than others' (*ibid.*: 12)? He claims that national agitation started earlier and made more progress in areas where the non-dominant ethnic groups lived under absolutist oppression. In such areas, the leaders of these groups – and the group as a whole – hardly had any political education and no political experience at all. Moreover, there was little room for alternative, more developed, forms of political discourse. Thus, it was easier to articulate hostilities in national categories, as was the case in Bohemia and Estonia. According to Hroch, this was precisely why these regions were different from Western Europe. The higher levels of political culture and experience in the West allowed the nationally relevant conflicts of interest to be articulated in political terms. This phenomenon was observed in the Flemish, Scottish and Welsh cases where the national programmes of the activists found it hard to win a mass following and in some cases never achieved a transition to Phase C. Hroch continues: 'The lesson is that it is not enough to consider only the formal level of social communication reached in a given society – one must also look at the complex of contents mediated through it' (*ibid.*). Phase C can be attained in a relatively short time if the goals articulated by agitators correspond to the immediate needs and aspirations of the majority of the non-dominant ethnic group. Let me conclude this brief review by a general observation from Hroch about the contemporary ethnic revival in Central and Eastern Europe:

> in a social situation where the old regime was collapsing, where old relations were in flux and general insecurity was growing, the members of the 'non-dominant ethnic group' would see the community of language and culture as the ultimate certainty, the unambiguously demonstrable value. Today, as the system or planned economy and social security breaks down, once again – the situation is analogous – language acts as a substitute for factors of integration in a disintegrating society. When society fails, the nation appears as the ultimate guarantee. (Cited in Hobsbawm 1996: 261)

Hroch's approach has been criticized on two grounds, namely for reifying nations and for downplaying the importance of political factors.

Hroch Reifies Nations

This criticism comes from Gellner who describes Hroch's approach as 'an interesting attempt to save . . . the nationalist vision of itself' by confirming that nations do really exist and express themselves through nationalist striving (1995a: 182). What lies behind this criticism is Hroch's distinction between established 'state-nations' and the 'non-dominant ethnic groups'. As we have seen above, Hroch argues that there were eight fully-fledged state-nations in Western Europe in the nineteenth century, which were the products of a long process of development that started in the Middle Ages. This argument led some scholars to suggest that Hroch's approach was a mixture of primordialism and modernism. Hence, for Hall, 'Hroch stands closer to Anthony Smith [the leading figure of ethno-symbolism] in insisting that nationalism would be ineffective were its appeal not directed at a pre-existing community' (1998: 6). Hroch, however, rejects such an interpretation, noting that he used the term 'revival' in a metaphorical sense – without implying that nations were eternal categories (1998: 94). Gellner's objections, Hroch comments, are based partly on misunderstanding and partly on an inadequate interpretation of the terms and concepts he used in his model (*ibid.*: 106, note 30). For him, the basic difference of opinion lies elsewhere:

> I cannot accept the view that nations are a mere 'myth', nor do I accept Gellner's global understanding of nationalism as an all-purpose explanation including categories of which the nation is a mere derivative. The relation between the nation and national consciousness (or national identity, or 'nationalism') is not one of unilateral derivation but one of mutual and complementary correlation, and the discussion about which of them is 'primary' can, at least for the present, be left to the philosophers and ideologues. (*Ibid.*: 104)

Hroch Downplays the Importance of Political Factors

Hroch's model was also criticized for ignoring the political determinants of nationalism (Hall 1993: 25). Hroch tries to redress the balance in his later work by focusing more on the political dimension. In a recent article on national self-determination, for example, he examines how the structure of national programmes was shaped by the political setting under which they operated and when political demands entered these national programmes

(1995). He basically argues that 'the strength and timing of the call for self-determination did not depend upon the intensity of political oppression and had no correlation with the level of linguistic and cultural demands'. Self-determination became more successful in movements 'which were based on a complete social structure of their non-dominant ethnic group and which could use some institutions or traditions of their statehood from the past' (*ibid.*: 79).

Further Reading

A stimulating (and highly critical) discussion of most theories reviewed in this chapter can be found in a recent book by Smith (1998). Smith's stated aim in this book is to provide an internal critique of what remains the dominant orthodoxy in the field, namely modernism. His unstated aim, however, is to promote his own 'ethnosymbolism'.

Where neo-Marxist theories are concerned, Nairn (1981) [1977] and Hechter (1975, 1985) are required reading. For a critical overview of Nairn's theory of 'uneven development' see James (1996), chapter 5. For other useful critiques of theories of economic transformation see Orridge (1981a, 1981b) and Brand (1985).

The most elaborate statement of Breuilly's approach is found in his *Nationalism and the State* (1993a) [1982]. For a concise summary see Breuilly (1996) [1994]. For an instrumentalist approach to ethnicity and nationalism see Brass (1991); for the theme of invention see Hobsbawm and Ranger (1983). Political theories of nationalism have been severely criticized by primordialist and ethno-symbolist writers. For an example of this critique, see Hastings (1997).

The earlier version of Gellner's theory appeared as chapter 7 of his *Thought and Change* (1964). Later, he expanded his theory to book length as *Nations and Nationalism* (1983). For a shorter and revised version of his theory see Gellner (1996a). On Gellner's theory, see also the books by Hall and Jarvie (1996b) and Hall (1998). The former is a general evaluation of the social philosophy of Gellner and contains articles which critically discuss his arguments on nationalism (see part II). The latter, on the other hand, is devoted solely to Gellner's theory of nationalism, and thus assesses every aspect of that theory.

For Anderson's theory see his *Imagined Communities* (1991) [1983]. For a critique of Anderson see the above-mentioned book by Smith (chapter 6) and an insightful essay by Chatterjee (1996) [1993]. An extended comparative review of Anderson and Gellner can be found in Breuilly (1985).

On Hroch's celebrated phase model see his *Social Preconditions of National Revival in Europe* (1985). For a concise statement of his theory see Hroch (1993). Hroch's work has been criticized most vigorously by Gellner (1995a). His reply to these criticisms can be found in Hroch (1998).

5

Ethno-symbolism

That is what the war is doing to us, reducing us to one dimension: the Nation. The trouble with this nationhood, however, is that whereas before, I was defined by my education, my job, my ideas, my character – and, yes, my nationality too – now I feel stripped of all that. I am nobody because I am not a person any more. I am one of 4.5 million Croats . . . I am not in a position to choose any longer . . . Something people cherished as part of their cultural identity has become their political identity and turned into something like an ill-fitting shirt. You may feel the sleeves are too short, the collar too tight. But there is no escape; there is nothing else to wear. One doesn't have to succumb voluntarily to this ideology of the nation – one is sucked into it. So right now, in the new state of Croatia, no one is allowed not to be a Croat.

Slavenka Drakulic, *The Balkan Express:*
Fragments from the Other Side of War

What is Ethno-symbolism?

Modernist arguments have been challenged in recent years by a number of scholars who focused on the role of pre-existing ethnic ties and sentiments in the formation of modern nations. In their determination to reveal the 'invented' or 'constructed' nature of nationalism, these scholars argued, modernists systematically overlooked the persistence of earlier myths, symbols, values and memories in many parts of the world and their continuing significance for large numbers of people (Smith 1996c: 361). We have already discussed the ethno-symbolist critique of modernism in the

167

preceding chapter. In this chapter, I will abstain from repeating these criticisms and concentrate instead on their own account of the rise of nations and nationalisms.

The term 'ethno-symbolist' seems to be a good starting point. Broadly speaking, this term is used to denote scholars who aim to uncover the symbolic legacy of pre-modern ethnic identities for today's nations (Smith 1998: 224). Uneasy with both poles of the debate, that is, primordialism/perennialism and modernism, ethno-symbolists like John Armstrong, Anthony D. Smith and John Hutchinson proposed a third position, a compromise or a kind of 'midway' between these two approaches. However, the term has not been appropriated by the writers in question until recently. For example Armstrong, considered by many as the pioneer of this approach, never mentions the term in his studies. For Smith, Armstrong is a 'perennialist', while for Hutchinson, both Smith and Armstrong are 'ethnicists' (Smith 1984; Hutchinson 1994: 7).

The term mostly appears in the writings of researchers who sympathize with such views. Hence, in an article on the theories of nationalism, Conversi defines 'ethno-symbolism' as an approach which rejects the axiom that nations may be *ipso facto* invented, claiming that they rely on a pre-existing texture of myths, memories, values and symbols and which, by so doing, tries to transcend the polarization between primordialism and instrumentalism (1995: 73–4). The modernists, on the other hand, ignore the term altogether and regard ethno-symbolism as a less radical version of 'primordialism' (for example Breuilly 1996: 150). This confusion came to an end recently, when Smith explicitly acknowledged – and defined – the term (1996c, 1998).

Ethno-symbolists form a more homogeneous category than both the primordialists and the modernists. Guided by a common reverence for the past, they lay stress on similar processes in their explanations of national phenomena. According to them, the formation of nations should be examined in *la longue durée*, that is, a 'time dimension of many centuries' (Armstrong 1982: 4), for the emergence of today's nations cannot be understood properly without taking their ethnic forebears into account. In other words, the rise of nations needs to be contextualized within the larger phenomenon of ethnicity which shaped them (Hutchinson 1994:

7). The differences between modern nations and the collective cultural units of earlier eras are of degree rather than kind. This suggests that ethnic identities change more slowly than is generally assumed. Once formed, they tend to be exceptionally durable under 'normal' vicissitudes of history (such as migrations, invasions, intermarriages) and to persist over many generations, even centuries (Smith 1986: 16). In short, the modern era is no *tabula rasa*:

> On the contrary, it emerges out of the complex social and ethnic formations of earlier epochs, and the different kinds of *ethnie* [ethnic community], which modern forces transform, but never obliterate. The modern era in this respect resembles a palimpsest on which are recorded experiences and identities of different epochs and a variety of ethnic formations, the earlier influencing and being modified by the later, to produce the composite type of collective cultural unit which we call 'the nation'. (Smith 1995: 59–60)

Ethno-symbolists reject the stark 'continuism' of the perennialists and accord due weight to the transformations wrought by modernity. They also reject the claims of the modernists by arguing that a greater measure of continuity exists between 'traditional' and 'modern' or 'agrarian' and 'industrial' eras. Hence the need for a wider theory of ethnic formation that will bring out the differences and similarities between contemporary national units and premodern ethnic communities (Smith 1986: 13).

Smith contends that such an approach is more helpful than its alternatives in at least three ways. First, it helps to explain which populations are likely to start a nationalist movement under certain conditions and what the content of this movement would be. Second, this approach enables us to understand the important role of memories, values, myths and symbols. Nationalism, Smith argues, mostly involves the pursuit of symbolic goals such as education in a particular language, having a TV channel in one's own language or the protection of ancient sacred sites. Materialist and modernist theories of nationalism fail to illuminate these issues as they are unable to comprehend the emotive power of collective memories. Finally, the ethno-symbolist approach explains why and how nationalism is able to generate such a widespread popular

support. 'The intelligentsia may "invite the masses into history"
. . . But why do "the people" respond?' For the sake of material
benefits? According to Smith, the answer cannot be that simple.
Ethno-symbolist approaches try to shed light on this process
(1996c: 362).

In the following sub-sections, I will discuss the contributions of
two leading figures of ethno-symbolism, namely John Armstrong
and Anthony D. Smith. I will end the chapter by considering the
major criticisms levelled against ethno-symbolist arguments.

John Armstrong and 'Myth–symbol Complexes'

Professor Emeritus of Political Science at the University of
Wisconsin-Madison and former President of the American Association for the Advancement of Slavic Studies, John Armstrong is a
leading specialist in East European politics. He is the author of the
classic *Ukrainian Nationalism* (1963). However, his most important
work in the field – his *magnum opus* in the words of Hutchinson
and Smith (1994: 362) – is the pioneering *Nations before Nationalism* (1982). Probing into the process of ethnic identity formation
in pre-modern Islamic and Christian civilizations, this book has the
quality of being the first study to cast a shadow of doubt on modernist assumptions.

Armstrong's stated aim is to explore 'the emergence of the
intense group identification that today we term a "nation"' by
adopting what he calls an 'extended temporal perspective' that
reaches back to antiquity (1982: 3). Having examined ethnic
groups in the course of their long historical journey, he stops at
the 'threshold of nationalism', that is before the period when
nationalism becomes the dominant political doctrine (the eighteenth century). He justifies this by noting that he is more concerned with the persistence rather than the genesis of particular
patterns (*ibid.*: 4). This led many scholars – including Smith – to
call his approach 'perennialist', or even 'primordialist'. Nevertheless, it can be asserted that the arguments put forward in this study,
particularly Armstrong's overall perspective, have laid the groundwork for ethno-symbolism which established itself more firmly with
the work of Smith. It is worth noting that Armstrong is still
regarded as the 'founding father' of ethno-symbolism by a con-

siderable number of scholars. However, the author himself refrains from using a term to describe his viewpoint.

Armstrong softens this stance in his recent work. While standing firm on his belief that nations did exist before nationalism, he nevertheless agrees with Anderson and Hobsbawm that, like other human identities, national identity had been an invention. The only remaining disagreement, Armstrong contends, is 'over the antiquity of some inventions and the repertory of pre-existing group characteristics that inventors were able to draw upon' (1995: 36). On this point, he seems to concur with Greenfeld (1992) who has located the origins of nationalism in the English Civil War. Unfortunately, Armstrong does not provide an explanation for this change. This in turn made him the target of a great deal of criticism (see for example Rizman 1996: 339). Before discussing this, however, it is necessary to summarize Armstrong's main arguments as articulated in *Nations before Nationalism*.

For Armstrong, ethnic consciousness has a long history: it is possible to come across its traces in ancient civilizations, for example in Egypt and Mesopotamia. In this sense, contemporary nationalism is nothing but the final stage of a larger cycle of ethnic consciousness reaching back to the earliest forms of collective organization. The most important feature of this consciousness, according to Armstrong, is its persistence. Therefore, the formation of ethnic identities should be examined in a time dimension of many centuries, similar to the *longue durée* emphasized by the *Annales* school of French historiography. Only an extended temporal perspective can reveal the durability of ethnic attachments and the 'shifting significance of boundaries for human identity' (1982: 4).

This emphasis on boundaries suggests Armstrong's stance *vis-à-vis* ethnic identities. Adopting the social interaction model of the Norwegian anthropologist Fredrik Barth, he argues that 'groups tend to define themselves not by reference to their own characteristics but by exclusion, that is, by comparison to "strangers"' (*ibid.*: 5). It follows that there can be no fixed 'character' or 'essence' for the group; the boundaries of identities vary according to the perceptions of the individuals forming the group. Thus, it makes more sense to focus on the boundary mechanisms that distinguish a particular group from others instead of objective group characteristics. For Armstrong, Barth's attitudinal approach affords many advantages. First, it makes room for changes in the cultural and the biological content of the group as long as the boundary mechanisms are maintained. Secondly, it shows that ethnic groups are not necessarily based on the occupation of particular, exclusive territories. The key to understanding ethnic identification is the 'uncanny experience of confronting others' who remained mute in response to attempts at communication, whether oral or through symbolic gestures (*ibid.*). Inability to communicate initiates the process of 'differentiation' which in turn brings a recognition of ethnic belonging.

Such a conception of ethnic group, that is a group defined by exclusion, implies that there is no definitional way of distinguishing ethnicity from other types of collective identity. Ethnic ties will often overlap with religious or class loyalties. 'It is precisely this complex, shifting quality that has repelled many social scientists from analyzing ethnic identity over long periods of time' (*ibid.*: 6). Drawing on this observation, Armstrong declares that he is more concerned with the shifting interaction among class, ethnic and religious loyalties than with 'compartmentalizing definitions'. To do that, however, the focus of investigation must shift from internal group characteristics to symbolic boundary mechanisms that differentiate these groups, without overlooking the fact that the mechanisms in question exist in the minds of the subjects rather than as lines on a map or norms in a rule book (*ibid.*: 7).

I have already noted that Armstrong lays special emphasis on the durability and persistence of these symbolic boundary mechanisms. For him, '[m]yth, symbol, communication, and a cluster of associated attitudinal factors are usually more persistent than purely material factors' (*ibid.*: 9). What, then, are the factors that ensure this persistence? Armstrong tries to specify and analyse these factors in the rest of his book.

He begins with the most general factor, namely ways of life and the experiences associated with them. Two fundamentally different ways of life, the nomadic and the sedentary, are particularly important in this context, because the myths and symbols they embody – expressed, notably, in nostalgia – create two sorts of identities based on incompatible principles. Thus, the territorial principle and its peculiar nostalgia ultimately became the predominant form in Europe, while the genealogical or pseudo-genealogical principle has continued to prevail in most of the Middle East. The second factor, religion, reinforced this basic distinction. The two great universal religions, Islam and Christianity, gave birth to different civilizations and the myths/symbols associated with them shaped the formation of ethnic identities in their own specific ways. Armstrong's third factor is the city. The analysis of the effect of towns on ethnic identification requires, Armstrong argues, examination of a host of factors, ranging from the impact of town planning to the unifying or centrifugal effects of various legal codes, especially the Lübeck and Magdeburg law. Then he moves to the role of imperial polities. At this point, the central question is 'how could the intense consciousness of loyalty and identity established through face-to-face contact in the city-state be transferred to the larger agglomerations of cities and countryside known as empires' (*ibid.*: 13)? Here, Armstrong stresses the diverse effects of the Mesopotamian myth of the polity – what he calls '*mythomoteur*' – as a reflection of heavenly rule. He argues that this myth was used as a vehicle for incorporating city-state loyalties in a larger framework. For him, this might constitute the earliest example of 'myth transference for political purposes' (*ibid.*). Finally, Armstrong introduces the question of language and assesses its impact on identity-formation in the pre-nationalist era. Contrary to commonsense assumptions, Armstrong concludes, 'the significance of language for ethnic identity is highly contingent' in pre-modern eras (*ibid.*: 282). Its significance depended in the long run on political and religious forces and allegiances.

Armstrong's work, despite its almost exclusive focus on the medieval European and Middle Eastern civilizations, offers a much more comprehensive overview of the process of ethnic identification than other comparable studies in the field. In the words of Smith,

> No other work attempts to bring together such a variety of evidence – administrative, legal, military, architectural, religious, linguistic, social and mythological – from which to construct a set of patterns in the slow formation of national identity . . . By doing so, Armstrong makes a strong case for grounding the emergence of modern national identities on these patterns of ethnic persistence, and especially on the long-term influence of 'myth-symbol complexes'. (1998: 185)

It was Smith who explored these issues further and elaborated the framework of analysis developed by Armstrong.

Anthony D. Smith and 'the Ethnic Origins of Nations'

One of the few scholars to specialize in the study of ethnicity and nationalism, Anthony D. Smith is the leading exponent of ethno-symbolism in the field. In his numerous books and articles on the subject, Smith focused especially on the pre-modern roots of contemporary nations, departing from the prevailing modernist interpretations that spurn the past. His three-decades-long intellectual engagement with nationalism led some scholars to call him 'the main guide' in the field for readers of the English language (Hobsbawm 1990: 2). Smith's contribution to the study of nationalism is not confined to his writings; he also played an important part in establishing ASEN, an association concerned with advancing the study of ethnicity and nationalism, at the London School of Economics and Political Science where he still teaches nationalism. In a way, then, Smith is the last representative of a chain of scholars who contributed to what Gellner calls the 'LSE debate' (1995a: 61), continuing a tradition bequeathed to him by such distinguished scholars as Elie Kedourie, Kenneth Minogue and Ernest Gellner.

Yet, Smith differs from the generation that preceded him in one important respect. Most participants of the LSE debate, including Kedourie, Minogue and Gellner, were proponents of the modernist paradigm. Smith, on the other hand, bases his approach on a critique of modernism. His central thesis is that modern nations cannot be understood without taking pre-existing ethnic components into account, the lack of which is likely to create a serious impediment to 'nation-building' (1986: 17). Smith concedes that there are a variety of cases where there was little in the way of a rich ethnic heritage. But, he continues, such extreme cases are rare. 'Usually, there has been some ethnic basis for the construction of modern nations, be it only some dim memories and elements of culture and alleged ancestry, which it is hoped to revive' (*ibid.*). It follows that the rise of contemporary nations should be studied in the context of their ethnic background. This means

grounding our understanding of modern nationalism on an historical base involving considerable time-spans, to see how far its
themes and forms were pre-figured in earlier periods and how
far a connection with earlier ethnic ties and sentiments can be
established. (*Ibid.*: 13)

According to Smith, if we are to move beyond the sweeping generalizations of both modernism and primordialism, we need to
formulate clear working definitions of key terms like nation,
nation-state and nationalism, thereby breaking out of an impasse
which bedevils progress in the field (1994). He begins by proposing the following definition of the nation, derived to a large extent
from the images and assumptions held by most or all nationalists:
a nation is 'a named human population sharing an historic territory, common myths and historical memories, a mass, public
culture, a common economy and common legal rights and duties
for all members' (1991a: 14). Smith holds that such a definition
reveals the complex and abstract nature of national identity which
is fundamentally multi-dimensional.

On the other hand, the origins of nations are as complex as its
nature. We might begin to look for a general explanation by asking
the following questions:

1. *Who* is the nation? What are the ethnic bases and models of
    modern nations? Why did these particular nations emerge?
2. *Why* and *how* does the nation emerge? That is, what are the
    general causes and mechanisms that set in motion the process
    of nation-formation from varying ethnic ties and memories?
3. *When* and *where* did the nation arise? (1991a: 19).

For Smith, the answer to the first question should be sought in
earlier ethnic communities (he prefers to use the French term
ethnie) since pre-modern identities and legacies form the bedrock
of many contemporary nations. He posits six main attributes for
such communities: a collective proper name, a myth of common
ancestry, shared historical memories, one or more differentiating
elements of a common culture, an association with a specific
homeland, a sense of solidarity for significant sectors of the
population (*ibid.*: 21). As this list reveals, most of these attributes

have a cultural and historical content as well as a strong subjective component. This suggests, contrary to the rhetoric of nationalist ideologies, that the *ethnie* is anything but primordial. According to Smith, as the subjective significance of each of these attributes waxes and wanes for the members of a community, so does their cohesion and self-awareness (*ibid.*: 23).

If the *ethnie* is not a primordial entity, then how does it come into being? Smith identifies two main patterns of *ethnie*-formation: coalescence and division. By coalescence he means the coming together of separate units, which in turn can be broken down into processes of amalgamation of separate units such as city-states and of absorption of one unit by another as in the assimilation of regions. By division he means subdivision through fission as with sectarian schism or through 'proliferation' (a term he borrows from Horowitz), when a part of the ethnic community leaves it to form a new unit as in the case of Bangladesh (*ibid.*: 23–4).

Smith notes that *ethnies*, once formed, tend to be exceptionally durable (1986: 16). However, this should not lead us to the conclusion that they travel across history without undergoing any changes in their demographic composition and/or cultural contents. In other words, we should try to eschew the polar extremes of the primordialist–instrumentalist debate when assessing the recurrence of ethnic ties and communities. Smith admits that there are certain events that generate profound changes in the cultural contents of ethnic identities. Among these, he singles out war and conquest, exile and enslavement, the influx of immigrants and religious conversion (1991a: 26). Nevertheless, what really matters is how far these changes reflect on and disrupt the sense of cultural continuity that binds successive generations together. For Smith, even the most radical changes cannot destroy this sense of continuity and common ethnicity. This is partly due to the existence of a number of external forces that help to crystallize ethnic identities and ensure their persistence over long periods. Of these, state-making, military mobilization and organized religion are the most crucial.

In the light of these observations, Smith sets out to specify the main mechanisms of ethnic self-renewal. The first such mechanism is 'religious reform'. The history of the Jews is replete with many instances of this. Conversely, groups who fell prey to religious conservatism tried to compensate for the failure to introduce reforms by turning to other forms of self-renewal. This was the dilemma faced by the Greeks at the beginning of the nineteenth century. When the Orthodox hierarchy failed to respond to popular aspirations, the Greek middle classes turned to secular ideological discourses to realize their goals. The second mechanism is 'cultural borrowing', in the sense of controlled contact and selective cultural exchange between different communities. Here again, examples can be found from Jewish history. The lively encounter between Jewish and Greek cultures, Smith holds, enriched the whole field of Jewish culture and identity. The third mechanism is 'popular participation'. The popular movements for greater participation in the political system saved many *ethnies* from withering away by generating a missionary zeal among the participants of these movements. The final mechanism of ethnic self-renewal identified by Smith is 'myths of ethnic election'. According to Smith, *ethnies* that lack such myths tended to be absorbed by others after losing their independence (*ibid.*: 35–6).

Together, these four mechanisms ensure the survival of certain ethnic communities across the centuries despite changes in their demographic composition and cultural contents. These mechanisms also lead to the gradual formation of what Smith terms 'ethnic cores'. These 'cohesive and self-consciously distinctive *ethnies*' form the basis of states and kingdoms in later periods. Thus, locating the ethnic cores helps us a great deal to answer the question 'who is the nation?' Smith observes that most latter-day nations are constructed around a dominant *ethnie*, which annexed or attracted other ethnic communities into the state it founded and to which it gave a name and a cultural character (*ibid.*: 38–9).

However, this observation is not sufficient to justify our quest for the origins of nations in the pre-modern era since there are many cases of nations formed without immediate ethnic antecedents. In other words, the relationship between modern nations and prior ethnic cores is problematic. At this point, Smith lists three more reasons to support his case. To begin with, the first nations were formed on the basis of ethnic cores. Being powerful and culturally influential, these nations provided models for subsequent cases of nation-formation. The second reason is that this model sat easily on the pre-modern 'demotic' kind of community (which will be explained below). In the words of Smith, 'the ethnic model was sociologically fertile'. Finally, even when there were no ethnic antecedents, the need to fabricate a coherent mythology and symbolism became everywhere paramount to ensure national survival and unity (*ibid.*: 40–1).

The existence of pre-modern ethnic ties helps us to determine which units of population are likely to become nations, but it does not tell us why and how this transformation comes about. To answer the second general question raised above, that is, 'why and how does the nation emerge?', we need to specify the main patterns of 'identity-formation' and the factors that triggered their development. Smith begins by identifying two types of ethnic community, the 'lateral' (aristocratic) and the 'vertical' (demotic), noting that these two types gave birth to different patterns of nation-formation.

'Lateral' *ethnies* were generally composed of aristocrats and higher clergy, though in some cases they might also include bureaucrats, high military officials and richer merchants. Smith explains why he chose the term 'lateral' by pointing out that these *ethnies* were at once socially confined to the upper strata and geographically spread out to form close links with the upper echelons of neighbouring lateral *ethnies*. As a result, their borders were 'ragged', but they lacked social depth, 'and [their] often marked sense of common ethnicity was bound up with [their] *esprit de corps* as a high status stratum and ruling class' (1991a: 53). On the contrary, 'vertical' *ethnies* were more compact and popular. Their culture was diffused to other sections of the population as well. Social cleavages were not underpinned by cultural differences; 'rather, a distinctive historical culture helped to unite different classes around a common heritage and traditions, especially when the latter were under threat from outside' (*ibid.*). As a result of this, the ethnic bond was more intense and exclusive, and the barriers to admission were much higher.

As noted above, these two types of ethnic communities followed different trajectories in the process of becoming a nation. Smith calls the first, lateral, route 'bureaucratic incorporation'. The survival of aristocratic ethnic communities depended to a large extent on their capacity to incorporate other strata of the population within their cultural orbit. This was most successfully realized in Western Europe. In England, France, Spain and Sweden, the dominant *ethnie* was able to incorporate the middle classes and peripheral regions into the elite culture. According to Smith, the primary vehicle in this process was the newly emerging bureaucratic state. Through a series of 'revolutions' in the administrative, economic and cultural spheres, the state was able to diffuse the dominant culture down the social scale. The major constituents of the 'administrative revolution' were the extension of citizenship rights, conscription, taxation and the build-up of an infrastructure that linked distant parts of the realm. These developments were complemented by parallel 'revolutions' in economic and cultural spheres. Smith singles out two such processes as relevant to nation-formation, namely the movement to a market economy and the decline of ecclesiastical authority. The latter was particularly important in that it allowed the development of secular studies and of university learning. This, in turn, led to a 'boom' in popular modes of communication – novels, plays and journals. An important role was played in these processes by the intellectuals and professionals (*ibid.*: 59–60).

The second route of nation-formation, what Smith calls 'vernacular mobilization', set out from a vertical *ethnie*. The influence of the bureaucratic state was more indirect in this case mainly because vertical *ethnies* were usually subject communities. Here, the key mechanism of ethnic persistence was organized religion. It was through myths of chosenness, sacred texts and scripts, and the prestige of the clergy that the survival of communal traditions were ensured. But demotic communities had problems of their own, which surfaced at the initial stages of the process of nation-formation. To start with, ethnic culture usually overlapped with the wider circle of religious culture and loyalty, and there was no internal coercive agency to break the mould. Moreover, the members of the community simply assumed that they already constituted a nation, albeit one without a political roof. Under these circumstances, the primary task of the secular intelligentsia was to alter the basic relationship between ethnicity and religion. In other words, the community of the faithful had to be distinguished from the community of historic culture. Smith identifies three different orientations among the intellectuals confronted with this dilemma: a conscious, modernizing return to tradition ('traditionalism'); a messianic desire to assimilate to Western modernity ('assimilation' or 'modernism'); and a more defensive attempt to synthesize elements of the tradition with aspects of Western modernity, hence to revive a pristine community modelled on a former golden age ('reformist revivalism') (*ibid.*: 63–4).

The solution adopted by the intellectuals had profound implications for the shape, pace, scope and intensity of the process of nation-formation. But whatever the solution espoused, the main task of an ethnic intelligentsia was 'to mobilize a formerly passive community into forming a nation around the new vernacular historical culture it has rediscovered' (*ibid.*: 64). In each case, they had to provide 'new communal self-definitions and goals', construct 'maps and moralities out of a living ethnic past'. This could be done in two ways: by a return to 'nature' and its 'poetic spaces' which constitute the historic home of the people and the repository of their memories; and by a cult of golden ages. These two methods were frequently used by the 'educator-intellectuals' to promote a national revival.

It needs to be noted in passing that Smith identifies a third route of nation-formation in his later work, that of the immigrant nations which consist largely of the fragments of other *ethnies*, particularly those from overseas:

> In the United States, Canada and Australia, colonist-immigrants have pioneered a providentialist frontier nationalism; and once large waves of culturally different immigrants were admitted, this has encouraged a 'plural' conception of the nation, which accepts, and even celebrates, ethnic and cultural diversity within an overarching political, legal, and linguistic national identity. (1998: 194; see also 1995: chapter 4)

This brings us to the final question guiding Smith's explanatory framework, namely 'where and when did the nation arise'? 'It is at this point that nationalism enters the political arena'. Nationalism, Smith contends, does not help us to determine which units of population are eligible to become nations, nor why they do so, but it plays an important part in determining when and where nations will emerge (1991a: 99). The next step, then, is to consider the (political) impact of nationalism in a number of particular cases. But this cannot be done without clarifying the concept of nationalism itself.

Smith begins by noting that the term 'nationalism' has been used in five different ways:

1. the whole process of forming and maintaining nations;
2. a consciousness of belonging to the nation;
3. a language and symbolism of the 'nation';
4. an ideology (including a cultural doctrine of nations); and
5. a social and a political movement to achieve the goals of the nation and realize the national will (1991a: 72).

Smith stresses the fourth and the fifth meanings in his own definition. Hence, nationalism is 'an ideological movement for attaining and maintaining autonomy, unity and identity on behalf of a population deemed by some of its members to constitute an actual or potential "nation"' (*ibid.*: 73). The key terms in this definition are autonomy, unity and identity. Autonomy refers to the idea of self-determination and the collective effort to realize the true, 'authentic', national will. Unity denotes the unification of the national territory and the gathering together of all nationals within the homeland. It also signifies the brotherhood of all nationals in the nation. Finally, identity means 'sameness', that is, that the members of a particular group are alike in those respects in which they differ from non-members, but it also implies the rediscovery of the 'collective self' (or the 'national genius') (*ibid.*: 74–7).

On the other hand, the 'core doctrine' of nationalism consists of four central propositions:

1. The world is divided into nations, each with its own peculiar character, history and destiny.
2. The nation is the source of all political and social power, and loyalty to the nation has priority over all other allegiances.
3. Human beings must identify with a nation if they want to be free and realize themselves.
4. Nations must be free and secure if peace is to prevail in the world (*ibid.*: 74).

Smith then moves on to the types of nationalism. Drawing on Kohn's philosophical distinction between a more rational and a more organic version of nationalist ideology, he identifies two kinds of nationalism: 'territorial' and 'ethnic' nationalisms (based on 'Western', civic-territorial, and 'Eastern', ethnic-genealogical models of the nation respectively). On this basis, he constructs a provisional typology of nationalisms, taking into account the overall situation in which the movements find themselves before and after independence:

1. Territorial nationalisms

   (a) *Pre-independence* movements based on a civic model of the nation will first seek to eject foreign rulers, then establish a new state-nation on the old colonial territory: these are 'anti-colonial' nationalisms.

   (b) *Post-independence* movements based on a civic model of the nation will try to bring together often disparate ethnic populations and integrate them into a new political community replacing the old colonial state: these are 'integration' nationalisms.

2. Ethnic nationalisms

   (a) *Pre-independence* movements based on an ethnic/genealogical model of the nation will seek to secede from a larger political unit and set up a new 'ethno-nation' in its place: these are 'secession' and 'diaspora' nationalisms.

   (b) *Post-independence* movements based on an ethnic/genealogical model of the nation will seek to expand by including ethnic kinsmen outside the present boundaries and establish a much larger 'ethno-nation' through the union of culturally and ethnically similar states: these are 'irredentist' and 'pan' nationalisms (1991a: 82–3).

Smith admits that the typology he develops is not an exhaustive one. It does not include some well-known examples of nationalism like Maurras' 'integral' nationalism. However, he insists that such a basic typology helps us to compare nationalisms within each category. Let me end this sub-section by a simple diagrammatic representation of the two main routes of nation-formation postulated by Smith:

   I. Lateral (aristocratic) ethnies → bureaucratic incorporation → civic-territorial nations → territorial nationalisms (from above; usually led by the elites).

II. Vertical (demotic) ethnies → vernacular mobilization → ethnic-genealogical nations → ethnic nationalisms (from below; usually led by the intelligentsia).

A Critique of Ethno-symbolism

A quick glance at the literature will reveal that the framework of analysis developed by Armstrong and Smith had its fair share of criticisms. There are six main objections to ethno-symbolist interpretations: ethno-symbolist writers are conceptually confused; they underestimate the differences between modern nations and earlier ethnic communities; it is not possible to speak of nations and nationalisms in pre-modern eras; ethno-symbolists underestimate the fluidity and malleability of ethnic identities; the relationship between modern national identities and the cultural material of the past is at best problematic; and their analysis of the process of ethnic consciousness-formation is misleading. Let us now consider each of these criticisms in more detail.

Ethno-symbolist Writers are Conceptually Confused

According to the proponents of this view, ethno-symbolist arguments constitute a typical illustration of the 'terminological chaos' that bedevils the study of nationalism. Connor, a stern critic of the conceptual licence in the field, notes that one of the most common manifestations of this confusion is the interutilization of the terms ethnicity, ethnic group and nation (1994: chapter 4). Smith and Armstrong are accused of falling into the same trap. O'Leary puts this very succinctly when he remarks that it is not too surprising to find nationalism in the 1500s if one grants the term such empirical range. According to him, 'most of those who discuss "nations" before "nationalism" are in fact establishing the existence of cultural precedents, and ethnic and other materials, which are subsequently shaped and re-shaped by nationalists in pursuit of nation-building' (1996: 90). Symmons-Symonolewicz makes a similar point, arguing that this confusion is partly caused by the lack of a generally acceptable definition of the nation. For him, a nation is not simply a large ethnic group, nor every large ethnic group is a nation. To become a nation, he maintains, an ethnic group must undergo many changes which transform its structure and mentality. Moreover, in the course of their journey through history, nations absorb many alien elements and a neverending flux of influences from other cultures and societies (1985a: 220). This observation brings us to the second criticism levelled against ethno-symbolism.

Ethno-symbolists Underestimate the Differences between Modern Nations and Earlier Ethnic Communities

Symmons-Symonolewicz claims that Smith eliminates the differences between ethnic and national phenomena by attributing to all ethnic groups a fully developed group consciousness and a deep sense of history (1985a: 219). However, most pre-modern groups were not aware of the cultural idiosyncrasies that differentiated them from others. Even when a consciousness of this kind existed, it was mostly confined to an intellectual elite as the stage was not yet set for the diffusion of ethnic sentiments to the wider public (1981: 152). Breuilly concurs with Symmons-Symonolewicz by arguing that it is impossible to know what meaning such sentiments had for the majority of the people (1996: 151; *cf.* Hobsbawm 1990: 11). The main reason for that is the near absence of data on the ideas, feelings and opinions of the masses.

Breuilly spots another difference between modern nations and earlier ethnic communities in the light of Smith's own arguments. This concerns pre-modern identities' lack of institutional basis. Smith argues that the three fundamental elements of modern nationality, that is legal, political and economic identity, are absent in pre-modern *ethnies*. According to Breuilly, however, 'these are the principal institutions in which national identity can achieve form'. This leads to a contradiction in Smith's arguments because, Breuilly maintains, identities established outside institutions, particularly those which can bind together people across wide social and geographical spaces, are necessarily fragmentary, discontinuous and elusive (1996: 150–1). He notes that there were only two institutions in pre-modern epochs that could provide an institutional basis to ethnic allegiances, namely the church and the dynasty. However, these institutions usually carried at their heart an alternative, ultimately conflicting sense of identity to that of the ethnic group.

Yet another difference is highlighted by Calhoun who notes that nationalism is not simply a claim of ethnic similarity, but a claim that certain similarities should count as *the* definition of political community. For this reason, nationalism needs rigid boundaries in a way pre-modern ethnicity does not: 'Nationalism demands internal homogeneity throughout a putative nation, rather than gradual continua of cultural variation or pockets of subcultural distinction' (1993: 229). Most distinctively, nationalists generally assert that national identities are more important than other personal or group identities (such as gender, family or ethnicity) and link individuals directly to the nation as a whole. In stark contrast to this, most ethnic identities flow from family membership, kinship or membership in other immediate groups (*ibid.*).

Smith rejects these criticisms in his recent book (1998). He concedes that his definitions of the nation and of the *ethnie* are closely aligned. But, he argues, it is precisely those features of nations that *ethnies* lack, that is a clearly delimited territory, a public culture, economic unity and legal rights and duties for everyone, that ultimately differentiate nations from earlier *ethnies* (1998: 196). Smith claims that those who raise the charge of 'retrospective nationalism' confuse a concern with *la longue durée* with perennialism. For him, ethno-symbolists clearly separate off a modern nationalism from pre-modern ethnic sentiments. What they try to do, he comments, is to trace in the historical record 'the often discontinuous formation of national identities back to their pre-existing cultural foundations and ethnic ties – which is a matter for empirical observation rather than *a priori* theorising'. Finally, Smith acknowledges the important role institutions play as carriers and preservers of collective identities. Nevertheless, he argues that Breuilly's understanding of such institutions is narrowly modernist. Significant numbers of people were included in schools, temples, monasteries and a host of legal and political institutions. More important was their inclusion 'in linguistic codes and in popular literature, in rituals and celebrations, in trade fairs and markets, and in ethnic territories or "homelands", not to mention the corvée and army service' (*ibid.*: 197). Obviously, not all these institutions reinforced a sense of common ethnicity, but many did. Smith concludes by asserting that there are many more cases of ethnic identities in pre-

modern periods than Breuilly allows and that some of them do
have 'political significance', such as the ethnic states of hellenistic
antiquity.

It is Not Possible to Speak of Nations and Nationalisms in Pre-modern Eras

Can we, then, claim that there were nations and nationalisms in
pre-modern eras? For scholars who subscribe to some form of
modernism, the answer to this question is negative. Eley and Suny
argue that Greeks in the classical period or Armenians in the fifth
century were not (and could not be) nations in the modern sense
of the term. Whatever their degree of cohesion and consciousness,
these ethnoreligious formations did not make claims to territory,
autonomy or independence, nor could they, since these political
claims were only authorized in the age of nationalism (1996a: 11).
Hall makes a similar point by noting that most of the conditions
that facilitated the growth of nations such as effective communication, cheap transport, increase in literacy rates, were the products of modernization processes (1993: 3).

Symmons-Symonolewicz claims that there were only three kinds
of collective sentiments in the Middle Ages: religious, political and
ethnic. The first contained loyalty to the church or to various
heretic movements; the second included feudal, city-state, dynastic, monarchical and imperial loyalties; and the third consisted of
loyalty to the neighbourhood or the region. Some of these loyalties faded away in time; others were replaced by new loyalties; still
others provided the 'bricks and mortar' out of which the cultural
unity of the future nation was built. However, it is not possible to
know with certitude which of these sentiments was dominant in a
particular situation (1981: 158–63).

What all these scholars share is a belief in the modernity of
nations and nationalisms. Nationalism involves a new form of
group identity or membership (Calhoun 1993: 229). In this sense,
earlier histories of nations should not be read simply as pre-
histories, but 'as varied historical developments whose trajectories
remained open' (Eley and Suny 1996a: 11). Smith tries to counter
these criticisms by conceding that nationalism 'both as an ideology and movement, is a wholly modern phenomenon', but insists

that 'the "modern nation" in practice incorporates several features of pre-modern *ethnie* and owes much to the general model of ethnicity which has survived in many areas until the dawn of the "modern era"' (1986: 18).

Ethno-symbolists Underestimate the Fluidity and Malleability of Ethnic Identities

Modernist scholars do not share the ethno-symbolist belief in the persistence of ethnic identities. According to Kedourie, for instance, ethnic identity is not an inert or stable object. He observes that it has proved to be highly plastic and fluid over the centuries, and has been subject to far-reaching changes and revolutions. Hence, 'the pagan Roman citizen of North Africa becomes, through his biological descendant, the Christian subject of a Christian emperor, then a member of the Muslim *u m m a*, and today perhaps a citizen of the People's Democratic Republic of Algeria or the Libyan *Jamahiriya*' (1994: 141).

Calhoun, on the other hand, argues that nationalism fundamentally transforms pre-existing ethnic identities and gives new significance to cultural inheritances (1997: 49). He supports this argument by noting that the social and cultural significance of ethnic traditions is dramatically changed when they are written down, and sometimes again when they are reproduced through visual media (*ibid.*: 50).

The Relationship between Modern National Identities and the Cultural Material of the Past is at best Problematic

Modernists also question the significance of the cultural material of the past. Breuilly admits that nationalist intellectuals and politicians seize upon myths and symbols of the past and use them to promote a particular national identity. But, he continues, 'it is very difficult to correlate their degree of success with the "objective" importance of such myths and symbols' (1996: 151). He points to the fact that in many cases nationalists invent myths. Moreover, they ignore those which cut across their purposes. Hence, for every national myth that has been used, there are many others that have disappeared in the mists of history. Moreover, myths and symbols of the past can be put to various, often conflicting, uses. Finally, there are also many nationalist movements that have succeeded without having a rich ethno-history to feed upon (*ibid.*).

Calhoun concurs with Breuilly and argues that noticing the continuity in ethnic traditions does not explain either which of these traditions last or which become the basis for nations or nationalist claims (1997: 49). Furthermore, traditions are not simply inherited, they have to be reproduced:

> stories have to be told over and again, parts of traditions have to be adapted to new circumstances to keep them meaningful, what seem like minor updatings may turn out to change meanings considerably, and the 'morals' to the stories – the lessons drawn from them – sometimes change even while the narratives stay the same . . . To say too simply that nationalism is grounded in ethnic traditions, thus, obscures from our view important differences in scale and mode of reproduction. (*Ibid.*: 50)

Ethno-symbolists' Analysis of the Process of Ethnic Consciousness-formation is Misleading

This criticism comes from Zubaida who focuses on Smith's definition of ethnic community (or *ethnie*), or, more precisely, the element of 'solidarity' which appears in that definition (1989). He argues that this 'sense of solidarity' is a problematic notion in the context of Western Europe. Solidarity was not generated spontaneously by common communal existence, nor by kinship, neighbourhood or religious networks. These pertained to much smaller communities. Solidarity, Zubaida contends, was generated by political and socioeconomic processes and remained for a long time conditional upon their operation. This has profound implications for Smith's argument because it reveals that

> 'common ethnicity' and solidarity are not the product of communal factors *given* to modernity, but are themselves the product of the socio-economic and political processes which, in the West, were institutionalized into state and civil society. (1989: 330)

Zubaida elaborates this argument by noting that every society offers to its members a number of possible identifications, of which the 'national', if and when it exists, is only one. Which identification becomes the basis of political solidarities at a given point in time, he argues, is contingent upon particular processes and events. Hence, one can speak of a French or English *ethnie* by the fifteenth century; but, 'the question is under what conditions these became the foci of political solidarity as against other possible identifications, for whom, and with what degree of success' (*ibid.*: 331). According to Zubaida, once national identification is achieved, it has to be maintained. The success and endurance of national identities depended on economic and political achievements such as intensification of the division of labour (which is very effective in breaking up the mould of 'primordial' solidarities), extension of state institutions (which will guarantee the security of citizens), prosperity (which gives citizens a stake in the national entity). The success of the old Western nation-states was based on a long process of centralization and institutionalization. Common ethnicity and cultural homogeneity were the products of these processes and not their determinants (*ibid.*).

Further Reading

As far as ethno-symbolism is concerned, the best introduction is again Smith (1998), chapter 8. The classic works in this category are Armstrong (1982) and Smith (1986). Other books of general importance include Llobera (1994) and Hastings (1997).

For a modernist critique of ethno-symbolism see Breuilly (1996) [1994]. Two other useful critiques are Calhoun (1997), chapter 2, and Zubaida (1989). Here, we should also mention the remarkable exchange between Gellner and Smith on the relative importance of ethnic pasts for modern nations: see Gellner (1996b) and Smith (1996b, 1996c).

6

New Approaches to Nationalism

Consuetudine oculorum assuescunt animi, neque admirantur, neque requirunt rationes earum semper vident.

[The habits of the eyes are conducive to mental habits: we are not surprised by the things we see all the time, nor do we look for their reasons.]

Cicero (quoted in Montaigne 1982: 194)

Why 'New'?

One of the arguments of this book is that we have entered a new stage in the theoretical debate on nationalism since the late 1980s. This rather assertive argument was introduced and briefly discussed in Chapter 2, where a historical overview of the debate was provided. It is indeed true that the claim looks like an overstatement of the present situation given that a series of independent studies are treated as a separate category, which is then differentiated qualitatively from the whole body of work hitherto produced. In that sense, the argument needs to be sustained with more concrete evidence. But before that, one point requires further clarification. This claim is not based on the presupposition that the interventions of the last decade offer completely new, or 'revolutionary', insights into nationalism, invalidating everything that had been previously said on the subject. On the contrary, most scholars of the period are generally sympathetic to modernist arguments (Smith 1998: 220, 224).

The distinctive characteristic of this constellation of studies is

190

their critical attitude *vis-à-vis* the mainstream scholarship on nationalism. Despite the fact that each highlights a different problem with earlier theories, they all question the fundamental assumptions of their predecessors, exploring the issues neglected (ignored?) by the latter. In short, the common denominator of these studies is their belief in the need to transcend the classical debate by proposing new ways of thinking about national phenomena. That explains the opening quotation from Cicero: scholars of the last decade question their visual habits and try to unearth what lies behind their commonsense assumptions. In a way, then, Cicero's words make up the slogan of the new era.

The rise of new theories was precipitated by a more general transformation in social sciences, which in turn reflected the developments in the real world, notably the rise of a women's movement, the writing of alternative histories which deny the homogeneity of national cultures and the changing nature of Western societies as a result of increasing migration. The growth of 'cultural studies' was particularly important in this context. The origins of this 'interdisciplinary incitement' go back to the late 1950s, when Richard Hoggart's *The Uses of Literacy* (1957) and Raymond Williams' seminal *Culture and Society* (1958) – among others – were published. The common aim of these scholars was to 'bring culture back' into social sciences (Eley and Suny 1996a: 20). In these studies, culture was not regarded as a coherent, harmonious whole, but as a deeply contested concept whose meaning is continually negotiated, revised and reinterpreted. In this sense, culture was not divorced from social fragmentation, class divisions, discrimination on the basis of gender and ethnicity, and relations of power: culture was more often not what people share, but what they choose to fight over (*ibid.*: 9).

The pioneering studies of Hoggart and Williams were soon followed by a rapidly growing body of work, focusing on questions of youth cultures and style, mass media, gender, race, popular memory and the writing of history. In Britain, it did not take long for cultural studies to acquire an institutional basis, first at the Birmingham Center for Contemporary Cultural Studies, then in various universities. In the United States, on the other hand, the impact of this emergent 'cross-disciplinary conversation' was more pronounced in areas like literary studies, film studies, anthropology and women's studies. The growing cultural studies literature made use of a wide range of theories, from Gramsci to psychoanalytic approaches, and incorporated the insights provided by alternative epistemological perspectives, notably feminism, postcolonialism and postmodernism (Eley and Suny 1996a; Eley 1996). How was the study of nationalism affected by all these developments? It is possible to identify two broad influences in this context. First, the gender-blind, Eurocentric character of the mainstream literature was criticized; greater emphasis was put on internal (within nations) and external (among nations) hierarchies of power. Second, the interaction of the studies of nationalism with such developing fields as migration, race, multiculturalism, diasporas and the like increased. In other words, there was a renewed emphasis on the interdisciplinary nature of nationalism as a subject of investigation (*cf.* Smith 1998: xiii). Let me now elaborate each of these influences.

The common feature of the theories and approaches I have reviewed in previous chapters is their involvement in the reproduction of the dominant discourses. None of these theories took account of the experiences of the 'subordinated', for example the former European colonies and their postcolonial successors, or women, ethnic minorities and the oppressed classes. Even the Marxist and neo-Marxist scholars, who based their theories on the experiences of nations occupying a dependent (or peripheral) position within the world political economy, fell prey to Eurocentrism, concentrating on the experiences of countries like Scotland and Ireland, and ignoring the disillusionments of the dozens of former colonies in Asia and Africa. Taking this 'theoretical blindness' as their starting point, a number of scholars tried to formulate frameworks of analysis that stress the experiences of the subordinated. Among these, approaches emphasizing the differential participation of women into nationalist projects, the experiences of postcolonial societies and the everyday dimension of nationalism, as well as postmodernist analyses were the most important.

As McClintock rightly observes, 'theories of nationalism have tended to ignore gender as a category constitutive of nationalism itself' (cited in Eley and Suny 1996b: 259). This important gap was filled by scholars like Nira Yuval-Davis, Floya Anthias, Sylvia Walby, Deniz Kandiyoti and Cynthia Enloe, among others, who explored the gendered character of membership in the nation. Actually, women were – and are – never absent from the nationalist discourse: they figure as 'conquerors' mistresses, wartime rape victims, military prostitutes, cinematic soldier-heroes, pin-up models on patriotic calendars' and of course, as workers, wives, girlfriends and daughters waiting dutifully at home (Enloe 1993, cited in Eley and Suny 1996a: 27). The nation is invariably imagined as a big family and the homeland as a 'vulnerable' woman needing protection. Rape becomes a weapon in war and sexual assault on women is often interpreted as a direct assault on the identity of the entire community (McCrone 1998: 125; Enloe 1995). As a result,

> [a]nxieties about the health of the nation, or its demographic future and productive efficiencies, or the stabilities of the social fabric, commonly translate into a politics directed to and against women, whether through systems of mother-and-child welfare, through rhetorics of family values, or by policy offensives around reproductive health, the regulation of sexuality, or the direct control of women's bodies. (Eley and Suny 1996a: 26)

Yet, despite their centrality to nationalist discourse, women are excluded from the public sphere and confined to their homes. Hence, to analyse the marginalization (and the silencing) of women by the national body politic, we have to look in the family and household, in the unspectacular details of everyday life. That was precisely what feminist scholars were trying to do. They explored how women participate in various national projects, which roles they play – or are forced to play – within them, revealing the political/ideological constellations which underlie these roles and their allocation. In a way, then, they revolted against women's confinement to a secondary, always subordinate, position.

Another fundamental characteristic of mainstream writings on nationalism is their Eurocentric, or to use Yuval-Davis' term 'Westocentric' (1997: 3), outlook. The origins of this attitude go back to the Enlightenment tradition from which many of the concepts and ideas we associate today with democracy first descended. Imperialism and colonialism were the main ingredients of this tradition from the beginning. In many respects, the advance of democracy in Europe, for example the spread of universal citizenship, was contingent on the exploitation of people elsewhere. This complex dialectical relationship between Europe and its 'others' was replicated inside Europe itself, between metropolitan and peripheral cultures, city and countryside, dominant and subordinate nationalities, East and West (Eley and Suny 1996a: 28).

The exploration of these relationships and the deconstruction of nationalism's negative codings, that is 'the ways in which even the nation's most generous and inclusively democratic imaginings entail processes of protective and exclusionary positioning against others', was one of the most important theoretical gains of the last decade (*ibid.*). Not surprisingly, this process of 're-reading' was initiated by scholars from outside Europe, notably by the Subaltern Studies Group coming out of Indian Marxism. Scholars like Partha Chatterjee and Ranajit Guha tried to reinterpret the history of South Asia from the vantage point of the subordinated. Their aim was to reveal how the hegemonic discourses of the West served to suppress the voices of the 'subalterns'. The most important Western instrument in this process was 'knowledge': thus, the various ways in which knowledge was used to dominate the world had to be unveiled. According to Chatterjee, Western ideas of rationality relegated non-Western cultures into 'unscientific traditionalism'. The relativist approach, on the other hand, which holds that every culture is unique, was based on an essentialist conception of culture that precludes understanding from outside. Both views, Chatterjee maintains, were reflections of power relations (Chatterjee 1986, 1990; see also Eley and Suny 1996a: 29). For him, anti/postcolonial nationalism, although a 'derivative discourse', was never totally dominated by Western models of nationhood. It could not imitate the West in every aspect of life, for then the very distinction between the West and the East would vanish and 'the self-identity of national culture would itself be threatened' (Chatterjee 1990: 237).

As explained in Chapter 4 (when considering Chatterjee's critique of Anderson), the nationalist resolution of this dilemma was to separate the domain of culture into two spheres, the material and the spiritual. 'What was necessary was to cultivate the material techniques of modern western civilization, while retaining and strengthening the distinctive spiritual essence of the national culture' (*ibid.*: 238). In short, the greatest contribution of scholars like Chatterjee and Guha was to offer a 'non-Westocentric' interpretation of anti/postcolonial nationalisms.

A third issue neglected by mainstream scholarship on nationalism concerns the familiar terrain of 'everyday life'. Seeking after macro-explanations, traditional approaches paid little attention to the micro-level, that is, the everyday manifestations of nationalism. Yet, as Billig (1995) contends, nationalism has to be reproduced daily if it is to persist (see also Essed 1991; van Dijk 1993, 1998). This process of reproduction is not consciously registered by the participants since everyday life is also the domain of the 'unconscious': in other words, 'everyday awareness is naive' (Blaschke 1980, cited in Eley and Suny 1996a: 22). In short, to understand the continuing hold of nationalism, we must probe into the process by which ordinary people continue to imagine themselves as an abstract community. As McClintock observes, 'national fetishes' play an important role in this process:

> More often than not, nationalism takes shape through the visible, ritual organization of fetish objects – flags, uniforms, airplane logos, maps, anthems, national flowers, national cuisines and architectures as well as through the organization of collective fetish spectacle – in team sports, military displays, mass rallies, the myriad forms of popular culture and so on. (1996: 274)

This continual reminding, taken for granted by most people, transforms national identity into a form of life, a way of seeing and interpreting the world, thereby securing the nation's existence (Yumul and Özkırımlı 1997).

The final stroke to the picture we have drawn so far comes from postmodernism. This is not the place to summarize all the debates around postmodernism or postmodernity, given that only a review of the definitions provided for these terms would require a separate volume. However, it is not possible to assess the impact of postmodernist approaches on the study of nationalism without first offering a working definition of the concept of postmodernity. Bauman's definition is quite helpful in this respect:

> Postmodernity is modernity coming of age: modernity looking at itself at a distance rather than from inside, making a full inventory of its gains and losses, psychoanalysing itself, discovering the intentions it never before spelled out, finding them mutually

cancelling and incongruous. Postmodernity is modernity coming to terms with its own impossibility: a self-monitoring modernity, one that consciously discards what it was once unconsciously doing. (1991: 272)

As with almost any definition, Bauman's formulation is not without its problems. It poses as many questions as it tries to answer: 'What is modernity?', 'Have we all gone through the modern era?' and so on. Nevertheless, it constitutes a good starting point in terms of considering the implications of postmodernism for the study of nationalism.

Broadly speaking, it is possible to distinguish two themes that recurrently appear in postmodernist analyses. The first of these is the production and reproduction of national identities through popular culture. This not only requires focusing on communication technologies and popular genres hitherto excluded from the academic agenda, but also 'deconstructing' the meanings and values promoted through these technologies – hence, unravelling the power relations that lie behind them. Accordingly, the visual technologies of film, photography, television and video are scrutinized; a wide range of popular cultural products from books and magazines to food, fashion and dress are dissected (Eley and Suny 1996a). In these studies, the texts are 're-read' and the meanings are 'reconstructed' because, the postmodernists contend, each text is a narrative and each narrative can be interpreted in myriads of different ways. The hegemonic discourses, or 'meta-narratives', are nothing but a sham; thus, they should be explicitly rejected.

In this context, a number of scholars problematized the notion of 'identity'. In the words of Stuart Hall,

[i]dentity is not as transparent or unproblematic as we think. Perhaps instead of thinking identity as an accomplished fact, which the new cultural practices then represent, we should think, instead, of identity as a 'production', which is never complete, always in process, and always constituted within, not outside, representation. (1990: 222)

In this perspective, identities are never fixed, essential or immutable. Rather, they are 'the unstable points of identification or suture, which are made within the discourses of history and culture. Not an essence, but a positioning' (*ibid.*: 226). History changes our conception of ourselves. Key to this change, argues Hall, is the concept of 'Other', because identity is also the relationship between us and the Other: 'only when there is an Other can you know who you are'. There is no identity 'without the dialogic relationship to the Other. The Other is not outside, but also inside the Self, the identity' (1996b: 345).

According to Hall, this 'de-centering' of identity is a consequence of the relativization of the Western world – 'of the discovery of other worlds, other peoples, other cultures, and other languages' (*ibid.*: 341). National identities are gradually eroded by the forces of globalization which increase the interdependence of the planet on the one hand and lead to the formation of strong local identities on the other (see also McCrone 1998: 34–5). In such a context, the idea of a 'unified' national identity – or a 'homogeneous' national culture – is no longer tenable.

Another theme explored by postmodernist scholars, notably Homi Bhabha, is the 'forms of contestation inside nationalism's dominant frame' (Eley and Suny 1996a: 29). Drawing on the writings of Derrida, Fanon, Foucault and Lacan, Bhabha emphasizes the role of the people on the national 'margins', that is ethnic minorities, foreign workers and immigrants, in the process of definition of national identities. According to Bhabha, 'hybrid' populations contest the dominant constructions of the nation by producing their own counter-narratives. These counter-narratives, he argues, 'disturb those ideological manoeuvres through which "imagined communities" are given essentialist identities' (1990a: 300). The resulting conflict among competing narratives, on the other hand, increases the porousness of national boundaries and intensifies the ambivalence of the nation as a cultural and political form (Bhabha 1990a; Rutherford 1990; see also Rattansi 1994).

This brings us to the second broad change generated by the developments in social sciences. This manifested itself in the form of a renewed emphasis on the interdisciplinary nature of the study of nationalism. Before elaborating this point, however, one qualification is in order. The term 'interdisciplinary' is usually taken to mean not being constrained by the boundaries of specific academic disciplines and adopting an eclectic approach in the study of a particular problem. In this sense, nationalism has always been an interdisciplinary subject. Scholars have made use of concepts and theories developed in a variety of disciplines, ranging from sociology and political science to international relations and psychology. However, the studies of the last decade differed from their predecessors in two respects. First, scholars no longer confined themselves to traditional disciplines and incorporated insights developed in such areas as women's studies, race relations theory, discourse analysis, postcolonial theories into their analyses. Second, special emphasis was laid on the multi-dimensional character of 'subjectivity' (Essed 1991; Anthias and Yuval-Davis 1989).

As I have briefly explained above, the studies in question challenged the orthodox conceptions which regarded individuals as coherent subjects with a unified sense of identity. They stressed the various dimensions of subjectivity, such as gender, race, ethnicity and class, noting that these dimensions are inextricably intertwined; hence, it makes no sense to treat them separately. What shapes an individual's preferences is an interaction of various dimensions that make up her/his subjectivity and not a particular dimension of that subjectivity. The experiences and reactions of a Black working class woman from an ethnic minority is different from that of a White middle class man from the dominant ethnic group. This point, which looks like a truism today, was largely overlooked by the participants of the classical debate. What the recent studies attempted to do was to bring these differences to the fore and draw our attention to the multi-dimensionality of the constructions of subjectivity. In short, the interaction between research on nationalism and that conducted in other, 'sister', areas increased in the last decade, which in turn made the study of nationalism more complicated, but also more rewarding.

So far I have tried to summarize the fundamental differences between the studies of the last decade and that of the earlier periods. This summary was intended to substantiate the claim that we have entered a new stage in the debate on nationalism since the late 1980s. The argument can be strengthened further by examining in detail a few studies that question orthodox theorizations about nations and nationalism. Thus, I will devote the following sections to Michael Billig's analysis of the daily reproduction of nationhood and Nira Yuval-Davis' survey of the relationship between gender and nationalist projects.

Reproduction of Nationhood: 'Banal Nationalism'

The reproduction of nations and nationalisms has generally been disregarded by mainstream writings on the subject. The issue was first taken up by scholars who attempted to provide a gendered understanding of nationalism. As we shall see in the next section, these scholars explored the contribution of women into several dimensions of nationalist projects, particularly their role in the biological, symbolic and ideological reproduction of nationalism (Jayawardena 1986; Yuval-Davis and Anthias 1989; Yuval-Davis 1997). Another important exception has been the French Marxist scholar Étienne Balibar who treated the nation as a social formation, in the sense of

a construction whose unity remains problematic, a configuration of antagonistic social classes that is not entirely autonomous, only becoming *relatively* specific in its opposition to others and via the power struggles, the conflicting interest groups and ideologies which are developed over the *longue durée* by this very antagonism. (1990: 334)

According to Balibar, the main problem posed by the existence of social formations was not that of their beginning or their end, but primarily that of their reproduction, that is, 'the conditions under which they can maintain this conflictual unity which creates their autonomy over long historical periods' (*ibid.*: 334–5). It is the British social psychologist Michael Billig who sets out to specify these conditions. Billig's influential *Banal Nationalism* (1995) can be considered as the first study that provides a systematic analysis of the reproduction of nationalism.

Billig's approach is based on a critique of orthodox theorizations that tend to associate nationalism with 'those who struggle to create new states or with extreme right-wing politics' (1995: 5). According to this view, nationalism is the property of 'others', the peripheral states which have yet to complete their nation-building processes, and not 'ours', the established 'nation-states' of the West. Nationalism is a temporary mood in the West, only manifesting itself under certain 'extraordinary' conditions, that is, in times of crises, suddenly disappearing once normal conditions are restored. In that sense, crises are like infections causing fever in a 'healthy body'. When the crisis abates, 'the temperature passes; the flags are rolled up; and, then, it is business as usual' (*ibid.*). Billig rejects this simplistic, even naive, picture. For him, the crises depend upon existing ideological foundations. They do not create nation-states as nation-states: '[i]n between times the United States of America, France, the United Kingdom and so on continue to exist. Daily, they are reproduced as nations and their citizenry as nationals'. However, 'this reminding is so familiar, so continual, that it is not consciously registered as reminding'. Billig introduces the term 'banal nationalism' to cover 'the ideological habits which enable the established nations of the West to be reproduced': 'The metonymic image of banal nationalism is not a flag which is being consciously waved with fervent passion: it is the flag hanging unnoticed on the public building' (*ibid.*: 6–8).

Such a conception casts doubt on standard interpretations which hold that nationalism becomes something surplus to everyday life once the nation-state is established, only to return when the orderly routines are broken down. According to Billig, nationalism does not disappear when the nation acquires a political roof: instead, it becomes absorbed into the environment of the established homeland (*ibid.*: 41). The symbols of nationhood (coins, bank notes, stamps) become a part of our daily lives. These small reminders turn the background space into 'national' space.

Billig maintains that it is not possible to explain all these routine habits or the popular reaction following the moments of crisis in terms of identity. National identity, he argues, is not a psychological accessory which people always carry with them, to be used whenever it is necessary. Like a mobile phone, this psychological equipment lies quiet for most of the time: '[t]hen the crisis occurs; the president calls; bells ring; the citizens answer; and the patriotic identity is connected' (*ibid.*: 7). According to Billig, this approach does not take us very far. For national identity to do its work, people must know what that identity is. In other words, they must have assumptions about what a nation is and, indeed, what patriotism is.

This information comes from different sources. For instance, national histories tell us the story of a people travelling across time – 'our' people, with 'our' ways of life. On the other hand, national community cannot be imagined without also imagining communities of foreigners which make 'our' culture unique: there can be no 'us' without a 'them' (*ibid.*: 78–9). It is at this stage that stereo-typed judgements come in. Stereotypes become means of distin-guishing 'them' from 'us': 'we' represent the standard, the normal, against which 'their' deviations appear notable. This unique com-munity of culture is also associated with a particular territory, a bounded geographical space which is 'our' homeland. Indeed, the whole world is composed of communities of culture like ours, each tied to a specific piece of land. 'If "our" nation is to be imagined in all its particularity, it must be imagined as a nation amongst other nations' (*ibid.*: 83). For Billig, this international conscious-ness is integral to the modern discourse of nationalism.

These observations raise another question: why do we, in estab-lished nations, not forget our national identity? For Billig, the short answer is that '"we" are constantly reminded that "we" live in nations; "our" identity is continually being flagged'. 'Routinely familiar habits of language' play an important role in this process of reminding. 'Small words, rather than grand memorable phrases' make our national identity unforgettable. To explore such matters, we should not only pay attention to words like 'people' (or 'society'), but also become 'linguistically microscopic' since the secret of banal nationalism lies in tiny words such as 'we', 'this' and 'here' (*ibid.*: 93–4). As might be expected, these words are most commonly used by politicians.

Politicians play an important part in the reproduction of nation-alism, but not because they are figures of great influence. On the contrary, many commentators argue that their weight in the key decision-making mechanisms is constantly declining – partly as a result of increasing globalization. 'Politicians are important because, in the electronic age, they are familiar figures'. Their faces appear regularly in the newspapers or on the television screens. In a way, they are the 'stars' of the modern age: their words daily reach millions (*ibid.*: 96). In such a context, what they say (and how they say it) is of utmost importance. The 'patriotic card' is played by almost all politicians. More importantly, however, politicians claim to speak for the nation. Evoking the whole nation as their audience, they rhetorically present themselves as repre-senting the national interest (*ibid.*: 106). By using a complex deixis of homeland, they invoke the national 'we' and place 'us' within 'our' homeland. When the homeland-making phrases are used regularly, '"we" are unmindfully reminded who "we" are and where "we" are. "We" are identified without even being mentioned'. Moreover, '[w]hat is "ours" is presented as if it were the objective world . . . The homeland is made both present and unnoticeable by being presented as *the* context' (*ibid.*: 109).

On the other hand, politicians are not the only actors contributing to the daily reproduction of nationhood. Their rhetorical forms and deixis are taken up by the newspapers. Like politicians, newspapers claim to stand in the eye of the nation. The opinion and editorial columns evoke a national 'we', including both readers and writers (as well as a universal audience). What unites the reader and the writer, what makes them 'we', is the national identity. The newspapers also contribute to the process of imagining a national 'we' by their internal organization and the structure of presentation of the news. 'Home' news is separated from 'foreign' news. And ' "[h]ome" indicates more than the contents of the particular page: it flags the home of the newspaper and of the assumed, addressed readers'. We, the readers, follow the directing signs and find our way around the familiar territory of the newspaper: 'As we do so, we are habitually at home in a textual structure, which uses the homeland's national boundaries, dividing the world into "homeland" and "foreign" ' (*ibid.*: 119).

One of the most original theses of Billig's study relates to social scientists' role in the reproduction of nationalism. According to Billig, scholars contribute to this process by:

- *Projecting nationalism* – these approaches define nationalism in a very restricted way, as an extreme/surplus phenomenon, thereby confining it to nationalist movements induced by irrational emotions. In this way, nationalism is projected on to 'others'; ' "ours" is overlooked, forgotten, even theoretically denied'.
- *Naturalizing nationalism* – some theorists reduce nationalism to a psychological need by arguing that contemporary loyalties to nation-states are instances of something general, or endemic to human condition. As such, ' "banal nationalism" not only ceases to be nationalism, but it ceases to be a problem for investigation' (*ibid.*: 16–17).

Billig notes that some scholars do both simultaneously. This leads to a theoretical (and rhetorical) distinction: 'our' nationalism is not presented as nationalism, something dangerously irrational, surplus and alien. A new label is found for it, 'patriotism', which is beneficial and necessary (*ibid.*: 55). Consequently, 'our patriotism' is presented as natural, therefore invisible, whereas 'nationalism' is seen as the property of 'others' (*ibid.*: 17).

If banal nationalism is so widespread, then, what should social scientists do? First and foremost, they should confess. Billig admits that he feels pleasure if a citizen from the homeland runs quicker or jumps higher than foreigners. Similarly, he confesses that he reads the 'home' news with greater interest. Generally speaking, we are all participants in the discourse of nationalism: 'it is present in the very words which we might try to use for analysis' (*ibid.*: 12). In that sense, it can be argued that all texts on nationalism – even the critical ones – contribute to its reproduction (see also Periwal 1995: 237). Calhoun sums this up succinctly: 'many of the categories and presumptions of this discourse are so deeply ingrained in our everyday language and our academic theories that it is virtually impossible to shed them, and we can only remind ourselves to take them into account' (1993: 214). We should at least do this because

... whatever else is forgotten in a world of information overload, we do not forget our homelands. ... If we are being routinely primed for the dangers of the future, then this is not a priming which tops up a reservoir of aggressive energy. It is a form of reading and watching, of understanding and of taking for granted. It is a form of life in which 'we' are constantly invited to relax, at home, within the homeland's borders. This form of life is the national identity, which is being renewed continually, with its dangerous potentials appearing so harmlessly homely. (Billig 1995: 127)

Gender and Nation

A key issue in the analysis of nations and nationalism has been the differential participation of various social groups in nationalist projects. It has been generally recognized that nationalist movements draw upon different constituencies, in uneven ways, and there has been a large body of work analysing various aspects of these movements, such as their class compositions, the levels of education of their participants and so on. However, this body of work has not engaged itself with the differential integration of women and men into national projects (Walby 1996: 235). As Yuval-Davis notes, most hegemonic theorizations about nations and nationalism, sometimes even those written by women (for example Greenfeld 1992), have ignored gender relations as irrelevant (1997: 1). Nationalism has been generally regarded as a male phenomenon, springing from masculinized memory, masculinized humiliation and masculinized hope (Enloe 1989: 44).

These assumptions have been increasingly questioned since the mid-1980s. McClintock, for example, argues that nationalism is constituted from the very beginning as a gendered discourse and cannot be understood without a theory of gender power (1996: 261). Our task, she continues, must be to formulate a feminist theory of nationalism, which might be strategically fourfold:

> (1) investigating the gendered formation of sanctioned male theories; (2) bringing into historical visibility women's active cultural and political participation in national formations; (3) bringing nationalist institutions into critical relation with other social structures and institutions; and (4) at the same time paying scrupulous attention to the structures of racial, ethnic and class power that continue to bedevil privileged forms of feminism. (*Ibid.*)

This was in a way what scholars like Kumari Jayawardena (1986), Cynthia Enloe (1989), Sylvia Walby (1996), Nira Yuval-Davis and Floya Anthias (1989; Yuval-Davis 1997) were attempting to do, namely to provide a gendered understanding of nations and nationalism. Among these, the work of Nira Yuval-Davis was particularly important. In an earlier intervention, Yuval-Davis and her co-editor Floya Anthias (1989) explored the various ways in which women affect and are affected by ethnic/national processes and how these relate to the state. Later, Yuval-Davis elaborated some of the theses developed in this book and expanded them to book length as *Gender and Nation* (1997).

The starting point of Anthias and Yuval-Davis, in the introduction to their seminal *Woman–Nation–State*, is the shortcomings of the feminist critique of the state. For them, the merit of feminists and socialist feminists was to reveal how the state constructs men and women differently. In this way, they were able to shed light on the ways in which the welfare state has constituted the 'state subject' in a gendered way, that is, as essentially male in its capacities and needs (Anthias and Yuval-Davis 1989: 6).

However, Anthias and Yuval-Davis contend, it is not enough to criticize the state's understanding of citizenship since this concept only relates to the way the state acts upon the individual and not the way in which the state forms its political project. Therefore, it cannot on its own explain the social forces that are dominant within the state. According to them, the notion of citizenship does not encapsulate adequately the relations of control and negotiation that take place in various areas of social life. What is required, then, is to identify the ways in which women participate in national and ethnic processes within civil society and to explore how these relate to the state. Before doing that, however, Anthias and Yuval-Davis stress that there is no unitary category of women which can be unproblematically conceived as the focus of ethnic, national and state policies: 'Women are divided along class, ethnic and life-cycle lines, and in most societies different strategies are directed at different groups of women' (*ibid.*: 7). In the light of these observations, Anthias and Yuval-Davis suggest five major ways in which women have tended to participate in ethnic and national processes:

(a) as biological reproducers of members of ethnic collectivities;
(b) as reproducers of the boundaries of ethnic/national groups;
(c) as participating centrally in the ideological reproduction of the collectivity and as transmitters of its culture;
(d) as signifiers of ethnic/national differences – as a focus and symbol in ideological discourses used in the construction, reproduction and transformation of ethnic/national categories; and
(e) as participants in national, economic, political and military struggles (*ibid.*).

As Biological Reproducers of Members of Ethnic Collectivities

Yuval-Davis notes that most discussions on women's reproductive rights have focused on the effects of the existence or absence of these rights on women as individuals. However, she argues, the pressures on women to have or not to have children often relate to them 'not as individuals, workers and/or wives, but as members of specific national collectivities': '[a]ccording to different national projects, under specific historical circumstances, some or all women of childbearing age groups would be called on, sometimes bribed, and sometimes even forced, to have more, or fewer, children' (1997: 22).

Yuval-Davis identifies three main discourses that tend to dominate nationalist policies of population control. The first is the 'people as power' discourse, in which the future of the nation is seen to depend on its continuous growth (*ibid.*: 29–31). Here, various policies are pursued to encourage women to have more children. In Israel, for example, there were calls for women to bear more children at times of slack immigration or national crisis. This encouragement was usually underpinned by religious discourses about the duty of women to produce more children. Politicians nurtured the fear of a 'demographic holocaust' by drawing attention to popular Palestinian sayings ('The Israelis beat us at the borders but we beat them in the bedrooms'), using it to increase the pressure on women. However, the state does not always rely on ideological mobilization and may adopt less radical measures such as the establishment of child benefit systems or the allocation of loans (maternal benefit schemes) for this purpose (Anthias and Yuval-Davis 1989: 8–9; Yuval-Davis 1989).

The second discourse identified by Yuval-Davis is the Eugenicist. The Eugenics were concerned not with the size of the nation, but with its 'quality' (1997: 31–2). This has given rise to various policies aimed at limiting the physical numbers of members of 'undesirable' groups. These policies may sometimes take the form of immigration controls; at other times, they may include more extreme measures such as the physical expulsion of particular groups or their actual extermination (for example Jews and Gypsies in Nazi Germany). Another strategy is to limit the number of people born in specific ethnic groups by controlling the reproductive capacity of women. Again various policies are pursued here, ranging from forced sterilization to the massive mobilization of birth control campaigns. A corollary of this strategy is the active encouragement of population growth of the 'right kind', that is of the dominant ethnic group (Anthias and Yuval-Davis 1989: 8–9).

Today, eugenistic policies are implemented most vigorously in Singapore, where the Prime Minister Lee Kuan Yew asked the highly educated women to produce more children – as part of their patriotic duty – while poor uneducated mothers were given a cash award of $ 10 000 if they agreed to be sterilized (Yuval-Davis 1997: 32). The final discourse identified by Yuval-Davis is the Malthusian. In stark contrast to the first discourse, the Malthusians see the reduction of the number of children as the way to prevent a future national disaster (1997: 32–5). This discourse is most visible in developing countries, where a number of policies aimed at reducing the overall rate of growth are adopted. 'Women are often the "captive" target population for such policies' (*ibid.*: 33). Yuval-Davis observes that the country which has gone furthest in this respect is China. Here, several measures were taken so that most families would not have more than one baby. Punishments for evading these measures ranged from unemployment for the parents to exclusion from education for the children. According to Yuval-Davis, the effect of Malthusian policies is highly gendered: '[w]here there is strong pressure to limit the number of children, and where male children are more highly valued for social and economic reasons, practices of abortions and infanticide are mainly directed towards baby girls' (*ibid.*: 34).

As Reproducers of the Boundaries of Ethnic/National Groups

Drawing on Armstrong's work, Yuval-Davis argues that the mythical unity of 'national imagined communities' is maintained and ideologically reproduced by a whole system of symbolic 'border guards' which classify people as members and non-members of a specific collectivity. These border guards are closely linked to 'specific cultural codes of style of dress and behaviour as well as to more elaborate bodies of customs, religion, literary and artistic modes of production, and, of course, language' (1997: 23). Gender relations and sexuality play a significant role in all this, as women are generally seen as embodiments and cultural reproducers of ethnic/national collectivities. According to Yuval-Davis, this dimension of women's lives is crucial to understanding their subjectivities as well as their relations with each other, with men and with children.

Given their centrality as symbolic border guards, it is easy to understand why women are controlled not only by being encouraged or discouraged from having children, but also in terms of the 'proper' way in which they should have them – that is, in ways which will reproduce the boundaries of their ethnic group or that of their husbands (Anthias and Yuval-Davis 1989: 9). Hence, in some cases they are not allowed to have sexual relations with men of other groups (as until recently in South Africa). This is particularly the case for women belonging to the dominant ethnic group. Legal marriage is generally a precondition for the child to be recognized as a member of the group. Often, religious and social traditions dictate who can marry whom so that the character and boundaries of the group can be maintained over generations (*ibid.*). In Israel, for example, it is the mother who determines the child's nationality. But if the mother is married to another man, then the child will be an outcast (even if she is divorced by civil, rather than religious law, because civil marriages are not recognized by the religious court) and not allowed to marry another Jew for ten generations (Yuval-Davis 1989: 103).

As Participating Centrally in the Ideological Reproduction of the Collectivity and as the Transmitters of its Culture

As noted above, women are usually seen as the 'cultural carriers' of the ethnic/national group. They are the main socializers of small children, and thus they are often required to transmit the rich heritage of ethnic symbols, traditions and values to the young members of the group (Anthias and Yuval-Davis 1989: 9). Here, Yuval-Davis stresses the need to treat 'culture' not as a reified fixed category, but rather 'as a dynamic process, continuously changing, full of internal contradictions which different social and political agents, differentially positioned, use in different ways' (1997: 67).

As Signifiers of Ethnic/National Differences

Women do not only transmit the cultural heritage of ethnic and national groups, but they also 'symbolize' it. The nation is often imagined as a loved woman in danger or as a mother who lost her sons in battle. It is supposedly for the sake of the 'womenandchildren' (sic) that men go to war (Enloe 1990, cited in Yuval-Davis 1997: 15). Yuval-Davis argues that this 'burden of representation' has brought about the construction of women as the bearers of the collectivity's honour (1997: 45). Hence, specific codes and regulations are usually developed, defining who/what is a 'proper woman' – and a 'proper man'. In the Hitler Youth movement, for example, the motto for girls was 'Be faithful; be pure; be German'. For boys it was 'Live faithfully; fight bravely; die laughing' (*ibid.*). Sometimes, the difference between two ethnic groups is determined by the sexual behaviour of women. For instance, a 'true' Cypriot girl should behave in sexually appropriate ways. If she does not, then neither herself nor her children may belong to the community (Anthias and Yuval-Davis: 10; see also Anthias 1989). In the words of Yuval-Davis,

> [o]ther women in many other societies are also tortured or murdered by their relatives because of adultery, flight from home, and other cultural breaches of conduct which are perceived as bringing dishonour and shame on their male relatives and community. (1997: 46)

As Participants in National, Economic, Political and Military Struggles

The category that is most commonly explored concerns women's role in national and ethnic struggles. Yuval-Davis argues that while women did not always participate directly in the fighting (although it was not uncommon for them to do so), they always had specific roles in the combat, 'whether it was to take care of the dead and wounded or to become the embodied possession of the victorious' (1997: 95). This 'sexual division of labour', however, usually disappears when there is no clear differentiation between the 'battle front' and the 'home front'. At this point, Yuval-Davis refers to the changing nature of warfare and the professionalization of militaries as having a positive impact on the incorporation of women into the military. But, she adds, 'it is only very rarely, if at all, that differential power relations between men and women have been erased, even within the most socially progressively organized national liberation armies or western professional militaries' (*ibid.*: 114).

In *Gender and Nation*, Yuval-Davis also offers a more detailed analysis of the absence of women from mainstream theorizing about nations and nationalism. She mentions two explanations that might be relevant in this respect. The first comes from Carole Pateman who traces the origins of this 'collective scholarly forgetting' back to the classical foundation theories which have shaped the commonsense understanding of Western political and social order. These theories divide the sphere of civil society into two domains, the public and the private, and locate women (and the family) in the private domain, which is not seen as politically relevant (Yuval-Davis 1997: 2). Rebecca Grant, on the other hand, argues that the foundation theories of both Hobbes and Rousseau portray the transition from the state of nature to an orderly society exclusively in terms of what they assume to be male characteristics – the aggressive nature of men (Hobbes) and the capacity for reason in men (Rousseau). Women are not part of this process, hence excluded from the 'social'. Later theories, Grant contends, took these assumptions for granted (*ibid.*).

Yuval-Davis notes that the gender-blindness of the mainstream literature continues unabated, despite a number of rare, thus welcome, exceptions. A recent reader on nationalism provides an excellent illustration of this. The editors of the Oxford Reader *Nationalism* (1994), John Hutchinson and Anthony D. Smith, placed the only extract (among 49) on nationalism and gender relations in the last section called 'Beyond Nationalism' and introduced it with the following words: 'The entry of women into the national arena, as cultural and biological reproducers of the nation and as transmitters of its values, has also redefined the content and boundaries of ethnicity and the nation' (1994: 287). Yuval-Davis' answer is concise: 'But, of course, women did not just "enter" the national arena: they were always there, and central to its constructions and reproductions!' (1997: 3)

Another theme developed in Yuval-Davis' recent study relates to the multi-dimensionality of nationalist projects. Noting that nationalist projects are often multiplex, Yuval-Davis argues that 'different members of the collectivity tend to promote contesting constructions which tend to be more or less exclusionary, more or less linked to other ideologies such as socialism and/or religion' (1997: 21). For her, attempts to classify all these different states and societies according to different types of nationalism would constitute an impossible and ahistorical task. Rather, we should treat these types as different dimensions of nationalist projects which are combined in different ways in specific historical cases. Drawing on this observation, Yuval-Davis differentiates between three major dimensions of nationalist projects. The first is the 'genealogical' dimension which is constructed around the specific origin of the people or their race (*Volknation*). The second is the 'cultural' dimension in which the symbolic heritage provided by language, religion and/or other customs and traditions is constructed as the 'essence' of the nation (*Kulturnation*). Finally, there is the 'civic' dimension that focuses on citizenship as determining the boundaries of the nation, relating it directly to notions of state sovereignty and specific territoriality (*Staatnation*) (*ibid.*). According to Yuval-Davis, gender relations play an important role in each of these dimensions and are crucial for any valid theorization of them.

Further Reading

The best starting point for anyone interested in recent approaches to nationalism is the excellent overview by Eley and Suny (1996a).

The issue of gender and nation has become the subject of a growing literature since the mid-1980s. The most useful introductions are McClintock (1996) [1991] and Walby (1996) [1992]. Other works which should be consulted are Jayawardena (1986), Yuval-Davis and Anthias (1989) and Yuval-Davis (1997). For an interesting collection of case studies see West (1997).

On postcolonial nationalisms, the works to consult are Chatterjee (1986, 1990). The reproduction of nationalism is analysed in Balibar (1990) and Billig (1995). For a 'deconstructionist' analysis of nationalism see Bhabha (1990b).

Other works of general use are Calhoun (1997) and Brubaker (1996, 1998), both of whom warn us against the dangers of reifying nations and treat nationalism first and foremost as a kind of discourse.

7

By Way of Conclusion

> A social formation only reproduces itself as a nation to the extent that, through a network of apparatuses and daily practices, the individual is instituted as homo *nationalis* from cradle to grave, at the same time he/she is instituted as homo *economicus, politicus, religiosus* . . .
>
> Étienne Balibar, 'The Nation Form: History and Ideology'

Summing up the Debate: A Critical Appraisal

In the preceding chapters, I have tried to provide a detailed overview of recent theories of nationalism. While doing this, I confined myself to sketching the main arguments of each theory/approach and the major criticisms levelled against them, and did not engage in a lengthy personal critique. This was, in a way, necessary since my first aim in writing this book was to offer as complete a picture of the theoretical debate as possible, with all viewpoints – more or less – equally represented. In this chapter, however, I will abandon my quest for objectivity (an endless and vain task) and present my own view of the debate. I will first expound my objections to the theories/approaches reviewed so far. For a more systematic presentation, I will divide these objections into two categories, those relating to the 'form' of the debate, that is, the way in which particular approaches are presented, and those relating to the 'content' of the debate, that is the specific arguments propounded by each theorist or group of theorists. I will then propose a framework of analysis that might be used in the study of nationalism on the basis of ideas put forward by various scholars. I will conclude the book by expressing a few, necessarily speculative, reflections on the future of the debate.

Criticisms with Regard to the Form of the Debate

As we have already seen, scholars of nationalism are generally divided into three categories in terms of the particular approach they espouse: primordialists, modernists and ethno-symbolists. I have adopted the same classification in this book. My choice, however, was conditioned by a concern for reflecting the general tendency in the field, not by a belief in the validity of the classification – although I admit that classifications cannot be empirically right or wrong (Breuilly 1993a: 9). There are a number of difficulties with this classification. First and foremost, the terms used to describe various theories/approaches are misleading, that is, they do not accurately represent the works concerned. This is mainly caused by the use of ambiguous, ill-defined criteria in the classification.

Let us begin with 'primordialism'. I have argued before, contrary to Eller and Coughlan's (1993) claims, that this term performs an important function by highlighting the role of perceptions and beliefs in guiding people's reactions. On the other hand, the concept is of limited use as a term describing a particular approach to nationalism and leads to serious confusions. Mostly employed to denote the nationalist standpoint, the term is wrongly stretched to cover the position of scholars like Geertz and Shils who focus on the ways in which ethnic identities are 'perceived' by individuals. As I have explained earlier, it makes more sense to call their approach 'constructivist' since both writers treat culture on the basis of meanings attached to it. In this view, culture is never 'given' or fixed: it is shaped by the perceptions and beliefs of those living in a particular community.

The concept of 'modernism' is even more problematic as it became a kind of catch-all term under which a number of quite divergent approaches are subsumed. The only 'apparent' point of intersection among these diverse interpretations is their belief in the modernity (in the sense of recent) of nations and nationalism; hence the term 'modernist', coined by Smith (1986; 1991b; 1994;

1998). However, apart from this shared conviction, there is little in common among the so-called modernists. Being stern critics of each other's work, they stress different, at times sharply conflicting, factors in their explanations. This point is overlooked by ethno-symbolist writers who tend to expand the common denominator joining these scholars. According to them, the modernists regard nations not only as a necessary concomitant of modernization processes, but also as 'invented', thus 'false' or 'artificial', constructions which become instruments of elites and leaders in their universal struggles for power. Moreover, they contend, the modernists believe that nationalism is an historically specific and transitory phenomenon (see for example Smith 1995: 35–7). Presenting these as the shared assumptions of the 'modernists', they then address their criticisms to all these scholars, treating them as a unitary, homogeneous category. This, however, constitutes an oversimplification of the theories concerned.

First, not all 'modernists' accept the 'falsity' of nations. We have already seen how this view, mostly associated with Gellner and Hobsbawm, is rejected by Anderson. His words are worth repeating here: 'Gellner is so anxious to show that nationalism masquerades under false pretences that he assimilates "invention" to "fabrication" and "falsity", rather than to "imagining" and "creation"' (1991: 6). In short, for Anderson, the fact that nations are 'imagined' does not imply that they are 'false' or 'artificial'. On the other hand, the role of elites in nurturing nationalism is explored by scholars like Brass who subscribe to some form of 'instrumentalism'. Gellner, Anderson or neo-Marxist writers do not dwell too much on this issue. Finally, the claim that nationalism is a transitory phenomenon which will disappear (or lose its virulence) once the nation is firmly established and achieves a high level of affluence is only made by Gellner and Hobsbawm. Clearly, these are not minor squabbles. How, then, could ethno-symbolists fail to notice these differences? Part of the answer might lie in ethno-symbolists' steadfast quest for an alternative interpretation. In an attempt to differentiate their position from available approaches, ethno-symbolists overlook the differences between various 'modernist' explanations and treat them as a coherent whole, thereby presenting us with a sharply dichotomized picture of the debate. This enables them to formulate an alternative interpretation by distancing themselves from both the primordialists and the modernists, and present it as a sensible 'middle way' between these polarized accounts. It needs to be noted, however, that any answer to this question, including this one, would be necessarily speculative.

As for ethno-symbolists, I concur with the view, prevalent among the modernists, that they should not be treated as a separate category (Breuilly 1996; Gellner 1996b; *cf.* Lieven 1997). However, it is not easy to decide where to place them given the rigidity of available categories. Ethno-symbolists make two different, in their view compatible, claims. On the one hand, they concede the modernity of nationalism as an ideology and a movement, incorporating many of the factors identified by the 'modernists' into their analyses. On the other hand, they hold that modern nations are built around pre-existing ethnic cores and that earlier ethnic cultures provide the material out of which today's national identities are forged. These claims point to the need to develop a new classification based on a redefinition of the existing categories.

In the light of these considerations, I will opt for a binary classification consisting of 'essentialist' and 'constructivist' approaches. Any attempt to defend this classification should begin by providing a working definition of these terms. Calhoun's definition of 'essentialism' seems to be a good starting point:

> 'Essentialism' refers to a reduction of the diversity in a population to some single criterion held to constitute its defining 'essence' and most crucial character. This is often coupled with the claim that the 'essence' is unavoidable and given by nature. It is common to assume that these cultural categories address really existing and discretely identifiable collections of people. More surprisingly, many also assume that it is possible to understand each category – Germans, say, or women, Blacks, or gays – by focusing solely on its primary identifier rather than on the way it overlaps with, contests and/or reinforces others (1997: 18)

According to this viewpoint, an individual belongs to one and only one nation, as s/he belongs to one and only one race and one gender. Each of these sharply demarcated (and indivisible) categories describes a particular aspect of the individual's being (Calhoun 1997: 18). This implies that the individual can have different self-definitions on the basis of different categories. In that sense, there is no interaction among the categories in question. Such a definition enables us to treat the primordialists and ethno-symbolists together. We have already seen that primordialists consider nationality as a 'natural' part of all human beings. In some cases, ethnic and national identities lay dormant for centuries because of treachery or oppression. But the national 'essence', unchanging and persistent, is always there to be 'reawakened'. Ethno-symbolist claims are not worlds apart. What unites Armstrong and Smith is their belief in the 'persistence' and 'durability' of ethnic ties. Both writers argue that the myths, symbols and values which form the basis of many modern national cultures 'tend to be *exceptionally* durable under "normal" vicissitudes and to persist over *many generations*, even *centuries*', setting limits to elite attempts at manipulation (Smith 1986: 16, emphasis added). In that sense, Smith's acceptance of the modernity of nationalism does not affect his essentialism. Nationalism is modern, but never 'contingent': every nationalism is constructed around 'particular' ethnic traditions. To put it in another way, there is a ethnic/national 'essence' (a 'myth–symbol complex') underlying many, if not all, contemporary nationalisms. And what impels so many people around the world to lay down their lives for their nation is precisely this 'essence'.

Some scholars have indeed recognized the essentialism inherent in Smith's analysis. According to Norval, for example, Smith's insistence on retaining a pre-existing, pre-modern form of ethnicity leads him to subject the theorization of nations (as imagined communities) to an objectivist reduction, 'a "ground" outside all forms of discursive construction':

> Imagined communities, on these readings, can be nothing other than ideological forms which cover over deeper, underlying objectivities, objectivities which may be revealed by drawing away the veil of manipulation which they seem to construct. (1996: 62)

Patrik Hall raises a similar point, arguing that cultural naturalism (the term he uses for ethno-symbolism) is of the same kind as the 'discovery' of culture during Romanticism:

> Herder's subjectivist notion of *Volkgeist* is of the same type as Smith's notion of the symbolical *Mythomoteur*. In both cases it is

imaginations, myths and symbols which are emphasised, not any 'objective' cultural markers. Both notions stress cultural unity instead of social and political contradictions. (1998: 40)

For both writers, the implications of such an approach can be quite dangerous. As Norval rightly argues,

[a] rejection of the symbolically constituted nature of certain forms of identification in favor of an uncovering of objective reality falls into a form of theorization which has been decisively problematized for its rationalism, its claims to a realm of truth not accessible to the consciousness of those engaged in the construction of their own identities, and, finally, its possible authoritarian consequences. (1996: 62)

Hall, on the other hand, claims that 'by making it dependent upon a cultural categorisation, nationalism becomes reified or conceived of as a natural expression of ethnicity or culture' (1998: 40). In that sense, 'it matters little that ethnicity or culture are constructions'. The argument, Hall concludes, runs the risk of being used as an apologetic political rhetoric.

These criticisms bring us to the second category, which consists of 'constructivists' who stress the intersubjective character of the process of ethnic/national identity-formation. The term 'socially constructed' is a recent contribution to the literature on nationalism. Tilley argues that this term permits recognition of two crucial points: first, that 'the logics, values and meanings which accrue to customs are interrelated and mutually informative'; and second, that 'such knowledge/value systems are continually reshaped as groups react to changing environmental and social conditions' (1997: 511). The second insight is more important for the purposes of our discussion. It implies that the meanings (and values) attributed to various constituents of the national culture, that is myths, symbols and traditions, are interminably negotiated, revised and redefined. In other words, ethnic membership is neither externally given, nor fixed: it is determined, consciously or unconsciously, by the group itself and varies according to changing circumstances.

This insight allows us to discover another commonality of the so-called 'modernists'. All scholars included in this category argue that it became possible and necessary to 'imagine' or 'invent' nations as a result of changing economic, political or social conditions. The transformation emphasized by each scholar and the underlying factors they identified display a great diversity: for Nairn, the key to understanding nationalism is 'uneven development'; for Hechter, it is 'internal colonialism'; for Breuilly, the rise of the modern state; for Gellner, industrialization; for Anderson, a series of interlinked factors, ranging from a revolution in the conceptions of time to 'print capitalism'. Moreover, they disagree on the degree of 'genuineness' of nations. What joins them, or what remains constant in their theories, is the belief that all human collectivities were subject to some fundamental changes at some point in history which disrupted the existing order, thereby forcing them to find new ways of organizing social/political life. The thread of their argument runs as follows: the older forms of organization become redundant under the impact of changes in economic, political and social life, which also create the conditions necessary to 'imagine' new forms (Anderson, Gellner, Hobsbawm, Breuilly, Nairn and Hechter); with the invention of new forms of collective organization, the concept of political legitimacy is redefined and the older principles of legitimacy, the dynastic and the religious, are abandoned (Anderson, Breuilly, Brass); the emerging elites 'invite the masses into history' in an attempt to get their support for the subsequent process of 'nation-building' (Brass, Breuilly, Nairn, Hroch); the improvements in communication technologies and corresponding increases in schooling and literacy rates help them to get their messages to ever-widening sections of the population (Anderson, Gellner, Hobsbawm, Breuilly, Brass); consequently, small-scale loyalties generated by face-to-face contact are gradually eroded and replaced by large-scale attachments felt for an 'impersonal' and 'anonymous' society the members of which will never meet, nor even hear of most of their fellow-members (Anderson, Gellner, Breuilly, Brass).

For the purposes of classification, it does not matter who 'creates' or 'imagines' the nation in the first place, nor how nationalism spreads among wider strata. Scholars opt for different scenarios to answer these questions. What matters for the classification is to determine the common denominator linking these different scenarios. The process I have sketched above catches this commonality. This process might not be as visible, or conspicuous, as the other criterion – the date of emergence of nations – used in classifying constructivist/modernist approaches; but it is more comprehensive and representative. Actually, the usefulness of the alternative principle of classification is quite debatable. We have already seen that constructivist/modernist scholars propose different dates for the emergence of nations. More importantly, this criterion leads to serious confusions in the case of scholars who are generally considered to be 'modernists', but who take the origins of nations as far back as the Middle Ages.

Liah Greenfeld is a good case in point. For Greenfeld, the modern idea of the nation emerged in sixteenth-century England, which was the first nation in the world and the only one for about two hundred years (1992: 14). On the other hand, Greenfeld, too, locates the origins of nationalism in a process of change (increasing upward or downward social mobility, the appearance of new roles) and people's reaction to it. Nationalism, she holds, was a response of individuals in elite sectors of society, who were personally affected by the contradictions of the society-of-orders. Upwardly-mobile commoners, who reached the top of the social ladder, found inacceptable the traditional image of society in which social mobility was an anomaly, and replaced it with that of a 'nation', making it synonymous with the 'people' of England. As a result of this redefinition, 'every member of the people was elevated to the dignity of the elite, becoming, in principle, equal to any other member' (1993: 49). The remarkable quality of national identity, for Greenfeld, is that 'it guarantees status with dignity to every member of whatever is defined as a polity or society' (*ibid.*). Again, the idea of 'constructivism' seems to be more useful than the alternative criterion of 'modernity' as a principle of classification since it enables us to place Greenfeld neatly within a particular category, that is, that of the 'constructivists'.

Criticisms with Regard to the Content of the Debate

Which of the theories/approaches we have reviewed enhances our understanding of nationalism? In other words, what is the most fruitful approach in terms of 'cracking the nut of nationalism' (Gellner 1995a: 61)? Let us consider each of these approaches in turn, following again the commonly adopted three-legged classification.

There is no need to dwell too much on the primordialist approach. As Brubaker observes, very few scholars today continue to subscribe to the view that nations are primordial, unchanging entities (1996: 15). Almost everybody admits that nations are born at a particular period in history, notwithstanding disagreements on the precise date of their emergence or the relative weight of pre-modern traditions and modern transformations in their formation. The pseudo-scientific, ideologically motivated belief that nations exist since time immemorial has little support in the academia.

This is largely to the credit of modernist studies which have been trying to show for the last four decades that the picture drawn by primordialists is far from representing the reality about nations and nationalism. The general assumptions of modernism seem to be fundamentally correct. Most of the nations that make up the world map today, including the old, 'historic' nations of Western Europe, are the products of the developments of the last two centuries. To substantiate this claim, it suffices to consider the case of 'language', the quintessential symbol of nationhood for many nationalists. Modernist scholars have revealed that in France, for example, 50 per cent of the people did not speak French at all and only 12–13 per cent spoke it correctly in 1789, the year of the Great Revolution. In the case of Italy, on the other hand, only 2.5 per cent of the population used Italian for everyday purposes at the moment of unification (Hobsbawm 1990: 60–1). Despite all efforts to the contrary, Norwegian never established itself as more than a minority language in Norway, which has been a bilingual country since 1947 with Norwegian confined to 20 per cent of the population (*ibid.*: 55). It is possible to multiply these examples. What is important for our purposes, however, is that in most cases nationalism becomes paramount after the state is established. As Pilsudski, the eventual liberator of Poland, recognized: 'It is the state which makes the nation and not the nation the state'. But perhaps the most forthright statement of this view comes from Massimo d'Azeglio who once said: 'We have made Italy, now we have to make Italians' (cited in *ibid.*: 44–5).

In my view, the general thrust of these arguments remains compelling despite the works of Armstrong and Smith. Nations are an outgrowth of the age of nationalism. Obviously, there is nothing modern about the attachments individuals feel for the communities of which they are a member. Throughout history, people felt attached to a great variety of groups or institutions such as city-states, empires, families or guilds. Given this, however, the crucial question is: why these attachments have disappeared or transformed into 'national' loyalties? And what is the degree of similarity between pre-modern attachments and contemporary collective ties felt for the abstract community of the nation which consists of millions of 'strangers'? It is indeed true that ethnic groups were salient and widespread in much of antiquity and the medieval era: but, to what extent do these groups resemble today's nations? Arguably, much less than ethno-symbolists would have us believe if we consider that myriads of 'unfavourable' events, for example migrations, conquests, genocides and intermarriages, have taken place in the course of history, altering the ethnic/cultural composition of any particular group.

Moreover, as Calhoun notes, ethnic identities are constituted, maintained and invoked in social processes involving diverse intentions, constructions of meaning and conflicts: 'not only are there claims from competing possible collective allegiances, there are competing claims as to just what any particular ethnic or other identity means' (1997: 36). In other words, dominant constructions of nationhood are continually challenged by alternative, often conflicting, definitions. The individual, then, has to make two choices: s/he has to decide not only to which community to belong, but also which particular communal definition to endorse. Some of these points are recognized by ethno-symbolist writers. For example, Smith admits that the traditions, customs and institutions of the past are 'reconstructed' and 'reinterpreted' (1991b: 358–9). However, he insists that ethnic cultures tend to persist over many generations, 'forming "moulds" within which all kinds of social and cultural processes can unfold and upon which all kinds of circumstances and pressures can exert an impact' (1986: 16). Then the question that awaits an answer is: to what extent a 'reconstructed' and 'reinterpreted' culture is the same culture? Smith does not address this question directly. The answer lies in the 'discourse' of nationalism. What reconstructs and reinterprets pre-modern cultures is the nationalist discourse. In the age of nationalism, the myths, symbols and traditions of the past are put to different and sometimes conflicting uses. Political concerns play a crucial role in this process since any particular definition will legitimate some claims and delegitimate others (Calhoun 1993: 215). All these attempts are guided by the 'exigencies' of state-building, which is a peculiarly modern phenomenon.

This brings us to another criticism raised against modernist explanations, generally expressed in the form of a question: why do so many people sacrifice their lives for their nations? Would they willingly lay down their lives for the products of the 'collective imagination' (Smith 1991b; 1998: 140)? This criticism, however, misses a crucial point. The fact that nations are 'invented' or 'imagined' does not make them 'less real' in the eyes of those who believe in them. As Halliday observes, the revelation of the falsity of a given myth does not affect its effectiveness because

> . . . once generated and expressed, [myths] can acquire a considerable life of their own. Myths of racist hatred, for example, may begin as lies invented by idle xenophobes, but once conveyed into the political realm and diffused in tense inter-ethnic contexts, they acquire a force and a reality they previously lacked. (1995: 7)

This point is also recognized by scholars who are sympathetic to nationalism. Thus, in his recent defense of nationality, Miller argues that national identities contain a considerable element of myth. Some of these myths are outright inventions; others place a particular interpretation on events whose occurrence is not in dispute (1995: 37–42). Miller continues with a quotation from Orwell: 'Myths which are believed tend to become true, because they set up a type or "persona", which the average person will do his best to resemble' (*ibid.*: 37).

Archard concurs with Miller and notes that national myths, which are deeply rooted within popular culture, will continue to be accepted as true insofar as they do serve important practical purposes: 'Their acceptance will probably depend less on evidence for their truth being compelling than on their meeting a populace's need to feel that they should be true' (1995: 478). This is precisely what ethno-symbolists overlook. The criticism may be valid in the case of Gellner and Hobsbawm who maintain that nations and the myths which go in their making are outright fabrications. However, neither Anderson, nor Breuilly, nor Brass claim that nations are 'false'. What matters is the perceptions and beliefs of the individuals that compose the nation. When believed in, myths become 'real' and nations are reified. In that sense, '*imagination* is not merely a "mental" or "intellectual" exercise; it is *material*, lived, tangible' (Sofos 1996: 251). And it is this reification process that needs to be explored, not the truth or falsity of national (or any other kind of) myths. As Ernst Cassirer observes,

> [t]o inquire into the 'truth' of the political myths is . . . as meaningless and as ridiculous as to ask for the truth of a machine gun or a fighter plane. Both are weapons; and weapons prove their truth by their efficiency. If the political myths could stand this test they needed no other and no better proof. . . . (Cited in Kapferer 1988: 27)

There is a second problem with this criticism. The view that individuals will not lay down their lives for the inventions of their imaginations (which impels Smith to look elsewhere, that is ethnic pasts, to account for the colossal sacrifices generated by nationalism) is based on the implicit assumption that every single member of the nation is completely aware of this process of imagination, in other words, that everybody has unrestricted and equal access to the truths about national myths. This is a highly dubious assumption, to say the least. How would an ordinary 'citizen', who is constantly faced with the 'reality' of the nation, discover that the community to which s/he belongs is in fact an 'imagined community'? By reading Benedict Anderson? Are we to assume that everybody reads Anderson or Hobsbawm? What would happen even if they do so? Would they all of a sudden realize that everything they have learned so far about their nation is nothing but a series of chimerical tales, reflecting the interests of a small number of elites? In my view, such a view will not take us too far. Calhoun summarizes this succinctly:

> What gives tradition (or culture generally) its force is not its antiquity but its immediacy and givenness. Some nationalist self-understandings may be historically dubious yet very real as aspects of lived experience and bases for action . . . People may even join in public rituals that affirm narratives they know to be problematic, but gain an identification with these as 'our stories', a sense of collusion in the production of these fictions,

and a recognition of them as background conditions of everyday life . . . It is thus not the antiquity of Eritrean nationalism
that mattered in mobilizing people against Ethiopian rule, for
example, but the *felt reality of Eritreanness.* (1997: 34–5, emphasis
added)

Another factor that explains the powerful emotions generated by
nationalism is concealed in the familiar terrain of everyday life
(Tilly 1994). The individuals that make up the nation engage in
myriads of 'non-national' social relations throughout their lives.
While doing this, they invest trust, resources and hopes for the
future. All these networks and resources depend directly or indirectly on the state's backing, or at least its existence. Thus, every
threat to the nation's survival reflects on the daily lives of millions
of 'nationals', imperilling everything they value. In other words,
'[t]o the extent that nationally and locally defined solidarities
actually coincide, threats and opportunities for national identities
therefore ramify into local affairs and impinge on the fates of many
people' (Tilly 1994: 18). In that sense, there is a strong connection
between the nation's existence and that of its individual members.
If the nation faces the threat of extinction, so too its citizens.

Otto Bauer was probably the first scholar to emphasize this point
when he defined the nation as a 'community of destiny'. For him,
'[c]ommunity of destiny does not mean just subjection to a
common fate, but rather common experience of the same fate in
constant communication and ongoing interaction with one
another' (1996: 51). Yuval-Davis argues that this factor can explain
the attachments people feel for their nations in settler societies or
postcolonial states in which there are no shared myths of common
origin (1997: 19). In short, making sacrifices for the nation often
means protecting one's own life – and the things one values –
which explains partly why nationalism is able to command such
powerful emotions (see also Smith 1998: 140).

The real problem with modernist explanations is their tendency
to explain nationalism in terms of a 'master variable'. Some of
these scholars, notably Nairn and Hechter, have been occasionally
subject to the charge of 'reductionism', but until quite recently
(Calhoun 1997: 20–3) this was not regarded as a problem common
to all modernist accounts. Nationalisms are too varied to be

explained by a single factor: chameleon-like, they take their colour from their context (Smith 1991a: 79). Theories and approaches which attempt to make sense of a phenomenon as protean as nationalism on the basis of a single process fall prey to reductionism, no matter how comprehensive this process is. I will explore this point further when presenting my own framework of analysis.

Here, one further point needs to be stressed, namely that scholars who try to avoid reductionism, or 'causal parsimony' to use Calhoun's term, commit the opposite error, incorporating as many variables as possible into their theory, thereby making it too general to be helpful. Anthony D. Smith's analysis of nationalism is a good case in point. The factors identified by Smith include state centralization, taxation, conscription, bureaucratization, extension of citizenship rights, improvements in communication networks, movement to a market economy, accumulation of capital, decline of ecclesiastical authority, development of secular education and of university learning, increase in the number of popular modes of communication such as novels, journals and plays, the entry of intellectuals and professionals into state appa-ratuses, rediscovery of ethnic cultures and so on – note that most of these factors are those identified by the modernists (Smith 1991a: 54–68). No wonder that nationalism is 'explained' when so many factors are invoked! It is indeed true that all these factors have contributed to the rise of nationalist movements in one way or the other. But herein lies the problem: 'at the level of practical activity, there are many diverse nationalisms' (Calhoun 1997: 21). It follows that when we are analysing 'nationalism', we are actually dealing with heterogeneous objects of analysis, not with a single, unitary phenomenon: hence the impossibility of 'macro' explana-tions or a general theory of nationalism.

As for recent studies, most of the criticisms they raised against the mainstream literature seem to be well-grounded. It is true that orthodox theories/approaches, with their Eurocentric and gender-blind outlook, presented us with a biased and incomplete picture of national phenomena. Given the general trends in social sci-ences, it was inevitable that the neglected issues (or the groups whose 'voices' have been suppressed) would be integrated into the study of nationalism. This task was largely accomplished by the studies of the last decade. In that sense, they filled an important gap in a field hitherto dominated by 'conventional' approaches. It should be stressed that the framework of analysis I will propose below is inspired to a great extent by the ideas developed in these works.

How to Study Nationalism? Towards an Analytical Framework

In the light of the criticisms articulated in the previous section, I will suggest a general framework of analysis for the study of nationalism. Before proceeding, however, two qualifications are in order. To start with, I am not advancing a 'theory of nationalism'. On the contrary, the first proposition of my 'analytical framework' is that there can be no such theory. Secondly, the five propositions that make up the framework are not born in a vacuum: they are a synthesis of the ideas put forward by various scholars. The originality of the framework lies in combining these ideas, distilled from a series of otherwise unrelated (sometimes even defending contradictory positions) works, into a coherent whole.

Proposition 1: There can be no 'General' Theory of Nationalism

This point, made two decades ago by Sami Zubaida (1978), may look like a 'truism' today. It can be asserted that a single, universal theory is not available in the case of most social phenomena, not only nationalism. Strikingly enough, however, the explicit recognition of this point by eminent scholars of nationalism dates only from the 1990s (Hall 1993; Smith 1996b, 1996c). I have already noted that nationalism is a protean phenomenon, capable of taking on a multiplicity of forms depending on the – historical, social and political – context over which it reigns. This diversity precludes the possibility of formulating an 'overarching theory' (Jenkins and Sofos 1996: 11). As Zubaida observes, a sociological theory of nationalism cannot content itself with the ideological homogeneity of nationalisms, but would also entail a sociological homogeneity, that is common social structures and processes which underlie the ideological/political phenomena. This is, for him, precisely what theories of nationalism assume and set out to demonstrate (1978: 56). But such assumptions are misleading and, in fact, ahistorical since nationalisms are born in different historical periods and in a variety of dissimilar settings:

> Why nationalism comes to dominate in those settings where it does – or for some people and not others within an ostensible national population – are questions that by and large can be answered only within specific contexts, with knowledge of local history, of the nature of the state (and other elite) power, and of what other potential and actual movements competed for allegiance. (Calhoun 1997: 25)

Moreover, historical contingencies play an important role in the formation of particular nationalisms. This point is articulated most cogently by Halliday (1997a, 1997b) and Brubaker (1996, 1998). Halliday, for example, observes that many of the ethnic groups who had claimed the status of 'nationhood' failed to obtain it and disappeared in the mists of history. He claims that the actual division of the world into 193 nations is not 'given', as the perennialists would argue, but a product of a series of contingent factors – wars, conflicts, treaties – that could have had very different outcomes. It follows that the world map, as we know it today, could have been very different (1997c).

What should we do then? Should we abandon all attempts at analysing or theorizing nationalisms? James, for instance, accuses Zubaida for falling prey to an 'overly exuberant' poststructuralism that is suspicious of any form of 'grand theory' (1996: 113). In my view, Zubaida does not deserve this criticism. Noting the 'impossibility' of a universal theory of nationalisms does not imply that nationalisms should not (or cannot) be theorized at all. Rather, we might formulate partial theories that account for different aspects of nationalisms. As Calhoun argues, 'grasping nationalism in its multiplicity of forms requires multiple theories' (1997: 8). To address the issue of the reproduction of nationhood will require a different theory from the question of the differential participation of women and men in nationalist projects. Yuval-Davis' (1997) attempt to analyse women's role in the reproduction of ethnic/national collectivities is a good case in point. These 'partial theories' that concentrate on particular aspects of nationalisms are more helpful than ambitious 'grand theories' which purport to explain all nationalisms (for a recent defense of 'grand theories' see Smith 1998: 219–20, 225).

Proposition 2: There is no 'One' Nationalism

The project of formulating an Euclidean theory is further impeded by the internal variations (and shifting contents) of particular nationalisms. Not only are there different types of nationalism, but different members of the nation promote different, often conflicting, constructions of nationhood (McClintock 1996: 264). A number of, at times quite divergent, ideologies and movements compete to capture the allegiance of the 'nationals'. In that sense, 'nationalism is rarely the nationalism of the nation, but rather represents the site where very different views of the nation contest and negotiate with each other' (Duara 1993: 2). Thus, it is not meaningful to speak of a single, unitary French nationalism or Turkish nationalism.

In Turkey, for example, Islamists, secular Kemalists, ultranationalists and liberals have different conceptions of nationhood. While Kemalists opt for (at least on the surface) a 'civic-territorial' national identity, ultra-nationalists deny any form of cultural pluralism, promoting instead the ethnic and cultural unity, even 'identity', of all those living in Turkey. Liberals subscribe to Western models of nationhood, whereas leftists espouse anti-imperialist Third World nationalisms which are largely inimical to the West. In short, there is no 'one' Turkish nationalism; rather, there are Turkish nationalisms. This shows clearly that we are faced with 'heterogeneous objects of analysis' (Calhoun 1997: 21). The differences among and within nationalisms cannot be embraced by a single Euclidean theory, however comprehensive and sophisticated its premises are. Therein lies the dilemma of conventional studies which take great pains to explain why there are so many exceptions to the particular approach they promote. The major source of this dilemma is their tendency to treat any particular nationalism as a coherent, homogeneous whole.

What, then, unites all these different nationalisms? In other words, how are we able to identify an enormous range of movements, policies and ideologies as 'nationalist'?

*Proposition 3: What Unites these Diverse Forms of Nationalism is the
'Discourse of Nationalism'*

The answer to these questions lies in the nationalist discourse: 'The
common denominator among Japanese economic protectionism,
Serbian ethnic cleansing and Americans singing the "Star-
Spangled Banner" before baseball games . . . is a discursive form
that shapes and links all of them' (Calhoun 1997: 21–2). A variety
of movements, ideologies and policies, arising in different contexts
and following different historical trajectories, are joined by the use
of a common rhetoric. Nationalism is first and foremost 'a form of
reading and watching, of understanding and of taking for granted'
that shapes our consciousness (Billig 1995: 127), or briefly, a way
of constructing the social reality we live (Calhoun 1997: 12; see
also Brubaker 1998: 291–2). Both the Japanese government and
the Serbian soldier would explain their deeds by resorting to a
common rhetoric, that is, the rhetoric of 'national interest'. In that
sense, the discourse of nationalism is the ultimate explanatory, and
legitimating, framework in today's world.

This also captures the 'modernity' of nationalisms. What defines
cultural collectivities as 'nations' and the members of these collectivities as 'citizens' is the discourse of nationalism. Nations can
only exist in the context of nationalism. And this is precisely what
separates earlier ethnic communities from contemporary nations.

On the other hand, the use of a common rhetoric enables us to
formulate an 'umbrella definition' of nationalism, that is 'a particular way of constructing the social reality we experience', which
is, in my view, more helpful than alternative objective or subjective
definitions of national phenomena. It is, of course, possible to
make a list of the objective characteristics which a collectivity
should possess to become a nation, such as common religion,
ethnicity, language, a specific territory and so on. However, formulating the 'perfect list' is a difficult, if not impossible, task – in
fact, as Yuval-Davis notes, some of these lists sound like a shopping
list (1997: 19). Most of today's nations lack one or more of the
characteristics commonly cited by scholars of nationalism. Furthermore, we will never be in a position to ascertain how many of
these characteristics a collectivity should possess – and which ones
– to become a nation. As for subjective characteristics like loyalty

or solidarity, they are necessary but not sufficient conditions to be a nation. Individuals feel attached to many other collectivities and institutions, including their families, kinsmen or regions. Thus, attachments *per se* cannot account for the existence of a nation or of nationalism. The key element of an 'umbrella definition', then, is the discourse of nationalism, which is shared by all movements, policies or ideologies we call 'nationalist' (Calhoun 1997: 21–2). All nations make use of this discourse to define, justify and reproduce themselves.

If the discourse of nationalism is the common denominator of all nationalisms, thus the most important element of an umbrella definition, then, we should be more specific about it. The nationalist discourse has three main characteristics:

- It claims that the interests and values of the nation override all other interests and values (Breuilly 1993a: 2; Smith 1991a: 74).
- It regards the nation as the only source of legitimacy. Here, I do not only mean 'political legitimacy'. The nation (or nationalism) can be used to justify all kinds of actions that would not otherwise be condoned or tolerated. As Löfgren observes, '[t]here is an empowering magic in the national prefix . . . This simple addition transforms its subject, makes it more official, more sacred, more emotional' (1993: 161).
- It operates through binary divisions – between 'us' and 'them', 'friends' and 'foes'. These categories are sharply separated from each other by 'mutually exclusive sets of assigned rights and duties, moral significance and behavioural principles' (Bauman 1992: 678; see also McCrone 1998: 116–19). It defines 'us' in terms of the Other: 'it is only through the relation to the Other, the relation to what it is not, to precisely what it lacks, to what has been called its *constitutive outside* that the "positive" meaning of [identity] can be constructed'. (Hall 1996a: 4–5)

Proposition 4: The Nationalist Discourse can Only be Effective if it is Reproduced on a Daily Basis

As Brubaker convincingly argues, 'nationalism is not a "force" to be measured as resurgent or receding. It is a heterogeneous set of "nation"-oriented idioms, practices, and possibilities that are continuously available or "endemic" in modern cultural and political life' (1996: 10). Why, then, is nationalism so essential to modern politics and culture? Or in Billig's words, 'why do "we", in established, democratic nations, not forget "our" national identity' (1995: 93)? The answers to these questions lie in the reproduction of nationhood on a daily basis. We cannot fully comprehend nationalism without taking its everyday manifestations into account since 'macro' structures, for example ideologies, are created and reproduced at a 'micro' level, that is through the social relations and routine practices of everyday life (Billig 1995; *cf.* Essed 1991; van Dijk 1993, 1998). In that sense, it would be misleading to confine nationalism to blatant racism, more subtle discourses of racial and ethnic domination or to aggressive ethnocentrism. Nationalism also involves the everyday, mundane opinions, attitudes and the seemingly naive acts of discrimination (van Dijk 1993: 5). The traces of nationalism can be found in all structures, institutions, processes and policies that perpetrate the hegemony of one (ethnic/national) group over another.

As Essed (1991) remarks, without a minimum knowledge of how to cope in everyday life, for example knowledge of language, norms, customs and rules, one cannot handle living in society. This knowledge is provided by a range of institutions, from family and school to media and workplace. Together, these institutions form the socialization process and transmit the stock of knowledge necessary to cope in everyday life from one generation to the next – thereby ensuring that the existing system is internalized. Inspired by Essed's notion of 'everyday racism', I will introduce the term 'everyday nationalism' and define it (paraphrasing Essed's concise definition) as 'the integration of nationalism into everyday situations through practices that activate underlying power relations' (1991: 50). When the nationalist discourse seeps into everyday life, its reproduction becomes inevitable. As long as the system reproduces itself, it reproduces 'everyday nationalism' (*ibid.*).

The implication of these observations is not hard to guess: the language we use in our everyday life and the attitudes that guide our social relations are not as innocent as they seem. Ostensibly naive statements such as 'Muslims have different cultural norms than ours' transform easily into stereotyping statements like 'Muslims are terrorists' under crisis situations. It is worth noting that this transformation is not generally registered consciously. We tend (or prefer) to forget that naive descriptions form the basis of many stereotypes and prejudices.

Proposition 5: As there are Different Constructions of Nationhood, any Study of Nationalism should Acknowledge the Differences of Ethnicity, Gender, Class or Place in the Life-cycle that Affect the Definition and Redefinition of National Identities

I have already argued that the nationalist discourse promotes categorical identities over relational ones. For Calhoun, this is not surprising because nationalism addresses 'large-scale collectivities in which most people could not conceivably enter into face-to-face relationships with most others' (1997: 46). However, identity is not a fixed and 'given' category: on the contrary, it is 'always mobile and processual, partly self-construction, partly categorization by others, partly a condition, a status, a label, a weapon, a shield, a fund of memories, et cetera' (Malkki 1996: 447–8). Individual self-definitions change according to one's differential positioning along the dimensions of gender, race, ethnicity, class or place in the life-cycle. The most important contribution of the studies of the last decade was to incorporate these dimensions into the study of nationalisms, hence presenting us with a more complete picture of the formation of national identities (Yuval-Davis and Anthias 1989; Yuval-Davis 1997).

Obviously, these are tentative propositions. New ones can be added to this list or the existing propositions can be elaborated further. In that sense, my 'embryonic' framework of analysis can be considered as a first step in the formulation of a more comprehensive approach to the study of nationalisms. But at least, I believe, it is a step in the right direction.

The Future?

It is clear that we have not yet reached 'the end of history' in a world torn apart by nationalist conflicts, cruel acts of ethnic cleansing and all kinds of fundamentalisms (for the thesis of the end of history see Fukuyama 1989). In fact, the revolutions of 1989 were not much of a watershed in terms of the incidence of conflict on the world political scene. In the meantime, we are 'inundated' by the discourse of the 'return of the repressed', which claims that the collapse of communism has unleashed a new wave of nationalist hatred, dashing hopes for a more peaceful new world order (see for example Ignatieff 1993: 2). The popular commentaries we encounter daily in the newspapers or on the television screens reproduce this discourse, maintaining that the ideological skirmish between communism and capitalism has been replaced by nationalist and religious wars, or by a 'clash of civilisations' (Huntington 1993). The value of these interpretations is open to question. Nationalism has never been absent from the inter*national* arena in the last two hundred years, forming the mould within which all kinds of political claims have been cast. Moreover, it is too early to proclaim the end of ideological conflicts in a world where thousands of people are living in hardship as a result of (ideologically motivated) embargoes. In short, the world we live in is as chaotic as ever.

Given that nationalism is one of the most important forces in this world, the need to understand it is all the more urgent. There are, I think, two fruitful ways of doing this. Both of them require us to reject the fundamental assumptions of the classical debate on nationalism. The first strategy is to address the issues neglected or ignored by the mainstream literature – without, however, ignoring the analytical gains of the past, particularly the insights provided by modernism. This would allow us to formulate a series of 'partial theories', each illuminating a particular aspect of national phenomena such as the reproduction of nationalisms, the differential participation of various groups into nationalist projects and so on. The second strategy, on the other hand, is inspired by another shortcoming of the classical debate, which is most cogently exposed by Halliday (1997b). For him, the debate on nationalism has already reached an impasse with an array of general theories offset against a mass of individual accounts, with relatively little interaction between the two. The way out of this impasse, argues Halliday, lies in producing 'theoretically informed' comparative histories, which will at the same time test the theories concerned against historical evidence. Whichever way we choose, there is still much to be done. Yet as Greenfeld notes, 'as long as history goes on, there is hope' (1993: 61).

Bibliography

Acton, Lord (1996) [1862] 'On Nationality', in Gopal Balakrishnan (ed.), *Mapping the Nation*, London: Verso, 17–38.

Agger, B. (1991) 'Critical Theory, Poststructuralism, Postmodernism', *Annual Review of Sociology*, 17, 105–31.

Agnew, J. (1989) 'Nationalism: Autonomous Force or Practical Politics? Place and Nationalism in Scotland', in C. H. Williams and E. Kofman (eds), *Community, Conflict, Partition and Nationalism*, London and New York: Routledge, 167–93.

Alp, T. [Moise Cohen] (1971) [1937] 'The Restoration of Turkish History', in E. Kedourie (ed.), *Nationalism in Asia and Africa*, London: Weidenfeld & Nicolson, 207–24.

Alter, P. (1989) *Nationalism*, London: Edward Arnold.

Anderson, B. (1991) [1983] *Imagined Communities: Reflections on the Origins and Spread of Nationalism*, London: Verso, 2nd edn.

Anderson, B. (1995) 'Ice Empire and Ice Hockey: Two *Fin de Siècle* Dreams', *New Left Review*, 214, 146–50.

Anderson, B. (1996) 'Introduction', in G. Balakrishnan (ed.), *Mapping the Nation*, London: Verso, 1–16.

Anderson, B. (1998) *Spectres of Comparison: Nationalism, Southeast Asia and the World*, London and New York: Verso.

Anderson, P. (1992) *A Zone of Engagement*, London: Verso.

Anthias, F. (1989) 'Women and Nationalism in Cyprus', in N. Yuval-Davis and F. Anthias (eds), *Woman–Nation–State*, London: Macmillan, 150–67.

Anthias, F. and N. Yuval-Davis (1989) 'Introduction', in N. Yuval-Davis and F. Anthias (eds), *Woman–Nation–State*, London: Macmillan, 1–15.

Archard, D. (1995) 'Myths, Lies and Historical Truth: A Defence of Nationalism', *Political Studies*, 43, 472–81.

Armstrong, J. (1982) *Nations before Nationalism*, Chapel Hill: University of North Carolina Press.

Armstrong, J. (1990) 'Contemporary Ethnicity: The Moral Dimension in Comparative Perspective', *The Review of Politics*, 52(2), 163–89.

Armstrong, J. (1992) 'The Autonomy of Ethnic Identity: Historic Cleavages and Nationality Relations in the USSR', in A. J. Motyl (ed.), *Thinking Theoretically about Soviet Nationalities: History and Comparison in the Study of the USSR*, New York: Columbia University Press, 23–44.

Armstrong, J. (1995) 'Towards a Theory of Nationalism: Consensus and Dissensus', in S. Periwal (ed.), *Notions of Nationalism*, Budapest: Central European University Press, 34–43.

Balakrishnan, G. (1996a) 'The National Imagination', in G. Balakrishnan (ed.), *Mapping the Nation*, London: Verso, 198–213.

Balakrishnan, G. (ed.) (1996b) *Mapping the Nation*, London: Verso.

Balibar, É. (1990) 'The Nation Form: History and Ideology', *New Left Review*, XIII(3), 329–61.

Barnard, F. M. (1983) 'National Culture and Political Legitimacy: Herder and Rousseau', *Journal of the History of Ideas*, XLIV(2), 231–53.

Barnard, F. M. (1984) 'Patriotism and Citizenship in Rousseau: A Dual Theory of Public Willing?', *The Review of Politics*, 46(2), 244–65.

Barth, F. (ed.) (1969) *Ethnic Groups and Boundaries*, Boston: Little, Brown & Co.

Bauer, O. (1996) [1924] 'The Nation', in G. Balakrishnan (ed.), *Mapping the Nation*, London: Verso, 39–77.

Bauman, Z. (1991) *Modernity and Ambivalence*, Cambridge: Polity Press.

Bauman, Z. (1992) 'Soil, Blood and Identity', *The Sociological Review*, 40, 675–701.

Baycroft, T. (1998) *Nationalism in Europe 1789–1945*, Cambridge: Cambridge University Press.

Bhabha, H. (1990a) 'DissemiNation: Time, Narrative and the Margins of the Modern Nation', in H. Bhabha (ed.), *Nation and Narration*, London: Routledge, 291–322.

Bhabha, H. (ed.) (1990b) *Nation and Narration*, London: Routledge.

Billig, M. (1995) *Banal Nationalism*, London: Sage.

Bloom, W. (1990) *Personal Identity, National Identity and International Relations*, Cambridge: Cambridge University Press.

Bourdieu, P. and J.-C. Passeron (1977) *Reproduction in Education, Society and Culture*, London and Beverly Hills, Cal.: Sage.

Brand, J. A. (1985) 'Nationalism and the Noncolonial Periphery: A Discussion of Scotland and Catalonia', in E. A. Tiryakian and R. Rogowski (eds), *New Nationalisms of the Developed West*, Boston: Allen & Unwin, 277–93.

Brass, P. R. (1977) 'A Reply to Francis Robinson', *Journal of Commonwealth and Comparative Politics*, 15(3), 230–4.

Brass, P. R. (1979) 'Elite Groups, Symbol Manipulation and Ethnic Identity among the Muslims of South Asia', in D. Taylor and M. Yapp (eds), *Political Identity in South Asia*, London: Curzon Press, 35–68.

Brass, P. R. (ed.) (1985) *Ethnic Groups and the State*, London: Croom Helm.

Brass, P. R. (1991) *Ethnicity and Nationalism: Theory and Comparison*, New Delhi and Newbury Park: Sage.

Breuilly, J. (1985) 'Reflections on Nationalism', *Philosophy of the Social Sciences*, 15, 65–75.

Breuilly, J. (1993a) [1982] *Nationalism and the State*, Manchester: Manchester University Press, 2nd edn.

Breuilly, J. (1993b) 'Nationalism and the State', in R. Michener (ed.),

Nationality, Patriotism and Nationalism in Liberal Democratic Societies, Minnesota: Professors World Peace Academy, 19–48.

Breuilly, J. (1996) [1994] 'Approaches to Nationalism', in G. Balakrishnan (ed.), *Mapping the Nation*, London: Verso, 146–74.

Brubaker, R. (1996) *Nationalism Reframed: Nationhood and the National Question in the New Europe*, Cambridge: Cambridge University Press.

Brubaker, R. (1998) 'Myths and Misconceptions in the Study of Nationalism', in J. A. Hall (ed.), *The State of the Nation: Ernest Gellner and the Theory of Nationalism*, Cambridge: Cambridge University Press.

Calhoun, C. (1991) 'Indirect Relationships and Imagined Communities: Large-Scale Social Integration and the Transformation of Everyday Life', in P. Bourdieu and J. S. Coleman (eds), *Social Theory for a Changing Society*, Boulder, Col.: Westview Press, 95–121.

Calhoun, C. (1993) 'Nationalism and Ethnicity', *Annual Review of Sociology*, 19, 211–39.

Calhoun, C. (1995) *Critical Social Theory: Culture, History, and the Challenge of Difference*, Oxford: Blackwell.

Calhoun, C. (1997) *Nationalism*, Buckingham: Open University Press.

Carr, E. H. (1945) *Nationalism and After*, London: Macmillan.

Chatterjee, P. (1986) *Nationalist Thought and the Colonial World: A Derivative Discourse?*, New Jersey: Zed Books.

Chatterjee, P. (1990) 'The Nationalist Resolution of the Women's Question', in K. Sanghari and S. Vaid (eds), *Recasting Women: Essays in Colonial History*, New Brunswick, N.J.: Rutgers University Press, 233–53.

Chatterjee, P. (1996) [1993] 'Whose Imagined Community?', in G. Balakrishnan (ed.), *Mapping the Nation*, London: Verso, 214–25.

Connor, W. (1984) *The National Question in Marxist–Leninist Theory and Strategy*, Princeton: Princeton University Press.

Connor, W. (1994) *Ethnonationalism: The Quest for Understanding*, Princeton: Princeton University Press.

Conversi, D. (1995) 'Reassessing Current Theories of Nationalism: Nationalism as Boundary Maintenance and Creation', *Nationalism and Ethnic Politics*, 1(1), 73–85.

Cordellier, S. (ed.) (1995) *Nations et Nationalismes*, Paris: La Découverte.

Dahbour, O. and M. R. Ishay (eds) (1995) *The Nationalism Reader*, New Jersey: Humanities Press International.

Delannoi, G. and P.-A. Taguieff (eds) (1991) *Théories du Nationalisme: Nation, Nationalité, Ethnicité*, Paris: Kimé.

Deutsch, K. W. (1966) [1953] *Nationalism and Social Communication: An Inquiry into the Foundations of Nationality*, Cambridge, Mass.: MIT Press, 2nd edn.

Duara, P. (1993) 'De-constructing the Chinese Nation', *The Australian Journal of Chinese Affairs*, 30, 1–26.

Eley, G. (1996) 'Is All the World a Text? From Social History to the History of Society Two Decades Later', in T. J. McDonald (ed.), *The Historic Turn in the Human Sciences*, Ann Arbor: The University of Michigan Press, 193–245.

Eley, G. and R. G. Suny (1996a) 'Introduction: From the Moment of Social History to the Work of Cultural Representation', in G. Eley and R. G. Suny (eds), *Becoming National: A Reader*, New York and Oxford: Oxford University Press, 3–38.

Eley, G. and R. G. Suny (eds) (1996b) *Becoming National: A Reader*, New York and Oxford: Oxford University Press.

Eller, J. D. and R. M. Coughlan (1993) 'The Poverty of Primordialism: The Demystification of Ethnic Attachments', *Ethnic and Racial Studies*, 16(2), 183–201.

Elshtain, J. B. (1991) 'Sovereignty, Identity, Sacrifice', *Millennium: Journal of International Studies*, 20(3), 395–406.

Enloe, C. (1989) *Bananas, Beaches, Bases: Making Feminist Sense of International Politics*, London: Pandora.

Enloe, C. (1995) 'Feminism, Nationalism and Militarism: Wariness Without Paralysis?', in C. R. Sutton (ed.), *Feminism, Nationalism and Militarism*, US: The Association for Feminist Anthropology/ American Anthropological Association, 13–32.

Eriksen, T. H. (1993a) 'Formal and Informal Nationalism', *Ethnic and Racial Studies*, 16(1), 1–25.

Eriksen, T. H. (1993b) *Ethnicity and Nationalism: Anthropological Perspectives*, London: Pluto Press.

Essed, P. (1991) *Understanding Everyday Racism*, Newbury Park and London: Sage.

Fine, R. (1994) 'The "New Nationalism" and Democracy: A Critique of *Pro Patria*', *Democratization*, 1(3), 423–43.

Finlayson, A. (1998) 'Ideology, Discourse and Nationalism', *Journal of Political Ideologies*, 3(1), 99–119.

Forgacs, D. (1989) 'Gramsci and Marxism in Britain', *New Left Review*, 176, 70–88.

Fukuyama, F. (1989) 'The End of History', *The National Interest*, 16(1), 3–18.

Geertz, C. (1993) [1973] *The Interpretation of Cultures: Selected Essays*, London: Fontana, 2nd edn.

Gellner, D. N. (1997) 'Preface', in E. Gellner, *Nationalism*, London: Weidenfeld & Nicolson.

Gellner, E. (1964) *Thought and Change*, London: Weidenfeld & Nicolson.

Gellner, E. (1979) *Spectacles and Predicaments: Essays in Social Theory*, Cambridge: Cambridge University Press.

Gellner, E. (1983) *Nations and Nationalism*, Oxford: Blackwell.

Gellner, E. (1987) *Culture, Identity and Politics*, Cambridge: Cambridge University Press.

Gellner, E. (1995a) *Encounters with Nationalism*, Oxford: Blackwell.

Gellner, E. (1995b) 'Introduction', in S. Periwal (ed.), *Notions of Nationalism*, Budapest: Central European University Press, 1–7.

Gellner, E. (1996a) [1993] 'The Coming of Nationalism and its Interpretation: The Myths of Nation and Class', in G. Balakrishnan (ed.), *Mapping the Nation*, London: Verso, 98–145.

Gellner, E. (1996b) 'Reply: Do Nations Have Navels?', *Nations and Nationalism*, 2(3), 366–71.

Gellner, E. (1996c) 'Reply to Critics', in J. A. Hall and I. Jarvie (eds), *The Social Philosophy of Ernest Gellner*, Atlanta and Amsterdam: Rodopi, 623–86.

Gellner, E. (1997) *Nationalism*, London: Weidenfeld & Nicolson.

Giddens, A. (1984) *The Constitution of Society*, Cambridge: Polity Press.

Giddens, A. (1985) *The Nation State and Violence*, Cambridge: Polity Press.

Greenfeld, L. (1992) *Nationalism: Five Roads to Modernity*, Cambridge, Mass.: Harvard University Press.

Greenfeld, L. (1993) 'Transcending the Nation's Worth', *Daedalus*, 122(3), 47–62.

Grewal, I. and C. Kaplan (eds) (1994) *Scattered Hegemonies: Postmodernity and Transnational Feminist Practices*, Minneapolis: University of Minnesota Press.

Grosby, S. (1994) 'The Verdict of History: The Inexpungeable Tie of Primordiality – a Response to Eller and Coughlan', *Ethnic and Racial Studies*, 17(1), 164–71.

Guibernau, M. (1996) *Nationalisms: The Nation-State and Nationalism in the Twentieth Century*, Cambridge: Polity Press.

Hall, J. A. (1993) 'Nationalisms: Classified and Explained', *Daedalus*, 122(3), 1–28.

Hall, J. A. (1998) 'Introduction', in J. A. Hall (ed.), *The State of the Nation: Ernest Gellner and the Theory of Nationalism*, Cambridge: Cambridge University Press, 1–20.

Hall, J. A. and I. Jarvie (1996a) 'The Life and Times of Ernest Gellner', in J. A. Hall and I. Jarvie (eds), *The Social Philosophy of Ernest Gellner*, Atlanta and Amsterdam: Rodopi, 11–21.

Hall, J. A. and I. Jarvie (eds) (1996b) *The Social Philosophy of Ernest Gellner*, Atlanta and Amsterdam: Rodopi.

Hall, P. (1998) *The Social Construction of Nationalism: Sweden as an Example*, Lund: Lund University Press.

Hall, S. (1990) 'Cultural Identity and Diaspora', in J. Rutherford (ed.), *Identity: Community, Culture and Difference*, London: Lawrence & Wishart, 222–37.

Hall, S. (1996a) 'Introduction: Who Needs "Identity"?', in S. Hall and P. du Gay (eds), *Questions of Cultural Identity*, London: Sage, 1–17.

Hall, S. (1996b) [1989] 'Ethnicity: Identity and Difference', in G. Eley and R. G. Suny (eds), *Becoming National: A Reader*, New York and Oxford: Oxford University Press, 339–51.

Halliday, F. (1992) 'Bringing the "Economic" Back in: The Case of Nationalism', *Economy and Society*, 21(4), 483–90.

Halliday, F. (1995) *Islam and the Myth of Confrontation: Religion and Politics in the Middle East*, London: I.B. Tauris.

Halliday, F. (1997a) 'The Nationalism Debate and the Middle East', *Kaller Public Lecture*, Dayan Centre for Middle Eastern and African Studies, Tel Aviv, 5 May.

Halliday, F. (1997b) 'The Formation of Yemeni Nationalism: Initial Reflections', in J. Jankowski and I. Gershoni (eds), *Rethinking Nationalism in the Middle East*, New York: Columbia University Press, 26–42.

Halliday, F. (1997c) 'Irish Nationalisms in Perspective', *Torkel Opsahl Lecture* (under the auspices of Democratic Dialogue), Belfast, 10 December.

Halliday, F. (1997d) 'Nationalism', in J. Baylis and S. Smith (eds), *The Globalization of World Politics*, Oxford: Oxford University Press, 359–73.

Handler, R. (1994) 'Is "Identity" a Useful Concept?', in J. R. Gillis (ed.), *Commemorations: The Politics of National Identity*, Princeton: Princeton University Press, 27–40.

Hastings, A. (1997) *The Construction of Nationhood: Ethnicity, Religion and Nationalism*, Cambridge: Cambridge University Press.

Hayes, C. (1926) *Essays on Nationalism*, New York: Macmillan.

Hayes, C. (1955) [1931] *The Historical Evolution of Modern Nationalism*, New York: Macmillan, 5th edn.

Hechter, M. (1975) *Internal Colonialism: The Celtic Fringe in British National Development, 1536–1966*, London and Henley: Routledge & Kegan Paul.

Hechter, M. (1985) 'Internal Colonialism Revisited', in E. A. Tiryakian and R. Rogowski (eds), *New Nationalisms of the Developed West*, Boston: Allen & Unwin, 17–26.

Hechter, M. and M. Levi (1979) 'The Comparative Analysis of Ethnoregional Movements', *Ethnic and Racial Studies*, 2(3), 260–74.

Herzfeld, M. (1997) *Cultural Intimacy: Social Poetics in the Nation-State*, New York and London: Routledge.

Hobsbawm, E. J. (1972) 'Some Reflections on Nationalism', in T. J. Nossiter, A. H. Hanson and S. Rokkan (eds), *Imagination and Precision in Social Sciences*, London: Faber & Faber, 385–406.

Hobsbawm, E. J. (1990) *Nations and Nationalism since 1780: Programme, Myth, Reality*, Cambridge: Cambridge University Press.

Hobsbawm, E. J. (1996) [1992] 'Ethnicity and Nationalism in Europe Today', in G. Balakrishnan (ed.), *Mapping the Nation*, London: Verso, 255–66.

Hobsbawm, E. J. and T. Ranger (eds) (1983) *The Invention of Tradition*, Cambridge: Cambridge University Press.

Hroch, M. (1985) *Social Preconditions of National Revival in Europe: A Comparative Analysis of the Social Composition of Patriotic Groups among the Smaller European Nations,* Cambridge: Cambridge University Press.

Hroch, M. (1993) 'From National Movement to the Fully-Formed Nation: The Nation-Building Process in Europe', *New Left Review,* 198, 3–20.

Hroch, M. (1995) 'National Self-Determination from a Historical Perspective', in S. Periwal (ed.), *Notions of Nationalism,* Budapest: Central European University Press, 65–82.

Hroch, M. (1996) 'Nationalism and National Movements: Comparing the Past and the Present of Central and Eastern Europe', *Nations and Nationalism,* 2(1), 35–44.

Hroch, M. (1998) 'Real and Constructed: The Nature of the Nation', in J. A. Hall (ed.), *The State of the Nation: Ernest Gellner and the Theory of Nationalism,* Cambridge: Cambridge University Press, 91–106.

Huntington, S. P. (1993) 'The Clash of Civilizations', *Foreign Affairs,* 72(3), 22–49.

Hutchinson, J. (1994) *Modern Nationalism,* London: Fontana.

Hutchinson, J. and A. D. Smith (1994) 'Introduction', in J. Hutchinson and A. D. Smith (eds), *Nationalism,* Oxford: Oxford University Press, 3–13.

Ignatieff, M. (1993) *Blood and Belonging,* London: Vintage.

Ishay, M. (1995) 'Introduction', in O. Dahbour and M. R. Ishay (eds), *The Nationalism Reader,* New Jersey: Humanities Press International, 1–21.

James, P. (1996) *Nation Formation: Towards a Theory of Abstract Community,* London: Sage.

Janowitz, M. (1983) *The Reconstruction of Patriotism: Education for Civic Consciousness,* Chicago and London: University of Chicago Press.

Jayawardena, K. (1986) *Feminism and Nationalism in the Third World,* London: Zed Books.

Jenkins, B. and S. A. Sofos (1996) 'Nation and Nationalism in Contemporary Europe: A Theoretical Perspective', in B. Jenkins and S. A. Sofos (eds), *Nation and Identity in Contemporary Europe,* London: Routledge, 9–32.

Jenkins, R. (1995) 'Nations and Nationalisms: Towards More Open Models', *Nations and Nationalism,* 1(3), 369–90.

Jordan, G. and C. Weedon (1995) *Cultural Politics: Class, Gender, Race and the Postmodern World,* Oxford: Blackwell.

Kamenka, E. (1976) 'Political Nationalism – The Evolution of an Idea', in E. Kamenka (ed.), *Nationalism: The Nature and Evolution of an Idea,* London: Edward Arnold, 2–36.

Kapferer, B. (1988) *Legends of People, Myths of State: Violence, Intolerance, and Political Culture in Sri Lanka and Australia,* Washington D.C. and London: Smithsonian Institution Press.

Kedourie, E. (ed.) (1971) *Nationalism in Asia and Africa,* London: Weidenfeld & Nicolson.

Kedourie, E. (1994) [1960] *Nationalism,* Oxford: Blackwell, 4th edn.

Kellas, J. G. (1991) *The Politics of Nationalism and Ethnicity*, London: Macmillan.

Kellner, D. (1988) 'Postmodernism as Social Theory: Some Challenges and Problems', *Theory, Culture and Society*, 5(2–3), 239–70.

Kemiläinen, A. (1964) *Nationalism: Problems Concerning the Word, the Concept and Classification*, Yvaskyla: Kustantajat Publishers.

Kitching, G. (1985) 'Nationalism: The Instrumental Passion', *Capital & Class*, 25, 98–116.

Kitromilides, P. M. (1989) ' "Imagined Communities" and the Origins of the National Question in the Balkans', *European History Quarterly*, 19, 149–94.

Koelble, T. A. (1995) 'Towards a Theory of Nationalism: Culture, Structure and Choice Analyses Revisited', *Nationalism and Ethnic Politics*, 1(4), 73–89.

Kohn, H. (1949) 'The Paradox of Fichte's Nationalism', *Journal of the History of Ideas*, x(3), 319–43.

Kohn, H. (1950) 'Romanticism and the Rise of German Nationalism', *The Review of Politics*, 12(4), 443–72.

Kohn, H. (1957) [1946] *Prophets and Peoples: Studies in Nineteenth Century Nationalism*, New York: Macmillan, 4th edn.

Kohn, H. (1967) [1944] *The Idea of Nationalism*, New York: Collier, 2nd edn.

Lerner, D. (1958) *The Passing of Traditional Society*, New York: Free Press.

Lieven, A. (1997) 'Qu'est-ce qu'une Nation?', *The National Interest*, 49, 10–22.

Lincoln, B. (1989) *Discourse and the Construction of Society: Comparative Studies of Myth, Ritual, and Classification*, New York: Oxford University Press.

Llobera, J. R. (1994) *The God of Modernity: The Development of Nationalism in Western Europe*, Oxford and Providence: Berg Publishers.

Llobera, J. R. (1998) 'The Concept of the Nation in French Social Theory: The Work of Dominique Schnapper', *Nations and Nationalism*, 4(1), 113–21.

Löfgren, O. (1993) 'Materializing the Nation in Sweden and America', *Ethnos*, 58(III–IV), 161–96.

Lutz, H., A. Phoenix and N. Yuval-Davis (eds) (1995) *Crossfires: Nationalism, Racism and Gender in Europe*, London: Pluto Press.

MacLaughlin, J. (1987) 'Nationalism as an Autonomous Social Force: A Critique of Recent Scholarship on Ethnonationalism', *Canadian Review of Studies in Nationalism*, xiv(1), 1–18.

Malkki, L. (1996) [1992] 'National Geographic: The Rooting of Peoples and the Territorialization of National Identity among Scholars and Refugees', in G. Eley and R. G. Suny (eds), *Becoming National: A Reader*, New York and Oxford: Oxford University Press, 434–55.

Mann, M. (1995) [1994] 'A Political Theory of Nationalism and its

Excesses', in S. Periwal (ed.), *Notions of Nationalism*, Budapest: Central European University Press, 44–64.

Mann, M. (1996) 'The Emergence of Modern European Nationalism', in J. A. Hall and I. Jarvie (eds), *The Social Philosophy of Ernest Gellner*, Atlanta and Amsterdam: Rodopi, 147–70.

Marx, K. and F. Engels (1976) *Collected Works*, vol. 6, London: Lawrence & Wishart.

Mayall, J. (1990) *Nationalism and International Society*, Cambridge: Cambridge University Press.

McClintock, A. (1996) [1991] ' "No Longer in a Future Heaven": Nationalism, Gender, and Race', in G. Eley and R. G. Suny (eds), *Becoming National: A Reader*, New York and Oxford: Oxford University Press, 260–85.

McCrone, D. (1998) *The Sociology of Nationalism*, London: Routledge.

McDonald, T. J. (ed.) (1996) *The Historic Turn in the Human Sciences*, Ann Arbor: The University of Michigan Press.

Mill, J. S. (1996) [1861] 'Nationality', in S. Woolf (ed.), *Nationalism in Europe, 1815 to the Present: A Reader*, London and New York: Routledge, 40–7.

Miller, D. (1995) *On Nationality*, Oxford: Oxford University Press.

Minogue, K. (1996) 'Ernest Gellner and the Dangers of Theorising Nationalism', in J. A. Hall and I. Jarvie (eds), *The Social Philosophy of Ernest Gellner*, Atlanta and Amsterdam: Rodopi, 113–28.

Montaigne, M. de (1982) *Denemeler*. İstanbul: Cem.

Mosse, G. L. (1985) *Nationalism and Sexuality: Middle Class Morality and Sexual Norms in Modern Europe*, Madison, Wisc.: University of Wisconsin Press.

Mouzelis, N. (1998) 'Ernest Gellner's Theory of Nationalism: Some Definitional and Methodological Issues', in J. A. Hall (ed.), *The State of the Nation: Ernest Gellner and the Theory of Nationalism*, Cambridge: Cambridge University Press, 158–65.

Munck, R. (1986) *The Difficult Dialogue: Marxism and Nationalism*, London: Zed Books.

Nairn, T. (1974) 'Scotland and Europe', *New Left Review*, 83, 92–125.

Nairn, T. (1981) [1977] *The Break-up of Britain: Crisis and Neo-Nationalism*, London: Verso, 2nd edn.

Nairn, T. (1993) 'Internationalism and the Second Coming', *Daedalus*, 122(3), 155–70.

Nairn, T. (1997) *Faces of Nationalism: Janus Revisited*, London: Verso.

Nairn, T. (1998) 'The Curse of Rurality: Limits of Modernisation Theory', in J. A. Hall (ed.), *The State of the Nation: Ernest Gellner and the Theory of Nationalism*, Cambridge: Cambridge University Press, 107–34.

The New International Webster's Comprehensive Dictionary of the English Language (1996 edn), Florida: Trident Press International.

Nimni, E. (1991) *Marxism and Nationalism: Theoretical Origins of a Political Crisis*, London: Pluto.

Norval, A. J. (1996) 'Thinking Identities: Against a Theory of Ethnicity', in E. N. Wilmsen and P. McAllister (eds), *The Politics of Difference: Ethnic Premises in a World of Power*, Chicago: The University of Chicago Press, 59–70.

O'Leary, B. (1996) 'On the Nature of Nationalism: An Appraisal of Ernest Gellner's Writings on Nationalism', in J. A. Hall and I. Jarvie (eds), *The Social Philosophy of Ernest Gellner*, Atlanta and Amsterdam: Rodopi, 71–112.

O'Leary, B. (1998) 'Ernest Gellner's Diagnoses of Nationalism: A Critical Overview, or, What is Living and What is Dead in Ernest Gellner's Philosophy of Nationalism', in J. A. Hall (ed.), *The State of the Nation: Ernest Gellner and the Theory of Nationalism*, Cambridge: Cambridge University Press, 40–88.

Orridge, A. W. (1981a) 'Uneven Development and Nationalism – 1', *Political Studies*, XXIX(1), 1–15.

Orridge, A. W. (1981b) 'Uneven Development and Nationalism – 2', *Political Studies*, XXIX(2), 181–90.

Page, E. (1978) 'Michael Hechter's Internal Colonial Thesis: Some Theoretical and Methodological Problems', *European Journal of Political Research*, 6, 295–317.

Parker, A., M. Russo, D. Sommer and P. Yaeger (eds) (1992) *Nationalisms and Sexualities*, London: Routledge.

Periwal, S. (1995) 'Conclusion' in S. Periwal (ed.), *Notions of Nationalism*, Budapest: Central European University Press, 228–40.

Rattansi A. (1994) ' "Western" Racisms, Ethnicities and Identities in a "Postmodern" Frame', in A. Rattansi and S. Westwood (eds), *Racism, Modernity and Identity: on the Western Front*, Cambridge: Polity Press, 15–86.

Renan, E. (1990) [1882] 'What is a Nation?', in H. Bhabha (ed.), *Nation and Narration*, London: Routledge, 8–22.

Reynolds, V., V. S. E. Falger and I. Vine (eds) (1987) *The Sociobiology of Ethnocentrism: Evolutionary Dimensions of Xenophobia, Discrimination, Racism and Nationalism*, London: Croom Helm.

Rizman, R. R. (1996) 'Book Review: *Notions of Nationalism*', *Nations and Nationalism*, 2(2), 338–40.

Robinson, F. (1977) 'Nation Formation: The Brass Thesis and Muslim Separatism', *Journal of Commonwealth and Comparative Politics*, 15(3), 215–30.

Robinson, F. (1979) 'Islam and Muslim Separatism', in D. Taylor and M. Yapp (eds), *Political Identity in South Asia*, London: Curzon Press, 78–107.

Rutherford, J. (1990) 'The Third Space: Interview with Homi Bhabha', in J. Rutherford (ed.), *Identity: Community, Culture and Difference*, London: Lawrence & Wishart, 207–21.

Safran, W. (1995) 'Nations, Ethnic Groups, States and Politics', *Nationalism and Ethnic Politics*, 1(1), 1–10.

Said, E. (1978) *Orientalism*, London: Routledge.

244   *Bibliography*

Samuel, R. and P. Thompson (eds) (1990) *The Myths We Live by*, London: Routledge.

Schnapper, D. (1994) *La Communauté des Citoyens*, Paris: Gallimard.

Scott, G. M., Jr. (1990) 'A Resynthesis of the Primordial and Circumstantial Approaches to Ethnic Group Solidarity: Towards an Explanatory Model', *Ethnic and Racial Studies*, 13(2), 147–71.

Shils, E. (1957) 'Primordial, Personal, Sacred and Civil Ties', *British Journal of Sociology*, 8(2), 130–45.

Shotter, J. (1993) *Cultural Politics of Everyday Life: Social Constructionism, Rhetoric and Knowing of the Third Kind*, Buckingham: Open University Press.

Smith, A. D. (1973) 'Nationalism: A Trend Report and Annotated Bibliography', *Current Sociology*, 21(3), 7–180.

Smith, A. D. (1983) [1971] *Theories of Nationalism*, London: Duckworth, 2nd edn.

Smith, A. D. (1984) 'Review Article: Ethnic Persistence and National Transformation', *British Journal of Sociology*, xxxv(3), 452–61.

Smith, A. D. (1986) *The Ethnic Origins of Nations*, Oxford: Blackwell.

Smith, A. D. (1991a) *National Identity*, London. Penguin.

Smith, A. D. (1991b) 'The Nation: Invented, Imagined, Reconstructed?', *Millennium: Journal of International Studies*, 20(3), 353–68.

Smith, A. D. (1992) 'Chosen Peoples: Why Ethnic Groups Survive?', *Ethnic and Racial Studies*, 15(3), 436–56.

Smith, A. D. (1993) 'The Ethnic Sources of Nationalism', in M. E. Brown (ed.), *Ethnic Conflict and International Security*, Princeton: Princeton University Press, 27–42.

Smith, A. D. (1994) 'The Problem of National Identity: Ancient, Medieval and Modern?', *Ethnic and Racial Studies*, 17(3), 375–99.

Smith, A. D. (1995) *Nations and Nationalism in a Global Era*, Cambridge: Polity Press.

Smith, A. D. (1996a) [1992] 'Nationalism and the Historians', in G. Balakrishnan (ed.), *Mapping the Nation*, London: Verso, 175–97.

Smith, A. D. (1996b) 'Memory and Modernity: Reflections on Ernest Gellner's Theory of Nationalism', *Nations and Nationalism*, 2(3), 371–88.

Smith, A. D. (1996c) 'Opening Statement: Nations and their Pasts', *Nations and Nationalism*, 2(3), 358–65.

Smith, A. D. (1996d) 'History and Modernity: Reflections on the Theory of Nationalism', in J. A. Hall and I. Jarvie (eds), *The Social Philosophy of Ernest Gellner*, Atlanta and Amsterdam: Rodopi, 129–46.

Smith, A. D. (1998) *Nationalism and Modernism*, London: Routledge.

Snyder, L. (1954) *The Meaning of Nationalism*, New Brunswick: Rutgers University Press.

Snyder, L. (1968) *The New Nationalism*, Ithaca, New York: Cornell University Press.

Snyder, T. (1997) 'Kazimierz Kelles-Krauz (1872–1905): A Pioneering Scholar of Modern Nationalism', *Nations and Nationalism*, 3(2), 231–50.

Sofos, S. A. (1996) 'Culture, Politics and Identity in Former Yugoslavia', in B. Jenkins and S. A. Sofos (eds), *Nation and Identity in Contemporary Europe*, London: Routledge, 251–82.

Somers, M. (1992) 'Narrativity, Narrative Identity, and Social Action: Rethinking English Working-Class Formation', *Social Science History*, 16(4), 591–630.

Stalin, J. (1994) [1973] 'The Nation', in J. Hutchinson and A. D. Smith (eds), *Nationalism*, Oxford: Oxford University Press, 18–21.

Stargardt, N. (1995) 'Origins of the Constructivist Theory of the Nation', in S. Periwal (ed.), *Notions of Nationalism*, Budapest: Central European University Press, 83–105.

Stern, P. C. (1995) 'Why do People Sacrifice for Their Nations?', in J. L. Comaroff and P. C. Stern (eds), *Perspectives on Nationalism and War*, Amsterdam: Gordon & Breach, 99–121.

Sugar, P. F. (1969) 'External and Domestic Roots of Eastern European Nationalism', in P. F. Sugar and I. J. Lederer (eds), *Nationalism in Eastern Europe*, Seattle: University of Washington Press.

Symmons-Symonolewicz, K. (1981) 'National Consciousness in Medieval Europe: Some Theoretical Problems', *Canadian Review of Studies in Nationalism*, VIII(1), 151–65.

Symmons-Symonolewicz, K. (1985a) 'The Concept of Nationhood: Toward a Theoretical Clarification', *Canadian Review of Studies in Nationalism*, XII(2), 215–22.

Symmons-Symonolewicz, K. (1985b) 'Book Review: *Nationalism and the State*', *Canadian Review of Studies in Nationalism*, XII(2), 359–60.

Tilley, V. (1997) 'The Terms of the Debate: Untangling Language about Ethnicity and Ethnic Movements', *Ethnic and Racial Studies*, 20(3), 497–522.

Tilly, C. (ed.) (1975) *The Formation of National States in Western Europe*, Princeton: Princeton University Press.

Tilly, C. (1990) *Coercion, Capital and European States, AD 990–1990*, Cambridge, Mass.: Oxford: Blackwell.

Tilly, C. (1993) 'National Self-Determination as a Problem for All of Us', *Daedalus*, 122(3), 29–36.

Tilly, C. (1994) 'A Bridge Halfway: Responding to Brubaker', *Contention*, 4(1), 15–19.

Tilly, C. (1995) 'States and Nationalism in Europe 1492–1992', in J. L. Comaroff and P. C. Stern (eds), *Perspectives on Nationalism and War*, Amsterdam: Gordon & Breach, 187–204.

Tiryakian, E. A. (1985) 'Introduction', in E. A. Tiryakian and R. Rogowski (eds), *New Nationalisms of the Developed West*, Boston: Allen & Unwin, 1–13.

Tiryakian, E. A. (1995) 'Nationalism and Modernity', in J. L. Comaroff and P. C. Stern (eds), *Perspectives on Nationalism and War*, Amsterdam: Gordon & Breach, 205–35.

van den Berghe, P. (1978) 'Race and Ethnicity: A Sociobiological Perspective', *Ethnic and Racial Studies*, 1(4), 401–11.

van den Berghe, P. (1979) *The Ethnic Phenomenon*, New York: Elsevier.

van Dijk, T. A. (1993) *Elite Discourse and Racism*, Newbury Park and London: Sage.

van Dijk, T. A. (1998) *Ideology*, London: Sage.

Verdery, K. (1993) 'Whither "Nation" and "Nationalism"?', *Daedalus*, 122(3), 37–46.

Walby, S. (1994) 'Is Citizenship Gendered?', *Sociology*, 28(2), 379–95.

Walby, S. (1996) [1992] 'Woman and Nation', in G. Balakrishnan (ed.), *Mapping the Nation*, London: Verso, 235–54.

West, L. A. (ed.) (1997) *Feminist Nationalism*, New York and London: Routledge.

Woolf, S. (ed.), *Nationalism in Europe, 1815 to the Present: A Reader*, London: Routledge

Yumul, A. and U. Özkırımlı (1997) 'Milliyetçiliğin Farkedilmeyen Yüzü' [The Hidden Face of Nationalism], *Varlık*, 1076, 6–11.

Yun, M. S. (1990) 'Ethnonationalism, Ethnic Nationalism, and Mini-Nationalism: A Comparison of Connor, Smith and Snyder', *Ethnic and Racial Studies*, 13(4), 527–41.

Yuval-Davis, N. (1989) 'National Reproduction and "the Demographic Race" in Israel', in N. Yuval-Davis and F. Anthias (eds), *Woman–Nation–State*, London: Macmillan, 92–108.

Yuval-Davis, N. (1997) *Gender and Nation*, London: Sage.

Yuval-Davis, N. and F. Anthias (1989) *Woman–Nation–State*, London: Macmillan.

Žižek, S. (1990) 'Eastern Europe's Republics of Gilead', *New Left Review*, 183, 50–63.

Zubaida, S. (1978) 'Theories of Nationalism', in G. Littlejohn, B. Smart, J. Wakefield and N. Yuval-Davis (eds), *Power and the State*, London: Croom Helm, 52–71.

Zubaida, S. (1989) 'Nations: Old and New. Comments on Anthony D. Smith's "The Myth of the Modern Nation and the Myths of Nations"', *Ethnic and Racial Studies*, 12(3), 329–39.

Index